Praise for
Songwriter's Market

A bounty of contacts. . . . Highly recommended for songwriters and music industry professionals of all levels.   **—Music Connection**

If you buy only one book on songwriting this year, . . . make sure that it's *Songwriter's Market*. If you are serious about becoming a songwriter, you *must* own the most recent edition.   **—Songwriter Magazine**

A sensational reference for songwriters.   **—Writers Write website**

A songwriter who applies the same level of perseverance and thoroughness that went into the compilation of *Songwriter's Market* will find it a very useful tool.   **—First Draft**

2000
SONG WRITER'S MARKET

1,600 PLACES TO MARKET YOUR SONGS

EDITED BY

TARA A. HORTON

WRITER'S DIGEST BOOKS
CINCINNATI, OHIO

If you would like to be considered for a listing in the next edition of *Songwriter's Market*, send a SASE (or SAE and IRC) with your request for a questionnaire to *Songwriter's Market*—QR, 1507 Dana Ave., Cincinnati OH 45207. Please indicate in which section you would like to be included. Questionnaires received after February 1, 2000, will be held for the 2002 edition.

Managing Editor, Annuals Department: Cindy Laufenberg
Production Editor: Pamala Shields

Writer's Digest website: http://www.writersdigest.com

International Standard Serial Number 0161-5971
International Standard Book Number 0-89879-914-7

Attention Booksellers: This is an annual directory of F&W Publications. Return deadline for this edition is December 31, 2000.

contents at a glance

Contents

The Markets

Resources

From the Editor

Does this ever happen to you? You hear or see something—the name of a person, place, or even just some random word—and then for the next few days it keeps popping up? As I was updating and editing this book, the word "professional" was unavoidable. I found it in several listings under "Tips" and it's all over the place in the business articles. You know what? I got sick of seeing that word after awhile.

An editor has to think up different ways of saying the same thing so her writing doesn't get boring or monotonous (as a songwriter, you can probably relate!). It's a challenge, especially working on a book each year with the same subject matter. If you use a word over and over again it begins to lose its meaning and starts to look foreign. And really, how many alternate ways can you think of to say "professional"? My computer's thesaurus suggests derivatives of "expert": master, pro, authority, specialist, veteran, maestro, genius, whiz. I didn't like any of these and couldn't think of another word with as much intrinsic strength or respect. Without an alternative, as I edited I kept "professional" wherever it appeared.

Being an expert/specialist/whiz is a vital part of being taken seriously in the music industry and is key if you want to get your songs heard. So, here's my challenge to you: while using this book, whenever you run across "professional" (Ugh! There it is again!)—whenever you run across THAT WORD, instead of glancing over it because you've seen it a million times, really read it and evaluate how it pertains to you. Don't allow THAT WORD to lose its meaning though it appears to be multiplying with every turn of the page. And to help you meet this challenge, be sure to take the Quiz: Are You Professional? on page 19. Your score may surprise you!

Some of the new elements that may pleasantly surprise you about this year's *Songwriter's Market* are the addition of new symbols (see the inside front and back covers of the book) and indexes (see Openness to Submissions Index on page 471 and Film & TV Index on page 481). These elements will allow you to quickly find companies open to your songs. The new articles and interviews in this edition are full of instruction and insight you can use to lift your songwriting to the next level. If this is your first time using this book, go directly to Quick-Start on page 3; it takes you step-by-step through the book's featrues and the song marketing process.

I hope this book makes your journey through the music business rewarding and a little less arduous. Along with your continued enthusiasm, *Songwriter's Market* will better prepare you to become a songwriter who is a profes—I mean, a *maestro*!

Tara A. Horton
songmarket@fwpubs.com
http://www.writersdigest.com

Songwriter's Market
Feedback

If you have a suggestion for improving *Songwriter's Market*, or would like to take part in a reader survey we conduct from time to time, please make a photocopy of this form (or cut it out of the book), fill it out, and return it to:

Songwriter's Market Feedback
1507 Dana Ave.
Cincinnati OH 45207
Fax: (513)531-2686

☐ Yes! I'm willing to fill out a short survey by mail or online to provide feedback on *Songwriter's Market* or other books on songwriting.

☐ Yes! I have a suggestion to improve *Songwriter's Market* (attach a second sheet if more room is necessary):

_____
_____
_____
_____
_____
_____
_____
_____
_____
_____
_____
_____

Name:_____
Address:_____
City:_____ State:_____ Zip:_____
Phone:_____ Fax:_____
E-mail:_____ Website:_____

I am a
☐ songwriter
☐ performing songwriter
☐ musician
☐ other_____

Quick-Start

If the business of marketing your songs is a new experience, this book may seem overwhelming. This "Quick-Start" will take you step by step through the process of preparing you and your songs to be heard by music industry professionals. It points you to the different places in *Songwriter's Market* that contain information on specific marketing and business subjects.

Use this as a guide to launch your songwriting career. When you are finished looking it over, read through the referred articles in their entirety. They will reinforce what you already know and introduce you to facets of the industry you have yet to encounter. Good luck!

1. Join a songwriting organization. This is the most important first step for a songwriter. Organizations provide opportunities to learn about the music business, polish your craft, and make indispensable contacts who can take you to the next level.
- Organizations, page 412

2. Educate yourself about the music business. Before you leap, read up on what you are getting yourself into. Attend songwriting workshops and music conferences. Don't learn the ins and outs the hard way.
- The Structure of the Music Business, page 12
- Royalties, page 13
- If You Write Lyrics, But Not Music sidebar, page 11
- Frequently Asked Questions About This Book sidebar, page 5
- The Business of Songwriting, page 21
- Understanding Performing Rights Organizations, page 51
- Workshops & Conferences, page 434
- Publications of Interest, page 454

3. Prepare yourself and your songs for marketing. Get letterhead, get criticism, make contacts and subscribe to songwriting/music magazines; then start building a following and a strong catalog.
- Improving Your Craft, page 11
- Organizations, page 412
- Workshops & Conferences, page 434
- Publications of Interest, page 454

4. Choose three songs you feel are ready to be marketed and make a demo.
- Submitting Your Songs, page 14
- What Music Professionals Look for In a Demo sidebar, page 15
- How to Make Your Submission Stand Out, page 35

5. Decide which arm(s) of the music business you will submit your songs to.
- Where Should I Send My Songs?, page 6

6. Find the companies open to your style of music and level of experience or use your contacts to get a referral and permission to submit. Be picky about where you send your material. It's a waste of your effort and money to send to every company listed in this book without regard to whether or not they want to hear your songs.
- Narrowing Your Search, page 8
- Openness to Submissions sidebar, page 8

7. Locate the companies closest to where you live. It's easier to have a relationship when the company is within driving distance.
- Geographic Index, page 483

8. Decide which companies you to want to submit your song to and whether they are appropriate markets for you (pay special attention to the information under the **Music** subhead and also the royalty percentage they pay). Do additional research through trade publications, Internet, other songwriters.
- The Markets, pages 55-410
- Publications of Interest, page 454
- Websites of Interest, page 460

9. Find out how to submit. Read the information under the **How to Contact** subhead.
- Using the Phone to Get a Solicited Submission, page 27
- Sample Reply Postcard, page 16
- How to Send Your Demos, page 9

10. Call the companies and verify that their submission policy has not changed; also check to make sure the contact person is still there.

11. Send out your submission package according to each company's directions.
- So You Got a Solicited Submission—Now What?, page 31
- Quiz: Are You Professional?, page 19
- Submitting Your Songs, page 14

12. Decide whether you want to sign with a company (if they reply and are interested in working with you). Just because they want to sign you doesn't mean you should.
- The Rip-Offs, page 24
- Is This the Right Company for Me?, page 39

13. Have an entertainment attorney look over any contract before you sign.
- Contracts, page 22
- Publishing Contracts, page 59
- Record Company Contracts, page 140

14. Wait for the royalties to arrive!
- Royalties, page 13

How to Use *Songwriter's Market* to Get Your Songs Heard

Songwriter's Market is designed to help you make good decisions about submitting your songs—whether you're approaching music publishers, record companies, producers, managers, chamber music groups, or theater companies.

If you're new to the business of marketing your music, a good place to start—after this article, but before you dive into the market listings—is with Quick-Start on page 3 and Getting Started, on page 11. If you're an old hand at this, you might wish to begin with a quick brush-up in The Business of Songwriting, on page 21. In either case, the other articles, Insider Report interviews, and section introductions throughout the book should prove informative and inspiring.

Getting to know this book. *Songwriter's Market* is divided into Markets and Resources. The Markets section contains all the companies (music publishers, record companies, etc.) seeking new material and is the part of the book you will concentrate on when submitting songs. If you're uncertain about which markets might have the most interest in your material, review the introductory explanations at the beginning of each section. They will clarify the various functions of each segment of the music industry and help you narrow your list of possible submissions. The Resources section contains listings and information on organizations, workshops, retreats/colonies, publications and websites to help you learn more about the music industry and the craft of songwriting.

Frequently Asked Questions About This Book

1. What's the deal with listing companies that don't take unsolicited submissions?

We want to provide you with the most complete songwriting resource. To do this, you should be aware of the companies that are not open to unsolicited submissions so you can take one of two actions: either 1) don't submit to them; or 2) work to establish a relationship with them to earn a solicited submission. If the major companies that are closed to submissions weren't in here, wouldn't you wonder what their policy was? Also, it's important to read these listings every year to keep informed about the industry.

2. How do these companies get listed in the book anyway?

No company pays to be included—all listings are free. Every company has to fill out a detailed questionnaire about their services. All questionnaires are screened to make sure the companies meet our requirements (see The Rip-Offs on page 24). Each year we contact every company in the book and have them update their information.

3. Why aren't other companies I know about listed in this book?

We may have sent these companies a questionnaire, but they never returned it. Or if they did return a questionnaire, we may have decided not to include them based on our requirements (see The Rip-Offs on page 24).

4. I sent a company a demo tape, and they said in their listing they take unsolicited submissions. My demo was returned unopened. What happened?

At the time we contacted the company they were open to submissions, but things change fast in this business and their policy may have changed by the time you sent your demo. It's always a good idea to call a company to check on their policy before sending them anything.

WHERE SHOULD I SEND MY SONGS?

It depends. Who are you writing your music for? Are you writing songs for an act you now belong to? Are you hoping to have your music accepted and recorded by an artist? Take a look at the How Songs Are Recorded and Released flow chart on page 7. It shows the different paths a songwriter can take to get her music recorded (the Key to this chart is below).

The performing songwriter. If you are writing songs for an existing group or for yourself as a solo artist, you're probably trying to advance the career of your act. If that's the case, and you're seeking a recording contract, the Record Companies section will be the place to start. Look also at the Record Producers section. Independent record producers are constantly on the lookout for up-and-coming artists. They may also have strong connections with record companies looking for acts, and will pass your demo on or recommend the act to a record company. And if your act doesn't yet have representation, your demo submission may be included as part of a promotional kit sent to a prospective manager listed in the Managers & Booking Agents section.

The nonperforming songwriter. If you are a songwriter seeking to have your songs recorded by other artists, you may submit to some of the same markets as the performing songwriter, but for different reasons. The Record Producers section contains mostly independent producers who work regularly with particular artists, rather than working fulltime for one record company. Because they work closely with a limited number of clients, they may be willing to consider songs written with a specific act in mind. The independent producer is often responsible for picking cuts for a recording project. The Managers & Booking Agents section may be useful for the same reason. Many personal managers are constantly seeking new material for the acts they represent, and a good song sent at the right time can mean a valuable cut for the songwriter. The primary market for songwriters not writing with particular artists in mind will be found in the Music Publishers section. Music publishers are the jacks-of-all-trades in the industry, having knowledge about and keeping abreast of developments in all other segments of the music business. They act as the first line of contact between the songwriter and the music industry.

Key to How Songs Are Recorded and Released (page 7)

A and B—options for non-performing songwriters
C—avenue for both performing and non-performing songwriters
D and E—processes for performing songwriters

Artist—band or singer who performs the music
Artist's Manager—works with the artist to manage her career; locates songs to record if the artist does not write her own material
Independent Producer—not affiliated with a record company; works in the studio and records songs; may have an affiliation with an artist
Producer—affiliated with a record company or music publisher; works in the studio and records songs
Publisher—evaluates songs for commercial potential, finds artists to record them, finds other uses (such as TV or film) for the songs, collects income generated by the songs and protects copyrights from infringement
Record Company—signs artists to its label, finances recording, promotion and touring, and releases songs/albums to radio and TV

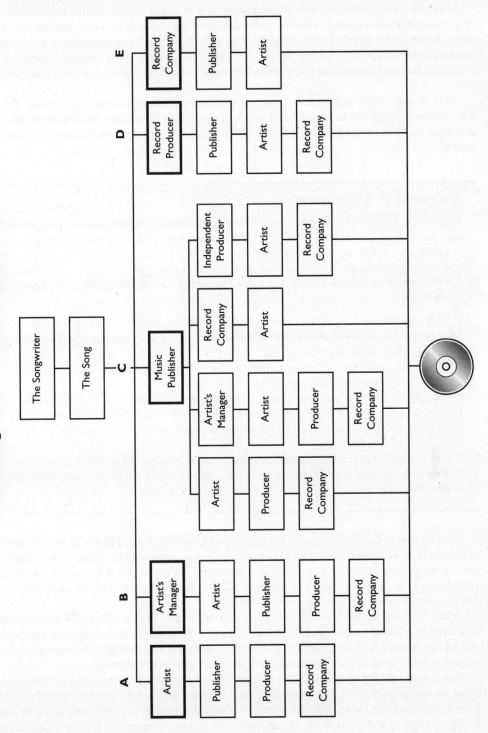

How Songs Are Recorded and Released

The Songwriter → **The Song**

A
Artist → Publisher → Producer → Record Company

B
Artist's Manager → Artist → Publisher → Producer → Record Company

C
Music Publisher
- Artist → Producer → Record Company
- Artist's Manager → Artist → Producer → Record Company
- Record Company → Artist
- Independent Producer → Artist → Record Company

D
Record Producer → Publisher → Artist → Record Company

E
Record Company → Publisher → Artist

NARROWING YOUR SEARCH

After you've identified the type of companies you're going to send demos to, the next step is to research each section to find the individual markets that will be most interested in your work. Refer to the sample listing on page 9 to see where specific information can be found. Most users of *Songwriter's Market* should first check three items in the listings: location of the company, the type of music the company is interested in hearing, and the company's submission policy.

Next, decide which best describes you as a songwriter: beginner or experienced. New to this edition, companies have indicated which type of songwriter they wish to work with by a symbol in front of their listing (☐ ◪ ◪ ◪). See the Openness to Submissions sidebar below.

Openness to Submissions

Improve the chances of getting your music heard by locating companies open to your level of experience. Listings in the Music Publishers, Record Companies, Record Producers, and Managers & Booking Agents sections were asked how open they are to submissions. You can quickly find listings open to your level of experience by checking one of two sources: 1. Openness to Submissions Index on page 471; or 2. the openness icon (☐ ◪ ◪ or ◪) at the beginning of the listing.

☐ indicates the company is open to beginners' submissions, regardless of past success.

◪ means the company is mostly interested in previously published songwriters/well-established acts*, but will consider beginners.

◪ these companies are not interested in submissions from beginners, only from previously published songwriters/well-established acts*.

◪ companies with this icon only accept material referred to them by a reputable industry source**. [Note: We still include these listings so you know *not* to send them material. You must get an industry referral in order for these companies to listen to your songs.]

* Well-established acts are those with a following, permanent gigs or previous record deal.
** Reputable industry sources include managers, entertainment attorneys, performing rights organizations, etc.

Each section of the book contains listings from all over the United States as well as the rest of the world. If location is important to you, check the Geographic Index at the back of the book for listings of companies by state and other countries. To quickly find those markets located outside the U.S., look for these two symbols: ▣ appears before the titles of all listings from Canada and ⊕ appears before all overseas listings.

Other important symbols are ☒ indicating a listing is new to this edition; ✔ meaning there is a change in contact name, address, phone, fax or e-mail; ☒ for award-winning companies; and ▣ for companies placing songs in film or TV (excluding commercials). For quick reference regarding these symbols, see the inside front and back covers of this book.

Don't mail blindly. Your music isn't going to be appropriate for submission to all companies. Most music industry firms have specific music interests and needs, and you want to be sure your submissions are being seen and heard by companies who have a genuine interest in them. Category Indexes at the end of the Music Publishers, Record Companies, Record Producers and Managers & Booking Agents sections will clue you in to which musical styles are being sought by which companies. (Keep in mind these are general categories. Some companies may not be listed in the Category Index because they either accept all types of music or the music they are looking for doesn't fit into any of the general categories.) Within each listing, under the **Music** subhead, you will find, in **bold** type, a more detailed list of the styles of music a company is seeking.

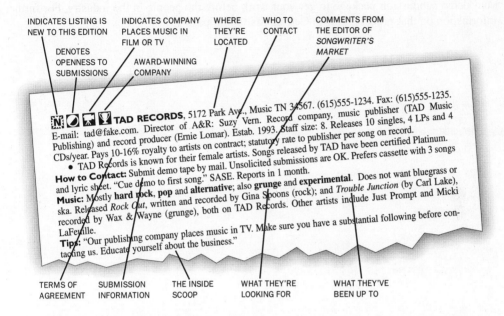

Pay close attention to the types of music described. For instance, if the music you write fits the category of "rock," there can be many variations on that style. Our sample above is interested in **hard rock**, another listing may be looking for **country rock**, and another, **soft rock**. These are three very different styles of music, but they all fall under the same general category. The Category Index is there to help you narrow down the listings within a certain music genre; it is up to you to narrow them down even further to fit the type of music you write. The music styles in each listing are *in descending order of importance*; if your particular specialty is country music, you may want to seek out those companies that list country as their first priority as your primary targets for submissions.

You will note that some market listings contain editorial comments and are marked by a bullet (●). Editorial comments give you additional information such as special submission requirements, any awards a company may have won, and other details that will be helpful in narrowing down your list of companies to submit to.

HOW TO SEND YOUR DEMOS

Finally, when you've placed the most likely listings geographically and identified their music preferences and openness to submissions, read the **How to Contact** subhead. As shown in the sample listing above, it will give you pertinent information about what to send as part of a demo submission, how to go about sending it and when you can expect to hear back from them.

Read carefully! Not all of the markets listed in *Songwriter's Market* accept unsolicited submissions (indicated by ⊘ in front of the listing), so it's important to read this information closely.

Most companies have carefully considered their submission policies, and packages that do not follow their directions are returned or discarded without evaluation. Follow the instructions: it will impress upon the market your seriousness about getting your work heard.

You've now identified markets you feel will have the most interest in your work. Read the complete listing carefully before proceeding. Many of the listings include individualized information important for the submitting songwriter. Then, it's time for you to begin preparing your demo submission package to get your work before the people in the industry. For further information on that process, turn to Getting Started on page 11.

Getting Started

Breaking in and thriving in the competitive music industry without being overwhelmed is perhaps the biggest challenge facing songwriters. Those who not only survive but also succeed have taken the time before entering the market to learn as much as they can about the inner workings of the music industry.

Reading, studying and using the information contained in sourcebooks such as *Songwriter's Market* will help you market yourself and your work professionally and effectively.

If You Write Lyrics, But Not Music

You must find a collaborator. The music business is looking for the complete package: music plus lyrics. If you don't write music, find a collaborator who does. The best way to find a collaborator is through songwriting organizations. Check the Organizations section (pages 412-433) for songwriting groups near you.

Don't get ripped-off. "Music mills" advertise in the back of magazines or solicit you through the mail. For a fee they will set your lyrics or poems to music. The rip-off is that they may use the same melody for hundreds of lyrics and poems, whether it sounds good or not. Publishers recognize one of these melodies as soon as they hear it. (Also see the Rip-Offs on page 24).

IMPROVING YOUR CRAFT

There is no magic formula for success in the music business. If you want to make it, you must begin by believing in yourself and your talent. Develop your own personal vision and stick with it. Why do you write songs? Is it because you want to be rich or because you love the process? Is every song you write an attempt to become famous or a labor of love? Every effort you make to discern your motives and clarify your goals will be a step in the right direction. Successful songwriters usually believe they have a talent that deserves to be heard, whether by 2 or 2,000 people. Songwriting is a craft, like woodworking or painting. Talent is involved, of course, but with time and practice the craft can be improved and eventually mastered.

Organizations. While working on songs, look for support and feedback wherever you can. A great place to start is a local songwriting organization, which can offer friendly advice, support from other writers, and a place to meet collaborators. (For more information on songwriting organizations in your area, see the Organizations section on page 412.) Many organizations offer song critique sessions to help you identify strengths and weaknesses in your material and give you guidance to improve your craft. Use the criticism you receive in such sessions to fine-tune your writing style. Your songwriting will improve, and you will be creating connections within the industry and continuing your education not only in the craft of songwriting but in the business as well.

Books. Books can also be helpful in matters of craft and business. Books are available to help you write better melodies, stronger lyrics and songs that sell. Many books cover the business side of music, explaining the intricacies of how the business works and giving valuable tips on how to network with people in the business. Music catalogs such as Music Books Plus (call (800)265-8481 for a catalog) or online booksellers like Amazon.com and barnesandnoble.com carry hundreds of books about songwriting and the music industry.

Magazines. Magazines can keep you up-to-date on the latest trends and happenings in today's ever-changing music business. From industry trade magazines like *Billboard* and *Variety* to more specific magazines such as *Performing Songwriter* and *JazzTimes*, there is a magazine catering to just about every segment of the industry and type of music you can imagine. Since this is a trend-oriented business, weekly and monthly magazines can help you stay abreast of what's hot and what's not. For some suggestions, see Publications of Interest on page 454.

The Internet. The Internet can be another valuable source of information. Not only are many record companies, publishers and magazines online, but an abundance of music sites exist where artists can showcase their songs for an unlimited audience, chat with other songwriters and musicians from all over the world, and even sell their product online. See Websites of Interest on page 460 for a list of some current music-oriented websites. New ones are popping up every day, so surfing the Web frequently will help you learn what's available.

THE STRUCTURE OF THE MUSIC BUSINESS

The music business in the U.S. revolves around three major hubs: New York, Nashville and Los Angeles. Power is concentrated in those areas because that's where most record companies, publishers, songwriters and performers are. Many people trying to break into the music business move to one of those three cities to be close to the people and companies they want to contact. From time to time a regional music scene will heat up in a non-hub city such as Austin, Chicago or Seattle. When this happens, songwriters and performers in that city experience a kind of musical Renaissance complete with better-paying gigs, a creatively charged atmosphere and intensified interest from major labels.

All this is not to say that a successful career cannot be nurtured from any city in the country, however. It can be, especially if you are a songwriter. By moving to a major music hub, you may be closer physically to major companies, but you'll also encounter more competition than you would back home. Stay where you're comfortable; it's probably easier (and more cost-effective) to conquer the music scene where you are than it is in Los Angeles or Nashville. There are many smaller, independent companies located in cities across the country. Most international careers are started on a local level, and some may find a local career more satisfying, in its own way, than the constant striving to gain the attention of major companies.

Making contact. If you are interested in obtaining a recording contract, you will need to make contact with A&R reps, producers, publishers and managers. Getting your material to these professionals and establishing relationships with as many people in the industry as you can should be your main goal as a songwriter. The more people who hear your songs, the better your chances of getting them recorded.

A&R reps, producers and managers. Consumer support, in the form of money spent on records, concert tickets and other kinds of musical entertainment, keeps the music industry in business. Because of that, record companies, publishers and producers are eager to give the public what they want. To stay one step ahead of public tastes, record companies hire people who have a knack for spotting musical talent and anticipating trends, and put them in charge of finding and developing new talent. These talent scouts are called A&R representatives. "A&R" stands for "artist and repertoire," which simply means they are responsible for discovering new talent and matching songs to particular artists. The person responsible for the recording artist's product—the record—is called the producer. The producer's job is to develop the artist's work and come out of the studio with a good-sounding, saleable product that represents the artist in the best way possible. His duties sometimes include choosing songs for a particular project, so record producers are also great contacts for songwriters. Managers are interested in developing an artist's career as a whole, and are typically on the prowl for material suitable for the performers they represent.

Music publishers. Producers, A&R reps, and managers are aided in their search for talent by the music publisher. A publisher works as a songwriter's advocate who, for a percentage of the profits (typically 50% of all earnings from a particular song), attempts to find commercially profitable uses for the songs he represents. A successful publisher stays in contact with several A&R reps, finding out what upcoming projects are in need of new material, and whether any songs he represents will be appropriate.

ROYALTIES

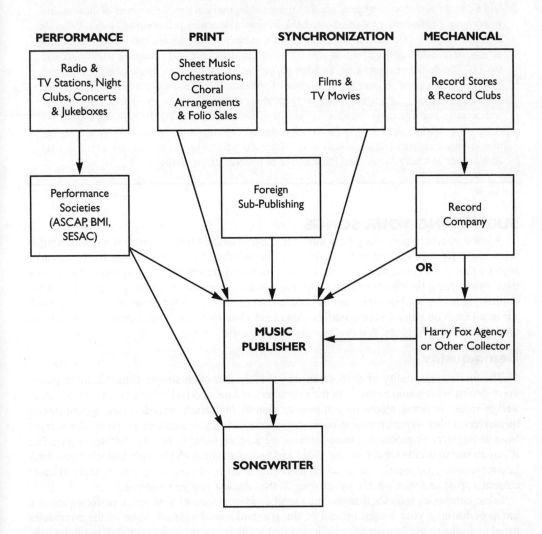

PERFORMANCE	PRINT	SYNCHRONIZATION	MECHANICAL
Radio & TV Stations, Night Clubs, Concerts & Jukeboxes	Sheet Music Orchestrations, Choral Arrangements & Folio Sales	Films & TV Movies	Record Stores & Record Clubs

Performance Societies (ASCAP, BMI, SESAC)

Foreign Sub-Publishing

Record Company

OR

MUSIC PUBLISHER

Harry Fox Agency or Other Collector

SONGWRITER

ROYALTIES

When a song is recorded and released to the public, the recording artist, songwriter, record company, producer and publisher all stand to profit. Recording artists earn a negotiated royalty from a record company based on the number of records sold. Producers are usually paid either a negotiated royalty based on sales or a flat fee at the time of recording. Publishers and songwriters earn mechanical royalties (money a record company pays a publisher based on record sales) and performance royalties, which are based on radio airplay and live performances. Look at the royalties flow chart above. It shows where royalties come from and where they go before landing in the songwriter's pocket. As the chart shows, a music publisher is an invaluable resource for songwriters to earn royalties (see the Music Publishers section on page 57).

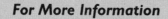

For More Information

Songwriter's Market lists music publishers, record companies, producers and managers (as well as advertising firms, play producers and classical performing arts organizations) along with specifications on how to submit your material to each. If you can't find a certain person or company you're interested in, there are other sources of information you can try. *The Recording Industry Sourcebook*, an annual directory published by Norris-Whitney Communications, lists record companies, music publishers, producers and managers, as well as attorneys, publicity firms, media, manufacturers, distributors and recording studios around the U.S. Trade publications such as *Billboard* or *Variety*, available at most local libraries and bookstores, are great sources for up-to-date information. These periodicals list new companies as well as the artists, labels, producers and publishers for each song on the charts. CD booklets and cassette j-cards can be valuable sources of information, providing the name of the record company, publisher, producer and usually the manager of an artist or group. Use your imagination in your research and be creative—any contacts you make in the industry can only help your career as a songwriter. See Publications of Interest on page 454.

SUBMITTING YOUR SONGS

When it comes to presenting your material, the tool of the music industry is a demonstration recording—a demo. Cassette tapes have been the standard in the music industry for decades because they're so convenient. Songwriters use demos to present their songs, and musicians use them to showcase their performance skills. Demos are submitted to various professionals in the industry, either by mail or in person. Be sure to read the sidebar What Music Professionals Look for in a Demo on page 15 for specifics. Also read How to Make Your Submission Stand Out on page 35 and Quiz: Are You Professional? on page 19.

Demo quality

The production quality of demos can vary widely, but even simple guitar/vocal or piano/vocal demos must sound clean, with the instrument in tune and lyrics sung clearly. Many songwriters invest in home recording equipment, such as multitrack recorders, and record demos themselves. Other writers prefer to book studio time, hire musicians, and get professional input from an engineer or producer. Demo services are also available to record your demo for a fee. It's up to you to decide what you can afford and feel most comfortable with, and what you think best represents your song. Once a master recording is made of your song, you're ready to make cassette copies and start pitching your song to the contacts you've researched.

Some companies indicate that you may send a videocassette of your act in performance or a group performing your songs, instead of the standard cassette demo. Most of the companies listed in *Songwriter's Market* have indicated that a videocassette is not required, but have indicated their preferred format should you decide to send one. Television systems vary widely from country to country, so if you're sending a video to a foreign listing check with them for the system they're using. For example, a VHS format tape recorded using the U.S. system (called NTSC) will not play back on a standard British VCR (using the PAL system), even if the recording formats are the same. It is possible to transfer a video from one system to another, but the expense in both time and money may outweigh its usefulness. Systems for some countries include: NTSC—U.S., Canada and Japan; PAL—United Kingdom, Australia and Germany; and SECAM—France.

What Music Professionals Look for in a Demo

- **Format**. The cassette is still the preferable format for demos. Music executives are busy people and whenever they have a chance, they will listen to demos. Cassette players are what they have the easiest access to, whether in their office, car or home. Cassettes are also cheaper to duplicate than CDs or DATs, and are cheaper and easier to mail. If they like what they hear on the cassette they can always ask you for a DAT or CD later.

- **Number, order and length of songs**. The consensus throughout the industry is that three songs is sufficient. Most music professionals don't have time to listen to more than three, and they figure if you can't catch their attention in three songs, your songs probably don't have hit potential.

   Put three complete songs on the tape, not just snippets of your favorites, and remember to put your best, most commercial song first on the tape. If it's an up-tempo number, that makes it even easier to catch someone's attention. All songs should be on the same side of the tape, and none of them should be longer than four minutes. Cue the tape to the beginning of the first song so no time will be wasted fast-forwarding or rewinding.

- **Production**. How elaborate a demo has to be lies in the type of music you write, and what an individual at a company is looking for. Usually, up-tempo pop, rock and dance demos need to be more fully produced than pop ballads and country demos. Many of the companies listed in *Songwriter's Market* tell you what type of demo they prefer to receive, and if you're not sure you can always call and ask what their preference is. Either way, make sure your demo is clean and clear, and the vocals are up front.

   If you are an artist looking for a record deal, obviously your demo needs to be as fully produced as possible to convey your talent as an artist. Many singer/songwriters record their demos as if they were going to be released as an album. That way, if they have already recorded three or four CD-quality demo tapes but haven't heard anything from the labels they've been submitting to, they can put those demos together and release a CD or cassette on their own. They end up with a professional-looking product, complete with album cover graphics and liner notes, to sell at shows and through mail order without spending a lot of money to re-record the songs.

- **Performance**. If you can't sing well, you may want to find someone who can. It pays to find a good vocalist and good musicians to record your demos, and there are many places to find musicians and singers willing to work with you. Check out local songwriting organizations, music stores and newspapers to find musicians in your area you can hire to play on your demo. Many singers who don't write their own songs will sing on demos in exchange for a copy of the tape they can use as their own demo to help further their performing careers.

   If you can't find local musicians, or don't want to go through the trouble of putting together a band just for the purposes of recording your demo, you may want to try a demo service. For a fee, a demo service will produce your songs in their studio using their own singers and musicians. Many of these services advertise in music magazines, songwriting newsletters and bulletin boards at local music stores. If you decide to deal with a demo service, make sure you can hear samples of work they've done in the past. Many demo services are mail-order businesses—you send them either a rough tape of your song or the sheet music and they'll produce and record a demo within a month or two. Be sure you find a service that will let you have creative control over how your demo is to be produced, and make sure you tell them exactly how you want your song to sound. As with studios, shop around and find the demo service that best suits your needs and budget.

SAMPLE REPLY POSTCARD

I would like to hear:
□ "Name of Song"   □ "Name of Song"   □ "Name of Song"

I prefer:
□ cassette   □ DAT   □ CD   □ videocassette

With:
□ lyric sheet   □ lead sheet   □ either   □ both

□ I am not looking for material at this time, try me in _____ weeks/months.
□ I am not interested.

_____   _____
Name   Title

Submitting by mail

When submitting material to companies listed in this book:

☑ Read the listing carefully and submit *exactly* what a company asks for in the exact way it asks that it be submitted. It's always a good idea to call first, just in case a company has changed its submission policy.

☑ Listen to each demo before sending to make sure the quality is satisfactory.

☑ Enclose a brief, typed cover letter to introduce yourself. Indicate what songs you are sending and why you are sending them. If you're a songwriter pitching songs to a particular artist, state that in the letter. If you're an artist/songwriter looking for a recording deal, you should say so. Be specific.

☑ Include typed lyric sheets or lead sheets if requested. Make sure your name, address and phone number appear on each sheet.

☑ Neatly label each tape with your name, address and phone number along with the names of the songs in the sequence in which they appear on the tape.

☑ If the company returns material (many do not; be sure to read each listing carefully), include a SASE for the return. Your return envelope to countries other than your own should contain a self-addressed envelope (SAE) and International Reply Coupon (IRC), available at your local post office. Be sure the return envelope is large enough to accommodate your material, and include sufficient postage for the weight of the package.

☑ Wrap the package neatly and write (or type on a shipping label) the company's address and your return address so they are clearly visible. Your package is the first impression a company has of you and your songs, so neatness is important.

☑ Mail first class. Stamp or write "First Class Mail" on the package and on the SASE you enclose. Don't send by registered or certified mail unless it is specifically requested by the company.

☑ Keep records of the dates, songs and companies you submit to.

If you are writing to inquire about a company's needs or to request permission to submit (many companies ask you to do this first), your query letter should be typed, brief and pleasant. Explain the kind of material you have and ask for their needs and submission policy.

To expedite a reply, enclose a self-addressed, stamped postcard requesting the information you are seeking. Your typed questions (see the Sample Reply Postcard on the previous page) should be direct and easy to answer. Place the company's name and address in the upper left hand space on the front of the postcard so you'll know which company you queried. Keep a record of the queries you send for future reference.

Simultaneous submissions and holds. It's acceptable to submit your songs to more than one person at a time (this is called simultaneous submission). The exception to this is when a publisher, artist or other industry professional asks if he may put a song of yours "on hold." This means he intends to record it and doesn't want you to give the song to anyone else. Your song may be returned to you without ever having been recorded, even if it's been on hold for months. Or, it may be recorded but not used on a album. If either of these things happens, you're free to pitch your song to other people again. (You can, and should, protect yourself from having a song on hold indefinitely. Establish a deadline for the person who asks for the hold, e.g., "You can put my song on hold for [number of] months." Or modify the hold to specify that you will pitch the song to other people, but you will not sign a deal without allowing the person who has the song on hold to make you an offer.) When someone publishes your song and you sign a contract, you grant that publisher exclusive rights to your song and you may not pitch it to other publishers. You can, however, pitch it to any artists or producers interested in recording the song without publishing it themselves.

Following up. If a company doesn't respond within several weeks after you've sent your demo, don't despair. As long as your demo is in their hands, there is a chance someone is reviewing it. If after a reasonable amount of time you still haven't received word on your submission (check the reporting time each company states in its listing), follow up with a friendly letter or phone call. Many companies do not return submissions, so don't expect a company that states "Does not return material" to send your materials back to you.

Submitting in person

Planning a trip to one of the major music hubs will give you insight into how the music industry works. Whether you decide to visit New York, Nashville or Los Angeles, have specific goals in mind and set up appointments to make the most of your time there. It will be difficult to get in to see some industry professionals as many of them are extremely busy and may not feel meeting out-of-town writers is a high priority. Other people are more open to, and even encourage, face-to-face meetings. They may feel that if you take the time to travel to where they are and you're organized enough to schedule meetings beforehand, you're more professional than many aspiring songwriters who blindly submit inappropriate songs through the mail. (For listings of companies by state, see the Geographic Index at the back of the book.)

What to take. Take several cassette copies and lyric sheets of each of your songs. More than one of the companies you visit may ask that you leave a copy to review. There's also a good chance that the person you have an appointment with will have to cancel (expect that occasionally) but wants you to leave a copy of the songs so he can listen and contact you later. Never give someone the last or only copy of your material—if it is not returned to you, all the hard work and money that went into making that demo will be lost.

Where to network. Another good place to meet industry professionals face-to-face is at seminars such as the yearly South by Southwest Music and Media Conference in Austin, the National Academy of Songwriters' annual Songwriters Expo in Los Angeles, or the Nashville Songwriters Association's Spring Symposium, to name a few (see the Workshops & Conferences section on page 434 for further ideas). Many of these conferences feature demo listening sessions, where industry professionals listen to demos submitted by songwriters attending the seminars.

Dealing with rejection. Many good songs have been rejected simply because they weren't what the particular publisher or record company was looking for at the time, so don't take rejection personally. Realize that if a few people don't like your songs, it doesn't mean they're not good. However, if there seems to be a consensus about your work—for instance, the feel of a song isn't right or the lyrics need work—give the advice serious thought. Listen attentively to what the reviewers say and use their criticism constructively to improve your songs.

Quiz: Are You Professional?

OK, everybody! Take out your submission package and let's take a look. Hmm . . . very interesting. I think you're well on your way, but you should probably change a few things.

We asked record companies, music publishers and record producers, "What do songwriters do in correspondence with your company (by phone, mail or demo) that screams 'amateur'?" Take this quiz and find out how professional you appear to those on the receiving end of your submission. The following are common mistakes songwriters make all the time. They may seem petty, but, really, do you want to give someone an excuse not to listen to your demo? Check off the transgressions you have committed.

BY MAIL YOU SENT:

☐ anything handwritten (lyrics, cover letters, labels for cassettes). Today there is no excuse for handwritten materials. Take advantage of your local library's typewriters or businesses that charge by the hour to use a computer. And don't even think about using notebook paper.

☐ materials without a contact name *and* phone number. Put this information on *everything*.

☐ lyrics only. Music companies want music and words. See the If You Write Lyrics, But Not Music sidebar on page 11.

☐ insufficient return postage, an envelope too small to return materials, no SASE at all, or a "certified mail" package. If you want materials returned, don't expect the company to send it back on their dime with their envelope—give them what they need. Certified mail is unnecessary and annoying; first class will suffice.

☐ long-winded, over-hyped cover letters, or no cover letter at all. Companies don't need (or want) to hear your life story, how many instruments you play, how many songs you've written, how talented you are or how all your songs are sure-fire hits. Briefly explain why you are sending the songs (e.g., your desire to have them published) and let the songs speak for themselves. Double check your spelling too.

☐ over-packaged materials. Do not use paper towels, napkins, foil or a mountain of tape to package your submission. Make the investment in bubble wrap or padded envelopes.

☐ photos of your parents or children. As much as you love them, your family's pictures or letters of recommendation won't increase your chances of success (unless your family is employed by a major music company).

☐ songs in the style the company doesn't want. Do not "shotgun" your submissions. Read the listings carefully to see if they want your style of music.

YOU CALLED THE CONTACT PERSON:

☐ to check on the submission only a couple days after it was received. Read the listings to see how soon (or if) they report back on submissions. Call them only after that time has elapsed. If they are interested, they will find a way to contact you.

☐ excessively. It's important to be proactive, but check yourself. Make sure you have given them enough time to respond before you call again. Calling every week is inappropriate.

☐ armed with an angry or aggressive tone of voice. A bad attitude will get you nowhere.

WITH THE DEMO YOU PROVIDED:

☐ no lyric sheet. A typed sheet of lyrics for each song is required.

☐ poor vocals and instrumentation. Spending a little extra for professionals can make all the difference.

☐ a poor-quality cassette. The tape should be new and have a brand name.

☐ long intros. Don't waste time—get to the heart of the song.

☐ buried vocals. Those vocals should be out front and clear as a bell.

☐ recordings of sneezes or coughs. Yuck.

SCORING

If you checked 1-3: Congratulations! You're well within the professional parameters. Remedy the unprofessional deeds you're guilty of and send out more packages.

If you checked 4 or more: Whoa! Overhaul your package, let someone check it over, and then fire away with those impeccably professional submissions!

The Business of Songwriting

Familiarizing yourself with standard music industry practices will help you toward your goal of achieving and maintaining a successful songwriting career. The more you know, the less likely you'll be to make a mistake when dealing with contracts, agreements and the other legal and business elements that make up the *business* side of your songwriting career.

COPYRIGHT

Copyright protection is extended to your songs the instant they are put down in fixed form. This protection lasts for your lifetime (or the lifetime of the last surviving author, if you co-wrote the song) plus 70 years. When you prepare demos, place notification of copyright on all copies of your song—the lyric sheets, lead sheets and cassette labels. The notice is simply the word "copyright" or the symbol © followed by the year the song was created (or published) and your name: © 2000 by John L. Public.

Registering your copyright

For the best protection, you may want to consider registering your copyright with the Library of Congress. Although a song is copyrighted whether or not it is registered, registration establishes a public record of your copyright and could prove useful in any future litigation involving the song. Registration also entitles you to a potentially greater settlement in a copyright infringement suit.

To register your song, request government form PA from the Copyright Office. Call the 24-hour hotline at (202)707-9100 and leave your name and address on the recorder. Once you receive the PA form, you will be required to return it, along with a registration fee and a tape or lead sheet of your song, to the Register of Copyrights, Copyright Office, Library of Congress, Washington DC 20559. It may take as long as four months to receive your certificate of registration from the Copyright Office, but your songs are protected from the date of creation, and the date of registration will reflect the date you applied for registration. For additional information about registering your songs, call the Copyright Office's Public Information Office at (202)707-3000 or visit their website at http://lcweb.loc.gov/copyright.

> ### For More Information
> The Library of Congress's copyright website is your best source for current, complete information on the subject of copyright. Not only can you learn all you could possibly wish to know about intellectual property rights and U.S. copyright law (the section of the U.S. Code dealing with copyright is reprinted there in its entirety), but you can also download copyright forms directly from the site. The site also includes links to other copyright-related web pages, many of which will be of interest to songwriters, including ASCAP, BMI, SESAC, and the Harry Fox Agency. Check it out at **http://lcweb.loc.gov/copyright**.

Copyright infringement is rarer than most people think, but if you ever feel that one of your songs has been stolen—that someone has unlawfully infringed on your copyright—you must prove that you created the work. Copyright registration is the best proof of a date of creation. You *must* have your copyright registered in order to file a copyright infringement lawsuit. One way writers prove a work is original is to keep their rough drafts and revisions of songs, either on paper or on tape.

CONTRACTS

You will encounter several types of contracts as you deal with the business end of songwriting. You may sign a legal agreement between you and a co-writer establishing percentages of the writer's royalties each of you will receive, what you will do if a third party (e.g., a recording artist) wishes to change your song and receive credit as a co-writer, and other things. As long as the issues at stake are simple and co-writers respect each other and discuss their business philosophy in advance of writing a song, they can write up an agreement without the aid of a lawyer. In other situations— when a publisher, producer or record company wants to do business with you—you should always have the contract reviewed by a knowledgeable entertainment attorney.

Single song contracts

This is a common contract and is likely to be the first you will encounter in your songwriting career. A music publisher offers a single song contract when he wants to sign one or more of your songs but doesn't want to hire you as a staff writer. You assign your rights to a particular song to the publisher for an agreed-upon number of years (usually the life of the copyright).

Typical components. Every single song contract should contain this basic information: the publisher's name, the writer's name, the song's title, the date and the purpose of the agreement. The songwriter also declares that the song is an original work and he is the creator of the work. The contract must specify the royalties the songwriter will earn from various uses of the song, including performance, mechanical, print and synchronization royalties.

Splits and royalties. The songwriter should receive no less than 50% of the income his song generates. That means that whatever the song earns in royalties, the publisher and songwriter should split 50/50. The songwriter's half is called the "writer's share" and the publisher's half is called the "publisher's share." If there is more than one songwriter, the songwriters split the writer's share. Sometimes successful songwriters will bargain for a percentage of the publisher's share, negotiating what is in fact a co-publishing agreement. For a visual explanation of royalties, see the flow chart on page 13.

"Holds" and reversion clauses. Songwriters should also negotiate for a reversion clause. This calls for the rights to the song to revert to the songwriter if some provision of the contract is not met. The typical reversion clause covers the failure to secure a commercial release of a song within a specified period of time (usually one or two years). If nothing happens with the song, the rights will revert back to the songwriter, who can then give the song to a more active publisher if he so chooses. Some publishers will agree to this, figuring that if they don't get some action on the song in the first year, they're not likely to ever have much luck with it. Other publishers are reluctant to agree to this clause. They may invest a lot of time and money in a song, re-demoing it and pitching it to a number of artists; they may be actively looking for ways to exploit the song. If a producer puts a song on hold for a while and goes into a lengthy recording project, by the time the record company (or artist or producer) decides which songs to release as singles, a year can easily go by. That's why it's so important to have a good working relationship with your publisher. You need to trust that he has your best interests in mind and be flexible if the situation calls for it.

Additional clauses. Other issues a contract should address include whether or not an advance will be paid to the songwriter and how much it will be; when royalties will be paid (quarterly or semiannually); who will pay for demos—the publisher, songwriter or both; how lawsuits against copyright infringement will be handled, including the cost of such lawsuits; whether the publisher has the right to sell the song to another publisher without the songwriter's consent; and whether the publisher has the right to make changes in a song, or approve of changes written by someone else, without the songwriter's consent. In addition, the songwriter should have the right to audit the publisher's books if the songwriter deems it necessary and gives the publisher reasonable notice. (For more information on music publishers, see the Music Publishers section introduction on page 57.)

SGA's Popular Songwriter's Contract. While there is no such thing as a "standard" contract, The Songwriters Guild of America (SGA) has drawn up a Popular Songwriter's Contract which it believes to be the best minimum songwriter contract available. The Guild will send a copy of the contract at no charge to any interested songwriter upon request (send a self-addressed stamped envelope to SGA, 1500 Harbor Blvd., Weehawken NJ 07087-6732). SGA will also review free of charge any contract offered to its members, checking it for fairness and completeness. For a thorough discussion of the somewhat complicated subject of contracts, see these two books published by Writer's Digest Books: *The Craft and Business of Songwriting*, by John Braheny and *Music Publishing: A Songwriter's Guide*, by Randy Poe.

Ten Basic Points Your Contract Should Include

The following list, taken from a Songwriters Guild of America publication, enumerates the basic features of an acceptable songwriting contract:

1. **Work for Hire.** When you receive a contract covering just one composition, you should make sure the phrases "employment for hire" and "exclusive writer agreement" are not included. Also, there should be no options for future songs.
2. **Performing Rights Affiliation.** If you previously signed publishing contracts, you should be affiliated with either ASCAP, BMI or SESAC. All performance royalties must be received directly by you from your performing rights organization and this should be written into your contract.
3. **Reversion Clause.** The contract should include a provision that if the publisher does not secure a release of a commercial sound recording within a specified time (one year, two years, etc.), the contract can be terminated by you.
4. **Changes in the Composition.** If the contract includes a provision that the publisher can change the title, lyrics or music, this should be amended so that only with your consent can such changes be made.
5. **Royalty Provisions.** You should receive fifty percent (50%) of all publisher's income on all licenses issued. If the publisher prints and sells his own sheet music, your royalty should be ten percent (10%) of the wholesale selling price. The royalty should not be stated in the contract as a flat rate ($.05, $.07, etc.).
6. **Negotiable Deductions.** Ideally, demos and all other expenses of publication should be paid 100% by the publisher. The only allowable fee is for the Harry Fox Agency collection fee, whereby the writer pays one half of the amount charged to the publisher for mechanical rights. The current rate charged by the Harry Fox Agency is 7.1 cents per cut for songs under 5 minutes; and 1.35 cents per minute for songs over 5 minutes.
7. **Royalty Statements and Audit Provision.** Once the song is recorded, you are entitled to receive royalty statements at least once every six months. In addition, an audit provision with no time restriction should be included in every contract.
8. **Writer's Credit.** The publisher should make sure that you receive proper credit on all uses of the composition.
9. **Arbitration.** In order to avoid large legal fees in case of a dispute with your publisher, the contract should include an arbitration clause.
10. **Future Uses.** Any use not specifically covered by the contract should be retained by the writer to be negotiated as it comes up.

THE RIP-OFFS

As in any business, the music industry has its share of dishonest, greedy people who try to unfairly exploit the talents and aspirations of others. Most of them use similar methods of attack that you can learn to identify and avoid. "Song sharks," as they're called, prey on beginners—those writers who are unfamiliar with ethical industry standards. Song sharks will take any songs—quality doesn't count. They're not concerned with future royalties, since they get their money upfront from songwriters who think they're getting a great deal.

Here are some guidelines to help you recognize these "song sharks":

- **Never pay to have your music "reviewed"** by a company that may be interested in publishing, producing or recording it. Reputable companies review material free of charge.
- **Never pay to have your songs published**. A reputable company interested in your songs assumes the responsibility and cost of promoting them, in hopes of realizing a profit once the songs are recorded and released.
- **Avoid paying a fee to have a publisher make a demo of your songs**. Some publishers may take demo expenses out of your future royalties, but you should reconsider paying upfront for demo costs for a song that is signed to a publisher. See the sidebar Publishers That Charge on the next page for more information.
- **No record company should ask you to make or pay for a demo**. Their job is to make records and decide which artists to sign *after* listening to demo submissions.
- **Never pay to have your lyrics or poems set to music**. "Music mills"—for a price—may use the same melody for hundreds of lyrics and poems, whether it sounds good or not. Publishers recognize one of these melodies as soon as they hear it (see the sidebar If You Write Lyrics, But Not Music on page 11.)
- **Avoid CD compilation deals where a record company asks you to pay a fee** to be included on a CD to be sent to radio stations, producers, etc. It's primarily a money-maker for the company involved, and radio station programmers and other industry professionals just don't listen to these things to find new artists.
- **Read all contracts carefully before signing** and don't sign any contract you're unsure about or that you don't fully understand. It is well worth paying an attorney for the time it takes him to review a contract if you can avoid a bad situation that may cost you thousands of dollars in potential income.
- **Don't pay a company to pair you with a collaborator**. A better way is to contact songwriting organizations that offer collaboration services to their members.
- **Don't sell your songs outright**. It's unethical for anyone to offer such a proposition.
- **If you are asked by a record company or other music-industry company to pay expenses upfront, be careful**. A record producer may charge upfront to produce your record, or a small indie label may ask you to pay recording costs. Each situation is different, and it's up to you to decide whether or not it will be beneficial. Talk to other artists who have signed similar contracts before signing one yourself. Research the company and its track record by finding out what types of product they have released, and what kind of distribution they have. Visit their website on the Internet, if they have one. Beware of any company that won't let you know what it has done in the past. If it has had successes and good working relationships with other writers and artists, it should be happy to brag about them.
- **Before participating in a songwriting contest, read the rules carefully**. Be sure that what you're giving up in the way of entry fees, etc., is not greater than what you stand to gain by winning the contest. See the Contests & Awards section introduction on page 395 for more advice on this.
- **Verify any situation about an individual or company if you have any doubts at all**. Contact the performing rights society with which it is affiliated. Check with the Better

Business Bureau in the town where it is located or the state's attorney general's office. Contact professional organizations you're a member of and inquire about the reputation of the company.

Publishers That Charge

Songwriter's Market feels if a publisher truly believes in you and your music, they will invest in a professional demo. This book only lists publishers that do not charge for this service. If you have found a publisher through this book that charges for demo services, write to the editor at: *Songwriter's Market*, 1507 Dana Ave., Cincinnati OH 45207.

There are smaller publishing companies with demo services as part of their organization. They may request a professional demo and give you the option of using their services or those of an outside company. This doesn't necessarily mean the publishing company is ripping you off. Use your best judgement and know there are many other publishing companies that will not charge for this service.

RECORD KEEPING

As your songwriting career continues to grow, you should keep a ledger or notebook containing all financial transactions relating to your songwriting. It should include a list of income from royalty checks as well as expenses incurred as a result of your songwriting business: cost of tapes, demo sessions, office supplies, postage, traveling expenses, dues to organizations, class and workshop fees and any publications you purchase pertaining to songwriting. It's also advisable to open a checking account exclusively for your songwriting activities, not only to make record keeping easier, but to establish your identity as a business for tax purposes.

Any royalties you receive will not reflect taxes or any other mandatory deductions. It is your responsibility to keep track of income and file the appropriate tax forms. Contact the IRS or an accountant who serves music industry clients for specific information.

INTERNATIONAL MARKETS

Everyone talks about the world getting smaller, and it's true. Modern communication technology has brought us to the point at which information can be transmitted around the globe instantly. No business has enjoyed the fruits of this progress more than the music industry. American music is heard in virtually every country in the world, and having a hit song in other countries as well as in the United States can greatly increase a songwriter's royalty earnings.

While these listings may be a bit more challenging to deal with than domestic companies, they offer additional avenues for songwriters looking for places to place their songs. To find international listings, see the Geographical Index at the back of the book. You might also flip through the pages and look for listings preceded by ⊕ which indicates an international market.

Using the Phone to Get a Solicited Submission

BY JOHN BRAHENY

In a business where people's time is at a premium and there are thousands of songwriters out there looking for a share of it, it becomes very important for A&R people and publishers to develop a way to screen which will allow maximum results for a minimum of time spent. It's sometimes difficult for new writers to understand that listening to new songs is not a publisher's main job. His most important job is to make money by exploiting the songs he has already published, especially the songs that are written by staff writers paid by advances. All publishers would agree that building their catalogs by signing new songs and writers is very important, but the priority given to that function differs from company to company and from week to week. A publishing executive may simply make the decision that "We won't accept any unsolicited tapes," or "We're not looking for any new songs at this time."

WHY A "NO UNSOLICITED SUBMISSIONS" POLICY?

There are many reasons for this decision. As an example, one major company went through a **change in management and personnel**. The new president brought in a team of people he'd worked with in the past and fired all but two songpluggers. That meant the new staff, with the help of the remaining original staff, was faced with the monumental task of familiarizing themselves with thousands of songs in the current catalog. Until they assessed that catalog there was really no point in spending valuable time looking for new songs.

A company also faces **legal jeopardy** when opening and listening to unsolicited tapes. The attorneys at many publishing and record companies advise representatives not to open them. Lawsuits frequently occur when a song is a hit and someone says, "I sent you a tape two years ago that had the same line, title, idea. I think you stole it from me." Since one of the major proofs needed for plagiarism is access to the song in question, if the plaintiff can prove it was in the publisher's possession at the right time, it can give a company attorney nightmares. Some publishers aren't too frightened by that prospect, but it remains a common excuse for not accepting unsolicited tapes.

Publishers, producers and A&R departments with continuous "open door" policies are few and far between. They usually hire people specifically to screen material and if the screener feels it's good, it's passed on to other ears. Other companies are small operations in which there are a limited number of person-hours available and most must be spent seeing producers, going to recording sessions, and performing other publishing duties, leaving **little time for screening**. Other publishing companies may be merely "holding companies" for a writer/artist's own catalog and don't accept demo submissions because they're genuinely **not interested in shopping other writers' songs**.

JOHN BRAHENY *has been a musician, performer, songwriter, recording artist, film composer, commercial jingle producer, educator, author and journalist. He conducts seminars on the music business throughout the U.S. Excerpted from* The Craft & Business of Songwriting © *1995 by John Braheny. Used with permission of Writer's Digest Books, a division of F&W Publications, Inc.*

THE SCREENING PROCESS

Regardless of the "we're not listening" policies and the reasons behind them, most publishers and A&R people still do listen to new songs, but very selectively. They want to weed out the writers who haven't learned anything about how the business works, or the hobbyists with two or three songs taking a quick shot at it, and then retreating. The pros size up a writer, his or her attitude and presentation, from the first contact and then decide whether to spend time listening or not. They know that even given all a writer's positive attributes, the odds are still minimal that they'll find something they can publish or a writer with genius-level raw talent they'd like to develop. That's why it's important to them to set up a tough screening process.

THE WRONG WAY

On the front lines of the screening process are receptionists, secretaries and assistants. Unless you have the name of a specific person at the company, your phone call won't get past that point. Even if you do have a name, you'll be referred to that person's secretary. She will say something like, "May I tell her what this is about?" or "He's not in right now. May I help you?" The worst thing you can say is, "Sorry, you can't help. I need to talk to the main man." That person's job is to save the main man's (or woman's) time. How you present yourself to a secretary or receptionist may determine whether or not your tape gets heard.

Here's a typical scenario:

Writer: Hi, I'm a songwriter and I've got a hit for Stevie Wonder and another one that would be great for Billy Joel. Actually, I've written over 20 songs. Could somebody there listen to them?

Receptionist: Could you please drop off a tape? [You'd be very lucky to get this request.]

Writer: No, I won't leave a tape—how do I know you won't steal my songs?

Receptionist: Who referred you to us?

Writer: I got your name out of the phone book. Could you connect me to the man in charge?

What do you think are the odds that the caller will get through? I'd say slim. An important part of a secretary's (and often a receptionist's) job is to screen out this type of call from songwriters. If they recognize your name or you've been referred by someone whose name they know and whose reputation they respect, your chances of getting through the door are much better. In other cases, it's pretty much up to their discretion who to accept tapes from or whose call to put through to their bosses. Consequently, the first encounter you have with the front desk is vital. If you present yourself as a rank amateur, they'll assume your writing is just as amateur and that their chances of finding a great song from you are zilch.

Every secretary or receptionist has his own criteria for figuring the odds in favor of the boss. Let's look at the call again. Only an amateur who has done no research doesn't know that Stevie Wonder and Billy Joel don't do outside songs. If you've written only 20 songs, you're obviously a beginner. You can't be on the scene long and not know you're going to have to leave tapes. Get them protected first so you won't have to worry about songs being stolen. You also haven't done your research if you don't have the name of a person at the company and have to resort to the phone book for the company name. If you don't know the name of "the man in charge" you just might be insulting the woman in charge. Do your homework.

THE RIGHT WAY

I asked the receptionist at a major publishing company how she screens unsolicited calls. She said she tells writers that the company is not listening to tapes now. If they ask when the company *will* be listening (and they seldom ask), she tells them to call back in a month. If she does get a call back from that writer, she accepts his or her tape. It shows her that writer is persistent, professional and organized enough to follow up the call.

I've gained a lot of insight into this process by going from being a struggling songwriter to the other side of the desk as a screener. It's taught me some important lessons that have been pretty much corroborated by my "other side of the desk" peers.

We always respect persistence, even though we may at times find it annoying and guilt-provoking. We know that no matter how talented you are, you need persistence to succeed. The hardest part of being persistent is continuing to be pleasant about it and not allowing yourself to become bitter or desperate from the rejection you'll experience. It turns people off when they sense that desperation in you.

A secretary I talked with said, "It's a real turn-off to have someone spill their guts out to me that this is their last chance or they need to pay their doctor bills or whatever. I don't want to subject my boss to that either. It's very unprofessional."

There's also a thin line between confidence and arrogance. We like to feel that you believe in yourself and are confident about your talent and abilities even though you're open to criticism and direction. If you come off arrogantly with the attitude, "I'm God's gift to the music world and if you can't recognize it, you're a Neanderthal," it will be difficult for you to find people to work with you.

"The squeaky wheel gets the grease" is a cliché that remains true. If someone calls me looking for a singer for a project "right now," I have no time to research and get to my lists, and you're a good singer I know who I just talked to a couple days ago, your name will jump out of my mouth. If I haven't heard from you in a year, it won't. The lesson here is never to assume that people will remember you and what you're doing if you don't periodically remind them.

Always be pleasant to the "gatekeepers." No matter how many times you call to talk to the boss and she won't return your call (she may have 50 calls to return that day and 49 of them are priorities) be polite, never abusive nor arrogant unless you want to be introduced to the boss as "that abusive, arrogant @#*!" Next year the person you abused may be the boss! Enlist his aid. Tell him your situation. Ask if *he* can help. Ask *him* to listen to your tape. He'll know what his boss likes or doesn't like. Empower assistants, secretaries and receptionists to help you by assuming they can.

Always follow up. Two weeks is an adequate amount of time to follow up once you know someone has your tape. That doesn't necessarily mean he should have listened to it in that time. He may have hundreds of tapes to hear, and listening to them is not a major part of his job in most cases. When you call, ask how soon you should call back. Don't get upset and demand your tape back. He'll be only too glad to get rid of it. Leaving a tape somewhere indefinitely means, at worst, you lose the cost of the tape. At best, a producer or publisher goes through a box of tapes in a couple of years, finds your tape, and calls you. Don't think it hasn't happened.

Say "thank you." If someone (a boss *or* gatekeeper) has given you his time, advice or help in any way, take the time to drop him a "thank you" card. It's another positive way to make contact, to acknowledge the value of his contribution, and to let him know that you're sensitive, caring, organized and taking care of business. If you knew how seldom it's done, you'd realize what an impact it has.

So You Got a Solicited Submission— Now What?

BY SCOTT MATHEWS

Congratulations! You made the calls and contacted the right people, and you've been given the green light to send your submission. Do you . . .

A) Start spending! You're headed straight to the top. Surely the industry professionals you have submitted your genius creations to will rise to the occasion and salute you with multitudes of fortune and fame.

B) Bury your head in the sand and realize there is no way on earth anyone in their right mind would ever care about the work of an unknown beginner. Therefore, it is wise to not follow your heart or attempt to get anywhere with it.

C) Congratulate yourself (ever so briefly) on clearing what may be the first of many hurdles in your musical career and carefully prepare for the opportunity presently at hand.

Photo by Jay Blakesberg

Scott Mathews

Answer: If you have chosen A or B you are not alone. I have known and worked with folks of similar bravado and fears. Who am I kidding? I have had tinges of both these demon thoughts my own bad self! However, if you have chosen C to better represent your outlook, I see you as having a few more ducks in a row.

Answer C speaks of preparing for the opportunity. And what exactly is that preparation? Call it Preparation H.Y.: Help Yourself. If you don't, who will? The following are lessons I have learned, and I encourage anyone faced with what feels like an uphill battle to use them to be heard far above the maddening crowd.

THE SHOT YOU'VE GOT

The moment you have been waiting for has finally come. You've got that invitation to bring forward the work that will usher you into your new life (and lifestyle) as a legitimate artist. You see it as your red carpet. Well, it very well might be, but you'd better make sure you check your fly one more time before you walk the walk. The first impression you make is going to be the one that sticks. Or stinks.

For people soliciting songs for publishing consideration, good (but simple) demo recordings showcasing the material in the style it is meant to be covered usually does the trick. Don't forget that lyric sheet and don't bury the vocal.

Now, for those seeking recording contracts, you're not gonna get off so easily. There was a time, not too many years back, when record companies were known to sign some artists on the basis of potential. Ladies and gentlemen, I am here to tell you those days are done. Potential

---

*It was recently brought to **SCOTT MATHEWS**'s attention that he is the only person to have a Platinum award from Barbra Streisand hanging next to a Gold award from John Lee Hooker, to which he grinned and replied, "Musically speaking, schizophrenic behavior can have its rewards!" See Scott's listing in the Record Producers section on page 247.*

has left the building. It is becoming common practice for today's artists to develop themselves into a force to be dealt with if there are to be any real expectations of getting signed. So, the days of doing rough demo recordings and sending them to labels are (for good or bad) over. I see most artists getting deals by taking the bull by the horns and providing a full-on, finished recording that can compete with what is currently selling or being played on the radio. Let's be honest, the first listening is the only listening a record company is going to give you unless you blow them away with that first shot.

So, to that end, aspiring artists need to either A) align themselves with a reputable producer who can understand and expand the artists' vision in the studio; or B) surround themselves with the right studio, musicians, etc. to help make a record to shop. (Option B is only viable if the artist is intent on self-producing and has the studio savvy to pull it off.)

No demo should be accompanied by disclaimers. Be prepared to put together a budget to fund this. How much you will need depends on many factors. If you can get to a producer with credits that appeal to you, is in demand and in the loop with hot-rod record company muckety-mucks, that might be a bigger price tag than doing it alone. Who knows? It might not be. I use a formula that allows me to produce new unsigned artists I believe in, get the record made and into the ears of A&R people while everyone keeps a fair piece of the pie. It can be done. This makes for good, long-term relations between artists and producers. Do your own investigating and (if necessary) fundraising—these are the costs of doing business.

Whatever you can do to get the best product made, do it. It might be more important than your hair. But, please beware of some "spec deals" that allow for free services at the moment but demand unreasonably large pieces on the back end. There are countless horror stories from bitter artists not aware of the downside. They signed agreements early on that ended up costing them valuable publishing and points on their records because "it sounded like a great deal at the time." Find an attorney who will help make sure the investment you put in now will earn you rightful profits if and when things happen.

SO DO YOU LOVE ME, OR WHAT?

I have become a big fan of e-mail as the primary source of corresponding with submissions. My assistant or myself can get back to artists quicker and easier by e-mail than snail mail or phone calls. There are not enough hours in the day for some executives to personally get back to everyone who sends in product. Why not make it easy on them? Include in your package a handy little self-addressed, stamped postcard with multiple choice responses available. Try something like:

A) Sorry, we are not at all interested in your so-called "music."

B) We don't feel you are ready yet, but you are welcome to submit future works (if, of course, it gets better).

C) Let's talk turkey, babe.

Word your card any way you like. The purpose is to make possible quick and simple responses that might otherwise not be forthcoming.

THICK SKIN

No matter how wonderful the package you send out happens to be, get yourself prepared for the inevitable rejections. I know, this is one of those easier-said-than-done kind of concepts, but you can do it and there is no time like the present to start working on it. Count on there being a host of useless bottom feeders with nothing to offer you but shattered dreams. That's a given. Now it's up to how you choose to handle it. I say treat them like water off a duck. Welcome those who offer constructive criticism. Check out their ideas. Who knows? They might be right. If they don't offer anything but a cold hard pass, they can still be character builders as opposed to dream stealers. Reject rejection. Just remember all it takes is one green light to get going and turn everything around. One person in a position to give a positive take on what you're doing can mean all the difference. One person! Go find him.

The truth is, everyone who has inspired you with their incredible music careers has also been passed on by "golden-eared industry pros" along the way. More than likely, several passed. If these artists had made the foolish decision to give up at the sign of the first rejection, the charts would be empty and those awards shows would be a whole lot shorter. (Actually, I often think the charts are a bit empty and that those award shows are much too long, but that's another story!) I defy you to show me one situation that was not passed on by someone else before being picked up by a major label. Did I hear you say, "Elvis?" OK, you win, but Sun Records wasn't *technically* a major label. The point is, the odds are kind of nutty but who cares? So are we!

I have to admit (through my tears) that I too have passed on some artists who have gone on to be gigantic (including one who stole my last name . . . you figure it out). All I can tell you is it hurts as much to pass on something that becomes huge as it does to be passed on. The trick for artists is having to be way sensitive to expose our heartfelt emotions and turn them into songs and then tough as nails when we put it out there for the masses to use and abuse. In my humble opinion, that's what you're going to be paid for once things happen for you. You thought it was just make music and cash checks? Oh no, it's make music, get humiliated, turn the other cheek, then (maybe) you get to cash the checks.

SUPPORT SYSTEMS

No matter what path you choose, this biz can be a hard road. Even harder if you are in it all alone. There are obviously things (such as mailing lists, setting up your web page, etc.) you might be able to do yourself. But for the time-consuming business necessary for your career to amount to anything, you need to gather a support team. They are out there.

I already mentioned attorneys. Promise me you'll get one before you sign anything regarding legal matters. You can audition them the same way you would musicians or a babysitter (Why would I possibly list those two together? Hmm . . .). Some will work on a percentage, others hourly. Shop around. Also important are (good) managers. Most labels prefer not to speak directly to the artists when things get to the point of a possible deal. I highly recommend finding someone trustworthy who believes in you to effectively guide the course with you. As a producer, I have a management team that is of paramount importance. I am in the music business. They are in the office doing business while I am in the studio doing music. I like that.

However, there is no telling how much damage the wrong person can do on your behalf. It can take years (if ever) to climb out of the deep dark holes some bad managers have caused their artists. So know the business side of the music industry and be cautious when entering into your agreements. But by all means be open to helping hands.

COUNTING CHICKENS

So far, we have mentioned ducks, turkeys and now chickens. Why this fowl metaphor for our lovely industry? I have absolutely no clue, but I do know there are tendencies to count blessings (if not birds) a wee bit early once we get a piece of good news regarding developments in our career. Why not get excited? We work very hard to make it happen and when it appears to be happening, we should be allowed to get worked up! True enough, but some people immediately turn into the "cock of the walk" (sorry, I can't stop) and make it impossible to work with them once they have been validated by the system to get started. I recently tried producing a band whose million-dollar advance was so mighty they could barely be bothered to show up to the studio and make their major label debut! Why sweat it? In their opinion (and pocketbooks) they were already stars. I guess getting the big deal was the goal, not taking the opportunity to make a great record and establishing themselves a real career in music. Wow, talk about your priorities.

Also, please be advised that a whole lot of what we hear and about half of what we see in this business is not to be believed. There are more than a few "excitable" folks who will lead you to believe you are the greatest thing since sliced bread, only to reveal later that you are in fact toast. Take everything with that obligatory grain of salt, keep your head and wits about you and remember who your friends are.

Well my dear *Songwriter's Market* future mega-stars, I do wish you all incredible careers in whatever area of the music business you pursue. I'm here to tell you it can be very good to you as it continues to be to me. I wake up every morning asking myself, "Uh oh, is today the day I'll have to get a real job?" And with every day I keep getting away with this I truly feel blessed. The records keep selling and I am more psyched than ever to keep making them.

So, now it's your turn. Take it! Go get that solicited submission, sail it off and let your career fly like an . . . you get the idea.

How to Make Your Submission Stand Out

BY MIKE PO

A common misconception is that, in order for a demo package to stand out, it must be the brightest, loudest, most attention-grabbing package of them all. In reality, this couldn't be further from the truth. Amidst a desk full of odd-shaped packages, fluorescent-colored paper and obnoxiously screaming press releases, what really shines is a demo submission presented in a concise, professional manner—one that says, "take me seriously."

The A&R rep, booking agent or radio programmer on the other end of your demo package is, above all, *busy*. With that in mind, then, the most successful way to make a first impression is to show you have done your homework, followed submission guidelines, and can present a complete package that needs no apologies—in short, to showcase your professionalism, as well as your musical talent!

Mike Po

MINIMIZE THE HYPE

Consider this: Yes, without question, the general public responds to hype, cheap gimmicks, fads, hucksterism and relentless hyperbole. For most performers, these are the key components of a successful rise to stardom (musical talent notwithstanding). Unfortunately, though, at this level the general public isn't your target audience—bored, jaded, "seen-it-all" music business professionals are. This is not to say everyone who receives your promo package is entirely immune to hype tactics. But, in addition to the countless unsolicited packages received from complete unknowns, nearly everyone at every level of the music business is constantly bombarded with press releases, gimmicks, the latest "hottest new act of the year," all crafted by some of the most clever advertising execs in the country.

This sort of hype is unstoppable, unbeatable and, frankly, numbing. You can gauge for yourself. Just consider how often you listen to glowing reviews and the like in magazines, on television and over the Internet. Now, can you put yourself in the position of someone who is immersed in this hype machine for a living, like a local club promoter, a disc jockey, an A&R rep for a big label? Face it, it's extremely difficult to compete with the big-label, big-money promotional machine!

More importantly, you've got to redefine your conception of who your target audience is. Music industry professionals are now prospective *business partners*, not potential new *fans*. This is, indeed, the music *business*, and that's exactly how it needs to be approached. You're not trying to sell tickets or T-shirts to your industry contacts; you are asking them to enter into a high-risk financial arrangement with you.

MIKE PO, *as president and A&R of Limited Potential Records, discovered acts such as Smashing Pumpkins, Brainiac and Catherine. He is a regular columnist for www.getsigned.com and is the author of his self-published book,* The Press Kit—A Rock Band's Survival Guide.

Just forget that concept of *hype* for a moment. Yes, like every other aspect of your career, there is plenty of room in your promotional presentation for sheer, unadulterated hype. For the most part, however, bear in mind that at this stage of your professional life, just getting out the raw *information* is absolutely crucial. This might be an entirely new way of thinking, compared to the "must be on stage all the time, must be a master showman" mentality, but: It's time to start thinking of yourself as more of a newscaster than a talk-show host.

COVER THE BASICS

The typical demo submission is centered around the *press kit*—a package of promotional materials generally accompanying a review copy of an album release or demo tape. Different versions of the press kit include materials suited for different recipients, as in music columnists, promoters, radio programmers or A&R reps. A typical press kit for a recording artist is composed of several basic components:

- artist biography
- fact sheet
- promotional photo
- reprints of press "clippings"

In addition, it's not unusual to include a song list, lyric sheet, gig sheet and reports of radio airplay and chart positions. These elements are almost always accompanied by a cassette or CD "demo," packaged in an outer folder or binder, along with a traditional, personalized cover letter.

The press kit

The goal of the press kit is twofold: The factual information within is sufficient for journalists to base an article or review upon, while the editorial content of the artist's biography leaves enough room for a certain element of *hype*. Above all else, the end result of the press kit is to generate interest for the artist. The press kit serves as the "mouthpiece," the salesman pitching the performer.

You can consider a press kit, then, to be either of two things: A) a promo package full of existing press clippings, or B) a promo package to be used by the press to produce clippings. For a larger, national act, a press kit contains reprints of interviews, reviews and articles—a representation of the overall persona of the performer. In this case, the purpose is more likely to promote a new release, a new tour, or perhaps put a new spin on the artist's public image— maybe even an attempt to completely overhaul an image.

For the as-yet-undiscovered act, though, the press kit is a much different animal. Rather than compiling review and interview clippings, its mission is to *generate* some of these write-ups. The press kit for a start-up act is also the promotional device used to get the first live bookings, radio play, reviews, and "shop" for the goal of every hungry artist: that huge record deal.

The fact sheet

This most useful element of the kit is also the easiest to compose. Just what the name implies, the fact sheet contains no hyperbole, no salesmanship and no filler. It's a concise overview of the factual information of who and what is involved. For a band or group project, it's the place to list individual members' names, instruments played and musical backgrounds (involvements in previous bands, side projects, awards, etc.). For solo artists, perhaps the focus will be on the specifics of a recent release or recording session. There are no hard and fast rules on what exactly should be in a fact sheet, but in general, it should at least contain:

- artist's hometown
- members' names and instruments played
- album release information
- touring, recent dates, upcoming shows of note

- management and record label (indie or otherwise) contact information
- producer and recording studios involved

The fact sheet can contain just about any relevant information you would like, as long as it is, indeed, *fact*. "We totally rocked every audience we played for last year" may or may not be entirely factual. However, "The band recently completed a 22-date Midwest college tour, supporting . . ." is verifiable information.

Why is the fact sheet so important? Basically, because numbers don't lie. If your act has been receiving consistent regional airplay, for example, it might serve you well to show the stations and chart positions, almost in spreadsheet format. The same rule applies to live performances. Show the attendance figures and capacities of venues played, rather than employing hype-filled statements such as "we consistently sell out shows" or "we're HUGE on the radio!" Music industry folks are surrounded by numbers, and pay attention to them: sales figures, attendance figures, chart positions, etc. If you can chart the progress of your act from playing to crowds of 50, all the way up to playing to crowds of 500, then you're able to show tangible proof of your act's audience appeal.

TOO MUCH? TOO LITTLE?

Generally, it's wise to avoid the temptation to cram absolutely everything relating to your act into the first promotional mailing. Attempts to "pad" the press kit with multiple pages of press clippings are usually taken as an amateur mistake, particularly if the enclosed clippings are repetitive or contain multiple mentions from the same publication. By and large, a well-written kit need not be more than several pages in length—particularly in the case of an unsolicited mailing. The old show biz adage of "leave 'em wanting more" is somewhat appropriate. While you don't want to leave out any of the vital information, the goal isn't to overwhelm with every imaginable detail. Quality, and not quantity, is the approach that will net the best results.

THE GIMMICK

Promotional gimmicks are another touchy issue. Again, most recipients of these tactics have seen it all, and aren't likely to be impressed. Worse than that, an ill-planned gimmick can work against you, by evidencing a desperation to be noticed, as opposed to letting the music speak for itself. From odd-shaped boxes, to glitter-covered cassette cases, to any sort of non-standard promotional item, there is no evidence gimmicks help get your music heard. In fact, if anything, these items are a hindrance, cluttering desks and making a mess, and more likely to be thrown away to make space.

SUBMISSION QUALITY

Above all else—above *anything* else—from the solo singer/songwriter to the full performing group, the single most important thing to consider in the promotional mailing is *"do I need to make apologies for any of this material?"* Ask yourself:

- Is the cassette or CD of the best quality?
- Is all of the necessary contact information clearly visible on EVERY element of the mailing (all pages of the press kit, the cassette or CD itself, the folder it's packaged in)?
- Are there any handwritten elements, or is everything clearly typewritten or laser printed?
- Have posted submission guidelines been followed *exactly*?
- Is the photo clean and sharp?
- Would you have any reservations about the material, from the performance, to the recording, if this was your only chance at being reviewed by a top A&R exec?

THE ALL-IMPORTANT CONTACT INFO

Lastly, if you are to read this, file it away, ignore it, forget it—do anything, but learn from it only this one tip: Put your contact info on EVERYTHING. Worse even than being summarily rejected, imagine if your band missed out on a prime opportunity if for no other reason than a promoter couldn't figure out how to call you! It can, and does, happen. Tapes and CDs are quickly separated from their packing in a messy, busy office, demos are often previewed in the car, and club promoters leave a stack of demos next to the tape deck on the mixing board. When your demo really does get its 15-second shot at glory, you had better hope that whoever is "discovering" it will know whom to call! The same principle applies to your press kit, in that you shouldn't assume your cover letter will stay attached, or even that all your pages will stay stapled together.

Follow these guidelines. Make your submission concise, fact-filled and keep the hype to a minimum. Prove you've taken a professional approach to your career, and your demo submission truly will stand out from the rest.

Is This the Right Company for Me?

BY DON GRIERSON

Don Grierson

The absolute ideal in asking the above question would be for you to have created such responsive music and an identifiable image that a multitude of record labels or publishers would be aware, excited and on the phone demanding you sign a deal immediately. Ideal, but not often the case, unfortunately!

THE "PERFECT" DEAL

Without question, the *perfect* record or publishing company does not exist. Sometimes, these deals are determined by relationships managers or attorneys have with label executives, connections which obviously can be valuable. But there are certain relevant criteria that should become part of any serious, decision-making process to find the "right" company for you. These include looking for a company that has a proven record for responding to the needs of its artists and writers, fostering innovation, planning wisely and following through with those plans to deliver results. It also means finding the company that will provide the most supportive "creative family" for you. Although many artists and writers may never have the luxury of making such choices, I hope you will pursue your dream no matter what. And when you are one of the lucky ones who must decide which dotted line to entrust your dream to, I hope you remember the following considerations.

ARTISTS & RECORD DEALS

Once a "buzz"—i.e., hype, media attention—has been created (various ways and means of getting to this point have been explored in previous editions of *Songwriter's Market*) and there are potential choices available to the artist, numerous questions need to be addressed and "red flags" to be watched out for.

Investigate the company track record

Let's assume that you as an artist are secure in your musical vision and have several labels interested in you. The first challenge is identifying the companies that, from known history, are most likely to best relate to your type of music and have a greater understanding of promoting, marketing and selling that creativity. Also crucial is evaluating the style and image of the label:

☑ Are they known to be a "big checkbook" company that might agree to a hefty contract but then lets the act end up just one of many names on a busy release schedule?

☑ Or, is the label more boutique in style and roster size with a reputation for selectivity and development of talent?

DON GRIERSON *has headed the A&R departments of Epic Records, Capitol Records and EMI-America Records. He is directly responsible for signing some of the world's most noted artists including Céline Dion, Kate Bush, Joe Cocker and George Clinton.*

Give serious consideration to the history of each label, whether they have, or don't have, proven successes in working with and maximizing talent similar to yours. Some labels have proven strengths with certain categories of music and not with others, even though they may have artists signed in several different genres. Arista Records, for example, has always been extremely successful with pop and R&B music but hasn't had the same level of success with rock. Warner Bros. Records has always been a label respected for being artist friendly with a long history of unique, self-defining talent, but lacks the same results with R&B. Research the style, strengths, history and even staff stability and reputation of any label showing interest in signing a deal.

Learn the position of your company contact

Is your initial connection to the label a junior A&R staff member or a senior A&R executive? The junior A&R person might be the daily go-to in-house champion and excitement trigger. However, the senior executive is more likely to be involved in the planning process for a new release and is included in the decision-making department meetings. In turn she is in a stronger position to speak on your behalf and help define the numerous, crucial commitments made.

Evaluate staff enthusiasm

I have, unfortunately, seen situations where artists have been lost in the shuffle after:

☑ being signed for political or other non-A&R reasons;

☑ not communicating or creating a "working" relationship with appropriate staff members; or

☑ lacking that daily in-house champion.

A key objective is having as many department heads as possible be knowledgeable about you and your music. The more excitement created within the company the better! It is not at all beneficial to sign with a label and be scheduled for release without the decision makers knowing and understanding your personality and vision. If these key decision makers at the label don't show legitimate interest in spending real time, or have to be pushed to do so, then perhaps this is not the company to do business with.

Meet with the creative departments

Ask questions of staff members of all the creative departments.

☑ How do they perceive the general imaging of your act and the type of approach they might take to establish you in the marketplace?

☑ What are their marketing philosophies? Get a feel for their "flair" and desire to bring innovation to their campaigns.

☑ Ask about their approach to video usage and their knowledge and exploitation via the ever-growing Internet.

Confer with the sales and press departments

Meet with the national sales staff. Analyze how they deal with the retail community and especially their understanding, and ability, to address nontraditional sales and distribution (e.g., a tie-in with a nontypical retail chain like The Gap or McDonald's). Again, see if they are idea-oriented people who consistently attempt to find new ways to reach potential customers. The same applies to the press department:

☑ How connected are they to key influential journalists?

☑ What kind of thinking goes into their planning of press campaigns if there is no unique story "hook" (which frequently happens)?

☑ Does it appear the staff involved has the time to personalize a campaign for each artist they are responsible for?

☑ Do they hire independent people to augment current staff?

I have seen the press folk definitely unable to spend necessary time working an artist, usually due to overload, but won't or can't outsource for help unless the artist pays for it.

Meet with the promotion department

Promotion is perhaps the most important segment of the company team, and also the most difficult to relate to. Promotion people usually concentrate on radio exposure and often lead the company on whether a record "has it" or not. I have never accepted the attitude that if a record doesn't make it at radio then all is lost. This is, unfortunately, often the case. A *good* record company will fight for radio exposure but will also strive to find other ways to connect to an audience. Try as best you can to relate with the promotion department but know they generally live and die by what radio tells them. There can be much more to the big picture than just that medium, making it critical to work with the other departments, to ensure *all* avenues for exposure are explored.

Ask about touring

Touring can be very important, depending on music style (see the When to Tour sidebar below). If touring is appropriate and will be beneficial in the early stages of an album's life, or even prior to release, ask about relationships the label has that can potentially enhance the right touring opportunities. Knowledgeable artist management and a good booking agency will be crucial in this mix. Check the label's ability to make things happen with agencies and what similar touring packages they have been involved with.

When to Tour

- Being able to play live and develop a "buzz" prior to a release can really enhance an act's interest level with labels, especially if the music is rock, alternative or metal. Once an album is released from those categories, touring becomes a very important part of the marketing plan.
- If the music is adult contemporary, dance or "pure pop"—singles driven—touring doesn't become part of the equation until after the hits have been established.
- Jazz artists can sometimes tour, usually clubs, without a label.
- Generally, R&B and rap artists don't use touring as a key element of a career until after a record has been exposed.
- With country music, touring has always, and probably always will be, a big part of an artist's life, contract or not. It's a lifestyle!

Determine commitment to international exposure

With the United States now only one-third of the world market, it is important to check the company's understanding and support for international exposure. Though it's usually necessary to jumpstart a successful release domestically before it has relevance overseas, it is smart to know about the various key markets outside the U.S. and the differentials that come into play in those locales.

With clever planning and the right timing, international presence and success can really extend your career. There is much more loyalty shown to artists overseas, and less emphasis on trends. Once you are accepted there and you show a commitment to them by a steady pattern of touring and doing the necessary press and promotion, an act can have a very long and rewarding career—U.S. longevity or not. For example, Tina Turner reigns as queen in Europe, selling out arenas and in some cases, stadiums, but cannot come close to matching that status here.

Making the decision

Once you and the label feel you want to partner, the attorneys (including your entertainment attorney) take over and then the "deal points" become part of the total package.

☑ If it is the biggest deal you are interested in, then much of the above philosophy won't apply. This article's overview is really about making creative decisions, not dollar ones.

☑ If it is the best "fair" offer that drives you, then your instincts and information gleaned from the relationships at the label and the belief in the staff's ability to identify with the act and its place in the market will be as important as the deal. A contract and no success is a very short term positive!

SONGWRITERS & PUBLISHING DEALS

For the songwriter in a similar situation to the artist (these days they can often be the same), the approach isn't so different. Usually a writer, and often the artist, enters into a separate agreement with a music publisher. Sometimes that contract is basically a collection agreement for all writer income for which the publisher takes an administration fee. That approach can be appropriate, but if you wish to have a professional team work on your behalf, this exercise will pertain to some of the elements that should be evaluated in considering a full publishing agreement. Assuming a record deal is in place, a publisher is likely to be anxious to lock in a relationship because it guarantees an album, and probably singles, will be released. Will the publisher support the label in any way to help promote the record upon release?

Inquire about song placement outlets

Some publishers will augment the record company's promotional efforts with added dollars to hire independent "consultants." How aggressive are they in working with the film and television community to create placement for songs, and sometimes exciting opportunities in upcoming movie and TV shows? In this era of heavy music involvement in these mediums, the more creative publishers spend a great deal of time and manpower attempting to initiate these types of usage, especially when a soundtrack is involved. Record labels are also active in this respect. It has become more difficult to work the traditional placement of songs with artists, primarily because the great majority is self-contained (country music being the obvious exception). A good publishing entity must seek additional ways to maximize usage of signed writers.

Ask about co-writing partnerships

The aggressive publisher will be active in generating co-write liaisons, sometimes with fellow signed writers, but more often with artists who are readying new material. Contemporary recording artists, in general, are very reluctant to record outside songs, but are more open to a creative co-write. Knowing schedules, who's interested, and whose music might fit with an outside writer's style is part of the publisher's day-to-day activity. Having the instincts to plan such combinations is a real expertise, as is the ability to actually make them happen.

Identify relationships with international markets

How interactive is the publisher with their overseas affiliates? As with record sales, the international marketplace constitutes approximately two thirds of the total publishing revenues earned. Does the publisher attempt to initiate co-writing opportunities with overseas artists and writers? This question applies much more to the basic songwriter than the recording artist whose publishing they represent. A big international hit can obviously stimulate serious cash flow, but it can also create new territories where your writing skills can be utilized, no matter your success, or lack of, at home.

Numerous songwriters have more success getting "cuts" overseas than here in the U.S. There are various international markets where the local recording scene is extremely active *and* where there is a very open mind to using "outside" songs. One Los Angeles-based songwriter I know has 20 songs (some co-written) recently recorded, or scheduled to be, by local artists in such diverse countries as Norway, Holland, England, Hungary, South Africa, Germany, Hong Kong and Japan. Many of these records create only small income but collectively it adds up. And, one big hit can mean not only a big payday but establish a much higher profile for future collaborations and covers.

Making the decision

A good publisher can open doors, make connections and initiate opportunities. Finding that publisher involves being proactive by asking questions and learning to trust your instincts. Remember, if a deal sounds fishy, it probably is. Do not enter into any agreement lightly and be sure to have an entertainment attorney look over any contract before signing. Understanding the possibilities and having a well-rounded overview of the broad spectrum of the music business will be invaluable in determining the right company to align with.

Managers Roundtable:
Taking Artists to the Next Level

BY TARA A. HORTON

Artists thank them in acceptance speeches and in album liner notes all the time, but what do managers do? If you read the introduction to the Managers & Booking Agents section on page 273, you'll see the text under "Booking Agents" is only a quarter of the size of information explaining "Managers." Because booking agents' responsibilities are apparent (booking gigs) they don't require an article unto themselves. But what about the managers? What do they actually manage? How can they further your career? How do you know you're ready to work with one?

Songwriter's Market rounded up three ambitious managers in different parts of the country to talk about their jobs. They explain what they look for in artists and offer advice on the qualities you should seek in a manager.

Cathy Gurley is the manager at Gurley & Company in Nashville. She currently handles eight acts, including Atlantic Records recording artist Matt King. Gurley & Company represents country and pop acts. See their listing on page 295.

Karen M. Smith manages two artists for Chicago's Conscience Music. Their client, percussionist Tal Bachman, is signed with Columbia Records. Conscience Music concentrates on rock and pop acts. See their listing on page 284.

Paul Filippone is one of two managers at Syndicate Management in Sherman Oaks, California. Currently, their roster consists of seven acts including Ice T (Explicit Records) and Body Count (Virgin Records). Syndicate Management's clients range from rappers to singer/songwriters, from major label to independent. See their listing on page 321.

What is the most important role of a manager?

Cathy Gurley: Depending on where an artist is in his career there are different things that are important. Matt King, for instance, is a new artist. My role is to work very closely with him and the record label. We are helping him develop a strong presence and positioning in the marketplace so people are able to identify him by his voice, by his look, by the type of material he does. That's how you enter into the consciousness of the consumer. We work with other artists like Lynn Anderson, who is at a different point in her career. After having slowed down for the last couple of years she decided she wants to become more active in the industry again. She has increased her performing and appearances, and we're also working on a book and television deal for her. Some of these things I brought up and other things she brought up. It's a combination and that's usually when it works best—when you have a really good relationship with the artist and sit and brainstorm different activities.

Karen M. Smith: To really capture what the artist envisions as a career and then determine if it is a viable choice. If the manager is enthusiastic she can actually enable that to happen. I am against managers developing artists the way they want the artist to be. Because I think later on in [an artist's] career there can be a lot of frustration and resentment. Usually what I do with my artists is have them come in on a consulting basis and we put together a game plan: What do you really want to do? What's important to you? Then we prioritize and I see if I can or can't do it. If I don't agree with the direction they're going in, and we can't come to a happy medium, then I don't work with them.

Paul Filippone: A manager has to "wear a lot of hats," so to narrow it down to one role isn't easy. The fact is that it varies depending on the artist in question and his particular career situation. The most important role might be getting the artist to work on his writing and songs, or motivating a label to work an artist's record, or protecting an artist's credibility. It depends. In a nutshell, a manager does whatever it takes to augment an artist's career.

What's the biggest misconception artists have about managers?

Paul Filippone: I talk to a lot of bands that believe a manager and a booking agent are the same person. Bands will call and say, "We're really big in our town and we're trying to get some out-of-town shows. Can you do that for us?" The fact is, no, I can't. You're looking for a booking agent. Another common misconception artists have about managers (as well as about record deals) is that once they get one, their lives will all of a sudden be easier and they can let up. This is absolutely not the case. Once you get a manager, or a record deal, the work is just beginning.

Cathy Gurley: Managers are not baby-sitters. It's a long-term vision for an artist offering guidance and assistance. We don't do their Christmas shopping. We don't take them to their hair appointments.

What should artists look for when shopping for a manager? What should they avoid?

Karen M. Smith: One of the things I encourage artists to do is get references. Find out what clients the manager has worked with. See how hesitant the manager is to release that information. I don't have any clients that I've worked with that I would not use as a reference. I feel it's very important that you talk to people who have worked with the manager to see what the manager's style really is. See what kind of releases she's been a part of. See what kind of touring she's overseen.

Paul Filippone: I believe an artist should look for someone who is passionate about the music. A manager should understand what you are doing and have a vision for what to do with it. The other thing that's critical is how an artist and a manager relate to one another. Technically, it's called personal management, and a manager and an artist are probably speaking with one another every day, if not more, and hanging out together. You will have more contact with your manager than anyone else in the business, so you should probably like him.

There is no school for music management, so anybody can decide to manage bands. That's not necessarily a bad thing, because every manager had to start somewhere, but it does mean that an act can wind up with someone who is not totally qualified. That person can either rise to the occasion or not. Ultimately, an act should decide if they believe in that person and his abilities. All the passion in the world isn't worth a thing if it is not focused, directed and effective.

Cathy Gurley: They should find somebody they feel comfortable with on a professional level. Someone who they think shares the same type of goals and values. It may be things you see and hear about somebody which is the same way you choose a client. You might see and get to know somebody or watch somebody and say, "I really like the way she does that. I think she's a real talent. I'd like to work with her." And then you would set up an appointment, maybe sit down and talk to other people who have either worked with or for them.

What do you look for in an artist's submission package?
Cathy Gurley: I look for a focus in the music, a realistic timetable and goals they are looking for. Also the desire to go for it at all costs—to have that drive, that "this is what I want" quality.

Karen M. Smith: The first thing I look at is the material. A lot of artists waste money on a lot of photos and bios and stickers and folders. All of that stuff, to be perfectly honest, ends up in the garbage. There's a time and a place for things like that. A photo is a good idea. You should always have a phone number and a mailing address on the photo—it should be a P.O. Box. You should never use your home address because it's always best to be guarded with your privacy. A one-page overview of what the band has done and a couple of press clippings is enough.

I don't necessarily look for quality in the [demo] recording because some of the most wonderful material I've heard has been off of cassettes with just an acoustic guitar and a mike. I'd have to say that I look for strong songs, and work with artists in a variety of genres.

Paul Filippone: Songs. First and foremost, it's all about the music. If I hear that and I'm interested, trust me, I'll call for the photo, bio, tour dates, website, what-have-you. I see bands that spend so much money on elaborate packaging, deluxe photos, etc. and that stuff winds up in the trash. Please save your money.

What do artists do when approaching you that turns you off?
Paul Filippone: Artists should understand that we are extremely busy. If you call to get permission to send in a package, be organized and prepared on the phone, e.g., if you don't have the mailing address already, have a pen and paper ready when you call. If you've sent in a package and haven't heard back, then you can either accept that we weren't into it, or you can follow up with a phone call to find out. But don't follow up 15 times looking for feedback. There's a fine line between being organized and on-the-ball and becoming a nuisance. Like I said, if I hear a tape and I like it, I'll find you.

Cathy Gurley: I get turned off when people tell me how much they're like someone else. Where nothing has gone right in their life because of everyone else: she'd be a better singer if her mother had let her take voice lessons; if his dad hadn't insisted he play basketball he'd probably play guitar better. Everybody has obstacles in their life and it's how you deal with them that determines whether you become successful or not.

Karen M. Smith: The one thing I hate that artists do is when they tell me to come out and see them, and right after they get done playing they come and ask me, "What do you think?". First of all, I like to go home and make notes and just absorb the music. Second of all, they've just gotten off stage and it's very uncomfortable. Or, they'll have a meeting with me and want to play the music right there and they want me to tell them what I think. It's much easier for me to get the material ahead of time or to go and see the band perform and have a meeting later in the week. So I'm not pressured to say what I think right then and there.

What should an artist do career-wise before approaching you?

Karen M. Smith: A lot of bands get managers before they really need one. So you're promising someone a percentage of nothing. You don't need a manager until you actually have product, and you're going to begin touring.

A lot of musicians don't want to make the phone calls and book the shows. Unfortunately, in order to get someone enthusiastic about you, you've got to have something. It's hard to go to a manager and say, "We've never recorded anything, we have five songs, and we've played at a few places."

Paul Filippone: I think there is a tendency for artists to think they need management before it's really necessary. An act can do a lot in their hometown and the surrounding markets without a manager's help. Quite frankly, there are bands releasing their own albums, getting them in stores and booking national and international tours on their own, so don't limit yourself. Run with the ball as far as you possibly can before you start looking for someone to pass it off to.

What's expected of artists once they sign with a manager?

Cathy Gurley: Once we decide to go in a direction, I expect that they will stay on track. If they are supposed to deliver ten songs to their publishing company that they will work on that. They will take care of themselves. It's like being in training—keeping yourself healthy—eating right, exercising physically, mentally, emotionally and spiritually.

Karen M. Smith: I start putting them out on small tours and seeing how resilient they are on a trip like that. Sometimes the reality is they can't deal with it. They can't give up their jobs, their families are getting upset, and the pressure is more than they anticipated. It's very idyllic, [the idea of] being on tour. And it isn't that way when you're actually out. It's important to not put a lot of energy into a group until you see that they actually are "road-worthy."

What can a manager do for songwriters who don't perform their own music?

Paul Filippone: There are several things: Try to get a songwriter's material to an appropriate artist to perform it, or hook that songwriter up with artists that may need someone to collaborate with, or look for a publisher who might want to do a deal.

Cathy Gurley: Sometimes what a manager can do is help them get tied in and positioned with songwriters who are perhaps more experienced than they are—broader than they are—to help them develop to the next level. Perhaps help them make contacts to get their songs published. Find other outlets for their songs: movies, TV, merchandising.

Karen M. Smith: The most important thing a manager can do is have songwriters get in a good habit of copyrighting their songs. You should also set up a publishing company. When you are a songwriter and you're going to performers to get them to perform your material, if you go in and you've already got a publishing company, then you are more established from a professional level and you're going to a better deal. If a manager starts soliciting material that's not copywritten, and you don't have a publishing company of your own, the label or the bigger publisher is going to try to take advantage of you. Really getting songwriters to understand how copyrighting and publishing works for them is very important.

What do you look for in a nonperforming songwriter's submission?

Cathy Gurley: A demo of three to four songs he considers best represent the type of writing he has done. A very simple demo of it and a letter outlining how he came to that point in his songwriting career and where he would like to be in the next year.

Paul Filippone: As long as the songs can be recorded in a way that is satisfactory to the song-writer, that's what's important. If the songwriter is comfortable with the way her songs are represented—whether that's by herself or by having someone else perform them—then that's what matters.

Do you have any additional advice for songwriters?

Cathy Gurley: You can't believe the timetables of every magazine you read. In the large scheme of somebody's life it feels like it just happened yesterday, but chances are it didn't. You are not going to get off the bus and have a deal. Garth [Brooks] found that out. He came to Nashville once and left and people tend to forget that! And then he realized it would take longer. Nothing happens overnight.

Remember it is entertainment. It is fun, but at the same time it's hard work. It's the same way football's a lot of fun—but those guys work hard to get there! There's a lot of sweat that goes before the glimmer. But it's worth it if that's what your dreams are made of.

Karen M. Smith: I cannot overemphasize that you stay true to yourself. Let's say you are writing country songs and you love country songs and a record company comes out and says, "Oh, your drummer should be a rock drummer and you'd be huge." And if that really isn't what your heart is telling you, stick with your heart. It's very, very hard to make it in this business. When you start trying to please other people and not yourself, you could become successful, but you're not going to be happy. It's important that along with success you have the opportunity to enjoy it. It's great to hear people critique your music and be open-minded to the comments they have, but stay true to yourself. Otherwise, you'll be changing your genre every six months, rather than developing and strengthening what you really are all about.

Paul Filippone: There are no hard and fast rules in this business, so think freely and creatively as you're working on your career.

Understanding Performing Rights Organizations

BY BILL PARSONS

As a kid who came of musical age in the '70s, I can remember hours spent in my room with a stack of new records, headphones on, devouring every little piece of information I could glean off the jacket covers. First, I scanned the song sequence and lyrics. Then the writers' credits to see which band members wrote which songs. Then a quick check to make sure I knew who was playing what and whether there were any session players on the recording. And finally, just as the music completely enveloped my medulla, I would quickly read the "special thanks" section for any inside jokes the band felt like sharing with its fans before losing myself completely in the graphics on the inside flaps of the double album. Ah, yes, the '70s.

There's one thing I never got, though. What was with those parenthesized letters that always seemed to follow the name of the band's publishing company: ASCAP, BMI, SESAC? Since every band did it, I assumed they had to. It was probably a legal thing. Or part of their publishing company. Or maybe it just looked cool. One thing I knew for sure: If I ever did an album, it was going to have those letters on it—just to make sure everyone knew it was for real.

As a professional songwriter in the '90s, I've learned that those letters are acronyms for the three major performing rights organizations (PROs) in the United States: the American Society of Composers, Authors and Publishers (ASCAP), Broadcast Music, Inc. (BMI) and the Society of European Stage Authors and Composers (SESAC). As it turns out, they are legal things, though they are not part of publishing companies. And, if you want to get paid for the public performance of your work, they are definitely cool.

This article is going to explain the basic official and unofficial functions of performing rights organizations, as well as give readers necessary information with which to make informed decisions about choosing a PRO.

THE BASICS: PERFORMING RIGHTS 101

A lot of people will tell you that copyright law is complicated. And they're right. It is. However, for the purposes of this article, it is possible to distill the basics of relevant copyright law into plain English. It goes something like this: When you write and copyright a song, it becomes your property. And, just as with any other piece of property, you have a right to be compensated when someone uses it.

There are two basic ways someone might use your song: They might put it on a recording or perform it publicly. If someone puts one of your songs on a recording, you are entitled to something called a mechanical royalty (a topic for another article). If someone performs your work publicly, you are entitled to something called a performance royalty. Enter the performing rights organizations.

BILL PARSONS *is a performing songwriter living in the Washington, D.C. area. He is the Industry Editor for* Performing Songwriter *magazine. This article is reprinted with permission from* Performing Songwriter. *Call (800)883-7664 for subscription information.*

GETTING PAID: THE OFFICIAL FUNCTION OF PROs

The basic, official function of PROs is to collect and distribute performance royalties to songwriters and publishers. They do this by licensing entities that use music (i.e., television, radio, clubs, bars, restaurants, malls, movie theaters, etc.) and then distributing the license fees they have collected to their member writers and publishers. Since it would be impossible for any individual writer or publisher to single-handedly monitor every television station, radio broadcast, and honky tonk in the country for an accurate record of where and how often their songs are being used, PROs do it for you. They are, in effect, a collection agency for performance royalties for songwriters and publishers. If one of your songs is performed publicly, their job is to make sure that you get paid. That, in theory, is how it is supposed to work.

THE PRO PAYMENT METHODOLOGY

Now, as it turns out, not even the PROs are able to track every public performance of every song at every musical outlet across the country. Instead, they focus primarily on public performances of musical works over television and radio and then make an assumption that what they find roughly approximates the frequency with which different works are being performed publicly everywhere else. It is admittedly an imprecise system, and the PROs are constantly deploying new technologies and refining their tracking techniques in order to produce the most representative sample possible. Additionally, some PROs have developed "special awards" for live performances in an effort to compensate writers whose works or chosen genre might be underrepresented on television and radio relative to its actual public performance. However, it is important for songwriters to realize that most PRO payments flow from television and radio airplay, not live performances.

OTHER OFFICIAL PRO FUNCTIONS AND SERVICES

In addition to collecting performance royalties, PROs are also advocates for their members in a variety of other ways. PROs organize showcases and workshops for their members. They help underwrite music festivals and songwriting contests. They can provide their members with access to a range of insurance products—from health to instrument insurance. And they represent songwriters' and publishers' interests before courts and legislatures on the state and federal levels. They are, by charter and instinct, the songwriter's ally in the rough and tumble world of the music biz.

MENTORING, NETWORKING AND GATEKEEPING: THE PROs' UNOFFICIAL ROLE

Every songwriter who works seriously at building their career knows that some doors are tough to open. You can't always get publishers to listen to your songs. Unless you already know them, most A&R people won't take your call. And no matter when you ask, that club manager always seems to be booked for the rest of the year. Such is life for the "unestablished" songwriter. However, all doors have keys if you know where to find them. And sometimes you can find them at a PRO.

"We're here to help," says Brendan Okrent, senior director of repertory at ASCAP. "We can pick up a phone and call a publisher or A&R people, or put them in a showcase. We're the people you can get to when you can't get to a record company."

Jeff Cohen, senior director of writer-publisher relations at BMI agrees, saying, "If we just paid [performance royalties], we'd be a bank. The cool thing is that BMI helps a little bit at all different levels—from questions about copyright to saying, 'I know a publisher who would go nuts for this'." Pat Rogers, SESAC's senior vice president for writer-publisher relations, maintains that SESAC's small size allows it to really focus on building its members' careers. "We take our personal service very seriously. Because we're small, we're able to give. We pitch songs, showcase our artists so that they can get record deals, and shop for publishing deals.

We're on their team. We're almost like the publishers of old: giving our writers support, feedback and a pat on the back."

Sound good? It is. But there are some caveats you should know about. First, though PROs try to be accessible to writers at all stages of development, they are often swamped with requests for assistance. "There are a lot more of you than there are of us," says ASCAP's Okrent, "so it can take some patience and follow through [to get our attention]." Moreover, PROs do not just recommend anybody who walks through the door to their industry contacts. If they did, they would lose their credibility as gatekeepers. In order to initiate an introduction, a PRO staffer has to love your material, think you're ready and find the right fit. "It can be detrimental to call an A&R rep with someone who's still developing," says BMI's Cohen. "It's important not to make promises you can't keep. We would rather work with someone over a long career than just go for the quick shot." As the smallest and only for-profit performing rights organization, SESAC's gatekeeping function begins at its own door. Whereas ASCAP and BMI have relatively easy membership criteria, SESAC has a far more involved application process. Explains SESAC's Rogers, "We have to be very selective when we sign writers so we don't overload the company with writers who can't make a living in the business. We take a look at writers with somewhat of a higher standard."

The bottom line here is that PROs can be enormously helpful allies to songwriters in building their careers if they are approached with patience, persistence and professionalism. The trick is to develop a relationship with a particular staffer in the writer relations department. Let them know what's going on with your career. Ask them questions. Respect their time and take their advice seriously. While you should not necessarily expect an immediate referral to the label of your choice, you should expect your phone calls to be returned. Over time, this kind of relationship with a PRO can be personally and professionally rewarding.

QUESTIONS TO ASK A PERFORMING RIGHTS ORGANIZATION BEFORE JOINING

OK, so now you understand why PROs exist, how they work, and what role they can play in helping to develop your career. Which one should you join? There is no right answer to that question. Each PRO has its own unique history, organizational structure, tracking methods, payout formulas and office staff. However, we can suggest some basic questions you can ask any PRO in order to make a truly informed decision before joining.

☑ What are your criteria for membership? How much does it cost to join? How long is the term of the membership? How and when can I end my membership if I feel things aren't working out?

☑ How and where do you track public performances? What is the likelihood that the style and level of music I play will appear in your tracking records? If none of my work turns up on your television and radio tracking, but I know it is being performed publicly, is there any other way I can be compensated for that performance? If my music is being performed publicly abroad, what kind of relationships do you have with foreign performing rights societies?

☑ What kind of showcases and workshops are you running? Which ones would I be eligible to participate in?

☑ What types of insurance plans do you offer?

☑ What distinguishes you from the other PROs?

Once you get the PROs' answers to these questions, ask your musician friends which PRO they belong to and why. Try to square the PROs' answers to these questions with your friends' experiences. Also think through whether there is somebody in particular you met or spoke with at one of the PROs who seemed to take an interest in what you're doing (or at least conveyed the impression that they would return your phone calls). Then make a decision. And try to make full use of all that performing rights organizations have to offer.

ASCAP

The American Society of Composers, Authors and Publishers (ASCAP) was established in 1914 and is the oldest performing rights organization in the United States. It operates on a not-for-profit basis and is governed by a Board of Directors comprised of writers and publishers elected every two years by its membership. In order to join ASCAP as a writer member, you must have any of the following 1) a commercially recorded music composition; 2) a published composition available for sale or rental; 3) proof that your music has been performed in any venue licensable by ASCAP.

BMI

Broadcast Music, Inc. (BMI) was established in 1940 and is the largest performing rights organization in the world. It operates on a not-for-profit basis and is governed by a Board of Directors comprised of twelve broadcasters and the organization's President. In order to join BMI as a writer affiliate, you must have musical compositions that are either being performed or likely to be performed by broadcasting stations or in other public performances.

SESAC

The Society of European Stage Authors and Composers (SESAC) was established in 1930 and is the second oldest performing rights organization in the United States. It operates as a for-profit, privately held company. In order to join SESAC as a writer affiliate, you must pass a screening process that includes an evaluation of your musical work and a personal meeting with a SESAC affiliation representative.

Editor's note: For more information on the PROs, including how to contact them, see the Organizations section on page 412.

The Markets

Important Information on Market Listings

- Although every listing in *Songwriter's Market* is updated, verified or researched prior to publication, some changes are bound to occur between publication and the time you contact any listing. You may want to call a company before sending them material to make sure their submission policy has not changed.
- Listings are based on interviews and questionnaires. They are not advertisements, nor are markets reported here necessarily endorsed by the editor.
- Every listing in *Songwriter's Market* is screened for unethical practices. If a listing does not meet our ethical requirements, they will be excluded from the book.
- Companies that appeared in the 1999 edition of *Songwriter's Market*, but do not appear this year, are listed in the General Index at the back of the book along with a code explaining why they do not appear in this edition.
- A word of warning. Don't pay to have your song published and/or recorded or to have your lyrics—or a poem—set to music. Read "Rip-Offs" in The Business of Songwriting section to learn how to recognize and protect yourself from the "song shark."
- If you have found a song shark through this book, write to us at 1507 Dana Ave., Cincinnati OH 45207, with an explanation and copies of documentation of the company's unethical practices.
- *Songwriter's Market reserves the right to exclude any listing which does not meet its requirements.*

Key to Abbreviations

SASE—self-addressed, stamped envelope
SAE—self-addressed envelope
IRC—International Reply Coupon, for use in countries other than your own.
- For definitions of terms and abbreviations relating specifically to the music industry, see the Glossary in the back of the book.
- For explanations of symbols, see the inside front and back covers of the book. Also see pages 8-9.

Complaint Procedure

If you feel you have not been treated fairly by a listing in *Songwriter's Market*, we advise you to take the following steps:
- First try to contact the listing. Sometimes one phone call or a letter can quickly clear up the matter.
- Document all your correspondence with the listing. When you write to us with a complaint, provide the details of your submission, including the date of your first contact with the listing, the nature of your subsequent correspondence, and copies of any documentation.
- We will enter your letter into our files and attempt to contact the listing.
- The number and severity of complaints will be considered in our decision whether or not to delete the listing from the next edition.

Music Publishers

Finding songs and getting them recorded—that's the main function of a music publisher. Working as an advocate for you and your songs, a music publisher serves as a song plugger, administrator, networking resource and more. The knowledge and personal contacts a music publisher can provide may be the most valuable resources available for a songwriter just starting in the music business.

HOW MUSIC PUBLISHERS WORK

Music publishers attempt to derive income from a song through recordings, use in TV and film soundtracks and other areas. While this is their primary function, music publishers also handle administrative tasks such as copyrighting songs, collecting royalties for the songwriter, negotiating and issuing synchronization licenses for use of music in films, arranging and administering foreign rights, and producing new demos of the music submitted to them. In a small, independent publishing company, one or two people may handle all these jobs. Larger publishing companies are more likely to be divided into the following departments: creative (or professional), copyright, licensing, legal affairs, royalty, accounting and foreign.

The *creative department* is responsible for finding talented writers and signing them to the company. Once a writer is signed, it is up to the creative department to develop and nurture the writer so he will write songs that create income for the company. Staff members often put writers together to form collaborative teams. And, perhaps most important, the creative department is responsible for securing commercial recordings of songs and pitching them for use in film and other media. The head of the creative department, usually called the professional manager, is charged with locating talented writers for the company. Once a writer is signed, the professional manager arranges for a demo to be made of the writer's songs. Even though a writer may already have recorded his own demo, the publisher will often re-demo the songs using established studio musicians in an effort to produce the highest-quality demo possible.

Once a demo is produced, the professional manager begins shopping the song to various outlets. He may try to get the song recorded by a top artist on his or her next album or get the song used in an upcoming film. The professional manager uses all the contacts and leads he has to get the writer's songs recorded by as many artists as possible. Therefore, he must be able to deal efficiently and effectively with people in other segments of the music industry, including A&R personnel, producers, distributors, managers and lawyers. Through these contacts, he can find out what artists are looking for new material, and who may be interested in recording one of the writer's songs.

WHERE THE MONEY COMES FROM

After a writer's songs are recorded, the other departments at the publishing company come into play.

- The *licensing and copyright departments* are responsible for issuing any licenses for use of the writer's songs in film or TV and for filing various forms with the copyright office.
- The *legal affairs department* works with the professional department in negotiating contracts with its writers.
- The *royalty and accounting departments* are responsible for ensuring the writer is receiving the proper royalty rate as specified in the contract and that statements are mailed to the writer promptly.

- Finally, the *foreign department*'s role is to oversee any publishing activities outside of the United States, and to make sure a writer is being paid for any uses of his material in foreign countries.

LOCATING A MUSIC PUBLISHER

How do you go about finding a music publisher that will work well for you? First, you must find a publisher suited to the type of music you write. If a particular publisher works mostly with alternative music and you're a country songwriter, the contacts he has within the industry will hardly be beneficial to you. Each listing in this section details, in order of importance, the type of music that publisher is most interested in; the music types appear in **boldface** to make them easier to locate. It's also very important to submit only to companies interested in your level of experience (see the Openness to Submissions sidebar on page 8). You will also want to refer to the Category Index at the end of this section, which lists companies by the type of music they work with. Publishers placing music in film or TV will be proceded by a ◪ (see the Film & TV Index for a complete list of these companies).

Additional Publishers

There are **MORE PUBLISHERS** located in other sections of the book! On page 125 use the list of Additional Publishers to find listings within other sections who are also music publishers.

Do your research!

It's important to study the market and do research to identify which companies to submit to.
- Are you targeting a specific artist to sing your songs? If so, find out if that artist even considers outside material. Get a copy of the artist's latest album, and see who wrote most of the songs. If they were all written by the artist, he's probably not interested in hearing material from outside writers. If the songs were written by a variety of different writers, however, he may be open to hearing new songs.
- Check the album liner notes, which will list the names of the publishers of each writer. These publishers obviously have had luck pitching songs to the artist, and they may be able to get your songs to that artist as well.
- If the artist you're interested in has a recent hit on the *Billboard* charts, the publisher of that song will be listed in the "Hot 100 A-Z" index. Carefully choosing which publishers will work best for the material you write may take time, but it will only increase your chances of getting your songs heard. "Shotgunning" your demo packages (sending out many packages without regard for music preference or submission policy) is a waste of time and money and will hurt, rather than help, your songwriting career.

Once you've found some companies that may be interested in your work, learn what songs have been successfully handled by those publishers. Most publishers are happy to provide you with this information in order to attract high-quality material. Ask the publisher for the names of some of their staff writers, and give them a call. Ask their opinion of how the publisher works. Keep in mind as you're researching music publishers how you get along with them personally. If you can't work with a publisher on a personal level, chances are your material won't be represented as you would like it to be. A publisher can become your most valuable connection to all other segments of the music industry, so it's important to find someone you can trust and feel comfortable with. Also read the article Is This the Right Company for Me? on page 39.

Independent or major company?

Also consider the size of the publishing company. The publishing affiliates of the major music conglomerates are huge, handling catalogs of thousands of songs by hundreds of songwriters. Unless you are an established songwriter, your songs probably won't receive enough attention from such large companies. Smaller, independent publishers offer several advantages. First, independent music publishers are located all over the country, making it easier for you to work face-to-face rather than by mail or phone. Smaller companies usually aren't affiliated with a particular record company and are therefore able to pitch your songs to many different labels and acts. Independent music publishers are usually interested in a smaller range of music, allowing you to target your submissions more accurately. The most obvious advantage to working with a smaller publisher is the personal attention they can bring to you and your songs. With a smaller roster of artists to work with, the independent music publisher is able to concentrate more time and effort on each particular project.

For More Information

For more instructional information on the listings in this book, including explanations of symbols ( ), read the article How to Use *Songwriter's Market* to Get Your Songs Heard on page 5.

SUBMITTING MATERIAL TO PUBLISHERS

When submitting material to a publisher, always keep in mind that a professional, courteous manner goes a long way in making a good impression. When you submit a demo through the mail, make sure your package is neat and meets the particular needs of the publisher. Review each publisher's submission policy carefully, and follow it to the letter. Disregarding this information will only make you look like an amateur in the eyes of the company you're submitting to. (For more detailed information on submitting your material, see the article Getting Started on page 11, What Music Professionals Look for in a Demo sidebar on page 15, Quiz: Are You Professional? on page 19 and the article How to Make Your Submission Stand Out on page 35.)

Listings of companies in Canada are preceded by a ✪, and international markets are designated with a ▣. You will find an alphabetical list of these companies at the back of the book, along with an index of publishers by state.

PUBLISHING CONTRACTS

Once you've located a publisher you like and he's interested in shopping your work, it's time to consider the publishing contract—an agreement in which a songwriter grants certain rights to a publisher for one or more songs. The contract specifies any advances offered to the writer, the rights that will be transferred to the publisher, the royalties a songwriter is to receive and the length of time the contract is valid.

- When a contract is signed, a publisher will ask for a 50-50 split with the writer. This is standard industry practice; the publisher is taking that 50% to cover the overhead costs of running his business and for the work he's doing to get your songs recorded.
- It is always a good idea to have a publishing contract (or any music business contract) reviewed by a competent entertainment lawyer.
- There is no "standard" publishing contract, and each company offers different provisions for their writers.

Make sure you ask questions about anything you don't understand, especially if you're new in the business. Songwriter organizations such as the Songwriters Guild of America (SGA) provide contract review services, and can help you learn about music business language and what constitutes a fair music publishing contract. Be sure to read The Business of Songwriting on page 21 for more information on contracts. See the Organizations section of this book for more information on the SGA and other songwriting groups.

When signing a contract, it's important to be aware of the music industry's unethical practitioners. The "song shark," as he's called, makes his living by asking a songwriter to pay to have a song published. The shark will ask for money to demo a song and promote it to radio stations; he may also ask for more than the standard 50% publisher's share or ask you to give up all rights to a song in order to have it published. Although none of these practices is illegal, it's certainly not ethical, and no successful publisher uses these methods. *Songwriter's Market* works to list only honest companies interested in hearing new material. (For more on "song sharks," see The Rip-Offs on page 24.)

☑ ◯ **ABALONE PUBLISHING**, 26257 Regency Club Dr., Suite 6, Warren MI 48089-4125. E-mail: jtrupi4539@aol.com. Website: http://members.aol.com/jtrupi4539/index.html. Music Director: Jack Timmons. Professional Manager: John Dudick. Music publisher and record company (L.A. Records). Estab. 1984. Publishes 20-30 songs/year; publishes 20-30 new songwriters/year. Staff size: 12. Hires staff songwriters. Pays standard royalty.
Affiliate(s): BGM Publishing, AL-KY Music and Bubba Music (BMI).
How to Contact: Submit demo tape by mail. Unsolicited submissions are OK. Prefers cassette with 1-5 songs and lyric sheet. "Include cover letter describing your goals." SASE for postage up to 33¢. All others, please include $1 to cover fluctuating postal rates. Reports in 3 months.
Music: Mostly **rock**, **pop** and **alternative**; also **dance**, **pop/rock** and **country**. Does not want rap, alternative or rave. Published *The Torch* (by Robbi Taylor/The Sattellites), recorded by The Sattellites (rock); "The Web" (by Jay Collins), recorded by The Net (rock); and "Passion" (by R. Gibb), recorded by Notta (blues), all on L.A. Records.
Tips: "Follow stipulations for submission 'to a tee.' Not conforming to our listing exactly constitutes return of your submission. Write what you feel; however, don't stray too far from the trends that are currently popular. Lyrical content should depict a definite story line and paint an accurate picture in the listener's mind."

📠 ◯ **AIM HIGH MUSIC COMPANY (ASCAP)**, 1300 Division St., Suite #200, Nashville TN 37203. (615)242-4722. Fax: (615)242-1177. E-mail: brokerhouse@msn.com. Producer: Robert Metzgar (country). Contact: Rebecca Waymack (pop); Spike Jones (all). Music publisher and record company (Platinum Plus Records). Estab. 1971. Publishes 250 songs/year; publishes 5-6 new songwriters/year. Staff size: 10. Hires staff writers. Pays standard royalty.
Affiliate(s): Bobby & Billy Music (BMI), Billy Ray Music (BMI), Club Platinum Music (BMI).
How to Contact: Submit demo tape by mail. Unsolicited submissions are OK. Prefers cassette or VHS videocassette with 5-10 songs and lyric sheet. "I like to get to know songwriters personally prior to recording their songs." Does not return material. Reports in 1 month.
Film & TV: Places 8 songs in film and 22 songs in TV/year. Music Supervisors: Mason Cooper (pop/rock); Spike Jones (all).
Music: Mostly **country**, **traditional country** and **pop country**; also **gospel**, **southern gospel** and **contemporary Christian**. Published *Honky Tonk Christmas* (by Bob Douglass), recorded by George Jones on MCA Records; *My Miss America* (by Bob Douglass), recorded by Carters on Curb Records; and "There By Now" (by T. Tucker), recorded by Le Clerc on Capitol Records.
Tips: "Please let us determine which songs you've written are commercial first and then get them formally recorded as demos."

📠 ◑ **MARCUS ALAN MUSIC (BMI)**, P.O. Box 128132, Nashville TN 37212. Phone/fax:)826-4141. E-mail: mamorbit@aol.com. Professional Managers: Marcus Alan (all styles); Susan ʳ (country); Scott (all styles). Music publisher, record company (Orbit Records) and record producer. 1993. Publishes 26 songs/year; 2 new songwriters/year. Staff size: 4. Hires staff writers. Pays royalty.
ˢ): Alan Marcus (ASCAP) and MAM (BMI).
ontact: Submit demo tape by mail. Unsolicited submissions are OK. Prefers cassette with 4 ᵣic sheet. "Try to make demos as clear as possible with good level. All the pro songwriters

have demos that sound like records or a guitar/piano vocal demo recorded with a professional demo singer." Does not return material. Reports in 6 weeks.
Film & TV: Places 3 songs in film and 3 songs in TV/year. Music Supervisor: Marcus Alan. Recently published "I Love Western Experience" (by Marcus Alan); "Betty's Beauty World" (by Marcus Alan/ Danny Simpson) and "Cain't Never Could" (by Adam Hughes/Marcus Alan), all recorded by Marcus Alan in *Western Experience*.
Music: Mostly **country**, **blues** and **alternative**; also **gospel** and **R&B**. Does not want rap. Published *I Know You Hear Me* (by Beverly Ross/Marcus Alan/Mark Gray), recorded by Engelbert Humperdink on Core (country/pop).
Tips: "Keep songs to three to three and a half minutes. Try to have your demos done in Nashville. The labels, producers and A&R reps are very sensitive to quality and production style."

  ALEXANDER SR. MUSIC (BMI), P.O. Box 8684, Youngstown OH 44507. (330)782-5031. Fax: (330)782-6954. A&R: LaVerne Chambers; Darryl Alexander. Music publisher, record company (LRG Records), music consulting, distribution and promotional services and record producer. Estab. 1992. Publishes 12-22 songs/year; publishes 2-4 new songwriters/year. Staff size: 3. Pays standard royalty.
How to Contact: Write first and obtain permission to submit. Prefers cassette with 4 songs and lyric sheet. "We will accept finished masters (cassette or CD) for review." SASE. Reports in 2 months. "No phone calls or faxes please."
Film & TV: Places 2 songs in TV/year. Music Supervisor: Darryl Alexander. Recently published "Maybe Tomorrow" for *Playing to Win* (NBC Movie of the Week), and "Don't Dis Me My Brother" for the *Maury Povich Show*, both written and recorded by Darryl Alexander.
Music: Mostly **contemporary jazz**, **urban Christian** and **urban gospel**; also **R&B**. Does not want rock, gangsta rap, heavy metal or country. Published "God is Good" and "Look Up," both written and recorded by Keith Logan (gospel); and "Let's Take A Chance" (by Darryl Alexander), recorded by Sheila Hayes (contemporary jazz), all on LRG Records.
Tips: "Send only music in styles that we review. Submit your best songs and follow submission guidelines. Finished masters open up additional possibilities. Lead sheets may be requested for material we are interested in. Must have SASE if you wish to have cassette returned. No phone calls, please."

  ALEXIS (ASCAP), P.O. Box 532, Malibu CA 90265. (323)463-5998. President: Lee Magid. Music publisher, record company, personal management firm, and record and video producer. Member AIMP. Estab. 1950. Publishes 50 songs/year; publishes 20-50 new songwriters/year. Pays standard royalty.
Affiliate(s): Marvelle (BMI), Lou-Lee (BMI), D.R. Music (ASCAP) and Gabal (SESAC).
How to Contact: Submit a demo tape by mail. Unsolicited submissions are OK. Prefers cassette or VHS videocassette with 1-3 songs and lyric sheet. "Try to make demo as clear as possible—guitar or piano should be sufficient. A full rhythm and vocal demo is always better." Does not return material. Reports in 6-8 weeks only if interested.
Music: Mostly **R&B**, **jazz**, **MOR**, **pop** and **gospel**; also **blues**, **church/religious**, **country**, **dance-oriented**, **folk** and **Latin**. Published "Jesus Is Just Alright" (by Reynolds), recorded by D.C. Talk on Forefront Records (pop); "Blues For the Weepers" (by Rich/Magid), recorded by Lou Rawls on Capitol Records (pop/blues); and "What Shall I Do" (by Q. Fielding), recorded by Tramaine Hawkins on EMI/Sparrow Records (ballad).
Tips: "Try to create a good demo, vocally and musically. A good home-recorded tape will do."

 ALIAS JOHN HENRY TUNES (BMI), 11 Music Square E. #601, Nashville TN 37203. (615)259-2012. Fax: (615)259-2148. E-mail: info@spencemanor.com. Website: http://spencemanor.com. Owner: Bobby John Henry. Music publisher, record producer and music hotel (The Spence Manor Suites). Estab. 1996. Publishes 3 songs/year; publishes 1 new songwriter/year. Staff size: 3. Pays standard royalty.
How to Contact: Call first and obtain permission to submit a demo. Prefers cassette with 3 songs and lyric sheet. Does not return material. Reports in 6 months only if interested.

FOR EXPLANATIONS OF THESE SYMBOLS,
SEE THE INSIDE FRONT AND BACK COVERS OF THIS BOOK.

Music: Mostly **country**, **rock** and **alternative**. Does not want rap. Published *Mr. Right Now* (by Kari Jorgensen), recorded by "Hieke" on Warner Bros. (rock); and *Nothing to Me* (by B.J. Henry), recorded by Millie Jackson on Spring.
Tips: "Focus and rewrite, rewrite, rewrite."

🌐 ⭕ **ALL ROCK MUSIC**, P.O. Box 2296, Rotterdam 3000 CG Holland. Phone: (31) 186-604266. Fax: (32) 1862-604366. President: Cees Klop. Music publisher, record company (Collector Records) and record producer. Estab. 1967. Publishes 40 songs/year; publishes several new songwriters/year. Staff size: 3. Pays standard royalty.
Affiliate(s): All Rock Music (England).
How to Contact: Submit demo tape by mail. Unsolicited submissions are OK. Prefers cassette. SAE and IRC. Reports in 1-2 months.
Music: Mostly **'50s rock**, **rockabilly** and **country rock**; also **piano boogie woogie**. Published *Parking In the Dark*, written and recorded by Charles Dean; and *A Little Bigger Rig*, written and recorded by Sammy Barr, both on Collector Records (50s rock); and *Roll Over Boogie*, written and recorded Erik Jan Overbeer and André Valkering on Down South (boogie).
Tips: "Send only the kind of material we issue/produce as listed."

⭕ **ALLEGHENY MUSIC WORKS**, 306 Cypress Ave., Johnstown PA 15902. (814)535-3373. Managing Director: Al Rita. Music publisher and record company (Allegheny Records). Estab. 1991. Staff size: 2. Pays standard royalty.
Affiliate(s): Allegheny Music Works Publishing (ASCAP) and Tuned on Music (BMI).
How to Contact: Submit demo tape by mail. Unsolicited submissions are OK. Prefers cassette with 3 songs and lyric or lead sheet. SASE. Reports in 2-4 weeks.
Music: Mostly **country**; also **pop**, **A/C**, **R&B** and **inspirational**. Does not want rap, metal or x-rated lyrics. Published *One Two Timer Too Many* (by William Wilkinson), recorded by Savanah Taylor on Ichiban (country); *Hound Dog Riding In a Pick-Up Truck* (by Craig Reeder/Tony Rast, recorded by Michael Hollomon on UAR (country); and *Shades of Gray* (by M.D. Carroll), recorded by Michael Dean on WIR (country).
Tips: "We would like to receive more material written for female artists. Currently, we are getting in on average ten 'male' songs to one 'female' song."

🎵 **ALLISONGS INC. (ASCAP, BMI)**, 1603 Horton Ave., Nashville TN 37212. (615)292-9899. President: Jim Allison. Professional Manager: Bill Renfrew. Music publisher, record company (ARIA Records) and record producer (Jim Allison). Estab. 1985. Publishes 50 songs/year. Staff size: 4. Pays standard royalty.
Affiliate(s): Jim's Allisongs (BMI) and Annie Green Eyes Music (BMI).
 ● Reba McEntire's "What Am I Gonna Do About You," published by AlliSongs, Inc., was included on her triple-platinum album, *Greatest Hits*.
How to Contact: Submit demo tape by mail. Unsolicited submissions are OK. Send chrome cassette and lyric sheet. Does not return material. Reports in 6 weeks only if interested.
Music: Mostly **country** and **pop**. Published "Fade To Blue" (by Reeves/Scott/Allison), recorded by LeAnn Rimes on Curb Records (country); "Preservation of the Wild Life" (by Allison/Young), recorded by Earl Thomas Conley on RCA Records (country); and "Cowboys Don't Cry" (by Allison/Simon/Gilmore/Raymond), recorded by Daron Norwood on Giant Records.
Tips: "Send your best—we will contact you if interested. No need to call us. It will be listened to."

📺 🎵 **ALLRS MUSIC PUBLISHING CO. (ASCAP)**, P.O. Box 422, Smithtown NY 11787. (718)767-8995. E-mail: allrsmusic@aol.com. Website: http://members.aol.com/allrsmusic/page6/index.htm. President: Renee Silvestri. Vice President/A&R: F. John Silvestri. Music publisher. Member NARAS (voting member), CMA (voting member), SGMA, SGA. Estab. 1994. Staff size: 5. Publishes 3 songs/year; publishes 2 new songwriters/year. Pays standard royalty.
Affiliate(s): Midi-Track Publishing Co. (BMI).
How to Contact: Submit demo tape by mail. Unsolicited submissions are OK. Prefers cassette with 3 songs and lyric sheet. "Make sure cassette tape is labeled with your name, address and telephone number." Does not return material. "Include SASE for reply . . . even if we decide to pass on your song, we will keep cassette on file. In the future there could be a need for your song." Reports in 4-6 weeks.
Film & TV: Places 1 song in film/year. Recently published "Why Can't You Hear My Prayer" (by F. John Silvestri), recorded by Iliana Medina in a documentary on anxiety disorders.
Music: Mostly **pop**, **country** and **gospel**; also **MOR**, **R&B** and **top 40**. Does not want jazz, classical or rap. Published *Because of You*, recorded by Terri Williams (gospel); and *It's Over*, recorded by Randy

Albright (country), both written by Leslie Silvestri/Fred John Silvestri on KMA Records; and "Why Can't You Hear My Prayer?" (by F. John Silvestri), recorded by Huey Dunbar of D.L.G. (Grammy nominee) on Trend Records (gospel/R&B), co-published with BOAM Publishing/ASCAP.
Tips: "Send us your song. We will listen to it several times. We are willing to work with you. When we pass on a song we will tell you what we think the song needs so you can re-write and re-submit it. Remember we also started from the bottom. We know what it feels like to get a rejection notice in the mail. We strongly believe if you have a love for music, attend workshops, seminars, join songwriters organizations and keep writing, you will achieve your goal."

ALPHA MUSIC INC. (BMI), 747 Chestnut Ridge Rd., Chestnut Ridge NY 10977. (914)356-0800. Fax: (914)356-0895. E-mail: trfemail@aol.com. Contact: Michael Nurko. Music publisher. Estab. 1931. Pays standard royalty.
Affiliate(s): Dorian Music Corp. (ASCAP) and TRF Music Inc.
How to Contact: Alpha Music does not accept unsolicited submissions.
Music: All categories, mainly **instrumental** and **acoustic**; also **theme music** for television and film. "Have published over 50,000 titles since 1931."

AMEN, INC., 2035 Pleasanton Rd., San Antonio TX 78221-1306. (210)932-AMEN. E-mail: amen@txdirect.net/. Music publisher and record company (AMC Records). Estab. 1963. Pays standard royalty.
Affiliate(s): CITA Music (BMI).
How to Contact: Submit demo tape by mail. Unsolicited submissions are OK. Prefers cassette and lyric sheet. "Allow three to four weeks before calling to inquire about submission." SASE. Reports in 12-16 weeks.
Music: Evangelical Christian gospel regardless of presentation, whether Spanish, English or bilingual. Published "Imponme Tus Manos" (by Jesus Yorba Garcia), recorded by Rudy Guerra; "Jesucristo" (by Enrique Alvarez), recorded by Kiko Alvarez; and "Hey, Hey, Hey" (by Manny R. Guerra), all on AMC Records.

AMERICAN HEARTSTRING PUBLISHING (ASCAP), 24632-C Brighton Dr., Valencia CA 91355. E-mail: amh@amhpublish.com. Website: http://www.amhpublish.com. President: Tim Howell. Music publisher. Estab. 1994. Publishes 10-20 songs/year; publishes 1-2 new songwriters/year. Staff size: 1. Pays standard royalty.
How to Contact: Submit demo tape by mail; or e-mail lyrics with lead sheet or midi file. Unsolicited submissions are OK. Prefers cassette, CD or videocassette. SASE. Reports in 1 month.
Music: Mostly **pop**, **contemporary Christian** and **country crossover**; also **MOR**, **R&B** and **duets any style**. Does not want rap. Published "Food for Thought," recorded by Rob Carter and the Blueprints on Salt Mine (contemporary Christian).
Tips: "Lyrics are king and good melodies make the magic happen. Make sure your song is 'singable' with a good hook and contemporary theme anyone can identify with."

ANTELOPE PUBLISHING INC., P.O. Box 55, Rowayton CT 06853. President: Tony LaVorgna. Music publisher. Estab. 1982. Publishes 5-10 new songs/year; publishes 3-5 new songwriters/year. Pays standard royalty.
How to Contact: Submit demo tape by mail. Unsolicited submissions are OK. Prefers cassette with lead sheet. Does not return material. Reports in 1 month "only if interested."
Music: Only **bebop** and **1940s swing**. Does not want anything electronic. Published *Inspiration*, written and recorded by T. LaVorgna (jazz); *Please Stay* (by Nicole Pasternak), recorded by Cathy Gale (1940s swing), both on Antelope; and *Nightcrawler* (by Tommy Dean), recorded by Swing Fever on Alto Sound (jazz).
Tips: "Put your best song first with a short intro."

ARAS MUSIC (ASCAP), P.O. Box 100215, Palm Bay FL 32910-0215. Phone/fax: (407)650-2589. E-mail: savmusic@juno.com. Website: http://www.zyworld.com/AYoung/SAV/htm. President (contemporary Christian, country): William D. Young. A&R (country, jingles, music for movies, Latin): Amy Young. Music publisher and record company (Outback Records). Member Academy of Country Music, Country Music Association. Estab. 1996. Staff size: 3. Pays standard royalty.
Affiliate(s): SAV Music (BMI) and PARDO Music (SESAC).
How to Contact: Submit demo tape by mail. Unsolicited submissions are OK. Prefers cassette or CD with 3 songs and typed (or neatly printed) lyric sheet. SASE. "Make sure enough postage is included to return demo." Reports in 4-6 weeks.

Music: Mostly **country, contemporary Christian** and **jazz**; also **jingles** and music suitable for motion pictures. Does not want rap or classical. Published "On Angels' Wings" (by Roland Caire, Jr.); "With You By My Side" (by Bob and Christina Marler); and "Send The Rain" (by Chris Eaton), all recorded by Kateena LeForge on Outback Records (Christian).
Tips: "When recording a demo, have an artist in mind. We pitch to major labels and major artists, so please submit studio-quality demos with typed lyric sheets. If you submit a marketable product, we will put forth 100% effort for you."

☑ ○ **AUDIO MUSIC PUBLISHERS (ASCAP)**, 449 N. Vista St., Los Angeles CA 90036. (213)653-0693. E-mail: unclelenny@aol.com. Professional Manager: Lew Weisman. Owner: Ben Weisman. Music publisher, record company and record producer (The Weisman Production Group). Estab. 1962. Publishes 25 songs/year; publishes 10-15 new songwriters/year. Staff size: 10. Pays standard royalty.
How to Contact: Submit demo tape by mail. Unsolicited submissions are OK. "No permission needed." Prefers cassette with 3-10 songs and lyric sheet. "We do not return unsolicited material without SASE. Don't query first; just send tape." Reports in 6 weeks. "We listen; we don't write back. If we like your material we will telephone you."
Music: Mostly **pop, R&B** and **rap**; also **dance, funk, soul** and **gospel**. Does not want heavy metal. "Crazy About You" and *Where Is Love*, both written by Curtis Womack; and *Don't Make Me Walk Away* (by Debe Gunn), all recorded by Valerie on Kon Kord (R&B).

◐ **BAGATELLE MUSIC PUBLISHING CO. (BMI)**, P.O. Box 925929, Houston TX 77292. (713)680-2160 or (800)845-6865. President: Byron Benton. Music publisher, record company and record producer. Publishes 40 songs/year; publishes 2 new songwriters/year. Pays standard royalty.
Affiliate(s): Floyd Tillman Publishing Co.
How to Contact: Submit demo tape by mail. Unsolicited submissions are OK. Prefers cassette (or videocassette) with any number of songs and lyric sheet. SASE.
Music: Mostly **country**; also **gospel** and **blues**. Published "Everything You Touch," written and recorded by Johnny Nelms; "This Is Real" and "Mona from Daytona," written and recorded by Floyd Tillman, all on Bagatelle Records.

🆕 ○ **BAITSTRING MUSIC (ASCAP)**, 2622 Kirtland Rd., Brewton AL 36426. (334)867-2228. President: Roy Edwards. Music publisher and record company (Bolivia Records). Estab. 1972. Publishes 20 songs/year; publishes 10 new songwriters/year. Hires staff songwriters. Pays standard royalty.
Affiliate(s): Cheavoria Music Co. (BMI)
How to Contact: Submit demo tape by mail. Unsolicited submissions are OK. Prefers cassette with 3 songs and lyric sheet. Does not return material. Reports in 1 month.
Music: Mostly **R&B, pop** and **easy listening**; also **country**. Published "Forever and Always," written and recorded by Jim Portwood (pop); and "Make Me Forget" (by Horace Linsley) and "Never Let Me Go" (by Cheavoria Edwards), both recorded by Bobbie Robertsen (country), all on Bolivia Records.

◐ **BAL & BAL MUSIC PUBLISHING CO. (ASCAP)**, P.O. Box 369, LaCanada CA 91012-0369. (818)548-1116. President: Adrian P. Bal. Music publisher, record company (Bal Records) and record producer. Member AGAC and AIMP. Estab. 1965. Publishes 2-6 songs/year; publishes 2-4 new songwriters/year. Staff size: 2. Pays standard royalty.
Affiliate(s): Bal West Music Publishing Co. (BMI).
How to Contact: Write or call first and obtain permission to submit. Prefers cassette with 3 songs and lyric sheet. SASE. Reports in 3 months.
Music: Mostly **MOR, country, rock** and **gospel**; also **blues, church/religious, easy listening, jazz, R&B, soul** and **top 40/pop**. Does not want heavy metal or rap. Published *Special Day*, written and recorded by Rhonda Johnson on Bal Records (gospel).
Tips: "Send what you believe to be commercial—who will buy the product?"

🆕 ◐ **BALMUR ENTERTAINMENT**, 1105 17th Ave. S., Nashville TN 37212-2203. (615)329-1431. Fax: (615)321-0240. E-mail: balmurent@aol.com. Creative Director: Richard Butler. Music publisher.

MARKET CONDITIONS are constantly changing! If you're still using this book and it is 2001 or later, buy the newest edition of *Songwriter's Market* at your favorite bookstore or order directly from Writer's Digest Books at (800)289-0963.

Publishes 100 songs/year; publishes 2-3 new songwriters/year. Hires staff songwriters. Pays standard royalty.
Affiliate(s): Willdawn Music, A Little Good News Music (ASCAP), Pugwash Music (BMI) and Paddy's Head Music (SOCAN).
How to Contact: Write first and obtain permission to submit a demo. Prefers cassette or DAT with 2 songs and lyric sheet. SASE. Reports in 3-4 months.
Music: Mostly **country, pop** and **rock**. Published "I Can Still Feel You," recorded by Collin Raye on Epic; and "Guys Do It All the Time," recorded by Mindy McCready on BNA (both written by Kim Tribble and Bobby Whiteside); and "That's Where You're Wrong" (by Jeff Crossan), recorded by Daryle Singletary on Giant (country).

BARKIN' FOE THE MASTER'S BONE, 1111 Elm St. #520, Cincinnati OH 45210-2271. Website: http://www.1stbook.com. Office Manager (rock, R&B): Kevin Curtis. Professional Managers: Shond Barr (country, jazz, pop, rap); Betty Barr (gospel, soul, soft rock). Music publisher. Estab. 1989. Publishes 4 songs/year; publishes 1 new songwriter/year. Staff size: 4. Pays standard royalty.
Affiliate(s): Beat Box Music (ASCAP) and Feltstar (BMI).
How to Contact: Submit demo tape by mail. Unsolicited submissions are OK. Prefers cassette (or VHS videocassette) with 3 songs. SASE. Reports in 2 weeks.
Music: Mostly **country, soft rock** and **pop**; also **soul, gospel, rap** and **jazz**. Does not want classical. Published "Close to the Son" (by Sean Stewart), recorded by Young Souls on God's Garden Records (gospel).

BARREN WOOD PUBLISHING (BMI), 180 Wallace Rd., #T12, Nashville TN 37211. Phone/fax: (615)315-9494. President: Jack Froschauer. Music publisher and record company (Emerald City Records). Estab. 1992. Publishes 5-6 songs/year; publishes 3-4 new songwriters/year. Staff size: 1. Pays standard royalty.
Affiliate(s): MerryGold Music Publishing (ASCAP).
How to Contact: Submit demo tape by mail. Unsolicited submissions are OK. Prefers cassette or DAT with 1-4 songs and lyric or lead sheet. "Studio quality demo cassette please." SASE. Reports in 2-3 months.
Music: Mostly **country, A/C** and **Christian**. Does not want alternative. Published *Rejoice in the Lord Always* (by J. Carolina/Mark Vanlurndor), recorded by 3 Kings & Caravan of Joy (Christmas); and *Come Out From the Storm* (by Kent Pritchard), recorded by Kent Pritchard & God's Will (rock), both on Emerald City Records.
Tips: "Recognize that songwriting is a business. Present yourself and your material in a professional, businesslike mannner."

BAY RIDGE PUBLISHING CO. (BMI), P.O. Box 5537, Kreole Station, Moss Point MS 39563-1537. (228)475-0059. Estab. 1974. President/Owner: Joe F. Mitchell. Music publisher and record company (Missile Records).
How to Contact: Write first and obtain permission to submit. Include #10 SASE. "No collect calls; not reviewing unsolicited material. Include sufficient return postage with all packages." Reports in 6-8 weeks.
Music: Mostly **country, hardcore, folk, contemporary, alternative, gospel, rap, heavy metal, jazz, bluegrass, R&B**; also **ballads, reggae, world, soul, MOR, blues, rock** and **pop**. Published *You Ran Away With My Heart* (by Leonard Eckhardt); *This New Life She's Living* (by James Hendricks); and *Hurt, Hurt Go Away* (by Diane Abbott/Eletta Sias), all recorded by Michael Pitts on Missile Records (country).
Tips: "We will give consideration to new exceptionally talented artists with a fan base and some backing."

BERANDOL MUSIC LTD. (BMI), 2600 John St., Unit 220, Markham, Ontario L3R 3W3 Canada. (905)475-1848. A&R Director: Ralph Cruickshank. Music publisher, record company (Berandol Records), music print publisher (Music Box Dancer Publications), record producer and distributor. Member CMPA, CIRPA, CRIA. Estab. 1969. Publishes 20-30 songs/year; publishes 5-10 new songwriters/year. Pays standard royalty.
How to Contact: Submit demo tape by mail. Unsolicited submissions are OK. Prefers cassette with 2-5 songs. Does not return material. Reports in 3 weeks.
Music: Mostly **instrumental, children's** and **top 40**.
Tips: "Strong melodic choruses and original-sounding music receive top consideration."

HAL BERNARD ENTERPRISES, INC., 2612 Erie Ave., P.O. Box 8385, Cincinnati OH 45208. (513)871-1500. Fax: (513)871-1510. E-mail: umbrella@one.net. President: Stan Hertzman. Professional Manager: Pepper Bonar. Music publisher, record company (Strugglebaby), record producer and management firm (Umbrella Artists Management). Publishes 12-24 songs/year; 1-2 new songwriters/year. Pays standard royalty.

Affiliate(s): Sunnyslope Music (ASCAP), Bumpershoot Music (BMI), Apple Butter Music (ASCAP), Carb Music (ASCAP), Saiko Music (ASCAP), Smorgaschord Music (ASCAP), Clifton Rayburn Music (ASCAP) and Robert Stevens Music (ASCAP).

How to Contact: Write or call first and obtain permission to submit. Prefers cassette with 3 songs and lyric sheet. SASE. Reports in 6 weeks only if interested.

Music: Mostly **rock**, **R&B** and **top 40/pop**. Published "Mattress," "Joy and Madness" and "Moaner," all recorded by psychodots on Strugglebaby Records; and "History," "Try," and "Blame Game" (by Rob Fetters/Adrian Belew), all recorded by Rob Fetters on Baby Ranch Records.

Tips: "Best material should appear first on demo. Cast your demos. If you, as the songwriter, can't sing it—don't. Get someone who can present your song properly, use a straight rhythm track and keep it as naked as possible. If you think it still needs something else, have a string arranger, etc. help you but still keep the *voice up* and the *lyrics clear*."

BETTER THAN SEX MUSIC (ASCAP), 110 W. 26th St., Third Floor South, New York NY 10001-6805. (212)645-3068. Fax: (212)989-6459. E-mail: citkovic@aol.com. President/Music Consultant: James Citkovic. Music publisher. Estab. 1996. Publishes 14 songs/year; publishes 2 new songwriters/year. Staff size: 3. Pays standard royalty.

Affiliate(s): Polysutra Music (ASCAP) and Deerbrook Music (ASCAP).

How to Contact: Submit demo tape by mail, "first class only." Unsolicited submissions are OK. Prefers cassette, DAT or VHS videocassette with 4 songs and lyric sheet. "No phone calls. Put the best song first on the tape. Include any information that can help us evaluate you and your music." Does not return material. Reports in 3 weeks.

Film & TV: Places 17 songs in film and 3 songs in TV/year.

Music: Mostly **pop**, **R&B** and **dance**; also **modern rock**, **electronica** and **acid house/hip-hop/funk**.

Tips: "We are looking for leaders, not followers."

BETTY JANE/JOSIE JANE MUSIC PUBLISHERS (ASCAP, BMI), 7400 N. Adams Rd., North Adams MI 49262-9713. E-mail: cereed@dmci.net. Website: http://cerrecordssimplenet.com. Professional Managers: Claude E. Reed (all styles); Eunice Reed (pop/choral). Music publisher, record company (C.E.R. Records) and record producer. Estab. 1980. Publishes 75-100 songs/year; 10 new songwriters/year. Staff size: 3-5. Pays standard royalty.

How to Contact: Submit demo tape by mail. Unsolicited submissions are OK. Prefers cassette or 7½ ips reel-to-reel with 1-5 songs and lyric or lead sheets. SASE. Reports in 2-4 weeks.

Music: Mostly **gospel** and **country western**; also **pop/R&B** and **MOR**. Published *Rebel Lee* and *No Doubt About It* (by Monique Doolittle), both recorded by Daniel Hodges on Wishbone (country); and *Making Christ Known* (by Paul Todd), recorded by Toni Walker on C.E.R. Records (gospel).

Tips: "Try to be original, present your music in a professional way, submit only your very best songs with accurate lyric sheets and well made demo tape. Be patient! Send SASE with a sufficient amount of postage if you want your material returned."

BIG FISH MUSIC PUBLISHING GROUP, 11927 Magnolia Blvd. #3, N. Hollywood CA 91607. (818)984-0377. CEO: Chuck Tennin. Professional Managers: Cathy Carlson (country, adult contemporary, pop); Lora Sprague (jazz/jazz instrumentals). Music publisher, record company (California Sun Records) and record producer. Estab. 1971. Publishes 10-20 songs/year; publishes 4-5 new songwriters/year. Staff size: 6. Pays standard royalty.

Affiliate(s): Big Fish Music (BMI) and California Sun Music (ASCAP).

How to Contact: Write first and obtain permission to submit. Include SASE for reply. "Please do not call." Prefers cassette with no more than 4 songs and lyric sheet. "Include a dated cover letter, with your source of referral (*Songwriter's Market*)." SASE. Reports in 2 weeks.

Film & TV: Places 1 song in TV/year. Recently published "Girls Will Be Girls" (by Cathy Carlson/John LeGrande), by Black River Girls in *All My Children*.

Music: Mostly **country**, including **country pop**, **country A/C** and **country crossover** with an edge; also **pop ballads**, **uplifting**, **inspirational contemporary gospel** with a message, **instrumental background**

TO HELP YOU UNDERSTAND and use the information in these listings, see "How to Use *Songwriter's Market* to Get Your Songs Heard," on page 5.

music for TV & films and **novelty type songs** for commercial use. Published "Stop That Train" (by Robert Porter), recorded by the Black River Girls on California Sun Records.
Tips: "Demo should be professional, high quality, clean, simple and dynamic, and must get the song across on the first listen. Good clear vocals, a nice melody, a good musical feel, good musical arrangement and strong lyrics and chorus. Looking for unique country songs with a different edge for ongoing Nashville music projects and songs for a female country trio."

☑ ▦ ⊘ **BIXIO MUSIC GROUP/IDM VENTURES, LTD. (ASCAP)**, 111 E. 14th St., Suite 140, New York NY 10003. (212)695-3911. Fax: (212)967-6284. E-mail: tomo@mail.idt.net or miriam@bixio. com or sales@bixio.com. Website: http://www.bixio.com. Professional Managers: Miriam Westercappel (all styles); Tomo (rock, R&B, dance); Karlene Evans (soundtracks). Music publisher and artist management. Estab. 1985. Publishes a few hundreds songs/year; publishes 2 new songwriters/year. Staff size: 4. Pays standard royalty.
How to Contact: Does not accept unsolicited material.
Music: Mostly **soundtracks**, **rock** and **R&B**; also **country**. Published "The Conformist" and "Commercial Lincoln Car," recorded by George Delereux on DRG Records; and "Big High T Sound Track" (by Bixio Cherubini/M. Salvatore) on TVT Records (jazz).

◐ **BLACK ROSE PRODUCTIONS**, P.O. Box 216, Cold Spring Harbor NY 11724. (516)367-8544. Fax: (516)692-4709. New Jersey office: 15 Gloria Lane, Suite 201, Fairfield NJ 07004. (973)227-3884. Fax: (973)575-2749. President: Tito Batista. A&R: Marc Lawrence. Subpublished through BMG Music Publishing (Japan, B.V., Hong Kong). Music publisher and record company. Estab. 1989. Publishes 200 songs/year; publishes 10 new songwriters/year. "We take 100% of publishing but can be negotiated based upon track history of composer."
Affiliate(s): One Hot Note Music Inc.
How to Contact: Submit demo tape by mail. Unsolicited submissions are OK. Prefers cassette or CD. Does not return material.
Music: Mostly **pop**, **rock** and **jazz**; also **dance**, **country** and **rap**. Published "Be My Baby," written and recorded by T.C. Kross on Reiter Records; "Ready or Not" (by Lange/Bastianelli), recorded by Yolanda Yan on Cinepoly Records and by Camille Nivens on BMG Records.
Tips: "Make the song as well produced and recorded as you can."

◐ **BLACK STALLION COUNTRY PUBLISHING (BMI)**, P.O. Box 368, Tujunga CA 91043. (818)352-8142. Fax: (818)352-2122. President: Kenn Kingsbury. Music publisher, management firm and book publisher (*Who's Who in Country & Western Music*). Member CMA, CMF. Publishes 2 songs/year; publishes 1 new songwriter/year. Pays standard royalty.
How to Contact: Submit demo tape by mail. Unsolicited submissions are OK. Prefers cassette with 3 songs and lyric sheet. SASE. Reports in 1 month.
Music: Mostly **bluegrass** and **country**.

🅽 ⊕ ⊘ **BME PUBLISHING**, P.O. Box 450224, Cologne Germany 50877. Phone: (049)221-9472000. Fax: (049)221-9502278. E-mail: bme.records@t-online.de. Contact: Dr. Dietmar Barzen. Music publisher, record company and record producer. Estab. 1993. Pays standard royalty to artists on contract.
How to Contact: Submit demo tape by mail. Unsolicited submissions are OK. Prefers cassette, DAT or CD-R with 3-5 songs and lyric sheet. SAE and IRC. Reports in 1 month.
Music: Mostly **pop/AC**, **rock** and **commercial dance/hip-hop**; also **MOR**.

☑ ⊘ **BMG MUSIC PUBLISHING**, 810 Seventh Ave., 36th Floor, New York NY 10019. (212)930-4000. Fax: (212)930-4096. Website: http://www.bmgentertainment.com. Beverly Hills office: 8750 Wilshire Blvd., Beverly Hills CA 90211. (310)358-4700. Fax: (310)358-4727. Contact: Danny Strick. Vice President of A&R: Bruce Flohr. Vice President of Film & Music: Art Ford. Nashville office: One Music Circle N., Suite 380, Nashville TN 37203. (615)780-5420. Fax: (615)780-5430. Music publisher.
How to Contact: BMG Music Publishing does not accept unsolicited submissions.
Music: Published "All Night Long" (by F. Evans/R. Lawrence/S. Combs/S. Crawford), recorded by Faith Evans featuring Puff Daddy on Bad Boy; and "Ain't Enough Roses" (by L. Brokop/S. Hogin/B. Reagan), recorded by Lisa Brokop on Columbia (country).

⊘ **BOURNE CO. MUSIC PUBLISHERS (ASCAP)**, 5 W. 37th St., New York NY 10018. (212)391-4300. Fax: (212)391-4306. E-mail: bournemusic@worldnet.att.net. Contact: Professional Manager. Music publisher. Estab. 1917. Publishes educational material and popular music.
Affiliate(s): ABC Music, Ben Bloom, Better Half, Bogat, Burke & Van Heusen, Goldmine, Harborn,

Lady Mac and Murbo Music.
How to Contact: Does not accept unsolicited submissions.
Music: Piano/vocal, **band pieces** and **choral pieces**. Published "Amen" and "Mary's Little Boy Child" (by Hairston); "When You Wish Upon a Star" (by Washington/Harline); and "Unforgettable" (by Irving Gordon).

DAVID BOWMAN PRODUCTIONS & W. DAVID MUSIC, 28 Park Lane, Feasterville PA 19053. (215)942-9059 or (215)322-8078. President: David Bowman. Music publisher, music library producers/music production house and orchestra. Estab. 1989. Publishes 10-20 songs/year; publishes 5-10 new songwriters/year. Staff size: 5. "Pays by the job."
How to Contact: Write first and obtain permission to submit. Prefers cassette. "We are looking for instrumental pieces of any length not exceeding 3 minutes for use in AV music library. Also looking for 30 and 60 second music spots for television, radio and all multimedia applications." Does not return material. Reports in 6-12 weeks.
Film & TV: Places 2 songs in film and 1 song in TV/year. Music Supervisors: David Bowman (instrumental, soundtracks, orchestrations); Marc McFadden (instrumental, commercial). Recently published "Kids on the Beat," in *Treasure Chest TV*; "The Devil's Theme," in *Fausta*; "Together As One," in *Fraternity Violence Education Program*, all written and recorded by W. David Bowman.
Music: All types. Published "Journalized," "The Streets of Longhorne" and "Claritronic," all written and recorded by W. David Bowman on Warren Records.
Tips: "Network. Get your name and your work out there. Let everyone know what you are all about and what you are doing. Be patient, persistent and professional. What are you waiting for? Do it!"

ALLAN BRADLEY MUSIC (BMI), 484 S. Grand, Orange CA 92866. Website: http://allanlicht.onth eweb.com. Owner: Allan Licht. Music publisher, record company (ABL Records) and record producer. Estab. 1993. Publishes 10 songs/year; publishes 5 new songwriters/year. Staff size: 2. Pays standard royalty.
Affiliate(s): Holly Ellen Music (ASCAP).
How to Contact: Submit demo tape by mail. Unsolicited submissions are OK. Prefers cassette with 3 songs and lyric sheet. "Send only unpublished works." Does not return material. Reports in 2 weeks only if interested.
Music: Mostly A/C, **pop** and **R&B**; also **country** and **Christian contemporary**. Does not want hard rock. Published *Time to Go*, written and recorded by Alan Douglass; *I'll Keep the Change* (by Betty Kay Miller/Marcia McCaslin), recorded by W. Alan Hall; and *Only In My Mind* (by Jonathon Hansew), recorded by Allan Licht, all on ABL Records.
Tips: "Be open to suggestions from well-established publishers. Please send only songs that have Top 10 potential. Only serious writers are encouraged to submit."

BRANCH GROUP MUSIC (SOCAN), 1067 Sherwin Rd., Winnipeg, Manitoba R3H 0T8 Canada. (204)694-3101. E-mail: oak@oakstreetmusic.ca. Website: http://www.oakstreetmusic.ca. Professional Manager: Arthur Pearson. Music publisher, record company (Oak Street Music), management firm (Paquin Entertainment) and record producer (Oak Street Music). Estab. 1987. Staff size: 8. Publishes 10 songs/year; publishes 2 new songwriters/year. Pays standard royalty.
Affiliate(s): Forest Group Music (SOCAN).
How to Contact: Submit demo tape by mail. Unsolicited submissions are OK. Prefers cassette or VHS videocassette with 2-3 songs and lyric and lead sheet. Does not return material. Reports in 2 months.
Film & TV: Places 10 songs in film and 5 songs in TV/year. Recently published "Something's Happened Here" (by Phil Deschambault/Jonah Store) in *The Clown At Midnight*; "The Simple Way," written and recorded by Fred Penner in *The Simple Way*; and "Take Good Care of Each Other," written and recorded by Fred Penner in *Fred Penner's Place*.
Music: Mostly **children's** and **novelty**; also **triple A**, **rock** and **ethnic**. Published "Fears Be Gone"; "Doctor Doctor"; and "I Love Night-Lullaby," all written and recorded by Fred Penner on Oak Street Music (children's).

BRANSON COUNTRY MUSIC PUBLISHING (BMI), P.O. Box 2527, Broken Arrow OK 74013. (918)455-9442. Fax: (918)451-1965. E-mail: bransoncm@aol.com. General Partners: Dee Branson

---

OPENNESS TO SUBMISSIONS: ☐ beginners; ☑ beginners and experienced; ☑ experienced only; ☑ industry referrals only.

and Betty Branson. Music publisher. Estab. 1997. Publishes 25 songs/year; publishes 4-5 new songwriters/year. Pays standard royalty.

How to Contact: Submit demo tape by mail with photo and bio. Unsolicited submissions are OK. Prefers cassette with 3-5 songs and lyric sheet. Does not return material. Reports in 2 weeks.

Music: Mostly **traditional country** and **upbeat country**. Published *One Prayer Away*, written and recorded by Jerry James (gospel); *The Picture*, written and recorded by Robert Beasley (country); and *Down and Next to Cryin* (by Garry McBryde/Bill Galloway), recorded by Garry McBryde (country), all on Richway.

Tips: "Send good quality demo of traditional or upbeat country songs capable of competing with current top 40. Put your 'attention getter' up front and build from that point as your listener will give you about 10-15 seconds to continue listening or turn you off. Use a good hook and keep comming back to it."

⊕ ◢ **KITTY BREWSTER SONGS**, "Norden," 2 Hillhead Rd., Newtonhill Stonehaven AB39 3TS Scotland. Phone: 01569 730962. MD: Doug Stone. Music publisher, record company (KBS Records), record producer and production company (Brewster & Stone Productions). Estab. 1989. Staff size: 6. Pays standard royalty.

How to Contact: Submit demo tape by mail. Unsolicited submissions are OK. Prefers cassette or VHS videocassette with any number of songs and lyric or lead sheet. Does not return material. Reports in 3-4 months.

Music: Mostly **AOR, pop, R&B** and **dance**; also **country, jazz, rock** and **contemporary**. Published *Sleepin' Alone* (by R. Donald); *I Still Feel the Same* (by R. Greig/K. Mundie); and *Your Love Will Pull Me Thru* (by R. Greig), all recorded by Kitty Brewster on KBS Records (AOR).

Ⓝ ◯ **BRIAN SONG MUSIC CORP. (BMI)**, P.O. Box 1376, Pickens SC 29671. E-mail: braines105@aol.com. Owner: Brian E. Raines. Music publisher, record company (Palmetto Records), record producer and artist management. Estab. 1985. Publishes 5 songs/year; publishes 2-3 new songwriters/year. Staff size: 3. Pays standard royalty.

How to Contact: Write first and obtain permission to submit a demo. Prefers cassette, CD or VHS videocassette with 3 songs and lyric sheet. "Unsolicited material not accepted, and will be returned. Demo must be good quality, lyrics typed. Send photo if an artist; send bio on writer or artist." Does not return material. Reports in 1 month.

Music: Mostly **country, gospel** and **country/gospel**; also **country/blues**. Published *I Wasn't There*, written and recorded by Dale Cassell on Mark V (gospel); and *From the Heart*, written and recorded by Jim Hubbard on Hubbitt (gospel).

Ⓝ ◢ **BRIGHTLY MUSIC PUBLISHING (PRS/MCPS)**, 231 Lower Clapton Rd., London ES 8EG United Kingdom. Phone: (0181)533-7994. Fax: (0181)986-4035. E-mail: abrightly@yahoo.com. Professional Managers: Anthony Brightly (reggae); Pat Rowe (gospel/R&B). Music publisher, record company (Sir George Records) and record producer. Estab. 1982. Publishes 24 songs/year; publishes 18 new songwriters/year. Staff size: 4. Pays standard royalty.

How to Contact: Write first and obtain permission to submit a demo. Prefers cassette or CD with 4 songs. SAE and IRC. Reports within 3 months.

Music: Mostly **reggae** and **gospel/R&B**. Published *I Won't Go On* (by Hendricks), recorded by Pure Silk on Sir George Records (reggae).

⊕ ✔ ◯ **THE BROTHERS**, The Music Village, 11b Osiers Rd., London SW8 1NL England. Phone: (0181)870-0011. Fax: (0181)870-2101. E-mail: info@thebrothers.co.uk. Director of A&R: Ian Titchener. Professional Managers: J. Underwood and Nick Titchener. Music publisher and record company. Estab. 1989. Publishes 20 songs/year. "Payment decided on a contract by contract basis."

How to Contact: Submit demo tape by mail. Unsolicited submissions are OK. Prefers CD-R. Does not return material. Reports in 2 weeks only if interested.

Music: Mostly **R&B/dance** and **pop**. Does not want rock, heavy rock, religious or country. Published "Rescue" (by Peter/Ward), recorded by Groove Generation (dance/pop) and "Apology," written and recorded by Love To Infinity (dance anthem), both on Brothers Records; and "Desailly" (by Kemper/Ward/Peter/Boff), recorded by Boff on Sans Branches (dance).

Tips: "Send no more than three tracks per submission. We are also interested in masters as well as publishing and have just had two national UK top 10 hits with a dance act 'The Course'."

Ⓝ ♈ ◯ **J. AARON BROWN & ASSOCIATES INC.**, 1508 16th Ave. S., Nashville TN 37212. (615)385-0022. Fax: (615)386-9988. Publisher Assistant: Becky Shirborne. Music publisher, record company and record producer. Estab. 1980. Publishes 30-50 songs/year; publishes 3-5 new songwriters/year. Hires staff songwriters. Pays standard royalty.

Affiliate(s): Prime Time Music (ASCAP), Mastercraft Music (BMI) and Snow Fox Music (SESAC).
- This company's songs won Grammys in 1990 and 1996 for Best Recording for Children.
How to Contact: Submit demo tape by mail. Unsolicited submissions are OK. Prefers cassette with 2 songs and lyric sheet. Does not return material. Reports in 1 month.
Music: Mostly **children's**, **country** and **pop**; also **R&B**. Published *Baby Your Baby* (by Hal Newman), recorded by George Strait on MCA (country); *Got A Hold On Me* (by Rachel Newman), recorded by Shania Twain on Mercury (country); and *Lullabyes*, recorded by various artists on Jaba (children's).
Tips: "Become a student of great songs."

[N] [ ] BSW RECORDS (BMI), P.O. Box 2297, Universal City TX 78148. (210)599-0022. Fax: (210)653-3989. E-mail: bswr18@txdirect.net. President: Frank Willson. Music publisher, record company and record producer (Frank Willson). Estab. 1987. Publishes 26 songs/year; publishes 14 new songwriters/year. Staff size: 7. Pays standard royalty.
Affiliate(s): WillTex Music and Universal Music Marketing (BMI).
- This company has been named Record Label of the Year ('94-'98) by the Country Music Association of America.
How to Contact: Submit demo tape by mail. Unsolicited submissions are OK. Prefers cassette or CD with 3 songs, lyric sheet and cover letter. SASE. Reports in 1-2 months.
Film & TV: Places 3 songs in film/year.
Music: Mostly **country**, **blues** and **soft rock**. Does not want rap. Published *When the Sun Began to Shine* (by Jimmy Roggers), recorded by S. Roggers; *Ole Gladys*, written and recorded by L. Butler; and *Now His Horse is Whiskey* (by Larry Butler/John Groeing), recorded by Larry Butler, all on BSW (country).

[N] [ ] BUG MUSIC, INC. (ASCAP, BMI), 6777 Hollywood, 9th Floor, Los Angeles CA 90028-4676. (323)466-4352. Fax: (323)466-2366. E-mail: bugmusicla@aol.com. Website: http://www.bugmusic.com. Creative Director: Eddie Gomez. Nashville office: 1026 16th Ave. S., Nashville TN 37212. (615)726-0782. Fax: (615)726-0784. Creative Director: Peter Cronin. London office: 31 Milson Rd., West Kensington, London W14 0LJ. Phone: 0171-602-0727. Fax: 0171-603-7483. Creative Manager: Paul Jordan. New York office: 1776 Broadway, Suite 1708, New York NY 10019. (212)765-2172. Fax: (212)765-2691. Creative Manager: Jeff Pachman. Music publisher. Estab. 1975. Other offices: Nashville contact Dave Durocher and London contact Paul Jordan. "We handle administration."
Affiliate(s): Bughouse (ASCAP).
How to Contact: Does not accept unsolicited submissions.
Music: All genres. Published "You Were Mine" (by E. Erwin/M. Seidel), recorded by Dixie Chicks on Monument.

[N] [ ] [ ] BUGLE PUBLISHING GROUP (ASCAP, BMI), 2410 Belmont Blvd., Nashville TN 37212-5504. (615)460-1112. Fax: (615)460-7300. Professional Manager: Roger Osborne. Music publisher. Estab. 1992. Publishes 5 songs/year. Staff size: 1. Hires staff songwriters. Pays standard royalty.
Affiliate(s): I.R.S. Songs/Firstars Music (ASCAP) and I.R.S. Music, Inc./Illegal Songs, Inc. (BMI).
- In 1996, "That's As Close As I'll Get to Loving You" (Aaron Tippin), published by Bugle Publishing, won a BMI Award for number one song.
How to Contact: Does not accept unsolicited submissions.
Music: Mostly **country** and **pop/rock**. Published *Love Or the Lack Of* (by Rich Wayland), recorded by Daryle Singeltary; and *Then There's You* (by Pat MacDonald), recorded by The Wilkinsons (country), both on Giant; and *The Reason* (by Greg Wells), recorded by Celine Dion on Sony (pop).
Tips: "Research the market and make sure your songs have a credible lyric; songs impact the listener and must be moving enough to cause excitement!"

[ ] BURIED TREASURE MUSIC (ASCAP), 524 Doral Country Dr., Nashville TN 37221. Executive Producer: Scott Turner. Music publisher and record producer (Aberdeen Productions). Estab. 1972. Publishes 30-50 songs/year; publishes 3-10 new songwriters/year. Pays standard royalty.
Affiliate(s): Captain Kidd Music (BMI).
How to Contact: Submit demo tape by mail. Unsolicited submissions are OK. Prefers cassette or VHS

REMEMBER: Don't "shotgun" your demo tapes. Submit only to companies interested in the type of music you write. For more submission hints, refer to Getting Started on page 11.

videocassette with 1-4 songs and lyric sheet. Reports in 2 weeks. "Always enclose SASE if answer is expected."
Music: Mostly **country**, **country/pop** and **MOR**. Does not want rap, hard rock, metal, hip-hop or alternative.
Tips: "*Don't* send songs in envelopes that are 15″x 20″, or by registered mail. The post office will not accept tapes in regular business-size envelopes."

○ CALIFORNIA COUNTRY MUSIC (BMI), 112 Widmar Pl., Clayton CA 94517. (510)833-4680. Owner: Edgar J. Brincat. Music publisher and record company (Roll On Records). Estab. 1985. Publishes 30 songs/year; publishes 2-4 new songwriters/year. Staff size: 1. Pays standard royalty.
Affiliate(s): Sweet Inspirations Music (ASCAP).
How to Contact: Submit demo tape by mail. Unsolicited submissions are OK. Do not call or write. Prefers cassette with 3 songs and lyric sheet. Any calls will be returned collect to caller. SASE. Reports in 4-6 weeks.
Music: Mostly **MOR**, **contemporary country** and **pop**; also **R&B**, **gospel** and **light rock**. Does not want rap, metal or rock. Published *For Realities Sake* (by F.L. Pittman/R. Barretta) and *Maddy* (by F.L. Pittman/ M. Weeks), both recorded by Ron Banks & L.J. Reynolds on Life & Bellmark Records; and *Quarter Past Love* (by Irwin Rubinsky/Janet Fisher), recorded by Darcy Dawson on NNP Records.

○ CAMEX MUSIC, 535 Fifth Ave., New York NY 10017. (212)682-8400. A&R Director: Alex Benedetto. Music publisher, record company and record producer. Estab. 1970. Publishes 100 songs/year; publishes 10 new songwriters/year. Query for royalty terms.
How to Contact: Submit demo tape by mail. Unsolicited submissions are OK. Prefers cassettes with 5-10 songs and lyric sheet or lead sheet. SASE. Reports in 3-6 months.
Music: Mostly **alternative rock**, **pop** and **hard rock**; also **R&B**, **MOR** and **movie themes**. Artists include Marmalade, SAM and Hallucination Station.

▧ ○ CAPP COMPANY (BMI), P.O. Box 150871, San Rafael CA 94915-0871. (415)457-8617. Fax: (415)453-6990. E-mail: capp@wco.com. Website: http://www.capprecords.com. Publisher/International Manager: Dominique Toulon (pop, dance, New Age); Creative Manager/A&R: Mark D'Elicio (dance, techno). Vice President/Publisher: Marc Oshry (pop, rock, dance). Music publisher and record company (CAPP Records). Member: NARAS, NCSA, Songwriter's Guild of America. Estab. 1993. Publishes 100 songs/year; publishes 25 new songwriters/year. Staff size: 8. Pays standard royalty.
Affiliate(s): Cary August Publishing Co./CAPP Records (BMI).
How to Contact: Submit demo by mail. Unsolicited submissions are OK. Prefers CD, NTSC videocassette or CD-R with 3 songs and cover letter. "E-mail us in advance for submissions, if possible." SASE. Reports in 2 weeks.
Film & TV: Places 20 songs in film and 7 songs in TV/year. Music Supervisors: Dominique Toulon (pop, dance, New Age); Mark D. D'Elicio (dance, techno). Recently published "Wish You Were Here" (by Cary August/Marc Oshry/Brian Wood/Tom Finch), recorded by Cary August for "Café Froth" TV/ad; "Indian Dream" and "Song For the Earth," both written and recorded by Steven Buckner in "Deep Encounters."
Music: Mostly **pop**, **dance** and **techno**; also **New Age** and **jazz**. Does not want country. Published "It's Not a Dream" (by Cary August/André Pessis), recorded by Cary August on CAPP Records (dance); "Where Do I Go" (by Andrew Lee), recorded by Andrew (pop); and "Don't Stop," written and recorded by DJ DuBois (house), both on Pro-Worldwide.

○ CASH PRODUCTIONS, INC. (BMI), 744 Joppa Farm Rd., Joppa MD 21085. (301)679-2262. President (country): Ernest W. Cash. A&R: Norma R. Cash (gospel); Debra L. Benedetta (country, R&B); Michael A. Benedetta (rock). Music publisher, record company (Continental Records, Inc.), national and international record distributor, artist management, record producer (Vision Music Group, Inc.) and video production. Estab. 1987. Publishes 30-60 songs/year; publishes 10-15 new songwriters/year. Staff size: 5. Pays standard royalty.
How to Contact: Call first and obtain permission to submit. Prefers cassette or VHS videocassette with 3 songs and lyric sheet. SASE. Reports in 2 weeks.
Music: Mostly **country**, **gospel** and **pop**; also **R&B** and **rock**. Published *Beer Drinkin' Belly Rubbin' Lyin' Cheatin' Songs* (by Patricia A. Smith); *A Man I Call Jones* (by Jimmy Peppers); and *Neon Angel* (by Leonard G. Eckhardt), all written and recorded by Randy Allen St. Claire on Continental (country).
Tips: "Be honest with me, and let's be successful together. Do the best job you can on your work—writing, arrangement and production. Demos are very important in placing material."

[N] Ⓓ CHERRI/HOLLY MUSIC (BMI), 1859 Acton Court, Simi Valley CA 93065-2205. (805)527-4082. Professional Managers: John G. Goske (MOR, pop, jazz); Holly Rose Lawrence (R&B, top 40, rock, country); Pat (Big Red) Silzer (gospel, Christian); John Wm. LaRocca (country, adult contemporary). Vice President: Helen Goske. Music publisher, record company (Whirlwind Label) and record producer (Helen and John G. Goske). Estab. 1961. Publishes 9 songs/year; publishes 9 new songwriters/year. Staff size: 5. Pays standard royalty.

Affiliate(s): Blue Sapphire Music (ASCAP).

How to Contact: Submit demo tape by mail. Unsolicited submissions are OK. Prefers cassette or CD with 3 songs and lyric sheet and cover letter. "Absolutely no phone calls. Extremely important to have name, address and phone number on cassette and titles of songs in order. Important to hear lyrics above music. Please submit cover letter overview with cassette. Lyrics should be typed. Photo would be good." Does not return material. Reports in 2 months only if interested.

Music: Mostly A/C, **top 40** and **country**; also **R&B** and **rock**. Published "These Are Your Tears" (by John Wm. LaRocca); "Don't Say Goodbye, Just Say Goodnight" (by Ron McManaman); and "I Can't" (by Viva Lewis), all recorded by Stephanie Sieggen on Whirlwind (country).

Tips: "Send only your best. Must be copyrighted with symbol and year. Uncopyrighted material will be discarded. No phone calls. A concise overview of songwriting career (with photo if possible—especially if writer is vocalist) on submission. Writer should be affiliated with BMI or ASCAP."

☑ 🖳 Ⓓ CHRISTMAS & HOLIDAY MUSIC (BMI), 3517 Warner Blvd., Suite 4, Burbank CA 91505. (323)849-5381. E-mail: justinwilde@christmassongs.com. Website: http://www.christmassongs.com. President (all styles): Justin Wilde. Music publisher. Estab. 1980. Publishes 8-12 songs/year; publishes 8-12 new songwriters/year. Staff size: 1. "All submissions must be complete songs (i.e., music and lyrics)." Pays standard royalty.

  • Christmas & Holiday Music is relocating their office this year. See their website for most current address before mailing.

Affiliate(s): Songcastle Music (ASCAP).

How to Contact: Submit demo tape by mail. Unsolicited submissions are OK. Do *not* call. "First class mail only. Registered or certified mail not accepted." Prefers cassette with no more than 3 songs and lyric sheet. "Professional demos a must." Do not send lead sheets or promotional material, bios, etc." SASE but does not return material out of the US. Reports in 1 month.

Film & TV: Places 1 song in TV/year. Recently published "Christmas Ain't Like It Used to Be," written and recorded by Joe Whistiny and Loren Barrigar in *ER* (Christmas episode).

Music: Strictly **Christmas music** (and a little Hanukkah and Halloween) in every style imaginable: easy listening, rock, R&B, pop, blues, jazz, country, reggae, rap, children's secular or religious. *Please do not send anything that isn't a holiday song.* Published "What Made the Baby Cry?" (by William J. Golay), recorded by Toby Keith on Mercury Records (country); "First Day of The Son" (by Derrick Procell), recorded by the Brooklyn Tabernacle Choir on Warner/Alliance Records (gospel); and "It Must Have Been The Mistletoe" (by Justin Wilde/Doug Konecky), recorded by Kathie Lee Gifford on Warner Bros. Records (pop).

Tips: "We only sign one out of every 100 submissions. Please be selective. If a stranger can hum your melody back to you after hearing it twice, it has 'standard' potential. Couple that with a lyric filled with unique, inventive imagery, that stands on its own, even without music. Combine the two elements, and workshop the finished result thoroughly to identify weak points. Only when the song is polished to perfection, then cut a master quality demo that sounds like a record or pretty close to it. Submit positive lyrics only. Avoid negative themes like 'Blue Christmas.' "

Ⓓ SONNY CHRISTOPHER PUBLISHING (BMI), P.O. Box 9144, Ft. Worth TX 76147-2144. (817)595-4655. Owner: Sonny Christopher. Music publisher, record company and record producer. Estab. 1974. Publishes 20-25 new songs/year; publishes 3-5 new songwriters/year. Staff size: 1. Pays standard royalty.

How to Contact: Write first, then call and obtain permission to submit. Prefers cassette with lyric sheet. SASE (#10 or larger). Reports in 3 months.

Music: Mostly **country, rock** and **blues**. Published *Did They Judge Too Hard* (by Sonny Christopher), recorded by Ronny Collins on Sonshine Records.

Tips: "Be patient. I will respond as soon as I can. A songwriter should have a studio-cut demo with a super vocal. I am one who can hear a song with just acoustic guitar. Don't be hesitant to do a rewrite. To the young songwriter: *never, never* quit."

N **Ø** **CHRYSALIS MUSIC**, 8500 Melrose Ave., Suite 207, Los Angeles CA 90069. (310)652-0066. Fax: (310)652-2024. Website: http://www.chrysalismusic.com. Vice President of Creative Services: Mark Friedman. Music publisher. Estab. 1968.
How to Contact: Chrysalis Music does not accept unsolicited submissions.
Music: Published "C'est La Vie" (by B*Witched/R. Hedges/Brannigan/Ackerman), recorded by B*Witched on Epic; "I Still Believe" (by A. Armato/B. Cantarelli), recorded by Mariah Carey on Columbia; and "Rosa Parks" (by A. Patton/A. Benjamin), recorded by Outkast on LaFace.

N **Ø** **CIMIRRON MUSIC (BMI)**, 607 Piney Point Rd., Yorktown VA 23692. (804)898-8155. E-mail: lpuckett@lx.netcom.com. President: Lana Puckett. Music publisher, record company (Cimirron/Rainbird Records) and record producer. Estab. 1986. Publishes 10-20 songs/year. "Royalty depends on song and writer."
How to Contact: Write or call first and obtain permission to submit. Prefers cassette with 1-3 songs and lyric sheet. Does not return material. Reports in 3 months.
Music: Mostly **country**, **acoustic**, **folk** and **bluegrass**. Published *Cornstalk Pony* (by Lana Puckett/K. Person), recorded by Lana Puckett; "This Box I'm Looking Through," written and recorded by Ron Fetner; and "Pictures," written and recorded by Stephen Bennett, all on Cimirron Records.

✓ **Ø** **CLEAR POND MUSIC (BMI)**, P.O. Box 148, Solana Beach CA 92075-9888. (619)350-8161. Publisher: Susan Pond. Music publisher and record producer (Crystal Clear Productions). Estab. 1992. Publishes 10-50 songs/year; publishes 1-5 new songwriters/year. Pays standard royalty.
How to Contact: Does not accept unsolicited material. "Demos must be submitted by a manager, attorney or paralegal. We are only interested in a singer/songwriter/artist, no exceptions!"
Music: Mostly **pop/rock**, **top 40**, **alternative** and **country** (all types). Published "Wish I Were In Love With You Again" written and recorded by Al Lancellotti (top 40); "Shaman's Song," written and recorded by MoonRage, both on Maxim Records (alternative); and "When All At Last" (by Steve Craig), recorded by Albert Hall on Metal Mind Records (pop/rock).
Tips: "We represent *Billboard* hit songwriters. We specialize in tracking and collecting royalties worldwide. Other areas of expertise are international music markets, encompassing publishing, distribution, licensing and radio markets."

N **Ø** **CLEARWIND PUBLISHING (SESAC)**, P.O. Box 42381, Detroit MI 48242-0381. Contact: A&R Department Director. Music publisher and management company (Clearwind Management). Estab. 1983. Publishes 12-15 songs/year; publishes 2-4 new songwriters/year. Staff size: 1. Pays standard royalty.
How to Contact: Write to obtain permission to submit. "Do NOT call! Unsolicited submissions will be returned unopened." Prefers cassette, CD or VHS videocassette with no more than 2 songs and lyric sheet. Does not return material. Reports in 3 months.
Music: Mostly **pop**, **highly commercial country** and **R&B**; also **highly commercial rock**. Published *Champion* and "What A Friend," written and recorded by Ron Moore on Morada Records.

⊕ **○** **R.D. CLEVÈRE MUSIKVERLAG (GEMA)**, Postfach 2145, D-63243 Neu-Isenburg, Germany. Phone: (6102)52696. Fax: (6102)52696. Professional Manager: Tony Hermonez. Music publisher. Estab. 1967. Publishes 700-900 songs/year; publishes 40 new songwriters/year. Pays standard royalty.
Affiliate(s): Big Sound Music, Hot Night Music, Lizzy's Blues Music, Max Banana Music, R.D. Clevère-Cocabana-Music, R.D. Clevère-Far East & Orient-Music, and R.D. Clevère-America-Today-Music.
How to Contact: Submit demo tape by mail. Unsolicited submissions are OK. Prefers cassette with "no limit" on songs and lyric sheet. SAE and 2 IRCs. Reports in 1-2 months.
Music: Mostly **pop**, **disco**, **rap**, **rock**, **R&B**, **country**, **ethno** and **folk**; also **musicals** and **classic/opera**. "No jazz, free style or instrumental music."

✓ **○** **CLIFFSIDE MUSIC INC. (ASCAP, BMI)**, P.O. Box 374, Fairview NJ 07022. (201)313-9112. Fax: (201)941-3987. E-mail: cliffmuinc@aol.com. Assistant: Carol Smallwood. Music publisher, record producer and artist management. Estab. 1982. Publishes 8-10 songs/year; publishes 2-3 new songwriters/year. Pays standard royalty.
Affiliate(s): Gloria Gaynor Music (ASCAP) and Wazuri Music (BMI).
How to Contact: Submit demo tape by mail. Unsolicited submissions are OK. Prefers cassette or DAT with 2-3 songs and lyric sheet. Does not return material. Reports in 1 month.

THE TYPES OF MUSIC each listing is interested in are printed in **boldface**.

Music: Mostly **dance/R&B/pop, ballads** and **message pop**; also **gospel**. Published *The Answer* (by Gloria Gaynor) (pop/gospel); *You* (by Oreallo/Snyder); and *Oh What A Life* (by G. Gaynor/Oreallo/Snyder), all recorded by Gloria Gaynor on Sony Records (dance).
Tips: "The writer should ask, 'Would I buy this song?' "

[N] [◐] CMI MUSIC GROUP, INC., 3840 W. Hillsboro Blvd. #210, Deerfield Beach FL 33442. Phone/fax: (954)574-9639. E-mail: cmimusic@aol.com. Professional Managers: Lee Covert (pop, MOR); Ken Hutnik (alternative); Steve Turman (rock, blues). Music publisher. Estab. 1998. Staff size: 3. Pays standard royalty.
How to Contact: Submit demo tape by mail. Unsolicited submissions are OK. Prefers cassette or CD with 3-4 songs and lyric sheets. Does not return material. Reports in 6 weeks.
Music: Mostly **pop, adult contemporary** and **rock**; also **country, jazz** and **blues**. Does not want rap.
Tips: "Good material is sent to Los Angeles for consideration, so be patient."

[N] [○] CO-CREATIONS MUSIC PUBLISHING (BMI), P.O. Box 644, Cameron SC 29030. (803)823-2225. Fax: (803)823-2203. E-mail: ccmp01@aol.com. Owner: David Durr. Music publisher and record producer (David Durr Productions). Estab. 1993. Publishes 3 songs/year; publishes 1 new songwriter/year. Staff size: 1. Pays standard royalty.
How to Contact: Write first and obtain permission to submit a demo. Prefers cassette with 3 songs, lyric sheet and cover letter. "In cover letter, give some insight on your background and vision for your career." Does not return material. Reports in 3-6 weeks.
Music: Mostly **pop/contemporary, contemporary Christian** and **crossover country**; also **standard country, reggae** and **R&B**.
Tips: "Be patient and steadfast."

[◐] COFFEE AND CREAM PUBLISHING COMPANY (ASCAP), 1138 E. Price St., Philadelphia PA 19138. (215)842-3450. President: Bolden Abrams, Jr. Music publisher and record producer (Coffee and Cream Productions). Publishes 20 songs/year; publishes 4 new songwriters/year. Pays standard royalty.
How to Contact: Submit demo tape by mail. Unsolicited submissions are OK. Prefers cassette or VHS videocassette with 1-4 songs and lyric or lead sheets. SASE. Reports in 2 weeks only if interested.
Music: Mostly **dance, pop** and **R&B**; also **gospel** and **country**. Published "If I Let Myself Go" (by Jose Gomez/Sheree Sano), recorded by Chuck Jackson and Dionne Warwick; "You Are My Life" (by Sean Chhangur), recorded by Chuck Jackson, both on RCA-BMG Records; and "Sweet Lover" (by Maxine Bachnia), recorded by Ron Hevener on RMB Records.

[N] [○] CORELLI'S MUSIC BOX (BMI), P.O. Box 2314, Tacoma WA 98401-2314. (253)573-1101. E-mail: cmb@telisphere.com. Professional Manager: Jerry Corelli. Music publisher. Estab. 1996. Publishes 10 songs/year; publishes 3 new songwriters/year. Staff size: 2. Pays standard royalty.
How to Contact: Submit demo tape by mail. Unsolicited submissions are OK. Prefers cassette or DAT with 1-3 songs and lyric sheet. "We want songs with a message and overtly Christian. Make sure all material is copyrighted." SASE. Reports in 2 months.
Music: Mostly **contemporary Christian** and **Christmas**. Does not want rap. Published *I Am Runnin'* (by Brett Helling); *Can You See Through the Sin* (by Ray Bennett); and *Angels Dance* (by Jerry Corelli/Kevin Mannarino), all recorded by Jerry Corelli on Omega III Records (contemporary Christian).

[◐] THE CORNELIUS COMPANIES (BMI, ASCAP), Dept. SM, 812 19th Ave. S., Suite 5, Nashville TN 37203. (615)321-5333. Website: http://www.corneliuscompanies.com. Owner/Manager: Ron Cornelius. Music publisher and record producer (Ron Cornelius). Estab. 1986. Publishes 60-80 songs/year; publishes 2-3 new songwriters/year. Occasionally hires staff writers. Pays standard royalty.
Affiliate(s): RobinSparrow Music (BMI), Strummin' Bird Music (ASCAP) and Bridgeway Music (SESAC).
How to Contact: Write or call first and obtain permission to submit. Submit demo tape by mail. Unsolicited submissions are OK. Prefers cassette with 2-3 songs. SASE. Reports in 6-8 weeks.
Music: Mostly **country** and **pop**; also **positive country** and **gospel**. Does not want instrumentals. Published songs by Confederate Railroad, Faith Hill, David Allen Coe, Alabama and over 50 radio singles in the positive Christian/country format.

[✓] [○] COUNTRY BREEZE MUSIC (BMI), 1715 Marty, Kansas City KS 66103. (913)596-1632. President: Ed Morgan Jr. A&R: Steve Russell (gospel); John Matthews (country). Music publisher and record company (Country Breeze Records, Walkin' Hat Records). Estab. 1984. Publishes 100 songs/year; publishes 25-30 new songwriters/year. Staff size: 2. Pays standard royalty.

Affiliate(s): Walkin' Hat Music (ASCAP).
How to Contact: Submit demo tape by mail. Unsolicited submissions are OK. Prefers cassette or VHS videocassette with 4-5 songs and lyric sheet. SASE. "The songwriter/artist should perform on the video as though on stage giving a sold-out performance. In other words put heart and soul into the project. Submit in strong mailing envelopes." Reports in 2 weeks.
Music: Mostly **country** (all types), **gospel (southern country** and **Christian country)** and **rock.** Does not want rap or metal. Published "Power on the Altar" (by Bill Cameron), recorded by Bill Cameron and Mills Family; "Open Up Your Heart" (by Jack Morris), recorded by Phil Cooley; and "Gonna Go Home" (by Allen Woliung), recorded by Lulu Roman, all on Angel Star (gospel).

◐ COUNTRY RAINBOW MUSIC (BMI), 9 Music Square S., Suite 225, Nashville TN 37203-3203. (513)489-8944. Owner: Samuel D. Rogers. Music publisher. Estab. 1995. Publishes 10-12 songs/year; publishes 4-6 new songwriters/year. Staff size: 1. Pays standard royalty.
Affiliate(s): Venture South Music (ASCAP).
How to Contact: "Please do not call first." Submit demo tape by mail. Unsolicited submissions are OK. Prefers cassette with 1-3 songs and lyric sheet. "No lead sheets." SASE. Reports in 2 weeks.
Music: Mostly **country** (contemporary and traditional). Published "Sleepwalking Avenue" (by Lionel deBernard), on Spree Productions.
Tips: "If you don't include a self-addressed stamped envelope we don't reply. Professional studio demos preferred . . . on good quality tape, please (not normal bias.) Your submission should sound better than what is currently on the charts."

◯ COUNTRY SHOWCASE AMERICA (BMI), 14134 Brighton Dam Rd., Clarksville MD 21029. (301)854-2917. Contact: Francis Gosman. Music publisher, record company and record producer. Estab. 1971. Publishes 9 songs/year; publishes 1 new songwriter/year. Pays standard royalty.
How to Contact: Submit demo tape by mail. Unsolicited submissions are OK. Prefers cassette with 2 songs and lyric sheet. Does not return material. Reports only if interested.
Music: Mostly **country.** Published "If You Think" (by J. Owens), recorded by Harry Wash on CSA Records (country).

⊕ ▨ ◐ CTV MUSIC (GREAT BRITAIN), Television Centre, St. Helier, Jersey JE1 3ZD Channel Islands Great Britain. Phone: (1534)816816. Fax: (1534)816817. Website: http://www.channeltv.co.uk. Managing Director: Gordon De Ste. Croix. Music publisher of music for TV commercials, TV programs and corporate video productions. Estab. 1986. Staff size: 1. Pays standard royalty.
How to Contact: Does not accept unsolicited submissions.
Music: Mostly **instrumental,** for TV commercials and programs.

Ⓝ ▨ ◯ CUPIT MUSIC (ASCAP, BMI), P.O. Box 121904, Nashville TN 37212. (615)731-0100. Fax: (615)731-3005. E-mail: jyoke@edge.net. Website: http://www.cupitmusic.com. Creative Assistant: Tracy Reynolds. Music publisher, record producer and recording studio. Estab. 1986. Staff size: 4. Pays standard royalty.
Affiliate(s): Cupit Memaries (ASCAP) and Cupit Music (BMI).
  ● Cupit Music's "Jukebox Junkie" won BMI's and ASCAP's awards for airplay in 1995.
How to Contact: Write first and obtain permission to submit. Prefers cassette with lyric sheet. "We will return a response card." SASE. Reports in 2 months.
Music: Mostly **country.** Does not want rap, hard rock or metal. Published *Ladies Night*, written and recorded by Ken Mellons (country); and *Bundle of Nerves* (by Jerry Cupit), recorded by Ken Mellons, both on Curb (country); and *I Smell Smoke* (by Lee Miller), recorded by Billy Yates on Almo (country).

◯ DAGENE MUSIC (ASCAP), P.O. Box 410851, San Francisco CA 94141. (415)822-1530. President: David Alston. Music publisher, record company (Cabletown Corp.), management firm (Golden City) and record producer (Classic Disc Production). Estab. 1988. Hires staff songwriters. Pays standard royalty.
Affiliate(s): 1956 Music.
How to Contact: Call first and obtain permission to submit. Prefers cassette with 2 songs and lyric sheet. "Be sure to obtain permission before sending any material." SASE. Reports in 1 month.

REFER TO THE CATEGORY INDEX (at the end of this section) to find exactly which companies are interested in the type of music you write.

Music: Mostly **R&B/rap, dance** and **pop**. Published "Maxin" (by Marcus Justice/Bernard Henderson), recorded by 2 Dominatorz on Dagene Records; "Love Don't Love Nobody" (by David Alston), recorded by Rare Essence on Cabletown Records; and "Why Can't I Be Myself," written and recorded by David Alston on E-lect-ric Recordings.

◯ DAPMOR PUBLISHING (ASCAP, BMI, SESAC), Box 121, Kenner LA 70065. (504)468-9820. President: Kelly Jones. Music publisher, record company and record producer. Estab. 1977. Publishes 10 songs/year. Publishes 3 new songwriters/year. Hires staff songwriters. Pays standard royalty.
How to Contact: Write first and obtain permission to submit. "Submit only through an attorney or another publisher." Prefers 10-song professionally-recorded CD. Does not return material. Reports in 6 weeks.
Music: Mostly **R&B, soul,** and **pop**; also **top 40, country** and **rap**. Published "Tell Me, Tell Me" (R&B); and "Sisco" (R&B), both written and recorded by Kelly Jones on Justice Recordings.

☑ ◯ THE EDWARD DE MILES MUSIC COMPANY (BMI), 117 W. Harrison Bldg., Suite S627, Chicago IL 60605-1709. (773)509-6381. Fax: (312)922-6964. Attn: Professional Manager. Music publisher, record company (Sahara Records), record producer, management, bookings and promotions. Estab. 1984. Publishes 50-75 songs/year; publishes 5 new songwriters/year. Hires staff songwriters. Pays standard royalty.
How to Contact: Write first and obtain permission to submit. Prefers cassette with 1-3 songs and lyric sheet. Does not return material. Reports in 1 month.
Music: Mostly **top 40 pop/rock, R&B/dance** and **country**; also **musical scores for TV, radio, films and jingles**. Published "Dance Wit Me" and "Moments," written and recorded by Steve Lynn on Sahara Records (R&B).
Tips: "Copyright all songs before submitting to us."

◼ ◯ DEL CAMINO MUSIC PUBLISHING (BMI), 5010 S. Twelfth Ave., Tucson AZ 85706. (520)573-7274. Fax: (520)573-3325. President: Luis Lopez. Music publisher and record producer. Estab. 1985. Pays standard royalty.
How to Contact: Submit demo tape by mail. Unsolicited submissions are OK. Prefers cassette with 3 songs and lyric and lead sheet. "Include copy of properly copyrighted form." Does not return material. Reports in 3-4 weeks.
Music: Mostly **Latin/Spanish, Tex-Mex/pop** and **country rock**. Published *La Risueña* (by Richard Garcia), recorded by MR-7 on Ponovisa Inc. Records; and *Me Da Verguenza* (by Epifanio Gonzalez), recorded by Los Recoditos on Musart.
Tips: "Make sure your songs have good commercial potential. Have a clean sounding demo and clearly typed lyric sheet."

◯ DELEV MUSIC COMPANY, 7231 Mansfield Ave., Philadelphia PA 19138-1620. (215)276-8861. President/CEO: W. Lloyd Lucas. A&R: Darryl Lucas. Music publisher and management. Publishes 6-10 songs/year; publishes 6-10 new songwriters/year. Pays standard royalty.
Affiliate(s): Sign of the Ram Music (ASCAP), Gemini Lady Music (SESAC) and Delev Music (BMI).
How to Contact: Write first and obtain permission to submit. Prefers cassette or VHS videocassette with 1-3 songs and lyric sheet. "Video must be in VHS format and as professionally done as possible. It does not necessarily have to be done at a professional video studio, but should be a very good quality production showcasing artist's performance. We will not accept certified mail." Does not return material. Reports in 2-3 months.
Music: Mostly **R&B ballads** and **dance-oriented**; also **pop ballads, crossover** and **country/western**. Published "Night Minds" and "When We're Alone" (by B. Heston/G. Fernandez), both recorded by Renee Francine on Transsonic Records (jazz); and "Good Things Come To Those Who Wait" (by Barbara Heston).
Tips: "Persevere regardless if it is sent to our company or any other company. Believe in yourself."

⊕ ◯ DEMI MONDE RECORDS & PUBLISHING LTD., Foel Studio, Llanfair Caereinion, PO-WYS, Wales. Phone/fax: (01938)810758. E-mail: demi-monde@dial.pipex.com. Website: http://www.demi.monde.co.uk/demimonde. Managing Director: Dave Anderson. Music publisher, record company (Demi Monde Records & Publishing Ltd.), record producer (Dave Anderson). Member MCPS. Estab. 1983. Publishes 50-70 songs/year; publishes 10-15 new songwriters/year. Pays standard royalty.
How to Contact: Submit demo tape by mail. Unsolicited submissions are OK. Prefers cassette or VHS videocassette with 3-4 songs. Does not return material. Reports in 6 weeks.
Music: Mostly **rock, R&B** and **pop**. Published "I Feel So Lazy" (by D. Allen), recorded by Gong (rock);

"Phalarn Dawn" (by E. Wynne), recorded by Ozric Tentacles (rock); and "Pioneer" (by D. Anderson), recorded by Amon Dual (rock), all on Demi Monde Records.

DENNY MUSIC GROUP, Dept. SM, 3325 Fairmont Dr., Nashville TN 37203-1004. (615)269-4847. E-mail: dennytunes@aol.com. Contact: Pandora Denny. Estab. 1983. Music publisher, record company (Dollie Record Co., Jed Record Production) and record producer. Publishes 100 songs/year; 20 new songwriters/year. Pays standard royalty.
How to Contact: Submit demo tape by mail. Unsolicited submissions are OK. Prefers cassette with 3 songs and lyric sheet. SASE. Reports in 6 weeks.
Music: Mostly **country, bluegrass** and **gospel.** Published "Angel Band" and "On the Other Side" (by Wes Homner).

DISNEY MUSIC PUBLISHING (ASCAP, BMI), 500 S. Buena Vista St., Burbank CA 91521-6182. (818)569-3228. Fax: (818)845-9705. Creative Director: Brian Rawlings. Music publisher.
Affiliate(s): Seven Peaks Music and Seven Summits Music.
How to Contact: Call first and obtain permission to submit. Does not return material.

BUSTER DOSS MUSIC (BMI), 341 Billy Goat Hill Rd., Winchester TN 37398. (931)649-2577. Fax: (615)649-2732. E-mail: cbd@edge.net. Website: http://www.a-page.com/cbd. President: Buster Doss. Music publisher, record producer, management firm and record company (Stardust). Estab. 1959. Publishes 500 songs/year; publishes 50 new songwriters/year. Staff size: 62. Pays standard royalty.
How to Contact: Write or call first and obtain permission to submit. Prefers cassette with 2 songs and lyric sheet. SASE. Reports in 1 week.
Music: Mostly **country**; also **rock.** Does not want rap or hard rock. Published *I Must Walk Away* (by Rooster Quantrell), recorded by Michael Apidgian; and *Flight of the Rooster* (by D. Bradley/T. Lewis), recorded by Border Raiders, both on Stardust (country); and *Key to Your Heart* (by Billy Martin), recorded by Bronco Buck Cody on Wizard (country).

DREAM SEEKERS PUBLISHING (BMI), 403 Brunswick Lane, Danville IL 61832. (615)822-1160. Professional Manager: Jerry Webb. President: Sally Sidman. Music publisher. Estab. 1993. Publishes 25-50 songs/year; publishes 15-20 new songwriters/year. Hires staff songwriters. Pays standard royalty.
Affiliate(s): Dream Builders Publishing (ASCAP).
How to Contact: Submit demo tape by mail. Unsolicited submissions are OK. "Please do not call to request permission—just submit your material. There are no code words. We listen to everything." Prefers cassette with 2 songs and lyric sheet. "If one of your songs is selected for publishing, we prefer to have it available on DAT for dubbing off copies to pitch to artist. Do not send your DAT until you have received a publishing contract." SASE. Reports in 4-6 weeks.
Music: Mostly **country** and **pop.** Does not want rap, jazz, classical, children's, hard rock, instrumental or blues. Published "Starting Tonight" (by Sam Storey), recorded by Wayne Horsburgh on Rotation Records (country); "I Can Still See it From Here" (by John Pearson), recorded by Matt Caldwell on RMC Records; and "An Elvis Night Before Christmas" (by Keith Collins), recorded by C.C. McCartney on Rotation Records (country).
Tips: "Be willing to work hard to learn the craft of songwriting. Be persistent. Nobody is born a hit songwriter. It often takes years to achieve that status."

DREAMWORKS SKG MUSIC PUBLISHING, 9268 W. 3rd St., Beverly Hills CA 90210. (310)234-7700. Contact: Chuck Kaye; Molly Kaye; Michael Badami; Ron Handler; Robert White. Music publisher and record company (DreamWorks Records).
How to Contact: DreamWorks SKG Music Publishing does not accept unsolicited submissions.

DRIVE MUSIC, INC. (BMI), 10451 Jefferson Blvd., Culver City CA 90232. (310)815-4900. Fax: (310)815-4908. E-mail: drive@earthlink.net. Website: http://www.driveentertainment.com. CEO: Stephen Powers. Music publisher and record company (Drive Entertainment). Estab. 1993. Publishes 25 songs/year. Pays negotiated royalty. "Seeks single songs for representation. Acquires catalogs, large and small."
Affiliate(s): Donunda Music (ASCAP), Fairyland Music (ASCAP) and Licette Music (ASCAP).

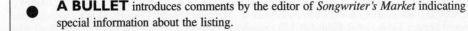

• **A BULLET** introduces comments by the editor of *Songwriter's Market* indicating special information about the listing.

How to Contact: Submit demo tape by mail. Unsolicited submissions are OK. Prefers 3 songs and lyric sheet. "Send regular mail only." SASE. Reports in 1 month.
Music: Mostly **dance, pop** and **rock**; also **R&B**. Published all Sharon, Lois and Bram products (children's).

□ DUANE MUSIC, INC. (BMI), 382 Clarence Ave., Sunnyvale CA 94086. (408)739-6133. President: Garrie Thompson. Music publisher and record producer. Publishes 10-20 songs/year; publishes 1 new songwriter/year. Pays standard royalty.
Affiliate(s): Morhits Publishing (BMI).
How to Contact: Submit demo tape by mail. Unsolicited submissions are OK. Prefers cassette with 1-2 songs. SASE. Reports in 1-2 months.
Music: Mostly **blues, country, disco** and **easy listening**; also **rock, soul** and **top 40/pop**. Published "Little Girl," recorded by The Syndicate of Sound & Ban (rock); "Warm Tender Love," recorded by Percy Sledge (soul); and "My Adorable One," recorded by Joe Simon (blues).

N □ EARITATING MUSIC PUBLISHING (BMI), P.O. Box 1101, Gresham OR 97030. Music publisher. Estab. 1979. Pays individual per song contract, usually greater than 50% to writer.
How to Contact: Submit demo tape by mail. Unsolicited submissions are OK. Prefers cassette with lyric sheet. "Submissions should be copyrighted by the author. We will deal for rights if interested." Does not return material. Reports only if interested.
Music: Mostly **rock, country** and **folk**. Does not want rap.
Tips: "Melody is most important, lyrics second. Style and performance take a back seat to these. A good song will stand with just one voice and one instrument. Also, don't use staples on your mailers."

□ EARTHSCREAM MUSIC PUBLISHING CO. (BMI), 8377 Westview Dr., Houston TX 77055. (713)464-GOLD. E-mail: sarsjef@aol.com. Website: http://www.soundartsrecording.com. Contact: Jeff Wells; Peter Verheck. Music publisher, record company and record producer. Estab. 1975. Publishes 12 songs/year; publishes 4 new songwriters/year. Pays standard royalty.
Affiliate(s): Reach For The Sky Music Publishing (ASCAP).
How to Contact: Submit demo tape by mail. Unsolicited submissions are OK. Prefers cassette or video-cassette with 2-5 songs and lyric sheet. Does not return material. Reports in 6 weeks.
Music: Mostly **new rock, country, blues** and **top 40/pop**. Published "Baby Never Cries" (by Carlos DeLeon), recorded by Jinkies on Surface Records (pop); "Telephone Road," written and recorded by Mark May on Icehouse Records (blues); and "Do You Remember" (by Barbara Pennington), recorded by Perfect Strangers on Earth Records (rock).

□ EAST COAST MUSIC PUBLISHING (BMI), P.O. Box 12, Westport MA 02790-0012. (508)679-4272. Fax: (508)673-1235. E-mail: eastcoastmusic@hotmail.com. Website: http://www.InsideTheWeb. com/mbs.cgi/mb329992. President: Mary-Ann Thomas. Professional Managers: Michael Thomas (hip-hop, rock, jazz); Lisa Medeiros (pop, electronic, dance, country); Noel James (R&B, rap, alternative). Music publisher. Estab. 1996. Publishes 20 songs/year; publishes 10 new songwriters/year. Staff size: 9. Pays standard royalty.
Affiliate(s): Eastern Musicals (BMI).
How to Contact: Submit demo tape by mail. Unsolicited submissions are OK. Prefers cassette with 3-5 songs and lyric or lead sheet. "If you send a SASE I will get back to you within one month. If no SASE I will only respond if interested. We keep submissions in case we decide to publish the song at a future date." Does not return material. Reports in 2 months.
Music: Mostly **pop, country** and **rock**; also **R&B, alternative, dance** and **rap**. Published "I Want More" (by Shana Keyser), recorded by Crying Inside (alternative); and *My Desire* (by La Pointe/Davis), recorded by Freedom (pop), both on Prolific Records; and *We Got Trouble* (by Jackson/Souza), recorded by Street Wize on East Coast Records (hip-hop).
Tips: "Please send current sounding music, not music that is already outdated. Our Internet message board is a free service. Songwriters, artists, producers, etc. will be posting and networking to move new projects forward."

⊕ □ EDITION ROSSORI, Hietzinger Hptstr 94, Vienna A-1130 Austria. Phone: (01)8762400. Fax: (01)8762400. E-mail: mario_rossori@compuserve.com. Manager: Mario Rossori. Music publisher and management agency. Estab. 1990. Publishes 150 songs/year; publishes 10 new songwriters/year. Staff size: 2. Pays negotiable royalty.

How to Contact: Submit demo tape by mail. Unsolicited submissions are OK. Does not return material. Reports in 2 months.
Music: Mostly **pop, dance** and **rock**. Does not want jazz. Published *Welsfischer au Wolpedelta*, written and recorded by Heinz on Universal (rock).

◖ ELECT MUSIC PUBLISHING (BMI), P.O. Box 22, Underhill VT 05489. (802)899-3787. Founder: Bobby Hackney. Music publisher, record producer and record company (LBI Records). Estab. 1980. Publishes 24 songs/year; publishes 3 new songwriters/year. Pays standard royalty.
How to Contact: Write first and obtain permission to submit. Prefers cassette and VHS videocassette with 3-4 songs and SASE. Reports in 4-6 weeks.
Music: Mostly **reggae**, **R&B** and **rap**; also **rock**, some **jazz** and **poetry**. Published "Spotlight on You" and "Carnival on Main St." (by B. Hackney), both recorded by Lambsbread on LBI Records.
Tips: "Send your best and remember, the amount of postage it took to get to the publisher is the same amount it will take to have your tape returned."

◖ EMANDELL TUNES, 10220 Glade Ave., Chatsworth CA 91311. (818)341-2264. Fax: (818)341-1008. President/Administrator: Leroy C. Lovett, Jr. Music Publisher. Estab. 1979. Publishes 6-12 songs/year; publishes 3-4 new songwriters/year. Pays standard royalty.
Affiliate(s): Ben-Lee Music (BMI), Birthright Music (ASCAP), Em-Jay Music (ASCAP), Northworth Songs, Chinwah Songs, Gertrude Music (all SESAC), Alvert Music (BMI) and Andrask Music, Australia (BMI).
How to Contact: Write first and obtain permission to submit. Prefers cassette or videocassette with 4-5 songs and lead or lyric sheet. Include bio of writer, singer or group. SASE. Reports in 4-6 weeks.
Music: Mostly **inspirational**, **contemporary gospel** and **choral**; also **strong country** and **light top 40**.
Tips: "We suggest you listen to current songs. Imagine how that song would sound if done by some other artist. Keep your ear tuned to new groups, bands, singers. Try to analyze what made them different, was it the sound? Was it the song? Was it the production? Ask yourself these questions: Do they have that 'hit' feeling? Do you like what they are doing?"

◖ EMF PRODUCTIONS, 1000 E. Prien Lake Rd., Suite D, Lake Charles LA 70601. Phone/fax: (318)474-0435. President: Ed Fruge. Music publisher and record producer. Estab. 1984. Pays standard royalty.
How to Contact: Submit demo tape by mail. Unsolicited submissions are OK. Prefers cassette or VHS videocassette with 4 songs and lyric sheet. Does not return material. Reports in 6 weeks.
Music: Mostly **R&B**, **pop** and **rock**; also **country** and **gospel**.

░N░ ◖ EMI CHRISTIAN MUSIC PUBLISHING, P.O. Box 5085, Brentwood TN 37024. (615)371-4400. Fax: (615)371-6897. Website: http://www.emicmg.com. Music publisher. Publishes 100 songs/year; publishes 2 new songwriters/year. Hires staff songwriters. Pays standard royalty.
• See the Insider Report interview with songwriter Ty Lacy on page 80.
Affiliate(s): Birdwing Music (ASCAP), Sparrow Song (BMI), His Eye Music (SESAC), Ariose Music (ASCAP), Straightway Music (ASCAP), Shepherd's Fold Music (BMI), Songs of Promise (SESAC), Dawn Treader Music (SESAC), Meadowgreen Music Company (ASCAP), River Oaks Music Company (BMI), Stonebrook Music Company (SESAC), Bud John Songs, Inc. (ASCAP), Bud John Music, Inc. (BMI), Bud John Tunes, Inc. (SESAC).
How to Contact: "We do not accept unsolicited submissions."
Music: Published "Concert of the Age" (by Jeffrey Benward), recorded by Phillips, Craig & Dean; "God Is In Control," written and recorded by Twila Paris, both on StarSong Records; and "Faith, Hope and Love" (by Ty Lacy), recorded by Point of Grace on Word Records.
Tips: "Come to Nashville and be a part of the fastest growing industry. It's nearly impossible to get a publisher's attention unless you know someone in the industry that is willing to help you."

☑ ◖ EMI MUSIC PUBLISHING, 1290 Avenue of the Americas, New York NY 10104. (212)830-2000. Fax: (212)245-4115. Santa Monica office: 2700 Colorado Ave., Suite 100, Santa Monica CA 90404.

OPENNESS TO SUBMISSIONS: ◻ beginners; ◓ beginners and experienced; ◖ experienced only; ◖ industry referrals only.

insider report

Ty Lacy: living his pop/R&B songwriting dream

The descendant of French Creoles who relocated from New Orleans during World War II, Ty Lacy grew up in Oakland, California, listening to white pop music. "All my cousins thought I was really strange—they were listening to Stevie Wonder and I was listening to James Taylor and Elton John," he says. Hearing Elton John's "Someone Saved My Life Tonight" when he was seven inspired Lacy to become a songwriter. "I didn't know what the song was about, but I remember getting goosebumps," says Lacy. "That amazing song moved me to say to myself, 'If I can make people feel like this song makes me feel, then that's what I want to do for a living.'"

Ty Lacy

But reaching his R&B dream did not come easily. After graduating from college, Lacy worked as a buyer for a chain of northern California record stores. From there, on the advice of several industry people, he went to Nashville. In Nashville, Lacy says, "I struggled. I didn't have a car and I was sleeping on my friend's porch." Several years later, in 1992, he was offered his first publishing deal to write contemporary Christian music (CCM) for Starsong Music, now EMI Christian Music. At EMI Lacy wrote over 200 songs, 20 of them number one hits on the CCM charts, including cuts by the popular Christian trio, Point of Grace.

In 1996, Lacy's R&B dream was realized when EMI signed him to a pop/R&B publishing contract. Along with songs he has written on his own, Lacy has co-written songs with Ellen Shipley, Darrell Brown, Desmond Child, Wendy Waldman and Dean Pitchford, to name a few. Artists cutting his songs include LeAnn Rimes, Bette Midler, Millennium and All for One. Here he shares insights about the music industry and gives some tips and encouragement for those who, like he, have a songwriting dream they just can't give up.

TY LACY

Songwriter/Artist
Music: Pop, R&B, Christian
Cuts by: Point of Grace, LeAnn Rimes, Bette Midler

What does a publishing deal really mean for a songwriter?

A publisher is your bank. They support your creative habits. They pay for your demos and give you money to live on. They obviously see some talent in you and think they can make a lot of money off that talent. It's a gamble; if it works, you both win. If it doesn't work, you're dropped. Luckily, I happen to be signed with one of the biggest publishing companies in the world. But the most important thing about a publishing deal is, even if the money is good, be sure you have a champion there. Have someone who believes in your talent and is willing to take your stuff to the next level, for instance to help develop you as an artist too.

You left the Oakland Bay area and went to Nashville. Since then, you have traveled between Nashville and Los Angeles and now live in New York City. As someone who has been a songwriter in all three music centers, how would you compare them?
Nashville is the only songwriters' community left in America. In Nashville, the writer is a star. Everywhere else it's all about the artists. New York is the old school—a lot of Broadway, but a lot of R&B and a lot of hip-hop, too. L.A. is the fast food of the music scene. In L.A., it's like, "let's write a hit by this afternoon." Nashville is like, "we'll take our time to really finish it and we'll have this amazingly crafted song—the lyric and melody."

But there's a part of all these places that I really love. I love the passion for pop that L.A. has—it's instant. I love the seriousness about musicianship that New York has—they're like, "how's your chops?" And I love the whole craft thing about the Nashville writers' community—it's wonderful and very embracing and nurturing. But, I think of all of them I like New York best. I love the diversity—culturally, racially, musically—in New York. You have the melting pot of the world there.

How does a beginning songwriter break into the music industry?
Immerse yourself in it. Go to musical events and conventions. Get involved with ASCAP or BMI or SESAC or whatever performing rights organization you're part of and meet other people. I started going to ASCAP meetings and networking that way. One person opens a door and says you need to meet other people. And you do your homework. You take notes. You look on album jackets and find people's names—who's doing what. You have to be a student of your art to make it. There's not a school that teaches you that. You just have to live it.

Once he's gotten through the door, how can a songwriter make it to the top as you have done?
Find what makes you unique. Then, amplify that, perfect it. Sharpen those skills, whether it be the music or the lyrics, whatever makes people see that there's only one like you around. This industry is full of talented people. If you don't stand out as being different, you'll just blend, and when you blend, you aren't successful. It's when you stand out that you're a success.

With the new millennium upon us, have you noticed any changes in the music industry songwriters need to be aware of?

Music in the next millennium, at least in the beginning, is going to definitely be more spiritual, more about real life and peace of mind. For instance, look at the Jewel album, *Spirit*. It's about healing and about coming to terms with your mortality. I think there's going to be a resurgence of emphasis on spirituality and faith. Baby Boomers are getting older and asking, "Is this what it's all about? What is the legacy I'm going to leave my kids? What do I want to accomplish? What's really important in life?" Of course, love will always be a theme, but I think people really want to know what's in store for them in the coming years. They want to talk about things that matter. We all need to realize what matters to us, to our hearts, to our souls. We need to refocus a lot of things. It's not all about the dollar. It's about peace of mind, it's about treasuring what we do have and our blessings around us.

Musically, I think it will always be about the song—a melody and a lyric. There was a time not long ago when a lot of people felt the songwriter was taking a back seat to all the other parts of the music industry. But they will always need songwriters because we dream and we share our souls and our hearts and we bleed. What we do touches a button in other people because we are all flesh and bone and we all need to be moved by the whole spiritual aspect of songs. It's still the same rule Irving Berlin had: It's about the heart, it's about the soul; if you can touch that, you can touch everyone. That's how you become a successful writer.

And if this is what you are called to do, if songwriting is really your dream, you can never give up. Your dream will always be there. If you don't do it, it's your problem, it's your loss. If you're going to do it, you've got to work on it until it happens. You can't give yourself another choice. And then you'll make it. I truly believe that. If I could be this black kid from Oakland, California, going to Nashville, Tennessee, and breaking in as a writer, anyone can do it.

What is your best piece of advice to aspiring songwriters to help them hold on until their songwriting dreams come true?

Before I ever got paid for writing songs, I did it because I couldn't help it—it was my passion; it burned in me. That's really how you've got to write, and if anything happens along the way, that's good. You have to write because you love it—or else you'll never make it. Failure comes when you give up too soon because if you keep knocking at that door, it's gonna open. You've got to be persistent. There are people who don't have the most amazing talent in the world, but they're persistent and determined to do it despite all the odds against them.

—*Barbara Kuroff*

(310)586-2762. Website: http://www.emimusic.com. Contact: Jodi Gerson; Sharona Sabbag; Big Jon; Carla Ondrasik. Music publisher.

How to Contact: EMI does not accept unsolicited material.

Music: Published "All Night Long" (by F. Evans/R. Lawrence/S. Combs), recorded by Faith Evans featuring Puff Daddy on Bad Boy; "You" (by C. Roland/J. Powell), recorded by Jesse Powell on Silas; and "I Was" (by C. Black/P. Vassar), recorded by Neal McCoy on Atlantic.

☐ EMSTONE, INC. MUSIC PUBLISHING (BMI), P.O. Box 1287, Hallandale FL 33008. (305)936-0412. E-mail: emstoneinc@yahoo.com. President: Mitchell Stone. Vice President: Madeline Stone. Music publisher. Estab. 1997. Pays standard royalty.

How to Contact: Submit demo tape by mail. Unsolicited submissions are OK. Prefers cassette with any number of songs and lyric sheet. Does not return material. Reports in 2-4 weeks.

Music: Mostly **pop**, **country** and **R&B**; also **gospel**, **dance** and **Christmas music**. Does not want classical, jazz or opera. Published *Ruby Slippers* (by Ken Cayea/Dave Ryan), recorded by Kimberley "KK" Short on BearKat Records (pop).

Tips: "Send the most polished-sounding demo you can, with songs that have clever hooks and memorable melodies. And make sure that all submissions have been registered with the U.S. Copyright Office."

☐ ESI MUSIC GROUP (BMI), 9 Music Square S., Suite 118, Nashville TN 37203-9336. (615)297-9336. Administrator: Curt Conroy. Professional Managers: Dave Wascher; Marcos Casiano. Music publisher. Estab. 1990. Publishes 50-60 songs/year. Staff size: 7. Pays standard royalty.

How to Contact: Submit demo tape by mail. Unsolicited submissions are OK. Prefers "good quality 3-4 song demo" and lyric sheet. "Guitar or piano-vocal OK. All envelopes must meet postal requirements for content." Does not return material. "To ensure reply, include stamped, self-addressed envelope with adequate postage attached." Reports within 3-4 weeks.

Music: Mostly **"new" country**, **country rock** and **country pop**; also **country blues**. Published *Next Year Better*, written and recorded by Pinto Bennett on Famous Motel Cowboy Records (Tex-Mex); *Hard Rain*, written and recorded by David Stewart on Santa Fe Records (country); and *Unlike You* (by Ricky Jenkins), recorded by Tom Rogers on Native Son Records (country).

Tips: "Research the artists you want to pitch to and match your songs to those artists. Listen carefully to current songs on the radio. This is your competition. Record the best demo that you can. Write for a list of songwriter information that is available through our company."

🌐 ◐ EVER-OPEN-EYE MUSIC (PRS), Wern Fawr Farm, Pencoed, MID, Glam CF356NB United Kingdom. Phone: (0656)860041. Managing Director: M.R. Blanche. Music publisher and record company (Red-Eye Records). Member PPL and MCPS. Estab. 1980. Publishes 6 songs/year. Staff size: 3. Pays negotiable royalty.

How to Contact: Submit demo tape by mail. Unsolicited submissions are OK. Prefers cassette or VHS videocassette. Does not return material. Reports in 2 months.

Music: Mostly **R&B**, **gospel** and **pop**; also **swing**. Published "Snake Hips" and "Eclection" (by Burton/Jones); and "Life Insurance" (by Steve Finn), all recorded by Tiger Bay on Red-Eye Records.

▦ ◐ FAMOUS MUSIC PUBLISHING COMPANIES, 10635 Santa Monica Blvd., Suite 300, Los Angeles CA 90025. (310)441-1300. Fax: (310)441-4722. Website: http://www.syncsit.com. President: Ira Jaffe. Senior Creative Director, Film and TV: Stacey Palm. Creative Coordinator: Lauren Roach. Senior Creative Director: Bobby Carlton. Creative Director, Urban Music: Brian Postelle. New York office: 1633 Broadway, 11th Floor, New York NY 10019. Creative Director: Laura Becker (rock/pop/alternative). Vice President, Standard Catalogue: Mary Beth Roberts. Nashville office: 65 Music Square East, Nashville TN 37212. Vice President: Pat Finch (country). Creative Director: Curtis Green. Music Publisher. Estab. 1929. Publishes 500 songs/year. Hires staff songwriters. Staff size: 100. Pays standard royalty.

Affiliate(s): Famous Music (ASCAP) and Ensign Music (BMI).

How to Contact: Write or call first and obtain permission to submit. Prefers cassette with 3 songs and lyric sheet. SASE. Reports in 1 month.

Film & TV: Famous Music is a Paramount Pictures' company. Music Supervisors: Stacey Palm and Laura Beecher. Published "My Heart Will Go On" (by James Homer/Wil Jennings), recorded by Celine Dion in *Titanic*.

Music: Mostly **rock**, **urban**, **R&B** and **country**. Published "Not An Addict" (by Sarah Bettens/Ger Bettens), recorded by K's Choice (modern rock), both on 550/Epic; and "When There's No One Around" (by Darrell Scott), recorded by Garth Brooks on Capitol (country).

🌐 🎬 💿 **FIRST TIME MUSIC (PUBLISHING) U.K. (PRS)**, Sovereign House, 12 Trewartha Road, Praa Sands, Penzance, Cornwall TR20 9ST United Kingdom. Phone: (01736)762826. Fax: (01736)763328. E-mail: panamus@aol.com. Website: http://www.lcn.co.uk/gisc.html. Managing Director: Roderick G. Jones. Music publisher, record company (First Time Records), record producer (Panama Music Library) and management firm (First Time Management and Production Co.). Member MCPS. Estab. 1986. Publishes 500-750 songs/year; 20-50 new songwriters/year. Staff size: 6. Hires staff writers. Pays standard royalty; "50-60% to established and up-and-coming writers with the right attitude."
Affiliate(s): Scamp Music Publishing.
How to Contact: Submit demo tape by mail. Unsolicited submissions are OK. Prefers cassette, 1⅞ ips cassette or VHS videocassette "of professional quality" with unlimited number of songs and lyric or lead sheets. Reports in 1 month. Does not return material.
Film & TV: Places 58 songs in film and TV/year. Recently published "Aimos," written and recorded by Bob Brimley for the BBC; "Maciek," written and recorded by Henryk Wozniacki for World Wide Pictures; and "Haunted House" (by Frank Millum), recorded by Colin Eade for Carlton Television.
Music: Mostly **country** and **folk, pop/soul/top 20/rock, country with an Irish/Scottish crossover**; also **gospel/Christian**. Published *My Limerick Vales* (by D. Barrow/J. Lennon), recorded by Corbett & Gaynor on Strings (MOR); *The Greenhills Are Rolling Still*, written and recorded by Charlie Landsborough on Telstar and Ritz Records (MOR); and *Blood Money* (by Neville Atkinson), recorded by Punishment of Luxury on Overground Records (new wave).
Tips: "Have a professional approach—present well produced demos. First impressions are important and may be the only chance you get. Writers are advised to join the Guild of International Songwriters and Composers in the United Kingdom."

💿 **FLEA CIRCUS MUSIC (ASCAP)**, 1820 Charles Yeargin Rd., Elberton GA 30635. Professional Managers: Greg Timms; Dee Dee. Music publisher. Member Harry Fox Agency. Estab. 1991. Staff size: 2. Pays standard royalty.
How to Contact: Submit demo tape by mail. Unsolicited submissions are OK. Prefers cassette with 3 songs and lyric sheet. SASE. Reports in 2-5 weeks.
Music: Mostly **rock, humorous** and **upbeat modern country**. Does not want depressing or negative songs.
Tips: "We are concentrating on movies and self contained ready-to-shop acts."

💿 **FLYING RED HORSE PUBLISHING (BMI)**, 2932 Dyer St., Dallas TX 75205. (214)691-5318. E-mail: barbe@texasmusicgroup.com. Website: http://texasmusicgroup.com. Contact: Barbara McMillen. Music publisher, record company (Remarkable Records) and record producer (Texas Fantasy Music). Estab. 1993. Publishes 15-30 songs/year; publishes 6-10 new songwriters/year. Pays standard royalty.
Affiliate(s): Livin' the Life Music (ASCAP).
How to Contact: Submit demo tape by mail. Unsolicited submissions are OK. Prefers cassette with 3 songs and lyric sheet. SASE. Reports in 6 months.
Music: Mostly **children's and special occasion songs and stories**. Published "Everybody's Special" (by Jeanie Perkins) on the Kid Rhino release, *Chicken Soup for Little Souls—You're a Special Person*; "I Was a Dinosaur" (by Bev Houston/Richard Theisen/Barbe McMillan); and "Off To School" (by Jeanie Perkins), on the Sirdar release, *Snow Monsters*.
Tips: "Even when a song is written for children, it should still meet the criteria for a well-written song—and be pleasing to adults as well."

✔ 💿 **MARK FOSTER MUSIC COMPANY**, Box 4012, Champaign IL 61824-4012. (217)398-2760. Fax: (217)398-2791. E-mail: info@markfostermusic.com. Website: http://www.markfoster.com. President: Jane C. Menkhaus. Assistant Editor: David Bohn. Music publisher. Estab. 1962. Publishes 30-40 songs/year; publishes 4-5 new songwriters/year. Pays negotiable royalty.
Affiliate(s): Marko Music Press (BMI) and Fostco Music Press (ASCAP).
How to Contact: Do not call. Write for full guidelines. Submit demo tape by mail accompanied by manuscripts. Unsolicited submissions are OK. Prefers cassette and 1 copy choral manuscript (must be legible). Include brief bio of composer/arranger if new. SASE. Reports in 5-8 weeks.
Music: Exclusively classical choral music: **sacred SATB, secular SATB** and **sacred and secular treble**

REFER TO THE GEOGRAPHIC INDEX (at the back of this book) to find listings of companies by state, as well as foreign listings.

& male choir; also **conducting books** and **Kodaly materials**. Published "O My Love Is Like a Red Red Rose" (by René Clausen); "Papa Nov" (by Emile Desamours); and "Friendly Frederick Fuddlestone" (by Daniel Kallman), all classical choral works.
Tips: "Write and request submission guidelines and sample package. We are always looking for strong choral music for church and/or school."

■ ○ FRESH ENTERTAINMENT (ASCAP), 1315 Simpson Rd., Atlanta GA 30314. (770)642-2645. A&R Director: Willie W. Hunter. Music publisher and record company. Publishes 5 songs/year. Staff size: 4. Hires staff songwriters. Pays standard royalty.
Affiliate(s): !Hserf Music (ASCAP), Blair Vizzion Music (BMI) and Santron Music (BMI).
How to Contact: Submit demo tape by mail. Unsolicited submissions are OK. Prefers cassette or video-cassette with 3 songs and lyric sheet. "Send photo if available." SASE. Reports in 4-6 weeks.
Film & TV: Places 1 song in TV/year. Recently published the theme song for BET's *Comic Vue* (by Charles E. Jones), recorded by Cirocco.
Music: Mostly **rap**, **R&B** and **pop/dance**. Published *Bass Me Down* (by F. Boddie/T. Houston), recorded by Wreck-N-Krew on Intersound (rap); "Throw Them Bows" (by Tino S. McIntosh), recorded by DJ Taz on Ichiban (rap); and "Girls" (by McIntosh/Kizzy/Smurf), recorded by Smurf on Ichiban (rap).

✓ ◑ FRICON MUSIC COMPANY (BMI), 11 Music Square E., Nashville TN 37203. (615)826-2288. Fax: (615)826-0500. E-mail: friconent@juno.com. President: Terri Fricon. Professional Manager: Madge Benson. Music publisher. Estab. 1981. Publishes 25 songs/year; publishes 1-2 new songwriters/year. Staff size: 6. Pays standard royalty.
Affiliate(s): Fricout Music Company (ASCAP) and Now and Forever Songs (SESAC).
How to Contact: Submit demo tape by mail. Unsolicited submissions are OK. Prefers cassette with 1-2 songs and lyric or lead sheet. "Prior permission must be obtained or packages will be returned." SASE. Reports in 6-8 weeks.
Music: Mostly **country**.

◑ FRO'S MUSIC PUBLISHING, 163 Tetreau St. #B, Thibodaux LA 70301. (504)446-8718. Fax: (504)455-7076. Owner: J. Roel Lungay. Music Editor: Vincent S. Tan. Lyrical Editor: Barbara Henry. Music publisher, record company (Fro's Records) and record producer. Estab. 1992. Publishes 5-8 songs/year; publishes 3-5 new songwriters/year. Staff size: 5. Pays standard royalty.
Affiliate(s): Telldem Records (Philippines), Foreign Brain Music (Philippines), Franz Music Production (Philippines) and PB Music.
How to Contact: "We're not accepting new/unsolicited materials this year due to backlog in our evaluation of previously submitted materials."
Music: Mostly **Christian**, **inspirational** and **church/religious**. Does not want secular or non-Christian. Published *The Greatest Gifts*, recorded on Fro's Records (pop).

✓ ◑ FROZEN INCA MUSIC, P.O. Box 20387, Atlanta GA 30325. (404)355-5580. Fax: (404)351-2786. E-mail: mrland@mindspring.com. Website: http://www.landsliderecords.com. President: Michael Rothschild. Professional Manager: Windy Balmore. Music publisher, record company (Landslide Records) and record producer. Estab. 1981. Publishes 12 songs/year; publishes 3 new songwriters/year. Pays standard royalty.
Affiliate(s): Landslide Records.
How to Contact: Submit demo tape by mail. Unsolicited submissions are OK. Prefers cassette with 3-12 songs. SASE. Reports in 2 months.
Music: Mostly **blues**, **swing**, **rock** and **roots music**. Published "Break My Rule" and "Change Your Mind," both written and recorded by Tinsley Ellis on Alligator Records (blues); and "I'm the One You Love" (by Buck Quigley), recorded by Steam Donkeys on Landslide Records (Americana).

○ FURROW MUSIC (BMI), P.O. Box 4121, Edmond OK 73083-4121. Owner/Publisher: G.H. Derrick. Music publisher, record company (Gusher Records) and record producer. Estab. 1984. Publishes 10-15 songs/year. Staff size: 1. Pays standard royalty.
How to Contact: Submit demo tape by mail. Unsolicited submissions are OK. Prefers cassette or VHS videocassette with 1 song and lyric sheet. "One instrument and vocal is OK for demo." SASE. Reports in 2 weeks.
Music: Mostly **country** and **cowboy**. Published "Texas Alphabet" (cowboy); "T.J. At the Alamo" (cowboy), both on Pelican; and "The Blues You Sent Me" on Gusher (blues), all written and recorded by Harvey Derrick.
Tips: "Have your song critiqued by other writers (or songwriter organizations) prior to making the demo.

Only make and send demos of songs that have a universal appeal. Make sure the vocal is out front of the music. Never be so attached to a lyric or tune that you can't rewrite it. Don't forget to include your SASE."

🅞 **ALAN GARY MUSIC (ASCAP, BMI)**, P.O. Box 179, Palisades Park NJ 07650. President: Alan Gary. Creative Director: Fran Levine. Creative Assistant: Harold Green. Music publisher. Estab. 1987. Publishes a varying number of songs/year. Staff size: 3. Pays standard royalty.
How to Contact: Submit demo tape by mail. Unsolicited submissions are OK. Prefers cassette or VHS videocassette with lyric sheet. SASE.
Music: Mostly **pop, R&B** and **dance**; also **rock, A/C** and **country**. Published "Liberation" (by Gary/Julian), recorded by Les Julian on Music Tree Records (A/C); "Love Your Way Out of This One" (by Gary/Rosen), recorded by Deborah Steel on Bad Cat Records (contemporary country); and "Dueling Rappers" (by Gary/Free), recorded by Prophets of Boom on You Dirty Rap! Records (rap/R&B).

🅝 🅞 **GLAD MUSIC CO. (ASCAP, BMI, SESAC)**, 14340 Torrey Chase, Suite 380, Houston TX 77014. (281)397-7300. E-mail: cwsong98@aol.com. Professional Managers: Wes Daily (modern country); Don Daily (traditional country); "Bud" Daily (traditional country). Music publisher, record company and record producer. Estab. 1958. Publishes 3 songs/year; publishes 3 new songwriters/year. Staff size: 4. Pays standard royalty.
Affiliate(s): Bud-Don (ASCAP) and Rayde (SESAC).
How to Contact: Write first and obtain permission to submit a demo or to arrange personal interview. Prefers cassette or CD with 6 songs, lyric sheet and cover letter. Does not return material. Reports in 2 weeks.
Music: Mostly **country**. Does not want weak songs.

🅞 **THE GOODLAND MUSIC GROUP INC.**, P.O. Box 24454, Nashville TN 37202. (615)269-7074. E-mail: jsprouse@aristomedia.com. Website: http://www.aristomedia.com. Contact: Publishing Dept. Music publisher. Estab. 1988. Publishes 50 songs/year; 5-10 new songwriters/year. Pays standard royalty.
Affiliate(s): Goodland Publishing Company (ASCAP), Marc Isle Music (BMI) and Gulf Bay Publishing (SESAC).
How to Contact: Submit demo tape by mail. Unsolicited submissions are OK. SASE. "Request inclusion of 33¢ SASE for reply only." Reports in 2-4 weeks.
Music: Mostly **contemporary country**. Published "Where Does Love Go When It's Gone?" (by Barton/Byram), recorded by Warren Johnson on MDL Records; "Swingin' for the Fences" (by Myers/Meier) and "The Best Mistake" (by Primamore), both recorded by Daniel Glidwell on Starborn Records.

🅰 🅞 **GOODNIGHT KISS MUSIC (BMI)**, 10153 1/2 Riverside Dr. #239, Toluca Lake CA 91602. (213)883-1518. Fax: (213)850-1964. E-mail: hlywdgrl@aol.com. Website: http://www.janetfisher.com. Managing Director: Janet Fisher. Music publisher. Estab. 1986. Publishes 8-10 songs/year; publishes 5-7 new songwriters/year. Pays standard royalty.
   ● Goodnight Kiss Music specializes in placing music in movies, but also pitches major label acts.
How to Contact: Write, call or e-mail first and obtain permission to submit. Prefers cassette, DAT or CD with 1-3 songs and lyric sheet. Send SASE for reply. Does not return material. Reports in 2-4 months.
Film & TV: Places 3 songs in film/year. Recently published "Dick and Jane" (by Irwin Rubinsky/Janet Fisher), recorded by Ricky Kershaw in HBO's *Ambushed*; "I Do, I Do, Love You" (by Joe David Curtis), recorded by Ricky Kershaw in *Road Ends*; and "Kiss Me" (by Janet Fisher), recorded by Christy Tierney in *The Sender*.
Music: **All modern styles**. Published *Take Your Shoulder From the Wheel* (by Mark Weigle), recorded by Candy Chase on Golden Records (ballad); and *Quarter Past Love* (by Irwin Rubinsky), recorded by Darcy Dawson on Calgary (ballad).
Tips: "Check out our 'song critique checklist' and 'how to submit material' on our website. We now offer classes and song reviews at the Songwriters Guild of America, in our offices, on the phone and online for beginners and intermediate writers. We will call you when possible, if we are interested. We use a basic SGA contract, with a few paragraphs excepted."

🅞 **GREEN ONE MUSIC (BMI)**, Rockin' Chair Center Suite 102, 1033 W. State Highway 76, Branson MO 65616. (417)334-2336. Fax: (417)334-2306. President: George J. Skupien. Music publisher, record

---

THE FILM & TV INDEX found at the back of this book lists companies placing music in film and TV (excluding TV commercials).

label and recording studio. Estab. 1992. Publishes 6-12 songs/year. Pays standard royalty.

How to Contact: Submit "professional studio" demo tape by mail. Unsolicited submissions are OK. Prefers cassette or DAT with 2-4 songs. "We *only* accept professional studio demo tapes. This means that your tape has been performed, recorded and produced by someone with music industry experience, who will represent your songs with the quality of a master recording." Does not return material. "For your protection, all tapes, lyrics or other material that is received, that are not accepted, are immediately destroyed to protect the songwriters." Reports in 3 months.

Music: Mostly country, MOR and **light rock**; also **American polka music, waltzes** and **comedy—fun songs**. Published "That Old Neighborhood I Left Behind" (by George Skupien/Gene Mikrut); "UFO's" (by Marty Nevers/Carla Elliott); and "We Seen A UFO" (by George Skupien/Marty Nevers/Carla Elliott).

Tips: "Always put your best song first on your tapes submitted. Be sure your vocal is clear!"

G-STRING PUBLISHING (BMI, SOCAN), P.O. Box 1096, Hudson, Quebec J0P 1H0 Canada. (613)780-1163. Fax: (514)458-2819. E-mail: larecord@total.net. Website: http://www.radiofreedom.com. Music Coordinator: Ms. Tanya Hart. Music publisher, record company (L.A. Records), record producer. Estab. 1991. Publishes 20 songs; publishes 5-10 new songwriters/year. Pays standard royalty.

How to Contact: Submit demo tape by mail. Unsolicited submissions are OK. Does not return material. Prefers cassette or DAT with 3 songs and lyric sheet. Reports in 4 months.

Music: Mostly **commercial rock, A/C** and **dance**; also **country**. Published "Sweet Sunshine" (pop) and "Where Am I?" (both by M. Lengies), recorded by Brittany; and "Risky Business" (by M. Mutulis/M. Lengies), recorded by Sonic Blast (pop).

Tips: "Know your craft; songs must have great lyrics and good melody, and create a strong emotional reaction. They must be under four minutes and must be radio friendly."

R.L. HAMMEL ASSOCIATES, INC., P.O. Box 531, Alexandria IN 46001-0531. (317)724-3900. Fax: (765)641-7270. E-mail: rlh@rlhammel.com. Website: http://www.rlhammel.com. President: Randal Hammel. Music publisher, record producer and consultant. Estab. 1974. Staff size: 3-5. Pays standard royalty.

Affiliate(s): Ladnar Music (ASCAP) and Lemmah Music (BMI).

How to Contact: Submit demo tape by mail. Unsolicited submissions are OK. Prefers cassette, DAT or VHS/8mm videocassette with 3 songs and typed lyric sheet. SASE. Reports ASAP.

Music: Mostly **pop, Christian** and **R&B**; also **MOR, rock** and **country**. Published *Lessons For Life* (by Kelly Hubbell/Jim Boedicker) and *I Just Want Jesus* (by Mark Condon), both recorded by Kelly Connor on Impact Records.

STEVIE RAY HANSEN MUSIC GROUP (ASCAP) (formerly Smokin' Cowboys Publishing Co.), P.O. Box 1246, Murrieta CA 92564. (909)677-8288. Fax: (909)677-0461. E-mail: srhhold@inland.net. Website: http://www.mediarecords.com. A&R: Stevie Ray Hansen. Music publisher and record company. Estab. 1985. Publishes 75 songs/year; publishes 10 new songwriters/year. Hires staff songwriters. Staff size: 3. Pays standard royalty.

Affiliate(s): Media Records, Smokin' Cowboys Publishing Co. (ASCAP), SRH Publishing (BMI) and Big Sound Publishing.

How to Contact: Submit demo tape by mail. Unsolicited submissions are OK. Prefers cassette with 1-3 songs and lyric sheet. "We prefer typewritten numbered lyric sheets and good professional quality demo tapes. Put name and phone number on all material. We will call if interested." Does not return material. Reports in 3 months.

Music: Mostly **country, country rock, surf music, gospel, rockabilly** and **blues**; also **R&B, top 40** and **MOR**. Does not want rap or metal. Published *I'm Not Shy* (by Molly Scheer), recorded by Molly & The Makers (Americana); *Forever Or Nothing*, written and recorded by Elvis Barker (country); and *Cold Hard Cash* (by Jack O'Neill), recorded by Rough Cuts (blues), all on Media Records.

Tips: "Our international division needs songs for Europe. We are interested in C&W and rockabilly artists. We request a bio with material."

HAPPY MELODY, (formerly Jump Music), VZW, Stationsstraat 146, Box 1, 9420 AAIGEM, Belgium. Phone: (053)62-73-77. General Manager: Eddy Van Mouffaert. Music publisher, record company (Jump Records) and record producer (Jump Productions). Member SABAM S.V., Brussels. Publishes 100 songs/year; publishes 8 new songwriters/year. Staff size: 2. Pays standard royalty via SABAM S.V.

How to Contact: Submit demo tape by mail. Unsolicited submissions are OK. Prefers cassette. Does not return material. Reports in 2 weeks.

Music: Mostly **easy listening, disco** and **light pop**; also **instrumentals**. Published *Dikke Berta* and *Da*

Da Da (by Ricky Mondes), both recorded by Guy Dumon on BM Studio (Flemish); and *Onze Vader* (by David Linton), recorded by De Korenaar on Korenaar (profane).
Tips: "Music wanted with easy, catchy melodies (very commercial songs)."

⊕ ⊠ ⊘ **HEUPFERD MUSIKVERLAG GmbH**, Ringwaldstr. 18, Dreieich 63303 Germany. Phone/fax: (06103)86970. E-mail: heupferd@t-online.de. General Manager: Christian Winkelmann. Music publisher and record company (Viva La Difference). GEMA. Publishes 60 songs/year. Staff size: 3. Pays "royalties after GEMA distribution plan."
Affiliate(s): Song Bücherei (book series).
How to Contact: Does not accept unsolicited submissions.
Film & TV: Places 1 song in film/year. Recently published "El Grito Y El Silencio" (by Thomas Hickstein), recorded by Tierra in *Frauen sind was Wunderbares*.
Music: Mostly **folk, jazz** and **fusion**; also **New Age**, **rock** and **ethnic music**. Published "Neddle Park," written and recorded by Mike Hanraham; and *Mozarts Mazurka*, written and recorded by Tom Daun, both on Wundertüte; and "West Coast of Clare" (by Andy Irvine), recorded by Geraldine MacGowan on Magnetic.

❖ ✔ ⊘ **HICKORY LANE PUBLISHING AND RECORDING (ASCAP, SOCAN)**, 19854 Butternut Lane, Pitt Meadown, British Columbia V3Y 2S7 Canada. E-mail: chrismichaels1@attcanada.net. Website: keywordsearch:HickoryLaneRecords. President: Chris Urbanski. A&R Manager: Dave Rogers. Music publisher, record company and record producer. Estab. 1988. Hires staff writers. Publishes 30 songs/year; publishes 5 new songwriters/year. Pays standard royalty.
How to Contact: Write first and obtain permission to submit. Prefers cassette, CD or VHS videocassette with 1-5 songs. Does not return material. Reports in 1-2 weeks.
Music: Mostly **country** and **country rock**. Published *Until Now* (by Steve Mitchell/Chris Michaels), recorded by Chris Michaels on Hickory Lane Records.
Tips: "Send us a professional quality demo with the vocals upfront. We are looking for hits, and so are the major record labels we deal with. Be original in your approach, don't send us a cover tune."

◻ **HICKORY VALLEY MUSIC (ASCAP)**, 10303 Hickory Valley, Ft. Wayne IN 46835. E-mail: alstraten@aol.com. President: Allan Straten. Music publisher, record company (Yellow Jacket Records) and record producer (Al Straten Productions). Estab. 1988. Publishes 10 songs/year; publishes 5 new songwriters/year. Staff size: 3. Pays standard royalty.
Affiliate(s): Straten's Song (BMI).
How to Contact: Submit demo tape by mail. Unsolicited submissions are OK. Prefers cassette with 3-4 songs and typed lyric sheets. Use a 6×9 envelope with no staples. Does not return material. Reports in 3-4 weeks.
Music: Mostly **country** and **MOR**. Does not want rap, hip-hop or hard/acid rock. Published "She's My Number One Fan" (by R. Hartman/S. Grogg/A. Straten); "She's My 'X' and I Know 'Y' " (by D. Crisman/S. Grogg/A. Straten); and "Kisa Marie" (by S. Grogg/A. Straten), all recorded by Tom Woodward on Pharoah Records (country).

◙ **HIGH-MINDED MOMA PUBLISHING & PRODUCTIONS (BMI)**, P.O. Box 959, Coos Bay OR 97420. President: Kai Moore Snyder. Music publisher and production company. Pays standard royalty.
How to Contact: Prefers 7½ ips reel-to-reel, CD or cassette with 4-8 songs and lyric sheet. SASE. Reports in 1 month.
Music: Mostly **country, MOR, rock (country), New Age** and **top 40/pop**.

Ⓝ ▣ ◻ **HIS POWER PRODUCTIONS AND PUBLISHING (ASCAP, BMI)**, 1304 Canyon, Plainview TX 79072-4740. (806)296-7073. Fax: (806)296-7111. E-mail: dcarter@o-c-s.com. Website: http://www.o-c-s.com/hispowerproductions. Professional Managers: Darryl Carter (R&B, gospel, country rock); T. Lee Carter (pop, new rock, classic rock). Music publisher, record company (Lion and Lamb), record producer and management and booking agency (End-Time Management & Booking Agency). Estab. 1995. Publishes 4-10 songs/year; publishes 3 new songwriters/year. Staff size: 9. Hires staff songwriters. Pays negotiable royalty.

MARKETS THAT WERE listed in the 1999 edition of *Songwriter's Market* but do not appear this year are listed in the General Index with a notation explaining why they were omitted.

Affiliate(s): Love Story Publishing (BMI).
● The song "Heal Me," published by His Power, was awarded a 1998 ASCAP Popular Award.
How to Contact: Write or call first and obtain permission to submit a demo. Prefers cassette, CD or DAT with 1-5 songs and lyric sheet. SASE. Reports in 2-6 weeks.
Music: Mostly **power gospel**, **country rock gospel** and **adult contemporary gospel**; also **R&B**, **jazz**, **Christ-oriented Christmas music**, **pro-life and family** and **southern gospel**. Does not want negative-based lyrics of any kind. Published "She Used to Be Me," written and recorded by Crystal Cartier on Love Story (blues); "America My Country," written and recorded by Randy Lee Williamson on Lion & Lamb (ballad); and *I'm Not Living In the Past*, written and recorded by Jack Stone on Stone (southern gospel).
Tips: "Be serious. We are only interested in those who have meaning and substance behind what is created. Music is an avenue to change the world. Submit what comes from the heart. Don't be in a hurry. Good music has no time limits. And yet, time will reward the desire you put into it. Be willing to embark on newly designed challenges that will meet a new century of opportunity and needs never before obtainable through conventional music companies."

☑ ⊘ HIT & RUN MUSIC PUBLISHING INC., 8938 Keith Ave., West Hollywood CA 90069. (310)724-5600. Fax: (310)724-5624. Vice President: Susan Koch. New York office: 1841 Broadway, Suite 411, New York NY 10023. (212)956-2882. Fax: (212)956-2114. Music publisher. Publishes 20-30 songs/year; publishes 2 new songwriters/year. Hires staff writers. Pays standard royalty.
Affiliate(s): Charisma Music Publishing USA Inc. Hidden Pun Music Publishing Inc. (BMI).
How to Contact: Hit & Run does not accept unsolicited material.
Music: Mostly **pop**, **rock** and **R&B**; also **dance**. Published "Almost Doesn't Count," recorded by Brandy on Atlantic Records; "Colour Everywhere," recorded by Deana Carter on Capitol Nashville; and "La Magia Del Ritmo," recorded by Olga Tanor on WEA Latina.

☑ ⊘ HITSBURGH MUSIC CO. (BMI), P.O. Box 1431, 233 N. Electra, Gallatin TN 37066. (615)452-0324. Promotional Director: Kimolin Crutcher. A&R Director: K'leetha Gilbert. Executive Vice President: Kenneth Gilbert. President/General Manager: Harold Gilbert. Music publisher. Estab. 1964. Publishes 12 songs/year. Staff size: 4. Pays standard royalty.
Affiliate(s): 7th Day Music (BMI).
How to Contact: Submit demo tape by mail. Unsolicited submissions are OK. Prefers cassette or quality videocassette with 2-4 songs and lead sheet. Prefers studio produced demos. SASE. Reports in 4-6 weeks.
Music: Mostly **country gospel** and **MOR**. Published "Blue Tears" (by H. Gilbert), recorded by Damon Gilbert; and "You Know I Really Love You" (by Bob Brinkley), recorded by The Fox Sex, both on Southern City Records (pop).

☒ ○ HOLY SPIRIT MUSIC (BMI), P.O. Box 31, Edmonton KY 42129. (502)432-3183. President: W. Junior Lawson. Music publisher. Member GMA, International Association of Gospel Music Publishers and Southern Gospel Music Association. Estab. 1973. Publishes 4 songs/year; publishes 2 new songwriters/year. Staff size: 1. Pays standard royalty.
How to Contact: Submit demo tape by mail. Unsolicited submissions are OK. Prefers cassette with 2 songs and lyric sheet. SASE. Reports in 3 weeks.
Film & TV: Places 1 song in film and 1 song in TV/year. Recently published "I'm Making Plans To See Jesus" (by Gregory A. Pollard), recorded by The Florida Boys in *Saved By Grace*.
Music: Mostly **Southern gospel** and **country gospel**. Does not want rock gospel or contemporary gospel. Published *Excuses* (by Harold S. Lecke), recorded by The Kingsmen on Horizon Records; and *Save the Children* (by Julie P. Routenberg), recorded by Interstate Quartet on Sims Records (southern gospel).
Tips: Send "good clear cut tape with typed copy of lyrics."

○ INHABITANTS MUSIC GROUP, P.O. Box 48864, Los Angeles CA 90048. (213)739-4824. E-mail: imgsongs4@aol.com. President: Larry Rosenblum. Contact: Sam Beglar. Professional Manager (rock, jazz, progressive): Sam Beglar. Professional Manager (punk, alternative): Scott Krantz. Professional Manager (film, TV, special projects): Manuel Saldana. Music publisher, record company (L.S. Disc) and record producer. Estab. 1987. Publishes 1-15 songs/year; publishes 1-5 new songwriters/year. Pays standard royalty.
Affiliate(s): Treasure Trove Music (BMI), Lazy Rose Music (ASCAP), J. Holmquist Music (BMI), L.A.C.A. Music (ASCAP), Straight From the Hip Music (BMI), Sniffaloadius Music (ASCAP) and Crankee Yankee Music (ASCAP).
How to Contact: Submit demo tape by mail. Unsolicited submissions are OK. Prefers cassette or CD with 1-10 songs and lyric sheet. SASE. Reports in 3 months.

Music: Mostly **rock, progressive rock** and **punk**; also **jazz, folk** and **psychedelic rock**. Published "Nobody for President" (by Fenson and Peri Traynor), recorded by The Bob Dole Band (punk) on L.S. Disc; "There Will Be Times" and "Waltzing Her Heartaches" (by Greg Andrews), both recorded by Route on Cruel World Records.

Tips: "Be original! Be unique! Don't pay attention to today's style because style is simply what you are wearing today! Style will change tomorrow, but a great melody and lyric will last forever."

🅐 ⊕ **INSIDE RECORDS/OK SONGS**, Bisschopstraat 25, 2060 Antwerp 6 Belgium. Phone: (32)+3+226-77-19. Fax: (32)+3+226-78-05. MD: Jean Ney. Music publisher and record company. Estab. 1989. Publishes 50 songs/year; publishes 30-40 new songwriters/year. Hires staff writers. Royalty varies "depending on teamwork."

How to Contact: Submit demo tape by mail. Unsolicited submissions are OK. Prefers cassette with complete name, address, telephone and fax number. SAE and IRC. Reports in 2 months.

Music: Mostly **dance, pop** and **MOR contemporary**; also **country, reggae** and **Latin**. Published *Fiesta De Bautiza* (by Andres Manzana); *I'm Freaky* (by Maes-Predu'homme-Robinson); and *Heaven* (by KC One-King Naomi), all on Inside Records.

⊡ **INTERPLANETARY MUSIC (BMI)**, 584 Roosevelt, Gary IN 46404. (219)886-2003. Fax: (219)886-1000. CEO: James R. Hall III. A&R Director (hip-hop, R&B, jazz): Martin Booker. A&R (R&B, gospel): Bryant Henderson. Music publisher, record company (Interplanetary Records) and record producer. Estab. 1972. Staff size: 5. Publishes 10 songs/year; publishes 4 new songwriters/year. Pays standard royalty.

How to Contact: Call first and obtain permission to submit. Prefers cassette. SASE. Reports in 1 month.

Music: Mostly **R&B, rap** and **Top 40/urban contemporary**. Does not want country. Published "Beneath the Sheets" (by James Hall) and "Good Times" (by Bernard Tucker), both recorded by Subliminal on Interplanetary Records.

Tips: "Please submit a good quality cassette recording of your best work."

🅽 ⊡ **IRON SKILLET MUSIC**, 229 Ward Circle, #A21, Brentwood TN 37027. (615)371-0646. Fax: (615)370-0353. President: Jack Schneider. Music publisher, record company (Rustic Records Inc.) and record producer. Estab. 1984. Publishes 20 songs/year. Pays standard royalty.

Affiliate(s): Covered Bridge Music (BMI), Town Square Music (SESAC).

How to Contact: Submit demo tape by mail. Unsolicited submissions are OK. Prefers cassette with 3 songs and lyric sheet. SASE. Reports in 3 months.

Music: Mostly **country**. Published "You Beat All I've Ever Seen," "If It's The Last Thing I Do," and "Crazy Heart," all written and recorded by T. Strawbridge on Rustic Records.

Tips: "Send three or four traditional country songs, story songs or novelty songs with strong hook. Enclose SASE (manilla envelope)."

⊕ ☑ ⊡ **ISLAND CULTURE MUSIC PUBLISHERS (BMI)**, Chateau Bordeaux, St. John U.S. Virgin Islands 00830. Phone/fax: (340)693-5544. E-mail: liston_m@hotmail.com. President: Liston Monsanto, Jr. Music publisher and record company (Island King Records). Estab. 1996. Publishes 10 songs/year; publishes 3 new songwriters/year. Hires staff songwriters. Staff size: 3. Pays standard royalty.

How to Contact: Submit demo tape by mail. Unsolicited submissions are OK. Prefers cassette with 8 songs and lyric sheet. Send bio and 8×10 glossy. Does not return material. Reports in 1 month.

Music: Mostly **reggae, calypso** and **zouk**; also **house**. Published *Take It Easy* (by Cindy Reuben), recorded by Hecky; *Garbage* (by Carl Martin), recorded by Lucinda Reid; and *You Know* (by Leonard Hill), recorded by Ras Ready, all on Island King (reggae).

☑ ⊡ **JANA JAE MUSIC (BMI)**, P.O. Box 35726, Tulsa OK 74153. (918)786-8896. E-mail: janajae@janajae.com. Website: http://www.janajae.com. Secretary: Kathleen Pixley. Music publisher, record company (Lark Record Productions, Inc.) and record producer (Lark Talent and Advertising). Estab. 1980. Publishes 5-10 songs/year; publishes 1-2 new songwriters/year. Staff size: 3. Pays standard royalty.

How to Contact: Submit demo tape by mail. Unsolicited submissions are OK. Prefers cassette or VHS videocassette with 3-4 songs and typed lyric and lead sheet if possible. Does not return material. Reports only if accepted for use.

FOR BOOKS ON THE CRAFT AND BUSINESS of songwriting, check out the website for Writer's Digest Books at http://www.writersdigest.com.

Music: Mostly **country, bluegrass, jazz** and **instrumentals** (**classical** or **country**). Published *Mayonnaise* (by Steve Upfold), recorded by Jana Jae; and *Bus 'N' Ditty* (by Steve Upfold), recorded by Hotwire, on Lark Records.

☑ ⬛ ◎ **JAELIUS ENTERPRISES (ASCAP, BMI)**, P.O. Box 459, Royse City TX 75189. (972)636-2600. E-mail: jaelius@flash.net. Owner: James Cornelius. Music publisher. Publishes 3-5 songs/year; publishes 3 new songwriters/year. Staff size: 2. Pays standard royalty.
Affiliate(s): Jaelius Music (ASCAP), Hitzgalore Music (BMI), Air Rifle Music (ASCAP) and Bee Bee Gun Music (BMI).
How to Contact: Write or call first and obtain permission to submit. Prefers cassette. SASE. Reports in 6 weeks.
Film & TV: Places 2 songs in film/year. Recently published "Night Has a Thousand Eyes" (by Wayne/Weisman/Garrett), recorded by Anita Kelsey in *Dark City*; and "Feeling in Love," written and recorded by J.J. Cale in *Lawn Dogs*.
Music: Mostly **pop, country** and **gospel**; also **R&B**. Does not want rap. Published "Dark Shadows of Night" (by Rich Wilbur/Penny Wigley), recorded by Nashville Bluegrass Band on Sugar Hill Records (bluegrass); "The Price Is Right," written and recorded by Joe Williams; and "Mama's Sunday Plates" (by Ann Cornelius/Wayne Ruff), recorded by Anne Hunter, both on Ascension Records (Christian).
Tips: "Today's market requires good demos. Strong lyrics are a must."

🆘 ⊕ ◯ **JA/NEIN MUSIKVERLAG GMBH**, Hallerstr. 72, D-20146 Hamburg Germany. Phone: (40)4102161. Fax: (040)448850. E-mail: janeinmv@aol.com. General Manager: Mary Dostal. Music publisher, record company and record producer. GEMA. Publishes 100 songs/year; publishes 20 new songwriters/year. Staff size: 3. Pays 60% royalty.
Affiliate(s): Pinorrekk Mv., Star-Club Mv., Wunderbar Mv. and Sempex Mv. (GEMA).
How to Contact: Submit demo tape by mail. Unsolicited submissions are OK. Prefers cassette, CD-R or VHS videocassette and lyric sheet. SAE and IRC. Reports in 2-8 weeks.
Music: Mostly **rock, pop, MOR** and **blues**. Does not want military. Published "Wenn Dugehst" (by Bernadette Hengst), recorded by Die Braut on RCA Records (pop); *Royte Pomarantsen* (by Michael Alpert), recorded by Brave Old World on Pinorrekk (Klezmer); and *A Yidishe Neshome* (by Kurt Bjorling), recorded by Chicago Klezmer Ensemble on Oriente (Klezmer).
Tips: "If IRC is not included, we only react if we fall in love. Single, A-Side songs only or extraordinary ideas, please. If artist, include photo. Leave three seconds between songs. Enclose lyrics. Be fantastic!"

◎ **JASPER STONE MUSIC (ASCAP)/JSM SONGS (BMI)**, 10 Deepwell Farms Rd., South Salem NY 10590. E-mail: gcrecords@aol.com. Website: http://members.aol.com/gcrecords. President: Chris Jasper. Vice President/General Counsel: Margie Jasper. Music publisher. Estab. 1986. Publishes 20-25 songs/year. "Each contract is worked out individually and negotiated depending on terms." Staff size: 5. Pays standard royalty.
How to Contact: Submit demo tape by mail. Unsolicited submissions are OK. Prefers cassette with maximum of 3 songs and lyric sheets. SASE. Reports in 6 weeks.
Music: Mostly **R&B/pop, rap** and **rock**. Does not want country, classical or children's. Published "And I Love Her" (by J. Lennon/P. McCartney), recorded by Brothaz By Choice on Gold City Records (R&B).
Tips: "Keep writing. Keep submitting tapes. Be persistent. Don't give up. Send your best songs in the best form (best production possible)."

☑ ◯ **JERJOY MUSIC (BMI)**, P.O. Box 1264, 6020 W. Pottstown Rd., Peoria IL 61654-1264. (309)673-5755. Fax: (309)673-7636. E-mail: uarltd@unitedcyber.com. Website: http://www.unitedcyber.com/uarltd. Professional Manager: Jerry Hanlon. Music publisher and record company (Universal-Athena Records). Estab. 1978. Publishes 4 songs/year; publishes 2 new songwriters/year. Staff size: 3. Pays standard royalty.
How to Contact: Write first and obtain permission to submit. "We do not return phone calls." Prefers cassette with 4-8 songs and lyric sheet. SASE. Reports in 2 weeks.
Music: Mostly **country** (modern or traditional), **gospel/Christian** and **Irish music**. Published *The Sweepstakes Song* (by Ranoy Saffell), recorded by B.J. Shawd; *Oowee-Oowee*, written and recorded by Steve Axley; and *Put My Buns In a Doggy Bag* (by Roger Gallagher), recorded by E. Sharpe, all on Universal-Athena Records (country).
Tips: "Compare, study and evaluate your music to the hit songs you hear on the radio. Let your songs tell a story. Choose your lyrics carefully and make every word count. Long and drawn-out songs don't seem to make it in writing. Every word should be chosen to its best commercial value. Don't submit any song that you don't honestly feel is well constructed and strong in commercial value. Be honest and sincere."

LITTLE RICHIE JOHNSON MUSIC (BMI), 2125 Willowmere Dr., Des Moines IA 50321. (505)864-7441. President: Tony Palmer. Manager: A.A. Chiodo. Music publisher and record company (LRJ Records). Estab. 1959. Publishes 50 songs/year; publishes 10 new songwriters/year. Pays standard royalty.
Affiliate(s): Little Cowboy Music (ASCAP).
How to Contact: Write first and obtain permission to submit. SASE. Reports in 6 weeks.
Music: Mostly **country** and **Spanish**. Published *Moonlight, Roses and the Wine* (by Jerry Jaramillo), recorded by Gabe Neoto; *Ship of Fools*, recorded by Reta Lee; and *Honky Tonk Cinderella*, written and recorded by Jerry Jaramillo, all on LRJ Records.

AL JOLSON BLACK & WHITE MUSIC (BMI), 116 17th Ave. S., Nashville TN 37203. (615)244-5656. President: Albert Jolson. Music publisher. Estab. 1981. Publishes 600 songs/year; publishes 50 new songwriters/year. Pays standard royalty.
Affiliate(s): Jolie House Music (ASCAP).
How to Contact: Submit a demo tape by mail. Unsolicited submissions are OK. Prefers cassette with 3 songs and lyric sheet. Send: Attn. Johnny Drake. SASE. Reports in 6 weeks.
Music: Mostly **country crossover**, **light rock** and **pop**. Published "Come Home to West Virginia" (by Scott Phelps), recorded by Kathy Mattea; "Ten Tiny Fingers, Ten Tiny Toes" (by David John Hanley), recorded by Kelly Dawn; and "Indiana Highway," recorded by Staggerlee, both on ASA Jolson Records (country).
Tips: "Make sure it has a strong hook. Ask yourself if it is something you would hear on the radio five times a day. Have good audible vocals on demo tape."

QUINCY JONES MUSIC, 3800 Barham Blvd., Suite 503, Los Angeles CA 90068. (213)882-1340. Fax: (213)874-0143. E-mail: kl@quincyjonesmusic.com. Contact: Judith Bright; Karen Lamberton. Music publisher.
How to Contact: Quincy Jones Music does not accept unsolicited submissions.

JOSENA MUSIC (SESAC), P.O. Box 566, Los Altos CA 94022. President: Joe Vilchez-Nardone. Music publisher and producer. Estab. 1983. Pays standard royalty.
Affiliate(s): Reigninme Music (SESAC).
How to Contact: Write first and obtain permission to submit. "Tapes sent without permission will not be listened to." Prefers cassette with 3 songs and lyric sheet. Does not return material. Reports in 2 months if interested.
Music: Mostly **pop** and **gospel**; also **modern rock** and **Latin Music** as well—**flamenco**, **rumba style** (Spanish) and **Spanish ballads**. Does not want trash music. Published "A Mi Lado," written and recorded by Joe Vilchez Nardone (Latin).
Tips: "Make sure it is a hot marketable tune—get unbiased opinions on your song—would it be playable on the radio? Keep working and perfecting your craft . . . we all do!"

JPMC MUSIC INC. (BMI), (formerly GlobeArt Inc.), 80 Pine St., 33rd Floor, New York NY 10005. (212)344-5588. Fax: (212)344-5566. E-mail: music@jpmc.com. Website: http://www.music@jpmc. com. President: Jane Peterer. Music publisher, record company (JPMC Records) and book publisher. Estab. 1989. Publishes 20 songs/year; publishes 10 new songwriters/year. Pays standard royalty.
Affiliate(s): GlobeSound Publishing (ASCAP) and GlobeArt Publishing Inc. (BMI).
How to Contact: Submit a demo tape by mail. Unsolicited submissions are OK. Prefers "professional" cassette or CD with 3 songs and lyric sheet. "If submitting a CD, indicate which three tracks to consider, otherwise only the first three will be considered." SASE. Reports in 2 months.
Music: Mostly **pop/R&B**, **jazz** and **gospel**; also **country** and **instrumental**. Published "Runnin' " (by Hank/Swan), recorded by Funky Bud on JPMC Records (funk); "Echoes," written and recorded by JoAnne Brackeen on DA Music Records (jazz); and "Woman Of the Sea" (by Breschi), recorded by Breschi/Cassidy on Pick Records (instrumental).
Tips: "We are in constant communication with record and film producers and will administer your work on a worldwide basis. We also publish songbooks for musicians and fans, as well as educational and method books for students and teachers."

SENDING TO A COUNTRY other than your own? Be sure to send International Reply Coupons (IRCs) instead of stamps for replies or return of your materials.

JUKE MUSIC (BMI), P.O. Box 121234, Nashville TN 37212. (615)383-7222. Songwriter Coordinator: Luke Sands. Professional Manager: Jack Cook. Music publisher. Estab. 1987. Publishes 60-150 songs/year; publishes 3-25 new songwriters/year. Pays standard royalty.
How to Contact: Submit demo tape by mail. Unsolicited submissions are OK. Prefers cassette with 3 songs and lyric sheet. "Send only radio-friendly material." Does not return material. Reports in 2 months.
Music: Mostly **country, pop** and **rock**; also **alternative adult** and **Christian**. Does not want theatrical, improperly structured, change tempo and feel, poor or music with no hook. Published *Our Road* (by Richard Jones), recorded by Johnny White on RAM (country); *Long Reach* (by Angie Chaney), recorded by Fish Heads & Rice on Asylum (country/AC); and *Still Bring a Thrill* (by Wayne Walton), recorded by Darlene Shadden on Phaedra (country/rock).
Tips: "Do your homework, craft the song, be sure you're willing to gamble your songwriting integrity on this song or songs you're sending. We recommend songwriters attend workshops or conferences before submitting material."

KANSA RECORDS CORPORATION, P.O. Box 1878, Frisco TX 75034. (214)335-8004. Secretary and Treasurer/General Manager: Kit Johnson. Music publisher, record company and record producer. Estab. 1972. Publishes 50-60 songs/year; publishes 8-10 new songwriters/year. Pays standard royalty.
Affiliate(s): Great Leawood Music, Inc. (ASCAP) and Twinsong Music (BMI).
How to Contact: Submit demo tape by mail. Unsolicited submissions are OK. Prefers cassette with 4 songs and lyric sheet. Does not return material. Reports in 2 months.
Music: Mostly **country, MOR** and **country rock**; also **R&B** (leaning to country) and **Christian**. Does not want hard rock. Published *Louisiana Hop*; *Big Hurt*; *Seasons of Our Love* (by Walter Leise), all recorded by Jerry Piper on Kansas Records.

☑ ◯ KAUPPS & ROBERT PUBLISHING CO. (BMI), P.O. Box 5474, Stockton CA 95205. (209)948-8186. Fax: (209)942-2163. E-mail: kauppmusic@calcentron.com. A&R Coordinator (all styles): Kristy Ledford. Production Manager (country, pop, rock): Rick Webb. Professional Manager (country, pop, rock): Bruce Boun. President: Nancy L. Merrihew. Music publisher, record company (Kaupp Records), manager and booking agent (Merri-Webb Productions and Most Wanted Bookings). Estab. 1990. Publishes 15-20 songs/year; publishes 5 new songwriters/year. Pays standard royalty.
How to Contact: Write first and obtain permission to submit. Prefers cassette or VHS videocassette (if available) with 3 songs maximum and lyric sheet. "If artist, send PR package." SASE. Reports in 3-6 months.
Music: Mostly **country, R&B** and **A/C rock**; also **pop, rock** and **gospel**. Published "Familiar Strangers" (by N. Merrihew/B. Bolin), recorded by Nanci Lynn; "Goin' Postal" (by N. Merrihew/B. Bolin), recorded by Bruce Bolin; and "Make-up My Mind" (by N. Merrihew/B. Bolin), recorded by Rick Webb, all on Kaupp Records (country/rock/pop).
Tips: "Know what you want, set a goal, focus in on your goals, be open to constructive criticism, polish tunes and keep polishing."

☑ ◯ KAREN KAYLEE MUSIC GROUP (BMI), R.D. #11, Box 360, Greensburg PA 15601. (724)836-0966. President (country): Karen Kaylee. Professional Manager (gospel): Den Hauk. Music publisher, record company (Ka-De Record Co.) and record producer. Estab. 1980. Publishes 15-20 songs/year; publishes 3 new songwriters/year. Hires staff writers. Pays standard royalty.
How to Contact: Submit demo tape by mail. Unsolicited submissions are OK. Prefers cassette or VHS videocassette with 3 songs and lyric sheet. "No phone calls please." SASE. Reports in 1 month.
Music: Mostly **country, gospel** and **traditional country**. Published "My Heart's Baby Blue," and "Fallen From Grace," both written and recorded by Karen Kaylee; and "Heart Be Still" (by Carlene), recorded by Haggerty, all on Ka-De Records (country).
Tips: "I am looking for top songs only. Write, rewrite, and listen to your tape. Only submit professional packages on clear tapes, recorded on one side only. Must include SASE."

◉ KOZKEEOZKO MUSIC (ASCAP), 928 Broadway, Suite 602, New York NY 10010. (212)505-7332. Professional Managers: Ted Lehrman and Libby Bush. Music publisher, record producer and management firm (Landslide Management). Estab. 1978. Publishes 5 songs/year; publishes 3 new songwriters/year. Pays standard royalty.
How to Contact: Write or call first and obtain permission to submit. Prefers cassette or VHS ½" videocassette with 2 songs maximum and typewritten lyric sheet for each song. SASE. Reports in 2 months.
Music: Mostly **soul/pop, dance, pop/rock, A/C** and **country**. Does not want heavy metal. Published "Ain't No Cure For You" (by Ed Chalfin/Tedd Lawson), recorded by Roger Clinton on Pyramid Records; "River of Love" (by Frank Scozzari/Tedd Lawson); "Music to My Eyes" (by Ed Chalfin/Ted Lehrman),

recorded by Emel on BMG Records; and "A Long Goodbye" (by Ed Chalfin/Ted Lehrman), recorded by Brothaz by Choice on Gold City Records.

N Ø LAKE TRANSFER PRODUCTIONS & MUSIC (ASCAP, BMI), 11300 Hartland St., Suite F, North Hollywood CA 91605. (818)508-7158. Professional Managers: Jim Holvay (pop, R&B, soul); Tina Antoine (hip-hop, rap); Steve Barri Cohen (alternative rock, R&B). Music publisher and record producer (Steve Barri Cohen). Estab. 1989. Publishes 11 songs/year; publishes 3 new songwriters/year. Staff size: 6. Pay "depends on agreement, usually 50% split."
Affiliate(s): Lake Transfer Music (ASCAP) and Transfer Lake Music (BMI).
How to Contact: Does not accept unsolicited submissions.
Music: Mostly **alternative pop, R&B/hip-hop** and **dance**. Does not want country & western, classical, New Age, jazz or swing.
Tips: "All our staff are songwriters/producers. Jim Holway has written hits like 'Kind of a Drag' and 'Hey Baby They're Playin our Song' for the Buckinghams. Steve Barri Cohen has worked with every one from Evelyn 'Champaigne' King, Patrice Rushen to Phantom Planets (Geffen)."

▣ Ø LARGO MUSIC PUBLISHING (ASCAP, BMI), 425 Park Ave., New York NY 10022. (212)756-5080. Fax: (212)207-8167. E-mail: largomp@aol.com. Website: http://www.largomusic.com. Creative Manager (all music genres): Peter Oriol. Professional Manager (hip-hop, rap, R&B): Walter Velesquez. A&R (A/C, pop): John M. Murro. Music publisher. Estab. 1980. Staff size: 10. Pays variable royalty.
Affiliate(s): Catharine Hiren Music, American Compass Music Corp., Diplomat Music Corp., Larry Shayne Enterprises (ASCAP), Largo Cargo Music (BMI), X-Square Music, Ros-World Music and Three White Boys Music, Rap Music (BMI), Rock-Logic Music (ASCAP).
How to Contact: Write first and obtain permission to submit or to arrange personal interview. Prefers cassette or CD with 4 songs and lyric sheet. "Spend money on recording well, not packaging." Does not return material. Reports in 2-4 weeks.
Film & TV: Places 10 songs in film and 10 songs in TV/year. Music Supervisors: Peter Oriol (all); Walter Velesquez (hip-hop, rap, R&B).
Music: Mostly **alternative rock, AOR** and **R&B**; also **hip-hop** and **rap**; "good music that transcends categories." Published "Drama" (by Ty Macklin), recorded by Erykah Badu on Universal (R&B); "Step Into a World" (by Jesse West), recorded by KRS-One on Jive (rap); and "24/7" (by Jesse West), recorded by 24/7 on Loud (rap).
Tips: "Good songs are not enough—you must be a complete artist and writer."

Ø LARI-JON PUBLISHING (BMI), 325 W. Walnut, Rising City NE 68658. (402)542-2336. Owner: Larry Good. Music publisher, record company (Lari-Jon Records), management firm (Lari-Jon Promotions) and record producer (Lari-Jon Productions). Estab. 1967. Publishes 20 songs/year; publishes 2-3 new songwriters/year. Staff size: 1. Pays standard royalty.
How to Contact: Submit demo tape by mail. Unsolicited submissions are OK. Prefers cassette with 5 songs and lyric sheet. "Be professional." SASE. Reports in 2 months.
Music: Mostly **country, Southern gospel** and **'50s rock**. Does not want rock, hip-hop, pop or heavy metal. Published "Glory Bound Train," written and recorded by Tom Campbell; "Nebraskaland" and "Jesus Is My Hero," written and recorded by Larry Good, all on Lari-Jon Records.

✓ Ø TRIXIE LEIGH MUSIC, (formerly Cherasny Elijah Entertainment Production Company), 1717 Crimson Tree Way #A, Edgewood MD 21040. (410)679-2545. Music publisher: Rick Solimini. Music publisher and record company (Cherasny Records). Estab. 1997. Publishes 4 songs/year; publishes 4 new songwriters/year. Hires staff writers. Staff size: 4. Pays standard royalty.
How to Contact: Write first and obtain permission to submit. Prefers cassette with 3 songs and lyric and lead sheets. SASE. Reports in 1 month.
Music: Mostly **contemporary Christian**. Does not want secular, rap, opera or hard rock. Published *Ol' Friend* (by Chris Ledgerwood); and *I Am Your Sheep* (by Ward Yont), both recorded by Redemption; and *Free* (by Chris Ledgerwood), recorded by Donna Bente, all on Cherasny Records (Christian).
Tips: "Be consistent in learning the craft of songwriting."

▧ ▣ Ø LILLY MUSIC PUBLISHING (SOCAN), 61 Euphrasia Dr., Toronto, Ontario M6B 3V8 Canada. (416)782-5768. Fax: (416)782-7170. President: Panfilo DiMatteo. Music publisher and record company (P. & N. Records). Estab. 1992. Publishes 20 songs/year; publishes 8 new songwriters/year. Staff size: 3. Pays standard royalty.
Affiliate(s): San Martino Music Publishing and Paglieta Music Publishing (CMRRA).

How to Contact: Submit demo tape by mail. Unsolicited submissions are OK. Prefers cassette (or videocassette if available) with 3 songs and lyric and lead sheets. "We will contact you only if we are interested in the material." Reports in 1 month.
Film & TV: Places 12 songs in film/year.
Music: Mostly **dance**, **ballads** and **rock**; also **country**. Published *Gift of Memories*, recorded by Anjelica Castro on P&N Records (dance).

DORIS LINDSAY PUBLISHING (ASCAP), P.O. Box 35005, Greensboro NC 27425. (336)882-9990. President: Doris Lindsay. Music publisher and record company (Fountain Records). Estab. 1979. Publishes 20 songs/year; publishes 4 songwriters/year. Pays standard royalty.
Affiliate(s): Better Times Publishing (BMI).
How to Contact: Submit demo tape by mail. Unsolicited submissions are OK. Prefers cassette with 2 songs. "Submit good quality demos." SASE. Reports in 2 months.
Music: Mostly **country, pop** and **contemporary gospel**. Published *Service Station Cowboy* (by Hoss Ryder), recorded by Ace Diamond on Sabre Records; and "Amusin' Cruisin' " by Susan and Frank Rosario; and "America's Song" (by Cathy Roeder), recorded by Terry Michaels, both on Fountain Records.
Tips: "Present a good quality demo (recorded in a studio). Positive clean lyrics and up-tempo music are easiest to place."

LINEAGE PUBLISHING CO. (BMI), P.O. Box 211, East Prairie MO 63845. (314)649-2211. Professional Manager: Tommy Loomas. Staff: Alan Carter and Joe Silver. Music publisher, record producer, management firm (Staircase Promotions) and record company (Capstan Record Production). Pays standard royalty.
How to Contact: Submit demo tape by mail. Unsolicited submissions are OK. Prefers cassette with 2-4 songs and lyric sheet; include bio and photo if possible. SASE. Reports in 1-2 months.
Music: Mostly **country, easy listening, MOR, country rock** and **top 40/pop**. Published "Let It Rain" (by Roberta Boyle), recorded by Vicarie Arcoleo on Treasure Coast Records; "Country Boy," written and recorded by Roger Lambert; and "Boot Jack Shuffle" (by Zachary Taylor), recorded by Skid Row Joe, both on Capstan Records.

LITTLE MILLER MUSIC CO., 97 Bow St., Arlington MA 02474-2722. Phone/fax: (781)641-0903. E-mail: minogue@earthlink.net. Website: http://www.minogue.com. Owner: Áine Minogue. Music publisher. Estab. 1994. Staff size: 2. Pays standard royalty.
How to Contact: Submit demo tape by mail. Unsolicited submissions are OK. Prefers CD or cassette with 5 songs and lyric and lead sheet. Does not return material. Reports in 2-3 months.
Music: Mostly **Celtic, New Age** and **world**; also **art music** and **acoustic**. Published "Fill It to the Brim" (by M. Simos) (folk); and "Across the Universe" (by John Lennon), both on BMG Classics (pop); and "Aifreann" (by Sean O-Riada) on North Star (world), all recorded by Áine Minogue.

LOLLIPOP FARM ENTERTAINMENT (BMI) (formerly Lonny Tunes Music), P.O. Box 460086, Garland TX 75046. E-mail: lonnyj@aol.com. President: Lonny Schonfeld. Music publisher, record company (Lollipop Farm) and record producer. Estab. 1988. Publishes 8-10 songs/year; publishes 2-3 new songwriters/year. Pays standard royalty.
How to Contact: Submit a demo tape by mail. Unsolicited submissions are OK. Prefers cassette with 3-5 songs and lyric sheet. "Professional quality only." Does not return material. Reports in 6-8 weeks.
Music: Mostly **country, children's** and **rock**; also **jazz** and **comedy**. Published "Baby With You" and "Lonliness," written and recorded by Randy Stout; and "You Put the Merry in My Christmas," recorded by Mary Massey (Christmas), all on Lollipop Farm.
Tips: "Make sure your lyrical content is contemporary. 'Old time' rhymes like moon and June will not work for us."

FOR EXPLANATIONS OF THESE SYMBOLS,
SEE THE INSIDE FRONT AND BACK COVERS OF THIS BOOK.

insider report

A good friend of Barney and Wishbone talks about children's music

Charles King

As Lyrick Studios's manager of music and copyright administration, Charles King oversees virtually every aspect of the company's operations where music is used—on both the publishing and the production sides of the business.

"Lyrick Studios produces and distributes entertainment products for families and children," King says. "Among the better known of our products are Barney, the purple dinosaur character beloved by millions of infants and toddlers, and Wishbone, the highly literary Jack Russell terrier who appeals to kids and those of us who are still 'kids at heart.' " Lyrick also represents the VeggieTales line, certain Shelley Duvall products and entertainers Joe Scruggs and Julie Chapman.

In the area of production, King oversees the administration of the company's music catalogs in the U.S. and Canada. He recommends selections for albums and for other programming and products, and prepares all artist and writer royalty statements.

Here King offers advice on writing songs for children, talks about a publisher's role in a songwriter's career and offers tips on contracts.

Tell me a little about your company.
Lyrick Studios's focus is on high-quality entertainment for families and children, and we are very selective about the properties we take on. We do not take on representation of properties inconsistent with our mission and standards, or for which our team doesn't truly have a passion.

Lyrick Studios itself produces and distributes television programming, videos, audio products, books and plush toys. We also produce live shows such as the *Barney's Big Surprise* concert tour, which won *Performance Magazine*'s Family Show Tour of the Year Award. With the production (in association with PolyGram Films) of *Barney's Great Adventure*, we have entered the world of feature film production. Lyrick Studios also handles

CHARLES KING

Title: Manager of Music and Copyright Administration
Company: Lyrick Studios
Music: Children's

domestic and international licensing of products for the Barney and Wishbone properties, as well as for other properties we represent. Lyrick Studios has 6 active music publishing catalogs with approximately 600 copyrights. Music is a particularly key element of the Barney character and programming, and Barney-related products are our primary audio products. The first three Barney albums were licensed to and released by EMI Records. However, in 1997, we brought that production and distribution in-house. Since that time, we have released five additional Barney albums.

As a music publisher, what is your role in the career of a songwriter?
My role is different than a typical music publisher. Since many of our arrangements with songwriters are done on a "work-for-hire" basis, there isn't much of a need to cultivate a songwriter's career. However, my impact usually comes in the form of meetings involving the songwriter with the production staff during the production phase of the television show. Here we discuss important music issues, what songs may or may not work, review any new material a songwriter has submitted for consideration, etc. The selection of compositions for our shows is a very detailed process.

My department usually performs research for public domain compositions the songwriters can use for new arrangements. Songwriters occasionally have performance rights society issues that may require some input from me as the publisher representative and I speak on their behalf with the societies. I'm very fortunate to have really great relationships with ASCAP, BMI and SESAC.

What's the best way for a songwriter to get their work heard by Lyrick?
First send a résumé with a list of songwriting accomplishments. It would help if the writer was represented by an agent. We've had to institute a strict protocol regarding the acceptance of material from songwriters for legal reasons. It is rare when the production staff is in a position to consider new material—and usually unannounced. When the consideration period occurs, production will review all submitted résumés and pare down the list of writers for demo tape consideration. We typically prefer to continue cultivating relationships with songwriters who have previously worked with us, especially if we have had success with them.

I would advise against writers calling proclaiming they have written a song that is "Barney appropriate." For me, that is an instant negative because there is no way for a person unfamiliar with the show or company to determine what is appropriate.

What makes you reject a song—what do you hear a lot that you dislike?
I dislike badly produced demo tapes. Having heard quite a few demos in my time, I can tell when attention to detail has been ignored in the production of a demo tape—that tape is a reflection of the songwriter's professionalism. My personal clue about the potential success of a children's song is if I play it for one of my younger nephews and he enjoys what he is hearing.

What are some special considerations songwriters should keep in mind when writing for children?

Keep it simple and keep it fresh. Significant portions of our music catalogs are arrangements of public domain works. However, a considerable number of original compositions have been created over the last three years. Children love the familiar—it gives them a sense of belonging to know the words or, at least, recognize the melody of a song. Therefore, it is important a composition stay simple, so it can be easily learned and repeated. The real challenge is to make simple songs have a fresh appeal. Some writers successfully address this challenge by including interactive elements, such as hand motions, which children love.

Can you offer songwriters advice on what to look for or avoid in a contract with a music publisher?

Try to maintain as much of your publishing as possible—never settle for less than 50 percent copyright control. If that is not possible, then make sure the retention periods are short. Also, make an effort to become personally involved in the business of music publishing. Your composition will be around much longer than any album it is on, and its profitability can be maximized in other royalty streams besides record sales. Therefore, a songwriter needs to maintain an acute business sense—pay attention to issues such as international subpublishing, synchronization rights, print rights, etc.

What is your advice for the beginning songwriter?

Keep your day job and maintain a sense of realism. Many beginning songwriters, as well as people starting out in other aspects of the music business, have a glamorized view of the industry. As happy as I am with the way my career has progressed, it has required hard work and there have been some hills and valleys to conquer along the way. Success can be fleeting, and is frequently wiped away in the blink of an eye. Therefore, if you maintain your focus toward your goal and stay grounded, success can and should happen.

Do you have any advice for songwriters interested in writing children's music?

Children's music is such an incredibly small genre in the music industry. Therefore, do not try to bank your success on trying to succeed in this genre. Good songwriters with solid training and background who have written for other genres can parlay their success in children's music by employing a little imagination, simplicity and freshness. For those who want to obtain a career on the business side of the industry, start early and take advantage of every opportunity handed to you.

—Alice Pope

☑ ⬛ ⭕ **LOVEY MUSIC, INC. (BMI)**, 3319 SW Woodcreek Trail, Palm City FL 34990. (561)219-7874. President: Jack Gale. Music publisher. Estab. 1981. Publishes 25 songs/year; publishes 10 new songwriters/year. Staff size: 5. Pays standard royalty.
Affiliate(s): Cowabonga Music, Inc. (ASCAP).
How to Contact: Submit demo tape by mail. Unsolicited submissions are OK. Prefers cassette or VHS videocassette with 2 songs max and lyric sheets. SASE. Reports in 2 weeks if interested.
Film & TV: Places 10 songs in film/year. Recently published "The Wish" and "Hitman" for *Prime Target*, "I'm A Honky Tonk Man" for *Eye of the Stanger*, all written and recorded by David Heavener.
Music: Mostly **country crossover** and **country**. Does not want rap, classical or alternative rock. Published "Old Dreams" (by Harris/Cannon), recorded by Charlie Louvin (country); "Second Time Around" (by Rocky Priola), recorded by Del Reeves (country); and "Angel in Disguise" (by Turney/Scherrer), recorded by Tommy Cash (country), all on Playback Records.

☑ ⭕ **HAROLD LUICK & ASSOCIATES MUSIC PUBLISHER (BMI)**, P.O. Box 368, Carlisle IA 50047. (515)989-3748. Fax: (515)989-0235. E-mail: haroldl@cmshowcase.org. Website: http://www.cm showcase.org. President (country, bluegrass, blues, contemporary Christian): Harold L. Luick. Vice President (cajun, gospel, country, blues): Barbara A. Luick. Professional Managers: Joe E. Harris (traditional country, gospel); Frank Gallagher (MOR, contemporary country). Music publisher, record company, record producer and music industry consultant. Publishes 25-30 songs/year; publishes 5-10 new songwriters/year. Pays standard royalty.
How to Contact: "We accept songs for publishing only from members of Country Music Showcase International (CMSI)." Write or call first about your interest, or for more information on CMSI. Prefers cassette with 3-5 songs and lyric sheet. SASE. Reports in 3 weeks.
   ● Harold Luick & Associates is now owned and operated by Country Music Showcase International Inc.
Music: Mostly **traditional country** and **hard core country**. Does not want hip-hop or rap. Published "Mrs. Used To Be," written and recorded by Joe E. Harris on River City Music Records (country); and "Ballad of Deadwood S.P.," written and recorded by Don Laughlin on Kajac Records (historical country).
Tips: "It takes just as much of your time and money to pitch a good song as a bad one, so concentrate on the potential of the good ones. Join nonprofit educational songwriters associations (like CMSI) that can help you write better songs through critiques, evaluations, seminars and workshops."

🅽 ⬛ ⭕ **LYRICK STUDIOS (ASCAP, BMI, SESAC)**, 2435 N. Central Expressway, Suite 1600, Richardson TX 75080-2734. (972)390-6084. Fax: (972)390-6001. E-mail: jslocum@lyrick.com. Website: http://www.wishbone.com. Manager/Copyright Administrator: Charles L. King. Music publisher and record company. Estab. 1996.
   ● Lyrick Studios produces and distributes music, products and TV programming for the characters Barney and Wishbone. See the Insider Report interview with Manager/Copyright Administrator Charles King on page 96.
How to Contact: "Send only a résumé with a list of songwriting accomplishments." Does not return material. Reports only if interested.
Music: Mostly **children's**. Published *Run, Jump, Skip & Sing*, *Barney's Favorites* and *Happy Holidays—Love, Barney*.

⭕ **M & T WALDOCH PUBLISHING, INC. (BMI)**, 4803 S. Seventh St., Milwaukee WI 53221. (414)482-2194. VP, Creative Management (rockabilly, pop, country): Timothy J. Waldoch. Professional Manager (country, top 40): Mark T. Waldoch. Music publisher. Estab. 1990. Publishes 2-3 songs/year; publishes 2-3 new songwriters/year. Staff size: 2. Pays standard royalty.
How to Contact: Submit demo tape by mail. Unsolicited submissions are OK. Prefers cassette with 3-6 songs and lyric or lead sheet. "We prefer a studio produced demo tape." SASE. Reports in 3 months.
Music: Mostly **country/pop**, **rock**, **top 40 pop**; also **melodic metal**, **dance**, **R&B**. Does not want rap. Published "It's Only Me" and "Let Peace Rule the World" (by Kenny LePrix), recorded by Brigade on SBD Records (rock).
Tips: "Study the classic pop songs from the 1950s through the present time. There is a reason why good songs stand the test of time. Today's hits will be tomorrow's classics. Send your *best* well-crafted, polished song material."

⭕ **MAGIC MESSAGE MUSIC (ASCAP)**, P.O. Box 9117, Truckee CA 96162. (530)587-0111. E-mail: alanred@telis.org. Website: http://www.alanredstone.com. Owner: Alan Redstone. Music publisher and record company (Sureshot Records). Estab. 1979. Publishes 6 songs/year; publishes 1 new songwriter/year. Staff size: 1. Pays standard royalty.

How to Contact: Write or call first and obtain permission to submit or submit demo tape by mail. Unsolicited submissions are OK. SASE. Reports in 1 week.
Music: Mostly **comedy**, **novelty** and **parody**; also **blues**. Does not want rap, soul, top 40, New Age or instrumental.

✅ 🖉 **MAJESTIC CONTROL (BMI)**, 331 W. 57th St. #173, New York NY 10019. (212)489-1500. Fax: (212)489-5660. CEO: Matt "Half Pint" Davis. President: Tatiana Sampson. Music publisher, promotions and public relations. Estab. 1983.
How to Contact: Submit demo tape by mail. Unsolicited submissions are OK. Prefers cassette with 3 songs. SASE. Reports in 2 months.
Music: Mostly **rap** and **R&B**. Artists include Soul IV Real, Big Daddy Kane and Kamakaze.

✅ 🖉 **MAKERS MARK GOLD (ASCAP)**, P.O. Box 42751, Philadelphia PA 19101. (215)236-4817. Website: http://www.prolificrecords.com. Producer: Paul Hopkins. Music publisher and record producer. Estab. 1991. Pays standard royalty.
How to Contact: Submit demo tape by mail. Unsolicited submissions are OK. Prefers cassette with 2-4 songs. Does not return material. Reports in 4-6 weeks if interested.
Music: Mostly **R&B**, **hip-hop**, **gospel**, **pop**, **country** and **house**. Published "Last Kiss," "Top of the World" (by C. Foreman/P. Hopkins), recorded by Rachel Scarborough; "All Eyes on the Philosopher" (by Norman Gilliam/P. Hopkins), recorded by Norman Gilliam; and "In the Still of the Night," recorded by Emerge, all on Prolific Records.
Tips: "I prefer to work with those with representation."

✅ 🖼 🖉 **MASTER SOURCE (ASCAP, BMI)**, 13903 Sherman Way #14, Van Nuys CA 91405. (818)994-3400. Fax: (818)994-3443. E-mail: mastersource@mastersource.net. Website: http://www.master source.net. Owner: Marc Ferrari. Professional Manager: Wendy Lubow. Music publisher. Estab. 1993. Publishes 100 songs/year; publishes 20 new songwriters/year. Pays standard royalty.
Affiliate(s): Red Engine Music (ASCAP) and Revision West (BMI).
How to Contact: Call first and obtain permission to submit. Prefers cassette with up to 5 songs and lyric sheet. SASE. Reports in 2 weeks.
Film & TV: Published music for *As Good As It Gets* (film); *Wag The Dog* (film); and *Touched By An Angel* (TV).
Music: Mostly **reggae/salsa**, **rap/urban** and **ethnic**; also **country**, **jazz** and **world beat**.
Tips: "We specialize in film and TV placements. Master quality recordings a must!"

🅽 🖉 **MAVERICK MUSIC**, 8730 Sunset Blvd., Suite 420, Los Angeles CA 90069. (310)652-6300. Contact: Lionel Conway. Music publisher and record company (Maverick).
How to Contact: Maverick Music does not accept unsolicited submissions.

🅽 🖰 **MAY PEACE BE UPON YOU MUSIC (ASCAP)**, 615 S. Hardy Dr., Suite 28, Tempe AZ 85281-3429. (602)967-4947. President/Owner: Carlos C. Muhammad. Music publisher. Estab. 1995. Publishes 20 songs/year; publishes 25 new songwriters/year. Pays standard royalty.
Affiliate(s): Egyptian Man Productions (ASCAP).
How to Contact: Submit demo tape by mail. Unsolicited submissions are OK. Prefers cassette or CD with 4 songs, lyric sheet, cover letter, 8 × 10 b&w glossy and bio. "Do not call. In cover letter say whether you are seeking a publishing or record deal." SASE. Reports in 1 month.
Music: Mostly **R&B/soul**, **hip-hop** and **pop**; also **soft rock**, **contemporary gospel** and **rap**. Published "Somewhere In My Heart" (by Joe Dunmore/Berris Bolton), recorded by Myra Jackson on Dumore Music (R&B).
Tips: "Listen to the radio to learn what's commercially current. Use a good quality tape and a clean recording for your demo. Never write songs that have already been written a thousand times."

MCA MUSIC PUBLISHING. MCA Music Publishing and PolyGram Music Publishing have merged into Universal Music Publishing. At press time they were going through restructuring.

TO HELP YOU UNDERSTAND and use the information in these listings, see "How to Use *Songwriter's Market* to Get Your Songs Heard," on page 5.

N ✎ ○ McCONKEY ARTISTS AGENCY MUSIC PUBLISHING (BMI), Hollywood Media Center Bldg., 1604 N. Cahuenga, Suite 108, Hollywood CA 90028-6267. (323)463-7141. Fax: (323)463-2558. Professional Managers: Mack K. McConkey (country); Steve Fazio (mainstream rock, R&B, jazz). Music publisher. Estab. 1998. Publishes 13 songs/year; publishes 5 new songwriters/year. Staff size: 10. Hires staff songwriters (part time only). Pays standard royalty.
Affiliate(s): Vinegower Music (ASCAP).
How to Contact: Submit demo tape by mail. Unsolicited submissions are OK. Prefers cassette or CD with 1-5 songs and lyric sheet and cover letter. "Please send us a professional tape or CD, as well as a typed or computer-printed lyric sheet and cover letter." Does not return material. Reports in 1-2 months.
Film & TV: Places 1 song in TV/year. Recently published "August" (by Em Kitterman), recorded by Pat Noland in an HBO Movie of The Month (untitled at press time).
Music: Mostly **country (all types)**; also **mainstream rock/R&B/jazz**. Does not want rap, heavy metal or ethnic. Published *Stuck In a Jam*, written and recorded by Kat Lester on Katalyst Records (country).
Tips: "Provide the best quality package on your songs. Also send the songs you feel are hits. Do not bother sending album filler material."

N ○ JIM McCOY MUSIC (BMI), Rt. 2, Box 2910, Berkeley Springs WV 25411. Owners: Bertha and Jim McCoy. Music publisher, record company (Winchester Records) and record producer (Jim McCoy Productions). Estab. 1973. Publishes 20 songs/year; publishes 3-5 new songwriters/year. Pays standard royalty.
Affiliate(s): New Edition Music (BMI).
How to Contact: Submit demo tape by mail. Unsolicited submissions are OK. Prefers cassette, 7½ or 15 ips reel-to-reel (or VHS or Beta videocassette) with 6 songs. SASE. Reports in 1 month.
Music: Mostly **country, country/rock** and **rock**; also **bluegrass** and **gospel**. Published "One Time" (by T. Miller), recorded by J.B. Miller on Hilton Records (country); and "Like Always" (by J. Alford), recorded by Al Hogan on Winchester Records (country).

N ○ McGIBONY PUBLISHING, 203 Mission Rdg. Rd., Rossville GA 30741. (706)861-2186. Fax: (706)866-2593. E-mail: mcgibonypub@webtv.net. Music Publisher: Richard McGibony. Music publisher, record company (R.R. & R. Music) and record producer. Estab. 1986. Publishes 20 songs/year; publishes 10-15 new songwriters/year. Pays standard royalty.
Affiliate(s): Sounds of Aicram (BMI) and Rich McGibone Music (ASCAP).
How to Contact: Write or call first and obtain permission to submit. Prefers cassette or VHS videocassette with 2 songs and lyric sheet. "Have a clear understandable tape with legible lyric sheets." SASE. Reports in 3 weeks.
Music: Mostly **country, gospel** and **R&B**. Published "Wings Wouldn't Change a Thing" (by Art, Al and Sharon Corey), recorded by Carl Towns (country); and *Party Hardy* (by Mike Lombardi/J. Mulrenan), recorded by Bunnie Mills (country), both on Greenback; and "My Life is Yours" (by J.C. Parham), recorded by Billy James on JP Records (pop).
Tips: "Present a good demo. Don't just throw something together. The competition is fierce."

✓ ○ MELLOW HOUSE MUSIC (BMI), P.O. Box 423618, San Francisco CA 94142. (415)776-8430. President: Darren Brown. Music publisher, record company (Mellow House Recordings) and record producer. Estab. 1992. Publishes 10 songs/year; publishes 10 new songwriters/year. Hires staff writers. Staff size: 7. Pays standard royalty.
How to Contact: Submit demo tape by mail. Unsolicited submissions are OK. Prefers cassette, DAT or CD with 3 songs and lyric sheet. SASE. Reports in 2 months.
Music: Mostly **funk, R&B** and **hip-hop**; also **pop/rock, alternative jazz** and **gospel**. Published "Soul Reflection" and "Love Parade," both written and recorded by Bobby Beale on Mellow House Recordings (jazz).

○ MELODY HILLS RANCH PUBLISHING CO. (BMI), 804 N. Trenton, Ruston LA 71270. (318)255-7127. Fax: (318)255-3050. E-mail: catmando@bayou.com. Owners: Jim Ball and Jane Ball. Music publisher. Estab. 1996. Publishes 2-3 songs/year; publishes 1-2 new songwriters/year. Staff size: 5. Pays standard royalty.
How to Contact: Write first and obtain permission to submit. Prefers cassette with 3-4 songs and lyric sheet. Does not return material. Reports in 4-6 weeks.
Music: Mostly **traditional country, southern rock** and **pop**. Does not want rap or rock. Recently published *I Can't Read Your Mind*; *Her Ring Is On My Finger*, both written and recorded by Jim Ball; and *Peter Filed Chapter 13* and *Lovin' On*, all written and recorded by Monty Russell on Melody Hills (traditional country).

⊕ ⊘ **MENTO MUSIC GROUP**, Winterhuder Weg 142, D-22085, Hamburg Germany. Phone: (040)22716552 + -53. Fax: (040)22716554. E-mail: mento_music@t-online.de. General Manager: Arno H. Van Vught. Professional Manager: Michael Frommhold. Music publisher and record company (Playbones Records). Estab. 1970. Pays standard royalty.
Affiliate(s): Auteursunie, Edition Lamplight, Edition Melodisc, Massimo Jauch Music Productions and Marathon Music.
How to Contact: Submit demo tape by mail. Unsolicited submissions are OK. Prefers cassette with 3-4 songs. "Put your strongest/best song first. Put your name and address on the inside sleeve of the tape. If you have a fax number, inform us. Tell us in a typed cover letter what you want/what you are looking for." Does not return material. Reports in 3 weeks.
Music: Mostly **instrumental, pop, MOR, country, background music** and **film music**. Does not want classical. Published *You and I* (by Claus Schneider), recorded by Yasmin (gospel); *Sunstorm*, written and recorded by Tom Jensen (MOR); and *On a Rainy Day* (by Roland Bankel), recorded by Ro Banks (MOR), all on Playbones Records.

N ⊘ **MERRY MARILYN MUSIC PUBLISHING (BMI)**, 33717 View Crest Dr., Wildomar CA 92595. (909)245-2763. Fax: (909)245-4423. Owner: Marilyn Hendricks. Professional Manager: James Hendricks. Music publisher. Estab. 1980. Publishes 5-10 songs/year; publishes 1-2 new songwriters/year. Staff size: 2. Pays standard royalty.
How to Contact: Submit demo tape by mail. Unsolicited submissions are OK. No more than 2 songs per submission. "Submit complete songs only. No lyrics without music." Does not return material. Reports in 3-12 weeks (depending on volume of submissions). "Don't call. If we like what we hear, we'll call you."
Music: Country. Does not want rap or rock. Published "Pushing Up Daisies," "Talk About the Weather" and "Betting on Love" (by J. Hendricks).

☑ ▢ **THE MIGHTY BLUE MUSIC MACHINE** (formerly Songs From Out of the Blue), 2016 Douglas Ave., Clearwater FL 33755. Fax: (727)736-TUNE. Vice President/Director of A&R: James C. Dina. President: Tony Blue. Music publisher. Estab. 1995. Staff size: 3-5. Pays standard royalty.
Affiliate(s): Earth Groovz (ASCAP) and Songs From Out of the Blue (BMI).
How to Contact: Submit demo tape by mail. Unsolicited submissions are OK. "No phone calls, please." Prefers cassette or CD with 1-3 songs and lyric sheets. "Send 'studio' quality demo with typed lyric sheets." SASE. Reports in 1-3 months.
Music: Mostly **rock (acoustic), country** and **pop;** also **blues, Christian/gospel, R&B, jazz** and **dance.** Does not want violent lyrics in regards to race.
Tips: "Submit only professional 'studio' quality demos (invest in your craft) and be very patient."

▟ ◐ **MONTINA MUSIC (SOCAN)**, Box 702, Snowdon Station, Montreal, Quebec H3X 3X8 Canada. Professional Manager: David P. Leonard. Music publisher and record company (Monticana Records). Estab. 1963. Pays negotiable royalty.
Affiliate(s): Sabre Music (SOCAN).
How to Contact: Write first and obtain permission to submit or submit demo tape by mail. Unsolicited submissions are OK. Prefers cassette, phonograph record or VHS videocassette and lyric sheet. SAE and IRC. Reports in 3 months.
Music: Mostly **top 40;** also **bluegrass, blues, country, dance-oriented, easy listening, folk, gospel, jazz, MOR, progressive, R&B, rock** and **soul.** Does not want heavy metal, hard rock, jazz, classical or New Age.
Tips: "Maintain awareness of styles and trends of your peers who have succeeded professionally. Understand the markets to which you are pitching your material. Persevere at marketing your talents. Develop a network of industry contacts, first locally, then regionally and nationally."

⊘ **MOODY MUSIC GROUP, INC.**, P.O. Box 23277, Charlotte NC 28227. (704)882-6134. Fax: (704)882-2063. Nashville office: 2994 Melbourne Terrace, Mt. Juliet TN 37122. Owners: The Moody Brothers. Estab. 1969. Music publisher and record producer (David Moody). Pays standard royalty.

MARKET CONDITIONS are constantly changing! If you're still using this book and it is 2001 or later, buy the newest edition of *Songwriter's Market* at your favorite bookstore or order directly from Writer's Digest Books at (800)289-0963.

Affiliate(s): Laymond Publishing (BMI), Mallie B. Music (BMI), Clayton Monday Publishing (BMI) and CDT Productions (ASCAP).
How to Contact: Submit demo tape by mail. Unsolicited submissions are OK. Prefers CD or cassette with 4 songs and lyric sheets. SASE. Reports in 2 months.
Music: Most **country, folk, gospel, rock,** and **New Age**; also **alternative, children's, R&B, instrumental** and **jazz**.

○ **MOON JUNE MUSIC (BMI)**, 4233 SW Marigold, Portland OR 97219. President: Bob Stoutenburg. Music publisher. Estab. 1971. Staff size: 1. Pays standard royalty.
How to Contact: Submit demo tape by mail. Unsolicited submissions are OK. Prefers cassette (or VHS videocassette) with 2-10 songs. SASE. Reports in 2-6 weeks.
Music: Mostly **country, top 40, blues, Christmas** and **novelty**. Does not want rap, Christian, world, folk or New Age.

◐ **MUSIC IN THE RIGHT KEYS PUBLISHING COMPANY (BMI)**, 9108 Arthur Ave., Crystal Lake IL 60014. (815)477-2072. President: Bert Swanson. Music publisher. Member CMA. Estab. 1985. Publishes 200-500 songs/year; publishes 50-100 new songwriters/year. Pays standard royalty.
Affiliate(s): High 'n Low Notes (ASCAP).
How to Contact: Submit a demo tape (professionally made) by mail. Unsolicited submissions are OK. Prefers cassette or CD with 3 songs and lyric sheets and proof of copyright. SASE. Reports in 5 weeks.
Music: Mostly **country, religious** and **MOR**. Published "Grandma's Shoes," recorded by Dainel on Wishbone Records; and "Don't Play Me No Sad Songs" (by D. Harmon/Cari Gregory), recorded by Cari Gregory on GoldBand Records.
Tips: "Always submit a good production. Good sound and good voice are very important. The better the demo, the better your chances for placement."

◐ **THE MUSIC ROOM PUBLISHING GROUP**, P.O. Box 219, Redondo Beach CA 90277. (310)316-4551. President/Owner: John Reed. Music publisher and record producer. Estab. 1982. Pays standard royalty.
Affiliate(s): MRP (BMI).
How to Contact: Write first and obtain permission to submit. Prefers cassette with 2 songs and lyric sheet. SASE. Reports in 2-4 weeks.
Music: Mostly **pop/rock/R&B** and **crossover**.

◐ **MUSIKUSER PUBLISHING (ASCAP)**, 15030 Ventura Blvd., Suite 425, Sherman Oaks CA 91403. (818)783-2182. Fax: (818)783-3204. E-mail: musikuser@aol.com. President: John Sloate. Music publisher. Estab. 1974. Publishes 20 songs/year; publishes 3 new songwriters/year. Pays standard royalty.
How to Contact: Write first and obtain permission to submit. "No phone calls." Prefers DAT with lyric and lead sheet. Does not return material.
Music: All styles. Published *Thief of Hearts* (by Hattler/Kraus), recorded by Tina Turner on Virgin Records.

✓ ○ **MYKO MUSIC (BMI)**, 1336 S. Avenida Polar 208, Tucson AZ 85710. (602)885-5931. E-mail: dukes@us.ibm.com. Website: http://www.geocities.com.ariana. President: James M. Gasper. Professional Managers: Scott Smith (pop, top 40); Tom Privett (funk, weird, space funk). Music publisher, record company (Ariana Records) and record producer (Future 1 Productions). Estab. 1980. Publishes 4 songs/year; publishes 2 new songwriters/year. Staff size: 3. Pays negotiable royalty.
How to Contact: Submit demo tape by mail. Unsolicited submissions are OK. Prefers cassette or ½″ VHS videocassette with 3 songs and lyric sheet. SASE. Reports in 3 months.
Music: Mostly **top 40, AOR, ambient** and **weird, space funk, electronic**. Does not want country, heavy metal or rap. Published "B.T.B.A." (by Scott Selany), recorded by Baby Fish Mouth (funk); "Tension" (by Bill Waters/Steve Lia), recorded by The Tool & Rod Club (AOR); and *It's Not Like the Feeling* (by Tom Priuett), recorded by JTiom (rock), all on Ariana.

◐ **CHUCK MYMIT MUSIC PRODUCTIONS (ASCAP)**, 9840 64th Ave., Flushing NY 11374. Professional Manager (pop, soft rock): Chuck Mymit. Professional Manager (A/C): Monte Mymit. Music publisher and record producer (Chuck Mymit Music Productions). Estab. 1978. Publishes 3-5 songs/year; publishes 2-4 new songwriters/year. Pays standard royalty.
Affiliate(s): Viz Music (BMI), Chargo Music (ASCAP) and Tore Music (BMI).

How to Contact: Submit demo tape by mail. Unsolicited submissions are OK. Prefers cassette or CD with 3-5 songs and lyric and lead sheets. "Bio and picture would be helpful." SASE. Reports in 4-6 weeks.
Music: Mostly **pop**, **soft rock**, **New Age** and **A/C**. Published *So Beautiful* (By Chuck Mymit), recorded by Bobby Chanel on Vista (soft rock); and *Foxy*, written and recorded by Monte Mymit on C&M (jazz).
Tips: "We are a small company. We have to be selective. Only send us your best work and make sure that it is as professional-sounding as possible. No cheap tapes. No weak productions."

☐ **NAUTICAL MUSIC CO. (BMI)**, Box 120675, Nashville TN 37212. (615)883-9161. Owner: Inez McGinnis. Music publisher and record company (Orbit Records). Estab. 1965. Publishes 25 songs/year; 10 new songwriters/year. Pays standard royalty.
How to Contact: Submit demo tape by mail. Unsolicited submissions are OK. Prefers cassette with 4 songs and lyric sheets. SASE. Reports in 4-6 weeks.
Music: Mostly **country ballads** and **country rock**. Published *Falling, Bad Reputation* and *Burning Love* (by Alan Warren), recorded by Bo Jest (rock), all on Orbit Records.

☑ ☐ **A NEW RAP JAM PUBLISHING**, P.O. Box 683, Lima OH 45802. (419)228-0691. Professional Managers: William Roach (rap, gangsta, hardcore); John Ward (soul, R&B); James Milligan (country, 70s music, pop). Contact (gospel, top 40): A&R Dept. Music publisher and record company (New Experience/Grand Slam Records and Pump It Up Records). Estab. 1989. Publishes 30 songs/year; publishes 2-3 new songwriters/year. Hires staff songwriters. Staff size: 6. Pays standard royalty.
Affiliate(s): Party House Publishing (BMI) and Creative Star Management.
How to Contact: Write first to arrange personal interview or submit demo tape by mail. Unsolicited submissions are OK. Prefers cassette with 3-5 songs and lyric or lead sheet. SASE. Reports in 5 weeks.
Music: Mostly **R&B**, **pop** and **rock/rap**; also **contemporary**, **gospel**, **country** and **soul**. Published "In My Room," written and recorded by Anthony Milligan; and "I'd Rather Be Lonely" (by Anthony Nagel), recorded by James Junior, both on Pump It Up Records; and "He Will Make a Way," written and recorded by James Junior on New Experience Records (gospel).
Tips: "We are a label that does not promote violence, drugs or anything that we feel is a bad example for our youth. Establish music industry contacts, write and keep writing and most of all believe in yourself. Use a good recording studio but be very professional. Just take your time and produce the best music possible. Sometimes you only get one listen. Make sure you place your best song on your demo first. This will increase your chances greatly. If you're the owner of your own small label and have a finished product, please send it. And if there is interest we will contact you."

☐ **NEWCREATURE MUSIC (BMI)**, P.O. Box 1444, Hendersonville TN 37077-1444. President: Bill Anderson, Jr. Professional Manager: G.L. Score. Music publisher, record company, record producer (Landmark Communications Group) and radio and TV syndicator. Publishes 25 songs/year; publishes 2 new songwriters/year. Pays standard royalty.
Affiliate(s): Mary Megan Music (ASCAP).
How to Contact: Submit demo tape by mail. Unsolicited submissions are OK. Prefers cassette or video-cassette with 4-10 songs and lyric sheet. SASE. Reports in 4-6 weeks.
Music: Mostly **country**, **gospel**, **jazz**, **R&B**, **rock** and **top 40/pop**. Published *Glory* and *Popcorn, Peanuts and Jesus* (by Harry Yates), both recorded by Joanne Cash Yates on Angel Too Records (gospel); and *Were You Thinkin' Of Me*, written and recorded by Jack Mosley on Landmark Records (country).

☐ **NSP MUSIC PUBLISHING INC. (ASCAP)**, 345 Sprucewood Rd., Lake Mary FL 32746-5917. (407)834-8555. Fax: (407)834-9997. President, A&R: Vito Fera. A&R: Mary Wayne. Office Manager: Rhonda Fera. Music publisher, record company (S.P.I.N. Records) and record producer (Vito Fera Productions). Estab. 1980. Publishes 10 songs/year; publishes 3 new songwriters/year. Hires staff writers "on agreement terms." Pays standard royalty.
Affiliate(s): Fera Music Publishing (BMI).
How to Contact: Submit demo tape by mail. Unsolicited submissions are OK. Prefers cassette (or VHS videocassette) with 3 songs maximum and lyric sheet. "Package song material carefully. Always label (name, address and phone) both cassette and lyric sheet. Copyright songs. If you need assistance or advice on submission procedures or packaging, please contact us." SASE. Reports in 1-2 months.

OPENNESS TO SUBMISSIONS: ☐ beginners; ☑ beginners and experienced; ☑ experienced only; ☑ industry referrals only.

Music: Mostly **modern jazz**, **instrumentals** and **Christian music**. Published "Moments With You, Lord," performed by Salvatore Cristiano on S.P.I.N. Records.

Tips: "Carefully follow each music publisher's review instructions. Always include lyrics and a SASE for reply. A professional package and music production will help your songs stand out amongst the crowd. Use short intros and 'quality' vocalists to record your demo. Supply us with your best songs, commercial styling and catchy lyrics but not too personal. If you are submitting yourself or band as the 'Artist or Act,' please specify your intentions. Finally, read every available songwriting book, music business manual and publication on the subject and inquire about songwriting organizations."

☑ ▣ ⦸ OLD SLOWPOKE MUSIC (BMI), P.O. Box 52681, Tulsa OK 74152. (918)742-8087. E-mail: cherryst@msn.com. Website: http://www.cherrystreetrecords.com. Professional Manager: Steve Hickerson. President: Rodney Young. Music publisher and record producer. Estab. 1977. Publishes 24-36 songs/year; publishes 2-3 new songwriters/year. Staff size: 2. Pays standard royalty.

How to Contact: Does not accept unsolicited submissions.

Film & TV: Places 1 song in film/year. Recently published "Samantha," written and recorded by George W. Carroll in *Samantha*.

Music: Mostly **rock**, **country** and **R&B**; also **jazz**. Published *Promise Land*, written and recorded by Richard Neville on Cherry Street Records (rock).

Tips: "Write great songs. We sign only artists who play an instrument, sing and write songs."

◻ OMNI 2000, INC., 413 Cooper St., Camden NJ 08102. (609)963-6400. President: Michael Nise. Music publisher, record company (Power Up-Sutra), recording studio (Studio 2000) and production company. Publishes 10 songs/year; publishes 5 new songwriters/year. Pays standard royalty.

How to Contact: Write or call first and obtain permission to submit. Prefers cassette or videocassette with 3 songs. Send Attention: Michael Nise. SASE. Reports in 1-3 months.

Music: Mostly **dance**, **R&B**, **country rock** and **pop**, all with pop crossover potential; also **children's**, **church/religious**, **easy listening**, **folk**, **gospel** and **jazz**.

◻ ONTRAX COMPANIES (ASCAP), P.O. Box 769, Crown Point IN 46307. (219)736-5815. Contact: Professional Manager. Music publisher and record producer. Estab. 1991. Publishes 30 songs/year; 7 new songwriters/year. Staff size: 7. Pays standard royalty.

How to Contact: Submit demo tape by mail. Unsolicited submissions are OK. Prefers cassette, DAT or CD with 1-6 songs. "Tapes should be mailed in as small a package as possible, preferrably in a 4×7 bubble mailer. All items must be labeled and bear the proper copyright notice. We listen to all submissions in the order they arrive. No phone calls please." Does not return submissions. Reports only if interested.

Music: Mostly **pop/rock**, **country** and **crossover country**. Does not want heavy metal or rap. Published "Here in My Heart" (by Peter Kostiois), recorded by Westwind on Southern Lies (country); *Digi* (by M. Leigh), recorded by 44.1K on Staff (pop) and "The Real Bottom Line" (by Edgar/Simms), recorded by Baby Turrett on Lisper (country crossover).

Tips: "Please do not include SASEs or response cards. We will not respond unless interested in publishing the song."

◪ ORCHID PUBLISHING (BMI), Bouquet-Orchid Enterprises, P.O. Box 1335, Norcross GA 30091. (770)814-2420. President: Bill Bohannon. Music publisher, record company, record producer (Bouquet-Orchid Enterprises) and artist management. Member: CMA, AFM. Publishes 10-12 songs/year; publishes 3 new songwriters/year. Pays standard royalty.

How to Contact: Submit demo tape by mail. Unsolicited submissions are OK. Prefers cassette or CD with 3-5 songs and lyric sheet. "Send biographical information if possible—even a photo helps." SASE. Reports in 1 month.

Music: Mostly **religious** ("Amy Grant, etc., contemporary gospel"); **country** ("Garth Brooks, Trisha Yearwood-type material"); and **top 100/pop** ("Bryan Adams, Whitney Houston-type material"). Published "Blue As Your Eyes," written and recorded by Adam Day; "Spare My Feelings" (by Clayton Russ), recorded by Terri Palmer; and "Trying to Get By" (by Tom Sparks), recorded by Bandoleers, all on Bouquet Records.

◻ OTTO PUBLISHING CO. (ASCAP), P.O. Box 16540, Plantation FL 33318. (305)741-7766. President (pop, gospel): Frank X. Loconto. Professional Manager (country western, bluegrass): Bill Dillon. Professional Manager (top 40, contemporary): Dennis Bach. Music publisher, record company (FXL Records) and record producer (Loconto Productions). Estab. 1978. Publishes 25 songs/year; publishes 1-5 new songwriters/year. Pays standard royalty.

Affiliate(s): Betty Brown Music Co. (BMI), Clara Church Music Co. (SESAC) and True Friends Music (BMI).
How to Contact: Submit demo tape by mail. Unsolicited submissions are OK. Prefers cassette with 1-4 songs and lyric sheet. SASE. Reports in 3-4 months.
Music: Mostly **country, MOR, religious** and **gospel**. Published "Silent Waters" (by various), recorded by Irena Kofman (inspirational); and "Holy Spirit" (by Frank X. Loconto), recorded by Kaye Stevens (gospel), both on FXL; and "Finally" (by various), recorded by Miracle Lights on RLB (gospel).
Tips: "The more you write the better you get. If you are a good writer, it will happen."

PAS MAL PUBLISHING SARL, 283 Fbg St. Antoine, Paris 75020 France. Phone: (33)1 43485151. Fax: (33)1 43485753. Website: http://www.theyounggods.com. Managing Director: Jammes Patrick. Music publisher. Estab. 1990. Staff size: 2. Publishes 5-10 songs/year. Pays 60% royalty.
How to Contact: Does not accept unsolicited submissions.
Film & TV: Places 3 songs in film and 2 songs in TV/year.
Music: Mostly **new industrial** and **metal**. Does not want country, pop or jazz. Published "Only Heaven" (by F. Treichler/A. Monod/U. Hiestand/R. Mosimann), recorded by The Young Gods on Interscope Records (alternative); and "Comet" (by A. Monod), recorded by Al Comet on Mutant Sound System (electronic).

PECOS VALLEY MUSIC (BMI), 2709 W. Pine Lodge, Roswell NM 88201. (505)622-0244. E-mail: pecos.valley.music@usa.net. President: Ray Willmon. Professional Managers: Jack Bush; Lance Law. Music publisher. Estab. 1989. Publishes 15-20 songs/year; publishes 4-5 new songwriters/year. Staff size: 3. Pays standard royalty.
How to Contact: Submit demo tape by mail. Unsolicited submissions are OK. "No phone calls please." Prefers cassette, CD or VHS videocassette with 1-2 songs and lyric sheet. SASE. Reports in 3 months.
Music: Mostly **country**. Does not want rock & roll. Published "Say When"; "Just Be With Me," both written and recorded by Jack Bush (country); and "Down That Way" (by Ray Williams), recorded by Jack Bush (country), all on SunCountry Records.
Tips: "Listen to what's playing on radio and TV and write with these in mind. Use proper song format (AAAA, ABAB, AABA, etc.) Also, please follow submission instruction. Do not phone. Learn proper song structure and proper meter."

PEERMUSIC (ASCAP, BMI), 8159 Hollywood Blvd., Los Angeles CA 90069. (323)656-0364. Fax: (323)656-3298. National Director, Talent Acquisition: John Lloyd. Music publisher and artist development promotional label. Estab. 1928. Publishes 600 songs/year (worldwide); publishes 1-2 new songwriters/year. Hires staff songwriters. Royalty standard, but negotiable.
Affiliate(s): Peer Southern Organization (ASCAP) and Peer International Corporation (BMI).
How to Contact: "We do NOT accept unsolicited submissions. We only accept material through agents, attorneys and managers." Prefers cassette and lyric sheet. Does not return material. Reports in 6 weeks.
Music: Mostly **pop, rock** and **R&B**. Published music by David Foster (writer/producer, pop); Robert Palmer (writer/producer, R&B, pop); London Jones (writer/producer, R&B, pop) and bands Jimmies Chicken Shack, Joe 90 and Jennifer Stills.

PEGASUS MUSIC, P.O. Box 127, Otorohanga 2564, New Zealand. Professional Manager (country, rock): Errol Peters. Professional Manager (gospel, pop): Ginny Peters. Music publisher and record company. Estab. 1981. Publishes 20-30 songs/year; publishes 5 new songwriters/year. Pays standard royalty.
How to Contact: Submit demo tape by mail. Unsolicited submissions are OK. Prefers cassette with 3-5 songs and lyric sheet. SAE and IRC. Reports in 1 month.
Music: Mostly **country**; also **bluegrass, easy listening** and **top 40/pop**. Published *I Only See You* (by Ginny Peters/Cliffie Stone), recorded by Reg McTaggart on Discovery (country); and *September Rain* (by Lynda Timmons Elvington), recorded by Basil Hall on Audio Link (country).
Tips: "Get to the meat of the subject without too many words. Less is better."

JUSTIN PETERS MUSIC (BMI), P.O. Box 271056, Nashville TN 37227. (615)331-6056. Fax: (615)831-0991. President: Justin Peters. Music publisher. Estab. 1981.
Affiliate(s): Platinum Planet Music and Tourmaline (BMI).

REMEMBER: Don't "shotgun" your demo tapes. Submit only to companies interested in the type of music you write. For more submission hints, refer to Getting Started on page 11.

How to Contact: Submit demo tape by mail. Unsolicited submissions are OK. Prefers cassette with 5 songs and lyric sheet. Does not return material. "Place code 'SM 2000' on each envelope submission."
Music: Mostly **religious**. Published "Saved By Love," recorded by Amy Grant on A&M Records; "Love Still Changing Hearts," recorded by Imperials on Starsong Records; and "Wipe a Tear," recorded by Russ Taff and Olanda Draper on Word Records, all written by Justin Peters.

◐ PLANET DALLAS RECORDING STUDIOS (ASCAP, BMI), P.O. Box 191447, Dallas TX 75219. (214)521-2216. Website: http://www.planetdallasstudios.com. Music publisher, record producer (Rick Rooney) and recording studio. Estab. 1985. Publishes 20 songs/year; 2-3 new songwriters/year. Pays standard royalty.
Affiliate(s): Stoli Music (BMI) and Planet Mothership Music (ASCAP).
How to Contact: Call first and obtain permission to submit. Prefers cassette with 1-3 songs and lyric sheet. Does not return material. Reports in 6-8 weeks.
Music: Mostly **modern rock**. Published "This Property is Condemned" (by P. Sugg), recorded by Maria McKee on Geffen Records (pop); *Ozone* (by various), recorded by MC 500 Ft. Jesus on Nettwerk/IRS Records; and *Scattered Remains/Poet*, written and recorded by the Blue Johnnies on Ganglion Records.

N̄ ◐ PLATINUM BOULEVARD PUBLISHING (BMI), 525 E. Moana Lane, Reno NV 89502. (702)827-4424. President: Lawrence Davis. Music publisher and record company. Estab. 1984. Publishes 12 songs/year; publishes 1 new songwriter/year. Pays standard royalty.
How to Contact: Submit a demo tape by mail. Unsolicited submissions are OK. Prefers CD, cassette or VHS videocassette, with unlimited songs and lyric or lead sheets. Does not return material. "We report only if interested."
Music: Mostly **rock**, **country** and **R&B**; also **jazz** and **New Age**. Published *Crazy Thing*, *Take My Heart* and *Lonely Lovers*, all written and recorded by Lawrence Davis on Platinum Boulevard Records.

☑ ◐ POLLYBYRD PUBLICATIONS LIMITED (ASCAP, BMI, SESAC), P.O. Box 8442, Universal CA 91608. (818)506-8533. Fax: (310)317-9993. E-mail: pplzmi@aol.com. Branch office: 333 Proctor St., Carson City NV 89703. (818)884-1946. Fax: (818)882-6755. Professional Managers: Maxx Diamond (country, pop, rock); Tedford Steele (hip-hop, R&B). Music publisher, record company (PPL Entertainment) and Management firm (Sa'mall Management). Estab. 1979. Publishes 100 songs/year; publishes 25-40 new songwriters/year. Hires staff writers. Pays standard royalty.
Affiliate(s): Kellijai Music (ASCAP), Pollyann Music (ASCAP), Ja'Nikki Songs (BMI), Velma Songs International (BMI), Lonnvanness Songs (SESAC), PPL Music (ASCAP), Zettitalia Music, Zett Two Music (ASCAP), Plus Publishing and Zett One Songs (BMI).
How to Contact: Write first and obtain permission to submit. Prefers cassette or VHS videocassette with 4 songs and lyric and lead sheet. SASE. Reports in 2 months.
Music: Published "Shakedown" (by J. Jarrett), recorded by The Band AKA (hip-hop/R&B); "American Dream," written and recorded by Riki Hendrix (rock); and "The Right Flavor" (by S. Cuseo/J. Jarrett), recorded by Fhyne (pop), all on PPL/Sony Records.
Tips: "Make those decisions—are you really a songwriter? Are you prepared to starve for your craft? Do you believe in delayed gratification? Are you commercial or do you write only for yourself? Can you take rejection? Do you want to be the best? If so, contact us—if not, keep your day job."

POLYGRAM MUSIC PUBLISHING. PolyGram Music Publishing and MCA Music Publishing have merged into Universal Music Publishing. At press time they were going through restructuring.

◻ PORTAGE MUSIC (BMI), 16634 Gannon W., Rosemount MN 55068. (612)432-5737. President: Larry LaPole. Music publisher. Publishes 5-20 songs/year. Pays standard royalty.
How to Contact: Submit demo tape by mail. Unsolicited submissions are OK. Prefers cassette with 3 songs and lyric sheet. Does not return material. Reports in 2-3 months.
Music: Mostly **country** and **country rock**. Published "Lost Angel," "Think It Over" and "Congratulations to Me" (by L. Lapole), all recorded by Trashmen on Sundazed.
Tips: "Keep songs short, simple and upbeat with positive theme."

☑ ◻ PREJIPPIE MUSIC GROUP (BMI), Box 312897, Penobscot Station, Detroit MI 48231. E-mail: zanda740@aol.com. Professional Manager: Victoria Henderson. Partner: Bruce Henderson. Music publisher, record company (PMG Records) and record producer (PMG Productions). Estab. 1990. Publishes 50-75 songs/year; publishes 2-3 new songwriters/year. Hires staff writers. Staff size: 3. Pays standard royalty.
How to Contact: Submit demo tape by mail. Unsolicited submissions are OK. Prefers cassette with 3-

4 songs and lyric sheet. "No phone calls please." SASE. Reports in 6 weeks.

Music: Mostly **alternative R&B**, **alternative rock**, **techno/house** and **experimental**. Does not want country, gospel, show tunes or lyrics only. Published "Everything" and "Work Your Spell on Me," written and recorded by Bourgeoisie Paper Jam (funk/rock); and "Webbslinger," written and recorded by Tony Webb, (jazz) all on PMG Records.

Tips: "We're always looking for new approaches to traditional genres. We want to hear vocals, lyrics and music that is passionate and takes a chance, but still keeps hooks that are solid."

PRESCRIPTION COMPANY (BMI), Box 222249, Great Neck NY 11021. (516)482-7697. E-mail: medmike525@aol.com. President: David F. Gasman. Vice President of Finance: Robert Murphy. Music publisher and record producer. Staff size: 11. Pays standard royalty.

How to Contact: Write or call first and obtain permission to submit. Prefers cassette with any number of songs and lyric sheet. "Send all submissions with SASE (or no returns)." Reports in 1 month.

Music: Mostly **bluegrass**, **blues**, **children's** and **country**, **dance-oriented**; also **easy listening**, **folk**, **jazz**, **MOR**, **progressive**, **R&B**, **rock**, **soul** and **top 40/pop**. Published "Good Lookin' Thing" (by Giant/Baum/Ray), recorded by Medicine Mike on Prescription Records (rock).

Tips: "Songs should be good and written to last. Forget fads—we want songs that'll sound as good in ten years as they do today. Organization, communication and exploration of form are as essential as message (and sincerity matters, too)."

PRITCHETT PUBLICATIONS (BMI), P.O. Box 725, Daytona Beach FL 32114-0725. (904)252-4848. Vice President: Charles Vickers. Music publisher and record company (King of Kings Record Co., Pickwick/Mecca/International Records). Estab. 1975. Publishes 21 songs/year; publishes 12 new songwriters/year.

Affiliate(s): Alison Music (ASCAP) and Charles H. Vickers Music Publishers (BMI).

How to Contact: Write first and obtain permission to submit. Prefers cassette with 6 songs and lyric or lead sheet. Does not return material.

Music: Mostly **gospel**, **rock-disco** and **country**.

PUBLISHING CENTRAL, (a subsidiary of Jackson Artists Corp.), 7251 Lowell Dr., Suite 200, Shawnee Mission KS 66204. (913)384-6688. E-mail: jacinc@ibm.net. CEO (all styles): Dave Jackson. Professional Manager (country, pop): Tom Zang. Music publisher, booking agency and producer (Drake/Jackson Productions). Staff size: 3. Pays standard royalty.

Affiliate(s): All Told Music (BMI), Zang/Jac Publishing (ASCAP) and Very Cherry (ASCAP).

How to Contact: Submit demo tape by mail. Unsolicited submissions are OK. Prefers cassette (or VHS videocassette of performance if available) with 2-4 songs and lead sheet. "List names of tunes on cassettes. May send up to 4 tapes. Although it's not necessary, we prefer lead sheets with the tapes—send 2 or 3 that you are proud of. We do most of our business by phone. We prefer good enough quality to judge a performance, however, we do not require that the video or cassettes be of professional nature." SASE.

Film & TV: Places 1 song in film/year. Recently published "Marvelous Marvo" (by Tom Zang), recorded by Herbert Khoney in *Blood Harvest*.

Music: Mostly **gospel**, **country** and **rock**; also **bluegrass**, **blues**, **easy listening**, **disco**, **MOR**, **progressive**, **soul** and **top 40/pop**.

QUARK, INC., P.O. Box 7320, New York NY 10150-7320. (212)838-6775. E-mail: quarkent@aol.com. Manager: Curtis Urbina. Professional Managers: Sergio Cossa (pop/soundtracks); Michelle Harris (alternative/pop). Music publisher, record company (Quark Records), record producer (Curtis Urbina). Estab. 1986. Publishes 12 songs/year; 2 new songwriters/year. Staff size: 4. Pays standard royalty.

Affiliate(s): Quarkette Music (BMI) and Freedurb Music (ASCAP).

How to Contact: Call first and obtain permission to submit. Prefers cassette with 2 songs. SASE. Reports in 2 months.

Film & TV: Places 10 songs in film/year. Music Supervisor: Curtis Urbina (pop/dance). Recently published the soundtrack for *The Versace Murder* (by Claudio Simonetti); and the soundtrack for *Tu Ridi* (by Nicola Provani).

Music: Mostly **New Age (instrumentals)**, **dance** and **pop/alternative**; also **storytelling** (all kinds—spoken word). Does not want anything short of a hit. Published "Luv-Thang" (by Simone Jay) (dance/pop); and "Mirage," written and recorded by Steve Quinzy (adult/pop), both on Pacific Time Ent.; and "Jet Set" (by Jeffrey Grafton/S. Moriwaki), recorded by Dat Oven on Jellybean Recordings (dance).

Tips: "Research—know what style of music or stories we release. If you have no clue, give us a call and we will tell you."

⊕ ⬤ **R.J. MUSIC**, 10A Margaret Rd., Barnet, Herts. EN4 9NP United Kingdom. Phone: (0181)440-9788. Managing Directors: Roger James and Susana Boyle. Music publisher and management firm (Roger James Management). PRS. Pays negotiable royalty (up to 50%).
How to Contact: Submit demo tape by mail. Unsolicited submissions are OK. Prefers cassette with 1 song and lyric or lead sheet. "Will return cassettes, but only with correct *full* postage!"
Music: Mostly **MOR**, **blues**, **country** and **rock**; also **chart material**. Does not want disco or rap.

⊕ ⬤ **R.T.L. MUSIC**, White House Farm, Shropshire TF9 4HA England. Phone: (01630)647374. Fax: (01630)647612. Professional Managers: Ron Lee (rock/rock 'n roll); Katrine LeMatt (MOR/dance); Xavier Lee (heavy metal); Tanya Lee (classical/other types). Music publisher, record company (Le Matt Music) and record producer. Estab. 1971. Publishes approximately 30 songs/year. Pays standard royalty.
Affiliate(s): Lee Music (publishing), Swoop Records, Grenouille Records, Check Records, Zarg Records, Pogo Records, R.T.F.M. (all independent companies).
How to Contact: Submit demo tape or CD by mail. Unsolicited submissions are OK. Prefers CD, cassette or DAT (also VHS 625/PAL system videocassette) with 1-3 songs and lyric and lead sheets; include still photos and bios. "Make sure name and address are on CD or cassette." SAE and IRC. Reports in 6 weeks.
Music: All types. Published *Sheriff*, recorded by Emmit Till; and *Dream Boat*, recorded by Orphan, both on Swoop; and *Great Balls of Fire*, recorded by Nightmare on Zarg.

⬤ **RAVING CLERIC MUSIC PUBLISHING/EUROEXPORT ENTERTAINMENT**, P.O. Box 4735, Austin TX 78765-4735. (512)452-2701. Fax: (512)452-0815. E-mail: rcmrecords@aol.com. President: L.A. Evans. Music publisher, record company (RCM Productions), record producer, artist management and development. Estab. 1985. Publishes 5-10 songs/year; publishes 6-8 new songwriters/year. Pays standard royalty.
Affiliate(s): Tripoli Inferno Music Publishing (BMI).
How to Contact: Write first and obtain permission to submit. Prefers cassette with 3 songs maximum and lyric sheet. "Submissions of more than 3 songs will not be listened to." Does not return material. Reports in 4-6 weeks.
Music: Mostly **rock**, **pop** and **R&B**. Published *Is It Hot?* (by Bernard/Rose/St. George); *Blue Ballet* and *Faster Than the Speed of Love* (by Epp/Van Hofwegen), all recorded by Tracy Mitchell on RCM Records.
Tips: "Unsolicited material is not accepted."

🅽 💟 ⬤ **REN ZONE MUSIC (ASCAP)**, P.O. Box 3153, Huntington Beach CA 92605. (714)846-4470. Fax: (714)846-2816. E-mail: rwmusic@aol.com. Website: http://www.renzonemusic.com. Professional Managers: Renah Wolzinger; Keith Wolzinger; Tyko Raboff. Music publisher. Estab. 1998. Publishes 14 songs/year; publishes 2 new songwriters/year. Staff size: 2. Pays standard royalty.
● This company won a Parents Choice 1998 Silver Honor Shield.
How to Contact: Submit demo tape by mail. Unsolicited submissions are OK. Prefers cassette or CD with 2 songs, cover letter and lyric sheet. SASE. Reports in 4-6 weeks.
Music: Mostly **children's**. Does not want rap or punk. Published *Power of Imagination*, written and recorded by Tyko Raboff; *Mysterious Pumpkin Man*, written and recorded by Stephanie Donatoni; and *Tumble-n-Tunes*, written and recorded by Dayle Lusk, all on Ren Zone (children's).
Tips: "Submit well-written lyrics that convey important concepts to kids on good quality demos with easy to understand vocals."

🅽 ⬤ **RHYTHMS PRODUCTIONS (ASCAP)**, P.O. Box 34485, Los Angeles CA 90034. President: Ruth White. Music and multimedia publisher. Member NARAS. Publishes 4 titles/year. Pays negotiable royalty.
Affiliate(s): Tom Thumb Music.
How to Contact: Submit tape with letter outlining background in educational children's music. SASE. Reports in 2 months.
Music: "We're only interested in **children's songs** and interactive programs that have educational value. Our materials are sold in schools and homes, so artists/writers with an 'edutainment' background would be most likely to understand our requirements." Published "Professor Whatzit®" series including "Adven-

---

REFER TO THE CATEGORY INDEX (at the end of this section) to find exactly which companies are interested in the type of music you write.

tures of Professor Whatzit & Carmine Cat"(cassette series for children); "Musical Math," "Musical Reading" and "Theme Songs."

N ○ RIDGE MUSIC CORP. (ASCAP, BMI), 38 Laurel Ledge Court, Stamford CT 06903. E-mail: ptannen@earthlink.net. President/General Manager: Paul Tannen. Music publisher. Estab. 1961. Member CMA. Publishes 6 songs/year. Pays standard royalty.
Affiliate(s): Tannen Music Inc. and Deshufflin, Inc.
How to Contact: Submit demo tape by mail. Unsolicited submissions OK. Prefers cassette with 3 songs and lyric sheet. SASE. Reports in 2 months.
Music: Mostly **country, rock, top 40/pop** and **jazz**. Published "Forever," written and recorded by Mark Whitfield on Verve Records (jazz).

N ▦ ○ RIVERHAWK MUSIC (BMI), 417 N. Pine Dr., Surfside Beach SC 29575. (843)238-1633. President: Arthur W. Byman. Professional Managers: Vivian Ulbrich (easy listening); Joanne Carothers (novelties). Music publisher, record company (Peregrine Records) and record producer. Estab. 1994. Publishes 10 songs/year; publishes 3 new songwriters/year. Staff size: 3. Pays standard royalty.
How to Contact: Submit demo tape by mail. Unsolicited submissions are OK. Prefers cassette with 3 songs and lyric sheet. "Follow submission guidelines exactly. Be neat." SASE. Reports in 1 month.
Film & TV: Places 1 song in TV/year. Recently published "Bald Men," written and recorded by Dee Braxton in *Inside Edition* and *Joan Rivers*.
Music: Mostly **MOR, country** and **A/C**; also **cowboy-type western** and **comedy**. Does not want rap, hip-hop, industrial, classical or instrumental. Published "Let Me Dance to the Beat" (by Yvonne Matthews), recorded by Queenie O-Shay (c/w); and "Santa, the Bandit" (by Bobby Duke), recorded by Arthur Jordan (Christmas), both on Perigrine; and "Summer in Myrtle Beach" (by Charles Brewer), recorded by Art Byman on Magenta Records.

N ▼ ○ ROADSHOW MUSIC CORP. (ASCAP, BMI), 13140 Lake Mary Jane Rd., Orlando FL 32822. (407)382-1701. Fax: (407)382-1741. E-mail: rsstudio1@aol.com. Vice President: Jane Frank. Music publisher and record company. Estab. 1974. Publishes 15 songs/year; publishes 5 new songwriters/year. Hires staff songwriters. Pays standard royalty.
Affiliate(s): JD Music (ASCAP) and Frankly Music (BMI).
  • Roadshow Music's songs—including those by B.T. Express and Brass Construction—have been certified Gold and Platinum by RIAA.
How to Contact: Submit demo tape by mail. Unsolicited submissions are OK. Prefers DAT with 5 songs, lyric sheet, bio and pictures. SASE. Reports in 1 month.
Music: Mostly **R&B, gospel** and **rap**; also **rock** and **country**. Published "Butt Naked," written and recorded by Guilbeaux on Priority (rap); and *B.T. Express*, written and recorded by B.T. Express on Collectables (disco).

N ▣ ROCK N METAL MUSIC PUBLISHING CO., P.O. Box 325, Fort Dodge IA 50501-0325. Owner: James E. Hartsell Jr. Music publisher. Estab. 1996. Publishes 1-4 songs/year. Pays standard royalty.
How to Contact: Write first and obtain permission to submit a demo. Prefers cassette and bio with 3 songs and lead sheet. SASE. Reports in 2-3 weeks.
Music: Mostly **heavy metal, hard rock** and **hard alternative**.
Tips: "This is a new company looking for new and established songwriters and artists who want to perform their own music. If lyrics are your weakness, we have hundreds available for collaboration. Come grow with us. Together we'll take the music industry by storm."

▣ ROCKER MUSIC/HAPPY MAN MUSIC (BMI, ASCAP), 4696 Kahlua Lane, Bonita Springs, FL 34134. (941)947-6978. Executive Producer: Dick O'Bitts. Estab. 1960. Music publisher, record company (Happy Man Records, Condor Records and Air Corp Records), record producer (Rainbow Collections Ltd.) and management firm (Gemini Complex). Publishes 25-30 songs/year; publishes 8-10 new songwriters/year. Staff size: 2. Pays standard royalty.
How to Contact: Submit demo tape by mail. Unsolicited submissions are OK. Prefers cassette or VHS videocassette with 4 songs and lyric or lead sheet. SASE. Do not call. Reports in 1 month.
Music: Mostly **country, rock, pop, gospel, Christian** and **off-the-wall**. Does not want hip-hop. Published *Love in a Pickup Truck*, written and recorded by Challengers on Tyneville.

▣ ROCKFORD MUSIC CO. (ASCAP, BMI), 150 West End Ave., Suite 6-D, New York NY 10023. (212)873-5968. Manager: Danny Darrow. Music publisher, record company (Mighty Records), record and

video tape producer (Danny Darrow). Publishes 1-3 songs/year; publishes 1-3 new songwriters/year. Staff size: 3. Pays standard royalty.
Affiliate(s): Corporate Music Publishing Company (ASCAP) and Stateside Music Company (BMI).
How to Contact: Submit demo tape by mail. Unsolicited submissions are OK. "No phone calls and do not write for permission to submit." Prefers cassette with 3 songs and lyric sheet. Does not return material. Reports in 1-2 weeks.
Music: Mostly **MOR** and **top 40/pop**; also **adult pop**, **country**, **adult rock**, **dance-oriented**, **easy listening**, **folk** and **jazz**. Does not want rap. Published *Falling In Love* (by Brian Dowen); *A Part of You* (by Brian Dowen/Randy Lakeman); and *For My Tomorrow* (by Steven Schoenberg/Michael Greer), all recorded by Danny Darrow on Mighty Records (easy listening).
Tips: "Listen to top 40 and write current lyrics and music."

○ **RUSTRON MUSIC PUBLISHERS (BMI)**, 1156 Park Lane, West Palm Beach FL 33417-5957. (561)686-1354. Professional Managers: Rusty Gordon (adult contemporary, acoustic, New Age, children's, cabaret); Ron Caruso (all styles); Davilyn Whims (folk fusions, country, blues). Music publisher, record company, management firm and record producer (Rustron Music Productions). Estab. 1972. Publishes 100-150 songs/year; publishes 10-20 new songwriters/year. Staff size: 9. Pays standard royalty.
Affiliate(s): Whimsong Publishing (ASCAP).
How to Contact: Submit demo tape by mail. Unsolicited submissions are OK. Prefers cassette with 1-3 songs and typed lyric or lead sheet. "Clearly label your tape and container. Include cover letter." SASE required for all correspondence. Reports in 4 months.
Music: Mostly **pop** (ballads, blues, theatrical, cabaret), **progressive country** and **folk/rock**; also **R&B** and **New Age** instrumental fusions with classical, jazz, pop themes and women's music. Does not want rap, youth music, hard rock, heavy metal or punk. Published *Happy Endings*, written and recorded by Lynn Thomas on Rustron (pop); *Carolina Sky*, written and recorded by Neal Phillips (country); and *The Rally*, written and recorded by Sandy Rapp on SRM Records (folk).
Tips: "Write strong hooks. Keep song length 3½ minutes or less. Avoid predictability—create original lyric themes. Tell a story. Compose definitive melody. Tune in to the trends and fusions indicative of the '90s."

○ **SABTECA MUSIC CO. (ASCAP)**, P.O. Box 10286, Oakland CA 94610. (415)465-2805. Professional Managers: Sean Herring (pop, R&B, jazz); Lois Shayne (pop, R&B, soul, country). President: Duane Herring. Music publisher and record company (Sabteca Record Co., Andre Romare). Estab. 1980. Publishes 8-10 songs/year; 1-2 new songwriters/year. Pays standard royalty.
Affiliate(s): Toyiabe Publishing (BMI).
How to Contact: Write first and obtain permission to submit a tape. Prefers cassette with 2 songs and lyric sheet. SASE. Reports in 2-4 weeks.
Music: Mostly **R&B**, **pop** and **country**. Published "Lost Somewhere Back in Time" (by Reggie Walker); and "What Can I Do" (by Thomas Roller), both recorded by Reggie Walker on Andre Romare Records (pop).
Tips: "Listen to music daily, if possible. Keep improving writing skills."

▓ ▓ ○ **SADDLESTONE PUBLISHING (BMI, SOCAN)**, 6260-130 St., Surrey British Columbia V3X 1R6 Canada. (604)572-4232. Fax: (604)572-4252. E-mail: saddles@sprint.ca. Website: http://saddlestone.ontheweb.nu. CEO: Candice James (country). President: Grant Lucas (rock). Professional Manager: Sharla Cuthbertson (pop, R&B). Music publisher, record company (Saddlestone) and record producer (Silver Bow Productions). Estab. 1988. Publishes 100 songs/year; publishes 12-30 new songwriters/year. Pays standard royalty.
Affiliate(s): Silver Bow Publishing (SOCAN, ASCAP).
How to Contact: Submit demo tape by mail. Unsolicited submissions are OK. Prefers cassette with 3 songs and lyric sheet. "Make sure vocal is clear." Does not return material. Reports in 3 months.
Film & TV: Places 1 song in film and 2 songs in TV/year. Music Supervisors: Janet York; John McCullough. Recently published "Midnite Ride" (by Cam Wagner), recorded by 5 Star Hillbillies in *North of Pittsburgh*.
Music: Mostly **country**, **rock** and **pop**; also **gospel** and **R&B**. Published *The Thrill Of It All* (by Billy

---

OPENNESS TO SUBMISSIONS: ○ beginners; ◑ beginners and experienced; ◉ experienced only; ⊘ industry referrals only.

O'Hara), recorded by Cathy Kramer on Blue Ridge Mountain Records (country); *Born in a Sign of Fire* (by Jean Paul Hunziker), recorded by Split on Liverpool Records (jazz); *If Love Has A Color* (by Melba Blake/Ray Barnette), recorded by Ray Grizzell on Independent Records (country).
Tips: "Submit clear demos, good hooks and avoid long intros or instrumentals. Have a good singer do vocals."

SCHMERDLEY MUSIC (BMI), 7560 Woodman Place #G3, Van Nuys CA 91405. (818)994-4862. Owner: Tom Willett. Music publisher. Estab. 1971. Publishes 2-6 songs/year; publishes 1 new songwriter/year. Staff size: 1. Pays standard royalty.
How to Contact: Submit demo tape by mail. Unsolicited submissions are OK. Prefers cassette with up to 3 songs. SASE. Reports in 1 month.
Music: Mostly **novelty comedy**.
Tips: "Avoid clichés."

SCI-FI MUSIC (SOCAN), P.O. Box 941, N.D.G., Montreal Quebec H4A 3S3 Canada. (514)487-8953. President: Gary Moffet (formerly guitarist/composer with April Wine). Music publisher and record producer. Estab. 1984. Publishes 10 songs/year; publishes 2 new songwriters/year. Pays standard royalty.
How to Contact: Submit demo tape by mail. Unsolicited submissions are OK. Submit cassette with 3-10 songs and lyric sheet. Does not return material.
Music: Mostly **rock** and **pop**.

TIM SCOTT MUSIC GROUP (BMI), 622 State St., Room 36, Springfield MA 01109. (413)731-6996. E-mail: tscottkiss@aol.com. Professional Managers: Mark Johson (pop, rock, rap); Sylvia Edson (country, R&B); Paul Williams (gospel). (gospel): Billy Smith. Music publisher and record company (Keeping It Simple and Safe). Estab. 1993. Publishes 20-50 songs/year. Staff size: 20. Hires staff writers. Pays standard royalty.
Affiliates: Tim Scott Music (ASCAP).
How to Contact: Submit demo tape by mail. Unsolicited submissions are OK. Prefers cassette with 3-5 songs and lyric sheet. SASE. Reports in 2-3 months.
Music: Mostly **R&B** and **pop**; also **country**, **rock** and **gospel**. Published "Just in Time," written and recorded by Willie Gray; "Everything You" (by Tim Scott), recorded by Loveworld; and "Sweet Music," written and recorded by Mike Johnson, all on Nightowl Records.

SDM (ASCAP, BMI), 740 N. La Brea, Los Angeles CA 90038. (323)933-9977. Fax: (323)933-0633. E-mail: sbe740@earthlink.net. A&R: Laurent Besencon. Music publisher, record company (Sunset Boulevard) and manager. Publishes 1,000 songs/year; publishes 5 new songwriters/year. Hires staff songwriters. Pays standard royalty.
Affiliate(s): Playhard Music and Plaything Music (ASCAP), Playful Music and Music Pieces (BMI).
• SDM has received BMI and ASCAP awards as well as several Gold and Platinum certifications.
How to Contact: Call first and obtain permission to submit a demo. Prefers CD with 3 songs and lyric sheet. SASE. Reports in 1 month.
Music: Mostly **pop**, **R&B** and **rock**. Published "Love Train" (by Felton Pilate), recorded by Dru Hill; and "A Little Bit of Love" (by Claude Glaubette), recorded by Celine Dion.

SEGAL'S PUBLICATIONS (BMI), P.O. Box 507, Newton MA 02159. (617)969-6196. Contact: Charles Segal. Music publisher and record producer (Segal's Productions). Estab. 1963. Publishes 80 songs/year; publishes 6 new songwriters/year. Pays standard royalty.
Affilate(s): Charles Segal's Publications (BMI) and Charles Segal's Music (SESAC).
How to Contact: Submit demo tape by mail. Unsolicited submissions are OK. Prefers CD or VHS videocassette with 3 songs and lyric or lead sheet. Does not return material. Reports only if interested.
Music: Mostly **rock**, **pop** and **country**; also **R&B**, **MOR** and **children's songs**. Published "A Time to Care" (by Brilliant/Segal), recorded by Rosemary Wills (MOR); "Go to Bed" (by Colleen Segal), recorded Susan Stark (MOR); and "Only In Dreams" (by Chas. Segal), recorded by Rosemary Wills (MOR), all on Spin Records.
Tips: "Besides making a good demo cassette, include a lead sheet of music—words, melody line and chords. Put your name and phone number on CD."

SELLWOOD PUBLISHING (BMI), 170 N. Maple, Fresno CA 93702. (209)255-1717. E-mail: tracsell@aol.com. Owner: Stan Anderson. Music publisher, record company (TRAC Record Co.) and record producer. Estab. 1972. Publishes 10 songs/year; publishes 3 new songwriters/year. Pays standard royalty.

How to Contact: Submit demo tape—unsolicited submissions are OK. Prefers cassette or VHS videocassette with 2 songs and lyric sheet. SASE. Reports in 3 weeks. "Submit professional studio demos only."

Music: Mostly **traditional country** and **country**. Does not want rock 'n' roll, rap or heavy metal. Published *Cowboy Cadillac* (by Brian D. McArdle/Donna Moody); *All Time Low* (by Jimmy Walker); and *Southern Cracker Boy* (by Joanne Mears), all recorded by Jimmy Walker on TRAC Records (country).

Tips: "We're looking for all styles of country, especially uptempo dance types."

✓ ▨ ◑ **SHAOLIN MUSIC (ASCAP)**, P.O. Box 900457, San Diego CA 92190. (801)595-1123. President: Richard O'Connor. Vice President, A&R: Don Dela Vega. Music publisher, record company (Shaolin Film and Records) and record producer (Richard O'Connor). Estab. 1984. Pays standard royalty.

How to Contact: Submit demo tape by mail. Unsolicited submissions are OK. Prefers cassette with 3-4 songs and lyric sheet. Include bio and press kit. Does not return material. Reports in 6 weeks.

Film & TV: Places 6 songs in film and 1 song in TV/year. Music Supervisors: Don De la Vega (all); Michelle McCourtys (easy listening). Recently published "Spring Rain" (by T.S. Coyote), recorded by American Zen for African television.

Music: Mostly **rock**, **hard rock** and **pop**; also **soundtracks**. Does not want hip-hop. Published *Peace of Mind* and *Black of Night* (by T. Coyote), recorded by American Zen (rock); and *Tai Chi Magic*, written and recorded by Zhen Shen-Lang, all on Shaolin Film and Records.

◑ **SHAWNEE PRESS, INC.** (formerly Harold Flammer Music), 49 Waring Dr., Delaware Water Gap PA 18327. (717)476-0550. Fax: (717)476-5247. E-mail: shawnerpress@noln.com. Website: http://www.shawneepress.com. Editor (church music): Lew Kirby. Professional Managers: Anne Austell (educational choral); Ed Esposito (instrumental); David Angerman (handbell music, organ-sacred only); Joseph Martin (piano). Music publisher. Estab. 1917. Publishes 50 songs/year. Staff size: 30. Pays negotiable royalty.

Affiliate(s): Glory Sound and Harold Flammer Music.

How to Contact: Submit demo tape by mail. Unsolicited submissions are OK. Prefers cassette with lyric and/or lead sheet. SASE. Reports in 3-4 months.

Music: Mostly **church/liturgical**.

▨ ◑ **SHU'BABY MONTEZ MUSIC**, 1447 N. 55th St., Philadelphia PA 19131. (215)473-5527. E-mail: schubaby@aol.com. Website: http://www.geocities.com/SunsetStrip/Cabaret/2810. President: Leroy Schuler. Music publisher. Estab. 1986. Publishes 25 songs/year; publishes 10 new songwriters/year. Pays standard royalty.

How to Contact: Submit demo tape by mail. Unsolicited submissions are OK. Prefers cassette with 3 songs and lyric sheet. SASE. Reports in 5 weeks.

Film & TV: Places 9 songs in film/year. Music Supervisor: Paul Roberts. Recently published "Sweaty and Nakey" (by Martin "Martygraw" Schuler), recorded by Color Blind and "Let Me Dreds Grow," written and recorded by Moses Livingston, both in *Temptation at Midnight*; and "Give It Up" (by Clint Washington), recorded by Felice in *A True American*.

Music: Mostly **R&B**, **dance**, **hip-hop** and **pop**. Does not want country. Published "Second Time With You" (by Wilson Lambert/Paul Columbo), recorded by Wilson Lambert on Urban Logic Records (R&B); "Have You Lost Something," written and recorded by Marie Olsen on Tornado Productions (pop); and "I Miss You" (by Tab Edwards), recorded by Cubby St. Charles on Kixx Records (R&B).

Tips: "Keep the music simple, but with nice changes. Don't be afraid to use altered chords."

✓ ◑ **SILICON MUSIC PUBLISHING CO. (BMI)**, 222 Tulane St., Garland TX 75043-2239. President: Gene Summers. Vice President: Deanna L. Summers. Public Relations: Steve Summers. Music publisher and record company (Front Row Records). Estab. 1965. Publishes 10-20 songs/year; publishes 2-3 new songwriters/year. Pays standard royalty.

How to Contact: Submit demo tape by mail. Unsolicited submissions are OK. Prefers cassette with 1-2 songs. Does not return material. Reports ASAP.

Music: Mostly **rockabilly** and **'50s material**; also **old-time blues/country** and **MOR**. Published "Almost

---

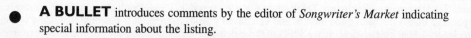

● **A BULLET** introduces comments by the editor of *Songwriter's Market* indicating special information about the listing.

Persuaded," "Someone Somewhere," and "Who Stole The Marker," all recorded by Gene Summers on Crystal Clear Records (rockabilly).
Tips: "We are very interested in '50s rock and rockabilly *original masters* for release through overseas affiliates. If you are the owner of any '50s masters, contact us first! We have releases in Holland, Switzerland, England, Belgium, France, Sweden, Norway and Australia. We have the market if you have the tapes! Our staff writers include James McClung, Gary Mears (original Casuals), Robert Clark and Dea Summers."

⚏ Ø SILVER BLUE MUSIC/OCEANS BLUE MUSIC, 3940 Laurel Canyon Blvd., Suite 441, Studio City CA 91604. (818)980-9588. E-mail: jdiamond2@aol.com. President: Joel Diamond. Music publisher and record producer (Joel Diamond Entertainment). Estab. 1971. Publishes 25 songs/year. Pays standard royalty.
How to Contact: Does not accept unsolicited material.
Film & TV: Places 4 songs in film and 6 songs in TV/year.
Music: Mostly **pop** and **R&B**; also **rap**. Does not want country, jazz or classical. Published "After the Lovin" (by Bernstein/Adams), recorded by Engelbert Humperdinck.

[N:] Ø SILVER THUNDER MUSIC GROUP, P.O. Box 41335, Nashville TN 37204. (615)391-5035. President: Rusty Budde. Music publisher and record producer (Rusty Budde Productions). Estab. 1985. Publishes 200 songs/year. Publishes 5-10 new songwriters/year. Hires staff songwriters. Pays standard royalty.
How to Contact: Write first and obtain permission to submit. Prefers cassette or VHS videocassette. Does not return material.
Music: Mostly **country, pop** and **R&B**. Published *Rock N Cowboys*, written and recorded by Jeff Samules on STR Records; *This Ain't the Real Thing* (by Rusty Budde), recorded by Les Taylor on CBS Records; and "Feel Again" (by Rusty Budde/Shara Johnson), recorded by Shara Johnson on Warner Bros. Records.
Tips: "Send clear, clean recording on cassette with lyric sheets."

Ø SIMPLY GRAND MUSIC, INC. (ASCAP, BMI), P.O. Box 41981, Memphis TN 38174-1981. (901)763-4787. Fax: (901)763-4883. E-mail: wahani@aol.com. President: Linda Lucchesi. Music publisher. Estab. 1965. Pays standard royalty.
Affiliate(s): Memphis Town Music, Inc. (ASCAP) and Beckie Publishing Co. (BMI).
How to Contact: Submit demo tape by mail. Unsolicited submissions are OK. Prefers cassette with 1-3 songs and lyric sheet. SASE. Reports in 3-4 weeks. "Please do not send demos by certified or registered mail. Include enough postage for return of materials."
Music: Mostly **pop, soul, country, soft rock, children's songs, jazz** and **R&B**.

⊕ Ø SINUS MUSIK PRODUKTION, ULLI WEIGEL, Geitnerweg 30a, D-12209, Berlin Germany. Phone: (0)30-715905-0. Fax: (0)30-715905-22. E-mail: ulli.weigel@t-online.de. Owner: Ulli Weigel. Music publisher, record producer and producer of radio advertising spots. Member: GEMA, GVL. Estab. 1976. Publishes 20 songs/year; publishes 6 new songwriters/year. Staff size: 3. Pays standard royalty.
Affiliate(s): Sinus Musikverlag H.U. Weigel GmbH.
How to Contact: Submit demo tape by mail. Unsolicited submissions are OK. Prefers cassette or CD-R with up to 10 songs and lyric sheets. SASE. Reports in 2 months.
Music: Mostly **rock, pop** and **New Age**; also **background music for movies/advertising**. Does not want hip-hop or techno. Published "Simple Story," recorded by MAANAM on RCA (Polish rock); *Die Musik Maschine* (by Klaus Lage), recorded by CWN Productions on Hansa Records (pop/German); and "Maanam" (by Jakowskyl/Jakowska), recorded by CWN Productions on RCA Records (pop/English).
Tips: "Take more time working on the melody than on the instrumentation."

◉ SISKATUNE MUSIC PUBLISHING CO., 285 Chestnut St., West Hempstead NY 11552. (516)489-0738. Fax: (516)565-9425. E-mail: platear1@aol.com. President: Mike Siskind. Music publisher. Estab. 1981. Publishes 10 songs/year; publishes 3 new songwriters/year. Staff size: 1. Pays standard royalty.
How to Contact: Submit demo tape by mail. Unsolicited submissions are OK. Prefers cassette with a maximum of 3 songs and lyric sheet. "Send any and all pertinent information." SASE. Reports in 3 months. "No phone calls."
Music: Mostly **R&B** and **country**; also **dance** and **ballads**. Published *More Than a Friend*, written and recorded by Michael Ellis on Storehouse Records (ballad).
Tips: "Send three songs maximum. Think songs that are coverable. Please don't check to see if we received the package unless it's been three months and you haven't heard from us. It is essential that demo is more than piano/vocal or guitar/vocal, as we send out those demos. Make sure songs are coverable. Be extremely harsh in your self criticism. Unless it's top-drawer, we'll be passing on the song."

● **SLANTED CIRCLE MUSIC (BMI)**, 13413 Delaney Rd., Woodbridge VA 22193. (703)670-8092. A&R Dept.: Pete Lawrence. Music publisher and record producer. Estab. 1993. Publishes 15 songs/year; publishes 10 new songwriters/year. Pays standard royalty.
How to Contact: Write first and obtain permission to submit. Prefers cassette or DAT with 2 songs and lyric sheet. "Only fully produced band demos." Does not return material. Reports in 6 weeks if interested.
Music: Mostly **go cat rockabilly**; also **Chicago blues**, **Christian pop** and **contemporary jazz**. Does not want country or bluegrass. Published *Monday Mornin'* (by Kingery/LaVey), recorded by Larry LaVey on RHM (blues); and "Another Empty Table For Two" (by LaVey/Kingery), recorded by Teri Schaeffer on Trend Records (blues).
Tips: "Have a good clear demo made and use the best tape when pitching material. A demo should sound authentic to the style the publisher wants. Research the style before sending."

N ● **SOLID DISCS**, 11328 Magnolia Blvd., Suite 3, N. Hollywood CA 91601. Fax: (818)508-1101. President: James Warsinske. Music publisher. Estab. 1988. Publishes 30-60 songs/year; publishes 10-20 new songwriters/year. Pays standard royalty.
Affiliate(s): Harmonious Music (BMI).
How to Contact: Submit demo tape by mail. Unsolicited submissions are OK. Prefers cassette or VHS videocassette with 2-5 songs and lyric sheet. "Clearly label tapes with phone numbers." SASE. Reports in 1 month.
Music: Mostly **hip-hop**, **rock** and **pop**.

● **SONG FARM MUSIC (BMI)**, P.O. Box 24561, Nashville TN 37202. (615)742-1557. President: Tom Pallardy. Music publisher and record producer (T.P. Productions). Estab. 1980. Publishes 2-5 songs/year; publishes 1-2 new songwriters/year. Pays standard royalty.
How to Contact: Write first and obtain permission to submit. Prefers cassette with maximum 2 songs and lyric or lead sheet. SASE required with enough postage for return of all materials. Reports in 2-6 weeks.
Music: Mostly **country** and **R&B**. Published "Mississippi River Rat" (by J. Hall/R. Hall/E. Dickey), recorded by Tom Powers on Fountain Records (Cajun country); "Today's Just Not the Day" (by J. Bell, E. Bobbitt), recorded by Liz Draper (country); and "In Mama's Time" (by T. Crone), recorded by Pat Tucker on Radioactive Records (country/pop).
Tips: "Material should be submitted neatly and professionally with as good quality demo as possible. Songs need not be elaborately produced (voice and guitar/piano are fine) but they should be clear."

● **SONY MUSIC PUBLISHING**, 550 Madison Ave., 27th Floor, New York NY 10022. (212)833-4729. Fax: (212)833-5552. Vice President of Film & TV (classical): Paul Cremo. Santa Monica office: 2100 Colorado Ave., Santa Monica CA 90404. (310)449-2100. Vice President of Film & TV: Jennifer Pyken. Nashville office: 34 Music Square E, Nashville TN 37203. (615)742-4321. Fax: (615)244-2549. Vice President of A&R: Blake Chancey. Director of Film & TV Music: Phillip Self. Music publisher.
How to Contact: Sony Music does not accept unsolicited submissions.
Music: Published "Angel" (by S. McLachlan/P. Marchand), recorded by Sarah McLachlan on Arista; "Doo Wop (That Thing)," written and recorded by Lauryn Hill on Ruffhouse; and "I Can't Get Over You" (by R. Dunn/T. McBride), recorded by Brooks & Dunn on Arista Nashville.

● **SOUND CELLAR MUSIC**, 116 N. Peoria, Dixon IL 61021. (815)288-2900. E-mail: tjoos@essexl.c om. Website: http://www.essex1/com/people/tjoos. President: Todd Joos (country, pop, Christian). Professional Managers: James Miller (folk, adult contemporary); Mike Thompson (metal, hard rock, alternative). Music publisher, record company (Sound Cellar Records), record producer and recording studio. Estab. 1987. Publishes 15-25 songs/year. Publishes 5 or 6 new songwriters/year. Staff size: 4. Pays standard royalty.
How to Contact: Submit demo tape by mail. Unsolicited submissions are OK. Prefers cassette with 3 or 4 songs and lyric sheet. Does not return material. "We contact by phone in 3-4 weeks only if we want to work with the artist."

REFER TO THE GEOGRAPHIC INDEX (at the back of this book) to find listings of companies by state, as well as foreign listings.

Music: Mostly **metal**, **country** and **rock**; also **pop** and **blues**. Published *Severed Lines* (by David Frazier), recorded by The Unknown (pop/rock); *One More Chance*, written and recorded by The Rumors (pop/rock); and *Kooler by the Lake* (by Dan Morel), recorded by The Kings (blues), all on Cellar Records.

☐ **SOUTHERN MOST PUBLISHING COMPANY (BMI)**, P.O. Box 1461446, Laurie MO 65038. (314)374-1111. President/Owner: Dann E. Haworth. Music publisher and record producer (Haworth Productions). Estab. 1985. Publishes 10 songs/year; 3 new songwriters/year. Hires staff songwriters. Pays standard royalty.
Affiliate(s): Boca Chi Key Publishing (ASCAP).
How to Contact: Submit demo tape by mail. Unsolicited submissions are OK. Prefers cassette with 3 songs and lyric sheet. SASE. Reports in 2 weeks.
Music: Mostly **rock**, **R&B** and **country**; also **gospel** and **New Age**.
Tips: "Keep it simple and from the heart."

☑ **SPRADLIN/GLEICH PUBLISHING (BMI)**, 4234 N. 45th St., Phoenix AZ 85018-4307. Managers: Lee Gleich (rock, pop, movie, country); Paul Spradlin (country). Music publisher. Estab. 1988. Publishes 4-10 songs/year; 2-4 new songwriters. Staff size: 2. Pays standard royalty.
Affiliate(s): Paul Lee Publishing (ASCAP).
How to Contact: Write first and obtain permission to submit. Prefers cassette with 3 songs and lyric or lead sheet. "It must be very good material, as I only have time for promoting songwriters who really care." SASE. Reports in 6 weeks.
Music: Mostly **country** geared to the US and European country markets; also **pop**, **rock** and **movie**. Published *Solo Act*, written and recorded by Kurt McFarland on Wild Sky (country); and *Go Slow and Wait* (by Paul Spradlin), recorded by the Goose Creek Symphony on Goose Records.
Tips: "I need radio type songs. Please send me only your best. I have pitches to major stars but need great songs. I cannot train writers!"

⛏☐ **STANDARD MUSIC PUBLISHING (BMI)**, 1131 Alta Loma Rd. #524, West Hollywood CA 90069. (310)854-0923. Fax: (310)854-0609. E-mail: rcmla@idt.net. Managers: Janine Kerr; Adrian Marchesoni. Music publisher and management company (RCM International). Estab. 1994. Publishes a variable number of songs/year; publishes a variable number of new songwriters/year. Staff size: 5. Pays negotiable royalty.
How to Contact: Write first and obtain permission to submit a demo. Prefers cassette with 6 songs and lyric sheet. Does not return material. Reports in 1 month.
Film & TV: Places 1 song in TV/year. Recently published "Burn" (by Redwick/Werfel/Arena), recorded by Tina Arena in *Baywatch*.
Music: Mostly **rock** and **pop**; also **country**. Published "Chains" (pop); *Wasn't It Good* (pop); and "Burn" (pop) (by Resnick/Wesfel/Arena), all recorded by Tina Arena on Epic (pop).

☑ **STARBOUND PUBLISHING CO. (BMI)**, Dept. SM, 207 Winding Rd., Friendswood TX 77546. (713)482-2346. E-mail: bh207@msn.com. President: Buz Hart. Music publisher, record company (Juke Box Records, Quasar Records and Eden Records) and record producer (Lonnie Wright and Buz Hart). Estab. 1970. Publishes 35-100 songs/year; publishes 5-10 new songwriters/year. Pays standard royalty.
How to Contact: Write or call first and obtain permission to submit. Prefers cassette with 3 songs and lyric sheet. SASE. Reports in 2 months.
Music: Mostly **country**, **R&B** and **gospel**. Does not want rap. Published "Butterfly" (by Pamela Parkins/Buz Hart), recorded by Frankie Laine on Score Records; "Let it Slide" (by James Watson/Buz Hart), recorded by Stan Steel on Gallery II Records; and "Country Boy's Dream" (by Gene Thomas/Buz Hart), recorded by Charlie Louvin, Waylon Jennings, and George Jones on Playback Records.

Ⓝ ⛯ ☑ **STARSTRUCK WRITERS GROUP (ASCAP, BMI)**, 40 Music Square W., Nashville TN 37203. (615)259-5300. Vice President: Mike Sebastian. Music publisher. Estab. 1991. Publishes 600 songs/year; publishes 5-8 new songwriters/year. Hires staff songwriters.
Affiliate(s): Starstruck Angel (BMI).
● "No News," published by Starstruck, won ASCAP's Song of the Year award.
How to Contact: Write first and obtain permission to submit a demo. Prefers cassette with 3 songs and lyric sheet. "List all co-writers if any." SASE. Reports in 3-4 weeks.
Music: Mostly **country/contemporary**, **R&B** and **alternative**. Published "No News," recorded by Lone Star on RCA; and "Blue Clear Sky," recorded by George Strait on MCA (both written by Mark Sanders/Ed Hill); and "Perfect Love" (by Sunny Russ/Stephanie Smith), recorded by Trisha Yearwood on MCA.

🖉 **STELLAR MUSIC INDUSTRIES (ASCAP, BMI)**, P.O. Box 54700, Atlanta GA 30308-0700. (770)454-1011. Fax: (770)454-8088. E-mail: goldwaxrec@aol.com. Website: http://www.goldwax.com. Vice President: James McClendon. Music publisher and record company (Goldwax Record Corporation). Estab. 1963. Staff size: 3. Publishes 100 songs/year; publishes 60 new songwriters/year. Hires staff songwriters. Pays standard royalty.
Affiliate(s): Rodanca Music (ASCAP) and Bianca Music (BMI).
How to Contact: Write or call first and obtain permission to submit a demo. Prefers cassette, DAT or videocassette with 4 songs and lyric sheet. SASE. Reports in 6 weeks.
Music: Mostly **R&B/hip-hop, pop/rock** and **jazz**; also **blues, contemporary country** and **contemporary gospel**. Published "Girls I Like," written and recorded by Courtney-Jahara Williams; *You Need A Job*, written and recorded by Cookie-D, both on Rap-N-Wax Records (rap); and "The ATL," written and recorded by Lanier/W. Gear/Charles M. on Urban Assault Records.

🆖 🖾 🖉 **RAY STEVENS MUSIC (BMI)**, 1707 Grand Ave., Nashville TN 37212. (615)327-4629. Fax: (615)321-5455. Assistant Manager: Ramona Smith. Professional Manager: Randy Cullers (country/pop/R&B). Music publisher. Publishes 40 songs/year; publishes 3 new songwriters/year. Staff size: 5. Hires staff songwriters. Pays standard royalty.
Affiliate(s): Ahab Music Co., Inc. (ASCAP) and Grand Ave. Music (BMI).
How to Contact: Does not accept unsolicited submissions.
Film & TV: Places 3 songs in film/year. Recently published "Injurin Joe" and "From The Very First Moment" (by Ray Stevens/C.W. Kalb, Jr.), recorded by Ray Stevens in *Tom Sawyer*.
Music: Mostly **country, pop** and **R&B**. Published *After Hours* (by Suzi Ragsdale), recorded by Pam Tillis on Arista (country); *Troublemaker* (by Suzi Ragsdale), recorded by Mila Mason on Atlantic (country); and *Bad Little Boy* (by C.W. Kalb Jr.), recorded by Ray Stevens on MCA (country).

🆖 🖾 🖉 **STILL WORKING MUSIC GROUP (ASCAP, BMI, SESAC)**, 1625 Broadway, Suite 600, Nashville TN 37203. (615)242-4201. Fax: (615)242-4202. Creative Director: Renee Thornton Browning (new writers). Music publisher and record company (Orby Records, Inc.). Estab. 1994. Publishes 1,000 songs/year. Staff size: 6. Hires staff songwriters. Pays standard royalty.
Affiliate(s): Still Working for the Woman Music (ASCAP), Still Working for the Man Music (BMI) and Still Working for All Music (SESAC).
How to Contact: Does not accept unsolicited submissions.
Film & TV: Places 6 songs in film and 20 songs in TV/year. Vice President of Film/TV: Tanja Crouch (country, pop, rock, dance, instrumentals). Recently published "First Noel," recorded by The Kelions in *Felicity*.
Music: Mostly **rock, country** and **pop**; also **dance** and **R&B**. Published "If You See Him/If You See Her" (by Tommy Lee James), recorded by Reba McIntire/Brooks & Dunn; "Round About Way" (by Wil Nance), recorded by George Strait on MCA; and "Wrong Again" (by Tommy Lee James), recorded by Martina McBride on RCA (country).
Tips: "If you want to be a country songwriter you need to be in Nashville where the business is. Write what is in your heart."

🖉 **JEB STUART MUSIC CO. (BMI)**, P.O. Box 6032, Station B, Miami FL 33101-6032. (305)547-1424. President: Jeb Stuart. Music publisher, record producer (Esquire International) and management firm. Estab. 1975. Publishes 4-6 songs/year. Pays standard royalty.
How to Contact: Submit demo tape by mail. Unsolicited submissions are OK. Prefers cassette or CD with 2-4 songs and lead sheet. SASE. Reports in 1 month.
Music: Mostly **gospel, jazz/rock, pop, R&B** and **rap**; also **blues, church/religious, country, disco** and **soul**. Published "Love in the Rough," "Guns, Guns (No More Guns)" and "Come On Cafidia," all written and recorded by Jeb Stuart on Esquire Int'l Records.

🆖 🌐 🖾 🖉 **SUCCES**, Pijnderslaan 84, 9200 Dendermonde Belgium. (052)21 89 87. Fax: (052)21 89 87. Director: Deschuyteneer Hendrik. Music publisher, record company and record producer. Estab. 1978. Publishes 400 songs/year. Hires staff songwriters. Staff size: 4. Pays standard royalty.
How to Contact: Submit demo tape by mail. Unsolicited submissions are OK. Prefers cassette or VHS videocassette with 3 songs. SAE and IRC. Reports in 2 months.
Film & TV: Places songs in TV. Recently released "Werkloos" (by Deschuyteneer), recorded by Jacques Vermeire in *Jacques Vermeire Show*.
Music: Mostly **pop, dance** and **variety**; also **instrumental** and **rock**. Published *Classical Experience*, written and recorded by Le Grand Julot on Arcade (instrumental); and *15 Country Songs*, written and recorded by Jimmy Lintou on Succes (country).

⦿ **SUN STAR SONGS**, P.O. Box 1387, Pigeon Forge TN 37868. (423)429-4121. Fax: (423)429-7090. E-mail: sunstarsng@aol.com. President: Tony Glenn Rast. Music publisher. Estab. 1965. Pays standard royalty.
How to Contact: Submit demo tape by mail. Unsolicited submissions are OK. Prefers cassette with 3 songs and lyric sheets. SASE. Reports in 2-3 weeks.
Music: Mostly **country, Christian country-gospel** and **bluegrass**; also **comedy**. Published *Let's Go Racing* (by Rast/Ruby/Rabbai), recorded by Nevada on SunStar Records (country); *If You Ain't Got Jesus* (by Jim Sales), recorded by Tommy Cash on Rejoice Records (gospel); and *You Are the Christ* (by Tony Glenn Rast/Betty Ross), recorded by Holly Robinson on Heartlight Records (gospel).
Tips: "Submit quality demos. Also interested in good lyrics for co-writing."

⦿ **SUNSONGS MUSIC (ASCAP, BMI, SESAC)**, 52 N. Evarts Ave., Elmsford NY 10523. (914)592-2563. E-mail: mberman438@aol.com. Professional Managers: Michael Berman (pop, country, rock); John Henderson (R&B, hip-hop). Music publisher, record producer and talent agency (Hollywood East Entertainment). Estab. 1981. Publishes 20 songs/year; publishes 10 new songwriters/year. Staff size: 6. Pays standard royalty; co-publishing deals available for established writers.
Affiliate(s): Media Concepts Music and Dark Sun Music (SESAC).
How to Contact: Submit demo tape by mail. Unsolicited submissions are OK. Prefers cassette with 3-4 songs and lyric sheet. SASE. Reports in 1 month.
Music: Mostly **dance-oriented, techno-pop** and **R&B**; also **rock (all styles)** and **top 40/pop**. Does not want hard core rap or heavy metal. Published "Where Will You Be on Christmas Day" (by Glenn Dorsey), and *Too Many Ain't Guts* (by Henderson/Mercadante), both recorded by The Joneses on Karoussell (R&B/dance); and *Cuando Piensoenti* (by Kevin Ceballo), recorded by Isidro Infante on RMM (Latin).
Tips: "Submit material with strong hook and know the market being targeted by your song."

[N] ⦿ **SUPREME ENTERPRISES INT'L CORP.**, 12304 Santa Monica Blvd., 3rd Floor, Los Angeles CA 90025. (818)707-3481. Fax: (818)707-3482. G.M. Copyrights: Lisa Lew. Music publisher, record company and record producer. Estab. 1979. Publishes 20-30 songs/year; publishes 2-6 new songwriters/year. Pays standard royalty.
Affiliate(s): Fuerte Suerte Music (BMI).
How to Contact: Submit demo tape by mail. Unsolicited submissions are OK. Prefers cassette. Does not return material. "Please copyright material before submitting." Reports in 2-3 weeks if interested.
Music: Mostly **Latin pop, reggae in Cumbias Spanish and English** and **ballads in Spanish**. Published "Paso La Vida Pensando," recorded by Jose Feliciano on Motown Records; "Cucu Bam Bam" (by David Choy), recorded by Kathy on Polydor Records (reggae/pop); and "El Marciano," recorded by Coco Man on M.P. Records.
Tips: "A good melody is a hit in any language."

⦿ **T.C. PRODUCTIONS/ETUDE PUBLISHING CO. (BMI)**, 121 Meadowbrook Dr., Somerville NJ 08876. (908)359-5110. Fax: (908)359-1962. E-mail: tcproductions@mindspring.com. Website: http://www.vmgmusic.com. President: Tony Camillo. Professional Manager (R&B): Jacqui Collins. Professional Manager (dance): Gene Serina. Music publisher and record producer. Estab. 1992. Publishes 25-50 songs/year; publishes 3-6 new songwriters/year. Pays negotiable royalty.
Affiliate(s): We Iz It Music Publishing (ASCAP) and Etude/Barcam (BMI).
How to Contact: Write or call first and obtain permission to submit a demo. Prefers cassette with 3-4 songs and lyric sheet. SASE. Reports in 3-4 weeks.
Music: Mostly **R&B** and **dance**; also **country** and **outstanding pop ballads**. Published "One of a Kind" (by Sandy Farina/Lisa Ratner), recorded by Vanessa Williams; "Waiting for Last Goodbye" and "I Feel a Song" (by Tony Camillo/Mary Sawyer), recorded by Gladys Knight, all on P.A.R. Records (R&B).

[N] ⦿ **TALBOT MUSIC GROUP (ASCAP, BMI)**, 2 Music Circle S., Nashville TN 37203. (615)244-6200. Fax: (615)254-8860. E-mail: talbotmusi@aol.com. Music publisher. Estab. 1984. Publishes 40 songs/year. Hires staff songwriters. Pays standard royalty.
Affiliate(s): Saheedron Music Publishing, Inc. (ASCAP) and Harbot (SESAC).
How to Contact: Talbot Music Group does not accept unsolicited submissions.

⦿ **DALE TEDESCO MUSIC CO. (BMI)**, 16020 Lahey St., Granada Hills CA 91344. (818)360-7329. Fax: (818)886-1338. President: Dale T. Tedesco. General Manager: Betty Lou Tedesco. Music publisher. Estab. 1981. Publishes 20-40 songs/year; publishes 20-30 new songwriters/year. Staff size: 2-3. Pays standard royalty.
Affiliate(s): Tedesco Tunes (ASCAP).

How to Contact: Submit demo tape by mail. Unsolicited submissions are OK. Prefers cassette with 1 song and lyric sheet. SASE or postcard for critique. "Dale Tedesco Music hand-critiques all material submitted. Only reviews 1 song. Free evaluation." SASE. Reports in 1 month.
Film & TV: Places 15 songs in film and 8 songs in TV/year. Recently published "Trouble on Your Mind," "Redneck Man" and "Logger Time," all written and recorded by Doug Ellis in *Sunset Beach*.
Music: Mostly **pop, R&B** and **A/C**; also **dance-oriented, instrumentals** (for TV and film), **jazz, MOR, rock, soul** and **ethnic instrumentals**. Does not want rap. Published *One Child* (by David Brisbin), recorded by Ernestine Anderson on Quest Records (jazz).

N ◯ **TEXAS CHEROKEE MUSIC,** 729 Grapevine Highway #308, Hurst TX 76053. Phone/fax: (817)590-0682. E-mail: T_C_M@email.com. Co-owners: Sarah Cate and Adrian Cate. Music publisher. Estab. 1995. Staff size: 2. Hires staff songwriters. Pays standard royalty.
How to Contact: Submit demo tape by mail. Unsolicited submissions are OK. Prefers cassette, CD or DAT with 3 songs, lyric sheet and cover letter. Does not return material. Reports in 1-2 weeks.
Music: Mostly **country, pop** and **Christian**; also **blues, western swing** and **lite rock**. Does not want alternative or heavy rock.
Tips: "Be flexible with your writing. Be willing to try changes to the song to improve its chances."

◯ **TEXAS TUFF MUSIC COMPANY (BMI),** P.O. Box 630555, Irving TX 75063-0555. (972)831-1272. Fax: (972)831-8644. E-mail: ttuffmuz@aol.com. Owner: Janice Matson. Music publisher. Estab. 1996. Publishes 20 songs/year; publishes 3-5 new songwriters/year. Staff size: 4. Pays standard royalty.
Affiliate(s): Jan Matson Publishing (ASCAP).
How to Contact: Submit demo tape by mail. Unsolicited submissions are OK. Prefers cassette with 3-5 songs and lyric sheet. Does not return material.
Music: Country only.

❖ ◯ **THIRD WAVE PRODUCTIONS LIMITED,** P.O. Box 563, Gander, Newfoundland A1V 2E1 Canada. (709)256-8009. Fax: (709)256-7411. President: Arch. Bonnell. Music publisher, record company (Third Wave/Street Legal), distribution and marketing company. Estab. 1986. Publishes 20 songs/year; publishes 2 new songwriters/year.
How to Contact: Submit demo tape by mail. Unsolicited submissions are OK. Prefers cassette or DAT with lyric sheet. SASE. Reports in 2 months.
Music: Mostly **traditional Newfoundland, Celtic/Irish, folk**; also **bluegrass, country** and **pop/rock**. Published *Salt Beef Junkie* and *He's a Part of Me* (by Buddy Wosisname), recorded by The Other Fellers (traditional); and *Nobody Never Told Me*, written and recorded by The Psychobilly Cadillacs (country), all on Third Wave Productions.

◯ **TIKI ENTERPRISES, INC. (ASCAP, BMI),** 195 S. 26th St., San Jose CA 95116. (408)286-9840. President (country, gospel, Mexican): Gradie O'Neal. Professional Manager (rock/pop, R&B, New Age): Jeannine O'Neil. Music publisher, record company (Rowena Records) and record producer (Jeannine O'Neal and Gradie O'Neal). Estab. 1967. Publishes 40 songs/year; publishes 12 new songwriters/year. Staff size: 3. Pays standard royalty.
Affiliate(s): Tooter Scooter Music (BMI), Janell Music (BMI) and O'Neal & Friend (ASCAP).
How to Contact: Submit demo tape by mail. Unsolicited submissions are OK. Prefers cassette with 3 songs and lyric or lead sheets. SASE. Reports in 2 weeks.
Music: Mostly **country, Mexican, rock/pop gospel, R&B** and **New Age**. Does not want atonal music. Published "So Far Away," written and recorded by Lisa Martens (alternative rock); and *Lord I Believe*, written and recorded by Dwight Bailey, Jr. (gospel), both on Rowena Records.
Tips: "Keep writing and sending songs in. Never give up—the next hit may be just around the bend."

◯ **TOPS AND BOTTOMS MUSIC (BMI),** P.O. Box 1341, New York NY 10113. (212)366-6636. Fax: (212)366-4646. Director: Richard Dworkin. Music publisher. Estab. 1988. Publishes 5 songs/year; publishes 1 new songwriter/year. Pays standard royalty.
How to Contact: Submit demo tape by mail. Unsolicited submissions are OK. Prefers cassette or VHS videocassette (if available) with 3-5 songs and lyric sheet. Does not return material. Reports in 4 months.

THE FILM & TV INDEX found at the back of this book lists companies placing music in film and TV (excluding TV commercials).

Music: Mostly **music relating to gay/lesbian life**. Published "Love Worth Fighting For"(by Callen/Malamet), recorded by Michael Callen; and "Oh Boy," written and recorded by David Downing, both on Significant; and "Love Don't Need A Reason" (by Callen/Allen/Malamet), recorded by Barbara Cook on DRG.

TOWER MUSIC GROUP (formerly Castle Music Group), 50 Music Square W., Suite 201, Nashville TN 37203. (615)320-7003. Fax: (615)320-7006. E-mail: castlerecord@earthlink.net. Website: http://www.castlerecords.com. Publishing Director: Dave Sullivan. Professional Managers: Ed Russell; Eddie Bishop. Music publisher, record company (Castle Records) and record producer. Estab. 1969. Publishes 50 songs/year; publishes 10 new songwriters/year. Staff size: 15. Pays standard royalty.
Affiliate(s): Cat's Alley Music (ASCAP) and Alley Roads Music (BMI).
How to Contact: Call first and obtain permission to submit or to arrange personal interview. Prefers cassette with 3 songs and lyric sheet. Does not return material. "You may follow up via e-mail." Reports in 2-3 months only if interested.
Film & TV: Places 2 songs in film and 26 songs in TV/year. Recently published "Run Little Girl" (by J.R. Jones/Eddie Ray), recorded by J.R. Jones in *Roadside Prey*.
Music: Mostly **country** and **R&B**; also **blues**, **pop** and **gospel**. Does not want rap. Published *Say When!* (by James House), recorded by Eileen Oturo (country); *Backyard Bar B Q* (by David Dunn), recorded by Adolfo Mayo (contemporary country); and "You Shoulda Known" (by Paul Sullivan), recorded by The Hoods (R&B), on all Castle Records.
Tips: "Please contact us via e-mail with any other demo submissions questions."

TRANSAMERIKA MUSIKVERLAG KG, Isestrasse 77, 20149 Hamburg, Germany. Phone: (0451)21530. E-mail: transamerika@online.de. Website: http://www.online.de/home/TRANSAMERIKA/. Professional Manager: Kirsten Kaminsky. General Manager: Pia Kaminsky. Member: GEMA, PRS, KODA, NCB, APRA. Music publisher and administrator. Estab. 1978. Publishes 2-4 songs/year; 1 new songwriter/year. Staff size: 3. Pays 50% royalty if releasing a record; 85% if only administrating.
Affiliate(s): MCI Ltd. (London, UK) and Leosong Music Australia Pty. Ltd., Sydney.
How to Contact: Submit demo tape by mail. Unsolicited submissions are OK. Prefers cassette, CD or VHS videocassette. Does not return material. Reports in 1-2 months only if interested.
Film & TV: Places 2 songs in film and 2 songs in TV/year. Recently published "Nice 'N' Nasty" (by Vincent Montana) in *La Verité si Qe Mens*; and "Wilde," written and recorded by Debbie Wiseman in *Oscar Wilde*.
Music: Mostly **pop**; also **rock**, **country**, **film music** and **reggae**. Published "T'estimo (I Love you")", written and recorded by José Carreras.
Tips: "We would like to have a partner in the U.S. to provide us with publishers who have released material in Europe but have no sub-publisher here. We are specializing in administering (filing, registering, licensing and finding unclaimed royalties, and dealing with counter-claims) publishers worldwide."

TRANSITION MUSIC CORPORATION (ASCAP, BMI, SESAC), 11328 Magnolia, N. Hollywood CA 91601. (818)760-1001. Fax: (818)760-7625. E-mail: onestopmus@aol.com. Director of Film and Television Music: Jennifer Brown. President: Donna Ross-Jones. Vice President: David Jones. Administration: Mike Dobson. Music publisher. Estab. 1988. Publishes 250 songs/year; publishes 20 new songwriters/year. Variable royalty based on song placement and writer.
Affiliate(s): Pushy Publishing (ASCAP), Creative Entertainment Music (BMI) and One Stop Shop Music (SESAC).
How to Contact: Submit demo tape by mail. Unsolicited submissions are OK. Prefers cassette, DAT or CD with 3 songs. SASE. Reports in 3 weeks.
Film & TV: "TMC provides music for television shows on a weekly basis. Credits include *Entertainment Tonight*, *Coach*, *Beverly Hills 90210* and *Melrose Place*. We also do music supervision for films such as *Blue Motel* starring Sean Young, *The Good Life* starring Dennis Hopper and *Back to Even* starring Lorenzo Lamas."
Music: All styles.
Tips: "Supply master quality material with great songs."

TRUSTY PUBLICATIONS (BMI), 8771 Rose Creek Rd., Nebo KY 42441. (502)249-3194. E-mail: trusty@wko.com. Website: http://www.wko.com/business/trusty/trusty.html. President: Elsie Childers. Music publisher, record company (Trusty Records and etc Records) and record producer. Member CMA. Estab. 1960. Publishes 2-3 songs/year; publishes 2 new songwriters/year. Pays standard royalty.
How to Contact: Submit demo tape by mail. Unsolicited submissions are OK. Prefers cassette or VHS

videocassette with 2-4 songs and lead sheet. Does not return material. "Will contact you if interested in songs you submit."
Music: Mostly **country, R&B, rock, contemporary Christian, Southern gospel, Christian country, jazz** and **line dancing**. Published *Heavens Bright Shore* (by Steve Holland), recorded by Stillwater on etc Records (Southern gospel); and *Red Barn's Rockin'*, written and recorded by Barry Russell on Trusty Records (country rock).

TWIN TOWERS PUBLISHING CO., Dept. SM, 8833 Sunset Blvd., Penthouse West, Los Angeles CA 90069. (310)659-9644. President: Michael Dixon. Music publisher and booking agency (Harmony Artists, Inc.). Publishes 24 songs/year. Pays standard royalty.
How to Contact: Call first and get permission to submit. Prefers cassette with 3 songs and lyric sheet. SASE. Reports only if interested.
Music: Mostly **pop, rock** and **R&B**. Published "Magic," from *Ghostbusters* soundtrack on Arista Records; and "Kiss Me Deadly" (by Lita Ford) on RCA Records.

ULTIMATE PEAK MUSIC (BMI), P.O. Box 707, Nashville TN 37076. Creative Manager: Danny Crader. Music publisher. Estab. 1992. Publishes 35 songs/year; publishes 4 new songwriters/year. Hires staff writers. Staff size: 4. Pays standard royalty.
How to Contact: Submit demo tape by mail. Unsolicited submissions are OK. Prefers cassette with 1-6 songs and lyric sheet. SASE. Reports in 6 weeks.
Music: Mostly **country** and **MTV pop/rock**. Published *Better* (by Billy Herzig/Anderson Page), recorded by Daryo (dance); and *Apathy* (by Billy Herzig/Darrell Yokochi), recorded by Eleven/Eleven on Green Zebra (rock).
Tips: "Listen to the radio and compare your songs to the hits—not for recording quality, but for substance and content and structure—and be objective and realistic and honest with yourself."

[N] UNIVERSAL MUSIC PUBLISHING, 12 Music Circle S., Nashville TN 37203.
• MCA Music Publishing and PolyGram Music Publishing have merged into Universal Music Publishing. At press time they were going through restructuring.
How to Contact: Does not accept unsolicited submissions.

UNKNOWN SOURCE MUSIC (ASCAP), 520 Washington Blvd., Suite 201, Marina Del Rey CA 90292-5442. A&R: Peter Johnson. Music publisher, record company (Smokin Ya Productions) and record producer. Estab. 1993. Publishes 5-10 songs/year; publishes 1-2 new songwriters/year. Hires staff songwriters. Staff size: 5. Pays standard royalty.
Affiliate(s): Sundance Records (ASCAP).
How to Contact: Submit demo tape by mail. Unsolicited submissions are OK. Prefers cassette with 3 songs. Does not return material. Reports in 6 weeks.
Music: Mostly **rap/hip-hop, R&B** and **alternative**. Published "Force of Tha Universe" (by DaForce/Edson Cr), recorded by DaForce; and "Tell Me What is in the Sky" (Antonio P/Sarah M/C.C.), recorded by Cluster, both on Unknown Source (hip-hop).
Tips: "Keep working with us, be patient, be willing to work hard. Send your very best work."

VAAM MUSIC GROUP (BMI), P.O. Box 29550, Hollywood CA 90029-0550. (323)664-7765. E-mail: vaampubl@aol.com or pmarti3636@aol.com. President: Pete Martin. Music publisher and record producer (Pete Martin/Vaam Productions). Estab. 1967. Publishes 9-24 new songs/year. Pays standard royalty.
Affiliate(s): Pete Martin Music (ASCAP).
How to Contact: Prefers cassette with 2 songs and lyric sheet. SASE. Reports in 1 month. "Small packages only."
Music: Mostly **top 40/pop, country** and **R&B**. "Submitted material must have potential of reaching top 5 on charts."
Tips: "Study the top 10 charts in the style you write. Stay current and up-to-date with today's market."

VALET PUBLISHING CO. (BMI), 2442 N.W. Market St., Suite 273, Seattle WA 98107. Administrative offices: 5503 Roosevelt Way NE, Seattle WA 98105. (206)524-1020. Fax: (206)524-1102. Publishing Director: Buck Ormsby. Music publisher, record producer (John "Buck" Ormsby) and record company (Etiquette/Suspicious Records). Estab. 1961. Publishes 5-10 songs/year. Pays standard royalty.

How to Contact: Call first and obtain permission to submit a demo tape. Prefers cassette with 3-4 songs and lyric sheets. Does not return material. "Responds only if interested."
Music: Mostly **R&B**, **rock** and **pop**; also **dance** and **country**.
Tips: "Production of tape must be top quality and lyric sheets professional."

VIRGINIA BORDEN RHYTHMS, 1502 18th Ave. S., Nashville TN 37212. (615)292-4602. Fax: (615)292-9117. COO: Everett Lowe. Music publisher and record company (Bridge Records, Inc.). Estab. 1994. Pays standard royalty.
Affiliate(s): King Author Publishing (BMI).
How to Contact: Write or call first and obtain permission to submit a demo. Prefers cassette with 3 songs and lyric sheet. SASE. Reports in 2 weeks.
Music: Mostly **country**, **alternative** and **pop**; also **bluegrass**. Published *Casualties of War* (by various artists), recorded by Barnstormer on Bridge (alternative).

VOKES MUSIC PUBLISHING (BMI), Box 12, New Kensington PA 15068-0012. (412)335-2775. President: Howard Vokes. Music publisher, record company, booking agency and promotion company.
How to Contact: Submit cassette with 3 songs and lyric or lead sheet. SASE. Reports within a week.
Music: Mostly **traditional country/bluegrass** and **gospel**. Published "A Million Tears" (by Duke & Null), recorded by Johnny Eagle Feather on Vokes Records; "I Won't Be Your Honky Tonk Queen" (by Vokes/Wallace), recorded by Bunnie Mills on Pot-Of-Gold Records; and "Break The News" (by Vokes/Webb), recorded by Bill Beere on Oakhill Records.
Tips: "We're always looking for country songs that tell a story, and only interested in hard-traditional-bluegrass, country and country gospel songs. Please no 'copy-cat songwriters.'"

WARNER/CHAPPELL MUSIC CANADA LTD. (SOCAN), 40 Sheppard Ave. W. #800, Toronto, Ontario M2N 6K9 Canada. (416)227-0566. Fax: (416)227-0573. E-mail: anne.marie.smith @warnerchappell.com. Creative Manager: Anne-Marie Smith. General Manager: Pat Campbell. Copyright Manager: Linda Worden. Film/TV Manager: Andrew Meck. Music publisher.
How to Contact: Call first and obtain permission to submit a demo. Prefers cassette with 3 songs with bio and lyric sheet. SAE and IRC. Reports in 2 months.
Music: **All genres** with music and lyrics completed. Published "If It Makes You Happy," written and recorded by Sheryl Crow on A&M Records (rock); "Wide Mouth Mason," written and recorded by Wide Mouth Mason on WEA (rock/blues); "Tea Party," written and recorded by Tea Party on EMI (rock).
Tips: "We are looking for hard-working people with honesty and professionalism."

WARNER/CHAPPELL MUSIC, INC., 10585 Santa Monica Blvd., Third Floor, Los Angeles CA 90025-4950. (310)441-8600. Fax: (310)470-3232. Vice President of Creative Services: Judy Stakee. New York office: 1290 Avenue of the Americas, 9th Floor, New York NY 10019. (212)399-6910. Fax: (212)644-1859. Music publisher.
How to Contact: Warner/Chappell does not accept unsolicited material.
Music: Published "Believe" (by B. Higgins/S. McLennen/P. Barry/S. Torch), recorded by Cher on Warner Bros. (pop); "Every Morning" (by Sugar Ray/D. Kahne/R. Bean/A. Zarate/P. Tellez), recorded by Sugar Ray on Lava; and "Save Tonight," written and recorded by Eagle-Eye Cherry on Work.

WEMAR MUSIC CORP. (BMI), 12403 Ventura Court, Studio City CA 91604. (818)980-8887. Fax: (818)980-9111. President: Stuart Wiener. Music publisher. Estab. 1940. Publishes 30 songs/year; publishes 30 new songwriters/year. Pays standard royalty.
Affiliate(s): Grand Music Corp. (ASCAP).
How to Contact: Submit demo tape by mail. Unsolicited submissions are OK. SASE. Reports in 2 months.
Music: Mostly **pop**, **R&B** and **dance**. Published "Pearl" and "Heavy Hitter," written and recorded by Geri Verdi on Mills Records (blues); and "Meat Street," written and recorded by Neal Fox on Gravity Records (Broadway Show).

BERTHOLD WENGERT (MUSIKVERLAG), Waldstrasse 27, D-76327, Pfinztal-Sollingen, Germany. Contact: Berthold Wengert. Music publisher. Pays standard GEMA royalty.

OPENNESS TO SUBMISSIONS: ☐ beginners; ◐ beginners and experienced; ● experienced only; ◉ industry referrals only.

How to Contact: Prefers cassette and complete score for piano. SAE and IRC. Reports in 1 month. "No cassette returns!"
Music: Mostly **light music** and **pop**.

✓ ◑ **WESTWOOD MUSIC GROUP (ASCAP, BMI)**, 1031 Amboy Ave., Suite 202, Edison NJ 08837. (732)225-8600. Fax: (732)225-8644. E-mail: music@westwoodgrp.com. Website: http://www.west woodgrp.com. President: Victor Kaply. Professional Manager: Steve Willoughby. Music publisher and management firm (Westwood Entertainment Group). Publishes 15 songs/year; publishes 2 new songwriters/year. Staff size: 3. Pays standard royalty.
How to Contact: Write first and obtain permission to submit. Prefers cassette with 3 songs and lyric sheet. SASE. Reports in 6 weeks.
Music: Mostly **rock**; also **pop**. Published "Every Step Of the Way" (by Bev O'Neill/Turner Battle), recorded by Buff-N-T; "What A Mess I'm In," written and recorded by Skip Denenberg, both on Westwood Records.
Tips: Submit a "neat promotional package with bio and lyrics."

◑ **WHITE CAT MUSIC**, 10603 N. Hayden Rd., Suite 114, Scottsdale AZ 85260. (602)951-3115. Fax: (602)951-3074. E-mail: songs@comstock-records.com. Website: http://www.comstock-records.com. Professional Manager: Frank Fara. Producer: Patty Parker. Music publisher, record company and record producer. Member CMA, CCMA, BCCMA and BBB. Estab. 1978. Publishes 30 songs/year; publishes 20 new songwriters/year. Staff size: 4. "50% of our published songs are from non-charted and developing writers." Pays standard royalty.
Affiliate(s): Rocky Bell Music (BMI), How The West Was Sung Music (BMI) and Crystal Canyon Music (ASCAP).
  • Fara and Parker are authors of the book *How to Open Doors in the Music Industry—the Independent Way.*
How to Contact: Submit demo tape by mail. Unsolicited submissions are OK. Prefers cassettes with 2-4 songs and include lyric sheet. SASE. Reports in 2 weeks.
Music: All styles of **country**—traditional to crossover. Published "Catch A Tiny Teardrop," written and recorded by R.J. McClintock; "Smooth Talker" (by Paul Gibson), recorded by Dakota Band; *Boogie Woogie Thang* (by Charles D. Ingram), recorded by Howdy, all on Comstock Records (country).
Tips: "Have an out front vocal presentation so lyric can be heard. Go easy on long instrumental intros and breaks which distract. Send only two to four songs—medium to up tempo are always in demand. This helps stack the odds in your favor for getting heard."

◑ **WHITEWING MUSIC (BMI)**, 413 N. Parkerson Ave., Crowley LA 70526. (318)788-0773. Fax: (318)788-0776. Owner: Georgia Miller. Music publisher and record company (Master-Trak, Showtime, Par T, MTE, Blues Unlimited, Kajun, Cajun Classics). Estab. 1946. Publishes 12-15 songs/year. Publishes 6 new songwriters/year. Pays standard royalty.
Affiliate(s): Jamil Music (BMI).
How to Contact: Submit demo tape by mail. Unsolicited submissions are OK. Prefers cassette (or videocassette) with 6 songs and lyric or lead sheets. Reports in 5-6 weeks.
Music: Mostly **country, R&B** and **MOR**; also **blues** and **cajun**. Published *Live at Vermilion Ville* (by Lee Benoit); and *Love On Me* (by Kenne Wayne).

◑ **WILCOM PUBLISHING (ASCAP)**, Box 4456, West Hills CA 91308. (805)789-5044. Owner: William Clark. Music publisher. Estab. 1989. Publishes 10-15 songs/year; publishes 1-2 new songwriters/year. Staff size: 2. Pays standard royalty.
How to Contact: Write or call first and obtain permission to submit a tape. Prefers cassette with 1-2 songs and lyric sheet. SASE. Reports in 3 weeks.
Music: Mostly **R&B, pop** and **rock**; also **country**. Does not want rap. Published "Girl Can't Help It" (by W. Clark/D. Walsh/P. Oland), recorded by Stage 1 on Rockit Records (top 40).

▣ ◑ **WINSTON & HOFFMAN HOUSE MUSIC PUBLISHERS (ASCAP, BMI)**, P.O. Box 1415, Burbank CA 91507-1415. President: Lynne Robin Green. Music publisher. Estab. 1958. Publishes 25 songs/year. Staff size: 2. Pays standard royalty.
Affiliate(s): Lansdowne Music Publishers (ASCAP), Bloor Music (BMI) and Ben Ross Music (ASCAP), "also administer 15 other firms."
How to Contact: Submit demo tape by mail. Unsolicited submissions are OK. "Do not query first. Do not call." Prefers cassette with 3 songs maximum and lyric sheet. "*Must* SASE, or *no* reply!" Reports in 1 month.

Film & TV: Places 45 songs in film and 25 songs in TV/year. Recently published "Groovin on the Bus" (by Lo-Cormier), recorded by Mr. Taboo in *Los Angeles Without a Map*; "The Roach" (by Alonzo Willis) in Conan O'Brien show; and "The Weave," written and recorded by Daniel Kane in *Death in America* (PBS).

Music: Mostly **R&B dance**, **ballads**, **hip hop**, **vocal jazz**, **alternative rock** and **R&B**; also **bluegrass**, **Spanish pop** and **pop ballads**. Published *So Goes Love* (by Benny Ray), recorded by Charles Brown on Verve (blues); *High Ground* (by G. Boatwright), recorded by Red White & Bluegrass on GMG (bluegrass); and *Doctor of Hearts* (by Williams/Williams/Quarles), recorded by The Chiffons on Warner Bros. (R&B).

Tips: "Be selective in what you send. Be realistic about which artist it suits! Be patient in allowing time to place songs. Be open to writing for films—be interesting lyrically and striking melodically."

N ⊕ ◐ WIPE OUT MUSIC LTD., P.O. Box 1NW, Newcastle-Upon-Tyne NE99 1NW England. Phone: (0191)2326700. Fax: (0191)2666073. E-mail: john@overground.co.uk. Managing Director (punk, indie, garage): John Esplen. Music publisher. Estab. 1995. Staff size: 3. Pays standard royalty.

How to Contact: Submit demo tape by mail. Unsolicited submissions are OK. Prefers cassette or CD with cover letter. SAE and IRC. Reports in 1 week.

Music: Mostly **punk**, **indie** and **garage**; also **lo-fi**, **power pop** and **instrumentals**. Does not want anything mainstream.

Tips: "As we are connected to a radio/TV plugging company, artists must have some potential in those areas."

☑ ◐ WITHOUT PAPERS MUSIC PUBLISHING INC., 7450 A Industrial Park, Lorain OH 44053. (440)282-8008, ext. 204. Fax: (440)282-8822. E-mail: michele@turtleplastics.com. President: Michele Norton. Music publisher. Estab. 1992. Publishes 4 songs/year; publishes 2 new songwriters/year. Staff size: 1. Pays standard royalty.

How to Contact: Write or call first and obtain permission to submit. Prefers cassette with lyric sheet. SASE. Reports in 1 week.

Music: Mostly **rock**, **R&B** and **children's** (with R&B or rock base); also **classical**, **different** and **commercial**. Does not want country. Published "Brown's Blues" (by Stutz Bearcat), recorded by Butch Armstrong on Doubleneck Records (blues).

Tips: "Be patient and be willing to work with us and the song."

◐ WOODRICH PUBLISHING CO. (BMI), P.O. Box 38, Lexington AL 35648. (205)247-3983. President: Woody Richardson. Music publisher, record company (Woodrich Records) and record producer. Estab. 1959. Publishes 20 songs/year; publishes 10 new songwriters/year. Pays standard royalty.

Affiliate(s): Mernee Music (ASCAP), Melstep Music (BMI) and Tennesse Valley Music (SESAC).

How to Contact: Submit demo tape by mail. Unsolicited submissions are OK. Prefers cassette with 2-4 songs and lyric sheet. Prefers studio produced demos. SASE. Reports in 2 weeks.

Music: Mostly **country** and **gospel**; also **bluegrass**, **blues**, **choral**, **church/religious**, **easy listening**, **folk**, **jazz**, **MOR**, **progressive**, **rock**, **soul** and **top 40/pop**. Does not want punk rock or rap. Published *Take Me* (by Bert Trenchard), recorded by Chris Gayle on Woodrich (country); *Wa Copenhagen* (by Johnny Russo) on WIR (jazz); and *You Sure Are Something*, written and recorded by J.R. Thompson on Woodrich (gospel).

Tips: "Use a studio demo if possible. If not, be sure the lyrics are extremely clear. Be sure to include a SASE with *sufficient* return postage. We will not respond otherwise."

N ◐ YORGO MUSIC (BMI), 615 Valley Rd., Upper Montclair NJ 07043. (473)746-2359. President: George Louvis. Affiliated with Warner/Chappell Music Publishing. Music publisher. Estab. 1987. Publishes 5-10 songs/year; publishes 3-5 new songwriters/year. Pays standard royalty.

How to Contact: Submit demo tape by mail. Unsolicited submissions are OK. Prefers cassette with 1-3 songs and lyric or lead sheets. "Specify if you are a writer/artist or just a writer." Does not return material. Reports in 2-3 months.

Music: Mostly **gospel**, **contemporary Christian**, **R&B** and **pop ballads**.

◐ YOUR BEST SONGS PUBLISHING, 1210 Auburn Way N., Suite P171, Auburn WA 98002. General Manager: Craig Markovich. Music publisher. Estab. 1988. Publishes 1-5 songs/year; publishes 1-3 new songwriters/year. Query for royalty terms.

FOR BOOKS ON THE CRAFT AND BUSINESS of songwriting, check out the website for Writer's Digest Books at http://www.writersdigest.com.

How to Contact: Write first and obtain permission to submit. Prefers cassette with 1-3 songs and lyric sheet. "Submit your 1-3 best songs per type of music. Use separate cassettes per music type and indicate music type on each cassette." SASE. Reports in 1-3 months.

Music: Mostly **country**, **rock/blues** and **pop/rock**; also **progressive**, **A/C**, some **heavy metal** and **New Age**. Published "Sea of Dreams," written and recorded by J.C. Mark on Cybervoc Productions (New Age).

Tips: "We just require good lyrics, good melodies and good rhythm in a song. We absolutely do not want music without a decent melodic structure. We do not want lyrics with foul language or lyrics that do not inspire some form of imaginative thought."

☑ ▨ ◑ **ZETTITALIA MUSIC INTERNATIONAL (ASCAP, BMI)**, P.O. Box 8442, Universal City CA 91618. (818)506-8533. Fax: (818)506-8534. E-mail: pplzmi@aol.com. Website: http://www.pplzmi.com. Professional Manager: Cheyenne Phoenix. Music publisher. Estab. 1995. Publishes 40 songs/year; publishes 2 new songwriters/year. Staff size: 2. Hires staff songwriters. Pays standard royalty.

Affiliate(s): Zett One Songs (ASCAP) and Zett Two Music (BMI).

How to Contact: Write or call first and obtain permission to submit. "Include SASE or e-mail." Prefers cassette with 3 songs and lyric sheet. SASE. Reports in 6 weeks.

Film & TV: Places 2 songs in film and 4 songs in TV/year.

Music: Mostly **pop**, **film music**, **country** and **R&B**. Does not want gangster rap or heavy metal. Published *High Dollar Wine* (by B. Heffernan), recorded by J. Sattiewhite on PPL Records (country).

Tips: "In art, be a good student and stay true to your instincts. In business, be thorough, realistic, flexible and straightforward. Finally, The Golden Rule rules."

◑ **ZOMBA MUSIC PUBLISHING (ASCAP, BMI)**, 137-139 W. 25th St., New York NY 10001. (212)824-1744. Fax: (212)242-7462. West Hollywood office: 9000 Sunset Blvd., Suite 300, West Hollywood CA 90069. (310)247-8300. Fax: (310)247-8366. Contact: Neil Portnow; Jeff Blue. Music publisher. Publishes 5,000 songs/year; publishes 25 new songwriters/year.

Affiliate(s): Zomba Enterprises, Inc. (ASCAP); Zomba Songs, Inc. (BMI).

How to Contact: Call first and obtain permission to submit a demo. Prefers cassette or DAT with no more than 4 songs and lyric sheet. SASE.

Music: Mostly **R&B**, **pop** and **rap**; also **rock** and **alternative**. Published ". . . Baby One More Time" (by M. Martin), recorded by Britney Spears on Jive; "Home Alone" (by R. Kelly/K. Price/K. Murray), recorded by R. Kelly featuring Keith Murray on Jive; and "Taking Everything" (by G. Levert/D. Allamby/L. Browder/A. Roberson), recorded by Gerald Levert on EastWest.

Additional Music Publishers

The following companies are also music publishers, but their listings are found in other sections of the book. See the General Index for page numbers, then read the listings for submission information.

Ikon Entertainment
J & V Management
Jag Studio, Ltd.
Jam Down Entertainment, LLC
Jay Jay Publishing & Record Co.
Joey Records
Katz Productions, Matthew
Keeping It Simple and Safe, Inc.
Kingston Records
Kleanza River Canyon Productions
KMA
Known Artist Productions
Kool Breeze Productions
Kuper Personal Management
L.A. Entertainment, Inc.
Lamar Music Marketing
Lamon Records
Lari-Jon Records
Lawrence, Ltd., Ray
Lazy Bones Productions/Recordings, Inc.
Legend Artists Management
Levy Management, Rick
Living Eye Productions Ltd.
Lowell Agency
Lucifer Records, Inc.
Mac-Attack Productions
Magnetic Oblivion Music Co.
Magnum Music Corp. Ltd.
Makeshift Music
Marsupial Management Ltd.
Martin, Pete/Vaam Music Productions
Mathes Productions, David
Mathews, Scott, d/b/a Hit or Myth Productions
May Music/Swift River Productions
Mayfly Record Productions, Ltd.
Mighty Records
Miller & Company, Thomas J.
Modern Tribe Records
Montgomery Management, Gary F.
Monticana Records
MSM Records
Mule Kick Records

Music Quest® Entertainment & Television
New Experience Records
NPO Records, Inc.
OCP Publications
Old School Records
Only New Age Music, Inc.
Orillyon Entertainment
Overstreet Music Companies, Tommy
P. & N. Records
Parker, Patty
Permanent Press Recordings/ Permanent Wave
Philly Breakdown Recording Co.
Pierce, Jim
Plastic Surgery
Platinum Groove Entertainment
Platinum Inc.
Playback Records
Prairie Fire Music Company
Precision Management
Presence Records
RA Records
Rampant Records
R&D Productions
Random Records
RAVE Records, Inc.
Red Dot/Puzzle Records
Regis Records Inc.
Riohcat Music
Rival Records
Robbeye Management Group, Inc.
Robbins Entertainment LLC
Ruf Records
Ruffhouse Records
Safire Records
Sanders Company, Ray
Satellite Music
Sea Cruise Productions, Inc.
Serge Entertainment Group
SM Recording/Hit Records Network
Sound Management Direction
Sound Works Entertainment Productions Inc.

Spiral-Wave
Spotlight Records
Stewart Music Group
Street Records
Strive Music
Stuart Audio Services
Studio Seven
Sweet June Music
T.J. Booker Ltd.
Tandem Records
Tangent Records
Tari, Roger Vincent
3rd Stone Ltd.
Thump Records, Inc.
Time-Out Productions/Bramla Music
TMC Productions
Touchwood Zero Hour Entertainment
Treasure Coast Records
Triplitt Production
Tutta Forza Music
TVT Records
Umpire Entertainment Enterprizes
Universal Music Marketing
Van Pol Management, Hans
Vickers Music Association, Charles
Walbash River and Broken Arrow Productions
Wall Street Music
Warehouse Creek Recording Corp.
Warner Productions, Cheryl K.
Wemus Entertainment
Westpark Music - Records, Production & Publishing
Wilder Artists' Management, Shane
Willett, Tom/Tommark Records
Williams Management, Yvonne
WIR (World International Records)
Wizards & Cecil B
World Wide Management
Worldwide Recordings Limited
X.R.L. Music/Music
Young Country Records/Plain Country Records

Category Index

The Category Index is a good place to begin searching for a market for your songs. Below is an alphabetical list of 20 general music categories. If you write country songs and are looking for a publisher to pitch them, check the Country section in this index. There you will find a list of music publishers interested in hearing country songs. Once you locate the entries for those publishers, read the music subheading *carefully* to determine which companies are most interested in the type of country music you write. Some of the markets in this section do not appear in the Category Index because they have not indicated a specific preference. Most of these said they are interested in "all types" of music. Listings that were very specific, or whose description of the music they're interested in doesn't quite fit into these categories, also do not appear here.

Adult Contemporary (also easy listening, middle of the road, AAA, ballads, etc.)

Alexis
Allegheny Music Works
ALLRS Music Publishing Co.
American Heartstring Publishing
Antelope Publishing Inc.
Baitstring Music
Bal & Bal Music Publishing Co.
Barkin' Foe the Master's Bone
Barren Wood Publishing
Bay Ridge Publishing Co.
Betty Jane/Josie Jane Music Publishers
Big Fish Music Publishing Group
BME Publishing
Bradley Music, Allan
Buried Treasure Music
California Country Music
Camex Music
Cherri/Holly Music
Clevère Musikverlag, R.D.
Cliffside Music Inc.
CMI Music Group, Inc.
Duane Music, Inc.
Emstone, Inc. Music Publishing
Gary Music, Alan
Green One Music
G-String Publishing
Hammel Associates, Inc., R.L.
Hansen Music Group, Stevie Ray
Happy Melody
Hickory Valley Music
High-Minded Moma Publishing & Productions
Hitsburgh Music Co.
Inside Records/OK Songs
Ja/Nein Musikverlag GmbH
Kansa Records Corporation
Kaupps & Robert Publishing Co.
Kozkeeozko Music
Largo Music Publishing
Lineage Publishing Co.
Mento Music Group
Montina Music
Music in the Right Keys Publishing Company
New Rap Jam Publishing, A
Omni 2000, Inc.
Otto Publishing Co.
Pegasus Music
Prescription Company
Publishing Central
R.J. Music
Riverhawk Music
Rockford Music Co.
Segal's Publications
Silicon Music Publishing Co.
Tedesco Music Co., Dale
Texas Cherokee Music
Whitewing Music
Woodrich Publishing Co.
Your Best Songs Publishing

Alternative (also modern rock, punk, college rock, new wave, hardcore, new music, industrial, ska, indie rock, garage, etc.)

Abalone Publishing
Alan Music, Marcus
Alias John Henry Tunes
Bay Ridge Publishing Co.
Camex Music
Clear Pond Music
East Coast Music Publishing
Flea Circus Music
Inhabitants Music Group
Josena Music
Juke Music
Lake Transfer Productions & Music
Largo Music Publishing
Moody Music Group, Inc.
Pas Mal Publishing Sarl
Planet Dallas Recording Studios
Prejippie Music Group
Prescription Company
QUARK, Inc.
Rock N Metal Music Publishing Co.

Starstruck Writers Group
Unknown Source Music
Virginia Borden Rhythms
Winston & Hoffman House Music Publishers
Wipe Out Music Ltd.
Zomba Music Publishing

Blues
Alan Music, Marcus
Alexis
Bagatelle Music Publishing Co.
Bal & Bal Music Publishing Co.
Bay Ridge Publishing Co.
Brian Song Music Corp.
BSW Records
Christopher Publishing, Sonny
CMI Music Group, Inc.
Duane Music, Inc.
Earthscream Music Publishing Co.
ESI Music Group
Frozen Inca Music
Hansen Music Group, Stevie Ray
Ja/Nein Musikverlag GmbH
Magic Message Music
Mighty Blue Music Machine, The
Montina Music
Moon June Music
Prescription Company
R.J. Music
Silicon Music Publishing Co.
Slanted Circle Music
Stellar Music Industries
Texas Cherokee Music
Tower Music Group
Whitewing Music
Woodrich Publishing Co.

Children's
Berandol Music Ltd.
Branch Group Music
Brown & Associates Inc., J. Aaron
Flying Red Horse Publishing
Lollipop Farm Entertainment
Lyrick Studios
Moody Music Group, Inc.
Omni 2000, Inc.
Prescription Company
Ren Zone Music
Rhythms Productions
Segal's Publications
Simply Grand Music, Inc.
Without Papers Music Publishing Inc.

Classical (also opera, chamber music, serious music, choral, etc.)
Clevère Musikverlag, R.D.
Jae Music, Jana
Without Papers Music Publishing Inc.

Country (also western, C&W, bluegrass, cowboy songs, western swing, honky-tonk, etc.)
Abalone Publishing
Aim High Music Company
Alan Music, Marcus
Alexis
Alias John Henry Tunes
All Rock Music
Allegheny Music Works
AlliSongs Inc.
ALLRS Music Publishing Co.
American Heartstring Publishing
ARAS Music
Bagatelle Music Publishing Co.
Baitstring Music
Bal & Bal Music Publishing Co.
Balmur Entertainment
Barkin' Foe the Master's Bone
Barren Wood Publishing
Bay Ridge Publishing Co.
Betty Jane/Josie Jane Music Publishers
Big Fish Music Publishing Group
Bixio Music Group/IDM Ventures, Ltd.
Black Rose Productions
Black Stallion Country Publishing
Bradley Music, Allan
Branson Country Music Publishing
Brewster Songs, Kitty
Brian Song Music Corp.
Brown & Associates Inc., J. Aaron
BSW Records
Bugle Publishing Group
Buried Treasure Music
California Country Music
Cash Productions, Inc.
Cherri/Holly Music
Christopher Publishing, Sonny
Cimirron Music
Clear Pond Music
Clearwind Publishing
Clevère Musikverlag, R.D.
CMI Music Group, Inc.
Co-Creations Music Publishing
Coffee and Cream Publishing Company
Cornelius Companies, The
Country Breeze Music
Country Rainbow Music
Country Showcase America
Cupit Music
Dapmor Publishing
De Miles Music Company, The Edward
Del Camino Music Publishing
Delev Music Company
Denny Music Group
Doss Music, Buster
Dream Seekers Publishing
Duane Music, Inc.

Whitewing Music
Wilcom Publishing
Winston & Hoffman House Music Publishers
Woodrich Publishing Co.
Your Best Songs Publishing
Zettitalia Music International

Dance (also house, hi-NRG, disco, club, rave, techno, trip-hop, trance, etc.)
Abalone Publishing
Alexis
Audio Music Publishers
Better Than Sex Music
Black Rose Productions
BME Publishing
Brewster Songs, Kitty
Brothers, The
CAPP Company
Clevère Musikverlag, R.D.
Cliffside Music Inc.
Coffee and Cream Publishing Company
Dagene Music
De Miles Music Company, The Edward
Delev Music Company
Drive Music, Inc.
Duane Music, Inc.
East Coast Music Publishing
Edition Rossori
Emstone, Inc. Music Publishing
Fresh Entertainment
Gary Music, Alan
G-String Publishing
Happy Melody
Hit & Run Music Publishing Inc.
Inside Records/OK Songs
Island Culture Music Publishers
Kozkeeozko Music
Lake Transfer Productions & Music
Lilly Music Publishing
M & T Waldoch Publishing, Inc.
Makers Mark Gold
Mighty Blue Music Machine, The
Montina Music
Omni 2000, Inc.
Prejippie Music Group
Prescription Company
Publishing Central
QUARK, Inc.
Rockford Music Co.
Shu'Baby Montez Music
Siskatune Music Publishing Co.
Still Working Music Group
Stuart Music Co., Jeb
Succes
Sunsongs Music
T.C. Productions/Etude Publishing Co.
Tedesco Music Co., Dale
Trusty Publications

Valet Publishing Co.
Wemar Music Corp.
Winston & Hoffman House Music Publishers

Folk (also acoustic, Celtic, etc.)
Alexis
Bay Ridge Publishing Co.
Cimirron Music
Clevère Musikverlag, R.D.
Earitating Music Publishing
First Time Music (Publishing) U.K.
Heupferd Musikverlag GmbH
Inhabitants Music Group
Jerjoy Music
Little Miller Music Co.
Montina Music
Moody Music Group, Inc.
Omni 2000, Inc.
Prescription Company
Rockford Music Co.
Rustron Music Publishers
Third Wave Productions Limited
Woodrich Publishing Co.

Instrumental (also background music, musical scores, etc.)
Alpha Music Inc.
Berandol Music Ltd.
Big Fish Music Publishing Group
Bowman Productions & W. David Music, David
CTV Music (Great Britain)
Happy Melody
Jae Music, Jana
JPMC Music Inc.
Mento Music Group
Moody Music Group, Inc.
Rustron Music Publishers
Succes
Tedesco Music Co., Dale
Wipe Out Music Ltd.

Jazz (also fusion, bebop, swing, etc.)
Alexander Sr., Music
Alexis
Antelope Publishing Inc.
ARAS Music
Bal & Bal Music Publishing Co.
Barkin' Foe the Master's Bone
Bay Ridge Publishing Co.
Black Rose Productions
Brewster Songs, Kitty
CAPP Company
CMI Music Group, Inc.
Elect Music Publishing Company
Heupferd Musikverlag GmbH
His Power Productions and Publishing
Inhabitants Music Group
Jae Music, Jana
JPMC Music Inc.

Lollipop Farm Entertainment
Master Source
McConkey Artists Agency Music Publishing
Mellow House Music
Mighty Blue Music Machine, The
Montina Music
Moody Music Group, Inc.
Newcreature Music
NSP Music Publishing Inc.
Old Slowpoke Music
Omni 2000, Inc.
Platinum Boulevard Publishing
Prescription Company
Ridge Music Corp.
Rockford Music Co.
Simply Grand Music, Inc.
Slanted Circle Music
Stellar Music Industries
Stuart Music Co., Jeb
Tedesco Music Co., Dale
Trusty Publications
Winston & Hoffman House Music Publishers
Woodrich Publishing Co.

Latin (also Spanish, salsa, Cuban, conga, Brazilian, cumbia, rancheras, Mexican, merengue, Tejano, Tex Mex, etc.)
Alexis
Amen, Inc.
Del Camino Music Publishing
Inside Records/OK Songs
Johnson Music, Little Richie
Josena Music
Supreme Enterprises Int'l Corp.

Metal (also thrash, grindcore, heavy metal, etc.)
Bay Ridge Publishing Co.
M & T Waldoch Publishing, Inc.
Pas Mal Publishing Sarl
Sound Cellar Music
Your Best Songs Publishing

New Age (also ambient)
CAPP Company
Heupferd Musikverlag GmbH
High-Minded Moma Publishing & Productions
Little Miller Music Co.
Moody Music Group, Inc.
Myko Music
Mymit Music Productions, Chuck
Platinum Boulevard Publishing
Rustron Music Publishers
Sinus Musik Produktion, Ulli Weigel
Southern Most Publishing Company
Tiki Enterprises, Inc.
Your Best Songs Publishing

Novelty (also comedy, humor, etc.)
Big Fish Music Publishing Group
Branch Group Music
Green One Music
Lollipop Farm Entertainment
Magic Message Music
Moon June Music
Riverhawk Music
Schmerdley Music
Sun Star Songs

Pop (also top 40, top 100, popular, chart hits, etc.)
Abalone Publishing
Alexis
Allegheny Music Works
AlliSongs Inc.
ALLRS Music Publishing Co.
American Heartstring Publishing
Audio Music Publishers
Baitstring Music
Bal & Bal Music Publishing Co.
Balmur Entertainment
Barkin' Foe the Master's Bone
Bay Ridge Publishing Co.
Berandol Music Ltd.
Bernard Enterprises, Inc., Hal
Better Than Sex Music
Betty Jane/Josie Jane Music Publishers
Big Fish Music Publishing Group
Black Rose Productions
BME Publishing
Bradley Music, Allan
Brewster Songs, Kitty
Brothers, The
Brown & Associates Inc., J. Aaron
Bugle Publishing Group
Buried Treasure Music
California Country Music
Camex Music
CAPP Company
Cash Productions, Inc.
Cherri/Holly Music
Clear Pond Music
Clearwind Publishing
Clevère Musikverlag, R.D.
Cliffside Music Inc.
Co-Creations Music Publishing
Coffee and Cream Publishing Company
Cornelius Companies, The
Dagene Music
Dapmor Publishing
De Miles Music Company, The Edward
Del Camino Music Publishing
Delev Music Company
Demi Monde Records & Publishing Ltd.
Dream Seekers Publishing
Drive Music, Inc.

Duane Music, Inc.
Earthscream Music Publishing Co.
East Coast Music Publishing
Edition Rossori
Emandell Tunes
EMF Productions
Emstone, Inc. Music Publishing
ESI Music Group
Ever-Open-Eye Music
First Time Music (Publishing) U.K.
Fresh Entertainment
Fro's Music Publishing
Gary Music, Alan
Hammel Associates, Inc., R.L.
Hansen Music Group, Stevie Ray
Happy Melody
High-Minded Moma Publishing & Productions
Hit & Run Music Publishing Inc.
Inside Records/OK Songs
Interplanetary Music
Jaelius Enterprises
Ja/Nein Musikverlag GmbH
Jasper Stone Music/JSM Songs
Jolson Black & White Music, Al
Josena Music
JPMC Music Inc.
Juke Music
Kaupps & Robert Publishing Co.
Kozkeeozko Music
Lake Transfer Productions & Music
Lindsay Publishing, Doris
Lineage Publishing Co.
M & T Waldoch Publishing, Inc.
Makers Mark Gold
May Peace Be Upon You Music
Mellow House Music
Melody Hills Ranch Publishing Co.
Mento Music Group
Mighty Blue Music Machine, The
Montina Music
Moon June Music
Music Room Publishing Group, The
Myko Music
Mymit Music Productions, Chuck
New Rap Jam Publishing, A
Newcreature Music
Omni 2000, Inc.
Ontrax Companies
Orchid Publishing
PeerMusic
Pegasus Music
Prescription Company
Publishing Central
QUARK, Inc.
R.J. Music
Raving Cleric Music Publishing/Euro Export Entertainment
Ridge Music Corp.

Rocker Music/Happy Man Music
Rockford Music Co.
Rustron Music Publishers
Sabteca Music Co.
Saddlestone Publishing
Sci-Fi Music
Scott Music Group, Tim
SDM
Segal's Publications
Shaolin Music
Shu'Baby Montez Music
Silver Blue Music/Oceans Blue Music
Silver Thunder Music Group
Simply Grand Music, Inc.
Sinus Musik Produktion, Ulli Weigel
Solid Discs
Sound Cellar Music
Standard Music Publishing
Stellar Music Industries
Stevens Music, Ray
Still Working Music Group
Stuart Music Co., Jeb
Succes
Sunsongs Music
T.C. Productions/Etude Publishing Co.
Tedesco Music Co., Dale
Texas Cherokee Music
Third Wave Productions Limited
Tiki Enterprises, Inc.
Tower Music Group
Transamerika Musikverlag KG
Twin Towers Publishing Co.
Ultimate Peak Music
Vaam Music Group
Valet Publishing Co.
Virginia Borden Rhythms
Warner/Chappell Music Canada Ltd.
Wemar Music Corp.
Wengert, Berthold (Musikverlag)
Westwood Music Group
Wilcom Publishing
Winston & Hoffman House Music Publishers
Wipe Out Music Ltd.
Woodrich Publishing Co.
Yorgo Music
Your Best Songs Publishing
Zettitalia Music International
Zomba Music Publishing

R&B (also soul, black, urban, etc.)

Alan Music, Marcus
Alexander Sr., Music
Alexis
Allegheny Music Works
ALLRS Music Publishing Co.
American Heartstring Publishing
Audio Music Publishers
Baitstring Music

Rap (also hip-hop, bass, etc.)
Audio Music Publishers
Barkin' Foe the Master's Bone
Bay Ridge Publishing Co.
Better Than Sex Music
Black Rose Productions
BME Publishing
Clevère Musikverlag, R.D.
Dagene Music
Dapmor Publishing
East Coast Music Publishing
Elect Music Publishing Company
Fresh Entertainment
Inhabitants Music Group
Interplanetary Music
Jasper Stone Music/JSM Songs
Lake Transfer Productions & Music
Largo Music Publishing
Majestic Control
Makers Mark Gold
Master Source
May Peace Be Upon You Music
Mellow House Music
New Rap Jam Publishing, A
Roadshow Music Corp.
Shu'Baby Montez Music
Silver Blue Music/Oceans Blue Music
Solid Discs
Stellar Music Industries
Stuart Music Co., Jeb
Unknown Source Music
Zomba Music Publishing

Religious (also gospel, sacred, Christian, church, hymns, praise, inspirational, worship, etc.)
Aim High Music Company
Alan Music, Marcus
Alexander Sr., Music
Alexis
Allegheny Music Works
ALLRS Music Publishing Co.
Amen, Inc.
American Heartstring Publishing
ARAS Music
Audio Music Publishers
Bagatelle Music Publishing Co.
Bal & Bal Music Publishing Co.
Barkin' Foe the Master's Bone
Barren Wood Publishing
Bay Ridge Publishing Co.
Betty Jane/Josie Jane Music Publishers
Big Fish Music Publishing Group
Bradley Music, Allan
Brian Song Music Corp.
Brightly Music Publishing
California Country Music
Cash Productions, Inc.

Cliffside Music Inc.
Co-Creations Music Publishing
Coffee and Cream Publishing Company
Corelli's Music Box
Cornelius Companies, The
Country Breeze Music
Denny Music Group
Emandell Tunes
EMF Productions
Emstone, Inc. Music Publishing
Ever-Open-Eye Music
First Time Music (Publishing) U.K.
Foster Music Company, Mark
Fro's Music Publishing
Hammel Associates, Inc., R.L.
Hansen Music Group, Stevie Ray
His Power Productions and Publishing
Hitsburgh Music Co.
Holy Spirit Music
Jaelius Enterprises
Jerjoy Music
Josena Music
JPMC Music Inc.
Juke Music
Kansa Records Corporation
Kaupps & Robert Publishing Co.
Kaylee Music Group, Karen
Lari-Jon Publishing
Leigh Music, Trixie
Lindsay Publishing, Doris
Makers Mark Gold
May Peace Be Upon You Music
McCoy Music, Jim
McGibony Publishing
Mellow House Music
Mighty Blue Music Machine, The
Montina Music
Moody Music Group, Inc.
Music in the Right Keys Publishing Company
New Rap Jam Publishing, A
Newcreature Music
NSP Music Publishing Inc.
Omni 2000, Inc.
Orchid Publishing
Otto Publishing Co.
Peters Music, Justin
Pritchett Publications
Publishing Central
Roadshow Music Corp.
Rocker Music/Happy Man Music
Saddlestone Publishing
Scott Music Group, Tim
Shawnee Press, Inc.
Southern Most Publishing Company
Starbound Publishing Co.
Stellar Music Industries
Stuart Music Co., Jeb
Sun Star Songs

Texas Cherokee Music
Tiki Enterprises, Inc.
Tower Music Group
Trusty Publications
Vokes Music Publishing
Woodrich Publishing Co.
Yorgo Music

Rock (also rockabilly, AOR, rock 'n' roll, etc.)
Abalone Publishing
Alias John Henry Tunes
All Rock Music
Bal & Bal Music Publishing Co.
Balmur Entertainment
Bay Ridge Publishing Co.
Bernard Enterprises, Inc., Hal
Better Than Sex Music
Bixio Music Group/IDM Ventures, Ltd.
Black Rose Productions
BME Publishing
Branch Group Music
Brewster Songs, Kitty
BSW Records
Bugle Publishing Group
California Country Music
Camex Music
Cash Productions, Inc.
Cherri/Holly Music
Christopher Publishing, Sonny
Clear Pond Music
Clearwind Publishing
Clevère Musikverlag, R.D.
CMI Music Group, Inc.
Country Breeze Music
De Miles Music Company, The Edward
Del Camino Music Publishing
Demi Monde Records & Publishing Ltd.
Doss Music, Buster
Drive Music, Inc.
Duane Music, Inc.
Earitating Music Publishing
Earthscream Music Publishing Co.
East Coast Music Publishing
Edition Rossori
Elect Music Publishing Company
EMF Productions
ESI Music Group
Famous Music Publishing Companies
First Time Music (Publishing) U.K.
Flea Circus Music
Frozen Inca Music
Gary Music, Alan
Green One Music
G-String Publishing
Hammel Associates, Inc., R.L.
Hansen Music Group, Stevie Ray
Heupferd Musikverlag GmbH
High-Minded Moma Publishing & Productions

Hit & Run Music Publishing Inc.
Inhabitants Music Group
Ja/Nein Musikverlag GmbH
Jasper Stone Music/JSM Songs
Jolson Black & White Music, Al
Juke Music
Kaupps & Robert Publishing Co.
Largo Music Publishing
Lari-Jon Publishing
Lilly Music Publishing
Lollipop Farm Entertainment
M & T Waldoch Publishing, Inc.
McConkey Artists Agency Music Publishing
McCoy Music, Jim
Melody Hills Ranch Publishing Co.
Mighty Blue Music Machine, The
Montina Music
Moody Music Group, Inc.
Music Room Publishing Group, The
Myko Music
Mymit Music Productions, Chuck
New Rap Jam Publishing, A
Newcreature Music
Old Slowpoke Music
Ontrax Companies
PeerMusic
Platinum Boulevard Publishing
Portage Music
Prejippie Music Group
Prescription Company
Pritchett Publications
Publishing Central
R.J. Music
Raving Cleric Music Publishing/Euro Export Enter-
    tainment
Ridge Music Corp.
Roadshow Music Corp.
Rock N Metal Music Publishing Co.
Rocker Music/Happy Man Music
Rockford Music Co.
Saddlestone Publishing
Sci-Fi Music
Scott Music Group, Tim
SDM
Segal's Publications
Shaolin Music
Silicon Music Publishing Co.
Simply Grand Music, Inc.
Sinus Musik Produktion, Ulli Weigel
Solid Discs
Sound Cellar Music
Southern Most Publishing Company
Standard Music Publishing
Stellar Music Industries
Still Working Music Group
Stuart Music Co., Jeb
Succes
Sunsongs Music

Tedesco Music Co., Dale
Third Wave Productions Limited
Tiki Enterprises, Inc.
Transamerika Musikverlag KG
Trusty Publications
Twin Towers Publishing Co.
Ultimate Peak Music
Valet Publishing Co.
Warner/Chappell Music Canada Ltd.
Westwood Music Group
Wilcom Publishing
Without Papers Music Publishing Inc.
Woodrich Publishing Co.
Your Best Songs Publishing
Zomba Music Publishing

World Music (also reggae, ethnic, calypso, international, world beat, etc.)
Aim High Music Company
Bay Ridge Publishing Co.
Branch Group Music
Brightly Music Publishing
Co-Creations Music Publishing
Elect Music Publishing Company
Heupferd Musikverlag GmbH
Inside Records/OK Songs
Island Culture Music Publishers
Little Miller Music Co.
Master Source
Supreme Enterprises Int'l Corp.
Tedesco Music Co., Dale
Transamerika Musikverlag KG

Record Companies

Record companies record and release records, cassettes and CDs—the tangible products of the music industry. They sign artists to recording contracts, decide what songs those artists will record, and determine which songs to release. They are also responsible for providing recording facilities, securing producers and musicians, and overseeing the manufacture, distribution and promotion of new releases.

MAJOR LABELS & INDEPENDENT LABELS

Major labels and independent labels—what's the difference between the two? Major labels are defined as those record companies distributed by one of the "Big 5" distribution companies: BMG Distribution, EMI Music Distribution (EMD), Sony Music Distribution, Warner/Elektra/Atlantic Distribution (WEA) and Universal Music and Video Distribution (UMVD). (UMVD is the result of the 1998 acquisition of PolyGram Distribution by Universal parent Seagram, making UMVD the world's largest record company.) Distribution companies are wholesalers that sell records to retail outlets. If a label is distributed by one of these major companies, you can be assured that any release coming out on that label has a large distribution network working behind it. It will most likely be sent to most major retail stores in the United States. Independent labels go through smaller distribution companies to distribute their product. They usually don't have the ability to deliver records in massive quantities as the major distributors do. However, that doesn't mean independent labels aren't able to have hit records just like their major counterparts. A record label's distributors are found in the listings after the **Distributed by** heading.

Many of the companies listed in this section are independent labels. They are usually the most receptive to receiving material from new artists. Major labels spend more money than most other segments of the music industry; the music publisher, for instance, pays only for items such as salaries and the costs of making demos. Record companies, at great financial risk, pay for many more services, including production, manufacturing and promotion. Therefore, they must be very selective when signing new talent. Also, the continuing fear of copyright infringement suits has closed avenues to getting new material heard by the majors. Most don't listen to unsolicited submissions, period. Only songs recommended by attorneys, managers and producers who record company employees trust and respect are being heard by A&R people at major labels (companies with a referral policy have a ⊘ preceding their listing). But that doesn't mean all major labels are closed to new artists. Several major labels listed in this year's *Songwriter's Market*, including Polydor Records, Relativity Records, TVT Records, Ruffhouse Records and London Records, accept unsolicited submissions. Following submission policies carefully and presenting a professional package could get you an attentive audience at a major label.

But the competition is fierce at the majors, so you shouldn't overlook independent labels. Since they're located all over the country, indie labels are easier to contact and can be important in building a local base of support for your music (consult the Geographic Index at the back of the book to find out which companies are located near you). Independent labels usually concentrate on a specific type of music, which will help you target those companies your submissions should be sent to. And since the staff at an indie label is smaller, there are fewer channels to go through to get your music heard by the decision makers in the company.

The Case for Independents

If you're interested in getting a major label deal, it makes sense to look to independent record labels to get your start. Independent labels are seen by many as a stepping stone to a major recording contract. Very few artists are signed to a major label at the start of their careers; usually, they've had a few independent releases that helped build their reputation in the industry. Major labels watch independent labels closely to locate up-and-coming bands and new trends. In the current economic atmosphere at major labels—with extremely high overhead costs for developing new bands and the fact that only 10% of acts on major labels actually make any profit—they're not willing to risk everything on an unknown act. Most major labels won't even consider signing a new act that hasn't had some indie success.

But independents aren't just farming grounds for future major label acts; many bands have long term relationships with indies, and prefer it that way. While they may not be able to provide the extensive distribution and promotion that a major label can (though there are exceptions), indie labels can help an artist become a regional success, and may even help the performer to see a profit as well. With the lower overhead and smaller production costs an independent label operates on, it's much easier to "succeed" on an indie label than on a major.

HOW RECORD COMPANIES WORK

Independent record labels can run on a small staff, with only a handful of people running the day-to-day business. Major record labels are more likely to be divided into the following departments: A&R, sales, marketing, promotion, product management, artist development, production, finance, business/legal and international.

- The *A&R department* is staffed with A&R representatives (reps) who search out new talent. They go out and see new bands, listen to demo tapes, and decide which artists to sign. They also look for new material for already signed acts, match producers with artists and oversee recording projects. Once an artist is signed by an A&R rep and a record is recorded, the rest of the departments at the company come into play.
- The *sales department* is responsible for getting a record into stores. They make sure record stores and other outlets receive enough copies of a record to meet consumer demand.
- The *marketing department* is in charge of publicity, advertising in magazines and other media, promotional videos, album cover artwork, in-store displays, and any other means of getting the name and image of an artist to the public.
- The *promotion department*'s main objective is to get songs from a new album played on the radio. They work with radio programmers to make sure a product gets airplay.
- The *product management department* is the ringmaster of the sales, marketing and promotion departments, assuring that they're all going in the same direction when promoting a new release.
- The *artist development department* is responsible for taking care of things while an artist is on tour, such as setting up promotional opportunities in cities where an act is performing.
- The *production department* handles the actual manufacturing and pressing of the record and makes sure it gets shipped to distributors in a timely manner.
- People in the *finance department* compute and distribute royalties, as well as keep track of expenses and income at the company.
- The *business/legal department* takes care of contracts, not only between the record company and artists but with foreign distributors, record clubs, etc.
- And finally, the *international department* is responsible for working with international companies for the release of records in other countries.

LOCATING A RECORD LABEL

With the abundance of record labels out there, how do you go about finding one that's right for the music you create? First, it helps to know exactly what kind of music a record label releases. Become familiar with the records a company has released, and see if they fit in with what you're doing. Each listing in this section details the type of music a particular record company is interested in releasing. You will want to refer to the Category Index, located at the end of this section, to help you find those companies most receptive to the type of music you write. You should only approach companies open to your level of experience (see the Openness to Submissions sidebar on page 8). Visiting a company's website can also provide valuable information about a company's philosophy, the artists on the label and the music they work with. Be sure to read the article Is This the Right Company for Me? on page 39.

Networking

Recommendations by key music industry people are an important part of making contacts with record companies. Songwriters must remember that talent alone does not guarantee success in the music business. You must be recognized through contacts, and the only way to make contacts is through networking. Networking is the process of building an interconnecting web of acquaintances within the music business. The more industry people you meet, the larger your contact base becomes, and the better are your chances of meeting someone with the clout to get your demo into the hands of the right people. If you want to get your music heard by key A&R representatives, networking is imperative.

Networking opportunities can be found anywhere industry people gather. A good place to meet key industry people is at regional and national music conferences and workshops. There are many held all over the country for all types of music (see the Workshops and Conferences section for more information). You should try to attend at least one or two of these events each year; it's a great way to increase the number and quality of your music industry contacts.

Creating a buzz

Another good way to attract A&R people is to make a name for yourself as an artist. By starting your career on a local level and building it from there, you can start to cultivate a following and prove to labels that you can be a success. A&R people figure if an act can be successful locally, there's a good chance they could be successful nationally. Start getting booked at local clubs, and start a mailing list of fans and local media. Once you gain some success on a local level, branch out. All this attention you're slowly gathering, this "buzz" you're generating, will not only get to your fans but to influential people in the music industry as well.

For More Information
For more instructional information on the listings in this book, including explanations of symbols (N ✓ Y ✿ ▦ ○ ⦶ ◖ ⦸), read the article How to Use *Songwriter's Market* to Get Your Songs Heard on page 5.

SUBMITTING TO RECORD COMPANIES

When submitting to a record company, major or independent, a professional attitude is imperative. Be specific about what you are submitting and what your goals are. If you are strictly a songwriter and the label carries a band you believe would properly present your song, state that in your cover letter. If you are an artist looking for a contract, showcase your strong points as a performer. Whatever your goals are, follow submission guidelines closely, be as neat as possible and include a top-notch demo. If you need more information concerning a company's requirements, write or call for more details. (For more information on submitting your material, see the article Getting Started on page 11, What Music Professionals Look for in a Demo sidebar on page 15, Quiz: Are You Professional? on page 19, and the article How to Make Your Submission Stand Out on page 35.)

Additional Record Companies

There are **MORE RECORD COMPANIES** located in other sections of the book! On page 218 use the list of Additional Record Companies to find listings within other sections who are also record companies.

RECORD COMPANY CONTRACTS

Once you've found a record company that is interested in your work, the next step is signing a contract. Independent label contracts are usually not as long and complicated as major label ones, but they are still binding, legal contracts. Make sure the terms are in the best interest of both you and the label. Avoid anything in your contract that you feel is too restrictive. It's important to have your contract reviewed by a competent entertainment lawyer. A basic recording contract can run from 40-100 pages, and you need a lawyer to help you understand it. A lawyer will also be essential in helping you negotiate a deal that is in your best interest.

Recording contracts cover many areas, and just a few of the things you will be asked to consider will be: What royalty rate is the record label willing to pay you? What kind of advance are they offering? How many records will the company commit to? Will they offer tour support? Will they provide a budget for video? What sort of a recording budget are they offering? Are they asking you to give up any publishing rights? Are they offering you a publishing advance? These are only a few of the complex issues raised by a recording contract, so it's vital to have an entertainment lawyer at your side as you negotiate.

N ☐ **A.P.I. RECORDS**, P.O. Box 7041, Watchung NJ 07061-0741. (908)753-1601. Fax: (908)753-3724. E-mail: apirecord@aol.com. Executive Vice President: Meg Poltorak. Vice President: Kevin Ferd. Record company, music publisher (Humbletunes, Inc.) and record producer (August Productions, Inc.). Estab. 1989. Staff size: 5. Releases 5 singles, 6 LPs and 6 CDs/year. Pays negotiable royalty to artists on contract; statutory rate to publisher per song on record.
How to Contact: Submit demo tape by mail. Unsolicited submissions are OK. Prefers cassette, CD, DAT or VHS videocassette with 3 songs and lyric sheet. Does not return material. Reports in 3-6 months if interested.
Music: Mostly **pop/rock**, **jazz** and **classical**. Released *Playground*, written and recorded by Tom Gavornik (jazz); *Historical St. Thomas Organ Series*, written and recorded by Duruflé (classical); and *On the Radio*, written and recorded by Tim Keyes (pop), all on API.
Tips: "Looking for well-crafted material. Packaging and production are not important."

☑ **A&M RECORDS**, 1416 N. LaBrea, Hollywood CA 90028. (213)469-2411. Fax: (213)856-7152. Website: http://www.amrecords.com. New York office: 825 Eighth Ave., New York NY 10019. (212)333-8000. Fax: (212)333-1301. Labels include Polydor Records. Record company.
● As a result of the PolyGram and Universal merger, A&M Records has been folded into Interscope Records. At press time the above contact information was still correct.

☐ **ABL RECORDS**, 484 S. Grand, Orange CA 92866. Website: http://allanlicht.ontheweb.com. Owner: Allan Licht. Record company and music publisher (Allan Bradley Music/BMI and Holly Ellen Music/ASCAP). Estab. 1993. Staff size: 2. Releases 10 singles/year. Pays 50% royalty to artists on contract; statutory rate to publisher per song on record.
How to Contact: Submit demo tape by mail. Unsolicited submissions are OK. Prefers cassette with 3

songs and lyric sheet. Does not return material. Reports in 1 month.

Music: Mostly **A/C**, **pop** and **R&B**; also **country** and **Christian contemporary**. Released *She's Not You*, written and recorded by Sam Morrison (country); *Better Things Than you* (by Marilyn Oakley), recorded by Donna West (country); and *Love 101*, written and recorded by Jill J. Switzer (pop/jazz), all on ABL Records. Other artists include Tracy Todd and Michael Cavanaugh.

Tips: "Submit top-notch material with great demos."

 AFTERSCHOOL RECORDS, INC., P.O. Box 14157, Detroit MI 48214. (313)894-8855. Director/ Producer: Genesis Act, MCP. Record company, music publisher (Afterschool Publishing Co., Inc.) and record producer (Feel Production, MCP). Estab. 1969. Releases 6 singles, 1 LP and a variable number of CDs/year. Pays negotiable royalty to artists on contract; statutory rate to publisher per song on record.

Distributed by: Afterschool, Fermata, Cancopy, CMRAA, NCB, AMRA, MCPS and BMG.

How to Contact: Submit demo tape by mail. Unsolicited submissions are OK. Prefers cassette, CD, DAT or videocassette with 1 song and lyric and lead sheets. SASE. Reports in 1 month.

Music: Mostly **pop**, **country** and **folk**; also **jazz**. Artists include P.M. Dawn and 2 Hyped Brothers and a Dog.

 THE AIRPLAY LABEL, P.O. Box 851, Asbury Park NJ 07712. Phone/fax: (732)681-0623. E-mail: airplaypete@hotmail.com. Website: http://www.evelynforever.com. President A&R: Peter P. Mantas. Vice President/Head of A&R: Jefferson Powers. Record company. Estab. 1995. Staff size: 3. Releases 6 singles, 3 LPs, 2 EPs and 4 CDs/year. Pays 20% royalty to artists on contract; statutory rate to publisher per song on record.

Distributed by: Music Source, Notlame.com and Carrot Top.

• This label received the Asbury Music Awards' 1997-98 Top Release.

How to Contact: Write first and obtain permission to submit. Prefers cassette, CD or videocassette. Does not return material. Reports in 1 month.

Music: Mostly **pop**, **acid jazz** and **jazz**; also **emo-core**. Released *Nightclub Jitters*, written and recorded by Evelyn Forever (pop); *Patrick Murphy*, written and recorded by Patrick Murphy (delta blues); and *12 Days* (by Adam Taylor), recorded by 12 Days (heavy), all on Airplay.

Tips: "Hard work pays off."

 AIRTRAX, 273 Chippewa Dr., Columbia SC 29210-6508. (803)750-5391. A&R Manager: Jackson Love. A&R: T.T. Morelli. Labels include Amethyst Records. Record company and promoter. Estab. 1985. Staff size: 3. Pays 5-15% royalty to artists on contract; statutory rate to publisher per song on record.

Distributed by: Plug Productions and International Music Media.

• AirTrax is known for test marketing and developing new talent around the world.

How to Contact: Submit demo by mail. Unsolicited submissions are OK. Prefers cassette, CD, DAT and videocassette with any number of songs. "We only return submission if requested in writing and accompanied by the proper postage—not one stamp!" Reports in 3-5 weeks.

Music: Mostly **pop**, **rock** and **alternative**; also **rap/R&B**, **gospel** and **country**. Released *Undercover*, written and recorded by Barry Duke (R&B); *Panic* (by Deloris Paradise), recorded by Blanche's Radio (pop); and *The Future* (by Gary Weisberg), recorded by Slither (rave/dance), all on Airtrax. Other artists include Chief ODY, Savasan, Toni Monet, Bodyshop, Ted Neil, Political Asylum and District 13.

Tips: "Don't expect anyone to hand you a hit, it's just not going to happen. Cooperate. Don't try to play like a big-time wheeler-dealer. Start somewhere with someone and be realistic. Being 'serious' and 'good' is not always enough. Be as helpful as possible."

 ALBATROSS RECORDS, P.O. Box 540102, Houston TX 77254-0102. (713)521-2616. E-mail: rpds2405@aol.com. Website: http://users.aol.com/rpds2405/Albatross.html. A&R: Jeff Troncoso. Labels include R&D Productions and Fanatic Records. Record company. Estab. 1990. Staff size: 4. Releases 20 singles, 10 LPs and 10 CDs/year. Pays negotiable royalty to artists on contract; statutory rate to publisher per song on record.

**FOR EXPLANATIONS OF THESE SYMBOLS,
SEE THE INSIDE FRONT AND BACK COVERS OF THIS BOOK.**

Distributed by: Select-O-Hits and Bayside.
How to Contact: Submit demo tape by mail. Unsolicited submissions are OK. Prefers cassette or CD and pictures. Does not return material. Reports in 3 weeks.
Music: Mostly **R&B**, **rap** and **Latino/TexMex**; also **jazz**, **country**, **rock** and **blues**. Released *Lines & Spaces*, recorded by Shades of Brown (jazz); *Remi n Alize*, recorded by Mr. International (rap); and *Screw Theory Vol. 2*, recorded by various (rap), all on Albatross Records. Other artists include D.G.I. Posse, Hollister Fraucus and 4-Deep.

○ ALLEGHENY MUSIC WORKS, 306 Cypress Ave,. Johnstown PA 15902. (814)535-3373. Managing Director: Al Rita. Labels include Allegheny Records. Record company and music publisher (Allegheny Music Works Publishing/ASCAP and Tuned on Music/BMI). Estab. 1991. Pays 10-12% royalty to artists on contract; statutory rate to publisher per song on record.
How to Contact: Submit demo tape by mail. Unsolicited submissions are OK. Prefers cassette with 2 songs and lyric sheet or lead sheet. SASE. Reports in 2-4 weeks.
Music: Mostly **country (all styles)**; also **pop**, **A/C**, **R&B** and **inspirational**. Released "If God Don't Like Country Music" (by T. Lenartz/C. Van Wey) (country); "Drive" (by K. McDermott), recorded by Gerry Moffett (beach rock); and "For An Hour or Two" (by A. Rita/D. Siegenthaler), recorded by Mark McLelland and Wanda Copier (country/MOR duet), all on Allegheny Records.

N ◐ ALMO SOUNDS, 360 N. LaCienega Blvd., Los Angeles CA 90048. (310)289-7070. Fax: (310)289-8662. E-mail: agrosky@unistudios.com. Website: http://www.almosounds.com. Vice President of A&R: Bob Bortnick. Record company.
How to Contact: Submit demo tape by mail. Unsolicited submissions are OK. Prefers cassette with 3 songs maximum and lyric sheet.
Music: Released *Version 2.0*, recorded by Garbage on Almo Sounds. Other artists include Herb Alpert, Lazlo Bane and Gillian Welch.

☑ ◐ ALYSSA RECORDS, 302 Bluepoint Rd. W., Holtsville NY 11742. President: Andy Marvel. Labels include Ricochet Records. Record company, music publisher (Andy Marvel Music/ASCAP, Bing Bing Bing Music/ASCAP and Andysongs/BMI) and record producer (Marvel Productions). Estab. 1981. Staff size: 3. Releases 12-15 singles, 1 12" single and 4 LPs/year. Pays standard royalty to artists on contract; statutory rate to publisher per song on record.
How to Contact: Submit demo tape by mail. Unsolicited submissions are OK. Prefers cassette or CD with 3 songs and lyric sheet. Does not return material. "Do not call." Reports in 2 months.
Music: Mostly **pop**, **R&B** and **top 40**; also **country**.

N ◐ AMERICAN RECORDINGS, 2100 Colorado Ave., Santa Monica CA 91505. (310)449-2100. Website: http://www.american.recordings.com. A&R: Dino Paredes. Labels include Too Pure, Infinite Zero, UBL, Venture and Onion. Record company.
Distributed by: WEA.
How to Contact: Submit demo tape by mail. Unsolicited submissions are OK. Prefers CD, cassette or videocassette with lyric and lead sheet.
Music: Released *Unchained*, recorded by Johnny Cash on American Recordings. Other artists include Slayer, The Black Crowes and Jayhawks.

☑ ◐ AMERICATONE RECORDS INTERNATIONAL USA, 1817 Loch Lomond Way, Las Vegas NV 89102-4437. (702)384-0030. Fax: (702)382-1926. E-mail: ameicaton@aol.com. Estab. 1985. Contact: A&R Director. Labels include The Rambolt Music International (ASCAP), Americatone (BMI) and Christy Records International. Record company, producer and music publisher. Releases 8 CDs and cassettes/year. Pays 10% royalty.
Distributed by: Big Band, Otter, World, North County, General, Harber Music Export, International, Twinbrook and Gibson.
How to Contact: Submit demo tape by mail. Unsolicited submissions are OK. Prefers cassette or CD. SASE. Reports in 1 month.
Music: Mostly **jazz**, **rock**, **Spanish** and **classic ballads**. Released *After All These Years*, written and recorded by Brent Blount; and *The Ramblers*, written and recorded by Brad Sauders, both on Americatone International Records. Other artists include Ladd McIntosh, Mark Masters, Penelope, Dick Shearer and Robert Martin.

N ⊕ ◐ AMP RECORDS & MUSIC, Box 387, 1A Buckingham Rd., London N22 GSF United Kingdom. Phone/fax: (0044)(0)181 889 0616. E-mail: info@ampmusic.demon.co.uk. Website: http://www.ampmusic.demon.co.uk. A&R: Mark Jenkins (New Age, instrumental, ambient, progressive, rock). Record company. Estab. 1985. Staff size: 10. Releases 12 CDs/year. Pays negotiable royalty to artists on contract; negotiable rate to publisher per song on record.

Distributed by: Magnum (UK), Eurock/ZNR/NSA (USA), MP (Italy) and Crystal Lake (France).

How to Contact: Submit demo tape by mail. Unsolicited submissions are OK. Prefers cassette, CD or DAT with cover letter and press clippings. Does not return material. Reports in 2 months.

Music: Mostly **New Age**, **instrumental** and **ambient**; also **progressive rock**, **synthesizer** and **ambient dance**. Does not want ballads, country or AOR. Released *Changing States*, recorded by Keith Emerson (progressive rock); *Tyranny of Beauty*, written and recorded by Tangerine Dream (synthesizer); and *Spirit of Christmas*, written and recorded by various artists (instrumental compilation), all on AMP Records.

Tips: "Send a relevant style of music."

☑ ⊘ **ANGEL/EMI RECORDS**, 304 Park Ave. S, New York NY 10010. (212)253-3200. Fax: (212)253-3011. Head of A&R: Steve Ferrera. Record company.

Distributed by: EMI.

How to Contact: Angel/EMI Records does not accept unsolicited submissions.

Music: Released *The Classical Album*, recorded by Vanessa Mae; and *Chant III*, recorded by The Benedictine Monks of Santo Domingo De Silos, both on Angel Records; and *Paul McCartney's Standing Stone*, recorded by the London Symphony Orchestra on MPL.

Ⓝ ◯ **ANISETTE RECORDS**, P.O. Box 74157, Los Angeles CA 90004. Phone/fax: (213)365-9495. E-mail: anisette@earthlink.net. Website: http://home.earthlink.net/~anisette. A&R Chief: M-K O'Connell. Record company. Estab. 1998. Staff size: 2. Releases 2 CDs/year. Pays negotiable royalty to artists on contract; statutory rate to publisher per song on record.

Distributed by: NAIL, Darla, Carrot Top, Surefire, Scratch and Parasol.

How to Contact: Submit demo tape by mail. Unsolicted submissions are OK. Prefers cassette or CD. Does not return material. Reports in 2 weeks.

Music: Mostly **rock**, **pop** and **rap**. Released *Greatest Moments of Doubt* (by Kevin Castillo), recorded by Retriever; and *The Miracle of Flight*, written and recorded by Stratotanker, both on Anisette (rock).

Tips: "Send the material and follow up with an e-mail."

❧ ◯ **ARIAL RECORDS**, Box 831, Black Diamond, Alberta T0L 0H0 Canada. E-mail: arial@cfreeyell ow.com/members3/arcorp. Website: http://www.freeyellow.com/members3/arcorp. Manager (country, instrumental, New Age): Tim Auvigne. Chief Executive Officer (country, rock): Brent McAthey. A&R Representative (pop, alternative): Charlotte Wiebe. Record company, management firm, booking agent and music publisher (Ster N' Ster Publishing). Estab. 1989. Staff size: 3. Pays standard royalty to artists on contract; statutory rate to publisher per song on record.

Distributed by: Spirit River Distribution.

How to Contact: Submit demo tape by mail. Unsolicited submissions are OK. Prefers cassette or VHS videocassette with 3 songs and lyric sheet. Does not return material. Reports in 2-8 weeks.

Music: Mostly **country**; also **pop**. Released "Chevy Blue Eyes" (by Bernie Nelson) (country); and "Slow Motion" (by Lonnie Ratliff/Lindy Gravelle) (country), both recorded by Brent McAthey on Arial Records. Other artists include Kickstart (trio) and Jessy Oakley (country singer/songwriter).

◯ **ARIANA RECORDS**, 1336 S. Avenida Polar #C-208, Tucson AZ 85710. (520)790-7324. E-mail: dukes@ibm.com. President: James M. Gasper. Vice President (pop, rock): Tom Dukes. Partners: Tom Privett (funk, experimental, rock); Scott Smith (pop, rock, AOR). Labels include Egg White Records. Record company, music publisher (Myko Music/BMI) and record producer. Estab. 1980. Staff size: 4. Releases 2 singles, 4 LPs and 4 CDs/year. Pays negotiable royalty to artists on contract; negotiable rate to publisher per song on record.

Distributed by: Impact Music Distributors and Care Free Music.

How to Contact: Submit demo tape by mail. Unsolicited submissions are OK. Prefers cassette or ½" VHS videocassette. SASE. Reports in 6 months.

Music: Mostly **rock**, **funk** and **jazz**; also **anything weird or strange**. Released "B.T.B.A." (by Scott Seleny), recorded by Baby Fish Mouth on Ariana (funk); and *Stompbox* (by Michael West/Tom James),

---

MARKET CONDITIONS are constantly changing! If you're still using this book and it is 2001 or later, buy the newest edition of *Songwriter's Market* at your favorite bookstore or order directly from Writer's Digest Books at (800)289-0963.

recorded by Larry's Limo on Egg White (space funk). Other artists include Radiant Grub, The Rakeheads and Mary's Purse.

Tips: "We're a small company, but working your material is our job. If we like it, we'll sell it!"

ARISTA RECORDS, 6 W. 57th St., New York NY 10019. (212)489-7400. Fax: (212)977-9843. Website: http://www.aristarec.com. Senior A&R Director: Peter Edge, Sr. Beverly Hills office: 9975 Santa Monica Blvd., Beverly Hills CA 90212. (310)789-3900. Fax: (310)789-3949. Manager of A&R: Jason Markey. A&R (sound tracks): John Rader. Nashville office: 1400 18th Ave. S., Nashville TN 37212. (615)846-9100. Fax: (615)846-9192. Director of A&R: Mike Sistad. Manager of A&R: Kerri Pauley Edwards. Labels include LaFace Records, Bad Boy Records, Arista Nashville and Time Bomb Recordings. Record company.

Distributed by: BMG.

How to Contact: Does not accept unsolicited material.

Music: Released *Harem World* by Mace on Bad Boy; *Surfacing* by Sarah McLachlan on Arista; and *Soul Food* soundtrack on LaFace. Other artists include Kenny G, Brooks & Dunn, Alan Jackson and OutKast.

ARKADIA ENTERTAINMENT CORP., 34 E. 23rd St., New York NY 10010. (212)533-0007. (212)979-0266. E-mail: songs@arkadiarecords.com. Website: http://www.arkadiarecords.com. Contact: A&R Song Submissions. Labels include Arkadia Jazz, Arkadia Classical, Arkadia Now and Arkadia Allworld. Record company, music publisher (Arkadia Music), record producer (Arkadia Productions) and Arkadia Video. Estab. 1995. Releases 6 singles, 12 LPs and 22 CDs/year. Pays statutory rate to publisher per song on record.

How to Contact: Write or call first and obtain permission to submit. Prefers cassette, DAT or VHS videocassette with 3-4 songs and lyric and lead sheets. SASE. Reports ASAP.

Music: Mostly **jazz** and **pop/R&B**; also **world**. Released *Velvet Moon*, recorded by Velvet Moon; and *Michel Gallois*, recorded by Michel Gallois, all on Arkadia Records. Other artists include Billy Taylor, Benny Golson, David Liebman and Nova Bossa Nova.

ASYLUM RECORDS NASHVILLE, 1906 Acklen Ave., Nashville TN 37212. (615)292-7990. Fax: (615)292-8219. A&R Director: Anthony Von Dollen. A&R Administrator: Vallerie Main. Labels include 143 Records. Record company.

Distributed by: WEA.

How to Contact: Call first and obtain permission to submit.

Music: Released *Between Now & Forever*, recorded by Bryan White; *Lila*, recorded by Lila McCann; and *Measure of a Man*, recorded by Kevin Sharp all on Asylum Records.

ATLAN-DEC/GROOVELINE RECORDS, 2529 Green Forest Court, Snellville GA 30078-4183. Phone/fax: (770)985-1686. E-mail: lyye71a@prodigy.com. Website: http://www.ATLAN-DEC.com. President/Senior A&R Rep: James Hatcher. A&R Rep: Wiletta J. Hatcher. Record company, music publisher and record producer. Estab. 1994. Staff size: 2. Releases 3-4 singles, 3-4 LPs and 3-4 CDs/year. Pays 10-25% royalty to artists on contract; statutory rate to publisher per song on record.

Distributed by: ATLAN-DEC Records and Baker & Taylor Entertainment.

How to Contact: Submit demo tape by mail. Unsolicited submissions are OK. Prefers cassette and lyric sheet. Does not return material. Reports in 2-3 months.

Music: Mostly **R&B/urban**, **hip-hop/rap** and **contemporary jazz**; also **soft rock**, **gospel**, **dance** and **new country**. Released *All Niggas Ain't Black* (by Davron Harmon), recorded by Furious D (rap/hip-hop); *Ecstatic*, written and recorded by Paul Carroll (jazz); and "Stepping Into The Light," written and recorded by Mark Cocker (new country), all on ATLAN-DEC Records. Other artists include R.I.P. and Family Tiez.

ATLANTIC RECORDS, 75 Rockefeller Plaza, New York NY 10019. (212)707-2000. Fax: (212)247-2303. Director of A&R: Gloria Gabriel. Los Angeles office: 9229 Sunset Blvd., 9th Floor, Los Angeles CA 90069. (310)205-7450. Fax: (310)205-7411. Vice President of A&R: Tom Storms. Vice President (soundtracks): Darren Higman. Vice President of A&R (rock): Kevin Williamson. Nashville office: 1906 Acklen, Nashville TN 37212. (615)327-9394. Fax: (615)327-9405. A&R: Al Cooley. Website: http://www.atlantic-records.com. Labels include Big Beat Records, Nonesuch Records, Atlantic Classics and Rhino Records. Record company. Pays negotiable royalty to artists on contract; negotiable rate to publisher per song on record.

Distributed by: WEA.

● Atlantic's Clannad won a 1998 Grammy Award for Best New Age Album; Gilberto Gil won for Best World Music Album.

How to Contact: Does not accept unsolicited material. "No phone calls please."

Music: Released *Yourself or Someone Like You*, recorded by Matchbox 20 on Lava; *Pieces of You*, recorded by Jewel on Atlantic; and *Greatest Hits*, recorded by John Michael Montgomery on Atlantic (Nashville). Other artists include Sugar Ray and Brandy.

○ **aUDIOFILE TAPES**, 209-25 18th Ave., Bayside NY 11360. E-mail: litlgrey@ix.netcom.com. Website: http://www.cnct.com/~litlgrey. Sheriff, aT County: Carl Howard. Record company. "Cassette-only label of alternative music." Estab. 1984. Produces about 25 cassettes/year. "Money is solely from sales. Some artists ask $1 per tape sold."
How to Contact: Write first and obtain permission to submit. Prefers cassette. "Relevant artist information is nice. Master copies accepted on hi-bias or metal analog tape, or DAT." SASE. Reports in 4-6 weeks.
Music: Mostly **psych/electronic rock**, **non-rock electronic music** and **progressive rock**; also **free jazz** and **world music**. Released *Beyond Tomorrow . . . High Energy!*, written and recorded by William Hooker; *Ankh*, written and recorded by LG Mair, Jr. (electronic); and *The Death of Leviticus*, written and recorded by Atomic Crash (rock improv), all on audiofile Tapes. Other artists include The Conspiracy, The Venus Fly Trap, Sphinx, Luster, Dachise, Bruce Atchinson and Blowhole.
Tips: "Please, no industrial music, no deliberately shocking images of racism and sexual brutality. And no New Age sleeping pills. Unfortunately, we are not in a position to help the careers of aspirant pop idols. Only true devotees *really* need apply. I mean it—money does not exist here. No artist has ever been under contract; this is real underground informal stuff."

○ **AVENUE COMMUNICATIONS**, P.O. Box 1432, Menlo Park CA 94026-1432. (650)321-8291 or (800)5AVENUE. Fax: (650)321-7491. Website: http://www.5avenue.com. Vice President: Erik Nielsen. Record company. Estab. 1989. Releases 5 singles and 3 CDs/year. Pays negotiable royalty to artists on contract; statutory rate to publisher per song on record.
Distributed by: CRD, Valley, Bayside and CD One-Stop.
How to Contact: Submit demo tape by mail. Unsolicited submissions are OK. Prefers cassette, CD, DAT or VHS videocassette. Does not return material. Reports "next day if we like it."
Music: Mostly **American/international**. Released "Got the Whole Night," recorded by Denny Brown.

N ○ **AWARE RECORDS**, P.O. Box 803817, Chicago IL 60680. (312)226-6335. Fax: (312)226-6299. E-mail: aware@awaremusic.com. Website: http://Awarerecords.com. A&R: Dan Sundt. President: Gregg Latterman. Record company. Estab. 1993. Staff size: 8. Releases 5 singles, 3 LPs, 1 EP and 3 CDs/year. Pays negotiable royalty to artists on contract; statutory rate to publisher per song on record.
Distributed by: Sony and RED.
How to Contact: Submit demo tape by mail. Unsolicited submissions are OK. Prefers CD with lead sheet, cover letter and press clippings. Does not return material. Reports back only if interested.
Music: Mostly **rock/pop**. Released *Train* (by Patrick Monahan), recorded by Train (pop/rock); *Level* (by Chuck Gladfelter), recorded by Dovetail Joint (alternative); and *Aware 6*, written and recorded by various artists (pop/rock), all on Aware Records.

○ **babysue**, P.O. Box 8989, Atlanta GA 31106. (404)320-1178. Website: http://www.babysue.com. President/Owner: Don W. Seven. Record company and management firm. Estab. 1983. Staff size: 1. Releases 2 singles, 5 LPs, 2 EPs and 7 CDs/year. Pays 5-20% royalty to artists on contract; varying royalty to publisher per song on record.
Distributed by: Not Lame Distribution.
How to Contact: Submit demo tape by mail. Unsolicited submissions are OK. Prefers cassette with any number of songs. Does not return material. Reports in 3 months. "We only report back if we are interested in the artist or act."
Music: Mostly **rock**, **pop** and **gospel**; also **heavy metal**, **punk** and **classical**. Released *Mnemonic*, recorded by LMNOP on babysue records (rock/pop). Other artists include the Mushcakes, The Shoestrings and The Mommy.
Tips: "Send us cash (just kidding). Actually, we're just into sincere, good stuff."

○ **BAGATELLE RECORD COMPANY**, P.O. Box 925929, Houston TX 77292. President: Byron Benton. Record company, record producer and music publisher (Bagatelle Music, Floyd Tillman Music

REMEMBER: Don't "shotgun" your demo tapes. Submit only to companies interested in the type of music you write. For more submission hints, refer to Getting Started on page 11.

Co.). Releases 20 singles and 10 LPs/year. Pays negotiable royalty to artists on contract.

How to Contact: Submit demo tape by mail. Prefers cassette and lyric sheet. SASE. Reports in 2 weeks.

Music: Mostly **country**; also **gospel**. Released "This is Real," by Floyd Tillman (country); "Lucille," by Sherri Jerrico (country); and "Everything You Touch," by Johnny Nelms (country). Other artists include Jerry Irby, Bobby Beason, Bobby Burton, Donna Hazard, Danny Brown, Sonny Hall, Ben Gabus, Jimmy Copeland and Johnny B. Goode.

[N] O BANANA RECORDS, 3115 Hiss Ave., Baltimore MD 21234. Phone/fax: (410)668-0892. President: Ronald Brown. A&R: Brian Batterdan. Record company, music publisher (Infinite Publishing) and record producer (Ronald Brown). Estab. 1990. Releases 30 singles, 20 LPs and 20 CDs/year. Pays standard royalty to artists on contract; statutory rate to publisher per song on record.

How to Contact: Submit demo tape by mail. Unsolicited submissions are OK. Prefers cassette with 3 songs and lyric sheet. SASE. Reports in 3 weeks.

Music: Mostly **top 40/commercial**, **pop/ballads** and **alternative**. Released "Crack of the Universe," written and recorded by Jesse Brown (pop) on Global.

Tips: "A good singer works hard at his craft. A hit song has good punch and a lot of talent."

O BELHAM VALLEY RECORDS, 5095 Napilihau St., Suite 177, Lahaina HI 96761. (808)669-9607. Fax: (808)669-5719. E-mail: bvrmusicnews@webtv.net. Website: http://24.3.19.68/montserrat/projmni/index.shtml. Owner/Producer: Gary Robilotta. Owner/Producer: Carrll Robilotta. A&R Director: Garbaldo. Lables include Isles Bay Music, Volcano, Montserrat Records and Rivermouth Records. Record company, music publisher (Belham Valley Records Publishing) and record producer (Gary Robilotta). Estab. 1993. Releases 1 LP and 1 CD every 2 years. Pays standard royalty to artists on contract; statutory rate to publisher per song on record.

Distributed by: Belham Valley Records.

How to Contact: Write first and obtain permission to submit. Prefers cassette or CD with any number of songs and lyric sheet. SASE. Reports in 3 weeks.

Music: Mostly **instrumental (pop/jazz/reggae)** and **neo-classical/jazz**; also **solo piano**. Released *Project: Montserrat*; *Once Around The Island*; and *Jungle Junge*, all written and recorded by Gary Robilotta on Belham Valley Records (instrumental).

Tips: "Be original but not to the point of sacrificing musical integrity. That is, there's lots of original stuff out there, but lots of it shouldn't really be called 'music.' Above all else, strive for mellifluousness—regardless of your chosen genre. We release music that transcends generational boundaries because it is music that speaks to the soul—the type of music Mannheim Steamroller is noted for."

O BELUGA RECORDS, P.O. Box 146751, Chicago IL 60614-6751. Website: http://www.belugarecords.com. Mastermind: Scott Beluga. Record company. Estab. 1994. Staff size: 1. Releases 4-8 CDs/year. Pays negotiable royalty to artists on contract; statutory rate to publisher per song on record.

Distributed by: Carrot Top, Southern, Choke and Lumberjack.

How to Contact: Submit demo tape by mail. Unsolicited submissions are OK. Prefers cassette or CD. "Please don't call." Does not return material. Reports back only if interested.

Music: Mostly **indie pop**, **indie rock** and **derivatives thereof**. Does not want heavy metal, goth, ska, country or singer/songwriters looking for publishing deals. Released *Hurray For Everything*, written and recorded by Cats and Jammers (garage pop); *13 Electric Turn-Ons*, written and recorded by Big Angry Fish (indie rock); and *Beluga . . . On the Rock (Round 2)*, written and recorded by various artists (double CD compilation), all on Beluga Records. Other artists include Zipperhead, Jupiter Down, Great Plains Gypsies, Today's My Super Spaceout Day and Mustache.

Tips: "Research the record company before wasting your time and product. For example, if you knew that Beluga Records only works with rock bands that write their own music, would it be appropriate to send us your music?"

O BIG BEAT RECORDS, 9229 Sunset Blvd., Los Angeles CA 90069. (310)205-5717. Fax: (310)205-5721. Director of A&R: Michael Caren. Record company. Labels include Undeas Records, CWAL and Slip-N-Slide.

Distributed by: WEA.

How to Contact: Submit demo tape by mail. Unsolicited submissions are OK. Prefers cassette, CD or DAT with bio and photo.

Music: Released *Hard Core*, recorded by Lil' Kim on Undeas Records; *All Day, All Night*, recorded by Changing Faces on Big Beat Records; and *Adrenaline Rush*, recorded by Twista on Creatures Way.

N **Y** **O** **BIG HEAVY WORLD**, P.O. Box 428, Burlington VT 05402-0428. (802)373-1824. E-mail: groundzero@bigheavyworld.com. Website: http://www.bigheavyworld.com. Founder/A&R Director: James Lockridge. Record company. Estab. 1996. Staff size: 4. Releases 3 CDs/year. Pays negotiable royalty to artists on contract; pay varies by project to publisher per song on record.
Distributed by: Dutch East India Trading Co.
  • This company was given the 1998 Visionary Award by the Women's Rape Crisis Center. Big Heavy World promotes the music of Burlington, Vermont, and its region. Their compilation CDs vary in genre and theme and often benefit humanitarian services.
How to Contact: Big Heavy World does not accept unsolicited submissions.
Music: Compilation projects vary in genre. Released *Pop Pie* (pop); *Pulsecuts Vol II* (alternative); and *No Secrets* (rock/alternative), all written and recorded by various artists on Big Heavy World.
Tips: "Vermont-based artists are welcome to contact us, both as a record label and online music retail venue."

N **Y** **O** **A BIG RICH MAJOR LABEL**, 151 First Ave., Suite 239, New York NY 10003. (212)560-2456. E-mail: majorcash@aol.com. Website: http://www.princesssuperstar.com. CEO: Concetta Kirschner. President: Louise Crane. Record company. Estab. 1997. Staff size: 5. Releases 2 singles, 2 LPs and 2 CDs/year. Pays negotiable royalty to artists on contract; statutory rate to publisher per song on record.
Distributed by: Carrot Top, Nail, Revolver, Sonic Unyon, Caroline and Darla.
  • This label's artist, Princess Superstar, won *Playboy*'s Hot Woman of the Year Award in Music.
How to Contact: Submit demo tape by mail. Unsolicited submissions are OK. Prefers cassette or CD with 3 songs. Does not return material. Reports in 3 weeks.
Music: Mostly **hip-hop**, **electronic** and **punk rock**; also **New Age** and **pornographic movie scores**. Released *CEO* and *Strictly Platinum*, both by Princess Superstar (hip-hop/punk rock) on A Big Rich Major Label. Other artists include The Sluts and The FWA's.
Tips: "Keep it innovative and hot!"

Y **O** **BIG WIG PRODUCTIONS**, 14088 W. Wrigley St., Boise ID 83713. Phone/fax: (208)938-1176. A&R Representative: Bryan Lass. Record company. Estab. 1992. Releases 3 singles and 2 CDs/year. Pays negotiable royalty to artists on contract; statutory rate to publisher per song on record.
How to Contact: Call first and obtain permission to submit. Prefers cassette or CD with 4 songs and lyric sheet. "Enclose any information regarding recent radio airtime and album sales if available." Does not return material. Reports in 2-6 weeks.
Music: Mostly **pop/top 40**, **contemporary** and **country**; also **gospel**, **folk** and **rock**. Released "Something's Missing" and "Day of Reckoning," both written and recorded by Memory Garden; and "Digital Madness" (by Bryan Lass), recorded by Hyperdigits on Big Wig Records (alternative).

O **BLACK DIAMOND RECORDS INC.**, P.O. Box 8073, Pittsburg CA 94565. (510)980-0893. Fax: (925)432-4342. E-mail: primeuse@aol.com. Website: http://www.primeuse.blackdiamond.com. President, A&R (all styles): Jerry "J." Vice President (R&B, hip-hop): Joe Brown. A&R President (rap, R&B, rock, country): Maurice Belcher. A&R Senior Director (blues, R&B, classical, jazz, rap): Raynard Thomas. Labels include "In The House" Records, Hittin' Hard Records, Flash Point Records, Stay Down Records and Jairus Records. Record company, music publisher, management firm (It's Happening Present Entertainment) and record producer (Bobelli Productions, In The House Productions). Estab. 1988. Pays 8-14% royalty to artists on contract; statutory rate to publisher per song on record.
Distributed by: Zomba, Sony Distribution and Bellmark/Life Records.
How to Contact: Call first and obtain permission to submit. Prefers cassette with 2-4 songs, photo and lyric sheet. Does not return material. Reports in 6 months.
Music: Mostly **R&B**, **hip-hop**, **country/jazz** and **hip-hop rap**; also **jazz**, **blues** and **rock**. Released "Bounce," written and recorded by Baby Rain on Big Bay Bee Records (R&B); "Every Which Way," written and recorded by Patchwork; and "12:00 Clock High," written and recorded by Deion Gladney, both on Pretty Peach (R&B).
Tips: "Be very simple and professional. Use clean (or your best) production tracks. Never say never or give out in your efforts."

N **O** **BLIND RECORDS**, P.O. Box 336, North Chili NY 14514. Phone/fax: (716)889-5641. E-mail: blindrec@aol.com. A&R: J.S. Smith. Record company and record producer. Estab. 1994. Staff size: 3. Releases 12 singles, 2 LPs and 2 CDs/year. Pays negotiable royalty to artists on contract; statutory rate to publisher per song on record.

Distributed by: Rare Necessities and TrueTunes.

How to Contact: Submit demo tape by mail. Unsolicited submissions are OK. Prefers cassette or CD with 3 songs, lyric sheet and cover letter. SASE. Reports in 2 months.

Music: Mostly **pop**, **rock** and **alternative**; also **Christian pop**, **rock**, **alternative** and **singer/songwriters**. Released *Dylan Casey Fades* (by John Bloomer/David Braming), recorded by Mojo Heroes (rock/pop); and *IRV 2*, written and recorded by various artists (pop/rock), both on Blind Records. Other artists include David Edwards, Perfect Tommy and Every Eye Closed.

Tips: "Persue your dream. Don't let anyone tell you it can't be done."

☑ ◖ BLUE GEM RECORDS, P.O. Box 29550, Hollywood CA 90029. (323)664-7765. E-mail: pmarti 3636@aol.com. Contact: Pete Martin. Record company, music publisher (Vaam Music Group) and record producer (Pete Martin/Vaam Productions). Estab. 1981. Pays 6-15% royalty to artists on contract; statutory rate to publisher per song on record.

How to Contact: Submit demo tape by mail. Unsolicited submissions are OK. Prefers cassette with 2 songs. SASE. Reports in 3 weeks.

Music: Mostly **country** and **R&B**; also **pop/top 40** and **rock**. Released "The Greener Years," written and recorded by Frank Loren (country); "It's a Matter of Loving You" (by Brian Smith), recorded by Brian Smith & The Renegades (country); and "Two Different Women" (by Frank Loren/Greg Connor), recorded by Frank Loren (country), all on Blue Gem Records. Other artists include Sherry Weston (country).

◖ BLUE WAVE, 3221 Perryville Rd., Baldwinsville NY 13027. (315)638-4286. President/Producer: Greg Spencer. Labels include Blue Wave/Horizon. Record company, music publisher (G.W. Spencer Music/ASCAP) and record producer (Blue Wave Productions). Estab. 1985. Staff size: 1. Releases 3 LPs and 3 CDs/year. Pays variable royalty to artists on contract; statutory rate to publisher per song on record.

Distributed by: MS Distribution, Select-O-Hits, United and Valley.

How to Contact: Submit demo tape by mail. Unsolicited submissions are OK. Prefers cassette or videocassette (live performance only) and as many songs as you like. SASE. Reports in 1 month only if interested.

Music: Mostly **blues/blues rock**, **roots rock** and **roots R&B/soul**; also **roots country/rockabilly** or **anything with "soul."** Released *Sunday Morning*, written and recorded by Kim Lembo (blues); *Dew Drop In* (by Chuck Jackson), recorded by Downchild Blues Band (blues); and *Just The Wind* (by Ron DeRollo), recorded by Ronnie D (blues), all on Blue Wave Records. Other artists include Kim Simmonds and Backbone Slip.

Tips: "Be able to put the song across vocally."

◖ BMX ENTERTAINMENT, P.O. Box 10857, Stamford CT 06904. (203)353-1400. Fax: (203)357-1676. Website: http://www.bmxrecordsgroup.com. President: Mauris Gryphon. Labels include Red Tape Records. Record company. Estab. 1984. Releases 7 singles, 7 12″ singles, 7 LPs, 7 EPs and 7 CDs/year. Pays 10-12% royalty to artists on contract.

How to Contact: Submit demo tape by mail. Unsolicited submissions are OK. Prefers cassette or VHS videocassette with 4 songs. "Send résumé, photo, management arrangements, if any." SASE. Reports in 3 weeks.

Music: Mostly **country**, **R&B** and **rock**; also **rap**, **pop**, **jazz**, **classical**, **children's**, **New Age**, **gospel** and **salsa**. Released "Just My Imagination" (by Jobete Music), recorded by Flipside on BMX Entertainment. Other artists include Jazreel and Hardcore Jollies.

Ⓝ ⊕ ◖ BOULEVARD MUSIC & PUBLISHING, 16 Limetrees, Llangattock, Crickhowell NP8 1IL Wales. Phone: (0044)(0)1873 810142. Fax: (0044)(0)1873 811557. A&R Directors: Kevin Holland-King (MOR/jazz); David Paramor (rock, R&B). Labels include Silverword, RP Media, Associate, Mirabean. Record company and music publisher (Boulevard Publishing). Estab. 1987. Staff size: 2. Releases 3 singles and 7 CDs/year. Pays negotiable royalty to artists on contract; statutory rate to publisher per song on record.

Distributed by: Else Distribution.

How to Contact: Submit demo tape by mail. Unsolicited submissions are OK. Prefers cassette, CD or VHS videocassette with 3 songs, lead sheet and cover letter. SAE and IRC. Reports in 1 month.

Music: Mostly **MOR**, **rock** and **R&B**; also **country** and **jazz**. Released *Back On Tracks* (by various

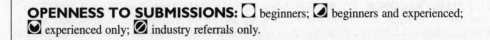

OPENNESS TO SUBMISSIONS: ◖ beginners; ◖ beginners and experienced; ◖ experienced only; ∅ industry referrals only.

artists), recorded by Guys 'n' Dolls on Associate (MOR); *Hidden Treasures*, written and recorded by Clifford T. Ward on RP Media (popular); and *Rick Wakeman*, written and recorded by Rick Wakeman on RP Media (rock). Other artists include Jeff Hooper, Southlanders, Screemer and Majik.
Tips: "A well-written song is like any masterpiece: hard to find—easy to recognize."

BOUQUET RECORDS, Bouquet-Orchid Enterprises, P.O. Box 1335, Norcross GA 30091. (770)814-2420. President: Bill Bohannon. Record company, music publisher (Orchid Publishing/BMI), record producer (Bouquet-Orchid Enterprises) and management firm (Bouquet-Orchid Enterprises). Releases 3-4 singles and 2 LPs/year. Pays 5-8% royalty to artists on contract; pays statutory rate to publishers for each record sold.
How to Contact: Submit demo tape by mail. Unsolicited submissions are OK. Prefers cassette or CD with 3-5 songs and lyric sheet. SASE. Reports in 1 month.
Music: Mostly **religious** (contemporary or country-gospel, Amy Grant, etc.), **country** ("the type suitable for Clint Black, George Strait, Patty Loveless, etc.") and **top 100** ("the type suitable for Billy Joel, Whitney Houston, R.E.M., etc."); also **rock** and **MOR**. Released *Blue As Your Eyes* (by Bill Bohannon), recorded by Adam Day (country); *Take Care of My World* (by Bob Freeman), recorded by Bandoleers (top 40); and *Making Plans* (by John Harris), recorded by Susan Spencer (country), all on Bouquet Records.
Tips: "Submit 3-5 songs on a cassette tape with lyric sheets. Include a short biography and perhaps a photo. Enclose SASE."

BRENTWOOD RECORDS, One Maryland Farms, Brentwood TN 37027. (615)373-3950. Fax: (615)221-3375. Website: http://providentmusic.com. Director of A&R: Ed Kee (Christian concept, instrumental). Co-Vice President/General Manager: Dean Diehl (A/C, Christian). Labels include Brentwood Jazz and Brentwood Kids Company. Record company and music publisher (Brentwood-Benson Publishing). Estab. 1981. Staff size: 9. Releases 18 CDs/year. Pays statutory rate to publisher per song on record "except when negotiated otherwise."
Distributed by: Provident Music Distribution and BMG.
• Music released by Brentwood Records has been certified Gold by the RIAA; and won the Gospel Music Association's Dove Award.
How to Contact: Does not accept unsolicited material.
Music: Mostly **Christian praise and worship**, **A/C** and **inspirational**; also **concept-driven projects**. Does not want country, rap, reggae, dance, hip-hop, etc. Released *First Love* (by various artists), recorded by Larnelle Harris (A/C); *Acoustic Worship* (praise and worship album); and *Brentwood Jazz Revival* (jazz concept album), all on Brentwood Records.

BROKEN RECORDS INTERNATIONAL, 305 S. Westmore Ave., Lombard IL 60148. (630)916-6874. E-mail: roy@mcguitar.com. Website: http://www.mcguitar.com. International A&R: Roy Bocchieri. Vice President: Jeff Murphy. Record company. Estab. 1984. Payment negotiable.
How to Contact: Write first and obtain permission to submit. Prefers cassette, CD or VHS videocassette with at least 2 songs and lyric sheet. Does not return material. Reports in 2 months.
Music: Mostly **rock**, **pop** and **dance**; also **acoustic** and **industrial**. Released *Figurehead* (by LeRoy Bocchieri), recorded by Day One (pop/alternative); and *Eitherway* (by Jeff Murphy/Herb Eimerman), recorded by The Nerk Twins (pop/alternative), both on Broken Records.

BSW RECORDS, P.O. Box 2297, Universal City TX 78148. (210)599-0022. Fax: (210)653-3989. E-mail: bswr18@txdirect.net. President: Frank Willson. Vice Presidents: Verdi Williams (pop); Frank Weatherly (country, jazz); Regina Willson (blues). Record company, music publisher (BSW Records/BMI), management firm (Universal Music Marketing) and record producer (Frank Willson). Estab. 1987. Staff size: 3. Releases 18 albums/year. Pays standard royalty to artists on contract; statutory rate to publisher per song on record.
How to Contact: Submit demo tape by mail. Unsolicited submissions are OK. Prefers cassette (or ¾″ videocassette) with 3 songs and lyric sheet. SASE. Reports in 4-6 weeks.
Music: Mostly **country**, **rock** and **blues**. Released *Follow the Roses*, written and recorded by Larry Butler; *Slow Dance* (by Joseph Mast), recorded by Paul Carter; and *I'll Get All the Sleep I Need When I Die*, written and recorded by Curtis Wayne, all on BSW Records (country). Other artists include Peter Coulton, Candee Land, Vince Hopkins, Shawn DeLorme, Buddy Hodges, Kenny Post, Davis Bueschler and Celeste.

C.P.R., 4 West St., Massapequa Park NY 11762. (516)797-1995. Fax: (516)797-1994. A&R: Denise Yannacone. Record company. Estab. 1997. Pays negotiable royalty to artists on contract; statutory rate to publisher per song on record.
How to Contact: Submit demo tape by mail. Unsolicited submissions are OK. Prefers cassette, CD or

DAT with 4 songs and lyric sheet. Does not return material. Reports in 2-4 weeks.
Music: Mostly **uptempos**, **R&B**, **rap**, **rock**, **pop** and **soundtrack**.
Tips: "There are no short cuts to success. So please submit songs that are well produced."

☑ ○ **CALLNER MUSIC**, 959 N. Cole Ave., Hollywood CA 90038. (323)465-8542. E-mail: info@call nermusic.com. Website: http://callnermusic.com. Owner: Dax Callner. Record company. Estab. 1994. Releases 4-5 CDs/year. Pays negotiable royalty to artists on contract; statutory rate to publisher per song on record.
How to Contact: Submit demo tape by mail. Unsolicited submissions are OK. Prefers cassette, CD, DAT or VHS videocassette with 3-4 songs. Does not return material. Reports in 1 month.
Music: Mostly **rock**, **pop** and **R&B**; also **dance** and **electronic**. Released *hi-fi junkie sonata*, written and recorded by blue van gogh (rock); *Dance With Your Ghost*, written and recorded by America Smith (rock), both on Callner.

◖ **CAMBRIA RECORDS & PUBLISHING**, P.O. Box 374, Lomita CA 90717. (310)831-1322. Fax: (310)833-7442. E-mail: cambruamus@aol.com. Director of Recording Operations: Lance Bowling. Labels include Charade Records. Record company and music publisher. Estab. 1979. Staff size: 3. Pays 5-8% royalty to artists on contract; statutory rate to publisher for each record sold.
Distributed by: Bayside Distribution.
How to Contact: Write first and obtain permission to submit. Prefers cassette. SASE. Reports in 1 month.
Music: Mostly **classical**. Released *Songs of Elinor Remick Warren* on Cambria Records. Other artists include Marie Gibson (soprano), Leonard Pennario (piano), Thomas Hampson (voice), Mischa Leftkowitz (violin), Leigh Kaplan (piano), North Wind Quintet and Sierra Wind Quintet.

◐ **CAPITOL RECORDS**, 1750 N. Vine St., Hollywood CA 90028-5274. (213)462-6252. Fax: (213)469-4542. Director of A&R: Craig Aaronson. Vice President of A&R: Ron Laffitte. New York office: 1290 Avenue of the Americas, 35th Floor, New York NY 10104. (212)492-5300. Website: http://www.holly woodandvine.com. Vice President of A&R: Dave Ayers; A&R Director: Juliet Panebianco. Nashville office: 3322 West End Ave., 11th Floor, Nashville TN 37203. (615)269-2000. Fax: (615)269-2062. Vice President of A&R: Mark Brown. A&R: Tracy Cox. Labels include Blue Note Records, Grand Royal, Pangaea Records, The Right Stuff Records and Capitol Nashville Records. Record company.
Distributed by: EMD.
How to Contact: Capitol Records does not accept unsolicited submissions.
Music: Released *Sevens*, recorded by Garth Brooks; *So Much for the Afterglow*, recorded by Everclear; and *OK Computer*, recorded by Radiohead, all on Capitol Records. Other artists include Bonnie Raitt and Beastie Boys.

☑ ◐ **CAPRICORN RECORDS**, 83 Walton St., Atlanta GA 30303. (404)954-6600. Fax: (404)954-6688. Website: http://www.capri.corn.com. A&R Director: Harvey Schwartz. Record company.
How to Contact: Write first and obtain permission to submit.
Music: Released *Fashion Nugget*, recorded by Cake; *311*, recorded by 311; and *Bombs & Butterflies*, recorded by Widespread Panic, all on Capricorn Records. Other artists include Fiji Mariners, Freddy Jones Band and Speaker.

◐ **CAPSTAN RECORD PRODUCTION**, P.O. Box 211, East Prairie MO 63845. (314)649-2211. Contact: Joe Silver or Tommy Loomas. Labels include Octagon and Capstan Records. Record company, music publisher (Lineage Publishing Co.), management firm (Staircase Promotion) and record producer (Silver-Loomas Productions). Pays 3-5% royalty to artists on contract.
How to Contact: Write first and obtain permission to submit. Prefers cassette or VHS videocassette with 2-4 songs and lyric sheet. "Send photo and bio." SASE. Reports in 1 month.
Music: Mostly **country**, **easy listening**, **MOR**, **country rock** and **top 40/pop**. Released "Country Boy" (by Alden Lambert); and "Yesterday's Teardrops" and "Round & Round," written and recorded by The Burchetts. Other artists include Bobby Lee Morgan, Skidrow Joe, Vicarie Arcole, Fleming and Scarlett Britoni.

REMEMBER: Don't "shotgun" your demo tapes. Submit only to companies interested in the type of music you write. For more submission hints, refer to Getting Started on page 11.

⬤ **CARMEL RECORDS**, 2331 Carmel Dr., Palo Alto CA 94303. (415)856-3650. Contact: Jeanette Avenida. Labels include Edgetone, Accoustic Moods, Rainin' Records Fountain, RMA, Canyon, Nightengale Music and Navarre Jazz. Record company and record producer. Estab. 1987. Staff size: 2. Releases 4 singles and 4 LPs/year. Pays statutory rate to publisher per song on record.
How to Contact: Write first and obtain permission to submit or submit demo tape by mail. Unsolicited submissions are OK. Prefers cassette or VHS videocassette and lyric sheet. Does not return material. Reports in 6 months.
Music: Mostly **A/C**, **folk/rock** and **classical**; also **instrumental**, **jazz**, **children's** and **light rock**.
Tips: "Send a complete demo with lyric sheet. Call to follow up. Be very nice—do something to make your submission different."

✓ ⊘ **CAROLINE RECORDS, INC.**, 104 W. 29th St., 4th Floor, New York NY 10001. (212)886-7500. Website: http://www.caroline.com. A&R Director: David Levine. Exclusive manufacturing and distribution of EG, Astralwerks (electronic) and Real World (world music), Vernon Yard (alternative rock), Instant Mayhem (alternative rock), Scamp (retrocool), Mercator (world) and Gyroscope (eclectic). Record company and independent record distributor (Caroline Records Inc.). Estab. 1979. Releases 10-12 12″ singles and 100 CDs/year. Pays varying royalty to artists on contract; statutory rate to publisher per song.
How to Contact: Does not accept unsolicited submissions.
Music: Mostly **alternative/indie/electronic**. Released *Three Sheets to the Wind*, written and recorded by Idaho on Caroline Records; *Whatever and Ever Amen*, written and recorded by Ben Folds Five on Passenger/Caroline Records; and *Fidelity*, written and recorded by Low Road on Vernon Yard/Caroline Records. Other artists include Meatmen, Adrian Belew and Dim Stars.
Tips: "We are open to artists of unique quality and enjoy developing artists from the ground up. We listen to all types of 'alternative' rock, metal, funk and rap but do not sign mainstream hard rock or dance. We send out rejection letters so do not call to find out what's happening with your demo."

🅽 ⊘ **CASARO RECORDS**, 932 Nord Ave., Chico CA 95926. (530)345-3027. Fax: (530)345-1266. E-mail: casaro@sunset.net. Website: http://www.casaro-records.com. Contact: Hugh Santos. A&R: John Peters; Dan Riley. Record company and record producer. Estab. 1988. Staff size: 3. Releases 5-8 LPs/year. Pays variable royalty to artists on contract; statutory rate to publisher per song on record.
How to Contact: Write or call first and obtain permission to submit. Prefers cassette or CD with full project demo and lyric sheet. Does not return material. Reports in 3 months.
Music: **Jazz** and **country**; also **R&B** and **pop**. Released *Gentle Rain* (by various artists), recorded by Roger Hogan Quintet on Casaro/Hill Top (easy standards); *Roger Hogan*, written and recorded by Roger Hogan on Casaro (jazz); and *Holly Taylor & Then Some* (by various artists), recorded by Holly Taylor on Casaro/Holly Taylor (standards). Other artists include Lesley McDaniel, King Cotton Jazz Band, Jeff Dixon, Lory Dobbs and Charlie Robinson.
Tips: "Produce your song well (in tune—good singer). It doesn't need to be highly produced—just clear vocals. Include lyric sheet."

⬤ **CELLAR RECORDS**, 116 N. Peoria, Dixon IL 61021. (815)288-2900. E-mail: tjoos@essex1.com. Website: http://www.essex1.com/people/tjoos. President (rock, pop, country): Todd Joos. Vice President (rock): Bob Brady. A&R: Mike Thompson (metal); Jim Miller (adult contemporary, pop, country). Record company, music publisher (Sound Cellar Music/BMI) and record producer (Todd Joos). Estab. 1987. Staff size: 3. Releases 4-6 singles, 12 cassettes, 6 EPs and 6-8 CDs/year. Pays 15-100% royalty to artists on contract; statutory rate to publisher per song on record. Charges in advance "if you use our studio to record."
Distributed by: V&R Distribution.
How to Contact: Submit demo tape by mail. Unsolicited submissions are OK. Prefers cassette or VHS videocassette with 3-4 songs and lyric sheet. Does not return material. Reports in 3-4 weeks only if interested. "If we like it we will call you."
Music: Mostly **metal**, **country** and **rock**; also **pop**, **rap** and **blues**. Released *Pacific*, written and recorded by The Rumors (pop); *Upon Waking*, written and recorded by Crush Ivy (rock); and *Guitar Strummin' Nobody* (by Matt Rogers), recorded by Noopy Wilson (folk/rock), all on Cellar Records. Other artists include Eric Topper, Haruspex, Roman, Jim Miller, John Stinson, Snap Judgment, Pull and Jimson Weed.
Tips: "Make sure that you understand that your band is business and you must be willing to self invest time, effort and money just like any other new business. We can help you but you must also be willing to help yourself."

⬤ **CEREBRAL RECORDS**, 1236 Laguna Dr., Carlsbad CA 92008. (619)434-2497. Publicist: Lincoln Kroll. Record company, music publisher (Cerebral Records/BMI) and record producer (Cerebral Records).

Estab. 1991. Releases 1-3 LPs and 1-3 CDs/year. Pays negotiable royalty.
How to Contact: Write first and obtain permission to submit. SASE. Reports in 2 months.
Music: Mostly **progressive rock**. Released *Sanctuary Much*, written and recorded by State of Mind on Cerebral Records.

○ **CHATTAHOOCHEE RECORDS**, 2544 Roscomare Rd., Los Angeles CA 90077. (818)788-6863. Contact: Chris Yardum. Music Director: Robyn Meyers. Record company and music publisher (Etnoc/Conte). Member NARAS. Releases 4 singles/year. Pays negotiable royalty to artists on contract.
How to Contact: Submit demo tape by mail. Unsolicited submissions are OK. Prefers cassette with 2-6 songs and lyric sheet. Does not return material. Reports in 6-8 weeks only if interested.
Music: Mostly **rock**. Artists include DNA.

○ **CHERRY STREET RECORDS**, P.O. Box 52681, Tulsa OK 74152. (918)742-8087. E-mail: cherryst @msn.com. Website: http://www.cherrystreetrecords.com. President: Rodney Young. Vice President: Steve Hickerson. Record company and music publisher. Estab. 1990. Staff size: 2. Releases 2 CD/year. Pays 50% royalty to artists on contract; statutory rate to publisher per song on record.
Distributed by: Focus Distribution and MS Distribution.
How to Contact: Write first and obtain permission to submit. Prefers cassette or videocassette with 4 songs and lyric sheet. SASE. Reports in 4 months.
Music: **Rock, country** and **R&B**; also **jazz**. Released *Promise Land*, written and recorded by Richard Neville on Cherry Street (rock). Other artists include George W. Carroll and Chris Blevins.
Tips: "We sign only artists who play an instrument, sing and write songs. Send only your best four songs."

○ **CHIAROSCURO RECORDS**, 830 Broadway, New York NY 10003. (212)473-0479. Fax: (914)279-5025. E-mail: jon@chiaroscurojazz.com. Website: http://www.ChiaroscuroJazz.com. A&R: Jon Bates. Labels include Downtown Sound. Record company and record producer (Hank O'Neal, Andrew Sordoni, Jon Bates). Estab. 1973. Releases 12 CDs/year. Pays negotiable royalty to artists on contract; statutory rate to publisher per song on record.
Distributed by: D.N.A., MS and Bayside.
How to Contact: Submit demo tape by mail. Unsolicited submissions are OK. Prefers cassette, CD, DAT or videocassette with 1-3 songs. SASE. Reports in 6 weeks.
Music: Mostly **jazz** and **blues**. Released *Dot's Cheesecake* (by John Bunch/Bob Haggar/Bucky Pizzarelli), recorded by New York Swing (jazz); *Maybe Someday*, written and recorded by Virginia Mayhew (jazz); and *Adam's Waltz*, written and recorded by Adam Makowicz (jazz), all on Chiaroscuro.
Tips: "We are not a pop label. Our average release sells between 3,000-5,000 copies in the first three years. We do not give cash advances or tour support, and our average budget per release is about $15,000 including all production, printing and manufacturing costs."

○ **CHROME DOME RECORDS**, 250 W. 57th St., New York NY 10019. (212)489-1500. Fax: (212)489-5660. A&R Department: Matt "½ Pint" Davis. Record company and music publisher (Majestic Control/BMI). Estab. 1997.
How to Contact: Submit demo tape by mail. Unsolicited submissions are OK. Prefers cassette with 3 songs. SASE. Reports in 2 months.
Music: Mostly **rap** and **R&B**. Artists include 1st Signings, Soul IV Real and Phatty Banks.

○ **CIMIRRON/RAINBIRD RECORDS**, 607 Piney Point Rd., Yorktown VA 23692. (757)898-8155. E-mail: lpuckett@ix.netcom.com. President: Lana Puckett (country, pop, gospel). Vice President: Kim Person (folk, bluegrass). Record company and music publisher (Cimirron Music). Releases 3-6 CDs and cassettes/year. Pays variable royalty to artists on contract; negotiable rate to publisher per song on record.
Distributed by: Peaches, Plan 9, Plan A and mail order.
How to Contact: Write first and obtain permission to submit. Prefers cassette or CD and lyric sheet. SASE. Reports in 2 months.
Music: Mostly **country/acoustic**, **bluegrass** and **singer/songwriter**. Released *Special Delivery*, written and recorded by Bill Parson (acoustic); *No Limit*, written and recorded by Mavis Holmes (instrumental);

THE TYPES OF MUSIC each listing is interested in are printed in **boldface**.

and *Harp Guitar*, written and recorded by Stephen Bennett, all on Cimirron/Rainbird Records. Other artists include Ron Fetner and Motely.

Tips: "Have a great song. Be hardworking and have a following."

☑ ○ **CITA COMMUNICATIONS INC.**, Dept. SM, 530 Pittsburgh Rd., Butler PA 16001. (724)586-6552. E-mail: citatb@citacomgroup.com. Website: http://www.citacomgroup.com. A&R/Producer: Mickii Taimuty. Labels include Phunn! Records and Tropē Records. Record company. Estab. 1989. Releases 3 singles, 2 EPs and 2 CDs/year. Pays artists 20% royalty on contract. Pays statutory rate to publisher per song on record.
How to Contact: Submit demo tape by mail. Unsolicited submissions are OK. Prefers cassette or VHS, Beta or ¾″ videocassette with up to 6 songs and lyric sheets. SASE. Reports in 6 weeks.
Music: Mostly **alternative**, **new country** and **rock gospel**; also **rock/dance**. Released "Hold Me Now" and "I Cross My Heart" (by Taimuty/Nelson), recorded by Melissa Anne on Phunn! Records; and "Fight the Fight," written and recorded by M.J. Nelson on Tropē Records. Other artists include Most High, Sister Golden Hair and Countdown.

◐ **CLEOPATRA RECORDS**, 8726 S. Sepulveda Blvd., Suite D-82, Los Angeles CA 90045. (310)577-1480. Fax: (310)821-4702. Contact: A&R. Labels include Hypnotic, Deadline, X-Ray, Cult and Purple Pyramid. Record company. Estab. 1991. Releases 5 singles, 10 LPs, 5 EPs and 100 CDs/year. Pays 10-14% royalty to artists on contract; negotiable rate to publisher per song on record.
How to Contact: Submit demo tape by mail. Unsolicited submissions are OK. Prefers CD with 3 songs. Does not return material. Reports in 1 month.
Music: Mostly **industrial**, **gothic** and **trance**; also **heavy metal**, **space rock** and **electronic**.

⊕ ☑ ○ **COLLECTOR RECORDS**, P.O. Box 1200, 3260 AE oud beyerland Holland. Phone: (31)186 604266. Fax: (31)186 604366. Research: Cees Klop. Labels include All Rock, Downsouth, Unknown, Pro Forma and White Label Records. Record company, music publisher (All Rock Music Publishing) and record producer (Cees Klop). Estab. 1967. Staff size: 4. Release 25 LPs/year. Pays 10% royalty to artist on contract.
How to Contact: Submit demo tape by mail. Unsolicited submissions are OK. Prefers cassette. SAE and IRC. Reports in 2 months.
Music: Mostly **'50s rock**, **rockabilly**, **hillbilly boogie** and **country/rock**; also **piano boogie woogie**. Released *Dixie Boogie* (by V. Laurentis), recorded by Rockin' Vincent on Down South; *The Milwaukee Road*, written and recorded by Larry Lee Phillipson; and *Let Me Go Baby*, written and recorded by Sunset Lenny, both on Collector Records. Other artists include Teddy Redell and Henk Pepping.

⛉ ☑ ◐ **COLUMBIA RECORDS**, 550 Madison Ave., New York NY 10022-3211. (212)833-8000. Fax: (212)883-4812. Director of A&R: John Day. Santa Monica office: 2100 Colorado Ave., Santa Monica CA 90404. (310)449-2100. Fax: (310)449-2071. A&R Director: John Weakland. Nashville office: 34 Music Square E., Nashville TN 37203. (615)742-4321. Fax: (615)244-2549. E-mail: sonymusiconline@sonymusic.com. Website: http://www.music.sony.com/Music/Columbia. Labels include So So Def Records and Ruffhouse Records. Record company.
Distributed by: Sony.
   • Columbia's Aerosmith won a 1998 Grammy Award for Best Rock Performance by a Duo or Group with Vocal and Will Smith won for Best Rap Solo Performance.
How to Contact: Columbia Records does not accept unsolicited submissions.
Music: Released *Big Willie Style*, recorded by Will Smith; *Savage Garden*, recorded by Savage Garden; and *Higher Ground*, recorded by Barbra Streisand, all on Columbia Records. Other artists include Mariah Carey, Aerosmith and Bob Dylan.

○ **COM-FOUR DISTRIBUTION**, 7 Dunham Place, Brooklyn NY 11211. (718)599-2205. Distribution Manager: Albert Garzon. Distribution company. Estab. 1985. Distributes over 100,000 different titles including imports.
How to Contact: "We are an independent distributor looking for independent artists with market-ready product (no cassettes please)." Submit product by mail. Unsolicited submissions are OK. Does not return material. "We only respond if we like material."
Music: All genres.
Tips: "Be original and have some talent. Be willing and ready to work hard touring, promoting, etc."

⊕ ☑ ◐ **COMMA RECORDS & TAPES**, Nachtigallenstr. 36, 63263 Neu-Isenburg, Germany. Phone: (6102)52696. Fax: (6102)52696. General Manager: Roland Bauer. Labels include Big Sound,

Comma International and Max-Banana-Tunes. Record company. Estab. 1969. Releases 50-70 singles and 20 LPs/year. Pays 7-10% royalty to artists on contract.

How to Contact: Submit demo tape by mail. Unsolicited submissions are OK. Prefers cassette, CD, DAT or MD and lyric sheet. Reports in 4-6 weeks, "if submission is accompanied by SAE and two IRCs." Does not return material.

Music: Mostly **pop**, **disco**, **rock**, **R&B** and **country**; also **musicals** and **classical**.

COMSTOCK RECORDS LTD., 10603 N. Hayden Rd., Suite 114, Scottsdale AZ 85260. (602)951-3115. Fax: (602)951-3074. E-mail: airplay@comstock-records.com. Website: http://www.comstock-records.com. Production Manager/Producer: Patty Parker. President: Frank Fara. Record company, music publisher (White Cat Music/ASCAP, Rocky Bell Music/BMI, How the West Was Sung Music/BMI), record producer (Patty Parker) and radio promotion. Member CMA, BBB, CCMA, BCCMA, British CMA and AF of M. "Comstock Records, Ltd. has three primary divisions: Production, Promotion and Publishing. We distribute and promote both our own Nashville productions, as well as already completed country or pop/rock CDs. We also offer CD design and mastering and manufacturing for products we promote. We can master from a copy of your DAT master or CD." Staff size: 2. Releases 24-30 CD singles, 10-12 albums/year and 5-6 international sampler CDs. Pays 10% royalty to artists on contract; statutory rate to publishers for each record sold. "Artists pay distribution and promotion fee to press and release their masters."

- Comstock Records was named indie Label of the Year at ECMA of Europe's Country Music Awards for 1998. Fara & Parker are also authors of the book *How To Open Doors in the Music Industry—The Independent Way.*

How to Contact: Submit demo tape by mail. Unsolicited submissions are OK. Prefers CD, DAT, cassette or VHS videocassette. SASE. "Enclose stamped return envelope if demo is to be returned." Reports in 2 weeks.

Music: Released *Strong Enough To Lean On*, written and recorded by Karen Cruise (country); "The Cowboy," written and recorded by Chuck Labelle (country); and "On My Knees" (by Grant Peterson/Lawrence Borg), recorded by Grant Peterson, all on Comstock Records. Other artists include Blazing Country, KC Jones, RJ McClintock, Karin Setter, Joanne Myrol and Vic Levac.

Tips: "Go global—good songs and good singers are universal. Country acts from North America will find a great response in the overseas radio market. Likewise U.S. Radio is open to the fresh new sounds that foreign artists bring to the airwaves."

CONTINENTAL RECORDS, 744 Joppa Farm Rd., Joppatowne MD 21085. (410)679-2262. Director (country): Ernest W. Cash. A&R: Norma R. Cash (gospel); Debra L. Benedetta (R&B, pop, jazz); Michael Benedetta (rock). Labels include Direct Response Records. Record company, management firm (Cash Productions) and music publisher (Ernie Cash Music/BMI). Estab. 1986. Staff size: 4. Pays 8% royalty to artists on contract; statutory rate to publisher per song on record.

Distributed by: Laurie, Inc. and Galgano Inc.

How to Contact: Write or call first and obtain permission to submit. Prefers cassette or VHS videocassette with 3 songs and lyric sheet. SASE. Reports in 2 weeks.

Music: Mostly **country** and **gospel**. Released *A Man I Call Jones* (by Jimmy Peppers), recorded by Randy Allen St. Clair; and *Give It Wings*, written and recorded by Johnny Duncan IV, both on Continental (country); and *Behind Your Lovely Eyes*, written and recorded by David R. Padrino on DRP Records (R&B).

Tips: "Do the best work possible when preparing your material and package. If you wish to compete in this industry, keep it clean, well-produced, commercial and simple. Be honest with yourself and everyone you expect to work with and you should be successful in your endeavors."

COUNTRY BREEZE RECORDS, 1715 Marty, Kansas City KS 66103. (913)596-1632. President: Ed Morgan, Jr. A&R Directors: John Matthews (rock); Steve Russell (gospel). Labels include Angel Star Records and Crusader Records. Record company and music publisher (Country Breeze Music/BMI and Walkin' Hat Music/ASCAP). Releases 15 7" singles and 20 cassettes and 15-20 CDs/year. Pays 30% royalty to artists on contract; statutory rate to publisher per song on record.

Distributed by: KAW Valley Distributors (country), Victory Mountain (gospel) and Screamin' Cat (rock).

REFER TO THE CATEGORY INDEX (at the end of this section) to find exactly which companies are interested in the type of music you write.

How to Contact: Submit demo tape by mail. Unsolicited submissions are OK. Prefers studio-produced demo with 3 songs and lyric sheet. SASE. Reports in 2 weeks.
Music: All types of **country**. Released "I Do" (by Buddy Davis), recorded by Frontier; and "Georgia Rain," written and recorded by Tommy Turner, both on Country Breeze (country); and "How Great Art Thou," written and recorded by David Dickerson on Angel Star (gospel). Other artists include Sky Hawk, Nicole Wilson, Mike Cooper, Wilma Bell, 65 MPH and Dirty Face.
Tips: "Do not submit material and call three days later to know if it's recorded yet. It takes time."

C CRANK! A RECORD COMPANY, 1223 Wilshire Blvd. #823, Santa Monica CA 90403. (310)264-0439. Fax: (310)264-0539. E-mail: fan@crankthis.com. Website: http://www.crankthis.com. Contact: Jeff Matlow. Record company and mail order/distribution company. Estab. 1994. Releases 6 singles, 5 LPs, 2 EPs and 5 CDs/year. Pays negotiable royalty to artists on contract.
Distributed by: RED, Southern, Dutch East, Lumberjack and Nail.
How to Contact: Submit demo tape by mail. Unsolicited submissions are OK. Prefers cassette or CD with 3 songs. "Send whatever best represents your abilities." Does not return material. Reports in 2-3 weeks.
Music: Mostly **indie/alternative rock** and **pop**. Released *The Power of Failing*, written and recorded by Mineral (rock); *Boys Life*, written and recorded by Boys Life (rock); and *Blinding Stars for Starving Eyes*, written and recorded by Cursive (rock), all on Crank! Other artists include Regrets, Far Apart and Silver Scooter.

C CREATIVE IMPROVISED MUSIC PROJECTS (CIMP) RECORDS, Cadence Building, Redwood NY 13679. (315)287-2852. Fax: 315)287-2860. Producer: Bob Rusch. Labels include Cadence Jazz Records. Record company and record producer (Robert D. Rusch). Estab. 1980. Releases 25-30 CDs/year. Pays negotiable royalty to artists on contract; pays statutory rate to publisher per song on record.
Distributed by: North Country Distributors.
  • CIMP specializes in jazz and creative improvised music.
How to Contact: Submit demo tape by mail. Unsolicited submissions are OK. Prefers cassette, CD or DAT. "We are not looking for songwriters but recording artists." SASE. Reports in 1 week.
Music: Mostly **jazz** and **creative improvised music**. Released *Mark 'N' Marshall*, recorded by Marshall Allen; and *Tag*, recorded by Yukofujiyama, both on CIMP (improvised jazz). Other artists include Kevin Norton Trio, John McPhee & David Prentice and Mark Whitecage Quartet.
Tips: "CIMP Records are produced to provide music to reward repeated and in-depth listenings. They are recorded live to two-track which captures the full dynamic range one would experience in a live concert. There is no compression, homogenization, eq-ing, post-recording splicing, mixing, or electronic fiddling with the performance. Digital recording allows for a vanishingly low noise floor and tremendous dynamic range. This compression of the dynamic range is what limits the 'air' and life of many recordings. Our recordings capture the dynamic intended by the musicians. In this regard these recordings are demanding. Treat the recording as your private concert. Give it your undivided attention and it will reward you. CIMP Records are not intended to be background music. This method is demanding not only on the listener but on the performer as well. Musicians must be able to play together in real time. They must understand the dynamics of their instrument and how it relates to the others around them. There is no fix-it-in-the-mix safety; either it works or it doesn't. What you hear is exactly what was played. Our main concern is music not marketing."

C CRESCENT RECORDING CORPORATION (CRC), P.O. Box 520195, Bronx NY 10452. (212)591-2148. Fax: (718)716-2963. E-mail: qsupreme@earthlink.net. Operations Officer: Leon G. Pinkston. Record company. Estab. 1994. Releases 2-4 singles, 1-2 LPs, 1-2 EPs and 1-2 CDs/year. Pays negotiable royalty to artists on contract; statutory rate to publisher per song on record.
How to Contact: Submit demo tape by mail. Unsolicited submissions are OK. Prefers cassette or CD

FOR EXPLANATIONS OF THESE SYMBOLS,
SEE THE INSIDE FRONT AND BACK COVERS OF THIS BOOK.

with 2-5 songs and lyric sheet. "Please include bio/résumé, cover letter, and/or any other material to strengthen your submission." Does not return material. Reports in 3-6 months if interested.

Music: Mostly **soul/R&B**, **rock/pop** and **rap**; also **dance/club** and **jazz**. Released *Crazytown*, written and recorded by Dodging Reality (rock); "Have You Ever (Been Hurt By Love)" written and recorded by Camille Watson (soul); and "Wait Until Tomorrow" (by Camille Watson), recorded by Charisma (pop), all on Crescent Records. Other artists include Sav'vy.

Tips: "Continue to grow and practice your skills and never quit reaching for your goals. Always be professional in handling your business."

☑ ⬤ CURB RECORDS, 47 Music Square E., Nashville TN 37203. (615)321-5080. Fax: (615)327-3003. Website: http://www.curb.com. Executive Vice President/General Manager: Dennis P. Hannon. Record company.

How to Contact: Curb Records does not accept unsolicited submissions; accepts previously published material only. Do not submit without permission.

Music: Released *Everywhere*, recorded by Tim McGraw; *Sittin' On Top of the World*, recorded by LeAnn Rimes; and *I'm Alright*, recorded by Jo Dee Messina, all on Curb Records. Other artists include Mary Black, Bananarama, Junior Brown, Merle Haggard, Kal Ketchum, David Kersh, Lyle Lovett, Wynonna and Sawyer Brown.

⬤ DAGENE/CABLETOWN COMPANY, P.O. Box 410851, San Francisco CA 94141. (415)822-1530. President: David Alston. Record company, music publisher (Dagene Music), management firm (Golden City International) and record producer (David-Classic Disc Productions). Estab. 1993. Pays standard royalty to artists on contract; statutory rate to publisher per song on record.

How to Contact: Write or call first and obtain permission to submit. Prefers cassette (or VHS videocassette) with 2 songs and lyric sheet. SASE. Reports in 1 month.

Music: Mostly **R&B/rap**, **dance** and **pop**; also **gospel**. Released "Maxin" (by Marcus Justice/Bernard Henderson), recorded by 2 Dominatorz on Dagene Records; "Love Don't Love Nobody" (by David Alston), recorded by Rare Essence on Cabletown Records; and "Why Can't I Be Myself," written and recorded by David Alston on E-lect-ric Recordings. Other artists include Chapter 1.

⬤ ALAN DALE PRODUCTIONS, 1630 Judith Lane, Indianapolis IN 46227. (317)786-1630. President: Alan D. Heshelman. Labels include ALTO Records. Record company. Estab. 1990. Pays 10% royalty to artists on contract.

How to Contact: Write or call first and obtain permission to submit or to arrange personal interview. Prefers cassette with 3 songs. Does not return material. Reports in 6-10 weeks.

Music: Mostly **A/C**, **country**, **jazz**, **gospel** and **New Age**.

Tips: "At the present time, we are only looking for vocalists to promote as we promote the songs we write and produce."

⬤ DANFORD ENTERTAINMENT GROUP/SISYPHUS RECORDS, 216 Third Ave. N., Minneapolis MN 55401. (612)337-6079. E-mail: info@danfordent.com. Website: http://danfordent.com. Vice President/Projects Coordinator: James Walsh (blues, country, rock, pop, R&B, jazz). President/Projects Coordinator: Tom Danford (pop, rock, R&B). Labels include Oarfin Records. Record company, record producer, artist management and development agency. Estab. 1998. Staff size: 6. Releases 4-6 singles, 2-3 EPs and 4-8 CDs/year. Pays 5-20% royalty to artists on contract; statutory rate to publisher per song on record.

Distributed by: Oarfin Records.

How to Contact: Write or call first and obtain permission to submit. Prefers cassette or CD with 3-4 songs and lyric sheet or lead sheet. SASE. Reports in 1 month.

Music: Mostly **pop**, **rock** and **country**; also **R&B** and **jazz**. Released *20 Years Ago Today*, (by Walsh/Challman), recorded by Gypsy (rock); *Buffalo Alice* (by Wilson/Sickels/Adams), recorded by Buffalo Alice (country); and *Night Life*, recorded by Down Right Tight (R&B).

⬤ DAPMOR RECORDS, 3031 Acorn St., Kenner LA 70065. (504)468-9820. Fax: (504)466-2896. President: Kelly Jones. Record company and music publisher (Dapmor Music). Estab. 1996.

OPENNESS TO SUBMISSIONS: ⬚ beginners; ⬤ beginners and experienced; ⬤ experienced only; ⬤ industry referrals only.

How to Contact: "Submit professionally done CDs through an attorney or another publisher."
Music: Mostly **R&B**, **jazz** and **country**; also **blues**, **rap**, **reggae** and **rock**.
Tips: "Learn to accept rejection and keep trying."

● **DEADEYE RECORDS**, P.O. Box 2607, Capistrano Beach CA 92624. (714)768-0644. E-mail: deade ye@deadeye.com. Website: http://www.deadeye.com. A&R: James Frank. Manager: Frank Jenkins. Record company, record producer and management firm (Danny Federici's Shark River Music). Estab. 1992. Staff size: 2. Releases 3 CDs/year. Pays varying royalty to artists on contract; statutory rate to publisher per song on record.
How to Contact: Write or e-mail first and obtain permission to submit. Prefers cassette or videocassette with 3 songs and lyric sheet. Does not return material. Reports in 3 months.
Music: Mostly **country**, **rock** and **blues**; also **R&B**. Released *Ragin' Wind* (by Frank Jenkins), recorded by Diamondback on Deadeye Records (country); and *Flemington*, recorded by Danny Federici (of the E Street Band).

◼️ ● **DEARY ME RECORDS**, P.O. Box 19315, Cincinnati OH 45219. (513)557-2930. E-mail: dearym e@one.net. Website: http://www.iac.net/~hubcap. Director of A&R: John Davis. Director of Business: Jim Farmer. Record company. Estab. 1995. Staff size: 2. Releases 1 single and 3 CDs/year. Pays 50% royalty "after we break even."
Distributed by: Lumberjack.
How to Contact: Submit demo tape by mail. Unsolicited submissions are OK. Prefers cassette or CD with 5-6 songs, lead sheet, cover letter, press clippings and photo. Does not return material. Reports in 1 month.
Music: Mostly **indie pop/rock**, **alternative** and **roots rock**; also **garage**, **surf** and **punk**. Does not want top 40. Released *Ka*, written and recorded by Big Soap (punk); *Wolverton Brothers*, written and recorded by Wolverton Brothers (alternative); and "End of the Night/No More," written and recorded by Greenhornes (garage), all on Deary Me Records.
Tips: "We are typically not impressed with gimmicks, or interested in trends. Be simple and direct. You have to be willing to work your album. You work for us, we will work for you. Touring is a major plus."

✓ ● **deCONSTRUCTION RECORDS**, (formerly dedicated records), 580 Broadway, Suite 504, New York NY 10012. (212)334-5959. Contact: A&R. Record company. Estab. 1994. Releases 4 singles, 6 LPs, 6 EPs and 8 CDs/year. Pays negotiable royalty to artists on contract (all deals via Arista Records).
How to Contact: Write first and obtain permission to submit. Prefers cassette. "Keep it simple with a tape or CD, bio and your best press." SASE. Reports in 1 month.
Music: Mostly **alternative rock**, **top 40/pop** and **singer/songwriter**; also **hippie/granola**, **jam bands** and **progressive**.
Tips: "Send only the songs/music you really like—don't send it and say, 'this isn't really representative/ good.' Have a great live performance, and build a local following."

◼️ ○ **DEEP SOUTH ENTERTAINMENT**, P.O. Box 17737, Raleigh NC 27619-7737. (919)676-2089. Fax: (919)844-1711. E-mail: kelly@deepsouthrec.com. Website: http://www.deepsouthrec.com. Director of Artist Relations: Kelly Watson. Director of A&R: Steve Williams. Record company and management company. Estab. 1996. Staff size: 7. Pays negotiable royalty to artists on contract; statutory rate to publisher per song on record.
Distributed by: Redeye Distribution, Valley, Select-O-Hits, City Hall, AEC/Bassin and Northeast One Stop.
How to Contact: Submit demo tape by mail. Unsolicited submissions are OK. Prefers cassette or CD with 3 songs, cover letter and press clippings. Does not return material. Reports in 2 months.
Music: Mostly **pop**, **modern rock** and **alternative**; also **swing**, **rockabilly** and **heavy rock**. Does not want rap, country or R&B. Released *El Baile de la Cobra* (by Ben Friedman), recorded by Cigar Store Indians (rockabilly); *The Chartreuse EP* (by Mike Garrigan), recorded by Collapsis (pop); and *Deep 3*, written and recorded by various artists (modern rock), all recorded on Deep South Records. Other artists include Laburnum, Radiostar and Mr. Henry.
Tips: "Send us a package, follow up with a call, and include lots of information about yourself—press, bios, etc. Presentation is a big part!"

✓ ♟ ● **DEF JAM RECORDS**, 8981 Sunset Blvd., Suite 309, Los Angeles CA 90069. (310)724-7233. Fax: (310)246-9779. New York office: 160 Varick St., 12th Floor, New York NY 10013. (212)229-5200. Fax: (212)627-3613. Vice President of A&R: Chris Lighty. A&R: Tina Davis. Labels include Roc-A-Fella, Oakland Hills Records and Ruff Ryders.

• Def Jam's Jay-Z won a 1998 Grammy Award for Best Rap Album.

How to Contact: Def Jam Records does not accept unsolicited submissions.

Music: Released *It's Dark and Hell Is Hot*, recorded by DMX on Ruff Ryders; and *In My Lifetime, Vol. 1*, recorded by Jay-Z on Roc-A-Fella. Other artists include Montell Jordan and Def Squad.

☑ ◯ **DEL-FI RECORDS, INC.**, 8271 Melrose Ave., Suite 103, Los Angeles CA 90046. (800)993-3534. Fax: (323)966-4805. E-mail: info@del-fi.com. Website: http://www.del-fi.com. Director of A&R: Bryan Thomas. Owner and President: Bob Keane. Labels include Del-Fi, Del-Fi Nashville, Donna, Mustang, Bronco and others. Record company. Estab. 1957. Releases 5-10 LPs and 40 CDs/year. Pays negotiable royalty to artists on contract; statutory rate to publisher per song on record.

Distributed by: Navarre Corporation.

• Del-Fi's open door policy is legendary.

How to Contact: Submit demo tape by mail. Unsolicited submissions are OK. Prefers cassette or CD. "Please enclose bio information and photo if possible. Send a résumé via fax." Does not return material "unless specified. Allow several weeks." Reports in 1 month.

Music: Mostly **rock**, **surf/drag** and **exotica**. Released several compilations including *Delphonic Sounds Today*; *Shots In the Dark*; and *Pulp Surfin!*, all on Del-Fi. Other artists include The El Caminos.

Tips: "Be sure you are making/writing music that specifically meets your own artistic/creative demands, and not someone else's. Write/play music from the heart and soul and you will always succeed on a personal rewarding level first. We are *the* surf label . . . home of the 'Delphonic' sound. We've also released many of the music world's best known artists, including Ritchie Valens and the Bobby Fuller Four."

⊕ ☑ ◐ **DEMI MONDE RECORDS AND PUBLISHING, LTD.**, Foel Studio, Llanfair Caereinion, Powys, Wales, United Kingdom. Phone/fax: (01938)810758. E-mail: demi.monde@dial.pipex.com. Website: http://www.demimonde.co.uk/demimonde. Managing Director: Dave Anderson. Record company, music publisher (Demi Monde Records & Publishing, Ltd.) and record producer (Dave Anderson). Estab. 1983. Releases 5 12" singles, 10 LPs and 6 CDs/year. Pays 10% royalty to artists on contract; statutory rate to publisher per song on record.

Distributed by: Pinnacle, Magnum and Shellshock.

How to Contact: Submit demo tape by mail. Unsolicited submissions are OK. Prefers cassette with 3-4 songs. Does not return material. Reports in 6 weeks.

Music: Mostly **rock**, **R&B** and **pop**. Released *Hawkwind*, *Amon Duul II & Gong* and *Groundhogs* (by T.S. McPhee), all on Demi Monde Records.

Ⓝ ◯ **DENTAL RECORDS**, P.O. Box 20058 DHCC, New York NY 10017. (212)486-4513. Fax: (212)832-6370. E-mail: rsanford@dentalrecords.com. Website: http://www.dentalrecords.com. Owner: Rick Sanford. Record company. Estab. 1981. Staff size: 2. Releases 3 CDs/year. Pays negotiable royalty to artists on contract; statutory rate to publisher per song on record.

Distributed by: Dutch East India Trading.

How to Contact: Submit demo tape by mail. Unsolicited submissions are OK. Prefers CD with any number of songs, lyric sheet and cover letter. "Check our website to see if your material is appropriate." SASE. Reports in 2 weeks.

Music: Mostly **weird pop**, **art pop** and **soda pop**. Does not want urban, heavy metal or hard core. Released *Add Corn Lester*, written and recorded by Les Izmor (pop); "Flotsam on the Water," written and recorded by Most Sordid Pies (pop); and *Arrows Thru the Heart*, written and recorded by Kevin Hayes (pop), all on Dental Records. Other artists include Moose Mason & the Oddfellows and Rick Sanford.

Ⓝ ◯ **DIRECT HIT RECORDS**, 470 Wildbriar Dr., Garland TX 75043. (972)279-0929. E-mail: direct-hit@home.com. Website: http://www.direct-hit.com. Owner: Kelly Handran. Record company. Estab. 1989. Staff size: 2. Releases 3 singles and 1 CD/year. Pays negotiable royalty to artists on contract; statutory rate to publisher per song on record.

Distributed by: Crystal Clear and Rhetoric Records.

How to Contact: Write first and obtain permission to submit a demo. Prefers cassette or CD with cover letter. Does not return material. Reports in 2 months.

Music: Mostly **rock**, **alternative** and **punk**; also **ska**, **experimental** and **ambient**. Does not want classical, jazz or folk.

◐ **DISC-TINCT MUSIC, INC.**, P.O. Box 5837, Englewood NJ 07631. (201)568-7066. President: Jeffrey Collins. Labels include Music Station, Echo USA, Dancefloor, Soul Creation and Soul Vibes. Record company, music publisher (Distinct Music, Inc./BMI, Distinct Echo Music/ASCAP) and record producer (Echo USA Productions). Estab. 1985. Releases 50 12" singles, 10 LPs, 4 EPs and 15 CDs/year.

Pays 5-8% royalty to artists on contract; ⅔ statutory rate to publisher per song on record.
How to Contact: Submit demo tape by mail. Unsolicited submissions are OK. Prefers cassette or VHS videocassette with up to 5 songs. SASE. Reports in 1 month.
Music: Mostly **hip-hop, R&B, dance** and **house/techno**. Released *Your Attitude* (by Jimmie Fox), recorded by Kim Cummings on Music Station Records; and "As Quiet As It's Kept" (by Elis Pacheco), recorded by Colonel Abrams on Soul Creation Records. Other artists include Debbie Blackwell/Cook, Eleanor Grant, Black Rebels, Ready for the World, Llake, George Kerr and Quincy Patrick.
Tips: "Cue your cassettes, which should be labeled clearly."

⚇ ◐ DOUBLE PLAY RECORDS, 41 Sutter St., Suite 1337, San Francisco CA 94104. (415)267-4837. Website: http://www.DoublePlay.com. President: Shawn Evans. Record company and music publisher (6-4-3 Publishing). Estab. 1994. Staff size: 4. Releases 2 CDs/year. Pays negotiable royalty to artists on contract; statutory rate to publisher per song on record.
Distributed by: NAIL, Revolver, Darla, Surefire, Dutch East and Caroline.
How to Contact: Call first and obtain permission to submit. Prefers cassette or CD with 5 songs, lyric sheet, lead sheet, cover letter and press clippings. Does not return material. Reports in 2 months.
Music: Mostly **alternative/rock** and **singer/songwriters**. Released *Walk A Lightyear Mile*, written and recorded by Dora Flood (rock); *Shut Up and Play*, written and recorded by Hissy Fit (pop/punk); and *In Orbit*, written and recorded by Snowmen (rock), all on Double Play Records.
Tips: "Don't submit material before it's ready and tour, tour, tour!"

♀ ◐ DREAMWORKS RECORDS, 9268 W. Third St., Beverly Hills CA 90210. (310)234-7700. Fax: (310)234-7750. Website: http://www.dreamworksrec.com. Vice President of A&R: Chris Douridas. A&R: Beth Halper. Nashville office: 1516 16th Ave. S., Nashville TN 37203. (615)463-4600. Fax: (615)244-2549. A&R: Allison Jones. New York office: 575 Broadway, 6th Floor, New York NY 10012. (212)219-2370. Fax: (212)219-2373. A&R: Will Langolf. Record company and music publisher (DreamWorks SKG Music Publishing).
● DreamWorks' John Williams won a 1998 Grammy Award for Best Instrumental Composition Written for a Motion Picture.
How to Contact: Material must be submitted through an agent or attorney. Does not accept unsolicited submissions.
Music: Released *Forces of Nature* (soundtrack); *XO*, recorded by Elliott Smith; and *The Sound of Wet Paint*, recorded by Forest for the Trees, all on DreamWorks Records.

✓ ◐ DRIVE ENTERTAINMENT, 10451 Jefferson Blvd., Culver City CA 90232. (310)815-4900. Fax: (310)815-4908. E-mail: drive@earthlink.net. Website: http://www.driveentertainment.com. CEO: Stephen Powers. Labels include Drive Archive, Pagoda Records, Golden Records. Record company and music publisher (Drive Music, Donunda Music). Estab. 1992. Releases 50 LPs and 50 CDs/year. Pays negotiable royalty to artists on contract; statutory rate to publisher per song on record.
Distributed by: Navarre, Fairyland Music, Licette Music, Dorton Music, Great American Gramophone Music, Blue Coast Music.
How to Contact: Submit demo tape by mail. Unsolicited submissions are OK. Prefers cassette or DAT with 3 songs and lyric sheet. SASE. Reports in 6 weeks.
Music: Mostly **pop, rock** and **Triple A**; also **dance**. Released *Swing Alive*, written and recorded by various artists (big band); *Singin' The Blues*, written and recorded by various artists (blues); *Talk Memphis to Me*, recorded by Cybill Sheperd; and *Drop Till You Dance*, written and recorded by various artists, all on Drive Entertainment.

◐ DRUMBEAT INDIAN ARTS, INC., 4143 N. 16th St., Suite 1, Phoenix AZ 85016. (602)266-4823. President: Bob Nuss. Labels include Indian House and Indian Sounds. Record company and distributor of American Indian recordings. Estab. 1984. Staff size: 2. Releases 50 cassettes and 20 CDs/year. Royalty varies with project.
● Note that Drumbeat Indian Arts is a very specialized label, and only wants to receive submissions by Native American artists.
How to Contact: Call first and obtain permission to submit. Prefers cassette or VHS videocassette.

● **A BULLET** introduces comments by the editor of *Songwriter's Market* indicating special information about the listing.

SASE. Reports in 2 months.

Music: Music by American Indians—any style (must be enrolled tribal members). Does not want New Age "Indian style" material. Other artists include Black Lodge Singers, R. Carlos Nakai, Lite Foot, Kashtin and Joanne Shenandoah.

Tips: "We deal only with American Indian performers. We do not accept material from others. Please include tribal affiliation."

🌐 ◯ **E.S.R. RECORDS**, 40 Camperdown Terrace, Exmouth, Devon EX8 1EQ United Kingdom. Phone: (01392)57880. M.D: John Greenslade. A&R: Pete Watkinson. Record company (P.R.S.) and record producer (E.S.R. Productions). Estab. 1965. Staff size: 2. Releases 4 singles and 10 LPs/year. Pays 50% royalty to artists on contract; statutory rate to publisher per song on records.

Distributed by: Nebo Records.

How to Contact: Submit demo tape by mail. Unsolicited submissions are OK. Prefers cassette with 4 songs and lyric sheet. Does not return material. Reports in 3 weeks.

Music: Mostly **country** and **MOR**. Released *Get In Line*, written and recorded by Solo and Watkinson (country); *May I Please*, written and recorded by Gerri Ellen (country); and *The Other Half*, written and recorded by The Other Half (MOR), all on E.S.R. Records. Other artists include Kar Barron, Barracuda, Gary Kane, Karaoke Bob and Storm Rivers.

📀 **ELEKTRA ENTERTAINMENT GROUP**, 345 N. Maple Dr., Suite 123, Beverly Hills CA 90210. (310)288-3800. Fax: (310)274-9491. Director of A&R: John Kirkpatrick. New York office: 75 Rockefeller Plaza, New York NY 10019. (212)275-4000. Fax: (212)581-4650. Website: http://www.elektra.com. Director of A&R: Darryl Williams. Labels include Elektra Records, Eastwest Records and Asylum Records. Record company.

Distributed by: WEA.

How to Contact: Elektra does not accept unsolicited submissions.

Music: Mostly **alternative/modern rock**. Released *Reload*, recorded by Metallica; *Ophelia*, recorded by Natalie Merchant; and *When Disaster Strikes*, recorded by Busta Rhymes, all on Elektra Entertainment. Other artists include Tracy Chapman, Bryan White, Phish, Björk, Spacehog, Pantera, The Cure, Silk and Natalie Cole.

◯ **EMERALD CITY RECORDS**, 180 Wallace Rd. #T12, Nashville TN 37211. Phone/fax: (615)315-9494. President: Jack Froschauer. Record company and publishing company (Barren Wood Publishing). Estab. 1992. Staff size: 1. Pays negotiable royalty to artists on contract; statutory rate to publisher per song on record.

Distributed by: Rotation Record Distributors, Dream Machine Entertainment and GEM.

How to Contact: Submit demo tape by mail. Unsolicited submissions are OK. Prefers cassette or DAT with 1-4 songs and lyric or lead sheet. "If sending cassette, studio quality please." SASE. Reports in 2-3 months.

Music: Mostly **A/C**, **country** and **contemporary Christian**. Released *Rejoicing on the Hillside* (by J. Carolina Vanluvender/M. Vanluvender/J. Ballard), recorded by 3 Kings & Caravan of Joy (Christmas); and *Come Out From the Storm* (by K. Pritchard), recorded by Kent Pritchard & God's Will (rock), all on Emerald City Records. Other artists include Cadillac Jack, Mark Vanluvender and Dale Walton.

📀 **EMF RECORDS & AFFILIATES**, 633 Post, Suite #145, San Francisco CA 94109. (415)263-5727. Fax: (415)752-2442. Director of Operations: Steven Lassiter. Vice President, A&R (all styles): Michael Miller. A&R Supervisor (commercial): Ed Jones. International Producer (world artists): Kimberly Nakamori. Producer/Writer (all or most styles): Joe Tsongo. Labels include Richland Communications, Sky Bent and Urbana Sounds. Record company. Estab. 1994. Staff size: 2-3. Releases 5 LPs and 5 CDs/year. Pays negotiable royalty to artists on contract; statutory rate to publisher per song on record.

Distributed by: GTI Marketing and Songs Publishing International.

How to Contact: Submit demo tape by mail. Unsolicited submissions are OK. Prefers cassette, CD or DAT with 3 songs and lyric and lead sheets. Does not return material. Reports in 3-4 months.

Music: Mostly **urban/pop/rock**, **jazz/Latin** and **New Age/classical (crossover)**; also **country, world beat** and **ethnic (world)**. Released *Mutual Impact*, written and recorded by Joe Tsongo on EMF Records (New Age); *If I Had Your Love*, written and recorded by Flamé on Richland Communications (soft jazz); and *From The Source* (by B. Flores/A. Jiminez), recorded by Orchestra de Sabor on Urbana Sounds (salsa/Latin jazz). Other artists include Slam Jam.

Tips: "Build your fan base and present good images or professional packages as much as possible."

N ○ ENTERPRIZE RECORDS-TAPES, 1507 Scenic Dr., Longview TX 75604-2319. (903)759-0300. Fax: (903)297-5864. Studio Manager/A&R: Johnny Patterson (country, gospel). Owner: Jerry Haymes (all styles). Record company and music publisher (Enterprize Entertainment). Estab. 1960. Staff size: 2. Releases 2 singles, 5 LPs and 5 CDs/year. Pays negotiable royalty to artists on contract.
Distributed by: Warner Bros Europe.
How to Contact: Write or call first and obtain permission to submit a demo. Prefers cassette, CD or videocassette with lyric and lead sheet, cover letter and press clippings. Does not return material. Reports in 1 month.
Music: Mostly **pop (AC)**, **country** and **gospel**; also **rock**. Does not want rap.

○ ENTOURAGE MUSIC GROUP, 11115 Magnolia Blvd., N. Hollywood CA 91601. (818)505-0001. (818)761-7956. E-mail: contact@entouragerecords.com. Website: http://www.entouragerecords.com/label. President: Guy Paonessa. Record company and recording studio. Estab. 1986 (studio); 1995 (label). Releases 4 CDs/year. Pays negotiable royalty to artists on contract; statutory rate to publisher per song on record.
Distributed by: Touchwood Distribution.
How to Contact: Submit demo tape by mail. Unsolicited submissions are OK. Prefers cassette, CD, DAT or ½" videocassette with 3-10 songs. "No phone calls please." SASE. Reports in 3 months.
Music: Mostly **rock**, **alternative** and **contemporary jazz**; also **alternative country**. Released *The Mustard Seeds*, written and recorded by The Mustard Seeds (alternative rock); *MacAnanys*, written and recorded by MacAnanys (alternative country); and *P.O.L. Sprockett*, recorded by P.O.L. (rock), all on Entourage Records.

✓ ∅ EPIC RECORDS, 550 Madison Ave., 22nd Floor, New York NY 10022. (212)833-6746. Fax: (212)833-7188. Senior Vice President/Head of A&R (urban): David McPherson. Director of A&R Epic Urban: Marvin Peart (rap, R&B); Senior Directors of A&R Epic Urban: Steve Prudholme and Martin Moore (rap, R&B). Santa Monica office: 2100 Colorado Ave., Santa Monica CA 90404. (310)449-2100. Fax: (310)449-2848. E-mail: sonymusiconline@sonymusic.com. Website: http://www.epiccenter.com. Vice President of A&R: Matthew Marshall. Nashville office: 34 Music Square E., Nashville TN 37203. (615)742-4321. Fax: (615)244-2549. Labels include Epic Soundtrax, LV Records, Immortal Records, Word Records, Work Records and 550 Music. Record company.
Distributed by: Sony Music Distribution.
How to Contact: Write or call first and obtain permission to submit (New York office only). Does not return material. Reports only if interested. Santa Monica and Nashville offices do not accept unsolicited submissions.
Music: Released "What's So Different" (by Timbaland/Ginuwine), recorded by Ginuwine (R&B); and "When I See You Smile" (by Diane Warren), recorded by Uncle Sam (R&B/pop), both on 550 Music; and "Horse & Carriage" (by Cam'Ron/Mase/Trackmasters), recorded by Cam'Ron on Untertainment/Epic (rap). Other artists include Ghostface Killah, Cappadonna, 7 Mile, Amel Larrieux, TQ and Cha Cha.
Tips: "Do an internship if you don't have experience or work as someone's assistant. Learn the business and work hard while you figure out what your talents are and where you fit in. Once you figure out which area of the record company you're suited for, focus on that, work hard at it and it shall be yours."

N ○ EVIL TEEN RECORDS, P.O. Box 651, Village Station, New York NY 10014. (212)337-0760. Fax: (212)337-0708. E-mail: info@evilteen.com. Website: http://www.evilteen.com. President: Stefani Scamardo. Record company. Estab. 1996. Releases 2 singles, 1 LP and 4-6 CDs/year. Pays negotiable royalty to artists on contract; statutory rate to publisher per song on record.
Distributed by: Symbiotic, MS, Nemesis and Baker & Taylor.
How to Contact: Submit demo tape by mail. Unsolicited submissions are OK. Prefers cassette, CD, DAT or VHS videocassette. "Send latest musical product with press kit and tour schedule." SASE. Reports in 1 month.
Music: Mostly **rock/alternative**, **drum & bass** and **Americana**. Released *Versatility*, written and recorded by various artists (drum & bass); *The Thrill of Gravity*, written and recorded by Dolly Varden (Americana); and *Small Wire*, written and recorded by VPN (alternative), all on Evil Teen. Other artists include Shaft, Benna, Pen Pal and Random.

REFER TO THE GEOGRAPHIC INDEX (at the back of this book) to find listings of companies by state, as well as foreign listings.

☑ ◖**FICTION SONGS**, 1540 Broadway, 28th Floor, New York NY 10036. (212)930-4910. Fax: (212)930-4736. E-mail: jdaniel@amplitude.org. Website: http://www.thecure.com. A&R (U.S.): Jonathan Daniel. A&R (U.K.): Kate Dale. Record company and music publisher. Estab. 1977. Staff size: 2. Pays 75% royalty to artists on contract.
Distributed by: Elektra, Universal and PolyGram.
How to Contact: Submit demo tape by mail. Unsolicited submissions are OK. Prefers cassette. SASE. "If we like it, we will respond immediately; if not, with SASE, we'll respond within 3 weeks."
Music: Mostly **alternative** and **rock**. Released *Sweet Charity* (by Jive), recorded by Rachid on Universal (R&B); *Wrong Number* (by Robert Smith), recorded by The Cure on Fiction/Elektra Records (alternative rock); and *Mr. Zoot Suit*, written and recorded by Flying Neutrinos on GRP/Universal (swing). Other artists include The Crocketts, Wilson, Primitive Radio Gods and The Kooks.

◖**FIRST POWER ENTERTAINMENT GROUP**, 5801 Riverdale Rd., Suite 105, Riverdale MD 20737. (301)277-1671. Fax: (301)277-0173. E-mail: powerpla@mail.erols.com. Vice President/A&R: Adrianne Harris. Labels include Power Play Records, First Power Records and Street Jam Records. Record company, recording studio and television show (StreetJam TV). Estab. 1992. Releases 3-5 singles, 2-3 LPs and a variable number of EPs and CDs/year. Pays negotiable royalty to artists on contract; statutory rate to publisher per song on record.
Distributed by: Great Bay Distributors.
How to Contact: Submit demo tape by mail. Unsolicited submissions are OK. Prefers cassette, CD, DAT or VHS videocassette. "Send name and contact number and address. Please write clearly." Does not return material. Reports in 3-4 weeks.
Music: Mostly **R&B**, **rap** and **rock**; also **alternative**, **gospel** and **children's**. "We do not accept 'gansta rap' artists or material. We prefer 'dance, love, reality and positive' song material and artists." Released *Bunwatcher* (by J. McCoy/M. Butler), recorded by Bad Influence on Power Play (rap/R&B). Other artists include Mothership, Provenwyze, Coffee, The Hylandas, Delana, The Chosen One and Da Foundation.
Tips: "Have patience, a professional attitude and devoted commitment to your career. You must also be creative, open to explore new ways to improve your songs from producers and appear at scheduled events in a timely manner. Artists should be focused and ready to work. We also love groups who have a creative and unique gimmick or image."

🌐 ◖**FIRST TIME RECORDS**, Sovereign House, 12 Trewartha Rd., Praa Sands, Penzance, Cornwall TR20 9ST England. Phone: (01736)762826. Fax: (01736)763328. E-mail: panamus@aol.com. Managing Director A&R: Roderick G. Jones. Labels include Pure Gold Records, Rainy Day Records and Mohock Records. Registered members of Phonographic Performance Ltd. (PPL). Record company, music publisher (First Time Music Publishing U.K./MCPS/PRS), management firm and record producer (First Time Management & Production Co.). Estab. 1986. Staff size: 6. Pays variable royalty to artists on contract; statutory rate to publisher per song on record subject to deal.
Distributed by: Media U.K. Distributors.
How to Contact: Submit demo tape by mail. Unsolicited submissions are OK. Prefers cassette with unlimited number of songs and lyric or lead sheets, but not necessary. SAE and IRC. Reports in 1-3 months.
Music: Mostly **country/folk**, **pop/soul/top 20** and **country with an Irish/Scottish crossover**; also **gospel/Christian** and **HI NRG/dance**. Released *Songwriters and Artistes Compilation Volume III*, on Rainy Day Records; "The Drums of Childhood Dreams," written and recorded by Pete Arnold on Mohock Records (folk); and *The Light and Shade of Eddie Blackstone*, written and recorded by Eddie Blackstone on T.W. Records (country).

Ⓝ ◖**FISH OF DEATH RECORDS**, P.O. Box 93206, Los Angeles CA 90093. (323)462-3404. E-mail: fod@earthlink.net. Website: http://www.fishofdeath.com. President: Michael D. Andelman. Record company, music publisher and management firm. Estab. 1994. Releases 2-4 singles, 1-2 EPs and 2-4 CDs/year. Pays 18% royalty to artists on contract; statutory rate to publisher per song on record.
Distributed by: MS Distributing, Carrot Top, Nail, Dutch East India and Surefire.
 • This label is noted for releasing fun, happy music.
How to Contact: Submit demo tape by mail. Unsolicited submissions are OK. Prefers cassette or CD with 3 songs. Does not return material. Reports in 3 weeks.
Music: Mostly **alternative**, **rock** and **hip-hop**; also **top 40**, **modern rock** and **AAA**. Released *American Made*, written and recorded by Hal Lovejoy Circus (alternative/rock); "Kitty Kat Max" (by Kevin Krakower), recorded by 1000 Clowns (rap/pop); and *430 N. Harper Ave* (by Jude Cristodal), recorded by Jude (folk), all on Fish of Death Records. Other artists include All Miserable Times, The Ghost of Tony Gold, Tiny Buddy and Brown Betty.
Tips: "Be persistent, professional, focused, and not too annoying."

▼ ◙ **550 MUSIC**, 550 Madison Ave., 21st Floor, New York NY 10022. (212)833-8000. Santa Monica office: 2100 Colorado Ave., Santa Monica CA 90404. (310)449-2100. Fax: (310)449-2932. Record company.
Distributed by: Sony.
• "My Heart Will Go On," recorded by Céline Dion and released by 550 Music and Sony Classical, won 1998 Grammy Awards for Record of the Year and Song of the Year, and Céline Dion won Best Female Pop Performance.
How to Contact: 550 Music does not accept demo tapes.
Music: Released *Whatever and Ever Amen*, recorded by Ben Folds Five on Caroline; *Falling Into You*, recorded by Celine Dion on 550 Music; and *Cool Relax*, recorded by Jon B. on Yab Yum.

Ⓝ ◖ **FLASH POINT RECORDS**, P.O. Box 8192, Pittsburg CA 94565. Phone/fax: (925)439-2040. E-mail: mmbflash@pacbell.net. President/CEO (hip-hop, R&B, pop): Maurice M. Belcher. Label Manager (jazz, gospel): Jennifer K. Hardin. Labels include Anzac Studio, CS Records, Black Diamond Records, Damage Records and Rickochet Records. Record company and record producer (MM&B Production Studio). Estab. 1994. Releases 1 single, 1 EP and 2 CDs/year. Pays 5% royalty to artists on contract; statutory rate to publisher per song on record.
Distributed by: MM&B Studio and Cosmic Blue Corp.
How to Contact: Submit demo tape by mail. Unsolicited submissions are OK. Prefers cassette, CD, DAT or VHS videocassette with 2-4 songs, lyric sheet, lead sheet, cover letter, press clippings, bio and photo. Does not return material. Reports in 1 month.
Music: Mostly **R&B/hip-hop, jazz/blues** and **rap/gospel**; also **rock/pop, country/alternative** and **reggae/techno**. Released "I Like the Way U Get Your Freak On," recorded by Angel (pop); *Big Big Balla*, recorded by I.N.D.O. (hip-hop); and "Find the Time to Find Me," recorded by Zsontana Golden (country), all written by various artists and recorded on Flash Point Records.
Tips: "Have more than one version of your songs recorded and have a well-executed demo."

◖ **FLIP RECORDS**, 8733 Sunset Blvd., Suite 205, W. Hollywood CA 90069. (310)360-8556. Fax: ✗ (310)360-8565. Website: http://www.flip-records.com. Record company. Estab. 1994.
How to Contact: Submit demo tape by mail. Unsolicited submissions are OK. Prefers cassette. Does not return material.
Music: Mostly **alternative**. Artists include Big Hate, SX-10, Fine, Staind, Cold, Jane Jensen, Limp Bizkit, D.J. Lethal and Dope.
Tips: "Have a hard, unique, fat sound."

◖ **FLYING HEART RECORDS**, Dept. SM, 4026 NE 12th Ave., Portland OR 97212. (503)287-8045. E-mail: flyheart@teleport.com. Website: http://www.teleport.com/~flyheart. Owner: Jan Celt. Record company and record producer (Jan Celt). Estab. 1982. Releases 2 LPs and 1 EP/year. Pays variable royalty to artists on contract; negotiable rate to publisher per song on record.
Distributed by: City Hall Records.
How to Contact: Submit demo tape by mail. Unsolicited submissions are OK. Prefers cassette with 1-10 songs and lyric sheets. Does not return material. "SASE required for *any* response." Reports in 3 months.
Music: Mostly **R&B, blues** and **jazz**; also **rock**. Released *Vexatious Progr.*, written and recorded by Eddie Harris (jazz); *Juke Music*, written and recorded by Thara Memory (jazz); and *Lookie Tookie*, written and recorded by Jan Celt (blues), all on Flying Heart Records. Other artists include Janice Scroggins, Tom McFarland, Obo Addy, Snow Bud and The Flower People.

◙ **FOUNTAIN RECORDS**, P.O. Box 35005 AMC, Greensboro NC 27425. (336))882-9990. President: Doris W. Lindsay. Record company, music publisher (Better Times Publishing/BMI, Doris Lindsay Publishing/ASCAP) and record producer. Estab. 1979. Releases 3 singles and 1 LP/year. Pays standard royalty to artists on contract; statutory rate to publisher per song on record.
How to Contact: Submit demo tape by mail. Unsolicited submissions are OK. Prefers cassette with 2 songs and lyric sheets. SASE. Reports in 2 months.
Music: Mostly **country, pop** and **gospel**. Released *Two Lane Life* (by D. Lindsay), recorded by Mitch

---

OPENNESS TO SUBMISSIONS: ◖ beginners; ◪ beginners and experienced; ◑ experienced only; ◙ industry referrals only.

Snow; "Grandma Bought A Harley" (by S. Rosario), recorded by Glenn Mayo; *Service Station Cowboy* (by Hoss Ryder), recorded by David Johnson, all on Fountain Records.
Tips: "Have a professional demo and include phone and address on cassette."

☐ **FRESH ENTERTAINMENT**, 1315 Simpson Rd. NW, Suite 5, Atlanta GA 30314. (770)642-2645. Vice President, Marketing/A&R: Willie Hunter. Record company and music publisher (Hserf Music/AS-CAP, Blair Vizzion Music/BMI). Releases 5 singles and 2 LPs/year. Pays 7-10% royalty to artists on contract; statutory rate to publisher per song on record.
Distributed by: Ichiban International and Intersound Records.
How to Contact: Submit demo tape by mail. Unsolicited submissions are OK. Prefers cassette or VHS videocassette with at least 3 songs and lyric sheet. SASE. Reports in 6-8 weeks.
Music: Mostly **R&B** and **pop**; also **jazz**, **gospel** and **rap**. Released "Throw Them Boes," written and recorded by DJ Taz on Ichiban (pop); *Bass Me Down*, written and recorded by Wreck-N-Krew on Intersound (rap); and *Nubian Woman*, written and recorded by Bob Miles on IFE Productions (jazz). Other artists include Cirocco and Invisible Men.

☐ **FRONT ROW RECORDS**, Ridgewood Park Estates, 222 Tulane St., Garland TX 75043. Website: http://www.athenet.net/~genevinc/GeneSummers.html. Contact: Gene or Dea Summers. Public Relations/Artist and Fan Club Coordinator: Steve Summers. A&R: Shawn Summers. Labels include Juan Records. Record company and music publisher (Silicon Music/BMI). Estab. 1968. Releases 5-6 singles and 2-3 LPs/year. Pays negotiable royalty to artists on contract; standard royalty to songwriters on contract.
Distributed by: Crystal Clear Records.
How to Contact: Submit demo tape by mail. Unsolicited submissions are OK. Prefers cassette or VHS videocassette with 1-3 songs. Does not return material. Reports ASAP.
Music: Mostly **'50s rock/rockabilly**; also **country**, **bluegrass**, **old-time blues** and **R&B**. Released "Domino," recorded by Gene Summers on Pollytone Records (rockabilly); "Goodbye Priscilla" and "Cool Baby," both recorded by Gene Summers on Collectables Records.
Tips: "If you own masters of 1950s rock and rockabilly, contact us first! We will work with you on a percentage basis for overseas release. We have active releases in Holland, Switzerland, Belgium, Australia, England, France, Sweden, Norway and the US at the present. We need original masters. You must be able to prove ownership of tapes before we can accept a deal. We're looking for little-known, obscure recordings. We have the market if you have the tapes! We are also interested in country and rockabilly *artists* who have not recorded for awhile but still have the voice and appeal to sell overseas. *We request a photo and bio with material submission.*"

☑ **MARTY GARRETT ENTERTAINMENT**, 111 E. Canton St., Broken Arrow OK 74012-7140. (800)210-4416. E-mail: bizbook@telepath.com. Website: http://www.telepath.com/bizbook. President: Marty R. Garrett. Labels include Lonesome Wind Records. Record company, record producer, music publisher and entertainment consultant. Estab. 1988. Releases 3-4 EPs and 1 CD/year. Pays negotiable royalty to artists on contract; statutory rate to publisher per song on record.
How to Contact: Call or check Internet site first and obtain permission to submit. Prefers cassette with 4-5 songs and lyric or lead sheet with chord progressions listed. Does not return material. Reports in 6 weeks.
Music: Mostly **Honky tonk**, **progressive** or **traditional country** or **scripturally-based gospel**. Released *I'm Not Over You* (by Drake/McGuire), recorded by Darla Drake on Comstock Records; *Too Free Too Long* (by Cliff Voss), recorded by Mark Cypert on Stormy Heart Records; and *Carry Me Over*, written and recorded by The Cripple Jimmi Band on Kid Mega Records.
Tips: "We help artists secure funding to record and release major label quality CD products to the public for sale through 1-800 television and radio advertising and on the Internet. Although we do submit finished products to major record companies for review, our main focus is to establish and surround the artist with their own long-term production, promotion and distribution organization. We do not require professional studio demos, but make sure vocals are distinct, up-front and up-to-date. I personally listen and respond to each submission received, so check website to see if we are reviewing for an upcoming project."

☑ ⊘ **GEFFEN/DGC RECORDS**, 9130 Sunset Blvd., Los Angeles CA 90069-6197. (310)278-9010. Fax: (310)278-4523. Director of A&R: Tony Berg. New York office: 1755 Broadway, New York NY 10019. (212)841-8600. Fax: (212)247-8852. Website: http://www.geffen.com. Record company.
• As a result of the PolyGram and Universal merger, Geffen has been folded into Interscope Records. At press time, the above information was still correct.

■ ○ **GEMINI RECORDS**, RR2, New Germany, Nova Scotia B0R 1E0 Canada. (902)543-5053. Fax: (902)527-1530. E-mail: joyce.seamone@ns.sympatico.ca. Website: http://www.lunco.com/jseamone. President: Gerald Seamone. Artist: Joyce Seamone. Record company. Estab. 1992. Releases 2 singles, 1 LP and 1 CD/year. Pays negotiable royalty to artists on contract; statutory rate to publisher per song on record.
Distributed by: Sam's.
How to Contact: Submit demo tape by mail. Unsolicited submissions are OK. Prefers cassette with 3 songs and lyric sheet. Does not return material. Reports in 3-4 weeks.
Music: Mostly **country** and **country/rock**. Released *The Other Side of Me*, written and recorded by Joyce Seamone on Gemini Records (country).
Tips: "Submit cassette with three of your best songs if you are a songwriter. If you are a singer, submit a cassette with as good a quality demo as possible. After listening to the product sent for consideration, be prepared to follow through for the long term commitments (photo shoots, interviews and concerts)."

○ **GENERIC RECORDS, INC.**, 433 Limestone Rd., Ridgefield CT 06877. (203)438-9811. E-mail: hifiadd@aol.com. President (pop, alternative, rock): Gary Lefkowith. A&R (pop, dance, adult contemporary): Bill Jerome. Labels include Outback, GLYN. Record company, music publisher (Sotto Music/BMI) and record producer. Estab. 1976. Staff size: 2. Releases 6 singles and 2 CDs/year. Pays 15% royalty to artists on contract; statutory rate to publisher per song on record.
Distributed by: Dutch East India.
How to Contact: Submit demo tape by mail. Unsolicited submissions are OK. Prefers cassette with 2-3 songs. SASE. Reports in 2 weeks.
Music: Mostly **alternative rock**, **rock** and **pop**; also **country** and **rap**. Released "Young Girls" (by Eric Della Penna/Dean Sharenow), recorded by Henry Sugar (alternative/pop); "Rock It," written and recorded by David Ruskay (rock/pop); and *Tyrus*, written and recorded by Tyris (alternative), all on Generic Records, Inc. Other artists include Hifi, Honest, Loose Change and John Fantasia.
Tips: "Love what you're doing. The music comes first."

○ **GOLD CITY RECORDS, INC.**, 10 Deepwell Farms Rd., S. Salem NY 10590. (914)533-5096. Fax: (914)533-5097. E-mail: gcrecords@aol.com. Website: http://members.aol.com/GCRecords. President: Chris Jasper. Vice President/General Counsel: Margie Jasper. Labels include Gold City Label. Record company. Estab. 1986. Staff size: 5. Releases 5-10 singles, 5-10 12″ singles, 3-5 LPs and 3-5 CDs/year. Pays negotiable royalty to artists on contract; statutory rate to publisher per song on record.
How to Contact: Submit demo tape by mail. Unsolicited submissions are OK. Prefers cassette with 3 songs and lyric sheets. SASE. Reports in 4-6 weeks.
Music: Mostly **R&B**, **contemporary gospel** and **pop**; also **rap**. Released "And I Love Her" (by P. McCartney/J. Lennon), recorded by Brothaz By Choice on Gold City Records (R&B).

☑ ○ **GOLDEN TRIANGLE RECORDS**, 5501 Camelia St., Pittsburgh PA 15201. E-mail: marcels@salsgiver.com. Website: http://www.geocities.com/Sunset Strip/6929/index.html. Producer: Sunny James Cvetnic. Labels include Rockin Robin and Shell-B. Music publisher (Golden Triangle/BMI) and record producer (Sunny James). Estab. 1987. Staff size: 1. Releases 8 singles, 6 12″ singles, 10 LPs and 19 CDs/year. Pays standard royalty to artists on contract; statutory rate to publishers per song on record.
How to Contact: Submit demo tape by mail. Unsolicited submissions are OK. Prefers cassette, 15 IPS reel-to-reel or ½″ VHS videocassette with 3 songs and lyric or lead sheets. Does not return material. Reports in 1 week.
Music: Mostly **progressive R&B**, **rock** and **A/C**; also **jazz** and **country**. Released "Burner Blues," written and recorded by T. Jack (blues); "Wip It Out," written and recorded by Weetman (R&B); and "Grek Fried" (by Bryan McClair), recorded by Sunny James (pop/rock), all on Golden Triangle. Other artists include the Marcels and the Bounty Hunters.
Tips: "Have patience."

○ **GOLDWAX RECORD CORPORATION**, P.O. Box 54700, Atlanta GA 30308-0700. (770)454-1011. Fax: (770)454-8088. E-mail: goldwaxrec@aol.com. Website: http://www.goldwax.com. A&R: Pamela Monique; Jimmy McClendon. Labels include Abec, Bandstand USA and Beale Street USA. Record company and music publisher (Stellar Music Industries). Estab. 1963. Staff size: 3. Releases 20 singles, 20 LPs, 5 EPs and 20 CDs/year. Pays negotiable royalty to artists on contract; statutory rate to publisher per song on record.
Distributed by: City Hall Records.
How to Contact: Write or call first and obtain permission to submit a demo. Prefers cassette, CD, DAT or VHS videocassette with 4 songs and lyric sheet. SASE. Reports in 6 weeks.
Music: Mostly **R&B/hip-hop**, **pop/rock** and **jazz**; also **blues**, **contemporary country** and **contemporary**

gospel. Released *You Need a Job* (by Cookie D/Cognal), recorded by Cookie D; and *Girls I Like* (by Jaharay Courtney Williams/L. Johnson), recorded by Ova/Unda, both on Rap-N-Wax (rap). Other artists include Double Deuce, 3-4-U and Margie Alexander.

Tips: "Songwriters need to provide great melodies; artists need to have commercial appeal."

☐ GONZO! RECORDS INC., P.O. Box 3688, San Dimas CA 91773. Phone/fax: (909)598-9031. E-mail: gonzorcrds@aol.com. Website: http://members.aol.com/gonzorcrds. President: Jeffrey Gonzalez. Vice President: Robb Schiltz. Record company. Estab. 1993. Staff size: 3. Releases 3 singles and 1-6 CDs/year. Pays negotiable royalty to artists on contract; statutory rate to publisher per song on record.

How to Contact: Submit demo tape by mail. Unsolicited submissions are OK. Prefers cassette or CD. "When submitting, please specify that you got the listing from *Songwriter's Market*." Does not return material. Reports in 4-6 weeks.

Music: Mostly **commercial industrial**, **dance** and **techno**; also **commercial alternative** and **synth pop**. Released *Hate Breeds Hate*, written and recorded by BOL (hard industrial); *Momentum*, written and recorded by Full Frequency (commerical industrial); and *Ruth in Alien Corn*, written and recorded by Pinch Point (alternative pop), all on Gonzo! Records. Other artists include Turning Keys.

Tips: "If you're going to submit music to me, it must be because you love to write music, not because you want to be a rockstar. That will eventually happen with a lot of hard work."

☑ ☐ GOTHAM RECORDS, P.O. Box 20188, New York NY 10014-0710. Phone/fax: (212)517-9192. E-mail: gothamrec@aol.com. Website: http://www.gothamrecords.com. Contact: A&R Dept. Record company. Estab. 1994. Staff size: 3. Releases 8 LPs and 8 CDs/year. Pays negotiable royalty to artists on contract; statutory rate to publisher per song on record.

Distributed by: Dutch East India and MS Distributing.

How to Contact: Submit demo tape by mail "in a padded mailer or similar package." Unsolicited submissions are OK. Prefers cassette or CD and bios, pictures and touring information. Does not return material. Reports in 6 weeks.

Music: Mostly **rock**, **pop**, **alternative** and **AAA**. Released *Nineteenth Soul*, recorded by Liquid Gang (rock); *Supafuzz*, written and recorded by Supafuzz (rock); and *Oh God! Help Our Fans!*, written and recorded by The Loose Nuts (ska), all on Gotham Records. Other artists include Love Huskies.

Tips: "Send all submissions in regular packaging. Spend your money on production and basics, not on fancy packaging and gift wrap."

☐ GREEN BEAR RECORDS, Rockin' Chair Center Suite 103, 1033 W. State Highway 76, Branson MO 65616. (417)334-2383. Fax: (417)334-2306. President: George J. Skupien. Labels include Green One Records and Bear Tracks Records. Record company, music publisher (Green One Music/BMI) and record producer (George Skupien). Estab. 1992. Releases 3-4 singles, 1-10 LPs and 2-6 CDs/year. Pays negotiable royalty to artists on contract; statutory rate to publisher per song on record.

How to Contact: Submit "professional studio" demo tape by mail. Unsolicited submissions are OK. Prefers cassette or DAT with 4-6 songs and lyric or lead sheet. Does not return material. "We only accept professional studio demo tapes. For your protection, all tapes, lyrics, or other material that is received, that are not accepted, are immediately destroyed to protect the songwriters." Reports in 6-8 weeks.

Music: Mostly **polkas**, **waltzes** and **country**; also **Southern gospel**, **MOR** and **light rock**. Released "Oh My Aching Back" and "Lotto Polka," written and recorded by George Skupien (country); and "Keep On Keepin' On," written and recorded by Matt Row'd (country), all on Green Bear Records. Other artists include D. Mack, B. Jackson, Ted Thomas, Rudy Negron and The Mystics.

Tips: "Submit a well-produced, studio quality demo of your material on cassette or DAT with a clean vocal up front. If possible, submit your demo with and without lead vocal for presentation to recording artists."

Ⓝ ☑ GRIFFIN MUSIC (a Division of Tango Music LLC), P.O. Box 1952, Lombard IL 60148. (630)424-0801. Fax: (630)424-0806. E-mail: grifmus@aol.com. Website: http://griffinmusic.com. A&R (Griffin Music): Ginger Lord (classic rock, pop). President (Chicago Lakeside Jazz Inc.): Ken Kirstner (jazz). Labels include Tango Music, Chicago Lakeside Jazz Inc., Lakeshore Jazz of Chicago. Record company. Estab. 1992. Staff size: 8. Releases 2 singles, 4 LPs and 24 CDs/year. Pays negotiable royalty

---

THE OPENNESS TO SUBMISSIONS INDEX at the back of this book lists all companies in this section by how open they are to submissions.

to artists on contract; pay to publisher per song on record "depends on artist."
Distributed by: Alliance, Baker & Taylor, Action, Norwalk, Pacific Coast, H.L. Distribution and Valley.
How to Contact: Submit demo tape by mail. Unsolicited submissions are OK. Prefers cassette or CD with cover letter and press clippings. Does not return material. Reports in 6 weeks.
Music: Mostly **classic rock**, **pop** and **various artists compilations**; also **jazz**, **blues** and **new world**. Does not want rap or dance. Released *BBC-Live in Concert*, written and recorded by Thin Lizzy on Griffin (rock); and *Soul Mates*, written and recorded by Joan Hickley on Chicago Lakeside Jazz Inc. (jazz).
Tips: "Have some sort of track history."

N O GROOVE MAKERS' RECORDINGS, P.O. Box 271170, Houston TX 77227-1170. Phone/fax: (281)403-6279. CEO: Ben Thompson (R&B, rap). Labels include Paid In Full Entertainment. Record company, music publisher and record producer (Crazy C). Estab. 1994. Staff size: 4. Releases 3 singles, 2 LPs and 2 CDs/year. Pays negotiable royalty to artists on contract; statutory rate to publisher per song on record.
Distributed by: S.O.H., Big Easy and Southwest Wholesale.
How to Contact: Submit demo tape by mail. Unsolicited submissions are OK. Prefers cassette or CD. Does not return material.
Music: Mostly **rap** and **R&B**. Released *Ph Factor*, written and recorded by Madd Hatta on GVM (rap). Other artists include S.O.U.L. and Heather Barrett.

✔ Ø GRP RECORDS, 825 Eighth Ave., New York NY 10019. (212)333-8000. Fax: (212)445-3470. Website: http://www.grp.com. A&R: Richard Seidel. Labels include Impulse! Records, Vervé and Blue Thumb Records. Record company.
How to Contact: GRP Records does not accept unsolicited submissions.
Music: Released *Road Scholars*, recorded by Spyro Gyra; *Serendipity*, recorded by Gregory Tardy; and *Live & More*, recorded by Marcus Miller, all on GRP Records. Other artists include George Benson, Danilo Perez, Groove Collective, Eric Reed, Keith Jarrett, Richard Page, The Crusaders, Candy Butchers, Nuyorcian Soul and Acoustic Alchemy.

N O GUESTSTAR RECORDS, INC., 17321 Ritchie Ave. NE, Sand Lake MI 49343-9475. President: Raymond G. Dietz, Sr. Record company, management firm (Gueststar Entertainment Agency), record producer and music publisher (Sandlake Music/BMI). Estab. 1967. Staff size: 3. Releases 8 singles, 2 LPs and 2 CDs/year. Pays variable royalty to artist on contract, "depending on number of selections on product; 3½¢/per record sold; statutory rate to publisher per song on record."
Distributed by: Guestar Worldwide Music Distributors.
How to Contact: Submit demo tape by mail. Unsolicited submissions are OK. Prefers cassette or VHS videocassette with lyric and lead sheet. "Send a SASE with submissions." Does not return material. Reports in 1 week.
Music: Mostly **country rock** and **traditional country**. Released "I've Been There" (by Eugene Calkins), recorded by Mountain Man on Gueststar Records (country). Other artists include Jamie "K" and Sweetgrass Band.
Tips: "Songwriters: send songs like you hear on the radio. Keep updating your music to keep up with the latest trends. Artists: send VHS video and press kit."

O HAMMERHEAD RECORDS, INC., 41 E. University Ave., Champaign IL 61820. (217)355-9052. Fax: (217)355-9057. E-mail: hammerhd@shout.net. Website: http://www.hammerheadrecords.com. A&R: Todd Thorstenson; Jeff Markland. Record company. Estab. 1993. Staff size: 2. Releases 6 CDs/year. Pays negotiable royalty to artists on contract; statutory rate to publisher per song on record.
Distributed by: MS Distributing.
How to Contact: Submit demo tape by mail. Unsolicited submissions are OK. Prefers cassette. "Include any press, bio, reviews, etc." SASE. Reports in 3 weeks.
Music: Mostly **rock—all forms**. Released *Solarshift*, written and recorded by Absinthe Blind; *Drive*, written and recorded by The Vibe Tribe; and *Gypped By Gyne* (by Rob McColley), recorded by Laurie McColley, all on Hammerhead Records (rock). Other artists include My Brother's Keeper and Funky Butt Drum Club.
Tips: "We work very closely with all of our artists and greatly appreciate honesty and integrity."

N O HEART MUSIC, INC., P.O. Box 160326, Austin TX 78716-0326. (512)795-2375. Fax: (512)795-9573. E-mail: info@heartmusic.com. Website: http://www.heartmusic.com. Promotions Director: Mimi Alidor. Record company and music publisher (Coolhot Music). Estab. 1989. Staff size: 2. Releases 3 CDs/year. Pays 75% royalty to artists on contract; statutory rate to publisher per song on record.

How to Contact: Call first and obtain permission to submit. Does not return material. Reports only if interested.

Music: Mostly **rock**, **pop** and **jazz**; also **blues**, **urban** and **contemporary folk**. Does not want New Age jazz, smooth jazz or Christian/religious. Released *1st & Repair*, written and recorded by Monte Montgomery (rock/pop); *Kicks Are for Kids*, written and recorded by Elias Haslanger (jazz); and *For You*, written and recorded by Joe Lo Cascio (jazz), all on Heart Music.

HI-BIAS RECORDS INC., 49 Beckett Ave., Toronto, Ontario MGL 2B3 Canada. (416)614-1581. Fax: (416)249-2799. E-mail: nick@hibias.ca. Website: http://www.hibias.ca/~hibias. Director: Nick Fiorucci. Labels include Toronto Underground, Remedy and Club Culture. Record company, music publisher (Bend 60 Music/SOCAN) and record producer (Nick Fiorucci). Estab. 1990. Staff size: 2. Releases 30-40 singles, 4-8 LPs, 10 EPs and 5-10 CDs/year. Pays negotiable royalty to artists on contract; statutory rate to publisher per song on record.

Distributed by: PolyGram/Universal.

How to Contact: Submit demo tape by mail. Unsolicited submissions are OK. Prefers cassette or DAT with 3 songs and lyric sheet. Does not return material. Reports in 6 weeks.

Music: Mostly **dance, pop** and **R&B**; also **acid jazz** and **house**. Released "Hands of Time" (by N. Fiorucci/B. Cosgrove), recorded by Temperance; "Now That I Found You" (by B. Farrinco/Cleopatra), recorded by YBZ; and "Lift Me Up," written and recorded by Red 5, all on Hi-Bias (dance/pop). Other artists include DJ's Rule.

HOLLYWOOD RECORDS, 500 S. Buena Vista St., Burbank CA 91521. Senior Vice President of A&R: Rob Cavallo. Senior Vice President of A&R (Latin): Cameron Randle. A&R Director: Julian Raymond. Vice President of A&R: Rob Seidenberg. New York office: 170 Fifth Ave., Penthouse, New York NY 10010. Website: http://www.hollywoodrec.com. Vice President of A&R: John Dee. A&R Assistant: Brendon Mendoza. Labels include Acid Jazz Records, Mountain Division Records and Bar/None Records. Record company.

How to Contact: Hollywood Records does not accept unsolicited submissions. Queries accepted only from a manager or lawyer.

Music: Released *All the Pain Money Can Buy*, recorded by Fastball. Other artists include Brian May, Khaleel, Caroline's Spine, Fishbone, Leroy & Loudmouth, Jesse Camp, Roger McGuinn and Pistoleros.

HORIZON RECORDS, INC., P.O. Box 610487, San Jose CA 95161-0487. E-mail: info@horizonrecords.com. (408)782-1501. Fax: (408)778-3567. Website: http://www.horizonrecords.com. Vice President: Jennifer Linn. Record company and music publisher (Horizon Music West). Estab. 1996. Staff size: 3. Pays negotiable royalty to artists on contract; statutory rate to publisher per song on record.

Distributed by: Big Daddy Distribution.

How to Contact: Horizon records does not accept unsolicited material.

Music: Mostly **rock/pop**, **singer/songwriter** and **blues**; also **jazz** and techno. Released *Bohemia*,written and recorded by Tommy Elskes on Horizon Records (rock/pop).

HOT WINGS ENTERTAINMENT, 429 Richmond Ave., Buffalo NY 14222. (716)884-0248. E-mail: dahotwings@aol.com. Manager, A&R: Dale Anderson. Record company and music publisher (Buffalo Wings Music/BMI). Estab. 1994. Staff size: 1. Releases 2 CDs/year. Pays 10-15% to artists on contract; statutory rate to publisher per song on record.

How to Contact: Call first and obtain permission to submit. Prefers cassette or CD with 3 or more songs. Does not return material. Reports in 6-8 weeks.

Music: Mostly **folk/acoustic, alternative rock** and **jazz**. (Preference to artists from Upstate New York.) Released *Like Being Born*, written and recorded by Alison Pipitone (folk/rock); *Flavor* (by Geoffrey Fitzhugh Perry), recorded by Fitzhugh and the Fanatics (blues/rock); and *Everything Counts*, written and recorded by Gretchen Schulz (pop/R&B), all on Hot Wings Records.

HOTTRAX RECORDS, 1957 Kilburn Dr., Atlanta GA 30324. (404)662-6661. E-mail: hotwax@hottrax.com. Website: http://www.hottrax.com. Vice President, A&R: Oliver Cooper. Labels include Dance-

THE FILM & TV INDEX found at the back of this book lists companies placing music in film and TV (excluding TV commercials).

A-Thon and Hardkor. Record company and music publisher (Starfox Publishing). Staff size: 3. Releases 12 singles and 3-4 CDs/year. Pays 5-15% royalty to artists on contract.
Distributed by: Get Hip Inc.
How to Contact: Write first and obtain permission to submit. Prefers cassette with 3 songs and lyric sheet. Does not return material. Reports in 3-6 months. "When submissions get extremely heavy, we do not have the time to respond/return material we pass on. We do notify those sending the most promising work we review, however."
Music: Mostly **top 40/pop**, **rock** and **country**; also **hardcore punk** and **jazz-fusion**. Released *New Nuclear Age*, written and recorded by Sheffield-Weff (rock); *No Regrets* (by R. Norris), recorded by Bullitthead (rock); and *Everything & Mo'*, written and recorded by Sammy Blue (blues), all on Hottrax Records. Other artists include Big Al Jano and The Blues Mafia.

✓ ☮ ◖ **HOUSE OF BLUES RECORDS**, 8439 Sunset Blvd., Suite 102, W. Hollywood CA 90069. (323)848-2508. Fax: (323)848-7211. Website: http://www.hobmusic.com. Contact: A&R Director.
• House of Blues Records' Otis Rush won a 1998 Grammy Award for Best Traditional Blues Album.
How to Contact: Write first and obtain permission to submit. Prefers CD with description of artist, press kit, bio and photo.
Music: Released *Paint It Blue—Songs of the Rolling Stones*, recorded by various artists on House of Blues Records.

Ⓝ ◯ **HOWDY RECORDS**, 1810 S. Pea Ridge Rd., Temple TX 76502. (817)773-8001 or (817)939-8000. Owner: Andy Anderson. A&R: Lannie Wright (country, religious); Jose Salinas (Tex-Mex). Labels include Border Serenade and Up Yonder. Record company, music publisher (Heart O' Country) and record producer (Lonnie Wright). Estab. 1960. Staff size: 3. Releases 18 singles, 6 EPs and 12 CDs/year. Pays 2.5% royalty to artists on contract; 2.5% rate to publisher per song on record.
Distributed by: Western Merchandising and Heart O' Country Distribution.
How to Contact: Submit demo tape by mail. Unsolicited submissions are OK. Prefers cassette with 10 songs and lyric sheet. Does not return material. Reports in 1 month.
Music: Mostly **country**, **religious** and **Tex-Mex**. Released *Blue Skies Up Above*, written and recorded by Robert Stack on Up Yonder (religious); and *Pancho Pete* (by Ron Al), recorded by Padro Valdez on Border Serenade (Tex-Mex). Other artists include Alan Andrews and Dick Jackson.

✿ ◑ **iHL RECORDS**, 5675 Giroux Ave., Charlesbourg, Quebec G1H 6X4 Canada. Fax: (418)626-7064. E-mail: yoopi@globetrotter.net. Website: http://www.microtec.net/~slam. Owner: Simon Lacroix. Record company. Estab. 1995. Staff size: 2. Releases 2-3 singles, 2-3 LPs, 1 EP and 1 CD/year. Pays negotiable royalty to artists on contract.
Distributed by: Sonic Unyon and FAB.
How to Contact: Submit demo tape by mail. Unsolicited submissions are OK. Prefers cassette or CD. Does not return material. Reports in 2 weeks.
Music: Mostly **indie rock/pop**, **power pop** and **new wave**; also **surf**, **pop/punk** and **space pop**. Released *Love With Fabio*, written and recorded by The Minipops (indie pop); *incessamment sous peu*, written and recorded by savonette (indie rock), both on iHL Records.
Tips: "Tour near Quebec City so we might get a chance to see your band live. If you used to be a Pearl Jam cover band, don't send us material."

✓ ☮ ◎ **INTERSCOPE RECORDS**, 10900 Wilshire Blvd., Suite 1230, Los Angeles CA 90024. (310)208-6547. A&R: Tom Whalley. New York office: 40 W. 57th St., 22nd Floor, New York NY 10019-4001. (212)957-9075. Fax: (212)328-9565. E-mail: interscope@interscoperecords.com. Website: http://www.interscoperecords.com. A&R (R&B): Tone Capone. Labels include Death Row Records, Nothing Records, Rock Land, Almo Sounds, Aftermath Records and Trauma Records. Record company.
• As a result of the PolyGram and Universal merger, Geffen and A&M Records have been folded into Interscope Records. At press time, the above contact information was correct. Interscope's Brian Setzer Orchestra won 1998 Grammy Awards for Best Pop Performance by a Duo or Group with Vocal and Best Pop Instrumental Performance.
How to Contact: Does not accept unsolicited submissions.
Music: Released *Fush Yu Mang*, recorded by Smash Mouth; *The Dirty Boogie*, recorded by The Brian Setzer Orchestra; and *Bulworth—The Soundtrack*, all on Interscope Records. Other artists include U2, Garbage, Marilyn Manson and Sparkle.

✓ ◑ **INTERSTATE RECORDS (ISR)**, P.O. Box 291991, Nashville TN 37229. (615)360-2331. Fax: (615)361-4438. E-mail: jbnisbett@aol.com. President, A&R: Jack Batey. Labels include Ameri-Star. Re-

cord company and record producer (Deke Little and Larry Duncan). Estab. 1993. Releases 10 singles and 2 CDs/year. Pays negotiable royalty to artists on contract; statutory rate to publisher per song on record.
How to Contact: Submit demo tape by mail. Unsolicited submissions are OK. Prefers cassette with 3-5 songs and lyric and lead sheet. "In screening artist we ask for original material only, thus we can listen for originality in vocal delivery and judge the strength of writing capabilities. (Please no cover songs or karaoke voice overs)." Does not return material. Reports in 2 months.
Music: Mostly **country**, **country/pop** and **country/R&B**; also **western swing**.
Tips: "Be original in both your vocal, lyrics and melodies. Submitting a full blown demo is not necessary as we prefer a tape with voice, acoustic guitar and bass, or voice, piano and bass. Click track optional to artist."

N ☐ **INTREPID RECORDS**, P.O. Box 5010, Lighthouse Point FL 33074. (713)225-5775. Director of Operations: Rick Eyk. Record company and record producer (Rick Eyk). Pays 50% royalty to artists on contract; statutory rate to publisher per song on record.
How to Contact: Submit demo tape by mail. Unsolicited submissions are OK. Prefers CDs ready for distribution. Does not return material. Reports in 1 month; include #10 SASE for response.
Music: Blues, **jazz**, **classical**, **standards**, **country**, **New Age** and **eclectic/folk**.

✓ ⊘ **ISLAND RECORDS**, 8920 Sunset Blvd., 2nd Floor, Los Angeles CA 90069. (310)276-4500. Fax: (310)278-5862. A&R: Jenny Price. Labels include T-Neck Records and Tuff Gong Records. Record company.
• As a result of the PolyGram and Universal merger, Island Records has been merged with Mercury Records. At press time the above information was correct.

☐ **JAM DOWN ENTERTAINMENT, LLC**, 2616 Southloop W., Suite 521, Houston TX 77054. (713)349-9968. Fax: (713)349-9972. Website: http://jamdownent.com. CEOs: Patrick Lewis and Vincent Perry. General Manager: Kirt Codrington (rap, R&B). COO: Gerard Mark (rap). Record company and music publisher (Came From Nowhere). Estab. 1992. Staff size: 4. Releases 3 LPs, 1 EP and 3 CDs/year. Pays 10% royalty to artists on contract; statutory rate to publisher per song on record.
Distributed by: South West Wholesale.
How to Contact: Submit demo tape by mail. Unsolicited submissions are OK. Prefers cassette with 3 songs and lyric and lead sheet. "Submit songs with an upbeat tempo. Include b&w picture and bio or letter of introduction." Does not return material. Reports in 6 weeks.
Music: Mostly **rap** and **R&B**. Released *The Commission*, written and recorded by Lil Keke; *No Rest for the Real*, written and recorded by The Most Hated; and *A Million Dollars Later*, written and recorded by Herschel Wood Hard Heads, all on Jam Down (rap). Other artists include Phaz.
Tips: "Be patient. Be consistent. Know what your expectations are and never give up. Submit songs that are well produced with in-depth lyrics and strong melody."

✓ ⊘ **JIVE RECORDS**, 137-139 W. 25th St., 9th Floor, New York NY 10001. (212)727-0016. Fax: (212)645-3783. Vice President of A&R: Faith Newman. Director of A&R: David Lighty. West Hollywood office: 9000 Sunset Blvd., Suite 300, West Hollywood CA 90069. (310)247-8300. Fax: (310)247-8366. A&R Director: Mike Nardone. Vice President of Creative Development: Jonathan McHugh. Chicago office: 700 N. Green St., Suite 200, Chicago IL 60622. (312)942-9700. Fax: (312)942-9800. Vice President of A&R: Wayne Williams. Nashville office: 914-916 19th Ave. S., Nashville TN 37212. (615)321-4850. Fax: (615)321-4616. London office: Zomba House, 165-167 High Rd., Willesden, London NW 10 2SG England. Phone: (44) 81-459-8899. Fax: (31) 2153-16785. Record company. Estab. 1982. Releases 23 singles and 23 CDs/year.
Distributed by: BMG.
How to Contact: Does not accept unsolicited material. "Contact us through management or an attorney."
Music: Mostly **R&B**, **pop** and **rap**. Artists include Backstreet Boys, Joe, KRS-One, R. Kelly, Britney Spears, Too Short and Imajin.
Tips: "Make the best material possible."

N ⛏ ⊘ **JOEY RECORDS**, 6707 W. Commerce, San Antonio TX 78227. (210)432-7893. Fax: (210)433-6520. National Promotions (Tejano): Joey Lopez. President (Mexican, regional): Joe S. Lopez.

MARKETS THAT WERE listed in the 1999 edition of *Songwriter's Market* but do not appear this year are listed in the General Index with a notation explaining why they were omitted.

Vice President (salsa, tropical, grupero): Dinah Perez. Labels include Zaz Records. Record company, music publisher (El Zaz Records) and record producer. Estab. 1968. Staff size: 72. Releases 500 LPs and 500 CDs/year. Pays negotiable royalty to artists on contract; statutory rate to publisher per song on record.
Distributed by: Anderson Merchandisers, FRD, Southwest Wholesale and Handleman Co.
• In 1998, Joey Records won Achievement of Excellence at the Tejano Music Awards.
How to Contact: Submit demo tape by mail. Unsolicited submissions are OK. Prefers CD or VHS videocassette with 10 songs, cover letter and press clippings. Does not return material. Reports in 1-3 months.
Music: Mostly **regional Mexican**, **Tejano** and **tropical/grupero**. Does not want country. Released *Carlo y los Cachorros*, written and recorded by Carlo y los Cachorros (Tejano); and *Michael Salgudo*, written and recorded by Michael Salgudo (Mexican regional), both on Joey Records. Other artists include Amanecer, Los Chacales and Trueno.
Tips: "Submit information and persist with letters and phone calls and even unexpected visit OK."

KAUPP RECORDS, Box 5474, Stockton CA 95205. (209)948-8186. President: Nancy L. Merrihew. Record company, music publisher (Kaupps and Robert Publishing Co./BMI), management firm (Merri-Webb Productions) and record producer (Merri-Webb Productions). Estab. 1990. Releases 1 single and 4 LPs/year. Pays standard royalty to artists on contract; statutory rate to publisher per song on record.
Distributed by: Merri-Webb Productions and Cal-Centron Distributing Co.
How to Contact: Write first and obtain permission to submit or to arrange personal interview. Prefers cassette or VHS videocassette with 3 songs. SASE. Reports in 3 months.
Music: Mostly **country**, **R&B** and **A/C rock**; also **pop**, **rock** and **gospel**. Released "He's Alive" and "Little Do You Know" (by N. Merrihew/B. Bolin), recorded by Nanci Lynn; and "(Since I Started to Believin') My Own B.S." (by N. Merrihew/B. Bolin), recorded by Bruce Bolin, all on Kaupp Records.

KEEPING IT SIMPLE AND SAFE, INC., 622 State St., Room 36, Springfield MA 01109. (413)731-6996. E-mail: tscottkiss@aol.com. A&R Directors: Tony Martin; Robert Perry. Labels include Night Owl Records, Grand Jury Records, Second Time Around Records and Southend-Essex Records. Record company and music publisher (Tim Scott Music Group). Estab. 1993. Releases 3 singles, 2 LPs and 2 CDs/year. Pays 12-20% royalty to artists on contract; statutory rate to publisher per song on record.
How to Contact: Write first to obtain permission to submit. Prefers cassette, CD or VHS videocassette with 3-5 songs and lyric sheet. SASE. Reports in 2 months.
Music: Mostly **pop**, **R&B**, and **rap**; also **country**, **rock** and **gospel**. Released "Just In Time," written and recorded by Willie Gray; "Everything You" (by Tim Scott), recorded by Loveworld; and "Sweet Music," written and recorded by Mike Johnson, all on Night Owl Records. Other artists include S.E.D., Sweet Tooth and DJ Smoothe.
Tips: "Always explain what you are asking for."

KILL ROCK STARS, 120 N.E. State #418, Olympia WA 98501. (360)357-9732. (360)357-6408. E-mail: krspromo@aol.com. Website: http://www.killrockstars.com. Owner: Slim Moon. Record company. Estab. 1991. Releases 6-8 singles, 6-8 LPs, 2-3 EPs and 6-8 CDs/year. Pays 50% of net profit to artists on contract; negotiated rate to publisher per song on record.
Distributed by: Mordam, Caroline, Cargo, Dutch East India, Revolver and Bayside.
How to Contact: Write first and obtain permission to submit. Prefers CD. Does not return material.
Music: Mostly **punk rock**, **neo-folk or anti-folk** and **spoken word**. Released *The Hot Rock*, written and recorded by Sleater-Kinney (pop guitar punk); *Julie Ruin*, written and recorded by Kathleen Hanna (punk); and *Frumpies One Piece*, written and recorded by Frumpies (punk), all on Kill Rock Stars. Other artists include Thrones, Emily's Sassy Lime, Long Hind Legs, Mocket and Free Kitten.
Tips: "Send a self-released CD. Prefer working with touring acts, so let us know if you are playing Olympia, Seattle or Portland. Particularly interested in young artists with indie-rock background."

KINGSTON RECORDS, 15 Exeter Rd., Kingston NH 03848. (603)642-8493. Coordinator: Harry Mann. Record company, record producer and music publisher (Strawberry Soda Publishing/ASCAP). Estab. 1988. Releases 3-4 singles, 2-3 12″ singles, 3 LPs and 2 CDs/year. Pays 3-5% royalty to artists on contract; statutory rate to publisher per song.
How to Contact: Write first and obtain permission to submit. Prefers cassette, DAT, 15 ips reel-to-reel or videocassette with 3 songs and lyric sheet. Does not return material. Reports in 2 months.
Music: Mostly **rock**, **country** and **pop**; "no heavy metal." Released *Two Lane Highway* and *Armand's Way*, written and recorded by Armand Learay on Kingston Records (rock).
Tips: "Working only with N.E. and local talent."

KSM RECORDS, 2305 Vista Court, Coquitlam, British Columbia V3J 6W2 Canada. (604)202-3644. Fax: (604)469-9359. E-mail: ksmrecords@infomatch.com. Website: http://www.infomatch.com/~ksmrecords/. A&R Rep: David London. Record company and record producer (David London). Estab. 1991. Releases 2-5 singles and 2-5 CDs/year. Pays negotiable rate to artists on contract; statutory rate to publisher per song on record.
Distributed by: Broken Seal (Germany), Factoria (Canada), Cri Du Chat (Brazil) and Dion Fortune (Germany).
How to Contact: Submit demo tape by mail. Unsolicited submissions are OK. Prefers cassette or VHS videocassette and press material. Does not return material. Reports in 1 month.
Music: Mostly **industrial**, **Gothic**, **techno**, **heavy/extreme**, **electronic** and **experimental**. Released *Oracle Pool*, written and recorded by various artists (industrial); *Jagd Wild* (by Bryan Kortness), recorded by Come Join the Hunt (industrial); and "KSM Split Single" (by David London), recorded by Violet Black Orchid (electro), all on KSM Records. Other artists include Daed21, Idiot Stare, Fourthman, Bytet, Colour Clique, Naked Wavelength, 162 and Multiplex.

L.A. RECORDS, P.O. Box 1096, Hudson, Quebec J0P 1H0 Canada. (514)869-3236. Fax: (514)458-2819. E-mail: larecord@total.net. Website: http://www.radiofreedom.com. Manager (alternative): Tonya Hart. Producer (rock): M. Lengies. A&R (dance, rap, AC): Vanessa B. A&R (country, blues): Scott N. Record company, management firm (M.B.H. Music Management), music publisher (G-String Publishing) and record producer (M. Lengies). Estab. 1991. Releases 20-40 singles and 5-8 CDs/year. Pays negotiable royalty to artists on contract; statutory rate to publishers per song on record.
Distributed by: Ozone Records, L.A. Records and Radiofreedom.com.
How to Contact: Submit demo tape by mail. Unsolicited submissions are OK. Prefers cassette or DAT with 3 songs and lyric sheet. Does not return material. Reports in 6 months.
Music: Mostly **commercial rock**, **alternative** and **A/C**; also **country** and **dance**. Released "Brittany," written and recorded by Brittany; and "Astral Guide," written and recorded by Ecclestone, all on L.A. Records. Other artists include Those Bloody Nigels, General Panic, Jessica Ehrenworth, Brittany and Joe King.

L.A. RECORDS, 26257 Regency Club Dr., Suite 6, Warren MI 48089. E-mail: jtrupi4539@aol.com. Website: http://www.abchosting.com/lotto or http://members.aol.com/jtrupi4539/index.html. Music Director: Jack Timmons. A&R: John Dudick. Labels include Stark Records, R.C. Records and Fearless. Record company, record producer and music publisher (Abalone Publishing). Estab. 1984. Staff size: 12. Releases 20-30 singles, 1-10 12" singles, 20-30 LPs, 1-5 EPs and 2-15 CDs/year. Pays 5% royalty to artists on contract; statutory rate to publisher per song on record.
How to Contact: Submit demo tape by mail. Unsolicited submissions are OK. Prefers cassette with 1-10 songs and lyric sheet. "It is very important to include a cover letter describing your objective goals." Reports in 3 months. "Due to fluctuation of postal rates include $1 to cover postage overage above 33¢. All others SASE is acceptable. Packages with 33¢ SASE are not acceptable."
Music: Mostly **rock/hard rock**, **heavy metal** and **pop/rock**; also **country/gospel**, **MOR/ballads**, **R&B**, **jazz**, **New Age**, **dance** and **easy listening**. Released *The Torch* (by Robbi Taylor/The Sattellites), recorded by The Sattellites (rock); "The Web" (by Jay Collins), recorded by The Net (rock); and "Passion" (by R. Gibb), recorded by Notta (blues), all on L.A. Records. Other artists include The Simmones, Kevin Stark, The Comets and Fearless.

LAFACE RECORDS, One Capitol City Plaza, 3350 Peachtree Rd., Suite 1500, Atlanta GA 30326-1040. (404)848-8050. Fax: (404)848-8051. A&R Director: Kawan Prather. Beverly Hills office: 8750 Wilshire Blvd., 3rd Floor, Beverly Hills CA 90211-2713. (310)358-4000. Fax: (310)858-4981. Website: http://www.peeps.com/laface/index.html. A&R Director: Pete Farmer. Record company.
Distributed by: BMG.
How to Contact: Does not accept unsolicited material.
Music: Released *Aquemini*, recorded by OutKast; *Soul Food* (soundtrack); and *My Way*, recorded by Usher, all on LaFace Records. Other artists include Az Yet and Donell Jones.

LAMAR MUSIC MARKETING, % 104 Pearsall Dr., Mt. Vernon NY 10552. (914)699-1744 or 973-7385. Fax: (914)668-3119. Associate Director: Darlene Barkley. Operations Director: Vernon Wilson.

FOR BOOKS ON THE CRAFT AND BUSINESS of songwriting, check out the website for Writer's Digest Books at http://www.writersdigest.com.

Labels include Lamar, MelVern, Wilson, Pulse Music and Co. Pub. Record company, music publisher and workshop organization. Estab. 1984. Staff size: 4. Releases 10-12 12″ singles and 2-4 LPs/year. Pays standard royalty to artists on contract; statutory rate to publisher per song. "We charge only if we are hired to do 'work-for-hire' projects."

How to Contact: Submit demo tape by mail. Unsolicited submissions are OK. Prefers cassette or VHS videocassette with 2 songs. SASE. Reports in 2 weeks. "Videotape submissions will get immediate response."

Music: Mostly **R&B**, **rap** and **pop**. Released "I Am So Confused," written and recorded by Eemense; and "Heavenly," recorded by Vern Wilson, both on Lamar Records; and "Feel Like a Woman" (by Wilson/Johnson), recorded by Sandra Taylor on MelVern Records (R&B/ballad). Other artists include Barry Manderson and Co/Vern.

Tips: "Must have managers or agents knowledgable in marketing with a promotional plan of action and the necessary funding to support the plan. Learn how the business works or you will get lost in the industry no matter what talent you believe you have!"

◐ LAMON RECORDS, P.O. Box 25371, Charlotte NC 28229. (704)882-6134. Fax: (704)882-2063. E-mail: mailbox@lamonrecords.com. Website: http://www.lamonrecords.com. A&R: David Moody. Nashville office: 9 Music Square S., Suite 284, Nashville TN 37203. International division office: 29 Kinfauns Ave., Hornchurch, Essex RM11 2AW England. A&R: Roy Sampson. Labels include Pan Handle, Plus Eight and Spotlight America. Record company and music publisher (Laymond Publishing Inc./BMI and CDT/ASCAP). Estab. 1962. Releases 12 singles and 12 CDs/year. Pays negotiable royalty to artists on contract; statutory rate to publisher per song on record.

Distributed by: Sound & Media/Virgin (England), Koch International (Germany and Austria), Supraphon (Czech Republic and Russia), Americana Records (Japan) and Intersound (US and Canada).

How to Contact: Submit demo tape by mail. Unsolicited submissions are OK. Prefers CD or cassette with 4 songs and lyric sheet. "Artists should also send bio information. Sending e-mail message first will ensure handling." SASE. Reports in 2 months.

Music: Mostly **country**, **folk**, **gospel**, **rock** and **New Age**; also **alternative**, **children's**, **R&B**, **instrumental** and **jazz**. Released *Cotton Eyed Joe* and *Great Train Song Medley*, both nominated for Grammys and recorded by The Moody Brothers (country); and *Jazzery Rhymes* (by Gary Marcus) (jazz). Other artists include Lynne Parker Wiggins, Committed, Lindy Miller, Old Time Radio Gang, Nicole McChele, Wayne Reynolds, Kristy Hoffman, The Briarhoppers and Jimm Mosher.

◐ LANDMARK COMMUNICATIONS GROUP, P.O. Box 1444, Hendersonville TN 37077. E-mail: lmarkcom@aol.com. President (all styles): Bill Anderson, Jr.. Professional Manager (western): Dylan Horse. Labels include Jana and Landmark Records. Record company, record producer, music publisher (Newcreature Music/BMI and Mary Megan Music/ASCAP) and management firm (Landmark Entertainment). Releases 10 singles, 8 LPs and 8 CDs/year. Pays 5-7% royalty to artists on contract; statutory rate to publisher for each record sold.

How to Contact: Submit demo tape by mail. Unsolicited submissions are OK. Prefers 7½ ips reel-to-reel or cassette with 4-10 songs and lyric sheet. SASE. Reports in 1 month.

Music: Mostly **country/crossover**, **gospel**, **jazz**, **R&B**, **rock** and **top 40/pop**. Released *The Gospel Truth* (by various artists), recorded by Vernon Oxford on Rocade (country); *The Yates Family 25 Year Anniversary* (by various artists), recorded by Joanne Cash Yates on Jana (gospel); and *Nothin' Else Feels Quite Like It*, written and recorded by various artists on Landmark (positive country).

Tips: "Be professional in presenting yourself."

☑ ◐ LANDSLIDE RECORDS, P.O. Box 20387, Atlanta GA 30325. (404)355-5580. E-mail: mrland @mindspring.com. Website: http://www.landsliderecords.com. President A&R: Michael Rothschild. Promotions Director/A&R: Windy Palmore. Record company, music publisher (Frozen Inca Music/BMI) and record producer. Estab. 1981. Releases 4 LPs and 4 CDs/year. Pays negotiable royalty to artists on contract; negotiable rate to publisher per song on record.

Distributed by: Rock Bottom, Action, Paul Starr and Twin Brook.

How to Contact: Submit demo tape by mail. Unsolicited submissions are OK. Prefers cassette with 6-12 songs and lyric sheet. SASE. Reports in 2 months.

Music: Mostly **blues** and **roots music**; also **jazz** and **swing**. Released *Derek Trucks Band* (by Derek Trucks), recorded by Derek Trucks Band (rock); *The Lost Continentals*, written and recorded by Amy Pike; and *New Orleans Big Beat*, written and recorded by Dave Bartholomew, all on Landslide Records. Other artists include The Steam Donkeys.

LARI-JON RECORDS, 325 W. Walnut, Rising City NE 68658. (402)542-2336. Owner: Larry Good. Record company, management firm (Lari-Jon Promotions), music publisher (Lari-Jon Publishing/BMI) and record producer (Lari-Jon Productions). Estab. 1967. Staff size: 1. Releases 15 singles and 5 LPs/year. Pays varying royalty to artists on contract.
How to Contact: Submit demo tape by mail. Unsolicited submissions are OK. Prefers cassette with 5 songs and lyric sheet. SASE. Reports in 2 months.
Music: Mostly **country**, **gospel-Southern** and **'50s rock**. Released "Glory Bound Train," written and recorded by Tom Campbell; *The Best of Larry Good*, written and recorded by Larry Good (country); and *Her Favorite Songs*, written and recorded by Johnny Nace (country), all on Lari-Jon Records. Other artists include Kent Thompson and Brenda Allen.

LARK RECORD PRODUCTIONS, INC., P.O. Box 35726, Tulsa OK 74153. (918)786-8896. E-mail: janajae@janajae.com. Website: http://www.janajae.com. Vice-President: Kathleen Pixley. Record company, music publisher (Jana Jae Music/BMI), management firm (Jana Jae Enterprises) and record producer (Lark Talent and Advertising). Estab. 1980. Staff size: 3. Pays negotiable royalty to artists on contract; statutory rate to publisher per song on record.
How to Contact: Submit demo tape by mail. Unsolicited submissions are OK. Prefers cassette or VHS videocassette with 3 songs and lead sheets. Does not return material. Reports only if interested.
Music: Mostly **country**, **bluegrass** and **classical**; also **instrumentals**. Released "Fiddlestix" (by Jana Jae); "Mayonnaise" (by Steve Upfold); and "Flyin' South" (by Cindy Walker), all recorded by Jana Jae on Lark Records (country). Other artists include Syndi, Hotwire and Matt Greif.

LBI RECORDS, P.O. Box 328, Jericho VT 05465. (802)899-3787. President: Bobby Hackney. Record company and record producer. Estab. 1986. Releases 12 singles, 2 LPs and 2 CDs/year. Pays negotiable royalty to artists on contract; statutory rate to publisher per song on record.
How to Contact: Submit demo tape by mail. Unsolicited submissions are OK. Prefers cassette with 3 songs and lyric sheet. SASE. Reports in 4-5 weeks.
Music: Mostly **reggae**, **R&B** and **jazz**; also **hip-hop/funk**. Artists include Trini.

LOCONTO PRODUCTIONS/SUNRISE STUDIO, 10244 NW 47 St., Sunrise FL 33351. (954)741-7766. President: Frank X. Loconto. Producer (country/western, gospel): Bill Dillon. Producer (pop, top 40): Dennis Bach. Labels include FXL Records. Record company, music publisher (Otto Music Publishing/ASCAP) and record producer. Estab. 1978. Releases 10 singles, 10 cassettes/albums and 5 CDs/year. Pays negotiable royalty to artists on contract; statutory rate to publisher per song on record.
Distributed by: FXL Record Distribution.
How to Contact: Submit demo tape by mail. Unsolicited submissions are OK. Prefers cassette with lyric sheet or lead sheet. SASE. Reports in 3-4 months.
Music: Released *Love Is In The Air* (by various), recorded by Michael Moog on FXL (disco); *Finally* (by various), recorded by Miracle Lights on RLB (gospel); and *Silent Waters* (by various), recorded by Irena Kofman on FXL (inspirational). Other artists include Roger Bryant, Bill Dillon and Bob Orange.
Tips: "Be sure to prepare a professional demo of your work and don't hesitate to seek 'professional' advice."

LONDON RECORDS, 825 Eighth Ave., 23rd Floor, New York NY 10019. (212)603-3999. Fax: (212)333-8030. Website: http://www.londonrecords.com. A&R Director: Neil Harris. Labels include London/Slash Records and FFRR Records. Record company.
• London's Renée Fleming won the 1998 Grammy Award for Best Classical Vocal Performance.
How to Contact: Submit demo tape by mail. Unsolicited submissions are OK. Prefers cassette, CD or DAT. "Send to Attn: A&R."
Music: Released *An Italian Songbook*, recorded by Cecilia Bartoli and James Levine on London Records.

LRJ, 2125 Willowmere Dr., Des Moines IA 50321. Manager: Tony Palmer. A&R (country, Spanish): A.A. Chiodo. Labels include Little Richie and Chuckie. Record company and music publisher (Little Richie Johnson Music). Estab. 1959. Releases 5 singles and 2 LPs/year.
How to Contact: Submit demo tape by mail. Unsolicited submissions are OK. Prefers cassette. Does

---

OPENNESS TO SUBMISSIONS: ◖ beginners; ◪ beginners and experienced; ◕ experienced only; ◙ industry referrals only.

not return material. Reports in 1 month.
Music: Mostly **country**. Released "Moonlight Roses and Wine," written and recorded by Gabe Nito; "Auction of My Life," written and recorded by Joe King; and "Helpless," recorded by Alan Godge, all on LRJ Records. Other artists include Reta Lee.

● **LUCIFER RECORDS, INC.**, P.O. Box 263, Brigantine NJ 08203-0263. (609)266-2623. President: Ron Luciano. Labels include TVA Records. Record company, music publisher (Ciano Publishing and Legz Music), record producer (Pete Fragale and Tony Vallo), management firm and booking agency (Ron Luciano Music Co. and TVA Productions). "Lucifer Records has offices in South Jersey; Palm Beach, Florida; and Las Vegas, Nevada."
How to Contact: Call or write to arrange personal interview. Prefers cassette with 4-8 songs. SASE. Reports in 3 weeks.
Music: Mostly **dance**, **easy listening**, **MOR**, **rock**, **soul** and **top 40/pop**. Released "I Who Have Nothing," by Spit-N-Image (rock); "Lucky," by Legz (rock); and "Love's a Crazy Game," by Voyage (disco/ballad). Other artists include Bobby Fisher, Jerry Denton, FM, Zeke's Choice, Al Caz, Joe Vee and Dana Nicole.

♣ ● **MAGNUM MUSIC CORP. LTD.**, 8607 128th Ave., Edmonton, Alberta T5E 0G3 Canada. (403)476-8230. Fax: (403)472-2584. General Manager: Bill Maxim. Record company, management firm and music publisher (High River Music Publishing/ASCAP and Ramblin' Man Music Publishing/BMI). Estab. 1982. Pays standard royalty.
How to Contact: Write or call first and obtain permission to submit. Prefers cassette or VHS videocassette with 3 songs and lyric sheet. Does not return material. Reports in 2 months.
Music: Mostly **country**, **gospel** and **contemporary**; also **pop, ballads** and **rock**. Published *Pray for the Family* and *Emotional Girl*, both written and recorded by C. Greenly (country); and *Don't Worry 'Bout It*, written and recorded by T. Anderson (country), all on Magnum Records.

⊕ ○ **MAKESHIFT MUSIC**, 13 Nowra St., Marayong 2148 Australia. Phone: (612)626-8991. E-mail: pbales@sia.net.au. Manager: Peter Bales. Record company and music publisher (Aria and Apra). Estab. 1980. Staff size: 1. "Makeshift Music is an administration and production company specializing within the recording and publishing fields of the music industry. Product and material is now leased out to third party companies such as BMG, Sony, Mushroom, etc." Pays statutory rate to publisher per song on record.
How to Contact: Submit demo tape by mail. Unsolicited submissions are OK. Prefers cassette or PAL/VHS videocassette with 2-3 songs and lyric sheet. Does not return material. Reports in 1 month only if interested and submission is accompanied by 2 IRCs.
Music: Mostly **rock/pop**. Released "Olympic 2000" (by Frank Seckold), recorded by Chimps on Makeshift; and "What You Do?" written and recorded by Fantasm on Right Music.

⋈ ⋈ ○ **MAKOCHÉ RECORDING COMPANY**, 208 N. Fourth St., Bismarck ND 58501. (701)223-7316. Fax: (701)255-8287. E-mail: makoche@aol.com. Website: http://www.makoche.com. A&R Assistant: Jennifer Swap. Labels include Chairmaker's Rush, Scoria and Tellurian. Record company and recording studio. Estab. 1995. Staff size: 2. Releases 3 singles, 4 LPs and 4 CDs/year. Pays negotiable royalty to artists on contract; statutory rate to publisher per song on record.
Distributed by: DNA, Music Design, Four Winds Trading, Zango Music and New Leaf Distribution.
   ● Makoché is noted for releasing music based in the Native American tradition, and fiddle and bluegrass. Winner of the 1998 New Age Voice Award for Best Album Cover and Best Contemporary Native American Album.
How to Contact: Submit demo tape by mail. Unsolicited submissions are OK. Prefers cassette or CD. "Please include an introductory letter and contact info. Please submit only fiddle, bluegrass, Native American, world and flute music." SASE. Reports in 2 months.
Music: Mostly **Native American**, **flute** and **fiddle**; also **world music** and bluegrass. Released *Wind River*, written and recorded by Andrew Vasquez on Makoché (Native American); *Cowboy Legacy* (by various), recorded by Fiddlin Johnny on Chairmakers Rush (fiddle); and *Nat'l Oldtime Fiddlers' Contest 1997*, written and recorded by various artists on Chairmakers Rush (fiddle). Other artists include Gary Stroutsos, Bryan Akipa, Keith Bear, Joseph Fire Crow, Sissy Goodhouse and Kevin Locke.
Tips: "We are a small label with a dedication to quality. We do contact every artist who submits work to us. Be persistent but patient."

⋈ ● **MAVERICK RECORDS**, 9348 Civic Center Dr., Beverly Hills CA 90210. (310)385-7800. Fax: (310)385-7711. Website: http://www.maverickrc.com. Director of Artist Development: Michael Pontecorvo. A&R: Guy Oseary. A&R: Jason Bentley. Record company.
Distributed by: WEA.

• Maverick's Madonna won three 1998 Grammy Awards including Best Dance Recording, Best Pop Album and Best Package.

How to Contact: Maverick Records does not accept unsolicited submissions.

Music: Released *The Wedding Singer Volume 2* (soundtrack); *Supposed Former Infatuation Junkie*, recorded by Alanis Morissette; and *Ray of Light*, recorded by Madonna. Other artists include Candlebox, Deftones, Love Spit Love, Me'shell Ndegeocello, Neurotic Outsiders, The Rentals, Rule 62 and Summercamp.

☑ ♟ ⬤ **MCA RECORDS**, 1755 Broadway, 8th Floor, New York NY 10019. (212)841-8000. Fax: (212)841-8146. A&R: Simon Collins; A&R: Carmen Cacciatore. Universal City office: 70 Universal City Plaza, Universal City CA 91608. (818)777-4000. Fax: (818)866-1406. Senior A&R Director: Gary Ashley. Nashville office: 60 Music Square E., Nashville TN 37203. (615)244-8944. Fax: (615)880-7447. Website: http://www.mcarecords.com. Vice President of A&R: Mark Wright. A&R Director: Larry Willoughby. A&R Manager: Renee White. Record company and music publisher (MCA Music).

• MCA's Vince Gill won a 1998 Grammy Award for Best Male Country Vocal Performance.

How to Contact: MCA Records cannot accept unsolicited submissions. Have your demo recommended to their A&R Department by a well-known manager, agent, producer, radio DJ or other music industry veteran. Create a buzz in your local community at the club label, through local music publications and at your local radio station.

Music: Released *Love Always*, recorded by K-Ci & JoJo; *Acquarium*, recorded by Aqua; and *Sublime*, recorded by Sublime, all on MCA Records. Other artists include Tracy Byrd, George Strait, Vince Gill, The Mavericks and Trisha Yearwood.

⬤ **MCB RECORDS**, 1437 Central G-1, Memphis TN 38104. (901)725-4940. E-mail: mcbrecord@aol.com. President: Ms. Boswell. Record company, music publisher (In the Green/BMI) and record producer (Ms. Boswell). Estab. 1991. Releases 4 singles, 2 LPs and 2 CDs/year. Pays standard royalty to artists on contract; statutory rate to publisher per song on record.

Distributed by: Select-O-Hits.

How to Contact: Write first and obtain permission to submit a demo. Prefers cassette with 3 songs and lyric sheet. "Full production, please. No home recordings." SASE. Reports in 3 months.

Music: Mostly **country**, **pop** and **alternative country**; also **rock**, **gospel** and **blues**. Released *It Must Be Love* (by Ben Shaw/Craig Clark), recorded by Alan Hall (pop); and *Gone to the Dogs*, written and recorded by Jeremiah Lucker (alternative county), both on MCB. Other artists include Gary Williams, Craig Wayne Clark and Scott Elwood.

Tips: "Read every book you can on songwriting."

⬤ **MEGAFORCE WORLDWIDE ENTERTAINMENT**, P.O. Box 779, New Hope PA 18938. (215)862-5411. Fax: (215)862-9470. E-mail: contact@megaforcerecords.com. Website: http://www.megaforcerecords.com. President: Marsha Zazula. CEO: Jon Zazula. Labels include Megaforce Records Inc. Record company. Estab. 1983. Staff size: 2. Releases 5 LPs, 2 EPs and 5 CDs/year. Pays various royalties to artists on contract; ¾ statutory rate to publisher per song on record.

Distributed by: Alternative Distribution Alliance.

How to Contact: Does not accept unsolicited material.

Music: Mostly **rock**. Released *Matinee Idols*, written and recorded by Ominous Seapods; and *Uncivilized Area*, written and recorded by The Disco Biscuits, both on Hydrophonics (rock); and *Let's Get It Right*, written and recorded by SNFU on Megaforce (rock). Other artists include Gouds Thumb and Juggling Suns.

☑ ⬤ **MERCURY RECORDS**, 825 Eighth Ave., 19th Floor, New York NY 10019. (212)333-8000. Fax: (212)333-8595. Los Angeles office: 11150 Santa Monica Blvd., Suite 1000, Los Angeles CA 90025-7226. (310)996-7200. Fax: (310)473-0380. Website: http://www.mercuryrecords.com/mercury. A&R Director: Jenny Price. Nashville office: 66 Music Square W., Nashville TN 37203. (615)320-0110. Fax: (615)327-4856. A&R Director: Gary Harrison. Labels include Mouth Almighty Records, Worldly/Triloka Records, Blackheart Records, Private Records, Slipdisc Records, Thirsty Ear, Blue Gorilla, Dubbly, Little Dog Records, Rounder, Capricorn Records and Mercury Nashville Records. Record company.

FOR BOOKS ON THE CRAFT AND BUSINESS of songwriting, check out the website for Writer's Digest Books at http://www.writersdigest.com.

• As a result of the PolyGram and Universal merger, Island Records has merged with Mercury Records. At press time the above contact information was correct.

How to Contact: Mercury Records does not accept unsolicited submissions. Do not send material unless requested.

Music: Released *Come On Over*, recorded by Shania Twain on Mercury Nashville. Other artists include Gina Thompson, Crystal Waters, Cardigans, James, Elvis Costello, Bon Jovi and downset.

MERLIN PRODUCTIONS, P.O. Box 5087, Vancouver British Columbia V6B 4A9 Canada. (604)434-9129. E-mail: zauber311@aol.com. President: Wolfgang Hamann. Vice Presidents of A&R: Martin E. Hamann (rock); Leslie Bishko (world, reggae). Record company, record producer and management firm (Merlin Management). Estab. 1979. Staff size: 3. Releases 5 singles, 3 LPs, 1 EP and 3 CDs/year. Pays negotiable royalty to artists on contract; statutory rate to publisher per song on record.

How to Contact: Write or call first and obtain permission to submit. Prefers cassette with 3 songs and lyric sheet. SAE and IRC. Reports in 2 weeks.

Music: Mostly **rock/pop**, **R&B** and **dance**; also **modern rock**. Released *20th Century Man*, written and recorded by The Defaids; and *Sounds of the Soul*, written and recorded by Xenobia Project (dance), both on Merlin Productions. Other artists include Wolfgang-Wolfgang.

Tips: "Learn what it takes to be a professional! Developing your art also means learning about the business side."

MHM RECORDINGS, 505 S. Beverly Dr., Beverly Hills CA 90212. (323)469-3399. Fax: (323)466-4717. E-mail: davenmad@usa.net. Vice President of A&R (hip-hop/rap): Chris Warner. President (R&B, dance): Daven Michaels. Vice President of A&R (R&B): Dave Steinberg. Record company, record producer (Daven Michaels) and management firm (Mad Hatter Management). Estab. 1990. Staff size: 10. Releases 8 singles, 5 LPs and 5 CDs/year. Pays negotiable royalty to artists on contract; statutory rate to publisher per song on record.

• In 1998, two releases by MHM received Gold certification by the Recording Industry Association of America, and one release received Platinum.

How to Contact: Submit demo tape by mail. Unsolicited submissions are OK. Prefers cassette, CD or VHS videocassette with 3 songs, lead sheet, cover letter and press clippings. Does not return material. Reports in 5 weeks.

Music: Mostly **R&B**, **hip-hop** and **dance**; also **rap**. Does not want country or rock. Released *Something About You* (by Denzel Foster/Tommy McElroy), recorded by Premier on Alien (R&B); *Ego Trip* (by Dave Ande), recorded by Superstar DJ Keoki on Moonshine (electronic); and "Color Of Joy" (by Ed Fox/Angel Sheppard), recorded by Angel Sheppard on MHM (R&B). Other artists include Cirrus, Daven the Mad Hatter and Suburban Parade.

MIGHTY RECORDS, 150 West End, Suite 6-D, New York NY 10023. (212)873-5968. Manager: Danny Darrow. Labels include Mighty Sounds & Filmworks. Record company, music publisher (Rockford Music Co./BMI, Stateside Music Co./BMI and Corporate Music Publishing Co./ASCAP) and record producer (Danny Darrow). Estab. 1958. Releases 1-2 singles, 1-2 12″ singles and 1-2 LPs/year. Pays standard royalty to artists on contract; statutory rate to publisher per song on record.

How to Contact: Submit demo tape by mail. Unsolicited submissions are OK. "No phone calls." Prefers cassette with 3 songs and lyric sheet. Does not return material. Reports in 2-4 weeks only if interested.

Music: Mostly **pop**, **country** and **dance**; also **jazz**. Released *Impulse* (by D. Darrow); *Corporate Lady* (by Michael Green); and *Falling In Love* (by Brian Dowen), all recorded by Danny Darrow on Mighty Records.

MISSILE RECORDS, Box 5537, Kreole Station, Moss Point MS 39563-1537. (228)475-0059. "No collect calls." President/Owner: Joe F. Mitchell. Record company, music publisher (Bay Ridge Publishing/BMI) and record producer. Estab. 1974. Releases 28 singles and 10 LPs/year. Pays "10-16¢ per song to new artists, higher rate to established artists"; statutory rate to publisher for each record sold.

Distributed by: Several national and international distributors. Some are: KY Imports/Exports, Curtis Wood, Dixie Rak Records & Tapes, Bogart Entertainment, Frank Music Distribution and KC/Saddlestone.

How to Contact: Write first and obtain permission to submit. Include #10 SASE. "All songs sent for review must include sufficient return postage. No collect calls." Prefers cassette with 3-6 songs and lyric sheet. Reports in 6-8 weeks.

Music: Mostly **country**, **alternative**, **gospel**, **rap**, **heavy metal**, **hardcore**, **folk**, **contemporary**, **jazz**, **bluegrass** and **R&B**; also **soul**, **MOR**, **blues**, **ballads**, **reggae**, **world**, **rock** and **pop**. Released "Hurt, Hurt Go Away" recorded by Michael Pitts; "Has Anyone Seen My Baby?," written and recorded by

Herbert Lacey (R&B); and "I'm Still Hanging On To Holding You" and "Dancing on the Moon" (by Jeremy Lee Sheppard), all on Missile Records.
Tips: "We will give consideration to new exceptionally talented artists with a fan base and some backing."

⦿ **MJJ MUSIC**, 2100 Colorado Ave., Santa Monica CA 90404. (310)449-2963. Fax: (310)449-2959.
Distributed by: Sony.
How to Contact: MJJ Music does not accept unsolicited submissions.
Music: Released "Anything," recorded by 3T on MJJ Records.

N ⦿ **MJM RECORDS**, P.O. Box 1731, La Mirada CA 90637. President (pop, rock, R&B, gospel): Mark Joseph. Manager (metal, rock): Ric Rodeheaver. Labels include Renaissance Recordings. Record company. Estab. 1991. Releases 3 CDs/year. Pays negotiable royalty to artists on contract; statutory rate to publisher per song on record.
How to Contact: Write first and obtain permission to submit.
Music: Mostly **pop**, **rock** and **R&B**; also **alternative**. Released *Love After All* (by Marre Ishii), recorded by Marre (pop); *Love Education*, written and recorded by Tom Gibson (pop); and *Behind Enemy Lines* (by George Ochoa), recorded by Recon (hard rock), all on MJM Records. Other artists include Saviour Machine, Sacred Warrior, Angelica, Mozart and Razzle.

⦿ **MODAL MUSIC, INC.**™, P.O. Box 6473, Evanston IL 60204-6473. (847)864-1022. President: Terran Doehrer. Assistant: J. Distler. Record company and agent. Estab. 1988. Staff size: 2. Releases 1-2 LPs/year. Pays negotiable royalty to artists on contract; negotiable rate to publisher per song on record.
How to Contact: Submit demo tape by mail. Unsolicited submissions are OK. Prefers cassette with bio, PR, brochures, any info about artist and music. Does not return material. Reports in 2-4 months.
Music: Mostly **ethnic** and **world**. Released *Dance The Night Away* (by T. Doehrer), recorded by Balkan Rhythm Band™; and *Sid Beckerman's Rumanian (D. Jacobs)*, recorded by Jutta & The Hi-Dukes™, both on Modal Music Records. Other artists include Ensemble M'Chaiya™, Nordland Band™ and Terran's Greek Band™.
Tips: "Please note our focus is ethnic. You waste your time and money by sending us any other type of music. If you are unsure of your music fitting our focus, please call us before sending anything. Put your name and contact info on every item you send!"

🕊 ⦿ **MONTICANA RECORDS**, P.O. Box 702, Snowdon Station, Montreal, Quebec H3X 3X8 Canada. General Manager: David P. Leonard. Labels include Dynacom. Record company, record producer (Monticana Productions) and music publisher (Montina Music/SOCAN). Estab. 1963. Staff size: 1. Pays negotiable royalty to artists on contract.
How to Contact: Submit demo tape by mail. Unsolicited submissions are OK. Prefers phonograph record or VHS videocassette and lyric sheet. SASE.
Music: Mostly **top 40**, **blues**, **country**, **dance-oriented**, **easy listening**, **folk** and **gospel**; also **jazz**, **MOR**, **progressive**, **R&B**, **rock** and **soul**.
Tips: "Be excited and passionate about what you do. Be professional."

⦿ **MOR RECORDS**, 17596 Corbel Court, San Diego CA 92128. (619)485-1550. Fax: (619)485-1883. E-mail: stulgsandca@webtv.net. President: Stuart L. Glassman. A&R (pop): Don Smith. Record company and record producer. Estab. 1980. Staff size: 2. Releases 3 singles/year. Pays 4% royalty to artists on contract; negotiable rate to publisher per song on record.
Affiliate(s): MOR Jazztime.
How to Contact: Submit demo tape by mail. Unsolicited submissions are OK. Prefers cassette or VHS videocassette. SASE. Reports in 2-4 weeks.
Music: Mostly **pop instrumental/vocal MOR**; also **novelty**.
Tips: "We are looking for commercially sounding product with a 'hook' and a clean lyric with 'outstanding' melody."

⤬ ⦿ **MOTION CITY RECORDS**, 1847 Centinela, Santa Monica CA 90404. (310)264-4870. Fax: (310)264-4871. E-mail: kcaetans@motioncity.com. Website: http://www.motioncity.com. A&R Director:

🕊 🌐 **SENDING TO A COUNTRY** other than your own? Be sure to send International Reply Coupons (IRCs) instead of stamps for replies or return of your materials.

Kevin Caetans. Record company. Estab. 1994. Releases 7 LPs and 7 CDs/year. Pays negotiable royalty to artists on contract; statutory rate to publisher per song on record.
Distributed by: CRD and BMG.
How to Contact: Submit demo tape by mail. Unsolicited submissions are OK. Prefers cassette, CD or DAT with 3 songs. Does not return material.
Music: Mostly **alternative, rock/metal** and **techno**. Released *Velvet*, recorded by Velvet (alternative); and *Mowed*, recorded by Voodoo (metal), both on Motion City Records. Other artists include Ten Pound Troy, UFO Bro and Brent David Fraser.

☑ ⬤ MOTOWN RECORDS, 825 Eighth Ave., New York NY 10019. (212)373-0600. Director of A&R: Shante Paige. Los Angeles office: 11150 Santa Monica Blvd. #1000, Los Angeles CA 90025. (310)996-7200. Website: http://www.motown40.com. Labels include BIV Records, Illtown Records and MoJazz Records. Record company.
   • See the Insider Report interview with A&R Director Shante Paige on page 180.
How to Contact: Motown Records does not accept unsolicited submissions.
Music: Released *Anytime*, recorded by Brian McKnight; and *Phoenix Rising*, recorded by The Temptations, both on Motown Records. Other artists include Erykah Badu and Chico DeBarge.

⬛ ⬤ MSM RECORDS, P.O. Box 101, Sutton MA 01590. Publisher/Owner: John Scott. Labels include Hālo Records and Bronco Records. Record company and music publisher (Mount Scott Music/BMI and Pick The Hits Music/ASCAP). Estab. 1979. Staff size: 3. Releases 3-4 LPs/year. Pays standard royalty to artists on contract; statutory rate to publisher per song on record.
How to Contact: Write first and obtain permission to submit. Prefers CD or DAT. "Professional demos only." Does not return material. Include SASE for response.
Music: Mostly **folk** and **theater/musical works**. Released Soundtrack for Historical Documentary (soundtrack); and *Stages* (theatre score), both written and recorded by John Gagne on Halo; and *Sutton Senior Choir* (by various artists), recorded by Sutton Choir on MSM (classical choral). Other artists include Cactus.
Tips: "Follow submission guidelines. Will discuss acceptance of theater works for review/possible collaboration. Write and include synopsis (two page maximum) if submitting theater works."

⬤ MULE KICK RECORDS, 3608 Sundance Trail, Placerville CA 95667. (818)343-3682 or (530)626-4536. Owner: Doug McGinnis, Sr. Record company and music publisher (Freewheeler Publishing/BMI). Estab. 1949. Pays 25% royalty to artists on contract; statutory rate to publisher.
Distributed by: Tower Records.
How to Contact: Submit demo tape by mail. Unsolicited submissions are OK. Prefers cassette or CD with 6-10 songs and lyric and lead sheet. SASE. Reports in 1-6 months.
Music: Mostly **country** and **c-rock**; also **pop**. Released *Pretending*, written and reported by Diana Blair; *Tribute to Joaquin*, written and recorded by Joaquin Murphy; and *Wild Country*, written and recorded by Don McGinnis, all on Mule Kick Records.

⬤ MUSIC QUEST® ENTERTAINMENT & TELEVISION, P.O. Box 822, Newark NJ 07102. (973)374-4421. Fax: (973)374-5888. E-mail: music@mqtv.com. Website: http://www.mqtv.com. Senior Vice President (urban, pop): Michael Feinstein. Vice President A&R (rap, hip-hop): Lasasha Sampson. Record company, music publisher (Music Quest® Publishing), record producer (Music Quest® Productions) and distribution (Music Quest® Distribution). Estab. 1994. Releases 20 singles, 10 LPs, 20 EPs and 10 CDs/year. Pays negotiable royalty to artists on contract; ¾ rate to publisher per song on record.
How to Contact: Submit demo tape (or finished product) by mail. Unsolicited submissions are OK. Prefers cassette, CD or VHS videocassette with picture, bio and letter. "Please include past experience, marketing plan, where you are and where you want to go. Include number of years of professional experience." Does not return material. Reports in 1-3 months.
Music: Mostly **pop (radio friendly)**, **hip-hop/R&B** and **jazz/urban/pop rock**; also **instrumental**, **children's/special** and **gospel/reggae**. Released *A Very Special Christmas Gift*, written and recorded by Melba Moore; *Can I Touch You*, written and recorded Synthia Saint James, both on Music Quest. Other artists include Hollywood, Majestic, Sonja, 4 Girls With No Name, Janice Dempsey (artist producer), B. Darius (formerly produced for the Fugees and the Refugee Camp) and Norman Bradley. "Dunn Pearson produced the soundtrack for the movie *Ride* on Mirimax Film."
Tips: "Know what the marketplace (consumers) wants because MQT is a very commercial-oriented label. MQT follows the trends and looks to break new and innovate ideas. Study your craft well, research your ideas to make sure they are what's happening in today's marketplace. We have exceptional, creative producers, and we are looking for youth oriented 'hot' artists to release."

insider report

For a Motown A&R Director, honesty is key

If there is one piece of advice artists breaking into the music business should heed, it is, "If one door slams, there is another one that will open, so just keep at it." That is Shante Paige's number one rule as a door slammer, or as she would prefer to be called, a door opener at Motown Records. As director of A&R, Paige is one who can furnish musical upstarts with guidance because it is her job to find fresh, new artists and sign them to Motown.

Shante Paige

So how do songwriters go about getting her or another A&R person's attention? "From a writer's standpoint, I think they should get with a producer or a band and have music behind their writing," Paige says. All too many times writers send only their songs on paper, and it is too difficult to "hear" how the writer wants the song to sound or to be arranged. "We don't know what they want to bring across. The best thing they can do is [record a demo], even if it is just an acoustic guitar, just so we know where the song is going."

Of course, getting signed to a label isn't as easy as just making and sending a demo. "Each company is different when it comes to unsolicited demos," says Paige. "Call the label and find out their policy for demo submission. Some companies, if they're not looking, won't accept anything at all. Other companies will tell you to put a specific code on [your demo package] for solicited materials so they don't throw it away." Each label varies, so don't waste time and money sending your demo to a label that has specifically said they don't take unsolicited demos. "They will literally throw into the garbage anything you send them."

Just call the labels open to your styles of music and ask. If calling a record label seems a bit old fashioned or outdated, technology has made it easy to find out the hows and wheres of demo submission. Just about every major record label has a website or e-mail address. "I get tons of e-mails through the Internet now because of our website," Paige says. "That's the easy part. The hard part is getting heard."

SHANTE PAIGE

Title: Director of A&R
Company: Motown Records

What an A&R person looks for in a submission is hard to describe. "Give me a little background history," Paige says. "Sincerity always works with me. I read the letters and if they sound sincere, I tend to be a little more biased to those artists. If somebody writes me and they're really cocky, saying 'I am better than any artist on your label,' that kind of thing, it immediately turns me off." Demos don't have to be elaborate with great pictures on glossy paper. "That doesn't matter to me. If it's hot, then I'm going to listen."

Once Paige hears a demo she likes, she involves her boss, Kedar Massenburg (whose label Kedar Entertainment was bought by Motown). "He will decide from there. He'll say to me, 'Are you really, really feeling this group?' Or if it's a writer or producer, 'Are you really feeling this person? If so, then we need to bring them here and have a meeting.' If they're a group, we'll probably have them perform here in a little rehearsal studio. If it's a producer, we'll have him come and play some of his stuff and just vibe with him—get a feel for him."

And then there is the deal—to sign or not to sign. Just like Motown songwriter Smokey Robinson wrote, "You better shop around," Paige wholeheartedly agrees. "Do not take your first offer. If I see something in you, take what I say and go to somebody else and see what they are offering. If you are shopping your deal, you should go to two or three labels and find the downfalls of each. Weigh your options. Talk to some of the artists and see how they feel, or talk to some of the writers or producers who are currently signed and [ask about] the problems they have."

It is understandable to be overzealous when a deal is offered. "You have to do your homework because this is your life," says Paige. "People just sign and hope it all comes together in the end. Don't sell yourself short. I honestly feel if one person signs you or feels they want to sign you, then there is going to be somebody else out there who sees the same vision. Getting screwed is a way to learn, but if you can, avoid it. Be cautious and don't prematurely take the first offer. It's not offensive to shop record labels as long as it is done with respect and honesty. What I don't like is if somebody comes to me and then they go to another label and try to get a bidding war going. I think that is what turns a lot of A&R people off."

Paige explains an artist needs to be upfront with the labels they deal with. "If [an artist] says, 'I really want to go with your label, but I feel like I owe it to myself to shop my idea around to other places. Then I'm going to get back to you and let you know,' that's cool. As long as we keep that constant communication open, it's OK."

It's just good business to be respectful to all the labels you're dealing with. "Remember, your first label may not be your only label," says Paige. "Your label could end up shelving you or dropping you, and then you may need to go to that other label. You don't ever want to burn a bridge."

Paige also advises artists to get a good lawyer. "A lot of artists have a tendency to take the first deal that comes their way because they're so anxious to get 'that deal.' Or they'll take the deal and not have an attorney sign it, scared the attorney will break the deal for them. Go with your gut. If you're comfortable with the company and you have a good attorney who has your best interest at heart, then it's a good situation for you and ultimately for everyone involved."

—*Diana Schlake*

❷ NATION RECORDS INC., 6351 W. Montrose #333, Chicago IL 60634. (773)736-9778. Fax: (312)458-5900. E-mail: agent@ripco.com. A&R: Phil Vaughan. Record company. Estab. 1996. Releases 5 CDs/year. Pays negotiable royalty to artists on contract; statutory rate to publisher per song on record.
Distributed by: MS Distributors.
How to Contact: Submit demo tape by mail. Unsolicited submissions are OK. Prefers cassette or CD with lyric sheet. Does not return material. Reports in 3 months.
Music: All types. Released *Morzat Street*, recorded by Pete Special (R&B); and *It's All About Christmas*, recorded by World Class Noise (pop), both on Nation Records Inc. Other artists include The Buckinghams, Dick Holiday and The Bamboo Gang.

❷ NIGHTMARE RECORDS, 7751 Greenwood Dr., St. Paul MN 55112. Phone/fax: (612)784-9654. E-mail: nightdiscs@aol.com. Website: http://www.nightmare-records.com. Contact: Lance King. Record company, distributor and management firm (Jupiter Productions). Estab. 1983. Pays 10-15% royalty to artists on contract.
Distributed by: Perris Records, Mega Rock, Lobel, Wildside and Dream Disc.
How to Contact: Submit demo tape by mail. Unsolicited submissions are OK. Prefers cassette or CD with 3 songs. Include brief bio, photo and press clippings (if available). Does not return material. Reports only if interested.
Music: Mostly **hard rock-metal**, with a special interest in **progressive metal**. Released *Untitled* (by King/ Barilla), recorded by The Kings Machine (rock); *From Cradle to Grave* (by Petrick/Cassidy), recorded by Malicious (rock); and *Pavlov's Dog's* (by Stevenson/Christensen), recorded by Conditioned Response (rock), all on Nightmare. Current acts include Godhead (Southern fried grunge), Visionary (progressive metal) and Sonic Boom (industrial dance).
Tips: "Be patient, persistent and positive! We're busy and we know what were looking for, if we like what we hear, we'll call you ASAP."

NOO TRYBE RECORDS. See the listing for Noo Trybe's parent company, Virgin Records, for submission and contact information.

❑ NORTH STAR MUSIC, 22 London St., E. Greenwich RI 02818. (401)886-8888. Website: http:// www.northstarmusic.com. President: Richard Waterman. Record company. Estab. 1985. Staff size: 1. Releases 5-10 LPs/year. Pays 9% royalty to artists on contract; ¾ statutory rate to publisher per song on record.
Distributed by: Valley Media Inc., Goldenrod and Lady Slipper.
How to Contact: Submit demo tape by mail. Unsolicited submissions are OK. Prefers cassette with 4-5 songs. Does not return material. Reports in 2 months.
Music: Mostly **instrumental**, **traditional** and **contemporary jazz**, **New Age**, **traditional world** and **classical**. Released *Mother*, written and recorded by Susan McKeown/Cathie Ryan/Robin Spielberg (instrumental); *Mysts of Time*, written and recorded by Aine Minogue (Celtic chant); and *Crossing the Waters* (by Steve Schuch), recorded by Steve Schuch and the Night Heron Consort (contemporary Celtic), all on North Star Music. Other artists include Judith Lynn Stillman, David Osborne, Emilio Kauderer, Gerry Beaudoin, Cheryl Wheeler and Nathaniel Rosen.

❑ NPO RECORDS, INC., P.O. Box 41251, Staten Island NY 10304. Phone/fax: (718)967-6121. E-mail: nporecords@hotmail.com. President/A&R: James Brody. Record company and music publisher (NPO Records and Music Publishing). Estab. 1996. Releases 6 singles, 2 LPs, 2 CDs/year. Pays negotiable royalty to artists on contract; statutory rate to publisher per song on record.
How to Contact: Submit demo tape by mail. Unsolicited submissions are OK. Prefers cassette with 3 songs and lyric sheet. SASE. Reports in 1 month.
Music: Mostly **hip-hop** and **dance**. Released "Love Will Come Again" (by M. Commorato), recorded by The Eggmen (top 40/rock); "Take Control of Love" (by A. Carrasquillo), recorded by Blak Aces (Latin/ dance); "Real Eyez," written and recorded by Anomos (rap); and "Diary of A Criminal," written and recorded by Gee Money (rap) on NPO Records.
Tips: "Be open minded and accepting of constructive criticism. Self-discipline and professionalism are essential."

REMEMBER: Don't "shotgun" your demo tapes. Submit only to companies interested in the type of music you write. For more submission hints, refer to Getting Started on page 11.

✿ ☑ ◗ **OAK STREET MUSIC**, 1067 Sherwin Rd., Winnipeg, Manitoba R3H 0T8 Canada. (204)694-3101. Fax: (204)697-0903. E-mail: peg@oakstreetmusic.ca. Website: http://www.oakstreetmusic.ca. A&R Director: Arthur Pearson. Labels include PEG Music. Record company, music publisher (Branch Group Music/SOCAN) and record producer (Oak Street Music). Estab. 1987. Staff size: 1. Releases 8 singles, 12 LPs and 12 CDs/year. Pays negotiable royalty to artists on contract; statutory rate to publisher per song on record.
Distributed by: Koch International and Acorn Distribution.
How to Contact: Submit demo tape by mail. Unsolicited submissions are OK. Prefers cassette, CD or VHS videocassette with 3 songs and lyric sheet. Does not return material. Reports in 2 months.
Music: Mostly **children's** and **novelty**; also **rock, A/C** and **triple A**. Released *All About Canada*; *All About Counting*; and *All About ABCs*, all written and recorded by various artists/composers on Oak Street Music (children's). Other artists include the Jonah Stone, Fred Penner and Al Simmons.
Tips: "Always include lyrics with submissions."

◗ **OCP PUBLICATIONS**, 5536 NE Hassalo, Portland OR 97213. (503)281-1191. Fax: (503)282-3486. Marketing Manager: Dave Island. Labels include Candleflame and NALR. Record company, music publisher and record producer. Estab. 1977. Releases 20 LPs and 10 CDs/year. Pays 10% royalty to artists on contract; negotiable rate to publisher per song on record.
How to Contact: Submit demo tape by mail. Unsolicited submissions are OK. Requires lead sheets (with chords, melody line and text minimum) with *optional* demo tape. Prefers cassette with lead sheet. "Detailed submission information available upon request." SASE. Reports in 3 months.
Music: Mostly **liturgical, Christian/listening** and **children's Christian**; also **choral Christian anthems** and **youth Christian anthems**. Released *Find Us Ready*, recorded by Tom Booth; *The Coming*, recorded by Leon Roberts; and *Table of Plenty*, recorded by John Michael Talbot, all on OCP. "There are over 80 artists signed by OCP."
Tips: "Know the Catholic liturgy and the music needs therein."

◗ **OGLIO RECORDS**, 507-A Pier Ave., Hermosa Beach CA 90254. (310)798-2252. Fax: (310)798-3728. Contact: Michael Byer. Record company. Estab. 1992. Releases 20 LPs and 20 CDs/year. Pays negotiable royalty to artist on contract; statutory rate to publisher per song on record.
How to Contact: Write first and obtain permission to submit. Accepts demos in all formats. Does not return material. Reports in 6 weeks.
Music: Mostly **alternative rock** and **comedy**.

◗ **OLD SCHOOL RECORDS**, 179 Prospect Ave., Wood Dale IL 60191-2727. E-mail: oldschrec@aol.com. Owner/President (experimental, jazz, creative/improvised, eclectic): Peter J. Gianakopoulos. A&R (alternative, pop): Desmond Whisp. Record company, music publisher (Old School Records/Goosongs/ASCAP). Estab. 1992. Staff size: 3. Releases 1-2 singles, 1-2 LPs, 1-2 EPs and 1-2 CDs/year. Pays 10-16% to artists on contract; statutory rate to publisher per song on record.
Distributed by: Dutch East India and Carrot Top.
How to Contact: Submit demo tape by mail. Unsolicited submissions are OK. Prefers cassette with 3-5 songs and lyric sheet. SASE. Reports in 3 weeks.
Music: Mostly **rock, pop** and **new music (jazz/classical)**; also **experimental/improvised or electronic based**. Released *Raymond Carverland*, written and recorded by Castle Broadway on Soutrane (experimental); and *Goo*, written and recorded by Goo on Old School (experimental). Other artists include The Now.
Tips: "Send something new that's not too derivative or trendy."

☑ ◗ **OMEGA RECORD GROUP, INC.**, 27 W. 72nd St., New York NY 10023. (212)769-3060. Fax: (212)769-3195. E-mail: info@omegarecords.com. Website: http://www.omegarecords.com. Sales Manager (pop, jazz, dance): Duane Martuge. Operations Manager (classical, jazz): Frank Burton. Labels include Vanguard Classics and Everest. Record company. Estab. 1989. Releases 5 singles and 60-70 CDs/year. Pays negotiable royalty to artists on contract.
Distributed by: Allegro Corporation.
How to Contact: Submit demo tape by mail. Unsolicited submissions are OK. Prefers cassette, CD or DAT. SASE. Reports in 3 weeks.
Music: Mostly **classical, jazz** and **dance**. Released *Tango, Tango*, written and recorded by Viveza on Omega; and *Awake Sweet Love* (by John Dowland), recorded by Alfred Deller on Vanguard Classics (classical).

◗ **OMNI 2000 INC.**, 413 Cooper St., Camden NJ 08102. (609)963-6400. Fax: (609)964-FAX-1. Website: http://www.omniplex413.com. President/Executive Producer: Michael Nise. Record company, music publisher and record producer. Estab. 1995. Pays 50% royalty to artists on contract; statutory rate to publisher per song on record.

Distributed by: Sutra and Sema.

How to Contact: Write first and obtain permission to submit. Prefers cassette. SASE. Reports in 2 months.

Music: Mostly **R&B**, **gospel** and **pop**; also **children's**.

Tips: "Send music with great hooks, magnetizing lyrics and commercial appeal. Quantity is not as important as quality."

✓ ○ **ONLY NEW AGE MUSIC, INC.**, 8033 Sunset Blvd. #472, Hollywood CA 90046. (323)851-3355. Fax: (323)851-7981. E-mail: info@newagemusic.com. Website: http://www.newagemusic.com. President: Suzanne Doucet. Record company and music publisher. Estab. 1987.

How to Contact: Call first and obtain permission to submit. Does not return material.

Music: Mostly **New Age**; also **world music**.

Tips: "You should have a marketing strategy and at least a small budget for markteing your product."

◑ **ORBIT RECORDS**, P.O. Box 120675, Nashville TN 37212. (615)883-9161. Owner: Inez McGinnis. Record company and music publisher (Nautical Music Co.). Estab. 1965. Releases 6-10 singles, 6 12″ singles and 4 CDs/year. Pays 5.25% royalty to artists on contract; statutory rate to publisher per song on record.

How to Contact: Submit demo tape by mail. Unsolicited submissions are OK. Prefers cassette with 4 songs and lead sheet. SASE. Reports in 4-6 weeks.

Music: Mostly **country (ballads)**, **country rock** and **R&B**. Released "Falling" (by Alan Warren), recorded by Bo Jest; "I'm Gonna Be Strong" (by Gene Pitney), recorded by Michael Storm; and "Southern Living" (by McGregory/Hughes), recorded by Sonny Martin, all on Orbit Records.

[N] ◑ **ORILLYON ENTERTAINMENT**, P.O. Box 8414, Washington DC 20336-8414. E-mail: orillyon @email.msn.com. Website: http://orillyon.com. President/CEO (rap, hip-hop): Lex Orillyon. Vice President A&R (R&B, blues, gospel): L. Blue. Record company, music publisher and record producer (Donneat B. [Lex Orillyon]). Estab. 1997. Releases 3 singles and 2 CDs/year. Pays 9-15% royalty to artists on contract; statutory rate to publisher per song on record.

How to Contact: Submit demo tape by mail. Unsolicited submissions are OK. Prefers cassette, CD or videocassette with 1-6 songs, lyric sheet, bio and picture. SASE. Reports in 3-6 weeks.

Music: Mostly **rap**, **hip-hop** and **R&B**; also **jazz**, **gospel** and **blues**.

Tips: "If you think your music is ready for the world, then it is. But it takes lots of time and preparation to be competitive on the next level."

◑ **ORINDA RECORDS**, P.O. Box 838, Orinda CA 94563. A&R Director: Harry Balk. Record company. Pays negotiable royalty to artists on contract; negotiable rate to publisher per song on record.

Distributed by: LB Enterprises.

How to Contact: Submit demo tape by mail. Unsolicited submissions are OK. Prefers cassette and lead sheet. Does not return material. Reports in 3 months.

Music: Mostly **pop**, **rock** and **jazz**.

Tips: "Follow what is now on the charts."

[N] 🔁 ◑ **OUTPOST RECORDINGS**, 689 Queen St. W., Suite 68, Toronto Ontario M6J 1E6 Canada. E-mail: outpost@outpostrec.com. Website: http://www.outpostrec.com. Record company.

● See the interview with Outpost recording artist Hayden on page 186.

How to Contact: Does not accept unsolicited submissions. "All unsolicited demos or other materials will be returned."

Music: Released *Eight Arms to Hold You* by Veruca Salt; *Strangers Almanac* by Whiskeytown; and *Everything I Long For* by Hayden, all on Outpost Recordings. Other artists include Home Grown, Vaganza and DJ Spooky.

MARKET CONDITIONS are constantly changing! If you're still using this book and it is 2001 or later, buy the newest edition of *Songwriter's Market* at your favorite bookstore or order directly from Writer's Digest Books at (800)289-0963.

○ **OVNI**, 1392 Rigsbee, Suite A, Plano TX 75074. (972)424-6750. A&R Director: Johnny V. Record company. Estab. 1997. Staff size: 1. Releases 1 LP and 1 CD/year. Pays negotiable royalty to artists on contract; statutory rate to publisher per song on record.
Distributed by: OVNI.
How to Contact: Submit demo tape by mail. Unsolicited submissions are OK. Prefers cassette or CD with 3 or more songs. "Please inlcude a bio with historical information about your act and a short summary of your future goals as a recording/performing artist/band." Does not return material. Reports in 3 months.
Music: Mostly **rock**, **alternative** and **dance**; also **pop**, **R&B**, **country**, **jazz** and **Latin**. Released *Eternity*, recorded by Dark Soul (alternative); and *Genitals on Fire*, written and recorded by Johnny Diamond (dance), both on OVNI.
Tips: "We are able to offer worldwide distribution over the Internet for artists who have retail-ready product."

🞉 ○ **P. & N. RECORDS**, 61 Euphrasia Dr., Toronto, Ontario M6B 3V8 Canada. (416)782-5768. Fax: (416)782-7170. Presidents, A&R: Panfilo Di Matteo and Nicola Di Matteo. Record company, record producer and music publisher (Lilly Music Publishing). Estab. 1993. Staff size: 2. Releases 10 singles, 20 12″ singles, 15 LPs, 20 EPs and 15 CDs/year. Pays 25-35% royalty to artists on contract; statutory rate to publisher per song on record.
How to Contact: Submit demo tape by mail. Unsolicited submissions are OK. Prefers cassette or videocassette with 3 songs and lyric or lead sheet. Does not return material. Reports in 1 month only if interested.
Music: Mostly **dance**, **ballads** and **rock**. Released *Only This Way* written and recorded by Angelica Castro; and *The End of Us*, written and recorded by Putz, both on P. & N. Records (dance).

🄽 ○ **P.M. RECORDS**, P.O. Box 19332, Indianapolis IN 46219-0100. (317)897-2545. E-mail: justtony @indy.net. Website: http://www.pmrecords.com. A&R Directors: John Pelfrey Jr. (country/blues); Tony Mansour (pop, rock). Assistant A&R: Lisa Jack (country); Lori Ellis (rock). Labels include Tomahawk Records. Record company and record producer. Estab. 1998. Staff size: 10. Releases 5 singles, 4 LPs and 4 CDs/year. Pays negotiable royalty to artists on contract; statutory rate to publisher per song on record.
How to Contact: Submit demo tape by mail. Unsolicited submissions are OK. Prefers cassette, CD or videocassette with 3 songs, lyric sheet and lead sheet. "Please specify music style on envelope. Vocals must be clear." SASE. Reports in 6 weeks.
Music: Mostly **rock**, **country** and **blues**; also **pop**. Does not want rap. Released *Neighborhood*, written and recorded by Simply Tony (rock); and *Wide Open Road* (by J.W. Bach), recorded by John Marshall (country), both on P.M. Records; and *Next Generation* (by Jerry Ashlock/Jason Ashlock/J.W. Bach), recorded by Tomahawk Records (pop).
Tips: "Remember, music is a business. Only serious-minded individuals need apply. Supply as much information as possible."

🞉 **PAINT CHIP RECORDS**, P.O. Box 12401, Albany NY 12212. (518)765-4027. E-mail: paintchipr@ aol.com. Owner/Producer: Dominick Campana. Record/production company. Estab. 1992. Staff size: 1. Releases 4 CDs/year. Pays negotiable royalty to artists on contract; statutory rate to publisher per song on record.
Distributed by: Dutch East India Trading.
How to Contact: Submit demo tape by mail. Unsolicited submissions are OK. Prefers cassette with 4 songs. Does not return material. Reports in several weeks only if interested.
Music: Mostly **"alternative" guitar rock** (bands). Released *Out of the Loop* (by Carlton/Sunday/Lilley), recorded by Dryer (alternative rock); *Pink As Hell* (by Conners/Campana), recorded by MK4 (alternative rock), both on Paint Chip; and *Take Her To The Zoo* (by Powell/Slater/Hogan), recorded by Vodkasonics on Cacophone (alternative rock). Other artists include Lughead, Bloom, Queer For Astroboy and Brett Rosenberg.
Tips: "Do not submit music if you haven't heard of any of the artists on this label. Do not submit music if you are not currently performing. Do not submit music if you don't think your work is absolutely amazing and will earn a spot in the top ten records of all time."

☑ 🞉 **PATTY LEE RECORDS**, 6034½ Graciosa Dr., Hollywood CA 90068. (213)469-5431 and 1920 Audubon St., New Orleans LA 70118. (504)866-4480. President: Patty Lee. Assistant to the President: Susan Neidhart. Record company and record producer. Estab. 1985. Releases 1-2 singles and 2-3 CDs/ year. Pays variable royalty to artists on contract.
Distributed by: Big Easy and Great Southern Records.
How to Contact: Does not accepted unsolicited material.
Music: Mostly **New Orleans rock**, **bebop jazz** and **cowboy poetry**; also **eclectic**, **folk** and **country**.

insider report

Performer's goal is great music, not rock stardom

Photo by Ann Giordano

Hayden

Hayden Desser grew up in Thornhill, Ontario, Canada, the suburban town where he was born in 1971. The quiet, gentle young man who puts 1970s Kodak Instamatic photos of his older brother and parents on his album covers still lives nearby, close to his family. When asked what he misses most when he's on the road he answers without pausing, "My girlfriend and my family."

It is this kind of sincerity that has snared the attention of both fans and record companies. While legions of male rock musicians have promoted their careers by playing tough, Hayden (as he is known professionally) has built his success by attracting fans—ranging in age from pre-teen to post-retirement—with his combination of live-show-friendliness, lyrical candor, melodic primitive folk and raw, throat-tearing rock.

Hayden names Neil Young, Tom Waits and Leonard Cohen as "the three biggies" who influenced him. "But," he adds, "as far as artists that influence me in the way I make music, there are tons: The Beatles, The Rolling Stones, Joni Mitchell and newer bands like Pavement, Sonic Youth and Sebadoh."

After studying radio and television in college, Hayden directed music videos for local bands. In his free time he wrote songs and began playing live. He opened for bands he admired, but was annoyed that people continually talked through his sets. In response, he cranked up the volume, screaming and never relenting until people paid attention. This became his signature vocal style for many songs, standing out like thunderstorms among his more folky, sotto-voce songs. A fan base developed, and Hayden soon played to sold-out clubs.

In 1995 Hayden self-released his debut CD *Everything I Long For*, which sold over 17,000 copies in Canada. "I did the album mostly at my house with my own money," he says. "I recorded it on a four track! And that's something that can be good information for someone starting out—the fact that if you have songs, you don't have to wait around 'til you get a record deal to have the money to do what you want. I'm living proof that you can record your songs at home with a Maxell tape and get attention in the music

HAYDEN

Singer/Songwriter
Hometown: Thornhill, Ontario, Canada
Label: Outpost Recordings

business. After a year of the CD being out in Canada, my manager sent it to different people in America. Once certain people responded, others found out about it."

Indeed they did respond. Hayden's CD became the object of a record company bidding war, and he selected Outpost Recordings to distribute his albums. In 1998 he released his second full-length CD, *The Closer I Get*, on Outpost.

In between releases, Hayden hardly stands still. He's toured coast to coast innumerable times as well as in Europe and Japan. He also played the H.O.R.D.E. Festival and Lollapalooza in Quebec City. The pinnacle, though, was playing the Bridge School Benefit (Neil Young's annual fundraiser for mentally and physically challenged children) because he played onstage with Patti Smith, David Bowie, Pearl Jam, and his royal idolness, Neil Young himself.

In between tours, Hayden released four recordings on vinyl and CD. His songs were included on four compilation albums, including the soundtrack for Steve Buschemi's 1997 movie *Trees Lounge*. Hayden wrote and recorded the title song which played during the film's end credits. "[Buschemi] was looking for songs to be on the soundtrack of his movie," says Hayden. "He was sent my CD and liked it, so we hooked up that way.

"For the *Trees Lounge* song, I actually watched the movie and took words right from the dialogue and fit them into the song. The writing process happens differently all the time. Sometimes I'll have written something down a month before and then I'll come up with a piece of music, and I'll fit them together. Sometimes I'll write music and write the words at the same time. It's totally different all the time. I'm always playing new things, whenever I have a spare moment."

His fans are pleased that he is so prolific, but Hayden seems surprised by his own success. "Success happens completely differently for everyone," he says. "But for me, I've always done things the way I think they should be done, and haven't done things just because I think they'll get me to some next level. I know a lot of bands that 'go for it,' you know. The main thing they're trying to achieve is to become rock stars. And that's a whole different way of going about a career in music. So, it sounds cheesy but I guess my advice is, just follow your instincts and your heart, and do things for the right reasons."

—*Jean Vickers*

Released *Louisiana Frenchman*, written and recorded by Armand St. Martin (New Orleans rock & roll) on Patty Lee Records. Other artists include Timm Daughtry and Angelyne.

Tips: "Our label is small, which gives us the ability to develop our artists at their own rate of artistry. We are interested in quality *only,* regardless of the genre of music or style. Keep in mind that Patty Lee Records is not Warner Bros.! So patience and a good query letter are great starts."

☑ ◗ **PENTACLE RECORDS,** P.O. Box 5055, Laguna Beach CA 92652. (949)494-3572. E-mail: pentaclerx@aol.com. Head Honcho: Bara Waters. Production Guru: Robert Cassard. Record company. Estab. 1991. Pays negotiable royalty to artists on contract.

How to Contact: Write first and obtain permission to submit. Prefers cassette or CD with lyric sheet. "We like photos and information (bio, etc.) about the artist. Have you performed live? Reviews?" Does not return material. Reports in 6 weeks.

Music: Mostly **AAA, modern rock** and **AOR**. Released *Get This* (by Waters/Cassard), recorded by Cassard (rock); *Roux* and "Trying Too Hard" (by Doug Rouhier), both recorded by Roux (rock/AAA), all on Pentacle Records. Other artists include Guillotine, Goose and Love Tribe.

Tips: "We are small and very selective. We look for music that is melodic and interesting with lyrics that reflect a unique point of view. Nothing typical please! If you think, "My stuff sounds as good as the stuff on the radio,' don't bother with us. Move forward until your music is better, different."

PERMANENT PRESS RECORDINGS/PERMANENT WAVE, 14431 Ventura Blvd. #311, Sherman Oaks CA 91423. Phone/fax: (818)981-7760. E-mail: permpress@earthlink.net. President/Director of A&R: Ray Paul Klimek. Labels include Permanent Wave. Record company, music publisher (Permanent Pop Music/BMI) and record producer (Ray Paul). Releases 0-1 singles and 8-10 CDs/year. Pays negotiable royalty to artists on contract; negotiable rate to publisher per song on record.

Distributed by: MS Distributing Co. and Not Lame Recording Co.

How to Contact: Does not accept unsolicited material.

Music: Mostly **pop/power pop**, **rock/pop reissues** and **alternative pop**; also **smooth jazz** and **modern instrumental**. Released "Love Songs To Myself" (by Walter Clevenger), recorded by Walter Clevenger & The Dairy Kings, and "Blow The Whistle" (by Thierry Dubois) recorded by the William Pears, both on Permanent Press Recordings (pop/rock); and "City of Lights" (by Joe Tansin), recorded by The City Beat (smooth jazz/instrumental) on Permanent Wave. Other artists include Klaatu, Brown Eyed Susans, Richard X. Heyman, The Spongetones, Badfinger, Chewy Marble, Ray Paul, Bobby Wells, The Van De-Lecki's, Bob Segarini, Terry Draper and The Carpet Frogs.

Tips: "Permanent Press is known for signing well-known or established artists. New artists are considered by referral and the strength of their songwriting and the recordings submitted. We are known to release high-quality product with excellent packaging. Permanent Press is a nationally distributed label with close ties to retail, industry trades, AAA and NAC radio. We service radio, most music publications, and the majority of weekly, daily and specialty newspapers."

PICKWICK/MECCA/INTERNATIONAL RECORDS, P.O. Box 725, Daytona Beach FL 32115. (904)252-4849. President: Clarence Dunklin. Record company and music publisher (Pritchett Publications). Estab. 1980. Releases 20 singles, 30 LPs and 30 CDs/year. Pays 5-10% royalty to artists on contract; negotiable rate to publisher per song on record.

How to Contact: Submit demo tape by mail. Unsolicited submissions are OK. Prefers cassette with 12 songs and lyric or lead sheet. Does not return material.

Music: Mostly **gospel**, **disco** and **rock/pop**; also **country**, **ballads** and **rap**. Released *Give It To Me Baby* (by Loris Doby), recorded by Gladys Nighte; *Baby I Love You*, written and recorded by Joe Simmon; and *I Love Sweetie* (by Doris Doby), recorded by Bobby Blane.

PLASTIC SURGERY, Coachhouse, Mansion Farm, Liverton Hill, Sandway, Maidstone, Kent ME172NJ England. Phone/fax: (01622)858300. E-mail: eddielock@plasticsurgery.demon.co.uk. A&R: Eddie Lock. Record company, music publisher (Lock 'n' S) and record producer (Carpe Diem). Estab. 1988. Staff size: 2. Releases 5 singles/year. Pays negotiable royalty to artists on contract; statutory rate to publisher per song on record.

Distributed by: "Varies, as we mainly license to majors."

How to Contact: Submit demo tape by mail. Unsolicited submissions are OK. Prefers cassette. Does not return material. Reports in 1 week.

Music: Mostly **dance**, **house** and **trance**. Released "Got To Get Up" (by Bambaataa/Lock/Burns), recorded by Atrika Bambaataa vs. Carpe Diem on Multiply (dance); "Can U Feel It," written and recorded by Parkride on Diverse (dance); and "Joker" (by Eddie Lock/John Davis/ Steve McGuire), recorded by Priest vs Eddie on Plastic Surgery (dance).

PLATEAU MUSIC, P.O. Box 947, White House TN 37188. (615)654-8131. Fax: (615)654-8207. E-mail: nuille93@aol.com. Owner: Tony Mantor. Record company and record producer. Estab. 1990. Staff size: 1. Pays negotiable royalty to artists on contract; statutory rate to publisher per song on record.

How to Contact: Submit demo tape by mail. Unsolicited submissions are OK. Prefers cassette with 4 songs and lyric sheet. Does not return material. Reports in 4-6 weeks.

Music: Mostly **country**, **gospel** and **rock/pop**. Released *Has She Gone Too Far*, recorded by Dobie Toms; and *I've Got Love* (by Sara Majors), recorded by The Weeds, both on PMI Records (country). Other artists include Mark Knight and Kris Denny.

Tips: "We are a music producer that develops talent and shops them to the major labels. We do independent releases, but our focus is on getting the artist ready to compete in the major arena. Have dedication and be prepared to work."

N ☑ ◐ **PLATINUM INC.**, P.O. Box 1724, Roswell GA 30077. (770)664-9262. Fax: (770)664-7316. A&R Rep (gospel): Rev. Suffewel; James Bullard; (rap): J.W. Sewell and Ron Patterson. Labels include Branson and So-Lo Jam. Record company, music publisher and distributor. Estab. 1982. Releases 6-10 singles and 150 CDs/year. Pays negotiable royalty to artists on contract; negotiable rate to publisher per song on record.
How to Contact: Write or call first and obtain permission to submit. Prefers cassette with 3 songs. "We will contact the songwriter when we are interested in the material." Does not return material. Reports in 2 months.
Music: Mostly **rock, gospel** and **country**; also **rap, swing** and **classical**. Released *Back to the Innocence*, written and recorded by Jonathan Cain (rock); *Ronnie James and the Jez Hot Swing Club*, written and recorded by Ronnie James (swing); and *Hold On* (by Michael Scott), recorded by Michael Scott and the Outreach Choir (gospel), all on Intersound Inc. Other artists include Way 2 Real (rap), Jennifer Holliday (gospel), The Gatlin Brothers (country) and The Bellamy Brothers (country).
Tips: "Intersound is only interested in non-signed, non-published writers."

N ◐ **PLATINUM BOULEVARD RECORDS**, 525 E. Moana Lane, Reno NV 89502. (702)827-4424. President: Lawrence Davis. Record company and music publisher. Estab. 1986. Releases 2 singles and 1 LP/year. Pays negotiable royalty to artists on contract; negotiable rate to publisher per song on record.
How to Contact: Submit demo tape by mail. Unsolicited submissions are OK. Prefers CD, cassette or VHS videocassette with lyric or lead sheets. Does not return material. Reports back only if interested.
Music: Mostly **rock, pop** and **R&B**; also **country, jazz** and **New Age**.
Tips: "When presenting material indicate which artists you have in mind to record it. If you desire to be the recording artist please indicate."

N ◐ **PLATINUM GROOVE ENTERTAINMENT**, P.O. Box 2877, Palm Beach FL 33480. (561)775-4561. Fax: (561)775-4562. E-mail: contact@sgi.net. Website: http://www.sgi.561.net or www.platinumgroove.com. Labels include Cloudy Records. Record company and music publisher (Advantage Lobb Music). Estab. 1993. Staff size: 5. Releases 8 singles, 8 LPs and 2 CDs/year. Pays negotiable royalty to artists on contract; statutory rate to publisher per song on record.
How to Contact: Submit demo tape by mail. Unsolicited submissions are OK. Prefers cassette or CD. Does not return material. Reports in 1 month.
Music: Mostly **dance, underground** and **hip-hop**; also **R&B, house/dance** and **drum-n-bass**. Does not want rock, country or garbage. Released *Double Platinum*, written and recorded by DJ X. Travagant on Groove Entertainment (funky breaks/dance).

☑ ◯ **PLAYBACK RECORDS**, 3319 SW Woodcreek Trail, Palm City FL 34990. Producer/A&R Director: Jack Gale. Labels include Gallery II Records and Ridgewood Records. Record company, music publisher (Lovey Music/BMI and Cowabonga Music/ASCAP) and record producer (Jack Gale). Estab. 1983. Staff size: 2. Releases 20 CDs/year. Pays negotiable royalty; statutory rate to publisher per song on record.
Distributed by: MS Distributing.
How to Contact: Submit demo tape by mail. Unsolicited submissions are OK. Prefers cassette VHS videocassette with 2 songs and lyric sheet. SASE. Reports in 2 weeks only if interested.
Music: Mostly **country**. Released *All The Way to Crazy* (by C. Allenson), recorded by Annette; *Waltz Across Texas* (by Billy Tubb), recorded by Sammi Smith; and *We Got Love* (by Lee-Hogin), recorded by Tommy Cash and Connie Smith, all on Playback Records (country). Other artists include Jimmy C. Newman, Del Reeves, Johnny Paycheck and Cleve Francis.

🌐 ◐ **PLAYBONES RECORDS**, Winterhuder Weg 142, D-22085 Hamburg Germany. Phone: (040)22716552 + -53. Fax: (040)22716554. E-mail: mentomusic@online.de. Head of A&R: Michael Frommhold. Producer: Arno van Vught. Labels include Rondo Records. Record company, music publisher

---

OPENNESS TO SUBMISSIONS: ◯ beginners; ◑ beginners and experienced; ◒ experienced only; ◐ industry referrals only.

(Mento Music Group) and record producer (Arteg Productions). Estab. 1975. Releases 30 CDs/year. Pays 8-16% royalty to artists on contract; statutory rate to publisher per song on record.

How to Contact: Submit demo tape by mail. Unsolicited submissions are OK. Prefers cassette with 3-4 songs. Put your strongest/best song first. "Put your name and address on the inside sleeve of the tape. If you have a fax number, inform us. Tell us in a typed cover letter what you want/what you are looking for." Does not return material. Reports in 3 weeks.

Music: Mostly **instrumentals**, **country** and **jazz**; also **background music**, **rock** and **gospel**. Released *Living Gospel* (by Claus Schneider), recorded by Yasmin (gospel); *Instrumentals, Vol. II*, written and recorded by various artists (MOR); and *Golden Light*, written and recorded by Ronald Hoth (relaxing), all on Playbones Records. Other artists include H.J. Knipphals, Gaby Knies, Jack Hals, H. Hausmann, Crabmeat and M. Frommhold.

O **PMG RECORDS**, P.O. Box 312897, Penobscot Station, Detroit MI 48231. E-mail: zanda740@aol.com. President: Bruce Henderson. Record company, music publisher (Prejippie Music Group/BMI) and record producer (PMG Productions, Prejippie Music Group). Estab. 1990. Staff size: 2. Releases 6-12 12″ singles, 2 LPs and 2 EPs/year. Pays 40% royalty to artists on contract; statutory rate to publisher per song on record.

Distributed by: Dancefloor and Win.

How to Contact: Submit demo tape by mail. Unsolicited submissions are OK. Prefers cassette or CD or VHS videocassette with 3-4 songs and lyric sheet. "Include photo if possible. No calls please." SASE. Reports in 6 weeks.

Music: Mostly **funk/rock**, **alternative R&B**, **alternative rock**, **experimental** and **techno/dance**. Released *Caleb's Cafe*, written and recorded by Bourgeoisie Paper Jam (alternative R&B) on PMG Records. Other artists include Urban Transit and the Prejippies.

Tips: "Be very original in your approach to a song: concentrate on creating an interesting arrangement; concentrate on having at least one good hook; and put some thought into creating interesting lyrical themes."

☑ ◐ **POLYDOR RECORDS**, 1416 N. La Brea Ave., Hollywood CA 90028. (323)856-6600. Fax: (323)856-6621. Director of A&R: Andrew Brightman. New York office: 825 Eighth Ave., 27th Floor, New York NY 10019. (212)603-3905. Fax: (212)603-3919. E-mail: otis@aol.com. Website: http://www.polydor.com. Vice President of A&R: Dennis McNamara. Labels include Rocket Records. Record company.

How to Contact: Submit demo tape with bio, press release, etc. by mail to California office. Unsolicited submissions are OK. Prefers CD. Does not return material. Reports only if interested.

Music: Released *The Healing Game*, recorded by Van Morrison; *Viva La Dreggs*, recorded by Hollowbodies; and *Lemon Parade*, recorded by Tonic, all on Polydor Records. Other artists include Moody Blues, Gene, The Badlees, Bee Gees, Big Back Forty, Goodfellaz and Senser.

◑ **PPL ENTERTAINMENT GROUP**, P.O. Box 8442, Universal City CA 91608. (818)506-8533. Fax: (818)506-8534. E-mail: pplzmi@aol.com. Vice President A&R: Jaeson Effantic. Vice President, A&R: Kaitland Diamond. General Manager: Jim Sellavain. President, Creative: Suzette Cuseo. Labels include Bouvier and Credence. Record company, music publisher (Pollybyrd Publications) and management firm (Sa'mall Management). Estab. 1979. Staff size: 3. Releases 10-30 singles, 12 12″ singles, 6 LPs and 6 CDs/year. Pays 10-15% royalty to artists on contract; statutory rate to publisher per song on record.

Distributed by: Sony and The Malibu Trading Company.

How to Contact: Call first and obtain permission to submit. Prefers cassette or videocassette with 2 songs. SASE. Reports in 6 weeks.

Music: Released *Change of Heart* (by B. Heffernan), recorded by Jay Sattiewhite (country); *Shakedown* (by J. Jarrett), recorded by The Band AKA (R&B); and *I Feel You* (by S. Cuseo/J. Jarrett), recorded by Fhyne (pop/hip-hop); all on Sony/PPL Records. Other artists include Phuntain, Buddy Wright, Riki Hendrix, Condottiere, BD Fuoco and D.M. Groove.

O **PRESENCE RECORDS**, 67 Candace Lane, Chatham NJ 07928-1115. (201)701-0707. President: Paul Payton. Record company, music publisher (Paytoons/BMI) and record producer (Presence Productions). Estab. 1985. Staff size: 1. Pays 1-2% royalty to artists on contract; statutory rate to publisher per song on record.

Distributed by: Clifton Music.

How to Contact: Submit demo tape by mail. Unsolicited submissions are OK. "No phone calls." Prefers cassette with 2-4 songs and lyric sheet. SASE. Reports in 2-4 weeks. "Tapes not returned without prepaid mailer."

Music: Mostly **doo-wop ('50s)**, **rock** and **new wave rock**. Released "Ding Dong Darling," "Bette Blue

Moon" and "Davilee/Go On" (by Paul Payton/Peter Skolnik), recorded by Fabulous Dudes (doo-wop), all on Presence Records.

✓ ⊘ **PRIORITY RECORDS**, 6430 Sunset Blvd., Suite 900, Hollywood CA 90028. (323)467-0151. Fax: (323)856-8796. Senior Vice President of A&R: Andrew Shack. A&R (rap): Marvin Watkins; Mark Brown. New York office: 32 W. 18th St., 12th Floor, New York NY 10011. (212)627-8000. Fax: (212)627-5555. A&R: Ray/Rae. Labels include No Limit Records, Rawkus Records, Hoo-Bangin' Records, Roc-A-Fella Record and Duck Down Records. Record company.
Distributed by: EMD.
How to Contact: Does not accept unsolicited submissions.
Music: Released *MP Da Last Don*, recorded by Master P; *Life or Death*, recorded by C-Murder; and *I Got the Hook-Up!* (soundtrack), all on No Limit. Other artists include Ice Cube, Young Bleed and Kane & Abel.

✓ ⊘ **QUARK RECORDS**, P.O. Box 7320, FDR Station, New York NY 10150 or 4 E. 12th St., New York NY 10003. Phone/fax: (212)741-2888. E-mail: quarkent@aol.com. President (pop, dance): Curtis Urbina. A&R: Michelle Harris (alternative); Sergio Cossa (movie soundtracks, pop). Labels include Pacific Time Entertainment. Record company and music publisher (Quarkette Music/BMI and Freedurb Music/ASCAP). Estab. 1984. Releases 20 singles and 12 LPs/year. Pays negotiable royalty to artists on contract; ¾ statutory rate to publisher per song on record.
How to Contact: Call first and obtain permission to submit. Prefers cassette with 2 songs. SASE. Reports in 4-6 weeks.
Music: Mostly **dance/pop**, **compilations** and **movie soundtracks**.

✓ ⊘ **QWEST RECORDS**, 3800 Barham Blvd., Suite 503, Los Angeles CA 90068. (323)874-7770. Fax: (323)874-5049. Vice President of A&R: Jay Brown. New York office: 75 Rockefeller Plaza, 20th Floor, New York NY 10019-6908. (212)275-4000. Fax: (212)258-3036. Senior A&R Director: Renee Bell. Website: http://www.qwestrecords.com. Record company.
Distributed by: WEA.
How to Contact: Qwest Records does not accept unsolicited submissions.
Music: Released *Tamia*, recorded by Tamia on Qwest Records.

Ⓝ ☑ ⊘ **RA RECORDS**, P.O. Box 72087, 1562 Danforth Ave., Toronto, Ontario M4J 5C1 Canada. (416)693-1609. Fax: (416)693-0688. E-mail: ra@ican.net. Contact: Josephine Nyholm. Record company and music publisher (Soda Jerks Melodies). Estab. 1993. Releases 1-2 singles and 1 CD/year. Pays negotiable royalty to artists on contract; statutory rate to publisher per song on record.
Distributed by: Indie Pool Toronto and Canyon Records U.S.A.
How to Contact: Write or call first and obtain permission to submit a demo. Prefers cassette or CD with 3 songs, lyric and lead sheet, press kit and bio information. SAE and IRC. Reports in 2 months.
Music: Mostly **world beat**, **women's** and **native/indigenous**. Released *Thirst* (by various artists), recorded by Jani Lauzon on RA (world beat jazz); and *Hearts of the Nations*, written and recorded by various artists on Sweetgrass (women's traditional).

☐ **RADICAL RECORDS**, 77 Bleecker St., Suite C2-21, New York NY 10012. (212)475-1111. Fax: (212)475-5676. E-mail: radical@idt.net. Website: http://www.radicalrecords.com. A&R: Eric Rosen. Record company. "We also do independent radio and retail promotion." Estab. 1986. Staff size: 1. Releases 5 singles, 1 LP and 4 CDs/year. Pays 14% royalty to artists on contract; statutory rate to publisher per song on record.
Distributed by: Rotz, Caroline, Newbury Comics, Action, City Hall, Revelation, Gallery of Sound, Ground Zero, Hot Topic, Mean Street, Select-O-Hits, Smash and Sound of California.
How to Contact: Submit demo tape by mail. Unsolicited submissions are OK. Prefers cassette or CD. Does not return material. Reports in 1 month.
Music: Mostly **modern rock**, **pop** and **ska**; also **punk** and **rock**. Released *For All the Massive*, written and recorded by The Agents (ska); *Bottoms Up*, written and recorded by The Cuffs (punk); and *Sound Formula*, written and recorded by Social Scare (hardcore), all on Radical Records. Other artists include Blanks 77, Sturgeon General, ICU and Inspector 7.
Tips: "Create the best possible demos you can and show a past of excellent self-promotion."

THE TYPES OF MUSIC each listing is interested in are printed in **boldface**.

RAMPANT RECORDS, 1447 12th St. #D, Manhattan Beach CA 90266. (310)546-2896. E-mail: rampant@earthlink.net. Website: http://www.rampantrecords.com. Vice President of A&R: Paul Grogan. Labels include Slinkey Recordings. Record company, music publisher (Nipple Fish Music Company) and record producer (Paul Grogan). Estab. 1993. Releases 32 LPs, 27 EPs and 2 CDs/year. Pays negotiable royalty to artists on contract; 75% rate to publisher per song on record.
Distributed by: Navarre, 3MV (UK), Watts Music, Nemesis Distribution, T.R.C., Gemini and Syntax.
How to Contact: Submit demo tape by mail. Unsolicited submissions are OK. Prefers cassette with 3 songs. "Supply contact info on cassette and cassette box cover." Does not return material. Reports in 3 weeks.
Music: Mostly **progressive house**, **trance** and **big beat**; also **techno**, **jungle** and **funky breaks**. Released *Tempest* (by J. Scotts/J. Blum), recorded by Deepsky (progressive house); and *Hush*, written and recorded by Joshua Ryan (trance), both on Slinkey; and *Fly Mutha Beatz* (by Chris Brown), recorded by Brownie on Rampant (big beat/funky breaks). Other artists include Flowtation, The Coffee Boys and Ascendance.
Tips: "We are looking for tracks that will rock a dance floor. Solid, well produced, energy tracks only."

RANDOM RECORDS, 22 Milverton Blvd., Toronto, Ontario M4J 1T6 Canada. (416)778-6563. E-mail: wprandall@dynacase.com. President (pop, folk, MOR): Peter Randall. A&R Director (rock, heavy rock): Shaun Firth. Record company, music publisher (Random Image Music) and record producer (Peter Randall). Estab. 1986. Staff size: 2. Releases 2 singles and 3 CDs/year. Pays 15% royalty to artists on contract; statutory rate to publisher per song on record.
How to Contact: Submit CD by mail. Unsolicited submissions are OK. Prefers CD, DAT or NTSC videocassette with no more than 2 songs and lyric sheet. Does not return material. Reports in 4 months.
Music: Mostly **pop**, **rock** and **country**; also **folk**. Released *Pipe Dreams* (by Allen/DeBrock/Louis/St. Croix), recorded by Quadras (rock); *Rebecca* (by DeJourney/Simpson), recorded by Rebecca DeJourney (MOR); and *Already Round the Bend* (by Farrar/Finerty/Lennon/McCartney), recorded by Fin Ran Far (pop), all on Random Records. Other artists include Timeline and Jeff Jackson.
Tips: "Songwriters would be much better off to rewrite and re-work one song until it's killer, than to try and submit 18 passable songs. We have no time or reason to rewrite them for you. We are accepting unsolicited submissions on CD only. If you can't invest a little in yourself, why should I? Don't send us your garbage. Give us something we can sink our teeth into."

RAVE RECORDS, INC., 13400 W. Seven Mile Rd., Detroit MI 48235. (248)540-RAVE. Fax: (248)338-0739. E-mail: info@raverecords.com. Website: http://www.raverecords.com. Production Managers: Carolyn and Derrick. Record company and music publisher (Magic Brain Music/ASCAP). Estab. 1992. Staff size: 2. Releases 2-4 singles and 2 CDs/year. Pays various royalty to artists on contract; statutory rate to publisher per song on record.
Distributed by: Action Music Sales.
How to Contact: Does not accept unsolicited submissions.
Music: Mostly **alternative rock** and **dance**. Artists include Cyber Cryst, Dorothy, Nicole and Bukimi 3.

RAW ENERGY, 0116-42-65 Front St. W, Toronto, Ontario M5J 1E6 Canada. (416)410-6749. E-mail: rawnrg@passport.ca. Website: http://rawenergy.passport.ca. Vice President: Chris Black (punk, hardcore). Record company. Estab. 1989. Staff size: 2. Releases 6 singles, 10 CDs/year. Pays negotiable royalty to artists on contract; standard SOCAN royalty rate to publisher per song on record.
Distributed by: Page (Canada), Choke, Get Hip, Very, Com Four and Revelation.
• Raw Energy's artists' music is also found in movies (*Naked City* and *White Lies*) and TV shows (*The Rez* and *Black Harbour*).
How to Contact: Submit demo tape by mail. Unsolicited submissions are OK. Prefers cassette or CD. "Include a bio and plans for the next year." Does not return material. Reports in 2 months.
Music: Mostly **punk** and **hardcore**. Released *Politics On the Dance Floor*, written and recorded by Marilyn's Vitamins (punk); *Throwin the Horns*, written and recorded by Trunk (punk); and *Canadian Gothic*, written and recorded by Out of Hand (punk), all on Raw Energy. Other artists include Jersey, Double Standard, Random Killing and Cut Off.
Tips: "We like it hard and fast, honest and passionate. Come to us with a detailed proposal. Don't come with a 'what can you do for me' attitude."

RAZOR & TIE ENTERTAINMENT, 214 Sullivan St., Suite 4A, New York NY 10012. E-mail: info@razorandtie.com. Website: http://www.razorandtie.com. Record company.
• See the interview with Razor & Tie recording artist Dar Williams on page 194.

How to Contact: Does not accept unsolicited material.
Music: Released *Cry, Cry, Cry* by Dar Williams; *The Sweetheart Collection* by Frankie & The Knockouts; and *Everybody's Normal But Me* by Stuttering John, all on Razor & Tie Entertainment. Other artists include Cledus T. Judd, Graham Parker and Mare Winningham.

☑ ☹ ⊘ **RCA RECORDS**, 1133 Avenue of the Americas, New York NY 10036. (212)930-4000. Fax: (212)930-4468. Website: http://www.bmg.com/labels/rca.html. Senior Vice President of A&R: Peter Robinson. Senior Vice President of A&R: David Bendeth. Beverly Hills office: 8750 Wilshire Blvd., Beverly Hills CA 90211. (310)358-4000. Fax: (310)358-4040. Senior Vice President of A&R: Bruce Flohr. Nashville office: 1 Music Circle N., Nashville TN 37203. (615)313-4300. Website: http://www.twangthis.c om. A&R Director: Sam Ramage. Director of Artist Development: Debbie Schwartz. Labels include Loud Records and Deconstruction Records. Record company.
Distributed by: BMG.
• RCA Records Nashville's Los Super Seven won a 1998 Grammy Award for Best Mexican-American Music Performance.
How to Contact: RCA Records does not accept unsolicited submissions.
Music: Released *'N Sync*, recorded by 'N Sync; and *Capitol Punishment*, recorded by Big Punisher, both on RCA Records. Other artists include Eve 6, Robyn and Dave Matthews Band.

◘ **RED DOT/PUZZLE RECORDS**, 1121 Market, Galveston TX 77550. (409)762-4590. President: A.W. Marullo, Sr. Record company, record producer and music publisher (A.W. Marullo Music/BMI). Estab. 1952. "We also lease masters from artists." Releases 14 12″ singles/year. Pays 8-10% royalty to artists on contract; statutory rate to publisher for each record sold.
How to Contact: Prefers cassette with 4-7 songs and lyric sheet. "Cassettes will not be returned. Contact will be made by mail or phone." Reports in 2 months.
Music: Mostly **rock/top 40 dance songs**. Released "Do You Feel Sexy" (by T. Pindrock), recorded by Flash Point (top 40/rock); "You Put the Merry in My Christmas," (by E. Dunn), recorded by Mary Craig (rock/pop country); and "Love Machine" (by T. Pindrock), recorded by Susan Moninger, all on Puzzle/ Red Dot Records. Other artists include Joe Diamond, Billy Wayde, Jerry Hurtado and Tricia Matula.
Tips: "All songs and masters must have good *sound* and be studio produced."

Ⓝ ⊕ ◖ **RED SKY RECORDS**, P.O. Box 27, Stroud, Glos. GL6 0YQ United Kingdom. Phone: 01453-836877. Producer: Johnny Coppin. Distributed by Direct, ADA and CM. Record company and record producer (Johnny Coppin). Estab. 1985. Staff size: 1. Releases 2 albums per year. Pays 8-10% to artists on contract; statutory rate to publisher per song on record.
How to Contact: Write first and obtain permission to submit. Does not return material. Reports in 6 months.
Music: Mostly **rock/singer-songwriters**, **modern folk** and **roots music**. Released *Edge of Day* (by Laurie Lee/Johnny Coppin), recorded by Laurie Lee (spoken word and music); and "Keep the Flame" (by J. Coppin/J. Brooman/M. Dolan), recorded by Johnny Coppin, both on Red Sky Records. Other artists include David Goodland.

◘ **REDEMPTION RECORDS**, P.O. Box 3244, Omaha NE 68103-0244. (712)328-2771. Fax: (712)328-9732. E-mail: rediscs@aol.com. Website: http://redemption.net. Vice President of A&R: Ryan D. Kuper (post hardcore, power pop). A&R (West): Nilo Naghdi (rock, punk). Labels include Chisel, Fahrenheit, Full Flavor and Mayhem. Record company. Estab. 1990. Staff size: 3. Releases 3-4 singles, 3-4 LPs, 2 EPs and 2 CDs/year. Pays 10-20% royalty to artists on contract; statutory rate to publisher per song on record.
Distributed by: Redemption Distribution Alliance, MS, MDI, PaulStarr and V&R.
How to Contact: Submit demo tape by mail. Unsolicited submissions are OK. Prefers cassette with 4 songs and lyric and/or lead sheet. "Include band's or artist's goals." Does not return material. Reports in 2-4 weeks only if interested.
Music: Mostly **alternative pop** and **hardcore**. Released *Gaia*, written and recorded by Grasshopper; "Not From Space," written and recorded by Not From Space; and "Red b/w Swan," written and recorded by Real, all on Redemption Records (rock). Other artists include Let's Rodeo, Downer, Anton Barbeau, Martin's Dau and Material Issue.
Tips: "Be prepared to tour to support the release. Make sure the current line-up is secure."

⊕ ◖ **RED-EYE RECORDS**, Wern Fawr Farm, Pencoed, Mid-Glam CF35 6NB United Kingdom. Phone: (0656)86 00 41. Managing Director: M.R. Blanche. Record company and music publisher (Ever-

insider report

Artist earns national attention through grassroots efforts

For Dar Williams, one of the most talked-about new artists in contemporary folk music, a career in the music industry has meant connecting with people in the local music scene and focusing on her music rather than worrying about how to get a major record label to represent her.

Dar Williams

Photo by C. Taylor Crothers

A New York native who dreamed of being an opera director and playwright, Williams "formally" began writing songs after moving to Boston to work as an assistant stage manager. "I would spend my afternoons writing dialogue for a play, then my brain would spin off and these little stories would come up—those were the songs," she says. As well as writing songs, Williams was also discovering the burgeoning Boston folk music community. "The music scene in Boston was just taking off and there was a real infrastructure of support for music—the radio, the press, the stages, the open mikes, the community. Everything was ripe for growing as an artist." The opposite was true about theater in Boston, where Williams found the audiences lacking and the press nasty. "I wanted to be a performer. I was also a part of a whole group of people trying to become full-time performers, so there was this community and camaraderie, a sort of kindling industry." For Williams, the choice became easy—music over theater.

To get feedback on her songs and hone her performing skills, Williams attended the numerous open mikes held every night throughout Boston. Moving from these open-mike performances to after-hours folk clubs to the coffeehouse circuit, Williams slowly learned the ins and outs of the local and regional music scene. "I went to radio stations and got to know all the DJs. Sometimes I would be asked to open for some of my friends or I would be on a split bill or would play at a café. Everything started very slowly."

In late 1993, with a couple of years of live performance experience under her belt, Williams took her music and her savings and recorded the album *The Honesty Room*. By selling the album at gigs, as well as sending it to the numerous contacts Williams had developed at radio stations, news about the album spread. The coffeehouse circuit word-of-mouth and folk-music chat

DAR WILLIAMS

Singer/Songwriter
Music: Folk
Label: Razor & Tie Entertainment

rooms on the Internet also helped garner interest in the album. Williams was even adopted as the personal cause of Alan Rowoth, the moderator for the Folk_Music list. "He put my name all over the Internet which gave me international exposure," she says. "I went on tour for a few months right after he took on my cause—literally driving around for three months in my car—and two or three of the shows I performed were set up by Internet contacts who said they would host house concerts." During the same road tour, Williams performed on several radio shows scheduled by people from another folk list. "I've had a lot of grassroots ways of getting my music out there: A lot of people taking responsibilty for helping artists get their work heard without all those questions of distribution, record labels and stuff like that."

Williams's music received an additional boost when she played an unofficial show-case at the Folk Alliance Conference in Boston in February 1994. "The Folk Alliance is a big convention for folk music, but it also includes people with long beards playing fiddle in the lobby until five o'clock in the morning," she explains. "It's a really unusual and wonderful thing. So I went there and played a showcase at three o'clock in the morning in a hotel room at the conference." In attendence at the showcase were Williams's future manager (Charlie Hunter of Young/Hunter Publicity), booking agent (Fleming/Tamulevich) and distributor (Waterbug Records, a small Chicago-based label). "Each of them heard one song they wanted to work with. It was nice because I was green and very nervous. I really was a mess, but they all nodded and said, 'You know, we don't know much about this person but she's been touring for a few years now and she works hard. How about [taking a chance on] Dar Williams?' I was a very lucky science experiment."

In early 1995, Williams found herself back at the Folk Alliance, but this time performing on the main stage to a standing ovation. She then signed a distribution arrangement with Razor & Tie Entertainment, an "artist-friendly" label from New York. Razor & Tie nationally released *The Honesty Room* in February 1995 with two additional songs and some remixing. Since then, Williams has recorded two more albums with Razor & Tie, *Mortal City* and *End of the Summer*. Both albums have garnered rave reviews and established Williams as a unique and accessible singer-songwriter of her generation.

Williams's music career has given her very little to offer beginning singer/songwriters who ask her advice about how to approach a major label. Rather, Williams recommends singer/songwriters look for a regional music scene they can become a part of. "I just don't know how people do the label thing on their own. But if you want to do a grassroots thing, I would recommend finding a scene that will help you feel like you are growing and going in the right direction. Sometimes it's very hard [to do this] because it takes a very special blend of groovy bookstores, record stores and music stores to have open mikes and support local artists." Williams also adds that artists interested in touring should look to the regional strength performers can obtain. By this she means investigating performance opportunities in neighboring towns—open mikes, clubs, cafés, outdoor venues, etc.—whatever is available to expose their music to an even wider audience. "If you want to get out into the world, you have to keep reaching your tendrils a little bit, but it only has to be a little bit at a time."

By focusing on her songs rather that that elusive major label deal, Williams feels her music career can have real staying power. "There is a lot people can do on their own without their processes or their actions being mediated by a record label. I don't know what I will do after I finish my contract with Razor & Tie, but I will have an understanding that you are not created by your label. I have so much of the audience-based, slow-growth career under my belt that my career seems pretty rock solid to me now. Even without a label, I can still make a living, make a connection and do good work."

—*Chantelle Bentley*

Open-Eye Music/PRS). Estab. 1979. Releases 4 singles and 2-3 LPs/year. Pays negotiable royalty to artists on contract; statutory rate to publisher per song on record.
How to Contact: Submit demo tape by mail. Unsolicited submissions are OK. Prefers cassette, VHS videocassette or 7½ or 15 ips reel-to-reel with 4 songs. SAE and IRC. Does not return material.
Music: Mostly **R&B**, **rock** and **gospel**; also **swing**. Released "River River" (by D. John), recorded by The Boys; and "Billy" (by G. Williams); and "Cadillac Walk" (by Moon Martin), both recorded by the Cadillacs, all on Red-Eye Records. Other artists include Cartoon and Tiger Bay.

N ○ **REGIS RECORDS INC.**, 122 E. 42nd St., Suite 1700, New York NY 10168. (212)551-7801. Fax: (212)551-1001. Vice President of A&R: Mark Rivers. Directors of A&R: Cherie Bacs (modern rock); Kennedy Atkinson (R&B); David Velazquez (rap). Vice President of Production/Management: Eric Curry. Record company and music publisher (Millen2/ASCAP and Servindio Music/BMI). Estab. 1994. Staff size: 15. Releases 3 LPs and 3 CDs/year. Pays negotiable royalty to artists on contract; statutory rate to publisher per song on record.
How to Contact: Write or call first and obtain permission to submit. Prefers cassette, CD or DAT with 3 songs, lyric sheet, cover letter, 8x10 b&w photo and press clippings. Does not return material. Reports in 3 months.
Music: Mostly **modern rock**, **adult top 40** and **R&B**; also **country**, **hip-hop** and **contemporary Christian**. Released *Up and Out*, written and recorded by The Real Cock Diesel (funk/rock); *Weekend*, (by Pearl), recorded by Sond (A/C); and *Barcelona*, written and recorded by David Rea (pop), all on Regis Records. Other artists include Pearl, Danielle and Laurell.
Tips: "Listen to your surroundings and then take it to the next phase. The industry is changing and you have to prepare and change with it."

✓ ○ **REITER RECORDS LTD.**, 308 Penn Estates, East Stroudsburg PA 18301. (570)424-9599. Fax: (570)424-0452. E-mail: stewrose@aol.com. Vice President of A&R: Greg Macmillan. Record company. Estab. 1990. Releases 5 singles, 5-10 LPs and 5-10 CDs/year. Pays negotiable royalty to artists on contract; 75% of statutory rate to publisher per song on record.
How to Contact: Submit demo tape by mail. Unsolicited submissions are OK. Does not return material.
Music: Mostly **pop**, **jazz** and **rock**. Released *Celtic Century Rock*, recorded by Owen Baxter; and *Unanswered Prayers*, recorded by Moon Children, both on Reiter Records.

✓ ○ **RELATIVITY RECORDS**, 79 Fifth Ave., 16th Floor, New York NY 10003. (212)337-5300. Senior Vice President, A&R: Cliff Cultreri. A&R Manager: Luxie Aquino. Website: http://www.relativityrecords.com. Labels include Ruthless Records. Record company.
Distributed by: Sony.

REFER TO THE CATEGORY INDEX (at the end of this section) to find exactly which companies are interested in the type of music you write.

How to Contact: Submit demo tape by mail. Unsolicited submissions are OK. Prefers cassette, CD or DAT. Submit to Attn: A&R Dept.
Music: Released *Heaven'z Movie*, recorded by Bizzy Bone on Mo Thugs Records.

REPRISE RECORDS, 3300 Warner Blvd., Burbank CA 91505. (818)846-9090. Fax: (818)840-2389. Vice President of A&R (R&B/hip-hop): Kris Parker. New York office: 75 Rockefeller Plaza, New York NY 10019. (212)275-4500. Fax: (212)275-4596. Website: http://www.repriserec.com. Vice President of A&R: Sue Drew. Labels include Duck. Record company.
Distributed by: WEA.
• Reprise's Eric Clapton won a 1998 Grammy Award for Best Male Pop Vocal Performance for "My Father's Eyes"; and Randy Scruggs and Vince Gill won for Best Country Instrumental Performance.
How to Contact: Reprise Records does not accept unsolicited submissions.
Music: Released *The Dance*, recorded by Fleetwood Mac; *Stunt*, recorded by Barenaked Ladies on Reprise; and *Pilgrim*, recorded by Eric Clapton on Duck. Other artists include Wilco, Paul Brandt, Eric Clapton, Chaka Khan, Brady Seals, Arkarna, Dinosaur Jr., Depeche Mode, Faith No More and Green Day.

RESTLESS RECORDS, 1616 Vista Del Mar, Hollywood CA 90028. (323)957-4357, ext. 223. Fax: (323)957-4355. Website: http://www.restless.com. A&R: Bill Hein. Labels include Medium Cool Records, Twin/Tone Records, Clean Records and On-U-Sound Records. Record company.
Distributed by: BMG.
How to Contact: Submit demo tape by mail. Unsolicited submissions are OK. Prefers cassette, DAT or CD with press kit.
Music: Artists include Econoline Crush, Reel Tight and Katalinn.

RHETORIC RECORDS, P.O. Box 82, Madison WI 53701. (608)223-9129. Fax: (608)223-0291. E-mail: rhetoric@execpc.com. Website: http://www.rhetoricrecords.com. Captain Demo: Jason Millard. President Demo: Brad Rhetoric. Labels include Anal Explosion Records. Record company. Estab. 1993. Staff size: 3. Releases 8 LPs, 8 EPs and 7 CDs/year. Pays negotiable royalty to artists on contract; statutory rate to publisher per song on record.
Distributed by: Revolver, Surefire, Green Hell (Germany), Helter Skelter (Italy), Very, Relapse, Blindspot and 1000 Flowers.
How to Contact: Submit demo tape by mail. Unsolicited submissions are OK. Prefers cassette, CD or VHS videocassette with any number of songs and lyric sheet. Does not return material. Reports in 1 month.
Music: Mostly **hardcore**, **grind** and **punk**; also **noise/real industrial**. Does not want country, rock, pop or anything religious. Released *Pez Core* (by Vinnie & The Boys), recorded by Less than Jake (ska/punk); *Train Station & Beyond* (by Dan), recorded by Cavity (HC/sludge); and *Cunt of God* (by Andrew), recorded by Rupture (HC/thrash), all on Rhetoric. Other artists include Kilara, Hellchild, Facade Burned Black and Mulligan Stu.
Tips: "Do not send us crap and cross your fingers."

RHIANNON RECORDS, 20 Montague Rd., London, E8 2HW United Kingdom. (0171)275-8292. Fax: (0171)503-8034. E-mail: rhiannon@enterprise.net. Website: http://www.rhiannonrecords.co.uk. Owner: Colin Jones. Record company, music publisher (Rhiannon Music) and record producer (Colin Jones). Estab. 1993. Releases 4-6 CDs/year. Pays negotiable royalty to artists on contract; pays according to agreement rate to publisher per song on record.
Distributed by: Direct and Vital.
How to Contact: Submit demo tape by mail. Unsolicited submissions are OK. "We only publish writers we also record. No separate publishing deals!" Prefers cassette or DAT with press writings, bio and photo. "Please ensure material submitted meets label requirements." SAE and IRC. Reports in 1 month.
Music: Mostly **acoustic**, **ethnic-based folk**, **folk rock**, **singer/songwriter**, **folk/country** and **contemporary**. Released *Wings of the Sphinx*, recorded by Barry Dransfield (British folk); *Sin É*, recorded by Sin É (contemporary Irish folk); and *By Heart*, by Maggie Holland (contemporary acoustic), all on Rhiannon Records. Other artists include Calico, Bob Pegg and Felicity Buirski.
Tips: "Don't imitate—originate! I'm not looking for imitation Chieftains or Nanci Griffith. I want to hear talented artists using their background and imagination to offer new ideas. One of my former artists said, 'Most singer/songwriters are putting down on record what they should be telling their therapist.' If this is you, please don't send me your material!"

RHINO RECORDS, 10635 Santa Monica Blvd., 2nd Floor, Los Angeles CA 90025. (310)474-4778. Fax: (310)441-6575. Website: http://www.rhino.com. Senior Vice President of A&R: Gary Stewart. Labels include Forward Records. Record company.

Distributed by: WEA.

● Rhino's Mel Brooks and Carl Reiner won a 1998 Grammy Award for Best Spoken Comedy Album.

How to Contact: Rhino is basically a reissue label, and is only interested in signing acts with long track records and who have an already-established audience.

Music: Released *The Very Best of Curtis Mayfield*, recorded by Curtis Mayfield; *Songs in the Key of Springfield*, recorded by The Simpsons; and Foxy Lady, recorded by RuPaul, all on Rhino Records.

☐ RISING STAR RECORDS, 52 Executive Park South, Suite 5203, Atlanta GA 30329. (404)636-2050. E-mail: info@ristar.com. Website: http://www.ristar.com. President: Barbara Taylor. Record company and record distributor. Estab. 1987. Releases 5-6 CDs/year. Pays negotiated royalty to artists on contract; negotiated rate to publisher per song on record.

Distributed by: Music Design, New Leaf, Goldenrod, Silo, Ladyslipper, Lifedance, LeFon, Mill City and Rivertown.

How to Contact: Write or call first and obtain permission to submit. SASE. Reports in 1-2 months.

Music: Mostly **contemporary instrumental**, **New Age**, **classical** and **comedy**. Released *Celestial Journey I & II*, written and recorded by various artists (space/ambient); *Classical Erotica I & II*, written and recorded by various artists (classical); and *Box Lunch*, written and recorded by Lea Delaria (comedy), all on Rising Star Records.

[N] ☐ RIVAL RECORDS, 204 W. Fifth St., Lorain OH 44052-1610. (440)244-5324. Fax: (440)244-5349. E-mail: scotti@anapmac.com. Website: http://www.RivalRecords.com. President: Scotti C. Campana. General Manager: Ray Calabrese. A&R: David Tolliver (urban, pop, hip-hop); Don Nicoloff (jazz). Record company, music publisher (Campana Music Publishing/ASCAP) and record producer. Estab. 1998. Staff size: 8. Pays 10% royalty to artists on contract; statutory rate to publisher per song on record.

Distributed by: Big Daddy Distributing.

How to Contact: Submit demo tape by mail. Unsolicited submissions are OK. Prefers CD with 3 songs, lyric sheet, cover letter, photo and press clippings. Does not return submissions. Reports in 6 weeks.

Music: Mostly **R&B**, **hip-hop** and **pop**; also **jazz**. Released "You Played Me" (by David Tolliver), recorded by Men at Large; and "Something About You" (by Scotti Campana), recorded by Soul, both on Rival Records (R&B). Other artists include Big T, Monatone Styles and Buddy Banks.

☐ RML RECORDS, P.O. Box 4835, Petaluma CA 94955. (707)766-8338. Fax: (707)766-8440. E-mail: baldieray@aol.com. Website: http://northbaymusic. com. Vice President of A&R (pop, A/C, MOR, R&B): Peter Finster. President (pop, A/C, rock, alternative, jazz): G.T. Albright. Record company, record producer (G.T. Albright) and merchandiser (RML Merchandise). Estab. 1991. Releases 1-4 singles, 1 LP, 1 EP and 1 CD/year. Pays negotiable royalty to artists on contract; statutory rate to publisher per song on record.

Distributed by: Comlink Narrowcast Systems and The Peoples Network.

How to Contact: Submit demo tape by mail. Unsolicited submissions are OK. Prefers cassette, CD, DAT or VHS videocassette with 1-15 songs and lyric sheet. "Voice and one instrument OK, produced demos preferred." Does not return material. Reports in 4-6 weeks.

Music: Mostly **pop**, **rock** and **R&B**; also **jazz/fusion**, **swing/big band** and **alternative rock**. Released *Courage*, written and recorded by G.T. Albright (pop); *Outer Limits* (by A. Jankauskas), recorded by Outer Limits (fusion); and *The Follenian Underground* (by Sherer/Albright), recorded by the Follenian Underground (blues/rock), all on RML Records.

Tips: "We are a small independent label with two very noteworthy producers in tow. James Fischer, associate producer on Grammy-nominated R&B LP *New World Order* (by Curtis Mayfield) and Steven Hart, internationally-acclaimed NAIRD Indie Award-winning producer on Alasdair Fraser's '95/'96 release *Dawn Dance*, are both producing for RML Records. We produce a first-class product. We serve the music!"

[N] ☐ ROBBEYE MANAGEMENT GROUP, INC., P.O. Box 95243, Atlanta GA 30347. (404)325-7829. Fax: (404)315-0011. President/CEO: Robb D. Cohen. Labels include Lucy Records. Record company and music publisher (Robbeye Music Group, Inc.). Estab. 1981. Staff size: 3. Releases 6 LPs and 6 CDs/year. Pays negotiable royalty to artists on contract; statutory rate to publisher per song on record.

How to Contact: Submit demo tape by mail. Unsolicited submissions are OK. Prefers cassette, CD or

---

● **A BULLET** introduces comments by the editor of *Songwriter's Market* indicating special information about the listing.

VHS videocassette with 3 songs, lyric and lead sheet, cover letter and press clippings. Does not return material. Reports in 2-3 weeks.
Music: Mostly **rock/alternative, jazz** and **blues**; also **reggae, swing** and **classical**. Does not want country twang.

⊘ ROBBINS ENTERTAINMENT LLC, 30 W. 21st St., 11th Floor, New York NY 10010-6905. (212)675-4321. Fax: (212)675-4441. E-mail: jpfine@robbinsent.com. Director of A&R: Jonathan P. Fine. Record company and music publisher (Rocks, No Salt). Estab. 1996. Staff size: 4. Releases 25 singles and 12-14 CDs/year. Pays negotiable royalty to artists on contract; statutory rate to publisher per song on record.
Distributed by: BMG.
How to Contact: Does not accept unsolicited submissions.
Music: Mostly **rap, dance, alternative rock, pop** and **R&B**. Released "This Kind of Love" (by Meg Hentges/Jude O'Nym), and *Brompton's Cocktail* (by Meg Hentges/Jude O'Nym/Adam Schlesinger), both recorded by Meg Hentges (modern rock); and "When I'm Gone" (by A. Hammond/H. Payne), recorded by Rockell (dance/pop), all on Robbins Entertainment. Other artists include Marco Polo, Nikisha Grier, Victoria Angeles and Lovatux.
Tips: "We are looking for original, but accessible music, with crossover potential."

◻ ROLL ON RECORDS®, 112 Widmar Pl., Clayton CA 94517. (510)833-4680. Owner: Edgar J. Brincat. Record company and music publisher (California Country Music). Estab. 1985. Releases 2-3 LPs/cassettes/year. Pays 10% royalty to artists on contract; statutory rate to publisher per song on record.
Distributed by: Tower.
How to Contact: Submit demo tape by mail. Unsolicited submissions are OK. Do not call or write. Prefers cassette with 3 songs and lyric sheet. SASE. Reports in 4-6 weeks.
Music: Mostly **contemporary/country, MOR** and **R&B**; also **pop, light rock** and **modern gospel**. Released "Broken Record" (by Horace Linsley/Dianne Baumgartner), recorded by Edee Gordon on Roll On Records; *Maddy* and *For Realities Sake* (both by F.L. Pittman/Madonna Weeks), recorded by Ron Banks/L.J. Reynolds on Life Records/Bellmark Records.
Tips: "Be patient and prepare to be in it for the long haul. A successful songwriter does not happen overnight. It's rare to write a song today and have a hit tomorrow. If you give us your song and want it back, then don't give it to us to begin with."

◻ ROTTEN RECORDS, P.O. Box 2157, Montclair CA 91763. (909)624-2332. Fax: (909)624-2392. E-mail: rotten@rottenrecords.com. Website: http://www.rottenrecords.com. President: Ron Peterson. Promotions/Radio/Video: Richard Shytlemeyer. Record company. Estab. 1988. Releases 3 LPs, 3 EPs and 3 CDs/year.
Distributed by: Shock (Australia), Sonic Rendezvous (UK), DNA, Smash (US) and St. Clair (Canada).
How to Contact: Submit demo tape by mail. Unsolicited submissions are OK. Prefers CD. Does not return material.
Music: Mostly **rock, alternative** and **commercial**; also **punk** and **heavy metal**. Released *Paegan Terrorism . . .*, written and recorded by Acid Bath; *Kiss the Clown* (by K. Donivon), recorded by Kiss the Clown; and *Full Speed Ahead* (by Cassidy/Brecht), recorded by D.R.T., all on Rotten Records.
Tips: "Be patient."

◻ ROWENA RECORDS, 195 S. 26th St., San Jose CA 95116. (408)286-9840. Fax: (408)286-9845. E-mail: onealproduction@juno.com. Owner/A&R (country, Mexican, gospel): Grady O'Neal. A&R (all styles): Jeannine O'Neal. Record company and music publisher (Tiki Enterprises). Estab. 1967. Staff size: 3. Releases 8-12 LPs and 8-12 CDs/year. Pays negotiable royalty to artists on contract; pays statutory rate to publisher per song on record.
How to Contact: Submit demo tape by mail. Unsolicited submissions are OK. Prefers cassette with 2 songs and lyric sheet. SASE. Reports in 2 weeks.
Music: Mostly **gospel, country** and **pop**; also **Mexican** and **R&B**. Released *Corazon De Niña*, recorded by Maria Dolores, and *Doble Vida*, recorded by Lupe Yepez, both written by Armando Sarabia (Mexican); and *Standing In The Night*, written and recorded by Khris Francis (pop), all on Rowena Records.

◻ ROYALTY RECORDS, 176 Madison Ave. 4th Floor, New York NY 10016. (212)779-0101. Fax: (212)779-3255. E-mail: royaltyrec@aol.com. Record company. Estab. 1994. Releases 5 singles and 5 CDs/year. Pays negotiable royalty to artists on contract; ¾ statutory rate to publisher per song on record.
How to Contact: Submit demo tape by mail. Unsolicited submissions are OK. Prefers CDs, cassette or videocassette. Does not return material. Reports in 2 months.

Music: Released *We Will Fall: The Iggy Pop Tribute*, recorded by 20 various artists; and *Speedealer*, written and recorded by Speedealer, both on Royalty Records.

☑ ◢ **RUF RECORDS**, 71 Newark Way, Maplewood NJ 07040. (973)275-1077. Fax: (973)275-1093. E-mail: intumg@aol.com. General Manager: Ira Leslie. Record company, music publisher and record producer (Thomas Ruf). Estab. 1993. Releases 12 CDs/year. Pays negotiable royalty to artists on contract; statutory rate to publisher per song on record.
Distributed by: Platinum Entertainment and PDG.
   • Ruf is known for releasing heavy blues.
How to Contact: Submit demo tape by mail. Unsolicited submissions are OK. Prefers CD with 4 songs. Does not return material. Reports in 1 week.
Music: Mostly **blues**, **rock** and **R&B**. Released *Fit To Serve*, written and recorded by A.J. Croce (pop); *Walter Trout*, written and recorded by Walter Trout (rock/blues); and *Taj Mahal* (by various), recorded by Taj Mahal (blues), all on Ruf Records. Other artists include Luther Allison, John Mooney, Larry Garner, Friends n Fellow, Hans Theessink, Hank Shizzoe and Joanna Connor.

N 💊 ◻ **RUFFHOUSE RECORDS**, 129 Fayette St., Conshohocken PA 19428. (610)940-9533. Fax: (610)940-6667. E-mail: rosep@ruffhouse.com. Website: http://www.ruffhouse.com. Ruffhouse Publishing: Dierdra O'hara. President: Joseph Nicolo. CEO: Chris Schwartz. Vice President of A&R: Rose Pierce. Record company, music publisher (Ruffhouse Publishing) and record producer (Joseph "The Butcher" Nicolo). Estab. 1989. Staff size: 12. Releases 20 singles and 6 LPs/year. Pays negotiable royalty to artists on contract.
Distributed by: Sony Distribution.
   • Ruffhouse's Lauryn Hill won five 1998 Grammys including Album of the Year, Best New Artist and Best R&B Album.
How to Contact: Submit demo tape by mail. Unsolicited submissions are OK. Prefers cassette, CD, DAT or videocassette. "Please place phone number on actual listening component." Does not return material. Reports in 1-3 months.
Music: Mostly **rap**, **R&B** and **rock artists**; also **songwriters of any music style**. Released *Miseducation of Lauryn Hill*, written and recorded by Lauryn Hill on Ruffhouse/Columbia/Sony (rap/R&B). Other artists include Pace Won, Sporty Thievz, Josh Wink, Pras, Wyclef Jean, John Forte, Cypress Hill and The Fugees.
Tips: "Be original, put your money into the production of the tape not the packaging. Have patience when shopping and let someone else help."

◢ **RUSTRON MUSIC PRODUCTIONS**, 1156 Park Lane, West Palm Beach FL 33417-5957. (561)686-1354. Executive Director (folk fusions, blues, women's music, adult contemporary, electric, acoustic, New Age instrumentals, children's, cabaret): Rusty Gordon. Director A&R: Ron Caruso. Associate Director of A&R (pop, country, blues, R&B, jazz): Kevin Reeves. Labels include Rustron Records and Whimsong Records. "Rustron administers 20 independent labels for publishing and marketing." Record company, record producer, management firm and music publisher (Whimsong/ASCAP and Rustron Music/BMI). Estab. 1970. Releases 5-10 cassettes and CDs/year. Pays variable royalty to artists on contract. "Artists with history of product sales get higher % than those with no sales track record." Pays statutory rate to publisher.
How to Contact: Write or call first to obtain permission to submit or submit demo tape or CD by mail. Unsolicited submissions are OK. Prefers cassette with 3 songs and typed lyric sheet. "If singer/songwriter has independent product (cassette or CD) produced and sold at gigs—send this product." SASE required for all correspondence, no exceptions. Reports in 4 months.
Music: Mostly **mainstream** and **women's music**, **A/C**, **electric acoustic**, **pop (cabaret, blues)** and **blues (R&B, country and folk)**; also **New Age fusions** (instrumentals), **modern folk fusions**, **environmental** and **socio-political**. Released "It's Almost Tomorrow" (by Jayne Margo-Reby/Vic Bersok), recorded by Jayne Margo-Reby; and "For Better or For Worse," written and recorded by Star Smiley, both on Rustron Records; and "Big Black Dog" (by Rusty Gordon), recorded by Anna Garber on Whimsong Records. Other artists include Star Smiley, Boomslang Swampsinger, Lisa Cohen, Jayne Margo-Reby, Ellen Hines and Robin Plitt.
Tips: "Find your own unique style; write well crafted songs with unpredictable concepts, strong hooks and definitive melody. New Age composers: evolve your themes and add multi-cultural diversity with instruments. Don't be predictable. Don't over-produce your demos and don't drown vocals. Send cover letter clearly explaining your reasons for submitting."

◻ **SABRE PRODUCTIONS**, P.O. Box 10147, San Antonio TX 78210. (210)533-6910. Producer: E.J. Henke. Labels include Fanfare, Satin and Legacy. Record company and record producer. Estab. 1965. Staff size: 2. Releases 48 singles, 5 LPs and 4 CDs/year. Pays 10% royalty to artists on contract; statutory rate to publisher per song on record.

How to Contact: Submit demo tape by mail. Unsolicited submissions are OK. Prefers cassette with 4 songs and lyric sheet. SASE. Reports in 1 month.

Music: Mostly **country** (all styles), **gospel** and **rock/R&B**. Released *Hills Of Helotes* (by Amos Ayala III), recorded by Robert Beckom; "May It Please the Court" (by Candie Lemare), recorded by Barry Watson; and *All This Love* (by Thelma Todd), recorded by Joe Terry, all on Sabre Productions (country western). Other artists include Suzie Rowles, Barry Watson, Brady Redding and Sunglows.

SABTECA RECORD CO., P.O. Box 10286, Oakland CA 94610. (510)465-2805. President: Duane Herring. Production Coordinator (pop, R&B, jazz): Sean Herring. Secretary (pop, R&B, country): Lois Shayne. Labels include André Romare Records. Record company and music publisher (Sabteca Music Co./ASCAP, Toyiabe Music Co./BMI). Estab. 1980. Releases 3 singles and 1 12″ single/year. Pays 10% royalty to artists on contract; statutory rate to publisher per song on record.

Distributed by: Sabteca.

How to Contact: Write first and obtain permission to submit. Prefers cassette with lyric sheet. SASE. Reports in 2-4 weeks.

Music: Mostly **R&B, pop** and **country**. Released "Lost Somewhere Back in Time," written and recorded by Reggie Walker; and "What Can I Do" (by Thomas Roller), recorded by Reggie Walker, both on André Romare (pop). Other artists include Walt Coleman, Lil Brown and Lois Shayne.

Tips: "Determination and persistence are vital."

SAFIRE RECORDS, 5617 W. Melvina, Milwaukee WI 53216. (414)444-3385. President: Darnell Ellis. A&R Representatives: Darrien Kingston (alternative, industrial, rock); Reggie Rodriqez (pop, contemporary country). Record company, music publisher (Ellis Enterprise Publishing), record producer (Darnell Ellis) and management firm (The Ellis International Talent Agency). Estab. 1997. Staff size: 2. Releases 3 singles, 3 LPs, 1 EP and 3 CDs/year. Pays negotiable royalty to artists on contract; statutory rate to publisher per song on record.

How to Contact: Submit demo tape by mail. Unsolicited submissions are OK. Prefers cassette with 3-4 songs. Does not return material. Reports in 1-2 months. "We will respond only if we are interested."

Music: Mostly **top 40/commercial hits, pop** and **country pop**. Artists include One Girl (AAA modern rock), Stacey Paul (contemporary country) and Derek Thevon (pop).

Tips: "Songwriters need to get back to the basics of songwriting: great hooklines, strong melodies. We would love to hear from artists and songwriters from all over the world. And remember, just because someone passes on a song it doesn't mean that it's a bad song. Maybe it's a song that the label is not able to market or the timing is just bad."

SAHARA RECORDS AND FILMWORKS ENTERTAINMENT, 117 W. Harrison Bldg. #S627, Chicago IL 60605-1709. (773)509-6381. Fax: (312)922-6964. President: Edward De Miles. Record company, music publisher (EDM Music/BMI, Edward De Miles Music Company) and record producer (Edward De Miles). Estab. 1981. Releases 15-20 CD singles and 5-10 CDs/year. Pays 9½-11% royalty to artists on contract; statutory rate to publishers per song on record.

How to Contact: Does not accept unsolicited submissions.

Music: Mostly **R&B/dance, top 40 pop/rock** and **contemporary jazz**; also **TV-film themes, musical scores** and **jingles**. Released "Hooked on U," "Dance Wit Me" and "Moments," written and recorded by Steve Lynn (R&B) on Sahara Records. Other artists include Lost in Wonder, Dvon Edwards and Multiple Choice.

Tips: "We're looking for strong mainstream material. Lyrics and melodies with good hooks that grab people's attention."

ST. FRANCIS RECORDS, 808¾ N. Detroit St., Los Angeles CA 90046. Phone/fax: (323)932-1040. Minister of Noise: Leland Leard. Record company. Estab. 1994. Releases 2 singles, 1 EP and 3 CDs/year. Pays negotiable royalty to artists on contract; statutory rate to publisher per song on record.

Distributed by: Nail, K, Darla, Bayside and Revolver.

How to Contact: Submit demo tape by mail. Unsolicited submissions are OK. Prefers cassette or CD

REFER TO THE GEOGRAPHIC INDEX (at the back of this book) to find listings of companies by state, as well as foreign listings.

with 4 songs and lead sheet. Does not return material. Reports in 2 months.
Music: Mostly **alternative, electronic** and **pop**; also **jazz**. Released *El Camino Real*, written and recorded by Carmaig de Forest (pop); *Strikes the Earth*, written and recorded by Deathstar (pop/alternative); and *Superwinners Summer Rock Academy*, written and recorded by various artists (alternative/pop), all on St. Francis Records.
Tips: "Commitment to performance is key."

○ **SALEXO MUSIC**, P.O. Box 18093, Charlotte NC 28218-0093. (704)536-0600. President: Samuel OBie. Record company. Estab. 1992. Releases 1 CD/year. Pays 2.5% royalty to artists on contract; variable rate to publisher per song on record.
How to Contact: Write first and obtain permission to submit. Prefers cassette with 3 songs and lyric sheet. SASE. Reports in 1 month.
Music: Mostly **contemporary gospel** and **jazz**. Released "Do You Know Him?" on Bellmark (gospel); and "The Blood," both recorded by Edwin Hawkins on Harmony (gospel); and "Psalms 34," recorded by Shirley Caesar on Word Records (gospel), all written by Samuel Obie.
Tips: "Make initial investment in the best production."

N ⊕ 🆅 ○ SATELLITE MUSIC, 34 Salisbury St., London NW8 8QE United Kingdom. Phone: (+44)171-402-9111. Fax: (+44)171-723-3064. Directors: Eliot Cohem; Ray Dorset. Labels include Saraja and Excalibur. Record company and music publisher. Estab. 1976. Staff size: 10. Releases 5 singles, 3 LPs and 3 CDs/year. Pays negotiable royalty to artists on contract; statutory rate to publisher per song on record.
Distributed by: S. Gold & Sons and Total Home Entertainment.
 • Satellite Music won two ASCAP awards in 1996 for Top R&B Song of the Year and Top Rap Song of the Year in the U.S.
How to Contact: Submit demo tape by mail. Unsolicited submissions are OK. Prefers cassette, CD, DAT or VHS videocassette with 4 songs, cover letter and press clippings. SAE and IRC. Reports in 6 weeks.
Music: Mostly **dance, disco** and **pop**. Does not want blues, jazz or country. Released "In the Show" (by Ray Dorset), recorded by Mungo Jerry on BME (pop).

N ○ SEALED FATE RECORDS, P.O. Box 9183, #120, Cambridge MA 02139. E-mail: ericm@sealedfate.com. Website: http://www.sealedfate.com. A&R: Eric Masunaga. Record company. Estab. 1995. Staff size: 1. Releases 3 singles, 5 LPs, 1 EP and 5 CDs/year. Pays 15% royalty to artists on contract; statutory rate to publisher per song on record.
Distributed by: Revolver, Nail, CTD, Choke and Bayside.
How to Contact: Submit demo tape by mail. Unsolicited submissions are OK. Prefers cassette or CD. Does not return material.
Music: Mostly **suburban underground rock, pop/techno** and **synth soul/mood**. Released *The Brighter Shore* (by Galinsky/McNally/O'Rourke), recorded by Sleepyhead (rock); *Black Box Diaries*, written and recorded by the Fly Seville (pastoral); and *Far Places* (by Moore Geretty), recorded by The Pushkings (pop/soul), all on Sealed Fate Records.
Tips: "Send quality material."

🆅 ○ SELECT RECORDS, 19 W. 21st St., Suite 1004, New York NY 10010. (212)691-1200. Fax: (212)691-3375. E-mail: selectrec@aol.com. Executive Assistant to President, A&R: Craig Davis. Record company and music publisher (ADRA/Hittage). Estab. 1980. Releases 8 singles, 3-4 LPs/year. Pays negotiable royalty to artists on contract; statutory rate to publisher per song on record.
Distributed by: MS Distribution.
How to Contact: Call first and obtain permission to submit a demo. Prefers cassette, CD or VHS videocassette with 3-4 songs and lyric sheet. "All bios/information should be typewritten." Does not return material.
Music: Mostly **rap, R&B** and **dance**; also **comedy**. Released *Life*, written and recorded by Chubb Rock (rap); "Da Medicine," written and recorded by The Veteranz (rap); and "Running 2 U," written and recorded by G-Man (R&B), all on Select.
Tips: "Submit strongest efforts only. Lyrical content is very important, as is the ability to construct strong hooks and being current, music should retain some original flavor."

N ○ SHAOLIN FILM & RECORDS, P.O. Box 58547, Salt Lake City UT 84158. (801)595-1123. President: Richard O'Connor. A&R: Don DelaVega. Labels include Shaolin Communications. Record company, music publisher (Shaolin Music/ASCAP) and record producer (Richard O'Connor). Estab. 1984. Releases 4 singles, 2 LP, 2 CDs and 2 EPs/year.

How to Contact: Submit demo tape by mail. Unsolicited submissions are OK. Prefers cassette with 3-4 songs and lyric sheet. Include bio and press kit. Does not return material. Reports in 6 weeks.
Music: Mostly **rock**, **hard rock** and **pop**; also **soundtracks**.

SILVER WAVE RECORDS, P.O. Box 7943, Boulder CO 80306. (303)443-5617. Fax: (303)443-0877. E-mail: info@silverwave.com. Website: http://www.silverwave.com. Contact: James Marienthal. Labels include Silver Planet Productions. Record company. Estab. 1986. Releases 6-8 CDs/year. Pays varying royalty to artists on contract and to publisher per song on record.
How to Contact: Write first and obtain permission to submit. Prefers CD. SASE. Reports only if interested.
Music: Mostly **world**, **New Age**, **Native American** and **contemporary instrumental**.

SILVERTONE RECORDS, 137-139 W. 25th St., New York NY 10001. (212)727-0016. Fax: (212)620-0048. Label Director: Michael Tedesco. Hollywood office: 9000 Sunset Blvd., Suite 300, W. Hollywood CA 90069. Fax: (213)247-8366. Director of Artist Development: Janet McQueeney. Labels include Essential Records. Record company.
Distributed by: BMG.
How to Contact: Submit demo tape by mail. Unsolicited submissions are OK. Any format acceptable, with lyric and lead sheets.
Music: Released *Jars of Clay*, recorded by Jars of Clay on Essential Records. Other artists include Chris Duarte, Buddy Guy, Hed, Livingstone, John Mayall, Metal Molly and Solar Race.

JERRY SIMS RECORDS, P.O. Box 648, Woodacre CA 94973. (415)789-7322. Fax: (415)456-9197. Owner: Jerry Sims. Record company. Estab. 1984. Releases 6-7 CDs/year. Pays negotiable royalty to artists on contract; statutory rate to publisher per song on record.
Distributed by: New Leaf, LeFon, DeVorss and Top (Hong Kong).
How to Contact: Submit demo tape by mail. Unsolicited submissions are OK. Prefers cassette or CD. Does not return material. Reports in 1 month only if interested.
Music: Mostly **instrumental**, **Celtic** and **pop**. Released *Viaggio* and *December Days*, both written and recorded by Coral (Celtic); and *King of California*, written and recorded by Chuck Vincent (rock), all on Jerry Sims Records. Other artists include Disfunctional Family, Kim Y. Han and Mike Lovelace.
Tips: "We are currently looking for ethnic music for movie soundtracks."

SIRE RECORDS, 2034 Broadway, Santa Monica CA 90404-2910. (800)377-9620. Fax: (310)828-1584. Website: http://www.sirerecords.com. A&R: Jonathon Paley, Andy Paley. New York office: 936 Broadway, New York NY 10010. (212)253-3900. A&R Manager: Scott Graves. Record company.
Distributed by: WEA.
How to Contact: Does not accept unsolicited submissions.
Music: Mostly **rock** and **alternative**. Artists include Spacehog, Morcheeba, The Derailers and Aphex Twins.

SMALL STONE RECORDS, P.O. Box 02007, Detroit MI 48202. (248)546-1206. Fax: (313)871-4840. E-mail: sstone@smallstone.com. Website: http://www.smallstone.com. Owner: Scott Hamilton. Record company. Estab. 1995. Staff size: 1. Releases 2 singles, 2 EPs and 10 CDs/year. Pays negotiable royalty to artists on contract; statutory rate to publisher per song on record.
Distributed by: Action, Parasol and Nail.
How to Contact: Submit demo tape by mail. Unsolicited submissions are OK. Prefers cassette, CD or VHS videocassette. Does not return material. Reports in 1-2 months.
Music: Mostly **alternative**, **rock** and **blues**; also **funk (not R&B)**. Released *Fat Black Pussy Cat*, written and recorded by Five Horse Johnson (rock/blues); *Wrecked & Remixed*, written and recorded by Morsel (indie rock, electronica); and *Only One Division*, written and recorded by Soul Clique (electronica), all on Small Stone Records. Other artists include 36-D, Roundhead, Wytchyker, K.O.B. and Walk on Water.
Tips: "Looking for esoteric music along the lines of Bill Laswell to Touch & Go/Thrill Jockey records material. Only send along material if it makes sense with what we do. Perhaps owning some of our records would help."

OPENNESS TO SUBMISSIONS: ○ beginners; ◐ beginners and experienced; ◑ experienced only; ◉ industry referrals only.

○ **SOLO RECORDS PRODUCTIONS**, 915 Cole St., Suite 137, San Francisco CA 94117. (415)282-4466. Fax: (415)282-4474. E-mail: solopro@aol.com. A&R: Jay Siegan. Record company. Estab. 1995. Releases 2-5 LPs and 2-5 CDs/year. Pays negotiable royalty to artists on contract; statutory rate to publisher per song on record.
Distributed by: ADA and BMG.
How to Contact: Submit demo tape by mail. Unsolicited submissions are OK. Prefers cassette or CD with 2-3 songs and lyric sheet. Does not return material. Reports only if interested.
Music: Mostly **pop**, **swing** and **ska**; also **alternative**. Released "We've Come for Your Daughter" (by Pat Smith/Bob Glynn), recorded by Undercover S.K.A. on Solo Records (ska).
Tips: "Please submit genre-specific songs. We particularly appreciate ska, swing and other horn-fueled genres."

◫ ○ **sonic unyon records canada**, P.O. Box 57347, Jackson Station, Hamilton, Ontario L8P 4X2 Canada. (905)777-1223. Fax: (905)777-1161. E-mail: jerks@sonicunyon.com. Website: http://www.sonicu nyon.com. Co-owners: Tim Potocic; Mark Milne; Andy McIntosh. Record company. Estab. 1992. Releases 2 singles, 2 EPs and 6 CDs/year. Pays negotiable royalty to artists on contract; statutory rate to publisher per song on record.
Distributed by: Caroline, Revolver and Smash.
How to Contact: Call first and obtain permission to submit. Prefers cassette or CD. "Research our company before you send your demo. We are small; don't waste my time and your money." Does not return material. Reports in 3-4 months.
Music: Mostly **rock**, **heavy rock** and **pop rock**. Released *Doberman*, written and recorded by Kittens (heavy rock); *What A Life*, written and recorded by Smoother; and *New Grand*, written and recorded by New Grand on sonic unyon records (pop/rock). Other artists include Siansphere, gorp, Hayden and Poledo.
Tips: "Know what we are about. Research us. Know we are a small company. Know signing to us doesn't mean that everything will fall into your lap. We are only the beginning of an artist's career."

𝗡 ◑ **SOUTHLAND RECORDS, INC.**, P.O. Box 1547, Arlington TX 76004-1547. (817)461-3280. E-mail: reedsteve@worldnet.att.net. Website: http://www.SouthlandRecords.com. President: Steve Reed. Record company and record producer (Steve Reed). Estab. 1980. Releases 3 CDs/year. Pays negotiable royalty to artists on contract; statutory rate to publisher per song on record.
How to Contact: Submit demo tape by mail. Unsolicited submissions are OK. Prefers cassette or CD with 4 songs, lyric and lead sheet, cover letter and press clippings. Does not return material. Reports in 2-3 months.
Music: Country only. Released *Close to You* (by Cindy Walker), recorded by Leon Rausch; and *Chip Off the Ole Block* (by various artists), recorded by Ron Gaddis, all Southland Records, Inc. (country).

𝗡 ◑ **SPOTLIGHT RECORDS**, 1387 Chambers Rd., Columbus OH 43212. Phone/fax: (614)487-1911. Owner: Jim Bruce. Distributed by J.H. Lennon Music Ltd. Record company, music publisher (James Paul Music), record producer (Jim Bruce) and artist management. Estab. 1994. Staff size: 2. Releases 1-3 singles, 1-3 LPs and 1-3 CDs/year. Pays 10% royalty to artists on contract; statutory rate to publisher per song on record.
How to Contact: Submit demo tape by mail. Unsolicited submissions are OK. Prefers cassette, DAT or VHS videotape with 1-3 songs. Does not return material. Reports in 4-6 weeks.
Music: Mostly **country**, **gospel** and **top 40/pop**; also **country rock**. Released *That's The Way* (by various), recorded by Debbie Collins on J. Paul Records; and *We Have Love* (by various artists), recorded by Brandi Lynn Howard (country) on Spotlight Records.
Tips: "Upbeat songs a must, ballads OK for songwriters. Artist must have professional package and band in place and working. Create that total package. Be persistent—it pays."

◑ **STARDUST**, 341 Billy Goat Hill Rd., Winchester TN 37398. (931)649-2577. Fax: (615)649-2732. President: Barbara Doss. Labels include Stardust, Wizard, Doss, Kimbolon, Thunder Hawk, Flaming Star. Record company, music publisher (Buster Doss Music/BMI), management firm (Buster Doss Presents) and record producer (Colonel Buster Doss). Estab. 1959. Releases 50 singles and 25 CDs/year. Pays 8-10% royalty to artists on contract; statutory rate to publisher per song on record.
How to Contact: Write first and obtain permission to submit. Prefers cassette with 2 songs and lyric sheet. SASE. Reports "on same day received."
Music: Mostly **country**; also **rock**. Released "Come On In," recorded by Duane Hall on Stardust Records

and "Rescue Me," recorded by Tommy D on Doss Records. Other artists include Linda Wunder, Rooster Quantrell, Don Sky, James Bryan, "Red" Reider, Holmes Bros., Donna Darlene, Jerri Arnold, "Bronco" Buck Cody and Dwain Gamel.

STARFISH RECORDS, P.O. Box 9441, Cincinnati OH 45209. E-mail: hubcap@iac.net. Website: http://w3.one.net/~hubcap. A&R: Matt Hart. President: Cindy Laufenberg. Record company. Estab. 1996. Staff size: 4. Releases 2 singles, 3 CDs/year. Pays negotiable royalty to artists on contract; negotiable rate to publisher per song on record.
How to Contact: "Starfish Records does not accept submissions. We only work with bands and artists from the Cincinnati area." Does not return material.
Music: Mostly **rock** and **pop**. Released *Topter Baster*, written and recorded by Clifford Nevernew (rock); *Hard Luck Din* (by Bench/Triger), recorded by 7 Speed Vortex (pop); and *Opus Oil Slick # Same Said*, written and recorded by Travel, all on Starfish Records. Other artists include Telegraph, Teenage Blackout, Little Billy Catfish & the Sodapops and The Middle Fingers.
Tips: "We only work with bands/artists from the Cincinnati area, so if you're not from Cincinnati, please don't contact us."

N **STREET RECORDS**, P.O. Box 1356, Folly Beach SC 29439. (843)588-4024. Fax: (843)588-6030. E-mail: rock@streetrecords.com. Website: http://www.streetrecords.com. Director of A&R: Tasos. A&R: Conner Lewis; MJ Shutrump; Bettina Torello. Labels include Kretan Sea Records. Record company, music publisher (Kretan Sea Music) and record producer (Tasos). Estab. 1983. Staff size: 5. Releases 4 singles, 2 EPs and 5 CDs/year. Pays negotiable or 13% royalty to artists on contract; statutory rate to publisher per song on record.
Distributed by: Southern Records (USA), Southern Studios (UK and parts of Europe), Sonic Unyon (Canada), Hitch-Hyke (Greece) and WEA (parts of Europe/select releases).
How to Contact: Submit demo tape by mail. Unsolicited submissions are OK. Prefers cassette, CD, DAT or VHS/NTSC videocassette with 3 songs and press clippings. Does not return material. Reports in 6 weeks.
Music: Mostly **rock**, **pop** and **punk**; also **folk**, **garage** and **indie**. Does not want rap, metal or country. Released *You Should Enjoy Getting Screamed At!* (by Thomas Crouch/Bryan Biggart), recorded by F13 (punk); *The Rock Garden* (by band collective), recorded by Eurogression (rock); and *Hutches of Gunch* (by Eric Baylies), recorded by Baylies Band (rock), all on Street Records. Other artists include Aberdeen Lizards, Desaru, the Cigs, Onassis and Wax American.
Tips: "Are you ready to tour and give up most luxuries for two years?"

N **STRIVE MUSIC**, P.O. Box 562, Youngstown OH 44501. Fax: (330)744-5778. President/CEO: George Ramey. Vice President (R&B, dance, rap): Tabitha Ramey. Senior A&R Representative (all styles): Elaine Walton. Labels include Dream Publishing. Record company. Estab. 1998. Staff size: 3. Releases 4 singles, 2 LPs, 2 EPs and 4 CDs/year. Pays 10% royalty to artists on contract; statutory rate to publisher per song on record.
Distributed by: National Record Mart.
How to Contact: Write or call first to obtain permission to submit or submit demo tape by mail. Unsolicited submissions are OK. Prefers cassette with 1-3 songs. SASE "or write/fax us for results." Reports in 1 week.
Music: Mostly **rap**, **R&B** and **hip-hop**; also **dance**. Released "Get On Down" and "Get cha Groove On," both written and recorded by G'DA Hustla; and "Money Makes the World Go Around," written and recorded by G'DA Hustla and Diamonds, all on Strive Music (rap). Other artists include 3X Nice.
Tips: "Never let anybody stop you from your dreams. Just keep following your goals and plans and you'll make it. We will try to help all our artists achieve success. Be optimistic on your way to the top."

STRUGGLEBABY RECORDING CO., 2612 Erie Ave., P.O. Box 8385, Cincinnati OH 45208. (513)871-1500. Fax: (513)871-1510. E-mail: umbrella@one.net or elaine@one.net. A&R/Professional Manager: Sam Richman. Record company, music publisher and record producer (Hal Bernard Enterprises). Estab. 1983. Releases 3-4 CDs/year. Pays negotiable royalty to artists on contract; statutory (per contract) rate to publisher per song on record.

THE OPENNESS TO SUBMISSIONS INDEX at the back of this book lists all companies in this section by how open they are to submissions.

How to Contact: Submit demo tape by mail. Unsolicited submissions are OK. Prefers cassette with 3 songs and lyric sheet. SASE. Reports in 3-4 weeks.

Music: Mostly **modern rock**, **rock** and **R&B**. Released *The Official Bootleg*, written and recorded by psychodots (modern rock); "Merry, Mary Christmas," recorded by Mary Ellen Tanner (seasonal); and "Solstice," recorded by David Todoran (Americana/AAA), all on Strugglebaby Recording Co.

Tips: "Keep it simple, honest, with a personal touch. Show some evidence of market interest and attraction and value as well as the ability to tour."

✓ ◯ SUISONIC RECORDS, 1245 W. Guadalupe Rd., Suite B6-290, Mesa AZ 85202. Phone/fax: (602)491-3642. E-mail: suisonic@primenet.com. A&R Director: Tony McFarland. Labels include Tremble Rose. Record company. Estab. 1996. Releases 2 singles, 4 LPs, 4 EPs and 4 CDs/year. Pays negotiable royalty to artists on contract; statutory rate to publisher per song on record.

How to Contact: Submit demo tape by mail. Unsolicited submissions are OK. Prefers CD. "Must fill out application at darkmusic.com. All music must be dark oriented." Does not return material. Reports in 2 weeks, "immediately if we like it a lot. Please do not call."

Music: Mostly **rock** and **dance**. "No glam metal, '80s metal, satanic worshipping music or gangsta please!" Released *Grace Overthrone*, written and recorded by Grace Overthrone (industrial); *Visual Purple*, written and recorded by Visual Purple (pop/punk), both on Suisonic Records; and *Ralene Baker*, written and recorded by Raylene Baker on Tremble Rose Records (goth rock). Other artists include NL9, Memory Pool and Six Sigma.

◯ SUNCOUNTRY RECORDS, 2709 W. Pine Lodge, Roswell NM 88201. (505)622-0244. E-mail: pecos.valley.musir@usa.net. Website: http://www.angelfire.com/wi/pecosvalleymusic/index.html. President, A&R: Ray Willmon. A&R: Jack Burns. Record company and music publisher (Pecos Valley Music). Estab. 1989. Releases 1-2 singles, 1 CD/year. Pays 2-10% royalty to artists on contract; statutory rate to publisher per song on record.

How to Contact: Submit demo tape by mail. Unsolicited submissions are OK. "No phone calls please—we will accept by mail." Prefers cassette, CD or VHS videocassette with 2 songs maximum and lyric sheet. SASE. Reports in 3 months.

Music: Mostly **C&W** and **gospel (country)**. Released "Say When" and "Just Be With," both written and recorded by Jack Bush; and "Down That Way" (by Ray Willmon), recorded by Jack Bush, all on SunCountry Records (country). Other artists include Sam Means and Jack Taylor.

N ◯ SUNDANCE RECORDS, 907 Baltimore St., Mobile AL 36605-4653. (334)3760. Fax: (334)433-8246. A&R Director: Mr. Antonio Pritchett. Record company. Estab. 1989. Staff size: 3. Releases 12 singles, 15 LPs, 6 EPs and 15 CDs/year. Pays negotiable royalty to artists on contract; statutory rate to publisher per song on record.

How to Contact: Submit demo tape by mail. Unsolicited submissions are OK. Prefers cassette, CD or VHS videocassette with 3-6 songs, lyric sheet, cover letter and press clippings. "Make sure you put your best effort in the product." SASE. Reports in 1-2 months.

Music: Mostly **R&B**, **rap** and **jazz**; also **blues**, **rock** and **gospel**. Released *Poverty to Riches* (by Domonic Laforce), recorded by Da Force (rap); *Alana* (by Antonio R. Pritchett), recorded by Alana (jazz/R&B); and *Messenger*, written and recorded by Messenger (Christian rock), all on SunDance. Other artists include Spice, O.G.K.B., Red T, Mob and Head Rush.

◯ SURESHOT RECORDS, P.O. Box 9117, Truckee CA 96162. (530)587-0111. E-mail: alanred@telis. org. Website: http://www.alanredstone.com. Owner: Alan Redstone. Record company, record producer and music publisher. Estab. 1979. Releases 1 LP/year. Pays statutory rate to publisher per song on record.

How to Contact: Submit demo tape by mail. Unsolicited submissions are OK. Write or call first and obtain permission to submit. SASE. Reports in 1 week.

Music: Mostly **country**, **comedy**, **novelty** and **blues**.

Tips: "Read up and learn to submit properly. Submit like a pro."

✓ ◯ SURFACE RECORDS, 8377 Westview, Houston TX 77055. (713)464-4653. Fax: (713)464-2622. E-mail: sarsjef@aol.com. Website: http://www.soundartsrecording. President: Jeff Wells. A&R: Peter Verkerk. Record company, music publisher (Earthscream Music Publishing Co./BMI) and record producer (Jeff Wells). Estab. 1996. Releases 4 CDs/year. Pays negotiable royalty to artists on contract; statutory rate to publisher per song on record.

Distributed by: Earth Records.

How to Contact: Submit demo tape by mail. Unsolicited submissions are OK. Prefers cassette with 4 songs and lyric sheet. Does not return material. Reports in 6 weeks.

Music: Mostly **country**, **blues** and **pop/rock**. Released *Everest*, recorded by The Jinkies; *Joe "King" Carrasco*, recorded by Joe "King" Carrasco; and *Perfect Strangers*, recorded by Perfect Strangers, all on Surface Records (pop). Other artists include Rosebud.

N! ◯ SWEET JUNE MUSIC, P.O. Box 669, Fulton TX 78358-0669. (512)729-4249. E-mail: musicdirector@classicctrymusicclub.com. Website: http://www.classicctrymusicclub.com. Owner: Tom Thrasher. Music Critiquer: Doris June. Labels include TBS Records and CMI Records. Record company, music publisher, record producer and music marketing. Estab. 1978. Staff size: 1. Releases 2 singles, 2 LPs and 2 CDs/year. Pays standard royalty to artists on contract; statutory rate to publisher per song on record.
Distributed by: World Wide Web.
How to Contact: Submit demo tape by mail. Unsolicited submissions are OK. Prefers cassette, CD or DAT with 3 songs, lyric sheet and cover letter. Does not return material. Reports in 1-2 months.
Music: Mostly **traditional country**, **bluegrass** and **gospel**; also **traditional Big Band**, **Dixieland** and **quartet (barbershop/gospel)**. Does not want rock or contemporary. Released *Texas Friends #2*, written and recorded by Scott Plant (old time fiddle); *Texas Friends #1* (by Tom Thrasher), recorded by various artists (classic country), both on TBS Records; and *Good News Guitar* (by public domain), recorded by Tom Thrasher on C-M-I Records (church classics).
Tips: "Looking for new artists. Must have marketing knowledge of who their customers are and what they buy or won't buy. Learn how to be a salesperson. All the exposure in the world won't do any good if the artist/songwriter drops the ball!"

◯ TANDEM RECORDS, 842 Stanton Rd., Burlingame CA 94010. (415)692-2866. Fax: (415)692-8800. E-mail: trcdist@trcdist.com. Website: http://www.trcdist.com. A&R Representative (gospel, R&B, dance): Dave Christian. A&R Representative (rock): Cindy Lui. Record company and music publisher (Atherton Music/ASCAP and Atherton Road Music/BMI). Estab. 1985. Pays statutory rate to publisher per song on record.
Affiliate(s): Speed Records.
How to Contact: Submit demo tape by mail. Unsolicited submissions are OK. Prefers cassette and lyric sheet. Does not return material. Reports in 1 month.
Music: Mostly **rap**, **R&B** and **gospel**; also **modern** and **dance**. Released *Pilot Me* (by Steven Roberts/D. Christian), recorded by Rev. Fleetwood Irving on Tandem Records (gospel); *Faith* (by Dave Sears), recorded by 7 Red 7; and *In Love Again*, written and recorded by Aria on Speed Records (dance). Other artists include Funklab All Stars, Rated X and Tenda Tee, What The Hell, Tabb Doe and Aria.

☑ ◯ TANGENT RECORDS, 1888 Century Park E., Suite 1900, Los Angeles CA 90067. (310)204-0388. Fax: (310)204-0995. E-mail: tangent@ix.netcom.com. President: Andrew Batchelor. Director of Marketing: Elisa Batchelor. Record company and music publisher (ArcTangent Music/BMI). Estab. 1988. Staff size: 2. Releases 10-12 CDs/year. Pays negotiable royalty to artists on contract; statutory rate to publisher per song on record.
How to Contact: Submit demo tape by mail. Unsolicited submissions are OK. Prefers cassette, CD, DAT or VHS videocassette with minimum of 3 songs and lyric or lead sheet if available. "Please include a brief biography/history of artist(s) and/or band, including musical training/education, performance experience, recording studio experience, discography and photos (if available)." Does not return material. Reports in 2-3 months.
Music: Mostly **alternative rock**, **artrock** and **contemporary instrumental/rock instrumental**; also **contemporary classical**, **world music**, **adult urban contemporary**, **smooth jazz**, **acid jazz**, **jazz/rock**, **ambient**, **electronic**, and **New Age**. Released *Shocking Blossom*, written and recorded by Electric Lotus on Tangent Records (art rock). Other artists include Andrew Batchelor.
Tips: "Take the time to pull together a quality cassette or CD demo with package/portfolio, including such relevant information as experience (on stage and in studio, etc.), education/training, biography, career goals, discography, photos, etc. Should be typed. We are *not* interested in generic sounding or 'straight ahead' music. We are seeking music that is innovative, pioneering and eclectic with a fresh, unique sound."

◯ TBS RECORDS, 611 N. Main St., Sweetwater TN 37874. (423)337-SONG. Fax: (423)337-7664. Owner (ballads, blues, rock, bluegrass, children's): Thomas B. Santelli. Vice President (ballads, blues, rock): Lucretia G. Santelli. A&R Department (R&B, ballads, rock): Julia L. Balsinger. Record company and record producer. Estab. 1995. Releases 4 singles, 4 LPs and 4 CDs/year. Pays 8% royalty (negotiable) to artists on contract; statutory rate to publisher per song on record.

How to Contact: Submit demo tape by mail. Unsolicited submissions are OK. Prefers cassette or DAT with 3 songs and lyric sheet. Does not return material. Reports in 2-3 months.
Music: Mostly **ballads, blues** and **rock**. Released *Hi Speed Banjo*, written and recorded by Tommy Santelli; "Little Brother," written and recorded by Joel Pilpilcher (ballad); and "No Hands," written and recorded by Joanie Woodby (children's), all on TBS Records.
Tips: "Know the business (no bull). Be a jack of all trades in the studio."

🌐 ☑ 🅿 **3RD STONE LTD.,** P.O. Box 8, Corby, Northants NM7 2XZ United Kingdom. (1536)202295. Fax: (1536)266246. Label Manager: Steve Kalidoski. Labels include Space Age Recordings and Them's Good Records. Record company and music publisher (Heavy Truth Music Publishing). Estab. 1987. Releases 6 singles, 6 LPs, 6 EPs and 20 CDs/year. Pays 50% of net receipts to artists on contract; statutory rate to publisher per song on record.
How to Contact: Submit demo tape by mail. Unsolicited submissions are OK. Prefers cassette or CD with 3-4 songs. "Include contact name and telephone number on CD/tape." SAE and IRC. Reports in 3 weeks.
Music: Mostly **alternative pop/ambient pop, space rock/post rock lo-fi** and **punk-melodic**; also **indie/ guitar bands, experimental electronic** and **psychedelic rock**. Released *Game Over*, written and recorded by Bark Psychosis on 3rd Stone (alternative/rock); *Forever Alien* (by Kember), recorded by Spectrum on Space Age (new electronica); and *Ext. Vacation* (by S.R. Sandall), recorded by Goober Patrol on Them's Good (punk). Other artists include Spacemen 3, Octal, Vanilla Pop, The Popguns, Mali Rain and No-Man.
Tips: "Send material stamped with your own strong identity. 3rd Stone Ltd. is a small, totally independent record label and publisher, signing and developing fledgling acts and looking to conclude world-wide licenses with their releases."

🍁 🔘 **THIRD WAVE PRODUCTIONS LTD.** P.O. Box 563, Gander Newfoundland A1V 2E1 Canada. (709)256-8009. Fax: (709)256-7411. Manager: Wayne Pittman. President: Arch Bonnell. Labels include Street Legal Records. Record company, music publisher, distributor and agent. Estab. 1986. Releases 2 singles, 2 LPs and 2 CDs/year. Pays negotiable royalty to artists on contract; statutory rate to publisher per song on record.
How to Contact: Submit demo tape by mail. Unsolicited submissions are OK. Prefers cassette, DAT and lyric sheet. SASE. Reports in 2 months.
Music: Mostly **folk/traditional, bluegrass** and **country**; also **pop, Irish** and **Christmas**. Published *Salt Beef Junkie*, written and recorded by Buddy Wasisname and Other Fellers (folk/traditional); *Newfoundland Bluegrass*, written and recorded by Crooked Stovepipe (bluegrass); and *Nobody Never Told Me*, written and recorded by The Psychobilly Cadillacs (rockabilly/country), all on Third Wave Productions. Other artists include Lee Vaughn.
Tips: "We are not really looking for songs but are always open to take on new artists who are interested in recording/producing an album. We market and distribute as well as produce albums. Not much need for 'songs' per se, except maybe country and rock/pop."

☑ 🅿 **THROWING STONES RECORDS**, P.O. Box 602, Columbus IN 47202. (812)372-6983. Fax: (812)372-3985. E-mail: tsr@ghp.net. Website: http://www.ghp.net/tsr. A&R, Artist Relations: Sandra Harris. Executive Producer (pop, blues, folk, acoustic): Suzanne Glass. Producer (rock, alternative): Paul Bultman. Assistant Producer (rock, hardcore, country, alternative): Jason Humphress. Record company, music publisher, record producer and management firm (Glass House Productions). Estab. 1995. Releases 10-12 singles, 1-5 EPs and 1-5 CDs/year. Pays negotiable royalty to artists on contract; "negotiable rate on our publishing, statutory to outside publishers."
How to Contact: Write first and obtain permission to submit. Prefers cassette or CD with picture, bio, play dates list, 3 songs and lyric sheet. "Do not call. You may e-mail. Please send stamped self-addressed postcard when writing for permission. Include goals, time commitment, etc. Tell us how much you are gigging." Does not return material. Reports in 1-3 months only if interested (varies with submission load).
Music: Mostly **alternative, acoustic (singer/songwriter), folk, acoustic rock (all types)** and **rock (mainstream, hard, metal, Christian, pop)**; also **blues/blues-rock, women artists** and **chorale/big band**. Does not want country. Released "Shake It Off" (by P. Ruffner), recorded by Tattoo Tribe (rock); and *No Flowers* (by Matt Askren), recorded by No Flowers (alternative), both on Throwing Stones; and *Start*

MARKETS THAT WERE listed in the 1999 edition of *Songwriter's Market* but do not appear this year are listed in the General Index with a notation explaining why they were omitted.

Smilin', written and recorded by Sally Webster on Family Connections Publishing (folk/children's). Other artists include Sacred Project, Swallow Tail, Fallen Empire and Suzanne Glass.

Tips: "Be professional, i.e., on time, easy to contact, able to be business-like when required, etc. We are looking for artists within 500 miles of our area. Most artists are signed to management contracts with our company, Glass House, before a full recording contract. A well developed song, unique singer and willingness to learn are most important."

THUMP RECORDS, INC., 3101 Pomona Blvd., Pomona CA 91768. (909)595-2144. Fax: (909)598-7028. E-mail: info@thumprecords.com. Website: http://www.thumprecords.com. President A&R: Bill Walker. Vice President of A&R and General Manager: Pebo Rodriguez. Labels include Thump Street. Record company and music publisher (Walk-Lo/ASCAP, On the Note/BMI). Estab. 1990. Releases 10 singles, 36 LPs, 6 EPs and 36 CDs/year. Pays 10% (negotiable) royalty to artists on contract; ¾ statutory rate to publisher per song on record.

How to Contact: Submit demo tape by mail. Unsolicited submissions are OK. Prefers cassette, lyric sheet, biography and 8×10 photo. SASE. Reports in 2-4 weeks.

Music: Mostly **dance**, **rap** and **ballads**; also **oldies**, **classic rock** and **Latin rock & soul**. Released "DJ Girl" (by Katalina). Other artists include Tierra, El Chicano and Malo.

Tips: "Provide Thump with positive upbeat music that has universal appeal."

TIME ART RECORDS, P.O. Box 87, Oak Lake, Manitoba R0M 1P0 Canada. (204)855-2929. Fax: (204)855-2197. E-mail: timeart@mb.sympatico.ca. President: Mike Hatfield. Record company. Estab. 1993. Staff size: 1. Releases 4-6 singles and 1 CD/year. Pays negotiable royalty to artists on contract; statutory rate to publisher per song on record.

Distributed by: Royalty Records, Page and EMI.

How to Contact: Write or call first and obtain permission to submit. Prefers cassette or CD with lyric sheet. Does not return material. Reports in 1-2 months.

Music: Mostly **country**. Released *You Oughta Know Love* and *Big News Back Home* (by various), both recorded by Curtis Grambo on Time Art (country).

Tips: "Send quality demos."

TOMMY BOY RECORDS, 902 Broadway, 13th Floor, New York NY 10010-6002. (212)388-8300. E-mail: mail@tommyboy.com. Website: http://www.tommyboy.com. A&R: Mr. Dave; Eddie O'Loughlin; Ian Steaman. Fax: (212)388-8400. Record company. Labels include Penalty Recordings, Outcaste Records, Timber and Tommy Boy Gospel.

Distributed by: WEA.

How to Contact: Call to obtain current demo submission policy.

Music: Released *Jock Jams Vol. 4*, recorded by various artists on Tommy Boy; and *N.O.R.E.*, recorded by Noreaga on Penalty. Other artists include Amber and Capone-N-Noreaga.

TON RECORDS, 6777 Hollywood Blvd., 3rd Floor, Hollywood CA 90028. (323)467-6002. Fax: (323)467-7737. E-mail: tonrecords@tonrecords.com. Website: http://www.tonrecords.com. Vice President: Jay Vasquez. Labels include 7″ collectors series and Ton Special Projects. Record company and record producer (RJ Vasquez). Estab. 1992. Releases 6-9 LPs, 1-2 EPs and 10-11 CDs/year. Pays negotiable royalty to artists on contract; statutory rate to publisher per song on record.

Distributed by: MS, Com Four, Rotz, Subterranean, Revelation, Get Hip, Impact, Page Canada and Disco Dial.

How to Contact: Submit demo tape by mail. Unsolicited submissions are OK. Prefers cassette or CD. SASE. Reports in 1 month.

Music: Mostly **new music**; also **hard new music**. Released *Intoxicated Birthday Lies*, recorded by shoegazer (punk rock); *The Good Times R Killing Me*, recorded by Top Jimmy (blues); and *Beyond Repair*, recorded by Vasoline Tuner (space rock), all on Ton Records. Other artists include Why? things burn, Hungry 5 and the Ramblers.

Tips: "Work as hard as we do."

TOPCAT RECORDS, P.O. Box 670234, Dallas TX 75367. (972)484-4141. Fax: (972)620-8333. E-mail: blueman@computek.net. Website: http://www.texasblues.com/topcat. President: Richard Chalk. Record company and record producer. Estab. 1991. Staff size: 1. Releases 3-4 CDs/year. Pays 10-15% royalty to artists on contract; statutory rate to publisher per song on record.

Distributed by: City Hall.

How to Contact: Call first and obtain permission to submit. Prefers cassette or CD. Does not return material. Reports in 1 month.

Music: Mostly **blues**, **swing** and **R&B**. Released *If You Need Me*, written and recorded by Robert Ealey (blues); *Texas Blueswomen* (by 3 Female Singers), recorded by various (blues/R&B); and *Jungle Jane*, written and recorded by Holland K. Smith (blues/swing), all on Topcat. Other artists include Grant Cook, Muddy Waters, Big Mama Thornton, Big Joe Turner, Geo. "Harmonica" Smith, J.B. Hutto and Bee Houston.

Tips: "Send me blues (fast, slow, happy, sad, etc.) or good blues oriented R&B. No pop."

☑ ⊘ TOUCHWOOD ZERO HOUR ENTERTAINMENT, (formerly Touchwood Records, LLC), 14 W. 23rd St., New York NY 10010. (212)337-3200. Fax: (212)337-3701. E-mail: cfinch@touchwood.c om. Website: http://www.touchwood.com. Director of A&R (pop, rock, R&B): Chris Finch. Managing Director (pop, jazz): Scott Schiff. Labels include After 9, Touchwood Classics and Before Dawn. Record company and music publisher (Touchwood Publishing). Estab. 1995. Staff size: 4. Releases 10 singles, 30 LPs, 20 EPs and 40 CDs/year. Pays 16.5% royalty to artist on contract; statutory rate to publisher per song on record.

Distributed by: ADA.

How to Contact: Write first and obtain permission to submit. Prefers CD. Does not return material. Reports in 2 months.

Music: Mostly **rock**, **popular** and **jazz**; also **R&B**, **cabaret** and **classical**. Released *Love Is the Key* (by Pele Kazir/Marvin Gunn/Bruce DeSchazer), recorded by Koko Blak (pop/R&B); *This Is the Way*, written and recorded by Eden White (pop), both on Touchwood; and *To Ella With Love* (by various artists), recorded by Ann Hampton Callaway on After 9 (jazz/cabaret). Other artists include Fraze, Neotone, Ann Hampton Callaway, Barbara Carrol, Frankie Laine, Christine Andreas and Billy Stritch.

Tips: "Do what comes naturally. Don't follow trends. Write from experience."

⊘ TRAC RECORD CO., 170 N. Maple, Fresno CA 93702. (209)255-1717. E-mail: tracsell@aol.com. Owner: Stan Anderson. Record company, record producer and music publisher (Sellwood Publishing/BMI). Estab. 1972. Staff size: 1. Releases 5 singles, 5 LPs and 2 CDs/year. Pays 13% royalty to artists on contract; statutory rate to publisher per song on record.

How to Contact: Submit demo tape by mail. Unsolicited submissions are OK. Prefers cassette or VHS videocassette with 2-3 songs and lyric sheet. "Demo must be clear and professionally recorded." SASE. Reports in 3 weeks.

Music: **Country**, all styles. Released *All Time Low* (by Jimmy Walker); *Cowboy Cadillac* (by Brian D. McArdle/Donna Moody); and *Southern Cracker Boy* (by Joanne Mears), all recorded by Jimmy Walker on TRAC Records (country). Other artists include Jessica James.

⊘ TREASURE COAST RECORDS (a division of Judy Welden Enterprises), 692 S.E. Port St. Lucie Blvd., Port St. Lucie FL 34984. Fax: (561)878-5755. E-mail: jwelden@flinet.com. Website: http://www.flin et.com/~jwelden. Labels include Heartfelt Records (Christian music only). President: Judy Welden. Record company, music publisher (Songrite Creations Productions/BMI, Sine Qua Non Music/ASCAP) and record producer. Estab. 1992. Staff size: 1. Releases 36 singles and 3 CDs/year. Pays 10-15% royalty to artists on contract; statutory rate to publisher per song on record.

Distributed by: World Records (Canada) and V.P.R. Distributing (Belgium, Germany, Holland).

How to Contact: Submit demo tape by mail. Unsolicited submissions are OK. "Send only your best unpublished songs (2 or 3 max), bio, press, number of songs written, releases, awards, etc." Prefers cassette with 2 or 3 songs and lyric sheet. SASE. Reports in 2-3 weeks.

Music: Mostly **contemporary country**, **crossover**, **traditional country** and most types of **Christian** music (from contemporary to country gospel). Released *Mitch Chanler*, written and recorded by Mitch Chanler (country/rock); and *Country Treasures #8*, written and recorded by various artists (compilation CD) (country), both on Treasure Coast; and *Heartfelt Hits #4*, written and recorded by various artists (compilation CD) on Heartfelt Records (country pop).

Tips: "We've had nine #1 songs on the indie charts in an 18-month period."

 TRIPLE X RECORDS, P.O. Box 862529, Los Angeles CA 90086-2529. (213)221-2204. Fax: (213)221-2778. E-mail: duffxxx@usa.net. Website: http://www.triple-x.com. A&R Director: Bruce Duff

---

FOR BOOKS ON THE CRAFT AND BUSINESS of songwriting, check out the website for Writer's Digest Books at http://www.writersdigest.com.

(pop, goth, rock). Co-owner (punk, skate, ska, reggae): Dean Naleway. Record company. Estab. 1986. Staff size: 3. Releases 25 CDs/year. Royalties not disclosed.
Distributed by: Navarre.
How to Contact: "See our web page for submission policy." Does not return material. Reports in 2 months.
Music: Mostly **rock**, **industrial/goth** and **punk**; also **blues**, **roots** and **noise**. Released *Everybody Knows the Monkey* (by Chris Bailey), recorded by Saints on Amsterdam (rock); *Trancendental Medication*, written and recorded by Inger Lorre on Triple X (rock); and *Songs of Betrayal* (by Johnny Indovina), recorded by Human Drama on Hollows Hill (rock). Other artists include Dickies and Epperley.
Tips: "Looking for self-contained units that generate their own material and are willing and able to tour."

☑ ◙ **TROPIKAL PRODUCTIONS**, (formerly Watusi Productions), 516 Storrs, Rockwall TX 75087. Phone/fax: (972)771-3797. E-mail: tropikalproductions@juno.com. Website: http://www.mammothartists. com/watusi. Producers: J. Towry (world beat, reggae, ethnic, jazz); Jembe (reggae, world beat, ethnic); Arik Towry (ska, pop, ragga, rock). Labels include World Beatnik Records. Record company and record producer (Jimi Towry). Estab. 1983. Staff size: 4. Releases 4 singles, 3 LPs, 4 EPs and 3 CDs/year. Pays negotiable royalty to artists on contract; statutory rate to publisher per song on record.
Distributed by: Midwest Records, Southwest Wholesale and Reggae OneLove.
How to Contact: Submit demo tape by mail. Unsolicited submissions are OK. Prefers cassette, DAT or VHS videocassette with 3 songs and lyric sheet. SASE. Reports in 2 weeks.
Music: Mostly **world beat, reggae** and **ethnic**; also **jazz, hip-hop/dance** and **pop**. Released *Cool Runner* (by Jembe), recorded by Watusi (reggae/world beat); "Big Up" (by Ragga D/Jembe), recorded by Ragga D (dancehall reggae); and *Standby* (by Jembe), recorded by WAVE (Latin jazz), all on World Beatnik Records. Other artists include Jimi Towry, Wisdom Ogbor (Nigeria), Joe Lateh (Ghana), Dee Dee Cooper, Ras Lyrix (St. Croix), Ras Kumba (St. Kitts), Gary Mon, Darbo (Gambia), Ricki Malik (Jamaica), Arik Miles, Narte's (Hawaii), Gavin Audagnotti (South Africa) and Bongo (Trinidad).

◙ **TRUSTY RECORDS**, 8771 Rose Creek Rd., Nebo KY 42441. (502)249-3194. E-mail: trusty@wko.c om. Website: http://www.wko.com/business/trusty/trusty.htm. President: Elsie Childers. Record company and music publisher (Trusty Publications/BMI). Member CMAA, CMA. Estab. 1960. Releases 2 CDs/ year. Pays negotiable royalty to artists on contract; statutory rate to publisher per song on record.
How to Contact: Submit demo tape by mail. Unsolicited submissions are OK. Prefers cassette with 2-4 songs and lead sheet. Does not return material. "We will contact you if interested in your songs or artist potential. No further correspondence will be made."
Music: Mostly **country, blues, contemporary Christian, country Christian, easy listening, gospel, MOR, soul** and **top 40/pop**. Released *We Can*, written and recorded by Just Cause on E.T.C. Records; and *Still Water* (by Steve Holland/Ken Dall), recorded by Still Water on Still Water Records. Other artists include Noah Williams, Barry Russell, Barry Howard and Billy Ray Harrison.

◙ **TVT RECORDS**, 23 E. Fourth St., New York NY 10003. (212)979-6410. Fax: (212)979-6489. Website: http://www.tvtrecords.com. Director of A&R: Adam Shore. Labels include Tee Vee Toons, Wax Trax! Records, TVT Soundtrax, 1001 Sundays, Building and Fuel Records. Record company and music publisher (TVT Music). Estab. 1986. Releases 25 singles, 20 12″ singles, 40 LPs, 5 EPs and 40 CDs/year. Pays varying royalty to artists on contract; statutory rate to publisher per song on record.
How to Contact: Send e-mail to demo-help@tvtrecords.com to receive information on how to submit your demo.
Music: Mostly **alternative rock, rap** and **techno**; also **jazz/R&B**. Released *Perversion*, recorded by Gravity Kills; *Still Life*, recorded by The Connells; and *Happy Birthday, Sabo!*, recorded by Royal Fingerbowl, all on TVT Records. Other artists include Catherine, DNote, EnEsch, Nine Inch Nails and Birdbrain.
Tips: "We look for seminal, ground breaking, genre-defining artists of all types with compelling live presentation. Our quest is not for hit singles but for enduring important artists."

◖ **28 RECORDS**, 19700 NW 86 Court, Miami FL 33015-6917. Phone/fax: (305)829-8142. E-mail: rec28@aol.com. President/CEO/A&R: Eric Diaz. Record company. Estab. 1994. Staff size: 1. Releases 2 LPs and 4 CDs/year. Pays 12% royalty to artists on contract; statutory rate to publisher per song on record.
Distributed by: Rock Bottom-USA.
How to Contact: Submit demo tape by mail. Unsolicited submissions are OK. Prefers cassette, VHS videocassette or CD (if already released on own label for possible distribution or licensing deals). If possible send promo pack and photo. "Please put Attn: A&R on packages." Does not return material. Reports in 6 weeks.
Music: Mostly **hard rock/modern rock, metal** and **alternative**; also **punk** and **death metal**. Released

Julian Day, recorded by Helltown's Infamous Vandal (modern/hard rock); *Near Life Experience*, written and recorded by Eric Knight (modern/hard rock); and *Mantra*, recorded by Derek Cintron (modern rock), all on 28 Records.

Tips: "Be patient and ready for the long haul. We strongly believe in nurturing you, the artist/songwriter. If you're willing to do what it takes, and have what it takes, we will do whatever it takes to get you to the next level. We are looking for artists to develop. We are a very small label but we are giving the attention that is a must for a new band as well as developed and established acts. Give us a call."

⊘ UNIVERSAL RECORDS, 1755 Broadway, 7th Floor, New York NY 10019. (212)373-0600. Fax: (212)373-0688. A&R Director: Tom Lewis. A&R Assistant/Coordinator: Jenny Jacobs. Universal City office: 70 Universal City Plaza, 3rd Floor, Universal City CA 91608. (818)777-1000. Contact: A&R Director. Labels include Uptown Records, Mojo Records, Republic Records, Bystorm Records and Gut Reaction Records. Record company.
  • As a result of the 1998 PolyGram and Universal merger, Universal is the world's largest record company.
How to Contact: Universal Records in California does not accept unsolicited submissions. The New York office *only* allows you to call first and obtain permission to submit.
Music: Released *Lost*, recorded by Eightball on Suave House; and *Spiders*, recorded by Space on Gut Reaction Records. Other artists include Boyz II Men and Merrill Bainbridge.

☑ ○ UNIVERSAL-ATHENA RECORDS (UAR Records), Box 1264, 6020 W. Pottstown Rd., Peoria IL 61654-1264. (309)673-5755. Fax: (309)673-7636. E-mail: uarltd@unitedcyber.com. Website: http://www.unitedcyber.com/uarltd. A&R Director: Jerry Hanlon. Record company and music publisher (Jerjoy Music/BMI). Estab. 1978. Staff size: 1. Releases 1-2 singles and 1 LP/year. Pays standard royalty to artists on contract; statutory rate to publisher for each record sold.
How to Contact: Write first and obtain permission to submit. Prefers cassette with 4-8 songs and lyric sheet. SASE. Reports in 2 weeks.
Music: Mostly **country**. Released *Oowee-Oowee*, written and recorded by Steve Axley; *Mama Was A Go-Go Girl*, written and recorded by Clint Miller; and *I Spy*, written and recorded by Eddie Grew, all on UAR Records (country). Other artists include Dan Follano.

☑ ⊘ VAI DISTRIBUTION, 109 Wheeler Ave., Pleasantville NY 10570. (914)769-3691. Fax: (914)769-5407. President: Ernest Gilbert. Record company, video label and distributor. Estab. 1983. Pays negotiable royalty to artists on contract; other amount to publisher per song on record.
How to Contact: Does not accept unsolicited material.
Music: Mostly **opera (classical vocal)**, **classical (orchestral)** and **classical instrumental/piano**. Released *Susannah* (by Carlisle Floyd), recorded by New Orleans Opera Orchestra and Chorus, on VAI Audio. Other artists include Jon Vickers, Rosalyn Tureck, Evelyn Lear and Thomas Stewart.

⊘ VALTEC PRODUCTIONS, P.O. Box 2642, Santa Maria CA 93457. (805)934-8400. Owner/Producers: J. Anderson and J. Valenta. Record company and record producer (Joe Valenta). Estab. 1986. Releases 20 singles, 15 LPs and 10 CDs/year. Pays negotiable royalty to artists on contract; statutory rate to publisher per song on record.
How to Contact: Submit demo tape by mail. Unsolicited submissions are OK. Prefers DAT with 4 songs and lyric sheet. Does not return material. Reports in 1-2 months.
Music: Mostly **country**, **top 40** and **A/C**; also **rock**. Released *Just Me* (by Joe Valenta) and *Hold On* (by Joe Valenta/J. Anderson), both recorded by Joe Valenta (top 40); and *Time Out (For Love)* (by Joe Valenta), recorded by Marty K. (country), all on Valtec Records.

♈ ⊘ THE VERVE GROUP, Worldwide Plaza, 825 Eighth Ave., 26th Floor, New York NY 10019. (212)333-8000. Fax: (212)333-8194. Senior Vice President of A&R: Richard Seidel. Los Angeles office: 11150 Santa Monica Blvd., 11th Floor, Los Angeles CA 90025. (310)996-7900. Fax: (310)477-7622. Record company.
  • Verve's Shirley Horn won a 1998 Grammy Award for Best Jazz Vocal Performance; and Herbie

---

⚫ 🌐 SENDING TO A COUNTRY other than your own? Be sure to send International Reply Coupons (IRCs) instead of stamps for replies or return of your materials.

Hancock won for Best Jazz Instrumental Performance, Individual or Group and Best Instrumental Arrangement with Accompanying Vocals.

How to Contact: Verve does not accept unsolicited submissions.

Music: Released *Measures of the Night*, recorded by Will Downing & Gerald Albright on Verve Records. Other artists include Mark Whitefield and Antonio Carlos Jobim.

N O VILLAGE RECORDS, 35 W. Fourth St., Suite 687, New York NY 10012. (212)998-5398. Fax: (212)995-4560. General Manager (alternative): Patrick Sullivan. Director (all styles): Catherine Moore. A&R: Gabrielle Rosen (alternative); Amanda Hale (alternative). Record company. Estab. 1988. Staff size: 27. Releases 3 singles, 3 LPs, 1 EP and 3 CDs/year. Pays negotiable royalty to artists on contract; negotiable rate to publisher per song on record.

Distributed by: Big Daddy.

How to Contact: Submit demo tape by mail. Unsolicited submissions are OK. Prefers CD with 2 songs, lyric sheet and cover letter. SASE. Reports in 3-6 months.

Music: Mostly **alternative**, **hip-hop** and **rock**. Does not want classical. Released *Massive Eclipse* (by Chris Allison/Makai Sakai), recorded by Conductor Z (drum & bass); and *Sounds of the Unknown*, written and recorded by Xandy Barry (alternative), both on Village Records; and *Ear to the Street* (by J. Saldaria/D. Jackson), recorded by Invisible Culture on MBT (alternative).

O VIRGIN RECORDS, 338 N. Foothill Rd., Beverly Hills CA 90210. (310)278-1181. Fax: (310)278-6231. A&R Director (hip-hop, R&B): Alexander Mejia. Vice Presidents, A&R: Danny Goodwin (rock); Gemma Corfield (pop, R&B); Andy Factor (alternative, rock); Todd Roberts (electronica). Vice President, A&R/Special Projects: John Wooler. New York office: 304 Park Ave. S., New York NY 10010. (212)253-3100. Fax: (212)253-3099. Senior Director of A&R: David Wolter. Executive Vice President, A&R: Keith Wood. Senior Vice President, A&R: Patrick Moxey. A&R Director: Collin Stanback. Website: http://www.virginrecords.com. Labels include Rap-A-Lot Records, Pointblank Records, SoulPower Records, AWOL Records, Astralwerks Records, Cheeba Sounds, Caroline Records and Noo Trybe Records. Record company.

Distributed by: EMD.

• Virgin Records' artist Lenny Kravitz won a 1998 Grammy Award for Best Male Rock Vocal Performance.

How to Contact: Virgin Records does not accept recorded material or lyrics unless submitted by a reputable industry source. "If your act has received positive press or airplay on prior independent releases, we welcome your written query. Send a letter of introduction accompanied by all pertinent artist information. Do not send a tape until requested. All unsolicited materials will be returned unopened."

Music: Released *Tribute*, recorded by Yanni; *Adore*, recorded by The Smashing Pumpkins; and *Bridges to Babylon*, recorded by The Rolling Stones, all on Virgin Records. Other artists include Tina Turner, The Verve, David Bowie, Isaac Hayes, Enigma, dc Talk and Boz Scaggs.

Y O VOKES MUSIC RECORD CO., P.O. Box 12, New Kensington PA 15068. (412)335-2775. President: Howard Vokes. Labels include Country Boy Records. Record company, booking agency (Vokes Booking Agency) and music publisher (Vokes Music Publishing). Releases 8 singles and 5 LPs/year. Pays 2½-4½% song royalty to artists and songwriters on contract.

• Mr. Whittaker is an inductee of the Country Music Organizations of America's American Eagle Awards' Hall of Fame.

How to Contact: Submit cassette only and lead sheet. SASE. Reports in 2 weeks.

Music: Mostly **country**, **bluegrass** and **gospel-old time**. Released "Cherokee Trail Of Tears" and "City Of Strangers," recorded by Johnny Eagle Feather; and "Portrait Of An Angel," recorded by Lenny Gee, all on Vokes Records.

O WALL STREET MUSIC, 1189 E. 14 Mile Rd., Birmingham MI 48009. (248)646-2054. Fax: (248)646-1957. E-mail: wallstmus@aol.com. A&R Director: Joe Sanders. Record company, record producer and music publisher (Burgundy Bros.). Estab. 1985. Releases 6 singles, 4 12" singles, 4 LPs, 4 EPs and 8 CDs/year. Pays 8-14% royalty to artists on contract; statutory rate to publisher per song on record.

How to Contact: Submit demo tape by mail. Unsolicited submissions are OK. Prefers cassette or VHS videocassette with 2 songs, photo, bio, performance history and sales history. "Label all items completely." Does not return material. Reports only if interested.

Music: Mostly **urban**, **rap** and **adult contemporary**; also **alternative**, **dance** and **gospel**. Released "Taste the Flava" (by Mike Buckholtz), recorded by Soulism; "Ooh LaLa" (by Lester Marlin), and *Nasty Sexual Thangs* (by Darell Campbell), both recorded by Simply Black, all on Wall Street Music. Other artists include Drueada and ANG.

Tips: "The most important attribute we look for is a track record of local performance and any product sales. We are motivated by artists who perform often and have produced and marketed their music locally. You should keep us informed of your success in the industry as a way of helping us keep an eye on you."

○ **THE WANSTAR GROUP**, P.O. Box 6283, Charleston SC 29405. (803)853-1962. Fax: (803)853-7224. E-mail: scolstoxl_111@hotmail.com. Website: http://www.wanstargroup.com. President/Executive Producer: Samuel W. Colston III. Associate Producer (R&B): Wanda Celston. Associate Producer (hip hop): Michael Falls. Labels include Tye Records (rap), Chela Records (R&B/hip-hop) and Surge Records (inspirational). Record company, music publisher (Out On A Limb Publishing/BMI), production house and record producer (S. Colston III). Estab. 1990. Staff size: 1. Releases 3 singles and 2 CDs/year. Pays 7% royalty to artists on contract; negotiable amount to publisher per song on record.
How to Contact: Submit demo tape by mail. Unsolicited submissions are OK. Prefers cassette or VHS videocassette with 3 songs. Does not return material. Reports in 3 weeks "by phone, fax or e-mail."
Music: Mostly **R&B**, **latin/pop** and **hip-hop**; also **inspirational** and **contemporary gospel**. Released *Personal Savior* (by S. Colstoni/D. Siler), recorded by Dena Siler on Surge (inspirational); and "Lyrics This Thick" (by S. Colstoni/T. Seabrook), recorded by T. Sorbrook on Tye Records (rap).

[N] ○ **WAREHOUSE CREEK RECORDING CORP.**, P.O. Box 102, Franktown, VA 23354. (757)442-6883. Fax: (757)442-3662. E-mail: warehouse@esva.net. Website: http://www.esva.net/~wareho use/. President: Billy Sturgis. Record company, music publisher (Bayford Dock Music) and record producer (Billy Sturgis). Estab. 1993. Staff size: 1. Releases 11 singles and 1 CD/year. Pays negotiable royalty to artists on contract; statutory rate to publisher per song on record.
Distributed by: City Hall Records.
How to Contact: Submit demo tape by mail. Unsolicited submissions are OK. Prefers cassette, CD, DAT or VHS videocassette with lyric sheet. Does not return material. Reports in 1 month.
Music: Mostly **R&B**, **blues** and **gospel**. Released *Greyhound Bus* (by Arthur Crudup); *Going Down in Style* (by Tim Drummond); and *Something On My Mind* (by George Crudup), all recorded by Crudup Brothers on Warehouse Creek Records (blues).

☑ ⬤ ⊘ **WARNER BROS. RECORDS**, 3300 Warner Blvd., 4th Floor, N. Bldg., Burbank CA 91505-4694. (818)846-9090. Fax: (818)953-3423. Vice President of A&R (urban): Alison Ball-Gabriel. New York office: 75 Rockefeller Plaza, New York NY 10019. (212)275-4500. Fax: (212)275-4595. Vice President of A&R: Joe McEwen. Nashville office: 20 Music Square E., Nashville TN 37203. (615)748-8000. Fax: (615)214-1523. Website: http://www.wbr.com. Senior Vice President of A&R: Paige Levy. A&R Director: Danny Kee. Labels include American Recordings, Eternal Records, Imago Records, Mute Records, Giant Records, Malpaso Records and Maverick Records. Record company.
Distributed by: WEA.
● Warner Bros.' Béla Fleck & the Flecktones won a 1998 Grammy Award for Best Instrumental Composition.
How to Contact: Warner Bros. Records does not accept unsolicited material. All unsolicited material will be returned unopened. Those interested in having their tapes heard should establish a relationship with a manager, publisher or attorney that has an ongoing relationship with Warner Bros. Records.
Music: Released *Van Halen 3*, recorded by Van Halen; *Evita* (soundtrack); and *Dizzy Up the Girl*, recorded by Goo Goo Dolls, both on Warner Bros. Records. Other artists include Faith Hill, Tom Petty & the Heartbreakers, Jeff Foxworthy, Porno For Pyros, Travis Tritt, Yellowjackets, Bela Fleck and the Flecktones, Al Jarreau, Joshua Redmond, Little Texas and Curtis Mayfield.

☑ ○ **WATERDOG RECORDS**, (formerly Whitehouse Records), 329 W. 18th St., #313, Chicago IL 60616-1120. (312)421-7499. Fax: (312)421-1848. E-mail: wthouse@housedog.com. Website: http://www.housedog.com. Label Manager: Rob Gillis. Labels include Whitehouse Records. Record company. Estab. 1994. Staff size: 1. Releases 1 EP and 6 CDs/year. Pays negotiable royalty to artists on contract; statutory rate to publisher per song on record.
Distributed by: Big Daddy Music.
How to Contact: Write first and obtain permission to submit. Prefers cassette or CD. Include cover letter, brief bio, itinerary and picture. Does not return material. Reports in 3 weeks.
Music: Mostly **rock**, **pop** and **folk**. Released "The Master Thief Has Been Murdered" (by Ralph Covert), recorded by The Bad Examples; "LNW (temporary love)" (by Andy Perostianis), recorded by Middle 8; and "When the Ends Don't Meet," written and recorded by Peter Bernas, all on Waterdog Records. Other artists include MysteryDriver, Joel Frankel, Bucky Halker, Al Rose, Coin, The Good and Spelunkers.
Tips: "We are primarily interested in artists who write their own material and perform live regularly."

WESTPARK MUSIC - RECORDS, PRODUCTION & PUBLISHING, P.O. Box 260227, Rathenauplatz 4, 50515 Cologne Germany. Phone: (49)221 247644. Fax: (49)221 231819. E-mail: westparc@aol.com. Website: http://www.westparkmusic.com. Contact: Ulli Hetscher. Record company and music publisher. Estab. 1986. Staff size: 2. Releases 3-4 singles and 10-12 CDs/year. Pays 9-18% royalty to artists on contract.

Distributed by: BMG Ariola and Indigo.

How to Contact: Write first and obtain permission to submit or submit demo tape by mail. Unsolicited submissions are OK. Prefers cassette with 5-6 songs and lyric sheets. Does not return material. Reports in 3-4 months.

Music: Everything apart from mainstream-pop, jazz, classical, country and hard rock/metal. "The only other criterion is: we simply should love it." Released *Passions For Klezmer*, recorded by Helmut Eisel (klezmer); *1848*, written and recorded by Rolly Brings (folk/pop); and *Guds Speleman*, recorded by Garmarna (world), all on Westpark. Other artists include Salsa Picante, Touch of Flamenco and Soul Cats.

Tips: "Check website first, if possible. Don't send country, mainstream rock/pop or MOR. Mark cassettes clearly. Save yourself money by sending just the CD and booklet (no box and no tray). Don't include stamps (we cannot use them). Send e-mail with brief description first."

   WHIRLYBIRD RECORDS, INC., 28 Decatur Ave., Annapolis MD 21403. (410)269-7651. Fax: (410)974-8362. E-mail: info@whirlybird-records.com. Website: http://www.whirlybird-records.com. Vice President of A&R: Simeon Coxe. Labels include Sybarite Records and Confusion Records. Record company and record producer (Whirlybird Productions, Inc.). Estab. 1997. Releases 3 singles, 6 LPs, 3 EPs and 6 CDs/year. Pays negotiable royalty to artists on contract; statutory rate to publisher per song on record.

Distributed by: "Will supply upon request."

• This company is noted for releasing electrospacepunkfunkdancerockmixjazzmojo. They won the Printing Industry of America Award of Excellence for the Silver Apples European tour poster.

How to Contact: Write first and obtain permission to submit a demo. Prefers cassette, CD or DAT with 3 songs and lyric sheet. Does not return material. Reports in 4-6 weeks.

Music: Mostly **experimental rock** and **electronic**; also **punkfunkspacerok**. Released *Beacon*, written and recorded by Silverabbles (rock); *Havy Baubaus*, written and recorded by Obliterati (rock); and *Synjasé*, written and recorded by Jake Bell (electronic), all on Whirlybird Records.

Tips: "Make me scratch my head."

  **WILD WHIRLED MUSIC GROUP**, 600 W. Dunlap, Phoenix AZ 85021-3527. (602)870-1788. Fax: (602)870-4165. E-mail: wwmg@amug.org. Website: http://www.amug.org/~wwmg. A&R: David Hilker. Labels include Fervor Records. Record company and music publisher (Mt. Pilot Music/BMI). Estab. 1990. Staff size: 3. Releases 2 CDs/year. Pays negotiable royalty to artists on contract; statutory rate to publisher per song on record.

Distributed by: Impact Music and Internet.

How to Contact: Submit demo tape by mail. Unsolicited submissions are OK. Prefers cassette, CD or DAT with 2 songs, lyric sheet, cover letter and press clippings. "Master quality demos, please." Does not return material. Reports in 4-6 weeks.

Music: Mostly **rap/hip-hop**, **R&B** and **rock/alternative**; also **country**. Released *Cooler Shade of Jazz*, written and recorded by John Costello on Fervor (smooth jazz); *Pure Bliss* (by London/Costello/Hilker), recorded by London on Blisstunes (R&B); and *Musicians For St. Mary's*, written and recorded by various artists of Fervor (R&B/jazz). Other artists include Phunklogistix, Dark Half and Mark Long.

Tips: "Send only your best work. Always looking for superb vocalists."

 WINDHAM HILL RECORDS, 8750 Wilshire Blvd., 3rd Floor, Beverly Hills CA 90211. (310)358-4800. Fax: (310)358-4804. Website: http://www.windham.com. New York office: 1540 Broadway, New

FOR EXPLANATIONS OF THESE SYMBOLS,
SEE THE INSIDE FRONT AND BACK COVERS OF THIS BOOK.

York NY 10036. Labels include Private Music, Windham Hill Jazz, Living Music, Peak Records, High Street Records and Dancing Cat Records. Record company.
Distributed by: BMG.
How to Contact: Windham Hill Records does not accept unsolicited submissions.
Music: Released *Celtic Christmas III*, recorded by various artists; *The Gift*, recorded by Jim Brickman; and *Conversations With God*, recorded by various artists, all on Windham Hill Records. Other artists include David Arkenstone, Patrick Cassidy, John Gorka, Patty Larkin, Liz Story, Keola Beamer, The Nylons, Nightnoise and Yanni.

■ WOODRICH RECORDS, P.O. Box 38, Lexington AL 35648. (205)247-3983. President: Woody Richardson. Record company, music publisher (Woodrich Publishing Co./BMI, Mernee Music/ASCAP and Tennessee Valley Music/SESAC) and record producer (Woody Richardson). Estab. 1959. Releases 12 singles and 12 LPs/year. Pays 10% royalty to artists on contract; statutory rate to publisher per song on record.
How to Contact: Submit demo tape by mail. Unsolicited submissions are OK. Prefers cassette with 4 songs and lyric sheet. "Be sure to send a SASE (not a card) with sufficient return postage." Reports in 2 weeks. "We prefer a good studio demo."
Music: Mostly **country**; also **gospel**, **comedy**, **bluegrass**, **rock** and **jazz**. Released *Till the Last Star Falls* (by Ricky L. Holden), recorded by Lenaye Pearson, and *If I Were to Fall in Love* (by Frank Kiley), recorded by Ray R. Jones, both on Woodrich (country); and *Wa Copenhagen*, written and recorded by Johnny Russo on WIR (jazz).
Tips: "Use a good studio with full band and vocals. Don't send a huge package. A business envelope will do. It's better to send a cassette *not in a box*."

☑ ⊘ WORD RECORDS & MUSIC, 3319 West End Ave., Suite 200, Nashville TN 37203-1074. (615)385-9673. Fax: (615)292-0606. Website: http://www.wordrecords.com. Director of A&R: Bubba Smith. Record company. Labels include Myrrh, Magnatone and Integrity.
Distributed by: Sony.
How to Contact: Word Records does not accept unsolicited submissions.
Music: Released *Blaze*, recorded by Code of Ethics; *Steady On*, recorded by Point of Grace; and *Past the Edges*, recorded by Chris Rice, all on Word.

☑ ⊘ WORK GROUP, 2100 Colorado Ave., Santa Monica CA 90404. (310)449-2666. Fax: (310)449-2095. New York office: 550 Madison Ave., 24th Floor, New York NY 10022. (212)833-8236. Fax: (212)833-4389. Website: http://www.workgroupnet.com. Labels include Clean Slate Records. Record company.
Distributed by: Sony.
How to Contact: Work Group does not accept unsolicited submissions.
Music: Released *Sun Machine*, recorded by Morley; *Siren*, recorded by Heather Nova; and *Desireless*, recorded by Eagle Eye Cherry, all on Work. Other artists include Mary Lou Lord, Youssou N' Dour, the Mighty Blue Kings, Cree Summer, Geneva, Andrew Darff, Jennifer Lopez, Dan Bern and Protein.

⊞ ⊕ ⊘ WORKERS PLAYTIME MUSIC CO., 64 Mount Grove Rd., London N5-2LT England. Phone/fax: (44)171-359-2232. E-mail: info@workers-mc.demon.co.uk. Head Honcho: Bill Gilliam. Record company. Estab. 1984. Staff size: 3. Releases 4 LPs, 4 EPs and 11 CDs/year. Pays negotiable royalty to artists on contract; statutory rate to publisher per song on record.
Distributed by: Pinnacle.
How to Contact: Submit demo tape by mail. Unsolicited submissions are OK. Prefers cassette, CD, DAT or PAL videocassette. SAE and IRC. Reports in 3 weeks.
Music: Mostly **political rock/dance** and **reissues**. Does not want jazz. Released *The Bloated Vegas Years*, written and recorded by Dr. Bison (rock); and *On thé Couch With . . .*, written and recorded by Serious Drinking, both on Workers Playtime Music.

⊞ ⊠ ⊘ WORLDWIDE RECORDINGS LIMITED, Box 38722, North Vancouver, British Columbia V7L 4T7 Canada. E-mail: info@worldrecords.com. Website: http://www.worldrecords.com. President: Jim Rota. Record company, music publisher, and Internet search engine. Estab. 1995. Staff size: 5. Releases 200 CDs/year.
How to Contact: Write first to obtain permission to submit, but we only accept packaged CDs, not cassette tapes. Prefers press kit, reviews and contact info. "If you have Internet access, please read the following page before sending CDs: http://www.worldrecords.com/aandr/index.html." Does not return material. Reports in 3 months.

Music: Mostly **rock**, **blues** and **jazz**; also **world**, **country** and **folk**. Released *Volumes I, II & III*, written and recorded by various artists on Worldwide Recordings Limited. Other artists include The Unified Theorists, Colourise, Ghost Like Sun, Daniel Rhodes, Shakamoraine, Moon Soup, Lyrical Eaze and others.

Tips: "Be patient. We promote each artist for free at our website which receives over 100,000 visitors per year. We create compilation CDs each year with those artists who sign our licensing and shipping agreement that gives us a 20% commission on deals we bring to the table, but, because we promote a lot of independent artists, we don't have the resources or interest in producing any one of them."

X.R.L. RECORDS/MUSIC, White House Farm, Stropshire TF9 4HA England. Phone: (01630)647374. Fax: (01630)647612. International A&R Manager: Xavier Lee. UK A&R Manager: Cathrine Lee. Labels include Swoop, Zarg Records, Genouille, Pogo and Check Records. Record company, record producer and music publisher (Le Matt Music, Lee Music, R.T.F.M. and Pogo Records). Member MPA, PPL, PRS, MCPS. Estab. 1972. Staff size: 11. Releases 30 12″ singles, 20 LPs and 20 CDs/year. Pays negotiable royalty to artists on contract; negotiable rate to publisher for each record sold. Royalties paid to US songwriters and artists through US publishing or recording affiliate.

Distributed by: Lematt Music.

How to Contact: Submit demo tape by mail. Unsolicited submissions are OK. Prefers CD, cassette, DAT or VHS 625 PAL standard videocassette with 1-3 songs and lyric sheet. Include bio and still photos. SAE and IRC. Reports in 6 weeks.

Music: Mostly **pop/top 40**; also **bluegrass**, **blues**, **country**, **dance-oriented**, **easy listening**, **MOR**, **progressive**, **R&B**, **'50s rock**, **disco**, **new wave**, **rock** and **soul**. Released "Borstal" (by M.J. Lawson), recorded by Husa on Swoop (rock blues); *Winter Time*, written and recorded by Sight 'N' Sound on Check (MOR); and *No Faith*, written and recorded by Suburban Studs on Pogo (punk). Other artists include Nightmare, Orphan, The Chromatics, Mike Sheriden and the Nightriders, Johnny Moon, Dead Fish, Sight 'N' Sound and Mush.

Tips: "Be original."

XEMU RECORDS, 34 W. 17th St., 5th Floor, New York NY 10011. (212)807-0290. Fax: (212)807-0583. E-mail: xemu@xemu.com. Website: http://www.xemu.com. Vice President A&R: Dr. Claw. Record company. Estab. 1992. Staff size: 1. Releases 4 CDs/year. Pays 11% royalty to artists on contract; statutory rate to publisher per song on record.

Distributed by: Sumthing Distribution.

How to Contact: Write first and obtain permission to submit. Prefers cassette with 3 songs. Does not return material. Reports in 2 months.

Music: Mostly **alternative**. Released *My March*, recorded by Poets & Slaves; *The Side Effects of Napalm*, recorded by The Neanderthal Spongecake; and *Top Dead Center*, recorded by Scary Chicken, all on Xemu Records (alternative rock). Other artists include Malvert P. Redd, Death Sandwich and Baby-Face Finster.

YAB YUM RECORDS, 1635 N. Cahenga Blvd., 6th Floor, Los Angeles CA 90028. (323)860-1520. Fax: (323)860-1537. A&R: Michael McQuarn. Record company.

Distributed by: Elektra Entertainment.

How to Contact: Submit demo tape by mail. Unsolicited submissions are OK. Any format accepted.

YELLOW JACKET RECORDS, 10303 Hickory Valley, Ft. Wayne IN 46835. E-mail: alstraten@aol.com. President: Allan Straten. Record company and music publisher (Hickory Valley Music). Estab. 1985. Staff size: 3. Releases 8-10 singles, 1 LP and 1 CD/year. Pays 10% royalty to artists on contract; statutory rate to publisher per song on record.

How to Contact: Submit demo tape by mail. Unsolicited submissions are OK. Prefers cassette with 3-4 songs and typed lyric sheet. Does not return material. Reports in 3-4 weeks.

Music: Mostly **country** and **MOR**. Released "She's My X and I Know Y" (by D. Crisman/S. Grogg/A. Straten), "Kisa Marie" (by S. Grogg/A. Straten) and "She's My Number One Fan" (by R. Hartman/S. Grogg/A. Straten), all recorded by Tom Woodard on Pharoah Records. Other artists include Roy Allan, Mike Vernaglia, Rick Hartman and Darin Crisman.

Tips: "Be professional. Be prepared to rewrite. When sending material use 6×9 envelope—no staples."

OPENNESS TO SUBMISSIONS: ☐ beginners; ☑ beginners and experienced; ☑ experienced only; ☑ industry referrals only.

ℕ ⬛ YOUNG COUNTRY RECORDS/PLAIN COUNTRY RECORDS, P.O. Box 5412, Buena Park CA 90620. (619)245-2920. Owner: Leo J. Eiffert, Jr. Labels include Eiffert Records and Napoleon Country Records. Record company, music publisher (Young Country Music Publishing Co./BMI, Eb-Tide Music/BMI) and record producer (Leo J. Eiffert, Jr). Releases 10 singles and 5 LPs/year. Pays negotiable royalty to artists on contract; negotiable rate to publishers per song on record.

How to Contact: Submit demo tape by mail. Unsolicited submissions are OK. "Please make sure your song or songs are copyrighted." Prefers cassette with 2 songs and lyric sheet. Does not return material. Reports in 3-4 weeks.

Music: Mostly **country**, **easy rock** and **gospel music**. Released *Like A Fool*, written and recorded by Pam Bellows; *Something About Your Love* (by Leo J. Eiffert, Jr.), recorded by Chance Waite Young (country); and *Cajunland*, written and recorded by Leo J. Eiffert, Jr., all on Plain Country Records. Other artists include Brandi Holland, Homemade, Crawfish Band and Larry Settle.

ℕ ⬛ ZEROBUDGET RECORDS, P.O. Box 2044, La Crosse WI 54602. (608)784-1422. President/ Director A&R: Stephen Harm. Distributed in Europe by Ché Records. "We distribute some titles on the Boat Records and Angry Seed labels." Record company. Estab. 1982. Pays negotiable royalty to artists on contract; negotiable rate to publisher per song on record.

How to Contact: Submit demo tape by mail. Unsolicited submissions are OK. Prefers cassette (or VHS ½″ videocassette if available) and lyric sheet. Does not return material. Reports in 3 months.

Music: Mostly **alternative** and **industrial**; also **rock** and **pop**. Released "Fly" (by Virock/Reinders); "Carnival" (by Virock/Reinders/Meusy); and "Losin' My Grip" (by Peterson), all recorded by Space Bike on Zerobudget Records. Other artists include Hick, Bombpop, Zero Dark Thirty, Hippie and Norm's Headache.

Tips: "Don't follow trends—set 'em. No cliché is ever OK."

Additional Record Companies

The following companies are also record companies, but their listings are found in other sections of the book. See the General Index for page numbers, then read the listings for submission information.

ACR Productions
Aim High Music Company
Alan Music, Marcus
Alert Music, Inc.
Alexander Sr. Music
Alexis
AlliSongs Inc.
Amen, Inc.
American Artists Entertainment
Angel Films Company
ARAS Music
Atch Records and Productions
Audio Music Publishers
Backstreet Booking
Baitstring Music
Bal & Bal Music Publishing Co.
Barrett Rock 'n' Roll Enterprises, Paul
Berandol Music Ltd.
Betty Jane/Josie Jane Music Publishers
Big Fish Music Publishing Group
Bird Entertainment Agency, J.
Birthplace Productions
Black Rose Productions
Blowin' Smoke Productions/Records
Blue Planet Music
Blues Alley Records
BME Publishing
Bojo Productions Inc.
Brewster Songs, Kitty
Brian Song Music Corp.
Brightly Music Publishing
Brothers, The
Brown & Associates Inc., J. Aaron
Camex Music

CAPP Company
Cherri/Holly Music
Christopher Publishing, Sonny
Coffee and Cream Productions
Conscience Music
Cool Records
Country Showcase America
Crawfish Productions
Denny Music Group
Dream Hatchery, Inc.
EAO Music Corporation of Canada
Elect Music Publishing Company
Erwin Music
Eternal Records/Squigmonster Management
Eternal Song Agency, The
Final Mix Music
Flying Red Horse Publishing
Furrow Music
GCI Inc.
Glad Music Co.
Golden Guru Entertainment
Hailing Frequency Music Productions
Hale Enterprises
Hansen Music Group, Stevie Ray
Happy Melody
Hardison International Entertainment Corporation
Heart Consort Music
Heupferd Musikverlag GmbH
Hickory Lane Publishing and Recording
His Power Productions and Publishing
Huge Production, Inc., A

Inhabitants Music Group
Inside Records/OK Songs
Interplanetary Music
Iron Skillet Music
Island Culture Music Publishers
Jag Studio, Ltd.
Ja/Nein Musikverlag GmbH
Jay Jay Publishing & Record Co.
John Productions, David
JPMC Music Inc.
JSB Groupe Management Inc.
Junquera Productions, C.
Katz Productions, Matthew
Kaylee Music Group, Karen
Kickstart Music Ltd.
Known Artist Productions
L.A. Entertainment, Inc.
Lazy Bones Productions/Recordings, Inc.
Legend Artists Management
Leigh Music, Trixie
Levy Management, Rick
Lollipop Farm Entertainment
Luick & Associates Music Publisher, Harold
Lyrick Studios
Magic Message Music
Magid Productions, Lee
Magnetic Oblivion Music Co.
Makers Mark Music Productions
May Music/Swift River Productions
Mayfly Record Productions, Ltd.
Mayo & Company, Phil
McCoy Music, Jim
McGibony Publishing
Mega Truth Records

Mellow House Music
Miller & Company, Thomas J.
Modern Tribe Records
Myko Music
Neu Electro Productions
New Experience Records
New Rap Jam Publishing, A
NSP Music Publishing Inc.
Outland Productions
Overstreet Music Companies,
    Tommy
Pacific North Studios Ltd.
Pegasus Music
Philly Breakdown Recording Co.
Pierce, Jim
Prairie Fire Music Company
PriceClub Productions
QUARK, Inc.
R.T.L. Music
Rainbow Collection Ltd.
R&D Productions
Raving Cleric Music Publishing/Euro
    Export Entertainment

Renaissance Entertainment Group
Riohcat Music
Riverhawk Music
Roadshow Music Corp.
Rocker Music/Happy Man Music
Saddlestone Publishing
Satkowski Recordings, Steve
SDM
Sea Cruise Productions, Inc.
Segal's Productions
Shute Management Pty. Ltd., Phill
Silver Bow Management
Silver Thunder Music Group
SM Recording/Hit Records Network
Sound Works Entertainment
    Productions Inc.
Southern Made Records
Spiral-Wave
Starbound Publishing Co.
Stewart Music Group
Still Working Music Group
Strictly Forbidden Artists
Studio Seven

Succes
Supreme Enterprises Int'l Corp.
Tari, Roger Vincent
Ten Ninety Nine Promotions
TMC Productions
Tower Music Group
Tutta Forza Music
Umpire Entertainment Enterprizes
Unknown Source Music
Up Front Management
Valet Publishing Co.
Van Pol Management, Hans
Vickers Music Association, Charles
Virginia Borden Rhythms
Walbash River and Broken Arrow
    Productions
Warner Productions, Cheryl K.
WE Records & Management
Whitewing Music
Willett/Tommark Records, Tom
Williams Management, Yvonne
WIR (World International Records)
World Records

Category Index

The Category Index is a good place to begin searching for a market for your songs. Below is an alphabetical list of 20 general music categories. If you write rock songs and are looking for a record company to submit your songs to, check the Rock section in this index. There you will find a list of record companies interested in hearing rock songs. Once you locate the entries for those record companies, read the music subheading *carefully* to determine which companies are most interested in the type of rock music you write. Some of the markets in this section do not appear in the Category Index because they have not indicated a specific preference. Most of these said they are interested in "all types" of music. Listings that were very specific, or whose description of the music they're interested in doesn't quite fit into these categories, also do not appear here.

Adult Contemporary (also easy listening, middle of the road, AAA, ballads, etc.)
ABL Records
Allegheny Music Works
Banana Records
Boulevard Music & Publishing
Brentwood Records
Capstan Record Production
Carmel Records
Dale Productions, Alan
E.S.R. Records
Emerald City Records
Enterprize Records-Tapes
Fish of Death Records
Golden Triangle Records
Green Bear Records
Kaupp Records
L.A. Records (Canada)
L.A. Records (Michigan)
Lucifer Records, Inc.
Missile Records
Monticana Records
MOR Records
Oak Street Music
Permanent Press Recordings/Permanent Wave
Regis Records Inc.
Roll On Records®
Rustron Music Productions
Tangent Records
Trusty Records
Valtec Productions
X.R.L. Records/Music
Yellow Jacket Records

Alternative (also modern rock, punk, college rock, new wave, hardcore, new music, industrial, ska, indie rock, garage, etc.)
Airtrax
AMP Records & Music
babysue
Banana Records
Big Rich Major Label, A
Blind Records
Caroline Records, Inc.
CITA Communications Inc.
Cleopatra Records
Crank! A Record Company
Creek Records
Deary Me Records
deConstruction Records
Deep South Entertainment
Direct Hit Records
Double Play Records
Elektra Entertainment Group
Entourage Music Group
Evil Teen Records
Fiction Songs
First Power Entertainment Group
Fish of Death Records
Flash Point Records
Flip Records
Generic Records, Inc.
Gonzo! Records Inc.
Gotham Records
Hot Wings Entertainment
Hottrax Records
iHL Records
KSM Records
L.A. Records (Canada)
Lamon Records
Merlin Productions
MJM Records
Motion City Records
Old School Records
Ovni
Paint Chip Records
Pentacle Records
PMG Records
Quark Records
Radical Records
RAVE Records, Inc.

Raw Energy
Redemption Records
Rhetoric Records
RML Records
Robbeye Management Group, Inc.
Robbins Entertainment LLC
Rotten Records
St. Francis Records
Sire Records
Small Stone Records
Solo Records Productions
Street Records
Strugglebaby Recording Co.
Tandem Records
Tangent Records
3rd Stone Ltd.
Throwing Stones Records
Ton Records
Triple X Records
TVT Records
28 Records
Village Records
Wall Street Music
Whirlybird Records, Inc.
Wild Whirled Music Group
Xemu Records
Zerobudget Records

Blues
Albatross Records
Black Diamond Records Inc.
Blue Wave
BSW Records
Cellar Records
Chiaroscuro Records
Dapmor Records
Deadeye Records
Flash Point Records
Flying Heart Records
Front Row Records
Goldwax Record Corporation
Griffin Music
Heart Music, Inc.
Horizon Records, Inc.
Intrepid Records
Landslide Records
MCB Records
Old School Records
Orillyon Entertainment
P.M. Records
Robbeye Management Group, Inc.
Ruf Records
Rustron Music Productions
Small Stone Records
SunDance Records
Sureshot Records
Surface Records
TBS Records

Throwing Stones Records
Ton Records
Topcat Records
Triple X Records
Trusty Records
Warehouse Creek Recording Corp.
Worldwide Recordings Limited
X.R.L. Records/Music

Children's
BMX Entertainment
Carmel Records
First Power Entertainment Group
Lamon Records
Music Quest® Entertainment & Television
Oak Street Music
Omni 2000 Inc.

Classical (also opera, chamber music, serious music, choral, etc.)
A.P.I. Records
babysue
Belham Valley Records
BMX Entertainment
Cambria Records & Publishing
Carmel Records
Comma Records & Tapes
Creek Records
EMF Records & Affiliates
Intrepid Records
Lark Record Productions, Inc.
North Star Music
Old School Records
Omega Record Group, Inc.
Platinum Inc.
Rising Star Records
Robbeye Management Group, Inc.
Tangent Records
Touchwood Zero Hour Entertainment
VAI Distribution

Country (also western, C&W, bluegrass, cowboy songs, western swing, honky-tonk, etc.)
ABL Records
Afterschool Records, Inc.
Airtrax
Albatross Records
Allegheny Music Works
Alyssa Records
Americatone Records International USA
Arial Records
Atlan-Dec/Grooveline Records
Bagatelle Record Company
Big Wig Productions
Black Diamond Records Inc.
Blue Gem Records
Blue Wave
BMX Entertainment

L.A. Records (Michigan)
Lucifer Records, Inc.
Merlin Productions
MHM Recordings
Mighty Records
Monticana Records
NPO Records, Inc.
Omega Record Group, Inc.
Ovni
P. & N. Records
Pickwick/Mecca/International Records
Plastic Surgery
Platinum Groove Entertainment
PMG Records
Quark Records
Rampant Records
RAVE Records, Inc.
Red Dot/Puzzle Records
Robbins Entertainment LLC
Sahara Records and Filmworks Entertainment
Satellite Music
Sealed Fate Records
Select Records
Strive Music
Suisonic Records
Tandem Records
Thump Records, Inc.
Tropikal Productions
Wall Street Music
Workers Playtime Music Co.
X.R.L. Records/Music

Folk (also acoustic, Celtic, etc.)
Afterschool Records, Inc.
Big Wig Productions
Carmel Records
First Time Records
Heart Music, Inc.
Hot Wings Entertainment
Intrepid Records
Kill Rock Stars
Lamon Records
Missile Records
Monticana Records
MSM Records
Patty Lee Records
Random Records
Red Sky Records
Rhiannon Records
Rustron Music Productions
Sims Records, Jerry
Street Records
Third Wave Productions Ltd.
Throwing Stones Records
Waterdog Records
Worldwide Recordings Limited

Instrumental (also background music, musical scores, etc.)
AMP Records & Music
Belham Valley Records
Carmel Records
Lamon Records
Lark Record Productions, Inc.
Makoché Recording Company
Music Quest® Entertainment & Television
North Star Music
Permanent Press Recordings/Permanent Wave
Playbones Records
Silver Wave Records
Sims Records, Jerry
Tangent Records

Jazz (also fusion, bebop, swing, etc.)
A.P.I. Records
A&M Records
Afterschool Records, Inc.
Airplay Label, The
Albatross Records
Americatone Records International USA
Ariana Records
Arkadia Entertainment Corp.
Atlan-Dec/Grooveline Records
audiofile Tapes
Belham Valley Records
Black Diamond Records Inc.
BMX Entertainment
Boulevard Music & Publishing
Carmel Records
Casaro Records
Cherry Street Records
Chiaroscuro Records
Creative Improvised Music Projects (CIMP)
    Records
Creek Records
Crescent Recording Corporation (CRC)
Dale Productions, Alan
Danford Entertainment Group/Sisyphus Records
Dapmor Records
EMF Records & Affiliates
Entourage Music Group
Flash Point Records
Flying Heart Records
Fresh Entertainment
Golden Triangle Records
Goldwax Record Corporation
Griffin Music
Heart Music, Inc.
Hi-Bias Records Inc.
Horizon Records, Inc.
Hot Wings Entertainment
Hottrax Records
Intrepid Records
L.A. Records (Michigan)
Lamon Records

Landmark Communications Group
Landslide Records
LBI Records
Mighty Records
Missile Records
Monticana Records
Music Quest® Entertainment & Television
North Star Music
Old School Records
Omega Record Group, Inc.
Orillyon Entertainment
Orinda Records
Ovni
Patty Lee Records
Permanent Press Recordings/Permanent Wave
Platinum Boulevard Records
Playbones Records
Reiter Records Ltd.
Rival Records
RML Records
Robbeye Management Group, Inc.
Sahara Records and Filmworks Entertainment
St. Francis Records
Salexo Music
Solo Records Productions
SunDance Records
Tangent Records
Topcat Records
Touchwood Zero Hour Entertainment
Tropikal Productions
TVT Records
Woodrich Records
Worldwide Recordings Limited

Latin (also Spanish, salsa, Cuban, conga, Brazilian, cumbia, rancheras, Mexican, merengue, Tejano, Tex Mex, etc.)
Albatross Records
Americatone Records International USA
BMX Entertainment
EMF Records & Affiliates
Howdy Records
Joey Records
Ovni
Thump Records, Inc.
Wanstar Group, The

Metal (also thrash, grindcore, heavy metal, etc.)
babysue
Cellar Records
Cleopatra Records
L.A. Records (Michigan)
Missile Records
Motion City Records
Nightmare Records
Rhetoric Records
Rotten Records
Throwing Stones Records

28 Records

New Age (also ambient)
AMP Records & Music
Big Rich Major Label, A
BMX Entertainment
Creek Records
Dale Productions, Alan
EMF Records & Affiliates
Intrepid Records
L.A. Records (Michigan)
Lamon Records
North Star Music
Only New Age Music, Inc.
Platinum Boulevard Records
Rising Star Records
Rustron Music Productions
Silver Wave Records
Tangent Records

Novelty (also comedy, humor, etc.)
MOR Records
Oak Street Music
Oglio Records
Rising Star Records
Select Records
Sureshot Records
Woodrich Records

Pop (also top 40, top 100, popular, chart hits, etc.)
A.P.I. Records
A&M Records
ABL Records
Afterschool Records, Inc.
Airplay Label, The
Airtrax
Allegheny Music Works
Alyssa Records
Anisette Records
Arial Records
Arkadia Entertainment Corp.
Aware Records
babysue
Banana Records
Belham Valley Records
Beluga Records
Big Wig Productions
Blind Records
Blue Gem Records
BMX Entertainment
Broken Records
C.P.R.
Callner Music
Capstan Record Production
Casaro Records
Cellar Records
Comma Records & Tapes
Crank! A Record Company

Crescent Recording Corporation (CRC)
Dagene/Cabletown Company
Danford Entertainment Group/Sisyphus Records
Deary Me Records
deConstruction Records
Deep South Entertainment
Demi Monde Records and Publishing, Ltd.
Dental Records
Drive Entertainment
EMF Records & Affiliates
Enterprize Records-Tapes
First Time Records
Fish of Death Records
Flash Point Records
Fountain Records
Fresh Entertainment
Generic Records, Inc.
Gold City Records, Inc.
Goldwax Record Corporation
Gonzo! Records Inc.
Gotham Records
Griffin Music
Heart Music, Inc.
Hi-Bias Records Inc.
Horizon Records, Inc.
Hottrax Records
iHL Records
Jive Records
Kaupp Records
Keeping It Simple and Safe, Inc.
Kingston Records
L.A. Records (Michigan)
Lamar Music Marketing
Landmark Communications Group
Lucifer Records, Inc.
Magnum Music Corp. Ltd.
Makeshift Music
MCB Records
Merlin Productions
Mighty Records
Missile Records
MJM Records
Monticana Records
MOR Records
Mule Kick Records
Music Quest® Entertainment & Television
Nation Records Inc.
Old School Records
Omni 2000 Inc.
Orinda Records
Ovni
P.M. Records
Permanent Press Recordings/Permanent Wave
Pickwick/Mecca/International Records
Plateau Music
Platinum Boulevard Records
Quark Records
Random Records

Red Dot/Puzzle Records
Redemption Records
Reiter Records Ltd.
Rival Records
RML Records
Robbins Entertainment LLC
Roll On Records®
Rowena Records
Rustron Music Productions
Sabteca Record Co.
Safire Records
Sahara Records and Filmworks Entertainment
St. Francis Records
Satellite Music
Sealed Fate Records
Shaolin Film & Records
Sims Records, Jerry
Solo Records Productions
sonic unyon records canada
Spotlight Records
Starfish Records
Street Records
SunDance Records
Surface Records
Third Wave Productions Ltd.
Throwing Stones Records
Touchwood Zero Hour Entertainment
Treasure Coast Records
Tropikal Productions
Trusty Records
Valtec Productions
Wall Street Music
Wanstar Group, The
Waterdog Records
X.R.L. Records/Music
Zerobudget Records

R&B (also soul, black, urban, etc.)
A&M Records
ABL Records
Airtrax
Albatross Records
Allegheny Music Works
Alyssa Records
Arkadia Entertainment Corp.
Atlan-Dec/Grooveline Records
Black Diamond Records Inc.
Blue Gem Records
Blue Wave
BMX Entertainment
Boulevard Music & Publishing
C.P.R.
Callner Music
Casaro Records
Cellar Records
Cherry Street Records
Chrome Dome Records
Comma Records & Tapes

Creek Records
Crescent Recording Corporation (CRC)
Dagene/Cabletown Company
Danford Entertainment Group/Sisyphus Records
Dapmor Records
Deadeye Records
Demi Monde Records and Publishing, Ltd.
Disc-tinct Music, Inc.
EMF Records & Affiliates
First Power Entertainment Group
First Time Records
Flash Point Records
Flying Heart Records
Fresh Entertainment
Front Row Records
Gold City Records, Inc.
Golden Triangle Records
Goldwax Record Corporation
Groove Makers' Recordings
Hi-Bias Records Inc.
Jam Down Entertainment, LLC
Jive Records
Kaupp Records
Keeping It Simple and Safe, Inc.
L.A. Records (Michigan)
Lamar Music Marketing
Lamon Records
Landmark Communications Group
LBI Records
Lucifer Records, Inc.
Merlin Productions
MHM Recordings
Missile Records
MJM Records
Monticana Records
Music Quest® Entertainment & Television
Nation Records Inc.
Omni 2000 Inc.
Orbit Records
Orillyon Entertainment
Ovni
Platinum Boulevard Records
Platinum Groove Entertainment
PMG Records
Red-Eye Records
Regis Records Inc.
Rival Records
RML Records
Robbins Entertainment LLC
Roll On Records®
Rowena Records
Ruf Records
Ruffhouse Records
Rustron Music Productions
Sabre Productions
Sabteca Record Co.
Sahara Records and Filmworks Entertainment
Sealed Fate Records

Select Records
Strive Music
Strugglebaby Recording Co.
SunDance Records
Tandem Records
Topcat Records
Touchwood Zero Hour Entertainment
TVT Records
Wanstar Group, The
Warehouse Creek Recording Corp.
Wild Whirled Music Group
X.R.L. Records/Music

Rap (also hip-hop, bass, etc.)
A&M Records
Airtrax
Albatross Records
Anisette Records
Atlan-Dec/Grooveline Records
Big Rich Major Label, A
Black Diamond Records Inc.
BMX Entertainment
C.P.R.
Cellar Records
Chrome Dome Records
Crescent Recording Corporation (CRC)
Dagene/Cabletown Company
Dapmor Records
Disc-tinct Music, Inc.
First Power Entertainment Group
Fish of Death Records
Flash Point Records
Fresh Entertainment
Generic Records, Inc.
Gold City Records, Inc.
Goldwax Record Corporation
Groove Makers' Recordings
Heart Music, Inc.
Jam Down Entertainment, LLC
Jive Records
Keeping It Simple and Safe, Inc.
Lamar Music Marketing
MHM Recordings
Missile Records
Music Quest® Entertainment & Television
NPO Records, Inc.
Orillyon Entertainment
Pickwick/Mecca/International Records
Platinum Groove Entertainment
Platinum Inc.
Rival Records
Robbins Entertainment LLC
Ruffhouse Records
Select Records
Strive Music
Tandem Records
Thump Records, Inc.
Triple X Records

Tropikal Productions
TVT Records
Village Records
Wall Street Music
Wanstar Group, The
Wild Whirled Music Group

Religious (also gospel, sacred, Christian, church, hymns, praise, inspirational, worship, etc.)
A&M Records
ABL Records
Airtrax
Allegheny Music Works
Atlan-Dec/Grooveline Records
babysue
Bagatelle Record Company
Big Wig Productions
Blind Records
BMX Entertainment
Bouquet Records
Brentwood Records
CITA Communications Inc.
Continental Records
Dagene/Cabletown Company
Dale Productions, Alan
Emerald City Records
Enterprize Records-Tapes
First Power Entertainment Group
First Time Records
Flash Point Records
Fountain Records
Fresh Entertainment
Garrett Entertainment, Marty
Gold City Records, Inc.
Goldwax Record Corporation
Green Bear Records
Howdy Records
Kaupp Records
Keeping It Simple and Safe, Inc.
L.A. Records (Michigan)
Lamon Records
Landmark Communications Group
Lari-Jon Records
Magnum Music Corp. Ltd.
MCB Records
Missile Records
Monticana Records
Music Quest® Entertainment & Television
OCP Publications
Omni 2000 Inc.
Orillyon Entertainment
Pickwick/Mecca/International Records
Plateau Music
Platinum Inc.
Playbones Records
Red-Eye Records
Regis Records Inc.

Roll On Records®
Rowena Records
Sabre Productions
Salexo Music
Spotlight Records
SunCountry Records
SunDance Records
Sweet June Music
Tandem Records
Throwing Stones Records
Treasure Coast Records
Trusty Records
Vokes Music Record Co.
Wall Street Music
Wanstar Group, The
Warehouse Creek Recording Corp.
Woodrich Records
Young Country Records/Plain Country Records

Rock (also rockabilly, AOR, rock 'n' roll, etc.)
A.P.I. Records
Airtrax
Albatross Records
Americatone Records International USA
Anisette Records
Ariana Records
Arkadia Entertainment Corp.
Atlan-Dec/Grooveline Records
audiofile Tapes
Aware Records
babysue
Beluga Records
Big Wig Productions
Black Diamond Records Inc.
Blind Records
Blue Gem Records
Blue Wave
BMX Entertainment
Boulevard Music & Publishing
Bouquet Records
Broken Records
BSW Records
C.P.R.
Callner Music
Capstan Record Production
Carmel Records
Cellar Records
Cerebral Records
Chattahoochee Records
Cherry Street Records
CITA Communications Inc.
Collector Records
Comma Records & Tapes
Creek Records
Crescent Recording Corporation (CRC)
Danford Entertainment Group/Sisyphus Records
Dapmor Records
Deadeye Records

World Music (also reggae, ethnic, calypso, international, world beat, etc.)
Arkadia Entertainment Corp.
audiofile Tapes
Belham Valley Records
Creek Records
Dapmor Records
EMF Records & Affiliates
Flash Point Records
Griffin Music
LBI Records
Makoché Recording Company
Missile Records
Modal Music, Inc.™
Music Quest® Entertainment & Television
North Star Music
Only New Age Music, Inc.
RA Records
Robbeye Management Group, Inc.
Silver Wave Records
Tangent Records
Tropikal Productions
Worldwide Recordings Limited

Record Producers

The independent producer can best be described as a creative coordinator. He's usually the one with the most creative control over a recording project and is ultimately responsible for the finished product. Although some larger record companies have their own in-house producers who work exclusively with artists signed to a particular label, it's common for a record company today to contract out-of-house, independent producers for recording projects.

WHAT RECORD PRODUCERS DO

Producers play a large role in deciding what songs will be recorded for a particular project and are always on the lookout for new songs for their clients. They can be valuable contacts for songwriters because they work so closely with the artists whose records they produce. They usually have a lot more freedom than others in executive positions and are known for having a good ear for potential hit songs. Many producers are songwriters and musicians themselves. Since they wield a great deal of influence, a good song in the hands of the right producer at the right time stands a good chance of being cut. And even if a producer is not working on a specific project, he is well-acquainted with record company executives and artists and can often get material through doors not open to you.

Additional Record Producers

There are **MORE RECORD PRODUCERS** located in other sections of the book! On page 265 use the list of Additional Record Producers to find listings within other sections who are also record producers.

SUBMITTING MATERIAL TO PRODUCERS

It can be difficult to get your tapes to the right producer at the right time. Many producers write their own songs and even if they don't write, they may be involved in their own publishing companies so they have instant access to all the songs in their catalogs. It's important to understand the intricacies of the producer/publisher situation. If you pitch your song directly to a producer first, before another publishing company publishes the song, the producer may ask you for the publishing rights (or a percentage thereof) to your song. You must decide whether the producer is really an active publisher who will try to get the song recorded again and again or whether he merely wants the publishing because it means extra income for him from the current recording project. You may be able to work out a co-publishing deal, where you and the producer split the publishing of the song. That means he will still receive his percentage of the publishing income, even if you secure a cover recording of the song by other artists in the future. Even though you would be giving up a little bit initially, you may benefit in the future.

The listings that follow outline which aspects of the music industry each producer is involved in, what type of music he is looking for, and what records and artists he's recently produced. Study the listings carefully, noting the artists each producer works with, and consider if any of your songs might fit a particular artist's or producer's style. Then determine whether they are open to your level of experience (see the Openness to Submissions sidebar on page 8). Be sure to read Quiz: Are You Professional? on page 19 as well.

Consult the Category Index at the end of this section to find producers who work with the type of music you write, and the Geographic Index at the back of the book to locate producers in your area.

For More Information

For more instructional information on the listings in this book, including explanations of symbols (🗎 ✓ 🡣 🡥 🌐 ◯ ◔ ◕ ◒), read the article How to Use *Songwriter's Market* to Get Your Songs Heard on page 5.

🡥 ◔ **"A" MAJOR SOUND CORPORATION**, 80 Corley Ave., Toronto, Ontario M4E 1V2 Canada. Phone/fax: (416)690-9552. E-mail: pmilner@sympatico.ca. Producer: Paul C. Milner. Record producer and music publisher. Estab. 1989. Produces 2 EPs and 12 CDs/year. Fee derived from sales royalty when song or artist is recorded, or outright fee from recording artist or record company, or investors.
How to Contact: Submit demo tape by mail. Unsolicited submissions are OK. Prefers cassette, DAT or VHS videocassette with 5 songs and lyric sheet (lead sheet if available). Does not return material. Reports in 3 months.
Music: Mostly **rock, A/C, alternative** and **pop**; also **Christian** and **R&B**. Produced *Orange Sky*, written and recorded by Orange Sky on Wildmeat Records (reggae); and *Phé Cullen* (by various artists), recorded by Norm Armadio Trio with Phé Cullen on Euphemia Records (contemporary jazz).

◯ **ABERDEEN PRODUCTIONS**, 524 Doral Country Dr., Nashville TN 37221. (615)646-9750. President: Scott Turner. Record producer and music publisher (Buried Treasure Music/ASCAP, Captain Kidd/BMI). Estab. 1971. Produces 10 singles, 15-20 12″ singles, 8 LPs and 8 CDs/year. Fee derived from outright fee from recording artist.
How to Contact: Submit demo tape by mail. Unsolicited submissions OK. Prefers cassette with maximum 4 songs and lead sheet. SASE. Reports in 2 weeks. No "lyrics only."
Music: Mostly **country, MOR** and **rock**; also **top 40/pop**. Produced *Just Wait 'Til Summer Comes* (by Herb Alpert/Scott Turner), recorded by Harry Nilsson on Retro (MOR). Other artists include Jimmy Clanton.
Tips: "Start out on an independent basis because of the heavy waiting period to get on a major label."

✓ ◔ **ACR PRODUCTIONS**, 505 N. A St., Midland TX 79701. (615)826-9233 or (915)687-2702. Owner: Dwaine Thomas. Record producer, music publisher (Joranda Music/BMI) and record company (ACR Records). Estab. 1986. Produces 120 singles, 8-15 12″ singles, 25 LPs, 25 EPs and 25 CDs/year. Fee derived from sales royalty when song or artist is recorded. "We charge for in-house recording only. Remainder is derived from royalties."
How to Contact: Submit demo tape by mail. Unsolicited submissions are OK. Prefers cassette or VHS videocassette with 5 songs and lyric sheet. Does not return material. Reports in 6 weeks if interested.
Music: Mostly **country swing, pop** and **rock**; also **R&B** and **gospel**. Produced "It's Never Easy," "Dreams," and "Forever Yours" (by Aaron Miller), recorded by Off Limitz on ACR Records (pop).
Tips: "Be professional. No living room tapes!"

◒ **AKO PRODUCTIONS**, Dept. SM, 20531 Plummer, Chatsworth CA 91311. (818)998-0443. President: A. Sullivan. Record producer and music publisher (Amiron Music). Produces 2-6 singles and 2-3 LPs/year. Fee derived from sales royalty when song or artist is recorded.
How to Contact: Write first and obtain permission to submit. Prefers cassette or videocassette and lyric sheet. SASE. Reports in 1 month.
Music: Mostly **pop/rock** and **modern country**. Produced *Ladies in Charge*, written and recorded by C. Ratliff on AKO Records.

◒ **STUART J. ALLYN**, Skylight Run, Irvington NY 10533. (212)486-0856. E-mail: adr.inc@ix.netcom. com. Associate: Jack Walker. General Manager: Jack Davis. President: Stuart J. Allyn. Record producer. Estab. 1972. Produces 6 singles and 3-6 CDs/year. Fee derived from sales royalty and outright fee from recording artist and record company.

How to Contact: Write first and obtain permission to submit. Prefers DAT, CD, cassette, 15 ips reel-to-reel or VHS videocassette with 3 songs and lyric or lead sheet. Does not return material. Reports in 6 months.
Music: Mostly **pop**, **rock**, **jazz** and **theatrical**; also **R&B** and **country**. Produced Dizzy Gillespie's "Winter in Lisbon" on Milan Records; *Mel Lewis & Jazz Orchestra* on Atlantic Records (jazz); and *Lickety Split* (by Jim McNeeley), recorded by Vangward Jazz Orchestra on New World (jazz). Other artists include Billy Joel, Aerosmith, Carole Demas, Harry Stone, Bob Stewart, The Dixie Peppers, Nora York, Buddy Barnes and various video and film scores.

☑ ◯ AMAJ RECORDS, (formerly London Brijj Productions), 815 E. Church Lane, Philadelphia PA 19138. (215)524-2900. Producer/engineer: Jae London. A&R: Jay Art. Record producer, music publisher (AMAJ Publishing Enterprise) and production company. Estab. 1984. Produces 7 singles, 3 12" singles, 3 LPs and 2 CDs/year. Fee derived from outright fee from record company.
How to Contact: Submit demo tape by mail. Unsolicited submissions are OK. Prefers cassette or VHS videocassette with 3 songs and lyric sheet. Does not return material. Reports in 1 month.
Music: Mostly **R&B**, **hip hop** and **ballads**; also **reggae** and **club/house**. Produced *Do What is Right* (by Horace Allen), recorded by Jah Bass; *Wild West* (by Lee Bonaparte), recorded by Wonder; and *What Goes Around Comes Around* (by Al Arthurs Jr.), recorded by J.L., all on AMAJ Records. Other artists include Nardo Ranks, IBO, Rickeeda.

◯ ANGEL FILMS COMPANY, 967 Hwy. 40, New Franklin MO 65274-9778. (573)698-3900. E-mail: angelfilm@aol.com. President: Arlene Hulse. Owner: William H. Hoehne, Jr. Record producer, motion picture company and record company (Angel One). Estab. 1980. Produces 5 LPs, 5 EPs and 5 CDs/year. Fee derived from sales royalty when song or artist is recorded.
How to Contact: Submit demo tape by mail. Unsolicited submissions are OK. Prefers cassette or VHS videocassette with 3 songs. "Send only original material, not previously recorded, and include a bio sheet on artist." SASE. Reports in 6 weeks.
Music: Mostly **pop**, **rock** and **rockabilly**; also **jazz** and **R&B**. Produced *Jim Dandy*, written and recorded by Kandy Kane (rock); *Love is a 4 Letter Word*, written and recorded by Linda G (pop), both on Angel One Records. Other artists include Julian James, Patrick Donovon, Euttland, B.D.K. and Teddies.
Tips: "Actually listen to what you're doing and ask, 'would I buy that?'"

☑ ◉ JONATHAN APPELL PRODUCTIONS, INC., 333 E. 23rd St. #9C, New York NY 10010. (212)725-5613. E-mail: appellproductions@newyorknet.net. Website: http://home.rmci.net/appellproducti ons. Producer/Engineer: Jonathan Appell. Record producer and audio engineer. Estab. 1989. Produces 2 singles and 5 LPs/year. Fee derived from sales royalty when song or artist is recorded, or outright fee from recording artist or record company.
How to Contact: Does not accept unsolicited submissions.
Music: Mostly **rock**, **pop** and **R&B**; also **jazz** and **reggae**. Produced *Piranha Brothers*, written and recorded by Piranha Brothers (rock); *Blue Eyed Soul* (by Chris and Tom O'Connor), recorded by Blue Eyed Soul (pop); and *Roseanne Drucker* (by Jan Polkson), recorded by Roseanne Drucker (pop), all on Reload. Other artists include Matt Cohler Band, Lee Drutman Band, YNot and Eric Fleischman.
Tips: "Learn your craft. Ask yourself (honestly), 'Am I good enough to perform alongside whomever the biggest stars are in my genre of music?' If you aren't convinced that you've attained that level of professionalism, you'll never convince a producer or a record company. If you're not ready, get back in there and practice, practice, practice!"

◉ BAL RECORDS, P.O. Box 369, LaCanada CA 91012-0369. (818)548-1116. Website: http://www.bus dir.com/balmusic/index.html. President: Adrian Bal. Vice President: Berdella M. Bal. Record producer and music publisher (Bal & Bal Music). Estab. 1965. Produces 1-3 CDs/year. Fee derived from sales royalty when song or artist is recorded.
How to Contact: Write or call first and obtain permission to submit. Prefers cassette with 3 songs and

**FOR EXPLANATIONS OF THESE SYMBOLS,
SEE THE INSIDE FRONT AND BACK COVERS OF THIS BOOK.**

lyric sheet. SASE. Reports in 3 months.
Music: Mostly **MOR, country, jazz, R&B, rock** and **top 40/pop**; also **blues, church/religious, easy listening** and **soul**. Produced "What's the Matter With Me?" and "Lord You Been So Good to Me," both written and recorded by Rhonda Johnson on BAL Records (gospel). Other artists include Kathy Simmons, Paul Richards and Terry Fischer.

HAL BERNARD ENTERPRISES, INC., P.O. Box 8385, Cincinnati OH 45208. (513)871-1500. Fax: (513)871-1510. E-mail: umbrella@one.net. President: Stan Hertzman. Record producer, record company (Strugglebaby Recording Co.), management firm (Umbrella Artists Management) and music publisher (Sunnyslope Music Inc. and Bumpershoot Music Inc.). Produces 5 singles and 3-4 LPs/year. Fee derived from sales royalty.
How to Contact: Prefers cassette with 1-3 songs and lyric sheet. SASE. Reports in 1 month only if interested.
Music: Produced *Merry, Mary Christmas*, recorded by Mary Ellen Tanner on Strugglebaby Records (holiday/seasonal).

BIG SKY AUDIO PRODUCTIONS, 1035 E. Woodland Ave. #2, Springfield PA 19064. (610)328-4709. Fax: (610)328-7728. Producer: Drew Raison. Record producer. Estab. 1990. Produces 5-7 EPs and 10-12 CDs/year. Fee derived from sales royalty when song or artist is recorded or outright fee from recording artist or record company.
How to Contact: Submit demo tape by mail. Unsolicited submissions are OK. Prefers cassette or VHS videocassette with 3 songs and lyric sheet. "Don't send it to us if it isn't copyrighted!" Does not return material. Reports in 4-6 weeks.
Music: Mostly **rock, R&B** and **New Age**; also **anything with strong vocals**. Produced *Speak On It* (by Syracuse/Gilham), recorded by Blue Noise; *Get It Right*, written and recorded by Johnny DeFrancesco, both on VAM Records; and *I Have Forgotten*, written and recorded by David E. Williamson on Ospedale Records. Other artists include Trash Planet, John Swiegart, Theodozia, Daniel Pry, Robert Hazzard, Joey DeFrancesco and Dreamlovers.

[N] BIRTHPLACE PRODUCTIONS, P.O. Box 1651, Bristol TN 37621. (423)878-3535. Fax: (423)878-9197. E-mail: tnqegsa@prodigy.com. President: Steve Patrick. Record producer and record company (Riverbend Records). Estab. 1994. Produces 12 singles, 10 LPs and 20 CDs/year. Fee derived from outright fee from recording artist or record company.
How to Contact: Write or call first and obtain permission to submit or to arrange personal interview. Prefers cassette or videocassette with 10 songs and lyric sheet. SASE. Reports in 3 weeks.
Music: Mostly **country, gospel** and **folk**. Produced *Paths Through Cedarville* (by Darrell Johnson), recorded by Garry Johnson (country); and *The Hour of Prayer*, written and recorded by Mike Reed (gospel), both on Riverbend; and "Be Kind" (by Duane Herring), recorded by Steve Warren on Andre Romare (country).
Tips: "Stay focused. Be willing to accept that the commitment you make is determined by your understanding of the business itself."

[N] BLUE PLANET MUSIC, P.O. Box 85671, Lincoln NE 68501. (402)441-9681. Fax: (402)476-7311. E-mail: hemant@world-vu.com. Producer/Publisher: Hemant Desai. Associate Producer: Milae. Assistant Producer: Roger Lambert. Record producer, record company and music publisher (Vu World Music/BMI). Estab. 1997. Produces 1-2 singles and 2 CDs/year. Fee derived from negotiated agreements for production and publishing.
How to Contact: Submit demo tape by mail. Unsolicited submissions are OK. Prefers cassette, DAT, VHS videocassette or minidisc with 3 songs and lyric sheet. "Please copyright your material with the Library of Congress before mailing it to us." SASE. Reports in 6-8 weeks.
Music: Mostly **soft rock/pop, R&B** and **reggae**; also **alternative rock, jazz** and **New Age/classical**. Produced *Love Sublime* (by Raj Alur), recorded by World-Vu on Blue Planet Music (reggae). Other artists include The Bombay Blues Band.
Tips: "We are looking for artists (performing and studio musicians) and songwriters who have a variety of material that is likely to prove 'radio-friendly.' We offer better than statutory rates for royalties and we also have original material that other artists/producers may be interested in. Please call to discuss your career goals and how we may help in that endeavor. All calls/letters returned ASAP."

BLUES ALLEY RECORDS, Rt. 1, Box 288, Clarksburg WV 26301. Producer: Joshua Swiger. Record producer, record company and music publisher (Blues Alley Publishing/BMI). Produces 2 singles, 1-2 LPs and 2 EPs/year. Fee derived from sales royalty when song or artist is recorded.
How to Contact: Submit demo tape by mail. Unsolicited submissions are OK. Prefers cassette with 4

songs and lyric and lead sheets. Does not return material. Reports in 6 weeks.
Music: Mostly **rock, country** and **Christian rock**; also **alternative**, **pop** and **R&B**. Produced *Imaginary Friends* (by Mike Arbogust), recorded by Imaginary Friends on Blues Alley Records (rock).

CACOPHONY PRODUCTIONS, 52-A Carmine St., Suite 544, New York NY 10014. (212)777-8763. Producer: Steven Miller. Record producer and music publisher (In Your Face Music). Estab. 1981. Fee derived from sales royalty when song or artist is recorded, or outright fee from recording artist or record company.
How to Contact: Call first and obtain permission to submit. Prefers cassette with 3 songs and lyric sheet. "Send a cover letter of no more than three paragraphs giving some background on yourself and the music. Also explain specifically what you are looking for Cacophony Productions to do." Does not return material. Reports only if interested.
Music: Mostly **progressive pop/rock**, **singer/songwriter** and **progressive country**. Produced Dar Williams, Suzanne Vega, John Gorka, Michael Hedges, Juliana Hatfield and Medeski-Martin & Wood.

JAN CELT MUSICAL SERVICES, 4026 NE 12th Ave., Portland OR 97212. (503)287-8045. E-mail: flyheart@teleport.com. Website: http://www.teleport.com/~flyheart. Owner: Jan Celt. Record producer, music publisher (Wiosna Nasza Music/BMI) and record company (Flying Heart Records). Estab. 1982. Produces 3-5 CDs/year.
How to Contact: Submit demo tape by mail. Unsolicited submissions are OK. Prefers high-quality cassette with 1-10 songs and lyric sheet. SASE. Reports in 4 months. "If calling, please check time zone."
Music: Mostly **R&B**, **rock** and **blues**; also **jazz**. Produced "Vexatious Progressions," written and recorded by Eddie Harris (jazz); "Bong Hit" (by Chris Newman), recorded by Snow Bud & the Flower People (rock); and "She Moved Away" (by Chris Newman), recorded by Napalm Beach, all on Flying Heart Records. Other artists include The Esquires and Janice Scroggins.

COACHOUSE MUSIC, P.O. Box 1308, Barrington IL 60011. (312)822-0305. Fax: (312)822-0267. E-mail: mickfreon@aol.com. President: Michael Freeman. Record producer. Estab. 1984. Produces 6-8 CDs/year. Fee derived from sales royalty when song or artist is recorded.
How to Contact: Write first and obtain permission to submit. Prefers cassette, DAT or CD with 3-5 songs and lyric sheet. SASE. Reports in 4-6 weeks.
Music: Mostly **rock**, **pop** and **blues**; also **alternative rock** and **country/roots**. Produced *Casque Nu*, written and recorded by Charlelie Couture on Chrysalis EMI France (contemporary pop); *Time Will Tell* (by various/John Grimaldi), recorded by Studebaker John on Blind Pig Records (blues); *Where Blue Begins* (by various/D. Coleman), recorded by Deborah Coleman on Blind Pig Records (contemporary blues) and *Floobie* (by Dan Ruprecht), recorded by The Pranks on Coachhouse Records (pop). Other artists include Maybe/Definitely, Eleventh Dream Day, Magic Slim, Amarillo Kings, The Tantrums, The Pranks, Allison Johnson, The Bad Examples, Mississippi Heat and Mick Freon.
Tips: "Be honest, be committed, strive for excellence."

COFFEE AND CREAM PRODUCTIONS, 1138 E. Price St., Philadelphia PA 19138. (215)842-3450. Producer: Bolden Abrams, Jr.. Record producer, music publisher (Coffee and Cream Publishing Company/ASCAP) and record company (Coffee and Cream Records). Produces 12 singles, 12 12″ singles and 6 LPs/year. Fee derived from sales royalty or outright fee from recording artist or record company.
How to Contact: Submit demo tape by mail. Unsolicited submissions are OK. Prefers cassette with 1-4 songs and lyric sheet. SASE. Reports in 2 weeks.
Music: Mostly **R&B**, **pop** and **country**; also **gospel** and **dance**. Produced "Si Me Dejo Llevar" (by Jose Gomez/Sheree Sano/Julio Hernandez); and "I Can't Wait" (by Abrams/Degrazio/Urbach), both recorded by Melissa Manjom on Misa Records; and "If I Let Myself Go" (by Gomez/Sano), recorded by Ron Hevener on RMB Records. Other artists include Michal Beckham, Robert Benjamin, Darrall Campbell, Elektra, Christopher Shirk, Tony Gilmore, Janine Whetstone, Kissie Darnell and Debra Spice.

COLLECTOR RECORDS, P.O. Box 1200, 3260 AE oud beyerland, Holland, The Netherlands. Phone: 186-604266. Fax: 186-604366. Research: Cees Klop. Record producer and music publisher (All Rock Music). Produces 25 CDs/year. Fee derived from outright fee from record company.

TO HELP YOU UNDERSTAND and use the information in these listings, see "How to Use *Songwriter's Market* to Get Your Songs Heard," on page 5.

How to Contact: Submit demo tape by mail. Unsolicited submissions are OK. Prefers cassette. SAE and IRC. Reports in 2 months.
Music: Mostly **'50s rock**, **rockabilly** and **country rock**; also **piano boogie woogie**. Produced *Parking in the Dark*, written and recorded by Charles Dean, and *Road Runner* (by Ellie Jaye), recorded by Ron & Ellie Jaye, both on Collector ('50s rock); and *Grand Hotel*, written and recorded by Vincent Laurentis on Down South Records (piano boogie). Other artists include André Valkering, Rob Hoeke, Eric Jan Overbeek and Teddy Redell.
Tips: "Only send the kind of music we produce."

N ⊕ ◪ JOHNNY COPPIN/RED SKY RECORDS, P.O. Box 27, Stroud, Glos. GL6 0YQ United Kingdom. Phone: 01453-836877. Record producer, music publisher (PRS) and record company (Red Sky Records). Estab. 1985. Produces 2 albums/year. Fee derived from sales royalty when song or artist is recorded.
How to Contact: Write first and obtain permission to submit. Does not return material. Reports in 6 months.
Music: Mostly **rock**, **modern folk** and **roots music**. Produced "A Country Christmas" and "Keep the Flame" written and recorded by Johnny Coppin; and "Dead Lively!," written and recorded by Paul Burgess, all on Red Sky Records. Other artists include David Goodland.

◪ DANO CORWIN, 5839 Silvercreek Rd., Azle TX 76020. (817)530-7942. Producer: Dano Corwin. Record producer, music video and sound production company. Estab. 1986. Produces 6 singles, 3 12" singles, 5 EPs and 2 CDs/year. Fee derived from sales royalty when song or artist is recorded.
How to Contact: Submit demo tape by mail. Unsolicited submissions are OK. Prefers cassette or VHS videocassette with 3 songs and lyric sheet. "Keep songs under five minutes. Only copyrighted material will be reviewed. Please do not send material without copyright notices." Does not return material. Reports in 6-8 weeks.
Music: Mostly **rock**; also **pop** and **dance**. Produced *Dimensions*, written and recorded by Silent Shame on MLM Records (rock); "Hello" (by W.J. Ross), recorded by RTIC; and "Early Dawn" (by T. Darren), recorded by Zeph, both on WW Records (rock). Other artists include Complete, Sir Gray Wolf and Drune.

N ◯ JERRY CUPIT PRODUCTIONS, Box 121904, Nashville TN 37212. (615)731-0100. E-mail: jyoke@edge.net. Website: http://www.cupitmusic.net. Creative Assistant: Tracy Reynolds. Record producer and music publisher (Cupit Music). Estab. 1984. Fee derived from sales royalty when song or artist is recorded or outright fee from artist.
How to Contact: Write first and obtain permission to submit. Prefers cassette with bio and photo. SASE. Reports in 2 months.
Music: Mostly **country**, **Southern rock** and **gospel**; also **R&B**. Produced "Jukebox Junkie" (by Ken Mellons/Jerry Cupit/Janice Honeycutt) and *Where Forever Begins*, both recorded by Ken Mellons on Epic Records. Other artists include Jack Robertson and Jon Nicholson.
Tips: "Be prepared to work hard and be able to take constructive/professional criticism."

◪ DALIVEN MUSIC, P.O. Box 398, Nolensville TN 37135. (615)776-5686. E-mail: daliven1@aol.c om. Owner/Operator: R. Steve Cochran. Producer: Robert Cochran. Record producer and music publisher. Produces 4 singles, 2 LPs and 2 CDs/year. Fee derived from outright fee from recording artist.
How to Contact: Submit demo tape by mail. Unsolicited submissions are OK. Prefers cassette or videocassette with 3 songs and lyric or lead sheet. "Can also send standard MIDI files of songs." Does not return material. Reports in 2 months.
Music: Mostly **A/C**, **R&B** and **rock**; also **jazz**, **dance** and **country**. Produced "Oye Amor" and "Baila Con Migo," written and recorded by Dalia on Polygram Records (pop); and "Catpaw," written and recorded by Rod Riley on Reggie (New Age). Other artists include Rex Sigmon and Tim Veazey.

◯ DAP PRODUCTIONS, P.O. Box 8684, Youngstown OH 44507. (330)782-5031. Fax: (330)782-6954. Producer: Darryl Alexander. Record Producer and music publisher (Alexander Sr. Music). Estab. 1997. Produces 12 singles and 2-4 CDs/year. Fee derived from sales royalty (producer points) when song or artist is recorded or outright fee from recording artist or record company.
How to Contact: Write first and obtain permission to submit. Prefers cassette with 2-4 songs and lyric sheet. SASE. Reports in 1 month. "No phone calls or faxes please."
Music: Mostly **contemporary jazz**, **urban contemporary Christian** and **gospel**; also **R&B**. Produced "Let's Take A Chance" (by Darryl Alexander), recorded by Sheila Hayes (contemporary jazz); "God Is Good," written and recorded by Keith Logan (gospel); and *Maybe Tomorrow* (in NBC Movie of the Week, *Playing to Win*), written and recorded by Darryl Alexander on LRG Records (contemporary jazz). Other artists include Kathryn Williams.

☑ DANNY DARROW, 150 West End Ave., Suite 6-D, New York NY 10023. (212)873-5968. Manager: Danny Darrow. Record producer, music publisher (Rockford Music Co.) and record company (Mighty Records). Estab. 1958. Produces 1-2 singles, 1-2 12″ singles and 1-2 LPs/year. Fee derived from sales royalty when song or artist is recorded.
How to Contact: Submit demo tape by mail. Unsolicited submissions are OK. "No phone calls. No requesting letters." Prefers cassette with 3 songs and lyric sheet. Does not return material. Reports in 2-4 weeks only if interested.
Music: Mostly **pop**, **country** and **dance**; also **jazz**. Produced *Wonderland of Dreams* (by Danny Darrow); *Look to the Wind* (by Peggy Stewart/Danny Darrow); and *Corporate Lady* (by Michael Barry Greer), all recorded by Danny Darrow on Mighty Records.
Tips: "At present, looking for songs like 'How Am I Supposed to Live Without You.' This type only!"

Ⓝ ☑ DAYLO MUSIC, 21604 Encino Rd., Topanga CA 90290. (310)455-0905. Producer: David Dale. Record producer and music publisher. Estab. 1998. Produces 4 singles and 3-4 CDs/year. Fee derived from sales royalty when song or artist is recorded, and outright fee from recording artist or record company.
How to Contact: Write or call first and obtain permission to submit. Prefers cassette, DAT or CD with 1-4 songs and lyric sheet. "Keep the demo production simple. Make sure the vocals are clear and it's as close to the way you wrote the song as possible, unless song is production-oriented and the atmosphere is essential to the presentation." Does not return material. Report in 1 month.
Music: Mostly **pop**, **alternative** and **world**. Produced *Transcendental Highway* (by Hay/Dale), recorded by Colin Hay on Lazy Eye/FMA (contemporary pop); *Your Backyard*, written and recorded by Brother on Rhubarb/FMA (celtic rock); and *9 Ways to Sunday* (by Robertson), recorded by 9 Ways to Sunday on Giant (alternative). Other artists include Reef, Bobby Bell and Celeste Prince.
Tips: "Just follow the song, it has its own voice. All you have to do is listen and stay open to where it will lead you. During the '80s I was chief engineer and producer of songwriter demos for C.B.S. Songs in New York City."

☑ ☑ EDWARD DE MILES, 117 W. Harrison Bldg. #S627, Chicago IL 60605-1709. (773)509-6381. Fax: (312)922-6964. A&R: Jason Woolridge. President: Edward De Miles. Record producer, music publisher (Edward De Miles Music Co./BMI) and record company (Sahara Records and Filmworks Entertainment). Estab. 1981. Produces 15-20 singles, 15-20 12″ singles, 5-10 LPs and 5-10 CDs/year. Fee derived from sales royalty when song or artist is recorded.
How to Contact: Does not accept unsolicited submissions.
Music: Mostly **R&B/dance**, **top 40 pop/rock** and **contemporary jazz**; also **country**, **TV and film themes—songs and jingles**. Produced "Moments" and "Dance Wit Me" (dance), both written and recorded by Steve Lynn; and "Games," written and recorded by D'von Edwards (jazz), all on Sahara Records. Other artists include D'von Edwards and Multiple Choice.
Tips: "Copyright all material before submitting. Equipment and showmanship a must."

☑ ☑ AL DELORY AND MUSIC MAKERS, 3000 Hillsboro Rd. #11, Nashville TN 37215. (615)292-2140. President: Al DeLory. Record producer and career consultant (DeLory Music/ASCAP). Estab. 1987. Fee derived from outright fee from recording artist.
• Al DeLory has won two Grammy Awards and has been nominated five times.
How to Contact: Write or call first and obtain permission to submit or to arrange personal interview. Prefers cassette or VHS videocassette. SASE. Reports in 1 month.
Music: Mostly **pop**, **country** and **Latin**. Produced "Gentle On My Mind," "By the Time I Get to Phoenix" and "Wichita Lineman," all recorded by Glen Campbell. Other artists include Letter Men and Gary Puckett.
Tips: "Seek advice and council only with professionals with a track record."

🌐 ☑ DEMI MONDE RECORDS & PUBLISHING LTD., Foel Studio, Llanfair Caereinion, Powys, SY21 ODS Wales. Phone/fax: 01938-810758. E-mail: demi.monde@dial.pipex.com. Website: http://www.demi.monde.co.uk/demimonde. Managing Director: Dave Anderson. Record producer, music publisher (PRS & MCPS) and record company (Demi Monde Records). Estab. 1982. Produces 5 singles, 15 12″ singles, 15 LPs and 10 CDs/year. Fee derived from sales royalty or outright fee from record company.

MARKET CONDITIONS are constantly changing! If you're still using this book and it is 2001 or later, buy the newest edition of *Songwriter's Market* at your favorite bookstore or order directly from Writer's Digest Books at (800)289-0963.

How to Contact: Submit demo tape by mail. Unsolicited submissions are OK. Prefers cassette with 3 or 4 songs and lyric sheet. Does not return material. Reports in 6 weeks.
Music: Mostly **rock, pop** and **blues**. Produced *Average Man*, recorded by Mother Gong (rock); *Frozen Ones*, recorded by Tangle Edge (rock); and *Blue Boar Blues* (by T.S. McPhee), recorded by Groundhogs (rock), all on Demi Monde Records. Other artists include Gong and Hawkwind.

⊘ **JOEL DIAMOND ENTERTAINMENT**, Dept. SM, 3940 Laurel Canyon Blvd., Suite 441, Studio City CA 91604. (818)980-9588. Fax: (818)980-9422. E-mail: jdiamond20@aol.com. Contact: Joel Diamond. Record producer, music publisher and manager. Fee derived from sales royalty when song is recorded or outright fee from recording artist or record company.
How to Contact: Does not accept unsolicited material.
Music: Mostly **dance, easy listening, country, R&B, rock, soul** and **top 40/pop**. Produced "One Night In Bangkok," by Robey; "Love is the Reason" (by Cline/Wilson), recorded by E. Humperdinck and G. Gaynor on Critique Records (A/C); and "After the Loving," recorded by E. Humperdinck.

☐ **PHILIP D. DIXON III, ATTORNEY AT LAW**, 2501 Parkview Dr. #500, Ft. Worth TX 76102. (817)332-8553. Fax: (817)332-2834. Attorney: Philip D. Dixon III. Record producer, artist representative; trademark/copyright protection for artists. Estab. 1995. Fee derived from sales royalty when song or artist is recorded or outright fee from record company. "We do charge for statutory payments made to third parties."
How to Contact: Write first and obtain permission to submit a demo or write first to arrange personal interview. Prefers cassette and videocassette with any number of songs and lyric sheet. SAE (they pay return postage). Reports in 1 month.
Music: Mostly **rock, country** and **Latino**.
Tips: "Protect your work from a legal standpoint before making any disclosures to anyone. Be vigilant in your creative and business affairs."

☐ **COL. BUSTER DOSS PRESENTS**, 341 Billy Goat Hill Rd., Winchester TN 37398. Producer: Col. Buster Doss. Fax: (931)649-2732. E-mail: cbd@edge.net. Website: http://www.a-page.com/colonelscorner. Record producer, record company (Stardust, Wizard), management firm and music publisher (Buster Doss Music/BMI). Estab. 1959. Produces 100 singles, 10 12″ singles, 20 LPs and 20 CDs/year. Fee derived from sales royalty when song or artist is recorded.
How to Contact: Write first and obtain permission to submit. Prefers cassette with 2 songs and lyric sheet. SASE. Reports in 1 week if interested.
Music: Mostly **pop, country** and **gospel**. Produced *The Man I Love* (by Buster Doss), recorded by Jerri Arnold; "Let's Go Dancing" (by Buster Doss), recorded by Mike "Doc" Holliday; and "You Can't Take Texas Out of Me" (by Barbara Doss), recorded by "Bronco" Buck Cody, all on Stardust Records. Other artists include Cliff Archer, Linda Wunder, Honey James, Don Sky, Shelly Streeter, Rooster Quantrell, Dwain Gamel, Donna Darlene and Jersey Outlaw.

DAVID DURR PRODUCTIONS. See David Durr's listing for Co-Creations Music in the Music Publishers section. Mr. Durr is focusing more on publishing.

🅽 ⊘ **LEO J. EIFFERT, JR.**, P.O. Box 5412, Buena Park CA 90620. (760)245-8473. Owner: Leo J. Eiffert, Jr. Record producer, music publisher (Eb-Tide Music/BMI, Young Country Music/BMI), management firm (Crawfish Productions) and record company (Plain Country). Estab. 1967. Produces 15-20 singles and 5 LPs/year. Fee derived from sales royalty when song or artist is recorded.
How to Contact: Submit demo tape by mail. Unsolicited submissions are OK. Prefers cassette with 2-3 songs, lyric and lead sheet. SASE. Reports in 3-4 weeks.
Music: Mostly **country** and **gospel**. Produced "Daddy I Know," written and recorded by Pam Bellows on Plain Country Records; "Little Miss," written and recorded by Johnny Horton; and "My Friend," written and recorded by Leo J. Eiffert Jr., both on Young Country Records. Other artists include Homemade, Crawfish Band, Brandi Holland, Mary T. Eiffert, Stiff Racoons, Steel Promises, Southern Spirit and David Busson.
Tips: "Just keep it real country."

⊘ **ESQUIRE INTERNATIONAL**, P.O. Box 6032, Station B, Miami FL 33101-6032. (305)547-1424. President: Jeb Stuart. Record producer, music publisher (Jeb Stuart Music) and management firm. Produces 6 singles and 2 LPs/year. Fee derived from sales royalty or independent leasing of masters and placing songs.

How to Contact: Submit demo tape by mail. Unsolicited submissions are OK. Prefers cassette or CD with 2-4 songs and lead sheet. SASE. Reports in 1 month.
Music: Mostly **blues**, **church/religious**, **country**, **dance**, **gospel**, **jazz**, **rock**, **soul** and **top 40/pop**. Produced "Go to Sleep, Little Baby" (by Jeb Stuart), recorded by Cafidia and Jeb Stuart; "Guns Guns (No More Guns)" and "No One Should Be Alone on Christmas," both written and recorded by Jeb Stuart, all on Esquire Int'l Records. Other artists include Moments Notice and Night Live.

◯ THE ETERNAL SONG AGENCY, 6326 E. Livingston Ave., Suite 153, Reynoldsburg OH 43068. (614)834-2830. E-mail: leopold@netexp.net. Website: http://www.Eternalsong.com. Executive Producer: Leopold Xavier Crawford. Record producer, record company and music publisher (Fragrance Records, Song of Solomon Records, Emerald Records, Lilly Records Ancient of Days Music and Anastacia Music). Estab. 1986. Produces 7-15 singles and 5 CDs/year. Fee derived from sales royalty when song or artist is recorded or outright fee from recording artist or record company.
How to Contact: Write first and obtain permission to submit. Prefers cassette or videocassette with 3 songs and lyric or lead sheet. "Send complete biography, pictures, tape. Type all printed material. Professionalism of presentation will get you an ear with us." SASE. Reports in 4-6 weeks.
Music: Mostly **pop music/top 40**, **country** and **instrumental**; also **contemporary Christian**, **Christian inspirational** and **southern gospel music**. Produced "Walking Out," written and recorded by Leopold Crawford; "Saul," written and recorded by Michael Higgins; and "Drink" (by Leopold Crawford), recorded by Streets of Gold, all on Fragrance Records. Other artists include Bloodbought, Yolanda Stewart, Greg Whightsell, Lynn Holloway and Seventh Dynasty.

✓ ◯ FINAL MIX MUSIC, 2219 W. Olive Ave., Suite 102, Burbank CA 91506. (818)840-9000. E-mail: finalmix@aol.com. A&R: Theresa Frank. Record producer/remixer/mix engineer, record company (3.6 Music, Inc.) and music publisher (Roachi World Music). Estab. 1989. Releases 12 singles and 3-5 LPs and CDs/year. Fee derived from sales royalty when song or artist is recorded.
How to Contact: Submit demo tape by mail. Unsolicited submissions are OK. Prefers cassette with 1 song. "No lyric sheets, no pictures or bios. Just the cassette. Have title, artist and contact info printed on cassette." Does not return material. Reports in 6 weeks only if interested.
Music: Mostly **pop**, **dance**, **R&B** and **rap**. Produced Michael Bolton, K-Ci and Jo Jo (of Jodeci), Will Smith, Janet Jackson, Ice Cube, Queen Latifah, Tatyana Ali, Jennifer Paige and The Corrs.

✓ ◯ JACK GALE, 3319 SW Woodcreek Trail, Palm City FL 34990. (305)935-4880. Fax: (305)933-4007. Producer: Jack Gale. Record producer, music publisher (Cowabonga Music/ASCAP and Lovey Music/BMI) and record company (Playback Records). Estab. 1983. Produces 48 singles and 20 CDs/year. Fee derived from sales royalty when song or artist is recorded.
How to Contact: Submit demo tape by mail. Unsolicited submissions are OK. Prefers cassette or VHS videocassette with 2 songs maximum and lyric sheet. SASE. Reports in 2 weeks only if interested.
Music: Mostly **contemporary country** and **country crossover**. Produced *Toast of the Town* (by Ash/Underwood), recorded by Johnny Paycheck; *My Love Belongs to You* (by R. Rogers), recorded by Del Reeves; and *Just Beyond the Pain* (by R. Simons), recorded by Charlie Louvin and Crystal Gayle, all on Playback Records (country). Other artists include Melba Montgomery, Cleve Francis, Margo Smith, Jimmy C. Newman, Tammy Wynette, Willie Nelson, Waylon Jennings, Charlie Daniels, Johnny Cash, Connie Smith and Jeanne C. Riley.

◯ GALLWAY BAY MUSIC, 580 Broadway, Suite 711, New York NY 10012. (212)925-1877. E-mail: gallbay@aol.com. Contact: Peter Gallway. Record producer and production company. Estab. 1983. Produces 4-5 CDs/year. Fee derived from sales royalty when song or artist is recorded or outright fee from recording artist or record company.
How to Contact: Write first and obtain permission to submit. Prefers cassette or DAT with 4 songs. Does not return material. "Responds only if interested in further information."
Music: Great songwriters of all kinds specializing in **contemporary folk** and **alternative pop**. Produced *Mona Lisa Cafe*, written and recorded by Cliff Eberhardt on Shanachie Records (folk/pop); *Industrial Twilight*, written and recorded by Devon Square on DEV Records (folk/pop); *Titanic*, recorded by Jim Infantino on Gadfly Records (alternative/folk); and *Time and Love (the music of Laura Nyro)*, featuring Suzanne Vega, Rosanne Cash, Jane Siberry, Jonatha Brooke and ten other contemporary women artists, on Astor Place Records.

THE TYPES OF MUSIC each listing is interested in are printed in **boldface**.

☑ ◙ **GLASS HOUSE PRODUCTIONS**, P.O. Box 602, Columbus IN 47202. (812)372-6983. Fax: (812)372-3985. E-mail: ghp@ghp.net. Website: http://www.ghp.net/ghp. Executive Producer: Suzanne Glass. Producer/Engineer: Paul Bultman. Producer/Arranger: Patrick Ruffner. A&R: Sandra Harris. Record producer, record company (Throwing Stones Records), music publisher and management firm. Estab. 1989. Produces 20 singles, 10 LPs and 10 CDs/year. Fee is negotiable.

How to Contact: Write first and obtain permission to submit. Prefers cassette or CD and promo materials with 3 songs and lyric sheet. "Include SAS query card when writing for permission and short cover letter." Does not return material. Reports in 1-3 months only if interested (depends on work load).

Music: Mostly **alternative**, **rock (all types)**, **pop** and **acoustic**; also **blues**, **women's** and **all types**. Produced "Purity" (by J. Humphress/B. Alexander), recorded by Dust to Dust (progressive rock); *Island Memories* (by various artists), recorded by Leigacy (folk/Hawaiian); and "Shake It Off" (by P. Ruffner/ S. Glass), recorded by Tattoo Tribe on Throwing Stones (rock). Other artists include Jr. Lewis, Sacred Project, Planet Caravan, Swallow Tail, Suzanne Glass and No Flowers.

Tips: "Be professional, timely, courteous and act with integrity. Work with us, not against. Don't have a closed mind on arrangements, listen to suggestions. Gig a lot, learn the business well enough to communicate, and focus on your art. If you've got talent and desire, contact us; we can help you succeed. Mostly interested in artists/bands from our region of the country. We are currently seeking management clients."

☑ ◙ **HAILING FREQUENCY MUSIC PRODUCTIONS**, 7438 Shoshone Ave., Van Nuys CA 91406. (818)881-9888. Fax: (818)881-0555. E-mail: blowinsmokeband@ktb.net. Website: http://www.blo winsmokeband.com. President: Lawrence Weisberg. Vice President: Larry Knight. Record producer, record company (Blowin' Smoke Records), management firm (Blowin' Smoke Productions) and music publisher (Hailing Frequency Publishing). Estab. 1992. Produces 3 LPs and 3 CDs/year. Fee derived from sales royalty when song or artist is recorded or outright fee from artist.

How to Contact: Write or call first and obtain permission to submit. Prefers cassette or VHS ½″ videocassette. "Write or print legibly with complete contact instructions." SASE. Reports in 1 month.

Music: Mostly **contemporary R&B**, **blues** and **blues-rock**; also **songs for film**, **jingles for commercials** and **gospel (contemporary)**. Produced *Beyond the Blues Horizon* (by various artists), recorded by Blowin' Smoke Rhythm & Blues Band (R&B); and *Got dem St. Louie Blues*, written and recorded by Larry "Fuzzy" Knight (blues), both on Blowin' Smoke Records. Other artists include Christina Vierra and the Fabulous Smokettes.

⚑ ◯ **HARLOW SOUND**, 31 Harlow Crescent, Rexdale, Ontario M9V 2Y6 Canada. (416)741-5007. Owner/Engineer: Gregory English. Record producer and recording studio. Estab. 1984. Produces 15-25 CDs/year. Fees derived from outright fee from recording artist.

How to Contact: Write or call first to arrange personal interview. Prefers cassette or DAT with 3-5 songs. SAE and IRC. Reports in 1-3 weeks.

Music: Produced *Sing or Die*, written and recorded by Courage of Lassie; *Beyond 7*, written and recorded by Gordon Deppe; and *Random Order*, written and recorded by Random Order. Other artists include Viciousphere, Andy Curren and Universal Honey.

Tips: "Be prepared for changes. Example: have three or four different choruses for any given song and be willing to try different things in the studio."

◯ **HAWORTH PRODUCTIONS**, Box 1446, Laurie MO 65038. (314)374-1111. President/Producer: Dann E. Haworth. Record producer and music publisher (Southern Most Publishing/BMI). Estab. 1985. Produces 5 singles, 3 12″ singles, 10 LPs, 5 EPs and 10 CDs/year. Fee derived from sales royalty when song or artist is recorded or outright fee from recording artist.

How to Contact: Submit demo tape by mail. Unsolicited submissions are OK. Prefers cassette or 7½ ips reel-to-reel with 3 songs and lyric or lead sheets. SASE. Reports in 2 weeks.

Music: Mostly **rock**, **country** and **gospel**; also **jazz**, **R&B** and **New Age**. Produced *Christmas Joy* (by Esther Kreak) on Serene Sounds Records. Other artists include The Hollowmen, Jordan Border, Jim Wilson, Tracy Creech and Tony Glise.

Tips: "Keep it simple and from the heart."

◙ **HEART CONSORT MUSIC**, 410 First St. W., Mt. Vernon IA 52314. (319)895-8557. Website: http://www.newmusiccentral.com/hrtcnsrtms.html. Manager: Catherine Lawson. Record producer, record company and music publisher. Estab. 1980. Produces 2-3 CDs/year. Fee derived from sales royalty when song or artist is recorded.

How to Contact: Submit demo tape by mail. Unsolicited submissions are OK. Prefers cassette or VHS videocassette with 3 songs and 3 lyric sheets. SASE. Reports in 3 months.

Music: Mostly **jazz**, **New Age** and **contemporary**. Produced "Irish Dancers," "Time Will Tell" and

"Elixer," all written and recorded by James Kennedy on Heart Consort Music (world/jazz).
Tips: "We are interested in jazz/New Age artists with quality demos and original ideas. We aim for an international audience."

HOUSE OF RHYTHM, 12403 Ventura Court, Suite G, Studio City CA 91604. (818)980-8887. Fax: (818)980-9111. President: Stuart Wiener. Producer: Mike Jett. Record producer and production company. Estab. 1991. Produces 3-5 singles, 3-5 12″ singles, 2 LPs, 2 EPs and 2 CDs/year. Fee derived from sales royalty when song or artist is recorded.
How to Contact: Submit demo tape by mail. Unsolicited submissions are OK. Prefers cassette with 3 songs and lyric sheet. "Do not call to follow up; if we like it we will call you." SASE. Reports in 1 month.
Music: Mostly **dance, pop, R&B** and **rock**; also **new artists** and **new producers**. Produced "The Truth" (by Mike Nally), recorded by SYSTM X on Innerkore Records (dance); "Nasty Groove" and "Lift Em" (by Mike Jett), both recorded by Cold Automatic Eyes on Crap Records (dance). Other artists include Natasha, Richard Grieco and L'Simone.

INTEGRATED ENTERTAINMENT, 3333 Walnut St. #209, Philadelphia PA 19104-3408. (215)417-6921. E-mail: gelboni@aol.com. President: Lawrence Gelburd. Record producer. Estab. 1991. Produces 6 EPs and 6 CDs/year. Fee derived from sales royalty when song or artist is recorded or outright fee from recording artist or record company.
How to Contact: Submit demo tape by mail. Unsolicited submissions are OK. Prefers cassette or CD with 3 songs. "Draw a guitar on the outside of envelope so we'll know it's from a songwriter." SASE. Reports in 2 months.
Music: Mostly **rock** and **AAA**. Produced *Gold Record*, written and recorded by Dash Rip Rock on Ichiban Records (rock); *Virus*, written and recorded by Margin of Error on Treehouse Records (modern rock); and *I Divide*, written and recorded by Amy Carr on Evil Twin Records (AAA). Other artists include Land of the Blind, Grimace, Harpoon, Sprawl, Lockdown and Tripe.

INTERSTATE RECORDS (ISR), P.O. Box 291991, Nashville TN 37229. (615)360-2331. Fax: (615)361-4438. E-mail: jbnisbett@aol.com. Director of A&R: Jack Batey. Record producer and record company. Estab. 1993. Produces 10 singles and 2 CDs/year. Fee derived from sales royalty when song or artist is recorded.
How to Contact: Submit demo tape by mail. Unsolicited submissions are OK. Prefers cassette with 3-5 songs and lyric and lead sheet. "Submit original material only. This allows an opportunity to listen for originality in vocal delivery and judge the strength of writing capabilities. (Please no cover songs or karaoke voice overs)." Does not return material. Reports in 2 months.
Music: Mostly **country, country/pop** and **country/R&B**; also **western swing**. Produced "Mirror-Mirror" (by Billy Powell/DeWayne Mize); "Hobo On a Wildcat Train" (by Jackson Smith); and "Touched By Angel Tears" (by David Lynn O'Connor), all recorded by Bart McEntire on Ameri-Star Records. Other artists include Tex Henley.
Tips: "Be original in your vocals, lyrics and melodies. Submitting a full-blown demo is not necessary as we prefer a tape with acoustic guitar and bass or piano and bass. Click track optional to artist."

JAG STUDIO, LTD., 3801-C Western Blvd., Raleigh NC 27606. (919)821-2059. General Manager: Joy Cook. Record producer, music publisher (Electric Juice Tunes/BMI), record company (JAG Records) and recording studio. Estab. 1981. Produces 12 singles and 8 CDs/year. Fee derived from outright fee from recording artist.
How to Contact: Write first and obtain permission to submit. Does not return material. Reports in 2 months.
Music: Mostly **pop/dance, rap** and **rock**; also **country** and **gospel**. Produced *Righteous*, written and recorded recorded by DAG (soul/rock); and *Brother*, written and recorded by Cry of Love (rock), both on Columbia; and "Waiting for Later" (by B. Guandolo), recorded by Dolo on As If Music. Other artists include Johnny Quest, Bad Checks, John Custer, Ellen Harlow, Stacy Jackson, Doug Jervey, Larry Hutcherson, Automatic Slim and Six String Drag.
Tips: "Be prepared. Learn something about the *business* end of music first."

REFER TO THE CATEGORY INDEX (at the end of this section) to find exactly which companies are interested in the type of music you write.

ALEXANDER JANOULIS PRODUCTIONS/BIG AL JANO PRODUCTIONS, 1957 Kilburn Dr., Atlanta GA 30324. (404)662-6661. E-mail: ajproductions@hottrax.com. Vice President of A&R: Oliver Cooper. CEO: Alex Janoulis. Record producer. Produces 6 singles and 2 CDs/year. Fee derived from sales royalty when song or artist is recorded or outright fee from recording artist or record company.
How to Contact: Write first and obtain permission to submit. "Letters should be short, requesting submission permission." Prefers cassette with 1-3 songs. Does not return material. Reports in 1-6 months.
Music: Mostly **top 40**, **rock** and **pop**; also **black** and **disco**. Produced *You Ain't Foolin*, written and recorded by Roger Hurrican Wilson (blues rock); *Poor Man Shuffle* (by Robert Page), recorded by The Bob Page Project (blues); and *Merry Christmas Rap*, written and recorded by Mike Lorenz (rap), all on Hottrax Records. Other artists include Bullitthead and Chesterfield Kings.

JAY JAY PUBLISHING & RECORD CO., 35 NE 62nd St., Miami FL 33138. (305)758-0000. Owner: Walter Jagiello. Record producer, music publisher (BMI) and record company (Jay Jay Record, Tape and Video Co.). Estab. 1951. Produces 12 singles, 12 LPs and 12 CDs/year. Fee derived from sales royalty when song or artist is recorded.
How to Contact: Submit demo tape by mail. Unsolicited submissions are OK. Prefers cassette or VHS videocassette with 6 songs and lyric and lead sheet. "Quality cassette or reel-to-reel, sheet music and lyrics." Does not return material. Reports in 2 months.
Music: Mostly **ballads**, **love songs**, **country music** and **comedy**; also **polkas** and **waltzes**. Produced *The Night of Christmas* (by Walter E. Jagiello), recorded by Sweet Marie Kubowski; and *Animal Ditties for the Kiddies* (by Al Trace), recorded by Capt. Stubby-Buccaneers, both on Jay Jay Records. Other artists include Eddie & The Slovenes, Johnny Vadnal and Wisconsin Dutchmen.

JAZMIN PRODUCTIONS, P.O. Box 92913, Long Beach CA 90809. (310)609-8723. E-mail: jazminpro@aol.com. Owner/Producer: Gregory D. Dendy. Record producer. Estab. 1991. Produces 2-4 LPs/year. Fee derived from sales royalty when song or artist is recorded or outright fee from record company.
How to Contact: Write or call first and obtain permission to submit. Prefers cassette with lyric sheet. Does not return material. Reports in 2 months.
Music: Mostly **urban gospel**. Produced *Broderick Rice Alive*, written and recorded by Broderick Rice on Born Again Records (gospel); and and *Make Us One* (by William Charles/Kevin Davis), recorded by Make Us One (contemporary gospel). Other artists include Enlightment, Kim & Dave, Rejoyce, Pentecostal Community Choir and Mary Floyd.

JERICHO SOUND LAB, Box 407, Jericho VT 05465. (802)899-3787. Owner: Bobby Hackney. Record producer, music publisher (Elect Music/BMI) and record company (LBI Records). Estab. 1988. Produces 5 singles, 2 12″ singles and 3 LPs/year. Fee derived from sales royalty when song or artist is recorded.
How to Contact: Write first and obtain permission to submit. Prefers cassette or VHS videocassette with 3-4 songs and lyric sheet. SASE. Reports in 4-6 weeks.
Music: Mostly **reggae**, **R&B** and **pop**; also **rock** and **jazz-poetry**. Produced "Spotlight on You" (by B. Hackney), and "Sharing and Caring," recorded by Lambsbread (reggae), both on LBI Records.
Tips: "Make it plain and simple. Send only your best. Most producers know within 10 to 15 seconds if a song catches their attention."

DAVID JOHN PRODUCTIONS, 26 Amidon Dr., Ashford CT 06278. (860)487-3613. Fax: (860)487-3614. E-mail: dmorascini@snet.net. Producer: David John. Vice President, A&R: Kirsten. Record producer and record company (Rock-It Records). Estab. 1983. Produces 2 singles, 8-12 LPs, 4 EPs and 10 CDs/year. Fee derived from outright fee from recording artist or record company.
How to Contact: Submit demo tape by mail. Unsolicited submissions are OK. Prefers cassette with 4 songs. Does not return material. Reports in 3-4 months.
Music: Mostly **original rock**, **alternative** and **computer-generated**; also **anything good**! Produced *Glass Houses* (by R. Rush), recorded by Jay Bird on Bird Song (alternative rock); *Metal Storm*, written and recorded by Jeff Weir on Hammer & Nail (metal); and *Smokin Weed*, written and recorded by Jane Long & Band on Inca's (alternative). Other artists include New Johnny 5, Silicone Safari and Guy Walker.

JSB GROUPE MANAGEMENT INC., 1307 Noire-Fontaine Place, Cap-Rouge, Quebec G1Y 3C9 Canada. Phone/fax: (418)651-4917. E-mail: jsbol@videotron.ca. President: Jean-Sebastien Boucher. Record producer, record company (Productions JSB) and management. Estab. 1994. Produces 1 LP and 1 CD/year. Fee derived from sales royalty when song or artist is recorded or outright fee from record company.
How to Contact: Submit demo tape by mail. Unsolicited submissions are OK. Prefers cassette, VHS videocassette or C.V. Does not return material. Reports in 2 months.

Music: Mostly **classical**, **children's** and **pop/rock**. Produced *Eric Laporte, The Tenor II*, recorded by Eric Laporte (classical) on JSB.

Tips: "We are very interested in classical music: tenors, instrumentalists and conductors. Be well prepared and have an independent structure of management."

JUNE PRODUCTIONS LTD., "Toftrees," Church Rd., Woldingham, Surrey CR3 7JH England. Producer: David Mackay. Record producer and music producer (Sabre Music). Estab. 1970. Produces 6 singles, 3 LPs and 3 CDs/year. Fee derived from sales royalty.

How to Contact: Submit demo tape by mail. Unsolicited submissions are OK. Prefers cassette with 1-2 songs and lyric sheet. SAE and IRC. Reports in 6-8 weeks.

Music: Mostly **MOR**, **rock** and **top 40/pop**. Produced *Web of Love* (by various), recorded by Sarah Jory on Ritz Records (country rock). Other artists include Bonnie Tyler, Cliff Richard, Frankie Miller, Johnny Hallyday, Dusty Springfield and Barry Humphries.

KAREN KANE PRODUCER/ENGINEER, 9 Wheatfield Rd., Toronto, Ontario M8V 2P5 Canada. (416)259-9177. Fax: (416)252-0464. E-mail: mixmama@total.net. Website: http://www.total.net/~mixmama. Producer/Engineer: Karen Kane. Record producer and recording engineer. Estab. 1978. Produces 5-10 singles and 5-10 CDs/year. Fee derived from sales royalty when song or artist is recorded or outright fee from recording artist or record company.

How to Contact: Write or call first and obtain permission to submit. Unsolicited submissions are *not* OK. Does not return material. Reports in 2-3 weeks.

Music: Mostly **pop**, **alternative**, **R&B/reggae** and **acoustic**. Produced *Can't Corner Me*, written and recorded by Ember Swift on Few'll Ignite Sound (alternative/folk/pop); *4 Blues* (by various artists), recorded by Big Daddy G on Reggie's Records (blues); and *Dance the Spiral Dance*, written and recorded by Ubaka Hill on Ladyslipper Records (African percussion with vocals). Other artists include Tracy Chapman (her first demo), Jack Grunsky, Kyn, Chad Mitchell and Kay Gardner.

Tips: "Get proper funding to be able to make a competitive, marketable product."

MATTHEW KATZ PRODUCTIONS, 29903 Harvester Rd., Malibu CA 90265. (310)457-4844. President: Matthew Katz. Record producer, music publisher (After You Publishing/BMI) and record company (San Francisco Sound and Malibu Records). Produces 6 singles, 6 12" singles and 2 CDs/year. Fee derived from sales royalty when song or artist is recorded, or outright fee from record company.

How to Contact: Submit demo tape by mail. Unsolicited submissions are OK. Prefers cassette or 8mm videocassette and lead sheet. Does not return material.

Music: Mostly **San Francisco rock** and **jazz**. Produced Jefferson Airplane, Moby Grape, It's A Beautiful Day, Indian Puddin' & Pipe, Fraternity of Man and Tim Hardin.

Tips: "We're interested in original New Age material for Malibu Records and message songs. Not interested in 'Why is she making it with some other guy, not me?' "

KILGORE PRODUCTIONS, 52323 Harrisburg, Chesterfield MI 48051. E-mail: ekilgore@email.msn.com. Chief Producer: Eric Kilgore. Record producer. Produces 6 EPs and 2-4 CDs/year. Fee derived from sales royalty when song or artist is recorded, or individual arrangements with artist.

How to Contact: Write first and obtain permission to submit. Prefers cassette with 1-3 songs and legibly printed lyric sheet. SASE. Reports in 6 weeks.

Music: Mostly **folk/rock**, **folk** and **acoustic rock**; also **novelty** and **hard to define style combinations**. Produced "The Morning After the Night Before," and *Lick Me & Mail Me*, both written and recorded by The Bouncing Perversions (novelty); and *Unclassified Ad*, written and recorded by various artists (compilation), all on Schizophrenic Records. Other artists include Pantheon June, reductive synthesis and O.C. Tolbert.

Tips: "We are a small company that works with a limited amount of acts. We work as hard as we can for our clients, but they must be willing to help themselves also!"

KINGSTON RECORDS AND TALENT, 15 Exeter Rd., Kingston NH 03848. (603)642-8493. Coordinator: Harry Mann. Record producer, music publisher (Strawberry Soda Publishing/ASCAP) and record company (Kingston Records). Estab. 1988. Produces 3-4 singles, 2-3 12" singles, 2-3 LPs and 1-2 CDs/year. Fee derived from sales royalty when song or artist is recorded. Deals primarily with NE and local artists.

How to Contact: Write first and obtain permission to submit. Prefers cassette with 1-2 songs and lyric sheet. Does not return material. Reports in 2 months.

Music: Mostly **rock**, **country** and **pop**; "no heavy metal." Produced *Ted Solovicus*, written and recorded by Ted Solovicus; *Billy Glynn*, written and recorded by Billy Glynn; and *Armond's Way*, written and recorded by Armand Lemay, all on Kingston Records (rock). Other artists include Bob Moore, Candy Striper Death Orgy, Pocket Band, Jeff Walker, J. Evans, NTM, Miss Bliss, Four On The Floor and Sumx4.

N ⦿ **KLEANZA RIVER CANYON PRODUCTIONS**, 2411 Pulaski Hwy., Columbia TN 38401. (931)840-5948. Owner/Producer: Gordon Thibideau. Record producer, music publisher (Wolf Paw Music) and artist development and management. Estab. 1999. Produces 15 singles, 10 LPs and 10 CDs/year. Fee derived from sales royalty when song or artist is recorded or outright fee from recording artist or record company.
How to Contact: Submit demo tape by mail. Unsolicited submissions are OK. Prefers cassette or video-cassette with 1-5 songs and lyric sheet. "For prospective artist, please submit promotional package with bio and photos." SASE. Reports in 2-3 weeks.
Music: Mostly **country**, **rock** and **pop**; also **blues**, **jazz** and **comedy**. Artists include Hal Wayne, Billie Jo Spears, Vic Chavez and Danny Mack (all produced in the '70s and '80s).
Tips: "Know that this is what you want to do. Understand there is a large amount of work and constructive criticism to deal with on the road to success."

⦿ **KMA**, 1650 Broadway, Suite 900, New York NY 10019-6833. (212)265-1570. A&R Director: Morris Levy. Record producer and music publisher (Block Party Music/ASCAP). Estab. 1987. Produces 2 12" singles, 3 LPs and 3 CDs/year. Fee derived from sales royalty or outright fee from recording artist or record company.
How to Contact: Does not accept unsolicited material.
Music: Mostly **R&B**, **dance** and **rap**; also **movie** and **ethnic**. Produced "I Found It," recorded by Daphne on Maxi Records; "Through the Day," recorded by Millenium on 143/Atlantic Records; and "I Want You for Me," recorded by Raw Stilo on dv8/A&M Records.
Tips: "*Original* lyrics a huge plus. We are starting a movie soundtrack. Send reggae and dance hall submissions."

N ⦿ **KNOWN ARTIST PRODUCTIONS**, 1219 Kerlin Ave., Brewton AL 36426. (334)867-2228. President: Roy Edwards. Record producer, music publisher (Cheavoria Music Co./BMI, Baitstring Music/ASCAP) and record company (Bolivia Records, Known Artist Records). Estab. 1972. Produces 10 singles and 3 LPs/year. Fee derived from sales royalty when song or artist is recorded.
How to Contact: Write first and obtain permission to submit. Prefers cassette with 3 songs and lyric sheet. Reports in 1 month. "All tapes will be kept on file."
Music: Mostly **R&B**, **pop** and **country**; also **easy listening**, **MOR** and **soul**. Produced "Got To Let You Know," "You Are My Sunshine" and "You Make My Life So Wonderful," all written and recorded by Roy Edwards on Bolivia Records (R&B). Other artists include Jim Portwood, Bobbie Roberson and Brad Smiley.

⦿ **KOOL BREEZE PRODUCTIONS**, N. 81 Lane, P.O. Box 120, Loxahatchee FL 33470. (407)795-4232. Executive Director: Kevin Reeves. Marketing Manager: Debbie Reeves. Record producer and music publisher. Estab. 1991. Produces 10 singles and 6 LPs-year. Fee derived from sales royalty when song or artist is recorded.
How to Contact: Submit demo tape by mail. Unsolicited submissions are OK. Prefers cassette and lyric sheet (typed and full size). "Commercially viable to industry standards. Strong hooks, definitive melody, uplifting lyrical concepts, SASE required for all correspondence, don't be predictable." SASE. Reports in 2 months.
Music: Mostly **pop contemporary (dance)**, **rock (pop, blues, folk, soft, jazz)**, **A/C** and **electric acoustic**; also **country (pop, blues)**, **blues (R&B, urban)** and **gospel**. Produced *Fatal Vision* (by Andy Atkins), recorded by Fatal Vision; *Dynamic Derrick and Boogie Brigade* (by Kevin Reeves), recorded by Dynamic Derrick and the Boogie Brigade, both on Kool Breeze Records; and *Jayne Reby*, written and recorded by Jayne Reby on Rustron Records.
Tips: "Always send SASE with proper postage if you want a reply."

⦿ **ROBERT R. KOVACH**, P.O. Box 7018, Warner Robins GA 31095-7018. (912)953-2800. Producer: Robert R. Kovach. Record producer. Estab. 1976. Produces 6 singles, 2 cassettes and 1 CD/year. Fee

REFER TO THE GEOGRAPHIC INDEX (at the back of this book) to find listings of companies by state, as well as foreign listings.

derived from sales royalty when song or artist is recorded, or outright fee from record company.

How to Contact: Submit demo tape by mail. Unsolicited submissions are OK. Prefers cassette with 4 songs and lyric sheet. SASE. Reports in 4 months.

Music: Mostly **country** and **pop**; also **easy listening**, **R&B**, **rock** and **gospel**. Produced "Pots & Pans," recorded by Theresa Justus (country); and "You Learn A Heart to Break," recorded by Wayne Little (country), both by Roy Robert Dunten (country); and "Lord I've Been Prayin" (by Robert R. Kovach), recorded by Napolean Starke (gospel), all on Scaramouche. Other artists include Little Rudy.

Tips: "Submit a demo and be patient."

☑ ◯ **L.A. ENTERTAINMENT, INC.**, 6367 Selma Ave., Hollywood CA 90028. (323)467-1496. Fax: (323)462-8562. E-mail: info@warriorrecords.com. Website: http://www.warriorrecords.com. A&R: Jim Ervin. Record producer, record company (Warrior Records) and music publisher (New Entity Music/ ASCAP). Estab. 1988. Fee derived from sales royalty when song or artist is recorded.

How to Contact: Submit demo tape by mail. Unsolicited submissions are OK. Prefers cassette or video-cassette with 3 songs, lyric and lead sheet if available. "All written submitted materials (e.g., lyric sheets, letter, etc.) should be typed." Does not return material. Reports in 2 months.

Music: Mostly **alternative** and **R&B**.

◐ **LANDMARK COMMUNICATIONS GROUP**, P.O. Box 1444, Hendersonville TN 37077. Producer: Bill Anderson Jr. Record producer, record company, music publisher (Newcreature Music/BMI) and TV/radio syndication. Produces 12 singles and 12 LPs/year. Fee derived from sales royalty.

How to Contact: Write first and obtain permission to submit. Prefers 7½ ips reel-to-reel, cassette or videocassette with 4-10 songs and lyric sheet. SASE. Reports in 1 month.

Music: Mostly **country crossover**; also **blues**, **country**, **gospel**, **jazz**, **rock** and **top 40/pop**. Produced "Good Love," written and recorded by Gail Score (R&B); "A Hero Never Dies," written and recorded by Joanne Cash Yates on Jana Records (gospel); and "Nothin' Else Feels Quite Like It" (by B. Nash/K. Nash/B. Anderson), recorded on TV Theme Records (country). Other artists include Skeeter Davis and Vernon Oxford.

◐ **LARI-JON PRODUCTIONS**, 325 W. Walnut, Rising City NE 68658. (402)542-2336. Owner: Larry Good. Record producer, music publisher (Lari-Jon Publishing/BMI), management firm (Lari-Jon Promotions) and record company (Lari-Jon Records). Estab. 1967. Produces 10 singles and 5 LPs/year. Fee derived from sales royalty when song or artist is recorded.

How to Contact: Submit demo tape by mail. Unsolicited submissions are OK. "Must be a professional demo." SASE. Reports in 2 months.

Music: Mostly **country**, **gospel-Southern** and **'50s rock**. Produced *Jesus is my Hero*, written and recorded by Larry Good on Lari-Jon Records (gospel). Other artists include Brenda Allen, Tom Campbell and Tom Johnson.

☑ ◯ **LARK TALENT & ADVERTISING**, P.O. Box 35726, Tulsa OK 74153. (918)786-8896. E-mail: janajae@janajae.com. Website: http://www.janajae.com. Vice President: Kathleen Pixley. Owner: Jana Jae. Record producer, music publisher (Jana Jae Music/BMI) and record company (Lark Record Productions, Inc.). Estab. 1980. Fee derived from sales royalty when song or artist is recorded.

How to Contact: Submit demo tape by mail. Unsolicited submissions are OK. Prefers cassette or VHS videocassette with 3 songs and lead sheet. Does not return material. Reports in 1 month only if interested.

Music: Mostly **country**, **bluegrass** and **classical**; also **instrumentals**. Produced "Fiddlestix" (by Jana Jae); "Mayonnaise" (by Steve Upfold); and "Flyin' South" (by Cindy Walker), all recorded by Jana Jae on Lark Records (country). Other artists include Sydni, Hotwire and Matt Greif.

☑ ◯ **LAZY BONES PRODUCTIONS/RECORDINGS, INC.**, 9594 First Ave. NE, Suite 230, Seattle WA 98115-2012. (206)447-0712. Fax: (425)821-5720. E-mail: lbrinc@earthlink.net. Website: http://www.lazybones.com. President: Scott Schorr. Record producer, record company and music publisher (Lazy Bones Music/BMI). Estab. 1992. Produces 5 singles, 3 EPs and 2-4 CDs/year. Fee derived from sales royalty when song or artist is recorded or outright fee from recording artist (if unsigned) or outright fee from record company (if signed) or publishing royalties when co-songwriting with artist.

How to Contact: Submit demo tape by mail. Unsolicited submissions are OK. Prefers cassette, DAT or CD with 3 songs (minimum) and lyric sheet. "If you honestly believe you can do better, improve your project to its greatest potential before submitting. With the number of projects received, if the material is not truly special and unique, it will not be taken seriously by a legitimate company." Does not return material. Reports in 1 month only if interested.

Music: Mostly **alternative** and **rock**; also **hip-hop**. Produced *No Samples* (by Da Blasta/Ratboy), recorded

by Turntable Bay (hip-hop); and *Headland II* (by Dave Hadland), recorded by Headland (pop), both on Lazy Bones. Other artists include Blackhead, MFTJ, B. Chestnut and Alan Charing.
Tips: "Have outstanding and unique talent!"

◐ LINEAR CYCLE PRODUCTIONS, P.O. Box 2608, Sepulveda CA 91393-2608. E-mail: lcp@west world.com. Website: http://www.westworld.com/lcp/. Producer: R. Borowy. Record producer. Estab. 1980. Produces 15-25 singles, 6-10 12″ singles, 15-20 LPs and 10 CDs/year. Fee derived from sales royalty when song or artist is recorded.
How to Contact: Submit demo tape by mail. Unsolicited submissions are OK. Prefers cassette, 7⅜ ips reel-to-reel or ½″ VHS or ¾″ videocassette. SASE. Reports in 1-6 months.
Music: Mostly **rock/pop**, **R&B/blues** and **country**; also **gospel** and **comedy**. Produced "Do The GAXe" (by Milk), recorded by Cheap Rotton Mallet on Drip Recordings (alternative); "She'll Leave The Beer Always Without You" (by T. Thumper), recorded by Pik Urp Trux on Sage Records (country); and "My Ice Isn't A Heart" (by Olif Spear), recorded by Reachie Feel on Mel-O Records (A/C).
Tips: "We only listen to songs and other material recorded on quality tapes and CDs. We will not accept anything that sounds distorted, muffled and just plain bad! If you cannot afford to record demos on quality stock, or in some high aspects, shop somewhere else!"

◻ LOCONTO PRODUCTIONS, 10244 NW 47 St., Sunrise FL 33351. (954)741-7766. (305)741-7766. President: Frank X. Loconto. Record producer, record company and music publisher. Estab. 1978. Produces 10 cassettes/albums and 10 CDs/year. Fee derived from sales royalty or outright fee from songwriter/artist and/or record company.
How to Contact: Submit demo tape by mail. Unsolicited submissions are OK. Prefers cassette. SASE. Reports in 3-4 months.
Music: Produced *Aurore* (by various), recorded by Aurore (gospel); *Vodec* (by various), recorded by Vodec (gospel); and *Total Package*, written and recorded by Jos. E. Ford, all on FXL Records. Other artists include Roger B. Bryant, Mark Goldman and Chris Risi.

✔ ◐ HAROLD LUICK & COUNTRY MUSIC SHOWCASE INTL. ASSOCIATES, Box #368, Carlisle IA 50047. (515)989-3748. Fax: (515)989-0235. E-mail: haroldl@cmshowcase.org. Website: http://www.cmshowcase.org. Producers: Robbie Wittkowski; Harold L. Luick. Artist Management: Aaron Kerns. Record producer, music industry consultant, music print publisher and music publisher. Produces 20 singles and 6 LPs/year. Fee derived from sales royalty, outright fee from artist/songwriter or record company, and from consulting fees for information or services.
How to Contact: Write or call first and obtain permission to submit. Prefers cassette with 3-5 songs and lyric sheet. SASE. Reports in 3 weeks.
Music: Mostly **traditional country**, **gospel**, **contemporary country** and **MOR**. Produced *I Want to Forget You* (by Bill Anderson/Sharon Rice/Al Anderson), recorded by Stacey Kerns on Kid Kody Records (country). "Over a 12-year period, Harold Luick has produced and recorded 412 singles and 478 albums, 7 of which charted and some of which have enjoyed independent sales in excess of 30,000 units."
Tips: "If you are looking to place a song with us and have it considered for a recording, make sure you have a decent demo, and all legals in order."

✔ ◻ MAC-ATTACK PRODUCTIONS, 8101 NE 8 Court, Miami FL 33138. (305)949-1422. E-mail: themacster@aol.com. Engineer/Producer: Michael McNamee. Record producer and music publisher (Mac-Attack Publishing/ASCAP). Estab. 1986. Fee derived from outright fee from recording artist or record company.
How to Contact: Submit demo tape by mail. Unsolicited submissions are OK. Prefers cassette or VHS videocassette with 3-5 songs, lyric sheet and bio. Does not return material. Reports in 1-4 weeks.
Music: Mostly **pop**, **alternative rock** and **dance**. Produced *Ocean of Love* (by Jordan Kahn), recorded by Jordan on JK Records (pop). Other artists include Blowfly, Forget the Name, Nine Llopis, The Lead and Girl Talk.

✔ ◻ LEE MAGID PRODUCTIONS, P.O. Box 532, Malibu CA 90265. (323)463-5998. President: Lee Magid. Record producer, music publisher (Alexis Music, Inc./ASCAP, Marvelle Music Co./BMI and

---

OPENNESS TO SUBMISSIONS: ◻ beginners; ◐ beginners and experienced; ◖ experienced only; ◒ industry referrals only.

Gabal Music Co./SESAC), record company (Grass Roots Records, LMI Records) and management firm (Lee Magid Management). Estab. 1950. Produces 4 singles, 4 12″ singles, 8 LPs and 8 CDs/year. Fee derived from sales royalty when song or artist is recorded.

How to Contact: Submit demo tape by mail. Unsolicited submissions are OK. "Send cassette giving address and phone number." Prefers cassette or VHS videocassette with 3-6 songs and lyric sheet. "Please only one cassette, and photos if you are an artist/writer." Does not return material. Reports in 6 weeks only if accepted.

Music: Mostly **R&B**, **rock**, **jazz** and **gospel**; also **pop**, **bluegrass**, **church/religious**, **easy listening**, **folk**, **blues**, **MOR**, **progressive**, **soul**, **instrumental** and **top 40**. Produced *I'll Be Seeing You Around* (by Lorna McGough/John Scott/Mark Newbar), recorded by 2AD on LMI Records (R&B); *It's Only Money* (by John M. Hides), recorded by J. Michael Hides on Grass Roots Records (pop); and *Blues For the Weepers* (by Lee Magid/Max Rich), recorded by Bob Stewart on VWC Records (jazz). Other artists include Tramaine Hawkins, Della Reese, Rod Piazza, "Big Joe" Turner, Tom Vaughn and Laura Lee.

✔ ◖ **MAGNETIC OBLIVION MUSIC CO.**, P.O. Box 1446, Eureka CA 95502. Phone/fax: (707)445-2698. E-mail: magob@aol.com. Website: http://magneticoblivion.com/go. Director of A&R: Eppilido Torres. President: Matthew Knight. Record producer, record company (Magnetic Oblivion Records) and music publisher. Estab. 1984. Produces 3 singles, 1 EP and 6-10 CDs/year. Fee derived from publishing royalty.

How to Contact: Submit demo tape by mail. Unsolicited submissions are OK. Prefers cassette, DAT or videocassette. "All material must be copyrighted. Non-copyrighted material will be trashed without review." Does not return material. Reports in 4-6 weeks.

Music: Mostly **experimental**, **early music** and **alternative**; also **Celtic**, **novelty** and **acid jazz**. Produced *The Fifth* (by M. Chan), recorded by The Fifth (alternative); *All For a Lark* (by various artists), recorded by All For a Lark (early); and *Negative Bouancy* (by Matty Dread), recorded by Troubled Loners (alternative), all on Magnetic Oblivion Records. Other artists include Goofus & Gallant, Country Matters, Chowderhead, Tama and Tim Fouts.

Tips: "Either the songwriting is there or it isn't. Don't send us trite material about your girlfriend leaving you—unless it's the best damn 'love lost' song ever written. Last year we received at least ten 'Fiona Apples.' It's great to admire successful performers—but there's only one Fiona (thank God!). Be yourself. Take some risks."

✔ ◖ **MAKERS MARK MUSIC PRODUCTIONS (ASCAP)**, P.O. Box 42751, Philadelphia PA 19101. (215)236-4817. Website: http://www.prolificrecords.com/. Producer: Paul E. Hopkins. Record producer, music publisher and record company (Prolific Records). Estab. 1991. Produces 15 singles, 5 12″ singles and 4 LPs/year. Fee derived from outright fee from recording artist or record company.

How to Contact: Submit demo tape by mail. Unsolicited submissions are OK. Prefers cassette with 2-4 songs and bio. "Explain concept of your music and/or style, and your future direction as an artist or songwriter." Does not return material. Reports in 4-6 weeks (if interested).

Music: Mostly **R&B**, **dance**, **pop**, **country** and **rap**. Produced "When Will My Heart Beat Again," and "Last Kiss" (by Cheryl Forman/Paul Hopkins), both recorded by Rachel Scarborough; and *All Eyes on the Philosopher* (by Norman Gilliam/Paul Hopkins), recorded by Norman Gilliam on Prolific Records. Other artists include Larry Larr, Paul Hopkins, Nardo Ranks (international Jamaican artist), Elaine Monk (R&B) and Andy Romano (R&B/pop).

◖ **COOKIE MARENCO**, P.O. Box 874, Belmont CA 94002. E-mail: otrstudios@aol.com. Record producer/engineer. Estab. 1981. Produces 10 CDs/year. Fee derived from sales royalty and outright fee from recording artist or record company.

• See the Insider Report interview with Cookie Marenco on page 248.

How to Contact: Write first and obtain permission to submit. Does not return material. Reports only if interested.

Music: Mostly **alternative modern rock**, **country**, **folk**, **rap**, **ethnic** and **avante-garde**; also **classical**, **pop** and **jazz**. Produced *Winter Solstice II*, written and recorded by various artists; *Heresay* (by Paul McCandless); and *Deep At Night* (by Alex DeGrassi), all on Windham Hill Records (instrumental). Other artists include Ladysmith Black Mambazo, Steve Owen, Tony Furtado, Oregon, Brain & Buckethead, Roy Hargrove, Monterey Jazz Festival, J.A. Deane, Mark Isham and Diamanda Galas.

✔ ◖ **PETE MARTIN/VAAM MUSIC PRODUCTIONS**, P.O. Box 29550, Hollywood CA 90029-0550. (323)664-7765. E-mail: vaampubl@aol.com or pmarti3636@aol.com. President: Pete Martin. Record producer, music publisher (Vaam Music/BMI and Pete Martin Music/ASCAP) and record company (Blue

Gem Records). Estab. 1982. Produces 12 singles and 5 LPs/year. Fee derived from sales royalty when song or artist is recorded.

How to Contact: Prefers cassette with 2 songs and lyric sheet. Send small packages only. SASE. Reports in 1 month.

Music: Mostly **top 40/pop**, **country** and **R&B**. Produced Shay Lynn, Sherry Weston, Vero, Frank Loren, Brian Smith & The Renegades, Victoria Limon, Brandy Rose and Cory Canyon.

Tips: "Study the market in the style that you write. Songs must be capable of reaching top 5 on charts."

◯ **DAVID MATHES PRODUCTIONS**, P.O. Box 22653, Nashville TN 37202. (615)252-6912. E-mail: music@gointer.net. Website: http://musicaccess.net. President: David W. Mathes. AF of M licensed. Record producer and music publisher (Mathes Company). Estab. 1962. Produces 6-10 singles, 4-16 12″ singles and 4-6 LPs/year. Fee derived from sales royalty when song or artist is recorded (for published material), or outright fee from record company (for production) or outright fee from recording artist (if custom recording).

How to Contact: Write first and obtain permission to submit. "No certified mail accepted." Prefers 7½ or 15 ips reel-to-reel, cassette or videocassette with 2-4 songs and lyric sheet. "Enclose correctly stamped envelope for demo return." Reports in 1 month.

Music: Mostly **country** and **gospel**; also **bluegrass**, **R&B** and **instrumental**. Produced *Jesus Loved the Devil Out of Me* (by Tommy and Ann Riggs), recorded by Hatchie Bottom Boys (bluegrass); and *Walking After Midnight Over You* (by Ernie Welch), recorded by Smokehouse Band (new grass), both on Nesak International. Other artists include Deanna, The Capitals, The Ballards, Johnny C. Newman, The Blackwood Singers and Eddie Albert Sings Americana.

Tips: "Be prepared. Time rehearsing in the studio is costly. Remember, Nashville's professional musicians will not delay the recording process. Allow the producer to make critical decisions concerning material selection and recording process."

� ◯ **SCOTT MATHEWS, D/B/A HIT OR MYTH PRODUCTIONS**, 36 Lisbon St., San Rafael CA 94901. Fax: (415)389-9682. E-mail: hitormyth@aol.com. President: Scott Mathews. Assistant: Mary Ezzell. Record producer, song doctor, studio owner and music publisher (Hang On to Your Publishing/ BMI). Estab. 1990. Produces 6-9 CDs/year. Fee derived from sales royalty when song or artist is recorded, or from recording artist or record company (with royalty points).

• Scott Mathews has several gold and platinum awards for sales of over 12 million records. He has worked on several Grammy and Oscar winning releases. See the article So You Got a Solicited Submission—Now What? on page 31 for more information from Scott Mathews.

How to Contact: Submit demo tape by mail. Unsolicited submissions are OK. Prefers DAT (cassette and CD accepted). SASE. Reports in 2 months. "Absolutely no phone calls, please."

Music: Mostly **rock/pop**, **alternative** and **singer/songwriters of all styles**. Produced "The Way We Make a Broken Heart" (by John Hiatt), recorded by John Hiatt with Rosanne Cash on Capitol (pop); *Succumb* (by Spets Ranson/Debbie Fox/Charlie Fulton), recorded by Virgin Whore Complex on Emperor Norton (alternative); and *How Else Can the Story Go?* (by Roger Clark), recorded by Lucy Lee on Island (pop). Has produced Roy Orbison, Rosanne Cash, John Hiatt and many more. Has recorded with everyone from Barbra Streisand to John Lee Hooker, including Keith Richards, Sammy Hagar, Van Morrison, Elvis Costello, Bonnie Raitt and Eric Clapton to name but a few.

Tips: "This year, we are putting more emphasis on finding new talent and developing unsigned artists who need an incredible 'finished' recording to land them the right deal. It is common knowledge that the days of sending rough demos to record companies are long gone. One has to blow away those finicky A&R ears with a product that competes with what is on the radio. I will find time to listen to any and all self-contained artists who are seriously looking for an established producer to collaborate with. Please, no publishing submissions."

◻ ◯ **MAY MUSIC/SWIFT RIVER PRODUCTIONS**, P.O. Box 231, Gladeville TN 37071. (615)453-0952. E-mail: maymusic@pobox.com. Producer: Andy May. Record producer, record company and music publisher. Estab. 1979. Produces 40 singles and 8 CDs/year. Fee derived from outright fee from recording artist or record company.

How to Contact: Write or call first and obtain permission to submit. Prefers cassette with 3 songs and

THE OPENNESS TO SUBMISSIONS INDEX at the back of this book lists all companies in this section by how open they are to submissions.

insider report

Producer empowers artists to be in control

Cookie Marenco's work as a recording engineer and producer came directly from her own love of music. Her career has been a model of the variety of work that *is* the music industry. Along with producing five Grammy-nominated albums and numerous hits on the Gavin charts, she has composed film scores, worked in A&R and been a pioneer in multimedia entertainment. A self-described "advocate of the indie artist," she has some often outspoken ideas about the future of music and the increasing importance of Internet technology to both emerging and established artists.

Photo by Andy Nozaka

Cookie Marenco

"I didn't even know what a producer was," Marenco admits when discussing the early stages of her career. She grew up surrounded by music, learning to read music before words. She began to study violin at age 10 and oboe at 13. She received the Art LaRatta Piano Scholarship and auditioned with the San Francisco Symphony, and went on to major in composition in college and studied jazz with Allaudin Bill Mathieu and Art Lande. This training has allowed her to score commercials for Nissan and AT&T, along with documentary and feature films.

While in college, she began teaching piano lessons. Though she loved all of the music she studied, she realized that, like many of her colleagues, she might only find work as a waitress or high school bandleader upon graduation. She continued to teach piano for ten years but began to look into engineering and producing. Her approach to teaching, she feels, led naturally to her current vocation. "When you produce," she says, "you're still in the role of teacher, especially with younger artists."

Another important part of working with younger artists is developing their patience and focus. Marenco feels part of a producer's job is to "keep them focused on the goal . . . and teach them what it takes." Often a band will send a demo tape with the belief that she will be able to make them sound great even if they aren't the most skilled musicians, get them a record deal, book gigs for them, and any number of other wonderful things. "If they're unrealistic, I can't work with them," she says.

COOKIE MARENCO

Producer
Worked with: Max Roach, Praxis,
  Mary Chapin Carpenter
Studio: OTR Studios, Belmont, CA

Before sitting down to record with a band, Marenco will ask artists for a list of influences and perhaps more importantly, who they want to be three albums from now. For the band that wants the "Big Hit" and a barrel full of fast money, that second question can be a deal-breaker with Marenco. She works with artists she likes and whose approach to music she respects. The critical thing when recording, she feels, is to set a goal. Often that goal is for the band to get the most out of themselves. "It's not some kind of get-rich-quick scheme."

Because Marenco has experience as an artist, she has many valuable lessons to impart to those she works with. She credits Lande with one of her basic theories as a producer and teacher: "When you're heading down a path, and it's not working, you have to be willing to try something out of the realm of possibility. You have to take a chance."

This attitude is crucial to the role of producer, says Marenco. Sometimes she acts solely as engineer, downplaying her own experience as a musician. More often, artists look to her for expert advice and sound opinions. When she does disagree with an artist's choice, she takes a diplomatic approach. Marenco respects their choices; she knows all too well how it is to be in that position. This also provides the chance for her to exercise one of her other talents, getting to know an artist. "The hardest thing is to keep the simplicity and space in the work, to discover the important aspect of this musician," she says. With all her training and education, Marenco must discover again and again the answer to the question: "How can I make artists perform at 300 percent of their ability?" This is perhaps one reason why many artists, even years after they have worked with Marenco, still consider their work with her to be their best. "The goal is to assemble the right group of people and create a great mood," Marenco says, describing the challenge of producing.

Marenco doesn't leave her responsibility to an artist at the console. She often helps those interested in the next step after the material has been recorded: the live show. As an example of how the role of producer can expand, she cites her work with Tony Furtado, an artist signed to Rounder Records. Furtado was a champion banjo player who also loved the slide guitar. Marenco, sensing where his true desire lay, told him he would be crazy not to play the slide guitar on his next record. All of this was, for Marenco, part of helping Furtado define who he was as an artist and how to best build a career. A year after working together, Furtado had booked 200 dates, was paying his band and refining his live show. Two years later, Furtado had sold out the Fox Theatre in Boulder, Colorado.

Along with playing, teaching and producing, Marenco has also worked in A&R with Windham Hill Records. This gives her an insight into the industry most artists (especially younger ones) don't have. As she has worked with more and more independent and developing artists, her experience has been valuable in helping them avoid some of the pitfalls of the industry.

Her experience has also fueled a growing disenchantment with some aspects of the music industry. With other independent musicians, producers and concerned talent, Marenco was part of what she referred to as "The Boston Tea Party." This celebration of independence was a turning point. "We weren't intimidated by not having a record deal," she says. "Nothing is settled with a record deal." As record labels become, in Marenco's opinion, glorified ad agencies, artists will turn to the ever-expanding electronic means available to them. Ani DiFranco and Leftover Salmon are just two examples of artists who use record companies as distribution outlets, and the Internet or other resources to retain power over their own careers.

"You are in control of your life," Marenco says of indie artists. "You won't be in control with a [major-label record] deal." For a newly signed band, or otherwise unproven talent, recording and publicity costs will often come out of their own pocket. They will have to book their own tour. A band will still have to develop their own marketing plan, advertising strategy, and incur many of those costs. What a label can do, Marenco feels, is provide the illusion that someone is there to help you.

"Ten years ago, a band had a year to make [something] of a record before the label would close the books," Marenco says. However, in an alarming trend over the last three years, that time has gone from three months to just less than one month from the date shipped. "In my estimation," she says, "it's like a movie which makes it in the first week or doesn't. If a record takes off, they [the label] push more." But if a record does not hit instantly, the support often isn't there. Marenco has found herself championing artists to form their own labels.

The record industry is in what Marenco refers to as a rebuilding phase. "Artists need to open themselves to all of the possibilities that are available to them." Marenco cites her work with Liquid Audio, a company providing 16-bit CD-quality sound on the Internet, as one of those possibilites. The songs are copyright protected, available for direct distribution, and allow consumers to audition songs before purchase.

In November of 1998, Marenco participated in an unprecedented recording session for Liquid Audio with Kristin Hersh, former lead singer of Throwing Muses. Hersh performed for an audience of 500, while Marenco recorded the concert. The recording was uploaded to the Internet and made available for sale and downloaded within an hour of the performance. With such technology readily available to bands and musicians, Marenco says, "It's OK to not have a record deal."

Marenco likens the changes in the music industry to the development of the NFL. In the '60s the NFL was an oft-snubbed sport; today, it is a national institution. The public spends six times as much on sports as they do on music. While the luxury of a constant reminder (á la weekly televised events) is not available to musicians, artists' websites make them a more consistent presence to fans and strangers alike. Just as people have a favorite team they follow from week to week, they can now keep track of their favorite band in a similar way. Continuing the sports analogy, Marenco mentions a study in which a crowd's noise and encouragement was shown to actually turn the tide of a football game to the home team's advantage. In a similar way, how an audience interacts with a band changes each performance. "The audience becomes a part of why the music happened that way, that night," Marenco says.

The shift in perception from the all-important record deal to an artist's ability to retain individual control of a career through new technology will also weed out less serious musicians. With such power comes responsibility, such as cultivating a loyal fan base and keeping up with changes in multimedia. Marenco supports these changes as more and more artists make live broadcasts, one-of-a-kind CDs, and special merchandise available to fans from their own websites. In this way, artists, not record companies or managers, will be in control of their work and careers.

—*Tricia Suit*

lyric sheet. "Demo should be clear and well thought out. Vocal plus guitar or piano is fine. Let us know your present goals and reason for contacting us and include a short bio." Does not return material. Reports in 3-4 weeks.

Music: Mostly **country, singer/songwriters** and **"roots" (folk, acoustic, bluegrass and rock)**; also **instrumental**. Produced *There's Talk About a Fence*, and *Natick* (by various artists), both recorded by Rick Lee on Waterbug; and *Old Friends*, recorded by Jeff Nourse on Caliente. Other artists include Marinda Flom, Robert Bromley, Lisa Green, Ron Young, Sterling Silver and Crossties.

Tips: "I'm interested in artists/writers who are accomplished, self-motivated and able to accept direction. I'm looking for music that is intelligent, creative and in some way contributes something positive."

☑ ◖ **MAYFLY RECORD PRODUCTIONS, LTD.**, 19523 Barwick Dr., Spring TX 77373. (281)288-5911. Fax: (281)288-5911. CEO: Monty Bodenhamer. A&R Rep: Jerald Gray. Record producer, record company (Blue DAT and Mon-Tee Records) and music publisher (Moan & Groan Publishing, Ltd.). Estab. 1991. Produces 30 singles, 5 LPs and 5 CDs/year. Fee derived from sales royalty when song or artist is recorded.

• Mayfly's A&R rep has performed with Ike & Tina Turner, Bobby Bland, B.B. King, Johnny Taylor, Buddy Ace and Johnny Copeland.

How to Contact: Submit demo tape by mail. Unsolicited submissions are OK. Prefers cassette. "Send original material only. Proof of ownership is required. Primitive recording is OK. Send all of your work on one tape. (This allows us to profile potential of artist). Do not send rap, Christian or country. Be sure to include a permanent address." Does not return material. Reports in 3 months.

Music: Mostly **blues, R&B** and **pop**. Produced "Zydeco Woman," written and recorded by Jerald Gray (blues); "Misery For Company" (by Monty Bodenhamer), recorded by Joe Mayfield (pop); and *We Goan Boogie* (by Bodenhamer-Gray), recorded by Mayfield/Gray (blues), all on Mon-Tee. Other artists include Robyn Mathis and Janis Boyer.

Tips: "You must be a team player willing to take constructive criticism from those who have 'been there' before you. We listen to what 'can be,' not 'what is.' A lot of talent, a little humility and a positive attitude will get you where you want to be."

◖ **MEGA TRUTH RECORDS**, P.O. Box 4988, Culver City CA 90231. E-mail: jonbare@aol.com. Website: http://users.aol.com/jonbare. CEO: Jon Bare. Record producer and record company. Estab. 1994. Produces 2 CDs/year. Fee negotiable.

How to Contact: Submit demo tape by mail. Unsolicited submissions are OK. Prefers cassette with 4 songs. "We specialize in recording world-class virtuoso musicians and bands with top players." Does not return material. Reports in 2 weeks only if interested.

Music: Mostly **rock, blues** and **country rock**; also **swing, dance** and **instrumental**. Produced *Party Platter* recorded by Hula Monsters (swing); and *Killer Whales* and *Shredzilla* (by Jon Bare) (rock), all on Mega Truth Records. Other artists include The Rich Harper Blues Band, Aeon Dream & the Dream Machine and Techno Dudes.

Tips: "Create a unique sound that blends great vocals and virtuoso musicianship with a beat that makes us want to get up and dance."

Ⓝ ◖ **MODERN TRIBE RECORDS**, 14550 W. Eight Mile Rd., Oak Park MI 48237. (248)968-2862. Fax: (248)968-2864. Producer: Juan Shannon. Record producer, record company and music publisher. Estab. 1990. Produces 4-12 singles and 2-4 LPs/year. "Fee varies depending on negotiation."

How to Contact: Submit demo tape by mail. Unsolicited submissions are OK. Prefers CD, cassette or

VHS videocassette with 3-4 songs, lyric sheet and photo for groups/artist wanting to be signed. "Include name, address and phone number on tape and cassette box. We won't listen to demo without photo or lyric sheet." SASE. Reports in 3 months.

Music: Mostly **pop, R&B, hip-hop, rap** and **alternative**; also **techno, house, gospel** and **country**. Produced "Get That Booty Up" (by J. Shannon/A. Brown), recorded by Raw (bass); *The Last Minute*, recorded by Mr. Scott (rap); and *Detroit Hip Hop, Volume 1* (by Mic Skillz 101 [Y. McKay]), recorded by Children of The Dust (rap), all on Modern Tribe Records. Other artists include 666 and Jack Housen.

Tips: "If you are not interested in a career and working with other individuals, don't call or send your tape. We are very serious and do this for a living. If you have good music and a good image we will call. If you have the right attitude and are marketable we will offer you a deal. If you are not ready at this time, why waste everyone's time by sending us a tape?"

⁑ ◑ GARY MOFFET, P.O. Box 941 N.D.G., Montreal, Quebec H4A 3S3 Canada. (514)487-8953. Contact: Gary Moffet. Record producer and music publisher (Sci-Fi Music). Estab. 1985. Produces 3 LPs, 4 EPs and 3 CDs/year. Fee derived from sales royalty when song or artist is recorded.

How to Contact: Submit demo tape by mail. Unsolicited submissions are OK. Prefers cassette with 6 songs and lyric sheet. SAE and IRC.

Music: Mostly **rock, pop** and **acoustic**. Produced *Back to Reality* (by T. Mitchell), recorded by Mindstorm on Aquarius Records (heavy rock); *See Spot Run* (by C. Broadbeck), recorded by See Spot Run on Primer Records (rock); and *The Storm*, written and recorded by Ray Lyell on Spy Records (rock). Other artists include Marie Carmen, Marjo and Manon Brunet.

Ⓝ ◯ MONA LISA RECORDS/BRISTOL STUDIOS, 169 Massachusetts Ave., Boston MA 02115. (617)247-8689. E-mail: bristol@thecia.net. Website: http://www.thecia.net/users/bristol. Producer: Ric Poulin. Record producer. Estab. 1987. Produces 50 singles and 10 CDs/year. Fee derived from outright fee from recording company or artist.

How to Contact: Submit through e-mail. Prefers cassette and lyric sheet. Reports in 6 weeks.

Music: Mostly **dance, R&B** and **pop**; also **jazz** and **rock**. Produced *Future Classics* (by Ric Poulin/Sean Cooper), recorded by various artists on Mona Lisa Records (dance); "Call the Doctor" (by Poulin/Yeldham/Poulin), recorded by Bijou on Critique/Atlantic Records (dance); and "Dance to the Rhythm of the Beat" (by Ric Poulin), recorded by Jennifer Rivers on Associated Artists Int'l (dance). Other artists include Never Never, Sherry Christian, Zina, Damien, Aaron Brown, Amy Silverman and Leah Langfeld.

Tips: "Develop the frame of mind that whatever you do, you are doing it as a professional."

⁑ ◑ MONTICANA PRODUCTIONS, P.O. Box 702, Snowdon Station, Montreal, Quebec H3X 3X8 Canada. Executive Producer: David Leonard. Record producer, music publisher (Montina Music) and record company (Monticana Records). Estab. 1963. Fee derived from sales royalty when song or artist is recorded.

How to Contact: Submit demo tape by mail. Unsolicited submissions are OK. Prefers cassette, phonograph record or VHS videocassette with maximum 10 songs and lyric sheet. "Demos should be as tightly produced as a master." SASE.

Music: Mostly **top 40**; also **bluegrass, blues, country, dance-oriented, easy listening, folk, gospel, jazz, MOR, progressive, R&B, rock** and **soul**.

Tips: "Work creatively and believe passionately in what you do and aspire to be. Success comes to those who persevere, have talent, develop their craft and network."

◑ DAVID MOODY, P.O. Box 23277, Charlotte NC 28227. (704)882-6134. Fax: (704)882-2063. E-mail: dmoody@moodymultimedia.com. Website: http://www.moodymultimedia.com. Record producer. Produces 6 singles and 6 CDs/year. Fees derived from sales royalty or outright fee from artist or record company.

How to Contact: Submit demo tape by mail. Unsolicited submissions are OK. "Sending e-mail message first will ensure handling." Prefers CD or cassette with 4 songs and lyric sheets. "Artists should also send bio information." SASE. Reports in 4-6 weeks, only if interested.

Music: Mostly **country, folk, gospel, rock** and **New Age**; also **alternative, children, R&B** and **instrumental**. Produced *Cotton Eyed Joe* and *Great Train Song Medley*, both nominated for Grammys, by The Moody Brothers; and *American Country Gothic* (by George Hamilton IV), co-produced with Chet Atkins. Other artists include Flaco Jimenez, Nicolette Larson, John Hartford, Radney Foster, Lou Christi, Paul Overstreet, Devante and many others. "I also shop artist masters to major and independent label contacts on a retainer basis. I have produced over 20 national top 100 singles."

◯ GARY JOHN MRAZ, 1324 Cambridge Dr., Glendale CA 91205. Producer: Gary Mraz. Record producer. Estab. 1984. Record producer. Produces 6-12 12″ singles and 2-6 LPs/year. Fee derived from sales royalty or outright fee from record company.
How to Contact: Submit demo tape by mail. Unsolicited submissions are OK. Prefers cassette or VHS videocassette if available with 3 songs and lyric sheet. Does not return material. Reports in 1-2 months.
Music: Mostly **dance**, **pop** and **R&B**. Produced "Studio Voodoo," recorded by Mraz Price on Radio Magic Records. Other artists include Bush Baby.
Tips: "Get your finished product to the untapped college radio market."

☑ ◯ MUSICLAND PRODUCTIONS, INC., 911 NE 17th Ave., Ocala FL 34470. (352)622-5529. E-mail: tempo@mfi.net. Website: http://www.musiclandproductions.com. Owner: Bobby Land. Record producer. Estab. 1986. Produces 2 singles and 2 CDs/year. Fee derived from associated producers.
How to Contact: Submit demo by mail. Unsolicited submissions are OK. Prefers cassette with 4 songs and lyric sheet. "Professional demos only." Does not return material. Reports in 2 weeks.
Music: Mostly **pop** and **gospel**. Produced "Cowboy Lady," written and recorded by Curt Powers on MPR Records.
Tips: "Don't get in such a hurry. It takes time."

◯ NEU ELECTRO PRODUCTIONS, P.O. Box 1582, Bridgeview IL 60455. (630)257-6289. Owner: Bob Neumann. Record producer and record company. Estab. 1984. Produces 16 singles, 16 12″ singles, 20 LPs and 4 CDs/year. Fee derived from outright fee from record company or recording artist.
How to Contact: Submit demo tape by mail. Unsolicited submissions are OK. Prefers cassette or CD with 3 songs and lyric sheet or lead sheet. "Provide accurate contact phone numbers and addresses, promo packages and photos." SASE. Reports in 2 weeks. "A production fee estimate will be returned to artist."
Music: Mostly **dance**, **house**, **techno**, **rap** and **rock**; also **experimental**, **New Age** and **top 40**. Produced "Juicy," written and recorded by Juicy Black on Dark Planet International Records (house); "Make Me Smile," written and recorded by Roz Baker (house); and *Reactovate-6* (by Bob Neumann), recorded by Beatbox-D on N.E.P. Records (dance). Other artists include Skid Marx and The Deviants.

☑ ◯ NEW EXPERIENCE RECORDS, P.O. Box 683, Lima OH 45802. Contact: A&R Department. Music Publisher: James L. Milligan Jr. Record producer, music publisher (A New Rap Jam Publishing), management firm (Creative Star Management) and record company (New Experience Records, Grand-Slam Records and Pump It Up Records). Estab. 1989. Produces 15-20 12″ singles, 2 LPs, 3 EPs and 2-5 CDs/year. Fee derived from sales royalty when song or artist is recorded or outright fee from record company, "depending on services required."
How to Contact: Write first to arrange personal interview. Address material to A&R Dept. or Talent Coordinator. Prefers cassette with a minimum of 3 songs and lyric or lead sheet (if available). "If tapes are to be returned, proper postage should be enclosed and all tapes and letters should have SASE for faster reply." Reports in 4-6 weeks.
Music: Mostly **pop**, **R&B** and **rap**; also **gospel**, **contemporary gospel** and **rock**. Produced "Brothers Always Striving" and "I Wanna Be Free," both written by William Roach, recorded by 419 Hustlers on Pump It Records (rap). Other artists include Sonya Koger, Qutina Milligan, Melquan Khalijah and Venesta Compton.
Tips: "Do your homework on the music business. There are too many sound alikes. Be yourself. I look for what is different, vocal ability, voice range and sound stage presence, etc."

◖ NEW HORIZON RECORDS, 3398 Nahatan Way, Las Vegas NV 89109. (702)732-2576. President: Mike Corda. Record producer. Fee derived from sales royalty when song or artist is recorded.
How to Contact: Submit demo tape by mail. Unsolicited submissions are OK. Prefers cassette with 1-3 songs and lyric sheet. Does not return material. Reports only if interested.
Music: Mostly **blues**, **easy listening**, **jazz** and **MOR**. Produced "Lover of the Simple Things," "Offa the Sauce" (by Corda & Wilson) and "Go Ahead and Laugh," all recorded by Mickey Rooney on Prestige Records (London). Other artists include Bob Anderson, Jan Rooney, Joe Williams, Robert Goulet and Bill Haley and the Comets.
Tips: "Send good musical structures, melodic lines and powerful lyrics."

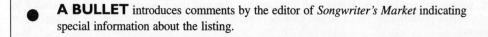 **A BULLET** introduces comments by the editor of *Songwriter's Market* indicating special information about the listing.

☑ ○ **THE NEW VIZION STUDIOS**, 14 Pinney, Unit 42, Corporate Center, Ellington CT 06029. (860)871-0178. Founder/Producer: Steve Sossin. Vice President/Artist Development: Aurore St. Germain. Executive Assistant: Caroline Hayes. Record producer. Estab. 1990. Produces 2-3 singles, 3-5 LPs and 3-5 CDs/year. Fee derived from outright fee from recording artist or producer/artist development contract.

How to Contact: Write or call first and obtain permission to submit. Prefers cassette or CD with 2-9 songs and lyric sheet. "We are an artist development company. Do not send photocopies or black and white promos. Originals and color promos only. Unlike most of the cliches in our industry, we are interested in the color of your eyes! Just because most people copy each other does not mean we all do. We set trends and break new ground." Does not return material. Reports in 1-2 months.

Music: Mostly **pop**, **A/C**, **pop/rock** and **crossover styles**; also **rock**, **R&B** and **New Age**. Produced "I Can't Find the Words," recorded by Dianne Glynn; and "She Was the Best," recorded by Memo Reese (both by Steve Sossin), on New Vizion Records (A/C).

Tips: "We are a 'rarity' in the recording industry. We are highly specialized as an artist development company and seek to work with emerging artists. All the talent in the world means nothing if you have a substance abuse problem. Attitude, professionality and quality of character count here. Our aim is to seek out truly gifted persons who are honest and dedicated to a goal and are willing to learn from experienced industry pros."

○ **NIGHTWORKS RECORDS**, 355 W. Potter Dr., Anchorage AK 99518. (907)562-3754. E-mail: smarket@surrealstudios.com. Website: http://www.surrealstudios.com. Owner: Kurt Riemann. Record producer and music licensor (electronic). Produces 2 singles, 8 LPs and 2 CDs/year. Fees derived from sales royalty when song or artist is recorded.

How to Contact: Submit demo tape by mail. Unsolicited submissions are OK. Prefers cassette or 15 ips reel-to-reel with 2-3 songs "produced as fully as possible. Send jingles and songs on separate reels." Does not return material. Reports in 1 month.

Music: Mostly **electronic**, **electronic jingles** and **Alaska-type music**. Produced *Rexskamation Point*, recorded by Nervis Rex (ska); *Second Face*, recorded by Rod Cook (show); and *Just In Time*, recorded by Stu Schulman (guitar), all on Nightworks.

◑ **OMNI 2000 INC.**, 413 Cooper St., Camden NJ 08102. (609)963-6400. Contact: A&R Director. Record producer, music publisher and record company. Estab. 1995. Produces 1-5 singles and 1-5 LPs/year. Fee derived from sales royalty when song or artist is recorded.

How to Contact: Write first and obtain permission to submit, "include SASE." Prefers cassette with 3 songs and lyric sheet. SASE. Reports in 1-3 months.

Music: Produced Brothers 2, Coalitions, Ghetto Children and Joy Stamford.

Tips: "Your music must have great hooks, imaginative lyrics and commercial appeal."

◑ **JOHN "BUCK" ORMSBY/ETIQUETTE PRODUCTIONS**, 2442 NW Market, Suite 273, Seattle WA 98107. (206)524-1020. Fax: (206)524-1102. Publishing Director: John Ormsby. Record producer and music publisher (Valet Publishing). Estab. 1980. Produces 1-2 singles, 3-5 LPs and 3-5 CDs/year. Fee varies.

How to Contact: Call first and obtain permission to submit. Prefers cassette or VHS videocassette with lyric or lead sheet. Does not return material. Reports in 6-8 weeks only if interested.

Music: Mostly **R&B**, **rock**, **pop** and **blues**; also **Latin**.

Tips: "Tape production must be top quality; lead or lyric sheet professional."

▧ ◑ **PACIFIC NORTH STUDIOS LTD.**, 257 W. 28th St., North Vancouver, British Columbia V7N 2H9 Canada. (604)990-9146. Fax: (604)990-9178. E-mail: djewer@direct.ca. Director: David Jewer. Contact: Don Bregg. Record producer and record company (Lynn Valley Music). Estab. 1993. Produces 4 CDs/year. Fee derived from sales royalty when song or artist is recorded or outright fee from recording artist.

How to Contact: Submit demo tape by mail. Unsolicited submissions are OK. Prefers cassette or CD. "Include a bio." Does not return material. Reports in 1 month.

Music: Mostly **world music**, **jazz** and **blues**; also **country** and **pop**. Produced *Songs From the Seahorse Hall*, written and recorded by David Cory (children's); *Mandala* (by J. Keating/D. Ritter), recorded by Locos Bravos (world), both on LVM; and *Change In the Weather*, written and recorded by Michael Dixon (country).

Tips: "Be a live performer."

○ **PANIO BROTHERS LABEL**, P.O. Box 99, Montmartre, Saskatchewan S0G 3M0 Canada. Executive Director: John Panio, Jr. Record producer. Estab. 1977. Produces 1 single and 1 LP/year. Fee derived from sales royalty or outright fee from artist/songwriter or record company.
How to Contact: Submit demo tape by mail. Unsolicited submissions are OK. Prefers cassette with any number of songs and lyric sheet. SAE and IRC. Reports in 1 month.
Music: Mostly **country**, **dance**, **easy listening** and **Ukrainian**. Produced *Ukranian Country*, written and recorded by Vlad Panio on PB Records.

○ **PATTY PARKER**, 10603 N. Hayden Rd., Suite 114, Scottsdale AZ 85260. (602)951-3115. Fax: (602)951-3074. E-mail: parker@comstock-records.com. Website: http://www.comstock-records.com. Producer: Patty Parker. Record producer, music publisher (White Cat Music) and record company (Comstock Records). Estab. 1978. Produces 10-12 CD singles and 4-5 albums/year. Fee derived from outright fee from recording artist or recording company.
How to Contact: Submit demo tape by mail. Unsolicited submissions are OK. Prefers CD, cassette or VHS videocassette with 2-4 songs and lyric sheet. Voice up front on demos. SASE. Reports in 2 weeks.
Music: Mostly **country—traditional** to **crossover**. Produced "Back On Track," written and recorded by R.J. McClintock; "Wait for the Dream," written and recorded by Maria Carmi; and *From Where I Sit I Can See Where I Stand* (by Dusty McKenny), recorded by Gary Mahnken, all on Comstock Records (country). Other artists include Colin Clark, Patti Mayo, Phil West and Pam Ferens.
Tips: "To catch the ears of radio programmers worldwide, I need good medium to uptempo songs for all the artists coming from Europe, Canada and the U.S. that I produce sessions on in Nashville."

○ **PHILLY BREAKDOWN RECORDING CO.**, 216 W. Hortter St., Philadelphia PA 19119. (215)848-6725. President: Matthew Childs. Music Director: Charles Nesbit. Record producer, music publisher (Philly Breakdown/BMI) and record company. Estab. 1974. Produces 3 singles and 2 LPs/year. Fee derived from sales royalty when song or artist is recorded.
How to Contact: Submit demo tape by mail. Unsolicited submissions are OK. Prefers cassette with 4 songs and lead sheet. Does not return material. Reports in 2 months.
Music: Mostly **R&B**, **hip hop** and **pop**; also **jazz**, **gospel** and **ballads**. Produced "My Sunshine" (by William Ross), recorded by Betty Carol (soul); *Hear It* (by Matt Lew Childs/Clarence Patterson), recorded by The H Factor (jazz); and *Jam On* (by M. Childs/C. Nesbitt), recorded by Four Buddies (R&B), all on Philly Breakdown Records. Other artists include Leroy Christy, Gloria Clark, Jerry Walker, Nina Bundy, Mark Adam and Emmit King.
Tips: "If you fail, just learn from your past experience and keep on trying, until you get it done right. Never give up."

◑ **JIM PIERCE**, Dept. SM, 101 Hurt Rd., Hendersonville TN 37075. (615)824-5900. Fax: (615)824-8800. President: Jim Pierce. Record producer, music publisher (Strawboss Music/BMI, Pier-Jac Music/ASCAP) and record company (Round Robin Records). Estab. 1974. Fee derived from sales royalty or outright fee from recording artist. "Some artists pay me in advance for my services." Has had over 200 chart records to date.
How to Contact: Write first and obtain permission to submit or to arrange personal interview. Prefers cassette with any number of songs and lyric sheet. Does not return material. Reports only if interested.
Music: Mostly **country**, **contemporary**, **country/pop** and **traditional country**. Artists include Tommy Cash, George Jones, Jimmy C. Newman, Margo Smith, Bobby Helms, Sammi Smith, Roy Drusky, Charlie Louvin and Melba Montgomery.
Tips: "Industry is seeking good singers who can write songs."

◑ **PLANET DALLAS**, P.O. Box 191447, Dallas TX 75219. (214)521-2216. Fax: (214)528-1299. President: Rick Rooney. Record producer and music publisher (Stoli Music/ASCAP and Planet Mothership/BMI). Estab. 1984. Produces 8-12 LPs, 5-12 EPs and 8-12 CDs/year. Fee derived from sales royalty when song or artist is recorded.
How to Contact: Call first and obtain permission to submit a demo. Prefers cassette or DAT. Does not return material. Reports in 2-4 weeks.
Music: Mostly **pop/rock**, **R&B** and **country**; also **soul** and **instrumental**. Produced albums by Gone By

---

MARKETS THAT WERE listed in the 1999 edition of *Songwriter's Market* but do not appear this year are listed in the General Index with a notation explaining why they were omitted.

Dawn on Burn Records (rock) and Tripping Daisy on Island Records (rock). Other artists include Fu Schnickens, Nixsons and MC 900 Ft. Jesus.

Tips: "There is no luck in this business, only the result of hard work, inspiration and determination."

⬛ 🔱 ⊘ POKU PRODUCTIONS, 176-B Woodridge Crescent, Nepran Ontario K2B 759 Canada. (613)820-5715. President: Jon E. Shakka. Record producer. Estab. 1988. Produces 1 single and 1 12″ single/year. Fee derived from sales royalty when song or artist is recorded.

How to Contact: Does not accept unsolicited submissions..

Music: Mostly **funk**, **rap** and **house music**; also **pop**, **ballads** and **funk-rock**. Produced "176-B" (by Jacob/Issac/Noah Poku), recorded by Shakka-Bro's (funk rap) on Poku Records. Other artists include Kim Warnock and James T. Flash.

⬛ PREJIPPIE MUSIC GROUP, P.O. Box 312897, Penobscot Station, Detroit MI 48231. E-mail: zanda 740@aol.com. President: Bruce Henderson. Record producer, music publisher and record company (PMG Records). Estab. 1990. Produces 5 12″ singles, 2 LPs and 2 EPs/year. Fee derived from sales royalty when song or artist is recorded.

How to Contact: Submit demo tape by mail. Unsolicited submissions are OK. No phone calls please. Prefers cassette with 3-4 songs and lyric sheet. SASE. Reports in 6 weeks.

Music: Mostly **alternative R&B**, **experimental**, **alternative rock** and **techno/house**. Produced *Caleb's Cafe* and *Sins of the Fathers*, written and recorded by Bourgeoisie Paper Jam, both on PMG Records (funk/rock). Other artists include Tony Webb and Synthetic Living Organism.

⬛ THE PRESCRIPTION CO., P.O. Box 222249, Great Neck NY 11021. (516)482-7697. President: David F. Gasman. Vice President A&R: Kirk Nordstrom. San Francisco office: 525 Ashbury St., San Francisco CA 94117. (415)553-8540. VP Sales: Bruce Brennan. Record producer and music publisher. Fee derived from sales royalty when artist or song is recorded or outright fee from record company.

How to Contact: Write or call first about your interest then submit demo. Prefers cassette with any number of songs and lyric sheet. SASE. "Does not return material without SASE and sufficient postage."

Music: Mostly **bluegrass**, **blues**, **children's**, **country**, **dance**, **easy listening**, **jazz**, **MOR**, **progressive**, **R&B**, **rock**, **soul** and **top 40/pop**. Produced "You Came In," "Rock 'n' Roll Blues" and *Just What the Doctor Ordered*, all recorded by Medicine Mike.

✔ ⬛ R&D PRODUCTIONS, P.O. Box 540102, Houston TX 77254-0102. (713)521-2616. Fax: (713)529-4914. Contact: Jeff Troncoso. Record producer, record company (Albatross Records) and music publisher (Ryedale Publishing). Estab. 1986. Produces 25 singles, 20 LPs, 4 EPs and 21 CDs/year. Fee derived from sales royalty when song or artist is recorded.

How to Contact: Submit demo tape by mail. Unsolicited submissions are OK. Prefers cassette or CD with 4 songs and lyric sheet. Does not return material. Reports in 2-4 weeks.

Music: Mostly **rap**, **rock** and **jazz**; also **country**.

⬛ REEL ADVENTURES, 9 Peggy Lane, Salem NH 03079. (603)898-7097. Chief Engineer/Producer: Rick Asmega. Record producer. Estab. 1972. Produces 45 singles, 1 12″ single, 23 LPs, 2 EPs and 6 CDs/year. Fee derived from sales royalty when song or artist is recorded, or outright fee from recording artist or record company.

How to Contact: Submit demo tape by mail. Unsolicited submissions are OK. Prefers cassette or CD. SASE. Reports in 4-6 weeks.

Music: Mostly **pop**, **funk** and **country**; also **blues**, **reggae** and **rock**. Produced *Funky Broadway*, recorded by Chris Hicks; *Testafye*, recorded by Jay Williams; and "Acoustical Climate" (by John G.). Other artists include Larry Sterling, Broken Men, Melvin Crockett, Fred Vigeant, Monster Mash, Carl Armand, Cool Blue Sky, Ransome, Backtrax, Push, Too Cool for Humans and Burn Alley.

⬛ MIKE ROSENMAN, 45-14 215 Place, Bayside NY 11361. (718)229-4864. E-mail: mkrosenman@ao l.com. Producer: Mike Rosenman. Record producer and arranger. Estab. 1984. Produces 12-24 singles/year. Fee derived from sales royalty when song or artist is recorded or outright fee from recording artist or record company.

How to Contact: Call first and obtain permission to submit. Prefers CD, cassette or VHS videocassette

---

🔱 🌐 SENDING TO A COUNTRY other than your own? Be sure to send International Reply Coupons (IRCs) instead of stamps for replies or return of your materials.

with 2-4 songs and lyric sheet. Include address and phone number. Put name and phone number on cassette. Will not return any tapes without SASE. Reports in 2-3 months.

Music: Mostly **pop**, **R&B** and **dance**. Produced "Tell Me Where It Hurts" (by Diane Warren), recorded by Jamaica on National (dance); "Mellow My Mind," written and recorded by Simply Red on Elektra/ East West (dance); and "Just Doin' What We Love" (by Alex Forbes/Michael Hacker/Michael Rosenman), recorded by Carole Sylvan on Champion UK (dance). Other artists include RH Factor, Tyrone Davis and Sara Parker.

Tips: "Don't worry about production on your demo, we are looking for a great song. Write a hook that's a real hook!"

RUSTRON MUSIC PRODUCTIONS, 1156 Park Lane, West Palm Beach FL 33417-5957. (561)686-1354. Executive Director: Rusty Gordon. A&R Director: Ron Caruso. Assistant A&R Director: Kevin Reeves. Record producer, record company, manager and music publisher (Rustron Music Publishers/ BMI and Whimsong Publishing/ASCAP). Estab. 1970. Produces 6-10 LP/cassettes and 6 CDs/year. Fee derived from sales royalty when song or artist is recorded or outright fee from record company. "This branch office reviews all material submitted for the home office in Ridgefield, CT."

How to Contact: Write or call first and obtain permission to submit or submit demo tape by mail. Unsolicited submissions are OK. Prefers cassette with 1-3 songs and typed lyric or lead sheet. Also send cover letter clearly explaining your reason for submitting. "Songs should be 3½ minutes long or less and must be commercially viable for today's market. Exception: New Age fusion compositions 3-10 minutes each, ½ hour maximum. Singer/songwriters and collaborators are preferred." SASE required for all correspondence. Reports in 4 months.

Music: Mostly **progressive country**, **pop** (ballads, blues, theatrical, cabaret), **folk/rock**, and **A/C electric acoustic**; also **R&B**, **New Age folk fusion**, **women's music** and **New Age instrumentals**. Produced *Happy Endings*, written and recorded by Lynn Thomas on Rustron (pop); *Carolina Sky*, written and recorded by Neal Phillips on Compilation (country); and *The Rally*, written and recorded by Sandy Rapp on SRM Records (folk). Other artists include Eric Shaffer, Bill Buck, Dianne Mower, Christian Camilo, Richard Collins and Diane Marra.

Tips: "Be open to developing your own unique style. Write well-crafted songs with unpredictable concepts, strong hooks and definitive melodies. New Age composers: evolve your themes and use multiculturally diverse instruments to embellish your compositions/arrangements. Don't be predictable. Experiment with instrumental fusion with jazz themes, pop themes and international styles."

RAY SANDERS COMPANY, 73-1052 Ahulani St., Kailua Kona HI 96740. Owner: Ray Sanders. Record producer and music publisher (Pacific Coast Music/BMI). Estab. 1954. Produces 4-5 CDs/ year. Fee derived from sales royalty when song or artist is recorded.

How to Contact: Submit lyrics *only*—must be typed! No cassettes. "If I want to hear a cassette, I'll request it." SASE. Reports in 1 week.

Music: Mostly **country**. Produced *I Forgot to Remember* (by Chet Klein), recorded by Ray Sanders on Sweet Sixteen (country). Other artists include Brad Ford, Janet Love, Raising Cane and Dennis O'Niel.

Tips: "Learn the basics of songwriting first! Try to find a successful co-writer who's had songs recorded. Or, if you live in a city with a college, check and see if they offer a basic songwriter program. It's hard to just wake up one day and say I'm going to be a songwriter, with no basic training."

STEVE SATKOWSKI RECORDINGS, (formerly Steve Satkowski Productions), P.O. Box 3403, Stuart FL 34995. (561)781-4657. Fax: (561)283-2374. Engineer/producer: Steven Satkowski. Record producer, recording engineer, management firm and record company. Estab. 1980. Produces 20 CDs/year. Fee derived from outright fee from recording artist or record company.

How to Contact Submit demo tape by mail. Unsolicited submissions are OK. Prefers cassette. Does not return material. Reports in 2 weeks.

Music: Mostly **classical**, **jazz** and **big band**. Produced recordings for National Public Radio and affiliates. Engineered recordings for Steve Howe, Patrick Moraz, Kenny G and Michael Bolton.

SEGAL'S PRODUCTIONS, 16 Grace Rd., Newton MA 02159. (617)969-6196. Contact: Charles Segal. Record producer, music publisher (Segal's Publications/BMI and Samro South Africa) and record company (Spin Records). Produces 6 singles and 6 LPs/year. Fee derived from sales royalty when song or artist is recorded.

How to Contact: Write first and obtain permission to submit or to arrange personal interview. Prefers cassette, CD or videocassette with 3 songs and lyric sheet or lead sheet of melody, words, chords. "Please record keyboard/voice or guitar/voice if you can't get a group." Does not return material. Reports in 3 months only if interested.

Music: Mostly **rock**, **pop** and **country**; also **R&B** and **comedy**. Produced "What Is This Love" (by Paul/Motou), recorded by Julia Manin (rock); "Lovely Is This Memory" (by Segal/Paul), recorded by Nick Chosn on AU.S. (ballad); and *There'll Come A Time* (by Charles Segal), recorded by Jill Kirkland on Spin Records (ballad). Other artists include Art Heatley, Dan Hill and Melanie.
Tips: "Make a good and clear production of cassette even if it is only piano rhythm and voice. Also do a lead sheet of music, words and chords."

SHU'BABY MONTEZ MUSIC, P.O. Box 28816, Philadelphia PA 19151. (215)473-5527. E-mail: schubaby@aol.com. Website: http://www.geocities.com/SunsetStrip/cabaret/2810/. General Manager: Leroy Schuler. Operations Officer: Martygraw. Record producer. Estab. 1986. Produces 6 singles, 25 12″ singles and 3 LPs/year. Fee derived from outright fee from record company.
How to Contact: Submit demo tape by mail. Unsolicited submissions are OK. Prefers cassette with 4 songs and lyric sheet. SASE. Reports in 5 weeks.
Music: Mostly **R&B**, **hip-hop** and **funk**. Produced "Silhouette of the Bells" (by Lou Leggieri/Dolores Leggier) on Urban Logic Records (pop), and "I Miss You" (by Tab Edwards) on Kixx Records (R&B), both recorded by Cubby St. Charles; and "It Was Only You," written and recorded by Camille Forest on Urban Logic Records (gospel). Other artists include Ralph Brown, Wilson Lambert, Martin "Martygraw" Schuler and Waller Wee.
Tips: "Be on time with all projects."

SILVER BOW PRODUCTIONS, 6260 130 St., Surrey, British Columbia V3X 1R6 Canada. (604)572-4232. Fax: (604)572-4252. E-mail: saddles@sprint.ca. A&R: Candice James. Record producer. Estab. 1986. Produces 16 singles, 4 LPs and 6 CDs/year. Fee derived from outright fee from recording artist.
How to Contact: Call first and obtain permission to submit. Prefers cassette with 2 songs and lyric sheet. Does not return material. Reports in 6 weeks.
Music: Mostly **country**, **pop**, and **rock**; also **gospel**, **blues** and **jazz**. Produced *Fragile-Handle With Care*, recorded by Razzy Bailey on SOA Records (country); *Sugar* (erotic mix) (by Martin Richmond), recorded by Martini (rock); and *Somewhere Downtown* (by Marsh Gardner), recorded by Clancy Wright on Saddlestone Records (country). Other artists include Rex Howard, Gerry King, Joe Lonsdale, Barb Farrell, Dorrie Alexander, Peter James, Matt Audette and Cordel James.

SILVER THUNDER MUSIC GROUP, P.O. Box 41335, Nashville TN 37204. (615)391-5035. President: Rusty Budde. Record producer, record company (Silver Thunder Records), music publisher (Silver Thunder Publishing) and management firm. Estab. 1982. Produces 20 singles, 5-7 LPs and 5-7 CDs/year. Fee derived from sales royalty when song or artist is recorded or outright fee from recording artist or record company.
How to Contact: Write first and obtain permission to submit or to arrange personal interview. Prefers cassette. "Artists should submit 8×10 photo along with demo tape." Does not return material. Reports in 6-16 weeks.
Music: Mostly **country**, **rock** and **R&B**; also **gospel** and **pop**. Produced *What's Not To Love* (by D.J. Music), recorded by Heather Hartsfield (country); and *Radio Active* (by G. McCorkel), recorded by J.D. Treece (country), both on STR Records. Other artists include Rod Woodson, Jeff Samules, Jodi Collins and Hank Thompson.

MIKE SISKIND PRODUCTIONS, 285 Chestnut St., West Hempstead NY 11552. (516)489-0738. Fax: (516)565-9425. E-mail: platear1@aol.com. Producer: Mike Siskind. Record producer. Estab. 1993. Produces 1-2 CDs/year. Fee derived from sales royalty when song or artist is recorded.
How to Contact: Submit demo tape by mail. Unsolicited submissions are OK. Prefers cassette or CD with 3 songs and lyric sheet. "Serious acts only." SASE. Reports in 3 months.
Music: Mostly **rock**, **folk** and **country** (work best with women singers); also **pop** and **A/C**. Produced

**FOR EXPLANATIONS OF THESE SYMBOLS,
SEE THE INSIDE FRONT AND BACK COVERS OF THIS BOOK.**

More Than a Friend, written and recorded by Michael Ellis on Storehouse Records (rock). Other artists include Georgi Smith.
Tips: "Be open to advice."

☑ ◯ **SM RECORDING/HIT RECORDS NETWORK**, (formerly S'N'M Recording/Hit Records Network), P.O. Box 6235, Santa Barbara CA 93160. (805)964-3035. E-mail: cms@silcom.com. Producers: Greg Lewalt; Ernie Orosco. Record producer, record company (Night City Records, Warrior Records and Tell International Records), radio and TV promotion and music publisher. Estab. 1984. Produces 4 singles, 2 12″ singles, 4 LPs, 2 EPs and 2-4 CDs/year. Fee derived from outright fee from record company.
How to Contact: Submit demo tape by mail. Unsolicited submissions are OK. Prefers cassette, CD or VHS videocassette with 4-8 songs, photos, bio and lyric sheet. Does not return material. Reports in 1-2 months.
Music: Mostly **pop-rock**, **country** and **top 40**; also **top 40 funk**, **top 40 rock** and **top 40 country**. Produced *Life of Illusion* (by Johny Podz), recorded by Johny Podz & Brian Faith Band (pop); *Diamond in the Rough* (by Doug Doherty), recorded by Doherty Brothers (rock); and *Do the Push* (by J.C. Martin), recorded by Traffic Jam (rock), all on Hit Records Network. Other artists include New Vision, Jade, Ernie and the Emperors, Hollywood Heros, Cornelius Bumpus (Doobie Brothers), Tim Bogert (Vanilla Fudge, Jeff Beck), Floyd Sneed (3 Dog Night), Peter Lewis, Jim Calire (America), Mike Kowalski, Ernie Knapp (Beach Boys) and Jewel.
Tips: "Keep searching for the infectious chorus hook and don't give up."

◑ **SOUND ARTS RECORDING STUDIO**, 8377 Westview Dr., Houston TX 77055. (713)464-GOLD. E-mail: sarsjef@aol.com. Website: http://soundartsrecording.com. President: Jeff Wells. Record producer and music publisher (Earthscream Music). Estab. 1974. Produces 12 singles and 3 LPs/year. Fee derived from sales royalty when song or artist is recorded.
How to Contact: Submit demo tape by mail. Unsolicited submissions are OK. Prefers cassette with 2-5 songs and lyric sheet. Does not return material. Reports in 6 weeks.
Music: Mostly **pop/rock**, **country** and **blues**. Produced *Texas Johnny Brown*, written and recorded by Texas Johnny Brown on Quality (blues). Other artists include Tim Nichols, Perfect Strangers, B.B. Watson, Jinkies, Joe "King" Carasco (on Surface Records), Mark May (on Icehouse Records), The Barbara Pennington Band (on Earth Records), Tempest Under the Sun and Attitcus Finch.

◯ **SOUND WORKS ENTERTAINMENT PRODUCTIONS INC.**, P.O. Box 26691, Las Vegas NV 89126-0691. (702)878-1870. Fax: (702)878-2284. E-mail: music@wizard.com. Website: http://musicforhope.org. President: Michael E. Jones. Record producer, record company (Sound Works Records) and music publisher (Sound Works Music). Estab. 1989. Produces 16 singles, 2 LPs and 20 CDs/year. Fee derived from sales royalty when song or artist is recorded or outright fee from recording artist or record company.
How to Contact: Submit demo tape by mail. Unsolicited submissions are OK. Prefers cassette with 3-6 songs and lyric sheet. "Please include short bio and statement of goals and objectives." Does not return material. Reports in 6 weeks.
Music: Mostly **country**, **folk** and **pop**; also **rock**. Produced "Lonelyville," and "Alabama Slammer," both written and recorded by Wake Eastman; and "Good Looking Loser," written and recorded by Renee Rubach, all on Sound Works Records (country). Other artists include Matt Dorman, Steve Gilmore, The Tackroom Boys, The Los Vegas Philharmonic and J.C. Clark.
Tips: "Put your ego on hold. Don't take criticism personally. Advice is meant to help you grow and improve your skills as an artist/songwriter. Be professional and business-like in all your dealings."

☑ ◑ **SPHERE GROUP ONE**, (formerly Sphere Productions), P.O. Box 991, Far Hills NJ 07931-0991. (908)781-1650. Fax: (908)781-1693. President: Tony Zarrella. Talent Manager: Louisa Pazienza. Record producer, artist development and management firm. Produces 5-6 singles and 3 CDs/year. Estab. 1986.
How to Contact: Submit demo tape by mail. Unsolicited submissions are OK. Prefers cassette, CD or VHS videocassette with 3-5 songs and lyric sheets. "Must include: photos, press, résumé, goals and specifics of project submitted, etc." Does not return material. Reports in 10-12 weeks.
Music: Mostly **pop/rock (mainstream)**, **progressive/rock**, **New Age** and **crossover country/pop**; also **film soundtracks**. Produced *Take This Heart*, *It's Our Love* and *You and I* (by T. Zarrella), recorded by 4 of Hearts (pop/rock) on Sphere Records. Other artists include Oona Falcon, Traveller, Forever More and Elexus Quinn & Ziggy True (the "Nothing is Meaningless Project").
Tips: "Be able to take direction and have trust and faith in yourself, your producer and manager. Currently seeking artists/groups incorporating various styles into a focused mainstream product."

SPIRAL-WAVE, 10 Reinhardt, Hull, Quebec J8Y 5V4 Canada. (819)778-6009. Fax: (819)777-7463. E-mail: ospirale@ondespirale.com. Website: http://www.spiralwave.com. Producer: Daniel Bouliane. Record producer, record company (OZMOZ Records) and music publisher (Atout Publishing). Estab. 1989. Produces 5-6 singles and 2-4 CDs/year. Fee depends on contract.
How to Contact: Submit demo tape by mail. Unsolicited submissions are OK. Prefers cassette with 3 songs and lyric sheet. "If looking for an artist contract, send résumé with photos. It is better to write by fax or e-mail before sending a demo." Does not return material. Reports in 3 weeks.
Music: Mostly **world ambiant**, **adult contemporary** and **dance**; also **soul**, **folk/pop** and **instrumental**. Produced "Love Set Us Free" (by Dan Murray/Josée Bélisle), recorded by Roxxy (dance); and *Kiss of destiny* (by various), recorded by Nadia (dance), both on Numozik; and "This is the Time" (by Pascal Lecoz), recorded by Nathalie Page on Major (dance). Other artists include Dak and Debbie Fredericks.
Tips: "In instrumental music we are looking for very well produced albums to license with our lab OZMOZ. Any electronic-only albums will not meet our requirements most of the time. Our company is always looking out for songs for our signed artists. We are looking for good dance, pop and adult contemporary songs."

STUART AUDIO SERVICES, 134 Mosher Rd., Gorham ME 04038. (207)892-0960. E-mail: jstuart105@aol.com. Producer/Owner: John A. Stuart. Record producer and music publisher. Estab. 1979. Produces 5-8 CDs/year. Fee derived from sales royalty when song or artist is recorded, outright fee from recording artist or record company, or demo and consulting fees.
How to Contact: Write or call first and obtain permission to submit or to arrange a personal interview. Prefers cassette with 4 songs and lyric sheet. SASE. Reports in 1-2 months.
Music: Mostly **alternative folk-rock**, **rock** and **country**; also **contemporary Christian**, **children's** and **unusual**. Produced *One of a Kind* (by various artists), recorded by Elizabeth Boss on Bosco Records (folk); *Toad Motel*, written and recorded by Rick Chaprette on Fine Point Records (children's); and *Holiday Portrait*, recorded by USM Chamber Singers on U.S.M. (chorale). Other artists include Noel Paul Stookey, Beavis & Butthead (Mike Judge), Don Campbell, Jim Newton and John Angus.

STUDIO D RECORDING, 425 Coloma, Sausalito CA 94965. (415)332-6289. Fax: (415)332-0249. Website: http://www.studiorecording.com. Manager/Co-owner: Joel Jaffe. Record producer and engineer. Estab. 1983. Produces 6-8 CDs/year. Fee derived from sales royalty when song or artist is recorded or outright fee from artist or record company.
How to Contact: Does not accept unsolicited material.
Music: Mostly **rock**, **alternative** and **pop**; also **country** and **R&B**. Produced *Starlight*, written and recorded by Lenny Williams on Ichiban (R&B). Other artists include Roberta Donnay, Ali Woodson, Fuse, Deborah Levoy, Far From Home and Micky Thomas's Starship.

STUDIO SEVEN, 417 N. Virginia, Oklahoma City OK 73106. (405)236-0643. Fax: (405)236-0686. E-mail: cope@okla.net. Website: http://www.onaxis.com/cope. Director of Production: Dave Copenhaver. Record producer, record company (Lunacy Records) and music publisher (DavenRon Music and Bo Kope Music). Estab. 1990. Produces 10 LPs and CDs/year. Fee is derived from sales royalty when song or artist is recorded or outright fee from recording artist or record company. "All projects are on a customized basis."
How to Contact: Submit demo tape by mail. Unsolicited submissions are OK. Prefers cassette with lyric sheet. SASE. Reports in 6 weeks.
Music: Mostly **rock**, **jazz-blues** and **world-Native American**; also **country** and **blues**. Produced *High Strung*, written and recorded by Burt Herrin on Lunacy (blues); *The Deviants*, written and recorded by Scott Keeton on J.S.P. (blues); and *Celtic Glory*, written and recorded by Jeff Fenholt on Fenholt (contemporary Christian). Other artists include Harvey Shelton, Steve Pryor and Ken Taylor.

SYNDICATE SOUND, INC., 475 Fifth St., Struthers OH 44471. (330)755-1331. President: Jeff Wormley. Producer: Billy Moyer. Record producer, audio and video production company and record and song production company. Estab. 1981. Produces 6-10 CDs and 15-20 singles/year. Fee derived from sales royalty when song or artist is recorded or outright fee from recording artist or record company.
How to Contact: Submit demo tape by mail. Unsolicited submissions are OK. "Please send a promo package or biography (with pictures) of artist, stating past and present concerts and records." Does not return material. Reports in 6 weeks.
Music: Mostly **rock**, **pop** and **Christian rock**; also **country**, **R&B**, **rap** and **alternative**. Produced "Time to Bowl" (by Gregg Wormley), recorded by Larry Shankman (rock); "The Shining" (by Jason Hairston), recorded by Jas the Ace (rap); and *Remember Me* (by Robert Noble), recorded by Lost Then Found (Christian rock), all on SS&VW. Other artists include Falling Down, Marc Tipton, Severence and Vessel.

🔳 ✓ ⭕ WILLIAM SZAWLOWSKI PRODUCTIONS & VENTURA MUSIC PUBLISHING, 7195 Mauriac, Brossard, Quebec J4Y 1T8 Canada. Phone/fax: (450)678-3629. E-Mail: ventura@pearle.net Website: http://www.pearle.net/~ventura/. President: Bill Szawlowski. Record producer. Estab. 1974. Produces 3 singles and 2 CDs/year. Fee derived from sales royalty when song or artist is recorded.
How to Contact: Submit demo tape by mail. Unsolicited submissions are OK. Prefers 4 songs and lyric/lead sheet. "Cassette clearly marked: title, date of composition. Include picture, bio and letter of intention." SASE. Reports in 2 months.
Music: Mostly **rock, MOR** and **country**; also **dance, heavy rock** and **pop**. Produced *If I Were* (by Habre/Eon), recorded by Anxiety on Musicor Records (rock); *Gypsy Road* (by Anthony/Vanderbol), recorded by Garry Anthony on 2M Records (rock); and *What You Mean to Me* (by Murray/Melanson/Szawlowski), recorded by Denise Murray on Loggerhead (country). Other artists include Sun City Rockers and Soul Stripper.

✓ ⭕ ROGER VINCENT TARI, P.O. Box 576, Piscataway NJ 08855. (201)583-0475. Fax: (908)287-1373. E-mail: mroze714@aol.com. A&R: Joseph Tsai. President/Producer: Roger Vincent Tari. Record producer, record company (VT Records) and music publisher (Vintari Music/ASCAP). Estab. 1979. Produces 6-8 singles/year. Fee derived from sales royalty when song or artist is recorded or outright fee from recording artist.
How to Contact: Submit demo tape by mail. Unsolicited submissions are OK. Prefers cassette or VHS videocassette with 3 songs and lyric sheet (videocassette is optional). "The artist should send any relevant literature and a simple black and white picture along with the 3-song cassette and lyric sheet." SASE. Reports in 1 month.
Music: Mostly **creative pop, electronic exotica** and **avant-jazz**; also **world music, J-pop, Korean pop**, and **indie rock**. Produced "10998/Conversation" (by Ecco), recorded by Heavenly Music Corp. on Osiris (pop); *Hawaiian Goodwill Mission*, written and recorded by various artists on World Groove Co. (variety); and "Cold Rocking the Fathoms" (by Benjamin Zavopnick), recorded by True Believer (electronic). Other artists include Mind Dope 63, Yaag Yang, Leeji Young, Fractured Glass, N.F. Inc., Ling Ling and East Coast Project (midi inc).
Tips: "We seek artists from around the world. The music should be new and creative regardless of style."

✓ 🖼 ⭕ TEXAS FANTASY MUSIC GROUP, 2932 Dyer St., Dallas TX 75205. (214)691-5318. Fax: (214)692-1392. E-mail: barbc@texasmusicgroup.com. Website: http://www.texasmusicgroup.com. Director of Film & TV Music: Don Ashley. Director of New Age, World and Classical: Richard Theisen. Director of Country, Rock and Classic Rock: Chris Albert. Creative Director: Barbara McMillen. Record producer and music publisher (Showcat Music and Flying Red Horse Publishing). Estab. 1982. Produces 35 singles/year. Fee derived from sales royalty when song or artist is recorded, or outright fee from record company or recording artist, also sync fees for film/TV.
How to Contact: Write first and obtain permission to submit. Prefers cassette with 2 songs and lyric sheet (if applicable). SASE. Reports in 6 months.
Music: Mostly **instrumental for film** and **all styles**. Produced *When I Was a Dinosaur*, written and recorded by various artists, and *Teardrops To Rainbows & Other New Classic Tales* (by Richard Theisen/Rollie Anderson), recorded by various artists, both on Remarkable Records (children's).

✓ ⭕ TEXAS MUSIC MASTERS/WRIGHT PRODUCTIONS, 11718 Hwy. 64 E., Tyler TX 75707. Owner: L. Wright. Record producer and management firm. 30 years in business. Fee derived from sales royalty when song or artist is recorded.
How to Contact: Submit demo tape. Unsolicited submissions are OK. Prefers cassette with 3 songs and lyric sheet. SASE. Reports in 6 weeks.
Music: Mostly **country, gospel** and **blues**. Produced *Time's Only Grace*, written and recorded by Marty Yale on Yale Song; *Waylon Adams* (by Hal Hatcher), recorded by Waylon on Silka Eden; and *I Feel Like Travelin On*, written and recorded by Dock Murdock. Other artists include Ron Whistler, Mickey Gilley, Roy Head, early George Strait, Gene Watson, Johnny Lee, Oscar Perry, Gene Thomas, David Houston and Freddy Fender.

MARKET CONDITIONS are constantly changing! If you're still using this book and it is 2001 or later, buy the newest edition of *Songwriter's Market* at your favorite bookstore or order directly from Writer's Digest Books at (800)289-0963.

TIME-OUT PRODUCTIONS/BRAMLA MUSIC, 69 Piccadilly Downs, Lynbrook NY 11563. (516)599-5025. Owner/Producer: Brian Albano. Record producer and music publisher (Bramla Music). Estab. 1989. Fee derived from sales royalty when song or artist is recorded, outright fee from record company or co-production with artist or label.
How to Contact: Call first and obtain permission to submit. Prefers cassette. SASE. Reports within 1 month. Does not return material.
Music: All types. Produced *Good Day* (by J. DeLair/R. Scott/W. Williams), recorded by Vicki Neville on T.L. Productions; *Balanchine Retrospective Sampler*, produced and recorded by Brian Albano on Hammerstein Archives/Lincoln Center (video release); and *Christine* (by various artists), recorded by Christine Lepera on Time-Out Productions. Other artists include Rocket 88, Sheer Magic, Joseph Dedominicis, Roger Calleo, David Bridges and Cheryl Padula.

TMC PRODUCTIONS, P.O. Box 12353, San Antonio TX 78212. (210)829-1909. Producer: Joe Scates. Record producer, music publisher (Axbar Productions/BMI, Scates & Blanton/BMI and Axe Handle Music/ASCAP), record company (Axbar, Trophy, Jato, Prince and Charro Records) and record distribution and promotion. Produces 3-4 LPs and 4-6 CDs/year. Fee derived from sales royalty.
How to Contact: Write or call first and obtain permission to submit. Prefers cassette with 1-5 songs and lyric sheet. Does not return material. Reports "as soon as possible, but don't rush us."
Music: Mostly **traditional country**; also **blues**, **comedy** and **rock (soft)**. Produced "Chicken Dance" (traditional), recorded by George Chambers and "Hobo Heart," written and recorded by Juni Moon, both on Axbar Records. Other artists include Jim Marshall, Caroll Gilley, Rick Will, Wayne Carter, Kathi Timm, Leon Taylor and Kenny Dale.

TRAC RECORD CO., 170 N. Maple, Fresno CA 93702. (209)255-1717. E-mail: tracsell@aol.com. Owners: Stan Anderson, Bev Anderson. Record producer, music publisher (Sellwood Publishing/BMI) and record company (TRAC Records). Estab. 1972. Produces 5 12″ singles, 5 LPs and 5 CDs/year. Fee derived from outright fee from recording artist or outside investor.
How to Contact: Submit demo tape by mail. Unsolicited submissions are OK. Prefers cassette with 3 songs and lyric sheet. "Send professional studio demo." SASE. Reports in 3 weeks.
Music: Mostly **country, all styles**. Produced *All Time Low*, written and recorded by Jimmy Walker on TRAC Records (country). Other artists include Jessica James.

[N] THE TRINITY STUDIO, P.O. Box 1417, Corpus Christi TX 78403. (512)854-SING. E-mail: trinitystudio@juno.com. Website: http://www.trinitystudio.rdirect.com. Owner: Jim Wilken. Record producer and recording studio. Estab. 1988. Fee derived from outright fee from recording artist or record company.
How to Contact: Submit demo tape by mail. Unsolicited submissions are OK. Prefers cassette, CD or VHS videocassette. Does not return material. Reports in 1 month.
Music: Mostly **Christian-country**. Produced *Miracle Man*, written and recorded by Merrill Lane on TC Records (country Christian); and *Childhood Dreams*, written and recorded by Patty Walker on Independent (country Christian). Other artists include Kerry Patton, Rod Raines, Leah, Lofton Kline, Jesse Bishop, Lovell and Charlotte McGee.

[N] TRIPLITT PRODUCTION, 120 Cloud Crest Dr., Henderson NV 89015. (702)564-3794. Producer: Vales Crossley. Record producer and music publisher. Estab. 1978. Produces 6 singles, 2 12″ singles, 3 LPs, 3 EPs and 2 CDs/year. Fee derived from sales royalty when song or artist is recorded.
How to Contact: Write or call first and obtain permission to submit. Prefers cassette or videocassette with 3-6 songs and lyric sheet. Does not return material. Reports in 4-6 weeks.
Music: Mostly **top 40**, **R&B**, **soul** and **rap**; also **New Age** and **rock**. Produced "Lapp Dog" (by S. Spann), recorded by Sweet Luie on Cryptic Records; "Hittin' Fo" (by R. Nullems), recorded by Baby Jon on Thump Records; and "Same Heart" (by V. Crossley/C. Burton), recorded by Twin Force on Dynasty Records. Other artists include Platters, Chrissie Zastrow and The Henleys.

TWIST TUNES, P.O. Box 181, Nanoose Bay, British Columbia V9P 9J9 Canada. (250)468-9484. E-mail: cabin@nanaimo.ark.com. Website: http://islandroots.com. Producer/Owner: Michael Donegani. Record producer. Estab. 1977. Produces 3 singles, 4 LPs, 1 EP and 20 CDs/year. Fee derived from outright fee from recording artist.
How to Contact: Submit demo tape by mail. Unsolicited submissions are OK. Prefers cassette with 3 songs and lyric sheet. SASE. Reports in 1 month.
Music: Mostly **personal**, **different** and **clear**; also **rock**, **pop** and **country**. Produced *Filth*, written and recorded by Filth (heavy metal); and *Spirit Childe* (by The Band), recorded by Spirit Childe, both on

Private Records; and *Lendahand* (by Michael Twist/A. Hasselgreen), recorded by Lendahand on Twist Tunes. Other artists include Damn the Diva, Hume, John Lynsley, 2:AM, Chris Otcasek, Hassel & Twist, Lendahand, Mean Streets, Danny Click and Jerry Jeff Walker.
Tips: "Be personal about your music as opposed to its market share, label or chart placement."

VALTEC PRODUCTIONS, P.O. Box 2642, Santa Maria CA 93457. (805)934-8400. Producer: Joe Valenta. Record producer. Estab. 1986. Produces 20 singles and 10 CDs/year. Fee derived from sales royalty when song or artist is recorded.
How to Contact: Submit demo tape by mail. Unsolicited submissions are OK. Prefers cassette, DAT or 8mm videocassette with 3 songs and lyric or lead sheet. Send photo. Does not return material (kept on file for 2 years). Reports in 3-6 weeks.
Music: Mostly **country**, **pop/AC** and **rock**. Produced *Lisa Sanchez*, written and recorded by Lisa Sanchez (country); *John Jacobson*, written and recorded by John Jacobson on Valtone Records (pop); and *Taxi*, written and recorded by Groupe Taxi on Tesoro Records (Spanish/pop).

CHARLES VICKERS MUSIC ASSOCIATION, P.O. Box 725, Daytona Beach FL 32015-0725. (904)252-4849. President: Harold Vickers. Manager: Loris Doby. President/Producer: Dr. Charles H. Vickers D.M. Record producer, music publisher (Pritchett Publication/BMI and Alison Music/ASCAP) and record company (King of Kings Records, L.A. International Records, Quicksilvers/Increase Records Inc. and Bell Records International). Produces 3 singles and 6 LPs/year. Fee derived from sales royalty when song or artist is recorded.
How to Contact: Call first and obtain permission to submit. Prefers 7½ ips reel-to-reel or cassette with 1-6 songs. Does not return material. Reports in 5-6 months.
Music: Mostly **church/religious**, **gospel** and **hymns**; also **bluegrass**, **blues**, **classical**, **country**, **easy listening**, **jazz**, **MOR**, **progressive**, **reggae (pop)**, **R&B**, **rock**, **soul** and **top 40/pop**. Produced *Run to Jesus While You Can*, written and recorded by Charles Vickers on Quicksilvers/Increase Records Inc. Other artists include James Franklin, Gladys Nighton and Charles Gardy.

WALBASH RIVER AND BROKEN ARROW PRODUCTIONS, 3200 Cypress Mill Rd. #917, Brunswick GA 31525-2863. (912)264-9837. E-mail: sgmarler@darientel.net. Executive Producer: Sammie Lee Marler. Vice President: Ginger Marler. Record producer, record company, music publisher and distributor. Estab. 1989. Produces 15 singles, 6 LPs, 2 EPs and 10 CDs/year. Fee derived from sales royalty when song or artist is recorded.
How to Contact: Submit demo tape by mail. Unsolicited submissions are OK. Prefers cassette or CD with 3 songs and lyric sheet. "Send cover letter with goals and history of your music career." SASE. Reports in 2 weeks.
Music: Mostly **country**, **gospel** and **traditional country**; also **Native American**, **rock**, **cowboy** and **pop**. Produced *The Borderland* (by Carl Ehrler), recorded by Dickey Minor (country); *I Want Your Truck*, written and recorded by Melody Knowles (country/pop); and *Blue*, written and recorded by Rebecca Howell (country). Other artists include John Moore, Sandy Moore, Steve Wallace, Sandra Davis, Mike Green, Dave Cole, Gary Usinger, Billy Green, Singing Sam, Ozark and Sammie Lee Marler.
Tips: "Send us a cover letter with your submission and tell us what you have going on with your music, and how we can help you."

THE WEISMAN PRODUCTION GROUP, 449 N. Vista St., Los Angeles CA 90036. (213)653-0693. E-mail: unclelenny@aol.com. Contact: Ben Weisman. Record producer and music publisher (Audio Music Publishers). Estab. 1965. Produces 10 singles/year. Fee derived from sales royalty when song or artist is recorded.
How to Contact: Submit demo tape by mail. Unsolicited submissions are OK. Prefers cassette with 3-10 songs and lyric sheet. SASE. "Mention *Songwriter's Market*. Please make return envelope the same size as the envelopes you send material in, otherwise we cannot send everything back. Just send tape." Reports in 6 weeks.
Music: Mostly **R&B**, **soul**, **dance**, **rap** and **top 40/pop**; also **gospel** and **all types of rock**.

WESTWIRES DIGITAL USA, 1042 Club Ave., Allentown PA 18103. (610) 435-1924. E-mail: westwire@voicenet.com. Website: http://www.voicenet.com/~westwire. Owner/Producer: Wayne Becker.

OPENNESS TO SUBMISSIONS: ○ beginners; ◐ beginners and experienced; ◑ experienced only; ◪ industry referrals only.

Producer: JJ Zeller. Record producer and production company. Fee derived from outright fee from record company or artist retainer.

How to Contact: Submit demo tape by mail. Unsolicited submissions are OK. Prefers cassette, CD or VHS videocassette with 3 songs and lyric sheet. Does not return material. Reports in 1 month.

Music: Mostly **R&B**, **dance**, **alternative**, **folk** and **improvisation**. Produced *A Survivor's Smile*, written and recorded by Gary Hassay on Dbops Records (jazz); *Twist*, written and recorded by Whirlwind Groove on Westwires (Christian rock); and *Another Shining Path*, written and recorded by Ye Ren on Drimala Records (jazz). Other artists include Elizabeth Jane and Nikki Hill.

Tips: "We are interested in singer/songwriters and alternative artists living in the mid-Atlantic area. Must be able to perform live and take chances."

WILBUR PRODUCTIONS, 159 W. Fourth St. #10, New York NY 10014. (212)255-5544. E-mail: will@pilotrecording.com. Website: http://www.pilotrecording.com. President: Will Schillinger. Record producer and recording engineer/studio owner. Estab. 1989. Produces 50 singles, 20 LPs and 20 CDs/year. Fee derived from sales royalty when song or artist is recorded or outright fee from record company.

How to Contact: Submit demo tape by mail. Unsolicited submissions are OK. Prefers cassette with 3-5 songs. Does not return material. Reports in 2 weeks.

Music: Mostly **rock** and **jazz**. Produced Marshall Crenshaw, Jack Walrath & Band and In The Groove.

Tips: "Don't worry about your demo quality. Send good songs. Very interested in new bands as well."

TOM WILLETT/TOMMARK RECORDS, 7560 Woodman Place, #G3, Van Nuys CA 91405. (818)994-4862. Owner: Tom Willett. Record producer, music publisher (Schmerdley Music/BMI) and record company. Estab. 1988. Produces 1 single and 1 CD/year.

How to Contact: Submit demo tape by mail. Unsolicited submissions are OK. Prefers cassette (or VHS videocassette if available) with any number of songs and lyric sheets. SASE. Reports in 1 month.

Music: Mostly **country** and **novelty**; also **folk**.

WIR (WORLD INTERNATIONAL RECORDS), A-1090 Vienna, Servitengasse 24, Austria. Phone: (+43)1-7684380. Fax: (+43)1-7677573. General Manager: Peter Jordan. Record producer, music publisher (Aquarius Publishing) and record company (WIR). Estab. 1986. Produces 5-10 singles and 5-8 LPs/year. Fee derived from sales royalty when song or artist is recorded.

How to Contact: Submit demo tape by mail. Unsolicited submissions are OK. Prefers cassette. Does not return material. Reports in 2-4 weeks.

Music: Produced *New River Run* (by W. Keese), recorded by Coldbrook Ramblers (country); *How Many Times* (by J. Collins), recorded by Teri Douglas (ballad); and *It's Over Baby* (by R. Hebein), recorded by Girly & The Blue Caps (rock 'n' roll), all on WIR Records. Other artists include Bill Roberts, Madmen, John Velora, Full Circle, Veronica Martell, Magaly, Ted Lang, Cindi Cain and John Lake.

WIZARDS & CECIL B, 1111 Second St., San Rafael CA 94901. (415)453-0335. Website: http://www.marinternet.com/wizard. Producer: Pete Slauson. Record producer and music publisher. Estab. 1978. Produces 10 singles, 10 12″ singles, 15 LPs and 15 CDs/year. Fee derived from sales royalty when song or artist is recorded.

How to Contact: See their website for submission policy.

Music: **All kinds**. Produced *San Francisco Maritime Hall Live* series recordings; *New Riders of Purple Sage*, recorded on MU Records; and *Reggae on the River* for Warner Brothers Records. Other artists include George Clinton & P-Funk, Jimmy Cliff, Gilberto Gil, Zero, Moby Grape, The Geezers, Caribbean All Stars with Carlos Santana, Shana Morrison and Caledonia.

WLM MUSIC/RECORDING, 2808 Cammie St., Durham NC 27705-2020. (919)471-3086. E-mail: wlm.musicrecording@worldnet.att.net. Owner: Watts Lee Mangum. Record producer. Estab. 1980. Fee derived from outright fee from recording artist. "In some cases, an advance payment requested for demo production."

How to Contact: Submit demo tape by mail. Unsolicited submissions are OK. Prefers cassette with 2-4 songs and lyric or lead sheet (if possible). SASE. Reports in 4-6 months.

Music: Mostly **country**, **country/rock** and **blues/rock**; also **pop**, **rock**, **blues**, **gospel** and **bluegrass**.

THE OPENNESS TO SUBMISSIONS INDEX at the back of this book lists all companies in this section by how open they are to submissions.

Produced "911," and "Petals of an Orchid," both written and recorded by Johnny Scoggins; and "Renew the Love" (by Judy Evans), recorded by Bernie Evans, all on Independent (country). Other artists include Southern Breeze Band and Heart Breakers Band.

◘ WORLD RECORDS, P.O. Box 422, Belmont MI 49306. Producer: Jack Conners. Record producer, engineer/technician and record company (World Records). Estab. 1984. Produces 1 CD/year. Fee derived from outright fee from recording artist.
How to Contact: Write first and obtain permission to submit. Prefers cassette with 1 or 2 songs. SASE. Reports in 6 weeks.
Music: Mostly **classical**, **folk** and **jazz**. Produced *Language of Love* (by James Mulholland), and *Roosevelt* (by Libby Larson), both recorded by Camerata Singers on World Records (chorus); and *Akulka*, written and recorded by SR Turner on North Cedar (folk). Other artists include The Murphy Brothers and The Burdons.

◙ STEVE WYTAS PRODUCTIONS, Dept. SM, 11 Custer St., West Hartford CT 06110. (860)953-2834. Contact: Steven J. Wytas. Record producer. Estab. 1984. Produces 4-8 singles, 3 LPs, 3 EPs and 4 CDs/year. Fee derived from outright fee from recording artist or record company.
How to Contact: Submit demo tape by mail. Unsolicited submissions are OK. Prefers cassette or VHS ¾″ videocassette with several songs and lyric or lead sheet. "Include live material if possible." Does not return material. Reports in 3 months.
Music: Mostly **rock**, **pop**, **top 40** and **country/acoustic**. Produced *Already Home*, recorded by Hannah Cranna on Big Deal Records (rock); *Under the Rose*, recorded by Under the Rose on Utter Records (rock); and *Sickness & Health*, recorded by Legs Akimbo on Joyful Noise Records (rock). Other artists include King Hop!, The Shells, The Gravel Pit, G'nu Fuz and Toxic Field Mice.

◙ Y-N-A/C.D.T. PRODUCTIONS, Dept. SM, 170 Rosedale Rd., Yonkers NY 10710. (914)961-1051. Fax: (914)961-5906. E-mail: niftrik@aol.com or rhythmjam@aol.com. Website: http://www.youthnasia.com. Producer: Rikk Angel. Record producer. Estab. 1984. Produces 30 singles, 5 LPs, 5 EPs and 5 CDs/year. Fee derived from outright fee from record company or contractual fees.
How to Contact: Write or call first to arrange personal interview or submit demo tape by mail. Unsolicited submissions are OK. Prefers DAT or VHS videocassette with 3 songs, photo and lyric or lead sheet. Does not return material. Reports in 2 weeks.
Music: Mostly **R&B/dance**, **soul** and **house**; also **underground** and **rock**. Produced "Sinoa's World" (by Sinoa/Y-N-A), recorded by Sinoa on T.O. Records (R&B/house). Other artists include Rikk Angel, Frank Jay, Tanya's Dream, Go For It, U & Me, Ray Tabano (formerly of Aerosmith), Tom Low and Creative You.

Additional Record Producers

The following companies are also record producers, but their listings are found in other sections of the book. See the General Index for page numbers, then read the listings for submission information.

Afterschool Records, Inc.
Alan Music, Marcus
Alias John Henry Tunes
AlliSongs Inc.
Alyssa Records
Ariana Records
Arkadia Entertainment Corp.
Atlan-Dec/Grooveline Records
Bacchus Group Productions, Ltd.
Backstage Entertainment/Loggins Promotion
Bagatelle Record Company
Banana Records
Barrett Rock 'n' Roll Enterprises, Paul
Belham Valley Records
Berandol Music Ltd.
Betty Jane/Josie Jane Music Publishers
Big Fish Music Publishing Group
Black Diamond Records Inc.

Blind Records
Blowin' Smoke Productions/Records
Blue Wave Productions
BME Publishing
Bouquet Records
Bradley Music, Allan
Branch Group Music
Brewster Songs, Kitty
Brian Song Music Corp.
Brightly Music Publishing
Brown & Associates Inc., J. Aaron
BSW Records
Camex Music
Capstan Record Production
Casaro Records
Cash Productions, Inc.
Cellar Records
Cerebral Records
Cherri/Holly Music
Chiaroscuro Records
Christopher Publishing, Sonny

Chucker Music Inc.
Cimirron Music
Clear Pond Music
Cliffside Music Inc.
Cornelius Companies, The
Country Showcase America
Creative Improvised Music Projects (CIMP) Records
Creek Records
Dagene Music
Danford Entertainment Group/ Sisyphus Records
Dapmor Publishing
Deadeye Records
Del Camino Music Publishing
Denny Music Group
Disc-tinct Music, Inc.
Duane Music, Inc.
E.S.R. Records
Ellis International Talent Agency
EMF Productions

Erwin Music
First Time Records
Flash Point Records
Flying Red Horse Publishing
Fountain Records
Frozen Inca Music
Furrow Music
Garrett Entertainment, Marty
GCI Inc.
Generic Records, Inc.
Glad Music Co.
Golden Triangle Records
Green Bear Records
Groove Makers' Recordings
G-String Publishing
Gueststar Records, Inc.
Hammel Associates, Inc., R.L.
Happy Melody
Hardison International Entertainment
    Corporation
Hickory Lane Publishing and
    Recording
Hickory Valley Music
His Power Productions and
    Publishing
Howdy Records
Inhabitants Music Group
Interplanetary Music
Intrepid Records
Iron Skillet Music
Ja/Nein Musikverlag GmbH
Joey Records
Josena Music
Kaupp Records
Kaylee Music Group, Karen
Kozkeeozko Music
KSM Records
L.A. Records (Canada)
L.A. Records (Michigan)
Lake Transfer Productions & Music
Landslide Records
Lark Record Productions, Inc.
Lineage Publishing Co.
Living Eye Productions Ltd.
Lollipop Farm Entertainment
Lucifer Records, Inc.
Marsupial Management Ltd.
Martin Productions, Rick

McCoy Music, Jim
McGibony Publishing
Mellow House Music
Merlin Productions
MHM Recordings
Missile Records
MOR Records
Music Quest® Entertainment &
    Television
Music Room Publishing Group, The
Myko Music
Mymit Music Productions, Chuck
NSP Music Publishing Inc.
Oak Street Music
OCP Publications
Ontrax Companies
Orchid Publishing
Orillyon Entertainment
Otto Publishing Co.
Outland Productions
P. & N. Records
P.M. Records
Patty Lee Records
Permanent Press Recordings/
    Permanent Wave
Plastic Surgery
Plateau Music
Playbones Records
Prairie Fire Music Company
Presence Records
PriceClub Productions
Publishing Central
QUARK, Inc.
R.T.L. Music
Rampant Records
Random Records
Raving Cleric Music Publishing/
    Euro Export Entertainment
Red Dot/Puzzle Records
Renaissance Entertainment Group
Rival Records
Riverhawk Music
RML Records
Rocker Music/Happy Man Music
Ruf Records
Ruffhouse Records
Saddlestone Publishing
Safire Records

Savage, Inc., T.E.
Sea Cruise Productions, Inc.
Shaolin Film & Records
Silver Blue Music/Oceans Blue
    Music
Sinus Musik Produktion, Ulli Weigel
Slanted Circle Music
Song Farm Music
Sound Cellar Music
Sound Management Direction
Southland Records, Inc.
Spotlight Records
Starbound Publishing Co.
Stardust
Street Records
Succes
Sunsongs Music
Supreme Enterprises Int'l Corp.
Sureshot Records
Surface Records
Sweet June Music
T.C. Productions/Etude Publishing
TBS Records
Tiger's Eye Entertainment Manage-
    ment & Consulting
Tiki Enterprises, Inc.
Ton Records
Topcat Records
Tower Music Group
Treasure Coast Records
Tropikal Productions
Trusty Publications
Twentieth Century Promotions
Universal Music Marketing
Unknown Source Music
Up Front Management
Wagner Agency, William F.
Wall Street Music
Warehouse Creek Recording Corp.
Warner Productions, Cheryl K.
Whirlybird Records, Inc.
White Cat Music
Wilder Artists' Management, Shane
Williams Management, Yvonne
Woodrich Records
World Entertainment Services, Inc.
X.R.L. Records/Music

Category Index

The Category Index is a good place to begin searching for a market for your songs. Below is an alphabetical list of 20 general music categories. If you write dance music and are looking for a record producer to pitch them, check the Dance section in this index. There you will find a list of record producers who work with dance music. Once you locate the entries for those producers, read the music subheading *carefully* to determine which companies are most interested in the type of dance music you write. Some of the markets in this section do not appear in the Category Index because they have not indicated a specific preference. Most of these said they are interested in "all types" of music. Listings that were very specific, or whose description of the music they're interested in doesn't quite fit into these categories, also do not appear here.

Adult Contemporary (also easy listening, middle of the road, AAA, ballads, etc.)
"A" Major Sound Corporation
Aberdeen Productions
Bal Records
Blue Planet Music
Daliven Music
Diamond Entertainment, Joel
Integrated Entertainment
June Productions Ltd.
Known Artist Productions
Kool Breeze Productions
Kovach, Robert R.
Luick, Harold, & Country Music Showcase Intl.
Magid Productions, Lee
Monticana Productions
New Horizon Records
New Vizion Studios, The
Panio Brothers Label
Planet Dallas
Prescription Co., The
Rustron Music Productions
Siskind Productions, Mike
Spiral-Wave
Szawlowski Productions, William, & Ventura Music Publishing
Valtec Productions
Vickers Music Association, Charles

Alternative (also modern rock, punk, college rock, new wave, hardcore, new music, industrial, ska, indie rock, garage, etc.)
"A" Major Sound Corporation
Blue Planet Music
Blues Alley Records
Coachouse Music
Daylo Music
Glass House Productions
John Productions, David
Kane, Karen, Producer/Engineer
L.A. Entertainment, Inc.
Lazy Bones Productions/Recordings, Inc.

Mac-Attack Productions
Magnetic Oblivion Music Co.
Marenco, Cookie
Mathews, Scott, d/b/a Hit or Myth Productions
Modern Tribe Records
Monticana Productions
Moody, David
Prejippie Music Group
Stuart Audio Services
Studio D Recording
Syndicate Sound, Inc.
Tari, Roger Vincent
Westwires Digital USA

Blues
Bal Records
Celt Musical Services, Jan
Coachouse Music
Demi Monde Records & Publishing Ltd.
Esquire International
Glass House Productions
Hailing Frequency Music Productions
Kleanza River Canyon Productions
Kool Breeze Productions
Landmark Communications Group
Linear Cycle Productions
Magid Productions, Lee
Mayfly Record Productions, Ltd.
Mega Truth Records
Monticana Productions
New Horizon Records
Ormsby, John "Buck"/Etiquette Productions
Pacific North Studios Ltd.
Prescription Co., The
Reel Adventures
Silver Bow Productions
Sound Arts Recording Studio
Studio Seven
Texas Music Masters
TMC Productions
Vickers Music Association, Charles
WLM Music/Recording

CATEGORY INDEX: RECORD PRODUCERS

Children's
JSB Groupe Management Inc.
Moody, David
Prescription Co., The
Stuart Audio Services

Classical (also opera, chamber music, serious music, choral, etc.)
Blue Planet Music
JSB Groupe Management Inc.
Lark Talent & Advertising
Marenco, Cookie
Satkowski Recordings, Steve
Vickers Music Association, Charles
World Records

Country (also western, C&W, bluegrass, cowboy songs, western swing, honky-tonk, etc.)
Aberdeen Productions
ACR Productions
AKO Productions
Allyn, Stuart J.
Bal Records
Birthplace Productions
Blues Alley Records
Cacophony Productions
Coachouse Music
Coffee and Cream Productions
Cupit Productions, Jerry
Daliven Music
Darrow, Danny
De Miles, Edward
DeLory, Al, and Music Makers
Diamond Entertainment, Joel
Dixon III, Philip D., Attorney at Law
Doss Presents, Col. Buster
Durr Productions, David
Eiffert, Jr., Leo J.
Esquire International
Eternal Song Agency, The
Gale, Jack
Haworth Productions
Interstate Records
Jag Studio, Ltd.
Jay Jay Publishing & Record Co.
Kingston Records and Talent
Kleanza River Canyon Productions
Known Artist Productions
Kool Breeze Productions
Kovach, Robert R.
Landmark Communications Group
Lari-Jon Productions
Lark Talent & Advertising
Linear Cycle Productions
Luick, Harold, & Country Music Showcase Intl. Associates
Magid Productions, Lee
Makers Mark Music Productions

Marenco, Cookie
Martin, Pete/Vaam Music Productions
Mathes Productions, David
May Music/Swift River Productions
Mega Truth Records
Modern Tribe Records
Monticana Productions
Moody, David
Pacific North Studios Ltd.
Panio Brothers Label
Parker, Patty
Pierce, Jim
Planet Dallas
Prescription Co., The
R&D Productions
Reel Adventures
Rustron Music Productions
Sanders Company, Ray
Segal's Productions
Silver Bow Productions
Silver Thunder Music Group
Siskind Productions, Mike
SM Recording/Hit Records Network
Sound Arts Recording Studio
Sound Works Entertainment Productions Inc.
Sphere Group One
Stuart Audio Services
Studio D Recording
Studio Seven
Syndicate Sound, Inc.
Szawlowski Productions, William, & Ventura Music Publishing
Texas Music Masters
TMC Productions
Trac Record Co.
Trinity Studio, The
Twist Tunes
Valtec Productions
Vickers Music Association, Charles
Walbash River and Broken Arrow Productions
Willett, Tom/Tommark Records
WLM Music/Recording
Wytas Productions, Steve

Dance (also house, hi-NRG, disco, club, rave, techno, trip-hop, trance, etc.)
AMAJ Records
Coffee and Cream Productions
Corwin, Dano
Daliven Music
Darrow, Danny
De Miles, Edward
Diamond Entertainment, Joel
Esquire International
Final Mix Music
House of Rhythm
Jag Studio, Ltd.

Janoulis Productions, Alexander/Big Al Jano
    Productions
KMA
Mac-Attack Productions
Makers Mark Music Productions
Mega Truth Records
Modern Tribe Records
Mona Lisa Records/Bristol
Monticana Productions
Mraz, Gary John
Neu Electro Productions
Panio Brothers Label
Poku Productions
Prejippie Music Group
Prescription Co., The
Rosenman, Mike
Spiral-Wave
Szawlowski Productions, William, & Ventura
    Music Publishing
Weisman Production Group, The
Westwires Digital USA
Y-N-A/C.D.T. Productions

Folk (also acoustic, Celtic, etc.)
Birthplace Productions
Coppin, Johnny/Red Sky Records
Durr Productions, David
Gallway Bay Music
Glass House Productions
Kilgore Productions
Magid Productions, Lee
Marenco, Cookie
May Music/Swift River Productions
Monticana Productions
Moody, David
Rustron Music Productions
Siskind Productions, Mike
Sound Works Entertainment Productions Inc.
Spiral-Wave
Westwires Digital USA
Willett, Tom/Tommark Records
World Records

Instrumental (also background music, musical scores, etc.)
Eternal Song Agency, The
Lark Talent & Advertising
Magid Productions, Lee
Mathes Productions, David
May Music/Swift River Productions
Mega Truth Records
Moody, David
Spiral-Wave
Texas Fantasy Music Group

Jazz (also fusion, bebop, swing, etc.)
Allyn, Stuart J.
Angel Films Company
Appell Productions, Inc., Jonathan

Bal Records
Blue Planet Music
Celt Musical Services, Jan
Daliven Music
DAP Productions
Darrow, Danny
De Miles, Edward
Durr Productions, David
Esquire International
Haworth Productions
Heart Consort Music
Katz Productions, Matthew
Kleanza River Canyon Productions
Landmark Communications Group
Magid Productions, Lee
Magnetic Oblivion Music Co.
Marenco, Cookie
Mona Lisa Records/Bristol
Monticana Productions
New Horizon Records
Pacific North Studios Ltd.
Philly Breakdown Recording Co.
Prescription Co., The
R&D Productions
Silver Bow Productions
Studio Seven
Tari, Roger Vincent
Vickers Music Association, Charles
Wilbur Productions
World Records

Latin (also Spanish, salsa, Cuban, conga, Brazilian, cumbia, rancheras, Mexican, merengue, Tejano, Tex Mex, etc.)
DeLory, Al, and Music Makers
Dixon III, Philip D., Attorney at Law
Ormsby, John "Buck"/Etiquette Productions
Satkowski Recordings, Steve

New Age
Big Sky Audio Productions
Durr Productions, David
Haworth Productions
Heart Consort Music
Moody, David
Neu Electro Productions
New Vizion Studios, The
Rustron Music Productions
Sphere Group One
Triplitt Production

Novelty (also comedy, humor, etc.)
Jay Jay Publishing & Record Co.
Kilgore Productions
Kleanza River Canyon Productions
Linear Cycle Productions
Magnetic Oblivion Music Co.
Segal's Productions
TMC Productions

Willett, Tom/Tommark Records

Pop (also top 40, top 100, popular, chart hits, etc.)
"A" Major Sound Corporation
Aberdeen Productions
ACR Productions
AKO Productions
Allyn, Stuart J.
Angel Films Company
Appell Productions, Inc., Jonathan
Bal Records
Blue Planet Music
Blues Alley Records
Cacophony Productions
Coachouse Music
Coffee and Cream Productions
Corwin, Dano
Darrow, Danny
Daylo Music
De Miles, Edward
DeLory, Al, and Music Makers
Demi Monde Records & Publishing Ltd.
Diamond Entertainment, Joel
Doss Presents, Col. Buster
Esquire International
Eternal Song Agency, The
Final Mix Music
Gallway Bay Music
House of Rhythm
Jag Studio, Ltd.
Janoulis Productions, Alexander/Big Al Jano
    Productions
Jericho Sound Lab
JSB Groupe Management Inc.
June Productions Ltd.
Kane, Karen, Producer/Engineer
Kingston Records and Talent
Kleanza River Canyon Productions
Known Artist Productions
Kool Breeze Productions
Kovach, Robert R.
Landmark Communications Group
Linear Cycle Productions
Mac-Attack Productions
Magid Productions, Lee
Marenco, Cookie
Martin, Pete/Vaam Music Productions
Mathews, Scott, d/b/a Hit or Myth Productions
Mayfly Record Productions, Ltd.
Modern Tribe Records
Moffet, Gary
Mona Lisa Records/Bristol
Monticana Productions
Mraz, Gary John
Musicland Productions, Inc.
Neu Electro Productions
New Experience Records

New Vizion Studios, The
Ormsby, John "Buck"/Etiquette Productions
Pacific North Studios Ltd.
Philly Breakdown Recording Co.
Planet Dallas
Poku Productions
Prescription Co., The
Reel Adventures
Rosenman, Mike
Rustron Music Productions
Segal's Productions
Silver Bow Productions
Silver Thunder Music Group
Siskind Productions, Mike
SM Recording/Hit Records Network
Sound Arts Recording Studio
Sound Works Entertainment Productions Inc.
Sphere Group One
Spiral-Wave
Studio D Recording
Syndicate Sound, Inc.
Szawlowski Productions, William, & Ventura
    Music Publishing
Tari, Roger Vincent
Triplitt Production
Twist Tunes
Valtec Productions
Vickers Music Association, Charles
Walbash River and Broken Arrow Productions
Weisman Production Group, The
WLM Music/Recording
Wytas Productions, Steve

R&B (also soul, black, urban, etc.)
"A" Major Sound Corporation
ACR Productions
Allyn, Stuart J.
AMAJ Records
Angel Films Company
Appell Productions, Inc., Jonathan
Bal Records
Big Sky Audio Productions
Blue Planet Music
Blues Alley Records
Celt Musical Services, Jan
Coffee and Cream Productions
Cupit Productions, Jerry
Daliven Music
DAP Productions
De Miles, Edward
Diamond Entertainment, Joel
Durr Productions, David
Esquire International
Final Mix Music
Hailing Frequency Music Productions
Haworth Productions
House of Rhythm

Janoulis Productions, Alexander/Big Al Jano
    Productions
Jericho Sound Lab
Kane, Karen, Producer/Engineer
KMA
Known Artist Productions
Kovach, Robert R.
L.A. Entertainment, Inc.
Lazy Bones Productions/Recordings, Inc.
Linear Cycle Productions
Magid Productions, Lee
Makers Mark Music Productions
Martin, Pete/Vaam Music Productions
Mathes Productions, David
Mayfly Record Productions, Ltd.
Modern Tribe Records
Mona Lisa Records/Bristol
Monticana Productions
Moody, David
Mraz, Gary John
New Experience Records
New Vizion Studios, The
Ormsby, John "Buck"/Etiquette Productions
Planet Dallas
Prejippie Music Group
Prescription Co., The
Rosenman, Mike
Rustron Music Productions
Segal's Productions
Shu'Baby Montez Music
Silver Thunder Music Group
Spiral-Wave
Studio D Recording
Syndicate Sound, Inc.
Triplitt Production
Vickers Music Association, Charles
Weisman Production Group, The
Westwires Digital USA
Y-N-A/C.D.T. Productions

Rap (also hip-hop, bass, etc.)
AMAJ Records
Final Mix Music
Jag Studio, Ltd.
KMA
Makers Mark Music Productions
Marenco, Cookie
Modern Tribe Records
Neu Electro Productions
New Experience Records
Philly Breakdown Recording Co.
Poku Productions
R&D Productions
Shu'Baby Montez Music
Syndicate Sound, Inc.
Triplitt Production
Weisman Production Group, The

**Religious (also gospel, sacred, Christian,
church, hymns, praise, inspirational,
worship, etc.)**
"A" Major Sound Corporation
ACR Productions
Bal Records
Birthplace Productions
Blues Alley Records
Coffee and Cream Productions
Cupit Productions, Jerry
DAP Productions
Doss Presents, Col. Buster
Durr Productions, David
Eiffert, Jr., Leo J.
Esquire International
Eternal Song Agency, The
Hailing Frequency Music Productions
Haworth Productions
Jag Studio, Ltd.
Jazmin Productions
Kool Breeze Productions
Kovach, Robert R.
Landmark Communications Group
Lari-Jon Productions
Linear Cycle Productions
Luick, Harold, & Country Music Showcase Intl.
    Associates
Magid Productions, Lee
Mathes Productions, David
Modern Tribe Records
Monticana Productions
Moody, David
Musicland Productions, Inc.
New Experience Records
Philly Breakdown Recording Co.
Silver Bow Productions
Silver Thunder Music Group
Stuart Audio Services
Syndicate Sound, Inc.
Texas Music Masters
Trinity Studio, The
Vickers Music Association, Charles
Walbash River and Broken Arrow Productions
Weisman Production Group, The
WLM Music/Recording

Rock (also rockabilly, AOR, rock 'n' roll, etc.)
"A" Major Sound Corporation
Aberdeen Productions
ACR Productions
AKO Productions
Allyn, Stuart J.
Angel Films Company
Appell Productions, Inc., Jonathan
Bal Records
Big Sky Audio Productions
Blues Alley Records
Cacophony Productions

Celt Musical Services, Jan
Coachouse Music
Collector Records
Coppin, Johnny/Red Sky Records
Corwin, Dano
Cupit Productions, Jerry
Daliven Music
Demi Monde Records & Publishing Ltd.
Diamond Entertainment, Joel
Dixon III, Philip D., Attorney at Law
Esquire International
Glass House Productions
Hailing Frequency Music Productions
Haworth Productions
House of Rhythm
Integrated Entertainment
Jag Studio, Ltd.
Janoulis Productions, Alexander/Big Al Jano
    Productions
Jericho Sound Lab
John Productions, David
JSB Groupe Management Inc.
June Productions Ltd.
Katz Productions, Matthew
Kilgore Productions
Kingston Records and Talent
Kleanza River Canyon Productions
Kool Breeze Productions
Kovach, Robert R.
Landmark Communications Group
Lari-Jon Productions
Lazy Bones Productions/Recordings, Inc.
Linear Cycle Productions
Magid Productions, Lee
Mathews, Scott, d/b/a Hit or Myth Productions
Mega Truth Records
Moffet, Gary
Mona Lisa Records/Bristol
Monticana Productions
Moody, David
Neu Electro Productions
New Experience Records
New Vizion Studios, The
Ormsby, John "Buck"/Etiquette Productions
Planet Dallas
Poku Productions

Prejippie Music Group
Prescription Co., The
R&D Productions
Reel Adventures
Rustron Music Productions
Segal's Productions
Silver Bow Productions
Silver Thunder Music Group
Siskind Productions, Mike
SM Recording/Hit Records Network
Sound Arts Recording Studio
Sound Works Entertainment Productions Inc.
Sphere Group One
Stuart Audio Services
Studio D Recording
Studio Seven
Syndicate Sound, Inc.
Szawlowski Productions, William, & Ventura
    Music Publishing
TMC Productions
Triplitt Production
Twist Tunes
Valtec Productions
Vickers Music Association, Charles
Walbash River and Broken Arrow Productions
Weisman Production Group, The
Wilbur Productions
WLM Music/Recording
Wytas Productions, Steve
Y-N-A/C.D.T. Productions

World Music (also reggae, ethnic, calypso, international, world beat, etc.)

AMAJ Records
Appell Productions, Inc., Jonathan
Blue Planet Music
Daylo Music
Durr Productions, David
Jericho Sound Lab
Kane, Karen, Producer/Engineer
KMA
Pacific North Studios Ltd.
Reel Adventures
Spiral-Wave
Studio Seven
Tari, Roger Vincent
Vickers Music Association, Charles

Managers & Booking Agents

Before submitting to a manager or booking agent, be sure you know exactly what you need. If you're looking for someone to help you with performance opportunities, the booking agency is the one to contact. They can help you book shows either in your local area or throughout the country. If you're looking for someone to help guide your career, you need to contact a management firm. Some management firms may also handle booking; however, it may be in your best interest to look for a separate booking agency. A manager should be your manager—not your agent, publisher, lawyer or accountant.

MANAGERS

Of all the music industry players surrounding successful artists, managers are usually the people closest to the artists themselves. The artist manager can be a valuable contact, both for the songwriter trying to get songs to a particular artist and for the songwriter/performer. Getting songs to an artist's manager is yet another way to get your songs recorded, since the manager may play a large part in deciding what material his client uses. For the performer seeking management, a successful manager should be thought of as the foundation for a successful career.

The relationship between a manager and his client relies on mutual trust. A manager works as the liaison between you and the rest of the music industry, and he must know exactly what you want out of your career in order to help you achieve your goals. His handling of publicity, promotion and finances, as well as the contacts he has within the industry, can make or break your career. You should never be afraid to ask questions about any aspect of the relationship between you and a prospective manager. Always remember that a manager works *for the artist*. A good manager is able to communicate his opinions to you without reservation, and should be willing to explain any confusing terminology or discuss plans with you before taking action. A manager needs to be able to communicate successfully with all segments of the music industry in order to get his client the best deals possible. He needs to be able to work with booking agents, publishers, lawyers and record companies. Keep in mind that you are both working together toward a common goal: success for you and your songs. Talent, originality, professionalism and a drive to succeed are qualities that will attract a manager to an artist—and a songwriter.

BOOKING AGENTS

The function of the booking agent is to find performance venues for their clients. They usually represent many more acts than a manager does, and have less contact with their acts. A booking agent charges a commission for his services, as does a manager. Managers usually ask for a 15-50% commission on an act's earnings; booking agents usually charge around 10%.

Additional Managers & Booking Agents

There are **MORE MANAGERS & BOOKING AGENTS** located in other sections of the book! On page 329 use the list of Additional Managers & Booking Agents to find listings within other sections who are also managers/booking agents.

SUBMITTING MATERIAL TO MANAGERS & BOOKING AGENTS

The firms listed in this section have provided information about the types of music they work with and the types of acts they represent. You'll want to refer to the Category Index at the end of this section to find out which companies deal with the type of music you write, and the Geographic Index at the back of the book to help you locate companies near where you live. Then determine whether they are open to your level of experience (see the Openness to Submissions sidebar on page 8). Each listing also contains submission requirements and information about what items to include in a press kit and will also specify whether the company is a management firm or a booking agency. Remember that your submission represents you as an artist, and should be as organized and professional as possible.

For More Information

For more instructional information on the listings in this book, including explanations of symbols ( ), read the article How to Use *Songwriter's Market* to Get Your Songs Heard on page 5.

○ **AFTERSCHOOL PUBLISHING COMPANY**, P.O. Box 14157, Detroit MI 48214. (313)894-8855. President: Herman Kelly. Manager: Genesis Act. Management firm, booking agency, record company (Afterschool Co.) and music publisher (Afterschool Pub. Co.). Estab. 1978. Represents individual artists, songwriters, producers, arrangers and musicians from anywhere; currently handles 20 acts. Reviews material for acts.
How to Contact: Submit demo tape by mail. Unsolicited submissions are OK. Prefers cassette with 3 songs and lyric or lead sheet. If seeking management, include cover letter, résumé, proposal, photo, demo tape, lyric sheets, press clippings, video and bio in press kit. SASE. Reports in 2 weeks.
Music: Mostly **pop**, **jazz**, **rap**, **country** and **folk**. Works primarily with small bands and solo artists. Current acts include L.L. Cool J, P.M. Dawn and Throw The D.

◑ **AIR TIGHT MANAGEMENT**, 115 West Rd., Winchester Center CT 06094. (860)738-9139. Fax: (860)738-9135. President: Jack Forchette. A&R: David Bengston. Management firm. Estab. 1969. Represents individual artists, groups or songwriters from anywhere; currently handles 5 acts. Receives 20% commission. Reviews material for acts.
How to Contact: Write first and obtain permission to submit. Prefers cassette or VHS videocassette. If seeking management, press kit should include photos, bio and recorded material. "Follow up with a fax, not a phone call." Does not return material. Reports in 2 weeks.
Music: Mostly **rock**, **country** and **jazz**. Current acts include Johnny Colla (songwriter/producer, and guitarist/songwriter for Huey Lewis and the News), Jason Scheff (lead singer/songwriter for the group "Chicago"), Gary Burr (Nashville songwriter/producer) and Cassandra Reed (R&B/pop singer/songwriter).

▚ ◑ **ALERT MUSIC INC.**, 41 Britain St., Suite 305, Toronto Ontario M5A 1R7 Canada. (416)364-4200. Fax: (416)364-8632. E-mail: alert@inforamp.net. Website: http://www.alertmusic.com. President: W. Tom Berry. Management firm and record company. Represents local and regional individual artists and groups; currently handles 4 acts. Receives 15% commission. Reviews material for acts.
How to Contact: Write first and obtain permission to submit. Prefers cassette or CD. If seeking management, press kit should include finished CD or 3-4 song cassette, photo, press clippings and bio. SASE. Reports in 6 weeks.
Music: **All types.** Works primarily with bands and singer/songwriters. Current acts include Holly Cole (pop vocalist), Kim Mitchell (rock singer/songwriter), Johnny Favourite Swing Orchestra (swing band).

◑ **ALL MUSICMATTERS**, P.O. Box 6156, San Antonio TX 78209. (210)651-5858. President: Jean Estes. Management firm. Represents artists from anywhere.
How to Contact: Call first and obtain permission to submit. Prefers cassette. Does not return material. Reports in 1 month.
Music: Mostly **jazz**. Current acts include True Diversity (jazz group) and Synergy Jazz.

☑ ◐ **ALL STAR MANAGEMENT**, 1229 S. Prospect St., Marion OH 43302-7267. (740)382-5939. E-mail: allstarmanage@acc-net.com. President: John Simpson. Management firm. Estab. 1990. Represents individual artists, groups and songwriters from anywhere; currently handles 9 acts. Receives 20% commission. Reviews material for acts.
How to Contact: Submit demo tape by mail. Unsolicited submissions are OK. Prefers cassette or videocassette with 3 songs and lyric or lead sheet. If seeking management, press kit should include audio cassette with 3 songs, bio, 8×10 photo or any information or articles written about yourself or group, and video if you have one. Does not return material. Reports in 2 months.
Music: Mostly **country** and **Christian country**; also **gospel**. Works primarily with bands and singers/songwriters. Current acts include Leon Seiter (country singer/songwriter), Debbie Robinson (country), Austin Rangers (country) and Corby LaCroix (country).

◐ **ALL STAR TALENT AGENCY**, P.O. Box 717, White House TN 37188. (615)643-4208. Owner/Agent: Joyce Kirby. Booking agency. Estab. 1966. Represents professional individuals, groups and songwriters; currently handles 6 acts. Receives 10% commission. Reviews material for acts.
How to Contact: Submit demo tape by mail. Unsolicited submissions are OK. Prefers cassette or VHS videocassette with 4 songs (can be cover songs) and lead sheet. If seeking management, press kit should include bios, cover letter, press clippings, demo and photos. Does not return material. Reports in 1 month.
Music: Mostly **country**; also **bluegrass, gospel, MOR, rock (country)** and **top 40/pop**. Works primarily with dance, show and bar bands, vocalists, club acts and concerts. Current acts include Alex Houston (MOR), Chris Hartley (country) and Jack Greene (country).

[N] 🖼 ◐ **AMERICAN ARTISTS ENTERTAINMENT**, 21 Chews Landing Rd., Clementon NJ 08021-3843. (609)566-1232. Fax: (609)435-7453. E-mail: ardept@aaeg.com. Website: http://www.aaeg.com. Contact: A&R Department. Management firm, music publisher (David Music, BMI), record company (East Coast Records) and record and motion picture distribution. Represents individual artists, groups, actors and models from anywhere; currently handles 3 acts. Receives 20% commission. Reviews material for acts.
How to Contact: Submit demo tape by mail. Unsolicited submissions are OK. Prefers cassette, videocassette or CD with 3 songs. If seeking management, press kit should include bio, press releases, photos, performing, training and background. SASE. Reports in 1 month.
Music: Mostly **R&B, top 40** and **rap**; also **modern** and motion picture scores. Current acts include The Blue Notes (R&B), Benjamin Falk (pop singer) and Derrick Simmons (actor/rapper).

[N] ◐ **AMERICAN BANDS MANAGEMENT**, P.O. Box 840607, Houston TX 77284. (713)783-1406. Fax: (713)789-7331. President: John Blomstrom. Management firm and booking agent. Estab. 1973. Represents groups from anywhere; currently handles 6 acts. Receives 15% commission, sometimes higher depending on need. Reviews material for acts.
How to Contact: Submit demo tape by mail. Unsolicited submissions are OK. Prefers cassette or VHS videocassette. If seeking management, press kit should include cover letter, bio, photo, demo tape/CD, press clippings, video, résumé and professional references with names and numbers. Does not return material. Reports in 2-4 weeks.
Music: Mostly **rock (all forms)** and **modern country**. Works primarily with bands. Current acts include Captain Pink (Motown style), Neal Zaza (guitarist) and Hamilton & Prime Time (blues/rock).

☑ ◑ **AMERICAN CLASSICS** (formerly Three Guys From Verona, Inc.), 5746 Rhodes Ave., Valley Village CA 91607. Partner: Danny Kessler. Estab. 1976. Represents individual artists, groups and songwriters from anywhere; currently handles 4 acts. Receives 15% commission. Reviews material for acts.
How to Contact: Submit demo tape by mail. Unsolicited submissions are OK. Prefers cassette, CD or VHS videocassette with 1-6 songs and lyric sheet. If seeking management, press kit should include bio, cover letter, CD or tape (audio and video if possible), photo and résumé. SASE. Reports in 3-4 weeks.
Music: Mostly **country, rock** and **R&B**; also **pop/rock**. Works primarily with singer/songwriters, bands and writers. Current acts include Sugar Bones (R&R), Lizzy (country) and Roy Gaines (blues).

🦋 ◐ **AMOK INC.**, Box 12, Fergus, Ontario N1M 2W7 Canada. (519)787-1100. Fax: (519)787-0084. E-mail: amok@sentex.net. Owner: Hugo Ranpen. Management firm and booking agency. Estab. 1985.

OPENNESS TO SUBMISSIONS: ◯ beginners; ◑ beginners and experienced; ◐ experienced only; ◒ industry referrals only.

Represents groups from anywhere; currently handles 13 acts. Receives 15-20% commission.
How to Contact: Submit demo tape by mail. Unsolicited submissions are OK. Prefers VHS videocassette or CD with lyric sheet. If seeking management, press kit should include bio, past performances, photo, cassette, CD or video. "Due to the large amount of submissions we receive we can only respond to successful applicants." Does not return material.
Music: Mostly **world beat**, **new roots** and **folk**. Works primarily with bands in the world music and new roots field; no mainstream rock/pop. Current acts include Amampondo (world beat, Melt 2000), Lester Quitzau (blues, Festival), Taxi Chain (Celtic), Kila (Celtic, Key Records) and Lucie Idlout (Inuit).

◑ ANDERSON ASSOCIATES COMMUNICATIONS GROUP, 9748 NW 14th St., Suite 31, Coral Spring FL 33071. (954)753-5440. Fax: (954)753-9715. E-mail: rjppny@aol.com. Website: http://andersona ssociates.com. CEO: Richard Papaleo. Management firm. Estab. 1992. Represents individual artists and groups from anywhere; currently handles 3 acts. Receives 15-20% commission. Reviews material for acts.
How to Contact: Submit demo tape by mail. Unsolicited submissions are OK. Prefers cassette, bio and/ or picture with 3 songs and lead sheet. If seeking management, press kit should include cassette with 3 songs (video OK), bio, cover letter and picture. Does not return material. Reports in 1-2 months.
Music: Mostly **R&B**, **pop/dance** and **pop/rock**; also **A/C**, **pop/mainstream** and **mainstream rock**. Current acts include Neutron Cafe (modern rock), Joyce Sims (R&B/dance) and Jim Walsh (pop/rock).

◑ AR MANAGEMENT, 1585 Via Parque, Thousand Oaks CA 91360. (805)529-0802. E-mail: armgmt @aol.com. President: Alan Rommelfanger. Management firm. Estab. 1995. Represents individual artists and groups from anywhere; currently handles 2 acts. Receives 20% commission.
How to Contact: Write first and obtain permission to submit. Prefers cassette with 5 songs and lyric sheet. If seeking management, press kit should include bio, photo, demo tape/CD, lyric sheets and press clippings. Does not return material.
Music: Mostly **rock**, **country** and **blues**. Current acts include The Rainmakers (rock) and Brewer & Shipley (folk duo).

❀ ◑ ARDENNE INT'L INC., 1800 Argyle St., Suite 444, Halifax, Nova Scotia B3J 3N8 Canada. (902)492-8000. Fax: (902)423-2143. E-mail: mardenne@ardenneinternational.com. Website: http://www.A rdenneInternational.com. President: Michael Ardenne. Management firm. Estab. 1988. Represents local, individual artists and songwriters from anywhere; currently handles 2 acts. Receives 20% commission. Reviews material for acts.
How to Contact: Write, call or fax first and obtain permission to submit. Prefers cassette with lyric sheet. "Put name, address, phone number and song list on the tape. Send maximum 3 songs." If seeking management, press kit should include cover letter, bio, photo, demo tape/CD, lyric sheets and video. Does not return material. Reports in 2 months.
Music: Mostly **country**, **pop** and **soft rock**. Works primarily with vocalists/songwriters. Current acts include Kris Taylor (pop/rock).
Tips: "Periodically we get asked to search for country material for independent artists."

Ⓝ ◑ ARIEL PUBLICITY ARTIST RELATIONS & BOOKING, 2999 Shady Hollow E., Boulder CO 80304. (303)443-0083. Fax: (303)443-0720. E-mail: info@arielpublicity.com. Website: http://www.arie lpublicity.com. President: Ariel Hyatt. Publicist: LaLêna Jamarusty. Booking agency and publicity firm. Estab. 1995. Represents individual artists and groups from anywhere; currently handles 24 acts. Receives 10% commission. Reviews material for acts.
How to Contact: Call first and obtain permission to submit a demo or call to arrange personal interview. Prefers cassette with 5 songs and press kit with photo. SASE. Reports in 6 weeks.
Music: "We work with all types from solo folk artists to ten piece ska bands." Current acts include Sally Taylor (folk singer/songwriter), Zuba (3 piece funk band) and Skavoovie & the Epitones (10 piece ska/ swing act).

Ⓝ ✿ ◑ ARPA MUSIK MANAGEMENT, 22970 Cass Ave., Woodland Hills CA 91364-3917. (818)591-9545. Fax: (818)591-7540. E-mail: arpamusik@msn.com. Owner: Marcelo Rey. Management firm and booking agency. Estab. 1994. Represents individual artists or groups from anywhere; currently handles 3 acts. Receives 15-20% commission. Reviews material for acts.
● One of Arpa Musik's artists has won *Billboard*'s award for Best Latin Rap Artist.
How to Contact: Submit demo tape by mail. Unsolicited submissions are OK. Prefers cassette or CD with 3 songs and lyric sheet. If seeking management, press kit should include bio and photos. "Try to be original." Does not return material. Reports back only if interested.
Music: Mostly **Latin pop**, **Latin rock** and **dance**. Works primarily with singers and groups. Current acts

include El General (dance), Anayka (pop/ballad) and Adore (rock), all for the Latin market.
Tips: "Never loose the feeling and don't try to copy anyone. Be yourself."

☑ ◑ **ARTIST MANAGEMENT SERVICES**, 48 Dogwood Lane, Springfield AR 72157. (501)354-3724. Fax: (501)354-3789. E-mail: musicedge@usa.net. Website: http://www.musicedge.net. Owner: Tam McClure. Management firm, promotion and press kit and web design. Estab. 1996. Represents individual artists, groups and songwriters from anywhere; currently handles 3 acts. Receives 15% commission. Reviews material for acts.
How to Contact: Call first to obtain permission to submit demo tape by mail or call first to arrange personal interview. Prefers cassette or CD with 3 songs and lyric sheet. If seeking management, press kit should include a typed bio, lyric sheets, press clippings and tour itinerary. "Also label everything so if parts get separated in the office among assistants we can still contact you. Always present a neat press kit, no handwritten, folded or stapled papers—looks unprofessional and is a mess to look at. If you don't care more about your career, why should we? If you don't have a computer or typewriter, then write it neatly and we will discuss press kit design services with you. The press kit is almost as important as the demo itself." SASE. Reports in 1 month.
Music: Mostly **rock**, **alternative/pop** and **hard rock**; also **industrial** and **folk**. Current acts include Two Thumbs (folk/rock), Heterodyne (dark alternative) and Elizabeth Price (folksinger/songwriter).
Tips: "Never sign a contract without having a lawyer read it. Never sign with a manager you don't feel 100% comfortable with. You will be working closely with them on one of the most important things to you, your music career. You have to like and trust them. We work closely with indie music distributors, the Independent Distribution Network."

☑ ◑ **ARTIST REPRESENTATION AND MANAGEMENT**, 1257 Arcade St., St. Paul MN 55106. (651)483-8754. Fax: (651)776-6338. E-mail: ra@armentertainment.com. Website: http://www.armentertain ment.com. Agent/Manager: Roger Anderson. Management firm and booking agency. Estab. 1983. Represents artists from anywhere; currently handles 10 acts. Receives 15% commission. Reviews material for acts.
How to Contact: Submit demo tape by mail. Unsolicited submissions are OK. Prefers cassette or videocassette with 3 songs and lyric sheet. If seeking management, press kit should include demo tape or videotape, cover letter, bio, photo, press clippings and résumé. "Priority is placed on original artists with product who are willing to tour." Does not return material. Reports in 2-4 weeks.
Music: Mostly **rock**, **heavy metal** and **R&B**; also **southern rock** and **pop**. Works primarily with bands. Current acts include Crow (R&B, rock), Austin Healy (southern rock), Knight Crawler (contemporary hard rock) and Touched (hard rock).

◑ **ATCH RECORDS AND PRODUCTIONS**, 10103 Fondren, Suite 380, Houston TX 77096-4502. (713)981-6540. Fax: (713)981-0083. Chairman/CEO: Charles Atchison. Management firm, recording studio and record company. Estab. 1989. Represents local, regional and international individual artists, groups and songwriters; currently handles 4 acts. Receives 20% commission. Reviews material for acts.
How to Contact: Submit demo tape by mail. Unsolicited submissions are OK. Prefers cassette with 2 songs and lyric sheet. If seeking management, include cover letter, bio, photo, demo and lyrics. Does not return material. Reports in 3 weeks.
Music: Mostly **R&B**, **country** and **gospel**; also **pop**, **rap** and **hip-hop**. Works primarily with vocalists and groups. Current acts include Demetris (R&B), Gotham Kidz (hip-hop) and Slamm (R&B).
Tips: "Send a good detailed demo with good lyrics. Looking for wonderful love stories, dance music, also songs for children."

◑ **ATLANTIC ENTERTAINMENT GROUP**, 1125 Atlantic Ave., 7th Floor, Atlantic City NJ 08401-4806. (609)823-6400. Fax: (609)823-4846. E-mail: aegshows@aol.com. Executive Director of Artist Services: Scott Sherman. Management, production firm and booking agency. Represents individual artists and groups from anywhere; currently handles over 20 acts. Receives 10-22% commission. Reviews material for acts and management.
How to Contact: Submit demo tape by mail. Unsolicited submissions are OK. Prefers cassette, CD or VHS videocassette with 3 songs. If seeking management, press kit should include bio, cover letter, photo,

---

TO HELP YOU UNDERSTAND and use the information in these listings, see "How to Use *Songwriter's Market* to Get Your Songs Heard," on page 5.

press clippings, video, résumé, previous listings, demo and reviews. SASE. Reports in 1-2 months if we may be able to offer services.

Music: Mostly **dance, R&B** and **contemporary**; also **house** and **specialty**. Current acts include Candace Jourdan (singer/writer), Candy J (singer), C&C Music Factory, Deborah Cooper (R&B vocalist), Candy Girls, Richard Skipper (vocal impersonator) and Sweet P. Pauline.

BACCHUS GROUP PRODUCTIONS, LTD., 5701 N. Sheridan Rd., Suite 8-U, Chicago IL 60660. (773)334-1532. Fax: (773)334-1531. E-mail: bacchusgrp@compuserve.com. Senior Vice President: M. Margarida Rainho. Management firm and record producer (D. Maximilian). Estab. 1990. Represents individual artists or groups from anywhere; currently handles 9 acts. Receives 15-25% commission. Reviews material for acts.

How to Contact: Submit demo tape by mail. Unsolicited submissions are OK. Prefers cassette, videocassette or CD with 5 songs and lead sheet. SASE. Reports in 1 month.

Music: Mostly **pop, R&B/soul** and **jazz**; also **Latin** and **world beat**. Works primarily with singer/songwriters, composers, arrangers, bands and orchestras. Current acts include Orchestra of the Americas (international dance orchestra), Sorcerers of Swing (big band jazz dance orchestra) and Samba Samba 2000 (Carnival/Mardi Gras worldbeat dance orchestra).

BACKSTAGE ENTERTAINMENT/LOGGINS PROMOTION, 26239 Senator Ave., Harbor City CA 90710. (310)325-2800. Fax: (310)325-2560. E-mail: logprod@aol.com. CEO: Paul Loggins. Management firm, record producer (Paul Loggins) and radio promotion. Represents individual artists, groups and songwriters from anywhere; currently handles 10 acts. Receives 15-25% commission. Reviews material for acts.

How to Contact: Write first and obtain permission to submit. If seeking management, press kit should include picture, short bio, cover letter, press clippings and audio cassette or CD (preferred). "Mark on cassette or CD which cut you, as the artist, feel is the strongest." Does not return material. Reports in 2 weeks.

Music: Mostly **adult, top 40** and **AAA**; also **urban, rap, alternative, college, smooth jazz** and **Americana**. Works primarily with bands and solo artists. Current acts include Andi Harrison (A/C/top 40 crossover solo musician), Kenny Loggins (Columbia Records), Silent Opera (Coast Records) and Joe's Band.

BACKSTREET BOOKING, 5658 Kirby Ave., Cincinnati OH 45239. (513)542-9544. Fax: (513)542-6780. E-mail: djppfb@aol.com. Website: http://www.holographicrecords.com/backstreet. President: James Sfarnas. Booking agency and record company (Holographic Records). Estab. 1992. Represents individual artists and groups from anywhere; currently handles 8 acts. Receives 10-15% commission. Reviews material for acts.

How to Contact: Call first and obtain permission to submit a demo. Prefers CD with 3-12 songs. "Make sure contact info is on CD and on packaging. Send press kit with bio and tour history." Does not return material. Reports in 1 month.

Music: Mostly **niche-oriented music** and **rock**. Current acts include The Miracles, Billy Preston and Acumen (progressive rock group).

Tips: "Build a base on your own."

BAMN MANAGEMENT, 25 Heathman's Rd., Ground Floor, London SW6 4TJ United Kingdom. (44)171 371 7223. Fax: (44)171 736 8041. General Manager: Will Stoppard. Management firm and music publisher (Junkbond Ltd.). Represents individual artists, groups and songwriters from anywhere; currently handles 8 acts. Reviews material for acts.

How to Contact: Submit demo tape by mail. Unsolicited submissions are OK. Prefers cassette, DAT or CD with 6 songs and lyric sheet. If seeking management, press kit should include photograph, demo, previous management details and record label/publisher (if any). SAE and IRC. Reports in 1 week.

Music: Mostly **pop, R&B** and **mainstream/radio friendly**; also **dance**. Works primarily with songwriters, bands, remixers and DJs. Current acts include Ian Green (songwriter/producer/mixer), Tim Laws (songwriter/producer/mixer) and Johnny Dollar (writer/producer/remixer/mixer).

Tips: "Identify a specific niche in the market and an emotion/empathy, and concentrate on one subject."

BARNARD MANAGEMENT SERVICES (BMS), 228 Main St., Venice CA 90291. (310)587-0771. Agent: Russell Barnard. Management firm. Estab. 1979. Represents artists, groups and songwriters; currently handles 3 acts. Receives 10-20% commission. Reviews material for acts.

How to Contact: Write first and obtain permission to submit. Prefers cassette with 3-10 songs and lead

sheet. Artists may submit VHS videocassette (15-30 minutes) by permission only. If seeking management, press kit should include cover letter, bio, photo, demo tape/CD, lyric sheets, press clippings, video and résumé. Does not return material. Reports in 2 months.
Music: Mostly **country crossover**, **blues**, **country**, **R&B**, **rock** and **soul**. Current acts include Helen Hudson (singer/songwriter), Mark Shipper (songwriter/author) and Kelly Tauper (R&B singer/songwriter).
Tips: "Semi-produced demos are of little value. Either save the time and money by submitting material 'in the raw,' or do a finished production version."

N ⊕ ⬮ **PAUL BARRETT ROCK 'N' ROLL ENTERPRISES**, 16 Grove Place, Penarth, Vale of Glamorgan CF64 2ND United Kingdom. Phone: 01222-704279. Fax: 01222-709989. Director: Paul Barrett. Management firm, booking agency, music publisher (October), record company (Rock 'n' Roll Records) and record producer (Paul Barrett and Ray Thompson). Estab. 1969. Represents individual artists and groups from anywhere; currently handles 30 acts. Receives 10% commission. Reviews material for acts.
• This company only represents acts who perform '50s rock 'n' roll.
How to Contact: Submit demo tape by mail. Unsolicited submissions are OK. Prefers cassette or DAT with picture and bio (for performers). SAE and IRC. Reports in 3 weeks.
Music: Mostly **50s rock 'n' roll**. Works primarily with "performers plus some writers." Current acts include The Jets (trio), Matchbox (P.B.) and Ray Campi (American rockabilly hero).

⬮ **BASSLINE ENTERTAINMENT, INC.**, P.O. Box 2394, New York NY 10185. (212)769-6956. Fax: (212)420-8231. E-mail: newbassinc@aol.com. Executive Director: Sharon Williams. General Manager: Oz Ithier. Management firm. Estab. 1993. Represents local and regional individual artists, groups and songwriters; currently handles 2 acts. Receives 20% commission. Reviews material for acts.
How to Contact: Submit demo tape by mail. Unsolicited submissions are OK. Prefers cassette, DAT or VHS videocassette. If seeking management, press kit should include cover letter, press clippings, bio (include physical description), demo (cassette, DAT or VHS video), picture and accurate contact telephone number. SASE. Reports in 2-3 weeks.
Music: Mostly **pop**, **R&B**, **club/dance** and **hip-hop/rap**; also **Latin**. Works primarily with singer/songwriters, rappers and bands. Current acts include 2 Wice Unique featuring Michael Anthony (pop/R&B vocalist) and Radames (rap artist).

⬮ **DICK BAXTER MANAGEMENT**, P.O. Box 1385, Canyon Country CA 91386. (805)268-1659. Owner: Dick Baxter. Management firm and music publisher. Estab. 1963. Represents individual artists and groups from anywhere; currently handles 1 act. Receives 15-20% commission. Reviews material for acts.
How to Contact: Write or call first and obtain permission to submit. Prefers cassette or VHS videocassette with 3 or more songs and lyric sheet. If seeking management, press kit should include photos, bio, cover letter, résumé, press clips, audio and video if available. Does not return material. Reports in 2-3 weeks.
Music: Mostly **country**, **gospel** and **pop**. Current acts include Ted & Ruth Reinhart (cowboy/western).

N ⬮ **BC PRODUCTIONS**, P.O. Box 2, Hughesville PA 17737. (717)584-4480. Fax: (717)584-4608. E-mail: bmtallman@aol.com. Artist Manager: Bonnie Tallman. Management firm and music publisher (Pixworld Music). Estab. 1989. Represents individual artists or groups from anywhere; currently handles 4 acts. Reviews material for acts.
How to Contact: Call first and obtain permission to submit a demo. Prefers cassette with 4 songs and lyric sheet. Does not return material. Reports in 1 month.
Music: Mostly **blues**, **pop** and **jazz**. Works primarily with "serious, full time musicians with good business sense—roots music in general, but not always." Current acts include Greg Piccolo (songwriter, tenor sax, lead vocals, band leader), Ann Rabson (boogie-woogie piano, singer) Saffire-the Uppity Blues Women (acoustic trio-blues) and Bob Margolin (blues, slide guitarist).
Tips: "Be patient."

⬮ **BIG J PRODUCTIONS**, 2516 S. Sugar Ridge, Laplace LA 70068. (504)652-2645. Agent: Frankie Jay. Booking agency. Estab. 1968. Represents individual artists, groups and songwriters; currently handles over 50 acts. Receives 15-25% commission. Reviews material for acts.
How to Contact: Call first and obtain permission to submit. Prefers cassette or VHS videocassette with 3-6 songs and lyric or lead sheet. "It would be best for an artist to lip-sync to a prerecorded track. The object is for someone to see how an artist would perform more than simply assessing song content." Artists

THE TYPES OF MUSIC each listing is interested in are printed in **boldface**.

seeking management should include pictures, biography, tape or CD and video. Does not return material. Reports in 2 weeks.

Music: Mostly **rock**, **pop** and **R&B**. Works primarily with groups with self-contained songwriters. Current acts include Zebra (original rock group), Crowbar (heavy metal) and Kyper (original dance).

J. BIRD ENTERTAINMENT AGENCY, 4905 S. Atlantic, Daytona Beach FL 32127. (904)767-1919. Fax: (904)767-1019. President: John Bird II. Management firm, booking agency and record company. Estab. 1963. Represents individual artists, groups and songwriters from anywhere; currently handles 55 acts. Receives 15-20% commission. Reviews material for acts.
How to Contact: Submit demo tape by mail. Unsolicited submissions are OK. Prefers cassette or VHS videocassette and photo with 3 songs and lyric sheet. Does not return material. Reports in 2 weeks.
Music: Mostly **rock**, **top 40** and **country**. Current acts include Hank Williams, Jr., Legendary Bama Band, Copperhead, Survivor, Starship, Collective Soul, Kansas, Little River Band and ELO.

BLACK STALLION COUNTRY, INC., P.O. Box 368, Tujunga CA 91043. (818)352-8142. E-mail: kennking@aol.com. President: Kenn E. Kingsbury, Jr.. Management firm, production company and music publisher (Black Stallion Country Publishing/BMI). Estab. 1979. Represents individual artists from anywhere; currently handles 20 acts. Receives 15-20% commission. Reviews material for acts.
How to Contact: Submit demo tape by mail. Unsolicited submissions are OK. Prefers cassette with 3 songs and lyric sheet. If seeking management, press kit should include picture/résumé and audio and/or video tape. "I would also like a one-page statement of goals and why you would be an asset to my company or me." SASE. Reports in 1-2 months.
Music: Mostly **country**, **R&B** and **A/C**. Works primarily with country acts, variety acts and film/TV pictures/actresses. Current acts include Lane Brody (singer country), Thom Bresh (musician) and Barbara Nickell (film/TV actress).

BLANK & BLANK, 1601 Market St., Suite 2560, Philadelphia PA 19103. (215)561-0800. Manager: E. Robert Blank. Management firm. Represents individual artists and groups. Reviews material for acts.
How to Contact: Submit demo tape by mail. Unsolicited submissions are OK. Prefers videocassette. If seeking management, press kit should include cover letter, demo tape/CD and video. Does not return material.

BLOWIN' SMOKE PRODUCTIONS/RECORDS, 7438 Shoshone Ave., Van Nuys CA 91406-2340. (818)881-9888. Fax: (818)881-0555. E-mail: blowinsmokeband@ktb.net. Website: http://www.blowinsmokeband.com. President: Larry Knight. Management firm and record producer. Estab. 1990. Represents local and West Coast individual artists and groups; currently handles 7 acts. Receives 15-20% commission. Reviews material for acts.
How to Contact: Write or call first and obtain permission to submit. Prefers cassette. If seeking management, press kit should include cover letter, demo tape/CD, lyric sheets, press clippings, video if available, photo, bios, contact telephone numbers and any info on legal commitments already in place. SASE. Reports in 1 month.
Music: Mostly **R&B**, **blues** and **blues-rock**. Works primarily with single and group vocalists and a few R&B/blues bands. Current acts include Larry "Fuzzy" Knight (blues singer/songwriter), King Floyd (R&B artist) and The Blowin' Smoke Rhythm & Blues Band.

THE BLUE CAT AGENCY/EL GATO AZUL AGENCY, P.O. Box 399, Novato CA 94948. Phone/fax: (415)507-9722. E-mail: klkindig@marin.kl2.ca.us. Website: http://www.ellensburg.com/~lupinus/bluecat/. Owner/agent: Karen Kindig. Management firm and booking agency. Estab. 1989. Represents individual artists and/or groups from anywhere; currently handles 4 acts. Receives 10-15% commission. Reviews material for acts.
How to Contact: Write or call first and obtain permission to submit. Prefers cassette or CD. If seeking management, press kit should include demo tape, bio and press clippings (photo optional). SASE. Reports in 6-8 weeks.
Music: Mostly **Latin jazz** and **rock/pop "en español."** Works primarily with singer/songwriters, instrumentalists and bands. Current acts include Alejandro Santos (flutist/composer), Ania Paz (pianist/composer), Dermis Tatú (rock-en-español) and La Muda (rock-en-español).

BLUE WAVE PRODUCTIONS, 3221 Perryville Rd., Baldwinsville NY 13027. (315)638-4286. Fax: (315)635-4757. Owner/president: Greg Spencer. Management firm, music publisher (G.W. Spencer Music/ASCAP), record company (Blue Wave Records) and record producer (Blue Wave Productions).

Estab. 1985. Represents individual artists and/or groups and songwriters from anywhere; currently handles 3 acts. Receives 15-20% commission. Reviews material for acts.
How to Contact: Submit demo tape by mail. Unsolicited submissions are OK. Prefers cassette or VHS videocassette with 3-6 songs. "Just the music first, reviews and articles are OK. No photos or lyrics until later." If seeking management, press kit should include cover letter and demo tape/CD. SASE. Reports in 1 month.
Music: Mostly **blues**, **blues/rock** and **roots rock**. Current acts include Kim Lembo (female blues vocalist), Kim Simmonds (blues guitarist and singer/songwriter) and Downchild Bluesband (blues).
Tips: "I'm looking for great singers with soul. Not interested in pop/rock commercial material."

N. ⦵ **BOHEMIA ENTERTAINMENT GROUP**, 8170 Beverly Hills Blvd., Suite 102, Los Angeles CA 90048. (323)651-5001. Contact: Susan Ferris. Management firm. Estab. 1992. Represents individual artists and groups from anywhere; currently handles 3 acts. Receives 15% commission. Reviews material for acts.
How to Contact: Submit demo tape by mail. Prefers cassette. If seeking management, press kit should include a tape (cassette) with a little blurb written about the band. Does not return material. Reports in 3 weeks.
Music: Mostly **alternative** and **adult alternative**. Works primarily with punk and alternative bands.

⦵ **BOJO PRODUCTIONS INC.**, 3935 Cliftondale Place, College Park GA 30349. (404)969-1913. Management firm and record company (Bojo Records). President: George J. Smith. Vice President: Julia E. Cage. Estab. 1982. Represents local, regional or international individual artists, groups and songwriters; currently handles 4 acts. Receives 15% commission. Reviews material for acts.
How to Contact: Submit demo tape by mail. Unsolicited submissions are OK. Prefers cassette or videocassette with 3 songs and lyric or lead sheets. If seeking management, press kit should include résumé, tape or video. SASE. Reports in 3 weeks.
Music: Mostly **R&B**, **gospel** and **country**; also **MOR**. Works primarily with vocalists and dance bands. Current acts include John Birdsong Quartet (jazz/pop), George Smith and his 18 piece orchestra and Arlene Smith (original lead for the Chantels).
Tips: "Send clean recording tape with lead sheets."

⦵ **BOUQUET-ORCHID ENTERPRISES**, P.O. Box 1335, Norcross GA 30091. (770)814-2420. President: Bill Bohannon. Management firm, booking agency, music publisher (Orchid Publishing/BMI) and record company (Bouquet Records). Represents individuals and groups; currently handles 4 acts. Receives 10-15% commission. Reviews material for acts.
How to Contact: Submit demo tape by mail. Unsolicited submissions are OK. Prefers cassette, CD or videocassette with 3-5 songs, song list and lyric sheet. Include brief résumé. If seeking management, press kit should include current photograph, 2-3 media clippings, description of act, and background information on act. SASE. Reports in 1 month.
Music: Mostly **country**, **rock** and **top 40/pop**; also **gospel** and **R&B**. Works primarily with vocalists and groups. Current acts include Susan Spencer, Jamey Wells, Adam Day and the Bandoleers.

⦵ **BREAD & BUTTER PRODUCTIONS**, P.O. Box 39, Seabrook TX 77586-0039. (713)623-8884. Fax: (409)938-7279. E-mail: steve@concerthill.com. Website: http://www.concerthill.com. Owner: Steve Gladson. Management firm and booking agency. Estab. 1969. Represents individual artists, songwriters and groups from anywhere; currently handles 5 acts. Receives 10-20% commission. Reviews material for acts.
How to Contact: Submit demo tape by mail. Unsolicited submissions OK. Prefers cassette, videocassette or CD and lyric sheet. If seeking management, press kit should include cover letter, demo tape/CD, lyric sheets, press clippings, video, résumé, picture and bio. Does not return material. Reports in 1 month.
Music: Mostly **alternative rock**, **country** and **R&B**; also **classic rock**. Works primarily with singer/songwriters and original bands. Current acts include K Moon-Winters (songwriter/singer), Duck Soup (band) and Jon Blondell (jazz musician/songwriter/arranger).
Tips: "Remember why you are in this biz. The art comes first."

REMEMBER: Don't "shotgun" your demo tapes. Submit only to companies interested in the type of music you write. For more submission hints, refer to Getting Started on page 11.

N ☑ ◐ CAPITAL ENTERTAINMENT, 1201 N St., N.W. #A, Washington DC 20005. (202)986-0693. Fax: (202)986-7992. E-mail: youngvince@capitalentertainment.com. Website: http://capitalentert ainment.com. Co-Founder: Vincent Young. Music publisher and Public Relations firm/entertainment services. Estab. 1996. Represents individual artists, groups or songwriters from anywhere; currently handles 15 acts. Receives 15-20% commission. Reviews material for acts.
• This company manages CeCe Winans, nine-time Grammy winner.
How to Contact: Submit demo tape by mail. Unsolicited submissions are OK. Prefers cassette and lyric sheet. "Not accepting management submissions." SASE. Reports in 3 weeks.
Music: Mostly **gospel** and **pop**. Current acts include CeCe Winans (gospel singer), Candi Staton (legendary soul singer of "Young Hearts Run Free" fame) and The Staple Singers (soul/gospel group who were inducted into the Rock & Roll Hall of Fame, March 1999).
Tips: "Learn as much as you can. Read about the music industry."

◐ CASH PRODUCTIONS, INC., 744 Joppa Farm Rd., Joppa Towne MD 21085. Phone/fax: (410)679-2262. President: Ernest W. Cash. Management firm, music publisher (Ernie Cash Music/BMI) and record company (Continental Records and Direct Response Records). Estab. 1988. Represents local, regional or international individual artists, groups and songwriters; currently represents 3 acts. Receives 20% commission. Reviews material for acts.
How to Contact: Write or call first and obtain permission to submit. Prefers cassette or VHS videocassette with 3 songs and lyric and lead sheet. If seeking management, press kit should include cover letter, bio, photo, demo tape/CD, lyric sheet, press clippings, video, résumé and available promotion material. SASE. Reports in 2 weeks.
Music: Mostly **country**, **pop** and **gospel**; also **contemporary**, **light rock** and **blues**. Works primarily with individual country artists and groups. Current acts include Randy Allen St. Clair (country), David R. Padrino (R&B) and Johnny Duncan IV.
Tips: "Above all be honest with me, and I will work with you. Please give me time to review your material and give it a justifiable chance with our music group."

N ⊕ ◐ CBA ARTISTS, P.O. Box 1495, Hilversum Netherlands 1200BL. Phone: (31)35 683 0515. Fax: (31)35 683 57 59. E-mail: dex_wessels@cba.nl. Management firm, booking agency and music publisher (Altitude Music). Estab. 1982. Represents individual artists, groups or songwriters from anywhere; currently handles 10 acts. Commission varies. Reviews material for acts.
How to Contact: Write or call first and obtain permission to submit a demo. Prefers cassette or videocassette with 5 songs and lyric and lead sheet. If seeking management, press kit should include bio, photo, reviews. Does not return material. Reports in 2 weeks.
Music: Mostly **dance**. Current acts include Shamrock Baskin (rapper/songwriter), T.O.F. (rapper/songwriter) and Face It (boy group).

◐ CHUCKER MUSIC INC., 345 E. 80th St., 15H, New York NY 10021. Fax: (212)879-9621. President: Chuck Dembrak. Management firm, music publisher (Cool 1) and record producer (Chuck Dembrak). Estab. 1984. Represents individual artists, groups and songwriters from anywhere; currently handles 5 acts. Receives 20% commission. Reviews material for acts.
How to Contact: Write first and obtain permission to submit. Prefers cassette, VHS videocassette or CD. If seeking management, press kit should include cover letter, bio, demo tape/CD, press clippings, video and photos. Does not return material. Reports in 2 months.
Music: Mostly **R&B**, **top 40** and **dance**; also **jazz**, **rock** and **A/C**. Works primarily with singer/songwriters. Current acts include Kim Waters (jazz), Dr. Zoot (swing) and Almighty (rap).

⊕ ◐ CIRCUIT RIDER TALENT & MANAGEMENT CO., 123 Walton Ferry Rd., Hendersonville TN 37075. (615)824-1947. Fax: (615)264-0462. E-mail: circuitridertalent@usa.net. President: Linda S. Dotson. U.K. office: 45 Gladstone Road, Melrose Villa House, Watford, Herts WD1 2RA UK. Phone: 011-44-1923-819415. Consultation firm, booking agency and music publisher (Channel Music, Cordial Music). Represents individual artists, songwriters and actors; currently handles 8 acts. Works with a large number of recording artists, songwriters, actors, producers. (Includes multi Grammy-winning producer/writer Skip Scarborough.) Receives 10-15% commission. Reviews material for acts (free of charge).
How to Contact: Write or call first and obtain permission to submit. Prefers cassette or videocassette with 3 songs and lyric sheet. If seeking consultation, press kit should include bio, cover letter, résumé, lyric sheets if original songs, photo and tape with 3 songs. Videocassettes required of artist's submissions. SASE. Reports in 6-8 weeks.
Music: Mostly **pop**, **country** and **gospel**; also **R&B** and **comedy**. Works primarily with vocalists, special concerts, movies and TV. Current acts include Shauna (R&B dance), Cam-Keyz (R&B), Willie John Ellison

(blues), Frank White (blues), Alton McClain (gospel), Trina Davis (urban gospel), Doug Swander (country) and Sheb Wooley (country).

Tips: "Artists, have your act together. Have a full press kit, videos and be professional. Attitudes are a big factor in my agreeing to work with you (no egotists). This is a business, and we will be building your career."

◐ CLASS ACT PRODUCTIONS/MANAGEMENT, P.O. Box 55252, Sherman Oaks CA 91413. (818)980-1039. E-mail: pkimmel@earthlink.net. President: Peter Kimmel. Management firm, music publisher and production company. Estab. 1985. Currently handles 3 acts. Receives 20% commission. Reviews material for acts.

How to Contact: Submit demo tape by mail. Unsolicited submissions are OK. Include cover letter, pictures, bio, lyric sheets (essential), cassette tape or CD and video in press kit. SASE. Reports in 1 month.

Music: All styles. Current acts include Terpsichore (cyber dance/pop), Don Cameron (new country) and Susie Piper (cutting edge pop/rock).

☑ ◐ CLOCKWORK ENTERTAINMENT MANAGEMENT AGENCY, 227 Concord St., Haverhill MA 01830. (508)373-5677. President: William J. Macek, esq., entertainment attorney. Management firm. Represents groups and songwriters throughout New England with mastered product who are looking for label deals and licensing in US and internationally. Fee is negotiated individually; currently handles multiple acts. Commissions vary. Reviews material for acts.

How to Contact: Submit demo tape by mail. Unsolicited submissions are OK. Prefers cassette or CD with 3-12 songs. "Also submit promotion and cover letter with interesting facts about yourself." If seeking management, press kit should include cover letter, tape or CD, photo, bio and press clippings. SASE. Reports in 1 month.

Music: Mostly **rock (all types)** and **top 40/pop**. Works primarily with bar bands and original acts.

◐ CLOUSHER PRODUCTIONS, P.O. Box 1191, Mechanicsburg PA 17055. (717)766-7644. Fax: (717)766-1490. E-mail: 17176081155@omnipoint.net. Owner: Fred Clousher. Booking agency and production company. Estab. 1972. Represents groups from anywhere; currently handles over 100 acts.

How to Contact: Submit demo tape by mail. Unsolicited submissions are OK. Prefers VHS videocassette. If seeking management, press kit should include press clippings, testimonials, letters, credits, glossies, video demo tape, references, cover letter, résumé and bio. Does not return material. "Performer should check back with us!"

Music: Mostly **country, old rock** and **ethnic** (German, Italian, etc.); also **dance bands** (regional) and **classical quartets**. "We work mostly with country, old time R&R, regional variety dance bands, tribute acts, and all types of variety acts." Current acts include Robin Right (country vocalist), Mike Bishop and Sweet & Sassy with Country Time (variety show) and Dixie's Three (original '60s Mercury recording artists).

Tips: "The songwriters we work with are entertainers themselves, which is the aspect we deal with. They usually have bands or do some sort of show, either with tracks or live music. We engage them for stage shows, dances, strolling, etc. We do not publish music or submit performers to recording companies for contracts. We strictly set up live performances for them."

◐ CODY ENTERTAINMENT GROUP, P.O. Box 456, Winchester VA 22604. Phone/fax: (540)722-4625. E-mail: codyent@visallink.com. President: Phil Smallwood. Management firm and booking agency. Estab. 1975. Represents individual artists and groups from anywhere; currently handles 11 acts. Receives 20% commission. Reviews material for acts.

How to Contact: Submit demo tape by mail. Unsolicited submissions are OK. Prefers cassette, DAT or videocassette with 3 songs and lead sheet. If seeking management, press kit should include cover letter, bio, photo, demo tape/CD and video. Does not return material. Reports in 2 months.

Music: Mostly **show acts** and **writers of love songs**. Current acts include The Hutchens (country), Daron Norwood (country) and Arlo Haines (writer/performer).

Ⓝ ◐ COLUMBIA MANAGEMENT CORP., 14600 S. Main St., Gardena CA 90248. (310)327-3725. Fax: (310)327-0342. E-mail: ewallenius@hbarc.com. President: Elizabeth Wallenius. Management

---

REFER TO THE CATEGORY INDEX (at the end of this section) to find exactly which companies are interested in the type of music you write.

firm. Estab. 1969. Represents individual artists or groups from anywhere; currently handles 3 acts. Receives 5-15% commission. Reviews material for acts.

How to Contact: Submit demo tape by mail. Unsolicited submissions are OK. Prefers cassette or videocassette with 4 songs and lyric sheet. If seeking management, press kit should include photo and bio. "Keep presentations clear, concise and brief." SASE. Reports in 6 weeks.

Music: Mostly **country, country-oriented swing** and **country blues**. Works primarily with singers, bands and duos with country styling. Current acts include Texas Troubadors (Texas swing), Roger Cook (mainline country) and Pure Country (Vegas show group).

✓ ◯ **CONCEPT 2000 INC.**, P.O. Box 2950, Columbus OH 43216-2950. (614)276-2000. Fax: (614)275-0163. Florida office: P.O. Box 2070, Largo FL 33779-2070. (727)585-2922. Fax: (727)585-3835. E-mail: info2k@concept2k.com. Website: http://www.concept2k.com. President: Brian Wallace. Management firm and booking agency. Estab. 1981. Represents international individual artists, groups and songwriters; currently handles 4 acts. Receives 20% commission. Reviews material for acts.

How to Contact: Submit demo tape by mail. Unsolicited submissions are OK. Prefers cassette with 4 songs. If seeking management, include demo tape, press clips, photo and bio. Does not return material. Reports in 2 weeks.

Music: Mostly **country, gospel** and **pop**; also **jazz, R&B** and **soul**. Current acts include Bryan Hitch (contemporary gospel), Shades of Grey (R&B/soul), Dwight Lenox (show group) and Gene Walker (jazz).

Tips: "Send quality songs with lyric sheets. Production quality is not necessary."

◯ **CONSCIENCE MUSIC**, P.O. Box 617667, Chicago IL 60661. (312)226-4858. E-mail: towrecords@aol.com. Consultant/Personal Manager: Karen M. Smith. Management firm and record company (TOW Records). Estab. 1985. Represents individual artists, groups and songwriters from anywhere; currently handles 4 acts. Receives 20% commission. Reviews material for acts.

• See the Managers Roundtable article on page 45 for more information from Karen M. Smith.

How to Contact: Write first and obtain permission to submit. Prefers cassette or current release with 2-3 songs and lyric sheet. If seeking management, press kit should include current reviews, demo tape/CD, lyric sheets, cover letter, bio or letter with band or artist objectives. "Cannot overemphasize the importance of having objectives you are ready to discuss with us." SASE. Reports in 4 months.

Music: Mostly **rock** and **pop**; also **visual artists, writers** and **models**. Works primarily with indie bands in the States and Great Britain. Currently represents Keith Kessinger (scattered pop/funk songwriter), Lance Porter (drummer with Tal Bachman) and PO! (U.K. pop band).

N ◯ **COOKE & ROSE ENTERTAINMENT & PRODUCTION, INC.**, 1107 S. Queen St., York PA 17403. (717)854-5541. Fax: (717)854-5543. E-mail: info@cookerose.com. Website: http://www.cookeandrose.com. President: Joyce Freeman. Vice President: Maria Wherley. Booking agency. Estab. 1945. Represents individual artists or groups from anywhere.

How to Contact: Submit demo tape by mail. Unsolicited submissions are OK. Prefers cassette or videocassette. If seeking management, press kit should include current bio, picture, tape or CD and video. Reports in 1 month.

Music: Mostly **swing bands**. Works primarily with bands, comedy acts, song and dance groups. Current acts include New Dawn Singers & Dancers (show group), Allison Wonderband (show band) and The Pixies Three (singers).

◯ **COOKMAN INTERNATIONAL**, 5625 Willowcrest Ave., North Hollywood CA 91601. Fax: (818)763-1398. E-mail: cookman@pacbell.net. Website: http://fabulosos-cadillacs.net. Contact: Peter Deantoni. Management firm and music publisher (El Leon Music). Estab. 1989. Represents individual artists, groups and songwriters from anywhere; currently handles 6 acts. Receives 15-20% commission. Reviews material for acts.

How to Contact: Submit demo tape by mail. Unsolicited submissions are OK. Prefers cassette with 3 songs and lyric sheet. Include a bio and photo. If seeking management, press kit should include cover letter, bio, photo, demo tape/CD, press clippings and video. SASE. Reports in 2 weeks.

Music: Mostly **Latin music**. Works primarily with bands and singer/songwriters. Current acts include Fabulosos Cadillacs (Grammy-winning Latin rock band), King Chango (Luaka Bop/Warner Bros.), Amigos Invisibles and Aterciopelados (Grammy nominated).

N ◯ **COOL RECORDS**, 12121 Wilshire Blvd., Suite 1201, Los Angeles CA 90025. (310)826-9363. Fax: (310)826-5450. E-mail: bruce@coolrecord.com. President: Bruce Peterson. Entertainment law firm and record company. Estab. 1978. Represents individual artists and/or groups from anywhere; currently handles 4 acts. Receives 10% commission.

How to Contact: Call first and obtain permission to submit. Prefers cassette or CD. If seeking management, press kit should include picture, bio, press clippings. SASE. Reports in 2 weeks.
Music: Mostly **alternative rock**, **folk** and **alternative country**.
Tips: "We are part of a team and it's a lot of hard work. Be diplomatic at all times."

 CORVALAN-CONDLIFFE MANAGEMENT, 1702 Clark Lane, Unit B, Redondo Beach CA 90278. (310)318-2574. Fax: (310)318-6574. E-mail: cdrv.cond@mcione.com. Manager: Brian Condliffe. Management firm. Estab. 1982. Represents individual artists, groups and songwriters from anywhere; currently handles 2 acts. Receives 15% commission.
How to Contact: Write or call first and obtain permission to submit. Prefers cassette with 4-6 songs. If seeking management, press kit should include bio, professional photo, press reviews and demo. SASE. Reports in 2 months.
Music: Mostly **pop** and **rock**; also **Latin**. Works primarily with alternative rock and pop/rock/world beat bands. Current acts include Ramiro Medina and Blue Tarantula.
Tips: "Be professional in all aspects of your kit and presentation. Check your grammar and spelling in your correspondence/written material. Know your music and your targeted market (rock, R&B, etc.)."

 COUNTDOWN ENTERTAINMENT, 109 Earle Ave., Lynbrook NY 11563. (516)599-4157. E-mail: citkovic@aol.com. President: James Citkovic. Management firm and consultants. Estab. 1983. Represents local, regional and international individual artists, groups, songwriters and producers; currently handles 3 acts. Receives 20-30% commission. Reviews material for acts.
How to Contact: Submit demo tape by mail. Unsolicited submissions are OK. "Please, no phone calls." Prefers cassette or VHS (SP speed) videocassette with lyric sheet. If seeking management, press kit should include cassette tape of best songs, 8×10 pictures, "live" VHS performance, lyrics, press and radio playlists. Does not return material. Reports in 3 weeks.
Music: Mostly **pop**, **modern rock** and **electronica/dance**; also **R&B**, **hip-hop** and **funk**. Deals with all styles of artists/songwriters/producers. Current acts include Jo Gabriel (modern female singer/songwriter).
Tips: "Leaders, not followers."

 COUNTRYWIDE PRODUCERS, 2466 Wildon Dr., York PA 17403. (717)741-2658. President: Bob Englar. Booking agency. Represents individuals and groups; currently handles 8 acts. Receives 10% commission. Reviews material for acts.
How to Contact: Query or submit demo tape by mail. Unsolicited submissions are OK. If seeking management, press kit should include photo and demo tape. SASE. Reports in 1 week.
Music: **Bluegrass**, **blues**, **classical**, **country** and **disco**; also **folk**, **gospel**, **jazz**, **polka**, **rock (light)**, **soul** and **top 40/pop**. Works primarily with show bands. Current acts include Lost & Found (bluegrass), The Meek Brothers (bluegrass) and The Groff Brothers (country variety).

 STEPHEN COX PROMOTIONS & MANAGEMENT, 6708 Mammoth Ave., Van Nuys CA 91405. (818)377-4530. Fax: (818)376-1283. E-mail: stephencox@earthlink.net. President: Stephen Cox. Management firm. Estab. 1993. Represents individual artists, groups or songwriters from anywhere; currently handles 5 acts. Receives 15% commission. Reviews material for acts.
How to Contact: Call first and obtain permission to submit a demo. Prefers cassette or CD. If seeking management, press kit should include biographies, performance history and radio play. "Include a clear definition of goals in a thoughtful presentation." SASE. Reports in 1-2 weeks.
Music: Mostly **rock**, **New Age/world** and **alternative**; also **blues**, **folk** and **progressive**. Works primarily with bands. Current acts include Joe Sherbanee (jazz), Val Ewell & Pulse (blues rock) and Paul Micich & Mitch Espe (New Age/jazz).
Tips: "Establish goals based on research, experience and keep learning about the music business. Start the business as though it will always be you as an independent. Establish a foundation before considering alternative commitments. We aim to educate and consult to a level that gives an artist the freedom of

FOR EXPLANATIONS OF THESE SYMBOLS,
SEE THE INSIDE FRONT AND BACK COVERS OF THIS BOOK.

choice to choose whether to go to the majors etc., or retain independence. Remember, promote, promote and promote some more. Always be nice to people, treat them as you would wish to be treated."

⊕ ✓ ◐ CRANIUM MANAGEMENT, P.O. Box 240, Annandale NSW 2038 Australia. E-mail: cranium@enternet.com.au. Manager: Peter "Skip" Beaumont-Edmonds. Management firm. Estab. 1992. Represents individual artists, groups and songwriters from anywhere; currently handles 5 acts. Receives 20% commission. Reviews material for acts.
How to Contact: Write, e-mail or call first and obtain permission to submit. Send "The minimum number of best songs—don't waste money on being elaborate. Talent will show through. Be sensible—if it doesn't suit us don't send it." If seeking management, press kit should include photo (optional), demo tape, press clippings (minimal), bio and cover letter. Does not return material. Reports in 1 month.
Music: Mostly **alternative** and **pop**; also **country**. Works primarily with pop/rock, alternative bands and singer/songwriters. Current acts include Mental As Anything (pop/rock), Dog Trumpet (alternative roots duo), Louis Tillett (blues/piano player/songwriter) and David Mason-Cox.

ℕ ◐ CRAWFISH PRODUCTIONS, P.O. Box 5412, Buena Park CA 90620. (619)245-2920. Producer: Leo J. Eiffert, Jr. Management firm, music publisher (Young Country/BMI), record producer (Leo J. Eiffert) and record company (Plain Country Records). Estab. 1968. Represents local and international individual artists and songwriters; currently handles 4 acts. Commission received is open. Reviews material for acts.
How to Contact: Submit demo tape by mail. Unsolicited submissions are OK. Prefers cassette with 2-3 songs and lyric sheet. SASE. Reports in 3 weeks.
Music: Mostly **country** and **gospel**. Works primarily with vocalists. Current acts include Brandi Holland, Teeci Clarke, Joe Eiffert (country/gospel), Mary T. Vertiz (songwriter), Crawfish Band (country) and Homemade.

◐ CRISS-CROSS INDUSTRIES, 24016 Strathern St., West Hills CA 91304. (818)710-6600. Fax: (818)719-0222. President: Doc Remer. Management firm and music publisher (Menachan's Music/ASCAP, Eyenoma Music/BMI). Estab. 1984. Represents individual artists, groups and songwriters from anywhere. Reviews material for acts.
How to Contact: Write first and obtain permission to submit. Prefers cassette or VHS videocassette with 3 songs and lyric sheet. If seeking management, press kit should include photo, bio, cover letter, demo tape/CD, video and credits. SASE. Reports in 3-4 weeks.
Music: Mostly **R&B** and **pop**. Works primarily with vocalists and self contained bands.
Tips: "You must currently be a working act. Make the words to the songs so they can be understood. The music should not be as loud as the vocals."

ℕ ◐ CROSSFIRE PRODUCTIONS, 1209 Baylor St., Austin TX 78703-4123. (512)457-8550. Fax: (512)442-1154. E-mail: vicky@wcclark.com. President: Vicky Moerbe. Management firm. Estab. 1990. Represents local, individual artists and songwriters; currently handles 3 acts. Receives 15% commission. Reviews material for acts.
How to Contact: Write or call first and obtain permission to submit a demo. Prefers cassette with any number of songs and lyric sheet. If seeking management, press kit should include biography, press releases/articles/reviews, photograph/discography and copy of current release or demo. SASE. Reports in 3-4 weeks.
Music: Mostly **blues**, **swing** and **country**; also **soul** and **contemporary rock**. Works primarily with singers and songwriters. Current acts include W.C. Clark (singer/songwriter/touring act; blues/soul), Seth Walker (singer/songwriter/touring act; blues/swing) and Joe Forlini & Mike Cross (singer/songwriter/touring act; blues/country/rock).
Tips: "Please submit only material to be considered for recordings for blues/soul, swing or country recordings. Our artists are looking for material to be considered for recordings for national releases."

◐ CROWE ENTERTAINMENT INC., 1009 17th Ave. S., Nashville TN 37212-2202. (615)327-0411. Fax: (615)329-4289. E-mail: jcrowe5349@aol.com. Owner: J. Crowe. Management firm and music publisher (Midnight Crow/ASCAP, Cro Jo/BMI). Estab. 1986. Represents individual artists and/or groups and songwriters from anywhere; currently handles 4 acts. Receives 25% commission. Reviews material for acts.
How to Contact: Call first and obtain permission to submit. Prefers DAT, CD or cassette with no more than 3 songs and lyric sheet. If seeking management, press kit should include cover letter and demo tape/CD. SASE. Reports in 2 months.
Music: Mostly **country**. Current acts include Johnny Scharch (traditional), Six Gun (pop/country) and Just Passin' Thru (positive country).

◑ **CYCLE OF FIFTHS MANAGEMENT, INC.**, 331 Dante Ct., Suite H, Holbrook NY 11741-3800. (516)467-1837. Fax: (516)467-1645. E-mail: fifths2@aol.com. President: James Reilly. Management firm. Represents individual artists and/or groups from anywhere. Receives 15-20% commission. Reviews material for acts.
How to Contact: Submit demo tape by mail. Unsolicited submissions are OK. Prefers cassette. If seeking management, press kit should include band's mission statement. Does not return material. Reports in 6-8 weeks, via e-mail only.
Music: Mostly **rock** and **alternative**. Works primarily with established groups.

◯ **FRANKIE DALE MANAGEMENT**, 2733 Riley Oaks Court, Las Vegas NV 89108. (702)645-7383. Fax: (702)645-7385. President/CEO: Frankie Dale. Management firm. Estab. 1989. Represents individual artists and groups from anywhere; currently handles 3 acts. Receives 20% commission. Reviews material for acts.
How to Contact: Submit demo tape by mail. Unsolicited submissions are OK. Prefers cassette or CD with 4 songs. If seeking management, press kit should include standard CD and/or cassette with 3-4 tracks, short bio, cover letter and photo. Does not return material. Reports in 2 months.
Music: Mostly **alternative**, **college radio** and **metal**. Works primarily with national acts along with opening acts. Current acts include Skillethead (alternative), Stranger (metal) and Chas Stumbo (musician/drummer).

✓◯ **D&M ENTERTAINMENT AGENCY**, P.O. Box 19242, Johnston RI 02919. (401)782-0239. President: Ray DiMillio. Management firm and booking agency. Estab. 1968. Represents local groups; currently handles 28 acts. Receives 15% commission. Reviews material for acts.
How to Contact: Submit demo tape by mail. Write or call to arrange personal interview. Unsolicited submissions are OK. Prefers cassette or VHS videocassette with 3 songs and lyric or lead sheet. If seeking management, include photo. Does not return material. Reports in 2-3 weeks.
Music: Mostly **R&B** and **pop**; also **rock**. Current acts include Sunshyne (top 40), Trilogy (top 40) and xpo (top 40).

⟦N⟧◯ **D&R ENTERTAINMENT**, 308 N. Park, Broken Bow OK 74728. (580)584-9429. President: Don Walton. Management firm. Estab. 1985. Represents individual artists from anywhere; currently handles 2 acts. Receives 15% commission. Reviews material for acts. Also reviews for other country singers.
How to Contact: Submit demo tape by mail. Unsolicited submissions are OK. Prefers cassette and videocassette with lyric and lead sheet. If seeking management, press kit should include brief background of artist, videotape of performance, cover letter, résumé, photo, press clippings and cassette or CD. "Indicate whether you have any financial or prospective financial backing." Does not return material. Reports in 3 months.
Music: Mostly **Christian country** and **country**; also **gospel** and **pop**. Works primarily with young beginning singers. Current acts include Melissa Hise (Christian country/gospel singer) and Jessica Slaybaugh (country/gospel singer).
Tips: "I need songs (country) that would fit a young singer under 16. In other words no drinking, cheating, marrying songs. A pretty tough choice. Also Christian country songs."

◍ **DAS COMMUNICATIONS, LTD.**, 83 Riverside Dr., New York NY 10024. (212)877-0400. Management firm. Estab. 1975. Represents individual artists, groups and producers from anywhere; currently handles 25 acts. Receives 20% commission.
How to Contact: Write first and obtain permission to submit. Reports in 2 months. Prefers demo with 3 songs, lyric sheet and photo. Does not return material.
Music: Mostly **rock**, **pop**, **R&B** and **alternative**. Current acts include Diana King (R&B/reggae), Joan Osborne (rock), Wyelef Jean (hip-hop) and Honkey Toast (rock).

✓◍ **DCA PRODUCTIONS**, 330 W. 38th St., Suite 303, New York NY 10018. (212)245-2063. Fax: (212)245-2367. E-mail: dcaplus@panix.com. E-mail: dcaplus@panix.com. Website: http://www.active-media.com/dca. Contact: Kate Magill. President: Daniel Abrahamsen. Vice President: Geraldine Abrahamsen. Management firm. Estab. 1975. Represents individual artists, groups and songwriters from anywhere; currently handles 24 acts.

REFER TO THE GEOGRAPHIC INDEX (at the back of this book) to find listings of companies by state, as well as foreign listings.

How to Contact: Call first and obtain permission to submit. Prefers cassette or VHS videocassette with 2 songs. If seeking management, press kit should include cover letter, bio, photo, demo tape/CD and video. "All materials are reviewed and kept on file for future consideration. Does not return material. We report back only if interested."

Music: Mostly **acoustic**, **rock** and **mainstream**; also **cabaret** and **theme**. Works primarily with acoustic singer/songwriters, top 40 or rock bands. Current acts include The Word (singers/songwriters), groovelily (melodic rock) and Fourth Avenue (a cappella).

Tips: "Please do not call for a review of material."

☑ ☑ **THE EDWARD DE MILES COMPANY**, 117 W. Harrison Bldg. #S627, Chicago IL 60605-1709. (773)509-6381. Fax: (312)922-6964. Management firm, booking agency, entertainment/sports promoter and TV/radio broadcast producer. Estab. 1984. Represents film, television, radio and musical artists; currently handles 15 acts. Receives 10-20% commission. Reviews material for acts. Regional operations in Chicago, Dallas, Houston and Nashville through marketing representatives. Licensed A.F. of M. booking agent.

How to Contact: Write first and obtain permission to submit or to arrange personal interview. Prefers cassette with 3-5 songs, 8x10 b&w photo, bio and lyric sheet. "Copyright all material before submitting." If seeking management, include cover letter, bio, demo cassette with 3-5 songs, 8×10 b&w photo, lyric sheet, press clippings and video if available in press kit. SASE. Does not return material. Reports in 1 month.

Music: Mostly **country**, **dance**, **R&B/soul**, **rock**, **top 40/pop** and **urban contemporary**; also looking for material for television, radio and film productions. Works primarily with dance bands and vocalists. Current acts include Steve Lynn (R&B/dance), Multiple Choice (rap) and D'vou Edwards (jazz).

Tips: "Performers need to be well prepared with their presentations (equipment, showmanship a must)."

☑ **BILL DETKO MANAGEMENT**, 127 Shamrock Dr., Ventura CA 93003. (805)644-0447. Fax: (805)644-0469. President: Bill Detko. Management firm. Estab. 1984. Represents individual artists, groups and songwriters from anywhere; currently handles 2 acts. Commission negotiable. Reviews material for acts.

How to Contact: Submit demo tape by mail. Unsolicited submissions are OK. "Artist must follow up by phone." Prefers CD or cassette, VHS videocassette (if available) with 3-6 songs and lyric sheet. If seeking management, press kit should include bio, cover letter, résumé, photo, plus above items and any press or radio action. Does not return material. Reports in 1-2 weeks.

Music: **All styles**. Current acts include Laurel Wiley (alternative) and Terry Hand (film composer).

⊕ ☑ **ANDREW DINWOODIE MANAGEMENT**, P.O. Box 5052, Victoria Point QLD 4165 Australia. Phone: (07)32070502. E-mail: adinwoodie@redland.net.au. Director: Andrew Dinwoodie. Management firm and booking agency. Estab. 1983. Represents regional (Australian) individual artists, groups and songwriters; currently handles 3 acts. Receives 10-20% commission. Reviews material for acts.

How to Contact: Submit demo tape by mail. Unsolicited submissions are OK. Prefers cassette or VHS PAL videocassette with lyric sheet. If seeking management, press kit should include cover letter, résumé, bio, photo, goals, audio or videotape and CD if available and anything the artist thinks will help. SAE and IRC. Reports in 1 month.

Music: Mostly **country**, **R&B** and **rock/pop**; also **bluegrass**, **swing** and **folk**. Current acts include Bullamakanka (good time Australian music), Donna Heke (blues/soul) and Bluey the Bastard (feral folk).

☑ **DIRECT MANAGEMENT**, 645 Quail Ridge Rd., Aledo TX 76008-2835. Owner: Danny Wilkerson. Management firm and booking agency. Estab. 1986. Represents individual artists and/or groups from anywhere; currently handles 4 acts. Receives 10-20% commission. Reviews material for acts.

How to Contact: Submit demo tape by mail. Unsolicited submissions are OK. Prefers CD, cassette or VHS videocassette with 3 songs. If seeking management, press kit should include bio, cassette or CD, photo, lyric sheets, press clippings and video. Does not return material. Reports in 1 month.

Music: Mostly **college rock**, **Christian** and **children's**. Current acts include Waltons (pop/rock), The EPs (rock) and Emily Rogers (country).

☐ **DMR AGENCY**, Galleries of Syracuse, Suite 250, Syracuse NY 13202-2416. (315)475-2500. E-mail: dmr@ican.net. Website: http://dmrbooking.net. Contact: David M. Rezak. Booking agency. Represents individuals and groups; currently handles 50 acts. Receives 15% commission.

How to Contact: Submit demo tape by mail. Unsolicited submissions are OK. Submit cassette or videocassette with 1-4 songs and press kit. Does not return material.

Music: Mostly **rock (all styles)**, **pop** and **blues**. Works primarily with cover bands. Current acts include

Joe Whiting (R&B), Little Georgie and the Shufflin' Hungarians (blues), Tryx (rock), Windsong (pop), Billionaires (blues) and Atlas (R&B).
Tips: "You might want to contact us if you have a cover act in our region. Many songwriters in our area have a cover group in order to make money."

☑ ◯ **JAMES R. DORAN, P.C.**, 1031 E. Battlefield Rd., Suite 224, Springfield MO 65807. (417)881-4174. Fax: (417)227-9404. Manager: Jim Doran. Management firm and booking agency. Estab. 1975. Represents individual artists, groups and songwriters from anywhere; currently handles 5 acts. Receives variable commission. Reviews material for acts.
How to Contact: Submit demo tape by mail. Unsolicited submissions are OK. Prefers cassette. If seeking management, press kit should include bio, photo and demo tape/CD. Does not return material. Reports in 2 weeks.
Music: Mostly **country**; also **rock**. Current acts include Ray Price (country artist), Johnny Paycheck (country artist), Ozark Jubilee (country variety show).

◐ **COL. BUSTER DOSS PRESENTS**, 341 Billy Goat Hill Rd., Winchester TN 37398. (931)649-2577. Fax: (615)649-2732. Producer: Col. Buster Doss. Management firm, booking agency, record company (Stardust Records), record producer and music publisher (Buster Doss Music/BMI). Estab. 1959. Represents individual artists, groups, songwriters and shows; currently handles 14 acts. Receives 15% commission. Reviews material for acts.
How to Contact: Write first and obtain permission to submit. Prefers cassette with 2-4 songs and lyric sheet. If seeking management, press kit should include demo, photos, video if available and bio. SASE. Reports back on day received.
Music: Mostly **country**, **gospel** and **progressive**. Works primarily with show and dance bands, single acts and package shows. Current acts include "Rooster" Quantrell, Linda Wunder, The Border Raiders, "Bronco" Buck Cody, Jerri Arnold, Bob Norman, Cindy Lee, John Hamilton and Brant Miller.

☑ ◐ **DREAM HATCHERY, INC.**, (formerly RNJ Productions, Inc.), 5701 N. Sheridan Rd., Suite 7M, Chicago IL 60660-4712. E-mail: manager@glennyarbrough.com. Website: http://www.glennyarbrough.com. Director: Marshall Tate. Management firm and record company (Brass Dolphin Records). Estab. 1967. Represents individual artists from anywhere; currently handles 5 acts. Receives negotiable commission. Reviews material for acts.
How to Contact: Submit demo tape by mail. Unsolicited submissions are OK. Prefers cassette with at least 3 songs and lyric and lead sheet. If seeking management, press kit should include photos, lyric sheets, bio, clips, demo with at least 3 songs or CD and a current telephone number. "Please indicate, in your cover letter, the nature of your material and the artists you write for. Also, please include a phone number. If your material is appropriate for our clients we will call you." Does not return material. Reports only if interested.
Music: Mostly **contemporary pop**, **contemporary folk** and **jazz**; also **New Age** and **gospel**. Works primarily with interpretive artists, acoustic musicians and vocalists. Current acts include Glenn Yarbrough (pop/folk singer), Holly Yarbrough (singer/songwriter) and Julie Adams (contemporary cellist).
Tips: "Write from the heart and don't be afraid to revise. Currently seeking material from singer-songwriters for a new radio show focusing on philosophy and spirituality. Looking for deeply meaningful songs about the human condition, and the true nature of love. Also seeking inspirational stories."

☑ ◐ **DREAM TEAM MANAGEMENT**, (formerly Sweet Pea Artist Management), P.O. Box 24884, Nashville TN 37202-9998. (615)321-0844. Fax: (615)356-7066. Co-Presidents: Julie Devereux and Kathi Mallec. Management firm. Estab. 1995. Represents individual artists and groups from anywhere; currently handles 3 acts. Receives 20% commission. Reviews material for acts.
How to Contact: Submit demo tape by mail. Unsolicited submissions are OK. Prefers cassette or CD with no more than 3 songs and lyric sheet. If seeking management, press kit should include cover letter, bio, itinerary, photo, lyric sheets, press clippings, video and 3 song demo. Does not return material. Reports in 1-2 months.
Music: Mostly **alternative**, **blues** and **country**. Works primarily with bands, lead vocalists and songwriters. Current acts include Tracy Nelson (blues) and Erin McCaffney (country).

THE OPENNESS TO SUBMISSIONS INDEX at the back of this book lists all companies in this section by how open they are to submissions.

N̄ ⮞ ◙ DUNNER TALENT MANAGEMENT, 4735 W. Fourth Ave., Vancouver, British Columbia V6T 1C3 Canada. (604)324-3764. Fax: (604)324-3744. E-mail: hoots@netcom.ca. Managing Director/owner: Chris Duncombe. Management firm. Estab. 1995. Represents groups or performance DJs from anywhere. Receives 10-15% commission. Reviews material for acts.
How to Contact: Call first and obtain permission to submit a demo. Prefers cassette with 3 songs and lyric sheet. If seeking management, press kit should include markets you have played in, touring info, past business history (prior management/agents), photo, music, bio, history and press articles. "Be creative. I need your characterization of what it is you do." Does not return material. Reports in 2 weeks.
Music: Mostly **rock/alternative** and **hip-hop/urban**. Works primarily with bands and hip-hop artists. "Singer-songwriters are a huge interest for us and we look forward to doing more of this." Current acts include Smokin Frogs (alternative ska/punk/funk), Fat Beats (experimental acid/reggae/funk/instrumental) and Sorce (producer/performer/DJ).
Tips: "Tell me what makes what you do your own. We often work projects that are off the wall and this is a mandate of ours. We represent artists and find their particular place in the music market. Be creative!"

⮞ ◙ EAO MUSIC CORPORATION OF CANADA, P.O. Box 1240, Station "M," Calgary, Alberta T2P 2L2 Canada. (403)228-9388. Fax: (403) 229-3598. E-mail: oliverio@istar.ca. President: Edmund A. Oliverio. Management firm and record company. Estab. 1985. Represents individual artists, groups and songwriters from western Canada (aboriginal artists); currently handles 52 acts. Receives 15-20% commission. Reviews material for acts.
How to Contact: Submit demo tape by mail. Unsolicited submissions are OK. Prefers cassette with 3 songs and lyric and lead sheets. If seeking management, press kit should include cover letter, résumé, b&w glossy photo, cassette tape, bio, media clippings and list of venues and festivals performed. SAE and IRC. Reports in 2 weeks.
Music: Mostly **country, folk** and **native (aboriginal)**; also **rock**. Works primarily with singer/songwriters. Current acts include Activate (funky reggae), Feeding Like Butterflies (folk rock/Celtic) and Katrina (country/folk).
Tips: "Be upfront and honest. Establish your long term goals and short term goals. Have you joined your music associations (i.e., CMA, etc.)? We are interested in native or aboriginal artists and songwriters. Recent demand for cowboy artists rather than country."

◙ EARTH TRACKS ARTISTS AGENCY, 4809 Ave. N., Suite 286, Brooklyn NY 11234. E-mail: enigpublus@aol.com. Managing Director-Artist Relations: David Krinsky. Management firm. Estab. 1990. Represents individual artists, groups and songwriters from anywhere; currently handles 1 act. Receives 10-15% commission. Reviews material for acts.
How to Contact: Submit demo tape by mail. Unsolicited submissions are OK. Prefers cassette with 3-6 songs and lyric sheet. If seeking management, press kit should include cover letter, bio, video (if available), 1 group photo, all lyrics with songs, a cassette/CD of original songs and the ages of the artists. Does not return material. Reports in 1 month. "We will contact artist if interested."
Music: Mostly **commercial rock** (all kinds), **pop** and **alternative**. No rap or metal. Works primarily with commercial, original, solo artists and groups, songwriters in the rock, pop, areas (no country, thrash or punk). Current act is The Nobody (alternative rock).
Tips: "Currently looking for the next Pink Floyd, Guns 'N Roses, Beatles, Nirvana or Doors, or singer/songwriter with potential (Bob Dylan, Elton John). Artists wanted, not commercial hacks. Note: I do not set up tours. No DAT submissions or computer disks."

N̄ ◙ EJJ MANAGEMENT, 3809 Brookline Ave., Rosemead CA 91770. Phone/fax: (626)350-1741. Manager: Patricia Louallen. Management firm. Estab. 1998. Represents individual artists, groups or songwriters from anywhere; currently handles 17 acts. Receives 20% commission. Reviews material for acts.
How to Contact: Write first and obtain permission to submit a demo. Prefers cassette with 5 songs and lyric sheet. If seeking management, press kit should include 8 × 10 b&w picture, 1 action shot and complete bio. "Artist must have passport and belong to a union." SASE. Reports in 1 month.
Music: Mostly **R&B, blues** and **rock**. Works primarily with songwriters, artists, bands (of organic music only), actors (mostly men). Current acts include Delaney Branulett (rock), Randell "Godson of Blues" (rock/blues) and Gal Costa (Latin).
Tips: "A songwriter is like a carpenter—it takes tools, but it starts with an idea. Don't throw away those little note pieces of lyrics! You could be your own worst critic."

◙ THE ELLIS INTERNATIONAL TALENT AGENCY, 5617 W. Melvina, Milwaukee WI 53216. (414)444-3385. President: Darnell Ellis. Management firm, booking agency, music publisher (Buzz Duzz Duzz Music/ASCAP) record company (Safire Records) and record producer (Darnell Ellis). Estab. 1997.

Represents individual artists, groups and songwriters from anywhere; currently handles 4 acts. Receives 10-20% commission. Reviews material for acts.
How to Contact: Submit demo tape by mail. Unsolicited submissions are OK. Prefers cassette or video-cassette with 4-6 songs and press kit. If seeking management, press kit should include cassette tape or CD with 4-6 songs (demo), 8×10 photo, video tape and reviews. Does not return material. Reports in 4-6 weeks. "We will respond only if we are interested."
Music: Mostly **top 40/pop hits, contemporary, country** and **alternative, metal**. Works primarily with singers, singer/songwriters, songwriters and bands. Current acts include NUNA (alternative-punk rock), One Girl (AAA modern rock), Kook (hardcore metal) and Derek Thevon (pop).

N ◢ ENDANGERED SPECIES ARTIST MANAGEMENT, 4 Berachah Ave., South Nyack NY 10960-4202. (914)353-4001. Fax: (914)353-4332. E-mail: endangers@aol.com or endangers@mjet.com. Website: http://www.endangers.com. Vice President: Suzanne Buckley. Management firm. Estab. 1979. Represents individual artists, groups and songwriters from anywhere; currently handles 3 acts. Receives 20% commission. Reviews material for acts.
How to Contact: Call first and obtain permission to submit. Prefers cassette or CD with 10 songs and lyric sheet. "Please include a demo of your music, a clear, recent photograph as well as any current press, if any. A cover letter indicating at what stage in your career you are and expectations for your future. Please label the cassette and/or CD with your name and address as well as the song titles." If seeking management, press kit should include cover letter, bio, photo, demo tape/CD, lyric sheet and press clippings. SASE. Reports in 2-6 weeks.
Music: Mostly **pop, rock** and **world**; also **R&B**, jazz and **instrumental**. Current acts include Jason Wilson & Tabarruk (pop/Celtic/folk/jazz/reggae), Reggie May (R&B performing songwriter), Terry Cole (pop/R&B with Eurodance feel).
Tips: "Listen to everything, classical to country, old to contemporary, to develop an understanding of many writing styles. Write with many other partners to keep the creativity fresh. Don't feel your style will be ruined by taking a class or a writing seminar. We all process moods and images differently and similar education always leads to uniqueness in individuals as we are all so very unique."

N ◢ ENTERCOM, 372 Richmond St. W. Suite 205, Toronto, Ontario M5V 1X6 Canada. (416)598-3330. Fax: (416)598-5428. Manager: James MacLean. Management firm. Estab. 1989. Represents groups from anywhere; currently handles 4 acts. Receives 20% commission. Reviews material for acts.
How to Contact: Submit demo tape by mail. Unsolicited submissions are OK. Prefers cassette. Does not return material. Reports in 6 weeks.
Music: Mostly **alternative, pop, rock** and **metal**. Works primarily with original cutting edge bands. Current acts include Doughboys (power punk pop, A&M Records), Voivod (cybermetal, Slipdisk/Mercury) and Made (MCA Records).
Tips: "Send to recommended people or companies. Random solicitation is useless. Research and educate yourself. If you come across as professional and down to earth you'll get a lot further. Forget what's popular at the moment. All music is current again or recycled, so write from the experience of your life, not anyone else's. Be true to yourself. Don't follow a trend, lead music into a new dimension. Create your own!"

N ◢ ERWIN MUSIC, P.O. Box 13525, Charleston SC 29422. (843)762-9125. Fax: (843)762-9124. E-mail: emusic@mindspring.com. Website: http://www.shrimpcityslim.com. Owner: Gary Erwin. Management firm, booking agency, music publisher (Blue Chasqui Music/BMI), record company and record producer. Estab. 1987. Represents regional artists from the southeast, individual artists, groups or songwriters; currently handles 5 acts.
How to Contact: Submit demo tape by mail. Unsolicited submissions are OK. Prefers cassette with 5 songs and lyric sheet. If seeking management, press kit should include video, audio, résumé and bio. Does not return material. Reports in 2 months.
Music: Mostly **blues, jazz** and **gospel**; also **world**. Works primarily with bands, solos. Current acts include Shrimp City Slim (blues and original music band), Big Boy Henry (bluesman) and Paul D. Kershaw (cajun artist).
Tips: "Write from the heart."

N ○ ETERNAL RECORDS/SQUIGMONSTER MANAGEMENT, 1598 E. Shore Dr., St. Paul MN 55106-1121. (612)771-0107. President/Owner: Robert (Squiggy) Yezek. Management firm and record company (PMS Records). Estab. 1983. Represents groups from anywhere; currently handles 25 acts. Receives 5-20% commission. Reviews material for acts.
How to Contact: Submit demo tape by mail. Unsolicited submissions are OK. Prefers CD (if available)

with any number of songs and lead sheet. If seeking management, press kit should include CD or tape, bio, cover letter, résumé and any press. Mail to attention: A&R Dept. Does not return material. Reports in 2-3 months.
Music: Mostly **alternative rock**, **heavy metal** and **hard rock**; also **comedy**, **R&B**, **rap** and **new pop**. Current acts include No Man's Land (alternative metal), Bad Boyz (R&B/rap) and Zombie (metal).

SCOTT EVANS PRODUCTIONS, P.O. Box 814028, Hollywood FL 33081-4028. (954)963-4449. Artistic Director: Scott Evans. Management firm and booking agency. Estab. 1979. Represents local, regional or international individual artists, groups, songwriters, comedians, novelty acts and dancers; currently handles 200 acts. Receives 25% commission. Reviews material for acts.
How to Contact: Submit demo tape by mail. Unsolicited submissions are OK. Prefers cassette or ½" videocassette with 3 songs. If seeking management, include picture, résumé, flyers, cassette or video tape. Does not return material.
Music: Mostly **pop**, **R&B** and **Broadway**. Deals with "all types of entertainers; no limitations." Current acts include Scott Evans and Company (variety song and dance), Dori Zinger (female vocalist), Jeff Geist, Actors Repertory Theatre, Entertainment Express, Perfect Parties and Joy Deco (dance act).
Tips: "Submit a neat, well put together, organized press kit."

FASTBACK MANAGEMENT, 1321 Sixth Ave., San Francisco CA 94122. (415)564-7404. Fax: (415)564-2927. E-mail: spydog2@well.com. Contact: Cathy Cohn. Management firm. Estab. 1992. Represents individual artists and groups; currently handles 2 acts.
How to Contact: Submit demo tape by mail. Unsolicited submissions are OK. Prefers cassette or VHS videocassette. If seeking management, press kit should include artist history (bio), press and tape. SASE.
Music: **Contemporary** only. Current acts include Meat Beat Manifesto and Freak Chakra.

S.L. FELDMAN & ASSOCIATES, 1505 W. Second Ave. #200, Vancouver, British Columbia V6H 3Y4 Canada. (604)734-5945. Fax: (604)732-0922. E-mail: feldman@slfa.com. Website: http://www.slfa.com. Management firm and booking agency. Estab. 1970. Represents individual artists and groups from anywhere; currently handles over 100 acts.
How to Contact: Submit demo tape by mail. Unsolicited submissions are OK. Prefers cassette and lyric sheet. If seeking management, include photo, bio, cassette and video (if available) in press kit. SAE and IRC. Reports in 6-8 weeks.
Music: Current acts include Bryan Adams, The Chieftains, Joni Mitchell, Anne Muuray, Odds, Sarah McLachlan and Spirit of the West.

FRED T. FENCHEL ENTERTAINMENT AGENCY, 2104 S. Jefferson Avenue, Mason City IA 50401. (515)423-4177. Fax: (515)423-8662. General Manager: Fred T. Fenchel. Booking agency. Estab. 1964. Represents local and international individual artists and groups; currently handles up to 10 acts. Receives 20% commission.
How to Contact: Submit demo tape by mail. Unsolicited submissions are OK. Prefers cassette or videocassette. Does not return material. Reports in 3 weeks.
Music: Mostly **country**, **pop** and some **gospel**. Works primarily with dance bands and show groups; "artists we can use on club dates, fairs, etc." Current acts include The Memories (vocal/musical trio), The Suby's (karaoke) and Black Diamonds (country group). "We deal primarily with established name acts with recording contracts, or those with a label and starting into popularity."
Tips: "Be honest. Don't submit unless your act is exceptional rather than just starting out, amateurish and with lyrics that are written under the pretense of coming from qualified writers."

FIRST TIME MANAGEMENT, Sovereign House, 12 Trewartha Rd., Praa Sands-Penzance, Cornwall TR20 9ST England. Phone: (01736)762826. Fax: (01736)763328. E-mail: panamus@aol.com. Managing Director: Roderick G. Jones. Management firm, record company (First Time Records) and music publisher (First Time Music). Estab. 1986. Represents local, regional and international individual aritsts, groups and songwriters; currently handles 114 acts. Commission varies. Reviews material for acts.
How to Contact: Submit demo tape by mail. Unsolicited submissions are OK. Prefers cassette, 15 ips reel-to-reel or VHS videocassette with 3 songs and lyric sheets. If seeking management, press kit should

---

MARKETS THAT WERE listed in the 1999 edition of *Songwriter's Market* but do not appear this year are listed in the General Index with a notation explaining why they were omitted.

include cover letter, bio, photo, demo tape/CD, press clippings and anything relevant to make an impression. Does not return material. Reports in 1 month.

Music: Mostly **dance**, **top 40**, **rap**, **country**, **gospel** and **pop**; also **all styles**. Works primarily with songwriters, composers, vocalists, groups and choirs. Current acts include Willow (pop), Colin Eade and Bob Brimley.

Tips: "Become a member of the Guild of International Songwriters and Composers. Keep everything as professional as possible. Be patient and dedicated to your aims and objectives."

FLINTER MUSIC, PB15, Antwerp 17, B-2018, Antwerp Belgium. Phone: +32(0)32480376. Fax: +32(0)32483186. E-mail: FlinterM@www.dma.be. President: Luc Nuitten. Management firm and booking agency. Estab. 1991. Represents artists from anywhere; currently handles 6 acts. Receives 15% commission. Reviews material for acts.

How to Contact: Write first and obtain permission to submit. Prefers CD or VHS videocassette (PAL) with 3 songs. If seeking management, press kit should include VHS video, CD, references, photos, bio, press book and financial dossier. "Always looking for new talent—please present a complete neat and self-explanatory promo kit." Does not return material. Reports once a year (August).

Music: Mostly **jazz** and **world music**. Works primarily with concert tour bands, festival bands and European touring acts. Current acts include the Brussels Jazz Orchestra (big band).

MITCHELL FOX MANAGEMENT INC., 209 10th Ave. S., Suite 322, Nashville TN 37203. (615)259-0777. Fax: (615)742-6333. E-mail: mitchell@mitchellfox.com. President: Mitchell Fox. Management firm. Estab. 1980. Represents individual artists, groups and songwriters from anywhere; currently handles 2 acts. Receives 10-15% commission. Reviews material for acts.

How to Contact: Submit demo tape by mail. Unsolicited submissions are OK. Prefers cassette with 2 songs and lyric sheet. If seeking management, press kit should include music, pictures and press clippings. Does not return material. Reports in 3-4 weeks.

Music: Mostly **country rock**, **1940-'50s country** and **world music**; also **jazz** and **rock**. Current acts include The Kentucky Head Hunters (country band) and Gary Nicholson (AAA artist, country songwriter).

FREEDMAN & SMITH ENTERTAINMENT, (formerly Peter Freedman Entertainment), 1790 Broadway, Suite 1316, New York NY 10019. (212)265-1776. Fax: (212)265-3678. E-mail: think007@aol.com. President: Peter Freedman. Partner: Steve Smith. Office Manager: Chris Hardin. Management firm. Estab. 1986. Represents individual artists, groups and songwriters from anywhere; currently handles 5 acts. Receives 10-20% commission. Reviews material for acts.

How to Contact: Write first and obtain permission to submit. Prefers cassette or VHS videocassette with 1-2 songs. If seeking management, press kit should include 2-3 song demo, short bio, press clippings, video and picture. Does not return material. Reports in 4-6 weeks.

Music: Mostly **alternative/pop/rock**. Works primarily with bands. Current acts include Live (modern rock), The Pound (modern rock) and Local H (alternative rock).

KEN FRITZ ENTERTAINMENT, (formerly Fritz/Byers Management), 451 N. Cañon Dr., Suite 1, Beverly Hills CA 90210. (310)888-0039. Fax: (310)271-3567. President: Ken Fritz. Associate Manager: Parker Bartlett. Management firm. Represents individual artists and groups.

How to Contact: Write or call first and obtain permission to submit. Prefers cassette, CD or VHS videocassette with 2-3 songs and lyric sheet. "Submissions should be short and to the point." If seeking management, press kit should include photo, bio, press clippings and cassette, CD or videocassette with lyric sheets. SASE. Reports in 1-2 months.

Music: All types.

FUTURE STAR ENTERTAINMENT, 315 S. Beverly Dr., Beverly Hills CA 90212. (310)553-0990. President: Paul Shenker. Management firm. Estab. 1982. Represents individual artists and groups from anywhere; currently handles 2 acts. Receives 20% commission. Reviews material for acts.

How to Contact: Call first and obtain permission to submit. Prefers cassette or VHS videocassette with 3-5 songs and lyric sheet. If seeking management, press kit should include cover letter, photo, bio, tape or CD and press material. Does not return material. Reports in 6 weeks.

Music: Mostly **rock**, **pop** and **R&B**. Works primarily with rock bands.

GCI, INC., P.O. Box 56757, New Orleans LA 70156. (504)299-9000. Fax: (504)299-9090. C.E.O.: John Shoup. Management firm, music publisher, record company, record producer and television producer (network). Estab. 1990. Represents groups and songwriters from anywhere; currently handles 1 act. Reviews material for acts.

How to Contact: Does not accept unsolicited material.
Music: Mostly **jazz**. Current acts include Bobby Short, Manhattan Transfer, Bela Fleck, Charlie Byrd, Bill Monroe, Silver Sage and Dukes of Dixieland.

☑ ◉ **THE GLOTZER MANAGEMENT CO.**, 9312 Nightingale Dr., Los Angeles CA 90069. Fax: (310)276-7330. E-mail: glotzer@hotmail.com. Partner: Michael Glotzer. Management firm. Estab. 1967. Represents individual artists, groups and songwriters from anywhere; currently handles 3 acts. Receives 20% commission. Reviews material for acts.
How to Contact: Submit demo tape by mail. Unsolicited submissions are OK. Prefers cassette or CD. If seeking management, press kit should include CD or cassette, picture, bio (optional) and contact information. Does not return material. Reports only if interested.
Music: All types, with an emphasis on **alternative**, **rock** and **roots rock**. Current acts include Calico, Gizmo (of Sweden) and Banned From Utopia (members of Frank Zappa's band).
Tips: "Past managed artists include Frank Zappa, Nina Hagen, Gang of Four, Janis Joplin, Bob Dylan, The Band, Sea Train, Gordon Lightfoot, Tom Rush, Orleans and many more. Practiced law for 10 years prior to managing bands."

◉ **GMI ENTERTAINMENT INC.**, 666 Fifth Ave. #302, New York NY 10103. (212)554-4000. Fax: (212)554-4150. President: Diane Gibson. Director, Artist Relations: Heather Moore. Management firm and music publisher. Estab. 1987. Represents individual artists and songwriters from anywhere; currently handles 1 act. Receives 20% commission. Reviews material for acts.
How to Contact: Write first and obtain permission to submit. Prefers cassette with 3 songs and lyric sheet. If seeking management, press kit should include photo, bio, cassette, press (if any) and lyrics. Does not return material. Reports in 3 months.
Music: Mostly **country, pop** and **R&B**; also **Broadway performers**. Works primarily with vocalists and singer/songwriters. Current acts include Deborah Gibson.
Tips: "Make sure the demos are clear and well-done. Spending a lot of money on production doesn't make the song any better. However, be sure the demos accurately reflect the feel and direction of the song. Use a professional singer if possible to avoid the listener being distracted by the vocal performance."

🆕 ◉ **ERIC GODTLAND MANAGEMENT, INC.**, 1108 Cole St., San Francisco CA 94117. (415)665-9985. Fax: (415)665-9986. Manager: Wayne Ledbetter. Management firm. Estab. 1995. Represents individual artists, groups or songwriters from anywhere; currently handles 5 acts. Reviews material for acts.
How to Contact: Submit demo tape by mail. Unsolicited submissions are OK. Prefers cassette, DAT or CD. If seeking management, press kit should include brief information on how to reach you. Does not return material.
Music: Mostly **pop**, **rock** and **hip-hop**. Works primarily with bands, producers and songwriters. Current acts include Third Eye Blind (rock band), Brougham (alternative/hip-hop group) and Snake River Conspiracy (rock band).

🆕 ◯ **GOLDEN CITY INTERNATIONAL**, Box 410851, San Francisco CA 94141. (415)822-1530. Fax: (415)695-1845. A&R Rep: Mr. Alston. Management firm, music publisher (Dagene Music/ASCAP) and record company (Dagene/Cabletown Records). Estab. 1993. Represents regional (California area) individual artists and groups; currently handles 3 acts. Receives 15-20% commission. Reviews material for acts.
How to Contact: Write or call first and obtain permission to submit. Prefers cassette or VHS videocassette with 2-3 songs. If seeking management, press kit should include a complete bio and current photo along with cassette or CD of recent material. SASE. Reports in 1 month.
Music: Mostly **R&B/dance, rap** and **pop**; also **gospel** and **dance**. Current clients include Rare Essence (vocal group), Marcus Justice (writer/artist) and David Alston (producer).

🆕 ◉ **GOLDEN GURU ENTERTAINMENT**, 765 Farnum Rd., Media PA 19063. (610)891-9766. Fax: (610)891-9316. Owners: Eric J. Cohen, Esq. and Larry Goldfarb. Management firm, music publisher

---

FOR BOOKS ON THE CRAFT AND BUSINESS of songwriting, check out the website for Writer's Digest Books at http://www.writersdigest.com.

and record company. Estab. 1988. Represents individual artists, groups and songwriters from anywhere; currently handles 5 acts. Reviews material for acts.

How to Contact: Call first and obtain permission to submit. Prefers cassette or VHS videocassette with 3-6 songs. If seeking management, press kit should include tape, press, photo, etc. SASE. Reports in 3-4 weeks.

Music: Mostly **rock**, **singer/songwriters**, **urban** and **pop**; "anything that is excellent!"

◯ **CHRIS GREELEY ENTERTAINMENT**, P.O. Box 593, Bangor ME 04402-0593. (207)947-8790. E-mail: brewer220@aol.com. General Manager: Christian D. Greeley. Management firm, shopping/contact service, security services and consultation. Estab. 1986. Represents local, regional and international individual artists, groups and songwriters; currently handles 5 acts. Receives variable commission. Reviews material for acts.

How to Contact: Submit demo tape by mail. Unsolicited submissions are OK. "Please don't call!" Prefers cassette or VHS videocassette with 1-4 songs. If seeking management, press kit should include business card, video and demo tape with return postage. SASE. Reports in 1 month.

Music: Mostly **rock**, **country** and **pop**. "I'm open to anything marketable." Wide range of musical styles. Current acts include Hey Mister (acoustic duo), Every Sunday (trio) and Chris Greeley (acoustic originals).

Tips: "Treat your music interests as a business venture. Don't be afraid to work hard and spend money to get where you want to go."

◢ **GREIF-GARRIS MANAGEMENT**, 2112 Casitas Way, Palm Springs CA 92264. (619)322-8655. Fax: (619)322-7793. Vice President: Sid Garris. Management firm. Estab. 1961. Represents individual artists and/or groups and songwriters from anywhere; currently owns 1 act. Reviews material for acts.

How to Contact: Write first to obtain permission to submit and/or to arrange a personal interview. Submit demo tape by mail. Unsolicited submissions are OK. Prefers cassette. If seeking management, press kit should include demo, cover letter, bio and photo. SASE. Reports in 3 weeks.

Music: **All types.** Current acts include The New Christy Minstrels.

◯ **GUESTSTAR ENTERTAINMENT AGENCY**, 17321 Ritchie Ave. NE, Sand Lake MI 49343-9475. (616)636-5068. President: Raymond G. Dietz, Sr. Management firm, booking agency, music publisher (Sandlake Music/BMI), record company (Gueststar Records, Inc.), record producer and record distributor (Gueststar Music Distributors). Represents individual artists, groups, songwriters and bands from anywhere; currently handles 3 acts. Receives 20% commission. Reviews material for acts.

• Mr. Dietz is also the editor of several music books, including *Everything You Should Know Before You Get into the Country Music Business.*

How to Contact: Submit demo tape by mail. Unsolicited submissions are OK. Prefers cassette or VHS videocassette with unlimited songs, but send your best with lyric or lead sheet. If seeking management, press kit should include photo, demo tape, bio, music résumé and VHS videocassette (live on stage) if possible and press clippings. Does not return material. Reports in 3 weeks.

Music: Mostly **hit country** and **traditional country**. Current acts include Mountain Man (singer), Jamie "K" (singer) and Sweetgrass (band).

[N] ◢ GURLEY & CO., P.O. Box 150657, Nashville TN 37215. (615)269-0474. Fax: (615)385-2052. E-mail: gurleybiz@aol.com. President: Cathy Gurley. Vice President: Meagan Gurley. Management firm and public relations/marketing. Estab. 1985. Represents individual artists, groups and songwriters from anywhere; currently handles 8 acts. Receives 15% commission. Reviews material for acts.

• See the Manager's Roundtable article on page 45 for more information from Cathy Gurley.

How to Contact: Submit demo tape by mail. Unsolicited submissions are OK. Prefers cassette with 3 songs and lyric sheet. Does not return material. Reports in 1 month.

Music: Mostly **country** and **pop**. Current acts include Matt King (country), Lynn Anderson (country), Andy Tubman (alternative rock) and Jay Clementi (country/pop).

Tips: "Stay on it. Keep writing."

◯ **HALE ENTERPRISES**, Rt. 1, Box 49, Worthington IN 47471-9310. (812)875-3664. E-mail: dakota @ncci.net. CEO: Rodger Hale. Management firm, booking agency and record company (Projection Unlimited). Estab. 1976. Represents artists, groups, songwriters and studio musicians; currently handles 15 acts. Receives 15% commission. Reviews material for acts.

How to Contact: Submit demo tape by mail. Unsolicited submissions are OK. Prefers cassette or videocassette with 2-10 songs and lyric sheet. If seeking management include cover letter, résumé, lyric sheets, press clippings, current promo pack *or* photo, video-audio tape, clubs currently performing, short performance history and equipment list (if applicable). Does not return material. Reports in 1 week.

Music: Mostly **country** and **top 40**; also **MOR**, **progressive**, **rock** and **pop**. Works primarily with show bands, dance bands and bar bands. Current acts include Indiana (country show band), Seventh Heaven (top 40 show) and Cotton (show band).

N ⬤ BILL HALL ENTERTAINMENT & EVENTS, 138 Frog Hollow Rd., Churchville PA 18966-1031. (215)357-5189. Fax: (215)357-0320. Contact: William B. Hall III. Booking agency and production company. Represents individuals and groups; currently handles 20-25 acts. Receives 15% commission. Reviews material for acts.
How to Contact: Submit demo tape by mail. Unsolicited submissions are OK. Prefers cassette or video-cassette of performance with 2-3 songs "and photos, promo material and record or tape. We need quality material, preferably before a 'live' audience." Does not return material. Reports only if interested.
Music: Marching band, **circus** and **novelty**. Works primarily with "unusual or novelty attractions in musical line, preferably those that appeal to family groups." Current acts include Fralinger and Polish-American Philadelphia Championship Mummers String Bands (marching and concert group), Erwin Chandler Orchestra (show band), "Mr. Polynesian" Show Band and Hawaiian Revue (ethnic group), the "Phillies Whiz Kids Band" of Philadelphia Phillies Baseball team, Paul Richardson (Phillies' organist/entertainer), Mummermania Musical Quartet, Philadelphia German Brass Band (concert band) and Vogelgesang Circus Calliope.
Tips: "Please send whatever helps us to most effectively market the attraction and/or artist. Provide something that gives you a clear edge over others in your field!"

⬛ ⬤ HANSEN ENTERPRISES, LTD., 855 E. Twain #123411, Las Vegas NV 89109. (702)896-8115. Fax: (702)792-1363. Contact: J. Malcom Baird. Management firm. Estab. 1971. Represents individual artists, groups and songwriters from anywhere; currently handles 3 acts. Receives 25% commission "or contracted fee arrangement." Reviews material for acts.
How to Contact: Submit demo tape by mail. Unsolicited submissions are OK. Prefers cassette. SASE. Reports in 3 weeks. We are looking for potential hit songs only: top 40, pop and Spanish. From time to time we need music for TV shows, commercials and films. Send SASE for requirements, which change from time to time depending upon the project(s).
Music: Mostly **'50s & '60s rock** and **Spanish adult contemporary**. Current acts include The Ronettes and Pilita Corrales (top selling female Spanish recording star).

N ⬤ HARDISON INTERNATIONAL ENTERTAINMENT CORPORATION, P.O. Box 1732, Knoxville TN 37901-1732. (423)673-3076. Fax: (423)637-2939. E-mail: alt1010@aol.com. CEO/President: Dennis K. Hardison. Management firm, booking agency, music publisher (Denlatrin Music), record company (Denlatrin Records) and record producer. Estab. 1984. Represents individual artists from anywhere; currently handles 3 acts. Receives 20% commission. Reviews material for acts.
• This company has promoted acts including New Edition, Freddie Jackson and M.C. Lyte.
How to Contact: Submit demo tape by mail. Unsolicited submissions are OK. Prefers cassette or CD with 3 songs. If seeking management, press kit should include bio, promo picture and cassette. Does not return material. Reports in 6 weeks.
Music: Mostly **R&B/hip-hop**, **contemporary pop** and **gospel**; also **country**. Current acts include Dynamo (hip-hop) and Linsey Williams (country).
Tips: "We have an in-house production staff to critique your music."

⬤ M. HARRELL & ASSOCIATES, 5444 Carolina, Merrillville IN 46410. (219)887-8814. Fax: (219)947-5255. Owner: Mary Harrell. Management firm and booking agency. Estab. 1984. Represents individual artists, groups, songwriters, all talents—fashion, dancers, etc.; currently handles 50-60 acts. Receives 10-20% commission. Reviews material for acts.
How to Contact: Call first and obtain permission to submit. Submit demo tape by mail. Unsolicited submissions OK. Prefers cassette or videocassette with 2-3 songs. If seeking management, press kit should include cover letter, résumé, bio, photo, demo tape/CD and press clippings. "Keep it brief and current." Does not return material. Reports in 3-4 weeks.
Music: All types, **country**, **R&B**, **jazz**, **gospel**, **Big Band** and **light rock**. Current acts include Bill Shelton ('50s music), 11th Ave. ('50s music) and Larger than Life (variety).

🔻 🌐 SENDING TO A COUNTRY other than your own? Be sure to send International Reply Coupons (IRCs) instead of stamps for replies or return of your materials.

◢**HORIZON MANAGEMENT INC.**, P.O. Box 8538, Endwell NY 13762. (607)785-9670. E-mail: hmi785@aol.com. Website: http://www.musicalonline.com/management/horizon. Contact: New Talent Department. Management firm, booking agency and concert promotion. Estab. 1967. Represents regional, national and international artists, groups and songwriters; currently handles 1,500 acts. Receives 20% commission. Reviews material for acts.

How to Contact: Call first and obtain permission to submit. Prefers CD, cassette or VHS videocassette with 1-4 songs and lead sheet. Send cover letter, résumé, lead sheets, photo, bio, lyric sheets, equipment list, demo tape/CD, video, press clippings, reviews, etc. Does not return material. Reports in 1 week.

Music: All styles, originals or covers. Current acts include the original cast of Beatlemania (Broadway show), Hardrive (original rock) and D Gerod (original rock).

N **⛏** ◢**A HUGE PRODUCTION, INC.**, P.O. Box 35765, Brighton MA 02135. (617)254-9660. Fax: (617)332-4756. E-mail: rippo@world.std.com. Website: http://www.rippo.com. President: Richard M. Gordon. Management firm, music publisher (Cat Butt Musik/BMI) and record company (2 Funky International Records). Estab. 1996. Represents regional groups from the northeast; currently handles 1 act. Receives negotiable commission.

• This company manages Rippopotamus, winner of 1996 Boston Music Award.

How to Contact: Write first and obtain permission to submit a demo. Prefers cassette with 3 songs and lyric sheet. If seeking management, press kit should include press, radio tracking, photo and CD. SASE. Reports in 3-4 weeks.

Music: Mostly **pop/rock** and **funk**. Works with bands exclusively. Current acts include Rippopotamus (8 piece funk band) and There (3 piece power rock).

Tips: "Always call first. Promo packages are expensive, and you should always make sure we're actively seeking material, especially since most modern bands do their own songwriting. Being artists ourselves, we strongly recommend that you be very sure of people you work with and that they have same level of faith and confidence in the project that you do. Never give away the store and always make sure that you are aware of what is transpiring with your career, even if you have someone you trust handling it for you. Ultimately, no one has your interests as much at heart as you do, and thus you should always have your finger on your career's pulse."

✓ ◯**JOE HUPP ENTERPRISES**, 4415 S. 449th St. W. Ave., Jennings OK 74038. (918)865-7026. Fax: (918)865-7403. E-mail: huppent@aol.com. Presidents: Joe Hupp or Patti Llovet Hughes. Management firm, booking agency and music publisher (Ol' Hippie Music). Estab. 1984. Represents individual artists, groups and songwriters from anywhere; currently handles 8 acts. Receives 10-20% commission. Reviews material for acts.

How to Contact: Call first to arrange personal interview or submit demo tape by mail. Prefers cassette or VHS videocassette with 1-4 songs. If seeking management, press kit should include photo, bio/fact sheet, cassette or CD and videocassette (if available). Does not return material. Reports in 1 month.

Music: Mostly **country**, **rock**, **alternative**; also **folk**, **R&B** and **pop**. Works primarily with bands singer/songwriters. Current acts include Kelly Spradlin, Patti Hughes and David Allan Coe (the original "Rhinestone Cowboy").

N ◯**IKON ENTERTAINMENT**, 1134 N. LaBrea Ave., Los Angeles CA 90038. (213)461-9755. Fax: (213)461-9787. E-mail: andrian1@msn.com. Contact: Andrian Adams. Management firm and music publisher (Ikon Music Limited). Estab. 1992. Represents individual artists, groups and songwriters from anywhere; currently handles 3 acts. Commission "varies from act to act. New acts are 20%. Reviews material for acts.

How to Contact: Submit demo tape by mail. Unsolicited submissions are OK. Prefers cassette with contact numbers. If seeking management, press kit should include photo and demo tape/CD. "Put strongest song first on the cassette." Does not return material. Reports in 2 weeks.

Music: Mostly **pop**, **urban** and **R&B**. Current acts include The Lucy Nation and Bond.

Tips: "Listen to the radio, try to write songs you would hear on the radio. Be realistic!"

N ◯**IMPERIAL ARTIST MANAGEMENT**, P.O. Box 4185, Huntington Beach CA 92605. (714)445-9193. President: James R. Wehmer, Jr. Management firm. Estab. 1995. Represents local individual artists and groups; currently handles 4 acts. Receives 15% commission. Reviews material for acts.

How to Contact: Submit demo tape by mail. Unsolicited submissions are OK. Prefers cassette, DAT or CD (prefers CD) with 4 songs and lyric sheet. If seeking management, press kit should include cover letter, demo tape/CD (prefer CD), band photo, brief history of band and lyric sheet. Does not return material. Reports within 1 month.

Music: Mostly **alternative rock**, **heavy metal** and **acoustics**. Works primarily with bands, and a few individual artists. Current acts include Filth (rockcore), Downercap (alternative rock), T-Roy (acoustic rock) and Sons of Jesus (alternative rock).

INTERNATIONAL ENTERTAINMENT BUREAU, 3612 N. Washington Blvd., Indianapolis IN 46205-3592. (317)926-7566. E-mail: intleb@prodigy.com. Booking agency. Estab. 1972. Represents individual artists and groups from anywhere; currently handles 135 acts. Receives 20% commission.

How to Contact: Submit demo tape by mail. Unsolicited submissions are OK. Prefers VHS videocassette. If seeking management, press kit should include cover letter, résumé, bio, picture, testimonials, demo tape/CD, video, sample song list and press clippings. "Do not call us, please." Does not return material. Reports in 6 months.

Music: Mostly **rock**, **country** and **A/C**; also **jazz**, **nostalgia** and **ethnic**. Works primarily with bands, comedians and speakers. Current acts include Five Easy Pieces (A/C), Doug Lawson (country) and Wray Brothers (gospel).

INTERNATIONAL PRODUCTION MANAGEMENT, 12 Dongan Place #201, New York NY 10040. Phone/fax: (212)304-8661. President: Lynn Manwell. Management firm and booking agency. Estab. 1990. Represents individual artists or groups from anywhere; currently handles 10 acts. Receives 15% commission. Reviews material for acts.

How to Contact: Submit demo tape by mail. Unsolicited submissions are OK. Prefers cassette or VHS videocassette with 3 songs and lyric sheet. If seeking management, press kit should include previous reviews and photos. SASE. Reports in 3 months.

Music: Mostly **pop**, **classical crossover** and **Broadway**. Works primarily with singers and groups. Current acts include The Cassidys (Irish band).

Tips: "Be thorough in submissions. Clarify your goals."

ITS HAPPENING PRESENT ENTERTAINMENT, P.O. Box 222, Pittsburg CA 94565. (510)980-0893. Fax: (510)432-4342. Management firm, booking agency and record company (Black Diamond Records, Flash Point Records, Triple Beam Records, Stay Down Records, Hitting Hard Records and D. City Records). Estab. 1989. Represents local, regional or international individual artists and songwriters; currently handles 9 acts. Receives 8-14% commission. Reviews material for acts.

How to Contact: Write first and obtain permission to submit. Prefers cassette with 2 songs and lyric sheet. If seeking management, press kit should include cover letter, 8×10 photo, bio, video, 3-song demo and demo voice tape. Does not return material.

Music: Mostly **pop**, **R&B** and **jazz**; also **rap** and **comedy**. Works primarily with vocalist songwriters, rap groups, bands and instrumentalists. Current acts include Baby Rain (rapper) and Patchwork (rapper).

Tips: "Please, copyright all your material as soon as possible. Don't let anyone else hear it until that's done first."

J & V MANAGEMENT, 143 W. Elmwood, Caro MI 48723. (517)673-2889. Manager/Publisher: John Timko. Management firm, booking agency and music publisher. Represents local, regional or international individual artists, groups and songwriters; currently handles 3 acts. Receives 10% commission. Reviews material for acts.

How to Contact: Write first and obtain permission to submit. Prefers cassette with 3 songs maximum and lyric sheet. If seeking management, include short reference bio, cover letter and résumé in press kit. SASE. Reports in 2 months.

Music: Mostly **country**. Works primarily with vocalists and dance bands. Current acts include John Patrick (country), Alexander Depue (fiddle) and Most Wanted (country).

**FOR EXPLANATIONS OF THESE SYMBOLS,
SEE THE INSIDE FRONT AND BACK COVERS OF THIS BOOK.**

☑ ○ **JACOBS MANAGEMENT**, 2611 S. Massey St., Philadelphia PA 19142. (215)492-5420. Fax: (215)492-1359. E-mail: midnitemgt@aol.com. Owner: Mitchell Jacobs. Management firm. Estab. 1988. Represents individual artists and groups from anywhere; currently handles 3 acts. Receives 20% commission. Reviews material for acts.
How to Contact: Submit demo tape by mail. Unsolicited submissions OK. Prefers cassette with 3 songs and lyric sheet. If seeking management, press kit should include cover letter, bio, photo and demo tape. SASE. Reports in 1 month.
Music: Mostly **rock**, **R&B** and **roots**. Works primarily with singer/songwriters, bands. Current acts include Loved Ones (jazz), Lizanne Fontana (jazz) and Stephanie Johnson (pop).

◑ **JACOBSON TALENT MANAGEMENT (JTM)**, P.O. Box 4097, Oceanside CA 92052-4097. (760)757-2683. Fax: (760)757-8176. E-mail: jake@jtm-ink.com. Website: http://www.jtm-ink.com. Owner: Jake Jacobson. Senior Associate: Randi Morgan. Management firm and online consultation service. Estab. 1981. Represents individual artists and groups from anywhere; currently handles 2 acts. Receives 20% commission. Reviews material for acts.
How to Contact: Call first and obtain permission to submit. Prefers cassette or CD with 5 songs and lyric sheet. If seeking management, press kit should include photo, bio and "anything else you think will help your cause." SASE. Reports in 2-3 weeks.
Music: Mostly **rock**, **R&B/hip-hop** and **country**; also **adult contemporary**. Works primarily with bands and singer/songwriters.
Tips: "Work hard. Hold up your end so we can do our jobs. In addition, we find it much easier to work with artists who have a basic working knowledge of the music industry and personal management. We also offer a unique service via the Internet. Our website provides online consulting services for artists and music industry entrepreneurs. It's real time and very secure. Perfect for someone who does not need full time management but is in need of occasional advice, counsel, or career direction."

⊕ ◑ **ROGER JAMES MANAGEMENT**, 10A Margaret Rd., Barnet, Herts EN4 9NP England. Phone: (0181)440-9788. Professional Manager: Susana Boyle. Management firm and music publisher (R.J. Music/PRS). Estab. 1977. Represents songwriters. Receives 50% commission (negotiable). Reviews material for acts.
How to Contact: Submit demo tape by mail. Unsolicited submissions are OK. Prefers cassette with 3 songs and lyric sheet. Does not return material.
Music: Mostly **pop**, **country** and "any good song."

⊕ ◑ **JAMPOP LTD.**, 27 Parkington Plaza, Kingston 10 W.I. Jamaica. Phone: (809)968-9235. Fax: (809)968-2199. E-mail: jampoptalent@hotmail.com. President: Ken Nelson. Contact: Claudia Nelson. Management firm and booking agency. Estab. 1990. Represents local, regional and international individual artists, groups and songwriters; currently handles 50 acts. Receives 15% commission. Reviews material for acts.
How to Contact: Write or call first and obtain permission to submit. Prefers cassette with lyric sheet. If seeking managment, press kit should include bio, photo, demo tape/CD and lyric sheets. Does not return material. Reports in 1 month.
Music: Mostly **R&B** and **pop**; also **gospel**. Works primarily with vocalists. Current artists include Sandra Brooks (Jamaica's leading female gospel artist), Sons and Daughters (gospel choir) and Ebony (female pop group).

○ **JANA JAE ENTERPRISES**, P.O. Box 35726, Tulsa OK 74153. (918)786-8896. E-mail: janajae@jana jae.com. Website: http://www.janajae.com. Agent: Kathleen Pixley. Booking agency, music publisher (Jana Jae Publishing/BMI) and record company (Lark Record Productions, Inc.). Estab. 1979. Represents individual artists and songwriters; currently handles 12 acts. Receives 15% commission. Reviews material for acts.
How to Contact: Submit demo tape by mail. Unsolicited submissions are OK. Prefers cassette or videocassette of performance. If seeking management, press kit should include cover letter, bio, photo, demo tape/CD, lyric sheets and press clippings. Does not return material.
Music: Mostly **country**, **classical** and **jazz instrumentals**; also **pop**. Works with vocalists, show and concert bands, solo instrumentalists. Represents Jana Jae (country singer/fiddle player), Matt Greif (classical guitarist), Sydni (solo singer) and Hotwire (country show band).

○ **C. JUNQUERA PRODUCTIONS**, P.O. Box 393, Lomita CA 90717. (310)325-2881. Consultant: Nikki Hornsby. Management consulting firm and record company (NH Records). Estab. 1987. Represents local, regional and international individual artists and songwriters; currently handles 1-5 acts. Receives a

flat fee for consulting, percentage for business management. Reviews material for acts.
How to Contact: Submit demo tape by mail. Unsolicited submissions are OK. Prefers CD or cassette with 1-4 songs and lyric sheet. If seeking management, include recent 8×10 photo, bio, photocopies of news articles, cover letter stating goals, résumé, lyric sheets and sample of product. SASE. Reports in 3-4 months.
Music: Mostly **traditional country** and **country pop**; also **easy listening** and **new Christian crossover**. Works primarily with songwriters and vocalists. Current recording acts include Nikki Hornsby (singer/songwriter), N. Kelel (songwriter) and Mary E. Ryan (songwriter).
Tips: "Be specific on goals you wish to obtain as artist or songwriter—submit a sample of your product and don't give up! Obtain outside financial support for production of your product—invest your talent, not your own money."

SHELDON KAGAN INTERNATIONAL, 35 McConnell, Dorval, Quebec H9S 5L9 Canada. (514)631-2160. Fax: (514)631-4430. E-mail: sheldon@sheldonkagan.com. Website: http://www.sheldonka gan.com. President: Sheldon Kagan. Booking agency. Estab. 1965. Represents local individual artists and groups; currently handles 17 acts. Receives 10-20% commission. Reviews materials for acts.
How to Contact: Submit demo tape by mail. Unsolicited submissions are OK. Prefers cassette or VHS videocassette with 6 songs. SASE. Reports in 4-5 weeks.
Music: Mostly **top 40**. Works primarily with vocalists and bands. Current acts include Quazz (jazz trio), City Lights (top 40 band) and Jeux de Cordes (violin and guitar duo).

KENDALL WEST AGENCY, P.O. Box 173776, Arlington TX 76003-3776. (817)468-7800. Fax: (817)468-7887. E-mail: vellucci@flash.net. Contact: Michelle Vellucci. Booking agency and television producer. Estab. 1994. Represents individual artists and groups from anywhere. Receives 10% commission. Reviews material for acts.
How to Contact: Write first and obtain permission to submit a demo or write to arrange personal interview. Prefers cassette with 5 songs and lead sheet. If seeking management, press kit should include bio, photo, cover letter, demo tape/CD and résumé. SASE. Reports in 1 month.
Music: Mostly **country**, **blues/jazz** and **rock**; also **trios**, dance and **individuals**. Works primarily with bands. Current acts include Way Out West (country band), Breckenridge (variety band) and Jaz-Vil (jazz/blues).

KICKSTART MUSIC LTD., 10 Park House, 140 Battersea Park Rd., London SW11 4NB England. Phone: (0171)498 9696. Fax: (0171)498 2063. E-mail: cms@cmsi.demon.co.uk. Directors: Ken Middleton and Frank Clark. Management firm and record company (BME). Estab. 1994. Represents individual artists, groups or songwriters from anywhere; currently handles 3 acts. Receives variable commission, "depends on contract." Reviews material for acts.
How to Contact: Submit demo tape by mail. Unsolicited submissions are OK. Prefers cassette, DAT or CD with 3 songs and lyric and lead sheet. If seeking management, press kit should include photograph and bio. SAE and IRC. Reports in 2 weeks.
Music: Mostly **pop**, **rock**, **country** and **blues**. Works primarily with bands who perform a live set of original music and talented singer/songwriters who can cross over to all types of music. Current acts include Pal Joey (rock band), Frank Clark (songwriter) and Simon Fox (songwriter).
Tips: "We prefer songwriters whose songs can cross over to all types of music, those who do not write in one style only."

KITCHEN SYNC, 8530 Holloway Dr. #208, West Hollywood CA 90069-2475. (310)855-1631. Fax: (310)657-7197. E-mail: ldg@hamptons.com. Contact: Laura Grover. Music production manager. Estab. 1990. Represents individual artists, groups and songwriters from anywhere. Reviews material for acts.
  • Kitchen Sync primarily manages the production of music.
How to Contact: Write first and obtain permission to submit. Prefers cassette with 3 songs and lyric sheet. If seeking management, press kit should include cover letter, résumé, bio, press clippings, discography and photo. SASE. Reports in 3-4 weeks.
Music: Mostly **pop/rock**, **country** and **R&B**. Works primarily with producers and singer/songwriters.
Tips: "Have a clear artistic mission statement and career goals. I'm mostly interested in overseeing/managing production of material, i.e., creating budgets and mapping out recording plan, booking studios, vendors, etc."

KKR ENTERTAINMENT GROUP, 1300 Clay St., 6th Floor, Oakland CA 94612. (510)464-8024. Fax: (510)769-8024 or 763-9004. E-mail: kkrentmnt@aol.com. Director of Operations: Keith Washington.

Management firm. Estab. 1989. Represents individual artists, groups and producers from anywhere; currently handles 5 acts. Receives 10-20% commission. Reviews material for acts.
How to Contact: Call first and obtain permission to submit. Prefers cassette. If seeking management, press kit should include bio, tape and photo (if available). "We do not accept unsolicited material." SASE. Reports in 1 month.
Music: Mostly **R&B**, **rap** and **rock**. Current acts include E-A-Ski & CMT (DreamWorks/Sony Music), CPO-Boss Hogg (Interscope) and Christion (R&B group, Def Jam Records).
Tips: "Always learn who you are working with and stay involved in everything."

⬛ **KUPER PERSONAL MANAGEMENT**, P.O. Box 66274, Houston TX 77266. (713)520-5791. Fax: (713)523-1048. E-mail: kuper@juno.com. Owner: Ivan Kuper. Management firm and music publisher (Kuper-Lam Music/BMI and Uvula Music/BMI). Estab. 1979. Represents individual artists, groups and songwriters from Texas; currently handles 3 acts. Receives 20% commission. Reviews material for acts.
How to Contact: Submit demo tape by mail. Unsolicited submissions are OK. Prefers cassette. If seeking management, press kit should include cover letter, press clippings, photo, bio (1 page) tearsheets (reviews, etc.) and demo tape/CD. Does not return material. Reports in 2 months.
Music: Mostly **singer/songwriters**, **triple AAA**, **hip-hop** and **Americana**. Works primarily with self-contained and self-produced artists. Current acts include Philip Rodriguez (singer/songwriter), Champ X (rap artist) and The Hit Squad (hip-hop).
Tips: "Create a market value for yourself, produce your own master tapes, create a cost-effective situation."

⬛ **L.D.F. PRODUCTIONS**, P.O. Box 406, Old Chelsea Station, New York NY 10011. (212)925-8925. President: Mr. Dowell. Management firm and booking agency. Estab. 1982. Represents artists and choirs in the New York area; currently handles 3 acts. Receives 20% commission. Reviews material for acts.
How to Contact: Write first and obtain permission to submit. Prefers cassette (or videocassette of performance—well-lighted, maximum 10 minutes) with 2-8 songs and lyric sheet. If seeking management, press kit should include résumé, cover letter, bio, demo tape/CD (prefer CD), lyric sheet, video and color photo. SASE. Reports in 3 weeks. "Do not phone expecting a return call unless requested by L.D.F. Productions. Videos should be imaginatively presented with clear sound and bright colors." Does not return material.
Music: Mostly **gospel**, **pop**, **rock** and **jazz**. Works primarily with inspirational and contemporary pop artists. Current acts include L.D. Frazier (gospel artist/lecturer), Peter Matthews (bassist) and Bernard Rosat (bassist).

◖ **LANDSLIDE MANAGEMENT**, 928 Broadway, New York NY 10010. (212)505-7300. Principals: Ted Lehrman and Libby Bush. Management firm and music publisher (Kozkeeozko Music). Estab. 1978. Represents singers, singer/songwriters and actor/singers; currently handles 15 acts. Receives 15% commission. Reviews material for acts.
How to Contact: Write or call first and obtain permission to submit. "Potential hit singles only." SASE. "Include picture, résumé and (if available) ½" videocassette if you're submitting yourself as an act." Reports in 6 weeks.
Music: Mostly **dance-oriented**, **MOR**, **rock (soft pop)**, **soul**, **top 40/pop** and **country/pop**.

⬛ **LARI-JON PROMOTIONS**, 325 W. Walnut, P.O. Box 216, Rising City NE 68658. (402)542-2336. Owner: Larry Good. Management firm, music publisher (Lari-Jon Publishing Co./BMI) and record company (Lari-Jon Records). Represents individual artists, groups and songwriters; currently handles 3 acts. Receives 15% commission. Reviews material for acts.
How to Contact: Submit demo tape by mail. Unsolicited submissions are OK. Prefers cassette with 5 songs and lyric sheet. If seeking management, press kit should include 8×10 photos, cassette, videocassette and bio sheet. SASE. Reports in 2 months.
Music: Mostly **country**, **gospel** and **'50s rock**. Works primarily with dance and show bands. Represents Kent Thompson (singer), Nebraskaland 'Opry (family type country show) and Brenda Allen (singer and comedienne).

⬛ **RAY LAWRENCE, LTD.**, P.O. Box 1987, Studio City CA 91614. (818)508-9022. Fax: (818)508-5672. President: Ray Lawrence. Management firm, booking agency and music publisher (Boha Music/

TO HELP YOU UNDERSTAND and use the information in these listings, see "How to Use *Songwriter's Market* to Get Your Songs Heard," on page 5.

BMI). Estab. 1963. Represents individual artists from anywhere; currently handles 15 acts. Receives 10-15% commission.

How to Contact: Submit demo tape by mail. Unsolicited submissions are OK. Prefers VHS videocassette. If seeking management, press kit should include 8 × 10 professional photographs and bio. Does not return material. Reports in 2 weeks.

Music: All types. Works primarily with musical and variety acts. Current acts include Trini Lopez (recording artist), Wayland Pickard (recording artist) and Glenn Ash (recording artist).

◙ LEGEND ARTISTS MANAGEMENT, 12 W. 37th St., 5th Floor, New York NY 10018-7404. (212)279-9288. Fax: (212)279-9666. E-mail: legend@crl.com. A&R: Michael Deputato. Management firm, music publisher (Harder Than Normal Music) and record company (RSA—Atlantic and Harder Than Normal—ADA). Estab. 1986. Represents individual artists, groups, songwriters and producers from anywhere; currently handles 7 acts. Receives up to 20% commission. Reviews material for acts.

How to Contact: Write or call first and obtain permission to submit. Prefers cassette or DAT. If seeking management, press kit should include tape, cover letter and photo. SASE. Reports in 6 weeks.

Music: Mostly **pop**, **R&B** and **rock**; also **all styles**. Current acts include Lynyrd Skynyrd (rock), Cuff (alt rock), Natalie Curtis (R&B).

☑ ◙ LEVINSON ENTERTAINMENT VENTURES INTERNATIONAL, INC., 1440 Veteran Ave., Suite 650, Los Angeles CA 90024. (323)663-6940. E-mail: leviinc@aol.com. President: Bob Levinson. Contact: Jed Leland, Jr. Management firm. Estab. 1978. Represents national individual artists, groups and songwriters; currently handles 4 acts. Receives 15-25% commission. Reviews material for acts.

How to Contact: Write first and obtain permission to submit. Prefers cassette or VHS videocassette with 6 songs and lead sheet. If seeking management, press kit should include bio, pictures and press clips. SASE. Reports in 2-4 weeks.

Music: Mostly **rock**, **MOR**, **R&B** and **country**. Works primarily with rock bands and vocalists.

Tips: "Should be a working band, self-contained and, preferably, performing original material."

◖ RICK LEVY MANAGEMENT, 2356 Commodores Club Blvd., St. Augustine FL 32084-6126. (904)460-1225. Fax: (904)460-1226. President: Rick Levy. Management firm, music publisher (Flying Governor Music/BMI) and record company (Luxury Records). Estab. 1985. Represents local, regional or international individual artists and groups; currently handles 7 acts. Receives 15-20% commission. Reviews material for acts.

How to Contact: Write or call first and obtain permission to submit. Prefers cassette or VHS videocassette with 3 songs and lyric sheet. If seeking management, press kit should include cover letter, bio, demo tape/CD, VHS video, photo and press clippings. SASE. Reports in 2 weeks.

Music: Mostly **R&B** (no rap), **pop**, **country** and **oldies**. Current acts include Jay & the Techniques ('60s hit group), The Original Box Tops ('60s), Tommy Roe ('60s) and The Limits (pop).

◙ LIVE-WIRE MANAGEMENT, P.O. Box 653, Morgan Hill, CA 95038. (408)778-3526. Fax: (408)453-3836. E-mail: bruce@L-WM.com. Website: http://www.L-WM.com. President: Bruce Hollibaugh. Management firm. Estab. 1990. Represents individual artists and groups from anywhere; currently handles 2 acts. Receives 15-25% commission. Reviews material for acts.

How to Contact: Submit demo tape by mail. Unsolicited submissions are OK. Prefers DAT with 3-6 songs and lyric sheet. If seeking management, press kit should include what region you are currently performing in; how often you are doing live shows; any reviews; photos. Does not return material. Reports in 1 month.

Music: Mostly **pop**, **acoustic pop** and **New Age**; also **jazz**, **R&B** and **country**. Works primarily with bands and singer/songwriters. Current acts include Tommy Elskes (singer/songwriter) and Janny Choi (jazz).

☑ ▢ LIVING EYE PRODUCTIONS LTD., P.O. Box 12956, Rochester NY 14612. (716)544-3500. Fax: (716)544-8860. E-mail: c.kings@worldnet.att.net. Secretaries: Monica or Carol. Managing Director: Andy Babiuk. Management firm, music publisher (Pussy Galore Publishing/BMI) and record producers (Andy Babiuk and Greg Prevost). Estab. 1982. Represents individual artists, groups and songwriters from anywhere; currently handles 4 acts. Receives 20% commission. Reviews material for acts.

How to Contact: Submit demo tape by mail. Unsolicited submissions are OK. Prefers cassette and "what the artist feels necessary." If seeking management, press kit should include cover letter, bio, photo, demo tape/CD, lyric sheet, press clippings, video and résumé. Does not return material. Reports in 2 weeks.

Music: Mostly **'60s rock**, **'50s rock** and **blues**; also **folk rock** and **surf**. Works primarily with bands that can tour to promote record releases. Current acts include The Chesterfield Kings (rock), The Mean Red

Spiders (rock), The Frantic Flattops ('50s rock) and the Moviees ('60s rock).
Tips: "We don't like trendy new stuff. Don't follow fads, create your own music by having good rock-n-roll influences."

◙ **LOWELL AGENCY**, 4043 Brookside Court, Norton OH 44203. (330)825-7813. Website: http://www.rfwm.com/leon/. Contact: Leon Seiter. Booking agency and song publisher (Lanies Pride/BMI). Estab. 1985. Represents regional (Midwest and Southeast) individual artists; currently handles 3 acts. Receives 10% commission. Reviews material for acts.
How to Contact: Submit demo tape by mail. Unsolicited submissions are OK. Prefers cassette with 4 songs and lyric sheet. If seeking management, press kit should include demo cassette tape, bio and picture. Does not return material. Reports in 2 months.
Music: Mostly **country**. Works primarily with country vocalists. Current acts include Leon Seiter (country singer/entertainer/songwriter), Tom Durden (country singer, co-writer of "Heartbreak Hotel") and Marvin Rainwater (country/songwriter).

◙ **RICHARD LUTZ ENTERTAINMENT AGENCY**, 5625 O St., Lincoln NE 68510. (402)483-2241. E-mail: r/94521@navix.net. General Manager: Cherie Worley. Management firm and booking agency. Estab. 1964. Represents individuals and groups; currently handles 50 acts. Receives 20% commission.
How to Contact: Submit demo tape by mail. Unsolicited submissions are OK. Prefers cassette or videocassette with 5-10 songs "to show style and versatility" and lead sheet. "Send photo, résumé, tape, partial song list and include references. Add comedy, conversation, etc., to your videocassette. Do not play songs in full—short versions preferred." If seeking management, press kit should include audio cassette and photo. SASE. Reports in 2 weeks.
Music: Mostly **top 40** and **country**; also **dance-oriented** and **MOR**. "Acts must be uniformed." Current acts include The Calhouns (country), Sweet 'N' Sassy (variety) and Endless Summer (nostalgia).

◙ **M.B.H. MUSIC MANAGEMENT**, P.O. Box 1096, Hudson, Quebec J0P 1H0 Canada. (613)780-1163. Fax: (514)458-2819. E-mail: larecord@total.net. Website: http://www.radiofreedom.com. Manager: Tanya Hart. Producer: M. Langies. Management firm, publishing company (G-String Publishing) and record company (L.A. Records). Estab. 1982. Works with individual artists and groups from anywhere; currently handles 5 acts. Receives 20-30% commission. Reviews material for acts.
How to Contact: Submit demo tape by mail. Unsolicited submissions are OK. Prefers cassette or DAT with 3 songs and lyric sheet. If seeking management, press kit should include demo, 8×10 glossy, bio/résumé and song list. Does not return material. Reports in 6 months.
Music: Mostly **commercial rock, alternative** and **A/C**; also **country** and **dance**. Works primarily with singer/songwriters and solo artists. Current acts include Jessica Ehrenworth (dream pop singer), Those Bloody Nigels (alternative pop), General Panic (alternative/new wave), Brittany (soda pop) and Luger (speed metal).

☑ ○ **M.E.G. MANAGEMENT**, 6255 Sunset Blvd. #1006, Hollywood CA 90028. (213)860-3430. Fax: (213)860-3435. Vice President Artist Development: Ty Ronald Supancic. Management firm. Estab. 1996. Represents individual artists, groups and songwriters from anywhere; currently handles 5 acts. Receives 20% commission. Reviews material for acts.
How to Contact: Submit demo tape by mail. Unsolicited submissions are OK. Prefers cassette or VHS videocassette and lyric sheet. If seeking management, press kit should include cover letter, demo tape/CD, lyric sheets, video, press clippings, photos and bio. "We believe in first impressions. Make it professional." Reports in 2-3 months.
Music: Mostly **alternative rock**. Current acts include ON (alternative/dance, signed to Warner Bros.), Nick Frost (folk/alternative), Sallie B (rap) and Simple Intrique (R&B).

◙ **KEVIN MABRY MINISTRIES**, 8 E. State, Box 385, Milford Center OH 43045. Phone/fax: (937)349-2971. Owner: Kevin Mabry. Booking agency. Estab. 1970. Represents individual artists, groups and songwriters from anywhere; currently handles 1 act. Receives 15-20% commission. Reviews material for acts.
How to Contact: Submit demo tape by mail. Unsolicited submissions are OK. Prefers cassette with 1-3 songs and lyric sheet. "Picture and bio is helpful." Does not return material. Reports in 4-5 weeks.
Music: Mostly **gospel songs (no rock)** and **positive country songs**. Works primarily with gospel and country artists, solo and groups. Current acts include Kevin Mabry (gospel artist).

◙ **MAGIC LAMP MANAGEMENT**, (201)493-9579. Fax: (201)493-1648. Contact: Karen Lampiasi. Management firm, marketing and industry consulting services. Estab. 1997. Represents individual artists,

groups and songwriters from anywhere. Receives negotiable commission. Reviews material for acts.
How to Contact: "Call or fax for address and for permission to submit. Will discuss submission requirements upon approval."
Music: All types.

✿ ◙ MAGNUM MUSIC CORPORATION LTD., 8607-128 Avenue, Edmonton, Alberta Canada T5E 0G3. (403)476-8230. Fax: (403)472-2584. Manager: Bill Maxim. Booking agency, music publisher (Ramblin' Man Music Publishing/PRO and High River Music Publishing/ASCAP) and record company (Magnum Records). Estab. 1984. Represents individual artists, groups and songwriters from anywhere; currently handles 5 acts. Receives 15% commission. Reviews material for acts.
How to Contact: Write or call first and obtain permission to submit. Prefers cassette with 3-4 songs. If seeking management, press kit should include tape or CD, photo, press clippings, bio, résumé and video. Does not return material. Reports in 2 months.
Music: Mostly **country** and **gospel**. Works primarily with "artists or groups who are also songwriters." Current acts include Catheryne Greenly (country), Thea Anderson (country) and Gordon Cormier (country).
Tips: "Prefers finished demos."

◙ MANAGEMENT BY JAFFE, 1560 Broadway, Suite 1103, New York NY 10036-0000. (212)869-6912. Fax: (212)869-7102. E-mail: jerjaf@aol.com. President: Jerry Jaffe. Management firm. Estab. 1987. Represents individual artists and groups from anywhere; currently handles 3-4 acts. Receives 20% commission. Reviews material for acts "sometimes."
How to Contact: Write or call first to arrange personal interview. Prefers CD or cassette and videocassette with 3-4 songs and lyric sheet. Does not return material. Reports in 2 months.
Music: Mostly **rock/alternative**, **pop** and **AAA**. Works primarily with groups and singers/songwriters. Current acts include Joe McIntrye (pop), Nancy Boy (rock/pop band) and Dirt Merchants (alternative rock band).
Tips: "Create some kind of 'buzz' first."

✓ ◙ MANAGEMENT PLUS, P.O. Box 65089, San Antonio TX 78265. (210)223-3251. Fax: (210)223-3251. Owner: Bill Angelini. Management firm and booking agency. Estab. 1980. Represents individual artists and groups from anywhere; currently handles 5 acts. Receives 10-15% commission. Reviews material for acts.
How to Contact: Submit demo tape by mail. Unsolicited submissions are OK. Prefers cassette, VHS videocassette and bio. If seeking management, press kit should include pictures, bio, résumé and discography. Does not return material. Reports in 3-4 weeks.
Music: Mostly **Latin American**, **Tejano** and **international**; also **Norteño** and **country**. Current acts include Jay Perez (Tejano), Ram Herrera (Tejano), Rodeo (Tejano) and Grupo Vida (Tejano).

N ✿ ◙ THE MANAGEMENT TRUST LTD., 309B, 219 Dufferin St., Toronto, Ontario M6K 3J1 Canada. (416)532-7080. Fax: (416)532-8852. Contacts: Sarah Barker Tonge; Bernie Breen; Jake Gold; Allan Gregg; Shelley Stertz. Management firm. Estab. 1986. Represents individual artists and/or groups; currently handles 4 acts.
How to Contact: Submit demo tape by mail. Unsolicited submissions are OK. If seeking management, press kit should include CD or tape, bio, cover letter, photo and press clippings. Does not return material. Reports in 2 months.
Music: All types. Current acts include The Tragically Hip (rock band), The Watchmen (rock band) and Colin Cripps (producer).

⊕ ✓ ◙ MARSUPIAL MANAGEMENT LTD., Roundhill Cottage, The Ridge, Cold Ash, Thatcham, Berks RG18 9HZ United Kingdom. Phone: 01635 862200. Fax: 01635 866449. Manager: John Brand. Management firm, music publisher and record producer. Estab. 1990. Represents individual artists and/or groups, songwriters, producers and remixers from anywhere; currently handles 4 acts. Receives 20% commission. Reviews material for acts.
How to Contact: Submit demo tape by mail. Unsolicited submissions are OK. Prefers cassette or PAL videocassette with 4 songs and lyric sheet. If seeking management, press kit should include cover letter, bio, lyric sheets, tape, photos, video (if possible) and any press. SAE and IRC. Reports in 1 month.
Music: All types. Current acts include Stereophonics (rock band).

THE TYPES OF MUSIC each listing is interested in are printed in **boldface**.

N. 🔘 **RICK MARTIN PRODUCTIONS**, 125 Fieldpoint Road, Greenwich CT 06830. (203)661-1615. E-mail: easywayric@aol.com. President: Rick Martin. Personal manager and independent producer. Holds the Office of Secretary of the National Conference of Personal Managers. Represents actresses and vocalists; currently handles 2 acts. Receives 15-25% commission. "Occasionally, we are hired as consultants, production assistants or producers of recording projects."
How to Contact: Write first and obtain permission to submit. SASE.
Music: Mostly **top 40, dance** and **easy listening**. Does not want rock or folk music. Produces vocal groups and female vocalists. Current acts include Marisa Mercedes (vocalist/pianist/songwriter) and Rob and Steve (songwriters/vocalists).
Tips: "The tape does not have to be professionally produced—it's really not important what you've done—it's what you can do now that counts."

🔘 **PHIL MAYO & COMPANY**, P.O. Box 304, Bomoseen VT 05732. (802)468-5011. E-mail: pmcamgp hil@aol.com. President: Phil Mayo. Management firm and record company (AMG Records). Estab. 1981. Represents individual artists, groups and songwriters from anywhere; currently handles 4 acts. Receives 20% commission. Reviews material for acts.
How to Contact: Submit demo tape by mail. Unsolicited submissions are OK. Prefers cassette and/or CD with 3 songs and lyric or lead sheet. If seeking management, include bio, photo and lyric sheet in press kit. Does not return material. Reports in 1-2 months.
Music: Mostly **rock, pop** and **country**; also **blues** and **Christian pop**. Works primarily with dance bands, vocalists and rock acts. Current acts include The Drive (R&B), Athena and Blind Date.

🔘 **MAZUR PUBLIC RELATIONS**, P.O. Box 360, E. Windsor NJ 08520. (609)426-1277. Fax: (609)426-1217. E-mail: mazurpr@aol.com. Website: http://www.mazurpr.com. Contact: Michael Mazur. Management and PR firm. Estab. 1987. Represents groups from anywhere; currently handles 12 acts. Commission varies. Reviews material for acts.
How to Contact: Submit demo tape by mail. Unsolicited submissions are OK. Prefers cassette, CD or VHS videocassette with 2 songs. If seeking management, press kit should include CD/cassette, photo, bio and video. SASE. "We try to reply." Reports in 1 month.
Music: Current acts include Bruce Dickinson (rock legend), Paul Plumery (blues, guitarist and vocalist) and The O.C. Supertones (ska).

🔘 **THE McDONNELL GROUP**, 27 Pickwick Lane, Newtown Square PA 19073. (610)353-8554. E-mail: fmcdonn@concentric.net. Contact: Frank McDonnell. Management firm. Estab. 1985. Represents individual artists, groups and songwriters from anywhere; currently handles 6 acts. Receives 20% commission. Reviews material for acts.
How to Contact: Write first and obtain permission to submit. Prefers cassette or VHS videocassette with 4 songs and lyric sheet. If seeking management, include cover letter, lyric sheets, press, tape or video, recent photos and bio. SASE. Reports in 1 month.
Music: Mostly **rock, pop** and **R&B**; also **country** and **jazz**. Current acts include Johnny Bronco (rock group), Mike Forte (producer/songwriter) and Pat Martino (jazz guitarist).

🔘 **MEGA MUSIC PRODUCTIONS**, 1108 Pine St., New Orleans LA 70118. Phone/fax: (504)862-6623. E-mail: megamusic1@aol.com. General Manager: Marco Vinicio Carvajal. Management firm and booking agency. Represents individual artists and groups from anywhere; currently handles 10 acts. Receives 15% commission. Reviews material for acts.
How to Contact: Submit demo tape by mail. Unsolicited submissions are OK. Prefers cassette, CD or VHS videocassette with 5 songs and lyric sheet. If seeking management, press kit should include cover letter, demo tape/CD, video, photos and bio. Does not return material. Reports in 1 month.
Music: Mostly **rock, techno-dance** and **Latin rock**; also **Latin** and **pop**. Works primarily with bands and singers. Current acts include David Summers & Hombres G (Latin pop), The Sacados (pop/Latin) and Enanitos Verdes (Latin).
Tips: "Send us compact information and describe your goals."

🔲 ✅ 🔘 **MERLIN MANAGEMENT CORP.**, P.O. Box 5087 V.M.P.O., Vancouver, British Columbia V6B 4A9 Canada. Phone/fax: (604)434-9129. E-mail: zauber311@aol.com. President: Wolfgang Hamman. Management firm, record company (Merlin) and record producer. Estab. 1979. Represents individual artists, groups, songwriters and producers from anywhere; currently handles 3 acts. Receives 20-25% commission. Reviews material for acts.
How to Contact: Write or call first and obtain permission to submit. Prefers cassette with 3 songs and

lyric and/or lead sheet. If seeking management, press kit should include photo, demo tape/CD, cover letter and bio. SASE. Reports in 2 weeks.

Music: Mostly **modern rock, dance** and **pop**; also **techno** and **alternative**. Current acts include The Defaids (modern rock), Wolfgang-Wolfgang (dance) and Xenobia (dance/R&B).

Tips: "Write daily, study successful writers."

✓ ○ **MERRI-WEBB PRODUCTIONS**, P.O. Box 5474, Stockton CA 95205. (209)948-8186. E-mail: merri-webb@calcentron.com. Contact: Kristy Ledford. Management firm, music publisher (Kaupp's & Robert Publishing Co./BMI) and record company (Kaupp Records). Represents regional (California) individual artists, groups and songwriters; currently handles 10 acts. Receives 10-15% commission. Reviews material for acts.

How to Contact: Write first and obtain permission to submit or to arrange personal interview. Prefers cassette or VHS videocassette with 3 songs maximum and lyric sheet. SASE. Reports in 3 months.

Music: Mostly **country, A/C rock** and **R&B**; also **pop, rock** and **gospel**. Works primarily with vocalists, bands and songwriters. Current acts include Bruce Bolin (rock/pop singer), Nanci Lynn (country/pop singer) and Rick Weber (country/pop singer).

🅽 ○ **METRO TALENT GROUP, INC.**, 3179 Maple Dr., Suite 29, Atlanta GA 30305. (404)237-9999. Fax: (404)237-4422. E-mail: brad@metrotalentgroup.com. Website: http://www.metrotalentgroup.c om. Booking Agent/Scout: Brad Broadrick. Booking agency. Represents individual artists and groups; currently handles 12 acts. Receives 10-15% commission. Reviews material for acts.

How to Contact: Write or call first and obtain permission to submit a demo. Prefers cassette or CD. Include clubs/venues played, guarantees for each show and who you've opened for. Does not return material. Reports in 2 weeks.

Music: Mostly **rock/alternative, blues** and **jazz**; also acoustic. Current acts include Edwin McCain fu(pop singer), Kevn Kinney (folk singer) and Warren Haynes (rock).

○ **MIDCOAST, INC.**, 1002 Jones Rd., Hendersonville TN 37075. (615)264-3896. E-mail: mid-coix@n etcom.com. Managing Director: Bruce Andrew Bossert. Management firm and music publisher (MidCoast, Inc./BMI). Estab. 1984. Represents individual artists, groups and songwriters; currently handles 2 acts. Reviews material for acts.

How to Contact: Submit demo tape by mail. Unsolicited submissions are OK. Prefers cassette, VHS videocassette or DAT with 2-4 songs and lyric sheet. If seeking management, press kit should include cover letter, "short" bio, tape, video, photo, press clippings and announcements of any performances in Nashville area. Does not return material. Reports in 6 weeks if interested.

Music: Mostly **rock, pop** and **country**. Works primarily with original rock and country bands and artists. Current acts include Room 101 (alternative rock).

✓ ○ **THOMAS J. MILLER & COMPANY**, 1802 Laurel Canyon Blvd., Los Angeles CA 90046. (323)656-7212. Fax: (323)656-7757. Artist Relations: Karen Deming. Management firm, music publisher and record company (Wilshire Park Records). Estab. 1975. Represents individual artists, groups and songwriters from anywhere; currently handles 12 acts. Reviews material for acts.

How to Contact: Submit demo tape by mail. Unsolicited submissions are OK. Prefers cassette or NTSC videocassette and lyric sheet. If seeking management, press kit should include photos, bio and video. Does not return material. Reports in 2-3 weeks.

Music: Mostly **rock, pop** and **jazz**; also **stage** and **country**. Current acts include Manowar.

○ **MONOPOLY MANAGEMENT**, 162 N. Milford, Highland MI 48357. E-mail: godzilli@aol.com. Vice President: Bob Zilli. Management firm. Estab. 1984. Represents songwriters from anywhere; currently handles 2 acts. Receives 10% commission. Reviews material for acts.

How to Contact: Submit demo tape by mail. Unsolicited submissions are OK. Prefers cassette or VHS videocassette with 4 songs and lyric sheet. If seeking management, press kit should include tape, photo, cover letter and résumé of live performances. SASE. Reports in 1 month.

Music: Mostly **country, alternative** and **top 40**. Works primarily with singer/songwriters. Current acts include Robert Richmond (songwriter) and The Nashville Sound.

REFER TO THE CATEGORY INDEX (at the end of this section) to find exactly which companies are interested in the type of music you write.

GARY F. MONTGOMERY MANAGEMENT, P.O. Box 5106, Macon GA 31208. (912)749-7259. Fax: (912)757-0002. E-mail: gfmmusic@mindspring.com. President: Gary F. Montgomery. Management firm, music publisher (g.f.m. Music/ASCAP and 12/31/49 Music/BMI) and production company. Estab. 1981. Represents individual artists, groups, songwriters, record producers and engineers; currently handles several acts. Receives 10-25% commission (it varies depending on the act). Reviews material for acts.
How to Contact: Write or call first and obtain permission to submit a demo. Prefers cassette with 3-5 songs and lyric sheet. If seeking management, press kit should include cover letter, bio, résumé, photo, demo tape/CD, lyric sheets, press clippings and video. "Call first to see if we are accepting new clients." Does not return material. Reports in 2 months only if interested.
Music: All types. Works primarily with singer/songwriters. Current acts include Otis Redding III (rock/ soul), Jerome "Bigfoot" Brailey (drummer/songwriter/funk) and Truckadelic (rock).

MUSIC MAN PROMOTIONS, P.O. Box 956, South Perth 6951 Australia. Phone: (618)9474 2300. Fax: (618)9474 1779. E-mail: mmp@global.net.au. Website: http://www.global.net.au/~mmp/. Executive Director: Eddie Robertson. Booking agency. Estab. 1991. Represents individual artists and/or groups; currently handles 100 acts. Receives 20% commission. Reviews material for acts.
How to Contact: Write first and obtain permission to submit or submit demo tape by mail. Unsolicited submissions are OK. Prefers cassette or videocassette with photo, information on style and bio. If seeking management, press kit should include photos, bio, cover letter, résumé, press clippings, video, demo, lyric sheets and any other useful information. Does not return material. Reports in 1 month.
Music: Mostly **top 40/pop, jazz** and **'60s-'90s punk**; also **reggae** and **blues**. Works primarily with show bands and solo performers. Current acts include Faces (dance band), N.R.G. (show band) and Key Largo (duo).
Tips: "Send as much information as possible. If you do not receive a call after four to five weeks, follow up with letter or phone call."

NASH-ONE MANAGEMENT, INC., 4555 Hickory Ridge Rd., Lebanon TN 37087. (615)449-7818. Fax: (615)443-3218. E-mail: bquisenb@bellsouth.net. President: Bill Quisenberry. Management firm and booking agency (Talent Group Intercontinental, Inc.). Estab. 1990. Represents local individual artists and groups; currently handles 1 act. Receives 5% commission. Reviews material for acts.
How to Contact: Call first and obtain permission to submit. Prefers cassette. If seeking management, press kit should include photo, cover letter, bio and 4-song tape. SASE. Reports in 2 weeks.
Music: Mostly **country** and **some rock**.

LOU NELSON PROMOTIONS & MANAGEMENT CO., P.O. Box 18943, Austin TX 78760. (512)268-0169. Fax: (512)268-1200. E-mail: lnpm@aol.com. Owner: Lou Nelson. Manager: Rose Mesa. Management firm and music promoter. Estab. 1995. Represents individual artists, groups and songwriters from anywhere; currently handles 2 acts. Receives 20% commission. Reviews material for acts.
How to Contact: Submit demo tape by mail. Unsolicited submissions are OK. Prefers cassette or VHS videocassette with 5 songs and lyric sheet. If seeking management, press kit should include CD, bio, 8×10 photo, press releases, last management company name, record company name/publisher name. If first time seeking management, please state so in writing. Does not return material. Reports in 6 weeks.
Music: Mostly **country, R&B** and **blues**; also **country gospel, jazz** and **rock**. Works primarily with bands, groups and songwriters. Current acts include Patty David (country/R&B), Sonny Christopher (songwriter) and Laura Bellomy (jazz).
Tips: "Be honest, hard working and open to suggestions. Also be willing to work with other songwriters."

NIK ENTERTAINMENT COMPANY, 274 N. Goodman St., Rochester NY 14607. (716)244-0331. Fax: (716)244-0356. E-mail: nikniceguy@aol.com. General Manager/President: Gary Webb. Management firm and booking agency. Estab. 1988. Represents groups from anywhere; currently handles 7 acts. Receives 15% commission. Reviews material for acts.
How to Contact: Submit demo tape by mail. Unsolicited submissions are OK. Prefers cassette or VHS videocassette with lyric or lead sheet. If seeking management, press kit should include photo, bio and demo tape. Does not return material. Reports in 3 weeks.
Music: Mostly **mainstream rock** and **pop**. Works primarily with bands. Current acts include Nik and the Nice Guys (pop show band), The Shag-adelics ('60s meets '90s) and The Bug Zapper (swing).

NORTHERN LIGHTS MANAGEMENT, 437 Live Oak Loop NE, Albuquerque NM 87122-1406. (505)856-7100. Fax: (505)856-2566. E-mail: nlightsmgt@aol.com. Website: http://www.super-charged.

com/nlightsmgt. Owner/Manager: Linda Bolton. Booking agency. Estab. 1989. Represents individual artists, groups and songwriters from anywhere; currently handles 4 acts. Receives 10-15% commission.
How to Contact: Write or call first and obtain permission to submit. Prefers cassette or CD with 3-4 songs and lyric sheet. "Please specify which artist the song(s) should be submitted to." Does not return material. Reporting time varies.
Music: Mostly **bluegrass** and **folk**. Works primarily with 1 "newgrass" band and 3 singer/songwriters. Current acts include Jonathan Edwards (folk/pop/rock singer), Dave Mallett (Maine singer/songwriter), Northern Lights (bluegrass/newgrass band) and Lisa McCormick (contemporary folk rock singer).

N ☉ NOTEWORTHY ENTERPRISES, 3741 Sunny Isles Blvd., N. Miami Beach FL 33160. (305)949-9192. Fax: (305)949-9492. E-mail: ss@noteworthy.net. Website: http://www.Noteworthy.net. President: Sheila Siegel. Booking agency, music publisher (On the Water Publications/BMI) and talent buyer. Estab. 1987. Represents individual artists, groups and songwriters from anywhere. Reviews material for acts.
How to Contact: Write first and obtain permission to submit. If seeking management, press kit should include photos, press clippings and bio. Does not return material.
Music: Mostly **big band**. Works primarily with jazz artists. Current acts include Noteworthy Orchestra (big band), Southlanders Traditional Jazz Band, David Siegel and Jack Siegel.

☉ NOTEWORTHY PRODUCTIONS, 124½ Archwood Ave., Annapolis MD 21401. (410)268-8232. Fax: (410)268-2167. E-mail: mcshane@songs.com. President: McShane Glover. Management firm and booking agency. Estab. 1985. Represents individual artists, groups and songwriters from everywhere; currently handles 6 acts. Reviews material for acts.
How to Contact: Write first and obtain permission to submit. Prefers cassette with lyric sheet. If seeking management, press kit should include cassette or CD, photo, bio, venues played and press clippings (preferably reviews). "Follow up with a phone call 3-5 weeks after submission." Does not return material. Reports in 3-4 weeks.
Music: Mostly **country**, **folk**, and **bluegrass**; also **pop**. Works primarily with performing singer/songwriters. Current acts include Seamus Kennedy (Celtic/contemporary), Debi Smith (contemporary acoustic) and Hot Soup! (swing harmony).

☉ ON STAGE MANAGEMENT, P.O. Box 679, Bronx NY 10469. (718)798-6980. E-mail: onstagemgt @aol.com. President: Paul M. Carigliano. Management firm and production. Estab. 1988. Represents individual artists and/or groups and songwriters from anywhere; currently handles 6 acts. Receives 15-20% commission. Reviews material for acts.
How to Contact: Write or call first for permission to submit. Prefers cassette or VHS videocassette with at least 2 songs, "the more the better." If seeking management, press kit should include cassette or VHS video tape, picture and bio. Does not return material. Reports in 2 weeks.
Music: Mostly **dance music**, **rock**, and **pop**; also **R&B**. Current acts include Choir of the Damned (rock group), Luna Eclipse (ambient dance) and Destiny (dance music).
Tips: "Our artists sing songs with positive messages. We don't want songs that glorify violence or are too risqué."

✔ ☉ ON THE LEVEL MUSIC!, P.O. Box 508, Owego NY 13827. CEO/President: Fred Gage. Management firm, booking agency and music publisher (On The Level Music! Publishing). Estab. 1970. Represents individual artists, groups and songwriters from anywhere; currently handles 15 acts. Receives 15% commission. Reviews material for acts.
How to Contact: Submit demo tape by mail. Unsolicited submissions are OK. Prefers cassette, DAT or VHS videocassette with 4 songs and lyric or lead sheet. If seeking management, press kit should include cover letter, bio, demo tape/CD, lyric sheets, press clippings, 8×10 photo and video. Does not return material. Reports in 1 month.
Music: Mostly **rock**, **alternative** and **jazz**. Current acts include Jane & Joy (alternative), Reynolds and Chase (rock).

N ☉ ORIGINAL ARTISTS' AGENCY, 1031 E. Battlefield Rd., Suite 224, Springfield MO 65807. (417)881-4174. Fax: (417)227-9404. Manager: James R. Doran. Management firm and booking agency. Estab. 1984. Represents individual artists, groups and songwriters from anywhere; currently handles 7 acts. Commission varies. Reviews materials for acts.
How to Contact: Submit demo tape by mail. Unsolicited submissions are OK. Prefers cassette. If seeking management, press kit should include demo tape, picture and bio. Does not return material.
Music: Mostly **country**, **blues** and **rock**. Works primarily with individual artists and bands. Current acts

include Ray Price (country artist), Johnny Paycheck (country artist) and Ozark Jubilee (country show).
Tips: "Please submit initial demo with your three top songs. We can go from there."

◐ **OUTLAND PRODUCTIONS**, 8511 Hurst Ave., Savannah GA 31406-6013. Phone/fax: (912)925-3205. Producer/Manager: John R. Brookshire. Management firm, record company (Outland Records) and record producer (John R. Brookshire). Estab. 1973. Represents individual artists and groups from anywhere; currently handles 4 acts. Receives 15% commission. Reviews material for acts.
How to Contact: Submit demo tape by mail. Unsolicited submissions are OK. Prefers cassette, videocassette or CD with 5 songs and lead sheet. If seeking management, press kit should include cover letter, demo tape/CD, lyric sheets, press clippings, résumé, bio and pictures or video. Does not return material. Reports in 8-10 weeks.
Music: Mostly **hard rock**, **heavy metal** and **hardcore**; also **punk rock**, **death metal** and **death black metal**. Works primarily with all metal bands. Current acts include Sickness (death metal), Requiem (hardcore trush) and Fist (death metal).

◆ ○ **OUTLAW ENTERTAINMENT INTERNATIONAL**, #101-1001 W. Broadway, Dept. 400, Vancouver, British Columbia V6H 4E4 Canada. (604)878-1494. Fax: (604)878-1495. E-mail: outlaw@istar.ca. Website: http://home.istar.ca/~outlaw. CEO/President: Tommy Floyd. Management firm. Estab. 1995. Represents individual artists, groups and songwriters from anywhere; currently handles 3 acts. Receives 20% commission. Reviews material for acts.
How to Contact: Submit demo tape by mail. Unsolicited submissions are OK. Prefers cassette with 2-3 songs and lyric sheet. If seeking management, press kit should include 8×10 photo, bio and written statement of goals. SAE and IRC. Reports in 1 month.
Music: Mostly **rock**, **metal** and **goth**; also **pop** and **dance**. Works primarily with bands, "but starting more towards singer/songwriters." Current acts include The Cartels (punk rock act), Bates Motel (goth rock act) and Shovel Head (heavy metal act).
Tips: "Clearly define your target market. Write simple, emotional, primal songs."

▣ ○ **TOMMY OVERSTREET MUSIC COMPANIES**, P.O. Box 14073, Springfield MO 65814-0073. (417)889-8080. Fax: (417)889-8090. Contact: Diane Elverud. Management firm, booking agency (On Stage Productions), recording studio, music publisher (Tommy Overstreet Music/BMI) and record company (De Ja Vu Records and Ram Records). Estab. 1969. Represents individual artists, groups and songwriters from anywhere; currently handles 3 acts. Receives 15% commission. Reviews material for acts.
How to Contact: Submit demo tape by mail. Unsolicited submissions are OK. Prefers cassette with 3 songs and lyric sheet. If seeking management, press kit should include pictures (8×10 or 5×7), short biography, tape (no more than 5 songs), lyric sheets and any information that might be helpful in promotion of the act. Does not return material. Reports "as soon as it's reasonably possible."
Music: Mostly **country** and **gospel**; also **light rock**. Current acts include Tommy Overstreet (established "classic country" artist), Scot Williams (country singer) and Eric Neznick (new young country/pop artist).

◑ **PERFORMERS OF THE WORLD INC. (P.O.W.)**, 8901 Melrose Ave., 2nd Floor, Los Angeles CA 90069-5605. E-mail: pow-stp@ix.netcom.com. President: Terry Rindal. Agents: Nita Scott, Bruce Eisenberg, Trip Brown. Booking agency. Estab. 1987. Represents individual artists and groups from anywhere; currently handles 50 acts. Receives 10-15% commission.
How to Contact: Write or call first and obtain permission to submit. Prefers cassette or VHS videocassette with several songs and lyric sheet. If seeking management, press kit should include cover letter, photo, bio, press clippings, demo tape/CD and video. Does not return material. Reports in 1 month (depends on quality).
Music: Mostly **rock**, **world music**, **alternative**, **jazz**, **R&B**, **folk** and **pop**. Current acts include Herbie Hancock (jazz legend), Joe Sample (jazz legend), Karla Bonoff (singer/songwriter) and John Cale.
Tips: "Don't harrass us after you submit. We are looking for artistry and quality—if you're not really prepared please don't waste your time (or ours)."

◆ ○ **PHIL'S ENTERTAINMENT AGENCY LIMITED**, 889 Smyth Rd., Ottawa Ontario K1G 1P4 Canada. (613)731-8983. President: Phyllis Woodstock. Booking agency. Estab. 1979. Represents artists and groups; currently handles 50 acts. Receives 10-15% commission.
How to Contact: "We are not accepting submissions at this time." Does not return material.
Music: Mostly **country**; also **country/rock**, **MOR jazz**, **Dixieland** and **old rock 'n' roll**. "We work with show bands, male and female vocalists, bar bands and dance bands on a regular basis." Current acts include

Elvis Aaron Presley Jr., Crystal Creek (new country/light rock) and Eddy & The Stingrays ('50s and '60s dance band).

Tips: "Be professional and business-like. Keep agency supplied with up-to-date promo material and develop entertainment ability. Videotape your live performance, then give yourself an honest review."

GORDON POOLE AGENCY LIMITED, The Limes, Brockley, Bristol BS48 3BB England. Phone: (1275)463222. Fax: (1275)462252. E-mail: gpents@aol.com. Managing Director: Gordon Poole. Booking agency. Estab. 1963. Represents individual artists and groups from anywhere; currently handles 100 acts. Receives 15-25% commission. Reviews material for acts.

How to Contact: Submit demo tape by mail. Unsolicited submissions are OK. Prefers cassette or videocassette and lyric sheet. If seeking management, press kit should include cv, tape/CD, cover letter, bio, photo, press clippings and video. SAE and IRC. Reports in 1 month.

Music: Mostly **MOR**. Works primarily with bands. Current acts include Fred Wedlock (composer/singer).

POWERPLAY ENTERTAINMENT, P.O. Box 243, Greenlawn NY 11740-0243. (516)271-4694. Fax: (516)271-4759. President: Theodore M. Weiner. Management firm and booking agency. Estab. 1996. Represents individual artists, groups and songwriters from anywhere; currently handles 10 acts. Receives 15-20% commission. Reviews material for acts.

How to Contact: Submit demo tape by mail. Unsolicited submissions are OK. Prefers cassette or videocassette with 3-5 songs and lyric sheet. If seeking management, press kit should include cover letter, demo tape/CD, video, photo, bio, résumé and ambitions. SASE. Reports in 2 weeks.

Music: Mostly **soul/R&B**, **pop/rock** and **all types**. Works primarily with singers, songwriters, bands, TV and media. Current acts include Freda Payne, The Miracles (Motown R&B), Billy Preston (pop/soul) and Billy J. Kramer (pop/rock).

Tips: "We are looking for talent plus persistence and the ability to follow direction. Stay focused. Never lose sight of your goals. Work hard and then harder. Our personal approach limits the amount of acts we can take on."

PRAIRIE FIRE MUSIC COMPANY, 2317 S. Pleasant Valley #716, Austin TX 78741-4657. (512)447-1650. President: Chris Stout. Management firm, booking agency, music publisher (Wild Prairie Publishing/BMI), record company (Prairie Fire Records) and record producer (Chris Stout). Estab. 1991. Represents midwest and southwest individual artists, groups and songwriters; currently handles 3 acts. Receives 15% commission. Reviews material for acts.

How to Contact: Submit demo tape by mail. Unsolicited submissions are OK. Prefers cassette with 3-15 songs and lyric and/or lead sheet. If seeking management, press kit should include bio, press releases, promotional materials, photograph, video and cassette/CD. Does not return material. Reports in 6 months.

Music: Mostly **country**, **alternative** and **rock**; also **folk**, **New Age** and **crossover**. Works primarily with singer/songwriters and bands. Current acts include Cosmic Cactus (roots/alternative/country band), Matt Pollock (original folk/country/blues singer/songwriter) and Duane Woner (original folk/rock singer/songwriter, bass guitarist).

Tips: "We consider all materials submitted. Don't be afraid to submit a low quality demo. Let us decide."

PRECISION MANAGEMENT, 2143-B Coliseum Dr., Suite 158, Hampton VA 23666-5902. Phone/fax: (757)875-0323. E-mail: pmmuzic@aol.com. Operations Director: Cappriccieo Scates. Management firm and music publisher (Mytrell/BMI). Estab. 1990. Represents individual artists and/or groups and songwriters from anywhere; currently handles 2 acts. Receives 20% commission. Reviews material for acts.

How to Contact: Submit demo tape by mail. Unsolicited submissions are OK. Prefers cassette or VHS videocassette with 3-4 songs and lyric sheet. If seeking management, press kit should include photo, bio, demo tape/CD, lyric sheets, press clippings and all relevant press information. SASE. Reports in 4-6 weeks.

Music: Mostly **R&B**, **rap** and **gospel**; also **all types**. Current acts include Surface (R&B act) and Joe'I Chancellor (rap artist).

PRESTIGE ARTISTES, "Foxhollow," West End, Nailsea Bristol BS19 2DB United Kingdom. E-mail: drees15066@aol.com. Proprietor: David Rees. Management firm and booking agency. Asso-

ciate company: Lintern Rees Organisation. Estab. 1983. Represents individual artists, groups, songwriters, comedians and specialty acts; currently handles 20 acts. Receives 10-15% commission. Reviews material for acts.
How to Contact: Submit demo tape by mail. Unsolicited submissions are OK. Prefers cassette with 3 songs and lyric sheet. If seeking management, press kit should include good demo tape, cover letter, any references, bio, press clippings, publicity photos and video if available (UK format). Artist should be based in the UK. Does not return material. Reports in 1 month.
Music: Mostly **MOR**, **pop**, **'60s style**, **country** and **rock**. Works primarily with vocal guitarists/keyboards, pop groups, pub/club acts and guitar or keyboard duos. Current acts include Legend (duo), Ocean (four-piece group), Elvis Presley Junior (vocalist), Steve James (keyboard/vocalist) and Ryan Turner (keyboard/vocalist).
Tips: "Do not send more than three songs, your best available. Tell us what you want in the UK—be realistic."

PRICECLUB PRODUCTIONS, 484 Lake Park Ave. #32, Oakland CA 94610. (510)834-0325. Fax: (510)834-3302. E-mail: music@melodia.com. Website: http://www.melodia.com. Director: Scott Price. Management firm, record company and record producer (Scott Price). Estab. 1995. Represents individual artists and groups from anywhere; currently handles 3 acts. Receives 20% commission. Reviews material for acts.
How to Contact: Submit demo tape by mail. Unsolicited submissions are OK. Prefers cassette, DAT or VHS videocassette with 5 songs and lyric sheet. If seeking management, press kit should include cover letter, bio, photo, demo tape/CD, press clippings, video and résumé. Does not return material. Reports in 2 months.
Music: Mostly **jazz**, **Latin** and **pop**. Works primarily with individual artists/groups. Current acts include Omar Sosa (Cuban pianist), Madhouse (jazz quartet) and Omar Sosa and John Santos (Latin duo).

PRO TALENT CONSULTANTS, P.O. Box 233, Nice CA 95464. (707)998-3587 or (707)274-2625. Coordinator: John Eckert. Management firm and booking agency. Estab. 1979. Represents individual artists and groups; currently handles 7 acts. Receives 20% commission. Reviews material for acts.
How to Contact: Submit demo tape by mail. Unsolicited submissions are OK. Prefers cassette or VHS videocassette with at least 4 songs and lyric sheet. "We prefer audio cassette (4 songs). Submit videocassette with live performance only." If seeking management, press kit should include an 8×10 photo, a cassette or CD of at least 4-6 songs, a bio on group/artist, references, cover letter, press clippings, video and business card or a phone number with address. Does not return material. Reports in 5 weeks.
Music: Mostly **country**, **country/pop** and **rock**. Works primarily with vocalists, show bands, dance bands and bar bands. Current acts include Jon Richards (country singer), The Leaders of the Rockin' '60s (variety show, various performers) and Jewel Akens (pop singer).

PROFESSIONAL ARTIST MANAGEMENT, LTD., P.O. Box 755, Shelburne VT 05482. (800)610-7625. Fax: (888)610-7625. E-mail: hughestj@together.net. Website: http://www.rockandrollacou ntant.com. General Manager: Tom Hughes. Management firm. Estab. 1994. Represents Northeast, New York and California individual artists and groups; currently handles 10 acts. Receives 10-15% commission. Reviews material for acts.
How to Contact: Submit demo tape by mail. Unsolicited submissions are OK. Prefers cassette, DAT, mini disc or CD with 4 or more songs. If seeking management, press kit should include cover letter, bio, demo tape/CD, any commercial releases, reviews and airplay. Does not return material. Reports in 6-8 weeks.
Music: Mostly **alternative metal** and **acoustic blues/folk**.

RADIOACTIVE, 350 Third Ave., Suite 400, New York NY 10010. (516)445-9595. E-mail: radiotv@aol.com. Website: http://radiotv.com. Agent: Kenjamin Franklin. Booking and talent agency. Estab. 1983. Represents individual artists, groups and broadcasters from anywhere; currently handles 20 acts. Receives 10% commission. Reviews material for acts.
How to Contact: Submit demo tape by mail. Unsolicited submissions are OK. "Please do not phone." Prefers cassette or video with 3 songs and lyric sheet. If seeking management, press kit should include bio, press clippings, photo, cover letter, résumé, video, e-mail and 3 radio-friendly original songs on cassettes/CD. "Label all cassettes with phone number." Does not return material. Reports in 3 weeks. "We only call upon further interest."
Music: Mostly **modern rock**, **ballads** and **AAA**; also **A/C** and **CHR/pop**. Current acts include Ambrosia, Les Lo Key (alternative) and Jim Lawson (adult contemporary).

RAINBOW COLLECTION LTD., 4696 Kahlua Lane, Bonita Springs FL 34134. (941)947-6978. Executive Producer: Richard (Dick) O'Bitts. Management firm, record company (Happy Man Records) and music publisher (Rocker Music and Happy Man Music). Represents individual artists, groups, songwriters and producers; currently handles 6 acts. Receives 10-20% commission. Reviews material for acts.
How to Contact: Submit demo tape by mail. Unsolicited submissions are OK. Prefers cassette or VHS videocassette of live performance with 4 songs and lyric sheet. If seeking management, press kit should include photos, bio and tapes. SASE. Reports in 1 month.
Music: Mostly **country**, **pop** and **rock**. Works primarily with writer/artists and groups of all kinds. Current acts include The Challengers (country pop), Jenny Wallace (gospel/pop) and Head Soup (rock band).

RENAISSANCE ENTERTAINMENT GROUP, P.O. Box 1222, Mountainside NJ 07092-1222. Director: Kevin A. Joy. Management firm, booking agency, record company (Suburan Records) and record producer (Onyx Music and Bo^{2}Legg Productions). Estab. 1992. Represents individual artists, groups and songwriters from anywhere; currently handles 20 acts. Receives 20% commission. Reviews material for acts.
How to Contact: Write first and obtain permission to submit. Prefers cassette with 3 songs and lyric or lead sheet. If seeking management, press kit should include cover letter, demo tape/CD, lyric sheets, press clippings, pictures and bio. Does not return material. Reports in 5 weeks.
Music: Mostly **R&B**, **rap** and **rock**. Works primarily with R&B groups, rap and vocalists. Current acts include Hillside Strangler (rap), Lori Stephens (R&B/pop) and A Mother's Child (rock).

JOEY RICCA, JR.'S ENTERTAINMENT AGENCY, 408 S. Main St., Milltown NJ 08850. (201)287-1230. Owner/President: Joseph Frank Ricca, Jr. Management firm and booking agency. Estab. 1985. Represents individual artists, groups and songwriters; currently handles 75-80 acts. Receives 15% commission. Reviews material for acts.
How to Contact: Submit demo tape by mail. Unsolicited submissions are OK. "We prefer that all material be copyrighted and that a letter be sent right before submitting material, but neither of these is essential." Prefers cassette or videocassette with 3-4 songs and lyric or lead sheets. If seeking management, press kit should include cover letter, résumé, tape (cassette, CD or video) 8×10 promo photo, bios, lead and lyric sheets and photocopy of news clippings of performances. SASE. Reports in 6-8 weeks.
Music: Mostly **love songs/ballads**, **songs for big band vocalists**, and **soft jazz/Latin**; also **good commercial material**. Works with show bands, dance bands and bar bands. Current acts include Stewart Ward, Donny "Z" and Angela Murcurri.
Tips: "Good lyrics and strong musical arrangements are essential if our vocalists are to select a song they would like to sing. I look for good love songs, ballads and Broadway play type compositions. No metal."

N **DIANE RICHARDS WORLD MANAGEMENT, INC.**, 530 Manhattan Ave., New York NY 10027. Phone/fax: (212)678-6746. E-mail: drworldmgm@aol.com. President: Diane Richards. Management firm. Estab. 1994. Represents individual artists, groups, songwriters and producers from anywhere; currently handles 8 acts. Receives 20% commission. Reviews material for acts.
How to Contact: Write first and obtain permission to submit. If seeking management, press kit should include cover letter, photograph, biography, cassette tape, telephone number and address. Does not return material. Reports in 1 month.
Music: Mostly **dance**, **pop** and **rap**; also **New Age**, **A/C** and **jazz**. Works primarily with pop and dance acts, and songwriters who also are recording artists. Current acts include Sappho (songwriter/artist), Menace (songwriter/producer/artist) and Babygirl (R&B/rap artist).

RIGHT-ON MANAGEMENT, P.O. Box 2627, Dearborn MI 48123. (313)274-7000. E-mail: nstarangel@aol.com. President: Angel Gomez. Management firm. Estab. 1979. Represents local and international individual artists, groups and songwriters; currently handles 9 acts. Receives 15-20% commission. Reviews material for acts.
How to Contact: Write first and obtain permission to submit. Prefers cassette or videocassette of performance with 3-5 songs. If seeking management, include photo, tape/CD, bio, cover letter, press clippings and itinerary of dates. Does not return material. Reports in 6-8 weeks.
Music: Mostly **rock**, **pop** and **top 40**; also **funk**. Works primarily with individual artists, groups (bar

---

THE OPENNESS TO SUBMISSIONS INDEX at the back of this book lists all companies in this section by how open they are to submissions.

bands) and songwriters. Current artists include Q (modern rock), The Rev. Right Time and the First Cuzins of Funk ('90s funk) and Greg Isles (alternative rock).

◉ RIOHCAT MUSIC, P.O. Box 764, Hendersonville TN 37077-0764. (615)824-9313. E-mail: tachoir @cris.com. Website: http://www.cris.com/~tachoir. Contact: Robert Kayne. Management firm, booking agency, record company (Avita Records) and music publisher. Estab. 1975. Represents individual artists and groups; currently handles 4 acts. Receives 20% commission.
How to Contact: Submit demo tape by mail. Unsolicited submissions are OK. Prefers cassette and lead sheet. If seeking management, press kit should include cover letter, bio, photo, demo tape/CD and press clippings. Does not return material. Reports in 6 weeks.
Music: Mostly **contemporary jazz** and **fusion**. Works primarily with jazz ensembles. Current acts include Group Tachoir (jazz), Tachoir/Manakas Duo (jazz) and Jerry Tachoir (solo vibraphone).

N ⊕ ◯ ROCK 'N' ROLL MANAGEMENT, Studio 2, Prospect Quay (108), Point Pleasant, London 8W18 1PR England. Phone: (00)44+1815166403. Fax: (00)44+1815161773. E-mail: rocknroll@mail.cy base.co.uk. Managers: Robert Swerdlow and David Nicoll. Management firm. Represents groups from anywhere; currently handles 5 acts. Reviews material for acts.
How to Contact: Submit demo tape by mail. Unsolicited submissions are OK. Prefers cassette. If seeking management, press kit should include cover letter, band history/biography, photo, demo tape, contact details (phone, etc.). SAE and IRC.
Music: Mostly **rock/pop** and **dance**. Works primarily with bands and 1 singer/songwriter. Current acts include Cast (4 members, band, rock/pop), Mansun (4 members, band, rock) and Manna (5 member rock band).

◯ ROCK OF AGES PRODUCTIONS, 517 Northlake Blvd. #4, N. Palm Beach FL 33408. (561)848-1500. Fax: (561)848-2400. President/Agency Director: Joseph E. Larson. Booking agent, literary agency and publisher. Estab. 1980. Represents individual artists and groups from anywhere; currently handles 500 acts. Receives 15-25% commission. Reviews material for acts.
How to Contact: Submit demo tape by mail. Unsolicited submissions are OK. Prefers cassette or VHS videocassette with 3 or more songs and lead sheet. If seeking management, press kit should include video-cassette and/or audio cassette, lyric sheets, relevant press, bio, cover letter, résumé and recent photo. SASE. Reports in 3 months.
Music: Mostly **top 40**, **country/western** and **rock**; also **gospel** and **opera**. Works primarily with bands, singers, singer/songwriters. Current acts include Andrew Epps (ballad singer/songwriter), John Michael Ferrari (singer/songwriter) and Paola Semprini (opera star).

N ◯ ROCK WHIRLED MUSIC MANAGEMENT, 1423 N. Front St., Harrisburg PA 17102. (717)236-2386. E-mail: philclark@rockwhirled.com. Website: http://www.rockwhirled.com. Director: Philip Clark. Management firm, booking agency, publicists. Estab. 1987. Represents individual artists and/ or groups from anywhere; currently handles 10 acts. Receives 10-25% commission. Reviews material for acts.
How to Contact: Submit demo tape by mail. Unsolicited submissions are OK. Prefers cassette. If seeking management, press kit should include bio, cover letter, demo tape/CD, photo, song list, venue list, description of performance frequency, equipment needed, goals. SASE. Reports in 3-6 weeks.
Music: Mostly **rock**, **alternative** and **folk**. Works primarily with soloist singer/instrumentalists, duo acoustic acts, bands. Current acts include Every Day @ Six (alternative fusion), Cameron Molloy (country fusion) and Diane Diachishin (folk).
Tips: "Be brief, clear, focused in approach. Approach a variety of other agents and managers to get a feel for which companies make the best match. We look for clients who wish to work specifically with us, not just any firm."

◙ ROGUE MANAGEMENT, 332 Naughton Ave., Staten Island NY 10305. Phone/fax: (718)351-8758. E-mail: xrogue@aol.com. President: Ralph Beauchamp. Management firm. Estab. 1992. Represents individual artists, groups and songwriters from anywhere; currently handles 2 acts. Receives 15% commission. Reviews material for acts.
How to Contact: Submit demo tape by mail. Unsolicited submissions are OK. Prefers cassette with 3-5 songs and lyric sheet. If seeking management, press kit should include cover letter, demo tape/CD, lyric sheets, press clippings, photo and bio. SASE. Reports in 2 weeks.
Music: Mostly **pop/rock**, **industrial** and **R&B/dance**; also **hard rock**. Works primarily with bands. Current acts include Head (pop/rock) and Requiem (industrial).
Tips: "Learn that the song comes first, not the image."

▣ ✔ ◐ **RPM MANAGEMENT SERVICES PTY LTD.**, 63 Fitzroy, Surry Hills, Sydney NSW Australia. Phone: (612)9331 7955. Fax: (612)9331 7827. E-mail: rpm@zip.com.au. Managers: Matthew Ellard and Jacinta Donnithorne. Management firm and business manager. Estab. 1991. Represents local groups; currently handles 3 acts. Receives 10-15% commission.
How to Contact: Submit demo tape by mail. Unsolicited submissions are OK. Prefers cassette with 3 songs. If seeking management, press kit should include cover letter, bio, demo tape/CD, press clippings and photo. SAE and IRC.
Music: Mostly **pop**, **rock** and **dance**; also **soundtrack**. Current acts include Angry Anderson (rock), Severed Heads (alternative dance) and Rose Tattoo (rock).
Tips: "Demos must be of professional quality. Have a clearly defined view of direction and/or market."

◐ **RUSTRON MUSIC PRODUCTIONS**, Send all artist song submissions to: 1156 Park Lane, West Palm Beach FL 33417-5957. (516)686-1354. Main Office: 42 Barrack Hill Rd., Ridgefield CT 06877. ("Main office does not review new material—only South Florida Branch office does.") Executive Director: Rusty Gordon. Artist Consultants: Rusty Gordon and Davilyn Whims. Composition Management: Ron Caruso. Management firm, booking agency, music publisher (Rustron Music Publishers/BMI and Whimsong Publishing/ASCAP), record company and record producer. Estab. 1970. Represents individuals, groups and songwriters; currently handles 22 acts. Commissions vary. Reviews material for acts.
How to Contact: Write first and obtain permission to submit. Send cassette with 3-6 songs (CD/cassette produced for sale preferred). Provide typed lyric or lead sheet for every song in the submission. If seeking management, press kit should include cover letter, bio, demo tape/CD, typed lyric sheets and press clippings. "SASE required for all correspondence." Reports in 4 months.
Music: Mostly **blues** (**country folk/urban, Southern**), **country** (**rock, blues, progressive**), **easy listening, soft rock** (**ballads**), **women's music, R&B, folk/rock**; also **New Age instrumentals** and **New Age folk fusion**. Current acts include Jayne Margo-Reby (folk fusions/soft rock), Star Smiley (country) and Lynn Thomas and Dorothy Hirsh (music comedy).
Tips: "Send cover letter, typed lyric sheets for all songs. Carefully mix demo, don't drown the vocals, 3-6 songs in a submission. Prefer independent CD/cassette (store-ready product). Send photo if artist is seeking marketing and/or production assistance. Very strong hooks, definitive melody, evolved concepts, unique and unpredictable themes. Flesh out a performing sound unique to the artist."

◯ **MIKE RYMKUS MANAGEMENT AND PROMOTIONS**, 21610 Park Wick Lane, Katy TX 77450. (713)492-0423. Owner: Mike Rymkus. Management firm. Estab. 1970. Represents local and regional (Texas) individual artists and songwriters; currently handles 1 act. Receives 20% commission. Reviews material for acts.
How to Contact: Submit demo tape by mail. Unsolicited submissions are OK. Prefers cassette. If seeking management, press kit should include cover letter, good bio, good picture, 3 of your best songs on cassette, press clippings and video (if available). "Can not have any management ties or record deals." Does not return material. Reports in 2 months.
Music: Mostly **country**. Works primarily with singer/songwriters. Current acts include Tommy Lee (country singer/songwriter).

✔ ◐ **SAFFYRE MANAGEMENT**, 17211 Lorne St., Van Nuys CA 91406. (818)842-4368. E-mail: ebsaffyre@aol.com. President: Esta G. Bernstein. Management firm. Estab. 1990. Represents individual artists, groups and songwriters from anywhere; currently handles 2 acts. Receives 15% commission.
How to Contact: Call first and obtain permission to submit. "We are not accepting any new material unless act is currently signed with a major label." If seeking management, press kit should include cover letter, bio, photo, cassette with 3-4 songs and lyric sheets. Does not return material. Reports in 2 weeks only if interested.
Music: Mostly **modern rock** and **top 40**. "We work only with bands and solo artists who write their own material; our main objective is to obtain recording deals and contracts, while advising our artists on their careers and business relationships." Current artists include JÖW (modern funk/rock) and Scott Moss (top 40 singer/songwriter).

✔ ◯ **ST. JOHN ARTISTS**, P.O. Box 619, Neenah WI 54957-0619. (920)722-2222. Fax: (920)725-2405. Website: http://www.St.John-Artists.com/. Agents: Jon St. John and Gary Coquo. Booking agency.

MARKETS THAT WERE listed in the 1999 edition of *Songwriter's Market* but do not appear this year are listed in the General Index with a notation explaining why they were omitted.

Estab. 1977. Represents local and regional individual artists and groups; currently handles 20 acts. Receives 15-20% commission. Reviews material for acts.

How to Contact: Call first and obtain permission to submit. Prefers cassette or VHS videocassette. If seeking management, press kit should include cover letter, bio, photo, demo tape/CD, video and résumé. SASE.

Music: Mostly **rock** and **MOR**. Current acts include Vic Ferrari Band (variety rock), The Groove Hogs (R&B/pop/classic rock) and Silent Illusion (light rock/classic rock).

SA'MALL MANAGEMENT, P.O. Box 8442, Universal City CA 91608. (818)506-8533. Fax: (818)506-8534. E-mail: pplzmi@aol.com. Managers: Nikki Ray, Cheyenne Phoenix, Sanra Albanese. Management firm, music publisher (Pollybyrd Publications) and record company (PPL Entertainment Group). Estab. 1990. Represents individual artists, groups and songwriters from anywhere; currently handles 10 acts. Receives 20-25% commission. Reviews material for acts.

How to Contact: Write or call first and obtain permission to submit. Prefers cassette with 2 songs and lyric and lead sheet. If seeking management, press kit should include picture, bio and tape. SASE. Reports in 2 months.

Music: **All types**. Current acts include Riki Hendrix, Fhyne, Suzette Cuseo, The Band Aka, LeJenz, B.D. Fuoco and Jay Sattiewhite.

T.E. SAVAGE, INC., 24 Wilton Crest, Wilton CT 06897. (203)834-1457. Fax: (203)761-8739. Account Manager: Xavier Egurbide. Management firm and record producer (Stephan Galfas). Represents individual artists and groups from anywhere; currently handles 10 acts. Receives 10-20% commission. Reviews material for acts.

How to Contact: Write first and obtain permission to submit or to arrange personal interview. Prefers cassette and VHS videocassette with 2-5 songs and lyric sheet. If seeking management, press kit should include photo, bio, past-present gig dates, intro letter and demo. Include some major or important press clippings. SASE. Reports in 3 weeks.

Music: Mostly **alternative rock**, **funk** and **Latin**; also **dance**, **rock**, **jazz** and **contemporary pop**. Current acts include GC & the P-Funk Allstars (funk Godfather) and KC & the Sunshine Band.

Tips: "Indicate which type of artist you are submitting material for with lyrics. Along with past work submitted and to whom."

CRAIG SCOTT ENTERTAINMENT, P.O. Box 1722, Paramus NJ 07653-1722. (201)587-1066. Fax: (201)587-0481. E-mail: scott@craigscott.com. Management firm. Estab. 1985. Represents individual artists and/or groups from anywhere. Commission varies. Reviews material for acts.

How to Contact: Submit demo tape by mail. Unsolicited submissions are OK. Prefers cassette or CD. If seeking management, press kit should include tape/CD, bio, picture, relevant press. Does not return material. Reports in 3-4 weeks.

Music: Current acts include Uptown Sounds and Impressions.

SEA CRUISE PRODUCTIONS, INC., P.O. Box 1875, Gretna LA 70054-1875. (504)392-4615. Fax: (504)392-4512. E-mail: kenkeene@aol.com. President/General Manager: Ken Keene. Management firm, booking agency, music publisher (Sea Cruise Music/BMI), record company (Briarmeade Records) and record producer (Sea Cruise Productions). Estab. 1970. Represents individual artists, groups and songwriters from anywhere; currently handles 12 acts. Receives 15% commission. Reviews material for acts.

How to Contact: Submit demo tape by mail. Unsolicited submissions are OK. Prefers cassette or VHS videocassette with 5-6 songs and lyric or lead sheet. If seeking management, press kit should include cassette, videocassette, CD, publicity photos, bio and press clipping, cover letter, résumé and lyric sheets. Does not return material. "No phone calls." Reports in 6-8 weeks "if we are interested in the act."

Music: Mostly **nostalgia '50s/'60s**, **country rock** and **R&B**; also **ballads**, **double entendre** and **novelty songs**. "Most of our acts are '50s, '60s and '70s artists, all of whom have had million selling records, and who are still very active on the concert/night club circuit." Current acts include Frankie Ford (legendary rock 'n' roll singer/pianist), Troy Shondell (singer/songwriter), Jean Knight (Grammy nominated R&B singer) and Narvel Felts (country/rockabilly legend).

SERGE ENTERTAINMENT GROUP, P.O. Box 672216, Marietta GA 30006-0037. (770)850-9560. Fax: (770)850-9646. E-mail: sergeent@aol.com. Website: http://www.serge.org. President: Sandy Serge. Management/shopping firm and song publishers. Estab. 1987. Represents individual artists, groups, songwriters from anywhere; currently handles 20 acts. Receives 15-25% commission. Reviews materials for acts.

How to Contact: Submit demo tape or CD by mail. Unsolicited submissions are OK. Prefers cassette,

CD or VHS videocassette with 4 songs and lyric sheet. If seeking management, press kit should include 8 × 10 photo, bio, cover letter, lyric sheets, max of 4 press clips, VHS videocassette, performance schedule and CD. "All information submitted must include name, address and phone number on each item." Does not return material. Reports in 4-6 weeks if interested.

Music: Mostly **rock, pop** and **country**; also **New Age**. Works primarily with singer/songwriters and bands. Current acts include The Moon (rock), Nine Dollar Melon Baller (rock) and Sweet Fancy Moses (rock).

Tips: "We have acquired numerous publishing deals for all clients. We have professional relationships with over 300 publishers and have connections at most major labels."

PHILL SHUTE MANAGEMENT PTY. LTD., Box 273, Dulwich Hill NSW 2203 Australia. Phone: (02)5692152. Managing Director: Phill Shute. Management firm, booking agency and record company (Big Rock Records). Estab. 1979. Represents local individual artists and groups; currently handles 8 acts. Receives 10% commission. Reviews material for acts.

How to Contact: Submit demo tape by mail. Unsolicited submissions are OK. Prefers cassette with 4 songs and lyric sheet. If seeking management, press kit should include cover letter, bio, photo, demo tape/CD, press clippings and résumé. Does not return material. Reports in 1 month.

Music: Mostly **rock, pop** and **R&B**; also **country rock**. Works primarily with rock bands, pop vocalists and blues acts (band and vocalists). Current acts include Phill Simmons (country), Two R More (pop/rock) and Now Hear This (rock).

Tips: "Make all submissions well organized (e.g. bio, photo and experience of the act). List areas in which the act would like to work, complete details for contact."

SIDDONS & ASSOCIATES, 584 N. Larchmont Blvd., Hollywood CA 90004. (323)462-6156. Fax: (213)462-2076. E-mail: siddons@earthlink.net. Contact: Erock. President: Bill Siddons. Management firm. Estab. 1972. Represents individual artists and groups from anywhere; currently handles 2 acts. Receives 15-20% commission. Reviews material for acts.

How to Contact: Write first and obtain permission to submit a demo. Prefers cassette or VHS videocassette with 3 songs and lyric sheet. If seeking management, press kit should include cassette of 3 songs, lyric sheet, VHS videocassette if available, biography, past credits and discography. Does not return material. Reports in 3 months.

Music: **All styles.** Current acts include Jonathan Butler (singer/songwriter) and Kaolin Thompson (alternative female rocker).

SIEGEL ENTERTAINMENT LTD., 101-1648 W. Seventh Ave., Vancouver British Columbia V6J 1S5 Canada. (604)736-3896. Fax: (604)736-3464. E-mail: jdudley@direct.ca. President: Robert Siegel. Management firm and booking agency. Estab. 1975. Represents individual artists, groups and songwriters from anywhere; currently handles 100 acts (for bookings). Receives 15-20% commission. Reviews material for acts.

How to Contact: Submit demo tape by mail. Unsolicited submissions are OK. Prefers cassette or VHS videocassette with 3 songs and lyric sheet. If seeking management, press kit should include 8 × 10 and cassette and/or video. Does not return material. Reports in 1 month.

Music: Mostly **rock, pop** and **country**; also **children's**. Current acts include Johnny Ferreira & The Swing Machine, Lee Aaron and Tim Brecht (pop/children's).

SILVER BOW MANAGEMENT, 6260 130 St., Surrey, British Columbia V3X 1R6 Canada. (604)572-4232. Fax: (604)572-4252. E-mail: saddles@sprint.ca. Website: http://saddlestone.ontheweb.net. President: Grant Lucas. Management firm, music publisher (Saddlestone Publishing, Silver Bow Publishing), record company (Saddlestone Records) and record producer (Silver Bow Productions, Krazy Cat Productions). Estab. 1988. Represents individual artists, groups, songwriters from anywhere; currently handles 8 acts. Receives 10% commission. Reviews material for acts.

How to Contact: Submit demo tape by mail. Unsolicited submissions are OK. Prefers cassette with 3 songs and lyric sheet. If seeking management, press kit should include 8 × 10 photo, bio, cover letter, demo tape or CD with lyric sheets, press clippings, video, résumé and current itinerary. "Visuals are everything—submit accordingly." Does not return material. Reports in 2 months.

Music: Mostly **country, pop** and **rock**; also **R&B, Christian** and **alternative**. Works primarily with bands, vocalists and singer/songwriters. Current acts include Darrell Meyers (country singer/songwriter), Nite Moves (variety band) and Gerry King (country singer/songwriter).

N O **SINGERMANAGEMENT, INC.**, 161 W. 54th St., Suite 1403, New York NY 10019. (212)757-1217. President: Robert Singerman. Management consulting firm. Estab. 1982. Represents local, regional or international individual artists and groups; currently handles 10-15 acts. Receives 5% fee. Reviews material for acts.
How to Contact: Write first and obtain permission to submit. Prefers CD, cassette or VHS videocassette. If seeking management consultation, include tape, lyric sheet, video (if available) cover letter, press clippings and bio in press kit. Does not return material. Reports in 1 month.
Music: Current acts include Lach ("anti-folk" songwriter), Bush Tetras (alt rock) and The Young Gods (industrial).

☑ O **SIRIUS ENTERTAINMENT**, 13531 Clairmont Way #8, Oregon City OR 97045-8450. (503)657-1813. E-mail: sirius1@teleport.com. Owner: Dan Blair. Management firm and booking agency. Estab. 1991. Represents individual artists and/or groups and songwriters from anywhere; currently handles 10 acts. Receives 10-15% commission. Reviews material for acts.
How to Contact: Submit demo tape by mail. Unsolicited submissions are OK. Prefers cassette with 3 songs and lyric sheet. If seeking management, press kit should include cover letter, bio, 8×10 photo, résumé, CD or cassette, video if available, copies of press clippings and a list of past performances and credits. "Résumé should include total career progress from beginning with all schooling listed." SASE. Reports in 2-5 weeks.
Music: Mostly **R&B** and **rock**; also **jazz**, **blues**, **classical** and **country**. Current acts include Linda Hornbuckle (R&B), Mac Charles (A/C rock) and Dorothy Moore (R&B).
Tips: "If you can't afford the services of a good studio and good studio musicians to play your material, then use one acoustic instrument (guitar or piano). Send lyric sheet with original material."

O **T. SKORMAN PRODUCTIONS, INC.**, 3660 Maguire Blvd., Suite 250, Orlando FL 32803. (407)895-3000. Fax: (407)895-1422. E-mail: ted@talentagency.com. Website: http://www.talentagency.c om. President: Ted Skorman. Management firm and booking agency. Estab. 1983. Represents groups; currently handles 40 acts. Receives 10-25% commission. Reviews material for acts.
How to Contact: Write or call first for permission to send tape. Prefers cassette with 3 songs, or videocassette of no more than 15 minutes. "Live performance—no trick shots or editing tricks. We want to be able to view act as if we were there for a live show." If seeking management, press kit should include cover letter, bio, photo and demo tape/CD. Does not return material. Reports in 1-2 months.
Music: Mostly **top 40**, **techno**, **dance**, **MOR** and **pop**. Works primarily with high-energy dance acts, recording acts, and top 40 bands. Current acts include Ravyn Dixon (country), Michelle Lynn (country), Stef Carse (country) and Big Daddy (R&B).
Tips: "We have many pop recording acts and are looking for commercial material for their next albums."

O **SLATUS MANAGEMENT**, 208 E. 51st St., Suite 151, New York NY 10022. (212)866-5371. E-mail: cpwrecds@aol.com. Website: http://johnnywinter.prohosting.com. Owner: Teddy Slatus. Management firm. Estab. 1981. Represents individual artists and groups from anywhere; currently handles 1 act. Reviews material for acts.
How to Contact: Submit demo tape by mail. Unsolicited submissions are OK. Prefers cassette. If seeking management, press kit should include cover letter, bio, press clippings, résumé, picture of artist and demo tape/CD if available. "If Slatus Management does not contact you within 60 days we have passed!" SASE. Reports in 2 months.
Music: Mostly **rock** and **blues**. Current acts include Johnny Winter (blues/rock artist).

O **GARY SMELTZER PRODUCTIONS**, 603 W. 13th #2A, Austin TX 78701. (512)478-6020. Fax: (512)472-3850. E-mail: gsptalent@aol.com. Owner: Gary Smeltzer. Management firm and booking agency. Estab. 1967. Represents individual artists and groups from anywhere. "We book about 100 different bands each year—none are exclusive." Receives 15-20% commission. Reviews material for acts.
How to Contact: Submit demo tape by mail. Unsolicited submissions are OK. Prefers cassette, videocassette or CD. If seeking management, press kit should include cover letter, résumé, cassette or CD, bio, picture, lyric sheets, press clippings and video. Does not return material. Reports in 1 month.
Music: Mostly **alternative**, **R&B** and **country**. Current acts include Ro Tel & the Hot Tomatoes (nostalgic '60s showband), Johnny Good and Dan Torosian (jazz).
Tips: "We prefer performing songwriters who can gig their music as a solo or group."

☑ ☺ **SOUND AND SERENITY MANAGEMENT**, P.O. Box 22105, Nashville TN 37202. (615)731-3100. Fax: (615)731-3005. E-mail: jyoke@cupitmusic.com. Website: http://www.cupitmusic.com. Manager: Eric Marcuse. Management firm. Represents individual artists from anywhere; currently handles 3 acts. Receives standard commission.
How to Contact: Call first and obtain permission to submit a demo. Prefers CD or cassette with lyric sheet. If seeking management, press kit should include photo, bio, cover letter and cassette. Does not return material; will reply with SASE. Reports in 3 months.
Music: Mostly **country**, **Americana**. Works primarily with individual artists. Current acts include Ken Mellons (traditional country singer/songwriter), Kevin Sharp (contemporary country singer/songwriter) and Gene Watson (country singer/songwriter).

☺ **SOUND MANAGEMENT DIRECTION**, (formerly Artists Only Inc.), 152-18 Union Turnpike, Flushing NY 11367. (718)969-0166. Fax: (718)969-8914. President: Bob Currie. Management firm, music publisher (Sun Face Music/ASCAP, Shaman Drum/BMI) and record producer. Estab. 1986. Represents individual artists and/or groups, songwriters, producers and engineers from anywhere; currently handles 6 acts. Receives 20% commission. Reviews material for acts.
How to Contact: Submit demo tape by mail. Unsolicited submissions are OK. Prefers cassette or VHS videocassette with 2 songs and lyric sheet. If seeking management, press kit should include 3 song demo, photo and contact information including phone numbers. "If you want material returned, include SASE." Reports in 2-3 weeks.
Music: Mostly **urban contemporary**, **dance** and **rap/rock**; also **popular (ballads)**, **Spanish** and **rock**. Works primarily with singer/songwriters and self-contained bands.
Tips: "We only want your best, and be specific with style. Quality, not quantity."

🅽 ☺ **SOUTHERN MADE RECORDS**, 4805 Cliff Wood Dr., Garland TX 75043. (972)504-8794. President: Johnny Bromsey. Management firm and record company (Southern Made). Estab. 1992. Represents local, regional, individual artists, groups and songwriters; currently handles 2 acts. Receives 20% commission. Reviews material for acts.
How to Contact: Write or call first and obtain permission to submit a demo. Submit demo by mail. Unsolicited submissions are OK. Prefers cassette with 3 songs. If seeking management, press kit should include bio, demo tape/CD, lyric sheet, a full length photo and indicate age. Does not return material. Reports in 1 month.
Music: Mostly **R&B**, **hip-hop** and **radio rap**. Works primarily with singer/songwriters. Current acts include Deep South (hip-hop/rap group) and Crystal (R&B singer).
Tips: "Tell a short story of your life or someone you know (poetic form)."

☺ **SP TALENT ASSOCIATES**, P.O. Box 475184, Garland TX 75047. Talent Coordinator: Richard Park. Management firm and booking agency. Represents individual artists and groups; currently handles 7 acts. Receives 15% commission. Reviews material for acts.
How to Contact: Submit demo tape by mail. Unsolicited submissions are OK. Prefers VHS videocassette with several songs. Send photo and bio. Does not return material. Reports back as soon as possible.
Music: Mostly **rock**, **nostalgia rock** and **country**; also **specialty acts** and **folk/blues**. Works primarily with vocalists and self-contained groups. Current acts include Joe Hardin Brown (country), Rock It! (nostalgia), Renewal (rock group) and Juan Madera & the Supple Grain Seeds.

☺ **SPHERE GROUP ONE**, P.O. Box 991, Far Hills NJ 07931-0991. (908)781-1650. Fax: (908)781-1693. President: Tony Zarrella. Talent Manager: Louisa Pazienza. Management firm and record producer. Estab. 1987. Represents individual artists, groups and singer/songwriters from anywhere; currently handles 4 acts. Receives 20-25% commission. Reviews material for acts.
How to Contact: Send all new submissions to Vision 2000. Submit demo tape by mail. Unsolicited submissions are OK. Prefers cassette or VHS videocassette with 3-5 songs. All submissions must include cover letter, lyric sheets, tape/CD, photo, bio and all press. SASE. Reports in 4-6 weeks.
Music: Mostly **pop/rock**, **pop/country** and **New Age**; also **R&B**. Works primarily with bands and solo singer/songwriters. Current acts include 4 of Hearts (pop/rock), Oona Falcon (pop/rock), Elexus Quinn and Ziggy True, The Nothing Is Meaningless Project (R&B) and Frontier 9 (pop/rock).

🔰 🌐 **SENDING TO A COUNTRY** other than your own? Be sure to send International Reply Coupons (IRCs) instead of stamps for replies or return of your materials.

Tips: "Develop and create your own style, focus on goals and work as a team and maintain good chemistry with all artists and business relationships. Timing is important."

● **STAIRCASE PROMOTION**, P.O. Box 211, East Prairie MO 63845. (573)649-2211. President: Tommy Loomas. Vice President: Joe Silver. Management firm, music publisher (Lineage Publishing) and record company (Capstan Record Production). Estab. 1975. Represents individual artists and groups from anywhere; currently handles 6 acts. Receives 25% commission. Reviews material for acts.
How to Contact: Submit demo tape by mail. Unsolicited submissions are OK. Prefers cassette with 3 songs and lyric sheet. If seeking management, press kit should include bio, photo, audio cassette and/or video and press reviews, if any. "Be as professional as you can." SASE. Reports in 2 months.
Music: Mostly **country, pop** and **easy listening**; also **rock, gospel** and **alternative**. Current acts include Skidrow Joe (country comedian, on Capstan Records), Vicarie Arcoleo (pop singer, on Treasure Coast Records) and Scarlett Britoni (pop singer on Octagon Records).

● **STARKRAVIN' MANAGEMENT**, 18075 Ventura Blvd., Encino CA 91316. (818)345-0311. Fax: (818)345-0340. E-mail: bcmclane@aol.com. Contact: B.C. McLane, Esq. Management and law firm. Estab. 1994. Represents individual artists, groups and songwriters. Receives 20% commission (management); $150/hour as attorney.
How to Contact: Submit demo tape by mail. Unsolicited submissions are OK. Does not return material. Reports in 2-4 weeks.
Music: Mostly **rock, pop** and **R&B**. Works primarily with bands.

● **STAY GOLD PRODUCTIONS**, 1611 S. Utica, Suite 144, Tulsa OK 74104-4909. (918)742-4141. Fax: (918)742-4554. E-mail: STAGOLD@aol.com. President: Joey Baker. Vice President: Julie Campbell. Management firm, booking agency, publicist and promoter. Estab. 1989. Represents individual artists, groups and songwriters from anywhere; currently handles 15 acts. Receives 15-20% commission. Reviews material for acts.
How to Contact: Write or call first and obtain permission to submit. Prefers cassette with 3 songs or complete CD. If seeking management, press kit should include cover letter, résumé, tape, bio, photo, press and references if available. Does not return material. Reports in 1-2 months.
Music: Mostly **jazz, rock** and **R&B**; also **funk, blues** and **alternative**. Works primarily with solo artists, bands and songwriters. Current acts include Dennis Mitcheltree (jazz saxophonist), Pay Kelley (contemporary jazz guitarist), Regulators (rock) and Herb Ellis (legendary jazz guitarist).
Tips: "Make sure your submissions are neat and complete. Realize that most agents and managers receive many submissions and are inclined to ignore those that arrive as a re-used demo with a hand-scrawled letter on notebook paper in a #10 envelope. Take yourself seriously and so will those you approach."

✓ ● **OBI STEINMAN MANAGEMENT**, 14531 Hamlin St., Suite 200, Van Nuys CA 91411. (818)787-4065. Fax: (818)787-4066. E-mail: obistmgmt@aol.com. Manager: Obi Steinman. Management firm. Represents individual artists and groups from anywhere; currently handles 4 acts.
How to Contact: Submit demo tape by mail. Unsolicited submissions are OK. Prefers cassette with 4 songs and lyric sheet. If seeking management, press kit should include 8×10 picture, press clippings and bio. "Concentrate more on the material enclosed than the flashy package." SASE. Reports in 5 weeks.
Music: Mostly **pop, alternative** and **hard rock**; also **dance** and **industrial**. Works primarily with bands and self-contained artists (write own material, have own backing band). Current acts include Warrant (hard rock), Jabberwocky (Jani Lane led AAA project) and Cyde (techno industrial).
Tips: "We are street level. We are looking for new acts."

● **JIM STEPHANY MANAGEMENT**, 1021 Preston Dr., Nashville TN 37206. (615)228-5638. President: Jim Stephany. Management firm. Estab. 1987. Represents individual artists and groups; currently handles 2 acts. Reviews material for acts.
How to Contact: Submit demo tape by mail. Unsolicited submissions are OK. Prefers cassette or VHS videocassette with 3 songs. If seeking management, press kit should include cover letter, bio and video. SASE. Reports in 1 month.
Music: Mostly **country**. Works primarily with single artists and bands. Current acts include Bobby Goldsboro (singer), Ric and Brian Butler (singers).

✓ ● **HARRIET STERNBERG MANAGEMENT**, 9100 Wilshire Blvd., East Tower, Suite 503, Beverly Hills CA 90212. (310)271-0600. President: Harriet Sternberg. Management firm. Estab. 1987.
How to Contact: Write first and obtain permission to submit. Prefers cassette or VHS videocassette with 3 songs and lyric sheet. If seeking management, press kit should include detailed history of the artist and

professional experience. "Industry referrals are crucial." SASE. Reports in 1 month.
Music: Works primarily with signed acts. Current acts include Delbert McClinton and Spinal Tap.
Tips: "Be knowledgeable about my artists and/or roster."

○ **STEVENS & COMPANY MANAGEMENT**, P.O. Box 6368, Corpus Christi TX 78411. (512)888-7311. Fax: (512)888-7360. E-mail: steveco@flash.net. Owner: Matt Stevens. Management firm. Estab. 1995. Represents individual artists from anywhere. Reviews material for acts.
How to Contact: Submit demo tape by mail. Unsolicited submissions are OK. Prefers cassette with lyric sheet. SASE. Reports in 3 weeks.
Music: Mostly **Latin**, **Mexican regional** and **tejano**; also **country**. Works primarily with singers and individual artists. Current acts include Fidel Hernandez (Mexican regional vocalist/PolyGram/Universal).
Tips: "Send material every time you have something new, always leave phone number on tapes."

✓ ◯ **STEVE STEWART MANAGEMENT**, 8225 Santa Monica Blvd., Los Angeles CA 90046. (323)650-9700. Fax: (323)650-2690. President: Steve Stewart. Management firm. Estab. 1993. Represents individual artists and/or groups from anywhere; currently handles 9 acts. Receives 20% commission.
How to Contact: Submit demo tape by mail. Unsolicited submissions are OK. Prefers cassette. If seeking management, press kit should include CD, photo and bio if available. "Mail first, call 4-6 weeks later. Cannot return any material." Reports in 2 months.
Music: Mostly **alternative** and **rock**. Works primarily with bands. Current acts include Stone Temple Pilots, Orbit, 10 Speed, Gordon, Loud Mouth, Sonic Chrome and Eleven.

○ **STEWART MUSIC GROUP**, P.O. Box 926302, Houston TX 77292-6302. (888)294-3294, ext. 7643. E-mail: stewmu@aol.com. Administrative Manager: Lisa Stewart. CEO: Patrick Stewart. Management firm, music publisher (SaMaritan Group Publishers) and record company (SMG Records). Estab. 1995. Represents local individual artists, groups and songwriters; currently handles 2 acts. Receives 25% commission. Reviews material for acts.
How to Contact: Submit demo tape by mail. Unsolicited submissions are OK. Prefers cassette with 4 songs and lead sheet. If seeking management, press kit should include cover letter, bio, photo, demo tape/CD, lyric sheets and press clippings. SASE. Reports in 1 month.
Music: Mostly **Christian contemporary** and **Christian gospel**. Works primarily with singers/songwriters and groups. Current acts include Patrick Stewart (gospel singer) and Grace (contemporary group).

✚ ✓ ◯ **STRICTLY FORBIDDEN ARTISTS**, 320 Avenue Rd., Suite 144, Toronto, Ontario M4V 2H3 Canada. (416)926-0818. Fax: (416)926-0811. E-mail: brad.black@sympatico.ca. Website: http://www.forbidden.com. Vice President of A&R: Brad Black. Management firm, booking agency and record company. Estab. 1986. Represents individual artists and groups from anywhere; currently handles 8 acts. Receives 20-30% commission. Reviews material for acts.
How to Contact: Submit demo tape by mail. Unsolicited submissions are OK. Prefers cassette with 3-6 songs and lyric sheet. If seeking management, press kit should include biography, press clippings, 8×10, photo and demo tape/CD. "Once you've sent material, don't call us, we'll call you." Does not return material. Reports in 4-6 weeks.
Music: Mostly **alternative rock, art rock** and **grindcore**; also **electronic, hip-hop** and **experimental**. Works primarily with performing bands, studio acts and performance artists. Current acts include Sickos (experimental/art-rock), Lazer (coldwave/electronica) and Andy Warhead (punk rock/noise).
Tips: "As long as you have faith in your music, we'll have faith in promoting you and your career."

Ⓝ ◯ **SURFACE MANAGEMENT INC.**, 2935 Church St. Station, New York NY 10008. Phone/fax: (212)468-2828. E-mail: patti@surfacemgmt.com. Website: http://www.surfacemgmt.com. President: Patti Beninati. Management firm. Estab. 1990. Represents local individual artists and groups; currently handles 3 acts. Receives 20% commission. Reviews material for acts.

FOR EXPLANATIONS OF THESE SYMBOLS,
SEE THE INSIDE FRONT AND BACK COVERS OF THIS BOOK.

How to Contact: Submit demo tape by mail. Unsolicited submissions are OK. Prefers cassette with 5 songs and lyric sheet. If seeking management, press kit should include cover letter, bio, photo, demo, lyric sheets and press clippings. Does not return material. Reports in 1 month.
Music: Mostly **alternative** and **heavy rock**. Current acts include Four Hundred (power punk rock).

✓ ○ **SYNDICATE MANAGEMENT** (formerly Rhyme Syndicate Management), 4902 Coldwater Canyon Ave., Sherman Oaks CA 91423-2221. (818)509-6700. Fax: (818)509-8883. Managers: Jorge Hinojosa and Paul Filippone. Management firm. Represents individual artists, groups and songwriters from anywhere; currently handles 7 acts. Receives 15-20% commission. Reviews material for acts.
 • See the Managers Roundtable article on page 45 for more information from Paul Filippone.
How to Contact: Submit demo tape by mail. Unsolicited submissions are OK. Prefers CD, cassette or DAT with 4 songs. If seeking management, press kit should include cover letter, photo, bio and press clippings, "although none of this is very important compared to the tape." Does not return material. Reports in 1-2 months (artist should call).
Music: Mostly **alternative rock**, **rock** and **folk/acoustic**; also **all types**. Works primarily with bands. Current acts include Ice-T (rapper, Coroner Records), Body Count (hard rock band, Coroner Records), Silver Jet (rock/pop band), Jimmy Eat World (band, Capitol Records), Ezra Holbrook (songwriter/singer, 7Seven Records) and Lael Alderman (songwriter/singer, Geffen Records).

✿ ○ **T.J. BOOKER LTD.**, P.O. Box 969, Rossland, British Columbia V0G 1Y0 Canada. (250)362-7795. Owner: Tom Jones. Management firm, booking agency and music publisher. Estab. 1976. Represents individual artists, groups and songwriters from anywhere; currently handles 6 acts. Receives 15% commission. Reviews material for acts.
How to Contact: Submit demo tape by mail. Unsolicited submissions are OK. Prefers cassette or videocassette with 3 songs. If seeking management, include demo tape or CD, picture, cover letter and bio in press kit. Does not return material. Reports in 1 month.
Music: Mostly **MOR**, **crossover**, **rock**, **pop** and **country**. Works primarily with vocalists, show bands, dance bands and bar bands. Current acts include Kirk Orr (folk/country), Mike Hamilton (rock/blues) and Larry Hayton (rock/blues).

◢ ○ **T.L.C. BOOKING AGENCY**, 37311 N. Valley Rd., Chattaroy WA 99003. (509)292-2201. Fax: (509)292-2205. E-mail: tlcagent@ix.netcom.com. Agent/Owners: Tom or Carrie Lapsansky. Booking agency. Estab. 1970. Represents individual artists and groups from anywhere; currently handles 15 acts. Receives 10% commission. Reviews material for acts.
How to Contact: Call first and obtain permission to submit. Prefers cassette with 3-4 songs. Does not return material. Reports in 3 weeks.
Music: Mostly **rock**, **country** and **variety**; also **comedians** and **magicians**. Works primarily with bands, singles and duos. Current acts include Nobody Famous (variety), Menagerie (variety-duo) and Celtic Knots (Irish).

○ **T.S.J. PRODUCTIONS**, 422 Pierce St. NE, Minneapolis MN 55413-2514. (612)331-8580. President/Artist Manager: Katherine J. Lange. Management firm and booking agency. Estab. 1974. Represents artists, groups and songwriters; currently handles varying number of acts. Receives 20% commission. Reviews material for acts.
How to Contact: Submit demo tape by mail. Unsolicited submissions are OK. Prefers "cassette tapes only for music audio with 4-6 songs and lyric sheets." If seeking management, press kit should include cover letter, bio, photo, demo tape, lyric sheets and press clippings. SASE. Reports in 1 month.
Music: Mostly **country rock**, **symphonic rock**, **easy listening** and **MOR**; also **blues**, **country**, **folk**, **jazz**, **progressive**, **R&B** and **top 40/pop**. Currently represents Thomas St. James (songwriter/vocalist) and a variety of other artists.
Tips: "We will view anyone who fits into our areas of music. However, keep in mind we work only with national and international markets. We handle those starting out as well as professionals, but all must be marketed on a professional level, if we work with you."

○ **TAKE OUT MANAGEMENT**, 5605 Woodman Ave. #206, Van Nuys CA 91401. (818)901-1122. Fax: (818)901-6513. E-mail: sclark@howiewood.com. Website: http://www.howiewood.com. Artist Relations: Steven Clark. Management firm. Estab. 1985. Represents individual artists, groups and songwriters from anywhere; currently handles 4 acts. Receives 15-20% commission. Reviews material for acts.
How to Contact: Submit demo tape by mail. Unsolicited submissions are OK. Prefers cassette or CD with any number of songs and lyric sheet. If seeking management, press kit should include tape or CD, picture, bio and cover letter. Does not return material. Reports in 1 week.

Music: Mostly **pop**, **A/C** and **rock**; also **R&B** and **dance**. Works primarily with singer/songwriters, arrangers and bands. Current acts include Dan Hill (A/C), Rodney Sheldon (R&B), Fran Lucci (singer/songwriter) and Julie Eisenhower.

⬤ **TAS MUSIC CO./DAVE TASSE ENTERTAINMENT**, N2467 Knollwood Dr., Lake Geneva WI 53147-9731. E-mail: baybreeze@idcnet.com. Website: http://www.baybreezerecords.com. Contact: David Tasse. Booking agency, record company and music publisher. Represents artists, groups and songwriters; currently handles 21 acts. Receives 10-20% commission. Reviews material for acts.
How to Contact: Submit demo tape by mail. Unsolicited submissions are OK. Prefers cassette with 2-4 songs and lyric sheet. Include performance videocassette if available. If seeking management, press kit should include tape, bio and photo. Does not return material. Reports in 3 weeks.
Music: Mostly **pop** and **jazz**; also **dance**, **MOR**, **rock**, **soul** and **top 40**. Works primarily with show and dance bands. Current acts include Dave Hulburt (blues), David Tasse (jazz) and Major Hamberlin (jazz).

TEN NINETY NINE PROMOTIONS, P.O. Box 21422, Washington DC 20009. Fax: (301)365-0803. E-mail: rov@dds.nl. Producer: Rob Verheij. A&R: Jaco van der Steen. P.O. Box 85824, 2508 CM Den Haag, The Netherlands. Management firm, booking agency and record company. Estab. 1982. Represents individual artists and groups from anywhere; currently handles 52 acts. Receives variable commission, "depends on the contract." Reviews material for acts.
How to Contact: Submit demo tape by mail. Unsolicited submissions are OK. Prefers CD if available, DAT or VHS videocassette. "Cassettes accepted from Caribbean, Asia and Africa only." If seeking management, press kit should include cover letter, demo CD, résumé, reviews, bio, photo and promotional material. SASE. Reports in 1-2 months.
Music: All types. Current acts include Rise (alternative), The Wailers (reggae) and Toure Kunda (African).

⬇✓⬤ **WILLIAM TENN ARTIST MANAGEMENT**, #431-67 Mowat Ave., Toronto, Ontario M6K 3E3 Canada. (416)534-7763. Fax: (416)534-9726. E-mail: pmwtm@ican.net. Office Assistant: Amanda Rowley. Management firm. Estab. 1981. Represents individual artists and groups in Canada, but not limited to that; currently handles 3 acts. Receives variable commission. Reviews material for acts.
How to Contact: Submit demo tape or CD by mail. Unsolicited submissions are OK. Prefers cassette or CD with at least 3 songs, lyric sheet optional. If seeking management, press kit should include cassette with minimum 3 songs, press clippings, reviews (live and/or album), photo (either b&w, color copied—to your discretion), cover letter, bio, lyric sheets, video, contact info and return address. "Please do not call for at least 3 weeks to check on your submission." SASE. Reports in 3 weeks.
Music: Mostly **rock/pop** and **alternative rock**. "We work with what we like. You don't need to be a certain type of artist." Current acts include Hayden (alternative/universal/rock), By Divine Right (alternative pop) and Merlin (pop).

⬤ **TIGER'S EYE ENTERTAINMENT MANAGEMENT & CONSULTING**, 1876 Memorial Drive, Green Bay WI 54303. (414)494-1588. Manager/CEO: Thomas C. Berndt. Management firm and record producer. Estab. 1992. Represents individual artists, groups and songwriters from anywhere; currently handles 1 act. Receives 20% commission. Reviews material for acts.
How to Contact: Submit demo tape by mail. Unsolicited submissions are OK. Prefers cassette or VHS videocassette with 3-4 songs and lyric sheet. If seeking management, press kit should include tape, lyric sheet, photo, relevant press and bio. "Artist should follow up with a call after 2 weeks." Does not return material. Reports in 2 weeks.
Music: Mostly **alternative**, **hard rock** and **R&B**; also **pop**, **rap** and **gothic groove**. Works primarily with vocalists, singer/songwriters and fresh alternative grunge. Current acts include Dusk (Ambient Gothic Groove).

▣⬤ **A TOTAL ACTING EXPERIENCE**, Dept. Rhymes-1, 20501 Ventura Blvd., Suite 399, Woodland Hills CA 91364. Agent: Dan A. Bellacicco. Talent agency. Estab. 1984. Represents vocalists, lyricists, composers and groups; currently handles 30 acts. Receives 10% commission. Reviews material for acts. Agency License: TA-0698.

MARKET CONDITIONS are constantly changing! If you're still using this book and it is 2001 or later, buy the newest edition of *Songwriter's Market* at your favorite bookstore or order directly from Writer's Digest Books at (800)289-0963.

How to Contact: Submit demo tape by mail. Unsolicited submissions are OK. Prefers cassette or VHS videocassette with 3-5 songs and lyric or lead sheets. Please include a revealing "self talk" at the end of your tape. "Singers or groups who write their own material must submit a VHS videocassette with photo and résumé." If seeking management, press kit should include VHS videotape, five 8×10 photos, cover letter, professional typeset résumé, bio, demo tape/CD, lyric sheets, press clippings and business card. Does not return material. Reports in 3 months only if interested. "Please include your e-mail address."
Music: Mostly **top 40/pop**, **jazz**, **blues**, **country**, **R&B**, **dance** and **MOR**; also "theme songs for new films, TV shows and special projects."
Tips: "No calls please. We will respond via your SASE. Your business skills must be strong. Please use a new tape and keep vocals up front. We welcome young, sincere talent who can give total commitment, and most important, *loyalty*, for a long-term relationship. We are seeking female vocalists (a la Streisand or Whitney Houston) who can write their own material, for a major label recording contract. Your song's story line must be as refreshing as the words you skillfully employ in preparing to build your well-balanced, orchestrated, climactic last note! Try to eliminate old, worn-out, dull, trite rhymes. A new way to write/ compose or sing an old song/tune will qualify your originality and professional standing. We welcome young fresh talent who appreciate old fashioned agency nurturing, strong guidance and honesty."

◉ **TOUGH GUY BOOKING**, 2217 Nicollet Ave. S., Minneapolis MN 55405. (612)874-2445 or 874-2475. Fax: (612)874-2430. E-mail: tguy@tt.net. Website: http://tt.net/tguy/index.html. Co-owners/agents: Christian Bernhardt and Brian Earle. Booking agent. Estab. 1994. Represents individual artists, groups and songwriters from anywhere; currently handles 41 bands. Receives 15% commission. Reviews material for acts.
How to Contact: Write or call first and obtain permission to submit. Prefers cassette or CD with lead sheet. If seeking management, press kit should include cover letter, photo, bio, press, CD and history. Does not return material. Reports in 1 month.
Music: Mostly **rock/pop**, **punk/noise**, **electronic** and **indie**. Works primarily with bands from established independent record labels. Current acts include Royal Trux, King Missile and Half Japanese.
Tips: "Be interesting, have a good touring history, established name and be signed to a good record label."

✓ ◯ **TRANSATLANTIC MANAGEMENT**, P.O. Box 2831, Tucson AZ 85702. (520)881-5880. Fax: (520)881-8001. E-mail: engcathy@euphoria.org. Website: http://www.rivergraphics.com/transmgt. Owner: English Cathy. A&R: Gina Inman. Management firm. Estab. 1979. Represents individual artists, groups and songwriters from anywhere; currently handles 10 acts. Receives 20% commission. "Transatlantic Management primarily showcase their artists through the use of compilation CDs presented at music conferences worldwide and also through their website." Reviews material for acts.
How to Contact: Submit demo tape by mail. Unsolicited submissions are OK. If seeking management, press kit should include tape/CD/bio/photo. Does not return material. Reports in 3-6 months.
Music: Mostly **all types** from **New Age to country to hard rock**. Current acts include Kathi McDonald (rock blues singer), Mary Ann Price (jazz singer), Mary Godfrey and Peter Subway (singer/songwriter).

◉ **TRIANGLE TALENT, INC.**, 10424 Watterson, Louisville KY 40299. (502)267-5466. Fax: (502)267-8244. President: David H. Snowden. Booking agency. Represents artists and groups; currently handles 85 acts. Receives 10-20% commission. Reviews material for acts.
How to Contact: Submit demo tape by mail. Unsolicited submissions are OK. Prefers cassette or VHS videocassette with 2-4 songs and lyric sheet. If seeking management, press kit should include photo, cassette of at least 3 songs, and video if possible. Does not return material. Reports in 3-4 weeks.
Music: Mostly **rock/top 40** and **country**. Current acts include Lee Bradley (contemporary country), Karen Kraft (country) and Four Kinsmen (Australian group).

◉ **TUTTA FORZA MUSIC**, 34 Haviland St. #310, Norwalk CT 06854. Phone/fax: (203)855-0095. Proprietor: Andrew Anello. Management firm, booking agency, music publisher (Tutta Forza Publishing/ ASCAP) and record company. Estab. 1990. Represents New York Metro Area artists; currently handles 6 acts. Receives 10% commission. Reviews material for acts.
How to Contact: Submit demo tape by mail. Unsolicited submissions are OK. Prefers cassette, VHS videocassette or CD with 3 songs. If seeking management, press kit should include recent press releases, music reviews, biography and cover letter. SASE. Reports in 3 weeks.
Music: Mostly **jazz fusion**, **classical** and **modal combat jazz**; also **instrumentalists**, **composers** and **improvisors**. Works primarily with single artists, composers, improvisors and instrumentalists. Current acts include Andrew Anello (clarinetist/composer) and The Jazz X-Centrix.
Tips: "Looking for self-sufficient individualists; musicians who bring their own unique artistic qualities to work with. Genre of music not nearly as important as quality and taste in their style!"

● **TWENTIETH CENTURY PROMOTIONS**, 155 Park Ave., Cranston RI 02905. (401)467-1832. Fax: (401)467-1833. President: Gil Morse. Management firm, booking agency and record producer (20th Century). Estab. 1972. Represents individual artists and groups from anywhere; currently handles 9 acts. Receives 15% commission. Reviews material for acts.
How to Contact: Call first and obtain permission to submit or to arrange personal interview. Prefers cassette. If seeking management, press kit should include photo and bio. Does not return material. Reports in 2-3 weeks.
Music: Mostly **country** and **blues**. Works primarily with individuals and groups. Current acts include Robbin Lynn, Charlie Brown's Costars and Bobby Buris Pickett (Monster Mash).
Tips: "Don't give up."

● **UMBRELLA ARTISTS MANAGEMENT, INC.**, 2612 Erie Ave., P.O. Box 8385, Cincinnati OH 45208. (513)871-1500. Fax: (513)871-1510. E-mail: umbrella@one.net. President: Stan Hertzman. Management firm. Represents artists and groups; currently handles 4 acts.
How to Contact: Submit demo tape by mail. Unsolicited submissions are OK. Prefers cassette with 3 songs and lyric sheet. SASE. If seeking management, press kit should include a short bio, reviews, photo and cassette. Reports in 2 months if interested.
Music: Mostly **progressive**, **rock** and **top 40/pop**. Works with contemporary/progressive pop/rock artists and writers. Current acts include The Blue Birds (R&B/rock band), Adrian Belew and The Greenhornes and Bandees.

◯ **UMPIRE ENTERTAINMENT ENTERPRIZES**, 1507 Scenic Dr., Longview TX 75604. (903)759-0300. Owner/President: Jerry Haymes. Management firm, music publisher (Golden Guitar, Umpire Music) and record company (Enterprize Records). Estab. 1974. Represents individual artists, groups, songwriters and rodeo performers from anywhere; currently handles 6 acts. Receives 15% commission. Reviews material for acts.
How to Contact: Submit demo tape by mail. Unsolicited submissions are OK. Prefers cassette with lyric and lead sheets. If seeking management, press kit should include cover letter, bio, picture, lyric sheets, video and any recordings. Does not return material. "Submissions become part of files for two years, then disposed of." Reports in 1 month.
Music: Mostly **country, pop** and **gospel**. Artists include Kelly Grant (country/pop artist), Over the Hill Gang (Golden Oldies group) and Jerry Haymes (cross-over country/rock-a-billy).

◯ **UNIVERSAL MUSIC MARKETING**, P.O. Box 2297, Universal City TX 78148. (210)599-0022. E-mail: bswrl8@txdirect.net. President: Frank Willson. Management firm, record company (BSW Records), booking agency, music publisher and record producer (Frank Wilson). Estab. 1987. Represents individual artists and groups from anywhere; currently handles 16 acts. Receives 15% commission. Reviews material for acts.
How to Contact: Submit demo tape by mail. Unsolicited submissions are OK. Prefers cassette or ¾″ videocassette with 3 songs and lyric sheet. If seeking management, include tape/CD, bio, photo and current activities. SASE. Reports in 4-6 weeks.
Music: Mostly **country** and **light rock**; also **blues** and **jazz**. Works primarily with vocalists, singer/songwriters and bands. Current acts include Candee Land, Bob Jares, Wes Wiginton and Peter Caulton.

◯ **UP FRONT MANAGEMENT**, 1906 Seward Dr., Pittsburg CA 94565. Phone/fax: (510)427-7210. CEO/President: Charles Coke. Vice President: Terry A. Pitts. Management firm, record company (Man Network) and record producer (Heavyweight Productions). Estab. 1977. Represents individual artists, groups, songwriters and producers from anywhere; currently handles 4 acts. Receives 20% commission. Reviews material for acts.
How to Contact: Submit demo tape by mail. Unsolicited submissions are OK. Prefers cassette, videocassette or CD with 3-5 songs and lyric sheet. If seeking management, press kit should include cover letter, bio, CD or cassette, phone number, photo, lyric sheets and press clippings. Does not return material. Reports in 6 weeks.
Music: Mostly **rock, country** and **R&B**. Works primarily with bands and singers. Current acts include Terrance B. (R&B), Ronnie Jeffers (country) and Jennifer Mancuso (country).

THE TYPES OF MUSIC each listing is interested in are printed in **boldface**.

🌐 ☑ ◑ **HANS VAN POL MANAGEMENT**, Utrechtseweg, 1381 G5, Weesp, Netherlands. Phone: (0)294-413-633. Fax: (0)294-480-844. E-mail: "hans"asgood-morely@wxs.nl. Managing Director: Hans Van Pol. Management firm, booking agency, consultant (Hans Van Pol Music Consultancy), record company (J.E.A.H.! Records) and music publisher (Blue & White Music). Estab. 1984. Represents regional (Holland/Belgium) individual artists and groups; currently handles 12 acts. Receives 15-25% commission. Reviews material for acts.
How to Contact: Submit demo tape by mail. Unsolicited submissions are OK. Prefers cassette or VHS videocassette with 3 songs and lyric sheets. If seeking management, press kit should include demo, possible video (VHS/PAL), bio, press clippings, photo and release information. SAE and IRC. Reports in 1 month.
Music: Mostly **dance**: **rap/swing beat/hip house/R&B/soul/c.a.r.** Current acts include Tony Scott (rap) and MC Miker "G" (rap/R&B).

◑ **RICHARD VARRASSO MANAGEMENT**, P.O. Box 387, Fremont CA 94537. (510)792-8910. Fax: (510)792-0891. E-mail: rvarrasso@aol.com. President: Richard Varrasso. A&R: Saul Vigil. Management firm. Estab. 1976. Represents individual artists, groups and songwriters from anywhere; currently handles several acts. Receives 10-20% commission. Reviews material for acts.
How to Contact: Submit demo tape by mail. Unsolicited submissions are OK. Prefers cassette. If seeking management, press kit should include photos, bios, cover letter, cassette, lyric sheets, press clippings, video, résumé and contact numbers. Good kits stand out. Does not return material. Reports in 1-2 months.
Music: Mostly **rock**, **electronica** and **young country**. Works primarily with concert headliners and singers. Current acts include Famous Hits, Jack LaSaud and Gary Cambra of the Tubes.

◑ **VOKES BOOKING AGENCY**, P.O. Box 12, New Kensington PA 15068-0012. (412)335-2775. President: Howard Vokes. Booking agency, music publisher (Vokes Music Publishing) and record company (Vokes Record Co.). Represents individual traditional country and bluegrass artists. Books name acts in on special occasions. For special occasions books nationally known acts from Grand Ole Opry, Jamboree U.S.A., Appalachian Jubliee, etc. Receives 10-20% commission.
How to Contact: New artists send 45 rpm record, cassette, LP or CD. Reports in 1 week.
Music: Mostly traditional **country**, **bluegrass**, **old time** and **gospel**; definitely no rock or country rock. Current acts include Howard Vokes & His Country Boys (country) and Mel Anderson.
Tips: "We work mostly with traditional country bands and bluegrass groups that play various bars, hotels, clubs, high schools, malls, fairs, lounges, or fundraising projects. We work at times with other booking agencies in bringing acts in for special occasions. Also we work directly with well-known and newer country, bluegrass and country gospel acts not only to possibly get them bookings in our area, but in other states as well. We also help 'certain artists' get bookings in the overseas marketplace."

◑ **WILLIAM F. WAGNER AGENCY**, 14343 Addison St. #221, Sherman Oaks CA 91423. (818)905-1033. Owner: Bill Wagner. Management firm and record producer (Bill Wagner). Estab. 1957. Represents individual artists and groups from anywhere; currently handles 2 acts. Receives 15% commission. Reviews materials for acts.
How to Contact: Submit demo tape by mail. Unsolicited submissions are OK. Prefers cassette or CD with 5 songs and lead sheet. If seeking management, press kit should include cover letter, bio, picture, tape or CD with 5 songs. "If SASE and/or return postage are included, I will reply in 30 days. I will not reply by telephone or fax." SASE. Reports in 1 month.
Music: Mostly **jazz**, **contemporary pop** and **contemporary country**; also **classical**, **MOR** and **film and TV background**. Works primarily with singers, with or without band, big bands and smaller instrumental groups. Current acts include Page Cavanaugh (jazz/pop/contemporary/pianist) and Sandy Graham (jazz singer).
Tips: "Indicate in first submission what artists you are writing for, by name if possible. Don't send material blindly. Be sure all material is properly copyrighted. Be sure package shows 'all material herein copyrighted' on outside."

🌐 ◑ **MR. WALKER'S COMPANY**, 13 Victoria Ave., Albert Park, Vic 3206 Australia. Phone: (+61)3 9645-7300. Fax: (+61)3 9645-7311. E-mail: mrwalkersco@peg.apc.org. Contact: Andrew Walker. Management firm, music publisher (Head Records Publishing) and record company (Head Records). Estab. 1995. Represents individual artists and groups from anywhere; currently handles 8 acts. Management company receives 20% commission.
How to Contact: Submit demo tape by mail. Unsolicited submissions are OK. Cassette or CD only. If seeking management, press kit should include CD, bio and history. "Processing takes time. Contact by fax or e-mail is best as it allows for time differences to be no obstacle." SAE and IRC. Reports in 1-2 months.
Music: Mostly **rock/pop**, **jazz** and **acoustic**; also **reggae**, **blues** and **world**. Works primarily with singers/

songwriters and bands. Current acts include Colin Hay (acoustic pop), Men At Work (Australian pop band) and Black Sorrows (blues and jazz).

Tips: "We have low need for songs to be supplied to our artists. We are mostly interested in recorded artists/writers looking for distribution/release in Australia/New Zealand."

N **WALLS & CO. MANAGEMENT**, 4237 Henderson Blvd., 2nd Floor, Tampa FL 33629. (813)948-6652. Fax: (813)289-9208. E-mail: prinkey@mindspring.com. President: M. Susan Walls. Management firm. Estab. 1988. Represents individual artists from anywhere; currently handles 7 acts. Receives 15% commission. Reviews material for acts.

How to Contact: Call first and obtain permission to submit a demo or submit demo tape by mail. Unsolicited submissions are OK. Prefers cassette or CD with up to 5 songs and lyric sheet. If seeking management, press kit should include appearance schedules, press releases, bio/picture, publicist's name, articles/reviews. Does not return material. Reports in 2 weeks.

Music: Mostly **country**, **jazz** and **pop**. Works primarily with bands with lead vocalists, individual artists and some songwriters. Current acts include Brandy Taylor (16-year-old country artist), Whitney Jordon (12-year-old country artist) and Amy Hartwig (15-year-old songwriter/singer).

Tips: "Listen, learn from experience and write every day."

N **CHERYL K. WARNER PRODUCTIONS**, P.O. Box 1721, Midland MI 48641-1721. Phone/fax: (517)839-5846. E-mail: davidsan@home.net. Owners: Cheryl K. Warner and David M. Warner. Management firm, booking agency, music publisher (Cheryl K. Warner Music), record company (CKW Records) and record producer (Cheryl K. Warner). Estab. 1988. Currently handles 3 acts. Receives 20% commission. Reviews material for acts.

How to Contact: Submit demo tape by mail. Unsolicited submissions are OK. Prefers cassette or VHS videocassette with 3 best songs, lyric or lead sheet, bio and picture. If seeking management, press kit should include CD or cassette with up-to-date bio, cover letter, lyric sheets, press clippings, video and picture. Does not return material. Reports in 4-6 weeks if interested.

Music: Mostly **country/traditional and contemporary**, **Christian/gospel** and **A/C/pop**. Works primarily with singer/songwriters and bands with original and versatile style. Current acts include Cheryl K. Warner (Nashville recording artist/entertainer), Cheryl Warner Band (support/studio alt) and Veronica (contemporary artist).

N **WE RECORDS & MANAGEMENT**, P.O. Box 751325, Houston TX 77275. (281)484-2964. E-mail: werecords@aol.com. Contact: Jason Whitmire. Management firm, booking agency and record company (WE Records). Estab. 1995. Represents individual artists and groups from anywhere; currently handles 6 acts. Receives 20% commission. Reviews material for acts.

How to Contact: Submit demo tape by mail. Unsolicited submissions are OK. Prefers CD. If seeking management, press kit should include cover letter, demo tape/CD, press clippings, photo and bio. "Explain, besides the music, what makes your act more appealing than others?" Does not return material. Reports in 2 months.

Music: Mostly **electronic**, **techno** and **progressive rock**; also **industrial**. Current acts include I-45 (hip-hop/slip-hop group), Secret Sunday (indie rock) and Joey Jaime aka Derrighan, Magic Fire Sheep (techno producer).

Tips: "Keep everyone updated on your status and keep your name in the public eye."

WEMUS ENTERTAINMENT, 4301 Arroyo, Suite 2, Midland TX 79707. (915)689-3687. Fax: (915)689-2665. President: Dennis Grubb. Management firm, booking agency and music publisher (Wemus Music, Inc.). Estab. 1983. Represents local and regional individual artists and groups; currently handles 10 acts. Receives 15-20% commission. Reviews material for acts.

How to Contact: Submit demo tape by mail. Unsolicited submissions are OK. Prefers cassette or VHS videocassette with 3-5 songs and lyric sheet. If seeking management, press kit should include glossy head and full body shots and extensive biography. "Make sure address, phone number and possible fax number is included in the packet, or a business card." Does not return material. Reports in 2-4 weeks.

Music: Mostly **country**, **pop** and **soul/R&B**; also **swing**. Current acts include Dallas Brass & Electric (variety), The Big Time (variety) and The Pictures (variety).

Tips: "We preview and try to place good songs with national artists who are in need of good materials. We have a very tough qualification process. We refuse to forward sub-par materials to major artists or artists management."

✓ **WESTWOOD ENTERTAINMENT GROUP**, 1031 Amboy Ave., Suite 202, Edison NJ 08820. (732)225-8600. Fax: (732)225-8644. E-mail: music@westwoodgrp.com. Website: http://www.west

woodgrp.com. Professional Manager: Steve Willoughby. Management agency and music publisher (Westunes Music). Estab. 1985. Represents regional artists and groups; currently handles 4 acts. Receives 15% commission. Reviews material for acts.
How to Contact: Write or call first and obtain permission to submit. Submit demo tape by mail. Unsolicited submissions are OK. Prefers cassette with 3 songs, lyric sheet, bio, press clippings, and photo. SASE. Reports in 6 weeks.
Music: Mostly **rock**; also **pop**. Works primarily with singer/songwriters, show bands and rock groups. Current acts include B.B. & The Stingers, Orville Davis (country) and Dave Baldwin (pop/rock).
Tips: "Present a professional promotional/press package with three song limit."

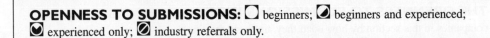 **WHITE HAT MANAGEMENT**, P.O. Box 896, Pine Brook NJ 07058. (973)227-7117. Fax: (973)808-1613. E-mail: aaron@aol.com. Manager: Aaron Van Duyne. Management firm. Estab. 1996. Represents individual artists, groups and record labels from anywhere. Receives 5% commission.
How to Contact: Write or call first to arrange personal interview. Prefers cassette or videocassette. If seeking management, press kit should include bio, contact details, tape or CD and video if possible. Does not return material.
Music: Mostly **rock/pop**, **blues** and **country**; also **alternative**. Current acts include Sam Taylor (blues singer/songwriter/guitarist), Gooding (alternative) and Eddie Brigati (singer/songwriter).
Tips: "Get a basic understanding of the music business, especially publishing."

SHANE WILDER ARTISTS' MANAGEMENT, P.O. Box 3503, Hollywood CA 90078. (805)251-7526. President: Shane Wilder. General Manager: Aaron Wilder. Management firm, music publisher (Shane Wilder Music/BMI) and record producer (Shane Wilder Productions). Represents artists and groups; currently handles 5 acts. Receives 15% commission. Reviews material for acts.
How to Contact: Submit demo tape by mail. Unsolicited submissions are OK. Prefers cassette or videocassette of performance with 4-10 songs and lyric sheet. If seeking management, send cover letter, bio, lyric sheets, cassette with 4-10 songs, photos of individuals or groups, video if possible and any press releases. "Submissions should be highly commercial." SASE. Reports in 2 weeks.
Music: **Country**. Works primarily with single artists and groups. Current acts include Billy O'Hara, Melanie Ray (country singer) and Sweden's #1 country music star Mia Hogland.

J.R. WILLIAMS & ASSOCIATES, P.O. Box 400, Catoosa OK 74015. (918)266-1191. Fax: (918)266-1040. E-mail: jeromew@worldnet.att.net. Owner: Jerome R. Williams. Booking agency. Estab. 1990. Represents individual artists and groups from anywhere; currently handles 4 acts. Receives 15% commission. Reviews material for acts.
How to Contact: Write or call first and obtain permission to submit. Prefers CD with 4 songs. If seeking management, press kit should include picture, cover letter, demo tape/CD, lyric sheets, video, résumé, bio and market you are looking for. Does not return material. Reports 2 weeks.
Music: Mostly **contemporary Christian** and **pop Christian**. Current acts include A Cross Between (alternative religion), Glorify Him (hip-hop religion) and Voice of Praise.

YVONNE WILLIAMS MANAGEMENT, 6433 Topanga Blvd. #142, Canoga Park CA 91303. (818)366-0510. Fax: (818)366-0520. E-mail: rawspitt@aol.com. President: Yvonne Williams. Management firm, music publisher (Jerry Williams Music), record company (S.D.E.G.) and record producer (Jerry Williams). Estab. 1978. Represents individual artists and songwriters from anywhere; currently handles 12 acts. Receives 10-20% commission. Reviews material for acts.
How to Contact: Submit demo tape by mail. Unsolicited submissions are OK. Prefers cassette or DAT with any number of songs and lyric sheet. If seeking management, press kit should include cover letter, bio, photo, demo tape/CD, press clippings, video and résumé. Include SASE, name, phone and any background in songs placed. Reports in 4-6 weeks.
Music: Mostly **R&B**, **rock** and **country**; also **gospel**. Works primarily with singer/songwriters and singers. Current acts include Dinah Mack (gospel), Swamp Dogg (rock) and Toussaint McCall (R&B).
Tips: "Make a good clean dub, with a simple pilot vocal that is understandable."

RICHARD WOOD ARTIST MANAGEMENT, 69 North Randall Ave., Staten Island NY 10301. (718)981-0641. Contact: Richard Wood. Management firm. Estab. 1974. Represents musical groups; cur-

---

OPENNESS TO SUBMISSIONS: ☐ beginners; ◐ beginners and experienced; ◑ experienced only; ⊘ industry referrals only.

rently handles 3 acts. Receives 20% commission. Reviews material for acts.

How to Contact: Submit demo tape by mail. Unsolicited submissions are OK. Prefers cassette and lead sheet. If seeking management, press kit should include demo tape, photo, cover letter and résumé. SASE. Reports in 1 month.

Music: Mostly **dance**, **R&B** and **top 40/pop**; also **MOR**. Works primarily with "high energy" show bands, bar bands and dance bands. Current acts include F.O.N. (rap).

N: **WORLD ENTERTAINMENT SERVICES, INC.**, 6830 N. Broadway, Unit J, Denver CO 80221. (303)428-5500. Fax: (303)428-5600. E-mail: oceanfree@aol.com. Vice President: Terri L. Fisher. Management firm, record producer (World Entertainment Services, Inc.) and artist development. Estab. 1992. Represents individual artists, groups and songwriters from anywhere; currently handles 2 acts. Receives 15-20% commission. Reviews material for acts.

How to Contact: Write or call first to obtain permission to submit. Unsolicited submissions are OK. Prefers cassette or CD with 3 songs and lyric sheet. If seeking management, press kit should include cover letter, bio, picture, demo tape/CD, lyric sheets and press clippings. "For bookings: include current references, song list, stage requirements, any other information you feel is necessary to be booked. Include: cassettes or CD, bio, picture, press kit." SASE. Reports in 2-4 weeks.

Music: Mostly **rock**, **country** and **R&B**; also **pop** and **alternative**. "All styles considered." Works primarily with bands, artists, songwriters. Current acts include Kindred (4 piece rock, alternative) and Millenium (4 piece rock).

Tips: "Be creative; willing to go the distance; have the drive, desire and patience it takes to move forward in a very competitive market."

WORLD PARK PRODUCTIONS, 384 Riverway, Suite #4, Boston MA 02115. Phone/fax: (617)278-9968. E-mail: worldpark@aol.com. Director/President: Eric Sanzen. Management firm and booking agency. Estab. 1985. Represents individual artists, groups and songwriters from anywhere; currently handles 8-15 acts. Receives 10-15% commission. Reviews material for acts.

How to Contact: Write first and obtain permission to submit. Prefers CD. If seeking management, press kit should include cover letter, press clippings, photo, bio, CD and video (if available). Does not return material. Reports in 2 months.

Music: Mostly **world/roots**, **jungle/techno** and **folk**; also **electronica**, **vocals** and **jazz**. Works primarily with established acts. Current acts include Vinx (singer/songwriter major releases), Capercaillie (Scottish/Celtic rock band) and Brian Hughes (jazz guitarist/producer).

Tips: "Have an organized presentation and attitude."

WORLD WIDE MANAGEMENT, P.O. Box 536, Bronxville NY 10708. (914)337-5131. Fax: (914)337-5309. Director: Steve Rosenfeld. Management firm and music publisher (Neighborhood Music/ASCAP). Estab. 1971. Represents artists, groups, songwriters and actors; currently handles 5 acts. Receives 15-20% commission. Reviews material for acts.

How to Contact: Write first and obtain permission to submit. Prefers CD, cassette or videocassete of performance with 3-4 songs. If seeking management, press kit should include cover letter, bio, reviews, press clippings, CD or cassette with lyrics and photo. Does not return material. Reports in 3-4 weeks.

Music: Mostly **contemporary pop**, **folk**, **folk/rock** and **New Age**; also **A/C**, **rock**, **jazz**, **bluegrass**, **blues**, **country** and **R&B**. Works primarily with self-contained bands and vocalists. Current acts include Small Things Big (alternative), Lena Koutrakas (adult contemporary) and Levi Byrd (blues).

WRIGHT PRODUCTIONS, 11718 Hwy. 64 E., Tyler TX 75707. Phone/fax: (903)566-5653. Owner: Lonnie Wright. Management firm, music publisher (Fer-De-Lance/BMI and Juke Box Music/ASCAP), record producer and studio owner. Estab. 1970. Represents individual artists and songwriters from anywhere; currently handles 4 acts. Receives 20% commission. Reviews material for acts.

How to Contact: Submit demo tape by mail. Unsolicited submissions are OK. Prefers cassette with 4 songs and lyric sheet. If seeking management, press kit should include cover letter, lyric sheets, picture, bio and tape. SASE. Reports in 6 weeks.

Music: Mostly **country**, **gospel** and **blues**. Works primarily with artist/writer combinations. Current acts include A.J. Dryman (country singer), Waylon Adams (country singer) and Jennifer Wright (playwright).

THE OPENNESS TO SUBMISSIONS INDEX at the back of this book lists all companies in this section by how open they are to submissions.

✓ ◎ **WYATT MANAGEMENT WORLDWIDE, INC.**, 17860 New Hope St., Fountain Valley CA 92708. (714)839-7700. Fax: (714)775-4300. E-mail: wmw@wyattworld.com. Website: http://www.wyattworld.com. President: Warren Wyatt and Julie Hines. Management firm. Estab. 1976. Represents individual artists, groups and songwriters from anywhere; currently handles 12 acts. Receives 20% commission. Reviews material for acts.

How to Contact: Submit demo tape by mail. Unsolicited submissions are OK. Prefers CD, cassette or VHS videocassette with 2-10 songs and lyric sheet. If seeking management, press kit should include band biography, photos, video, members' history, press and demo reviews. SASE. Reports in 1 month.

Music: Mostly **rock**, **pop** and **world**; also **heavy metal**, **hard rock** and **top 40**. Works primarily with pop/ rock groups. Current acts include Saigon Kick (hard rock), Carmine Appice (rock), Keali'i Reichel (world music), Armadillo Man and Mike Tramp (pop/rock).

Tips: "Always submit new songs/material, even if you have sent material that was previously rejected; the music biz is always changing."

◎ **ZANE MANAGEMENT, INC.**, 1608 Walnut St., Suite 703, Philadelphia PA 19103. (215)772-3010. Fax: (215)772-3717. President: L.Z. Remick, Esq. Entertainment/sports consultants and managers. Represents artists, songwriters, producers and athletes; currently handles 6 acts. Receives 10-15% commission.

How to Contact: Submit demo tape by mail. Unsolicited submissions are OK. Prefers cassette and lyric sheet. If seeking management, press kit should include cover letter, bio, photo, demo tape and video. Does not return material. Reports in 3 weeks.

Music: Mostly **dance**, **easy listening**, **folk**, **jazz** (fusion), **MOR**, **rock** (hard and country), **soul** and **top 40/pop**. Current acts include Bunny Sigler (disco/funk), Peter Nero and Philly Pops (conductor) and Cast in Bronze (rock group).

Additional Managers & Booking Agents

The following companies are also managers/booking agents, but their listings are found in other sections of the book. See the General Index for page numbers, then read the listings for submission information.

Bernard Enterprises, Inc., Hal
Bixio Music Group/IDM Ventures
Branch Group Music
Brian Song Music Corp.
Capstan Record Production
Clearwind Publishing
Cliffside Music Inc.
Danford Entertainment Group/
   Sisyphus Records
Deadeye Records
Deep South Entertainment
Delev Music Company
Diamond Entertainment, Joel
Edition Rossori
Esquire International
Fish of Death Records

Glass House Productions
Hailing Frequency Music
   Productions
His Power Productions and
   Publishing
JSB Groupe Management Inc.
Kleanza River Canyon Productions
L.A. Records (Canada)
Lineage Publishing Co.
Lucifer Records, Inc.
Magid Productions, Lee
MHM Recordings
New Experience Records
Nightmare Records
Orchid Publishing
Pollybyrd Publications Limited

PPL Entertainment Group
Publishing Central
Raving Cleric Music Publishing/Euro
   Export Entertainment
Rowena Records
Satkowski Recordings, Steve
SDM
Silver Thunder Music Group
Standard Music Publishing
Stuart Music Co., Jeb
Texas Music Masters
Third Wave Productions Ltd.
Throwing Stones Records
Twin Towers Publishing Co.

Category Index

The Category Index is a good place to begin searching for a market for your songs. Below is an alphabetical list of 20 general music categories. If you write pop songs and are looking for a manager or booking agent to submit your songs to, check the Pop section in this index. There you will find a list of managers and booking agents who work with pop performers. Once you locate the entries for those publishers, read the music subheading *carefully* to determine which companies are most interested in the type of pop music you write. Some of the markets in this section do not appear in the Category Index because they have not indicated a specific preference. Most of these said they are interested in "all types" of music. Listings that were very specific, or whose description of the music they're interested in doesn't quite fit into these categories, also do not appear here.

Adult Contemporary (also easy listening, middle of the road, AAA, ballads, etc.)

All Star Talent Agency
Anderson Associates Communications Group
Backstage Entertainment/Loggins Promotion
Black Stallion Country, Inc.
Bojo Productions Inc.
Chucker Music Inc.
Gueststar Entertainment Agency
Hale Enterprises
International Entertainment Bureau
Jacobson Talent Management (JTM)
Junquera Productions, C.
Levinson Entertainment Ventures International, Inc.
Lutz Entertainment Agency, Richard
M.B.H. Music Management
Management by Jaffe
Martin Productions, Rick
Merri-Webb Productions
Phil's Entertainment Agency Limited
Poole Agency Limited, Gordon
Prestige Artistes
RadioActive
Richards World Management, Inc., Diane
Rustron Music Productions
St. John Artists
Skorman Productions, Inc., T.
Staircase Promotion
T.J. Booker Ltd.
T.S.J. Productions
Take Out Management
Tas Music Co./Dave Tasse Entertainment
Total Acting Experience, A
Wagner Agency, William F.
Warner Productions, Cheryl K.
World Wide Management
Zane Management, Inc.

Alternative (also modern rock, punk, college rock, new wave, hardcore, new music, industrial, ska, indie rock, garage, etc.)

American Artists Entertainment
Artist Management Services
Bohemia Entertainment Group
Bread & Butter Productions
Cool Records
Countdown Entertainment
Cox Promotions & Management, Stephen
Cranium Management
Cycle of Fifths Management, Inc.
Dale Management, Frankie
DAS Communications, Ltd.
Detko Management, Bill
Direct Management
Dream Team Management
Dunner Talent Management
Earth Tracks Artists Agency
Entercom
Eternal Records/Squigmonster Management
Freedman & Smith Entertainment
Glotzer Management Co., The
Hupp Enterprises, Joe
Imperial Artist Management
Kuper Personal Management
M.B.H. Music Management
M.E.G Management
Management by Jaffe
Merlin Management Corp.
Metro Talent Group, Inc.
Monopoly Management
Music Man Promotions
On the Level Music!
Outland Productions
Outlaw Entertainment International
Performers of the World Inc. (P.O.W.)
Prairie Fire Music Company
RadioActive
Rock Whirled Music Management

Greeley Entertainment, Chris
Gueststar Entertainment Agency
Gurley & Co.
Hale Enterprises
Hardison International Entertainment Corporation
Harrell & Associates, M.
Hupp Enterprises, Joe
International Entertainment Bureau
J & V Management
Jacobson Talent Management (JTM)
Jae Enterprises, Jana
James Management, Roger
Junquera Productions, C.
Kendall West Agency
Kickstart Music Ltd.
Kitchen Sync
Landslide Management
Lari-Jon Promotions
Levinson Entertainment Ventures International, Inc.
Levy Management, Rick
Live-Wire Management
Lowell Agency
Lutz Entertainment Agency, Richard
M.B.H. Music Management
Mabry Ministries, Kevin
Magnum Music Corporation Ltd.
Management Plus
Mayo & Company, Phil
McDonnell Group, The
Merri-Webb Productions
Midcoast, Inc.
Miller & Company, Thomas J.
Monopoly Management
Nash-One Management Inc.
Nelson Promotions & Management Co., Lou
Nik Entertainment Company
Northern Lights Management
Noteworthy Productions
Original Artists' Agency
Overstreet Music Companies, Tommy
Phil's Entertainment Agency Limited
Prairie Fire Music Company
Prestige Artistes
Pro Talent Consultants
Rainbow Collection Ltd.
Rock of Ages Productions
Rustron Music Productions
Rymkus Management and Promotions, Mike
Serge Entertainment Group
Siegel Entertainment Ltd.
Silver Bow Management
Smeltzer Productions, Gary
Sound and Serenity Management
SP Talent Associates
Sphere Group One
Staircase Promotion
Stephany Management, Jim
Stevens & Company Management

T.J. Booker Ltd.
T.L.C. Booking Agency
T.S.J. Productions
Total Acting Experience, A
Triangle Talent, Inc.
Twentieth Century Promotions
Umpire Entertainment Enterprizes
Universal Music Marketing
Up Front Management
Varrasso Management, Richard
Vokes Booking Agency
Wagner Agency, William F.
Walls & Co. Management
Warner Productions, Cheryl K.
Wemus Entertainment
White Hat Management
Wilder Artists' Management, Shane
Williams Management, Yvonne
World Entertainment Services, Inc.
World Wide Management
Wright Productions

Dance (also house, hi-NRG, disco, club, rave, techno, trip-hop, trance, etc.)
Anderson Associates Communications Group
Arpa Musik Management
Atlantic Entertainment Group
Bamn Management
Bassline Entertainment, Inc.
CBA Artists
Chucker Music Inc.
Clousher Productions
Countdown Entertainment
Countrywide Producers
De Miles Company, The Edward
First Time Management
Golden City International
Kendall West Agency
Landslide Management
Lutz Entertainment Agency, Richard
M.B.H. Music Management
Martin Productions, Rick
Mega Music Productions
Merlin Management Corp.
On Stage Management Inc.
Outlaw Entertainment International
Richards World Management, Inc., Diane
Rock 'N' Roll Management
Rogue Management
RPM Management Services Pty Ltd.
Savage, Inc., T.E.
Skorman Productions, Inc., T.
Sound Management Direction
Steinman Management, Obi
Take Out Management
Tas Music Co./Dave Tasse Entertainment
Total Acting Experience, A
Van Pol Management, Hans

Varrasso Management, Richard
WE Records & Management
Wood Artist Management, Richard
World Park Productions
Zane Management, Inc.

Folk (also acoustic, Celtic, etc.)
Afterschool Publishing Company
Amok Inc.
Artist Management Services
Cool Records
Countrywide Producers
Cox Promotions & Management, Stephen
Dinwoodie Management, Andrew
Dream Hatchery, Inc.
EAO Music Corporation of Canada
Hupp Enterprises, Joe
Living Eye Productions Ltd.
Northern Lights Management
Noteworthy Productions
Performers of the World Inc. (P.O.W.)
Prairie Fire Music Company
Professional Artist Management, Ltd.
Rock Whirled Music Management
Rustron Music Productions
SP Talent Associates
Syndicate Management
T.S.J. Productions
Tiger's Eye Entertainment Management &
    Consulting
World Park Productions
World Wide Management
Zane Management, Inc.

**Instrumental (also background music,
musical scores, etc.)**
Endangered Species Artist Management
Jae Enterprises, Jana
Tutta Forza Music
Wagner Agency, William F.

Jazz (also fusion, bebop, swing, etc.)
Afterschool Publishing Company
Air Tight Management
All Musicmatters
Bacchus Group Productions, Ltd.
Backstage Entertainment/Loggins Promotion
BC Productions
Blue Cat Agency, The/El Gato Azul Agency
Chucker Music Inc.
Concept 2000 Inc.
Cooke & Rose Entertainment & Production, Inc.
Countrywide Producers
Crossfire Productions
Dream Hatchery, Inc.
Endangered Species Artist Management
Erwin Music
Flinter Music
Fox Management, Inc., Mitchell

GCI Inc.
Harrell & Associates, M.
International Entertainment Bureau
Its Happening Present Entertainment
Jae Enterprises, Jana
Kendall West Agency
L.D.F. Productions
Live-Wire Management
McDonnell Group, The
Metro Talent Group, Inc.
Miller & Company, Thomas J.
Music Man Promotions
Nelson Promotions & Management Co., Lou
Noteworthy Enterprises
On the Level Music!
Performers of the World Inc. (P.O.W.)
Phil's Entertainment Agency Limited
PriceClub Productions
Ricca, Jr.'s Entertainment Agency, Joey
Richards World Management, Inc., Diane
Riohcat Music
Savage, Inc., T.E.
Sirius Entertainment
Stay Gold Productions
T.S.J. Productions
Tas Music Co./Dave Tasse Entertainment
Tiger's Eye Entertainment Management &
    Consulting
Total Acting Experience, A
Tutta Forza Music
Universal Music Marketing
Wagner Agency, William F.
Walker's Company, Mr.
Walls & Co. Management
Wemus Entertainment
World Park Productions
World Wide Management
Zane Management, Inc.

**Latin (also Spanish, salsa, Cuban, conga,
Brazilian, cumbia, rancheras, Mexican,
merengue, Tejano, Tex Mex, etc.)**
Arpa Musik Management
Bacchus Group Productions, Ltd.
Bassline Entertainment, Inc.
Blue Cat Agency, The/El Gato Azul Agency
Cookman International
Corvalan-Condliffe Management
Hansen Enterprises, Ltd.
Management Plus
Mega Music Productions
PriceClub Productions
Ricca, Jr.'s Entertainment Agency, Joey
Savage, Inc., T.E.
Sound Management Direction
Stevens & Company Management

Metal (also thrash, grindcore, heavy metal, etc.)

Artist Representation and Management
Dale Management, Frankie
Entercom
Eternal Records/Squigmonster Management
Imperial Artist Management
Outland Productions
Outlaw Entertainment International
Professional Artist Management, Ltd.
Right-On Management
Wyatt Management Worldwide, Inc.

New Age (also ambient)

Cox Promotions & Management, Stephen
Dream Hatchery, Inc.
Live-Wire Management
Prairie Fire Music Company
Richards World Management, Inc., Diane
Rustron Music Productions
Serge Entertainment Group
Sphere Group One
World Wide Management

Novelty (also comedy, humor, etc.)

Circuit Rider Talent & Management Co.
Eternal Records/Squigmonster Management
Hall Entertainment & Events, Bill
Its Happening Present Entertainment
Sea Cruise Productions, Inc.

Pop (also top 40, top 100, popular, chart hits, etc.)

Afterschool Publishing Company
Alert Music, Inc.
All Star Talent Agency
American Artists Entertainment
American Classics
Anderson Associates Communications Group
Ardenne Int'l Inc.
Arpa Musik Management
Artist Management Services
Artist Representation and Management
Atch Records and Productions
Bacchus Group Productions, Ltd.
Backstage Entertainment/Loggins Promotion
Bamn Management
Bassline Entertainment, Inc.
Baxter Management, Dick
BC Productions
Big J Productions
Bird Entertainment Agency, J.
Blue Cat Agency, The/El Gato Azul Agency
Bouquet-Orchid Enterprises
Capital Entertainment
Cash Productions, Inc.
Chucker Music Inc.
Circuit Rider Talent & Management Co.
Clockwork Entertainment Management Agency

Concept 2000 Inc.
Conscience Music
Corvalan-Condliffe Management
Countdown Entertainment
Countrywide Producers
Cranium Management
Criss-Cross Industries
D&M Entertainment Agency
D&R Entertainment
DAS Communications, Ltd.
De Miles Company, The Edward
Dinwoodie Management, Andrew
DMR Agency
Dream Hatchery, Inc.
Earth Tracks Artists Agency
Ellis International Talent Agency, The
Endangered Species Artist Management
Entercom
Eternal Records/Squigmonster Management
Evans Productions, Scott
Fenchel Entertainment Agency, Fred T.
First Time Management
Freedman & Smith Entertainment
Future Star Entertainment
GMI Entertainment Inc.
Godtland Management, Inc., Eric
Golden City International
Golden Guru Entertainment
Greeley Entertainment, Chris
Gurley & Co.
Hale Enterprises
Hardison International Entertainment Corporation
Huge Production, Inc., A
Hupp Enterprises, Joe
Ikon Entertainment
International Production Management
Its Happening Present Entertainment
Jae Enterprises, Jana
James Management, Roger
Jampop Ltd.
Junquera Productions, C.
Kagan International, Sheldon
Kickstart Music Ltd.
Kitchen Sync
L.D.F. Productions
Landslide Management
Legend Artists Management
Levy Management, Rick
Live-Wire Management
Lutz Entertainment Agency, Richard
Management by Jaffe
Martin Productions, Rick
Mayo & Company, Phil
McDonnell Group, The
Mega Music Productions
Merlin Management Corp.
Merri-Webb Productions
Midcoast, Inc.

Miller & Company, Thomas J.
Monopoly Management
Music Man Promotions
Nik Entertainment Company
Noteworthy Productions
On Stage Management Inc.
Outlaw Entertainment International
Performers of the World Inc. (P.O.W.)
Powerplay Entertainment
Prestige Artistes
PriceClub Productions
Pro Talent Consultants
RadioActive
Rainbow Collection Ltd.
Richards World Management, Inc., Diane
Right-On Management
Rock 'N' Roll Management
Rock of Ages Productions
Rogue Management
RPM Management Services Pty Ltd.
Saffyre Management
Savage, Inc., T.E.
Serge Entertainment Group
Shute Management Pty. Ltd., Phill
Siegel Entertainment Ltd.
Silver Bow Management
Skorman Productions, Inc., T.
Sound Management Direction
Sphere Group One
Staircase Promotion
Starkravin' Management
Steinman Management, Obi
T.J. Booker Ltd.
T.S.J. Productions
Take Out Management
Tas Music Co./Dave Tasse Entertainment
Tenn Artist Management, William
Total Acting Experience, A
Tough Guy Booking
Triangle Talent, Inc.
Umbrella Artists Management, Inc.
Umpire Entertainment Enterprizes
Wagner Agency, William F.
Walker's Company, Mr.
Walls & Co. Management
Warner Productions, Cheryl K.
Wemus Entertainment
Westwood Entertainment Group
White Hat Management
Williams & Associates, J.R.
Wood Artist Management, Richard
World Entertainment Services, Inc.
World Wide Management
Wyatt Management Worldwide, Inc.
Zane Management, Inc.

R&B (also soul, black, urban, etc.)
American Artists Entertainment
American Classics

Anderson Associates Communications Group
Artist Representation and Management
Atch Records and Productions
Atlantic Entertainment Group
Bacchus Group Productions, Ltd.
Bamn Management
Barnard Management Services (BMS)
Bassline Entertainment, Inc.
Big J Productions
Black Stallion Country, Inc.
Blowin' Smoke Productions/Records
Bojo Productions Inc.
Bouquet-Orchid Enterprises
Bread & Butter Productions
Chucker Music Inc.
Circuit Rider Talent & Management Co.
Concept 2000 Inc.
Countdown Entertainment
Countrywide Producers
Criss-Cross Industries
D&M Entertainment Agency
DAS Communications, Ltd.
De Miles Company, The Edward
Dinwoodie Management, Andrew
EJJ Management
Endangered Species Artist Management
Eternal Records/Squigmonster Management
Evans Productions, Scott
Future Star Entertainment
GMI Entertainment Inc.
Golden City International
Hardison International Entertainment Corporation
Harrell & Associates, M.
Hupp Enterprises, Joe
Ikon Entertainment
Its Happening Present Entertainment
Jacobs Management
Jacobson Talent Management (JTM)
Jampop Ltd.
Kitchen Sync
KKR Entertainment Group
Landslide Management
Legend Artists Management
Levinson Entertainment Ventures International, Inc.
Levy Management, Rick
Live-Wire Management
McDonnell Group, The
Merri-Webb Productions
Nelson Promotions & Management Co., Lou
On Stage Management Inc.
Performers of the World Inc. (P.O.W.)
Powerplay Entertainment
Precision Management
Renaissance Entertainment Group
Rogue Management
Rustron Music Productions
Sea Cruise Productions, Inc.
Shute Management Pty. Ltd., Phill

Silver Bow Management
Sirius Entertainment
Smeltzer Productions, Gary
Southern Made Records
Sphere Group One
Starkravin' Management
Stay Gold Productions
T.S.J. Productions
Take Out Management
Tas Music Co./Dave Tasse Entertainment
Total Acting Experience, A
Up Front Management
Van Pol Management, Hans
Wemus Entertainment
Williams Management, Yvonne
Wood Artist Management, Richard
World Entertainment Services, Inc.
World Wide Management
Zane Management, Inc.

Rap (also hip-hop, bass, etc.)
Afterschool Publishing Company
American Artists Entertainment
Atch Records and Productions
Bassline Entertainment, Inc.
Dunner Talent Management
Eternal Records/Squigmonster Management
First Time Management
Godtland Management, Inc., Eric
Golden City International
Hardison International Entertainment Corporation
Its Happening Present Entertainment
Jacobson Talent Management (JTM)
KKR Entertainment Group
Precision Management
Renaissance Entertainment Group
Richards World Management, Inc., Diane
Sound Management Direction
Southern Made Records
Strictly Forbidden Artists
Van Pol Management, Hans

Religious (also gospel, sacred, Christian, church, hymns, praise, inspirational, worship, etc.)
All Star Management
All Star Talent Agency
Atch Records and Productions
Baxter Management, Dick
Bojo Productions Inc.
Bouquet-Orchid Enterprises
Capital Entertainment
Cash Productions, Inc.
Circuit Rider Talent & Management Co.
Concept 2000 Inc.
Countrywide Producers
Crawfish Productions
D&R Entertainment
Direct Management

Doss Presents, Col. Buster
Dream Hatchery, Inc.
Erwin Music
Fenchel Entertainment Agency, Fred T.
First Time Management
Golden City International
Gueststar Entertainment Agency
Hardison International Entertainment Corporation
Harrell & Associates, M.
Jampop Ltd.
Junquera Productions, C.
L.D.F. Productions
Lari-Jon Promotions
Mabry Ministries, Kevin
Magnum Music Corporation Ltd.
Mayo & Company, Phil
Merri-Webb Productions
Nelson Promotions & Management Co., Lou
Overstreet Music Companies, Tommy
Precision Management
Rock of Ages Productions
Silver Bow Management
Staircase Promotion
Stewart Music Group
Umpire Entertainment Enterprizes
Vokes Booking Agency
Warner Productions, Cheryl K.
Williams & Associates, J.R.
Williams Management, Yvonne
Wright Productions

Rock (also rockabilly, AOR, rock 'n' roll, etc.)
Air Tight Management
Alert Music, Inc.
All Star Talent Agency
American Bands Management
American Classics
Anderson Associates Communications Group
AR Management
Ardenne Int'l Inc.
Arpa Musik Management
Artist Management Services
Artist Representation and Management
Backstreet Booking
Barnard Management Services (BMS)
Barrett Rock 'n' Roll Enterprises, Paul
Big J Productions
Bird Entertainment Agency, J.
Blowin' Smoke Productions/Records
Blue Cat Agency, The/El Gato Azul Agency
Blue Wave Productions
Bouquet-Orchid Enterprises
Bread & Butter Productions
Cash Productions, Inc.
Chucker Music Inc.
Clockwork Entertainment Management Agency
Clousher Productions
Conscience Music

Advertising, Audiovisual & Commercial Music Firms

It's happened a million times—you hear a jingle on the radio or television and can't get it out of your head. That's the work of a successful jingle writer, writing songs to catch your attention and make you aware of the product being advertised. But the field of commercial music consists of more than just memorable jingles. It also includes background music that many companies use in videos for corporate and educational presentations, as well as films and TV shows.

SUBMITTING MATERIAL

More than any other market listed in this book, the commercial music market expects composers to have made an investment in the recording of their material before submitting. A sparse, piano/vocal demo won't work here; when dealing with commercial music firms, especially audiovisual firms and music libraries, high quality production is important. Your demo may be kept on file at one of these companies until a need for it arises, and it may be used or sold as you sent it. Therefore, your demo tape or reel must be as fully produced as possible.

The presentation package that goes along with your demo must be just as professional. A list of your credits should be a part of your submission, to give the company an idea of your experience in this field. If you have no experience, look to local television and radio stations to get your start. Don't expect to be paid for many of your first jobs in the commercial music field; it's more important to get the credits and exposure that can lead to higher-paying jobs.

Commercial music and jingle writing can be a lucrative field for the composer/songwriter with a gift for writing catchy melodies and the ability to write in many different music styles. It's a very competitive field, so it pays to have a professional presentation package that makes your work stand out.

Three different segments of the commercial music world are listed here: advertising agencies, audiovisual firms and commercial music houses/music libraries. Each looks for a different type of music, so read these descriptions carefully to see where the music you write fits in.

ADVERTISING AGENCIES

Ad agencies work on assignment as their clients' needs arise. Through consultation and input from the creative staff, ad agencies seek jingles and music to stimulate the consumer to identify with a product or service.

When contacting ad agencies, keep in mind they are searching for music that can capture and then hold an audience's attention. Most jingles are short, with a strong, memorable hook. When an ad agency listens to a demo, it is not necessarily looking for a finished product so much as for an indication of creativity and diversity. Many composers put together a reel of excerpts of work from previous projects, or short pieces of music that show they can write in a variety of styles.

AUDIOVISUAL FIRMS

Audiovisual firms create a variety of products, from film and video shows for sales meetings, corporate gatherings and educational markets, to motion pictures and TV shows. With the increase of home video use, how-to videos are a big market for audiovisual firms, as are spoken word educational videos. All of these products need music to accompany them. For your quick reference, companies working to place music in movies and TV shows (excluding commercials) have a 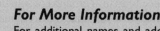 preceding their listing (also see the Film & TV Index for a complete list of these companies).

Like ad agencies, audiovisual firms look for versatile, well-rounded songwriters. When submitting demos to these firms, you need to demonstrate your versatility in writing specialized background music and themes. Listings for companies will tell what facet(s) of the audiovisual field they are involved in and what types of clients they serve. Your demo tape should also be as professional and fully produced as possible; audiovisual firms often seek demo tapes that can be put on file for future use when the need arises.

COMMERCIAL MUSIC HOUSES & MUSIC LIBRARIES

Commercial music houses are companies contracted (either by an ad agency or the advertiser) to compose custom jingles. Since they are neither an ad agency nor an audiovisual firm, their main concern is music. They use a lot of it, too—some composed by inhouse songwriters and some contributed by outside, freelance writers.

Music libraries are different in that their music is not custom composed for a specific client. Their job is to provide a collection of instrumental music in many different styles that, for an annual fee or on a per-use basis, the customer can use however he chooses.

In the following listings, commercial music houses and music libraries, which are usually the most open to works by new composers, are identified as such by **bold** typeface.

The commercial music market is similar to most other businesses in one aspect: experience is important. Until you develop a list of credits, pay for your work may not be high. Don't pass up opportunities if a job is non- or low-paying. These assignments will add to your list of credits, make you contacts in the field, and improve your marketability.

Money and rights

Many of the companies listed in this section pay by the job, but there may be some situations where the company asks you to sign a contract that will specify royalty payments. If this happens, research the contract thoroughly, and know exactly what is expected of you and how much you'll be paid.

Depending on the particular job and the company, you may be asked to sell one-time rights or all rights. One-time rights involve using your material for one presentation only. All rights means the buyer can use your work any way he chooses, as many times as he likes. Be sure you know exactly what you're giving up, and how the company may use your music in the future.

I **For More Information**

For additional names and addresses of ad agencies that may use jingles and/or commercial music, refer to the *Standard Directory of Advertising Agencies* (National Register Publishing). For a list of audiovisual firms, check out the latest edition of *AV Marketplace* (R.R. Bowker). Both these books may be found at your local library. To contact companies in your area, see the Geographic Index at the back of this book.

THE AD AGENCY, P.O. Box 470572, San Francisco CA 94147. Creative Director: Michael Carden. Advertising agency and **jingle/commercial music production house**. Clients include business, industry and retail. Estab. 1971. Uses the services of music houses, independent songwriter/composers and lyricists for scoring of commercials, background music for video production, and jingles for commercials. Commissions 20 composers and 15 lyricists/year. Pays by the job or by the hour. Buys all or one-time rights.

How to Contact: Submit demo tape of previous work. Prefers cassette with 5-8 songs and lyric sheet. SASE. Reports in 2-3 weeks.
Music: Uses variety of musical styles for commercials, promotion, TV, video presentations.
Tips: "Our clients and our needs change frequently."

☑ **ADVERTEL, INC.**, P.O. Box 18053, Pittsburgh PA 15236-0053. (412)886-1400. Fax: (412)886-1411. President/CEO: Paul Beran. Telephonic/Internet production company. Clients include small and multi-national companies. Estab. 1983. Uses the services of music houses and independent songwriters/composers for scoring of instrumentals (all varieties) and telephonic production. Commissions 3-4 composers/year. Pay varies. Buys all rights and phone exclusive rights.
How to Contact: Submit demo tape of previous work. Prefers CD or cassette. "Most compositions are 2 minutes strung together in 6, 12, 18 minute length productions." Does not return material; prefers to keep on file. Reports "right away if submission fills an immediate need."
Music: Uses all varieties, including unusual; mostly subdued music beds. Radio-type production used exclusively in telephone and Internet applications.
Tips: "Go for volume. We have continuous need for all varieties of music in two minute lengths."

☑ ⊠ **AGA COMMUNICATIONS**, 2557C N. Terrace Ave., Milwaukee WI 53211-3822. (414)962-9810. E-mail: greink@juno.com. CEO: Arthur Greinke. Advertising agency, public relations/music artist management and media relations. Clients include small business, original music groups and special events. Estab. 1984. Uses the services of music houses, independent songwriters/composers and lyricists for scoring of motion picture and video productions; background music for special events; jingles for TV and radio. Commissions 4-6 composers and 4-6 lyricists/year. Pays on a per job basis. Buys all rights and one-time rights.
How to Contact: Submit demo tape of previous work. Prefers CD, cassette, DAT or VHS videocassette with any number of songs and lyric sheet. "We will contact only when job is open, but will keep submissions on file." Does not return material. Reports in 2-48 weeks.
Music: Uses original rock, pop and heavy rock for recording groups, commercials and video projects.
Tips: "Try to give as complete a work as possible without allowing us to fill in the holes. High energy, unusual arrangements, be creative, different and use strong hooks!"

☑ ⊠ **ALLEGRO MUSIC**, 3990 Sunsetridge, Suite 203, Moorpark CA 93021-3756. E-mail: dannymuse@aol.com. Website: http://www.danielobrien.com. Owner: Daniel O'Brien. Scoring service, **jingle/commercial music production house**. Clients include film-makers, advertisers, network promotions and aerobics. Estab. 1991. Uses the services of independent songwriters/composers and lyricists for scoring of films, TV and broadcast commercials, jingles for ad agencies and promotions, and commercials for radio and TV. Commissions 3 composers and 1 lyricist/year. Pays 50% royalty. Buys one-time rights.
How to Contact: Query with résumé of credits or submit demo tape of previous work. Do not call first. Prefers CD, cassette and lyric sheet. SASE. Reports in 1-4 weeks (if interested).
Music: Varied: Contemporary to orchestral.

⊠ **ANDERSON COMMUNICATIONS**, Dept. SM, 2245 Godby Rd., Atlanta GA 30349. (404)766-8000. President: Al Anderson. Producer: Vanessa Vaughn. Advertising agency and syndication operation. Estab. 1971. Clients include major corporations, institutions and media. Uses the services of music houses, independent songwriters/composers and lyricists for background music for commercials and jingles for syndicated radio programs. Commissions 5-6 songwriters or composers and 6-7 lyricists/year. Pays by the job. Buys all rights.
How to Contact: Write first to arrange personal interview or submit demo tape of previous work. Prefers cassette. Does not return material. Reports in 2 weeks or "when we have projects requiring your services."
Music: Uses a variety of music for music beds for commercials and jingles for nationally syndicated radio programs and commercials targeted at the black consumer market.
Tips: "Be sure the composition plays well in a 60-second format."

⊠ **ANGEL FILMS COMPANY**, 967 Hwy. 40, New Franklin MO 65274-9778. Phone/fax: (573)698-3900. E-mail: angelfilm@aol.com. President: Arlene Hulse. Motion picture and record production company (Angel One Records). Estab. 1980. Uses the services of music houses, independent songwriters/composers and lyricists for scoring of feature films, animation, TV programs and commercials, background music for TV and radio commercials and jingles for commercials. Commissions 12-20 composers and 12-20 lyricists/year. Payment depends upon budget; each project has a different pay scale. Buys all rights.
How to Contact: Submit demo tape of previous work or query with résumé of credits. Prefers cassette

or VHS videocassette with 3 pieces and lyric and lead sheet. "Do not send originals." SASE, but prefers to keep material on file. Reports in 6 weeks.
Music: Uses basically MOR, but will use anything (except country and religious) for record production, film, television and cartoon scores. Uses jazz—modern, classical for films.
Tips: "Don't copy others, just do the best you can. We freelance all our work for our film and television production company, and are always looking for that one break-through artist for Angel One Records."

BLUMENTHAL CADY & ASSOCIATES, INC., 10040 Regency Circle, Omaha NE 68114. (402)397-2077. Fax: (402)397-1958. E-mail: bcadver@earthlink.net. Executive Vice President/Creative Director: Bob Blumenthal. Advertising agency. Clients include financial, bank, health services, computer software design, retail, legal, other business to business. Estab. 1989. Uses the services of music houses, independent songwriters/composers and lyricists for background music for AV and shows (infomercials), jingles for commercials and commercials for radio and TV. Commissions 3-5 composers and 3-5 lyricists/year. Pays by the job. Buys all rights.
How to Contact: Submit demo tape of previous work. Prefers cassette or VHS videocassette. Prefers to keep submitted material on file. Reports back "if work matches our proposals to clients."
Music: Uses up-tempo, jazz, New Age for jingles, commercials and videos.

DAVID BOWMAN PRODUCTIONS, 28 Park Lane, Feasterville PA 19053. (215)942-9059 or (215)322-8078. Fax: (215)396-8693. President/Artistic Director: W. David Bowman. Scoring service, **jingle/commercial music production house**, music library producers/music production house and music publisher. Clients include television, radio, video production houses, computer/video game manufacturers, music production houses and multimedia developers, compositions and arrangements for symphony orchestras and various other ensembles. Estab. 1989. Uses the services of independent songwriters/composers and own team of music staff writers for scoring of films, documentaries and video productions, background music for television, radio, video productions and all multimedia applications, commercials for radio and TV, and background instrumental works for use in their music library. Commissions 5-10 composers/year. Pays by the job. Buys all rights or one-time rights.
How to Contact: Write first and obtain permission to submit. Prefers cassette with 3-5 songs. "We are looking for instrumental pieces of any length not exceeding three minutes for use in our music library." Does not return material. Reports in 1-2 months.
Music: Uses all styles for TV and radio commercials, video productions, various multimedia applications.
Tips: "Network. Get your name and your work out there. Let everyone know what you are all about and what you are doing. Be patient, persistent and professional. What are you waiting for? Do it!"

BRg MUSIC WORKS, P.O. Box 202, Bryn Mawr PA 19010. (610)825-5656. E-mail: jandron@erols.com. Creative Director: Doug Reed. Contact: Lee Napier. **Jingle producers/music library producers**. Uses independent composers and music houses for background music for radio, TV and commercials and jingles for radio and TV. Commissions 20 songwriters/year. Pays per job. Buys all rights.
How to Contact: Submit demo tape of previous work. Prefers cassette. "We are looking for quality jingle tracks already produced, as well as instrumental pieces between 2 and 3 minutes in length for use in AV music library." SASE. Reports in 2 weeks.
Music: All types.
Tips: "Send your best and put your strongest work at the front of your demo tape."

BRYAN/DONALD INC. ADVERTISING, 2345 Grand, Suite 1625, Kansas City MO 64108. (816)471-4866. Fax: (816)421-7218. Creative Director: Don Funk. Advertising agency. Clients include food, business to business. Estab. 1966. Uses the services of independent songwriters/composers and lyricists for background music, jingles and commercials for radio. Commissions 1-2 composers and 1 lyricist/year. Pays negotiable. Buys all rights.
How to Contact: Submit demo tape of previous work. Prefers cassette. Prefers to keep material on file.

BUTWIN & ASSOCIATES, INC., 8700 Westmoreland Lane, Minneapolis MN 55426. Phone/fax: (612)545-3886. President: Ron Butwin. Advertising agency. Clients include restaurants, banks, manufacturers, retail. Estab. 1977. Uses the services of music houses, independent songwriters/composers and lyricists

LISTINGS OF COMPANIES within this section which are either commercial music production houses or music libraries will have that information printed in **boldface** type.

for background music for videos and corporate presentations, jingles for radio and TV commercials and shows and commercials for radio and TV. Commissions 6-8 composers and 6-8 lyricists/year. Pays per job. Buys all rights "generally."

How to Contact: Submit demo tape of previous work. Prefers cassette or VHS videocassette with 8-12 songs and lyric sheet. Does not return material. Prefers to keep submitted material on file. "We only respond if we're interested and either want more information or have a project in place."

Music: Uses up-tempo, pop, jazz, classical and New Age for slide presentations, jingles and commercials.

Tips: "Send us good, clean work that is truly representative of your skills. We are interested in knowing your experience and skill level. Give us some background on you and your business."

CALDWELL VANRIPER, 1314 N. Meridian, Indianapolis IN 46202. (317)632-6501. Website: http://www.cw.com. Vice President/Executive Producer: Sherry Boyle. Advertising agency and public relations firm. Clients include industrial, financial and consumer/trade firms. Uses the services of music houses for scoring of radio, TV and A/V projects, jingles and commercials for radio and TV.

How to Contact: Submit demo tape of previously aired work on audio cassette. Does not return material. "Sender can follow up on submission. Periodic inquiry or demo update is fine."

Tips: "We do not work directly with composers, we work with music production companies. Composers should contact the production companies directly."

☑ 🎞 **CANTRAX RECORDERS**, Dept. CM, 2119 Fidler Ave., Long Beach CA 90815. (562)498-6492. E-mail: cantrax@earthlink.net. Owner: Richard Cannata. Recording studio. Clients include anyone needing recording services (i.e., industrial, radio, commercial). Estab. 1980. Uses the services of independent songwriters/composers and lyricists for scoring of independent features and films and background music for radio, industrials and promotions, commercials for radio and TV and jingles for radio. Commissions 10 composers/year. Pays fees set by the artist. "We take 15%."

How to Contact: Query with résumé of credits or submit demo tape of previous work. Prefers 7½/15 ips reel-to-reel, DAT or CD with lyric sheets. "Indicate noise reduction if used." Does not return material. Reports in 3 weeks.

Music: Uses jazz, New Age, rock, easy listening and classical for slide shows, jingles and soundtracks.

Tips: "Send a 7½ or 15 ips reel, CD or DAT tape for us to audition; you must have a serious, professional attitude."

☑ **CASANOVA-PENDRILL PUBLICIDAD**, 3333 Michelson, Suite 300, Irvine CA 92612. (949)474-5001. Production: Anna Wilkinson. Advertising agency. Clients include consumer and corporate advertising—Hispanic markets. Estab. 1985. Uses the services of music houses, independent songwriters/composers and lyricists for radio, TV and promotions. Pays by the job or per hour. Buys all rights or one-time rights.

How to Contact: Submit demo tape of previous work, tape demonstrating composition skills and manuscript showing music scoring skills. Prefers cassette (or ¾ videocassette). "Include a log indicating spot(s) titles." Does not return material; prefers to keep on file.

Music: All types of Hispanic music (e.g., salsa, merengue, flamenco, etc.) for TV/radio advertising.

🅽 **CEDAR CREST STUDIO**, P.O. Box 28, Mountain Home AR 72653. (870)488-5777. Fax: (870)488-5255. E-mail: cedarcrest@oznet.com. Website: http://www.oznet.com/cedarcrest. Owner: Bob Ketchum. Audiovisual firm and **jingle/commercial music production house**. Clients include corporate, industrial, sales, music publishing, training, educational, legal, medical, music and Internet. Estab. 1973. Uses the services of independent songwriters/composers for background music for video productions, jingles for TV spots and commercials for radio and TV. Pays by the job or by royalties. Buys all rights or one-time rights.

How to Contact: Query with résumé of credits or submit demo tape of previous work. Prefers cassette, DAT, 3.25, 7.5 or 15 IPS reel-to-reel, videocassette or CD. Does not return material. "We keep it on file for future reference." Reports in 2-8 weeks.

Music: Uses up-tempo pop (not too "rocky"), unobtrusive—no solos for commercials and background music for video presentations.

Tips: "Hang, hang, hang. Be open to suggestions. Improvise, adapt, overcome."

🎞 **CINEVUE/STEVE POSTAL PRODUCTIONS**, P.O. Box 428, Bostwick FL 32007. (904)325-9356. Website: http://www.caisa.com/worstfilms. Director/Producer: Steve Postal. Motion picture production company. Estab. 1955. Serves all types of film distributors. Uses the services of music houses, independent songwriters, composers and lyricists for scoring and background music for films and nature documentaries. Commissions 10 composers and 5 lyricists/year. Pays by the job. Buys all and one-time rights.

How to Contact: Query with résumé of credits or submit demo tape of previous work ("good tape only!"). Submit manuscript showing music scoring skills. Prefers cassette with 10 pieces and lyric or lead sheet. Does not return material. "Send good audio-cassette, then call me in a week." Reports in 2 weeks.
Music: Uses all styles of music for features (educational films and slide presentations). "Need horror film music on traditional instruments—no electronic music."
Tips: "Be flexible, fast—do first job free to ingratiate yourself and demonstrate your style. Follow up with two phone calls."

☑ **COAKLEY HEAGERTY**, 1155 N. First St., San Jose CA 95112. (408)275-9400. Creative Director: Ray Bauer. Advertising agency. Clients include consumer, business to business and high-tech firms. Estab. 1966. Uses the services of music houses for jingles for commercials for radio and TV. Commissions 15-20 songwriters/year. Pays by the job. Buys all rights.
How to Contact: Submit demo tape of previously aired work. Prefers cassette with 8-10 pieces. Does not return material; prefers to keep on file. Reports in 6 months.
Music: All kinds of music for jingles and music beds.
Tips: "Send only commercials of past clients. Please don't be pushy and call over and over again. I'll call when I have something I like. Please include costs for creative and final production in a cover letter, address issues of talent availability if you are not located in a major ad market."

COMMUNICATIONS ELECTRONICS INC., P.O. Box 1045-SWM, Ann Arbor MI 48106. (734)996-8888. Fax: (734)663-8888. Website: http://www.usascan.com. Ad Director: Ken Ascher. Advertising agency. Clients include electronic and hi-tech firms. Estab. 1969. Uses the services of music houses for jingles for the Web, commercials for radio and TV and background music for music on hold. Commissions 20-50 composers and 5 lyricists/year. Pays $500-3,000/job or $15-75/hour. Buys all rights.
How to Contact: Submit demo tape of previous work. Prefers cassette or CD. Prefers to keep submitted material on file. Reports in 3 weeks.
Music: Uses jazz, New Age, synthesized, MOR for music-on-hold, Internet music beds and commercials.

COMMUNICATIONS FOR LEARNING, 395 Massachusetts Ave., Arlington MA 02174. (781)641-2350. E-mail: comlearn@thecia.net. Executive Producer/Director: Jonathan L. Barkan. Audiovisual and design firm. Clients include multi-nationals, industry, government, institutions, local, national and international nonprofits. Uses services of music houses and independent songwriters/composers for background music for videos and multimedia. Commissions 1-2 composers/year. Pays $2,000-3,000/job and one-time fees. Rights purchased varies.
How to Contact: Submit demo tape of previous work. Prefers cassette, CD, DAT or 7½ or 15 ips reel-to-reel (or ½" or ¾" videocassette). Does not return material; prefers to keep on file. "For each job we consider our entire collection." Reports in 2-3 months.
Music: Uses all styles of music for all sorts of assignments.
Tips: "Please don't call. Just send good material and when we're interested, we'll be in touch. Make certain name and phone number are on all submitted work itself, not only cover letter."

CREATIVE ASSOCIATES, Dept. SM, 44 Park Ave., Madison NJ 07940. (973)377-4440. Production Coordinator: Susan Graham. Audiovisual/multimedia firm and web content provider. Clients include commercial, industrial firms. Estab. 1975. Uses the services of music houses and independent songwriters/composers for scoring of video programs, background music for press tours and jingles for new products. Pays $300-5,000/job. Buys all or one-time rights.
How to Contact: Submit demo tape of previous work demonstrating composition skills or query with résumé of credits. Prefers cassette, CD-ROM or ½" VHS videocassette. Prefers to keep material on file.
Music: Uses all styles for many different assignments.

FOR EXPLANATIONS OF THESE SYMBOLS, SEE THE INSIDE FRONT AND BACK COVERS OF THIS BOOK.

CREATIVE HOUSE ADVERTISING, INC., 30777 Northwestern Hwy., Suite 301, Farmington Hills MI 48334. (248)737-7077. Executive Vice President/Creative Director: Robert G. Washburn. Marketing/advertising agency and graphics studio. Serves commercial, retail, consumer, industrial, medical and financial clients. Uses the services of songwriters and lyricists for jingles, background music for radio and TV commercials and corporate sales meeting films and videos. Commissions 3-4 songwriters/year. Pays $1,500-10,000/job depending on job involvement. Buys all rights.
How to Contact: Query with résumé of credits or submit tape demo showing jingle/composition skills. Submit cassette or ¾″ videocassette with 6-12 songs. SASE, but would prefer to keep material on file. "When an appropriate job comes up associated with the talents/ability of the songwriters/musicians, then they will be contacted."
Music: "The type of music we need depends on clients. The range is multi: contemporary, top 40, rock, MOR and traditional."
Tips: "Be fresh, innovative and creative. Provide good service and costs."

✅ **CREATIVE SUPPORT SERVICES**, 1950 Riverside Dr., Los Angeles CA 90039. (323)666-7968. E-mail: info@mail.cssmusic.com. Website: http://www.cssmusic.com. Creative Director: Michael M. Fuller. **Music/sound effects library**. Clients include audiovisual production houses. Estab. 1978. Uses the services of independent songwriters and musicians for production library. Commissions 3-5 songwriters and 1-2 lyricists/year. Buys all rights.
How to Contact: Submit demo tape of previous work. Prefers cassette ("chrome or metal only") or 7½ ips reel-to-reel with 3 or more pieces. Does not return material; prefers to keep on file. "Will call if interested."
Music: Uses "industrial music predominantly, but all other kinds or types to a lesser degree."
Tips: "Don't assume the reviewer can extrapolate beyond what is actually on the demo."

🔳 **D.S.M. PRODUCERS INC.**, 161 W. 54th St., Suite 803, New York NY 10019. (212)245-0006. President, CEO: Suzan Bader. CFO, CPA: Kenneth R. Wiseman. Submit to: Elba T. Maldonado, Director A&R. Vice President, National Sales Director: Doris Kaufman. Scoring service, **jingle/commercial music production house** and original stock library called "All American Composers Library (administered world wide except USA by Warner/Chappell Music, Inc.)" Clients include networks, corporate, advertising firms, film and video, book publishers (music only). Estab. 1979. Uses the services of independent songwriters/composers for scoring of TV and feature films, background music for feature films and TV, jingles for major products and commercials for radio and TV. Pays 50% royalty. Buys all rights.
How to Contact: Write first and enclose SASE for return permission. Prefers cassette or VHS videocassette with 2 songs and lyric or lead sheet. "Use a large enough return envelope to put in a standard business reply letter." Reports in 2-3 months.
Music: Uses all styles including alternative, dance, New Age, country and rock for adventure films and sports programs.
Tips: "Carefully label your submissions. Include a short bio/résumé of your works. Lyric sheets are very helpful to A&R. Only send your best tapes and tunes. Invest in your profession and get a local professional to help you produce your works. A master quality tape is the standard today. This is your competition so if you really want to be a songwriter, act like the ones who are successful—get a good tape of your tune. This makes it easier to sell overall. Never use 'samples' or any other copyrighted material in your works without a license."

✅ **dbF A MEDIA COMPANY**, P.O. Box 2458, Waldorf MD 20604. (301)843-7110. Website: http://dbfmedia.com. Creative Director: Jan Ivie. Advertising agency, audiovisual and media firm and audio and video production company. Clients include business and industry. Estab. 1981. Uses the services of music houses, independent songwriters/composers and lyricists for background music for industrial, training, educational and promo videos, jingles and commercials for radio and TV. Commissions 5-12 composers and 5-12 lyricists/year. Pays by the job. Buys all rights.
How to Contact: Submit demo tape of previous work. Prefers cassette or 7½ ips reel-to-reel or VHS videocassette with 5-8 songs and lead sheet. SASE, but prefers to keep material on file. Reports in 1-6 months.
Music: Uses up-tempo contemporary for industrial videos, slide presentations and commercials.
Tips: "We're looking for commercial music, primarily A/C."

✅ **DELTA DESIGN GROUP, INC.**, Dept. SM, 409 Washington Ave., Greenville MS 38701. (601)335-6148. E-mail: dmb@tecinfo.com. President: Debbie McBride. Advertising agency. Serves industrial, health care, agricultural, casino and retail commercial clients. Uses the services of music houses and independent

songwriters and composers for jingles, background music and commercials for radio and TV. Commissions 3-6 pieces/year. Pays by the job. Buys all rights.
How to Contact: Submit demo tape of previous work. Prefers cassette or CD with 3-6 songs. "Include typed sequence of cuts on tape on the outside of the box." Does not return material. Reports in 3 weeks.
Music: Needs "30- and 60-second jingles for agricultural, health care, gambling casinos, vacation destinations, auto dealers and chambers of commerce."

DISK PRODUCTIONS, 1100 Perkins Rd., Baton Rouge LA 70802. (504)343-5438. Director: Joey Decker. **Jingle/production house.** Clients include advertising agencies, slide production houses and film companies. Estab. 1982. Uses the services of music houses, independent songwriters/composers and lyricists for scoring and background music for TV spots, films and jingles for radio and TV. Commissions 7 songwriters/composers and 7 lyricists/year. Pays by the job. Buys all rights.
How to Contact: Submit demo tape of previous work. Prefers cassette or DAT (or ½" videocassette). Does not return material. Reports in 2 weeks.
Music: Needs all types of music for jingles, music beds or background music for TV and radio, etc.
Tips: "Advertising techniques change with time. Don't be locked in a certain style of writing. Give me music that I can't get from pay needle-drop."

EAST TEXAS HOSPITALITY CENTERS, P.O. Box 789, Marshall TX 75671-0789. (903)935-5524. Fax: (903)935-6789. Sales/Marketing: H.A. (Tony) Bridge, Jr. Hotel, restaurant and bar operator. Clients include hospitality industry. Estab. 1970. Uses the services of music houses, independent songwriters/composers and lyricists for jingles and commercials for radio and TV. Pays per job. Buys all rights.
How to Contact: Submit demo tape of previous work. Prefers cassette with lyric sheet. "No phone calls, please." SASE. Reports in 3 weeks.
Music: Uses various styles of music for commercials and jingles.
Tips: "Develop a good track record with radio/TV, ad agencies and hospitality industry."

ENSEMBLE PRODUCTIONS, P.O. Box 2332, Auburn AL 36831. (334)703-5963. E-mail: mcconbj@mail.auburn.edu. Owner: Barry J. McConatha. Interactive multimedia and video production/post production. Clients include corporate, governmental and educational. Estab. 1984. Uses services of music houses and independent songwriters/composers for background music for corporate public relations, educational and training videos. Commissions 0-5 composers/year. Pays $25-250/job depending upon project. Buys one-time rights or all rights.
How to Contact: Submit demo tape of previous work demonstrating composition skills. "Needs are sporadic, write first if submission to be returned." Prefers cassette or VHS videocassette with 3-5 songs. "Most needs are up-beat industrial sound but occasional mood setting music also. Inquire for details." Does not return material; prefers to keep on file. Reports in 3 months if interested. "Usually does not reply unless interested."
Music: Uses up-beat, industrial, New Age, and mood for training, PR, education and multi-media.
Tips: "Make sure your printed material is as precise as your music."

ENTERTAINMENT PRODUCTIONS, INC., 2118 Wilshire Blvd. #744, Santa Monica CA 90403. (310)456-3143. Fax: (310)456-8950. President/Producer: Edward Coe. Motion picture and television production company. Clients include motion picture and TV distributors. Estab. 1972. Uses the services of music houses and songwriters for scores, production numbers, background and theme music for films and TV and jingles for promotion of films. Commissions/year vary. Pays by the job or by royalty. Buys motion picture and video rights.
How to Contact: Query with résumé of credits. Demo should show flexibility of composition skills. "Demo records/tapes sent at own risk—returned if SASE included." Reports by letter in 1 month, "but only if SASE is included."
Tips: "Have résumé on file. Develop self-contained capability."

FIERCE MUSIC GROUP, 705 King St. W. #1715, Toronto, Ontario M5V 2W8 Canada. (416)860-9797. Fax: (416)955-9197. E-mail: fierce@io.org. Executive Producer: Derek Brin. Scoring service, **music sound effect library, jingle/commercial music production house** and record producer. Clients

---

REMEMBER: Don't "shotgun" your demo tapes. Submit only to companies interested in the type of music you write. For more submission hints, refer to Getting Started on page 11.

include film production companies and record companies. Estab. 1987. Uses the services of lyricists for jingles for radio, commercials for radio. Commissions 20 lyricists/year. Pays negotiable amount per job.
 • Fierce Music Group is the recipient of three Juno Awards.
How to Contact: Query with résumé of credits or submit demo tape of previous work. Prefers cassette or CD with 3-5 songs. Prefers to keep submitted material on file. Reports in 2 weeks.
Music: Uses R&B, hi energy and pop for radio spots, remixes and record production.

FILM CLASSIC EXCHANGE, 143 Hickory Hill Circle, Osterville MA 02655-1322. Phone/fax: (508)428-7198. Vice President: Elsie Aikman. Motion picture production company. Clients include motion picture industry/TV networks and affiliates. Estab. 1916. Uses the services of music houses, independent songwriters/composers and lyricists for scoring and background music for motion pictures, TV and video projects. Commissions 10-20 composers and 10-20 lyricists/year. Pays by the job. Buys all rights.
How to Contact: Submit demo tape of previous work. Prefers cassette or VHS videocassette. SASE, but prefers to keep material on file. Reports in 3 weeks to 2 months.
Music: Uses pop and up-tempo for theatrical films/TV movies.
Tips: "Be persistent."

FINE ART PRODUCTIONS/RICHIE SURACI PICTURES, MULTIMEDIA, INTERAC-TIVE, 67 Maple St., Newburgh NY 12550-4034. Phone/fax: (914)561-5866. E-mail: rs7.fap@mhv.net. Website: http://www.woodstock69.com or http://www.mhv.net/~rs7.fap/OPPS5.html or http://indyjones.si mplenet.com/Kunda.htm. Director: Richard Suraci. Advertising agency, audiovisual firm, scoring service, **jingle/commercial music production house**, motion picture production company (Richie Suraci Pictures) and **music sound effect library**. Clients include corporate, industrial, motion picture and broadcast firms. Estab. 1987. Uses services of independent songwriters/composers for scoring, background music and jingles for various projects and commercials for radio and TV. Commissions 1-10 songwriters or composers and 1-10 lyricists/year. Pays by the job. Buys all rights.
How to Contact: Submit demo tape of previous work or tape demonstrating composition skills, query with résumé of credits or write or call first to arrange personal interview. Prefers cassette (or ½″, ¾″, or 1″ videocassette) with as many songs as possible and lyric or lead sheets. SASE, but prefers to keep material on file. Reports in 1 year.
Music: Uses all types of music for all types of assignments.

FREDRICK, LEE & LLOYD, 235 Elizabeth St., Landisville PA 17538. (717)898-6092. Vice President: Dusty Rees. **Jingle/commercial music production house**. Clients include advertising agencies. Estab. 1976. Uses the services of independent songwriters/composers and staff writers for jingles. Commissions 2 composers/year. Pays $650/job. Buys all rights.
How to Contact: Submit tape demonstrating composition skills. Prefers cassette, CD or 7½ ips reel-to-reel with 5 jingles. "Submissions may be samples of published work or original material." SASE. Reports in 3 weeks.
Music: Uses pop, rock, country and MOR.
Tips: "The more completely orchestrated the demos are, the better."

GETER ADVERTISING INC., 75 E. Wacker Dr. #410, Chicago IL 60601-3708. (312)782-7300. Creative Director: Rosemary Geter. Advertising agency. Clients include retail-direct response. Estab. 1978. Uses the services of music houses, independent songwriters/composers and lyricists for jingles for clients, commercials for radio and TV. Pays per job. Buys all rights.
How to Contact: Write or call first to arrange personal interview or submit demo tape of previous work. Prefers cassette, ¾″ or ½″ videocassette with 8 songs. Does not return material.
Music: Uses all styles of music for jingles, commercials.

GOLD & ASSOCIATES, INC., 6000 Sawgrass Village Circle #C, Ponte Vedra Beach FL 32082. (904)285-5669. Fax: (904)285-8186. E-mail: gold@strikegold.com. Website: http://strikegold.com. Creative Director: Keith Gold. Marketing, design and advertising firm. Clients include Time-Warner, Disney, Mercury Records, Time-Life Music. Estab. 1988. Uses the services primarily of music houses, but also independent songwriters/composers. Agency develops its own lyrics for scoring background music for films, presentations, games, websites, etc., radio and TV commercials, special events and CDs. Commissions 5-10 music projects/year. "We pay 2-3 firms $500-1,000 for demos. For the final production, we pay between $5,000 and $35,000. We normally buy all rights. However, sometimes one time rights, for a year or specific markets."
 • Gold & Associates, Inc. has won over 750 regional, national and international awards, including Clio Awards, American Music Awards and London International Awards.

It's who you know that counts in commercial music

"Connections are everything," says composer Mike Levine. And he should know. Through networking, he has procured an impressive collection of credits, including the score for CNN's *Saturday/Sunday Morning*, as well as numerous commercials for national companies like 3M, Kool Aid, Days Inn and MCI. "Generally speaking," says Levine, "people don't give you a break unless they know you or you've been recommended by somebody."

Levine, who became interested in the commercial music business as a way to earn additional income as a musician, says getting that first break is "never easy. It took a lot of effort and perseverance—sending out tapes and getting rejected—but I finally got my foot in the door of a couple of places. From that point, I was able to get work."

Mike Levine

For beginners feeling discouraged or far removed from the industry, Levine suggests some creative approaches to finding networking opportunities. "If you went to college, check your alumni list. If anybody is working in the part of the music business you want to get into—boom! There's an instant contact." A friend from Hampshire College, where Levine received a B.A. in Communications, turned out to be an invaluable acquaintance when his friend later owned a music production company.

Maintaining relationships with people you meet along the way is also important. "You never know," says Levine. "Someone who was a drummer in your band might end up being a producer and will be able to hire you. The key is to be out there in as many music situations as you can, making as many contacts as you can." One way Levine established contacts was through a course on jingle writing at the New School in New York. Not only was the professor a jingle producer, but "a lot of people in the class were working studio musicians or involved in the commercial industry."

Through this class, as well as his own personal experience, Levine learned the three main approaches a composer can take to obtain commercial work. "The hardest way is to get the job directly from an advertising agency. Another possibility is to get on the staff of a music company in a low-level position—such as the person who makes tape dubs—and work your way up to where

MIKE LEVINE

Composer
Commercials: Kool Aid, 3M, MCI
Book: How to Be a Working Musician

they're giving you composing assignments."

The third, and most common, method is to be "subcontracted" by a music production company. The company, originally hired by an advertising agency, commissions "a number of freelancers to write versions of a commercial," says Levine. "There are a lot of situations where you end up competing against 15 other demos." At that point, the agency and its client pick one version. If yours is chosen, then you complete a finished production for the commercial.

Freelancers can work on commercials in one of two ways. "Usually you do what is called 'post-scoring,'" says Levine, "which is writing to an existing video, or a voice-over for radio that gives you the structure. Not only do you have to make your music fit the picture, but there are certain visual events that have to be accentuated by the music. You have to do a lot of calculating and experimenting with tempos." If the commercial has not been previously shot, the composer is often given "a storyboard, which is a set of drawings showing sequentially what goes on in the commercial. They end up cutting the picture to your music."

Levine, who has written a book entitled *How to Be a Working Musician* (Watson-Guptill), enjoys writing ad music because "it's creative, challenging and fun work. I love working with the gear in my studio, and it pays pretty well. As a freelancer in New York, you get paid anywhere from $150 to $300 for a demo. If your version gets picked, you typically get about 30 percent of what is called the creative fee or what the agency pays the music company. Usually that translates to two to three thousand dollars, although on some spots you can make even more."

Nevertheless, there can be drawbacks to composing for commercials. "It's very competitive, and you are often working under the gun. If you are lucky, you have three days to do a job. Most of the time it's two days, and occasionally a video is sent to me one afternoon and I need to have something in the next morning. You end up staying up half the night, and you can't have anything major go wrong because you'll run out of time." And even though composing can be a great creative outlet, Levine adds, "you still have a limited amount of freedom. No matter what musical style they ask you to write in, you have to make it work in a 30-second format."

Through his experience with commercial writing, Levine has garnered an abundance of advice for beginning freelancers. "I would suggest making a reel (which is usually recorded on a CD) of short examples of the different types of music you can write and produce. You have to decide on a strategy. You can show your abilities in different styles of music or concentrate on one area and hope they'll think of you for that area when something comes up. It's a tough call.

"Also, bear in mind that commercials are generally 30 seconds, so you want your [reel] to be short, featuring your best stuff. Edit so there is not a lot of space in between the examples. People in this business have a notoriously short attention span when it comes to listening to somebody's reel. If they are listening to your reel and there is a five-second pause between pieces, they might just turn it off."

After making a reel of music samples, the next step, says Levine, is to "call the various music production companies, such as those listed in *Songwriter's Market*. If you live in New York, Los Angeles or Chicago, you'll find more of these companies in your area. Try to get appointments to play your reel for people or mail it in with a letter addressed to a specific person at each company. Wait a couple of weeks and follow up with a phone call. Be persistent and be willing to get a lot of turn-downs."

Levine also advises songwriters to explore any possible connection they can find. "Think of all the people you know, your relatives, your friends, your college buddies—anyone who is involved in the commercial world. You have to use the 'throw it against the wall and hope something sticks' method."

When searching for work, always keep an open mind to nontraditional possibilities. "There are new opportunities opening up," says Levine, "including multimedia music opportunities and stuff for the Web. As the Internet grows, people will be able to hear music more easily. There will be more opportunities for composers to write music that will go on the Net or on websites. Ads are [on the Internet] already and when [advertisers] can add music, I'm sure they will." Understanding the importance of exploring new technologies, Levine uses his website (http://www.mikelevine.com) to list his clients as well as to provide sample clips of his work for future employers.

Finally, Levine stresses professionalism in order to succeed. "You have to take this business seriously. Look at [your career] as a business person rather than a musician. And don't give up. You have to put up with the negative stuff—almost anybody is going to get that. If you are talented, someone will give you a shot."

—*Donya Dickerson*

How to Contact: Submit demo tape of previous work. Prefers audio cassette, videocassette or CD. Will keep submitted material on file. "Sorry, but we contact writers and music houses only when we are ready to have music developed."
Music: Uses any and every style.
Tips: "Keep sending demos—at least one a year. Most of the time, we select and pay three companies to take our lyrics, and produce a rough demo. We select companies or individuals who have the 'sound' we are looking for. We then choose one for final production."

GROUP X, INC., P.O. Box 65, Reynoldsburg OH 43068-0065. (614)755-9565. Fax: (614)866-2636. President: Eddie Powell. Advertising agency. Clients include retail accounts. Estab. 1990. Uses the services of independent songwriters/composers for background music, jingles and commercials for radio and TV. Pays by the job. Buys all rights.
How to Contact: Submit demo tape of previous work. Prefers cassette, ips reel-to-reel or VHS videocassette with lyric or lead sheet. SASE. Reports in 3 months.
Music: Uses country and contemporary for jingles and educational projects.
Tips: "Be patient—work available on an 'as needed' basis only!"

HAMMOND & ASSOCIATES, 11307 Tawinee, Houston TX 77065. (281)955-5029. Fax: (281)890-8784. E-mail: jambeaux@swbell.net. Creative Directors: Michael Hammond and J.B. Strange. Audiovisual firm, **jingle/commercial music production house**, motion picture production company and recording studio. Clients include food store chains, land development, auto dealers, television stations. Estab. 1985. Uses the services of independent songwriters/composers and lyricists for movie scores, background music for educational/training films, jingles for TV, auto dealers, grocery stores etc., background music for educational and training films, and commercials for radio and TV. Pays per job. Buys all or one-time rights.
How to Contact: Query with résumé of credits. Submit cassette or VHS videocassette with 3 songs and lyric sheet. Does not return material. Prefers to keep submitted material on file. Reports in 3 weeks.
Music: Uses up tempo, R&B, country and gospel for jingles, educational and commercial songs.

HEPWORTH ADVERTISING CO., 3403 McKinney Ave., Dallas TX 75204. (214)526-7785. President: S.W. Hepworth. Advertising agency. Clients include financial, industrial and food firms. Estab. 1952. Uses services of songwriters for jingles for commercials for radio and TV. Pays by the job. Buys all rights.
How to Contact: Query with résumé of credits. Prefers cassette. SASE. Reports as need arises.

HEYWOOD FORMATICS & SYNDICATION, 1103 Colonial Blvd., Canton OH 44714. (330)456-2592. Owner: Max Heywood. Advertising agency and consultant. Clients include radio, TV, restaurants/lounges. Uses the services of music houses for commercials for radio and TV. Payment varies per project. Buys all rights.
How to Contact: Submit demo tape of previous work. Prefers cassette or 7½ or 15 ips reel-to-reel or VHS/Beta videocassette. Does not return material.
Music: Uses pop, easy listening and CHR for educational films, slide presentations and commercials.

THE HITCHINS COMPANY, 22756 Hartland St., Canoga Park CA 91307-2604. (818)715-0510. E-mail: hitchins@soca.com. President: W.E. Hitchins. Advertising agency. Estab. 1985. Uses the services independent songwriters/composers for jingles and commercials for radio and TV. Commissions 1-2 composers and 1-2 lyricists/year. Will negotiate pay. Buys all rights.
How to Contact: Query with résumé of credits. Prefers cassette, CD or VHS videocassette. "Check first to see if we have a job." Does not return material; prefers to keep on file.
Music: Uses variety of musical styles for commercials.

HODGES ASSOCIATES, INC., P.O. Box 53805, 912 Hay St., Fayetteville NC 28305. (910)483-8489. President/Production Manager: Chuck Smith. Advertising agency. Clients include industrial, retail and consumer. ("We handle a full array of clientele.") Estab. 1974. Uses the services of music houses and independent songwriters/composers for background music for industrial films and slide presentations, and commercials for radio and TV. Commissions 1-2 composers/year. Pays by the job. Buys all rights.
How to Contact: Submit demo tape of previous work. Prefers cassette. Does not return material; prefers to keep on file. Reports in 2-3 months.
Music: Uses all styles for industrial videos, slide presentations and TV commercials.

HOME, INC., 731 Harrison Ave., Boston MA 02118. (617)266-1386. Director: Alan Michel. Audiovisual firm and video production company. Clients include cable television, nonprofit organizations, pilot programs, entertainment companies and industrial. Uses the services of music houses and independent songwriters/composers for scoring of music videos, background music and commercials for TV. Commissions 2-5 songwriters/year. Pays up to $200-600/job. Buys all rights and one-time rights.
How to Contact: Submit demo tape of previous work. Prefers cassette with 6 pieces. Does not return material; prefers to keep on file. Reports as projects require.
Music: Mostly synthesizer. Uses all styles of music for educational videos.
Tips: "Have a variety of products available and be willing to match your skills to the project and the budget."

N IZEN ENTERPRISES, INC., 2809 Bentree Court, Las Vegas NV 89134. (702)233-4473. President: Ray Izen. Video services. Estab. 1980. Uses the services of music houses and independent songwriters/composers. Commissions 2 composers and 2 lyricists/year. Pays by the job. Buys all rights.
How to Contact: Submit demo tape of previous work. Prefers cassette or VHS videocassette. Does not return material; prefers to keep on file.

N JEWELITE INC., 106 Reade St., New York NY 10013. (212)233-1900. Fax: (212)233-1998. E-mail: jewelite@eclipse.net. Website: http://www.jewelite.com. Vice President: Robert Bank. Advertising agency. Estab. 1934. Uses the services of independent songwriters/composers, lyricists and arrangers for jingles, commercials for radio and TV and features. Pays by the job. Buys one-time rights.
How to Contact: Query with résumé of credits or submit demo tape of previous work. Prefers cassette. SASE. Reports in 2 weeks.
Tips: "Continue to work anywhere. The music industry changes so you never know where the hits are going to come from."

LISTINGS OF COMPANIES within this section which are either commercial music production houses or music libraries will have that information printed in **boldface** type.

☑ **JUNIPER MUSIC PRODUCTIONS**, 3227 McKinney Ave., Suite 100, Dallas TX 75204. (214)979-9424. Fax: (214)979-9492. Website: http://www.junipermusic.com. Senior Composer: John Hunter. Executive Producer: Jon Slott. Scoring service, **jingle/commercial music production house** and sound design. Clients include advertising agencies. Estab. 1994. Uses the services of independent songwriters/composers for scoring of industrial films and commercials for radio and TV. Pay varies per job. Buys all rights.
How to Contact: Query with résumé of credits. Prefers CD, cassette, DAT or ½″ or ¾″ videocassette with 5 songs and lead sheet. "Send only your best work. Don't make any excuses for your reel." Prefers to keep submitted material on file. Reports in 2 weeks.
Music: Uses all styles of music for commercial music.
Tips: "Be flexible. Don't waste your time or ours if you're only fluent in one style of writing. We are looking for people who can write well in all genres of music. Be quick. In this business you don't have time to be 'inspired.' We work with short time lines. Be good. We only want to hear from composers with real talent."

☑ **K&R'S RECORDING STUDIOS**, 28533 Greenfield, Southfield MI 48076. (248)557-8276. E-mail: recordav@flash.net. Website: http://www.knr.net. Contact: Ken Glaza. Scoring service and **jingle/commercial music production house**. Clients include commercial and industrial firms. Services include sound for pictures (music, dialogue). Uses the services of independent songwriters/composers and lyricists for scoring of film and video, commercials and industrials and jingles and commercials for radio and TV. Commissions 1 composer/month. Pays by the job. Buys all rights.
How to Contact: Submit demo tape of previous work. Prefers CD or VHS videocassette with 5-7 short pieces. We rack your tape for client to judge. Does not return material.
Tips: "Keep samples short. Show me what you can do in five minutes. Go to knr.net 'free samples' and listen to the sensitivity expressed in emotional music."

☑ **KATSIN/LOEB ADVERTISING INC.**, 100 Sansome St., San Francisco CA 94111. (415)399-9960. Fax: (415)399-9264. Head of Production: Pamela Zellers. Co-Creative Directors: Jef Loeb and Carlton Taylor. Production Director: Pamela Zellers. Advertising agency. Clients include travel, health care and entertainment. Estab. 1989. Uses the services of music houses and independent songwriters/composers for background music for commercials for radio and TV. Commissions 3-6 composers/year. Pays by the job. Buys all rights.
How to Contact: Submit demo tape of previous work. Does not return material; prefers cassette or ¾″ videocassette. Prefers to keep submitted material on file.
Music: Uses all kinds for commercials.
Tips: "We look for great musical ideas that work in harmony with the commercials we produce. If you've got a reel filled with same, we may be able to do business."

☑ **KEATING MAGEE ADVERTISING**, 2223 Magazine, New Orleans LA 70130. (504)523-2121. CEO: Jennifer Magee. Advertising agency. Clients include retail, consumer products and services, business-to-business. Estab. 1981. Uses the services of music houses and independent songwriters/composers and lyricists for scoring of, background music and jingles for radio and TV commercials. Commissions 4 composers/year. Pays by the job. Buys all or one time rights.
How to Contact: Submit demo tape of previous work. Prefers cassette or VHS videocassette. Does not return material; prefers to keep on file. Reports in 2 weeks.
Music: Uses all types for commercials, presentations.
Tips: "Send reel of actual work and references."

KEN-DEL PRODUCTIONS INC., First State Production Center, 1500 First State Blvd., Wilmington DE 19804-3596. (302)999-1164. Estab. 1950. Contact: Edwin Kennedy. A&R Director: Shirl Lotz. General Manager: Edwin Kennedy. Clients include publishers, industrial firms and advertising agencies, how-to's and radio/TV. Uses services of songwriters for radio/TV commercials, jingles and multimedia. Pays by the job. Buys all rights.
How to Contact: "Submit all inquiries and demos in any format to general manager." Does not return material. Will keep on file for 3 years. Generally reports in 1 month.

KJD ADVERTISING & TELEPRODUCTIONS, INC., 30 Whyte Dr., Voorhees NJ 08043. (609)751-3500. Fax: (609)751-7729. E-mail: mactoday@earthlink.net. President/Executive Producer: Larry Scott. Audio-video production and media buyers. Clients are varied. Estab. 1989. Uses the services of music houses, independent songwriters/composers or lyricists for background music for commercials, industrials, TV programming themes and jingles; also commercials for radio and TV. Commissions 1-2 composers and 1-2 lyricists/year. Pay varies. Buys all rights.

How to Contact: Query with résumé of credits or submit demo tape of previous work. Prefers cassette, DAT, ips reel-to-reel or ½″ or ¾″ Beta SP videocassette. SASE; but prefers to keep material on file. Reports in 6 weeks.

LAPRIORE VIDEOGRAPHY, 86 Allston Ave., Worcester MA 01604. (508)755-9010. Owner: Peter Lapriore. Video production company. Clients include corporations, retail stores, educational and sports. Estab. 1985. Uses the services of music houses, independent songwriters/composers for background music for marketing, training, educational videos and TV commercials and for scoring video. "We also own several music libraries." Commissions 2 composers/year. Pays $150-1,000/job. Buys all or one-time rights.
How to Contact: Submit demo tape of previous work. Prefers cassette or VHS videocassette with 5 songs and lyric sheet. Does not return material; prefers to keep on file. Reports in 3 weeks.
Music: Uses slow, medium, up-tempo, jazz and classical for marketing, educational films and commercials.
Tips: "Be very creative and willing to work on all size budgets."

N̄ McCANN-ERICKSON WORLDWIDE, Dept. SM, 1360 Post Oak Blvd., Suite 1900, Houston TX 77056. (713)965-0303. Creative Director: Mark Daspit. Advertising agency. Serves all types of clients. Uses services of music houses and independent songwriters for background music for television, jingles for radio, commercials for radio and TV, and videos. Commissions 10 songwriters/year. Pays production cost and registrated creative fee. Arrangement fee and creative fee depend on size of client and size of market. "If song is for a big market, a big fee is paid; if for a small market, a small fee is paid." Buys all rights.
How to Contact: Submit demo tape of previously aired work. Prefers 7½ ips reel-to-reel. "There is no minimum or maximum length for tapes. Tapes may be of a variety of work or a specialization. We are very open on tape content; agency does own lyrics." Does not return material. Responds by phone when need arises.
Music: All types.

MEDIA CONSULTANTS, INC., P.O. Box 130, Sikeston MO 63801. (573)472-1116. E-mail: media@ld d.net. Owner: Richard Wrather. Advertising agency. Clients are varied. Estab. 1979. Uses the services of music houses, independent songwriters/composers and lyricists for jingles and commercials for radio and TV. Commissions 10-15 composers and 10-15 lyricists/year. Pays varying amount/job. Buys all rights.
How to Contact: Submit a demo tape or CD of previous work demonstrating composition skills. Prefers cassette, CDs or ½″ or ¾″ videocassette. Does not return material; prefers to keep on file. "Send samples and prices."
Music: Uses all styles of music for varied assignments.

◪ PATRICK MOORE COMPOSITIONS, 91 Cambermere Dr., North York, Ontario M3A 2W4 Canada. (416)446-2974. Owner/President: Patrick Moore. Scoring service and **jingle/commercial music production house**. Clients include producers of documentaries/films (educational). Estab. 1988. Uses the services of orchestrators for scoring of orchestral scores. Commissions 1 composer/year. Pays by royalty. Buys synchronization rights.
How to Contact: Write first to arrange personal interview. Prefers cassette. Does not return material. Prefers to keep submitted material on file. Reports in 1 month.
Music: "I specialize in combining ethnic music with current music for educational films/documentaries."
Tips: "My needs are very specific and must meet the requirements of the producer and music editor on each project. It is not unusual for me to work with film producers and music writers from all over the world. I do a great deal of work by mailing video tapes and cassette tapes of rough drafts to producers and other professionals involved in a film production."

N̄ ◪ MULTI IMAGE PRODUCTIONS, Dept. SM, 8849 Complex Dr., San Diego CA 92123. (619)560-8383. Website: http://www.multiimage.com. Contact: Mark Maisonneuve. Audiovisual firm and motion picture production company. Serves business, corporate, industrial, commercial, military and cultural clients. Uses the services of independent songwriters/composers and lyricists for scoring of video and motion pictures, background music for videos, jingles and commercials for radio and TV, as well as corporate videos. Commissions 2-10 composers and 2-5 lyricists/year.

FOR BOOKS ON THE CRAFT AND BUSINESS of songwriting, check out the website for Writer's Digest Books at http://www.writersdigest.com.

How to Contact: Submit demo tape of previous work. Prefers DAT with 2-5 pieces. SASE. Reports in 2-3 weeks.

Music: Uses "contemporary, pop, specialty, regional, ethnic, national and international" styles of music for "background scores written against script describing locales, action, etc. We try to stay clear of stereotypical 'canned' music and prefer a more commercial and dramatic (film-like) approach."

Tips: "We have established an ongoing relationship with a local music production/scoring house with whom songwriters would be in competition for every project; but an ability to score clean, full, broad, contemporary commercial and often 'film score' type music, in a variety of styles, would be a benefit."

NORTON RUBBLE & MERTZ, INC. ADVERTISING, 205 W. Walker Dr., Suite 400, Chicago IL 60606. (312)422-9500. Fax: (312)422-9501. Contact: Jason Lambert. Advertising agency. Clients include consumer products, retail, business to business. Estab. 1987. Uses the services of music houses and independent songwriters/composers for jingles and background music for radio/TV commercials. Commissions 2 composers/year. Pays by the job.

How to Contact: Submit tape of previous work; query with résumé of credits. Prefers cassette. Does not return materials; prefers to keep on file.

Music: Uses up-tempo and pop for commercials.

NOVUS VISUAL COMMUNICATIONS INC., 18 W. 27th St., New York NY 10001-6904. Phone/fax: (212)696-9676. E-mail: novuscom@aol.com. President/Creative Director: Robert Antonik. Advertising agency. Clients include corporations, interactive products. Estab. 1986. Uses the services of music houses, independent songwriters/composers and lyricists for scoring and background music for documentaries, commercials, multimedia applications, film shorts, and commercials for radio and TV. Commissions 2 composers and 4 lyricists/year. Pay varies per job. Buys one-time rights.

How to Contact: Write first to arrange personal interview. Query with résumé. Submit demo of previous work. Prefers cassette or VHS videocassette with 2-3 songs. "Submissions should be short and to the point." Prefers to keep submitted material on file, but will return material if SASE is enclosed. Reports in 6 weeks.

Music: Uses all styles for a variety of different assignments.

Tips: "Always present your best and don't add quantity to your reel, cassette, DAT or other submission. Novus is a full service marketing and communications agency. We work with various public relations, artists managements and legal advisors. We create multimedia events to album packaging and promotion."

OMNI COMMUNICATIONS, Dept. SM, 12955 Old Meridian St., P.O. Box 302, Carmel IN 46032-0302. (317)844-6664. E-mail: winston@omniproductions.com. Website: http://omniproductions.com. President: W. H. Long. Creative Director: S.M. Long. Production Manager: Jim Mullet. Television production and audiovisual firm. Estab. 1978. Serves industrial, commercial and educational clients. Uses the services of music houses and songwriters for scoring of films and television productions, CD-ROMs and Internet streams; background music for voice overs; lyricists for original music and themes. Pays by the job. Buys all rights.

How to Contact: Submit demo tape of previous work. Prefers reel-to-reel, cassette or videocassette. Does not return material. Reports in 2 weeks.

Music: Varies with each and every project; from classical, contemporary to commercial industrial.

Tips: "Submit good demo tape with examples of your range to command the attention of our producers."

ON-Q PRODUCTIONS, INC., 618 Gutierrez St., Santa Barbara CA 93103. (805)963-1331. President: Vincent Quaranta. Audiovisual firm. Clients include corporate accounts/sales conventions. Uses the services of music houses, independent songwriters/composers and lyricists for scoring, background music and jingles for AV shows. Commissions 1-5 composers and 1-5 lyricists/year. Buys all or one-time rights.

How to Contact: Query with résumé of credits. Prefers cassette or 15 ips reel-to-reel or VHS videocassette. Prefers to keep material on file.

Music: Uses up-tempo music for slide, video and interactive presentations.

PHOTO COMMUNICATION SERVICES, INC., 6055 Robert Dr., Traverse City MI 49684. (616)943-5050. E-mail: lesnmore@aol.com. President: M'Lynn Hartwell. Audiovisual firm and motion picture production company. Serves commercial, industrial and nonprofit clients. We provide the following services: advertising, marketing, design/packaging, distribution and booking. Uses services of music houses, independent songwriters/composers for jingles and scoring of and background music for multi-image, film and video. Negotiates pay. Buys all or one-time rights.

How to Contact: Submit demo tape of previous work, demonstrating composition skills or query with resume of credits. Prefers cassette. Does not return material; prefers to keep on file. Reports only if interested.

Music: Uses mostly industrial/commercial themes.

RH POWER AND ASSOCIATES, INC., 6616 Gulton Court NE, Albuquerque NM 87109. (505)761-3150. Fax: (505)761-3153. E-mail: rhpowr@aol.com. Website: http://rhpower.com. Creative Director: Roger L. Vergara. Advertising agency. Clients include RV, boat and automotive manufacturers. Estab. 1988. Uses the services of music houses and independent songwriters/composers for background music, and jingles and commercials for radio and TV. Pay varies per job. Buys all rights or one-time rights.

How to Contact: Submit résumé or circular by mail or fax only. "No need to include a submission package unless contacted from initial résumé or letter contact. Save on costs!" SASE. Reports in 1 week.

Music: Uses contemporary, jazz and up-tempo for jingles, TV and radio, commercials and music-on-hold.

PRICE WEBER MARKETING COMMUNICATIONS, INC., Dept. SM, P.O. Box 99337, Louisville KY 40223. (502)499-9220. E-mail: cfrank@priceweber.com. Website: http://www.priceweber.com. Producer/Director: Charles Frank. Advertising agency and audiovisual firm. Estab. 1968. Clients include Fortune 500, consumer durables, light/heavy industrials and package goods. Uses services of music houses and independent songwriters/composers for scoring of long format videos and corporate shows, jingles for radio and commercials for radio and TV. Commissions 6-8 composers/year. Pays by the job ($5,000-20,000). Buys all or one-time rights.

How to Contact: Submit demo tape of previous work demonstrating composition skills. Prefers cassette with 10 pieces. "Enclose data sheet on budgets per selection on demo tape." SASE. Reports in 2 weeks.

Music: Uses easy listening, up-tempo, pop, jazz, rock and classical for corporate image industrials and commercials.

Tips: "We want fresh music. Budgets run from $5,000 to $20,000. Your music must enhance our message."

QUALLY & COMPANY INC., 2238 Central St. #3, Evanston IL 60201-1457. (847)864-6316. Creative Director: Robert Qually. Advertising agency. Uses the services of music houses, independent songwriters/composers and lyricists for scoring, background music and jingles for radio and TV commercials. Commissions 2-4 composers and 2-4 lyricists/year. Pays by the job. Buys various rights depending on deal.

How to Contact: Submit demo tape of previous work or query with résumé of credits. Prefers cassette or ¾" Beta videocassette. SASE, but prefers to keep material on file. Reports in 2 weeks.

Music: Uses all kinds of music for commercials.

✓ 🖻 **RS MUSIC PRODUCTIONS**, 318A Acacia Ave., Carlsbad CA 92008. (760)434-0815. E-mail: coral@sd.znet.com. Website: http://www.richardsamuels.com. President: Richard Samuels. Creative Director: Mike Davies. Scoring service, **jingle/commercial music production house**. Clients include songwriters (private sector), ad agencies, direct retailers and communications companies. Estab. 1989. Uses the services of independent songwriters/composers and lyricists for background music for TV and corporate video and scoring of music for film. Commissions 2-3 composers and 4-6 lyricists/year. Pays by the job. Buys all or one-time rights.

How to Contact: Submit demo tape of previous work. Prefers cassette or VHS videocassette with 4 songs and lyric sheet. SASE. Reports in 1 month.

Music: Uses up-tempo and pop for jingles, corporate video underscore.

Tips: "Be exact in what you want to accomplish by contacting our company, i.e., what area of composition your forté is. Be professional with your submissions."

✓ **SMITH MULTIMEDIA, LLC**, 205 Thomas St., P.O. Box 190, Glen Ridge NJ 07028. (973)429-2177. Fax: (973)429-7119. E-mail: assoc@smithdesign.com. Website: http://www.smithdesign.com. Contact: Laraine Blauvelt. Multimedia design firm. Clients include corporations. Uses the services of music

THE FILM & TV INDEX found at the back of this book lists companies placing music in film and TV (excluding TV commercials).

houses and independent songwriters/composers for scoring and background music for CD-ROMs, presentations and videos. Commissions 3 composers/year. Buys all rights.
How to Contact: Submit demo tape of previous work. Prefers cassette. Prefers to keep submitted material on file. Reports in 1 month.
Music: Uses all styles of music for CD-ROMs, laptop presentations and videos.

SORIN PRODUCTIONS INC., 919 Highway 33, Suite 46, Freehold NJ 07728. (732)462-1785. Fax: (732)462-8411. E-mail: mail@sorinvideo.com. Website: http://www.sorinproductions.com. President: David Sorin. Audiovisual firm. Clients include corporations. Estab. 1982. Uses the services of music houses and independent songwriters/composers for background music for industrials, corporate sales, training and image, and commercials for radio and TV. Commissions 2-3 composers/year. Pays negotiable amount/job. Buys all rights.
How to Contact: Query with résumé of credits or send e-mail. Does not return material.
Music: Uses contemporary, upbeat, corporate for video, educational and local spots.

⌐N⌐ SOTER ASSOCIATES INC., 209 N. 400 W., Provo UT 84601. (801)375-6200. President: N. Gregory Soter. Advertising agency. Clients include financial, health care, municipal, computer hardware and software. Estab. 1970. Uses services of music houses, independent songwriters/composers and lyricists for background music for audiovisual presentations and jingles for radio and TV commercials. Commissions 1 composer, 1 lyricist/year. Pays by the job. Buys all rights.
How to Contact: Submit tape demonstrating previous work and composition skills. Prefers cassette or VHS videocassette. Does not return submissions; prefers to keep materials on file.

NATE STEWART ADVERTISING, 401 S. Main St., Cleburne TX 76031. (817)641-4389. Fax: (817)641-7446. Owner: Nate Stewart. Advertising agency and recording studio. Clients include "top musicians for work on the projects we are involved in and songwriters." Estab. 1983. Uses the services of music houses and independent songwriters/composers for background music for videos, "music for release on CD and tapes for specific purposes such as spiritual, political, educational and romantic." Commissions 4 composers and 2 lyricists/year. Pays by the job or the hour.
How to Contact: Query with résumé of credits. "If the résumé of credits fits the needs of the project, then current material may be requested." Prefers cassette with 3 songs and lyric sheet. "Please send an introductory letter if no résumé is available. Please send both introductory letter and résumé if possible." Prefers to keep submitted material on file. Reports in 4-6 weeks.
Music: Top 40 crossover.

⌐N⌐ TIERNEY & PARTNERS, Dept. SM, 200 S. Broad St., Philadelphia PA 19102. (215)790-4100. Broadcast Business Manager: Rebecca O'Leary. Advertising agency. Serves industrial and consumer clients. Uses music houses for jingles and background music in commercials. Pays creative fee asked by music houses.
How to Contact: Submit demo tape of previously aired work, all types of music. "You must send in previously published work. We do not use original material." Prefers cassette. Will return with SASE if requested, but prefers to keep on file.

☑ ▣ TRF PRODUCTION MUSIC LIBRARIES, Dept. SM, 747 Chestnut Ridge Rd., Chestnut Ridge NY 10977. (914)356-0800. E-mail: trfemail@aol.com. Contact: Anne Marie Russo. **Music/sound effect libraries.** Estab. 1931. Uses the services of independent composers for all categories of production music for television, film and other media. Pays 50% royalty.
How to Contact: Submit demo tape of new compositions. Prefers audio cassette with 3-7 pieces. Does not return material. Reports in 2-3 months.
Music: Primarily interested in instrumental and acoustic music for TV, film and AV/multimedia.

VIDEO I-D, INC., Dept. SM, 105 Muller Rd., Washington IL 61571. (309)444-4323. E-mail: videoid@videoid.com. Website: http://www.VideoID.com. Manager, Marketing Services: Gwen Wagner. Post production/teleproductions. Clients include industrial and business. Estab. 1977. Uses the services of music houses and independent songwriters/composers for background music for video productions. Pays per job. Buys one-time rights.
How to Contact: Submit demo tape of previous work. Prefers cassette or VHS videocassette with 5 songs and lyric sheet. Does not return material. Reports in 3-4 weeks.

▣ VIS/AID MARKETING/ASSOCIATES, P.O. Box 4502, Inglewood CA 90309-4502. (310)399-0696. Manager: Lee Clapp. Advertising agency. Clients include "companies in 23 SIC codes (workable)."

Estab. 1965. Uses the services of music houses, independent songwriters/composers and lyricists for background music for films, and commercials, TV jingles for radio/TV and scoring new material. Commissions 1-2 composers and 1-2 lyricists/year. Pay is negotiable. Buys all or one-time rights.

How to Contact: Call first to arrange personal interview or submit demo tape of previous work. Prefers cassette with 1-2 songs and lyric and lead sheet. "Do not send original material that if misplaced/lost cannot be duplicated." SASE. Reports in 2 weeks.

Music: Uses up-tempo, pop, jazz and classical for educational films, slide presentations and commercials.

 EVANS WYATT ADVERTISING, 346 Mediterranean Dr., Suite 220, Corpus Christi TX 78418. (512)939-7200. Fax: (512)939-7999. E-mail: evwyatt@webtv.net. Contact: D. Spaller. Advertising agency. Clients are general/all types. Estab. 1975. Uses the services of independent songwriters/composers for background music for commercial/video, jingles for advertising, commercials, radio and TV and interactive video. Commissions 10-12 composers/year. Pays by the job. Buys all rights.

How to Contact: Submit demo tape of previous work demonstrating composition skills, query with resume of credits or write first to arrange personal interview. Prefers cassette. Does not return material. Reports in 2 months.

Music: Uses all types for commercials and videos.

 GREG YOUNGMAN MUSIC, P.O. Box 381, Santa Ynez CA 93460. (805)688-1136. Advertising agency/audio production. Serves all types of clients. Local, regional and national levels. Uses the services of music houses and independent composers/lyricists for commercials, jingles and audiovisual projects. Commissions 12-20 composers/year. Pays $500-10,000/project. Buys all or one-time rights.

How to Contact: Submit demo tape of previously aired work. Prefers cassette, R-DAT or reel-to-reel. Does not return material; prefers to keep on file. Reports in 1 month.

Music: Uses all types for radio commercials, film cues.

Tips: "Keep demos to ten minutes."

**FOR EXPLANATIONS OF THESE SYMBOLS,
SEE THE INSIDE FRONT AND BACK COVERS OF THIS BOOK.**

Play Producers & Publishers

Finding a theater company willing to invest in a new production can be frustrating for an unknown playwright. But whether you write the plays, compose the music or pen the lyrics, it is important to remember not only where to start but how to start. Theater in the U.S. is a hierarchy, with Broadway, Off Broadway and Off off Broadway being pretty much off limits to all but the Stephen Sondheims of the world.

Aspiring theater writers would do best to train their sights on nonprofit regional and community theaters to get started. The encouraging news is there is a great number of local theater companies throughout the U.S. with experimental artistic directors who are looking for new works to produce, and many are included in this section. This section covers two segments of the industry: theater companies and dinner theaters are listed under Play Producers, and publishers of musical theater works are listed under the Play Publishers heading (beginning on page 373). All these markets are actively seeking new works of all types for their stages or publications.

BREAKING IN

Starting locally will allow you to research each company carefully and learn about their past performances, the type of musicals they present, and the kinds of material they're looking for. When you find theaters you think may be interested in your work, attend as many performances as possible, so you know exactly what type of material each theater presents. Or volunteer to work at a theater, whether it be moving sets or selling tickets. This will give you valuable insight into the day-to-day workings of a theater and the creation of a new show. On a national level, you will find prestigious organizations offering workshops and apprenticeships covering every subject from arts administration to directing to costuming. But it could be more helpful to look into professional internships at theaters and attend theater workshops in your area. The more knowledgeable you are about the workings of a particular company or theater, the easier it will be to tailor your work to fit its style and the more responsive they will be to you and your work. (See the Workshops & Conferences section for more information.) As a composer for the stage, you need to know as much as possible about a theater and how it works, its history and the different roles played by the people involved in it. Flexibility is the key to successful productions, and knowing how a theater works will only help you in cooperating and collaborating with the director, producer, technical people and actors.

If you're a playwright looking to have his play published in book form or in theater publications, see the listings under the Play Publishers section (page 373). To find play producers and publishers in your area, consult the Geographic Index at the back of this book.

Play Producers

ACTORS ALLEY, 5269 Lankershim, North Hollywood CA 91601. (818)508-4234. Fax: (818)508-5113. Director of Administration: Jill Jones. Play producer. Estab. 1968. Produces 4-6 plays and 1 musical/year. Performance space includes a 40-seat equity waiver and a 99-seat theater. Pay varies.
How to Contact: Query with synopsis, character breakdown and set description. SASE. Reports in 2 months.
Musical Theater: Two-act plays for actors who sing and dance. Cast limit of 12.
Productions: *The World Goes Round*, by Kander/Ebb; *Room Service*, by Murray/Boretz (comedy); and *Denial*, by Peter Sagal (drama).

ALCAZAR THEATRE, 650 Geary St., San Francisco CA 94102. (415)441-6655. Fax: (415)441-9567. Artistic Director: Steve Dobbins. Play producer. Estab. 1990. Produces 4 plays and 2 musicals (2 new musicals)/year. Audience is upper middle class, 40% are from the area, 60% are tourists. Performance space is a 500-seat procenium theatre. Pays 3-5% royalty or $50-100/performance.
How to Contact: Query with synopsis, character breakdown and set description. SASE. Reports in 4 months.
Musical Theater: Open to all types of musicals. Cast size limit is 16.
Productions: *Fab!*, by Heather Bros. (1964 rock and roll); *Tango*, by Rafael Nicolau (history of tango).
Tips: "Have patience and creativity. Take chances. Interest the 20 and 30 year olds in coming to the theatre."

☑ **ALLIANCE THEATRE COMPANY**, 1280 Peachtree St., Atlanta GA 30309. (404)733-4650. Fax: (404)733-4625. Website: http://www.alliancetheatre.org. Literary Associate: Megan Schultz. Play producer. Estab. 1969. Produces 9-10 plays and 1 new musical/year. Audience is diverse, regional and young. Two performing spaces: 800-seat proscenium and a 200-seat flexible black box. Pays negotiable amount per performance.
How to Contact: Query with synopsis, character breakdown and set description. SASE. Reports in 6 weeks.
Musical Theater: They are primarily interested in new musicals, but also will consider works for children's theatre. Musicals for young audiences must be no longer than 1 hour in length and have a cast of 8 or fewer.
Productions: *Hot Mikado*, by David Bell/Rob Bowman/Marjorie B. Kellogg (Gilbert & Sullivan's *The Mikado* updated); *Livin' in the Garden*, music by Melanie Hammett (children's theatre piece about urban garden); and *Little Me*, by Neil Simon/Cy Coleman/Carolyn Leigh.

AMAS MUSICAL THEATRE, INC., 450 W. 42nd St., Suite 2J, New York NY 10036. (212)563-2565. Fax: (212)268-5501. E-mail: amas@westegg.com. Website: http://www.westegg.com/amas. Producing Director: Donna Trinkoff. Play producer. Estab. 1968. Produces 2 musicals/year and musical development series (AMAS Six O'clock Musical Theatre Lab) produces 5-6 concert versions of new musicals. "We seek to reach a wide and diverse audience by presenting musicals that speak to different cultures." Performance space is on Off-off Broadway theater with 76-99 seats. Payment is standard agreement.
How to Contact: Submit complete manuscript, score and tape of songs. SASE. Reports in 3-6 months.
Musical Theater: Seeks "innovative, well-written, good music. We seek musicals that lend themselves to multiracial casting."
Productions: *Barrio Babies*, by Luis Santeiro/Fernando Rivas (Latino musical satire); *Rolling on the T.O.B.A.*, by Ronald Stevens/Langston Hughes (black vaudeville); and *Delphi or Bust*, by Gerald Jay Markoe/Michael Colby (Greek romp).
Tips: "Submit works that speak to and about racial and cultural themes using a fresh, new, fun style."

AMERICAN LIVING HISTORY THEATER, Box 752, Greybull WY 82426. (307)765-9449. President and Artistic Director: Dorene Ludwig. Play producer. Estab. 1975. Produces 1-2 plays/year. Performs all over U.S.—conventions, schools, museums, universities, libraries, etc. Pays by royalty.
How to Contact: Query first. SASE. Reports in 6-12 months.
Musical Theater: "We use only primary source, historically accurate material: in music—*Songs of the Civil War* or *Songs of the Labor Movement*, etc.—presented as a program rather than play would be the only use I could foresee. We need music historians more than composers."
Tips: "Do not send fictionalized historical material. We use primary source material only."

☑ **AMERICAN MUSIC THEATER FESTIVAL**, 100 S. Broad St., Suite 650, Philadelphia PA 19110. (215)972-1000. Fax: (215)972-7020. E-mail: amtf@philly.infi.net. Website: http://members.aol.com/lou d82/amtfpage.html. Artistic Director: Ben Levit. Play producer. Estab. 1984. Produces 4 new musicals/year. "Our average audience member is in their mid-40s. We perform to ethnically diverse houses." Plays performed at "Plays and Players theater, an old turn-of-the-century vaudeville house." 320 seats in Center City, Philadelphia." Pays advance plus royalties.
How to Contact: Query with synopsis and character breakdown with scene and lyric samples and sample

---

FOR BOOKS ON THE CRAFT AND BUSINESS of songwriting, check out the website for Writer's Digest Books at http://www.writersdigest.com.

tape (4 songs). SASE. Reports in 6 months.

Music: "We seek musicals ranging from the traditional to very experimental. We encourage multimedia and technological applications. Topics can range. We are interested in music theater/opera that comments on current life. Musical styles can vary from folk pop through opera. Orchestra generally limited to a maximum of 9 pieces; cast size maximum of 10-12."

Musical Theater: *Band in Berlin*, by Susan Feldman (comedian harmonist vocal group of pre-Facist Germany); *Floyd Collins*, by Adam Gueltel/Tina Landau (true story of a man trapped in a cave, 1925, and media blitz exp. around him); and *Somewhere Over the Rainbow*, by Deena Rosenberg/Mel Marvin (yip Hamburg review).

Tips: "We only produce pieces that are music/lyric driven, not merely plays with music."

☑ **AMERICAN MUSICAL THEATRE OF SAN JOSE**, 1717 Technology Dr., San Jose CA 95110-1305. (408)453-7100. Fax: (408)453-7123. E-mail: mjacobs@amtsj.org. Website: http://www.amtsj.org. Associate Artistic Director: Marc Jacobs. Play producer. Estab. 1935. Produces 4 mainstage musicals/year (just starting New Works program). "Our season subscribers are generally upper-middle class families. However, we plan to open a second stage where we can do works which would appeal to a more eclectic audience. Our main season is in the 2,500-seat San Jose Center for the Performing Arts. This is a state-of-the-art theatre. We are currently looking for a flexible 200-800 seat space to be a second stage which would be partially dedicated to producing new works." Pays variable royalty.

How to Contact: Submit complete manuscript and tape of songs. SASE. Reports in 3-6 months.

Musical Theater: "We are not looking for children's musicals, Christmas shows or puppet shows. We are looking for high quality (professional caliber) musicals to develop for either our 2,500-seat main stage theatre or a proposed smaller second stage, a national tour or possible Broadway production. Submissions from composers and writers with some previous track record only, please. We are especially interested in works which are presented in non-traditional (non-linear) styles. The first thing we look for is quality and originality in the music and lyrics. Next we look for librettos that offer exciting staging possibilities. If writing original music to a pre-existing play please be sure all rights have been cleared."

Productions: *The Hot Mikada*, by David Bell (G&S to swing); *La Cage aux Follies*, by Jerry Herman (traditional musical); *Biz River*; and *South Pacific*.

Tips: "We are a company with a $6 million per season operating budget and one of the largest subscription audiences in the country. We are looking for shows we can develop for possible main stage or Broadway productions. Therefore it is advisable that any composers or writers have some professional production history before submitting to us."

N **ARIZONA THEATRE COMPANY**, P.O. Box 1631, Tucson AZ 85702. (520)884-8210. Artistic Director: David Goldstein. Professional regional theater company. Members are professionals. Performs 6 productions/year, including 1 new work. Audience is middle and upper-middle class, well-educated, aged 35-64. "We are a two-city operation based in Tucson, where we perform in a 603-seat newly renovated, historic building, which also has a 100-seat flexible seating cabaret space. Our facility in Phoenix, the Herberger Theater Center, is a 712-seat, proscenium stage." Pays 4-10% royalty.

How to Contact: Submit through agent only. SASE. Reports in 4 months.

Musical Theater: Musicals or musical theater pieces. 15-16 performers maximum including chorus. Instrumental scores should not involve full orchestra. No classical or operatic.

Productions: *Five Guys Named Moe*, by Clarke Peters (musical theatre); *The Gershwins' Fascinating Rhythm*, conceived by Mark Lamos/Mel Marvin (musical theatre); and *Candide*, by Sondheim/Bernstein (musical theatre).

Tips: "As a regional theater, we cannot afford to produce extravagant works. Plot line and suitability of music to further the plot are essential considerations."

N **ARKANSAS REPERTORY THEATRE**, 601 Main, P.O. Box 110, Little Rock AR 72203. (501)378-0445. Contact: Brad Mooy. Play producer. Estab. 1976. Produces 8 plays and 4 musicals (1 new musical)/year. "We perform in a 354-seat house and also have a 99-seat blackbox." Pays 5-10% royalty or $75-150 per performance.

How to Contact: Query with synopsis, character breakdown and set description. SASE. Reports in 6 months.

MARKETS THAT WERE listed in the 1999 edition of *Songwriter's Market* but do not appear this year are listed in the General Index with a notation explaining why they were omitted.

Musical Theater: "Small casts are preferred, comedy or drama and prefer shows to run 1:45 to 2 hours maximum. Simple is better; small is better, but we do produce complex shows. We aren't interested in children's pieces, puppet shows or mime. We always like to receive a tape of the music with the book."
Productions: *Radio Gals*, by Mike Craver/Mark Hardwick; and *Always . . . Patsy Cline*, by Ted Swindley (bio-musical).
Tips: "Include a *good* cassette of your music, *sung well*, with the script."

ASOLO THEATRE COMPANY, Dept. SM, 5555 N. Tamiami Trail, Sarasota FL 34243. (941)351-9010. E-mail: bruce_rodgers@asolo.org. Website: http://www.asolo.org. Associate Artistic Director: Bruce E. Rodgers. Play producer. Produces 7-8 plays (1 musical)/year. Plays are performed at the Asolo Mainstage (500-seat proscenium house). Pays negotiated royalty.
How to Contact: Query with synopsis, character breakdown, set description and one page of dialogue. SASE. Reports in 6 months.
Musical Theater: "We want small to mid-size non-chorus musicals only. They should be full-length, any subject. There are no restrictions on production demands; however, musicals with excessive scenic requirements or very large casts may be difficult to consider."
Productions: *Oh What A Lovely War*, by Joan Littlewood (WWI); and *Jane Eyre*, by Ted Davis/David Clark.

N: BAILIWICK REPERTORY, Bailiwick Arts Center, 1229 W. Belmont, Chicago IL 60657. (773)883-1091. Director: David Zak. Artistic/Managing Director: Patrizia Acerra. Play producer. Estab. 1982. Produces 5 mainstage, 5 one-act plays and 1-2 new musicals/year. "We do Chicago productions of new works on adaptations that are politically or thematically intriguing and relevant. We also do an annual director's festival which produces 50-75 new short works each year." Pays 5-8% royalty.
How to Contact: "Send SASE (business size) first to receive manuscript submission guidelines. Material returned if appropriate SASE attached." Reports in 6 months.
Musical Theater: "We want innovative, dangerous, exciting material."
Productions: *The Christmas Schooner*, by John Reeger and Julie Shannon (holiday musical); *Pope Joan*, by Christopher Moore (dark ages); and *In The Deep Heart's Core*, by Joseph Sobel (Yeats).
Tips: "Be creative. Be patient. Be persistent. Make me believe in your dream."

BARTER THEATRE, P.O. Box 867, Abingdon VA 24212. (540)628-2281. Fax: (540)628-4551. E-mail: barter@naxs.com. Website: http://www.bartertheatre.com. Artistic Director: Richard Rose. Play producer. Estab. 1933. Produces 12 plays and 2-3 musicals (1 new musical)/year. Audience "varies; middle American, middle age, tourist and local mix." 500-seat proscenium stage, 150-seat thrust stage. Pays 5% royalty.
How to Contact: Query with synopsis, character breakdown and set description. SASE. Reports in 9-12 months.
Musical Theater: "We investigate all types. We are not looking for any particular standard. Prefer sellable titles with unique use of music. Prefer small cast musicals, although have done large scale projects with marketable titles or subject matter. We use original music in almost all of our plays." Does not wish to see "political or very urban material, or material with very strong language."
Productions: *Alice . . . Through the Picture Tube*, by Michael Hirsel and Ed Stuller; *Girl of My Dreams*, by Peter Ekstrom and David DeBoy; and *WMKS*, by Frank Higgins (old time folk and country music).
Tips: "Be patient. Be talented. Don't be obnoxious. Be original and make sure subject matter fits our audience."

BROADWAY ON SUNSET, 10800 Hesby St., North Hollywood CA 91601. (818)508-9270. E-mail: brdwyonsunst@earthlink.net. Website: http://members.aol.com/BrdwyonSS. Play producer. Estab. 1981. Executive Director: Kevin Kaufman. Artistic Director: Allison Bergman. "Sponsored by the National Academy of Songwriters (NAS), Broadway on Sunset is devoted exclusively to developing original material through various classes, workshops and staging opportunities."
How to Contact: Query first. SASE. Reports in 3 months.
Musical Theater: "Seeking original, unproduced musicals, only, for mainstream audience. This is not the place for experimental, controversial material, although challenging themes and concepts are encouraged."
Productions: *American Twistory*, by Kevin Kaufman/John Everst (satirical revue); and *Mates: The Pirate Musical*, by Don Hale/Jimmy Horawitz.

WILLIAM CAREY COLLEGE DINNER THEATRE, William Carey College, Hattiesburg MS 39401-5499. (601)582-6218. E-mail: thecom@wmcarey.edu. Managing Director: O.L. Quave. Play producer. Produces 2 musicals/year. "Our dinner theater operates only in summer and plays to family audiences." Payment negotiable.

How to Contact: Query with synopsis, character breakdown and set description. Does not return material. Reports in 1 month.
Musical Theater: "Plays should be simply-staged, have small casts (8-10 maximum), and be suitable for family viewing; two hours maximum length. Score should require piano only, or piano, synthesizer."
Productions: *Smoke on the Mountain*; *Schoolhouse Rock Live*; and *Pump Boys and Dinettes*.

CENTENARY COLLEGE, Theatre Dept., Shreveport LA 71134-1188. (318)869-5011. Fax: (318)869-5760. E-mail: rbuseick@beta.centenary.edu. Chairman: Robert R. Buseick. Play producer. Produces 6 plays (1-2 new musicals)/year. Plays are presented in a 350-seat playhouse to college and community audiences. Pay is negotiable.
How to Contact: Query with synopsis, character breakdown and set description. Does not return material. Reports as soon as possible.
Productions: *Blood Brothers*; *Grand Hotel*; and *Funny Girl*.
Tips: "Keep trying. It's not easy."

CENTER THEATER, 1346 W. Devon, Chicago IL 60660. (312)508-0200. Contact: Literary Manager. Play producer. Estab. 1984. Produces 6 plays and 1 musical (1 new musical)/year. "Our 60-seat flexible theater has produced 3 original musicals, based on novels or plays." Royalty negotiable.
How to Contact: Query with synopsis, character breakdown and set description. SASE. "Have a complete script and a demo tape with professional singers." Reports in 3 months.
Musical Theater: 12 person cast maximum.
Productions: *The Black Tulip*, by Tracy Friedman/Brian Lasser (adaptation of Dumas novel); *Two Many Bosses*, by Dan La Morte/Donald Coates (musical adaptation of *Servant of Two Masters*); and *Lysistrata 2411 A.D.*, by Dale Calandra/Donald Coates (futuristic musical adaptation).
Tips: "We also host an annual international play contest which includes plays/musicals of all genres and subject matter. SASE for contest guidelines."

THE COTERIE, 2450 Grand Ave., Kansas City MO 64108. (816)474-6785. Artistic Director: Jeff Church. Play producer. Estab. 1979. Produces 7-8 plays/year. Plays produced at Hallmark's Crown Center in downtown Kansas City in The Coterie's resident theater (capacity 240). Musicals are produced for adventurous families and schools K-12. A typical performance run is 1 month in length. "We retain some rights on commissioned plays. Writers are paid a royalty for their work per performance or flat fee."
How to Contact: Query with synopsis and character breakdown. Submit complete manuscript and score, "if established writer in theater for young audiences. We will consider musicals with smaller orchestration needs (3-5 pieces), or a taped score." SASE. Reports in 10 months.
Musical Theater: "Types of plays we produce: pieces which are universal in appeal; plays for all ages. They may be original or adaptations of classic or contemporary literature. Limitations: typically not more than 12 in a cast—prefer 5-9 in size. No fly space or wing space. No couch plays. Prefer plays by seasoned writers who have established reputations. Groundbreaking and exciting scripts from the youth theater field welcome. It's perfectly fine if your musical is a little off center."
Productions: *I Can't Eat Goat Head*, by Sylvia Gonzales S. (Latino journey); *The Little Prince*, by Jeff Church (adaptation of classic literature); and *A Woman Called Truth*, by Sandra Asher (life of Sojourner Truth).
Tips: "Make certain your submitted musical is very theatrical and not cinematic. Writers need to see how far the field of youth and family theater has come—the interesting new areas we're going—before sending us your query or manuscript. We like young protagonists in our plays, but make sure they're not romanticized or stereotyped good-and-bad like the children's theater playwrights of yesterday would have them."

CROSSROADS THEATRE, 7 Livingston Ave., New Brunswick NY 08901. (732)249-5800. Fax: (732)249-1861. E-mail: crossroads@iop.com. Website: http://www.crossroadstheatre.org. Literary Manager: Lenora Inez Brown. Play producer. Estab. 1978. Produces 4 plays/year. 250-300 seat thrust stage. Pay depends on the piece.
How to Contact: Submit synopsis, 10 page sample of book and lyrics/tape. SASE. Reports in 1 month on synopsis; 6-9 months on full manuscript.

MARKET CONDITIONS are constantly changing! If you're still using this book and it is 2001 or later, buy the newest edition of *Songwriter's Market* at your favorite bookstore or order directly from Writer's Digest Books at (800)289-0963.

Musical Theater: "We tend to produce material for adults and young adults. We focus on works by and about African-Americans. We also produce works that show the intersection of cultures especially with African-American culture." Considers original music for use in a play being developed or for use in a pre-existing play.

Productions: *Lost Creek Township*, by Charlotte Gibson (family drama); *Blues For An Alabama Sky*, by Pearl Cleage (drama); *Ain't Nothing But the Blues*, by Charles Bevel/Lita Gaithers/Dan Wheetman/Ron Taylor/Randal Mylen; and *Ali*, by Geoffry C. Ewing/Graydon Royce.

N: GEOF ENGLISH, PRODUCER, SADDLEBACK CIVIC LIGHT OPERA, Saddleback College, 28000 Marguerite Pkwy., Mission Viejo CA 92692. (714)582-4763. E-mail: genglish@saddleback.cc.ca.us. Producer: Geofrey English. Play producer for musical theater. Produces 4 musicals/year. Community audience of mostly senior citizens. Pays by royalty and performance.

How to Contact: Submit complete manuscript, score and tape of songs. Does not return material. Reports in 2-3 months.

Musical Theater: "Looking for mainly family musicals. No limitations, open to options. It is important that music must be sent along with scripts. Best not to call. Just send materials."

Productions: Hello Dolly; Once Upon a Mattress; and Musical Revues (Rodgers/Hart/various).

Tips: "Submit materials in a timely manner—usually at least one year in advance."

ENSEMBLE THEATRE, 1127 Vine St., Cincinnati OH 45210. (513)421-3555. Fax: (513)421-8002. Website: http://www.Cincinnati.com/etc./etc.html. Producing Artistic Director: D. Lynn Meyers. Play producer. Estab. 1986. Produces 14 plays and 1 musical (1 new musical)/year. Audience is multi-generational and multi-cultural. 202 seats, ¾ stage. Pays 5-8% royalty (negotiable).

How to Contact: Query with synopsis, character breakdown and set description. SASE. Reports in 6 months.

Musical Theater: "All types of musicals are acceptable. Cast not over ten; minimum set, please."

Productions: *Cars, Dogs, Money and the Moon*, by David Kisor (musical about growing up in West Virginia); *Hi Hat Hattie*, by Larry Parr; and *The Frog Princess*, by David Kisor/Joseph McDonough (musical adaptation of the classic fairy tale).

Tips: Looking for "creative, inventive, contemporary subjects or classic tales. Send materials as complete as possible."

✓ FOOLS COMPANY, INC., 423 W. 46th, New York NY 10036. (212)307-6000. E-mail: foolsco@att. net. Website: http://www.foolsco.org. Artistic Director: Martin Russell, Ph.D. Collaborative new works producer. Estab. 1970. Produces 4 plays and 1-2 musicals (1-2 new musicals)/year. "Audience is comprised of hip, younger New Yorkers. Plays are performed at our own mid-Manhattan theater." Pay is negotiable.

How to Contact: Query first. SASE. Reports in 1 month.

Musical Theater: "We seek new and unusual, contemporary and experimental material. We would like small, easy-to-tour productions. Nothing classical, folkloric or previously produced." Would also consider working with composers in collaboration or original music for use in plays being developed.

Productions: *Eden Arcade Nights* (alternative cabaret).

Tips: "Come work in NYC!"

THE FOOTHILL THEATRE COMPANY, P.O. Box 1812, Nevada City CA 95959. (530)265-9320. E-mail: ftc@foothilltheatre.org. Website: http://www.foothilltheatre.org. Artistic Director: Philip Charles Sneed. Literary Manager: Gary Wright. Play producer. Estab. 1977. Produces 6-10 plays and 1-2 musicals/year. Rural audience, with some urban visitors to the area. 250-seat historic proscenium house; built in 1865 (oldest in CA). Payment is negotiated.

How to Contact: Query with synopsis, character breakdown and set description. SASE. Reports in 6-12 months.

Musical Theater: "We're particularly interested in works which deal with the region's history or with issues relevant to the area today. We are also interested in one-act musicals and children's musicals. We have limited space backstage, especially in the wings. We also have very limited fly space. We're interested in original ideas, nothing derivative (except in an adaptation, of course). A good rock musical would be nice. Will consider original music for use in a play being developed, or for use in a pre-existing play. The use will depend upon the play: could be *pre-show*, or underscoring, or scene change, or any combination."

Productions: *Quilters*, by Damaschek and Newman (pioneer story with music); *The Robber Bridegroom*, by Alfred Uhry/Robert Waldman; and *Man of La Mancha*, by Dale Wasserman/Mitch Leigh/Joe Darion.

Tips: "Know something about our region and its history."

THE GASLIGHT THEATRE, 7010 E. Broadway, Tucson AZ 85710. (520)886-9428. General Manager: Nancy LaViola. Play producer. Estab. 1976. Produces 5 musical melodramas (2 new musicals)/year. "We cater to family audiences. Our musical melodramas are always fun and never sad. Ages from toddlers to senior citizens come to our shows." Performance space is 20'w × 15'd (not including the apron). Pays for outright purchase.
How to Contact: Query with synopsis, character breakdown and set description. SASE. Reports in 1 month.
Musical Theater: Prefers musical melodramas of 1 hour and 30 minutes; with an olio of 18-20 minutes. "Our shows always have a hero and villain." Cast size is usually 3 women and 5-6 men. Does not wish to see anything violent or sad. "Family entertainment only." Looking for slapstick comedy. "We always use fun sets, i.e., rolling rocks, underwater adventure, camels that move, horses, etc. Our musical melodrama is followed by a themed olio (song and dance show with jokes). Include lots of music to accompany the show."
Productions: *Cisco Kid* (western); *Secret Agent Man*, by Peter Van Slyke (spy spoof); and *Give My Regards to Santa*, by Carol Calkins/Bobby Joyce Smith (holiday).
Tips: "Think fun and comedy! Our productions always have a villian and a hero. In the conflict the hero always wins. Always fun and family entertainment. Lots of music."

THE WILL GEER THEATRICUM BOTANICUM, P.O. Box 1222, Topanga CA 90290. (310)455-2322. E-mail: theatricum@aol.com. Artistic Director: Ellen Geer. Literary Director: Isreal Baran. Play producer. Produces 4 plays, 1 new musical/year. Plays are performed in "large outdoor amphitheater with 60'x 25' wooden stage. Rustic setting." Pays negotiable royalty.
How to Contact: Query with synopsis, tape of songs and character breakdown. SASE. Reports as soon as can be read.
Musical Theater: Seeking social or biographical works, children's works and full length musicals with cast of up to 10 equity actors (the rest non-equity). Requires "low budget set and costumes. We emphasize paying performers." Would also consider original music for use in a play being developed. Does not wish to see "anything promoting avarice, greed, violence or apathy."
Productions: *Three Penny Opera*, by Brecht; *Robber Bridegroom*, by VHRY/Waldman (country folktale); and *Pie in the Sky*, by Alsop (nuclear/3 Mile Island).

HARTFORD STAGE COMPANY, 50 Church St., Hartford CT 06103. (860)525-5601. Fax: (860)525-4420. Literary Associate: Shawn René Graham. Play producer. Estab. 1963. Produces 6 plays and 1-2 musicals/year. "Mainly white-collar, upper middle-class audience; plays performed on a thrust stage, seats 489 people." Pays royalty.
How to Contact: Submit through agent. SASE. Reports in 3-6 months.
Musical Theater: Looking for "any kind of musicals except for children's theater. Musicals are preferred to be 2-2½ hours in length, but longer ones accepted also. We are mainly interested in small to medium-sized casts, up to 12 actors, although larger ones are also accepted." Does not wish to see "anything in the vein of the typical Broadway musical—*Phantom of the Opera*, *Miss Saigon*, etc."
Productions: *Herringbone*, by Tom Cone (one-man show); *Martin Guerre*, by Laura Harrington (adaptation of French film); and *March of the Falsettos* and *Falsettolands*, by William Finn (gay man's journey among friend's family).

LA JOLLA PLAYHOUSE, P.O. Box 12039, La Jolla CA 92039. (619)550-1070. Fax: (619)550-1075. Literary Manager: Elizabeth Bennett. Play producer. Estab. 1947. Produces 6 plays and 1-2 musicals (1-2 new musicals)/year. Audience is University of California students to senior citizens. Performance space is a large proscenium theatre with 480 seats.
How to Contact: Query with synopsis, character breakdown and set description. SASE. Reports in 6-9 months.
Musical Theater: "We prefer contemporary music but not necessarily a sturdy set in contemporary times. Retellings of classic stories can enlighten us about the times we live in. For budgetary reasons, we'd prefer a smaller cast size."
Productions: *Dogeaters*, by Jessica Hagedorn (life in the Philippines); *70 Hill Lane*, by Improbable Theater (influence of paranormal experience); and *The Captain's Tiger*, by Athol Fugard (a young man's voyage around the world).

REFER TO THE GEOGRAPHIC INDEX (at the back of this book) to find listings of companies by state, as well as foreign listings.

☑ **LOS ANGELES DESIGNERS' THEATRE**, P.O. Box 1883, Studio City CA 91614-0883. (323)650-9600. T.D.D.: (323)654-2700. Fax: (323)654-3260. E-mail: ladesigners@juno.com. Artistic Director: Richard Niederberg. Play producer. Estab. 1970. Produces 20-25 plays and 8-10 new musicals/year. Audience is predominantly Hollywood production executives in film, TV, records and multimedia. Plays are produced at several locations, primarily Studio City, California. Pay is negotiable.
How to Contact: Query first. Does not return material. Reports in 4 months.
Musical Theater: "We seek out controversial material. Street language OK, nudity is fine, religious themes, social themes, political themes are encouraged. Our audience is very 'jaded' as it consists of TV, motion picture and music publishing executives who have 'seen it all'." Does not wish to see bland, "safe" material. "We like first productions. In the cover letter state in great detail the proposed involvement of the songwriter, other than as a writer (i.e., director, actor, singer, publicist, designer, etc.). Also, state if there are any liens on the material or if anything has been promised."
Productions: *St. Tim*, by Fred Grab (historical '60s musical); *Slipper and the Rose* (gang musical); and *1593—The Devils Due* (historical musical).
Tips: "Make it very 'commercial' and inexpensive to produce. Allow for non-traditional casting. Be prepared with ideas as to how to transform your work to film or videotaped entertainment."

N **MAGIC THEATRE**, Ft. Mason Center, Bldg. D, San Francisco CA 94123. (415)441-8001. Fax: (415)771-5505. Literary Manager: Kent Nicholson. Play producer. Estab. 1968. Produces 5-6 plays/year. Audience is educated/intelligent, willing to take risks. Two performance spaces: 155-seat modified thrust and 155-seat proscenium. Pays negotiable royalty.
How to Contact: Query with synopsis, character breakdown and set description. SASE. Reports in 6-8 weeks.
Musical Theater: Plays are innovative in form and structure. Chamber musicals are best. Cast size of 6-8. "We have only recently decided to start producing musicals. We are interested in stories with a strong book as well as music." Considers original music for use in a play being developed or for use in a pre-existing play.
Productions: *Mules*, by Winsome Pinnock (Drug Trade); *Pharmacist's Daughter*, by Monika Monika (genetic engineering); and *A Question of Mercy*, by David Rabe (assisted suicide).

☑ **MILL MOUNTAIN THEATRE**, 1 Market Square, 2nd Floor, Roanoke VA 24011-1437. (540)342-5730. Fax: (540)342-5745. E-mail: mmtmail@intrlink.com. Website: http://www.millmountain.org. Resident Director: Doug Zschiegner. Play producer. Estab. 1964. Produces 11-14 plays and generally 3 established musicals (1-2 new musicals)/year. General theater audience on mainstage; a more open minded audience in Theatre B; also children's musicals. 400-seat proscenium mainstage; 125-seat alternate space. Pays variable royalty.
How to Contact: Query with synopsis, character breakdown and demo tape. SASE. Reports in 6 months.
Musical Theater: "We seek children's musicals (especially those adapted from recognizable children's works); we also accept contemporary musicals which explore new forms and themes, especially those which encourage diversity of life experiences. Smaller cast musicals with a minimum of technical requirements are encouraged. We have, in the past, used original music for existing plays (*Midsummer Night's Dream*, *To Kill A Mockingbird*), usually to set the production's mood and emphasize the action on stage."
Productions: *Shiniest Rock of All*, by Jere Hodgin/Ron Barnett (original young people's musical); *Uh-Oh, Here Comes Christmas*, by Ernie Zulia/David Caldwell (adaptation of Robert Fulghum's work); and *Blackbirds of Broadway*, by Marion Caffrey/David Coffman (original review of African-American music of '20s and '30s).

MIXED BLOOD THEATRE CO., 1501 S. Fourth St., Minneapolis MN 55454. (612)338-0937. E-mail: mixedblood@wavetech.net. Script Czar: David Kunz. Play producer. Estab. 1976. Produces 4-5 plays/year and perhaps 1 new musical every 2 years. "We have a 200-seat theater in a converted firehouse. The audience spans the socio-economic spectrum." Pays royalty or per performance.
 • See the listing for the We Don't Need No Stinkin' Dramas playwriting contest in the Contests & Awards section.
How to Contact: Query first (1-page cover letter, 1-page synopsis). SASE. Reports on queries in 1-2 months.
Musical Theater: "We want full-length, non-children's works with a message. Always query first. Never send unsolicited script or tape."
Productions: *Black Belts II*, musical revue (black female vocalists and their music); *A . . . My Name Is Still Alice* and *Birth of the Boom* (do-wop/hip hop extravaganza).
Tips: "Always query first. The direct approach is best. Be concise. Make it interesting. Surprise us. Contemporary comedies, politically-edged material and sports-oriented shows are usually of interest."

NEW YORK STATE THEATRE INSTITUTE, 155 River St., Troy NY 12180. (518)274-3200. E-mail: nysti@crisny.org. Website: http://www.crisny.org/not-for-profit/nysti. Producing Artistic Director: Patricia Di Benedetto Snyder. Play producer. Produces 5 plays (1 new musical)/year. Plays performed for student audiences grades K-12, family audiences and adult audiences. Theater seats 900 with full stage. Pay negotiable.

How to Contact: Query with synopsis, character breakdown, set description and tape of songs. SASE. Reports in 3-4 weeks for synopsis, 3-4 months for manuscript.

Musical Theater: Looking for "intelligent and well-written book with substance, a score that enhances and supplements the book and is musically well-crafted and theatrical." Length: up to 2 hours. Could be play with music, musical comedy, musical drama. Excellence and substance in material is essential. Cast could be up to 20; orchestra size up to 8.

Productions: *A Tale of Cinderella*, by W.A. Frankonis/Will Severin/George David Weiss (adaptation of fairy tale); *The Silver Skates*, by Lanie Robertson/Byron Janis/George David Weiss (adaptation of book); and *The Snow Queen*, by Adrian Mitchell/Richard Peaslee (adaptation of fairy tale).

Tips: "There is a great need for musicals that are well-written with intelligence and substance which are suitable for family audiences."

☑ **NORTHERN LIGHTS PLAYHOUSE**, P.O. Box 256, Dept. SMV, Hazelhurst WI 54531-0256. (715)356-7173, ext. 958. Fax: (715)356-1851. E-mail: nlplays@newnorth.net. Producer: Michael D. Cupp. Play producer. Estab. 1976. Produces 5 plays and 8 musicals/year. Audience consists of conservative, wealthy, retired senior citizens. Performance space includes a proscenium and three-quarter. Pays per performance or per royalty.

How to Contact: Query with synopsis, character breakdown and set description. SASE. Reports in 3-6 months.

Musical Theater: Prefers family oriented musical comedies, 2 hours in length; children's theatre 1 hour in length. "We would love to receive a Christmas musical and/or revue." Cast limit is 12-16. "I am also in search of small musicals with 4-6 people for our smaller space." Does not wish to see anything racy or profane.

Productions: *Grease!*; *Forever Plaid*; and *Jesus Christ Superstar*.

Tips: "Consider the audience. Think commercial."

ODYSSEY THEATRE ENSEMBLE, Dept. SM, 2055 S. Sepulveda Blvd., Los Angeles CA 90025. (310)477-2055. Director of Literary Programs: Sally Essex-Lopresti. Play producer. Estab. 1969. Produces 9 plays and 1 musical (1-2 new musicals)/year. "Our audience is predominantly over 35, upper middle-class and interested in eclectic brand of theater which is challenging and experimental." Pays negotiable royalty.

How to Contact: Query with synopsis, character breakdown, 8-10 pages of libretto, cassette of music and set description. Query should include résumé(s) of artist(s) and tape of music. SASE. "Unsolicited material is not read or screened at all." Reports on query in 1 month; manuscript in 6 months.

Musical Theater: "We want nontraditional forms and provocative, unusual, challenging subject matter. We are not looking for Broadway-style musicals. Comedies should be highly stylized or highly farcical. Works should be full-length only and not requiring a complete orchestra (small band preferred). Political material and satire are great for us. We're seeking interesting musical concepts and approaches. The more traditional Broadway-style musicals will generally not be done by the Odyssey. If we have a work in development that needs music, original music will often be used. In such a case, the writer and composer would work together during the development phase. In the case of a pre-existing play, the concept would originate with the director who would select the composer."

Productions: *Frauleins In Underwear*, by various (Germany in the '30s); *Avenue X*, by John Jiler/Ray Leslee; and *Lucky Stiff*, by Lynn Ahrens/Stephen Flaherty.

Tips: "Stretch your work beyond the ordinary. Look for compelling themes or the enduring questions of human existence. If it's a comedy, go for broke, go all the way, be as inventive as you can be."

THE OPEN EYE THEATER, P.O. Box 959, Margaretville NY 12455. (914)586-1660. E-mail: openeye@catskill.net. Website: http://www.theopeneye.com (select: Arts Centers). Producing Artistic Director: Amie Brockway. Play producer. Estab. 1972. Produces approximately 3 full length or 3 new plays for multi-generational audiences. Pays on a fee basis.

How to Contact: Query first. "A manuscript will be accepted and read only if it is a play for multi-generational audiences and is: 1) Submitted by a recognized literary agent; 2) Requested or recommended by a staff or company member; or 3) Recommended by a professional colleague with whose work we are familiar. Playwrights may submit a one-page letter of inquiry including a very brief plot synopsis. Please enclose a self-addressed (but not stamped) envelope. We will reply only if we want you to submit the script (within several months)."

Musical Theater: "The Open Eye Theater is a not-for-profit professional company working in a community context. Through the development, production and performance of plays for all ages, artists and audiences are challenged and given the opportunity to grow in the arts. In residence, on tour, and in the classroom, The Open Eye Theater strives to stimulate, educate, entertain, inspire and serve as a creative resource."

Productions: *Selkie*, by Laurie Brooks Gollobin, music by Elliot Sokolov (Selkie legend); *A Midsummer Night's Dream*, by Shakespeare, music by Robert Cucinotta; and *The Nightingale*, by William E. Black/ Annie Brockway, music by Elliot Sokolov (freedom and nature vs. technology).

PLAYHOUSE ON THE SQUARE, 51 S. Cooper, Memphis TN 38104. (901)725-0776. Executive Producer: Jackie Nichols. Play producer. Produces 12 plays and 4 musicals/year. Plays are produced in a 260-seat proscenium resident theater. Pays $500 for outright purchase.

How to Contact: Submit complete manuscript, score and tape of songs. Unsolicited submissions OK. SASE. Reports in 6 months.

Musical Theater: Seeking "any subject matter—adult and children's material. Small cast preferred. Stage is 26′ deep by 43′ wide with no fly system." Would also consider original music for use in a play being developed.

Productions: *Chess*; *Children of Eden*; and *Tommy*, by The Who.

PLAYWRIGHTS' ARENA, 1531 N. Bronson Ave., Hollywood CA 90028. (323)469-7156. E-mail: jrivera923@juno.com. Website: http://writeaway.net/playrena. Artistic Director: Jon Lawrence Rivera. Play producer. Estab. 1992. Produces 4 plays and 1 musical (1 new musical)/year. Audience is in their early 20s to 50s. Performance space is 12′×16′×10′. Pays 6% royalty.

How to Contact: Submit complete manuscript, score and tape of songs. SASE. Reports in 6 months.

Musical Theater: Seeking new musicals like *Rent*. Does not want old fashioned musicals.

Productions: *Moscow*, by Nick Salamone/Maury McIntyre (musical of 3 sisters with 3 men); *The Next Step*, by Jean Colonomos (Martha Graham); and *The Demented Slave of Love*, by Robert Harder (Arabian Nights).

PLAYWRIGHTS HORIZONS, 416 W. 42nd St., New York NY 10036. (212)564-1235. Musical Theater Resident: Matt Morrow. Play producer. Estab. 1971. Produces about 4 plays and 1 new musical/ year. "Adventurous New York City theater-going audience." Pays general Off-Broadway contract.

How to Contact: Submit complete manuscript and tape of songs. Attn: Musical Theater Program. SASE. Reports in 6-10 months.

Musical Theater: American writers. "No revivals, one-acts or children's shows; otherwise we're flexible. We have a particular interest in scores with a distinctively contemporary and American flavor. We generally develop work from scratch; we're open to proposals for shows and scripts in early stages of development."

Productions: *Assassins*, by Stephen Sondheim/John Weidman; *Floyd Collins*, by Adam Guettel/Tina Landau; and *Violet*, by Brian Crawley/Jeanine Tesorie.

PRIMARY STAGES, 584 Ninth Ave., New York NY 10036. (212)333-7471. Fax: (212)333-2025. Literary Manager: Tricia McDermott. Play producer. Estab. 1984. Produces 4 plays and 1 musical/year. "New York theater-going audience representing a broad cross-section, in terms of age, ethnicity, and economic backgrounds. 99-seat, Off-Broadway theater." Pays a fee for production.

How to Contact: Query first with synopsis, character breakdown, set description and tape. "No unsolicited scripts accepted. Submissions by agents only." SASE. Reports in 4-6 months.

Musical Theater: "We are looking for work of heightened theatricality, that challenges realism—musical plays that go beyond film and televisions standard fare. We are looking for small cast shows, with limited sets. We are interested in original works, that have not been produced in New York."

Productions: *I Sent a Letter to My Love*, by Melissa Manchester/Jeffrey Sweet; and *Nightmare Alley*, by Jonathan Brielle.

THE REPERTORY THEATRE OF ST. LOUIS, P.O. Box 191730, St. Louis MO 63119. (314)968-7340. Associate Artistic Director: Susan Gregg. Play producer. Estab. 1966. Produces 9 plays and 1 or 2

MARKETS THAT WERE listed in the 1999 edition of *Songwriter's Market* but do not appear this year are listed in the General Index with a notation explaining why they were omitted.

musicals/year. "Conservative regional theater audience. We produce all our work at the Loretto Hilton Theatre." Pays by royalty.
How to Contact: Query with synopsis, character breakdown and set description. Does not return material. Reports in 2 years.
Musical Theater: "We want plays with a small cast and simple setting. No children's shows or foul language. After a letter of inquiry we would prefer script and demo tape."
Productions: *Almost September* and *Esmeralda*, by David Schechter and Steve Lutvak; and *Jack*, by Barbara Field and Hiram Titus.

SECOND STAGE THEATRE, P.O. Box 1807, Ansonia Station, New York NY 10023. (212)787-8302. Dramaturg/Literary Manager: Christopher Burney. Play producer. Estab. 1979. Produces 4 plays and 1 musical (1 new musical)/year. Plays are performed in a small, 108-seat Off Broadway House. Pays per performance.
How to Contact: Query with tape of 5 songs (no more). No unsolicited manuscripts. SASE. Reports in 6 months.
Musical Theater: "We are looking for innovative, unconventional musicals that deal with sociopolitical themes."
Productions: *In a Pig's Valise*, by Eric Overmyer/Kid Creole (spoof on '40s film noir); *A . . . My Name Is Still Alice*, by various (song/sketch revue); and *Little Fish*, by Michael John La Chusa (woman's journey for fulfillment).
Tips: "Submit through agent; have strong references; always submit the best of your material in small quantities: 5 outstanding songs are better than 10 mediocre ones."

☑ **SHAKESPEARE SANTA CRUZ**, Performing Arts, U.C.S.C., Santa Cruz CA 95064. (831)459-2121. Fax: (831)459-3552. E-mail: iago@cats.ucsc.edu. Website: http://arts.ucsc.edu/Shakespeare/cruz. Artistic Director: Paul Whitworth. Play producer. Estab. 1982. Produces 4 plays/year. Performance spaces are an outdoor redwood grove; and an indoor 540-seat thrust. Pay is negotiable.
  • Although Shakespeare Santa Cruz does not produce musicals, they are open to original music for pre-existing plays.
How to Contact: Query first. SASE. Reports in 2 months.
Musical Theater: Does not wish to see musical theatre. "We are usually interested in composers' original music for pre-existing plays—including songs, for example, for Shakespeare's plays."
Productions: *The Two Gentlemen of Verona*, by Shakespeare; *Romeo & Juliet*, by Shakespeare; and *Cinderella*, by Hawley.
Tips: "Always contact us before sending material."

Ⓝ **SHENANDOAH INTERNATIONAL PLAYWRIGHTS RETREAT (A Project of Shenan Arts, Inc.)**, Rt. 5, Box 167-F, Staunton VA 24401. (540)248-1868. E-mail: shenarts@cfw.com. Director of Playwriting and Screenwriting Programs: Robert Graham Small. Play producer. Estab. 1976. Develops 10-12 plays/year for family audience. Pays royalty for full production.
How to Contact: Submit complete manuscript, score and tape of songs. SASE. Reports in 4 months.
Productions: *Starting Here Starting Now*, by Maltby Shire (cabaret); *The Who's Tommy*, by Pete Townsend (rock opera); and *The Gift of the Magi*, by St. Germaint Cross.
Tips: "Submit full materials by January 1."

STAGE ONE, 5 Riverfront Plaza, Louisville KY 40202. (502)589-5946. E-mail: kystageone@aol.com. Website: http://www.stageone.org. Producing Director: Moses Goldberg. Play producer. Estab. 1946. Produces 7-8 plays and 0-2 new musicals/year. "Audience is mainly young people ages 5-18, teachers and families." Pays 3-6% royalty, flat fee or $25-75 per performance.
How to Contact: Submit complete manuscript and tape of songs (cassette preferred). SASE. Reports in 4 months.
Musical Theater: "We seek stageworthy and respectful dramatizations of the classic tales of childhood, both ancient and modern. Ideally, the plays are relevant to young people and their families, as well as related to school curriculum. Cast is rarely more than 12."
Productions: *The Great Gilly Hopkins*, by David Paterson/Steve Liebman (foster home); *Pinocchio*, by Moses Goldberg/Scott Kasbaum (classic tale); and *Jack & the Beanstalk*, by Goldberg/Corrett (fairytale).
Tips: "Stage One accepts unsolicited manuscripts that meet our artistic objectives. Please do not send plot summaries or reviews. Include author's résumé, if desired. In the case of musicals, a cassette tape is preferred. Cast size is not a factor, although, in practice, Stage One rarely employs casts of over 12. Scripts will be returned in approximately 3-4 months, if SASE is included. No materials can be returned without the inclusion of a SASE. Due to the volume of plays received, it is not possible to provide written evaluations."

STAGES REPERTORY THEATRE, 3201 Allen Parkway, Houston TX 77019. (713)527-0220. Fax: (713)527-8669. Artistic Director: Rob Bundy. Play producer. Estab. 1979. Produces 6 plays and 1 musical/ year. Performance space includes 170-seat thrust and 230-arena theatre. Pays negotiable royalty.
How to Contact: Query with synopsis, character breakdown and set description. SASE. Reports in 6-7 months.
Musical Theatre: Prefers edgy, theatrical, non-realistic stories, with a maximum cast size of 10, and single unit set with multiple locations.
Productions: *Nixon's Nixon*, by Russell Lees; *Funny Girl*, by Jules Styne; and *The Pitchfork Disney*, by Philip Ridley.

 STRAWBERRY PRODUCTIONS, INC., 432 Front St., Chicopee MA 01013. (413)592-4184. Fax: (413)594-7758. E-mail: strawberryproductions.com. Website: http://www.strawberryproductions.com. President/Producer: Jack Desroches. Play producer. Estab. 1976. Produces 3-6 plays and 3-6 musicals (2 new musicals)/year. Audience is children and families. Strawberry Productions is a touring company. Pays for outright purchase.
How to Contact: Query first. SASE. Reports in 2-3 months.
Musical Theater: Seeking children's theater of 70-80 minutes in length, children's puppet theater of 30 minutes in length and educational shows. Normal touring limits vary from production to production.
Productions: *Scholastic's* "Bright Idea" (light); *Scholastic's* "Recycles" (recycling); and *Alvin & The Chipmunks* "Rockin through the Decades" (music), all by John Michael Burke.
Tips: "Creativity and the ability to entertain young and old alike is very important."

TAPROOT THEATRE, P.O. Box 30946, Seattle WA 98103-0946. (206)781-9705. Fax: (206)706-1502. E-mail: taproot@taproottheatre.org. Website: http://www.taproot.org/taproot. Managing Director: Sean Gaffney. Play producer. Estab. 1976. Produces 13-15 plays and 1-3 musicals (1-3 new musicals)/year. Mainstage is for a general audience. Touring is for a church audience or grade/high school students. Intimate 225-seat thrust stage with a balcony. Pays $20-30/performance.
How to Contact: Query with synopsis, character breakdown and set description. SASE. Reports in 3-6 months.
Musical Theater: Primarily full-length, for general adult audience. "Taproot is guided by a belief in the integrity of values rooted in the historic Judeo Christian worldview. Taproot productions reflect a respect for people, a belief in the virtues of faith and hope." Maximum cast size 15 (prefers 6-12). Does not wish to see "anything in direct opposition to the values shown above. We only want to see music that is part of a musical; we will not evaluate, comment on or consider individual songs."
Productions: *Godspell*, by John Michael Tebelak/Stephen Schwartz (general); *Christmas on the Orpheum Circuit*, by S. Gaffney/G. Gaffney (Christmas); and *Kick It!*, by Karen Lund/Samuel Vance (elementary).

 THE TEN-MINUTE MUSICALS PROJECT, P.O. Box 461194, West Hollywood CA 90046. (323)651-4899. Producer: Michael Koppy. Play producer. Estab. 1987. All pieces are new musicals. Pays $250 advance.
How to Contact: Submit complete manuscript, score and tape of songs. SASE. Reports in 3 months.
Musical Theater: Seeks complete short stage musicals of 8-15 minutes in length. Maximum cast: 9. "No parodies—original music only."
Productions: *Away to Pago Pago*, by Jack Feldman/Barry Manilow/John PiRoman/Bruce Sussman; *The Bottle Imp*, by Kenneth Vega (from the story of the same title by Robert Louis Stevenson); and *The Furnished Room*, by Saragail Katzman (from the story of the same title by O. Henry).
Tips: "Start with a *solid* story—either an adaptation or an original idea—but with a solid beginning, middle and end (probably with a plot twist at the climax). We caution that it will surely take much time and effort to create a quality work. (Occasionally a clearly talented and capable writer and composer seem to have almost 'dashed' something off, under the misperception that inspiration can carry the day in this format. Works selected in previous rounds all clearly evince that considerable deliberation and craft were

invested.) We're seeking short contemporary musical theater material, in the style of what might be found on Broadway, Off-Broadway or the West End. Think of shows like *Candide* or *Little Shop of Horrors*, pop operas like *Sweeney Todd* or *Chess*, or chamber musicals like *Once on this Island* or *Falsettos*. (Even small accessible operas like *The Telephone* or *Trouble in Tahiti* are possible models.) All have solid plots, and all rely on sung material to advance them. Of primary importance is to start with a strong story, even if it means postponing work on music and lyrics until the dramatic foundation is complete."

THEATRE WEST VIRGINIA, P.O. Box 1205, Beckley WV 25802. (800)666-9142. E-mail: twv@cwv.n et. Website: http://wvweb.com/www/TWV. Artistic Director: Marina Dolinger. Play producer. Estab. 1955. Produces 5 plays and 2 musicals/year. "Audience varies from mainstream summer stock to educational tours (ages K-high school)." Pays 3-5% royalty.
How to Contact: Query with synopsis, character breakdown and set description; should include cassette tape. SASE. Reports in 3 months.
Musical Theater: "Theatre West Virginia is a year-round performing arts organization that presents a variety of productions including community performances and statewide educational programs on primary, elementary and secondary levels. This is in addition to our summer, outdoor dramas of *Hatfields & McCoys* and *Honey in the Rock*, now in their 39th year." Anything suitable for school tours. No more than 6 in cast. Play should be able to be accompanied by piano/synthesizer.
Productions: *The Apple Tree*; *Honey in the Rock*, by Kermit Hunter/L. Frank Baum; and *The Story of King Midas*.

THEATREVIRGINIA, 2800 Grove Ave., Richmond VA 23221-2466. (804)353-6100. E-mail: tva@erols. com. Website: http://www.theatreva.com. Artistic Director: Dr. George Black. Play producer. Estab. 1955. Produces 5-9 plays and 2-5 musicals/year. "Plays are performed in a 500-seat LORT-C house for the Richmond-area community." Payment negotiable.
How to Contact: Query first. "If material seems to be of interest to us, we will reply with a solicitation for a complete manuscript and cassette. SASE. Reports in 3 months for synopsis.
Musical Theater: "We do not deal in one-acts or in children's material. We would like to see full length, adult musicals. There are no official limitations. We would be unlikely to use original music as incidental/ underscoring for existing plays, but there is potential for adapting existing plays into musicals."
Productions: *A Closer Walk with Patsy Cline*, by Dean Regan (Patsy Cline); *The Mikado*, by Gilbert and Sullivan; and *Gypsy*, by Arthur Laurents.
Tips: "Read plays. Study structure. Study character. Learn how to concisely articulate the nature of your work. A beginning musical playwright wishing to work for our company should begin by writing a wonderful, theatrically viable piece of musical theater. Then he should send us the material requested in our listing, and wait patiently."

N. THUNDER BAY THEATRE, 400 N. Second Ave., Alpena MI 49707. (517)354-2267. Artistic Director: Thom Fielder. Play producer. Estab. 1967. Produces 12 plays and 6 musicals (1 new musical)/year. Performance space is thrust/proscenium stage. Pays variable royalty or per performance.
How to Contact: Submit complete manuscript, score and tape of songs. SASE. Reports in 3 months.
Musical Theater: Small cast. Not equipped for large sets. Considers original background music for use in a play being developed or for use in a pre-existing play.
Productions: *Wonderful Life*, by Holmes/Knoner/Willison (Christmas); *Smoke On the Mountain* (gospel); and *Fantasticks*, by Jones/Shmidt.

UNIVERSITY OF ALABAMA NEW PLAYWRIGHTS' PROGRAM, P.O. Box 870239, Tuscaloosa AL 35487-0239. (205)348-9032. Fax: (205)348-9048. E-mail: pcastagn@woodsquad.as.ua.edu. Website: http://www.as.va.edu/theatre/npp.htm. Director/Dramaturg: Dr. Paul Castagno. Play producer. Estab. 1982. Produces 8-10 plays and 1 musical/year; 1 new musical every other year. University audience. Pays by arrangement. Stipend is competitive. Also expenses and travel.
How to Contact: Submit complete manuscript, score and tape of songs. Submit only August-March. SASE. Reports in 4-6 months.
Musical Theater: Any style or subject (but no children's or puppet plays). No limitations—just solid

---

MARKET CONDITIONS are constantly changing! If you're still using this book and it is 2001 or later, buy the newest edition of *Songwriter's Market* at your favorite bookstore or order directly from Writer's Digest Books at (800)289-0963.

lyrics and melodic line. Drama with music, musical theater workshops, and chamber musicals.
Productions: *Gospels According to Esther*, by John Erlanger.
Tips: "Take your demos seriously. We really want to do something small scale, for actors, often without the greatest singing ability. While not ironclad by any means, musicals with Southern themes might stand a better chance."

VIRGINIA STAGE COMPANY, P.O. Box 3770, Norfolk VA 23514. (757)627-6988. Fax: (757)628-5958. E-mail: chops2000@erols.com. Artistic Director: Charlie Hensley. Play producer. Estab. 1978. Produces 7-10 plays and 1-2 musicals (0-1 new musical)/year. "We have a diverse audience. As home to a large, well-traveled population from NATO and the U.S. Navy, we serve many sophisticated theatregoers as well as those for whom theatre is not yet a habit. Located in Southeastern Virginia, we also play to a number of people from Southern backgrounds." Performance space is a 670-seat, Beaux-Arts proscenium theatre built in 1913—a national historic landmark. This hemp house features a proscenium opening 36' wide and 28' high with a stage depth of 28'. Pay is negotiable.
How to Contact: Query with synopsis, character breakdown and set description. SASE. Reports in 6 months.
Musical Theater: "We have produced the world premieres of *The Secret Garden* and *Snapshots* (with music by Stephen Schwartz). Our tastes are eclectic and have covered a number of styles. We have recently expanded our programming for young audiences." At this time, shows with less than 20 in the cast have a better chance of production. They have commissioned original music and adaptations for plays including *Hamlet*, *Twelfth Night*, *Terra Nova* and *A Christmas Carol*.
Productions: *Appalachian Strings*, by Randal Myler/Dan Wheetman (social history of the Appalachian region); *Snapshots*, by David Stern/Michael Scheman, music by Stephen Schwartz (a middle-aged couple trying to save their marriage); and *Twelfth Night*, by Shakespeare (set in 18th century Ireland with live musicians playing Celtic music).
Tips: "Be patient. We review material as quickly as possible. It also takes time to establish the relationships and resources needed to lead us into full, top-quality productions."

WATERLOO COMMUNITY PLAYHOUSE, P.O. Box 433, Waterloo IA 50704. (319)235-0367. E-mail: wcpbhct@cedarnet.org. Website: http://www.cedarnet.org. Managing Artistic Director: Charles Stilwill. Play producer. Estab. 1917. Produces 12 plays (1-2 musicals)/year. "Our audience prefers solid, wholesome entertainment, nothing risqué or with strong language. We perform in Hope Martin Theatre, a 366-seat house." Pays $15-150/performance.
How to Contact: Submit complete manuscript, score and cassette tape of songs. SASE. Reports in 10 months.
Musical Theater: "Casts may vary from as few as 6 people to 54. We are producing children's theater as well. We're *especially* interested in new adaptations of classic children stories."
Productions: *Joseph and the Amazing Technicolor Dreamcoat* (traditional); *State Fair*; and *Annie*..
Tips: "The only 'new' musicals we are likely to produce are adaptations of name shows that would fit in our holiday slot or for our children's theater."

WEST COAST ENSEMBLE, P.O. Box 38728, Los Angeles CA 90038. (310)449-1447. Artistic Director: Les Hanson. Play producer. Estab. 1982. Produces 4-8 plays and 1 new musical/year. "Our audience is a wide variety of Southern Californians. Plays will be produced in our theater in Hollywood." Pays $35-50 per performance.
● See the listing for West Coast Ensemble—Musical Stairs in the Contests & Awards section.
How to Contact: Submit complete manuscript, score and tape of songs. SASE. Reports in 6-8 months.
Musical Theater: "There are no limitations on subject matter or style. Cast size should be no more than 12 and sets should be simple. If music is required we would commission a composer; music would be used as a bridge between scenes or to underscore certain scenes in the play."
Productions: *The Human Comedy*, by Galt McDermott (adaptation of the Saroyan novel); *The Much Ado Musical*, by Tony Tanner (adaptation of Shakespeare); *Company*; and *Cabaret*.
Tips: "Submit work in good form and be patient. We look for musicals with a strong book and an engaging score with a variety of styles."

☑ **WEST END ARTISTS**, 18034 Ventura Blvd. #291, Encino CA 91316. (818)766-9381. Fax: (818)766-1090. E-mail: egaynes@pacbell.net. Artistic Director: Edmund Gaynes. Associate Artistic Director: Pamela Hall. Play producer. Estab. 1983. Produces 5 plays and 3 new musicals/year. Audience "covers a broad spectrum, from general public to heavy theater/film/TV industry crowds. Pays negotiable royalty.
How to Contact: Submit complete manuscript, score and tape of songs. SASE. Reports in 3 months.
Musical Theater: "Prefer small-cast musicals and revues. Full length preferred. Interested in children's

shows also." Cast size: "Maximum 12; exceptional material with larger casts will be considered."
Productions: *The Taffetas*, by Rick Lewis ('50s nostalgia, received 3 Ovation Award nominations); *Songs the Girls Sang*, by Alan Palmer (songs written for women now sung by men, received 1 Ovation Award nomination); and *Broadway Sings Out!*, by Ray Malvani (Broadway songs of social significance).
Tips: "If you feel every word or note you have written is sacred and chiseled in stone and are unwilling to work collaboratively with a professional director, don't bother to submit."

WESTBETH THEATRE CENTER, 151 Bank St., New York NY 10014. (212)691-2272. E-mail: wbetht c@aol.com. Artistic Associate: Steven Bloom. Play producer. Estab. 1978. Produces 1-2 musicals/year. Audience consists of New York theater professionals and Village neighborhood. "We have five performance spaces, including a music hall and cafe theater." Pay varies. Uses usual New York showcase contract.
How to Contact: Query with synopsis, character breakdown and tape. SASE. Does not return material from outside the US. Reports in 3-5 months. "Artists must be accessible to NYC."
Musical Theater: "Full-length musicals, all Broadway styles. Small, ensemble casts the best." Does not wish to see "one character musicals, biographies and historical dramas. Musicals selected for development will undergo intense process. We look for strong collaborators."
Productions: *20th Century Man*, by Ray Davies (bio of rock group The Kinks); *I'm Still Here, Dammit*, by Sandra Bernhardt (contemporary, hip with music); and *Exactly Like You*, by Cy Coleman/E. Hutchner (musical comedy).
Tips: "Be open to the collaborative effort. We are a professional theater company, competing in the competitive world of Broadway and off-Broadway, so the work we present must reach for the highest standard of excellence."

✅ **THE WILMA THEATER**, 265 S. Broad St., Philadelphia PA 19107. (215)893-9456. Fax: (215)893-0895. E-mail: info@wilmatheater.org. Website: http://www.wilmatheater.org. Literary Manager: Emily Morse. Play producer. Produces 4 shows/year. Performance space is a 300-seat, state of the art proscenium theater, with full fly system and large backstage area. Pays royalty negotiated between managing director and agent.
How to Contact: Submit through agent only. SASE. Reports in 6 months.
Musical Theater: "We seek to produce the most adventurous work possible. Because this is a director-driven theater, the full-length projects must pose creative challenges that engage the imaginations of our two artistic directors. The eclectic tastes of the artistic directors make it almost impossible to identify specific styles or topics. We look for work that is original, bold, challenging and stimulating."
Productions: *The Psychic Life of Savages*, by Amy Freed; *Love and Anger*, by George F. Walker; and *Bed and Sofa*, by Polly Pen/Laurence Klavan.
Tips: "Please be familiar with the Wilma's production history before submitting your material."

WOMEN'S PROJECT AND PRODUCTIONS, 55 West End Ave., New York NY 10023. (212)765-1706. E-mail: wpp@earthlink.net. Website: http://www.womensproject.org. Literary Manager: Lisa Mc-Nulty. Artistic Director: Julia Miles. Estab. 1978. Produces 3 plays/year. Pays by outright purchase.
How to Contact: Query with synopsis, character breakdown and set description. SASE. Reports in 2 months for query and 6 months for full submission. "Adult audience. Plays by women only."
Musical Theater: "We usually prefer a small to medium cast of 3-6. We produce few musicals and produce *only* women playwrights."
Productions: *Ladies*, by Eve Ensler (homelessness); *O Pioneers!*, by Darrah Cloud (adapted from Willa Cather's novel); and *Frida: The Story of Frida Kahlo*, by Hilary Blecher/Migdalia Cruz (biography of Frida Kahlo).
Tips: "Resist sending early drafts of work."

🆕 **WOOLLY MAMMOTH THEATRE CO.**, M, 1401 Church St. NW, Washington DC 20005. (202)234-6130. Literary Manager: Mary Resing. Play producer. Estab. 1978. Produces 4 plays/year. Royalties vary.
How to Contact: Submit through agent only. We do not accept unsolicited manuscripts. SASE. Reports in 6 months.
Musical Theater: "We do unusual works. We have done 1 musical, the *Rocky Horror Show* (very

FOR BOOKS ON THE CRAFT AND BUSINESS of songwriting, check out the website for Writer's Digest Books at http://www.writersdigest.com.

successful). 8-10 in cast. We do not wish to see one-acts."
Productions: *Wanted*, by Al Carmines (J. Edgar Hoover); and *Rocky Horror Picture Show* (monsters/sex).
Tips: "Know what we do. Read or see our plays."

Play Publishers

AMELIA MAGAZINE, 329 "E" St., Bakersfield CA 93304. (805)323-4064. Editor: Frederick A. Raborg, Jr. Play publisher. Estab. 1983. Publishes 1 play/year. General audience; one-act plays published in *Amelia Magazine*. The annual Frank McClure One-Act Play Award awards $150 plus publication. Deadline May 15 annually.
How to Contact: Submit complete manuscript and score. Reports in 6-8 weeks. "We would consider publishing musical scores if submitted in clean, camera-ready copy—also single songs. Best bet is with single songs complete with clear, camera-ready scoresheets, for regular submissions. We use only first North American serial rights. All performance and recording rights remain with songwriter. Payment same as for fiction—$35 plus copies for regular acceptance. Write for guidelines for McClure Award with SASE." Sample copy: $9.95 ppd.
Tips: "Be polished, professional, and submit clear, clean copy."

☑ BAKER'S PLAYS, 100 Chauncy St., Boston MA 02111. (617)482-1280. Fax: (617)482-7613. E-mail: info@bakersplays.com. Website: http://www.bakersplays.com. Associate Editor: Ray Pape. Play publisher. Estab. 1845. Publishes 15-22 plays and 0-3 new musicals/year. Plays are used by children's theaters, junior and senior high schools, colleges and community theaters. Pays negotiated book and production royalty.
   • See the listing for Baker's Plays High School Playwriting Contest in the Contests & Awards section.
How to Contact: Submit complete manuscript, score and cassette tape of songs. SASE. Reports in 3-4 months.
Musical Theater: "Seeking musicals for teen production and children's theater production. We prefer large cast, contemporary musicals which are easy to stage and produce. Plot your shows strongly, keep your scenery and staging simple, your musical numbers and choreography easily explained and blocked out. Music must be camera-ready, or at least clean and legible." Would consider original music for use in a play being developed or in a pre-existing play.
Productions: *Broadway Cafe*, by Jennie Cohen/Cat Spencer; and *Rivercide, P.I.*, by Lauren Marshall/Edd Rey.
Tips: "As we publish musicals that can be produced by high school theater departments with high school talent, the writer should know if their play can be done on the high school stage. I recommend that the writer go to performances of original high school musicals whenever possible."

I.E. CLARK PUBLICATIONS, P.O. Box 246, Schulenburg TX 78956-0246. E-mail: ieclark@cvtv.net. General Manager: Donna Cozzaglio. Play publisher. Estab. 1956. Publishes 10 new plays and 1-3 new musicals/year. Pays negotiable royalty.
How to Contact: Submit complete manuscript, score and tape of songs. SASE. Reports in 3-4 months.
Musical Theater: "Musicals for children's theater and for high school and community theater, adaptations of well-known stories and novels. We do not publish puppet shows. We seek plays that appeal to a wide spectrum of producers—professional, community, college, high school, junior high, elementary schools, children's theater, etc. The more of these groups a play will appeal to, the better the sales—and the better the chance that we will accept the play for publication." Does not wish to see plays with obscenities or blasphemous material. Prefers plays for more than 1-3 characters. "We feel that the songs and musical numbers in a play should advance the plot and action, rather than interrupting the flow of the play for the sake of the music."
Publications: *Peter Pan in Neverland*, by R. Eugene Jackson/David Ellis (a "non-flying" adaptation); *Nutcracker—the Musical*, by Debbie Meyer (the story of the Nutcracker without ballerinas); and *The Homework Conspiracy*, by Dave Cockley/Louis Lunenberg (high school students use the Internet to avoid doing homework).
Tips: "We demand originality and high literary quality. Avoid clichés, both in plot and music."

CONTEMPORARY DRAMA SERVICE, 885 Elkton Dr., Colorado Springs CO 80907. (719)594-4422. E-mail: merpcds@aol.com. Executive Editor: Arthur Zapel. Play publisher. Estab. 1979. Publishes 40-50 plays and 4-6 new musicals/year. "We publish for young children and teens in mainstream Christian churches and for teens and college level in the secular market. Our musicals are performed in churches, schools and colleges." Pays 10% royalty (often up to fixed amount).

How to Contact: Submit complete manuscript, score and tape of songs. SASE. Reports in 2 months.

Musical Theater: "For churches we publish musical programs for children and teens to perform at Easter, Christmas or some special occasion. Our school musicals are for teens to perform as class plays or special entertainments. Cast size may vary from 5-25 depending on use. We prefer more parts for girls than boys. Music must be written in the vocal range of teens. Staging should be relatively simple but may vary as needed. We are not interested in elementary school material. Elementary level is OK for church music but not public school elementary. Music must have full piano accompaniment and be professionally scored for camera-ready publication."

Publications: *Lucky Lucky Hudson & the 12th St. Gang*, words and music by Tim Kelly/Bill Francoeur (gangster musical); *Oz!*, words and music by Bill Francoeur/Tim Kelly (*The Wizard of Oz* set to music); and *Operation Angel Undercover*, by Melanie White (children's Christmas musical).

Tips: "Familiarize yourself with our market. Try to determine what would fit in, yet still be unique."

☑ THE DRAMATIC PUBLISHING COMPANY, 311 Washington St., Woodstock IL 60098. (815)338-7170. E-mail: plays@dramaticpublishing.com. Website: http://dramaticpublishing.com. Music Editor: Dana Wolworth. Play publisher. Publishes 35 plays and 3-5 musicals/year. Estab. 1885. Plays used by community theaters, high schools, colleges, stock and professional theaters and churches. Pays negotiable royalty.

How to Contact: Submit complete manuscript, score and tape of songs. SASE. Reports in 10-12 weeks.

Musical Theater: Seeking "children's musicals not over 1¼ hours, and adult musicals with 2 act format. No adaptations for which the rights to use the original work have not been cleared. If directed toward high school market, large casts with many female roles are preferred. For professional, stock and community theater small casts are better. Cost of producing a play is always a factor to consider in regard to costumes, scenery and special effects." Would also consider original music for use in a pre-existing play, "if we or the composer hold the rights to the non-musical work."

Publications: *The Little Prince*, by Rick Cummins/John Scoullar; *Hans Brinker*, by Gayle Hudson/Bobbe Bramson; and *Bubbe Meises, Bubbe Stories*, by Ellen Gould/Holly Gewandter (all are full-length family musicals).

Tips: "A complete score, ready to go is highly recommended. Tuneful songs which stand on their own are a must. Good subject matter which has wide appeal is always best but not required."

☑ ELDRIDGE PUBLISHING CO., INC., P.O. Box 1595, Venice FL 34284. (800)HI-STAGE. E-mail: info@histage.com. Website: http://www.histage.com. Musical Editor: Scott Keys. Play publisher. Estab. 1906. Publishes 40 plays and 2-3 musicals/year. Seeking "large cast musicals which appeal to students. We like variety and originality in the music, easy staging and costuming. Also looking for children's theater musicals which have smaller casts and are easy to tour. We serve the school and church market, 6th grade through 12th; also Christmas and Easter musicals for churches." Would also consider original music for use in a play being developed; "music that could make an ordinary play extraordinary." Pays 50% royalty and 10% copy sales in school market.

How to Contact: Submit manuscript, score or lead sheets and tape of songs. SASE. Reports in 3-4 weeks.

Publications: *Hoola Hoops & Halos*, by Jeffrey Smart/Scott Keys ('50s heavenly musical comedy); *Lagooned!*, by Tim Kelly/Lee Ahlin (tropical-pop musical spoof); and *Katastrophe Kate*, by Stephen Murray (a wild-west melodrama).

Tips: "We're always looking for talented composers but not through individual songs. We're only interested in complete school or church musicals. Lead sheets, cassette tape and script are best way to submit. Let us see your work!"

☑ ENCORE PERFORMANCE PUBLISHING, P.O. Box 692, Orem UT 84059. (801)225-0605. E-mail: encoreplay@aol.com. Website: http://www.encoreplay.com. Editor: Michael C. Perry. Play publisher. Estab. 1979. Publishes 20-30 plays (including musicals)/year. "We are interested in plays which emphasize strong family values and play to all ages." Pays 10-50% royalty.

How to Contact: Query with synopsis, character breakdown, set description and production history. SASE. Reports in 2-3 months.

Musical Theater: Musicals of all types for all audiences. Can be original or adapted. "We tend to favor shows with at least an equal male/female cast." Do not wish to see works that can be termed offensive or vulgar. However, experimental theater forms are also of interest.

Publications: *Boy Who Knew No Fear*, by Mark Levenson and Gary Mills (youth quest); *Right Around the Corner*, by Joe Bell/Hope Hommers/Nate Herman (Twain adaptation); and *Carpenter's Son*, by Al Viola (Christian).
Tips: "Always write with an audience in mind."

SAMUEL FRENCH, INC., 45 W. 25th St., New York NY 10010. (212)206-8990. Hollywood office: 7623 Sunset Blvd., Hollywood CA 90046. (323)876-0570. Fax: (323)876-6822. Website: http://www.samu elfrench.com. President: Charles R. Van Nostrand. Play publisher. Estab. 1830. Publishes 40-50 plays and 2-4 new musicals/year. Amateur and professional theaters.
How to Contact: Query first. SASE. Reports in minimum 10 weeks.
Musical Theater: "We publish primarily successful musicals from the NYC, London and regional stage."
Publications: *Eating Raoul*, by Paul Bartel; *Hello Muddah Hello Faddah*, by Bernstein/Krause; and *Love and Shrimp*, by Judith Viorst.

HEUER PUBLISHING CO., P.O. Box 248, Cedar Rapids IA 52406. (319)364-6311. E-mail: editor@hitp lays.com. Website: http://www.hitplays.com. Publisher: C. Emmett McMullen. Play publisher. Estab. 1928. Publishes plays and musicals for the amateur market including middle schools, junior and senior high schools and church groups. Pays by outright purchase or percentage royalty.
How to Contact: Query with synopsis, character breakdown and set description or submit complete manuscript and score. SASE. Reports in 2 months.
Musical Theater: "We prefer two or three act comedies or mystery-comedies with a large number of characters."
Publications: *Brave Buckaroo*, by Renee J. Clark (musical melodrama) and *Pirate Island*, by Martin Follose (musical comedy).
Tips: "We sell almost exclusively to junior and smaller senior high schools. Thus flexible casting is extremely important. We need plays with large, predominantly female casts and if you are writing a musical, we need more choral numbers and solos for girls than boys."

PIONEER DRAMA SERVICE, P.O. Box 4267, Englewood CO 80155. (303)779-4035. E-mail: piodrama @aol.com. Website: http://www.pioneerdrama.com. Assistant Editor: Beth Somers. Play publisher. Estab. 1963. "Plays are performed by junior high and high school drama departments, church youth groups, college and university theaters, semi-professional and professional children's theaters, parks and recreation departments." Playwrights paid 50% royalty (10% sales).
How to Contact: Query first with character breakdown, synopsis and set description. SASE. Reports in 4-6 months.
Musical Theater: "We seek full length children's musicals, high school musicals and one act children's musicals to be performed by children, secondary school students, and/or adults. As always, we want musicals easy to perform, simple sets, many female roles and very few solos. Must be appropriate for educational market. We are not interested in profanity, themes with exclusively adult interest, sex, drinking, smoking, etc. Several of our full-length plays are being converted to musicals. We edit them, then contract with someone to write the music and lyrics."
Publications: *Groovy*, by Tim Kelly/Bill Francoeur ('60s musical); *Tales of Terror from Nightmare High School*, by Patrick Rainville Dorn/Stephen Murray (musical spoof); and *The Real Story of Little Red Riding Hood*, by Judy Wolfman/David Reser (children's musical).
Tips: "Research and learn about our company. Our website and catalog provide an incredible amount of information."

PLAYERS PRESS, INC., P.O. Box 1132, Studio City CA 91614. (818)789-4980. Associate Editor: Karen Flathers. Vice President: Robert W. Gordon. Play publisher. Estab. 1965. Publishes 20-70 plays and 1-3 new musicals/year. Plays are used primarily by general audience and children. Pays variable royalty and variable amount/performance.
How to Contact: Query first. SASE. Reports in 1 year (3 weeks on queries).
Musical Theater: "We will consider all submitted works. Presently musicals for adults and high schools are in demand. When cast size can be flexible (describe how it can be done in your work) it sells better."
Publications: *Rapunzel n' The Witch*, by William-Alan Landes (children's musical); *Song of Love*, by

REFER TO THE GEOGRAPHIC INDEX (at the back of this book) to find listings of companies by state, as well as foreign listings.

William Alan Landes (musical); and *Curse of the Mummy's Tomb*, by J. Harries/P. Witymark (musical).
Tips: "Have your work produced at least twice. Be present for rehearsals and work with competent people. Then submit material asked for in good clear copy with good audio tapes."

N THIS MONTH ON STAGE, P.O. Box 62, Hewlett NY 11557-0062. (800)536-0099. E-mail: tmosmai l@aol.com. Associate Editor: Eric Harris. Play publisher. Estab. 1991. Publishes 4-6 plays and 0-1 musicals/ year. "Musical must read well on paper (we don't publish the score). TMOS readers are theater lovers and members of the professional theater industry." Pays $150 for outright purchase.
How to Contact: Submit complete manuscript and score. SASE. Reports in 12-16 months.
Musical Theater: "Open to various styles and themes, children's also. Short and one-act musicals especially welcome." No "non-linear, visual-oriented material or religious pageant plays."
Publications: *Truck Stop Parking Lot*, by Wm. S. Leavengood (one-act drama); *Miracle Teller*, by Trisha L. Frankhart (one-act comedy); and *When the Twain Met*, by Matt K. Miller (absurdist one-act).
Tips: "Neat readable submission. Proper SASE (or recycle instructions). Have patience during our lengthy consideration process."

Classical Performing Arts

Finding an audience is critical to the composer of orchestral music. Fortunately, baby boomers are swelling the ranks of classical music audiences and bringing with them a taste for fresh, innovative music. So the climate is fair for composers seeking their first performance.

Finding a performance venue is particularly important because once a composer has his work performed for an audience and establishes himself as a talented newcomer, it can lead to more performances and commissions for new works.

BEFORE YOU SUBMIT

Be aware that most classical music organizations are nonprofit groups, and don't have a large budget for acquiring new works. It takes a lot of time and money to put together an orchestral performance of a new composition, therefore these groups are quite selective when choosing new works to perform. Don't be disappointed if the payment offered by these groups is small or even non-existent. What you gain is the chance to have your music performed for an appreciative audience. Also realize that many classical groups are understaffed, so it may take longer than expected to hear back on your submission. It pays to be patient, and employ diplomacy, tact and timing in your follow-up.

In this section you will find listings for classical performing arts organizations throughout the U.S. But if you have no prior performances to your credit, it's a good idea to begin with a small chamber orchestra, for example. Smaller symphony and chamber orchestras are usually more inclined to experiment with new works. A local university or conservatory of music, where you may already have contacts, is a great place to start.

All of the groups listed in this section are interested in hearing new works from contemporary classical composers. Pay close attention to the music needs of each group, and when you find one you feel might be interested in your music, follow submission guidelines carefully. To locate classical performing arts groups in your area, consult the Geographic Index at the back of this book.

☑ **ACADIANA SYMPHONY ORCHESTRA**, P.O. Box 53632, Lafayette LA 70505. (318)232-4277. Fax: (318)237-4712. Executive Director: Geraldine Hubbel. Symphony orchestra. Estab. 1984. Members are amateurs and professionals. Performs 20 concerts/year, including 1 new work. Commissions 1 new work/year. Performs in 2,230-seat hall with "wonderful acoustics." Pays "according to the type of composition."
How to Contact: Query first. Does not return material. Reports in 2 months.
Music: Full orchestra: 10 minutes at most. Reduced orchestra, educational pieces: short, up to 5 minutes.
Performances: Quincy Hilliard's *Universal Covenant* (orchestral suite); James Hanna's *In Memoriam* (strings/elegy); and Gregory Danner's *A New Beginning* (full orchestra fanfare).

ADRIAN SYMPHONY ORCHESTRA, 110 S. Madison St., Adrian MI 49221. (517)264-3121. E-mail: aso@lni.com. Website: http://www.aso.org. Music Director: David Katz. Symphony orchestra and chamber music ensemble. Estab. 1981. Members are professionals. Performs 25 concerts/year including 2-3 new works. Commissions 1 new composer or new work/year. 1,200 seat hall—"Rural city with remarkably active cultural life." Pays $200-1,000 for performance.
How to Contact: Query first. Does not return material. Reports in 6 months.
Music: Chamber ensemble to full orchestra. "Limited rehearsal time dictates difficulty of pieces selected." Does not wish to see "rock music or country—not at this time."
Performances: Michael Pratt's *Dancing on the Wall* (orchestral—some aleatoric); Sir Peter Maxwell Davies' *Orkney Wedding* (orchestral); and Gwyneth Walker's *Fanfare, Interlude, Finale* (orchestral).

CLASSICAL PERFORMING ARTS

☑ 🏆 **AMERICAN JAZZ PHILHARMONIC**, 10811 Washington Blvd., Suite 300, Culver City CA 90232. (310)845-1900. Fax: (310)845-1909. Website: http://www.amjazzphil.org. Executive Director: Mitch Glickman. Symphonic jazz orchestra (72 piece). Estab. 1979. Members are professionals. Performs 8 concerts/year, including 10 new works. Commissions 2-5 composers or new works/year. Performs in major concert halls nationwide: Avery Fisher (New York), Karen & Richard Carpenter Performing Arts Center (Long Beach), Royce Hall (Los Angeles), Pick-Staiger (Chicago). Pays $2,500-5,000 for commission.

How to Contact: Query first then submit complete score and tape of piece(s) with résumé. SASE. "Newly commissioned composers are chosen each July. Submissions should be sent by June 15th, returned by August 15th."

Music: "The AJP commissions 1-2 new symphonic jazz works annually. Decisions to commission are based on composer's previous work in the symphonic jazz genre. The AJP is a 72-piece symphonic jazz ensemble that includes a rhythm section and woodwinds who double on saxophones, plus traditional symphonic orchestra."

Performances: John Clayton's *Three Shades of Blue* (solo tenor sax and orchestra); Lennie Niehaus' *Tribute to Bird* (solo alto sax and orchestra); and Eddie Karam's *Stay 'N See* (symphonic jazz overture).

Tips: "The AJP has been a recipient of a Reader's Digest/Meet the Composer grant and has received awards from ASCAP and the American Symphony Orchestra League for its programming. The ensemble has also received a Grammy Award nomination for its debut album on GRP Records featuring Ray Brown and Phil Woods. The AJP has recently established the Henry Mancini Institute—a four week summer educational music program for talented young musicians and composer/arrangers chosen from auditions held nationally. Participants study and perform with the principal players of the AJP and guest artists and composers/conductors. Program includes private lessons, ensemble rehearsals, panel discussions/clinics, master classes, soloist opportunities and performances in orchestra, big band, chamber ensembles and combos."

AMERICAN OPERA MUSICAL THEATRE CO., 400 W. 43rd St. #19D, New York NY 10036. Phone/fax: (212)594-1839. E-mail: corto@mindspring.com. Artistic Director: Diana Corto. Chamber music ensemble, chamber opera and musical theatre producing/presenting organization. Estab. 1994. Members are professionals with varying degrees of experience. Performs 5 concerts/year; 1 or 2 are new works. Audience is sophisticated and knowledgeable about music and theatre. "We rent different performance spaces." Pays negotiable royalty.

How to Contact: Submit tape. Does not return material. Reports in 2-3 weeks.

Music: "Must be vocal (for opera or for music theatre) with chamber groups. Cast should not exceed 10. Orchestration should not exceed 22, smaller chamber groups preferred. No rock 'n' roll, brassy pop or theatre material."

Performances: P. Griffith's *Jewel Box* (opera), Paisiello's *La Molinara* (opera); and *Stars of the Bolshoi Opera* (opera).

AMHERST SAXOPHONE QUARTET, 137 Eagle St., Williamsville NY 14221-5721. (716)632-2445. E-mail: rosenthl@acsu.buffalo.edu. Website: http://www.acsu.buffalo.edu/~rosenthl/asqs.html. Director: Steve Rosenthal. Chamber music ensemble. Estab. 1978. Performs 80 concerts/year including 10-20 new works. Commissions 1-2 composers or new works/year. "We are a touring ensemble." Payment varies.

How to Contact: Query first. SASE. Reports in 1 month.

Music: "Music for soprano, alto, tenor and baritone (low A) saxophone. We are interested in great music of many styles. Level of difficulty is commensurate with full-time touring ensembles."

Performances: Lukas Foss's *Saxophone Quartet* (new music); David Stock's *Sax Appeal* (new music); and Chan Ka Nin's *Saxophone Quartet* (new music).

Tips: "Professionally copied parts help! Write what you truly want to write."

N̄ **ANDERSON SYMPHONY ORCHESTRA**, P.O. Box 741, Anderson IN 46015. (765)644-2111. Conductor: Dr. Richard Sowers. Symphony orchestra. Estab. 1968. Members are professionals. Performs 7 concerts/year. Performs for typical mid-western audience in a 1,500-seat restored Paramount Theatre. Pay negotiable.
How to Contact: Query first. SASE. Reports in several months.
Music: "Shorter lengths better; concerti OK; difficulty level: mod high; limited by typically 3 full service rehearsals."

✿ ✓ **ARCADY**, (formerly The Norfolk Singers' Chorus and Orchestra), P.O. Box 955, Simcoe, Ontario N3Y 5B3 Canada. (519)428-3185. Fax: (519)426-1573. Director: Ronald Beckett. Administrator: Naomi O'Neill. Semi-professional chorus and orchestra. Estab. 1983. Members are professionals and amateurs. Performs 12 concerts/year including 1-2 new works. Commissions 1 composer or new work/year. Pay negotiable.
How to Contact: Submit complete score and tape of piece(s). Does not return material. Reports in 3 months.
Music: "Compositions appropriate for ensemble accustomed to performance of chamber works, accompanied or unaccompanied, with independence of parts. Specialize in repetoire of 17th, 18th and 20th centuries. Number of singers does not exceed 45. Orchestra is limited to strings, supported by a professional quartet. No popular, commercial or show music."
Performances: Ronald Bechett's *I Am . . .* (opera); Ronald Bechett's *John* (opera); and David Lenson's *Prologue to Dido and Aeneas* (masque).
Tips: "Write for conservative resources (i.e., small ensembles). Performance level must take into account the limited amount of time available for rehearsal. Small-scale is generally more effective than large-scale. Ensemble is very interested in and capable of performance of new music, is very experienced with stage performance, and is available for hire."

AUGSBURG CHOIR, Augsburg College, 731 21st Ave. S., Minneapolis MN 55454. E-mail: hendricp@a ugsburg.edu. Website: http://www/augsburg.edu. Director of Choral Activities: Peter A. Hendrickson. Vocal ensemble (SATB choir). Members are amateurs. Performs 25 concerts/year, including 1-6 new works. Commissions 0-2 composers or new works/year. Audience is all ages, "sophisticated and unsophisticated." Concerts are performed in churches, concert halls and schools. Pays for outright purchase.
How to Contact: Query first. SASE. Reports in 1 month.
Music: Seeking "sacred choral pieces, no more than 5-7 minutes long, to be sung a cappella or with obbligato instrument. Can contain vocal solos. We have 50-60 members in our choir."
Performances: Carol Barnett's *Spiritual Journey*; Steven Heitzeg's *Litanies for the Living* (choral/orchestral); and Morton Lanriclsen's *O Magnum Mysteries* (a cappella choral).

AUREUS QUARTET, 22 Lois Ave., Demarest NJ 07627-2220. (201)767-8704. E-mail: llyandra2@aol.c om. Artistic Director: James J. Seiler. Vocal ensemble (a cappella). Estab. 1979. Members are professionals. Performs 75 concerts/year, including 12 new works. Commissions 5 composers or new works/year. Pay varies for outright purchase.
How to Contact: Query first. SASE. Reports in 2 months.
Music: "We perform anything from pop to classic—mixed repertoire so anything goes. Some pieces can be scored for orchestras as we do pops concerts. Up to now, we've only worked with a quartet. Could be expanded if the right piece came along. Level of difficulty—no piece has ever been too hard." Does not wish to see electronic or sacred pieces. "Electronic pieces would be hard to program. Sacred pieces not performed much. Classical/jazz arrangements of old standards are great!"
Tips: "We perform for a very diverse audience—luscious, four part writing that can showcase well-trained voices is a must. Also, clever arrangements of old hits from '20s through '50s are sure bets. (Some pieces could take optional accompaniment)."

✓ **BILLINGS SYMPHONY**, 201 N. Broadway., Suite 350, Box 7055, Billings MT 59101-1936. (406)252-3610. Fax: (406)252-3353. E-mail: symphony@mcn.net. Website: http://www.mcn.net/~sympho ny. Music Director: Dr. Uri Barnea. Symphony orchestra, orchestra and chorale. Estab. 1950. Members are professionals and amateurs. Performs 15 concerts/year, including 6-7 new works. Traditional audience. Performs at Alberta Bair Theater (capacity 1,416). Pays by outright purchase (or rental).
How to Contact: Query first. SASE. Reports in 2-3 months.
Music: Any style. Traditional notation preferred.
Performances: Jerod S. Tate's *Winter Moons* (ballet suite); Alberto Ginastera's *Harp Concerto* (concerto); and Olga Victorova's *Compliments to American Audience* (orchestral piece).
Tips: "Write what you feel (be honest) and sharpen your compositional and craftsmanship skills."

BIRMINGHAM-BLOOMFIELD SYMPHONY ORCHESTRA, 1592 Buckingham, Birmingham MI 48009. (248)645-2276. Fax: (248)645-22760. Music Director and Conductor: Felix Resnick. Executive Director: Carla Lamphere. Symphony orchestra. Estab. 1975. Members are professionals. Performs 6 concerts including 1 new work/year. Commissions 1 composer or new work/year "with grants." Performs for middle-to-upper class audience at Temple Beth El's Sanctuary. Pays per performance "depending upon grant received."
How to Contact: Query first. Does not return material. Reports in 1-2 months.
Music: "We are a symphony orchestra but also play pops. Usually 3 works on program (2 hrs.) Orchestra size 65-75. If pianist is involved, they must rent piano."
Performances: Brian Belanger's *Tuskegee Airmen Suite* (symphonic full orchestra); and Larry Nazer & Friend's *Music from "Warm" CD* (jazz with full orchestra).

BRAVO! L.A., 16823 Liggett St., North Hills CA 91343. (818)892-8737. Fax: (818)892-1227. Director: Dr. Janice Foy. An umbrella organization of recording/touring musicians, formed in 1994. Includes the following musical ensembles: Trio of the Americas (piano, clarinet, cello); the New American Quartet (string quartet); Festive Strings! (string trio); The Ascending Wave (harp, soprano, cello or harp/cello duo); and the Sierra Chamber Players (piano with strings or mixed ensemble). Performs 8 concerts/year, including 1-2 new works.
How to Contact: Submit complete score and tape of piece(s). SASE. Reports in 1-2 months.
Music: "Classical, Romantic, Baroque, Popular (including new arrangements done by Shelly Cohen, from the 'Tonight Show Band'), ethnic (including gypsy) and contemporary works (commissioned as well). The New American Quartet has a recording project which features music of Mozart's *Eine Kleine Nachtmusik*, Borodin's *Nocturne*, a Puccini Opera Suite (S. Cohen), Strauss' *Blue Danube Waltz*, *Trepak* of Tschaikovsky, *'El Choclo'* (Argentinian tango), *Csardas!* and arrangements of Cole Porter, Broadway show tunes and popular classics."
Performances: Paul Schoenfield's *Café Music* (piano trio); Lee Hildridge's *Fantasy Sonata* (piano and cello piece); and Aurelio de la Vega's *Leyenda del Ariel Criollo* (piano and cello).
Tips: "Please be open to criticism/suggestions about your music and try to appeal to mixed audiences. We also look for innovative techniques, mixed styles or entertaining approaches, such as classical jazz or Bach and pop."

CALGARY BOYS CHOIR, 2521 Dieppe Ave. SW, Calgary, Alberta T3E 7J9 Canada. (403)217-7790. Fax: (403)217-7796. E-mail: cbchoir@telusplanet.net. Website: http://www.telusplanet.net/public/cbchoir/Home.html. Artistic Director: Jean-Louis Barbier. Boys choir. Estab. 1973. Members are amateurs age 5 and up. Performs 50 concerts/year including 1-2 new works. Pay negotiable.
How to Contact: Query first. SASE. Reports in 1 month.
Music: "Style fitting for boys choir. Lengths depending on project. Orchestration preferable a cappella/for piano/sometimes orchestra."
Performances: G. Wirth's *Sadhaka* and *Our Normoste*; and Shri Mataji Nirmala Devi's *Binati Suniye*.

CANADIAN OPERA COMPANY, 227 Front St. E., Toronto, Ontario M5A 1E8 Canada. (416)363-6671. E-mail: sandrag@coc.ca. Website: http://www.coc.ca. Associate Artistic Administrator: Sandra J. Gavinchuk. Opera company. Estab. 1950. Members are professionals. 50-55 performances, including a minimum of 1 new work/year. Pays by contract.
How to Contact: Submit complete score and tapes of vocal and/or operatic works. "Vocal works please." SASE. Reports in 5 weeks.
Music: Vocal works, operatic in nature. 12 singers maximum, 1½ hour in duration and 18 orchestral players. "Do not submit works which are not for voice. Ask for requirements for the Composers-In-Residence program."
Performances: Randolph Peters' *The Golden Ass* (opera).
Tips: "We have a Composers-In-Residence program which is open to Canadian composers or landed immigrants."

MARKET CONDITIONS are constantly changing! If you're still using this book and it is 2001 or later, buy the newest edition of *Songwriter's Market* at your favorite bookstore or order directly from Writer's Digest Books at (800)289-0963.

CARMEL SYMPHONY ORCHESTRA, P.O. Box 761, Carmel IN 46032. (317)844-9717. Fax: (317)844-9916. Website: http://www.ci.carmel.in.us/. Executive Director: Alicia McMahon. Symphony orchestra. Estab. 1976. Members are professionals and amateurs. Performs 15 concerts/year, including 1-2 new works. Audience is "40% senior citizens, 85% white." Performs in a 1,500-seat high school performing arts center. Pay is negotiable.
How to Contact: Query first. SASE. Reports in 3 months.
Music: "Full orchestra works, 10-20 minutes in length. Can be geared toward 'children's' or 'Masterworks' programs. 65-70 piece orchestra, medium difficulty."
Performances: Jim Becket's *Glass Bead Jane* (full orchestra); Percy Grainger's *Molly on the Shore* (full orchestra); and Frank Glover's *Impressions of New England* (full orchestra and jazz quartet).

☑ **CARSON CITY SYMPHONY**, P.O. Box 2001, Carson City NV 89702-2001 or 191 Heidi Circle, Carson City NV 89701-6532. (775)883-4154. Fax: (775)883-4371. E-mail: dcbugli@aol.com. Website: http://members.aol.com.CCSymphony. Music Director/Conductor: David C. Bugli. Amateur community orchestra. Estab. 1984. Members are amateurs. Performs 5 concerts, including 2 new works/year. Audience is largely Carson City/Reno area retirees. "Most concerts are performed in the Carson City Community Center Auditorium, which seats 816." Pay varies for outright purchase.
How to Contact: Submit complete score and tape of works. Does not return material. Reports in 2 months.
Music: "We want classical, pop orchestrations, orchestrations of early music for modern orchestras, concertos for violin or piano, holiday music for chorus and orchestra (children's choirs and handbell ensemble available), music by women, music for brass choir. Most performers are amateurs, but there are a few professionals who perform with us. Available winds and percussion: 2 flutes and flute/piccolo, 2 oboes (E.H. double), 2 clarinets, 1 bass clarinet, 2 bassoons, 3 or 4 horns, 3 trumpets, 3 trombones, 1 tuba, timpani, and some percussion. Harp and piano. Strings: 8-10-6-6-3. Avoid rhythmic complexity (except in pops) and music that lacks melodic appeal. Composers should contact us first. Each concert has a different emphasis. Note: Associated choral group, Carson Chamber Singers, performs several times a year with the orchestra and independently."
Performances: Thomas Svoboda's *Overture of the Season* (minimalist overture); Gwyneth Walker's *A Concerto of Hymns and Spirituals for Trumpet and Orchestra*; and Ronald R. Williams' *Noah: Suite After Andre Obey*.
Tips: "It is better to write several short movements well than to write long, unimaginative pieces, especially when starting out. Be willing to revise after submitting the work, even if it was premiered elsewhere."

CASCADE SYMPHONY ORCHESTRA, P.O. Box 550, Edmonds WA 89020. (425)778-4688. E-mail: cso@eskimo.com. Website: http://www.eskimo.com/~csol. Musical Director: Gregory Sullivan Isaacs. Symphony orchestra. Estab. 1960. Members are professionals and amateurs. Performs 7 concerts/year including 3-4 new works. Commissions 1 composer or new work/year. Performs in 900-seat theater. Pays rental and royalty.
How to Contact: Query first. SASE. Reports in 3 months.
Music: Full orchestra. No choral works.
Performances: Samuel Jones's *Fanfare and Celebration (orchestral); and Gregory Sullivan Issacs' Song Without Words (English horn and orchestra).*
Tips: "Don't send a large oversized score."

[N] **CHAMBER ORCHESTRA OF SOUTH BAY/CARSON-DOMINIQUEZ HILLS SYMPHONY**, 21 La Vista Verde, Rancho Palos Verdes CA 90275. (310)243-3947. E-mail: fsteiner@dhvxzo.csabh.edu. Music Director: Dr. Frances Steiner. Symphony orchestra. Estab. 1972. Members are professionals (chamber orchestra); professionals and amatuers (symphony). Performs 10-11 concerts/year including 3-4 new works. Commissions 0-1 new works/year. Chamber orchestra audience is conservative in musical taste; symphony has an ethnically diverse and new student audience. Performance spaces seat 450-480. Pays ASCAP/BMI royalty or rental fee to publisher.

[N] ☑ **CHARLOTTE PHILHARMONIC ORCHESTRA**, P.O. Box 470987, Charlotte NC 28247-0987. (704)846-2788. Fax: (704)847-6043. E-mail: charphilor@aol.com. Website: http://www.charlottephilharmonic.org. Music Director: Albert Moehring. Symphony orchestra. Estab. 1991. Members are professionals. Performs 12 concerts/year including 2-4 new works. Audience consists of music lovers, educated and uneducated. "We regularly perform Broadway/movie soundtracks, also standard classical repertoire." Performance spaces are up to 2,500 seats. Pay is negotiable.
   ● The Charlotte Philharmonic Orchestra was voted Charlotte's Best Entertainment in 1998.
How to Contact: Submit complete score and tape of piece(s). Does not return material. Reports in 4-6 weeks.

Music: Seeks full orchestrations, lush strings always popular. Maximum 8-10 minutes. Would review classical styles, but also interested in Boston Pops type selections. Require lyrical music with interesting melodies and good rhythms. "We are not interested in atonal, dissonat styled music. We will neither perform it, nor bother to review it. Our audiences do not like it." Players are professional. Limited rehearsals. String passages playable in limited time. Full orchestra sound—excellent brass players. 75 piece orchestra. Always interested in fine Broadway styled arrangements. Look for strong, smooth transpositions/modulations.

Performances: Davis Brown's *Dance of the Moryak* (bright, interesting Russian sailor dance); Davis Brown's arrangement of *Jesu, Bambino* (lush, orchestra/choral); and Ron Kickasola's *Appalachian Spring* (folk, melodic tunes woven in tone poem).

Tips: "With a new composer, we recommend pieces under 10 minutes, lyrical basis with definite melodies. Full use of 75 piece orchestra. Lush strings without exceedingly difficult passages for limited rehearsals. Variety of materials welcomed. Enjoy standard classics, bib band, ballroom dance-type music, ballet style. Also enjoy operatic arrangements. Use our own Philharmonic Chorus as well as regular vocalists. Good choral arrangements with full orchestra always of interest. Appreciate a tape when possible. If a composer submits during a really busy period of performances, please be patient. If there is no response in 4-6 weeks, they may contact us again."

☑ **CHASPEN OPERA THEATER**, 27819 NE 49th St., Redmond WA 98053. Phone/fax: (425)880-6035. E-mail: chaspen@aol.com. Website: http://members.aol.com/chaspen. Executive Director: Penny Orloff. Symphony orchestra, chamber music ensemble and opera/music theater ensemble. Estab. 1991. Members are professionals. Performs 6-10 concerts/year including 2-3 new works. Commissions 1-2 composers or new works/year. Audience is generally upper-middle class families and seniors. Performs in space with 250-600 seats, depending upon space requirements. Pay is negotiable.

How to Contact: Query first by e-mail only. SASE. Reports immediately.

Music: "Thematic revues for 6-8 singers, pianist, auxiliary keyboard; accessible symphonic pieces for voice and 40-50 piece symphony orchestra on contemporary themes; small chamber works for narrator/voice(s), and mixed chamber ensemble. 12-tone or serial pieces are NOT considered, nor are symphonic works using more players than a standard Mozart symphony orchestration. We do not wish to see any work which may not be performed for a family audience. Keep it clean!"

Performances: P. Orloff's *Lone Star Ladies*; Menotti's *Amahl and the Night Visitors* (opera); C. Fraley's *Frog Prince* (opera for young audiences); and A Shawn's *The Ant & the Grasshopper* (opera for young audiences).

Tips: "Flexibility, imagination, economy: If you are difficult to work with and your piece requires a lot of extras, we won't be producing it. Have a heart. Have a sense of humor."

CHATTANOOGA GIRLS CHOIR, P.O. Box 6036, 612 Maclellan Building, Chattanooga TN 37401. (423)266-9422. E-mail: girlschoir@mindspring.com. Artistic Director: Ed Huey. Vocal ensemble. Estab. 1986. Members are amateurs. Performs 2 concerts/year including at least 1 new work. Audience consists of cultural and civic organizations and national and international tours. Performance space includes concert halls and churches. Pays for outright purchase.

How to Contact: Query first. SASE. Reports in 6 weeks.

Music: Seeks renaissance, baroque, classical, romantic, twentieth century, folk and musical theatre for young voices of up to 8 minutes. Performers include 5 treble choices: 4th grade (2 pts.); 5th grade (2 pts.) (SA); grades 6-9 (3 pts.) (SSA); grades 10-12 (3-4 pts.) (SSAA); and a combined choir: grades 6-12 (3-4 pts.) (SSAA). Medium level of difficulty. "Avoid extremely high Tessitura Sop I and extremely low Tessitura Alto II."

Performances: Jan Swafford's *Iphigenia Book: Meagher* (choral drama); Penny Tullock's *How Can I Keep from Singing* (Shaker hymn).

Ⓝ **THE CHICAGO STRING ENSEMBLE**, 410 S. Michigan Ave., Chicago IL 60605. (312)332-0567. Fax: (847)501-5348. E-mail: cse@interaccess.com. Website: http://homepage.interaccess.com/~cse/. President: Virginia Graham. Professional string orchestra. Estab. 1977. Members are professionals. Performs 20 concerts/year, including 1-2 new works. Commissions 1 new work/year. Audience is a Chicago and suburban cross-section. Performance space: 3 large, acoustically favorable area churches and a library. Composers possibly paid $100-200 for producing parts.

How to Contact: Submit complete score and tape of piece. Does not return material. Reports in 6 months.

Music: "Open to any work for string orchestra, with or without a solo instrument. Additional instrumentation (e.g., harp, keyboard, percussion, a few winds) is possible but not encouraged. Must be possible to 6-6-4-4-2 or fewer strings. 10-15 minutes long. No electronics."

Performances: Daniel Dorff's *Summer Solstice* (clarinet & strings); William Ferris' *Bristol Hills* (string orchestra); and Franz Thürauer's *Cello Concerto* (cello and strings-world premiere).

☑ **CIMARRON CIRCUIT OPERA COMPANY**, P.O. Box 1085, Norman OK 73070. Phone/fax: (405)364-8962. E-mail: ccoc@telepath.com. Music Director: Kevin Smith. Opera company. Estab. 1975. Members are semi professional. Performs 75 concerts/year including 1-2 new works. Commissions 1 or less new work/year. "CCOC performs for children across the state of Oklahoma and for a dedicated audience in central Oklahoma. As a touring company, we adapt to the performance space provided, ranging from a classroom to a full raised stage." Pay is negotiable.
How to Contact: Query first. Does not return material. Reports in 6 months.
Music: "We are seeking operas or operettas in English only. We would like to begin including new, American works in our repertoire. Children's operas should be no longer than 45 minutes and require no more than a synthesizer for accompaniment. Adult operas should be appropriate for families, and may require either full orchestration or synthesizer. CCOC is a professional company whose members have varying degrees of experience, so any difficulty level is appropriate. There should be a small to moderate number of principals. Children's work should have no more than four principals. Our slogan is 'Opera is a family thing to do.' If we cannot market a work to families, we do not want to see it."
Performances: Mozart's *Cosi Fan Tutte*; Barab's *Little Red Riding Hood*; and Gilbert & Sullivan's *The Mikado*.
Tips: "45-minute fairy tale-type children's operas with possibly a 'moral' work well for our market. Looking for works appealing to K-8 grade students. No more than four principles."

☑ **COLORADO CHILDREN'S CHORALE**, 518 17th St., Suite 760, Denver CO 80202. (303)892-5600. Fax: (303)892-0828. Artistic Director: Deborah DeSantis. Vocal ensemble and highly trained children's chorus. Estab. 1974. Members are professionals and amateurs. Performs 150 concerts/year including 3-5 new works. Commissions 2-5 composers or new works/year. "Our audiences' ages range from 5-80. We give school performances and tour (national, international). We give subscription concerts and sing with orchestras (symphonic and chamber). Halls: schools to symphony halls to arenas to outdoor theaters." Pays $100-500 outright purchase (more for extended works).
How to Contact: Submit complete score and tapes of piece(s). Does not return material. Reports in 1-3 months. "No guarantee of report on unsolicited material."
Music: "We want short pieces (3-5 minutes): novelty, folk arrangement, serious; longer works 5-20: serious; staged operas/musicals 30-45 minutes: piano accompaniment or small ensemble; or possible full orchestration if work is suitable for symphony concert. We are most interested in SA, SSA, SSAA. We look for a variety of difficulty ranges and encourage very challenging music for SSA-SSAA choruses (32 singers, unchanged voices). We don't want rock, charts without written accompaniments or texts that are inappropriate for children. We are accessible to all audiences. We like some of our repertoire to reflect a sense of humor, others to have a message. We're very interested in well crafted music that has a special mark of distinction."
Performances: John Kuzma's *O, Excellence* (virtuosit encore); Normand Lockwood's *Thought of Him I Love* (15-minute series with chamber orchestra); and Samuel Lancaster's *Stocking Stuffer 1994* (8-minute comic number with full symphony orchestra).
Tips: "Submit score and tape with good cover letter, résumé and record of performance. Wait at least three weeks before a follow-up call or letter. Materials should be in excellent condition. We review a great quantity of material that goes through several channels. Please be patient. Sometimes excellent material simply doesn't fit our current needs and is put in a 'future consideration file.' "

☑ **COMMONWEALTH OPERA INC.**, 140 Pine St., Florence MA 01062. (413)586-5026. E-mail: commopr1@aol.com. Artistic Director: Richard R. Rescia. Opera company. Estab. 1977. Members are professionals and amateurs. Performs 4 concerts/year. "We perform at the Academy of Music at Northampton in an 800-seat opera house. Depending on opera, audience could be family oriented or adult." Pays royalty.
How to Contact: Query first. Does not return material. Reports will take months.
Music: "We are open to all styles of opera. We have the limitations of a regional opera company with local chorus. Principals come from a wide area. We look only at opera scores."
Performances: Arnold Black's *The Phantom Tollbooth* (children's opera).

REFER TO THE GEOGRAPHIC INDEX (at the back of this book) to find listings of companies by state, as well as foreign listings.

Tips: "We're looking for opera that is accessible to the general public and performable by a standard opera orchestra."

DÚO CLÁSICO, 87 N. Fullerton Ave., Montclair NJ 07042. (973)655-1126. E-mail: wittend@saturn.mo ntclair.edu. Website: http://www.montclair.edu/pages/music/Faculty/witten.html. Contact: David Witten. Chamber music ensemble. Estab. 1986. Members are professionals. Performs 16 concerts/year including 4 new works. Commissions 1 composer or new work/year. Performs in small recital halls. Pays 10% royalty.
How to Contact: Query first. SASE. Reports in 6 weeks.
Music: "We welcome scores for flute solo, piano solo or duo. Particular interest in Latin American composers."
Performances: Diego Luzuriaga's *La Múchica* (modern, with extended techniques); Robert Starer's *Yizkor & Anima Aeterna* (rhythmic); and Piazzolla's *Etudes Tanguistiques* (solo flute).
Tips: "Extended techniques, or with tape, are fine!"

GREATER GRAND FORKS SYMPHONY ORCHESTRA, P.O. Box 7084, Grand Forks ND 58202-7084. (701)777-3359. Fax: (701)777-3395. Music Director: Timm Rolek. Symphony orchestra. Estab. 1908. Members are professionals and/or amateurs. Performs 6 concerts/year. "New works are presented in 4-6 of our programs." Audience is "a mix of ages and musical experience. In 1997-98 we moved into a renovated, 450-seat theater." Pay is negotiable, depending on licensing agreements.
How to Contact: Submit complete score or complete score and tape of pieces. SASE. Reports in 3-6 months.
Music: "Style is open, instrumentation the limiting factor. Music can be scored for an ensemble up to but not exceeding: 3,2,3,2/4,3,3,1/3 perc./strings. Rehearsal time limited to 3 hours for new works."
Performances: Michael Harwood's *Amusement Park Suite* (orchestra); Randall Davidson's *Mexico Bolivar Tango* (chamber orchestra); and John Corigliano's *Voyage* (flute and orchestra).

HASTINGS SYMPHONY ORCHESTRA, Fuhr Hall, Ninth & Ash, Hastings NE 68901. (402)461-7361. E-mail: jjohnson@hastings.edu. Conductor/Music Director: Dr. James Johnson. Symphony orchestra. Estab. 1926. Members are professionals and amateurs. Performs 7-8 concerts/year including 1 new work. Commissions 0-1 new works/year. "Audience consists of conservative residents of mid-Nebraska who haven't heard most classics." Concert Hall: Masonic Temple Auditorium (950). Pays per performance.
How to Contact: Submit complete score and tapes of piece(s). SASE. Reports in 4-6 months.
Music: "We are looking for all types of music within the range of an accomplished community orchestra. Write first and follow with a phone call."
Performances: Richard Wilson's *Silhouette*; and James Oliverio's *Pilgrimage* (symphonic).
Tips: "Think about the size, ability and budgetary limits. Confer with our music director about audience taste. Think of music with special ties to locality."

HENDERSONVILLE SYMPHONY ORCHESTRA, P.O. Box 1811, Hendersonville NC 28793. (704)697-5884. Fax: (704)697-5765. E-mail: hvlso@juno.com. General Manager: Sandie Salvaggio-Walker. Symphony orchestra. Estab. 1971. Members are professionals and amateurs. Performs 6 concerts/year. "We would welcome a new work per year." Audience is a cross-section of retirees, professionals and some children. Performance space is a 857-seat high school audiorium.
How to Contact: Query first. SASE. Reports in 1 month.
Music: "We use a broad spectrum of music (classical concerts and pops)."
Performances: Nelson's *Jubilee* (personal expression in a traditional method); Britten's "The Courtly Dances" from Glorina (time-tested); and Chip Davis' arrangement for Mannheim Steamroller's *Deck the Halls* (modern adaptation of traditional melody).
Tips: "Submit your work even though we are a community orchestra. We like to be challenged. We have the most heavily patronized fine arts group in the county. Our emphasis is on education."

HERSHEY SYMPHONY ORCHESTRA, P.O. Box 93, Hershey PA 17033. (800)533-3088. E-mail: drdackow@aol.com. Music Director. Dr. Sandra Dackow. Symphony orchestra. Estab. 1969. Members are professionals and amateurs. Performs 8 concerts/year, including 1-3 new works. Commissions "possibly 1-2" composers or new works/year. Audience is family and friends of community theater. Performance space is a 1,900 seat grand old movie theater. Pays commission fee.
How to Contact: Submit complete score and tape of piece(s). SASE. Reports in 3 months.
Music: "Symphonic works of various lengths and types which can be performed by a non-professional orchestra. We are flexible but like to involve all our players."
Performances: Paul W. Whear's *Celtic Christmas Carol* (orchestra/bell choir) and Linda Robbins Cole-

man's *In Good King Charlie's Golden Days* (overture).

Tips: "Please lay out rehearsal numbers/letter and rests according to phrases and other logical musical divisions rather than in groups of ten measures, etc., which is very unmusical and wastes time and causes a surprising number of problems. Also, please do not send a score written in concert pitch; use the usual transpositions so that the conductor sees what the players see; rehearsal is much more effective this way. Cross cue all important solos; this helps in rehearsal where instruments may be missing."

N THE PAUL HILL CHORALE (AND) THE WASHINGTON SINGERS, 5630 Connecticut Ave. NW, Washington DC 20015. (202)364-4321. E-mail: singing@paulhillchorale.com. Website: http://paulhill chorale.com. Music Director: Donald McCullough. Vocal ensemble. Estab. 1967. Members are professionals and amateurs. Performs 8 concerts/year including 1-3 new works. Commissions one new composer or work every 2 years. "Audience covers a wide range of ages and economic levels drawn from the greater Washington DC metropolitan area. Kennedy Center Concert Hall seats 2,400." Pays by outright purchase.
How to Contact: Submit complete score and tape of piece(s). SASE. Reports in 6-9 months.
Music: Seeks new works for: 1) large chorus with or without symphony orchestras; 2) chamber choir and small ensemble.
Performances: Jeffrey Van's *Road to Aringnon* (choral with guitar, small professional ensemble); Joonas Kokkonen's *Requiem* (symphonic choral with orchestra); and Donald McCullough's *Holocaust Cantata* (chorus, piano and cello).

KITCHENER-WATERLOO CHAMBER ORCHESTRA, Box 34015, Highland Hills P.O., Kitchener, Ontario N2N 3G2 Canada. (519)744-3828. Music Director: Graham Coles. Chamber Orchestra. Estab. 1985. Members are professionals and amateurs. Performs 5-6 concerts/year including 1-2 new works. "We perform mainly baroque and classical repertoire, so any contemporary works must not be too dissonant, long or far fetched." Pays per performance.
How to Contact: "It's best to query first so we can outline what not to send. Include: complete cv—list of works, performances, sample reviews." Does not return material. Reports in 2 months.
Music: "Musical style must be accessible to our audience and players (3 rehearsals). Length should be under 20 minutes. Maximum orchestration 2/2/2/2 2/2/0/0 Timp/or 1 Percussion String 5/5/3/4/2. We have limited rehearsal time, so keep technique close to that of Bach-Beethoven. We also play chamber ensemble works—octets, etc. We do not want choral or solo works."
Performances: James Grant's *Lament* (string orchestra) and Reynaldo and Hahn's *La Fete Chez Therese* (ballet suite).
Tips: "If you want a first-rate performance, keep the technical difficulties minimal."

KNOX-GALESBURG SYMPHONY, Box 31, Knox College, Galesburg IL 61401. (309)343-0112, ext. 208. E-mail: bpolay@knox.edu. Website: http://www.knox.edu/knoxweb/kgs/home.html. Music Director: Bruce Polay. Symphony orchestra. Estab. 1951. Members are professionals and amateurs. Performs 7 concerts/year including 2-5 new works. Commissions 1 composer or new work/year. High diverse audience; excellent, recently renovated historical theater. Pay is negotiable.
How to Contact: Submit complete score and tapes of piece(s). "Pops material also welcome." SASE. Reports in 6-8 months.
Music: Moderate difficulty 3222/4331/T piano, harpsichord, celesta and full strings. No country.
Performances: Winstin's *5th Symphony* (orchestral); Pann's "Bullfight" from "Two Portraits of Barcelona" (orchestral); and Polay's Concerto-Fantasie (piano and orchestra).
Tips: "Looking for moderately difficult, 8-10 minute pieces for standard orchestra."

LAKESIDE SUMMER SYMPHONY, 236 Walnut Ave., Lakeside OH 43440. (419)798-4461. Contact: G. Keith Addy. Conductor: Robert L. Cronquist. Symphony orchestra. Members are professionals. Performs 8 concerts/year. Performs "Chautauqua-type programs with an audience of all ages (2-102). Hoover Auditorium is a 3,000-seat auditorium."
How to Contact: Query first. SASE.
Music: Seeking "classical compositions for symphony composed of 50-55 musicians. The work needs to have substance and be a challenge to our symphony members. No modern jazz, popular music or hard rock."

MARKETS THAT WERE listed in the 1999 edition of *Songwriter's Market* but do not appear this year are listed in the General Index with a notation explaining why they were omitted.

LAMARCA AMERICAN VARIETY SINGERS, 2655 W. 230th Place, Torrance CA 90505. (310)325-8708. E-mail: kandelpris@hotmail.com. Director: Priscilla Kandel. Youth to high school vocal ensembles. Estab. 1979. Members are professionals and amateurs. Performs 10 concerts/year including 3 new works. Performs at major hotels, conventions, community theaters, fund raising events, cable TV, community fairs and Disneyland. Pays showcase only.
How to Contact: Query first. SASE. Reports in 2 weeks.
Music: "Seeks 3-10 or 15 minute medleys; a variety of musical styles from Broadway—pop styles to humorous specialty songs. Top 40 dance music, light rock and patriotic themes. No hip-hop or anything not suitable for family audiences."
Performances: Priscilla LaMarca's *Hip Hop Alphabet* (upbeat educational); Mariah Carey's *Hero* (inspirational); and *Colors of the Wind* (ballad).

N LEHIGH VALLEY CHAMBER ORCHESTRA, Box 20641, Lehigh Valley PA 18002-0641. (610)266-8555. Music Director: Donald Spieth. Symphony orchestra. Estab. 1979. Performs 25 concerts/year including 2-3 new works. Members are professionals. Commissions 1-2 composers or new works/year. Typical orchestral audience, also youth concerts. Pays commission for first 2 performances, first right for recording.
How to Contact: Submit complete score and tape of piece(s). SASE. Reports in 4 months.
Music: "Classical orchestral; works for youth and pops concerts. Duration 10-15 minutes. Chamber orchestra 2222-2210 percussion, strings (76442). No limit on difficulty."
Performances: David Stock's *String Set* (4 dances for strings); and John Scully's *Letters from Birmingham Jail* (soprano and orchestra).
Tips: "Send a sample tape and score of a work(s) written for the requested medium."

LITHOPOLIS AREA FINE ARTS ASSOCIATION, 3825 Cedar Hill Rd., Canal Winchester OH 43110-8929. (614)837-8925. Series Director: Virginia E. Heffner. Performing Arts Series. Estab. 1973. Members are professionals and amateurs. Performs 6-7 concerts/year including 2-3 new works. "Our audience consists of couples and families 30-80 in age. Their tastes run from classical, folk, ethnic, big band, pop and jazz. Our hall is acoustically excellent and seats 400. It was designed as a lecture-recital hall in 1925." Composers "may apply for Ohio Arts Council Grant under the New Works category." Pays straight fee to ASCAP.
How to Contact: Query first. SASE. Reports in 2-3 weeks.
Music: "We prefer that a composer is also the performer and works in conjunction with another artist, so they could be one of the performers on our series. Piece should be musically pleasant and not too dissonant. It should be scored for small vocal or instrumental ensemble. Dance ensembles have difficulty with 15' high 15' deep and 27' wide stage. We do not want avant-garde or obscene dance routines. No ballet (space problem). We're interested in something historical—national or Ohio emphasis would be nice. Small ensembles or solo format is fine."
Performances: Dana Mengel's *O Come, Come Away* (choral SSA 1998); and Hagemann/Licks' *Fruitcake* (choral SATB).
Tips: "Call in September of '99 for queries about our 1999-2000 season. We do a varied program. We don't commission artists. Contemporary music is used by some of our artist or groups. By contacting these artists, you could offer your work for inclusion in their program."

N MESQUITE COMMUNITY BAND, 1527 North Galloway, Mesquite TX 75149-2327. (972)216-8125. Conductor: Dale Y. Coates. Community band. Estab. 1986. Members are both professionals and amateurs. Performs 9 (4 formal, 5 outdoor) concerts/year. Commissions 1 composer or new work/year. Audience is young-to-mature adult. Performance space is concert hall (Mesquite Arts Center). Pays variable rate for outright purchase.
How to Contact: Query first. SASE. Reports in 1 month.
Music: Seeks full orchestration for band, approximately 4-5 minutes. "At this time we have approximately thirty-five members with the top level being level four." Does not want modern style.
Performances: James Curnow's *Olympic Fanfare & Theme*.
Tips: "Know the capability of the performing group."

✓ THE MIRECOURT TRIO, 50 Orchard St., Jamaica Plain MA 02130. (617)524-2495. E-mail: terryk @tiac.net. Contact: Terry King. Chamber music ensemble; violin, cello, piano. Estab. 1973. Members are professionals. Performs 2-4 concerts/year including 1 new work. Commissions 1 composer or new work/year. Concerts are performed for university, concert series, schools, societies and "general chamber music audiences of 100-1,500." Pays for outright purchase, percentage royalty or per performance.
How to Contact: Query first. SASE. Reports in 6 months.

Music: Seeks "music of short to moderate duration (5-20 minutes) that entertains, yet is not derivative or clichéd. Orchestration should be basically piano, violin, cello, occasionally adding voice or instrument. We do not wish to see academic or experimental works."
Performances: Otto Leuning's *Solo Sonata* (solo cello); Lukas Foss's *Three American Pieces* (cello, piano premiere); and Coolidge's *Dialectic No. 1 for piano trio.*
Tips: "Submit works that engage the audience or relate to them, that reward the players as well."

N. MOHAWK TRAIL CONCERTS, P.O. Box 75, Shelburne Falls MA 01370. (413)625-9511. 1-888-MTC-MUSE. E-mail: concerts@crocker.com. Website: http://www.mohawktrailconcers.org. Director: Polesny Baitali. Artistic Director: Arnold Black. Chamber music presenter. Estab. 1969. Members are professionals. Performs 22 concerts/year including 3-5 new works. Conducts school performances. "Audience ranges from farmers to professors, children to elders. Concerts are performed in Federated Church, Charlemont, MA." Pays by variable rate.
How to Contact: Query first. (Attention: Arnold Black, Artistic Director). SASE. Reports in months.
Music: "We want chamber music, generally not longer than 30 minutes. We are open to a variety of styles and orchestrations for a maximum of 8 performers. We don't want pop, rock or theater music."
Performances: Michael Cohen's *Fantasia for Flute, Piano and Strings* (chamber); William Bolcom's *Nes Songs* (piano/voice duo); and Arnold Black's *Laments & Dances* (string quartet and guitar duo).
Tips: "We are looking for artistic excellence, a committment to quality performances of new music, and music that is accessible to a fairly conservative (musically) audience."

N. ☪ MONTREAL CHAMBER ORCHESTRA, 800 René Lévesque Blvd. W, Suite 450, Montreal, Quebec H3B 1X9 Canada. (514)871-1224. Fax: (514)871-8967. Conductor and Music Director: Wanda Kaluzny. Chamber orchestra. Estab. 1974. Members are professionals. Performs 6 concerts including 1-3 new works/year. Commissions various new works/year (Canadian composers only). Audience is mixed ages, mixed income levels. Orchestra performs in Pollack Hall, seating 600. Pays "through the composer's performing arts organization."
How to Contact: Submit complete score. Does not return material. Reports "only if performing the work."
Music: Works with string orchestra (6 / 4 / 2 / 2 / 1), 8-12 min. duration. Strings (6 / 4 / 2 / 2 / 1).
Performances: Stewart Grant's *Chawnne* (string orchestra); Jene René's *Sonata à trois* (string orchestra); and Elegy (string orchestra).

N. MOORES OPERA CENTER, Moores School of Music, University of Houston, Houston TX 77204-4201. (713)743-3162. E-mail: bross@www.music.uh.edu. Director of Opera: Buck Ross. Opera/music theater program. Members are professionals, amateurs and students. Performs 12-14 concerts/year including 1 new work. Performs in a proscenium theater which seats 800. Pit seats approximately up to 75 players. Audience covers wide spectrum, from first time opera-goers to very sophisticated. Pays per performance.
How to Contact: Submit complete score and tapes of piece(s). SASE. Reports in 6 months.
Music: "We seek music that is feasible for high graduate level student singers. Chamber orchestras are very useful. No more than two and a half hours. No children's operas."
Performances: John Corigliano's *The Ghosts of Versailles*; Carlisle Floyd's *Bilby's Doll*; and Robert Nelson's *A Room With a View.*

MOZART FESTIVAL ORCHESTRA, INC., 33 Greenwich Ave., New York NY 10014. (212)675-9127. Conductor: Dr. Baird Hastings. Symphony orchestra. Estab. 1960. Members are professionals. Performs 1-4 concerts/year including 1-2 new works. Audience members are Greenwich Village professionals of all ages. Performances are held at the First Presbyterian Church, Fifth Ave. and 12th St., ("wonderful acoustics"). Pays for outright purchase.
How to Contact: Query first. SASE. Reports in 2 weeks.
Music: "We are an established chamber orchestra interested in *unusual* music of all periods, but not experimental. Orchestra size usually under 20 performers."
Performances: Gary Sunden's *Sganarelle* (prelude); and Virgil Thomson's *Portrait* (strings).

NATIONAL ASSOCIATION OF COMPOSERS/USA (NACUSA), P.O. Box 49256, Los Angeles CA 90049. (310)541-8213. Website: http://www.thebook.com/nacusa. President: Marshall Bialosky. Cham-

---

FOR BOOKS ON THE CRAFT AND BUSINESS of songwriting, check out the website for Writer's Digest Books at http://www.writersdigest.com.

ber music ensemble and composers' service organization. Estab. 1932. Members are professionals. Performs 3-4 concerts/year in L.A.; 10-11 nationally with other chapters—all new works. Usually perform at universities in Los Angeles and at a mid-town church in New York. Paid by ASCAP or BMI (NACUSA does not pay composers).

How to Contact: To submit, you must be a member of NACUSA. Submit complete score and tape of pieces. SASE. Reports in 6 months.

Music: Chamber music for five or fewer players; usually in the 5-20 minute range. "Level of difficulty is not a problem; number of performers is solely for financial reasons. We deal in serious, contemporary concert hall music. No 'popular' music."

Performances: Bruce Taub's *Sonata for Solo Viola*; Tom Flaherty's *Quartet for Viola, Cello, and Digital Synthesizer*; and Maria Newman's *Sonata for Bass Trombone and Piano*.

Tips: "Send in modest-sized pieces—not symphonies and concertos."

N: NEW WORLD YOUTH SYMPHONY ORCHESTRA, 10815 Brenda Court, Fortville IN 46040. (317)485-6022. Fax: (317)485-5247. Music Director: Susan Kitterman. Youth orchestra. Estab. 1982. Members are amateurs. Performs 6 concerts/year including 1 or 2 new works. Commissions 1 composer or new work every other year. "Typically 500-1,500 in attendance, broad spectrum of arts patrons and educators." Performs at Circle Theatre, downtown Indianapolis, home of Indianapolis Symphony; also at the Warren Performing Arts Center. Pay variable for outright purchase.

How to Contact: Query first. SASE. Reports in 2 months.

Music: "Innovative, creative works for full or string orchestra, brass or woodwind or percussion ensemble—may be with vocal or instrumental soloist. Any length."

Performances: David Baker's *Alabama Landscape* (orchestral with narration); Robert Ward's *Jubilation* (orchestral overture); and Paul Hindemith's *Symphonic Metamorphoses* (orchestral).

Tips "Come hear and meet our ensemble. Make the creative process highly individualized and one all can participate in."

N: OCEAN CITY POPS ORCHESTRA, P.O. Box 931, Ocean City NJ 08226. (609)398-9585. Fax: (609)398-8589 or (215)722-7356. E-mail: billnoc@aol.com. Website: http://www.oceancitypops.org. Artistic Director: William Scheible. 24-piece all professional orchestra (occasionally augmented). Estab. 1928. Members are professionals. Performs 50 concerts/year including "very few" new works. Audience is mature and affluent and young professionals. Performance space is 900-seat inside auditorium over the ocean. Pays variable rate for outright purchase.

How to Contact: Submit complete score and tape of piece(s). SASE. Reports in 2 months.

Music: Seeks for orchestra: strings (1 clarinet, 1 french horn, 2 trumpets, 2 trombones), percussion and piano/keyboard. Pops format includes some serious/educational, desired length 6-12 minutes. "No pieces esoteric in nature—this is a summer pops series."

Performances: Seymour Barab's *Little Red Riding Hood* (children's work operetta).

Tips: "We are looking for new overtures to open concerts and would like something interesting! We would like to pursue some contemporary pieces for future programming."

✓ OPERA FESTIVAL OF NEW JERSEY, 228 Alexander St., Princeton NJ 08540. (609)279-1750. Fax: (609)279-1832. General Director: Ms. Karen Tiller. Professional opera company. Estab. 1983. Members are professionals. Performs 3 productions/year. "Performances for mainstage season are held in the McCarter Theater Center for the Performing Arts in Princeton. Small proscenium stage with approximately 1,000 seats. Intimate hall with great acoustics."

How to Contact: Query first. SASE.

Performances: Peter Maxwell Davies' *The Lighthouse* (opera); Dominick Argento's *Postcard from Morocco* (opera); and Floyd's *Susannah* (opera).

Tips: "Have an interest in workshopping or producing new American opera."

OPERA MEMPHIS, Campus Box 526331, Memphis TN 38152. (901)678-2706. Fax: (901)678-3506. E-mail: operamemboxman@juno.com. Website: http://gray.music.rhodes.edu/operahtmls/opera.html. Artistic Director: Michael Ching. Opera company. Estab. 1955. Members are professionals. Performs 8-12 concerts/year including 1 new work. Commissions 1 composer or new work/year. Audience consists of older, wealthier patrons, along with many students and young professionals. Pay is negotiable.

How to Contact: Query first. SASE. Reports in 1 year.

Music: Accessible practical pieces for educational or main stage programs. Educational pieces should not exceed 90 minutes or 4-6 performers. We encourage songwriters to contact us with proposals or work samples for theatrical works. We are very interested in crossover work.

Performances: Mike Reid's *Different Fields* (one act opera); David Olney's *Light in August* (folk opera);

and Sid Selvidge's *Riversongs* (one act blues opera).
Tips: "Spend many hours thinking about the synopsis (plot outline)."

OPERA ON THE GO, 184-61 Radnor Rd., Jamaica Estates NY 11432. (718)380-0665. E-mail: operaont
hego@banet.net. Website: http://operaonthego.org. Artistic Director: Jodi Rose. American opera chamber
ensemble. Estab. 1985. Members are professionals. Performs about 60-80 operas/year including 1-2 new
works. Commissions variable number of new works/year. "We perform primarily in schools and community
theaters. We perform only American contemporary opera. It must be lyrical in sound and quality as we
perform for children as well as adults. We prefer pieces written for children based on fairy tales needing
2-4 singers." Pays royalties of $20-30 per performance. "We also help composers acquire a 'Meet the
Composer' grant."
How to Contact: Query first, then submit complete score and tapes of piece(s). SASE. Reports in 2
months.
Music: Need works in all age groups including adults. For older ages the pieces can be up to 60 minutes.
Rarely use orchestra. "Keep the music about 45 minutes long since we do a prelude (spoken) and postlude
involving the children's active participation and performance. If it is totally atonal it will never work in
the schools we perform in."
Performances: Arne Christiansen's *Tumbleweeds* (performed by children); Noel Katz's *Pirate Captains*
(opera for 6 grade-adult); and Seymour Barab's *Little Red Riding Hood* (children's opera).
Tips: "Be flexible. Through working with children we know what works best with different ages. If this
means editing music to guarantee its performance, don't get offended or stubborn. All operas must have
audience participatory sections."

☑ **OPERAWORKS**, 170 W. 73rd St., New York NY 10023. (212)873-9531. E-mail: operaworks@juno.c
om. Website: http://www.operaworks.org. Music Director: David Leighton. Opera producers. Estab. 1983.
Members are professionals. Performs 50 times including 5 new works/year. Commissions new composers
or new works each year. Diverse audience—classical music enthusiasts and avant-garde art scene. Spaces:
100-400 seat theaters, traditional and experimental. Pay is negotiable.
How to Contact: Submit complete score and tape of piece(s). SASE. Reports in 2-3 months.
Music: The Virtual Orchestra-realistic orchestral sound produced by state-of-the-art electronic technology.
Performances: Steven Paulus' *The Village Singer*; and Penderecki's *The Devils*.

OREGON SYMPHONY, 711 SW Alder, Portland OR 97205. (503)228-4294. E-mail: symphony@orsym
phony.org. Website: http://www.orsymphony.org. General Manager: Tony Beadle. Symphony orchestra.
Estab. 1896. Members are professionals. Performs 110 concerts/year including 5-10 new works. Commissions 1 composer or new work/every other year. "Classical concerts are attended predominantly by 35-60
year olds. Hall seats 2,776—renovated vaudeville house." Pay varies for outright purchase.
How to Contact: Query first. Does not return material. Reports in 1 month.
Music: "Classical 10-20 min.: 3333-5331 3 perc, 1 tmp, 1 harp, 1 keyboard, strings: 16-14-12-10-8; pops,
jazz: same, except strings 12-10-8-6-4. No country. Send a list of other orchestras with whom you have
performed."
Performances: John Adam's *Violin Concerto* (classical); Aaron Vernis' *New Era Dance* (classical); and
George Rochberg's *Oboe Concerto* (classical).

PICCOLO OPERA COMPANY INC., 24 Del Rio Blvd., Boca Raton FL 33432-4737. (800)282-3161.
Executive Assistant: Lee Merrill. Opera company. Estab. 1962. Members are professionals. Performs 1-
50 concerts/year including 1-2 new works. Commissions 0-1 composer or new work/year. Operas are
performed for a mixed audience of children and adults. Pays by performance or outright purchase.
How to Contact: Query first. SASE.
Music: "Musical theater pieces, lasting about one hour, for adults to perform for adults and/or youngsters.
Performers are mature singers with experience. The cast should have few performers (up to 10), no chorus
or ballet, accompanied by piano or orchestra. Skeletal scenery. All in English."
Performances: Menotti's *The Telephone* and *The Old Maid and the Thief*; and Puccini's *La Boheme*
(repertoire of more than a dozen productions).

RIDGEWOOD SYMPHONY ORCHESTRA, P.O. Box 176, Ridgewood NJ 07451. (201)612-0118.
Fax: (201)445-2762. E-mail: drdackow@aol.com. Website: http://www.ridgewoodsymphony.org. Music
Director: Dr. Sandra Dackow. Symphony orchestra. Estab. 1939. Members are professionals and amateurs.
Performs 4 concerts/year and 2-3 children's concerts including 1-2 new works. Commissions possibly
1 new work/year. Audience is "sophisticated." Performance space is 800-seat school auditorium. Pays
commission fee.

How to Contact: Submit complete score and tape of piece(s). SASE. Reports in 3 months ("it depends on how busy we are").

Music: "Symphonic works of various lengths and types which can be performed by a nonprofessional orchestra. We are flexible but would like to involve all of our players; very restrictive instrumentations do not suit our needs."

Performances: Otar Gordeli's *Concertino for Flute* (flute concerto); and Howard Hanson's *Serenade for Strings, Flute & Harp* (short work).

Tips: "Please lay out rehearsal numbers/letters and rests according to phrases and other logical musical divisions rather than in groups of ten measures, etc., which is very unmusical, wastes time and causes a surprising number of problems. Also, please *do not* send a score written in concert pitch; use the usual transpositions so that the conductor sees what the players see. Rehearsal is much more effective this way. Cross cue all important solos; this helps in rehearsal where instruments may be missing."

SACRAMENTO MASTER SINGERS, P.O. Box 215501, Sacramento CA 95821. (916)338-0300. Fax: (916)334-1808. E-mail: rehchoir@aol.com. Website: http://www.mastersingers.org. Conductor/Artistic Director: Ralph Hughes. Vocal ensemble. Estab. 1984. Members are professionals and amateurs. Performs 9 concerts/year including 5-6 new works. Commissions 2 new works/year. Audience is made up of mainly high school age and older patrons. Performs mostly in churches with 500-900 seating capacity. Pays $200 for outright purchase.

How to Contact: Submit complete score and tape of piece(s). SASE. Reports in 5 weeks.

Music: "A cappella works; works with small orchestras or few instruments; works based on classical styles with a 'modern' twist; multi-cultural music; shorter works probably preferable, but this is not a requirement. We usually have 38-45 singers capable of a high level of difficulty, but find that often simple works are very pleasing."

Performances: Schnittke's *Requiem*; John Taverner's *Thunder Entered Her*; and Linda Dawson's *Deck the Hall* and *Away in a Manger* (holiday).

Tips: "Keep in mind we are a chamber ensemble, not a 100-voice choir."

ST. LOUIS CHAMBER CHORUS, P.O. Box 11558, Clayton MO 63105. (314)458-4343. E-mail: maltworm@inlink.com. Website: http://www.iwc.com/slcc/index.html. Artistic Director: Philip Barnes. Vocal ensemble, chamber music ensemble. Estab. 1956. Members are professionals and amateurs. Performs 6 concerts/year including 5-10 new works. Commissions 1-2 new works/year. Audience is "diverse and interested in unaccompanied choral work and outstanding architectural/acoustic venues." Performances take place at various auditoria noted for their excellent acoustics—churches, synagogues, schools and university halls. Pays by arrangement.

How to Contact: Query first. Does not return material. "Panel of 'readers' submit report to Artistic Director. Reports in 3 months. 'General Advice' leaflet available on request."

Music: "Only *a cappella* writing; no contemporary 'popular' works; historical editions welcomed. No improvisatory works. Our programs are tailored for specific acoustics—composers should indicate their preference."

Performances: Charles Collins' *Missa St. Louis* (a cappella mass); Ernst Widmer's *Salmo 150* (Brazilian psalm); and Almeida Prado's *Oraculo* (avant garde madrigal), all a cappella.

Tips: "We only consider a cappella works which can be produced in five rehearsals. Therefore pieces of great complexity or duration are discouraged."

 SAN FRANCISCO GIRLS CHORUS, P.O. Box 15397, San Francisco CA 94115-0397. (415)673-1511. Fax: (415)673-0639. E-mail: sfgc@worldnet.att.net. Website: http://www.citysearch.com/sfo/sfgirlschorus. Artistic Director: Dr. Sharon J. Paul. Vocal ensemble. Estab. 1978. Volunteer chorus with a core of paid professionals. Performs 8-10 concerts/year including 3-4 new works. Commissions 2-3 composers or new works/year. Concerts are performed for "choral/classical music lovers of all ages, plus family audiences; audiences interested in international repertoire. Season concerts are performed in a 900-seat church with excellent acoustics; one concert is performed in San Francisco's Davies Symphony Hall, a 2,800-seat state-of-the-art auditorium." Pay negotiable for outright purchase.

• The San Francisco Girls Chorus was a featured guest performer on the San Francisco Symphony's recording of Carl Orff's *Carmina Burana*, which won a 1993 Grammy Award for best choral recording.

How to Contact: Submit complete score. Does not return material. Reports in 6 months.

Music: "Music for treble voices (SSAA); a cappella, piano accompaniment, or small orchestration; 3-10 minutes in length. Wide variety of styles; 45 singers; challenging music is encouraged."

Performances: Lisa Bielawa's *Letter to Anna (1998)* (a cappella); Stephen Leek's *Australian Bush Bird Songs* (a cappella); and Jake Heggie's *Patterns* (piano, mezzo-soprano soloist, chorus).

Tips: "Choose excellent texts and write challenging and beautiful music! The San Francisco Girls Chorus has pioneered in establishing girls choral music as an art form in the United States. The Girls Chorus is praised for its 'stunning musical standard' (*San Francisco Chronicle*) in performances in the San Francisco Bay Area and on tour. SFGC's annual concert season showcases the organization's concert/touring ensembles, Chorissima and Virtuose, in performances of choral masterworks from around the world, commissioned works by contemporary composers, and 18th-century music from the Venetian Ospedali which SFGC has brought out of the archives and onto the concert stage. Chorissima and Virtuose tour through California with partial support provided by the California Arts Council Touring Program and have represented the U.S. and the City of San Francisco nationally and abroad. The choruses provide ensemble and solo singers for performances and recordings with the San Francisco Symphony and San Francisco Opera, Women's Philharmonic, and many other music ensembles. SFGC's discography includes two 1996 CD recordings, *I Never Saw Another Butterfly* (20th Century music); *A San Francisco Christmas* (Benjamin Britten's *A Ceremony of Carols* and other holiday music) and a 1998 release, *Music of the Venetian Ospedali* (18th-century works for girls chorus)."

☑ **SINGERS FORUM**, 39 W. 19th St., New York NY 10011. (212)366-0541. Fax: (212)366-0546. E-mail: nysings@aol.com. Website: http://singersforum.org. Executive Director: Phil Campanella. Administrative Director: Jeff Biegaiek. Vocal school and presenting organization. Estab. 1978. Members are professionals and amateurs. Performs more than 50 concerts/year including 5-10 new works. Commissions variable number of composers or new works/year. 75-seat performance space with varied audience. Pays through donations from patrons.

How to Contact: Submit complete score and tape of piece(s). SASE. Reports in 2-3 months.

Music: "All popular music, art songs, full musicals and small operas with minimal orchestration."

Performances: Jeffrey Middleton's *Movement 3* (classical); Bill Daniels' *Cold December* (new music); and Sidney Lippman's *Fables* (children's).

Tips: "Think of the voice."

☑ **SOUTHERN ARIZONA SYMPHONY ORCHESTRA**, P.O. Box 43131, Tucson AZ 85733-3131. (520)323-7166. Fax: (602)494-0328. E-mail: secomb@u.arizona.com. Website: http://www.Tucson.com/saso. Musical Director: Warren Cohen. Symphony orchestra. Estab. 1979. Members are amateurs. Performs 9 concerts/year including 6 new works. We want to have at least 2 every year. Commissions 1 composer or new work/year. Audience is a cross-section of Tucson as well as retirees. Perfoms in the 400-seat Berger Performing Arts Center, the 800-seat Tucson High School Auditorium, and the 700-seat Saddlebrooke Arts Center. Pay varies. "We arrange each case differently, usually pay per performance."

How to Contact: Submit complete score and tape of piece(s). SASE. Reports in 1-4 months "or longer."

Music: Seeking works for a full symphony or chamber orchestra. Open to all styles of music, and will consider works of any length under 30 minutes. "Concertos are harder to program, as are works with chorus, but we will consider them. We have an amateur orchestra, but we have played a good deal of fairly difficult music. We could not, however, do Bruckner or Mahler symphonies. Most contemporary music has been fairly conservative in style, but we are open to things that are different, as long as it's not extremely difficult. Please keep orchestration fairly standard; no bass oboes or theremins."

Performances: 1998-99 season included 6 world premieres, including Michael Kimball's Arcadian Symphony. Other performances include Richard Arnell's *Overture 1940* (orchestral); and Warren Cohen's *Sinfonetta Giocoso* (orchestral).

Tips: "Send a nice clean score. Don't get discouraged as we only have limited performance options. We appreciate knowing if you have orchestral parts available. We are especially excited by the possibility of discovering talented, unknown composers who have not had the opportunities available to those who are well-connected."

☑ **SPACE COAST POPS, INC.**, P.O. Box 3344, Cocoa FL 32924 or 2150 Lake Dr., Cocoa FL 32926. (407)632-7445. Website: http://community.insidecentralflorida.com/spacecoastpops. Music Director and

Conductor: Dr. Chandler Schaffer. Pops orchestra and chamber music ensemble. Estab. 1986. Members are professionals. Performs 7 concerts/year, including 3-4 new works. Concerts are performed for "average audience—they like familiar works and pops. Concert halls range from 600 to 2,000 seats."
How to Contact: Query first. SASE. Reports in 6 months.
Music: Seeks "pops and serious music for full symphony orchestra, but not an overly large orchestra with unusual instrumentation. We use about 60 musicians because of hall limitations. Works should be medium difficulty—not too easy and not too difficult—and not more than ten minutes long." Does not wish to see avant-garde music.
Performances: Dussich's *First March* (march).
Tips: "If we would commission a work it would be to feature the space theme in our area."

SUSQUEHANNA SYMPHONY ORCHESTRA, P.O. Box 485, Forest Hill MD 21050. (410)838-6465. E-mail: sbzbair@erols.com. Music Director: Sheldon Bair. Symphony orchestra. Estab. 1978. Members are amateurs. Performs 6 concerts/year including 1-2 new works. Composers paid depending on the circumstances. "We perform in 1 hall, 600 seats with fine acoustics. Our audience encompasses all ages."
How to Contact: Query first. SASE. Reports in 3-6 or more months.
Music: "We desire works for large orchestra, any length, in a 'conservative 20th century' style. Seek fine music for large orchestra. We are a community orchestra, so the music must be within our grasp. Violin I to 7th position by step only; Violin II—stay within 5th position; English horn and harp are OK. Full orchestra pieces preferred."
Performances: Theldon Myers' *People Look East* (Christmas); Henry Cowell's *Vox Humana* (orchestral); and Henry Cowell's *Slow Jig* (orchestral).

SYMPHONY OF THE AMERICAS, 3300 N. Federal Highway, Suite 214, Ft. Lauderdale FL 33306. (954)561-5882. Fax: (954)561-5884. Conductor: Dr. James Brooks-Bruzzese. Symphony orchestra and chamber music ensemble (strings). Estab. 1988. Members are professionals. Performs 10 concerts/year including 2 new works. Commissions 1 composer or new work/year. Audience is very conservative. Performance space is the 600-seat Broward Center for the Arts. Pays by performance.
How to Contact: Query first or submit complete score and tape of piece(s). SASE. Reports in 2-3 weeks.
Music: Seeking contemporary neo-romantic and classical for a small classical size orchestra. "At times we add trombones, extra percussion and harp but we prefer not to do this. It is too costly. No 12-tone music. Must be pleasing to the ear."
Performances: Villa-bobos's *Mono Precoce* (piano concerto); Robert Beaser's *Song of the Bells* (flute concerto); and *Everglades Symphony #3*.
Tips: "Make it cost effective, pleasing to the ear and dramatic."

☑ **TOURING CONCERT OPERA CO. INC.**, 228 E. 80th, New York NY 10021. (212)988-2542. Fax: (518)851-6778. E-mail: tcoc@mhonline.net. Director: Anne DeFigols. Opera company. Estab. 1971. Members are professionals. Performs 30 concerts/year including 1 new work. Payment varies.
How to Contact: Submit complete score and tape of piece(s). Does not return material. Reporting time varies.
Music: "Operas or similar with small casts."
Tips: "We are a touring company which travels all over the world. Therefore, operas with casts that are not large and simple but effective sets are the most practical."

UNIVERSITY OF UTAH ORCHESTRAS, 1425 E. Presidents Circle, Salt Lake City UT 84112. (801)581-6692. Fax: (801)581-5683. E-mail: robert.debbaut@music.utah.edu. Website: http://www.music. utah.edu/faculty/debbaut. Contact: Music Director. Symphony orchestra and chamber music ensemble. Estab. 1920. Members are amateurs. Performs 15 concerts/year including 3 new works. Audience is classical music lovers. Performance space is currently being renovated. Pays variable amount per performance.
How to Contact: Submit complete score and tape of piece(s). SASE.
Music: Seeking orchestration 3333/4331/7 + 4/H or less; length of generally 12-15. "Will consider longer works." No pointalism or concertos.
Performances: Henry Working's *Saturnian Verses* (symphony); David Carlson's *Rhapsodies*; and Tracy Cathey's *Disposable City*.
Tips: "I like colorful, emotionally charged music. I hate fixing scene and part errors."

☒ **VANCOUVER CHAMBER CHOIR**, 1254 W. Seventh Ave., Vancouver, British Columbia V6H 1B6 Canada. E-mail: vcc@dowco.com. Website: http://www.sitegeist.com/vcc. Artistic Director: Jon Washburn. Vocal ensemble. Members are professionals. Performs 40 concerts/year including 5-8 new works. Commissions 2-4 composers or new works/year. Pays SOCAN royalty or negotiated fee for commissions.

How to Contact: Submit complete score and tape of piece(s). Does not return material. Reports in 6 months if possible.

Music: Seeks "choral works of all types for small chorus, with or without accompaniment and/or soloists. Concert music only. Choir made up of 20 singers. Large or unusual instrumental accompaniments are less likely to be appropriate. No pop music."

Performances: The VCC has commissioned and premiered over 110 new works by Canadian and international composers, including Alice Parker's *That Sturdy Vine* (cantata for chorus, soloists and orchestra); R. Murray Schafer's *Magic Songs* (SATB a cappella); and Jon Washburn's *A Stephen Foster Medley* (SSAATTBB/piano).

Tips: "We are looking for choral music that is performable yet innovative, and which has the potential to become 'standard repertoire.' Although we perform much new music, only a small portion of the many scores which are submitted can be utilized."

N: VIRGINIA OPERA, P.O. Box 2580, Norfolk VA 23501. (804)627-9545. Fax:(804)622-0058. E-mail: hcsoped@eeols.com. Website: http://www.vaopera.com. Director of Education: Helen Stevenson. General Director: Peter Mark. Opera company. Estab. 1974. Members are professionals. Performs more than 560 concerts/year. Commissions vary on number of composers or new works/year. Concerts are performed for school children throughout Virginia, grades K-5, 6-8 and 9-12 at the Harrison Opera House in Norfolk, and at public/private schools in Virginia. Pays on commission.

How to Contact: Query first. SASE. Reports vary.

Music: "Audience accessible style approximately 45 minutes in length. Limit cast list to three vocal artists of any combination. Accompanied by piano and/or keyboard. Works are performed before school children of all ages. Pieces must be age appropriate both aurally and dramatically. Musical styles are encouraged to be diverse, contemporary as well as traditional. Works are produced and presented with sets, costumes, etc." Limitations: "Three vocal performers (any combination). One keyboardist. Medium to difficult acceptable, but prefer easy to medium. Seeking only pieces which are suitable for presentation as part of an opera education program for Virginia Opera's education and outreach department. Subject matter must meet strict guidelines relative to Learning Objectives, etc. Musical idiom must be representative of current trends in opera, musical theater. Extreme dissonance, row systems not applicable to this environment."

Performances: Seymour Barab's *Snow White and the Seven Dwarfs*; John David Earnest's *The Legend of Sleepy Hollow*; and Seymour Barab's *The Pied Piper of Hamelin*.

Tips: "Theatricality is very important. New works should stimulate interest in musical theater as a legitimate art form for school children with no prior exposure to live theatrical entertainment. Composer should be willing to create a product which will find success within the educational system."

N: THE DALE WARLAND SINGERS, 119 N. Fourth St., Minneapolis MN 55401-1792. (612)339-9707. Fax: (612)339-9826. E-mail: dwsinger@aol.com. Website: http://www.winternet.com/~webpage/warland.html. Composer in Residence: Carol Barnett. Choral ensemble. Estab. 1972. Members are professionals. Performs 20-25 concerts/year including 5-10 new works. Commissions 4-8 composers or new works/year. Audience is a typical classical music concert audience; also college and high school students and occasional "popular Christmas" audience. Performance spaces vary, including concert halls, high school/college auditoriums and churches. Pays commission.

How to Contact: Submit complete score and tape of piece(s). SASE. Reports in 2-4 months.

Music: "A cappella or with small accompanying forces; texts primarily secular; works for concert choir; 5-15 minutes in length (semi-extended)." Does not wish to see "show choir material or gospel."

Performances: Steven Stucky's *Three Cradle Songs*; Frank Ferko's *Hildegard Tryptch*; and Stephen Paulus' *Three Nativity Carols*.

Tips: "Keep in mind that there will never be enough rehearsal time. Be clear and concise in notation, and write for the capabilities of the choral voice. We seek from our composers not only craft, but a certain 'magic' quality."

WESTMINSTER PRESBYTERIAN CHURCH, 724 Delaware Ave., Buffalo NY 14209-2294. (716)884-9437. Fax: (716)884-3450. E-mail: thomasswan@aol.com. Organist and Choirmaster: Thomas Swan. Vocal ensemble. Estab. 1976. Members are professionals and amateurs. Performs 4 concerts/year

---

MARKET CONDITIONS are constantly changing! If you're still using this book and it is 2001 or later, buy the newest edition of *Songwriter's Market* at your favorite bookstore or order directly from Writer's Digest Books at (800)289-0963.

including 1 new work. Commissions 1 composer or new work/year. Performs in Kleinhans Music Hall (2,800) and church (1,000). Pays up to $1,500 for outright purchase.

How to Contact: Query first. SASE. Reports in 2 months.

Music: Choral/orchestral-SATB, with or without soloists. A cappella SATB—sacred or secular. Chamber orchestra/choral. Both 3-5 minute motets for worship and larger/longer works for concert with or without orchestra. "My semi-professional church choir numbers 50."

Performances: Libby Larsen's *Three Summer Scenes*; Fred Thayer's *Three Motets* (a cappella); and Mack Wilberg's *Tres Cantus Laudeni* (SATB/large brass and percussion).

Tips: "Composers writing for the church should carefully consider text and instrumentation. Music written for a cappella singing is especially useful."

✓ WHEATON SYMPHONY ORCHESTRA, 344 Spring Ave., Glen Ellyn IL 60137. (630)790-1430. Fax: (630)790-9703. Manager: Donald C. Mattison. Symphony orchestra. Estab. 1959. Members are professionals and amateurs. Performs 5 summer concerts/year including 1 new work. Pays $200/per performance.

How to Contact: Query first. SASE. Reports in 1 month.

Music: "This is a *good* amateur orchestra that wants pieces in a traditional idiom. Large scale works for orchestra only. No avant garde, 12-tone or atonal material. Pieces should be 20 minutes or less and must be prepared in 3 rehearsals. Instrumentation is woodwinds in 3s, full brass 4-3-3-1, 4-5 percussion and strings—minimum instrumentation only."

Performances: John Biggs's *Pastiche* (25 composers in 8 minutes); Frank Proto's *The Voyage that Johnny Never New* (variations on "Johnny Comes Marching Home"); and Norman Dello-Joio's *Variations Chaccome and Finale* (neo-classical).

Contests & Awards

Participating in contests is a great way to gain exposure for your music. Prizes vary from contest to contest, from cash to musical merchandise to studio time, and even publishing and recording deals. For musical theater and classical composers, the prize may be a performance of your work. Even if you don't win, valuable contacts can be made through contests. Many times, contests are judged by music publishers and other industry professionals, so your music may find its way into the hands of key industry people who can help further your career.

HOW TO SELECT A CONTEST

It's important to remember when entering any contest to do proper research before signing anything or sending any money. We have confidence in the contests listed in *Songwriter's Market*, but it pays to read the fine print. First, be sure you understand the contest rules and stipulations once you receive the entry forms and guidelines. Then you need to weigh what you will gain against what they're asking you to give up. If a publishing or recording contract is the only prize a contest is offering, you may want to think twice before entering. Basically, the company sponsoring the contest is asking you to pay a fee for them to listen to your song under the guise of a contest, something a legitimate publisher or record company would not do. For those contests offering studio time, musical equipment or cash prizes, you need to decide if the entry fee you're paying is worth the chance to win such prizes.

Be wary of exorbitant entry fees, and if you have any doubts whatsoever as to the legitimacy of a contest, it's best to stay away. Songwriters need to approach a contest, award or grant in the same manner as they would a record or publishing company. Make your submission as professional as possible; follow directions and submit material exactly as stated on the entry form.

Contests in this section encompass all types of music and levels of competition. Read each listing carefully and contact them if the contest interests you. Many contests now have websites that offer additional information and even entry forms you can print. Be sure to read the rules carefully and be sure you understand exactly what a contest is offering before entering.

AARON ENTERPRISES SUMMERTIME SONG FESTIVAL, 4411 Red Gate Dr., Disputanta VA 23842. (804)733-5908. Song Contest Director: Cham Laughlin. Estab. 1997. For songwriters in the US and Canada. Annual award sponsored by the Aaron Enterprises Songwriters Group, Cham's Music (BMI) and Red Gate Recordings.
Requirements: "Entries are accepted from May 1st through the postal deadline of June 30th in each contest year. Categories available for entry are: new country, traditional country, folk, rock, pop and R&B, instrumental, humorous and song lyric." Deadline: June 30. Send SASE for application. Entry fee: $10 per song.
Awards: "Prizes include cash, T-shirts, certificates of merit, memberships in our songwriter's group, newsletter subscriptions, songwriter's kits, and more." Entries judged by industry professionals.
Tips: "Prepare your entry properly and follow guidelines to make responses speedy and accurate."

AGO/ECS PUBLISHING AWARD IN CHORAL COMPOSITION, American Guild of Organists, 475 Riverside Dr., Suite 1260, New York NY 10115. (212)870-2310. Fax: (212)870-2163. E-mail: info@agohq.org. Website: http://www.agohq.org. Program Assistant: Paul Wolfe. For citizens of US, Canada and Mexico. Biannual award.
Requirements: Work submitted must be unpublished. Approximately 4-8 minutes in length. Competitors must be citizens of the United States, Canada or Mexico. There is no age restriction. Deadline: TBA. Send for application.
Awards: AGO/ECS Publishing Award in Choral Composition. Details TBA.

ALEA III INTERNATIONAL COMPOSITION PRIZE, 855 Commonwealth Ave., Boston MA 02215. (617)353-3340. E-mail: kaloger@fas.harvard.edu. Executive Administrator: Synneve Carlino. For composers. Annual award.

Purpose: To promote and encourage young composers in the composition of new music.

Requirements: Composers 40 years of age and younger may apply; 1 score per composer. Works may be for solo voice or instrument or for chamber ensemble up to 15 members lasting between 6 and 15 minutes. All works must be unpublished. Deadline: March 15. Send for application. Submitted work required with application. "Real name should not appear on score; a nom de plume should be signed instead. Sealed envelope with entry form should be attached to each score."

Awards: ALEA III International Composition Prize: $2,500. Awarded once annually. Between 8-10 finalists are chosen and their works are performed in a competition concert by the ALEA III contemporary music ensemble. One grand prize winner is selected by a panel of judges.

Tips: "Emphasis placed on works written in 20th century compositional idioms."

ALL AMERICAN SONGWRITER/COMPOSER CONTEST, 460 Carlton St., Brazoria TX 77422. E-mail: songcontest@hotmail.com. Contest Director: Tracie Williams. Estab. 1995. For songwriters and composers. Annual award.

Purpose: "To encourage and promote American songwriters/composers through recognition of excellence in their work."

Requirements: Applicants must be American citizens, but may live in any country. Deadline: June 30. Send for application or send correctly marked cassettes and lyric sheets with entry fees. Samples of work are required with application. Submit cassette with lyric sheet with $10 entry fee per entry in any of the following catagories: country/bluegrass, gospel/inspirational, blues/R&B, rock/pop, folk, heavy metal, children's, novelty, instrumental and lyric only. Unlimited entries allowed. Cassettes and lyric sheets should have name, address, title and phone number on them. Catagory of entry should also be on tape and lyric sheet.

Awards: $600 Grand Prize; $300 1st Prize; $150 2nd Prize; $75 3rd Prize; 3 Honorable Mentions. Applications are judged by impartial industry professionals, for marketability, originality and creativity.

Tips: "If you send for application, please include SASE. Make sure your vocals are upfront and can be easily heard over the music. Cue tape to beginning, no long introductions; entries are judged on marketability in today's market as well as originality and creativity. For contest results include SASE with your entry."

☑ **AMERICAN SONGWRITER LYRIC CONTEST**, 1009 17th Ave. S., Nashville TN 37212-2201. (615)321-6096. Fax: (615)321-6097. E-mail: asongmag@aol.com. Website: http://www.songnet.com/ason gmag/. Editor: Vernell Hackett. Administration: Diana Black. Estab. 1984. For songwriters and composers. Award for each bimonthly issue of *American Songwriter* magazine, plus grand prize at year-end.

Purpose: To promote the art of songwriting and to allow readers the opportunity to be actively involved.

Requirements: Lyrics must be typed and a check for $10 (per entry) must be enclosed. Deadlines: January 22, March 26, May 21, July 23, September 24, November 19. Samples are not required. Call for required official form or get it from our website. Lyrics only, no cassettes.

Awards: A Martin guitar to each contest winner. Awards airfare to Nashville and a demo session for yearly winner; certificates to all winners; and top 5 winning lyrics reprinted in each magazine. Lyrics judged by 5-6 industry people—songwriters, publishers, journalists.

Tips: "You do not have to be a subscriber to enter or win. Pick your best lyric (limit three), don't just send them at random."

◼Ｎ◼ ARTISTS' FELLOWSHIPS, New York Foundation for the Arts, 155 Avenue of Americas, 14th Floor, New York NY 10013. To receive an application, or contact the fellowship's department, call: (212)366-6900, ext. 217. Fax: (212)366-1778. E-mail: nyfaafp@artswire.org. Website: http://www.tmn. com/Artswire/www/nyfa.html. Director of Programs: Penelope Dannenberg. For songwriters, composers and musical playwrights. Annual award, but each category funded biennially. Estab. 1984.

Purpose: "Artists' Fellowships are $7,000 grants awarded by the New York Foundation for the Arts to

REFER TO THE GEOGRAPHIC INDEX (at the back of this book) to find listings of companies by state, as well as foreign listings.

individual originating artists living in New York State. The Foundation is committed to supporting artists from all over New York State at all stages of their professional careers. Fellows may use the grant according to their own needs; it should not be confused with project support."

Requirements: Must be 18 years of age or older; resident in New York State for 2 years prior to application; and cannot be enrolled in any graduate or undergraduate degree program. Applications will be available in July. Deadline: October. Samples of work are required with application. 1 or 2 original compositions on separate audiotapes and at least 2 copies of corresponding scores or fully harmonized lead sheets.

Awards: All Artists' Fellowships awards are for $7,000. Payment of $6,300 upon verification of NY State residency, and remainder upon completion of a mutually agreed upon public service activity. Nonrenewable. "Fellowships are awarded on the basis of the quality of work submitted and the evolving professional accomplishments of the applicant. Applications are reviewed by a panel of 5 composers representing the aesthetic, ethnic, sexual and geographic diversity within New York State. The panelists change each year and review all allowable material submitted."

Tips: "Please note that musical playwrights may submit only if they write the music for their plays—librettists must submit in our playwriting category."

☑ BAKER'S PLAYS HIGH SCHOOL PLAYWRITING CONTEST, Baker's Plays 100 Chauncy St., Boston MA 02111. (617)482-1280. Fax: (617)482-7613. E-mail: info@bakersplay.com. Website: http://www.bakersplays.com. Associate Editor: Raymond Pape. Estab. 1990. For high school students. Annual award.

Requirements: Plays should be about the "high school experience," but may also be about any subject and of any length, so long as the play can be reasonably produced on the high school stage. Plays must be accompanied by the signature of a sponsoring high school drama or English teacher, and it is recommended that the play receive a production or a public reading prior to the submission. Multiple submissions and co-authored scripts are welcome. Teachers may not submit a student's work. The manuscript must be firmly bound, typed and come with a SASE. Include enough postage to cover the return of the manuscript. Scripts that do not come with an SASE will not be returned. Do not send originals; copies only. Deadline: January 30th. Send for guidelines.

Awards: 1st Place: $500 and the play will be published by Baker's Plays; 2nd Place: $250 and an Honorable Mention; 3rd Place: $100 and an Honorable Mention.

☑ BILLBOARD SONG CONTEST, P.O. Box 60628, Oklahoma City OK 73146-0628. (405)523-4814. Fax: (405)523-4815. E-mail: jimh@theshop.net. Website: http://www.billboard.com/songcontest. Director: Deanie Williams. Estab. 1988. For songwriters, composers and performing artists. Annual international contest.

Purpose: "To reward deserving songwriters and performers for their talent."

Awards: To be announced. For entry forms and additional information send SASE to the above address or visit website.

Tips: "Participants should understand popular music structure."

☑ BUSH ARTIST FELLOWS PROGRAM, E-900 First National Bank Bldg., 332 Minnesota St., St. Paul MN 55101. (651)227-5222. E-mail: kpolley@bushfound.org. Program Assistant: Kathi Polley. Estab. 1976. For songwriters, composers and musical playwrights. Applications in music composition are accepted in alternate years.

Purpose: "To provide artists with significant financial support that enables them to further their work and their contribution to their communities."

Requirements: Applicant must be a Minnesota, North Dakota, South Dakota or western Wisconsin resident for 12 of preceeding 36 months, 25 years or older, not a student. Deadline: late October. Send for application. Samples of work on cassette required with application. "Music composition applications will not be taken again until the fall of 2000. Applications will be taken in the fall of 2000 in the following areas: music composition, scriptworks (screenwriting and playwriting), literature (creative non-fiction, fiction, poetry) and film/video.

Awards: Fellowships: $40,000 stipend for a period of 12-18 months. "Five years after completion of preceeding fellowship, one may apply again." Applications are judged by peer review panels.

COLUMBIA ENTERTAINMENT COMPANY'S JACKIE WHITE MEMORIAL PLAYWRITING CONTEST, 309 Parkade Blvd., Columbia MO 65202. (573)874-5628. Director, CEC Contest: Betsy Phillips. For musical playwrights. Annual award.

Purpose: "We are looking for top-notch scripts for theater school use to challenge and expand the talents of our students, ages 10-15. We want good plays with large casts (20-30 characters) suitable for use with our theater school students."

Requirements: "Must be large cast plays, original story lines and cannot have been previously published. Because theater school enrollment is typically composed of more girls than boys, scripts should have at least 50% of characters female. Please write or call for complete rules." Send SASE for application; then send scripts to address above. Full-length play, neatly typed. No name on title page, but name, address and name of play on a 3×5 index card. Cassette tape of musical numbers required. $10 entry fee. SASE for entry form.

Awards: $250 1st Prize. Production likely but play may not be produced at discretion of CEC. If produced, partial travel expenses will be available to author. Award given after any revisions required are completed. "The judging committee is taken from members of Columbia Entertainment Company's Executive and Advisory boards, and from theater school parents. Readings by at least eight members, with at least three readings of all entries, and winning entries being read by entire committee. We are looking for plays that will work with our theater school students."

Tips: "Remember the play we are looking for will be performed by 10-15 year old students with normal talents—difficult vocal ranges, a lot of expert dancing and so forth will eliminate the play. We especially like plays that deal with current day problems and concerns. However, if the play is good enough, any suitable subject matter is fine. It should be fun for the audience to watch."

COMPOSERS COMMISSIONING PROGRAM, ACF, 332 Minnesota St., #E-145, St. Paul MN 55101. (612)228-1407. Fax: (612)291-7978. E-mail: pblackburn@composersforum.org. Website: http://www.composersforum.org. Program Director: Philip Blackburn. Estab. 1979. For songwriters, musical playwrights, composers and performers. Annual award.

Purpose: "CCP provides grants to support the commissioning of new works by emerging composers."

Requirements: Not for students. Deadline: end of July. Send for application. Samples of work are required with application. Send score/tape.

Awards: 18-22 commissioning grants of $1,500-8,000; each grant good for 5 years. Applications are judged by peer review panel (anonymous).

Tips: "Composers pair up with performers: one party must be based in Minnesota or New York City."

COMPOSERS GUILD ANNUAL COMPOSITION CONTEST, P.O. Box 586, Farmington UT 84025. (801)451-2275. President: Ruth B. Gatrell. Estab. 1963. For songwriters, musical playwrights and composers. Annual award.

Purpose: "To stimulate musical composition and help composers through judge's comments on each composition submitted. Composers can broaden their creative skills by entering different categories. Categories: Arrangements (original in public domain or with composer's permission); music for children; choral; instrumental; jazz/New Age; keyboard; orchestra/band; popular (all types); vocal solo; young composer (18 or under on August 31)."

Requirements: Score and/or cassette. Entry fee: $20 for work 7 minutes or more in length (may include multimovements on compositions), $15 for work less than 7 minutes. Dues are $25/year. Member entry fees: $10 for work 7 minutes or more, $5 less than 7 minutes. Deadline: August 31. Send or call for application.

Awards: Award of Excellence $500; 1st Prize in each category except Award of Excellence category $100; 2nd Prize in each category $50; 3rd Prize in each category $25; Honorable Mention certificate. Judge has a doctorate in music, plus compositions published and performing (usually has vast teaching experience). Same judge never used in successive years.

Tips: "Submit good clear copies of score. Have cassette cued up. Only one composition per cassette (each entry requires separate cassette). No composer names to appear on score or cassette. Enter as many categories and compositions as you wish. Separate entry for each. One check can cover all entries and dues."

CRS NATIONAL COMPOSERS COMPETITION, 724 Winchester Rd., Broomall PA 19008. (610)544-5920. Fax: (215)544-5921. E-mail: crsnews@erols.com. Website: http://www.erols.com. Administrative Assistant: Caroline Hunt. Senior Representative: Jack Shusterman. Estab. 1981. For songwriters, composers and performing artists. College faculty. Annual award.

Requirements: For composers: The work submitted must be non-published (prior to acceptance) and not

FOR EXPLANATIONS OF THESE SYMBOLS,
SEE THE INSIDE FRONT AND BACK COVERS OF THIS BOOK.

commercially recorded on any label. The work submitted must not exceed nine performers. Each composer may submit one work for each application submitted. (Taped performances are additionally encouraged.) Composition must not exceed twenty-five minutes in length. CRS reserves the right not to accept a First Prize Winner. Write with SASE for application. Add $3 for postage and handling. Deadline: October 28. Send a detailed résumé with application form. Samples of work required with application. Send score and parts on cassette or DAT. Application fee $50.
Awards: 1st Prize: Commercial recording grant. Applications are judged by panel of judges determined each year.

CUNNINGHAM PRIZE FOR PLAYWRITING, The Theatre School, DePaul University, 2135 N. Kenmore Ave., Chicago IL 60614. (773)325-7938. Fax: (773)325-7920. E-mail: lgoetsch@wppost.depaul.e du. Website: http://theatreschool.depaul.edu. Director of Marketing/Public Relations: Lara Goetsch. Estab. 1990. For musical playwrights. Annual award.
Purpose: "To recognize and encourage the writing of dramatic works which affirm the centrality of religion, broadly defined, and the human quest for meaning, truth and community. It is the intent of the endowment to consider submissions of new dramatic writing in all genres, including works for children and young people."
Requirements: "The focus for the awarding of the prize is metropolitan Chicago. The candidates for the award must be writers whose residence is in the Chicago area, defined as within 100 miles of the Loop." Deadline: December 1. Send for application with SASE.
Awards: $5,000. "Winners may submit other work for subsequent prize year. The Selection Committee is composed of distinguished citizens including members of DePaul University, representatives of the Cunningham Prize Advisory Committee, critics and others from the theater professions, and is chaired by the Dean of The Theatre School."

FUTURE CHARTERS, 332 Eastwood Ave., Feasterville PA 19053. (800)574-2986. Phone/fax: (215)953-0952. E-mail: a1foster@aol.com. Website: http://www.geocities.com/TimesSquare/Labyrinth/19 17. Editor/Publisher: Allen Foster. Estab. 1993. For songwriters, composers and any aspiring songwriters and composers. Monthly award.
Requirements: To enter, send a clean demo tape of one song with vocals up front, a photo, a bio, lyric sheet, contact information and a SASE (if you'd like your tape returned).
Awards: Winners will receive a writeup in an upcoming issue of *Songwriter's Monthly*, plus a portion of your song will be placed on our 1-800 number so interested parties will be able to call up and listen to your song.
Tips: "There is no application form or entry fee. Just send your best song. It doesn't have to be an expensive demo, but it does have to sound clean. Also, be sure to include all materials listed under requirements, as incomplete entry packages will be disqualified."

N COLONEL ARNOLD D. GABRIEL AWARD, The United States Air Force Band, 201 McChord St., Bolling AFB DC 20332-0202. (202)404-8363. Contact: Master Sergeant Lawrence Ink. For composers. Biennial award (odd-numbered years).
Requirements: Must be American citizens born after April 30, 1964 except those currently involved in a military music program or who have been commissioned to write a composition for an Air Force band. Compositions must be unpublished and can't be under rental contract with a publisher. Each composer may enter only 1 composition. The composition must be a work for standard band instrumentation. Send for rules and information. Samples of work are required with application.
Awards: Awards a performance by The United States Air Force Band and a $3,000 follow-on commission for an additional work. Applications are judged by a judging committee.

HENRICO THEATRE COMPANY ONE-ACT PLAYWRITING COMPETITION, P.O. Box 27032, Richmond VA 23273. (804)501-5100 or (804)501-5138. Fax: (804)501-5284. Cultural Arts Coordinator: Amy A. Perdue. Cultural Arts Assistant: Debbie Nolan. For musical playwrights, songwriters, composers and performing artists. Annual award.
Purpose: Original one-act musicals for a community theater organization.
Requirements: "Only one-act plays or musicals will be considered. The manuscript should be a one-act original (not an adaptation), unpublished, and unproduced, free of royalty and copyright restrictions. Scripts with smaller casts and simpler sets may be given preference. Controversial themes should be avoided. Standard play script form should be used. All plays will be judged anonymously; therefore, there should be two title pages; the first must contain the play's title and the author's complete address and telephone number. The second title page must contain only the play's title. The playwright must submit two excellent quality copies. Receipt of all scripts will be acknowledged by mail. Scripts will be returned if SASE is included. No scripts will be returned until after the winner is announced. The HTC does not assume

responsibility for loss, damage or return of scripts. All reasonable care will be taken." Deadline: July 1st. Send for application first.
Awards: 1st Prize $250; 2nd Prize $125; 3rd Prize $125.

HOLTKAMP-AGO AWARD IN ORGAN COMPOSITION, American Guild of Organists, 475 Riverside Dr., Suite 1260, New York NY 10115. E-mail: info@agohq.org. Website: http://www.agohq.org. Program Coordinator: Paul Wolfe. For composers and performing artists. Biannual award.
Requirements: Organ solo, no longer than 8 minutes in duration. Specifics vary from year to year. Composer must be a citizen of the United States, Canada or Mexico. Deadline: May 31 (odd-numbered years). Send for application.
Award: $2,000 provided by the Holtkamp Organ Company; publication by Hinshaw Music Inc.; performance at the biennial National Convention of the American Guild of Organists.

I WRITE THE SONGS, 2250 Justin Rd., Suite 108-208, Highland Village TX 75067. (972)317-2760. Fax: (972)317-4737. E-mail: info@cqkmusic.com. Website: http://www.cqkmusic.com. President: Mary Dawson. Estab. 1998. For songwriters. Annual award.
Purpose: To encourage aspiring songwriters to develop their craft.
Requirements: Open to all amateur songwriters (who have earned less than $5,000 over the past year from songwriting-related royalties). Send for application. Samples of work are required with application. Send cassette and typed lyric sheet.
Awards: Prizes vary from year to year. First prize ranges from $500-1,000 in value—usually recording equipment.

INDIANA OPERA THEATRE/MACALLISTER AWARDS FOR OPERA SINGERS, 7530 E. 30th St., Indianapolis IN 46226. (317)253-1001. Fax: (317)253-2008. E-mail: opera@iquest.net. Website: http://www.iquest.net/~opera/. Artister/General Director: E. Bookwalter. Estab. 1980. For college and professional opera singers.
Requirements: For professional and amateurs. New works for high school/college students. Send for application.

INNER CITY CULTURAL CENTER'S AUGUSTIN LARA COMPETITION FOR COMPOSERS & SONGWRITERS, P.O. Box 272, Los Angeles CA 90028. (213)627-7670. Contact: Talent Fest Coordinator. For songwriters, composers. Annual award.
Purpose: "Named in honor of famed Mexican composer of 'Granada,' the primary purpose of the competition is to bring songwriters, composers and those who perform original music into contact with those in the music and entertainment industry who are in a position to hire them and to bring to public prominence the role played by creators of original music."
Requirements: One entry per participant, maximum length 7 minutes. Entry must be performed live, may not have been previously published. Deadline: March. Send SASE for application. Samples are not required.
Awards: 1st Place $1,000, 2nd Place $500, 3rd Place $250. Additional prizes to be announced at time of competition. Criteria: 1. originality, 2. overall presentation (performance), 3. thematic development, 4. structural unity, 5. fullfillment of functional intent. Judges are recruited from the ranks of music industry professionals. Members of the audience cast ballots during a series of 3 elimination rounds to determine which entries proceed to the final round.
Tips: "Have a sponsor capable of providing the support necessary to gather resources needed to make an effective performance presentation (performers, transportation to competition site, rehearsal space, on-site accommodations, special equipment, etc.). This is done LIVE! Competition is open to all. There are NO categories or distinctions made based on genre (classical, jazz, country western, reggae, etc.). Lyrics or librettos may be in any language. There is no citizenship or U.S. residency requirement. Compositions designed to support other media (dance, film, etc.) must be presented in their original context. Keep in mind that the goal of the competition is to develop employment opportunities for gifted writers and to bring attention to the craft in all of its diversity. The competition is divided into 2 divisions: Adult (over 18) and youth (under 18). ICCC has successfully conducted competitions resulting in professional employment and production for actors over the past 13 years as well as for playwrights and performers."

INTERNATIONAL CLARINET ASSOCIATION COMPOSITION COMPETITION, Dept. of Music, Miami University, Oxford OH 45056. Fax: (513)529-3027. E-mail: gingram@muohio.edu. Website: http://miavxl@muohio.edu/~gingram. Professor: Michèle Gingras. Estab. 1992. For composers. Annual award.
Purpose: To expand the clarinet repertoire.

Requirements: Unpublished work, no age limit, no length limit. Legit repertoire or legit neo-jazz OK. Submit a tape and score. Entries must be labeled with composer's name, address and phone number on the score and tape. Deadline: mid-April every year. Send score and tape.
Awards: $1,000 and a performance at the annual clarinet congress run by ICA. Applications judged by international jury.
Tips: "Submit recent compositions which would enrich the present clarinet repertoire."

☑ **L.A. DESIGNERS' THEATRE MUSIC AWARDS**, P.O. Box 1883, Studio City CA 91614-0883. (323)650-9600. (323)654-2700 (T.D.D.). Fax: (323)654-3260. E-mail: ladesigners@juno.com. Artistic Director: Richard Niederberg. For songwriters, composers, performing artists, musical playwrights and rights holders of music.
Purpose: To produce new musicals, operettas, opera-boufes and plays with music, as well as new dance pieces with new music scores.
Requirements: Submit nonreturnable cassette, tape, CD or any other medium by first or 4th class mail. "We prefer proposals to scripts." Acceptance: continuous. Submit nonreturnable materials with cover letter. No application form or fee is necessary.
Awards: Music is commissioned for a particular project. Amounts are negotiable. Applications judged by our artistic staff.
Tips: "Make the material 'classic, yet commercial' and easy to record/re-record/edit. Make sure rights are totally free of all 'strings,' 'understandings,' 'promises,' etc. ASCAP/BMI/SESAC registration is OK, as long as 'grand' or 'performing rights' are available."

☑ **THE JOHN LENNON SONGWRITING CONTEST**, 459 Columbus Ave., Box 120, New York NY 10024. Fax: (212)579-4320. E-mail: info@jlsc.com. Website: http://www.jlsc.com. Associate Director: Gregg Ross. Estab. 1996. For songwriters. Annual award.
• See the Insider Report interview with Executive Director Brian Rothschild on page 402.
Purpose: "The purpose of the John Lennon Songwriting Contest is to promote the art of songwriting by assisting in the discovery of new talent as well as providing more established songwriters with an opportunity to advance their careers."
Requirements: Each entry must consist of the following: completed and signed application; audio cassette containing one song only, 5 minutes or less in length; lyric sheet typed or printed legibly (English translation is required when applicable); $30 entry fee. Deadline: August 31, 2000. Applications can be found in various music-oriented magazines. Prospective entrants can send for an application or contact the contest via e-mail at info@jlsc.com.
Awards: Entries are accepted in the following 12 categories: rock, country, jazz, pop, world, gospel/inspirational, R&B, hip-hop, Latin, dance, folk and a special category of children's music. 1998 prize packages: Grand Prize winners received $2,000 in cash, $5,000 in Yamaha project studio equipment, and a $5,000 advance from EMI Music Publishing. One Grand Prize winner received an additional $20,000 for the "Song of the Year" courtesy of Maxell. Finalists received $1,000. 72 winners received portable CD players. Winners will be chosen by an Executive Committee comprised of noted songwriters, producers and recording artists. Songs will be judged based upon melody, composition and lyrics (when applicable). The quality of performance and production will not be considered.

☑ **MAXIM MAZUMDAR NEW PLAY COMPETITION**, One Curtain Up Alley, Buffalo NY 14202-1911. (716)852-2600. E-mail: alleywayth@aol.com. Website: http://www.alleyway.com. Literary Manager: Kevin Stevens. For musical playwrights. Annual award.
Purpose: Alleyway Theatre is dedicated to the development and production of new works. Winners of the competition will receive production and royalties.
Requirements: Unproduced full-length work not less than 90 minutes long with cast limit of 10 and unit or simple set, or unproduced one-act work less than 40 minutes long with cast limit of 6 and simple set; prefers work with unconventional setting that explores the boundaries of theatricality; limit of submission in each category; guidelines available, no entry form. $5 playwright entry fee. Script, résumé, SASE optional. Cassette mandatory. Deadline: July 1.
Awards: $400, production with royalty and travel and housing to attend rehearsals for full-length play or musical; $100 and production for one-act play or musical.

MARKETS THAT WERE listed in the 1999 edition of *Songwriter's Market* but do not appear this year are listed in the General Index with a notation explaining why they were omitted.

insider report

Contest promotes the vocation of songwriting

"As an innovator, freedom fighter, artist and father, John Lennon serves as a tremendous inspiration to so many songwriters," says Brian Rothschild, executive director of the John Lennon Songwriting Contest (JLSC). The contest aims to sustain this inspiration by assisting in the discovery of new talent and helping more established songwriters further their careers.

Rothschild has been involved since the first contest in 1997. "I speak with the entrants all the time," he says. "I'm responsible for every aspect of the project: the contest, the educational tour bus, working with our executive committee of judges, sponsors, etc." Rothschild knows what it's like to make a name for yourself in the music industry.

Brian Rothschild

He traces his musical background to the age of four when he began playing piano. Later he became interested in songwriting, wrote music for theatre, scored commercials, and in the '80s was an artist on Columbia Records.

Yoko Ono Lennon, who established the contest, receives frequent updates about the contest and its side projects. "Yoko has been very supportive of the whole idea of trying to provide songwriters with new opportunities," says Rothschild. As she envisioned, the benefit of the contest goes beyond the winning.

The Executive Committee judging the entries includes recording artists Paula Cole, Enrique Iglesias, Busta Rhymes, Elton John and Luther Vandross, among others. "We're giving songwriters an opportunity to have their music listened to by artists and top industry professionals," Rothschild says.

The JLSC averages over 20,000 entries each year—quite a lot of tapes and entry forms to manage, much less judge. Rothschild stresses that when you enter the contest, you are not giving up any rights to your song. Songwriters can enter their music in 12 different musical categories. By far, the category receiving the most entries is "Pop."

BRIAN ROTHSCHILD

Title: Executive Director
Contest: John Lennon Songwriting Contest

"The prize packages have been designed to help songwriters further their careers," says Rothschild. Twelve Grand Prize winners (one in each category) receive cash, recording equipment, and an advance on an EMI Music Publishing contract. In addition, one of the Grand Prize winning entries is selected as the "Song of the Year" with a cash prize of $20,000.

"As you can imagine, our winners represent a broad range of people," says Rothschild. "However, most of them seem to be involved in many different activities." Winners are announced on the contest's website (http://www.jlsc.com) and in press releases throughout the world. Additionally, all winners are notified by telephone. "This year we are concentrating on providing winners with some real opportunities to present their music, such as the performance at the NAMM (National Association of Music Merchants) show by this year's rock winner, Brad Mitchell, and the upcoming press we'll be doing for our pop winner, Chris Lowe, in Austin at South by Southwest.

The JLSC also works to promote the vocation of songwriting. In 1998, in an effort to advocate music education, the JLSC launched a multimedia "tour bus." Painted with the contest's trademark clouds, blue sky and a Lennon self-portrait, this mobile research and recording studio visits high schools, colleges, festivals and outdoor music venues and music conferences. Onboard, visitors see how computer hardware and innovative software programs aid today's songwriter. When the bus stops at schools, students witness demonstrations of song composition and recording. To the delight of visitors on the bus, many of the artists on the Executive Committee have agreed to appear at different stops on the "tour."

The JLSC website goes beyond explaining the vital statistics of the contest. It also features the "Songwriter's Forum." Here songwriters post messages about every aspect of writing music: questions, tips, the songwriting process and complaints about the music business. Topics include "What makes a good song?", "What if all you can do is sing?" and "The sorry state of A&R." The forum's benefits aren't limited to advice and information, it's a source of networking. Occasionally, members of the Executive Committee will join in and express their thoughts.

Through the efforts of the John Lennon Songwriting Contest, songwriters are provided the opportunity to be proactive in their craft and, for 120 winners, given global affirmation of their talent.

—*Tara A. Horton*

Tips: "Entries may be of any style, but preference will be given to those scripts which take place in unconventional settings and explore the boundaries of theatricality. No more than ten performers is a definite, unchangeable requirement."

☑ **McKNIGHT VISITING COMPOSER PROGRAM**, ACF, 332 Minnesota St., #E-145, St. Paul MN 55101. (612)228-1407. Fax: (631)291-7978. E-mail: pblackburn@composersforum.org. Website: http://www.composersforum.org. Program Director: Philip Blackburn. Estab. 1994. For songwriters, musical playwrights and composers. Annual award.
Purpose: "Up to 2 annual awards for non-Minnesota composers to come to Minnesota for a self-designed residency of at least 2 months."
Requirements: Not for Minnesota residents or students. American Composers Forum membership required. Deadline: March. Send for application. Samples of work are required with application. Send score/tape.
Awards: McKnight Visiting Composer $11,000 stipend. Each award good for 1 year. Applications are judged by peer review panel.
Tips: "Find committed partners in Minnesota with whom to work, and explore diverse communities."

McLAREN COMEDY PLAYWRITING COMPETITION, 2000 W. Wadley, Midland TX 79705. (915)682-2544. Fax: (915)682-6136. Estab. 1990. For musical playwrights. Annual award.
Purpose: "The purpose of The McLaren Competition is to develop new comedy scripts suitable for production by community theaters and other nonprofit theaters. The competition honors Mike McLaren, a writer, actor and radio personality, who often appeared in Midland Community Theatre productions."
Requirements: "We are seeking comedy scripts only. Plays submitted should be unproduced. We do not count previous 'readings' as productions; we will consider plays produced once in a nonprofit setting. Length, number of characters, setting is not limited. The playwright retains all rights to the work submitted." Deadline: January 31. Send for guidelines. Scripts should be submitted between December 1 and January 31 with a $5 entry fee.
Awards: The four finalists will be presented in a staged reading at Midland Community Theatre in July or August of the year selected. The winning playwright will receive a cash prize. Scripts are judged by a committee.

☑ **MID-ATLANTIC SONG CONTEST**, 4200 Wisconsin Ave., NW, Box 100-137, Washington DC 20016. (800)218-5996. E-mail: president@saw.org. Website: http://www.saw.org. For songwriters, performing artists and composers. Estab. 1982. Sponsored by BMI and the Songwriters of Washington. Annual award.
Purpose: "Contest is designed to afford rising songwriters the opportunity of receiving awards/exposure/ feedback of critical nature in an environment of peer competition." Applicants must send for application to Mid-Atlantic Song Contest at above address. Rules and regulations explained—amateur status is most important requirement. Samples of work are required with application: cassette, entry form and 3 copies of lyrics. "Deadline for entries is usually late fall—awards given in spring."
Awards: "Awards usually include free recording time, merchandise and cash. Awards vary from year to year. Awards must be used within one calendar year. Winning songs will be placed on a winners CD, which will be distributed to major music publishers. Grand Prize is $1,000. Winners can perform their songs at the Awards Night Gala.
Requirements: Applications are judged by a panel of 3 judges per category, for 3 levels, to determine top winners in each category and to arrive at the Grand Prize winner. Reduced entry fees are offered for SAW members. Membership also entitles one to a newsletter and reduced rates for special events/seminars.
Tips: "Keep intros short; avoid instrumental solos; get to the chorus quickly and don't bury vocals."

☑ **THELONIOUS MONK INSTITUTE OF JAZZ INTERNATIONAL JAZZ COMPOSERS COMPETITION**, 5225 Wisconsin Ave. #605, Washington DC 20016. (202)364-7272. Fax: (202)364-0176. E-mail: sfischer@tmonkinst.org. Website: http://www.monkinstitute.com. Executive Producer: Shelby Fischer. Estab. 1993. For songwriters and composers. Annual award.
Purpose: The award is given to an aspiring jazz composer who best demonstrates originality, creativity and excellence in jazz composition.
Requirements: Deadline: August 1. Send for application. Samples of work are required with application. Send cassette. The composition features a different instrument each year.
Awards: $10,000. Applications are judged by panel of jazz musicians. "The Institute will provide piano, bass, guitar, drum set, tenor saxophone, and trumpet for the final performance. The winner will be responsible for the costs of any different instrumentation included in the composition."

☑ **MUSEUM IN THE COMMUNITY COMPOSER'S AWARD**, P.O. Box 423, Hurricane WV 25526. (304)562-0484. Fax: (304)562-4733. E-mail: mitc@newwave.net. Managing Director: Mark Payne. Programming Assistant: Sharon Antoine. For composers. Biennial award.
Purpose: The Composer's Competition is to promote the writing of new works. "Specific type of competition changes. Past competitions have included string quartet, full orchestra and nonet."
Requirements: Work must not have won any previous awards nor have been published, publicly performed or used commercially. Requires 3 copies of the original score, clearly legible and bound. Title to appear at the top of each composition, but the composer's name must not appear. Entry forms must be filled out and a SASE of the proper size enclosed for return of entry. "If you happen to move while competition is underway please let us know." Enclose $25 entry fee (non-refundable). Send for application.
Awards: "Next competition will open in fall 2000. Winning composition announced January 2001 with concert in Spring 2001." Jurors will be 3 nationally known musicologists. Winning composer will be awarded a cash prize of $2,500 and a premiere concert of the composition. Transportation to the premiere from anywhere in the continental United States will be provided by the Museum.
Tips: "Applicants can contact the museum to be put on our mailing list to receive prospectus. Read *and* follow rules listed in Prospectus. Neatness still counts! Enclose SASE if you wish to have your score returned. Please write legibly. Please let us know if you move after you've sent in your entry!"

NACUSA YOUNG COMPOSERS' COMPETITION, Box 49256 Barrington Station, Los Angeles CA 90049. (310)541-8213. Fax: (310)373-3244. Website: http://www.thebook.com/nacusa. President, NACUSA: Marshall Bialosky. Estab. 1978. For composers. Annual award.
Purpose: To encourage the composition of new American concert hall music.
Requirements: Deadline: October 30. Send for application. Samples are not required.
Awards: 1st Prize: $200; 2nd Prize: $50; and possible Los Angeles and New York performances. Applications are judged by a committee of experienced NACUSA composer members.

NATIONAL SONGWRITER'S NETWORK CONTESTS, 3870 La Sierra #101, Riverside CA 92505. (909)422-3539. Editor: Andrew Inglese. For songwriters. Monthly song and lyric contests.
Purpose: To promote the craft of songwriting and lyric writing.
Requirements: For the Song Contest: send song on cassette with typed or neatly printed lyric sheet; include $5/song; materials are not returned. For the Lyric Contest: send typed or neatly printed lyric; include $3/lyric; materials are not returned. Deadline: 1st of the month.
Awards: Cash, T-shirts, newsletter subscriptions; lyric writer's workbooks and certificates.
Tips: "Make sure the lyric storyline is well thought out. The melody of each verse should be consistent. Also, the N.S.N. Hotsheet Newsletter is available. A one-year subscription is $18."

NEW FOLK CONCERTS FOR EMERGING SONGWRITERS, P.O. Box 1466, Kerrville TX 78029. (830)257-3600. E-mail: info@kerrville-music.com. Website: http://www.kerrville-music.com. Attn: New Folk. For songwriters. Annual award.
Purpose: "To provide an opportunity for unknown songwriters to be heard and rewarded for excellence."
Requirements: Songwriter enters 2 previously unrecorded songs on same side of cassette tape with entry fee; no more than one tape may be entered; 6-8 minutes total for 2 songs. No written application necessary; no lyric sheets or press material needed. Deadline: April 1st. Call to request rules.
Awards: New Folk Award Winner. 32 semi-finalists invited to sing the 2 songs entered during The Kerrville Folk Festival. 6 writers are chosen as award winners. Each of the 6 receives a cash award of $150 or more and performs at a winner's concert during the Kerrville Folk Festival, May 27-28, 2000. Initial round of entries judged by the Festival Producer. 32 finalists judged by panel of 3 performer/songwriters.
Tips: "Make certain cassette is rewound and ready to play. Do not allow instrumental accompaniment to drown out lyric content. Don't enter without complete copy of the rules. Former winners and finalists include Lyle Lovett, Nanci Griffith, Hal Ketchum, John Gorka, David Wilcox, Lucinda Williams and Robert Earl Keen, David Wilcox, Tish Hinojosa, Carrie Newcomer, Jimmy Lafave, etc."

☑ **OMAHA SYMPHONY GUILD INTERNATIONAL NEW MUSIC COMPETITION**, 1605 Howard St., Omaha NE 68102-2705. (402)342-3836. E-mail: bravo@omahasymphony.org. Website: http://www.omahasymphony.org. Guild Office Representative: Kimberly Mettenbrink. For composers with an annual award. Estab. 1976.
Purpose: "The objective of the competition is to promote new music scored for chamber orchestra."
Requirements: Competition open to applicants 25 and up for entry fee of $30. "Follow competition guidelines including orchestration and length of composition." Deadline: April 15, 2000. Write or call for application. Each fall new guidelines and application forms are printed. Follow application guidelines.
Awards: "Monetary award is $2,500. Winners composition will possibly be included in the Omaha Symphony 1999-2000 season. Applications are screened by Omaha Symphony Music Director." Scores will be judged by a panel of respected composers and musicologists.
Tips: "This is an annual competition and each year has a new Symphony Guild chairman; all requests for extra information sent to the Omaha Symphony office will be forwarded. Also, 1,700-1,800 application information brochures are sent to colleges, universities and music publications each fall."

PLAYHOUSE ON THE SQUARE NEW PLAY COMPETITION, 51 S. Cooper, Memphis TN 38104. (901)725-0776. Executive Director: Jackie Nichols. For musical playwrights. Annual award. Estab. 1983.
Requirements: Send script, tape and SASE. "Playwrights from the South will be given preference." Open to full-length, unproduced plays. Musicals must be fully arranged for piano when received. Deadline: April 1.
Awards: Grants may be renewed. Applications judged by 3 readers.

FOR BOOKS ON THE CRAFT AND BUSINESS of songwriting, check out the website for Writer's Digest Books at http://www.writersdigest.com.

☑ **PORTLAND SONGWRITERS ASSOCIATION ANNUAL SONGWRITING COMPETITION**, P.O. Box 16985, Portland OR 97292-0985. (503)727-9072. E-mail: psa@teleport.com. Website: http://www.teleport.com/~psa/. President: Wayne Richards. Vice President: Julie Adams. Estab. 1991. For songwriters. Annual award.

Purpose: To provide opportunities for songwriters to improve their skills in the art and craft of songwriting, to connect our performing songwriters with the public through PSA sponsored venues and to create a presence and an avenue of approach for members' songs to be heard by industry professionals.

Requirements: For information, send SASE. All amateur songwriters may enter.

Awards: Multiple awards totaling $1,500 in prizes. All songs will be reviewed by at least three qualified judges, including industry pros. Finalists may have their songs reviewed by celebrity judges.

PULITZER PRIZE IN MUSIC, 709 Journalism, Columbia University, New York NY 10027. (212)854-3841. Website: http://www.pulitzer.org. Music Secretary: Elizabeth Mahaffey. For composers and musical playwrights. Annual award.

Requirements: "For distinguished musical composition of significant dimension by an American that has had its American premiere between March 2 and March 1 of the one-year period in which it is submitted for consideration." Deadline: March 1. Samples of work are required with application, biography and photograph of composer, date and place of performance, score or manuscript and recording of the work, entry form and $50 entry fee.

Awards: "One award: $5,000. Applications are judged first by a nominating jury, then by the Pulitzer Prize Board."

☑ **ROCHESTER PLAYWRIGHT FESTIVAL CONTEST**, Midwest Theatre Network, 5031 Tongen Ave. NW, Rochester MN 55901. (507)281-8887. Executive Director/Dramaturg: Joan Sween. Estab. 1994. For any person who has created a work that is musical theater. Biennial award.

Purpose: To provide exposure, support and promotion of new works for the theatre.

Requirements: Plays must be previously unpublished or never professionally produced. Send SASE for guidelines and required entry form. An audio tape is required with submission of libretto.

Awards: Full production, playwright travel expenses and possible cash. 4-8 plays produced and awarded by a coalition of differing theatres.

Tips: "The closer to performance values the audio tape is, the better."

ROCKY MOUNTAIN FOLKS FESTIVAL SONGWRITER SHOWCASE, 500 W. Main St., Lyons CO 80540. (800)624-2422. Fax: (303)823-0849. E-mail: steve@bluegrass.com. Website: http://www.bluegrass.com. Director: Steve Szymanski. Estab. 1993. For songwriters, composers and performers. Annual award.

Purpose: Award based on having the best song and performance.

Requirements: Finalists notified by July 14. Send for rules. Samples of work are required with application. Send cassette with $10 entry fee.

Awards: 1st Place is a custom Breedlove Concert Guitar and Festival Main Stage Set; 2nd: $400; 3rd: $300; 4th: $200; 5th: $100. Applications judged by panel of judges.

Tips: "Relax and have fun."

RICHARD RODGERS AWARDS, American Academy of Arts and Letters, 633 W. 155th St., New York NY 10032. (212)368-5900. E-mail: artslet@aol.com. Coordinator: Lydia Kaim. Estab. 1978. "The Richard Rodgers Awards subsidize full productions, studio productions, and staged readings by nonprofit theaters in New York City of works by composers and writers who are not already established in the field of musical theater. The awards are only for musicals—songs by themselves are not eligible. The authors must be citizens or permanent residents of the United States." Guidelines for this award may be obtained by sending a SASE to above address.

ROME PRIZE FELLOWSHIP IN MUSICAL COMPOSITION, American Academy in Rome, 7 E. 60th St., New York NY 10022-1001. (212)751-7200. Fax: (212)751-7220. E-mail: aainfo@aol.com. Website: http://www.aarome.org. Contact: Programs Department. For composers. Annual award.

Purpose: "Rome Prize winners pursue independent projects which vary in content and scope."

Requirements: "Applicants for one-year fellowships must hold a bachelor's degree in music, musical

---

REFER TO THE GEOGRAPHIC INDEX (at the back of this book) to find listings of companies by state, as well as foreign listings.

composition or its equivalent." Deadline: November 15. Application guidelines are available to download through the Academy's website. Samples of work are required with application; send CDs and/or tapes and scores.

Awards: Fellowship stipend is up to $15,000 for one year. "Juries convene from January through March to review all work submitted in the competition. In all cases, excellence is the primary criterion for selection, based on the quality of the materials submitted."

LOIS AND RICHARD ROSENTHAL NEW PLAY PRIZE, % Cincinnati Playhouse in the Park, P.O. Box 6537, Cincinnati OH 45206-0537. (513)345-2242. Website: http://www.cincyplay.com Contact: Associate Artistic Director. For playwrights and musical playwrights. Annual award.

Purpose: The Lois and Richard Rosenthal New Play Prize was established in 1987 to encourage the development of new plays that are original, theatrical, strong in character and dialogue, and make a significant contribution to the literature of American theatre. Residents of Cincinnati, the Rosenthals are committed to supporting arts organizations and social agencies that are innovative and foster social change.

Requirements: "Plays must be full-length in any style: comedy, drama, musical, etc. Translations, adaptations, individual one-acts and any play previously submitted for the Rosenthal Prize are not eligible. Collaborations are welcome, in which case the prize benefits are shared. Plays must be unpublished prior to submission and may not have received a full-scale, professional production. Plays that have had a workshop, reading or non-professional production are still eligible. Playwrights with past production experience are especially encouraged to submit new work. Submit a two-page maximum abstract of the play including title, character breakdown, story synopsis and playwright information (bio or résumé). Also include up to five pages of sample dialogue. If submitting a musical, please include a tape of selections from the score. All abstracts and dialogue samples will be read. From these, selected manuscripts will be solicited. Do not send a manuscript with or instead of the abstract. All unsolicited manuscripts will be returned unread. Submitted materials, including tapes, will be returned only if a SASE with adequate postage is provided. The Rosenthal Prize is open for submission from July 1st to December 31st. Only one submission per playwright each year."

Awards: The Rosenthal Prize play receives a full production at Cincinnati Playhouse in the Park as part of the theater's annual season and is given regional and national promotion. The playwright receives a $10,000 award plus travel and residency expenses for the Cincinnati rehearsal period.

SONG SPREE SONGWRITER COMPETITION, 2417 Pinewood Rd. W., Dept. 97, Nunnelly TN 37137. E-mail: spree@earthlink.net. Website: http://home.earthlink.net/~spree/. President: Lynda Bostwick. Vice President: John Gitter. Estab. 1995. For songwriters, lyricists and composers. Annual award.

Purpose: "Seeking best songs in four categories: rock/pop, country, blues and R&B, and soft alternatives. (Note: gospel accepted in all categories.) Winners to be recorded and released on CD at our expense. Winners are also widely promoted to industry."

Requirements: Send lyrics, separate cassette and entry blank (or 3×5 card) for each song along with entry fee ($20 first song, $15 each additional song). For complete rules and prize info send #10 SASE.

Awards: "Song Category winners receive trip to Nashville, get recorded or remastered on CD and earn royalties. Publishing contracts are offered, but signing with us is not mandatory. Resulting songs will be presented on our CD. We promote our winners in every way possible. All entrants receive a free CD of winning songs. Honorable Mention winners receive an additional CD from a prior contest year and their songs are also held for possible industry pitches."

Tips: "Visit our website. All pertinent information—and more—is there. Or send an SASE (#10 long) to us and we'll send a brochure out."

MARVIN TAYLOR PLAYWRIGHTING AWARD, P.O. Box 3030, Sonora CA 95370. (209)532-3120. Fax: (209)532-7270. E-mail: srt@mlode.com. Website: http://www.sierrarep.com. Producing Director: Dennis Jones. Estab. 1981. For all musical playwrights. Annual award.

Purpose: "To encourage new voices in American theater."

Requirements: "Any new plays and unpublished scripts with no more than 2 previous productions are eligible." Deadline: August 31. Send for application with SASE. Samples of work are required with application. Scripts should be typed.

Awards: $500. "Applications are read by our Dramaturg and the Producing Director."

TELLURIDE TROUBADOUR CONTEST, 500 W. Main St., Lyons CO 80540. (800)624-2422. Fax: (303)823-0849. E-mail: steve@bluegrass.com. Website: http://www.bluegrass.com. Director: Steve Szymanski. Estab. 1991. For songwriters, composers and performers. Annual award.

Purpose: Award based on having best song and performance.

Requirements: Deadline: must be postmarked by May 1; notified May 15, if selected. Send for rules.

Send cassette and $10 entry fee.
Awards: 1st: custom Shanti Guitar and main stage set; 2nd: $400 and Crate acoustic amp; 3rd: $300 and Martin backpacker guitar; 4th: $200 and Martin backpacker guitar; 5th: $100. Applications judged by panel of judges.

✅ THE TEN-MINUTE MUSICALS PROJECT, P.O. Box 461194, West Hollywood CA 90046. (323)651-4899. Producer: Michael Koppy. For songwriters, composers and musical playwrights. Annual award.
Purpose: "We are building a full-length stage musical comprised of complete short musicals, each of which play for between 8-14 minutes. Award is $250 for each work chosen for development towards inclusion in the project, plus a share of royalties when produced."
Requirements: Deadline: August 31. For guidelines, write or phone. Final submission should include script, cassette and lead sheets.
Awards: $250 for each work selected. "Works should have complete stories, with a definite beginning, middle and end."

✅ U.S.A. SONGWRITING COMPETITION, Dept A.W. 98, Box 15711, Boston MA 02215-5711. (781)397-0256. E-mail: asn@tiac.net. Website: http://www.songwriting.net. Contact: Contest Manager. Estab. 1994. For songwriters, composers, performing artists and lyricists. Annual award.
Purpose: "To honor good songwriters/composers all over the world, especially the unknown ones."
Requirements: Open to professional and beginner songwriters. No limit on entries. Each entry must include an entry fee, a cassette tape of song(s) and lyric sheet(s). Judged by music industry representatives. Past judges have included record label representatives and publishers from Arista Records, EMI and Warner/Chappell. Deadline: To be announced. Send SASE with request or e-mail for entry forms at any time. Samples of work are not required.
Awards: Prizes include cash and merchandise in 15 different categories: pop, rock, country, Latin, R&B, gospel, folk, jazz, "lyrics only" category, instrumental and many others.
Tips: "Judging is based on lyrics, originality, melody and overall composition. CD quality production is great but not a consideration in judging."

Ⓝ U.S.-JAPAN CREATIVE ARTISTS EXCHANGE FELLOWSHIP PROGRAM, Japan-U.S. Friendship Commission, 1120 Vermont Ave., NW, Suite 925, Washington DC 20005-3523. (202)275-7712. Fax: (202)275-7413. E-mail: jusfc@compuserve.com. Website: http://www2.dgsys.com/~jusfc. Executive Assistant: Roberta Stewart. Estab. 1980. For all creative artists. Annual award.
Purpose: "For artists to go as seekers, as cultural visionaries, and as living liaisons to the traditional and contemporary life of Japan."
Requirements: "Artists' works must exemplify the best in U.S. arts." Deadline: June. Send for application. Samples of work are required with application. Requires 2 pieces on cassette or CD, cued to the 3-5 minute section to be reviewed.
Awards: Five artists are awarded a six-month residency anywhere in Japan. Awards monthly stipend for living expenses, housing and professional support services; up to $6,000 for pre-departure costs, including such items as language training and economy class roundtrip airfare. Residency is good for 1 year. Applications are judged by a panel of previous recipients of the awards, as well as other arts professionals with expertise in Japanese culture.
Tips: "Applicants should anticipate a highly rigorous review of their artistry and should have compelling reasons for wanting to work in Japan."

Ⓝ 🌐 U.S.-MEXICO FUND FOR CULTURE, Londres 16-PB, Col. Juarez Mexico City Mexico 06600. (525)592-5386. Fax: (525)577-8071. E-mail: usmexcult@laneta.apc.org. Website: http://www.fidei comisomexusa.org.mx. Program Officer: Beatriz E. Nava. Estab. 1991. For composers, choreographers, musical playwrights and performers. Annual award.
Purpose: "The U.S.-Mexico Fund for Culture, an independent body created through a joint initiative of the Bancomer Cultural Foundation, The Rockefeller Foundation and Mexico's National Fund for Culture and the Arts, provides financial support for the development of cultural binational projects in music, theater, dance, visual arts, cultural studies, literary and cultural publications, media arts and libraries."
Requirements: Deadline: March 31. Send for application with SASE (8½×11 envelope) or contact us at our website. Samples of work are required with application in duplicate.
Awards: Range from $2,500-25,000. Award is good for 1 year. Judged by binational panel of experts in each of the disciplines, one from Mexico and one from the USA.
Tips: "Proposals must be binational in character and have a close and active collaboration with artists from Mexico. The creation of new works is highly recommendable."

"UNISONG" INTERNATIONAL SONG CONTEST, 7095 Hollywood Blvd. #1015, Hollywood CA 90028. (213)673-4067. Fax: (818)704-1597. E-mail: entry@unisong.com. Website: http://www.unison g.com. Co-Founder: Alan Roy Scott. London office: P.O. Box 13383, London, NW3 5ZR United Kingdom. (44)236-4197. Co founder: David Stark. Estab. 1997. For songwriters, composers and lyricists. Annual songwriting contest.

Purpose: "This contest is designed for songwriters by songwriters. We help songwriters around the world by making donations from every entry fee to songwriter organizations internationally and Amnesty International."

Requirements: Deadline: September 1. Send for application or download application from website or request one by phone. Samples of work are required with application. Send cassette or CD only. No DATs.

Awards: Grand Prize in 1999 was an all expenses paid trip to Australia to participate in the next "Music Bridges" retreat in conjunction with the Sydney 2000 Olympics. 1st Prize in all 11 categories: $2,000. 2nd Prize in all 11 categories: $500 and publishing contract with EMI, MCA, Peermusic or Global Music. 3rd Prize: various services. First level judging by Taxi (professional screening service); second level by National Academy of Songwriters. Final level by top professionals and celebrities (artists, A&R, publishers, etc.) Songs judged on song quality only, not demo.

Tips: "Please make sure your song is professionally presented. Make sure lyrics can be clearly understood. Make sure you are entering song in most appropriate categories."

N UNISYS AFRICAN AMERICAN COMPOSER'S RESIDENCY AND NATIONAL SYMPO-SIUM, 3663 Woodward Ave., Detroit MI 48201-2403. (313)576-5162. Fax: (313)576-5101. Director of Education: Daisy Newman. Estab. 1989. For composers. Annual award.

Purpose: "Program was designed to identify and perform significant orchestral works by contemporary African American Composers."

Requirements: Send for application. Samples of work upon request.

Awards: Applications are judged by Adjudication Committee (conductor and resident conductor).

WE DON'T NEED NO STINKIN' DRAMAS, 1501 S. Fourth St., Minneapolis MN 55454. (612)338-0937. E-mail: mixedblood@wavetech.net. Script Czar: Dave Kunz. For musical playwrights. Annual award. Estab. 1998.

Purpose: To encourage emerging musical playwrights.

Requirements: "We Don't Need No Stinkin' Dramas" (comedy) playwriting contest. Deadline February 1. Always query first. Queries responded to within 4-8 weeks. Send SASE for copy of contest guidelines. Samples are not required. No translations or adaptations.

Awards: The winning musical will receive a cash prize of $2,000 if Mixed Blood Theatre Company chooses to produce the musical and $1,000 if Mixed Blood Theatre Company decides not to produce the winning musical.

Tips: "Professionalism is always a plus. Surprise us. Political satires and shows involving sports (baseball, golf, etc.) always of interest."

WEST COAST ENSEMBLE–MUSICAL STAIRS, P.O. Box 38728, Los Angeles CA 90038. (310)449-1447. Artistic Director: Les Hanson. For musical playwrights. Annual award.

Purpose: To provide an arena and encouragement for the development of new musicals for the theater.

Requirements: Submit book and a cassette of the score to the above address.

Awards: The West Coast Ensemble Musical Stairs Competition Award includes a production of the selected musical and $500 prize. Panel of judges reads script and listen to cassette. Final selection is made by Artistic Director.

Tips: "Submit libretto in standard playscript format along with professional sounding cassette of songs."

WORDS BY, 332 Eastwood Ave,. Feasterville PA 19053. (800)574-2986. Phone/fax: (215)953-0952. E-mail: alfoster@aol.com. Website: http://www.geocities.com/TimeSquare/Labyrinth/1917. Editor/Publisher: Allen Foster. Estab. 1992. For lyricists. Monthly contest.

Requirements: To enter, send your best lyrics and contact information.

MARKET CONDITIONS are constantly changing! If you're still using this book and it is 2001 or later, buy the newest edition of *Songwriter's Market* at your favorite bookstore or order directly from Writer's Digest Books at (800)289-0963.

Awards: Winning lyrics will be published along with your address so interested parties may contact you directly. Also, the top lyric for each month receives a voucher for a free book compliments of Writer's Digest Books.

Tips: "Due to the large number of submissions we receive each month, you may resubmit a lyric, after two months, if you really believe in that work."

Y.E.S. FESTIVAL OF NEW PLAYS, Northern Kentucky University Dept. of Theatre, FA-206, Highland Heights KY 41099-1007. (606)572-6362. E-mail: forman@nku.edu. Project Director: Sandra Forman. Estab. 1983. For musical playwrights. Biennial award.

Purpose: "The festival seeks to encourage new playwrights and develop new plays and musicals. Three plays or musicals are given full productions and one is given a staged reading."

Requirements: "Submit a script with a completed entry form. Musicals should be submitted with a piano/conductor's score and a vocal parts score. Scripts may be submitted May 1 through Oct. 31, 2000, for the New Play Festival occuring April 2001. Send for application. Samples of work are required with application."

Awards: Four awards of $400. "The four winners are brought to NKU at our expense to view late rehearsals and opening night." Applications are judged by a panel of readers.

Tips: "Plays/musicals which have heavy demands for mature actors are not as likely to be selected as an equally good script with roles for 18-25 year olds."

Resources

Organizations

One of the first places a beginning songwriter should look for guidance and support is a songwriting organization. Offering encouragement, instruction, contacts and feedback, these groups of professional and amateur songwriters can help a songwriter hone the skills needed to compete in the ever-changing music industry.

The type of organization you choose to join depends on what you want to get out of it. Local groups can offer a friendly, supportive environment where you can work on your songs and have them critiqued in a constructive way by other songwriters. They're also great places to meet collaborators. Larger, national organizations can give you access to music business professionals and other songwriters across the country.

Most of the organizations listed in this book are non-profit groups with membership open to specific groups of people—songwriters, musicians, classical composers, etc. They can be local groups with a membership of less than 100 people, or large national organizations with thousands of members from all over the country. In addition to regular meetings, most organizations occasionally sponsor events such as seminars and workshops to which music industry people are invited to talk about the business, and perhaps listen to and critique demo tapes.

Check the following listings, bulletin boards at local music stores and your local newspapers for area organizations. If you are unable to locate an organization within an easy distance of your home, you may want to consider joining one of the national groups. These groups, based in New York, Los Angeles and Nashville, keep their members involved and informed through newsletters, regional workshops and large yearly conferences. They can help a writer who feels isolated in his hometown get his music heard by professionals in the major music centers.

In the following listings, organizations describe their purpose and activities, as well as how much it costs to join. Before joining any organization, consider what they have to offer and how becoming a member will benefit you. To locate organizations close to home, see the Geographic Index at the back of this book.

AARON ENTERPRISES SONGWRITERS GROUP, 4411 Red Gate Dr., Disputanta VA 23842. (804)733-5908. Founder: Cham Laughlin. Estab. 1997. "Songwriters of all ages, all styles and all skill levels are welcome to join. Applicants must have an interest in songwriting—music writing, lyric writing or co-writing. The main purpose of this organization is to educate songwriters about the business of songwriting, the art and craft of songwriting, lyric writing and structure, musical composition, song structure or arranging and professional presentation of your songs." Offers newsletter, evaluation services, seminars, discounts on demos and leads to publishers. Applications accepted year-round. Membership fee: $25/year with discounts for multiple years.
Tips: "Networking is a very important part of this business. Members are offered a large amount of information and that information is explained to them through free seminars, the newsletter or one-on-one phone consultations to ensure the best possible support network for their songwriting careers."

☑ **ACADEMY OF COUNTRY MUSIC**, 6255 Sunset Blvd., #923, Hollywood CA 90028. (323)462-2351. E-mail: acmoffice@value.net. Website: http://www.acmcountry.com. Executive Director: Fran Boyd. Estab. 1964. Serves producers, artists, songwriters, talent buyers and others involved with the country music industry. Eligibility for professional members is limited to those individuals who derive some portion of their income directly from country music. Each member is classified by one of the following categories: artist/entertainer, club operator/employee, musician/trend leader, DJ, manager/booking agent, composer, music publisher, promotion, publications, radio, TV/motion picture, record company or affiliated (general). The purpose of ACM is to promote and enhance the image of country music. The Academy is involved year-round in activities important to the country music community. Some of these activities include charity fund-raisers, participation in country music seminars, talent contests, artist showcases, assistance to producers in placing country music on television and in motion pictures and backing legislation that benefits the interests of the country music community. The ACM is governed by directors and run by officers elected annually. Applications are accepted throughout the year. Membership is $60/year.

N ALABAMA SONGWRITER'S GUILD, P.O. Box 272, Garden City AL 35070. (256)352-4873. Fax: (256)352-5755. Contact: Dennis N. Kahler. Estab. 1992. "The Alabama Songwriter's Guild is comprised of songwriters and their supporters, with no restrictions. We have members who are just beginning to write, and others who have number one hits under their belts on the *Billboard* charts. We welcome all genres of songwriting, and count several non-writers as members of our network efforts. The main purpose of the ASG is to help link Alabama and outside songwriters to information on seminars, showcases, publishing and song-plugging opportunities, local associations, workshops, and other events from one end of the state to the other. We help spread word of the induction ceremonies and other events at the Alabama Music Hall of Fame, report on the annual Frank Brown International Songwriter's Festival in Gulf Shores/ Orange Beach every November, and help link writers together with like-minded individuals for co-writes. Any purpose that serves the songwriter is of interest to us." Offers competitions, instruction, workshops, performance opportunities and evaluation services. Applications accepted year-round.
Tips: "Networking is crucial! Wherever you live, develop your network. If you need songwriting contacts in Alabama, contact us."

✓ AMERICAN MUSIC CENTER, INC., 30 W. 26th St., Suite 1001, New York NY 10010-2011. (212)366-5260. Fax: (212)366-5265. E-mail: center@amc.net. Website: http://www.amc.net. Executive Director: Richard Kessler. Administrative Assistant: Ann Marie Taylor. The American Music Center, founded by a consortium led by Aaron Copland in 1939, is the first-ever national service and information center for new music in the world. The Center approaches its 60th anniversary with the creation of a variety of innovative new programs and services, including a montly Internet magazine for new American music, an online catalog of new music for educators specifically targeted to young audiences, regular networking meetings for composers, performers and presenters, and a series of professional development workshops. Each month, AMC provides its over 2,500 members with a listing of opportunities including calls for scores, competitions, and other new music performance information. Last year, AMC's Information Services Program fielded over 35,000 requests concerning composers, performers, data, funding, and support programs. The AMC Library circulates throughout the world and presently includes over 60,000 scores and recordings, many unavailable elsewhere. AMC also continues to administer several grants programs: the Aaron Copland Fund for Music; the Mary Flagler Cary Charitable Trust/Live Music for Dance; and its own program, The Margaret Fairbank Jory Copying Assistance Program. Members are also eligible to link their artists' pages to the center's website. The American Music Center is not-for-profit and has an annual membership fee.

AMERICAN SOCIETY OF COMPOSERS, AUTHORS AND PUBLISHERS (ASCAP), One Lincoln Plaza, New York NY 10023. (212)621-6000 (administration); (212)621-6240 (membership). E-mail: info@ascap.com. Website: http://www.ascap.com. President and Chairman of the Board: Marilyn Bergman. CEO: John Lofrumento. Contact: Member Services at (800)95-ASCAP. Regional offices: 7920 Sunset Blvd., 3rd Floor, Los Angeles CA 90046, (213)883-1000; 2 Music Square W., Nashville TN 37203, (615)742-5000; 1608 W. Belmont Ave., Suite 200, Chicago IL 60657, (773)472-1157; 541-400 10th St. NW, Atlanta GA 30318, (404)753-4679; 844 Alton Rd., Miami Beach FL 33139, (305)673-3446; 8 Cork St., London WIX IPB England, 011-44-171-439-0909; Puerto Rico, (787)281-0782. ASCAP is a membership associate of over 80,000 composers, lyricists, songwriters, and music publishers, whose function is to protect the right of its members by licensing and collecting royalties for the nondramatic public performance of their copyrighted works. ASCAP licensees include radio, television, cable, live concert promoters, bars, restaurants, symphony orchestras, new media, and other users of music. ASCAP is the leading performing right society in the world, with 1998 revenues of more than $500 million. All revenues, less operating expenses, are distributed to members (about 84 cents of each dollar, $400 million, in 1998). ASCAP was the first US performing rights organization to distribute royalties from the Internet. Founded in 1914, ASCAP is the only society created and controlled by writers and publishers. The ASCAP Board of Directors consists of 12 writers and 12 publishers, elected by the membership. ASCAP offers a variety

---

REFER TO THE GEOGRAPHIC INDEX (at the back of this book) to find listings of companies by state, as well as foreign listings.

of tailor-made benefits to its members, including medical, dental and term insurance, instrument and equipment insurance, and credit union access. ASCAP's Member Benefit cards offers new insurance benefits including studio and tour liability, retail, financial, travel benefits and discounts. A foreign tax credit opportunity saves members over $3 million annually. ASCAP hosts a wide array of showcases and workshops throughout the year, and offers grants, special awards, and networking opportunities in a variety of genres. Visit their website listed above for more information.

AMERICAN SONGWRITERS NETWORK (ASN), Dept A95, Box 15711, Boston MA 02215. (617)576-8836. E-mail: asn@tiac.net. Website: http://www.tiac.net/users/asn. Contact: Network Manager. Estab. 1995. Serves "professional level songwriters/composers with monthly music industry leads tipsheet. The tipsheet includes the most current listing of producers, A&R managers, record labels, entertainment attorneys, agents and publishing companies looking for specific material for their projects/albums. Any songwriter from any part of the country or world can be a member of this organization. The purpose of this organization is to foster a better professional community by helping members to place their songs." Membership fee: $140/year.
Tips: "Please send SASE or e-mail for application form."

N **ARIZONA SONGWRITERS ASSOCIATION**, P.O. Box 678, Phoenix AZ 85001-0678. (602)973-1988. Membership Director: Gavan Wieser. Estab. 1977. Members are all ages with wide variety of interests; beginners and those who make money from their songs. Most members are residents of Arizona. Purpose is to educate about the craft and business of songwriting and to facilitate networking with business professionals and other local songwriters. Offers instruction, newsletter, lectures, workshops and performance opportunities. Applications accepted year-round. Membership fee: $25/year.

N **ARKANSAS SONGWRITERS**, 6817 Gingerbread, Little Rock AR 72204. (501)569-8889. E-mail: pvining@aristotle.net. Counselor: Peggy Vining. Estab. 1979. Serves songwriters, musicians and lovers of music. Anyone interested may join. The purpose of this organization is to promote and encourage the art of songwriting. Offers competitions, instruction, lectures, newsletter, performance opportunities, social outings and workshops. Applications accepted year-round. Membership fee: $20/year.
Tips: "We also contribute time, money and our energies to promoting our craft in other functions. Meetings are held monthly. Notices sent."

N **ARTISTS' LEGAL & ACCOUNTING ASSISTANCE (ALAA)**, P.O. Box 2577, Austin TX 78768-2577. (512)407-8980. Fax: (512)407-8981. E-mail: mpolgar@realtime.net. Website: http://www.real time.net/alaa. Executive Director: Michelle Polgar. Estab. 1979. "ALAA provides *pro bono* legal and accounting assistance to low income artists and arts organizations on arts-related business matters. We present 4 to 7 educational programs each year on various topics of interest to the local arts community. We provide speakers on arts-related business topics to classes and other arts groups, maintain an arts reference library and generally serve as an informative referral service for arts-related legal, accounting and management questions." Offers instruction, newsletter, library and workshops. Applications accepted year-round. Membership fee: $25 artist membership; $35 business or organization membership/year.

ASSOCIATED MALE CHORUSES OF AMERICA, RR1, 773 Cedar Glen Rd., Dunsford, Ontario K0M 1L0 Canada. E-mail: wbates@peterboro.net. Website: http://www.tc.umn.edu/nlhome/M042/thoma 075/scholar.html. Executive Secretary: William J. Bates. Estab. 1924. Serves musicians and male choruses of US and Canada. "Our members are people from all walks of life. Many of our directors and accompanists are professional musicians. Age ranges from high school students to members in their '70s and '80s. Potential members must be supportive of Male Chorus Singing. They do not have to belong to a chorus to join. We have both Associate and Affiliate memberships. Our purpose is to further the power of music, not only to entertain and instruct, but to uplift the spirit, arouse the finest instincts, and develop the soul of man. With so little male chorus music being written, we as a 1,500 member organization provide a vehicle for songwriters, so that the music can be performed." Offers competitions, instruction, lectures, library, newsletter, performance opportunities, social outings and workshops. Also sponsors annual Male Chorus Songwriters Competition Contest. Applications accepted year-round. Membership fees are Chorus Members: $7 (per singer); Affiliate (Individual or Organization) Members: $10; Student Members: $2; Life Members: $125 (one time fee).

ASSOCIATION DES PROFESSIONEL.LE.S DE LA CHANSON ET DE LA MUSIQUE, 225 ch. Montréal, Suite 200, Ontario K1L 6C4 Canada. (613)745-5642. Fax: (613)745-1733. E-mail: apcm@sympatico.ca. Website: http://www.francoculture.ca/musique/apcm. Director of Commercial Development: Mélany Gauvin. Estab. 1989. Members are French Canadian signers and musicians. Members must be French signing and may have a CD/cassette to be distributed. Purpose is to gather French speaking artists (outside of Quebec, mainly in Ontario) to distribute their material, other workshops, instructions, lectures, etc. Offers instruction, newsletter, lectures, workshops, distribution and recording. Applications accepted year-round. Membership fee: $40 (Canadian).

N: AUSTIN SONGWRITERS GROUP, P.O. Box 2578, Austin TX 78768. (512)442-TUNE. Fax: (512)422-8863. President: Reneé French. Vice President of Membership: John Hudson. Estab. 1986. Serves all ages and all levels, from just beginning to advanced. Perspective members should have an interest in the field of songwriting, whether it be for profit or hobby. The main purpose of this organization is "to educate members in the craft and business of songwriting; to provide resources for growth and advancement in the area of songwriting; and to provide opportunities for performance and contact with the music industry." The primary benefit of membership to a songwriter is "exposure to music industry professionals, which increases contacts and furthers the songwriter's education in both craft and business aspects." Offers competitions, instruction, lectures, library, newsletter, performance opportunities, evaluation services, workshops and "contact with music industry professionals through special guest speakers at meetings, plus our yearly 'Austin Songwriters Conference,' which includes instruction, song evaluations, and song pitching direct to those pros currently seeking material for their artists, publishing companies, etc." Applications accepted year-round. Membership fee: $40/year.
Tips: "Our newsletter is top-quality—packed with helpful information on all aspects of songwriting—craft, business, recording and producing tips, and industry networking opportunities."

BERMUDA SONGWRITERS ASSOCIATION, P.O. Box 2857, Hamilton HM LX Bermuda. Phone: (441)296-5774. Fax: (441)238-6874. E-mail: djonz@bsabermuda.com. Website: http://www.bsaber muda.com. President: Dwight Jones. Estab. 1995. "Ages range from 20 to approximately 60 years. Interest ranges from hobbyists to persons seeking publishing and record deals. Skill levels range from amateur to professional musician/recording artists. BSA is open to all writers at all skill levels. BSA's objectives are to provide local and international songwriting networking and collaborative opportunities and to provide education that will help develop songwriting skills through seminars and workshops. It was formed for the advancement of creative songwriting and to provide talent discovery opportunities for Bermuda-based songwriters." Offers lectures, performance opportunities, instruction, newsletter and workshops. Applications accepted year-round. Membership fee: $75/full year.

N: THE BLACK COUNTRY MUSIC ASSOCIATION, 629 Shady Lane, Nashville TN 37206. (615)227-5570. Co-Founder/Chair: Frankie Staton. Estab. 1997. Members are all ages and all people who perform or support country music. "Purpose is to have a platform for African Americans who love and perform country music in an industry that does not realize how much African-Americans want to participate in this genre." Offers instruction, newsletter, workshops, performance opportunities and evaluation services. Applications accepted year-round. Membership fee: $40.
Tips: "With respect to the Black country artist and songwriter, the BCMA acts as an introduction to artist development. We have a quarterly newsletter. Send all promotional material (picture, bio, tape) to J.J. Jones, 235 Ross Ave., Gallatin TN 37066 (he's the talent co-ordinator)."

THE BOSTON SONGWRITERS WORKSHOP, 14 Skelton Rd., Burlington MA 01803. (617)499-6932. E-mail: elliott_a._jacobowitz@bostonbbs.org. Website: http://www.dcreators.com/bsw. Executive Director: Elliott Jacobowitz. Estab. 1988. "The Boston Songwriters Workshop is made up of a very diverse group of people, ranging in age from late teens to people in their sixties, and even older. The interest areas are also diverse, running the gamut from folk, pop and rock to musical theater, jazz, R&B, dance, rap and classical. Skill levels within the group range from relative newcomers to established veterans that have had cuts and/or songs published. By virtue of group consensus, there are no eligibility requirements other than a serious desire to pursue one's songwriting ventures, and availability and interest in volunteering for the various activities required to run the organization. The purpose of the BSW is to establish a community of songwriters and composers within the greater Boston area, so that its members may better help each other to make further gains in their respective musical careers." Offers performance opportunities, instruction, newsletter, workshops and bi-weekly critique sessions. Applications accepted year-round. Membership: $35/year; newsletter subscription only: $10/year; guest (nonmember) fees: free, "limited to two meetings."

MARKETS THAT WERE listed in the 1999 edition of *Songwriter's Market* but do not appear this year are listed in the General Index with a notation explaining why they were omitted.

BROADCAST MUSIC, INC. (BMI), 320 W. 57th St., New York NY 10019. (212)586-2000; 8730 Sunset Blvd., Los Angeles CA 90069, (310)659-9109; and 10 Music Square East, Nashville TN 37203, (615)291-6700. President and CEO: Frances W. Preston. Senior Vice President, Performing Rights: Del R. Bryant. Vice President, California: Rick Riccobono. Vice President, New York: Charlie Feldman. Vice President, Nashville: Roger Sovine. BMI is a performing rights organization representing over 200,000 songwriters, composers and music publishers in all genres of music, including pop, rock, country, R&B, rap, jazz, Latin, gospel and contemporary classical. "Applicants must have written a musical composition, alone or in collaboration with other writers, which is commercially published, recorded or otherwise likely to be performed." Purpose: BMI acts on behalf of its songwriters, composers and music publishers by insuring payment for performance of their works through the collection of licensing fees from radio stations, broadcast and cable TV stations, hotels, nightclubs, aerobics centers and other users of music. This income is distributed to the writers and publishers in the form of royalty payments, based on how the music is used. BMI also undertakes intensive lobbying efforts in Washington D.C. on behalf of its affiliates, seeking to protect their performing rights through the enactment of new legislation and enforcement of current copyright law. In addition, BMI helps aspiring songwriters develop their skills through various workshops, seminars and competitions it sponsors throughout the country. Applications accepted year-round. There is no membership fee for songwriters; a one-time fee of $100 is required to affiliate a publishing company.

BROADWAY ON SUNSET, 10800 Hesby, Suite 9, North Hollywood CA 91601. (818)508-9270. Fax: (818)508-1806. Artistic Director: Allison Bergman. Estab. 1981. Sponsored by the National Academy of Songwriters. Members are musical theater writers (composers, lyricists, librettists) at all skill levels. All styles of music and musicals accepted. Participants should have access to the Los Angeles area to attend our programs. "We provide writers of new musicals with a structured development program that gives them a full understanding of the principles and standards of Broadway-level craft, and provide them with opportunities to test their material in front of an audience." We produce an annual West Coast Musical Theatre Conference. Offers lectures, symposia, interviews with Broadway writers and other crafts, production opportunities, evaluation and consultation services, workshops and instruction. Co-produces full productions of developed original musicals in various local theaters. Applications accepted year-round. No membership fee per se; writers pay nominal fees to participate in classes and workshops. Certain scholarships are available.

CALIFORNIA LAWYERS FOR THE ARTS, 1641 18th St., Santa Monica CA 90404. (310)998-5590. Fax: (310)998-5594. E-mail: usercla@aol.com. Website: http://sirius.com/~cla. Associate Director: Dorian Dawson. Systems Coordinator: Josie Porter. Estab. 1974. "For artists of all disciplines, skill levels, and ages, supporting individuals and organizations, and arts organizations. Artists of all disciplines are welcome, whether professionals or amateurs. We also welcome groups and individuals who support the arts. We work most closely with the California arts community. Our mission is to establish a bridge between the legal and arts communities so that artists and art groups may handle their creative activities with greater business and legal competence; the legal profession will be more aware of issues affecting the arts community; and the law will become more responsive to the arts community." Offers newsletter, lectures, library, workshops, mediation service, attorney referral service, housing referrals, publications and advocacy. Membership fee: $20 for senior citizens and full-time students; $25 for working artists; $40 for general individual; $55 for panel attorney; $100 to $1,000 for patrons. Organizations: $45 for small organizations (budget under $50,000); $80 for large organizations (budget of $50,000 or more); $100 to $1,000 for corporate sponsors.

CANADA COUNCIL FOR THE ARTS/CONSEIL DES ARTS DU CANADA, 350 Albert St., P.O. Box 1047, Ottawa, Ontario K1P 5V8 Canada. (613)566-4414, ext. 5060. Website: http://www.canadacouncil.ca. Information Officers: Maria Martin and Lise Rochon. Estab. 1957. An independent agency that fosters and promotes the arts in Canada by providing grants and services to professional artists including songwriters and musicians. "Individual artists must be Canadian citizens or permanent residents of Canada, and must have completed basic training and/or have the recognition as professionals within their fields. The Canada Council offers grants to professional musicians to pursue their own personal and creative development. There are specific deadline dates for the various programs of assistance." Call or write for more details.

CANADIAN ACADEMY OF RECORDING ARTS & SCIENCES (CARAS), 124 Merton St., Suite 305, Toronto, Ontario M4S 2Z2 Canada. (416)485-3135 or (800)440-JUNO. Fax: (416)485-4978. E-mail: caras@juno-awards.ca. Website: http://www.juno-awards.ca. President: Daisy C. Falle. Coordinator, Membership Services: Lesley Wakefield. Membership is open to all employees (including support staff) in broadcasting and record companies, as well as producers, personal managers, recording artists, recording engineers, arrangers, composers, music publishers, album designers, promoters, talent and booking agents, record retailers, rack jobbers, distributors, recording studios and other music industry related professions (on approval). Applicants must be affliliated with the Canadian recording industry. Offers newsletter, Canadian artist record discount program, nomination and voting privileges for Juno Awards and discount tickets to Juno awards show. Also discount on trade magazines. "CARAS strives to foster the development of the Canadian music and recording industries and to contribute toward higher artistic standards." Applications accepted year-round. Membership fee is $50/year. Applications accepted from individuals only, not from companies or organizations.

N **CANADIAN COUNTRY MUSIC ASSOCIATION (CCMA)**, 5 Director Court, Unit 102, Woodbridge, Ontario L4L 4S5 Canada. (905)850-1144. Fax: (905)856-1330. E-mail: country@ccma.org. Executive Director: Sheila Hamilton. Estab. 1976. Members are songwriters, musicians, producers, radio station personnel, managers, booking agents and others. Offers newsletter, workshops, performance opportunities and annual awards. "Through our newsletters and conventions we offer a means of meeting and associating with artists and others in the industry. During our workshops or seminars (Country Music Week), we include a songwriters' seminar. The CCMA is a federally chartered, nonprofit organization, dedicated to the promotion and development of Canadian country music throughout Canada and the world and to providing a unity of purpose for the Canadian country music industry." Send for application.

N **CENTER FOR THE PROMOTION OF CONTEMPORARY COMPOSERS**, P.O. Box 131030, Tyler TX 75713. E-mail: cpcc@under.org. Website: http://www.under.org/cpcc. Director: Dr. Stephen Lias. Estab. 1996. "Our members range from student composers to composers with international reputations." Purpose is to promote the works and activities of contemporary composers by creating custom composer web pages, posting composer opportunities (competitions, calls for scores, grants, faculty openings, etc.), maintaining a catalogue of members' works and a calendar of upcoming performances of new music. Offers competitions, newsletter, performance opportunities and custom web pages and listings in online catalog. Applications accepted year-round. Membership fee: $20 regular; $10/month resident.

☑ **CENTRAL CAROLINA SONGWRITERS ASSOCIATION (CCSA)**, 1144 Amber Acres Lane, Knightdale NC 27545. (919)266-5791. Website: http://www.NCneighbors.com. Founder: Shantel R. Davis. Vice President: Jacques Chenet. Estab. 1996. "CCSA welcomes all songwriters and musicians, regardless of age. Our members vary in musical interests, and we cover all types of music. From the beginning songwriter to the experienced professional, all songwriters and musicians can find benefit in joining CCSA. Our headquarters are located just outside of Raleigh, NC. We are open to all songwriters who could possibly make it to our meetings, or those who are too far away could use our Critique-By-Mail service. All members must be active participants in CCSA for the benefit of the group, as well as for their own benefit, dedicated songwriters/musicians. The main purpose of the CCSA is to provide each songwriter and musician a resourceful organization where members can grow musically by learning and sharing with one another. We want to reach every songwriter we can and attend to his/her musical needs. Members are eligible for a discount when they use the services of Synth-Sational Productions, a local music company." Offers instruction, newsletter, library, workshops, evaluation services and musicians/collaborators network. Applications accepted year-round. Dues are $15 per year.

THE COLLEGE MUSIC SOCIETY, 202 W. Spruce St., Missoula MT 59802. (406)721-9616. Fax: (406)721-9419. E-mail: cms@music.org. Website: http://www.music.org. Estab. 1959. Serves college, university and conservatory professors, as well as independent musicians. "It is dedicated to gathering, considering and disseminating ideas on the philosophy and practice of music as an integral part of higher education, and to developing and increasing communication among the various disciplines of music." Offers journal, newsletter, lectures, workshops, performance opportunities, job listing service, databases of organizations and institutions, music faculty and mailing lists. Applications accepted year-round. Membership fee: $65 (regular dues).

COMPOSERS GUILD, 40 N. 100 West, Box 586, Farmington UT 84025. (801)451-2275. President: Ruth Gatrell. Estab. 1963. Serves all ages, including children. Musical skill varies from beginners to professionals. An interest in composing is the only requirement. The purpose of this organization is to

FOR BOOKS ON THE CRAFT AND BUSINESS of songwriting, check out the website for Writer's Digest Books at http://www.writersdigest.com.

"help composers in every way possible through classes, workshops and symposiums, concerts, composition contests and association with others of similar interests." Offers competitions, instruction, lectures, newsletter, performance opportunities, evaluation services and workshops. Applications accepted year-round. Membership fee is $25/year. Associate memberships for child, spouse, parent, grandchild or grandparent of member: $15. "Holds four concerts/year. See our listing in the Contests & Awards section for details."

CONNECTICUT SONGWRITERS ASSOCIATION, P.O. Box 1292, Glastonbury CT 06033. (860)659-8992. E-mail: ddcsa@aol.com. Website: http://www.ctsongs.com. President: Don Donegan. Vice President: Ric Speck. "We are an educational, nonprofit organization dedicated to improving the art and craft of original music. Founded in 1979 by Don Donegan, CSA has grown to over 250 active members and has become one of the best known songwriters' associations in the country. Membership in the CSA admits you to 12-18 seminars/workshops/song critique sessions per year at 3 locations in Connecticut. Out of state members may mail in songs for free critique at our meetings. Noted professionals deal with all aspects of the craft and business of music including lyric writing, music theory, music technology, arrangement and production, legal and business aspects, performance techniques, song analysis and recording techniques. CSA offers 2-3 song screening sessions per year for members (songs which are voted on by the panel). Songs that 'pass' are then eligible for inclusion on the CSA sampler anthology cassette series. Seven 16-20 song tapes have been released so far and are for sale at local retail outlets and are given to speakers and prospective buyers. CSA also offers showcases and concerts which are open to the public and designed to give artists a venue for performing their original material for an attentive, listening audience. CSA benefits help local soup kitchens, group homes, hospice, world hunger, libraries, nature centers, community centers and more. CSA shows encompass ballads to bluegrass and Bach to rock. Our monthly newsletter, *Connecticut Songsmith*, offers free classified advertising for members, and has been edited and published by Bill Pere since 1980. Annual dues: $40; senior citizen and full time students $30; organizations $80. Memberships are tax-deductible as business expenses or as charitable contributions to the extent allowed by law."

COUNTRY MUSIC ASSOCIATION OF TEXAS, P.O. Box 549, Troy TX 76579. (254)938-2454. Founder/Director: Bud Fisher. Estab. 1989. Open to songwriters, singers, pickers and other professionals of all ages from all over the world. Members are interested in country music, especially traditional, classics. Purpose is to promote traditional and independent country music. Offers newsletter, workshops, performance opportunities and evaluation services. Applications accepted year-round. Membership fee: $23.95/year.
Tips: "Membership has grown to over 4,000 fans, musicians and songwriters, making it one of the largest state organizations in America. We hold numerous functions throughout the year and we have helped many local recording artists chart their releases nationwide and in Europe. Texas country music is hot!"

COUNTRY MUSIC SHOWCASE INTERNATIONAL, INC., P.O. Box 368, Carlisle IA 50047. (515)989-3748. Fax: (515)989-0235. E-mail: haroldl@cmshowcase.org. Website: http://www.cmshowcase.org. President: Harold L. Luick. "We are a nonprofit, educational performing arts organization and an independent entertainment trade association for songwriters, musicians, recording artists and entertainers. The organization showcases songwriters at different seminars and workshops held at the request of its members in many different states across the nation. It also showcases recording artists/entertainer members at many Fair Association showcases held across the United States. When a person becomes a member they receive a membership card, newsletters, an educational information packet (about songwriting/entertainment business), a question and answer service by e-mail, mail or phone, a song evaluation and critique service, info on who's looking for song material, songwriters who are willing to collaborate, and songwriting contests. Members can submit one song per month for a critique. We offer good constructive criticism and honest opinions. Also, we offer our information provider packets on songwriting, copyrights, etc. This is done free as part of a membership. We maintain that a songwriter, recording artist or entertainer should associate himself with professional people and educators who know more about the business of music than they do; otherwise, they cannot reach their musical goals." Membership donation: $100/year. For free information, brochure or membership application send SASE to the above address.

✅ **DALLAS SONGWRITERS ASSOCIATION**, Sammons Center for the Arts, 3036 Harry Hines, Box 20, Dallas TX 75219. E-mail: info@dallassongwriters.org. Website: http://www.dallassongwriters.org. President: Joni Ringo. Founding President Emeritis: Barbara McMillen. Estab. 1988. Serves songwriters and lyricists of Dallas/Ft. Worth metroplex. Members are adults ages 18-65, Dallas/Ft. Worth area songwriters/lyricists who are or aspire to be professionals. Purpose is to provide songwriters an opportunity to meet other songwriters, share information, find co-writers and support each other through group discussions at monthly meetings; to provide songwriters an opportunity to have their songs heard and critiqued by peers and professionals by playing cassettes and providing an open mike at monthly meetings and by offering contests judged by publishers; to provide songwriters opportunities to meet other music business professionals by inviting guest speakers to monthly meetings and the Dallas Songwriters Seminar; and to provide songwriters opportunities to learn more about the craft of songwriting and the business of music by presenting mini-workshops at each monthly meeting. "We offer a chance for the songwriter to learn from peers and industry professionals and an opportunity to belong to a supportive group environment to encourage the individual to continue his/her songwriting endeavors." Offers competitions, field trips, instruction, lectures, newsletter, performance opportunities, social outings, workshops and seminars. "Our members are eligible for discounts at several local music stores and seminars." Applications accepted year-round. Membership fee: $45. "When inquiring by phone, please leave complete mailing address and phone number where you can be reached day and night."

DETROIT MUSIC ALLIANCE, P.O. Box 24323, Detroit MI 48224. (313)730-SONG. Fax: (313)886-7860. E-mail: suestatic@aol.com. Website: http://www.detroitmusic.com/dma. Vice President: Sue Summers. Estab. 1992. Ages 18-40. Members are bands, musicians, songwriters, poets, artists, managers, engineers and music fans. Purpose is to expose Detroit and indie talent, and to educate musicians just starting out as well as musicians who are already in the game. "We are open to helping performers out of state as well." Offers competitions, instruction, newsletter, lectures, library, workshops, performance opportunities, UPC codes, compilation series and evaluation services. Applications accepted year-round. Membership fee: $15/year for individual; $50/year for band.
Tips: "We are looking to network with other music alliances or like-minded organizations across the country."

☑ **THE DRAMATISTS GUILD, INC.**, 1501 Broadway, Suite 701, New York NY 10036. (212)398-9366. Fax: (212)944-0240. Website: http://www.dramaguild.com. Executive Director: Christopher C. Wilson. "For over three-quarters of a century, The Dramatists Guild has been the professional association of playwrights, composers and lyricists, with more than 6,000 members across the country. All theater writers, whether produced or not, are eligible for Associate membership ($75/year); those who are engaged in a drama-related field but are not a playwright are eligible for Subscribing membership ($50/year); students enrolled in writing degree programs at colleges or universities are eligible for Student membership ($35/year); writers who have been produced on Broadway, Off-Broadway or on the main stage of a resident theater are eligible for Active membership ($125/year). The Guild offers its members the following activities and services: use of the Guild's contracts (including the Approved Production Contract for Broadway, the Off-Broadway contract, the LORT contract, the collaboration agreements for both musicals and drama, the 99 Seat Theatre Plan contract, the Small Theatre contract, commissioning agreements, and the Underlying Rights Agreements contract; advice on all theatrical contracts including Broadway, Off-Broadway, regional, showcase, Equity-waiver, dinner theater and collaboration contracts); a nationwide toll-free number for all members with business or contract questions or problems; advice and information on a wide spectrum of issues affecting writers; free and/or discounted ticket service; symposia led by experienced professionals in major cities nationwide; access to two health insurance programs and a group term life insurance plan; a reference library; and a spacious and elegant meeting room which can accommodate up to 50 people for readings and auditions on a rental basis. The Guild's publications are: *The Dramatist*, a bimonthly journal containing articles on all aspects of the theater (which includes *The Dramatists Guild Newsletter*, with announcements of all Guild activities and current information of interest to dramatists); and an annual resource directory with up-to-date information on agents, grants, producers, playwriting contests, conferences and workshops (with off-year addendum including information updates).

☑ **THE FIELD**, 161 Sixth Ave., New York NY 10013. (212)691-6969. (212)255-2053. E-mail: thefield@aol.com. Website: http://www.thefield.org. Program Director: Maureen Brennan. Program Assistant: Heather Trautwein. Estab. 1986. "The Field gives independent performing artists the tools to develop and sustain their creative and professional lives, while allowing the public to have immediate, direct access to a remarkable range of contemporary artwork. The organization was started by eight emerging artists who shared common roots in contemporary dance and theater. Meeting regularly, these artists created a structure to help each other improve their artwork, and counter the isolation that often comes with the territory of an artistic career. The Field offers a comprehensive program structure similar to an urban artists' residency or graduate program. Participants select from a broad array of services focused in three basic areas: Art, Career and Exploration. These include: workshops and performance opportunities; management training and career development; fundraising consultations, fiscal sponsorship, and informational publications; and residencies. Our goal is to help artists develop their best artwork by deepening the artistic process and finding effective ways to bring that art into the marketplace. Most of our programs cost under $75, and tickets to our performance events average $8. In addition, since 1992, we have coordinated a network of satellite sites in Atlanta, Chicago, Dallas, Houston, Miami, Philadelphia, San Francisco, Seattle, Toronto, Washington D.C. and most recently, Japan. The Field is the only organization in New York that provides comprehensive programming for independent performing artists on a completely non-exclusive basis. This means our programs are open to artists from all disciplines, aesthetic viewpoints, and levels of development." Offers newsletter, workshops and performance opportunities. Applications accepted year-round. Membership fee: $75/year.

FILM MUSIC NETWORK, 1146 N. Central Ave. #103, Glendale CA 91202. (818)771-7778. E-mail: info@filmmusic.net. Website: http://www.filmmusic.net. Contact: Mark Northam. Estab. 1997. "We welcome all professionals from the film music business including songwriters, composers, music editors and music supervisors, publishers, musicians and filmmakers. A member must be active in the film music business." Purpose is to provide an opportunity for networking, communication and education via networking events and workshops. Offers monthly magazine, lectures, workshops and monthly networking events. Applications accepted year-round. Call or write the California office for membership fee information.
  • At press time, the Film Music Network had formed a New York chapter, and plans to add regional chapters during the year.
Tips: "Networking events are held the first Monday of every month in Los Angeles. Call for more information. Visitors and guests are welcome."

☑ **THE FOLK ALLIANCE (North American Folk Music and Dance Alliance)**, 1001 Connecticut Ave. NW, #501, Washington DC 20036. (202)835-3655. Fax: (202)835-3656. E-mail: fa@folk.org. Website: http://www.folk.org. Executive Director: Phyllis Barney. Programs and Services: Janet Brown. Estab. 1989. Members are organizations and individuals involved in traditional and contemporary folk music and dance in the US and Canada (in any genre—blues, bluegrass, Celtic, Latino, old-time, singer/songwriter, etc.). The Folk Alliance hosts its annual conference (which includes performance showcases) in late February at different locations in the US and Canada. The conferences include workshops, panel discussions, the largest all folk exhibit hall and showcases. The Folk Alliance also serves members with their newsletter and through education, advocacy and field development. Memberships accepted year-round. Membership fee: $40/year for individual (voting); $100-400/year for organizational. Upcoming conference sites: 2000: Cleveland OH. 2001: Vancouver BC, Canada. "We *do not* offer songwriting contests. We are *not* a publisher—no demo tapes, please."

☑ **GOSPEL MUSIC ASSOCIATION**, 1205 Division St., Nashville TN 37203. (615)242-0303. E-mail: holly@gospelmusic.org. Website: http://www.gospelmusic.org. Membership Coordinator: Holly Zabka. Estab. 1964. Serves songwriters, musicians and anyone directly involved in or who supports gospel music. Professional members include advertising agencies, musicians, agents/managers, composers, retailers, music publishers, print and broadcast media, and other members of the recording industry. Associate members include supporters of gospel music and those whose involvement in the industry does not provide them with income. The primary purpose of the GMA is to promote the industry of gospel music, and provide professional development series for industry members. Offers library, newsletter, performance opportunities and workshops. Applications accepted year round. Membership fee: $75/year (professional) and $50/year (associate).

🅽 **🌐** **THE GUILD OF INTERNATIONAL SONGWRITERS & COMPOSERS**, Sovereign House, 12 Trewartha Rd., Praa Sands, Penzance, Cornwall TR20 9ST England. Phone: (01736)762826. Fax: (01736)763328. E-mail: songmag@aol.com. Website: http://www.icn.co.uk/gisc.html. Secretary: C.A. Jones. Serves songwriters, musicians, record companies, music publishers, etc. "Our members are amateur and professional songwriters and composers, musicians, publishers, studio owners and producers. Membership is open to all persons throughout the world of any age and ability, from amateur to professional. The Guild gives advice and services relating to the music industry. A free magazine is available upon request with an SAE or 3 IRCs. We provide contact information for artists, record companies, music publishers,

**FOR EXPLANATIONS OF THESE SYMBOLS,
SEE THE INSIDE FRONT AND BACK COVERS OF THIS BOOK.**

industry organizations; free copyright service; *Songwriting & Composing Magazine*; and many additional free services." Applications accepted year-round. Annual dues: £38 in the U.K.; £50 in E.E.C. countries; £50 overseas (subscriptions in pounds sterling only).

THE INDIANAPOLIS SONGWRITERS ASSOCIATION, INC., P.O. Box 44724, Indianapolis IN 46244-0724. (317)862-3366 or 862-4922. E-mail: jumpstam@iquest.net. President: Nancy J. Seibert. Estab. 1983. Purpose is "to create an affiliation of serious-minded songwriters, promote the artistic value of the musical composition, the business of music and recognition for the songwriter and his craft." Sponsors quarterly newsletter, monthly meetings, periodic showcases and periodic seminars and workshops. "The monthly critiques are helpful for improving songwriting skills. The meetings offer opportunities to share information concerning publishing, demos, etc. Also offers monthly tip sheets. In addition, it provides the opportunity for members to meet co-writers." Membership fee: $20/year.

☑ INTERNATIONAL BLUEGRASS MUSIC ASSOCIATION (IBMA), 207 E. Second St., Owensboro KY 42303. (502)684-9025. E-mail: ibma1@occ-uky.campus.mci.net. Website: http://www.ibma.org. Member Services: Susan Cooke. Estab. 1985. Serves songwriters, musicians and professionals in bluegrass music. "IBMA is a trade association composed of people and organizations involved professionally and semi-professionally in the bluegrass music industry, including performers, agents, songwriters, music publishers, promoters, print and broadcast media, local associations, recording manufacturers and distributors. Voting members must be currently or formerly involved in the bluegrass industry as full or part-time professionals. A songwriter attempting to become professionally involved in our field would be eligible. We promote the bluegrass music industry and unity within it. IBMA publishes bimonthly *International Bluegrass*, holds an annual trade show/convention in the fall, represents our field outside the bluegrass music community, and compiles and disseminates databases of bluegrass related resources and organizations. Market research on the bluegrass consumer is available and we offer Bluegrass in the Schools information and matching grants. The primary value in this organization for a songwriter is having current information about the bluegrass music field and contacts with other songwriters, publishers, musicians and record companies." Offers social outings, workshops, liability insurance, rental car discounts, consultation and databases of record companies, radio stations, press, organizations and gigs. Applications accepted year-round. Membership fee: for a non-voting patron $25/year; for an individual voting professional $50/year; for an organizational voting professional $125/year.

🆕 INTERNATIONAL COUNTRY GOSPEL MUSIC ASSOCIATION, 200 N. Holly, Sherman TX 75092. Phone/fax: (903)893-9562. E-mail: gospel2@gte.net. President: Wendy Duvall. Offers instruction, newsletter, workshops, performance opportunities, evaluation services and Annual Gold Cross Awards. Applications accepted year-round. Membership fee: $50/year.

🌐 INTERNATIONAL SONGWRITERS ASSOCIATION LTD., 37b New Cavendish St., London WI England. (0171)486-5353. E-mail: jliddane@songwriter.iol.ie. Website: http://www.songwriter.co.uk. Membership Department: Anna M. Sinden. Serves songwriters and music publishers. "The ISA headquarters is in Limerick City, Ireland, and from there it provides its members with assessment services, copyright services, legal and other advisory services and an investigations service, plus a magazine for one yearly fee. Our members are songwriters in more than 50 countries worldwide, of all ages. There are no qualifications, but applicants under 18 are not accepted. We provide information and assistance to professional or semi-professional songwriters. Our publication, *Songwriter*, which was founded in 1967, features detailed exclusive interviews with songwriters and music publishers, as well as directory information of value to writers." Offers competitions, instruction, library, newsletter and a weekly e-mail newsletter *Songwriter Newswire*. Applications accepted year-round. Membership fee for European writers is £19.95; for non-European writers, US $30.

☑ KERRVILLE MUSIC FOUNDATION INC., P.O. Box 1466, Kerrville TX 78029-1466. (830)257-3600. E-mail: festivals@kerrville-music.com. Website: http://www.kerrville-music.com. Executive Director: Rod Kennedy. The Kerrville Music Foundation was "founded in 1975 for the recognition and promotion of original music and has awarded more than $28,000 to musicians over the last 25 years through open competitions designed to recognize and encourage excellence in songwriting. Annually, 32 new folk finalists are selected to sing their 2 songs entered and 6 new folk Award Winners receive $150 prize money each and are invited to share 20 minutes of their songs at the Kerrville Folk Festival with 1 or more selected to perform on the main stage the next year." Opportunities include: The New Folk Concerts for Emerging Songwriters at the Kerrville Folk Festival (do not send entries without requesting complete rules first). Also offers booking and management seminar. A 3-day intensive with 4 of the nation's outstanding managers and agents working in the folk music field, the seminar includes 12 hours of booking seminars and discussions;

12 hours of management seminars and discussions; 3 lunches; free camping at Quiet Valley Ranch during the Kerrville Folk Festival 3 weekdays in June. Also offers the annual Folk Cruise of the Caribbean. Call (800)435-8429 for information or check their website.

THE LAS VEGAS SONGWRITERS ASSOCIATION, P.O. Box 42683, Las Vegas NV 89116-0683. (702)223-7255. President: Betty Kay Miller. Secretary: Barbara Jean Smith. Estab. 1980. "We are an educational, nonprofit organization dedicated to improving the art and craft of the songwriter. We want members who are serious about their craft. We want our members to respect their craft and to treat it as a business. Members must be at least 18 years of age. We offer quarterly newsletters, monthly information meetings, workshops three times a month and quarterly seminars with professionals in the music business. We provide support and encouragement to both new and more experienced songwriters. We critique each song or lyric that's presented during workshops, we make suggestions on changes—if needed. We help turn amateur writers into professionals. Several of our songwriters have had their songs recorded on both independent and major labels." Dues: $30/year.

☑ LOS ANGELES MUSIC NETWORK, P.O. Box 8934, Universal City CA 91618-8934. (818)769-6095. E-mail: lamnetwork@aol.com. Website: http://www.lamn.com. Membership Coordinator: Shirleen Talavera. Estab. 1988. "Ours is an association of music industry professionals, i.e., people who work at record companies, in publishing, management, entertainment law, etc. Members are ambitious and interested in advancing their careers. We prefer people who are employed full-time in some capacity in the music business, not so much singers and songwriters because there already exist so many organizations to meet and promote their needs. LAMN is an association created to promote career advancement, communication and continuing education among music industry professionals and top executives. LAMN sponsors industry events and educational panels held bi-monthly at venues in the Hollywood area." Offers instruction, newsletter, lectures, seminars, music industry job listings and many professional networking opportunities. See our website for current job listings and a calendar of upcoming events. Applications accepted year-round. Membership fee is $75.

☑ LOUISIANA SONGWRITERS ASSOCIATION, P.O. Box 80425, Baton Rouge LA 70898-0425. (225)924-0804. E-mail: pvida@intersurf.com. Website: http://www.tyrell.net/~pvida/lsa. President, Baton Rouge chapter: Janice Calvert. President, New Orleans chapter: Linda Torres. Serves songwriters. "LSA has been organized to educate songwriters in all areas of their trade, and promote the art of songwriting in Louisiana. We are of course honored to have a growing number of songwriters from other states join LSA and fellowship with us. LSA membership is open to people interested in songwriting, regardless of age, musical ability, musical preference, ethnic background, etc. One of our goals is to work together as a group to establish a line of communication with industry professionals in order to develop a music center in our area of the country. LSA offers competitions, lectures, library, newsletter, directory, marketing, performance opportunities, workshops, discounts on various music-related books and magazines, discounts on studio time, and we are developing a service manual that will contain information on music related topics, such as copyrighting, licensing, etc." Also offers regular showcases in Baton Rouge and New Orleans. General membership dues: $25/year.

Ⓝ M.O.-H.A.M. (Members Organization-Helping All Musicians), 1601 W. Apache Trail, Suite 2-5, Apache Junction AZ 85220. (602)288-8622. Fax: (602)288-7733. E-mail: mohamm@doitnow.com. President/CEO: Terri Barker. Estab. 1997. Active Entertainers are up and coming performers, ages 9-60 (country, bluegrass, R&B, etc.). Booster members are active in the art of music. Members must be committed to the music industry and active participants in concerts, shows, etc. "This organization is dedicated to the education and career development of the music artist." Offers competitions, instruction, newsletter, lectures, workshops, performance opportunities, evaluation services and promotions (bios, demos, press kits, etc.). Applications accepted year-round. Membership fee: $50/year (entertainers); $15/year (booster members).

♦ ☑ MANITOBA AUDIO RECORDING INDUSTRY ASSOCIATION (MARIA), 407-100 Arthur St., Winnipeg, Manitoba R3B 1H3 Canada. (204)942-8650. Fax: (204)956-5780. E-mail: info@man audio.mb.ca. Website: http://www.manaudio.mb.ca. Executive Director: Gaylene Dempsey. Estab. 1987. Organization consists of "songwriters, producers, agents, musicians, managers, retailers, publicists, radio,

REFER TO THE GEOGRAPHIC INDEX (at the back of this book) to find listings of companies by state, as well as foreign listings.

talent buyers, media, record labels, etc. (no age limit, no skill level minimum). Must have interest in the future of Manitoba's sound recording industry." The main purpose of MARIA is to foster growth in all areas of the Manitoba music industry primarily through education, promotion and lobbying. Offers newsletter, lectures, directory of Manitoba's music industry, workshops and performance opportunities; also presents demo critiquing sessions. MARIA also presents the Prairie Music Weekend festival, conference and awards show (September 30 to October 3, 1999). Applications accepted year-round. Membership fee: $25 (Canadian funds).

☑ **MEET THE COMPOSER**, 2112 Broadway, Suite 505, New York NY 10023. (212)787-3601. Fax: (212)787-3745. E-mail: mtc@meetthecomposer.org. Website: http://www.meetthecomposer.org. Public Information Coordinator: Fard Johnson. Estab. 1974. "Meet the Composer serves all American composers working in all styles of music, at every career stage, through a variety of grant programs and information resources. A nonprofit organization, Meet the Composer raises money from foundations, corporations, individual patrons and government sources and designs programs that support all genres of music—from folk, ethnic, jazz, electronic, symphonic, and chamber to choral, music theater, opera and dance. Meet the Composer awards grants for composer fees to non-profit organizations that perform, present, or commission original works. This is not a membership organization; all composers are eligible for support. Meet the Composer was founded in 1974 to increase artistic and financial opportunities for American composers by fostering the creation, performance, dissemination, and appreciation of their music." Offers grant programs and information services. Deadlines vary for each grant program.

☑ **MEMPHIS SONGWRITERS' ASSOCIATION**, 1494 Prescott St., Memphis TN 38111. (901)577-0906. Fax: (901)743-4987. President: Dennis Nelson. Estab. 1973. "MSA is a nonprofit songwriters organization serving songwriters nationally. Our mission is to dedicate our services on a monthly basis to promote, advance, and help songwriters in the composition of music, lyrics and songs; to work for better conditions in our profession; and to secure and protect the rights of MSA songwriters. We offer a correspondence course for all members outside of Memphis. MSA provides a monthly Basic Lyric Writing Course for beginners with a focus on commercial songwriting. We also supply copyright forms, pitch sheets and a collaborator's guide. We offer critique sessions for advanced writers at our monthly meetings. We also have monthly jam sessions to encourage creativity, networking and co-writing. We host an annual songwriter's seminar and an annual songwriter's showcase, as well as a bi-monthly guest speaker series, which provide education, competition and entertainment for the songwriter. In addition, our members receive a monthly newsletter to keep them informed of MSA activities, demo services and opportunities in the songwriting field." Annual fee: $35.

☑ **MICHIGAN SONGWRITERS ASSOCIATION**, P.O. Box 26044, Fraser MI 48026. (810)498-7673. E-mail: senecal@earthlink.net. Manager: Terri Senecal. Estab. 1990. Serves songwriters, musicians, artists and beginners. "Members are from NY, IL, MI, OH, etc. with interests in country, pop, rock and R&B. The main purpose of this organization is to educate songwriters, artists and musicians in the business of music." MSA offers performance opportunities, song critique services, instruction, quarterly newsletter and 4 workshops/year. Applications accepted year-round. Membership fee: $50/year. Newsletter subscription available for $20/year.

MINNESOTA ASSOCIATION OF SONGWRITERS, P.O. Box 581816, Minneapolis MN 55458. (612)649-4636. E-mail: mas@mndir.com. Website: http://www.isc.net/mas. President: Gigi Marie Byrd. "Includes a wide variety of members, ranging in age from 18 to 60; types of music are very diverse ranging from alternative rock to contemporary Christian; skill levels range from newcomers to songwriting to writers with published material and songs on CDs in various parts of the country. Main requirement is an interest in songwriting—although most members come from the Minneapolis-St. Paul area, others come in from surrounding cities and nearby Wisconsin. Some members are fulltime musicians, but most represent a wide variety of occupations. MAS is a nonprofit community of songwriters which informs, educates, inspires and assists its members in the art and business of songwriting. Members are able to have their own web page on the MAS website." Offers instruction, newsletter, lectures, library, workshops, performance opportunities, evaluation services, MAS compilation CDs and bimonthly meetings. Applications accepted year-round. Membership fee: $25.
Tips: "Through a monthly newsletter and announcements at bimonthly meetings, members are kept current on resources and opportunities. Original works are played at meetings and are critiqued by the group. Through this process, writers hone their skills and gain experience and confidence in submitting their works to others. Members vote to endorse the songs critiqued at meetings. The MAS assists writers of endorsed songs by selectively marketing the compositions and by providing access to an expanding pool of industry contacts."

MISSOURI SOCIETY OF SONGWRITERS AND MUSICIANS, HCR1 Box 157E, Eminence MO 65466. (573)226-5620. E-mail: daveslt@aol.com. Co-Founder: Susan Brinkley. Estab. 1995. "Members live all over Missouri and include amateur and professional songwriters and musicians as well as recording studio owners, music instructors, booking agents, managers, venue owners, video producers, music publishers, radio personnel and record producers. We have several members who have recently self-released CDs. Out-of-state members are welcome—anyone with an interest in the music industry is invited to join. Those unable to travel to bimonthly meetings will still benefit from joining: our bimonthly newsletter is full of insider tips, industry information, and interviews with today's singer/songwriters and industry professionals. Each issue also contains an in-depth recap of the previous meeting's guest speaker's presentation. We offer members a great opportunity to network and share knowledge with colleagues from all over the state in a friendly, creative atmosphere. We meet in centrally located Rolla on the first Saturday of every other month. Guest speakers have ranged from music publishers to voice instructors to singer/songwriters with gold records. Our Songwriter's Workshops allow members to play an original work (live or demo cassette) and receive constructive feedback and criticism from a supportive audience of their peers." Offers competitions, instruction, newsletter, lectures, library, workshops, performance opportunities, evaluation services, networking and discounts. Send $1 for a sample newsletter. Membership fee: $27/year; $20/year out-of-state.
Tips: "MSSM has been gaining recognition and attracting the attention of music industry professionals, including publishers and producers, from around the country. There is an incredible amount of talent in Missouri, and by coming together we can create a strong enough voice to be heard from L.A. to Nashville and beyond. MSSM also gives songwriters and musicians in rural areas a chance to meet one another. Anyone serious about their music should join."

MUSICIANS CONTACT, P.O. Box 788, Woodland Hills CA 91365. (818)347-8888. Fax: (818)227-5919. Website: http://www.musicianscontact.com. President: Sterling. Estab. 1969. "A referral service for bands and musicians seeking each other. Job openings updated online, as well as a 24-hour hotline. Offers industry contacts for complete acts seeking representation. Bands and collaborators phone in to hear voice classified ads of available players, many with demo tapes."

☑ **NASHVILLE SONGWRITERS ASSOCIATION INTERNATIONAL (NSAI)**, 1701 W. End Ave., 3rd Floor, Nashville TN 37203. (615)256-3354. Fax: (615)256-0034. E-mail: nsai@song.org. Website: http://www.songs.org/nsai. Executive Director: Barton Herbison. Purpose: a not-for-profit service organization for both aspiring and professional songwriters in all fields of music. Membership: Spans the United States and several foreign countries. Songwriters may apply in one of four annual categories: Active ($75—for songwriters who have at least one song contractually signed to a publisher affiliated with ASCAP, BMI or SESAC); Associate ($75—for songwriters who are not yet published or for anyone wishing to support songwriters); Student ($50—for full-time college students or for students of an accredited senior high school); Professional ($100—for songwriters who derive their primary source of income from songwriting or who are generally recognized as such by the professional songwriting community). Membership benefits: music industry information and advice, song evaluations by mail, quarterly newsletter, access to industry professionals through weekly Nashville workshop and several annual events, regional workshops, use of office facilities, discounts on books and discounts on NSAI's three annual instructional/awards events. There are also "branch" workshops of NSAI. Workshops must meet certain standards and are accountable to NSAI. Interested coordinators may apply to NSAI.

NATIONAL ACADEMY OF POPULAR MUSIC (NAPM), 330 W. 58th St., Suite 411, New York NY 10019-1827. (212)957-9230. Fax: (212)957-9227. E-mail: 73751.1142@compuserve.com. Website: http://www.songwritershalloffame.org. Projects Director: Bob Leone. Managing Director: April Anderson. Estab. 1969. "The majority of our members are songwriters, but also on NAPM's rolls are music publishers, producers, record company executives, music attorneys, and lovers of popular music of all ages. Professional members are affiliated with ASCAP, BMI and/or SESAC; or are employed by music industry firms. Associate membership, however, merely requires a completed application and $25 dues. NAPM was formed to determine a variety of ways to celebrate the songwriter (e.g., induction into the Songwriters' Hall of Fame). We also provide educational and networking opportunities to our members through our workshop and showcase programs." Offers newsletter, workshops, performance opportunities and scholarships for excellence in songwriting. Applications accepted year-round. Membership fee: $25.
Tips: "Our priority at this time is to locate a site for the re-establishment of the Songwriters' Hall of Fame Museum in New York City."

☑ **NATIONAL ACADEMY OF SONGWRITERS (NAS)**, 6255 Sunset Blvd., Suite 1023, Hollywood CA 90028. (323)463-7178 or (800)826-7287. Fax: (323)463-2146. E-mail: nassong@aol.com. Website: http://www.nassong.org. Executive Director: Dawn Dagucon. A nonprofit organization dedicated to the education and protection of songwriters. Estab. 1974. Offers group legal discount; toll free hotline; *Songwriters Musepaper* newspaper with songwriter interviews; collaborators network; song evaluation workshops; song screening sessions; open mics; and more. Also produces the highly acclaimed "Acoustic Underground" Showcase, "Writers In The Round," the annual "Songwriter's Expo" (international song-writers event), annual Lifetime Achievement Awards dinner and the annual "Salute to the American Songwriter." "We offer services to all songwriter members from street-level to superstar: song evaluation through the mail, health and dental insurance program and mail-in publisher pitches for members. Our services provide education in the craft and opportunities to market songs." Membership fees: $110 general; $125 professional (written proof of monies earned from songwriting); $200 gold (RIAA certification gold record or single on a gold album). Additional $20 fee for members outside US.

THE NATIONAL ASSOCIATION OF COMPOSERS/USA (NACUSA), P.O. Box 49256, Barring-ton Station, Los Angeles CA 90049. (310)541-8213. President: Marshall Bialosky. Estab. 1932. Serves songwriters, musicians and classical composers. "We are of most value to the concert hall composer. Members are serious music composers of all ages and from all parts of the country, who have a real interest in composing, performing, and listening to modern concert hall music. The main purpose of our organization is to perform, publish, broadcast and write news about composers of serious concert hall music—mostly chamber and solo pieces. Composers may achieve national notice of their work through our newsletter and concerts, and the fairly rare feeling of supporting a non-commercial music enterprise dedicated to raising the musical and social position of the serious composer." Offers competitions, lectures, performance opportunities, library and newsletter. Applications accepted year-round. Membership fee: $20; $40 for Los Angeles and New York chapter members.
Tips: "99% of the money earned in music is earned, or so it seems, by popular songwriters who might feel they owe the art of music something, and this is one way they might help support that art. It's a chance to foster fraternal solidarity with their less prosperous, but wonderfully interesting classical colleagues at a time when the very existence of serious art seems to be questioned by the general populace."

☑ NATIONAL SOCIETY OF MEN AND WOMEN OF THE MUSIC BUSINESS (WOMB), P.O. Box 5170, Beverly Hills CA 90209-5170. (323)464-4300. Fax: (323)467-8468. E-mail: wombaccess@aol.com. Contact: Director. Estab. 1996. "WOMB is a non-profit organization of top music industry profes-sionals keeping music education and dreams alive for kids who attend inner-city high schools and commu-nity organizations around the U.S. Music industry professionals are encouraged to participate and make a difference in a child's life!" Programs include "WOMB's School Music Network": top music industry professionals volunteer 2-3 hours to visit inner-city high schools; "WOMB's Music for Music": organizes music instrument and material donation drives for schools through corporate sponsorships and events; "WOMB's Internship Program": available for students who can gain work experience credit through their school or community organization. Offers corporate sponsorships, events, performance opportunities and an e-mail newsletter. Future programs include afterschool music programs, college scholarships and special events. Volunteers, music instrument, material donations and corporate sponsorships accepted year-round.

NORTH FLORIDA CHRISTIAN MUSIC WRITERS ASSOCIATION, P.O. Box 61113, Jackson-ville FL 32236. (904)786-2372. E-mail: justsongs@aol.com. Website: http://www.geocities.com/Eureka/concourse/5120/NFCMWA.html. President: Jackie Hand. Estab. 1974. "Members are people from all walks of life who promote Christian music—not just composers or performers, but anyone who wants to share today's message in song with the world. No age limit. Anyone interested in promoting Christian music is invited to join. If you are talented in several areas you might be asked to conduct a training session or workshop. Your expertise is wanted and needed by our group. The group's purpose is to serve God by using our God-given talents and abilities and to assist our fellow songwriters, getting their music in the best possible form to be ready for whatever door God chooses to open for them concerning their music. Members' works are included in songbooks published by our organization—also biographies." Offers competitions, performance opportunities, field trips, instruction, newsletter, workshops and critiques. This year we offer a new website featuring song clips by members as well as a short bio. Also featured is a special "Memorial Members" list honoring deceased members by keeping their music alive. The one time fee of $100 to place loved ones on the list includes a song clip on our website and entry privileges in our songwriting contest. Applications accepted year-round. Membership fee: $15/year ($20 for outside US),

MARKETS THAT WERE listed in the 1999 edition of *Songwriter's Market* but do not appear this year are listed in the General Index with a notation explaining why they were omitted.

$20 for husband/wife team ($25 for outside US). Make checks payable to Jackie Hand.

Tips: "If you are serious about your craft, you need fellowship with others who feel the same. A Christian songwriting organization is where you belong if you write Christian songs."

NORTHERN CALIFORNIA SONGWRITERS ASSOCIATION, 1724 Laurel St., Suite 120, San Carlos CA 94070. (650)654-3966. Fax: (650)654-2156, or (800)FORSONG (California and Nashville only). E-mail: info@ncsasong.org. Website: http://www.ncsasong.org. Executive Director: Ian Crombie. Serves songwriters and musicians. Estab. 1979. "Our 1,200 members are lyricists and composers from ages 16-80, from beginners to professional songwriters. No eligibility requirements. Our purpose is to provide the education and opportunities that will support our writers in creating and marketing outstanding songs. NCSA provides support and direction through local networking and input from Los Angeles and Nashville music industry leaders, as well as valuable marketing opportunities. Most songwriters need some form of collaboration, and by being a member they are exposed to other writers, ideas, critiquing, etc." Offers annual Northern California Songwriting Conference, "the largest event in northern California. This 2-day event held in September features 16 seminars, 50 screening sessions (over 1,200 songs listened to by industry profesionals) and a sunset concert with hit songwriters performing their songs." Also offers monthly visits from major publishers, songwriting classes, seminars conducted by hit songwriters ("we sell audio tapes of our seminars—list of tapes available on request"), mail-in song-screening service for members who cannot attend due to time or location, a monthly newsletter, monthly performance opportunities and workshops. Applications accepted year-round. Dues: $40/year, student; $75/year, regular membership; $150/year, pro-membership; $250/year, contributing membership.

Tips: "NCSA's functions draw local talent and nationally recognized names together. This is of a tremendous value to writers outside a major music center. We are developing a strong songwriting community in Northern California. We serve the San Jose, Monterey Bay, East Bay, San Francisco and Sacramento areas and we have the support of some outstanding writers and publishers from both Los Angeles and Nashville. They provide us with invaluable direction and inspiration."

☑ OKLAHOMA SONGWRITERS & COMPOSERS ASSOCIATION, P.O. Box 57043, Oklahoma City OK 73157. 24 hour info line: (405)949-2938. E-mail: arf-n-annie@juno.com. Website: http://www.davelaurence.com/osca. President: Tom Marshall. Treasurer: Ann Wilson. Estab. 1983. Serves songwriters, musicians, professional writers, amateur writers, college and university faculty, musicians, poets and others. "A nonprofit, all-volunteer organization sponsored by Rose State College providing educational and networking opportunities for songwriters, lyricists, composers and performing musicians. All styles of music. Each month we sponsor major workshops, open-mic nights, demo critiques and the *OSCA News*. Throughout the year we sponsor contests and original music showcases." Applications accepted year-round. Membership fee: $25 for new members, $15 for renewal, $15 for out of state newsletter only.

☑ OPERA AMERICA, 1156 15th St., NW, Suite 810, Washington DC 20005-1704. (202)293-4466. Fax: (202)393-0735. E-mail: frontdesk@operaam.org. Website: http://www.operaam.org. Membership Coordinator: Elizabeth Stager. Administrative Assistant: Monica Kibler. Estab. 1970. Members are composers, librettists, musicians and opera/music theater producers. "OPERA America maintains an extensive library of reference books and domestic and foreign music periodicals, and the most comprehensive operatic archive in the United States. OPERA America draws on these unique resources to supply information to its members." Offers conferences. Publishes directories of opera/music theater companies in the US and Canada. Publishes directory of opera and musical performances world-wide and US. Publishes a directory of new works created and being developed by current-day composers and librettists. This publication is sent to all general directors of member companies in order to encourage the performance of new works. Applications accepted year-round. Membership fee is on a sliding scale.

☒ OZARK NOTEWORTHY SONGWRITERS ASSOCIATION, INC., 2303 S. Luster, Springfield MO 65804. (417)883-3385. President: Betty Hickory. Vice President: Mary Hickory. Estab. 1992. Purpose is to help songwriters find co-writers, give them updated tip sheets, keep writers updated about what is selling in the music world and explain the copyright law." Offers instruction, newsletter, workshops and performance opportunities. Applications accepted year-round. Membership fee: $30/year.

Tips: Sponsors showcases second and fourth Tuesday of each month at McSalty's Pizza, Springfield MO.

☒ PACIFIC MUSIC INDUSTRY ASSOCIATION, 400-177 W. Seventh Ave., Vancouver, British Columbia V5Y 1L8 Canada. (604)873-1914. Fax: (604)876-4104. E-mail: ellieo@pmia.org. Website: http://www.pmia.org. Executive Director: Ellie O'Day. Estab. 1990. Serves "mostly young adults and up from semi-pro to professional. Writers, composers, performers, publishers, engineers, producers, broadcasters, studios, retailers, manufacturers, managers, publicists, entertainment lawyers and accountants, etc.

Must work in some area of music industry." The main purpose of this organization is "to promote B.C. music and music industry; stimulate activity in B.C. industry; promote communication and address key issues." Offers competitions, newsletters, monthly managers forum, library and workshops. Applications accepted year-round. Membership fee: $50 Canadian (plus 7% sales tax).
Tips: "We also administer the Pacific Music/Fraser MacPherson Music Scholarship Fund for young B.C. instrumentalists (up to age 25). The fund awards $2,000 bursaries to further their music education."

PACIFIC NORTHWEST SONGWRITERS ASSOCIATION, P.O. Box 98564, Seattle WA 98198. (206)824-1568. "PNSA is a nonprofit organization, serving the songwriters of the Puget Sound area since 1977. Members have had songs recorded by national artists on singles, albums, videos and network television specials. Several have released their own albums and the group has done an album together. For only $35 per year, PNSA offers monthly workshops, a quarterly newsletter and direct contact with national artists, publishers, producers and record companies. New members are welcome and good times are guaranteed. And remember, the world always needs another great song!"

THE PHILADELPHIA SONGWRITERS FORUM, 332 Eastwood Ave., Feasterville PA 19053. Phone/fax: (215)953-0952. E-mail: a1foster@aol.com. Chairman: Allen Foster. Estab. 1986. Membership consists of all ages and levels; an interest in songwriting is the common bond. The main purpose of this organization is to provide support and instruction for songwriters. Offers instruction, newsletter, lectures, workshops and performance opportunities. Applications accepted year-round. Membership fee: $10/year.

PITTSBURGH SONGWRITERS ASSOCIATION, 124 W. Edgewood Dr., McMurray PA 15317-3354. E-mail: psa@trfn.clpgh.org. Website: http://trfn.clpgh.org/psa. President: Deborah J. Berwyn. Estab. 1983. "We are a non-profit organization dedicated to helping its members develop and market their songs. Writers of any age and experience level welcome. Current members are from 20s to 50s. All musical styles and interests are welcome. Our organization wants to serve as a source of quality material for publishers and other industry professionals. We assist members in developing their songs and their professional approach. We provide meetings, showcases, collaboration opportunities, instruction, industry guests, library and social outings. Annual dues: $30. We have no initiation fee. Prospective members are invited to attend two free meetings. Interested parties please call Van Stragand at (412)751-9584."

☑ **PORTLAND SONGWRITERS ASSOCIATION**, P.O. Box 16985, Portland OR 97292-0985. (503)727-9072. E-mail: psa@teleport.com. Website: http://www.teleport.com/~psa/. Estab. 1991. President: Wayne Richards. "The PSA is a nonprofit organization providing education and opportunities that will assist writers in creating and marketing their songs. The PSA offers an annual National Songwriting Contest, monthly workshops, songwriter showcases, special performance venues, monthly newsletter, mail-in critique service, discounted legal services and seminars by music industry pros." Annual dues: $35. Associate memberships: $15 (no eligibility requirements).
Tips: "Although most of our members are from the Pacific Northwest, we offer services that can assist songwriters anywhere. Our goal is to provide information and contacts to help songwriters grow artistically and gain access to publishing, recording and related music markets. For more information, please call or write."

N: RHODE ISLAND SONGWRITERS' ASSOCIATION (RISA), 159, Elmgrove Ave., Providence RI 02906. E-mail: rhodysong@aol.com. Co-Chairs: Deb DoVale and David Fontaine. Founder: Mary Wheelan. Estab. 1993. "Membership consists of novice and professional songwriters. RISA provides opportunities to the aspiring writer or performer as well as the established regional artists who have recordings, are published and perform regularly. The only eligibility requirement is an interest in the group and the group's goals. Non-writers are welcome as well." The main purpose is to "encourage, foster and conduct the art and craft of original musical and/or lyrical composition through education, information, collaboration and performance." Offers instruction, newsletter, lectures, workshops, performance opportunities and evaluation services. Applications accepted year-round. Membership fee: $25/year. "The group holds twice monthly critique sessions; twice monthly performer showcases (one performer featured) at a local coffeehouse; songwriter showcases (usually 6-8 performers); weekly open mikes; and a yearly songwriter festival called 'Hear In Rhode Island,' featuring approximately 50 acts, over two days."

FOR BOOKS ON THE CRAFT AND BUSINESS of songwriting, check out the website for Writer's Digest Books at http://www.writersdigest.com.

SAN DIEGO SONGWRITERS GUILD, 3368 Governor Dr., Suite F-326, San Diego CA 92122. (619)225-2131. E-mail: sdsongwriters@hotmail.com. Website: http://www.sdsongwriters.org. President: Tony Taravella. Vice President: Dave English. Membership/correspondence: Evan Sun Wirt. Estab. 1982. "Members range from their early 20s to senior citizens with a variety of skill levels. Several members perform and work full time in music. Many are published and have songs recorded. Some are getting major artist record cuts. Most members are from San Diego county. New writers are encouraged to participate and meet others. All musical styles are represented." The purpose of this organization is to "serve the needs of songwriters and artists, especially helping them in the business and craft of songwriting through industry guest appearances." Offers competitions, newsletter, workshops, performance opportunities, in-person song pitches and evaluations by publishers, producers and A&R executives. Applications accepted year-round. Membership dues: $45 full; $25 student; $135 corporate sponsorship. Meeting admission for non-members: $20 (may be applied toward membership if joining within 30 days).
Tips: "Members benefit most from participation in meetings and concerts. Generally, one major meeting held monthly on a Monday evening, at the Doubletree Hotel, Hazard Center, San Diego. Call for meeting details. Can join at meetings."

SESAC INC., 421 W. 54th St., New York NY 10019. (212)586-3450; 55 Music Square East, Nashville TN 37203. (615)320-0055. Website: http://sesac.com. President and Chief Operating Officer: Bill Velez. Coordinator-Writer/Publisher Relations: Cindy Brown. Assistant Coordinator: Gwen Davey. SESAC is a selective organization taking pride in having a repertory based on quality rather than quantity. Serves writers and publishers in all types of music who have their works performed by radio, television, nightclubs, cable TV, etc. Purpose of organization is to collect and distribute performance royalties to all active affiliates. As a SESAC affiliate, the individual and the individual's family may obtain group medical and equipment insurance at competitive rates. Tapes are reviewed upon invitation by the Writer/Public Relations dept.

☑ **THE SINGER SONGWRITER INFORMATION LINE**, 9 Music Square S. #145, Nashville TN 37203. Information Hotline: (800)345-2694. Office: (615)792-2222. Fax: (615)792-1509. E-mail: cjstarlit@aol.com. Owner: C.J. Reilly. Estab. 1988. Purpose is to give advice over a free 1-800 number to anyone who writes music. All callers will receive a free publisher's list. Offers instruction, newsletter, performance opportunities and evaluation services.
Tips: "We are a Nashville-based company. When people call, we try to answer questions regarding music publishing and record production."

🌐 **SOCIETY FOR THE PROMOTION OF NEW MUSIC (spnm)**, Francis House, Francis St., London SW1P 1DE United Kingdom. Phone: (+44)171 828 9696. Fax: (+44)171 931 9928. E-mail: spnm@spnm.org.uk. Website: http://www.spnm.org.uk. Executive Director: Gill Graham. Administrator: Katy Bignold. Estab. 1943. "All ages and backgrounds are welcome, with a common interest in the innovative and unexplored. We enable new composers to hear their works performed by top-class professionals in quality venues." Offers newsletter, lectures, workshops, special offers and concerts. Annual selection procedure, deadline July 31. "From contemporary jazz, classical and popular music to that written for film, dance and other creative media, spnm is one of the main advocates of new music in Britain today. Through its eclectic program of concerts, workshops, education projects and collaborations and through its two publications, *new notes* and *Beat Magazine*, spnm brings new music in all guises to many, many people." Other calls for specific events throughout year. Membership fee: Ordinary: £18 sterling, concessions: £5, friend: £30.
Tips: "Most calls for pieces are restricted to those living and/or studying in UK/Ireland, or to British composers living overseas."

Ⓝ **SOCIETY OF COMPOSERS & LYRICISTS**, 400 S. Beverly Dr. #124, Beverly Hills CA 90217. (310)281-2812. Fax: (818)990-0601. E-mail: info@filmscore.org. Website: http://www.filmscore.org. Members are engaged in writing music/lyrics for films or TV, or are students of film composition or songwriting. Purpose is to advance the interests of the film and TV music community. Offers instruction, lectures, and annual conference. Applications accepted year-round. Membership fee: $75 associate member; $125 full member.

📺 **SOCIETY OF COMPOSERS, AUTHORS AND MUSIC PUBLISHERS OF CANADA (SOCAN)**, Head Office: 41 Valleybrook Dr., Don Mills, Ontario M3B 2S6 Canada. Manager, Member Services (Toronto): Lynn Foster. Director, West Coast Office (Vancouver): Kent Sturgeon. Director, Quebec Office (Montreal): France Lafleur. (416)445-8700, (800)55 SOCAN. Fax: (416)445-7108. E-mail: socan.ca. Website: http://www.socan.ca. General Manager: Michael Rock. The purpose of the society is to collect music user license fees and distribute performance royalties to composers, lyricists, authors and music publishers. The SOCAN catalogue is licensed by ASCAP, BMI and SESAC in the US.

  SODRAC INC., 759 Victoria Square, Suite 420, Montreal, Quebec H2Y 2J7 Canada. (514)845-3268. Fax: (514)845-3401. E-mail: sodrac@mlink.net. Website: http://www.sodrac.com. Membership Department: George Vuotto. Estab. 1985. "In Canada, SODRAC represents the musical repertoire of about 60 countries and more than 3,500 Canadian members." Serves those with an interest in songwriting and music publishing no matter what their age or skill level is. "Members must have written or published at least one musical work that has been reproduced on an audio (CD, cassettte, LP) or audio-visual support (TV, video). The main purpose of this organization is to administer the reproduction rights of its members: author/composers and publishers. The new member will benefit of a society working to secure his reproduction rights (mechanicals)." Applications accepted year-round. "There is no membership fee or annual dues. SODRAC retains a commission currently set at 10% for amounts collected in Canada and 5% for amounts collected abroad. SODRAC is the only Reproduction Rights Society in Canada where both songwriters and music publishers are represented, directly and equally."

THE SONGWRITERS ADVOCATE (TSA), 47 Maplehurst Rd., Rochester NY 14617. (716)266-0679. E-mail: jerrycme@aol.com. Director: Jerry Englerth. "TSA is a nonprofit educational organization that is striving to fulfill the needs of the songwriter. We offer opportunities for songwriters which include song evaluation workshops to help songwriters receive an objective critique of their craft. TSA evaluates tapes and lyric sheets via the mail. We do not measure success on a monetary scale, ever. It is the craft of songwriting that is the primary objective. If a songwriter can arm himself with knowledge about the craft and the business, it will increase his confidence and effectiveness in all his dealings. However, we feel that the songwriter should be willing to pay for professional help that will ultimately improve his craft and attitude." One-time membership dues: $15. Must be member to receive discounts or services provided.

 SONGWRITERS & LYRICISTS CLUB, % Robert Makinson, P.O. Box 23304, Brooklyn NY 11202-3304. Director: Robert Makinson. Estab. 1984. Serves songwriters and lyricists. Gives information regarding songwriting: creation of songs, collaboration and reality of market. Only requirement is ability to write lyrics or melodies. Beginners are welcome. The club currently specializes in country songs, gospel songs and novelty songs. The primary benefits of membership for the songwriter are opportunities to collaborate and assistance with creative aspects and marketing of songs through publications and advice. Offers newsletter and assistance with lead sheets and demos. Songwriters & Lyricists Club Newsletter will be mailed semi-annually to members. Other publications, such as "Climbing the Songwriting Ladder" and "Roster of Songs by Members," are mailed to new members upon joining. Applications accepted year-round. Dues: $35/year, remit to Robert Makinson. Write with SASE for more information.

 SONGWRITERS AND POETS CRITIQUE, 2804 Kingston Ave., Grove City OH 43125. E-mail: spcmusic@yahoo.com. Website: http://www.freeyellow.com/members2/spcmusic. Founder/Publicity Director: Ellis Cordle. Treasurer: Pat Adcock. Estab. 1985. Serves songwriters, musicians, poets, lyricists and performers. Meets second and fourth Friday of every month to discuss club events and critique one another's work. Offers seminars and workshops with professionals in the music industry. Has established Nashville contacts. "We critique mail-in submissions from long-distance members. We have over 200 members from the U.S. and Canada. Our goal is to provide support, opportunity and community to anyone interested in creating songs or poetry." Applications are accepted year-round. Write (please include legal size SASE) or e-mail for more information. Annual dues: $25.

  SONGWRITERS ASSOCIATION OF NOVA SCOTIA, P.O. Box 1543, HfX CRO, Halifax, Nova Scotia B3J 2Y3 Canada. (902)465-7174. E-mail: bkershaw@supercity.ns.ca. Website: http://sans.cjb. net. President: Stephen Bordl. Newsletter Coordinator: Becky Kershaw. Estab. 1989. Members are professionals, apprentices and hobbyists, age 18-98. "Must be a songwriter living in Nova Scotia; however, we

**FOR EXPLANATIONS OF THESE SYMBOLS,
SEE THE INSIDE FRONT AND BACK COVERS OF THIS BOOK.**

do accept membership from songwriters who reside in the province part time." Purpose is to create and promote a support base for Nova Scotia songwriters through workshops, song circles, concerts and networking opportunities. Offers newsletter, membership directory, workshops, performance opportunities and evaluation services. Applications accepted year-round. Membership fee: $20.

SONGWRITERS ASSOCIATION OF WASHINGTON, 4200 Wisconsin Ave. NW, Box 100-137, Washington DC 20016. (301)654-8434. E-mail: president@saw.org. Website: http://www.saw.org. President: Eric Eckl. Vice President: Brian Parks. Coordinator: Tuckey Requa. Marketing: Jill Strachan. Estab. 1979. "S.A.W. is a nonprofit organization committed to providing its members with the means to improve their songwriting skills, learn more about the music business and gain exposure in the industry. S.A.W. sponsors various events to achieve this goal, such as workshops, open mics, song swaps, seminars, meetings, member directory with sound bites, showcases and the Mid-Atlantic song contest. S.A.W. publishes *S.A.W. Notes*, a bimonthly newsletter containing information on the music business, upcoming events around the country, tip sheets and provides free classifieds to its members. Joint membership is available with the Washington Area Music Association. For more information regarding membership write or call." Contest information: (800)218-5996.

☑ **THE SONGWRITERS GUILD OF AMERICA (SGA)**, 1500 Harbor Blvd, Weehawken NJ 07087-6732. (201)867-7603. E-mail: songnews@aol.com. Website: http://www.songwriters.org. West Coast: Suite 705, 6430 Sunset Blvd., Hollywood CA 90028, (323)462-1108; Nashville: 1222 16th Ave. S., Nashville TN 37203, (615)329-1782. "The Songwriters Guild of America is the nation's largest, oldest, most respected and most experienced songwriters' association devoted exclusively to providing songwriters with the services, activities and protection they need to succeed in the business of music." President: George David Weiss. Executive Director: Lewis M. Bachman. National Projects Director: George Wurzbach. West Coast Regional Director: Aaron Meza. Southern Regional Director: Rundi Ream. "A full member must be a published songwriter. An associate member is any unpublished songwriter with a desire to learn more about the business and craft of songwriting. The third class of membership comprises estates of deceased writers. The Guild contract is considered to be the best available in the industry, having the greatest number of built-in protections for the songwriter. The Guild's Royalty Collection Plan makes certain that prompt and accurate payments are made to writers. The ongoing Audit Program makes periodic checks of publishers' books. For the self-publisher, the Catalogue Administration Program (CAP) relieves a writer of the paperwork of publishing for a fee lower than the prevailing industry rates. The Copyright Renewal Service informs members a year in advance of a song's renewal date. Other services include workshops in New York and Los Angeles, free Ask-A-Pro sessions with industry pros, critique sessions, collaborator service and newsletters. In addition, the Guild reviews your songwriter contract on request (Guild or otherwise); fights to strengthen songwriters' rights and to increase writers' royalties by supporting legislation which directly affects copyright; offers a group medical and life insurance plan; issues news bulletins with essential information for songwriters; provides a songwriter collaboration service for younger writers; financially evaluates catalogues of copyrights in connection with possible sale and estate planning; operates an estates administration service, and a nonprofit educational foundation (The Songwriters Guild Foundation)."

SONGWRITERS OF OKLAHOMA, P.O. Box 4121, Edmond OK 73083-4121. (405)348-6534. President: Harvey Derrick. Offers information on the music industry: reviews publishing/artist contracts, where and how to get demo tapes produced, presentation of material to publishers or record companies, royalties and copyrights. Also offers information on the craft of songwriting: co-writers, local songwriting organizations, a written critique of lyrics, songs and compositions on tapes as long as a SASE is provided for return of critique. A phone service is available to answer any questions writers, composers or artists may have. "Calls accepted between 10 and 11 pm CST Tuesday through Thursday only." All of these services are provided at no cost; there is no membership fee.

☑ **SONGWRITERS OF WISCONSIN INTERNATIONAL**, P.O. Box 1027, Neenah WI 54957-1027. (920)725-1609. E-mail: sowtoner@aol.com. President: Tony Ansems. Workshop Coordinator: Mike Heath. Estab. 1983. Serves songwriters. "Membership is open to songwriters writing all styles of music. Residency in Wisconsin is recommended but not required. Members are encouraged to bring tapes and lyric sheets of their songs to the meetings, but it is not required. We are striving to improve the craft of

---

MARKETS THAT WERE listed in the 1999 edition of *Songwriter's Market* but do not appear this year are listed in the General Index with a notation explaining why they were omitted.

songwriting in Wisconsin. Living in Wisconsin, a songwriter would be close to any of the workshops and showcases offered each month at different towns. The primary value of membership for a songwriter is in sharing ideas with other songwriters, being critiqued and helping other songwriters." Offers competitions, field trips, instruction, lectures, newsletter, performance opportunities, social outings, workshops and critique sessions. Applications accepted year-round. Membership dues: $20/year.
Tips: "Songwriters of Wisconsin now offers three critique meetings each month. For information call: Fox Valley chapter, Mike Heath (920)722-0122; Milwaukee chapter, Joe Warren (414)475-0314; La Crosse chapter, Jeff Cozy (608)784-4332."

SONGWRITERS RESOURCE NETWORK, 6327-C SW Capitol Hill #135, Portland OR 97201-1937. (503)515-9025. E-mail: info@songpro.com. Website: http://www.songpro.com. Executive Director: Steve Cahill. Estab. 1998. Members are songwriters and lyricists of every kind, from beginners to advanced. No eligibility requirements. Purpose is to help songwriters develop their craft and market their songs and to provide education and helpful information. Offers competitions, marketing tips and access to the music industry through website. "We provide leads to publishers, producers and other music industry professionals." Applications accepted year-round. Send SASE for more information.

SOUTHEAST TEXAS BLUEGRASS MUSIC ASSOCIATION, 7110 Lewis Dr., Beaumont TX 77708-1017. (409)892-5767. Editor: Edy Mathews. Estab. 1976. Members are musicians and listeners of all ages. Purpose is to promote bluegrass, gospel and old time music. Offers newsletter and monthly shows which are free. Applications accepted year-round. Membership fee: $10/year.

[N] SOUTHWEST CELTIC MUSIC ASSOCIATION, 4340 N. Central Expressway, Suite E104, Dallas TX 75206-6550. (214)821-4173. Fax: (214)824-1009. Website: http://www.cyberramp.net/~scma. President: Betsy Ener. Estab. 1983. Persons interested in promotion and preservation of Celtic music. Musicians and Celtic music lovers are members (not necessary to be a musician to join). No eligibility requirements, although membership is primarily in Texas and surrounding states. Purpose is to promote, preserve and provide education about Celtic music, dance and culture in Texas and the Southwest region of the US. Offers instruction, newsletter, lectures, workshops, performance opportunities and sponsorships and scholarships. Applications accepted year-round. Membership fee: $12/single; $15/family; $25/organization; $50/sponsor; $300/lifetime member.
Tips: "We are the producers of the second largest Irish Festival in the U.S."

THE TENNESSEE SONGWRITERS INTERNATIONAL, P.O. Box 2664, Hendersonville TN 37077-2664. TSA Hotline: (615)969-5967. (615)824-4555. Fax: (615)822-2048. E-mail: asktsai@aol.com Website: http://www.clubnashville.com/tsai.htm. Executive Director: Jim Sylvis. Serves songwriters. "Our membership is open to all ages and consists of both novice and experienced professional songwriters. The only requirement for membership is a serious interest in the craft and business of songwriting. Our main purpose and function is to educate and assist the songwriter, both in the art/craft of songwriting and in the business of songwriting. In addition to education, we also provide an opportunity for camaraderie, support and encouragement, as well a chance to meet co-writers. We also critique each others' material and offer suggestions for improvement, if needed. We offer the following to our members: Informative monthly newsletters; 'Pro-Rap'—once a month a key person from the music industry addresses our membership on their field of specialty. They may be writers, publishers, producers and sometimes even the recording artists themselves; 'Pitch-A-Pro'—we schedule a publisher, producer or artist who is currently looking for material to come to our meeting and listen to songs pitched by our members; Annual Awards Dinner—honoring the most accomplished of our TSAI membership during the past year; Tips—letting our members know who is recording and how to get their songs to the right people. Other activities—a TSAI summer picnic, parties throughout the year, and opportunities to participate in music industry-related charitable events." Applications accepted year-round. Membership runs for one year from the date you join. Membership fee is $45/year.

[N] TEXAS ACCOUNTANTS & LAWYERS FOR THE ARTS, 1540 Sul Ross, Houston TX 77006-4730. (713)526-4876. Fax: (713)526-1299. E-mail: info@talarts.org. Executive Director: Jane S. Lowery. Estab. 1979. TALA's members include accountants, attorneys, museums, theatre groups, dance groups, actors, artists, musicians and filmmakers. Our members are of all age groups and represent all facets of their respective fields. TALA is a nonprofit organization that provides pro bono legal and accounting services to income-eligible artists from all disciplines and to nonprofit arts organizations. TALA also provides mediation services for resolving disputes as a low cost-nonadversarial alternative to litigation. Offers newsletter, lectures, library and workshops. Applications accepted year-round. Membership fee: $25.

Tips: TALA's speakers program presents low-cost seminars on topics such as The Music Business, Copyright and Trademark, and The Business of Writing. These seminars are held annually at a location in Houston. TALA's speaker's program also provides speakers for seminars by other organizations.

TEXAS MUSIC OFFICE, P.O. Box 13246, Austin TX 78711. (512)463-6666. (512)463-4114. E-mail: music@governor.state.tx.us. Website: http://www.governor.state.tx.us/music. Director: Casey Monahan. Estab. 1990. "The main purpose of the Texas Music Office is to promote the Texas music industry and Texas music, and to assist music professionals around the world with information about the Texas market. The Texas Music Office serves as a clearinghouse for Texas music industry information using their seven databases: Texas Music Industry (5,800 Texas music businesses in 94 music business categories); Texas Music Events (700 Texas music events); Texas Talent Register (900 Texas recording artists); Texas Radio Stations (733 Texas stations); U.S. Record Labels; Classical Texas (detailed information for all classical music organizations in Texas); and International (450 foreign businesses interested in Texas music). Provides referrals to Texas music businesses, talent and events in order to attract new business to Texas and/ or to encourage Texas businesses and individuals to keep music business in-state. Serves as a liaison between music businesses and other government offices and agencies. Publicizes significant developments within the Texas music industry." Publishes the *Texas Music Industry Directory* (see the Publications of Interest section for more information).

N TEXAS SONGWRITERS ASSOCIATION, Rt. 1, Box 160AA, Pickton TX 75471. (903)866-3002. President: Kay Mayfield. Estab. 1986. "Writing songs and learning how to improve on writing skills is the main reason people join T.S.A. Some members have written songs for many years, whereas, some have only written a few. Age varies from teenage to senior citizens. Purpose is to educate the songwriter to become better writers; to know the business of songwriting; and to learn how to properly pitch their songs. Offers instruction, lectures, library, workshops, performance opportunities and evaluation services. Applications accepted year-round. Membership fee: $25/year.
Tips: "We encourage those who join TSA to take seriously their gift of songwriting. We also believe that TSA is a valuable asset to our community as well as to each writer. We recognize and respect all forms of music and promote each other as fellow members."

✓ TREASURE COAST SONGWRITERS ASSN. (TCSA), P.O. Box 7382, Port St. Lucie FL 34985-7382. E-mail: gpboley@aol.com. Director: George Boley. Founder/Advisor: Judy Welden. Estab. 1993. A service organization for and about songwriters. Age range of members, 15-80; varying levels of ability, from beginning writer to professional writers with substantial catalogs, publishing track records, radio airplay and releases. Offers competitions, lectures, performance opportunities, evaluation services, instruction, newsletter and workshops. Applications accepted year-round. Send SASE. Membership fee: $25.

✓ VICTORY MUSIC, P.O. Box 2254, Tacoma WA 98401. (253)428-0832. E-mail: victory@nwlink.com. Website: http://www.victory.org. Director: Patrice O'Neill. Estab. 1969. All-volunteer organization serves songwriters, audiences and local acoustic musicians of all music styles. Victory Music provides places to play, showcases, opportunities to read about the business and other songwriters, referrals and seminars. Produced 6 albums of NW songwriters. Offers library, magazine, newsletter, performance opportunities, business workshops, music business books and a musician referral service. Applications accepted year-round. Membership fee: $30/year single; $80/year business; $40/family; $250 lifetime.

✓ VOLUNTEER LAWYERS FOR THE ARTS, 1 E. 53rd St., 6th Floor, New York NY 10022. (212)319-ARTS (2787) (Monday-Friday 9:30-12 and 1-4 EST). E-mail: vlany@bway.net. Director of Membership: Marguerite Day. Estab. 1969. Serves songwriters, musicians and all performing, visual, literary and fine arts artists and groups. Offers legal assistance and representation to eligible individual artists and arts organizations who cannot afford private counsel and a mediation service. VLA sells publications on arts-related issues and offers educational conferences, lectures, seminars and workshops. In addition, there are affiliates nationwide who assist local arts organizations and artists. Call for information.
Tips: "VLA now offers a monthly copyright seminar, 'Copyright Basics,' for songwriters and musicians as well as artists in other creative fields."

REFER TO THE GEOGRAPHIC INDEX (at the back of this book) to find listings of companies by state, as well as foreign listings.

☑ **WOMEN IN MUSIC**, P.O. Box 441, Radio City Station, New York NY 10101. (212)459-4580. Website: http://www.womeninmusic.org. President: Gina Andriolo. Executive Director: Karen Laupiasi. Estab. 1985. Members are professionals in the business and creative areas: record company executives, managers, songwriters, musicians, vocalists, attorneys, recording engineers, agents, publicists, studio owners, music publishers and more. Purpose is to support, encourage and educate as well as provide networking opportunities. Offers newsletter, lectures, workshops, performance opportunities and business discounts. Presents annual "Touchstone Award" luncheon helping to raise money to support other organizations and individuals through WIM donations and scholarships. Applications accepted year-round. Membership fee: Professional $75; Associate $45; Student $25.

Workshops & Conferences

For a songwriter just starting out, conferences and workshops can provide valuable learning opportunities. At conferences, songwriters can have their songs evaluated, hear suggestions for further improvement and receive feedback from music business experts. They are also excellent places to make valuable industry contacts. Workshops can help a songwriter improve his craft and learn more about the business of songwriting. They may involve classes on songwriting and the business, as well as lectures and seminars by industry professionals.

Get the Most From a Conference

Before You Go:
- **Save money.** Sign up early for a conference and take advantage of the early registration fee. Don't put off making hotel reservations either—the conference will usually have a block of rooms reserved at a discounted price.
- **Become familiar with all the pre-conference literature.** Study the maps of the area, especially the locations of the rooms in which your meetings/events are scheduled.
- **Make a list of three to five objectives you'd like to obtain**, e.g., what you want to learn more about, what you want to improve on, how many new contacts you want to make.

At the Conference:
- **Budget your time.** Label a map so you know where, when and how to get to each session. Note what you want to do most. Then, schedule time for demo critiques if they are offered.
- **Don't be afraid to explore new areas.** You are there to learn. Pick one or two sessions you wouldn't typically attend. Keep your mind open to new ideas and advice.
- **Allow time for mingling.** Some of the best information is given after the sessions. Find out "frank truths" and inside scoops. Asking people what they've learned at the conference will trigger a conversation that may branch into areas you want to know more about, but won't hear from the speakers.
- **Attend panels.** Panels consist of a group of industry professionals who have the capability to further your career. If you're new to the business you can learn so much straight from the horse's mouth. Even if you're a veteran, you can brush up on your knowledge or even learn something new. Whatever your experience, the panelist's presence is an open invitation to approach him with a question during the panel or with a handshake afterwards.
- **Collect everything**: especially informational materials and business cards. Make notes about the personalities of the people you meet to later remind you who to contact and who to avoid.

After the Conference:
- **Evaluate.** Write down the answers to these questions: Would I attend again? What were the pluses and minuses, e.g., speakers, location, food, topics, cost, lodging? What do I want to remember for next year? What should I try to do next time? Who would I like to meet?
- **Write a thank-you letter** to someone who has been particularly helpful. They'll remember you when you later solicit a submission.

Each year, hundreds of workshops and conferences take place all over the country. Songwriters can choose from small regional workshops held in someone's living room to large national conferences such as South by Southwest in Austin, Texas, which hosts more than 6,000 industry people, songwriters and performers. Many songwriting organizations—national and local—host workshops that offer instruction on just about every songwriting topic imaginable, from lyric writing and marketing strategy to contract negotiation. Conferences provide songwriters the chance to meet one on one with publishing and record company professionals and give performers the chance to showcase their work for a live audience (usually consisting of industry people) during the conference. There are conferences and workshops that address almost every type of music, offering programs for songwriters, performers, musical playwrights and much more.

This section includes national and local workshops and conferences with a brief description of what they offer, when they are held and how much they cost to attend. Write or call any that interest you for further information. To find out what workshops or conferences take place in specific parts of the country, see the Geographic Index at the end of this book.

✅ **APPEL FARM ARTS AND MUSIC FESTIVAL**, P.O. Box 888, Elmer NJ 08318. (609)358-2472. E-mail: appelarts@aol.com. Website: http://www.rowan.edu/appel. Artistic Director: Sean Timmons. Estab. Festival: 1989; Series: 1970. "Our annual open air festival is the highlight of our year-round Performing Arts Series which was established to bring high quality arts programs to the people of South Jersey. Festival includes acoustic and folk music, blues, etc." Past performers have included Indigo Girls, John Prine, Ani DiFranco, Randy Newman, Nanci Griffith, Shawn Colvin, Arlo Guthrie and Madeleine Peyroux. In addition, our Country Music concerts have featured Toby Keith, Joe Diffie, Ricky Van Shelton, Doug Stone and others. Programs for songwriters and musicians include performance opportunities as part of Festival and Performing Arts Series. Programs for musical playwrights also include performance opportunities as part of Performing Arts Series. Festival is a one-day event held in June, and Performing Arts Series is held year-round. Both are held at the Appel Farm Arts and Music Center, a 176-acre farm in Southern New Jersey. Up to 20 songwriters/musicians participate in each event. Participants are songwriters, individual vocalists, bands, ensembles, vocal groups, composers, individual instrumentalists and dance/mime/movement. Participants are selected by demo tape submissions. Applicants should send a press packet, demonstration tape and biographical information. Application materials accepted year round. Faculty opportunities are available as part of residential Summer Arts Program for children, July/August.

ARCADY MUSIC FESTIVAL, P.O. Box 780, Bar Harbor ME 04609. (207)288-3151. E-mail: mwilson@ acadia.net. Website: http://www.acadia.net/arcadymusic. Executive Director: Dr. Melba Wilson. Artistic Director: Masanobu Ikemiya. Estab. 1980. Promotes classical chamber music, chamber orchestra concerts, master classes and a youth competition in Maine. Offers programs for performers. Workshops take place year-round in several towns in Eastern Maine. 30-50 professional, individual instrumentalists participate each year. Performers selected by invitation. Fee: $15. "Sometimes we premiere new music by songwriters but usually at request of visiting musician."

ASCAP MUSICAL THEATRE WORKSHOP, 1 Lincoln Plaza, New York NY 10023. (212)621-6234. Fax: (212)724-9064. Website: http://www.ascap.com. Director of Musical Theatre: Michael A. Kerker. Estab. 1981. Workshop is for musical theatre composers and lyricists only. Its purpose is to nurture and develop new musicals for the theatre. Offers programs for songwriters. Offers programs annually, usually April through May. Event took place in New York City. Six musical works are selected. Others are invited to audit the workshop. Participants are amateur and professional songwriters, composers and musical playwrights. Participants are selected by demo tape submission. Send for application. Deadline: mid-March.

ASCAP WEST COAST/LESTER SILL SONGWRITER'S WORKSHOP, 7920 Sunset Blvd., 3rd Floor, Los Angeles CA 90046. (213)883-1000. Fax: (213)883-1048. E-mail: rgrimmett@ascap.com. Website: http://www.ascap.com. Director of Repertory: Randy Grimmett. Estab. 1963. Offers programs for songwriters. Offers programs annually. Event takes place mid-January through mid-February. 14 songwriters/musicians participate in each event. Participants are amateur and professional songwriters. Participants are selected by demo tape submission or by invitation. "Send in two songs with lyrics, bio and brief explanation why you'd like to participate." Deadline: November 30.

ASPEN MUSIC FESTIVAL AND SCHOOL, 2 Music School Rd., Aspen CO 81611. (970)925-3254. Fax: (970)925-3802. E-mail: school@aspenmusic.org. Website: http://www.aspen.com/musicfestival. Associate Artistic Administrator: Jeremy Geffen. Estab. 1949. Promotes classical music by offering programs for composers, including an advanced master class in composition which meets weekly during the nine-week season. Offers several other music programs as well. School and Festival run June 16 to August 22 in Aspen CO. Participants are amateur and professional composers, individual instrumentalists and ensembles. Send for application. Deadline: February 22. Charges $2,150 for full 9 weeks, $1,425 for one of two 4½ week sessions. Fee: $80 until February 5, $100 February 5-22. Scholarship assistance is available.

N. BLUESTOCK INTERNATIONAL MUSIC CONVENTION AND FESTIVAL, P.O. Box 41858, Memphis TN 38174-1858. (901)526-4280. Fax: (901)766-0976. E-mail: info@bluestock.org. Website: http://www.bluestock.org. Office Manager: Adrienn Mendonca. Estab. 1997. Bluestock's main purpose is to showcase unsigned music talent (blues, soul, blues-based rock, R&B, gospel, etc.) to a host of industry executives and luminaries. Offers programs for songwriters and performers. Offers programs annually. Event takes place in historic downtown Memphis on Beale Street in autumn. "In addition to showcasing over 100 acts, Bluestock offers educational panels, industry workshops and clinics, heritage and cultural arts, and plenty of networking opportunities." Participants are amateur and professional songwriters, vocalists, insturmentalists and bands. Call for dates and application information.

✓ BMI-LEHMAN ENGEL MUSICAL THEATRE WORKSHOP, 320 W. 57th St., New York NY 10019. (212)830-2508. Website: http://Jbanks.com. Director of Musical Theatre: Jean Banks. Estab. 1961. "BMI is a music licensing company which collects royalties for affiliated writers. We have departments to help writers in jazz, concert, Latin, pop and musical theater writing." Offers programs "to musical theater composers and lyricists. The BMI-Lehman Engel Musical Theatre Workshops were formed in an effort to refresh and stimulate professional writers, as well as to encourage and develop new creative talent for the musical theater." Each workshop meets 1 afternoon a week for 2 hours at BMI, New York. Participants are professional songwriters, composers and playwrights. "BMI-Lehman Engel Musical Theatre Workshop Showcase presents the best of the workshop to producers, agents, record and publishing company execs, press and directors for possible option and production." Call for application. Tape and lyrics of 3 compositions required with application. "BMI also sponsors a jazz composers workshop. For more information call Burt Korall at (212)586-2000."

BROADWAY TOMORROW PREVIEWS, % Science of Light, Inc., 191 Claremont Ave., Suite 53, New York NY 10027. E-mail: solight@worldnet.att.net. Website: http://home.att.net/~solight. Artistic Director: Elyse Curtis. Estab. 1983. Purpose is the enrichment of American theater by nurturing new musicals. Offers series in which composers living in New York city area present scores of their new musicals in concert on New Age or transpersonal themes only. 2-3 composers/librettists/lyricists of same musical and 1 musical director/pianist participate. Participants are professional singers, composers and opera/musical theater writers. Submission is by audio cassette of music, synopsis, cast breakdown, résumé, reviews, if any, acknowledgement postcard and SASE. Participants selected by screening of submissions. Programs are presented in fall and spring with possibility of full production of works presented in concert. Membership fee: $50.

CMJ MUSIC MARATHON®, MUSICFEST & FILMFEST, 11 Middle Neck Rd., Suite 400, Great Neck NY 11021-2301. (516)498-3150. Fax: (516)466-7161. E-mail: marathon@cmj.com. Website: http://www.cmj.com/marathon. Convention Coordinator: Kevin McCullough. Estab. 1981. Premier annual alternative music gathering of more than 7,000 performers and music business and film professionals. Fall, NYC. Features 4 days and nights of more than 50 panels and workshops focusing on every facet of the industry; exclusive film screenings; keynote speeches by the world's most intriguing and controversial voices; exhibition area featuring live performance stage; over 1,000 of music's brightest and most visionary talents (from the unsigned to the legendary) performing over 4 evenings at more than 60 of NYC's most important music venues. Participants are selected by submitting demonstration tape. Send for application.

N. COUNTRY MUSIC EXPO & SHOWCASE, 24 Music Square W., Nashville TN 37203. (615)256-4263. Fax: (615)259-0199. Website: http://www.allycatmusic.com/showcase. Assistant to Vice President: Sheri Malloy. Estab. 1994. Conference of country and Christian music. Offers programs for songwriters

REFER TO THE GEOGRAPHIC INDEX (at the back of this book) to find listings of companies by state, as well as foreign listings.

and performers. Offers programs annually. Event takes place September 3-6 at Opryland Hotel in Nashville. 600 songwriters/musicians participate in each event. Participants are amateur and professional songwriters, vocalists and bands. Anyone can participate. Send or call for application. Deadline: September 1. Fee: $300. "Each attendee has an opportunity to showcase in front of publishers or record company A&R."

N̄ CUTTING EDGE MUSIC BUSINESS CONFERENCE, 1524 N. Claiborne Ave., New Orleans LA 70119. (504)945-1800. Fax: (504)945-1873. E-mail: cut_edge@bellsouth.net. Website: http://www.ikoi ko.com/cuttingedge/. Executive Producer: Eric L. Cager. Showcase Producer: Nathaniel Franklin. Estab. 1993. "The conference is a five-day international conference which covers the business and educational aspects of the music industry. As part of the conference, the New Works showcase features over 200 bands and artists from around the country and Canada in showcases of original music. All music genres are represented." Offers programs for songwriters and performers. "Bands and artists should submit material for consideration of entry into the New Works showcase." Event takes place late August in New Orleans. 1,000 songwriters/musicians participate in each event. Participants are songwriters, vocalists and bands. Send for application. Deadline: June 1. Fee: $175 general registration; $25 showcase registration. "The Music Business Institute offers a month-long series of free educational workshops for those involved in the music industry. The workshops take place each October."

PETER DAVIDSON'S WRITER'S SEMINAR, P.O. Box 497, Arnolds Park IA 51331. Seminar Presenter: Peter Davidson. Estab. 1985. "Peter Davidson's Writer's Seminar is for persons interested in writing all sorts of materials, including songs. Emphasis is placed on developing salable ideas, locating potential markets for your work, copyrighting, etc. The seminar is not specifically for writers of songs, but is very valuable to them, nevertheless." Offers programs year-round. One-day seminar, 9:00 a.m.-4:00 p.m. Event takes place on various college campuses. In even-numbered years offers seminars in Minnesota, Iowa, Nebraska, South Dakota, Kansas, Colorado and Wyoming. In odd-numbered years offers seminars in Minnesota, Iowa, South Dakota, Nebraska, Missouri, Illinois, Arkansas and Tennessee. Anyone can participate. Send SASE for schedule. Deadline: day of the seminar. Fee: $40-59. "All seminars are held on college campuses in college facilities—various colleges sponsor and promote the seminars."

EMERGING ARTISTS & TALENT IN MUSIC (EAT'M) CONFERENCE AND FESTIVAL, 2030 E. Flamingo Rd. #110, Las Vegas NV 89119. (702)792-9430. Fax: (702)792-5748. E-mail: ltenner@aol.c om. Website: http://EAT-M.com. Co-director: Sue Shifrin-Cassidy. Director: Lisa Tenner. Estab. 1998. A music conference which addresses both recording and touring. Offers programs for songwriters and performers. Offers 3 days of educational panels, mentor sessions, continuing legal education, also the David Cassidy Celebrity Golf Tournament benefitting Special Olympics, and the Rock & Roll Demolition Derby. Event took place May 19-22 (1999) at The Desert Inn in Las Vegas. 2,000-3,000 songwriters/musicians participate in each event. Participants are amateur and professional songwriters, vocalists, composers, bands and instrumentalists. Participants are selected by demo tape submission. Send for application. Deadline: February 28. Fee: $50. Artists will appear on 10 stages in and around the Las Vegas Strip.

FOLK ALLIANCE ANNUAL CONFERENCE, 1001 Connecticut Ave. NW, Suite 501, Washington DC 20036. (202)835-3655. Fax: (202)835-3656. E-mail: fa@folk.org. Website: http://www.folk.org. Estab. 1989. Conference/workshop topics change each year. Conference takes place mid-February and lasts 4 days at a different location each year. 1,500 attendees include artists, agents, arts administrators, print/ broadcast media, folklorists, folk societies, merchandisers, presenters, festivals, recording companies, fans, etc. Artists wishing to showcase should contact the office for a showcase application form. Closing date for application is June 1. Application fee is $35 for members, $75 for nonmembers. Charges $200 on acceptance. Additional costs vary from year to year. Housing is separate for the event, scheduled for Feb. 9-13, 2000 in Cleveland, OH and Feb. 15-18, 2001 in Vancouver, B.C., Canada.

KERRVILLE FOLK FESTIVAL, Kerrville Festivals, Inc., P.O. Box 1466, Kerrville TX 78029. (830)257-3600. E-mail: festivals@kerrville-music.com. Website: http://www.kerrville-music.com. Executive Director: Rod Kennedy. Estab. 1972. Hosts 3-day songwriters' school, a 3-day advanced songwriters school, a booking and management seminar and New Folk concert competition sponsored by the Kerrville Music Foundation. Programs held in late spring and late summer. Spring festival lasts 18 days and is held outdoors at Quiet Valley Ranch. Around 120 artists participate. Performers are professional songwriters and bands. Participants selected by submitting demo, by invitation only. Send cassette, or CD, promotional material and list of upcoming appearances. "Songwriter schools include lunch, experienced professional instructors, camping on ranch and concerts. Rustic facilities—no electrical hookups. Food available at reasonable cost. Audition materials accepted at above address. Added is a booking and management seminar to teach newcomers and bring additional insight to established agents and managers. These three-day seminars include noon meals, handouts and camping on the ranch. Usually held during Kerrville Folk Festival, first week in June. Write for contest rules, schools and seminars information, and festival schedules. Also establishing a Phoenix Fund to provide assistance to ill or injured singer/songwriters who find themselves in distress."

N LAMB'S RETREAT FOR SONGWRITERS, P.O. Box 304, Royal Oak MI 48068-0304. (800)530-9955. E-mail: jdlamb@jdlamb.com. Website: http://www.jdlamb.com. Director: John D. Lamb. Estab. 1995. Offers programs for songwriters. Offers programs annually. Event takes place first weekend in November (Thursday-Sunday) at The Birchwood Inn, Harbor Springs, MI. 60 songwriters/musicians participate in each event. Participants are amateur and professional songwriters. Anyone can participate. Send for application or e-mail. Deadline: day before event begins. Fee: $140-265, includes all meals; price varies according to lodging arrangements. Facilities are single/double occupancy lodging with private baths; 2 conference rooms and hospitality lodge. Offers song assignments, 10 hours of songwriting workshops, song swaps, open mike and one-on-one mentoring. Faculty are noted performing songwriters, such as Michael Smith. Partial scholarships may be available by writing: Blissfest Music Organization, % Jim Gillespie, P.O. Box 441, Harbor Springs, MI 49740; deadline is first Tuesday in October.

N LMNOP (Louisiana Music—New Orleans' Pride), P.O. Box 3469, New Orleans LA 70177-3469. (504)592-9800. Fax: (504)592-9809. E-mail: lmnopinfo@aol.com. Website: http://www.offbeat.com/lmnop. Executive Director: Louis Jay Meyers. LMNOP focuses on regional and independent music. Features a showcase, networking and marketing opportunities, and panel discussions. Offers programs for songwriters, composers and performers. Offers programs annually. Event takes place in April at Le Meridien Hotel in New Orleans. Participants are amateur and professional songwriters, composers, vocalists, bands and instrumentalists. Send for application or obtain via website. Fee: $60-100.

MANCHESTER MUSIC FESTIVAL, P.O. Box 1165, Manchester Center UT 05255. (802)362-1956. Fax: (802)362-0711. E-mail: mmf@vermontel.com. Website: http://www.utweb.com/mmf. Business Manager: Michele Sargent. Estab. 1974. School for young professional instrumentalists with a concert series of mainly chamber music. Offers programs for composers and performers and commissions some new music. Offers programs year-round at area schools and concerts in New York City. Event is held at various venues in Manchester. 50 songwriters/musicians participate in each event. Participants are professional vocalists, composers and instrumentalists. Participants are selected by audition in person, demo tape submission or by invitation. Auditions are held at various locations on the east and west coasts. Send for application. Deadline: April 1. Fee: $40. Housing is rented by the festival (several concert halls, churches). "This is a full scholarship program."

✓ MUSIC BUSINESS SOLUTIONS/CAREER BUILDING WORKSHOPS, P.O. Box 266, Boston MA 02123-0266. (781)639-1971. E-mail: success@mbsolutions.com. Website: http://www.mbsolutions.com. Director: Peter Spellman. Estab. 1991. Workshop titles include "How to Succeed in Music Without Overpaying Your Dues," "How to Release an Independent Record" and "Promoting and Marketing Music Toward the Year 2000." Offers programs for music entrepreneurs, songwriters, musical playwrights, composers and performers. Offers programs year-round, annually and bi-annually. Event takes place at various colleges, recording studios, hotels, conferences. 10-100 songwriters/musicians participate in each event. Participants are both amateur and professional songwriters, vocalists, music business professionals, composers, bands, musical playwrights and instrumentalists. Anyone can participate. Call or write (regular or e-mail) for application. Fee: $50-125. "Music Business Solutions offers a number of other services and programs for both songwriters and musicians including: private music career counseling, business plan development and internet marketing; publication of *Music Biz Insight: Power Reading for Busy Music Professionals*, a bimonthly infoletter chock full of music management and marketing tips and resources."

MUSICAL THEATRE WORKS, INC., 440 Lafayette St., New York NY 10003. (212)677-0040. Artistic Director: Lonny Price. Executive Director: Jacqueline Anne Siegel. Estab. 1983. "We develop and present new works for the musical theater: informal readings, staged readings and workshops of new musicals." Functions year-round. Participants are emerging and established composers and songwriters and opera/

MARKETS THAT WERE listed in the 1999 edition of *Songwriter's Market* but do not appear this year are listed in the General Index with a notation explaining why they were omitted.

musical theater writers. Participants are selected through a critique/evaluation of each musical by the Literary Manager and his staff. Call or write for submission guidelines.

NATIONAL ACADEMY OF POPULAR MUSIC SONGWRITING WORKSHOP PROGRAM, 330 W. 58th St. Suite 411, New York NY 10019. (212)957-9230. Fax: (212)957-9227. E-mail: 73751.1142 @compuserve.com. Website: http://www.songwritershalloffame.org. Projects Director: Bob Leone. Managing Director: April Anderson. Estab. 1969. "For all forms of pop music, from rock to R&B to dance." Offers programs for member lyricists and composers including songwriting workshops (beginning to master levels) and songwriters showcases. "The Abe Olman Scholarship for excellence in songwriting is awarded ($1,200) to a student who has been in our program for at least 4 quarters." Offers programs 3 times/year: fall, winter and spring. Event takes place mid-September to December, mid-January to April, mid-April to July (10 2-hour weekly sessions) at New York Spaces, 131 W. 72nd St., New York. 50 students involved in 4 different classes. Participants are amateur and professional lyricists and composers. Some participants are selected by submitting demonstration tape (pro-song class), and by invitation (master class). Send for application. Deadline: first week of classes. Annual dues: $25. Sponsors songwriter showcases in March, June, September and December.

N: NEMO MUSIC SHOWCASE & CONFERENCE, Zero Governors Ave. #6, Boston MA 02155. (781)306-0441. Fax: (781)306-0442. E-mail: cavery@ultranet.com. Website: http://www.nemo99.com. Founder/Director: Candace Avery. Estab. 1996. Music showcase and conference, featuring the Kahlua Boston Music Awards and 3 days/nights of a conference with trade show and more than 200 nightly showcases in Boston. Offers programs for songwriters. Offers music awards show with over 40 categories with many for singer/songwriters. Offers programs annually. Event takes place in April. 1,500 songwriters/ musicians participate at conference; 3,000 at awards show; 20,000 at showcases. Participants are professional songwriters, vocalists, composers, bands and instrumentalists. Participants are selected by invitation. Send for application or visit website. Fee: $20.

THE NEW HARMONY PROJECT, 613 N. East St., Indianapolis IN 46202. (317)464-9405. Fax: (317)635-4201. Artistic Director: James Houghton. Estab. 1986. Selected scripts receive various levels of development with rehearsals and readings, both public and private. "Our mission is to nurture writers and their life-affirming scripts. This includes plays, screenplays, musicals and TV scripts." Offers programs for musical playwrights. Offers programs year-round. Event takes place in southwest Indiana. Participants are amateur and professional writers and media professionals. Send for application.

NEW MUSIC WEST, P.O. Box 308, Delta, British Columbia V4K 343 Canada. (604)684-9338. Fax: (604)684-9337. E-mail: info@newmusicwest.com. Website: http://www.newmusicwest.com/. Producer: John Donnelly. Associate Producer: Barbara Ivor. Estab. 1990. A four day music festival and conference held May each year in Vancouver, B.C. The conference offers songwriter intensive workshops; demo critique sessions with A&R and publishers; information on the business of publishing; master producer workshops: "We invite established hit record producers to conduct 3 hour intensive hands-on workshops with 30 young producers/musicians in studio environments." The festival offers songwriters in the round and 250 original music showcases. Largest music industry event in the North Pacific Rim. $150 for 3 day passes; fee varies depending on conference/festival options preference.

N: NEW YORK MUSIC AND INTERNET EXPO, (212)592-4095. E-mail: hal@hbpr.com. Website: http://www.nyrock.com/expo. Press Contact: Hal Bringman. Purpose is to bring new music and new media together. Focuses on promotional productivity for the music industry as well as securing customer loyalty to existing music industry websites. Offers programs for songwriters, composers and performers. Annual event held in March at the New Yorker Hotel in New York City. Participants are amateur and professional songwriters, composers, vocalists and bands. Entry fee: $12-15.

N: NORFOLK CHAMBER MUSIC FESTIVAL, September-May address: 435 College St., Box 208246, New Haven CT 06520. (203)432-1966. Fax: (203)432-2136. June-August address: Ellen Battell, Stoeckel Estate, Box 545, Norfolk CT 06058. (860)542-3000. Fax: (860)542-3004. E-mail: norfolk@yale.e du. Website: http://www.yale.edu/norfolk. Festival Manager: Elaine C. Carroll. Estab. 1941. Festival of seniors chamber music. Offers programs for composers and performers. Offers programs summer only. Approximately 70 fellows participate in each event. Participants are professional vocalists, composers and instrumentalists. Participants are selected by audition in person or demo tape submission. Auditions are held in New York and New Haven, CT. Send for application. Deadline: February 15. Fee: $35. Situated on the elegant Ellen Battell Stoeckel Estate, the Festival offers a magnificent Music Shed with seating for

1,000, practice facilities, music library, dining hall, laundry and art gallery. Nearby are hiking, bicycling and swimming.

✂ NORTH BY NORTHEAST MUSIC FESTIVAL AND CONFERENCE (NXNE), 185A Danforth Ave., 2nd Floor, Toronto, Ontario M4K 1N2 Canada. (416)469-0986. Fax: (416)469-0576. E-mail: inquire@nxne.com. Website: http://www.nxne.com. Festival Coordinator: Leslie Goldthorpe. Estab. 1995. "Our festival takes place mid-June at 26 venues and 2 outdoor stages in downtown Toronto, drawing over 1,700 conference delegates, 400 bands and 50,000 music fans. Musical genres include everything from folk to funk, roots to rock, polka to punk and all points in between, bringing exceptional new talent, media front-runners, music business heavies and music fans from all over the world to Toronto." Participants include emerging and established songwriters, vocalists, composers, bands and instrumentalists. Festival performers are selected by submitting a demo tape and package. Send for an application form, or call, fax or e-mail. Submission accepted from November 1 to January 19, 2000. Submissions fee: $15. Conference registration fee: $115-195 (US), $145-250 (Canadian). "The program includes mentor sessions—15-minute one-on-one opportunities for songwriters and composers to ask questions of industry experts."

✓ NORTHERN CALIFORNIA SONGWRITERS ASSOCIATION CONFERENCE, 1724 Laurel St., Suite 120, San Carlos CA 94070. (650)654-3966 or (800)FOR-SONG. Fax: (650)654-2156. E-mail: info@ncsasong.org. Website: http://www.ncsasong.org. Executive Director: Ian Crombie. Estab. 1980. "Conference offers opportunity and education. 16 seminars, 50 song screening sessions (1,500 songs reviewed), performance showcases, one on one sessions and concerts." Offers programs for lyricists, songwriters, composers and performers. "During the year we have competitive open mics. Winners go into the playoffs. Winners of the playoffs perform at the sunset concert at the conference." Event takes place second weekend in September at Foothill College, Los Altos Hills, CA. Over 500 songwriters/musicians participate in this event. Participants are songwriters, composers, musical playwrights, vocalists, bands, instrumentalists and those interested in a career in the music business. Send for application. Deadline: September 1. Fee: $90-175. "See our listing in the Organizations section."

✓ NSAI SPRING SYMPOSIUM, 1701 West End Ave., Nashville TN 37203. (615)256-3354. Fax: (615)256-0034. E-mail: nsai@songs.org. Website: http://www.songs.org/nsai. Membership Director: Richard Nord. Events Coordinator: Erika Wollam-Nichols. Covers "all types of music. Participants take part in publisher and professional songwriter evaluations, as well as large group sessions with different guest speakers." Offers annual programs for songwriters. Event takes place in April at Doubletree Hotel Downtown in Nashville. 350 amateur songwriters/musicians participate in each event. Send for application. Deadline: late March. Fee: $225, member; $275, non-member.

⧈ PHILADELPHIA MUSIC CONFERENCE, P.O. Box 30288, Philadelphia PA 19103. (215)587-9550. E-mail: gopmc@aol.com. Website: http://www.gopmc.com. Showcase Director: Michael Kunze. Estab. 1992. "The purpose of the PMC is to bring together rock, hip hop and acoustic music for three days of panels and four nights of showcases. Offers programs for songwriters, composers and performers, including one-on-one sessions to meet with panelists and song evaluation sessions to have your music heard. "We present 45 panels on topics of all facets of the music industry; 350 showcases at clubs around the city. Also offer a DJ cutting contest." Held annually at the Doubletree Hotel in Philadelphia in October. 3,000 amateur and professional songwriters, composers, individual vocalists, bands, individual instrumentalists, attorneys, managers, agents, publishers, A&R, promotions, club owners, etc. participate each year. "As per showcase application, participants are selected by independent panel of press, radio and performing rights organizations." Send for application. Deadline: September 1. Fee: $15 showcase application fee. "The Philadelphia Music Conference is one of the fastest-growing and exciting events around. Our goal is not just to make the Philadelphia Music Conference one of the biggest in America, but to make it one of the best. 23 artists were signed to major label deals in the first four years of the conference. We will continue to build upon our ideas to keep this an event that is innovative, informative and fun."

⧈　✓　✂　⊕　✴　♆　○　⊘　♋　⊘

FOR EXPLANATIONS OF THESE SYMBOLS,
SEE THE INSIDE FRONT AND BACK COVERS OF THIS BOOK.

✄ **RIVER'S EDGE SONGWRITER'S RETREAT WITH PAT PATTISON**, hosted by REO Rafting Adventure Resort, 355-535 Thurlow St., Vancouver, British Columbia V6E 3L2 Canada. (604)684-4438 or (800)736-7238. Fax: (604)684-9536. E-mail: info@reorafting.com. Website: http://www.reorafting.com. President: Bryan Fogelman. Reservations Manager: Helen Sheehan. Estab. 1996. "A two-day songwriter's workshop with Writer's Digest author Pat Pattison. Evening object writing and campfire sessions included. Relevant to all musical styles with lyrics." Event takes place September, 2000 at Nahatlatch River Resort, a wilderness retreat 3 hours from Vancouver, B.C. Up to 25 songwriters can participate. Participants are amateur and professional songwriters, vocalists and composers. Send or call for application. Deadline: when full at 25 participants or 1 week prior. Fee: For 2000, $295 US or $245 US with early registration. "This unique workshop with Pat Pattison is a wilderness retreat in a beautiful setting on a jade-green river. Includes 7 delicious meals; beverages; 2 nights accommodation in tent cabins; scenic hot tub and sauna; private beach on river; hot showers, etc. Includes your choice of adventure activities such as whitewater rafting, hiking and horseback riding. Songwriting critiques and special services can be arranged with Pat Pattison by calling (603)964-5181."

THE SHIZNIT MUSIC CONFERENCE, P.O. Box 1881, Baton Rouge LA 70821. (504)231-2739. Fax: (504)926-5055. E-mail: staffers@sprynet.com. Website: http://www.theshiznit.com. Public Relations: Lee Williams. Vice President: Sedrick Hills. Purpose is to provide performance and networking opportunities for a wide variety of music and music related businesses, from urban to country, from blues to zydeco. Showcases, networking, trade shows and seminars offer information about the music industry. Offers programs annually for songwriters and performers. Event takes place in April at over 40 venues in Baton Rouge and New Orleans. 400 songwriters/musicians participate in each event. Participants are amateur and professional songwriters, vocalists and bands. Participants are selected by demo tape audition. Fee: $185. Send for application.

☑ **SONGWRITERS EXPO**, 6255 Sunset Blvd. #1023, Hollywood CA 90028. (323)463-7178. Fax: (323)463-2146. E-mail: nassong@aol.com. Director of Programs: John Feins. Director of Educational Services: Sekou Olatunji. Estab. 1976. Offers programs for songwriters, composers and performers. Offers programs annually. Event takes place in October in Los Angeles, CA. Over 500 songwriters/musicians participate in each event. Participants are amateur and professional songwriters, vocalists, composers and bands. Anyone can participate. Send or call for application. Deadline: October. Fee: $200 members; $300 general. Offers classes, panels, workshops, song-pitches/evaluations and showcases involving all aspects of the music business.

☑ **THE SONGWRITERS GUILD FOUNDATION**, 6430 Sunset Blvd., Suite 705, Hollywood CA 90028. (323)462-1108. E-mail: lasga@aol.com. Website: http://www.songwritersorg.com. West Coast Regional Director: B. Aaron Meza. Assistant West Coast Regional Director: Phyllis Osman.
Ask-A-Pro/Song Critique: SGA members are given the opportunity to present their songs and receive constructive feedback from industry professionals. A great chance to meet industry people, make contacts, ask questions and get your song heard! Free to SGA members. Reservations required. Call for schedule.
Jack Segal's Songshop: This very successful 9-week workshop focuses on working a song through to perfection, including title, idea, rewrites and pitching your songs. Please call for more information regarding this very informative workshop. Dates to be announced. Fee.
Phil Swan Country Music Workshop: This 6-week workshop is perfect for those writers who want an inside look into the world of country music. Fee.
Special Seminars and Workshops: Held through the year. Past workshops included Sheila Davis on lyrics, tax workshops for songwriters, MIDI workshops, etc. Call for schedule.
Dr. George Gamez's Creativity Workshop: A 4-week class designed to help songwriters discover their creative possibilities and give them the tools and techniques they need to increase their creative abilities. Fee.
SGA Story Night: Featuring interviews with top guild members. Learn about their experiences in songwriting and perhaps hear a live performance from the pros. Fee.
Vocal Performance Workshop for Singer/Songwriters: Conducted by Berklee College of Music Grad, Phyllis R. Osman, this 4-week performance workshop is held on Saturday mornings at The Songwriters Foundation Office in Hollywood. The class is for all levels of singers and focuses on fundamental breathing exercises and techniques that help the singer/songwriter build stamina and control and help them achieve the sound they desire. Repitoire is also worked on.
Building a Songwriting Career: A 1-day workshop for songwriters, musicians and recording artists, etc. to help them discover how they can establish a career in the exciting world of songwriting. Features

SGA professional songwriters and music business executives in panel discussions about intellectual property, creativity, the craft and business of songwriting and more. No charge for this event.

THE SONGWRITERS GUILD OF AMERICA (SGA), 1560 Broadway #1306, New York NY 10036. (212)768-7902. Nashville office: 1222 16th Ave. S., Suite 25, Nashville TN 37212. LA office: 6430 Sunset Blvd., Hollywood CA 90028. E-mail: songnews@aol.com. Website: http://www.songwriters.org. National Projects Director: George Wurzbach. Estab. 1931.
Song Critique: New York's oldest ongoing song critique. Guild songwriters are invited to either perform their song live or present a cassette demo for feedback. A Guild moderator is on hand to direct comments. Nonmembers may attend and offer comments. Free.
Pro-Shop: For each of 6 sessions an active publisher, producer or A&R person is invited to personally screen material from professional Guild writers. Participation is limited to 10 writers, and audit of 1 session. Audition of material is required. Coordinator is producer/musician/award winning singer, Ann Johns Ruckert. Fee; $75 (SGA members only).
SGA Week: Held in spring and fall of each year, this is a week of scheduled events and seminars of interest to songwriters. Events include workshops, seminars and showcases. For schedule and details contact the SGA office beginning several weeks prior to SGA Week.

☑ **SONGWRITERS PLAYGROUND**®, 1085 Commonwealth Ave. #323, Boston MA 02215. (617)926-8766. E-mail: bljjms@tiac.net. Director: Barbara Jordan. Estab. 1990. "To help songwriters, performers and composers develop creative and business skills through the critically acclaimed programs *Songwriters Playground*®, *The 'Reel' Deal on Getting Songs Placed in Film and Television*, and the *Mind Your Own Business* Seminars. We offer programs year-round. Workshops last anywhere from 2-15 hours. Workshops are held at various venues throughout the United States. Prices vary according to the length of the workshop." Participants are amateur and professionals. Anyone can participate. Send or call for application.

SOUTH BY SOUTHWEST MUSIC CONFERENCE AND FESTIVAL, P.O. Box 4999, Austin TX 78765. (512)467-7979. Fax: (512)451-0754. E-mail: sxsw@sxsw.com. Website: http://sxsw.com/sxsw. Estab. 1987. "We have over 800 bands perform in over 40 venues over 5 nights featuring every genre of alternative-based music." Offers programs for songwriters and performers. Annual event takes place in March, at the Austin Convention Center, Austin, TX. Participants are songwriters, vocalists, bands, instrumentalists and representatives of almost all areas of the music business. Participants are selected by demo tape audition. Submissions accepted September through mid-November. Fee: $10 early fee; $20 late fee. Application is required. Forms are available by request or on the SXSW website. "We have a mentor program during the conference where participants can have a one-on-one with professionals in the music business. Also of interest to musicians are the SXSW film and interactive/multimedia festivals held the week before the music conference, and the North By Northwest music conference held annually in Autumn in Portland, OR. For more information, see the website."
 ● See the Insider Report interview with Operations Manager Eve McArthur on page 443.

☑ **THE SWANNANOA GATHERING—CONTEMPORARY FOLK WEEK**, Warren Wilson College, P.O. Box 9000, Asheville NC 28815-9000. (828)298-3434 or (828)298-3325, ext. 426. Fax: (828)299-3326. E-mail: gathering@warren-wilson.edu. Website: http://www.swangathering.org. Director: Jim Magill. Coordinator: Eric Garrison. "For anyone who ever wanted to make music for an audience, we offer a comprehensive week in artist development, divided into four major subject areas: Songwriting, Performance, Sound & Recording and Vocal Coaching, along with daily panel discussions of other business matters such as promotion, agents and managers, logistics of touring, etc. 1999 staff includes Tom Paxton, Cosy Sheridan, Chuck Pyle, Steve Seskin, Caroline Aiken, Reggie Harris, Leslie Ritter, Scott Petito, Bob Franke, Sloan Wainwright and Eric Garrison. For a brochure or other info contact Jim Magill, Director, The Swannanoa Gathering, at the phone number/address above. Tuition: $300. Takes place last week in July. Housing (including all meals): $225. Annual program of The Swannanoa Gathering Folk Arts Workshops."

☑ **THE TEN-MINUTE MUSICALS PROJECT**, P.O. Box 461194, West Hollywood CA 90046. (323)651-4899. Producer: Michael Koppy. Estab. 1986. Promotes short complete stage musicals. Offers programs for songwriters, composers and musical playwrights. "Works selected are generally included in full-length 'anthology musical'—11 of the first 16 selected works are now in the show *Stories*, for instance." Awards a $250 royalty advance for each work selected. Participants are amateur and professional songwriters, composers and musical playwrights. Participants are selected by demonstration tape, script, lead sheets. Send for application. Deadline: August 31st annually.

insider report

Opportunities abound at Austin conference

For Eve McArthur, operations director for South by Southwest Music Conference and Festival (SXSW), a love of music, and most particularly songwriters, steered her into a new and exciting career. "I have many friends in the arts community in Austin," she says. "When I decided to make a career change in 1989, South by Southwest was one of my first thoughts." McArthur feels her ten years in nonprofit organizing prepared her for working with the conference. Initially, she volunteered her time, and eventually the volunteer job grew into a full-time position.

Eve McArthur

McArthur has seen many changes since she has been with SXSW. "Steady growth and growing respect within the industry are the perceptual ones," she says. "These are assets for our registrants as well as for organizations." SXSW also produces North by Northwest in Portland, Oregon and manages the U.S. staff for North by Northwest in Toronto. According to McArthur this activity and growth correlate to major changes for SXSW. The volunteer staff has grown from 30 to nearly 900 solely for the Austin conference.

Six years ago the Film Conference and Festival and the Interactive/Multimedia Festival were added as separate, but simultaneous, synergistic events, offering songwriters high-tech avenues to pursue. Additionally, the conference has linked with the electronic resources now available. Their website is of utmost importance in facilitating the efficient dispersal of information to inquiring songwriters, performers and musicians. McArthur goes on to say, "Change seems constant and my learning curve often seems near vertical, which is probably the reason I'm still here after 12 years."

Austin may at first seem an unlikely location for a growing alternative music scene. McArthur explains it is a party town with many nightclubs featuring original music and a variety of musicians. The party atmosphere is due largely to the influence of 50,000 University of Texas students along with legislators and lobbyists from the state capitol. "Austin is considered to be the 'liberal oasis' in a mostly conservative state." When the conference began in the late '80s, "most of the music industry conventions and major music media were on either coast. So,

EVE MCARTHUR

Title: Operations Director
Event: South by Southwest Music
   Conference and Festival

there was a void to be filled."

And fill the void they do. The 13-year-old conference features every aspect of alternative-based music with more than 750 bands performing in over 40 showcases during 5 nights. SXSW offers a multitude of programs for the songwriter including panels, credit courses, interviews, focus group discussions, happy hours for various affinity groups, mentor sessions, roundtables, case studies and more. "We strive to offer programs of interest to many levels of experience and sections of the industry," McArthur says. However, the conference is not all work and no play. "We also like to have fun. So, the mix usually includes some stimulating but humorous programs. We once held a musician's workshop in the parking lot of the host hotel, called 'Dead Van by the Side of the Road,' which had a mechanic showing ways to get the band van to limp to the next gig."

For songwriters looking for a stimulating and productive atmosphere to foster business, networking and creative contacts, SXSW is a must. Response from conference goers has been extremely positive. "The annual feedback forms we get indicate the vast majority of attendees are professionally refreshed and attain many career targets as a result of efforts made at South by Southwest. That same feedback demonstrates the warm weather, good food, creative zaniness and Austin friendliness are major reasons entertainment industry pros return year after year."

McArthur relates the most valuable assets attendees can take away from the conference are new contacts, face-to-face meetings with music industry professionals, renewed energy and new ideas for success. "Whether someone who is a star now made their first record deal at South by Southwest or a road manager or publicist got a new client, most attendees will have grown professionally as a result of the conference."
—*Pamala Shields*

UNDERCURRENTS, P.O. Box 94040, Cleveland OH 44101-6040. (216)397-9921. Fax: (216)932-1143. E-mail: musicatucs@aol.com. Website: http://www.undercurrents.com. Director: John Latimer. Estab. 1989. A yearly music industry expo featuring seminars, trade show, media center and showcases of rock, alternative, metal, folk, jazz and blues music. Offers programs for songwriters, composers, music industry professionals and performers. Dates for Undercurrents '99 were May 20-22. Deadline for showcase consideration is February 1. Participants are selected by demo tape, biography and 8×10 photo audition. Send for application. Fee: $100 for 3-day event.

WINTER MUSIC CONFERENCE INC., 3450 NE 12 Terrace, Ft. Lauderdale FL 33334. (305)563-4444. Fax: (305)563-6889. E-mail: wmcconfab@aol.com. Website: http://www.wmcon.com/wmc.html. President: Margo Possenti. Estab. 1985. Features educational seminars and showcases for dance, hip hop, alternative and rap. Offers programs for songwriters and performers. Offers programs annually. Event takes place March of each year in Miami, Florida. 3,000 songwriters/musicians participate in each event. Participants are amateur and professional songwriters, composers, musical playwrights, vocalists, bands and instrumentalists. Participants are selected by submitting demo tape. Send or call for application. Deadline: February. Event held at either nightclubs or hotel with complete staging, lights and sound. Fee: $200-350.

Retreats & Colonies

This section provides information on retreats and artists' colonies. These are places for creatives, including songwriters, to find solitude and spend concentrated time focusing on their work. While a residency at a colony may offer participation in seminars, critiques or performances, the atmosphere of a colony or retreat is much more relaxed than that of a conference or workshop. Also, a songwriter's stay at a colony is typically anywhere from one to twelve weeks (sometimes longer), while time spent at a conference may only run from one to fourteen days.

Like conferences and workshops, however, artists' colonies and retreats span a wide range. Yaddo, perhaps the most well-known colony, limits its residencies to artists "working at a professional level in their field, as determined by a judging panel of professionals in the field." The Brevard Music Center offers residencies only to those involved in classical music. Despite different focuses, all artists' colonies and retreats have one thing in common: They are places where you may work undisturbed, usually in nature-oriented, secluded settings.

SELECTING A COLONY OR RETREAT

When selecting a colony or retreat, the primary consideration for many songwriters is cost, and you'll discover that arrangements vary greatly. Some colonies provide residencies as well as stipends for personal expenses. Some suggest donations of a certain amount. Still others offer residencies for substantial sums but have financial assistance available.

When investigating the various options, consider meal and housing arrangements and your family obligations. Some colonies provide meals for residents, while others require residents to pay for meals. Some colonies house artists in one main building; others provide separate cottages. A few have provisions for spouses and families. Others prohibit families altogether.

Overall, residencies at colonies and retreats are competitive. Since only a handful of spots are available at each place, you often must apply months in advance for the time period you desire. A number of locations are open year-round, and you may find planning to go during the "off-season" lessens your competition. Other colonies, however, are only available during certain months. In any case, be prepared to include a sample of your best work with your application. Also, know what project you'll work on while in residence and have alternative projects in mind in case the first one doesn't work out once you're there.

Each listing in this section details fee requirements, meal and housing arrangements, and space and time availability, as well as the retreat's surroundings, facilities and special activities. Of course, before making a final decision, send a SASE to the colonies or retreats that interest you to receive their most up-to-date details. Costs, application requirements and deadlines are particularly subject to change.

For More Information

For other listings of songwriter-friendly colonies, see *Musician's Resource* (available from Watson-Guptill Publications, 1695 Oak St., Lakewood NJ 08701, 1-800-451-1741), which not only provides information about conferences, workshops and academic programs but also residencies and retreats. Also check the Publications of Interest section in this book for newsletters and other periodicals providing this information.

☑ **BREVARD MUSIC CENTER**, P.O. Box 312, Brevard NC 28712-0312. (828)884-2975. Fax: (828)884-2036. E-mail: brevardmusic@citcom.net. Website: http://www.brevardmusic.org. Admissions Coordinator: Lynn Johnson. Estab. 1936. Offers 6-week residencies from the last week in June through the first week of August. Open to professional and student composers, classical guitarists, pianists, vocalists and instrumentalists of classical music. A 1-week advanced conducting workshop (orchestral and opera) with David Effron and Gunther Schuller is offered, as well as a collaborative pianist program. Accommodates 400 at one time. Personal living quarters include cabins. Offers rehearsal, teaching and practice cabins.
Costs: $3,050 for tuition, room and board.
Requirements: Call for application forms and guidelines. $50 application fee. Participants are selected by audition or demonstration tape and then by invitation. There are 60 audition sites throughout the US.

BYRDCLIFFE ARTS COLONY, 34 Tinker St., Woodstock NY 12498. (914)679-2079. Fax: (914)679-4529. E-mail: wguild@ulster.net. Website: http://www.woodstockguild.org. Executive Director: Carla T. Smith. Estab. 1980. Offers 1-month residencies June-September. Open to composers, writers and visual artists. Accommodates 10 at one time. Personal living quarters include single rooms, shared baths and kitchen facilities. Offers separate private studio space. Composers must provide their own keyboard with headphone. Activities include open studio, readings, followed by pot luck dinner once a month. The parent organization offers music and dance performances, gallery exhibits and book signings.
Costs: $500/month. Residents are responsible for own meals and transporation.
Requirements: Send SASE for application forms and guidelines. Accepts inquiries via fax or e-mail. $5 application fee. Submit a score of at least 10 minutes with 2 references, résumé and application.

DORLAND MOUNTAIN ARTS COLONY, P.O. Box 6, Temecula CA 92593. (909)676-5039. Fax: (909)696-2855. E-mail: dorland@ez2.net. Website: http://www.ez2.net/dorland. Contact: Director. Estab. 1979. Offers 1- or 2-month residencies, year-round, on availability. Open to composers, playwrights, writers, visual artists, sculptors, etc. Personal living quarters include 6 individual rustic cottages with private baths and private kitchen facilities. Propane gas is provided for cooking, refrigeration and hot water. Lighting is by kerosene lamps and heat is by wood stoves. There is no electricity. Two Composer studios are equipped with pianos, including 1 concert grand Steinway, and 1 baby grand Chickering.
• See the Insider Report interview with Director of Operations Karen Parrott on page 448.
Costs: $50 non-refundable scheduling fee. Cabin donation: $300 per month (½ non-refundable).
Requirements: Send SASE for application forms and guidelines. Accepts inquiries via fax or e-mail. Deadline: March 1 and September 1.

☑ **DORSET COLONY HOUSE**, P.O. Box 510, Dorset VT 05251-0510. (802)867-2223. Fax: (802)867-0144. E-mail: theatre@sover.net. Website: http://www.theatredirectories.com. Executive Director: John Nassivera. Estab. 1980. Offers up to 1-month residencies September-October and April-May. Open to writers, composers, directors, designers and collaborators of the theatre. Accommodates 8 at one time. Personal living quarters include single rooms with desks with shared bath and shared kitchen facilities.
Costs: $120/week. Meals not included. Transportation is residents' responsibility.
Requirements: Send SASE for application forms and guidelines. Accepts inquiries via fax or e-mail. Submit letter with requested dates, description of project and résumé of productions.

🌐 ☑ **THE TYRONE GUTHRIE CENTRE**, Annaghmakerrig, Newbliss, County Monaghan, Ireland. Phone: (353)(47)54003. Fax: (353)(47)54380. E-mail: thetgc@indigo.ie. Director: Bernard Loughlin. Estab. 1981. Offers year-round residencies. Artists may stay for anything from 1 week to 3 months in the Big House, or for up to a year at a time in one of the 5 self-catering houses in the old farmyard. Open to artists of all disciplines. Accommodates 15 at one time. Personal living quarters include bedroom with bathroom en suite. Offers a variety of workspaces. There is a music room for composers and musicians, a large rehearsal and performance space for theatre groups and music ensembles. Activities include informal readings and performances. At certain times of the year it is possible, by special arrangement, to accommodate groups of artists, symposiums, master classes, workshops and other collaborations.
Costs: Artists who are not Irish must pay £600 per week, all found, for a residency in the Big House and £300 per week for one of the self-catering farmyard houses. To qualify for a residency, it is necessary to show evidence of a significant level of achievement in the relevant field. "We are happy to help successful applicants find funding for the fees."
Requirements: Send SAE and IRC for application forms and guidelines. Accepts inquiries via fax or e-mail. Fill in application form with cv to be reviewed by the board members at regular meetings.

ISLE ROYALE NATIONAL PARK ARTIST-IN-RESIDENCE PROGRAM, 800 E. Lakeshore Dr., Houghton MI 49931-1869. (906)482-0984. Fax: (906)482-8753. E-mail: isro_parkinfo@nps.gov. Website: http://www.nps.gov/ISRO/. Coordinator: Greg Blust. Estab. 1991. Offers 2-3 week residencies from mid-June to mid-September. Open to all artists. Accommodates 1 artist with 1 companion at one time. Personal living quarters include cabin without electricity; shared outhouse. A canoe is provided for transportation. Offers a guest house at the site that can be used as a workroom. The artist is asked to contribute a piece of work representative of their stay at Isle Royale, to be used by the park in an appropriate manner. During their residency, artists will be asked to share their experience (1 presentation per week of residency, about 1 hour/week) with the public by demonstration, talk, or other means.
Requirements: Send SASE for application forms and guidelines. Accepts inquiries via fax or e-mail. A panel of professionals from various disciplines, and park representatives will choose the finalists. The selection is based on artistic integrity, ability to reside in a wilderness environment, a willingness to donate a finished piece of work inspired on the island, and the artist's ability to relate and interpret the park through their work.

☑ **KALANI OCEANSIDE RETREAT**, RR 2 Box 4500, Pahoa-Beach Road HI 96778-9724. (808)965-7828. Fax: (808)965-9613. E-mail: kalani@kalani.com. Website: http://www.kalani.com. Director: Richard Koob. Estab. 1980. Offers 2-week to 2-month residencies. Open to all artists who can verify professional accomplishments. Accommodates 80 at one time. Personal living quarters include private cottage or lodge room with private or shared bath. Full (3 meals/day) dining service, also shared kitchens available. Offers shared studio/library spaces. Activities include opportunity to share works in progress, ongoing yoga, hula and other classes; beach, thermal springs, Volcanos National Park nearby; olympic pool/spa on 113-acre facility.
Cost: $33-65/night lodging with 50% stipend. Meals separate at $25/day. Transportation by rental car from $20/day or taxi $70/trip. 50% discount ("stipend") on lodging only.
Requirements: Send SASE for application forms and guidelines. Accepts inquiries via fax or e-mail. $10 application fee.

N THE MACDOWELL COLONY, 100 High St., Peterborough NH 03458. (603)924-3886. Fax: (603)924-9142. Website: http://www.macdowellcolony.org. Admissions Coordinator: Patricia Dodge. Estab. 1907. Offers year-round residencies of up to 2 months (average length is 6 weeks). Open to writers, composers, film/video makers, visual artists, architects and interdisciplinary artists. Personal living quarters include single rooms. Offers private studios on 450-acre grounds.
Cost: "Only after acceptance for residency is one asked to indicate what contribution one is able to make."
Requirements: Send SASE for application forms and guidelines. Composers should send 2 clearly reproduced scores and corresponding tapes with application form. "One should be a work in a large form, e.g., a string quartet, sonata, orchestral piece." Application deadline: January 15, April 15 and September 15.

N MEDICINE WHEEL ARTISTS' RETREAT, 54 Nod Rd., Groton MA 01450-3088. (978)448-3717. E-mail: medwheel@tiac.net. Estab. 1989. Offers 1-4 week residencies in May and September. Open to all artists over 18 years old. Accommodates less than 15 at one time. Personal living quarters vary: some single rooms with private bath, some single cabins with use of bathhouse. Artists must bring portable piano.
Cost: $60-250/week including meals. Artists may work in kitchen to reduce fees.
Requirements: Send SASE for application forms and guidelines. Accepts inquiries via e-mail. Supply example of work. No application fee. Application deadline: April 10 (for May); August 7 (for September).

N NORTHWOOD UNIVERSITY ALDEN B. DOW CREATIVITY CENTER, 3225 Cook Rd., Midland MI 48640-2398. (517)837-4478. Fax: (517)837-4468. E-mail: creativity@northwood.edu. Director: Ron Koenig. Estab. 1979. Offers 10-week summer residencies (mid-June through mid-August). Fellowship Residency is open to individuals in all fields (the arts, humanities or sciences) who have innovative, creative projects to pursue. Accommodates 4 at one time. Each Fellow is given a furnished apartment on campus, complete with 2 bedrooms, kitchen, bath and large living room. Fellows' apartments serve as their work space as well as their living quarters unless special needs are requested. "Fellows are invited to lunch weekdays at the Creativity Center on campus."
Cost: $10 application fee. Room and board is provided plus a $750 stipend to be used toward project costs or personal needs. "We also provide travel to and from the residency. We look for projects which are innovative, creative, unique. We ask the applicant to set accomplishable goals for the 10-week residency."
Requirements: Send for application forms and guidelines. Accepts inquiries via fax or e-mail. Applicants submit 2-page typed description of their project; cover page with name, address, phone numbers plus summary (30 words or less) of project; support materials such as tapes, CDs; personal résumé; facilities or equipment needed; and $10 application fee. Application deadline: December 31 (postmarked).

Colony furnishes "unexpected concepts and directions"

California's Dorland Mountain Arts Colony is not for those who wish to be catered to, nor those prone to panicking without the trappings of technology. It is certainly not a place to mingle, let alone network. But for the most dedicated of artists and musicians, these qualities are what make Dorland so attractive and successful. As one of the most widely known and respected artist colonies in the U.S., Dorland offers relief from the sometimes harried environment of a workshop or conference. Karen Parrott, director of operations at Dorland, describes it as "a respite from the glitz and noise of the day-to-day world, a quiet, natural environment conducive to contemplation and the flow of creative energy."

German novelist Berthold Auerbach said "music washes away from the soul the dust of everyday life," and clearly a composer or musician's experience at Dorland can achieve the same goal. Established in 1930, Dorland Mountain Arts Colony was the brainchild of Ellen Babcock Dorland, a concert pianist and highly regarded music instructor. Dorland was enamored with the East Coast artist colonies she had attended and hoped to establish a similar community on the West Coast. She envisioned a safe space for artists to work undisturbed, to absorb and utilize nature as a muse, and to convene for opportunities to collaborate, and with help from co-founder (and noted environmentalist) Barbara Horton, Dorland's vision became a reality. The colony, which had at first simply been a gathering place for Dorland's friends, eventually became a hermitage where composers, visual artists, and writers could experience what Parrott calls a "Walden-like existence." Set amidst 300 acres of unspoiled wilderness, the colony indeed provides residents seclusion and inspiration that would have made Thoreau green with envy.

Dorland Mountain Arts Colony could easily be called rustic—its six cottages are heated by wood stoves, lit by kerosene lamps, sans television and telephone—and privacy is clearly a priority. Residents are asked to contact each other by placing notes in on-site mailboxes and are never contacted in their cottages except in an emergency. This "natural atmosphere of solitude," Parrott says, "seems to foster an introspection that often results in the artist finding a surprising new direction for his work." However, those with cabin fever can venture into the local town of Temecula, and those who really want to satiate their city craving can make the 60-mile trip to San Diego or the 100-mile trip to Los Angeles.

KAREN PARROTT

Title: Director of Operations
Colony: Dorland Mountain Arts Colony

Parrott stresses that although the Dorland staff "imposes no structured socializing or collaboration," there are studio sessions providing artists in residence a chance to join forces, an opportunity for musicians to perform non-performing songwriters' songs, or poets to provide lyrics for instrumental pieces. In addition, there is a monthly "Works-in-Progress" evening staged at a local gallery where artists can "share and explain their work to each other as well as to the local community."

To suit the needs of composers and musicians, the colony features two pianos, including a concert grand Steinway once played by composer/pianist/conductor Rachmaninoff, and a baby grand Chickering. Those not wishing to take advantage of the colony's resources must provide their own instruments and other working materials. Parrott admits the colony has, in the past, accommodated fewer composers in relation to the number of visual artists, poets and writers. Because of this, she encourages more composers, both fledgling and those with established careers, to apply. "Dorland has always encouraged emerging artists," she says. "Our review board makes selections based not only on credentials but also their promise and commitment to their art." Composers, no matter how experienced, can expect to have a similar experience. "Living in what is most likely a very different environment, the majority of Dorland residents experience fresh, unexpected concepts and directions."

Although shorter residencies are available, Parrott recommends artists plan at least a two-week visit at Dorland and suggests the average stay of one month proves the most beneficial. This longer time frame allows the artist a necessary period of adjustment to what is, for some, a very foreign environment, and once the adjustment is made, once residents are free from the "dust of everyday life," they can focus intensively on their projects.

Upon admission, the colony requires a $50 scheduling fee to confirm the residency and monthly "cabin donations" of $300 (half of which is due 6 months prior to the artist's stay). A modest price, perhaps, for a composer to be alone with her music, to escape the numbing hum of the computer or the din of traffic. Parrott agrees the Dorland experience—which offers endless opportunities for revelation, regardless of a composer's musical genre be it alternative, classical or folk—is priceless. "Nature has been the inspiration for many of the greatest works of art in all disciplines," Parrott says, "and the sounds of nature certainly seem to delight and inspire every composer who has had a residency at Dorland."

—*Amanda Heele*

N **SITKA CENTER FOR ART & ECOLOGY**, P.O. Box 65, Otis OR 97368-0065. (541)994-5485. Fax: (541)994-8024. Executive Director: Randall Koch. Estab. 1971. Offers 4-month residencies in October through January or February through May; shorter residencies are available upon arrangement. Open to artists or naturalists who have earned a BA, BS, BFA and/or MA, MS, MFA, PhD degree, or equivalent professional experience. Personal living quarters include 2 living quarters, each self-contained with a sleeping area, kitchen and bathroom. Offers 3 studios. Workshops or presentations are encouraged; an exhibition/presentation to share residents' works is held in January and May.

Cost: The resident is encouraged to hold an open studio or community outreach program at Sitka one day per month during the residency, exceptions by arrangements with the director. The resident is asked to provide some form of community service on behalf of Sitka.

Requirements: Send SASE for application forms and guidelines. Accepts inquiries via fax. Send completed application with résumé, 2 letters of recommendation, work samples and SASE.

N: VILLA MONTALVO ARTIST RESIDENCY PROGRAM, P.O. Box 158, Saratoga CA 95071-0158. (408)961-5818. Fax: (408)961-5850. E-mail: kfunk@villamontalvo.org. Website: http://www.villam ontalvo.org. Artist Residency Program Director: Kathryn Funk. Estab. 1942. "Offers 1- to 3-month residencies year-round. Open to writers (prose, poetry, playwrights, screen writers, etc.), visual artists, musicians and composers, architects, filmmakers. Residents are provided with fully equipped apartments/cottages, with kitchens and baths. Four to five apartments/cottages have pianos. The composer's apartment has a grand piano. Activities include weekly gatherings of the residents.
Cost: Residencies are free, but artists must provide food, materials and transportation. There are 7 fellowships ($400) awarded to highest ranking artists based on panelist's review of work samples.
Requirements: Send self addressed label and 55¢ postage. Accepts inquiries via fax or e-mail. $20 application fee plus work samples as defined by discipline. Application deadline: March 1 and September 1.

VIRGINIA CENTER FOR THE CREATIVE ARTS, Box VCCA, Sweet Briar VA 24595. (804)946-7236. Fax: (804)946-7239. E-mail: vcca@vcca.com. Website: http://www.vcca.com. Director of Artists' Services: Sheila Gulley Pleasants. Estab. 1971. Offers residencies year-round, typical residency lasts 1 month. Open to originating artists: composers, writers and visual artists. Accommodates 22 at one time. Personal living quarters include 20 single rooms, 2 double rooms, bathrooms shared with one other person. All meals are served. Kitchens for fellows' use available at studios and residence. Activities include trips in the VCCA van twice a week into town. Fellows share their work regularly.
Cost: No transportation costs are covered. The suggested daily fee is $30 which includes meals.
Requirements: Send SASE for application forms and guidelines or call the above number. Applications are reviewed by a panel of judges. Application fee: $20. Deadline: May 15 for September-December residency; September 15 for January-April residency; January 15 for May-August residency.

YADDO ARTISTS' COMMUNITY, P.O. Box 395, Union Ave., Saratoga Springs NY 12866-0395. (518)584-0746. Fax: (518)584-1312. E-mail: yaddo@yaddo.org. Website: http://www.yaddo.org. Centennial and Public Affairs Coordinator: Lesley M. Leduc. Estab. 1900. Offers residencies of 2 weeks to 2 months, year-round except for a brief 2-3 week period in September. Open to those working at a professional level in their field, as determined by a judging panel of professionals in the field. Accommodates 12-15 in winter, up to 35 in spring and summer at one time. Personal living quarters include private rooms and studios, some with private baths and some with shared baths. All meals are provided; breakfast and dinner are communal; lunches packed in lunch pails. Offers composers' studios equipped with pianos. Several small libraries are available on the grounds; guests have access to a college and municipal library nearby.
Cost: No fees are charged for any services, transportation costs are not provided.
Requirements: Send SASE with 55¢ postage for application forms and guidelines. Accepts inquiries via fax or e-mail. $20 non-refundable filing fee, work samples required (2 musical scores and audio cassette of one of the scores) and 2 letters of support sent directly to Yaddo by the sponsors. Deadline: January 15 and August 1.

State & Provincial Grants

This section lists arts councils in the United States and Canada. Councils provide assistance to artists (including songwriters) in the form of fellowships or grants. These grants can be substantial and confer prestige upon recipients; however, **only state or province residents are eligible**. Because deadlines and available support vary annually, query first with a SASE.

UNITED STATES ARTS AGENCIES

Alabama State Council on the Arts, *201 Monroe St., Montgomery AL 32530-1800. (334)242-4076. E-mail: staff@arts.state.al.us. Website: http://www.arts.state.al.us.*

Alaska State Council on the Arts, *411 W. Fourth Ave., Suite 1-E, Anchorage AK 99501-2343. (907)269-6610. E-mail: info@aksca.org. Website: http://www.aksca.org.*

Arizona Commission on the Arts, *417 W. Roosevelt, Phoenix AZ 85003. (602)255-5882. E-mail: general@arizonaarts.org. Website: http://az.arts.asu.edu/artscomm/.*

Arkansas Arts Council, *1500 Tower Bldg., 323 Center St., Little Rock AR 72201. (501)324-9766. E-mail: info@dah.state.ar.us. Website: http://www.heritage.state.ar.us/acc/index.html.*

California Arts Council, *1300 I St., Suite 930, Sacramento CA 95814. (916)322-6555. E-mail: cac@cwo.com. Website: http://www.cac.ca.gov/.*

Colorado Council on the Arts and Humanities, *750 Pennsylvania St., Denver CO 80203-3699. (303)894-2617. E-mail: coloarts@artswire.org. Website: http://www.state.co.us/gov_dir/arts/.*

Connecticut Commission on the Arts, *1 Financial Plaza, 755 Main St., Hartford CT 06103. (860)566-4770. Website: http://www.cslnet.ctstateu.edu/cca/.*

Delaware State Arts Council, *Carvel State Office Building, 820 N. French St., Wilmington DE 19801. (302)577-8278. E-mail: delarts@artswire.org. Website: http://www.artsdel.org/about/delaware.htm.*

District of Columbia Commission on the Arts & Humanities, *410 Eighth St. NW, 5th Floor, Washington DC 20004. (202)724-5613. E-mail: carrien@tmn.com. Website: http://www.capaccess.org/ane/dccah/.*

Florida Arts Council, *Division of Cultural Affairs, Florida Dept. of State, The Capitol, Tallahassee FL 32399-0250. (850)487-2980. Website: http://www.dos.state.fl.us/dca/general/html.*

Georgia Council for the Arts, *530 Means St. NW, Suite 115, Atlanta GA 30318-5793. (404)651-7920.*

Hawaii State Foundation on Culture & Arts, *44 Merchant St., Honolulu HI 96813. (808)586-0300. E-mail: sfca@sfca.state.hi.us. Website: http://www.state.hi.us/sfca.*

Idaho Commission on the Arts, *P.O. Box 83720, Boise ID 83720-0008. (208)334-2119. E-mail: mcknight@ica.state.id.us. Website: http://www2.state.id.us/arts.*

Illinois Arts Council, *100 W. Randolph, Suite 10-500, Chicago IL 60601. (312)814-6750. E-mail: info@arts.state.il.us. Website: http://www.state.il.us/agency/iac.*

Indiana Arts Commission, *402 W. Washington St., Indianapolis IN 46204-2741. (317)232-1268. Website: http://www.state.in.us/iac/.*

Iowa Arts Council, *600 E. Locust, Capitol Complex, Des Moines IA 50319-0290. (515)281-4451.*

Kansas Arts Commission, *Jay Hawk Tower, SW 700 Jackson, Suite 1004, Topeka KS 66603. (785)296-3335.*

Kentucky Arts Council, *31 Fountain Place, Frankfort KY 40601-1942. (502)564-3757.*

Louisiana State Arts Council, *P.O. Box 44247, Baton Rouge LA 70804-4247. (225)342-8180. E-mail: arts@crt.state.la.us. Website: http://www.crt.state.la.us/arts/.*

Maine State Arts Commission, *55 Capitol St., 25 State House Station, Augusta ME 04333-0025. (207)287-2724. E-mail: jan.poulin@state.me.us. Website: http://www.mainearts.com.*

Maryland State Arts Council, *601 N. Howard St., Baltimore MD 21201. (410)767-6555. E-mail: tcolvin@mdbusiness.state.md.us. Website: http://www.msac.org/.*

Massachusetts Cultural Council, *120 Boylston St., Boston MA 02116. (617)727-3668. Website: http://www.massculturalcouncil.org/.*

Michigan Council for Arts & Cultural Affairs, *1200 Sixth St., Executive Plaza, Detroit MI 48226-2461. (313)256-3735. E-mail: mcacal@artswire.org. Website: http://www.commerce.state.mi.us/arts/home.htm.*

Minnesota State Arts Board, *Park Square Court, 400 Sibley St., Suite 200, St. Paul MN 55101-1928. (651)215-1600. E-mail: msab@state.mn.us. Website: http://www.state.mn.us/ebranch/msab.*

Mississippi Arts Commission, *239 N. Lamar St., Suite 207, Jackson MS 39201. (601)359-6030. E-mail: bradley@arts.state.ms.us. Website: http://www.arts.state.ms.us/.*

Missouri Arts Council, *111 N. Seventh St., Suite 105, St. Louis MO 63101-2188. (314)340-6845. E-mail: mhunt01@mail.state.mo.us. Website: http://www.missouriartscouncil.org.*

Montana Arts Council, *316 N. Park Ave., Room 252, Helena MT 59620-2201. (406)444-6430. E-mail: mac@state.mt.us. Website: http://www.art.state.mt.us.*

Nebraska Arts Council, *3838 Davenport St., Omaha NE 68131-2329. (402)595-2122. E-mail: mskomal@cwis.unomaha.edu. Website: http://www.gps.k12.ne.us/nac_web_site/nac.htm.*

Nevada State Council on the Arts, *602 N. Curry, Carson City NV 89703. (702)687-6680. Website: http://www.clan.lib.nv.us/docs/ARTS.*

New Hampshire State Council on the Arts, *40 N. Main St., Concord NH 03301-4974. (603)271-2789. Website: http://www.state.nh.us/nharts.*

New Jersey State Council on the Arts, *CN 306, 20 W. State St., Trenton NJ 08625. (609)292-6130. Website: http://www.artswire.org/Artswire/njsca/.*

New Mexico Arts Division, *228 E. Palace Ave., Santa Fe NM 87501. (505)827-6490.*

New York State Council on the Arts, *915 Broadway, New York NY 10010. (212)387-7000. E-mail: pinfo@nysca.org. Website: http://www.nysca.org.*

North Carolina Arts Council, *221 E. Lane St., Raleigh NC 27601-2807. (919)733-2111. Website: http://www.ncarts.org/home.html.*

North Dakota Council on the Arts, *418 E. Broadway, Suite 70, Bismark ND 58501-4086. (701)328-3954. E-mail: thompson@pioneer.state.nd.us. Website: http://www.state.nd.us/arts/index.html.*

Ohio Arts Council, *727 E. Main St., Columbus OH 43205. (614)466-2613. E-mail: wlawson@mail.oac.ohio.gov. Website: http://www.oac.ohio.gov/.*

Oklahoma Arts Council, *P.O. Box 52001-2001, Oklahoma City OK 73152-2001. (405)521-2931. E-mail: okarts@oklaosf.state.ok.us. Website: http://www.oklaosf.state.ok.us/~arts/.*

Oregon Arts Commission, *775 Summer St. NE, Floor 2, Salem OR 97310. (503)986-0088. E-mail: oregon.artscomm@state.or.us.*

Pennsylvania Council on the Arts, *Room 216, Finance Bldg., Harrisburg PA 17120. (717)787-6883. Website: http://artsnet.heinz.cmu.edu/pca/.*

Institute of Puerto Rican Culture, *P.O. Box 9024184, San Juan PR 00902-4184. (787)725-5137.*

Rhode Island State Council on the Arts, *95 Cedar St., Suite 103, Providence RI 02903. (401)222-3880. E-mail: info@risca.state.ri.us. Website: http://www.risca.state.ri.us/.*

South Carolina Arts Commission, *1800 Gervais St., Columbia SC 29201. (803)734-8696. Website: http://www.state.sc.us/arts/.*

South Dakota Arts Council, *800 Governors Dr., Pierre SD 57501. (605)773-3131. E-mail: sdac@stlib.state.sd.us. Website: http://www.state.sd.us/state/executive/deca/sdarts/sdarts.htm.*

Tennessee Arts Commission, *401 Charlotte Ave., Nashville TN 37243-0780. (615)741-1701. Website: http://www.arts.state.tn.us/index.html.*

Texas Commission on the Arts, *P.O. Box 13406, Austin TX 78711-3406. (512)463-5535. E-mail: front.desk@arts.state.tx.us. Website: http://www.arts.state.tx.us/.*

Utah Arts Council, *617 E. South Temple, Salt Lake City UT 84102-1177. (801)236-7555. Website: http://www.ce.ex.state.ut.us/arts/.*

Vermont Arts Council, *136 State St., Drawer 33, Montpelier VT 05633-6001. (802)828-3291. E-mail: info@arts.vca.state.vt.us. Website: http://www.state.vt.us/vermont-arts/.*

Virgin Islands Council on the Arts, *41-42 Norre Gada, P.O. Box 103, St. Thomas VI 00804. (340)774-5984. E-mail: vicouncil@islands.vi.*

Virginia Commission for the Arts, *Lewis House, 2nd Floor, 223 Governor St., Richmond VA 23219. (804)225-3132. E-mail: vacomm@artswire.org. Website: http://www.artswire.org/~vacomm/.*

Washington State Arts Commission, *P.O. Box 42675, Olympia WA 98504-2675. (360)753-3860. E-mail: wsac@artswire.org.*

West Virginia Arts Commission, *Cultural Center, 1900 Kanawha Blvd. E., Charleston WV 25305-0300. (304)558-0220. Website: http://www.wvlc.wvnet.edu/culture/arts.html.*

Wisconsin Arts Board, *101 E. Wilson St., 1st Floor, Madison WI 53702. (608)266-0190. E-mail: artsboard@arts.state.wi.us. Website: http://www.arts.state.wi.us.*

Wyoming Arts Council, *2320 Capitol Ave., Cheyenne WY 82002. (307)777-7742. Website: http://commerce.state.wy.us/cr/arts/index.htm.*

CANADIAN PROVINCES ARTS AGENCIES

Alberta Foundation for the Arts, *901 Standard Life Centre, 10405 Jasper Ave., 9th Floor, Edmonton, Alberta T5J 4R7. (403)427-9968. E-mail: afa@mcd.gov.ab.ca. Website: http://www.affta.ab.ca.*

British Columbia Arts Council, *800 Johnson St., 5th Floor, Victoria, British Columbia V8V 1X4. (250)356-1728.*

Manitoba Arts Council, *525 - 93 Lombard Ave., Winnipeg, Manitoba R3B 3B1. (204)945-0421. E-mail: manart1@mb.sympatico.ca. Website: http://www.artscouncil.mb.ca.*

New Brunswick Department of Economic Development, Tourism & Culture, *Arts Branch, P.O. Box 6000, Fredericton, New Brunswick E3B 5H1. (506)453-2555. Website: http://www.gov.nb.ca/edit/index.htm.*

Newfoundland & Labrador Arts Council, *P.O. Box 98, St. John's, Newfoundland A1C 5H5. (709)726-2212. E-mail: nlacmail@newcomm.net. Website: http://www.nlac.nf.ca/.*

Nova Scotia Arts Council, *1660 Hollis St., Suite 302, P.O. Box 1559, CRO, Halifax, Nova Scotia B3J 2Y3. (902)422-1123.*

The Canada Council, *350 Albert St., P.O. Box 1047, Ottawa, Ontario K1P 5V8. (613)566-4414. Website: http://www.canadacouncil.ca/.*

Ontario Arts Council, *151 Bloor St. W., 6th Floor, Toronto, Ontario M5S 1T6. (416)961-1660. E-mail: info@arts.on.ca. Website: http://www.arts.on.ca/.*

Prince Edward Island Council of the Arts, *115 Richmond, Charlottetown, Prince Edward Island C1A 1H7. (902)368-4410. Website: http://www.peisland.com/arts/council.htm.*

Saskatchewan Arts Board, *3475 Albert St., Regina, Saskatchewan S4S 6X6. (306)787-4056.*

Yukon Arts Branch, *Box 2703, Whitehorse, Yukon Y1A 2C6. (867)667-8589. Website: http://www.artsyukon.com.*

Publications of Interest

Knowledge about the music industry is essential for both creative and business success. Staying informed requires keeping up with constantly changing information. Updates on the evolving trends in the music business are available to you in the form of music magazines, music trade papers and books. There is a publication aimed at almost every type of musician, songwriter and music fan, from the most technical knowledge of amplification systems to gossip about your favorite singer. These publications can enlighten and inspire you and provide information vital in helping you become a more well-rounded, educated, and, ultimately, successful musical artist.

This section lists all types of magazines and books you may find interesting. From songwriters' newsletters and glossy music magazines to tip sheets and how-to books, there should be something listed here that you'll enjoy and benefit from.

PERIODICALS

THE ALBUM NETWORK, 120 N. Victory Blvd., Burbank CA 91502. (818)955-4000. Website: http://www.musicbiz.com. *Weekly music industry trade magazine.*

AMERICAN SONGWRITER MAGAZINE, 1009 17th Ave. S., Nashville TN 37212-2201. (615)321-6096. E-mail: asongmag@aol.com. Website: http://www.songnet.com/asongmag. *Bimonthly publication for and about songwriters.*

BACK STAGE and BACK STAGE WEST, P.O. Box 5026, Brentwood TN 37024. (800)437-3183. Website: http://www.backstage.com. *Weekly East and West Coast performing artist trade papers.*

BILLBOARD, 1515 Broadway, New York NY 10036. (800)745-8922. E-mail: bbstore@billboard.com. Website: http://www.billboard.com. *Weekly industry trade magazine.*

CANADIAN MUSICIAN, 23 Hannover Dr., Suite 7, St. Catharines, Ontario L2W 1A3 Canada. (877)746-4692. Website: http://www.canadianmusician.com. *Bimonthly publication for amateur and professional Canadian musicians.*

CHART, 200-41 Britain St., Toronto, Ontario M5A 1R7 Canada. (416)363-3101. E-mail: chart@chartnet.com. Website: http://www.chartnet.com. *Monthly magazine covering the Canadian and international music scenes.*

CMJ NEW MUSIC REPORT, 11 Middle Neck Rd., Suite 400, Great Neck NY 11021-2301. (800)CMJ-WKLY or (516)466-6000. E-mail: subscriptions@cmj.com. Website: http://www.cmjmusic.com. *Weekly college radio and alternative music tip sheet.*

COUNTRY LINE MAGAZINE, P.O. Box 17245, Austin TX 78760. (512)292-1113. E-mail: editor@countrylinemagazine.com. Website: http://countrylinemagazine.com. *Monthly Texas-only country music cowboy and lifestyle magazine.*

DAILY VARIETY, 5700 Wilshire Blvd., Suite 120, Los Angeles CA 90036. (323)857-6600. Website: http://www.variety.com. *Daily entertainment trade newspaper.*

THE DRAMATISTS GUILD QUARTERLY, 1501 Broadway, Suite 701, New York NY 10036. (212)398-9366. *The quarterly journal of the Dramatists Guild, the professional association of playwrights, composers and lyricists.*

Get Your 2001 Edition Delivered Right to Your Door—and Save!

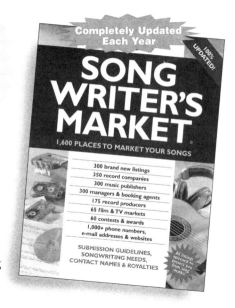

Finding the right markets for your songs is crucial to your success! With constant changes in the music industry, staying informed as to who, where and why is a challange. That's why every year the most savvy songwriters turn to the new edition of *Songwriter's Market* for the most up-to-date information on the people and places that will get their songs heard. This indispensable guide includes over 2,000 listings of music publishers, record producers, managers, booking agents and more. You'll also find insider tips from successful industry professionals which will further increase your opportunities.

Through this special offer, you can reserve your *2001 Songwriter's Market* now at the 2000 price—just $23.99— no matter how much the price may increase. Order today and save!
#10664/$23.99/528 pgs/pb

2001 Songwriter's Market will be published and ready for shipment in September 2000.

Turn Over for More Great Books to Help Market Your Songs!

☐ **Yes!** I want the most current edition of *Songwriter's Market*. Please send me the 2001 edition at the 2000 price—$23.99. (NOTE: *2001 Songwriter's Market* will be ready for shipment in September, 2000.) #10664

Additional books from the back of this card:

Book	Price
#	$
#	$
#	$
#	$
Subtotal	$

*Add $3.50 postage and handling for one book; $1.50 for each additional book.

Postage & Handling	$

Payment must accompany order. Ohioans add 6% sales tax. Canadians add 7% GST.

Total	$

VISA/MasterCard orders call TOLL FREE 1-800-289-0963
8:30 to 5:00 Mon.-Fri. Eastern Time
or FAX 1-888-590-4082

☐ Payment enclosed $_____ (or)

Charge my: ☐ Visa ☐ MasterCard Exp._____

Account #_____

Signature_____

Name_____

Address_____

City_____

State/Prov._____ Zip/PC _____

30-Day Money Back Guarantee on every book you buy!

☐ **FREE CATALOG!** Ask your bookstore about other fine Writer's Digest Books, or mail this card today for a complete catalog.

☐ Check here if you do not want your name added to our mailing list

6559

Mail to: Writer's Digest Books • 1507 Dana Avenue • Cincinnati, OH 45207

More Great Books to Help You Market Your Songs!

Music Publishing: A Songwriter's Guide
by Randy Poe
Make the most of yourself and your songs in the music industry! From a wide range of royalty options, to a large range of publishing options, you'll get all the facts you need to make the right publishing decisions.
#10505/$18.99/144 pages/paperback

The Musician's Guide to Making & Selling Your Own CDs & Cassettes
by Jana Stanfield
Learn how to produce the kind of recordings that will launch your music career. It doesn't take a major label to be successful in the music industry. Stanfield shows you how she made it to the top, and how you can, too.
#10522/$18.99/160 pages/paperback

Songwriter's Market Guide to Song and Demo Submission Formats
by the editors of Songwriter's Market
Get your foot in the door with knock-out query letters, a slick demo presentation, and the best advice for dealing with every player in the industry!
#10401/$19.99/160 pages/hard cover

The Craft and Business of Songwriting
by John Braheny
From generating a song idea to signing a record deal, you'll discover how to create and market artistically and commercially successful songs in today's market.
#10429/$21.99/322 pages/paperback

Writing Better Lyrics
by Pat Pattison
Make every song sizzle using this unique, in-depth approach to lyric writing. You'll examine extraordinary songs to determine what makes them so effective; work through more than 30 language exercises to find snappy rhymes; and create meaningful metaphors and similes.
#10453/$19.99/192 pages/hard cover

Books are available at your local bookstore, or directly from the publisher using the order card on the reverse.

ENTERTAINMENT LAW & FINANCE, New York Law Publishing Co., 345 Park Ave. S., 8th Floor, New York NY 10010. (917)256-2115. E-mail: leader@ljextra.com. *Monthly newsletter covering music industry contracts, lawsuit filings, court rulings and legislation.*

EXCLAIM!, 7-B Pleasant Blvd., Suite 966, Toronto, Ontario M4T 1K2 Canada. (416)535-9735. E-mail: exclaim@exclaim.ca. Website: http://exclaim.ca. *Canadian music monthly covering all genres of non-mainstream music.*

FAST FORWARD, Disc Makers, 7905 N. Rt. 130, Pennsauken NJ 08110-1402. (800)468-9353. Website: http://www.discmakers.com/music/ffwd. *Quarterly newsletter featuring companies and products for performing and recording artists in the independent music industry.*

THE GAVIN REPORT, 140 Second St., San Francisco CA 94105. (415)495-1990. Website: http://www.gavin.com. *Weekly listing of radio charts.*

HITS MAGAZINE, 14958 Ventura Blvd., Sherman Oaks CA 91403. (818)501-7900. *Weekly music industry trade publication.*

JAZZTIMES, P.O. Box 99050, Collingswood NJ 08108. (888)279-7444. E-mail: jtimes@aol.com. *10 issues/year magazine covering the American jazz scene.*

THE LEADS SHEET, Allegheny Music Works, 306 Cypress Ave., Johnstown PA 15902. (814)535-3373. *Monthly tip sheet.*

LYRICIST REVIEW, P.O. Box 2167, North Canton OH 44720-0167. (330)305-9130. E-mail: lyricaslit@aol.com. Website: http://www.lyricistreview.com. *Quarterly commentaries on song lyrics and previously unpublished lyrics available to performing musicians.*

MUSIC BOOKS PLUS, 23 Hannover Dr., Suite 7, St. Catharines, Ontario L2W 1A3 Canada. (800)265-8481. E-mail: mail@nor.com. Website: http://www.musicbooksplus.com.

MUSIC BUSINESS INTERNATIONAL MAGAZINE, 460 Park Ave. S., 9th Floor, New York NY 10016. (212)378-0400. *Bimonthly magazine for senior executives in the music industry.*

MUSIC CONNECTION MAGAZINE, 4731 Laurel Canyon Blvd., N. Hollywood CA 91607. (818)755-0101. E-mail: muscon@earthlink.net. Website: http://www.musicconnection.com. *Biweekly music industry trade publication.*

MUSIC MORSELS, P.O. Box 672216, Marietta GA 30006-0037. (770)850-9560. E-mail: musmorsels@aol.com. Website: http://www.serge.org/musicmorsels.htm. *Monthly songwriting publication.*

THE MUSIC PAPER, Sound Resources Ltd., P.O. Box 5167, Bay Shore NY 11706. (516)666-4892. E-mail: musicpaper@hotmail.com. Website: http://www.musicpaper.com. *Monthly music magazine for musicians.*

MUSIC ROW MAGAZINE, Music Row Publications, Inc., 1231 17th Ave. S., Nashville TN 37212. (615)321-3617. E-mail: news@musicrow.com. Website: http://www.musicrow.com. *Biweekly Nashville industry publication.*

NATIONAL SONGWRITER'S NETWORK, 3870 La Sierra Ave. #101, Riverside CA 92505. (909)422-3539. *National monthly news update for songwriters.*

OFFBEAT MAGAZINE, OffBeat Publications, 421 Frenchman St., Suite 200, New Orleans LA 70116-2056. (504)944-4300. Website: http://www.offbeat.com. *Monthly magazine covering Louisiana music and artists.*

PERFORMANCE MAGAZINE, 1101 University Dr., Suite 108, Fort Worth TX 76107. (817)338-9444. Fax: (817)877-4273. E-mail: performmag@aol.com. Website: http://www.performancemag.com. *Weekly publication on touring itineraries, artist availability, upcoming tours, and production and venue news.*

THE PERFORMING SONGWRITER, 6620 McCall Dr., Longmont CO 80503. (800)883-7664. E-mail: perfsong@aol.com. Website: http://www.performingsongwriter.com. *Bimonthly songwriters' magazine.*

PRODUCER REPORT, 415 S. Topanga Canyon Blvd., Suite 114, Topanga CA 90290. (310)455-0888. Fax: (310)455-0894. E-mail: pr@mojavemusic.com. Website: http://www.mojavemusic.com. *Semimonthly newsletter covering which producers are working on which acts, and upcoming, current and recently completed projects.*

PROFESSIONAL SOUND, 23 Hannover Dr., Suite 7, St. Catharine's, Ontario L2W 1A3 Canada. (877)746-4692. E-mail: info@nor.com. Website: http://www.professional-sound.com. *Bimonthly publication for professionals in the sound and light industry.*

PUBLIC DOMAIN REPORT, P.O. Box 3102, Margate NJ 08402. (609)822-9401. Website: http://www.p ubdomain.com. *Monthly guide to significant titles entering the public domain.*

RADIO AND RECORDS, 10100 Santa Monica Blvd., 5th Floor, Los Angeles CA 90067-4004. (310)788-1625. E-mail: moreinfo@rronline.com. Website: http://www.rronline.com. *Weekly newspaper covering the radio and record industries.*

RADIR, Radio Mall, 2412 Unity Ave. N., Dept. WEB, Minneapolis MN 55422. (888)852-4747. E-mail: mediamall@aol.com. Website: http://www.bbhsoftware.com. *Quarterly radio station database on disk.*

SING OUT!, P.O. Box 5253, Bethlehem PA 18015-0253. (888)SING-OUT. E-mail: info@singout.org. Website: http://www.singout.org. *Quarterly folk music magazine.*

SONGCASTING, 15445 Ventura Blvd. #260, Sherman Oaks CA 91403. (818)377-4084. *Monthly tip sheet.*

SONGLINK INTERNATIONAL, 23 Belsize Crescent, London NW3 5QY England. E-mail: david@son glink.demon.co.uk. Website: http://www.songlink.com. *10 issues/year newsletter including details of recording artists looking for songs; contact details for industry sources; also news and features on the music business.*

SONGWRITER MAGAZINE, P.O. Box 25879, Colorado Springs CO 80936. *Monthly magazine especially for songwriters.*

SONGWRITER PRODUCTS, IDEAS AND NECESSITIES, NSP Music Publishing, P.O. Box 952063, Lake Mary FL 32795-2063. (407)834-8555. Fax: (407)834-9997. Website: http://www.songwriterp roducts.com. *Free semi-annual catalog of songwriting tips, tools and accessories, including tapes, CDs, duplication products and music business career packages.*

SONGWRITER'S MONTHLY, The Stories Behind Today's Songs, 332 Eastwood Ave., Feasterville PA 19053. (215)953-0952. E-mail: a1foster@aol.com. *Monthly songwriters' magazine.*

THE TEXAS POLKA NEWS, P.O. Box 800183, Houston TX 77280. (713)468-2494. Fax: (713)462-7213. *Monthly publication on Texas dancehalls, record releases, festival and dance listings, and radio station information.*

VARIETY, 5700 Wilshire Blvd., Suite 120, Los Angeles CA 90036. (323)857-6600. Website: http://www. variety.com. *Weekly entertainment trade newspaper.*

WORDS AND MUSIC, 41 Valleybrook Dr., Don Mills, Ontario M3B 2S6 Canada. (416)445-8700. Website: http://www.socan.ca. *Monthly songwriters' magazine.*

BOOKS & DIRECTORIES

88 SONGWRITING WRONGS & HOW TO RIGHT THEM, by Pat & Pete Luboff, Writer's Digest Books, 1507 Dana Ave., Cincinnati OH 45207. (800)289-0963. Website: http://www.writersdigest.com.

THE A&R REGISTRY, by Ritch Esra, SRS Publishing, 7510 Sunset Blvd. #1041, Los Angeles CA 90046-3418. (800)377-7411 or (800)552-7411. E-mail: musicregistry@compuserve.com.

ATTENTION: A&R, by Teri Muench and Susan Pomerantz, Alfred Publishing Co. Inc., P.O. Box 10003, Van Nuys CA 91410-0003. (818)892-2452. Website: http://www.alfredpub.com.

THE BILLBOARD GUIDE TO MUSIC PUBLICITY, revised edition, by Jim Pettigrew, Jr., Billboard Books, 1695 Oak St., Lakewood NJ 08701. (800)344-7119.

BREAKIN' INTO NASHVILLE, by Jennifer Ember Pierce, Madison Books, University Press of America, 4720 Boston Way, Lanham MD 20706.

CMJ DIRECTORY, 11 Middle Neck Rd., Suite 400, Great Neck NJ 11021-2301. (516)466-6000. Website: http://www.cmj.com.

CONTRACTS FOR THE MUSIC INDUSTRY, P.O. Box 952063, Lake Mary FL 32795-2063. (407)834-8555. E-mail: info@songwriterproducts.com. Website: http://www.songwriterproducts.com. *Book and computer software of a variety of music contracts.*

THE CRAFT AND BUSINESS OF SONGWRITING, by John Braheny, Writer's Digest Books, 1507 Dana Ave., Cincinnati OH 45207. (800)289-0963. Website: http://www.writersdigest.com.

THE CRAFT OF LYRIC WRITING, by Sheila Davis, Writer's Digest Books, 1507 Dana Ave., Cincinnati OH 45207. (800)289-0963. Website: http://www.writersdigest.com.

CREATING MELODIES, by Dick Weissman, Writer's Digest Books, 1507 Dana Ave., Cincinnati OH 45207. (800)289-0963. Website: http://www.writersdigest.com.

DIRECTORY OF INDEPENDENT MUSIC DISTRIBUTORS, by Jason Ojalvo, Disc Makers, 7905 N. Rt. 130, Pennsauken NJ 08110. (800)468-9353. E-mail: discman@discmakers.com. Website: http://www.discmakers.com.

FILM/TV MUSIC GUIDE, by Ritch Esra, SRS Publishing, 7510 Sunset Blvd. #1041, Los Angeles CA 90046-3418. (800)552-7411. E-mail: musicregistry@compuserve.com or srspubl@aol.com.

FINDING FANS & SELLING CDs, by Veronique Berry and Jason Ojalvo, Disk Makers, 7905 N. Rt. 130, Pennsauken NJ 08110-1402. (800)468-9353. E-mail: discman@diskmakers.com. Website: http://www.discmakers.com.

GUIDE TO INDEPENDENT MUSIC PUBLICITY, by Veronique Berry, Disc Makers, 7905 N. Rt. 130, Pennsauken NJ 08110-1402. (800)468-9353. E-mail: discman@discmakers.com.

GUIDE TO MASTER TAPE PREPARATION, by Dave Moyssiadis, Disk Makers, 7905 N. Rt. 130, Pennsauken NJ 08110-1402. (800)468-9353. E-mail: discman@discmakers.com.

HOLLYWOOD CREATIVE DIRECTORY, 3000 W. Olympic Blvd. #2525, Santa Monica CA 90404. (800)815-0503. Website: http://www.hcdonline.com. *Lists producers in film and TV.*

THE HOLLYWOOD REPORTER BLU-BOOK PRODUCTION DIRECTORY, 5055 Wilshire Blvd., Los Angeles CA 90036. (323)525-2150. Website: http://www.hollywoodreporter.com.

HOT TIPS FOR THE HOME RECORDING STUDIO, by Hank Linderman, Writer's Digest Books, 1507 Dana Ave., Cincinnati OH 45207. (800)289-0963. Website: http://www.writersdigest.com.

HOW YOU CAN BREAK INTO THE MUSIC BUSINESS, by Marty Garrett, Lonesome Wind Corporation, P.O. Box 2143, Broken Arrow OK 74013-2143. (800)210-4416. Website: http://www.telepath.com/bizbook.

LOUISIANA MUSIC DIRECTORY, OffBeat, Inc., 421 Frenchmen St., Suite 200, New Orleans LA 70116. (504)944-4300. Website: http://www.offbeat.com.

MUSIC ATTORNEY LEGAL & BUSINESS AFFAIRS REGISTRY, by Ritch Esra and Steve Trumbull, SRS Publishing, 7510 Sunset Blvd. #1041, Los Angeles CA 90046-3418. (800)552-7411. E-mail: musicregistry@compuserve.com or srspubl@aol.com.

MUSIC DIRECTORY CANADA, seventh edition, Norris-Whitney Communications Inc., 23 Hannover Dr., Suite 7, St. Catherines, Ontario L2W 1A3 Canada. (877)RING-NWC. E-mail: mail@nor.com. Website: http://nor.com.

MUSIC LAW: HOW TO RUN YOUR BAND'S BUSINESS, by Richard Stin, Nolo Press, 950 Parker St., Berkeley CA 94710-9867. (510)549-1976. Website: http://www.nolo.com.

MUSIC, MONEY AND SUCCESS: THE INSIDER'S GUIDE TO THE MUSIC INDUSTRY, by Jeffrey Brabec and Todd Brabec, Schirmer Books, 1633 Broadway, New York NY 10019. Website: http:// w3.mlr.com/mlr/schirmer.

THE MUSIC PUBLISHER REGISTRY, by Ritch Esra, SRS Publishing, 7510 Sunset Blvd. #1041, Los Angeles CA 90046-3418. (800)552-7411. E-mail: musicregistry@compuserve.com or srspubl@aol.com.

MUSIC PUBLISHING: A SONGWRITER'S GUIDE, revised edition, by Randy Poe, Writer's Digest Books, 1507 Dana Ave., Cincinnati OH 45207. (800)289-0963. Website: http://www.writersdigest.com.

THE MUSICIAN'S GUIDE TO MAKING & SELLING YOUR OWN CDs & CASSETTES, by Jana Stanfield, Writer's Digest Books, 1507 Dana Ave., Cincinnati OH 45207. (800)289-0963. Website: http://www.writersdigest.com.

MUSICIANS' PHONE BOOK, THE LOS ANGELES MUSIC INDUSTRY DIRECTORY, Get Yourself Some Publishing, 28336 Simsalido Ave., Canyon Country CA 91351. (805)299-2405. E-mail: mpb@earthlink.net. Website: http://www.musiciansphonebook.com.

NASHVILLE MUSIC BUSINESS DIRECTORY, by Mark Dreyer, NMBD Publishing, P.O. Box 120675, Nashville TN 37212. Phone/Fax: (615)826-4141. E-mail: nashvillemusicbusinessdirectory@juno. com.

NASHVILLE'S UNWRITTEN RULES: INSIDE THE BUSINESS OF THE COUNTRY MUSIC MACHINE, by Dan Daley, Overlook Press, 2568 Rt. 212, Woodstock NY 12498. (914)679-6838.

NATIONAL DIRECTORY OF INDEPENDENT RECORD DISTRIBUTORS, P.O. Box 452063, Lake Mary FL 32795-2063. (407)834-8555. E-mail: info@songwriterproducts.com. Website: http://www. songwriterproducts.com.

THE OFFICIAL COUNTRY MUSIC DIRECTORY, P.O. Box 7000, Rancho Mirage CA 92270. (760)773-0995.

RADIO STATIONS OF AMERICA: A NATIONAL DIRECTORY, P.O. Box 452063, Lake Mary FL 32795-2063. (407)834-8555. E-mail: info@songwriterproducts.com. Website: http://www.songwriterpr oducts.com.

THE REAL DEAL—HOW TO GET SIGNED TO A RECORD LABEL FROM A TO Z, by Daylle Deanna Schwartz, Billboard Books, 1695 Oak St., Lakewood NJ 08701. (800)344-7119.

RECORDING INDUSTRY SOURCEBOOK, Music Books Plus, P.O. Box 670, 240 Portage Rd., Lewiston NY 14092. (800)265-8481. Website: http://www.musicbooksplus.com.

THE SONGWRITERS IDEA BOOK, by Sheila Davis, Writer's Digest Books, 1507 Dana Ave., Cincinnati OH 45207. (800)289-0963. Website: http://www.writersdigest.com.

SONGWRITER'S MARKET GUIDE TO SONG & DEMO SUBMISSION FORMATS, Writer's Digest Books, 1507 Dana Ave., Cincinnati OH 45207. (800)289-0963. Website: http://www.writersdigest. com.

SONGWRITER'S PLAYGROUND—INNOVATIVE EXERCISES IN CREATIVE SONGWRITING, by Barbara L. Jordan, Creative Music Marketing, 1085 Commonwealth Ave., Suite 323, Boston MA 02215. (617)926-8766.

SONGWRITING AND THE CREATIVE PROCESS, by Steve Gillette, Sing Out! Publications, P.O. Box 5253, Bethlehem PA 18015-0253. (888)SING-OUT. E-mail: singout@libertynet.org. Website: http:// www.singout.org/sopubs.html.

THE SOUL OF THE WRITER, by Susan Tucker with Linda Lee Strother, Journey Publishing, P.O. Box 92411, Nashville TN 37209. (800)776-4231. Website: http://www.journeypublishing.com.

SUCCESSFUL LYRIC WRITING, by Sheila Davis, Writer's Digest Books, 1507 Dana Ave., Cincinnati OH 45207. (800)289-0963. Website: http://www.writersdigest.com.

TIM SWEENEY'S GUIDE TO RELEASING INDEPENDENT RECORDS, by Tim Sweeney, TSA Books, 21213-B Hawthorne Blvd. #5255, Torrance CA 90503. (310)542-1322. Website: http://www.tsa-music.com.

TIM SWEENEY'S GUIDE TO SUCCEEDING AT MUSIC CONVENTIONS, by Tim Sweeney, TSA Books, 21213-B Hawthorne Blvd. #5255, Torrance CA 90503. (310)542-1322. Website: http://www.ts amusic.com.

TEXAS MUSIC INDUSTRY DIRECTORY, Texas Music Office, Office of the Governor, P.O. Box 13246, Austin TX 78711. (512)463-6666. E-mail: music@governor.state.tx.us. Website: http://www.govern or.state.tx.us/music.

TUNESMITH: INSIDE THE ART OF SONGWRITING, by Jimmy Webb, Hyperion, 114 Fifth Ave., New York NY 10011. (800)343-9204.

VOLUNTEER LAWYERS FOR THE ARTS GUIDE TO COPYRIGHT FOR MUSICIANS AND COMPOSERS, One E. 53rd St., 6th Floor, New York NY 10022. (212)319-2787.

WRITING BETTER LYRICS, by Pat Pattison, Writer's Digest Books, 1507 Dana Ave., Cincinnati OH 45207. (800)289-0963. Website: http://www.writersdigest.com.

THE YELLOW PAGES OF ROCK, The Album Network, 120 N. Victory Blvd., Burbank CA 91502. (818)955-4000.

Websites of Interest

The Internet can provide a wealth of information for songwriters and performers, and the number of sites devoted to music grows each day. Below is a list of some websites that can offer you information, links to other music sites, contact with other songwriters and places to showcase your songs. Since the online world is changing and expanding at such a rapid pace, this is hardly a comprehensive list, and some of these addresses may be obsolete by the time this book goes to print. But it gives you a place to start on your journey through the Internet to search for opportunities to get your music heard.

AMERICAN MUSIC CENTER: http://www.amc.net
Classical/jazz archives, includes a list of composer organizations and contacts.

AMERICAN SOCIETY OF COMPOSERS, AUTHORS AND PUBLISHERS (ASCAP)
http://www.ascap.com
Database of performed works in ASCAP's repertoire. Also includes songwriter, performer and publisher information, ASCAP membership information and industry news.

ARCANA, Artist Research, Composer's Aid & Network Access: http://www.arcananet.org
Reference site for classical composers and musicians, including collaboration opportunities, contests and music archives, in addition to industry news.

BANDSTAND: http://www.bandstand.com
Music news and links.

THE BLUES FOUNDATION: http://www.blues.org
Information on the foundation, its membership and events.

BROADCAST MUSIC, INC. (BMI): http://www.bmi.com
Offers lists of song titles, songwriters and publishers of the BMI repertoire. Also includes BMI membership information, and general information on songwriting and licensing.

CHILDREN'S MUSIC WEB: http://www.childrensmusic.org
Website dedicated to music for kids.

CHORUS AMERICA: http://www.libertynet.org/chorusam
The website of Chorus America, a national service organization for professional and volunteer choruses, including job listings and professional development information.

COMPOSERS CONCORDANCE: http://arcananet.org
The website of the ARCANA-sponsored group which promotes performance of new American music through concert series and public awareness.

COUNTRY SONGWRITER: http://www.country-songwriter.com
Monthly online music magazine with articles on the music business and the songwriting process.

CPCC: http://www.under.org/cpcc
Website for the Center for the Promotion of Contemporary Composers.

CREATIVE MUSICIANS COALITION (CMC): http://www.aimcmc.com
Website of the CMC, an international organization dedicated to the advancement of independent musicians, links to artists, and tips and techniques for musicians.

THE DELIVERY ROOM: http://metaverse.com/droom
A biweekly, hour-long radio show for unsigned bands.

ENSEMBLE 21: http://woof.music.columbia.edu/~jke4/e21.html
Website of the New York contemporary music performance group dedicated to promotion and performance of new orchestral compositions.

FILM MUSIC: http://www.filmmusic.com
Website relating to film and TV music composition.

GETSIGNED.COM: http://www.getsigned.com
Interviews with industry executives, how-to business information and more.

INDEPENDENT ARTISTS' SERVICES: http://www.idiom.com/~upend/
Full of information including searchable databases of bands and booking/touring information and other resources.

INDEPENDENT DISTRIBUTION NETWORK: http://www.ivs.net/IDN
Website of independent bands distributing their music, with advice on everything from starting a band to finding labels.

INDEPENDENT SONGWRITER WEB MAGAZINE: http://www.independentsongwriter.com
Independent music reviews, classifieds, message board and chat sessions.

INDIE CENTRE: http://www.indiecentre.com
An independent label information site created to share ideas on releasing albums, including creating a label, distribution and touring.

JAZZ CENTRAL STATION: http://www.jazzcentralstation.com
Jazz-related information, including reviews, magazines, a listing of jazz record labels and contacts, managers and more.

JAZZ COMPOSERS COLLECTIVE: http://www.jazzcollective.com
Industry information on composers, projects, recordings, concerts and events.

JAZZ CORNER: http://www.jazzcorner.com
Website for musicians and organizations featuring links to 70 websites for jazz musicians and organizations and the Speakeasy, an interactive conference area.

LAW CYBERCENTER: http://www.hollywoodnetwork.com/Law/music/survival2.html
Tips on negotiating and dealing with songwriting contracts.

LI'L HANK'S GUIDE FOR SONGWRITERS IN L.A.: http://www.halsguide.com
Website for songwriters with information on clubs, publishers, books, etc. as well as links to other songwriting sites.

LIVECONCERTS.COM: http://www.liveconcerts.com
Features interactive interviews with artists, concert dates and industry news.

LOS ANGELES GOES UNDERGROUND: http://www.primenet.com/~matthew/lagu/lagu.html
Website dedicated to underground rock bands from Los Angeles and Hollywood.

LOS ANGELES MUSIC ACCESS (LAMA): http://lama.com
Database of Los Angeles bands, clubs and resources sponsored by a group that promotes independent artists.

LYRICAL LINE: http://www.lyricalline.com
Offers places to market your songs, critique service, industry news and more.

LYRICIST.COM: http://www.lyricist.com
Jeff Mallet's songwriter site offering contests, tips and job opportunities in the music industry.

MEDIA BUREAU: http://www.mediabureau.com
Live Internet radio programs where guests perform and talk about songwriting.

THE MUSE'S MUSE: http://www.musesmuse.com
Classifieds, catalog of lyric samples, songwriting articles, organizations and chat room.

MUSIC & AUDIO CONNECTION: http://www.vaxxine.com/music
Guide to Canadian artists, associations and other resources from Norris-Whitney Communications, Inc.

MUSIC INDUSTRY PAGES: http://www.musicindustry.com
Listings of labels, magazines, products, music schools, retailers, etc.

MUSIC PUBLISHERS ASSOCIATION: http://host.mpa.org
Provides a copyright resource center, directory of member publishers and information on the organization.

MUSIC YELLOW PAGES: http://www.musicyellowpages.com
Phone book listings of music-related businesses.

NASHVILLE PUBLISHERS NETWORK: http://www.songnet.com/npn
Website dedicated to networking in the Nashville music community.

NATIONAL ASSOCIATION OF COMPOSERS USA (NACUSA): http://www.thebook.com/nacusa
Website of the organization dedicated to promotion and performance of new music by Americans, featuring a young composers' competition, concert schedule, job opportunities and more.

NATIONAL MUSIC PUBLISHERS ASSOCIATION: http://www.nmpa.org
The organization's online site with information about copyright, legislation and other concerns of the music publishing world.

OPERA AMERICA: http://www.operaam.org
Website of Opera America, featuring information on advocacy and awareness programs, publications, conference schedules and more.

OUTERSOUND: http://www.outersound.com
Information on finding a recording studio, educating yourself in the music industry, and a list of music magazines to advertise in or get reviewed by.

RES ROCKET SURFER: http://www.resrocket.com
Offers collaboration opportunities and industry news.

RHYTHM NET: http://www.rhythmnet.com
Information on artists, labels, entertainment establishments and more.

SESAC INC.: http://www.sesac.com
Includes SESAC performing rights organization information, songwriter profiles, organization news, licensing information and links to other sites.

SONG SHARK: http://www.geocities.com/SunsetStrip/Venue/2838/main
Website of information on known song sharks.

SONGLINK: http://www.songlink.com
Offers opportunities to pitch songs to music publishers for specific recording projects, also industry news.

SONGSCAPE: http://www.genoagrp.com/genoagrp/sngscape.html
Music database and music industry news service.

SONGWRITER'S GUILD OF AMERICA (SGA): http://www.songwriters.org
Offers industry news, members services information, newsletters, contract reviews and more.

SONGWRITER'S RESOURCE NETWORK: http://www.songpro.com
Online information and services designed especially for songwriters.

SONIC NET: http://www.sonicnet.com
Music news, chat and reviews.

STUDIO FINDER: http://www.studiofinder.com
Locate more than 5,000 recording studios anywhere in the U.S.

TAXI: http://www.taxi.com
Independent A&R vehicle that shops tapes to A&R professionals.

ULTIMATE BAND LIST: http://www.ubl.com
Lists record labels and their artists, posts calendar of events, festivals and club dates for artists nationwide; also includes chart information and artist news.

UNFURLED: http://www.unfurled.com
Search engine for music-related sites.

UNITED STATES COPYRIGHT OFFICE: http://lcweb.loc.gov/copyright
The homepage for the U.S. copyright office, offering information on registering songs.

YAHOO!: http://www.yahoo.com/Entertainment/Music/
Use this search engine to retrieve over 20,000 music listings.

ONLINE SHOWCASES

These sites offer places for you to post your music for a fee as a way of marketing your songs to music executives.

ARTIST UNDERGROUND: http://www.aumusic.com

BILLBOARD TALENT NET: http://www.billboardtalentnet.com

INDEPENDENT ARTIST NETWORK: http://www.ian-net.com/index.htm

INTERNET UNDERGROUND MUSIC ARCHIVE (IUMA): http://www.iuma.com.

KALEIDOSPACE: http://kspace.com

MUSIC SPOTLIGHT WEB: http://www.musicspotlight.com

ONLINE AUDITIONS, INC.: http://newbands.net

ROCKTROPOLIS: http://www.rocktropolis.com

SONGS.COM: http://songs.som/noma

SOUND ARTIST: http://www.soundartist.com

Contributors to the Insider Reports

CHANTELLE BENTLEY

Chantelle Bentley is editor of *Poet's Market*. She has also contributed articles to *Novel & Short Story Writer's Market, Guide to Literary Agents* and *Writer's Digest* magazine.

DONYA DICKERSON

Donya Dickerson is editor of *Guide to Literary Agents* and assistant editor of *Writer's Market*.

AMANDA HEELE

Amanda Heele is a writer living in Cincinnati. She teaches college composition at Miami University in Oxford, Ohio.

BARBARA KUROFF

Barbara Kuroff is editor of *Novel & Short Story Writer's Market*. She was editor of *Songwriter's Market* from 1981 to 1984.

ALICE POPE

Alice Pope is editor of *Children's Writer's & Illustrator's Market*. She has a large collection of picture books and a genuine appreciation for all things "kid."

DIANA SCHLAKE

Diana Schlake, a native of Cincinnati, is a freelance writer whose work has been published in *The Cincinnati Enquirer* and other local publications.

PAMALA SHIELDS

Pamala Shields is production editor for *Photographer's Market* and *Children's Writer's & Illustrator's Market*. Her poetry has been published in *Cameo, Venetian, Colorblind* and *MM Review*.

TRICIA SUIT

Tricia Suit is a dilettante pop culture historian with a collection of shot glasses and matchbooks acquired from her travels in the Continental 48.

JEAN VICKERS

Jean Vickers is a writer, artist and designer living in Ridgway, Colorado. She writes for the magazines *Colorado West Style* and *Telluride Style*.

Glossary

A cappella. Choral singing without accompaniment.

AAA form. A song form in which every verse has the same melody; often used for songs that tell a story.

AABA, ABAB. A commonly used song pattern consisting of two verses, a bridge and a verse, or a repeated pattern of verse and bridge, where the verses are musically the same.

A&R Director. Record company executive in charge of the Artists and Repertoire Department who is responsible for finding and developing new artists and matching songs with artists.

A/C. Adult contemporary music.

Advance. Money paid to the songwriter or recording artist before regular royalty payment begins. Sometimes called "up front" money, advances are deducted from royalties.

AFIM. Association for Independent Music (formerly NAIRD). Organization for independent record companies, distributors, retailers, manufacturers, etc.

AFM. American Federation of Musicians. A union for musicians and arrangers.

AFTRA. American Federation of Television and Radio Artists. A union for performers.

AIMP. Association of Independent Music Publishers.

Airplay. The radio broadcast of a recording.

AOR. Album-Oriented Rock. A radio format that primarily plays selections from rock albums as opposed to hit singles.

Arrangement. An adaptation of a composition for a recording or performance, with consideration for the melody, harmony, instrumentation, tempo, style, etc.

ASCAP. American Society of Composers, Authors and Publishers. A performing rights society. (See the Organizations section.)

Assignment. Transfer of rights of a song from writer to publisher.

Audiovisual. Refers to presentations that use audio backup for visual material.

b&w. Black and white.

Bed. Prerecorded music used as background material in commercials.

Black box. Theater without fixed stage or seating arrangements, capable of a variety of formations. Usually a small space, often attached to a major theater complex, used for workshops or experimental works calling for small casts and limited sets.

BMI. Broadcast Music, Inc. A performing rights society. (See the Organizations section.)

Booking agent. Person who schedules performances for entertainers.

Business manager. Person who handles the financial aspects of artistic careers.

Buzz. Attention an act generates through the media and word of mouth.

b/w. Backed with. Usually refers to the B-side of a single.

C&W. Country and western.

Catalog. The collected songs of one writer, or all songs handled by one publisher.

CD. Compact Disc (see below).

CD-R. A recordable CD.

CD-ROM. Compact Disc-Read Only Memory. A computer information storage medium capable of holding enormous amounts of data. Information on a CD-ROM cannot be deleted. A computer user must have a CD-ROM drive to access a CD-ROM.

Chamber music. Any music suitable for performance in a small audience area or chamber.

Chamber orchestra. A miniature orchestra usually containing one instrument per part.

Chart. The written arrangement of a song.

Charts. The trade magazines' lists of the best-selling records.

CHR. Comtemporary Hit Radio. Top 40 pop music.

Collaboration. Two or more artists, writers, etc., working together on a single project; for instance, a playwright and a songwriter creating a musical together.

Compact disc. A small disc (about 4.7 inches in diameter) holding digitally encoded music that is read by a laser beam in a CD player.

Co-publish. Two or more parties own publishing rights to the same song.

Copyright. The exclusive legal right giving the creator of a work the power to control the publishing, reproduction and selling of the work. Although a song is technically copyrighted at the time it is written, the best legal protection of that copyright comes through registering the copyright with the Library of Congress.

Copyright infringement. Unauthorized use of a copyrighted song or portions thereof.

Cover recording. A new version of a previously recorded song.

Crossover. A song that becomes popular in two or more musical categories (e.g., country and pop).

Cut. Any finished recording; a selection from a LP. Also to record.

DAT. Digital Audio Tape. A professional and consumer audio cassette format for recording and playing back digitally-encoded material. DAT cassettes are approximately one-third smaller than conventional audio cassettes.

DCC. Digital Compact Cassette. A consumer audio cassette format for recording and playing back digitally-encoded tape. DCC tapes are the same size as analog cassettes.

Demo. A recording of a song submitted as a demonstration of a writer's or artist's skills.

Distributor. Marketing agent responsible for getting records from manufacturers to retailers.

Donut. A jingle with singing at the beginning and end and instrumental background in the middle. Ad copy is recorded over the middle section.

E-mail. Electronic mail. Computer address where a company or individual can be reached via modem.

Engineer. A specially-trained individual who operates recording studio equipment.

Enhanced CD. General term for an audio CD that also contains multimedia computer information. It is playable in both standard CD players and CD-ROM drives.

EP. Extended play record or cassette containing more selections than a standard single, but fewer than a standard album.

Exploit. To seek legitimate uses of a song for income.

Final mix. The art of combining all the various sounds that take place during the recording session into a two-track stereo or mono tape. Reflects the total product and all of the energies and talents the artist, producer and engineer have put into the project.

Fly space. The area above a stage from which set pieces are lowered and raised during a performance.

Folio. A softcover collection of printed music prepared for sale.

Following. A fan base committed to going to gigs and buying albums.

Foreign rights societies. Performing rights societies other than domestic which have reciprocal agreements with ASCAP and BMI for the collection of royalties accrued by foreign radio and television airplay and other public performance of the writer members of the above groups.

Harry Fox Agency. Organization that collects mechanical royalties.

Grammy. Music industry awards presented by the National Academy of Recording Arts and Sciences.

Hip-hop. A dance oriented musical style derived from a combination of disco, rap and R&B.

Hit. A song or record that achieves top 40 status.

Hook. A memorable "catch" phrase or melody line that is repeated in a song.

House. Dance music created by remixing samples from other songs.

Hypertext. Words or groups of words in an electronic document that are linked to other text, such as a definition or a related document. Hypertext can also be linked to illustrations.

Indie. An independent record label, music publisher or producer.

Internet. A worldwide network of computers that offers access to a wide variety of electronic resources.

ips. Inches per second; a speed designation for tape recording.

IRC. International reply coupon, necessary for the return of materials sent out of the country. Available at most post offices.

Jingle. Usually a short verse set to music designed as a commercial message.

Lead sheet. Written version (melody, chord symbols and lyric) of a song.

Leader. Plastic (non-recordable) tape at the beginning and between songs for ease in selection.

Libretto. The text of an opera or any long choral work. The booklet containing such text.

Listing. Block of information in this book about a specific company.

LP. Designation for long-playing record played at 33⅓ rpm.

Lyric sheet. A typed or written copy of a song's lyrics.

Market. A potential song or music buyer; also a demographic division of the record-buying public.

Master. Edited and mixed tape used in the production of records; the best or original copy of a recording from which copies are made.

MD. MiniDisc. A 2.5 inch disk for recording and playing back digitally-encoded music.

Mechanical right. The right to profit from the physical reproduction of a song.

Mechanical royalty. Money earned from record, tape and CD sales.

MIDI. Musical instrument digital interface. Universal standard interface that allows musical instruments to communicate with each other and computers.

Mix. To blend a multi-track recording into the desired balance of sound.

Modem. MOdulator/DEModulator. A computer device used to send data from one computer to another via telephone line.

MOR. Middle of the road. Easy-listening popular music.

MP3. File format of a relatively small size that stores audio files on a computer. Music saved in a MP3 format can be played only with a MP3 player (which can be downloaded onto a computer).

Ms. Manuscript.

Multimedia. Computers and software capable of integrating text, sound, photographic-quality images, animation and video.

Music jobber. A wholesale distributor of printed music.

Music library. A business that purchases canned music, which can then be bought by producers of radio and TV commercials, films, videos and audiovisual productions.

Music publisher. A company that evaluates songs for commercial potential, finds artists to record them, finds other uses (such as TV or film) for the songs, collects income generated by the songs and protects copyrights from infringement.

Music Row. An area of Nashville, TN, encompassing Sixteenth, Seventeeth and Eighteenth avenues where all of the publishing houses, recording studios, mastering labs, songwriters, singers, promoters, etc. practice their trade.

NARAS. National Academy of Recording Arts and Sciences.

The National Academy of Songwriters (NAS). The largest U.S. songwriters' association. (See the Organizations section.)

Needle-drop. Refers to a type of music library. A needledrop music library is a licensed library that allows producers to borrow music on a rate schedule. The price depends on how the music will be used.

Network. A group of computers electronically linked to share information and resources.

NMPA. National Music Publishers Association.

One-off. A deal between songwriter and publisher which includes only one song or project at a time. No future involvement is implicated. Many times a single song contract accompanies a one-off deal.

One-stop. A wholesale distributor of records representing several manufacturers to record stores, retailers and jukebox operators.

Operetta. Light, humorous, satiric plot or poem, set to cheerful light music with occasional spoken dialogue.

Overdub. To record an additional part (vocal or instrumental) onto a basic multi-track recording.

Payola. Dishonest payment to broadcasters in exchange for airplay.

Performing rights. A specific right granted by U.S. copyright law protecting a composition from being publicly performed without the owner's permission.

Performing rights organization. An organization that collects income from the public performance of songs written by its members and then proportionally distributes this income to the individual copyright holder based on the number of performances of each song.

Personal manager. A person who represents artists to develop and enhance their careers. Personal managers may negotiate contracts, hire and dismiss other agencies and personnel relating to the artist's career, review material, help with artist promotions and perform many services.

Piracy. The unauthorized reproduction and selling of printed or recorded music.

Pitch. To attempt to solicit interest for a song by audition.

Playlist. List of songs a radio station will play.

Points. A negotiable percentage paid to producers and artists for records sold.

Producer. Person who supervises every aspect of a recording project.

Production company. Company specializing in producing jingle packages for advertising agencies. May also refer to companies specializing in audiovisual programs.

Professional manager. Member of a music publisher's staff who screens submitted material and tries to get the company's catalog of songs recorded.

Proscenium. Permanent architectural arch in a theater that separates the stage from the audience.

Public domain. Any composition with an expired, lapsed or invalid copyright.

Purchase license. Fee paid for music used from a stock music library.

Query. A letter of inquiry to an industry professional soliciting his interest.

R&B. Rhythm and blues.

Rate. The percentage of royalty as specified by contract.

Release. Any record issued by a record company.

Residuals. In advertising or television, payments to singers and musicians for use of a performance.

RIAA. Recording Industry Association of America.

Royalty. Percentage of money earned from the sale of records or use of a song.

RPM. Revolutions per minute. Refers to phonograph turntable speed.

SAE. Self-addressed envelope (with no postage attached).

SASE. Self-addressed stamped envelope.

SATB. The abbreviation for parts in choral music, meaning Soprano, Alto, Tenor and Bass.

Score. A complete arrangement of all the notes and parts of a composition (vocal or instrumental) written out on staves. A full score, or orchestral score, depicts every orchestral part on a separate staff and is used by a conductor.

Self-contained. A band or recording act that writes all their own material.

SESAC. A performing rights organization, originally the Society of European Stage Authors and Composers. (See the Organizations section.)

SFX. Sound effects.

Shop. To pitch songs to a number of companies or publishers.

Single. 45 rpm record with only one song per side. A 12″ single refers to a long version of one song on a 12″ disc, usually used for dance music.

Ska. Fast tempo dance music influenced primarily by reggae and punk, usually featuring horns, saxophone and bass.

SOCAN. Society of Composers, Authors and Music Publishers of Canada. A Canadian performing rights organization. (See the Organizations section.)

Solicited. Songs or materials that have been requested.

Song plugger. A songwriter representative whose main responsibility is promoting uncut songs to music publishers, record companies, artists and producers.

Song shark. Person who deals with songwriters deceptively for his own profit.

Soundtrack. The audio, including music and narration, of a film, videotape or audiovisual program.

Space stage. Open stage that features lighting and, perhaps, projected scenery.

Split publishing. To divide publishing rights between two or more publishers.

Statutory royalty rate. The maximum payment for mechanical rights guaranteed by law that a record company may pay the songwriter and his publisher for each record or tape sold.

Subpublishing. Certain rights granted by a U.S. publisher to a foreign publisher in exchange for promoting the U.S. catalog in his territory.

Synchronization. Technique of timing a musical soundtrack to action on film or video.

Take. Either an attempt to record a vocal or instrument part, or an acceptable recording of a performance.

Tejano. A musical form begun in the late 1970s by regional bands in south Texas, its style reflects a blended Mexican-American culture. Incorporates elements of rock, country, R&B and jazz, and often features accordion and 12-string guitar.

Thrust stage. Stage with audience on three sides and a stagehouse or wall on the fourth side.

Top 40. The first 40 songs on the pop music charts at any given time. Also refers to a style of music which emulates that heard on the current top 40.

Track. Divisions of a recording tape (e.g., 24-track tape) that can be individually recorded in the studio, then mixed into a finished master.

Trades. Publications covering the music industry.

12″ Single. A 12-inch record containing one or more remixes of a song, originally intended for dance club play.

Unsolicited. Songs or materials that were not requested and are not expected.

VHS. ½″ videocassette format.

Vocal score. An arrangement of vocal music detailing all vocal parts, and condensing all accompanying instrumental music into one piano part.

Website. An address on the World Wide Web that can be accessed by computer modem. It may contain text, graphics and sound.

Wing space. The offstage area surrounding the playing stage in a theater, unseen by the audience, where sets and props are hidden, actors wait for cues, and stagehands prepare to chance sets.

World music. A general music category which includes most musical forms originating outside the U.S. and Europe, including reggae and calypso. World music finds its roots primarily in the Caribbean, Latin America, Africa and the south Pacific.

World Wide Web (WWW). An Internet resource that utilizes hypertext to access information. It also supports formatted text, illustrations and sounds, depending on the user's computer capabilities.

Indexes

Openness to Submissions Index

Use this index to find companies open to your level of experience. Be sure to read the Openness to Submissions sidebar on page 8 for more information. It is recommended to use this index in conjunction with the Category Indexes found at the end of the following sections: Music Publishers, Record Companies, Record Producers, Managers & Booking Agents. Once you have compiled a list of companies open to your experience and music, read the information in these listings, paying close attention to **How to Contact**.

☐ OPEN TO BEGINNERS

Music Publishers
Abalone Publishing
Aim High Music Company
Alexander Sr., Music
Alexis
Alias John Henry Tunes
All Rock Music
Allegheny Music Works
American Heartstring Publishing
Antelope Publishing Inc.
ARAS Music
Audio Music Publishers
Baitstring Music
Barren Wood Publishing
Bay Ridge Publishing Co.
Berandol Music Ltd.
Black Rose Productions
Black Stallion Country Publishing
Bradley Music, Allan
Brian Song Music Corp.
Brothers, The
Brown & Associates Inc., J. Aaron
Buried Treasure Music
California Country Music
Clevère Musikverlag, R.D.
Cliffside Music Inc.
Co-Creations Music Publishing
Corelli's Music Box
Country Breeze Music
Country Showcase America
Cupit Music
Dagene Music
Dapmor Publishing
Delev Music Company
Doss Music, Buster
Dream Seekers Publishing
Duane Music, Inc.
Earitating Music Publishing
East Coast Music Publishing
Edition Rossori
Emstone, Inc. Music Publishing
ESI Music Group
Flea Circus Music
Fresh Entertainment

Furrow Music
Gary Music, Alan
Glad Music Co.
Hammel Associates, Inc., R.L.
Hickory Valley Music
His Power Productions and Publishing
Holy Spirit Music
Inhabitants Music Group
Interplanetary Music
Iron Skillet Music
Island Culture Music Publishers
Jae Music, Jana
Ja/Nein Musikverlag GmbH
Jerjoy Music
JPMC Music Inc.
Kaupps & Robert Publishing Co.
Kaylee Music Group, Karen
Little Miller Music Co.
Lollipop Farm Entertainment
Lovey Music, Inc.
M & T Waldoch Publishing, Inc.
May Peace Be Upon You Music
McConkey Artists Agency Music Publishing
McCoy Music, Jim
Mellow House Music
Melody Hills Ranch Publishing Co.
Mighty Blue Music Machine, The
Moon June Music
Myko Music
Nautical Music Co.
Newcreature Music
NSP Music Publishing Inc.
Omni 2000, Inc.
Ontrax Companies
Otto Publishing Co.
Portage Music
Prejippie Music Group
R.T.L. Music
Ridge Music Corp.
Riverhawk Music
Roadshow Music Corp.
Saddlestone Publishing
Schmerdley Music
Scott Music Group, Tim
SDM

Gueststar Entertainment Agency
Hale Enterprises
Hupp Enterprises, Joe
Ikon Entertainment
Imperial Artist Management
Jacobs Management
Jae Enterprises, Jana
Junquera Productions, C.
Kuper Personal Management
L.D.F. Productions
Living Eye Productions Ltd.
M.E.G Management
Merlin Management Corp.
Merri-Webb Productions
Midcoast, Inc.
Monopoly Management
Montgomery Management, Gary F.
On Stage Management Inc.
On the Level Music!
Outlaw Entertainment International
Prairie Fire Music Company
Precision Management
Pro Talent Consultants
Renaissance Entertainment Group
Rock 'N' Roll Management
Rock of Ages Productions
Rock Whirled Music Management
Rymkus Management and Promotions, Mike
St. John Artists
Sea Cruise Productions, Inc.
Silver Bow Management
Singermanagment, Inc.
Slatus Management
Smeltzer Productions, Gary
Southern Made Records
Stevens & Company Management
Stewart Music Group
Syndicate Management
T.J. Booker Ltd.
T.S.J. Productions
Take Out Management
Tenn Artist Management, William
Total Acting Experience, A
Transatlantic Management
Umpire Entertainment Enterprizes
Universal Music Marketing
Up Front Management
Wagner Agency, William F.
WE Records & Management
Wilder Artists' Management, Shane
Williams & Associates, J.R.
Wood Artist Management, Richard
World Entertainment Services, Inc.
Wright Productions

☑ PREFERS EXPERIENCED, BUT OPEN TO BEGINNERS

Music Publishers
Alan Music, Marcus
AlliSongs Inc.
ALLRS Music Publishing Co.
Amen, Inc.
Bagatelle Music Publishing Co.
Bal & Bal Music Publishing Co.
Balmur Entertainment
Barkin' Foe the Master's Bone
Bernard Enterprises, Inc., Hal
Better Than Sex Music
Betty Jane/Josie Jane Music Publishers
Big Fish Music Publishing Group
BME Publishing
Bowman Productions, David, & W. David Music
Branch Group Music
Branson Country Music Publishing
Brewster Songs, Kitty
Brightly Music Publishing
BSW Records
Camex Music
CAPP Company
Cash Productions, Inc.
Cherri/Holly Music
Christmas & Holiday Music
Christopher Publishing, Sonny
Cimirron Music
Clearwind Publishing
CMI Music Group, Inc.
Coffee and Cream Publishing Company
Cornelius Companies, The
Country Rainbow Music
De Miles Music Company, The Edward
Del Camino Music Publishing
Demi Monde Records & Publishing Ltd.
Denny Music Group
Earthscream Music Publishing Co.
Emandell Tunes
EMF Productions
Ever-Open-Eye Music
Famous Music Publishing Companies
First Time Music (Publishing) U.K.
Flying Red Horse Publishing
Foster Music Company, Mark
Fricon Music Company
Frozen Inca Music
Goodland Music Group Inc., The
Goodnight Kiss Music
Green One Music
G-String Publishing
Hansen Music Group, Stevie Ray
Happy Melody
Hickory Lane Publishing and Recording
High-Minded Moma Publishing & Productions
Hitsburgh Music Co.
Inside Records/OK Songs

Record Companies

Coppin, Johnny/Red Sky Records
Daliven Music
Darrow, Danny
De Miles, Edward
DeLory, Al, and Music Makers
Demi Monde Records & Publishing Ltd.
Eiffert, Jr., Leo J.
Esquire International
Eternal Song Agency, The
Final Mix Music
Gale, Jack
Gallway Bay Music
Glass House Productions
Hailing Frequency Music Productions
Heart Consort Music
House of Rhythm
Integrated Entertainment
Interstate Records
Jag Studio, Ltd.
Janoulis Productions, Alexander/Big Al Jano
    Productions
Jazmin Productions
John Productions, David
JSB Groupe Management Inc.
June Productions Ltd.
Kane, Karen, Producer/Engineer
Kilgore Productions
Kingston Records and Talent
Kleanza River Canyon Productions
Known Artist Productions
Kovach, Robert R.
Landmark Communications Group
Lari-Jon Productions
Linear Cycle Productions
Luick, Harold, & Country Music Showcase Intl.
    Associates
Magnetic Oblivion Music Co.
Makers Mark Music Productions
Martin, Pete/Vaam Music Productions
Mathes Productions, David
May Music/Swift River Productions
Mega Truth Records
Modern Tribe Records
Moffet, Gary
Monticana Productions
Moody, David
New Horizon Records
Omni 2000 Inc.
Ormsby, John "Buck"/Etiquette Productions
Pacific North Studios Ltd.
Pierce, Jim
Planet Dallas
Prescription Co., The
R&D Productions
Rosenman, Mike
Rustron Music Productions
Segal's Productions
Silver Thunder Music Group

Sound Arts Recording Studio
Sphere Group One
Spiral-Wave
Stuart Audio Services
Texas Fantasy Music Group
Texas Music Masters
Time-Out Productions/Bramla Music
Trac Record Co.
Valtec Productions
Westwires Digital USA
Wilbur Productions
WIR (World International Records)
Wizards & Cecil B
Y-N-A/C.D.T. Productions

Managers & Booking Agents
Air Tight Management
Alert Music, Inc.
All Musicmatters
All Star Management
American Artists Entertainment
American Bands Management
Amok Inc.
Anderson Associates Communications Group
AR Management
Ardenne Int'l Inc.
Ariel Publicity Artist Relations & Booking
Arpa Musik Management
Artist Management Services
Artist Representation and Management
Atlantic Entertainment Group
Bacchus Group Productions, Ltd.
Backstage Entertainment/Loggins Promotion
Backstreet Booking
Bamn Management
Barrett Rock 'n' Roll Enterprises, Paul
Baxter Management, Dick
BC Productions
Big J Productions
Bird Entertainment Agency, J.
Blank & Blank
Blowin' Smoke Productions/Records
Blue Cat Agency, The/El Gato Azul Agency
Bohemia Entertainment Group
Bouquet-Orchid Enterprises
Capital Entertainment
Cash Productions, Inc.
CBA Artists
Chucker Music Inc.
Circuit Rider Talent & Management Co.
Class Act Productions/Management
Clockwork Entertainment Management Agency
Clousher Productions
Cody Entertainment Group
Columbia Management Corp.
Concept 2000 Inc.
Cooke & Rose Entertainment & Production, Inc.
Corvalan-Condliffe Management
Countdown Entertainment

◙ ONLY OPEN TO PREVIOUSLY PUBLISHED SONGWRITERS/WELL-ESTABLISHED ACTS

◙ ONLY ACCEPTS MATERIAL REFERRED BY AN INDUSTRY SOURCE—DOES NOT ACCEPT UNSOLICITED MATERIAL

Atlantic Records
Big Heavy World
Brentwood Records
Capitol Records
Caroline Records, Inc.
Columbia Records
Curb Records
Dapmor Records
deConstruction Records
Def Jam Records
DreamWorks Records
Elektra Entertainment Group
Epic Records
550 Music
Geffen/DGC Records
GRP Records
Hollywood Records
Horizon Records, Inc.
Interscope Records
Island Records
Jive Records
LaFace Records
Maverick Records
MCA Records
Megaforce Worldwide Entertainment
Mercury Records
MJJ Music
Motown Records
Outpost Recordings
Patty Lee Records
Permanent Press Recordings/Permanent Wave

Priority Records
Qwest Records
RAVE Records, Inc.
Razor & Tie Entertainment
RCA Records
Reprise Records
Rhino Records
Robbins Entertainment LLC
Sahara Records and Filmworks Entertainment
Sire Records
Starfish Records
Tommy Boy Records
Universal Records
VAI Distribution
Verve Group, The
Virgin Records
Warner Bros. Records
Windham Hill Records
Word Records & Music
Work Group

Record Producers
Appell Productions, Inc., Jonathan
Diamond Entertainment, Joel
KMA
Poku Productions
Studio D Recording

Managers & Booking Agents
Entercom
GCI Inc.
Phil's Entertainment Agency Limited
Stay Gold Productions

Film & TV Index

This index lists companies who place music in motion pictures and TV shows (excluding commercials). To learn more about their film/TV experience, read the information under **Film & TV** in their listings. It is recommended to use this index in conjunction with the Openness to Submissions Index on page 471.

Music Publishers
Alan Music, Marcus
Alexander Sr., Music
ALLRS Music Publishing Co.
Alpha Music Inc.
Better Than Sex Music
Big Fish Music Publishing Group
Bixio Music Group/IDM Ventures, Ltd.
Bowman Productions, David, & W. David Music
Branch Group Music
BSW Records
CAPP Company
Christmas & Holiday Music
CTV Music (Great Britain)
Famous Music Publishing Companies
First Time Music (Publishing) U.K.
Fresh Entertainment
Goodnight Kiss Music
Heupferd Musikverlag GmbH
Holy Spirit Music
Jaelius Enterprises
Largo Music Publishing
Lilly Music Publishing
Lovey Music, Inc.
Lyrick Studios
Master Source
McConkey Artists Agency Music Publishing
Old Slowpoke Music
Pas Mal Publishing Sarl
Publishing Central
QUARK, Inc.
Riverhawk Music
Saddlestone Publishing
Shaolin Music
Shu'Baby Montez Music
Silver Blue Music/Oceans Blue Music
Standard Music Publishing

Still Working Music Group
Succes
Tedesco Music Co., Dale
Tower Music Group
Transamerika Musikverlag KG
Transition Music Corporation
Warner/Chappell Music Canada Ltd.

Record Producers
Texas Fantasy Music Group

Managers & Booking Agents
American Artists Entertainment
Hansen Enterprises, Ltd.
Total Acting Experience, A

Advertising, Audiovisual & Commercial Music Firms
AGA Communications
Allegro Music
Angel Films Company
Bowman Productions, David
Cantrax Recorders
Cinevue/Steve Postal Productions
D.S.M. Producers Inc.
Disk Productions
Entertainment Productions, Inc.
Fierce Music Group
Film Classic Exchange
Gold & Associates, Inc.
Hammond & Associates
Multi Image Productions
Photo Communication Services, Inc.
RS Music Productions
TRF Production Music Libraries
Vis/Aid Marketing/Associates

Geographic Index

This Geographic Index will help you locate companies by state, as well as those in countries outside of the U.S. It is recommended to use this index in conjunction with the Openness to Submissions Index on page 471. Once you find the names of companies in this index you are interested in, check the listings within each section for addresses, phone numbers, contact names and submission details.

Odyssey Theatre Ensemble
Players Press, Inc.
Playwrights' Arena
Shakespeare Santa Cruz
Ten-Minute Musicals Project, The
West Coast Ensemble
West End Artists

Classical Performing Arts
American Jazz Philharmonic
BRAVO! L.A.
Chamber Orchestra of South Bay/Carson-
  Dominiquez Hills Symphony
Lamarca American Variety Singers
National Association of Composers/USA
  (NACUSA)
Sacramento Master Singers
San Francisco Girls Chorus

Contests & Awards
Inner City Cultural Center's Augustin Lara
  Competition for Composers & Songwriters
L.A. Designers' Theatre Music Awards
NACUSA Young Composers' Competition
National Songwriter's Network Contests
Taylor Playwrighting Award, Marvin
Ten-Minute Musicals Project, The
"Unisong" International Song Contest
West Coast Ensemble—Musical Stairs

Organizations
Academy of Country Music
American Society of Composers, Authors and
  Publishers (ASCAP)
Broadway On Sunset
California Lawyers for the Arts
Film Music Network
Los Angeles Music Network
Musicians Contact
National Academy of Songwriters
National Association of Composers/USA
  (NACUSA), The
National Society of Men and Women of the
  Music Business (WOMB)
Northern California Songwriters Association
San Diego Songwriters Guild
Society of Composers & Lyricists
Songwriters Guild of America (SGA), The

Workshops & Conferences
ASCAP West Coast/Lester Sill Songwriter's
  Workshop
Northern California Songwriters Association
  Conference
Songwriters Expo
Songwriters Guild Foundation, The
Ten-Minute Musicals Project, The

Retreats & Colonies
Dorland Mountain Arts Colony
Villa Montalvo Artist Residency Program

COLORADO
Record Companies
Silver Wave Records

Managers & Booking Agents
Ariel Publicity Artist Relations & Booking
World Entertainment Services, Inc.

Play Producers & Publishers
Contemporary Drama Service
Pioneer Drama Service

Classical Performing Arts
Colorado Children's Chorale

Contests & Awards
Rocky Mountain Folks Festival
Telluride Troubadour Contest

Workshops & Conferences
Aspen Music Festival and School
Bluestock International Music Convention and
  Festival

CONNECTICUT
Music Publishers
Antelope Publishing Inc.
Ridge Music Corp.

Record Companies
BMX Entertainment
Generic Records, Inc.

Record Producers
John Productions, David
New Vizion Studios, The
Wytas Productions, Steve

Managers & Booking Agents
Air Tight Management
Martin Productions, Rick
Rustron Music Productions
Savage, Inc., T.E.
Tutta Forza Music

Play Producers & Publishers
Hartford Stage Company

Organizations
Connecticut Songwriters Association

Workshops & Conferences
Norfolk Chamber Music Festival

DELAWARE
Advertising, Audiovisual &
Commercial Music Firms
Ken-Del Productions Inc.

DISTRICT OF COLUMBIA
Record Companies
Orillyon Entertainment

Managers & Booking Agents
Capital Entertainment

Play Producers & Publishers
Woolly Mammoth Theatre Co.

Classical Performing Arts
Hill Chorale, The Paul, (and) The Washington
    Singers

Contests & Awards
Gabriel Award, Colonel Arnold D.
Mid-Atlantic Song Contest
Monk Institute of Jazz International Jazz
    Composers Competition, Thelonious
U.S.-Japan Creative Artists Exchange Fellowship
    Program

Organizations
Folk Alliance
Opera America
Songwriters Association of Washington

Workshops & Conferences
Folk Alliance Annual Conference

FLORIDA
Music Publishers
ARAS Music
CMI Music Group, Inc.
Emstone, Inc. Music Publishing
Lovey Music, Inc.
Mighty Blue Music Machine, The
NSP Music Publishing Inc.
Otto Publishing Co.
Pritchett Publications
Roadshow Music Corp.
Rocker Music/Happy Man Music
Rustron Music Publishers
Stuart Music Co., Jeb

Record Companies
Intrepid Records
Loconto Productions/Sunrise Studio
Pickwick/Mecca/International Records
Platinum Groove Entertainment
Playback Records
Rustron Music Productions
Treasure Coast Records
28 Records

Record Producers
Esquire International
Gale, Jack
Jay Jay Publishing & Record Co.
Kool Breeze Productions
Loconto Productions
Mac-Attack Productions
Musicland Productions, Inc.
Rustron Music Productions
Satkowski Recordings, Steve
Vickers Music Association, Charles

Managers & Booking Agents
Bird Entertainment Agency, J.
Concept 2000 Inc.
Evans Productions, Scott
Levy Management, Rick
Noteworthy Enterprises
Rainbow Collection Ltd.
Rock of Ages Productions
Rustron Music Productions
Skorman Productions, Inc., T.
Walls & Co. Management

*Advertising, Audiovisual &
Commercial Music Firms*
Cinevue/Steve Postal Productions
Gold & Associates, Inc.

Play Producers & Publishers
Asolo Theatre Company
Eldridge Publishing Co., Inc.

Classical Performing Arts
Piccolo Opera Company Inc.
Space Coast Pops, Inc.
Symphony of the Americas

Organizations
North Florida Christian Music Writers
    Association
Treasure Coast Songwriters Assn. (TCSA)

Workshops & Conferences
Winter Music Conference Inc.

GEORGIA
Music Publishers
Flea Circus Music
Fresh Entertainment
Frozen Inca Music
McGibony Publishing
Orchid Publishing
Stellar Music Industries

Record Companies
Atlan-Dec/Grooveline Records
babysue
Bouquet Records
Capricorn Records
Fresh Entertainment
Goldwax Record Corporation
Hottrax Records
LaFace Records
Landslide Records
Platinum Inc.
Rising Star Records
Robbeye Management Group, Inc.

Record Producers
Janoulis Productions, Alexander/Big Al Jano
    Productions
Kovach, Robert R.
Walbash River and Broken Arrow Productions

Managers & Booking Agents
Bojo Productions Inc.
Bouquet-Orchid Enterprises
Metro Talent Group, Inc.
Montgomery Management, Gary F.
Outland Productions
Serge Entertainment Group

*Advertising, Audiovisual &
Commercial Music Firms*
Anderson Communications

Play Producers & Publishers
Alliance Theatre Company

HAWAII
Record Companies
Belham Valley Records

Record Producers
Sanders Company, Ray

Retreats & Colonies
Kalani Oceanside Retreat
Virginia Center for the Creative Arts

IDAHO
Record Companies
Big Wig Productions

ILLINOIS
Music Publishers
De Miles Music Company, The Edward
Dream Seekers Publishing
Foster Music Company, Mark
Jerjoy Music
Music in the Right Keys Publishing
    Company
Sound Cellar Music

Record Companies
Aware Records
Beluga Records
Broken Records
Cellar Records
Griffin Music
Hammerhead Records, Inc.
Modal Music, Inc.™
Nation Records Inc.
Old School Records
Sahara Records and Filmworks Entertainment
Universal-Athena Records
Waterdog Records

Record Producers
Coachouse Music
De Miles, Edward
Neu Electro Productions

Managers & Booking Agents
Bacchus Group Productions, Ltd.
Conscience Music

Dream Hatchery, Inc.

*Advertising, Audiovisual &
Commercial Music Firms*
Geter Advertising Inc.
Norton Rubble & Mertz, Inc. Advertising
Qually & Company Inc.
Video I-D, Inc.

Play Producers & Publishers
Bailiwick Repertory
Center Theater
Dramatic Publishing Company, The

Classical Performing Arts
Chicago String Ensemble, The
Knox-Galesburg Symphony
Wheaton Symphony Orchestra

Contests & Awards
Cunningham Prize for Playwriting

Organizations
American Society of Composers, Authors and
    Publishers (ASCAP)

INDIANA
Music Publishers
Hammel Associates, Inc., R.L.
Hickory Valley Music
Interplanetary Music
Ontrax Companies

Record Companies
Dale Productions, Alan
P.M. Records
Throwing Stones Records
Yellow Jacket Records

Record Producers
Glass House Productions

Managers & Booking Agents
De Miles Company, The Edward
Hale Enterprises
Harrell & Associates, M.
International Entertainment Bureau

*Advertising, Audiovisual &
Commercial Music Firms*
Caldwell Vanriper
Omni Communications

Classical Performing Arts
Anderson Symphony Orchestra
Carmel Symphony Orchestra
New World Youth Symphony Orchestra

Contests & Awards
Indiana Opera Theatre/MacAllister Awards for
    Opera Singers

Organizations
Indianapolis Songwriters Association, Inc., The

Workshops & Conferences
New Harmony Project, The

IOWA
Music Publishers
Johnson Music, Little Richie
Luick & Associates Music Publisher, Harold
Rock N Metal Music Publishing Co.

Record Companies
LRJ

Record Producers
Heart Consort Music
Luick & Country Music Showcase Intl.
   Associates, Harold

Managers & Booking Agents
Fenchel Entertainment Agency, Fred T.

Play Producers & Publishers
Heuer Publishing Co.
Waterloo Community Playhouse

Organizations
Country Music Showcase International, Inc.

Workshops & Conferences
Davidson's Writer's Seminar, Peter

KANSAS
Music Publishers
Country Breeze Music
Publishing Central

Record Companies
Country Breeze Records

KENTUCKY
Music Publishers
Holy Spirit Music
Trusty Publications

Record Companies
Trusty Records

Managers & Booking Agents
Triangle Talent, Inc.

*Advertising, Audiovisual &
Commercial Music Firms*
Price Weber Marketing Communications, Inc.

Play Producers & Publishers
Stage One

Contests & Awards
Y.E.S. Festival of New Plays

Organizations
International Bluegrass Music Association
   (IBMA)

LOUISIANA
Music Publishers
Dapmor Publishing
EMF Productions
Fro's Music Publishing
Melody Hills Ranch Publishing Co.

Record Companies
Dapmor Records
Patty Lee Records

Managers & Booking Agents
Big J Productions
GCI Inc.
Mega Music Productions
Sea Cruise Productions, Inc.

*Advertising, Audiovisual &
Commercial Music Firms*
Disk Productions
Keating Magee Advertising

Play Producers & Publishers
Centenary College

Classical Performing Arts
Acadiana Symphony Orchestra

Organizations
Louisiana Songwriters Association

Workshops & Conferences
Cutting Edge Music Business Conference
LMNOP
Shiznit Music Conference, The

MAINE
Record Producers
Stuart Audio Services

Managers & Booking Agents
Greeley Entertainment, Chris

Workshops & Conferences
Arcady Music Festival

MARYLAND
Music Publishers
Cash Productions, Inc.
Country Showcase America
Leigh Music, Trixie

Record Companies
Banana Records
Continental Records
First Power Entertainment Group
Whirlybird Records, Inc.

Managers & Booking Agents
Cash Productions, Inc.
Noteworthy Productions

GEOGRAPHIC INDEX

MINNESOTA

Music Publishers
Portage Music

Record Companies
Danford Entertainment Group/Sisyphus
    Records
Nightmare Records

Managers & Booking Agents
Artist Representation and Management
Eternal Records/Squigmonster Management
T.S.J. Productions
Tough Guy Booking

Advertising, Audiovisual &
Commercial Music Firms
Butwin & Associates, Inc.

Play Producers & Publishers
Mixed Blood Theatre Co.

Classical Performing Arts
Augsburg Choir
Warland Singers, The Dale

Contests & Awards
Bush Artist Fellows Program
Composers Commissioning Program
McKnight Visiting Composer Program
Rochester Playwright Festival Contest
We Don't Need No Stinkin' Dramas

Organizations
Minnesota Association of Songwriters

MISSISSIPPI

Music Publishers
Bay Ridge Publishing Co.

Record Companies
Missile Records

Advertising, Audiovisual &
Commercial Music Firms
Delta Design Group, Inc.

Play Producers & Publishers
Carey College Dinner Theatre, William

MISSOURI

Music Publishers
Green One Music
Lineage Publishing Co.
Southern Most Publishing Company

Record Companies
Capstan Record Production
Green Bear Records

Record Producers
Angel Films Company
Haworth Productions

Managers & Booking Agents
Doran, P.C., James R.
Original Artists' Agency
Overstreet Music Companies, Tommy
Staircase Promotion

Advertising, Audiovisual &
Commercial Music Firms
Angel Films Company
Bryan/Donald Inc. Advertising
Media Consultants, Inc.

Play Producers & Publishers
Coterie, The
Repertory Theatre of St. Louis, The

Classical Performing Arts
St. Louis Chamber Chorus

Contests & Awards
Columbia Entertainment Company's Jackie
    White Memorial Children's Playwriting
    Contest

Organizations
Missouri Society of Songwriters and Musicians
Ozark Noteworthy Songwriters Association, Inc.

MONTANA

Classical Performing Arts
Billings Symphony

Organizations
College Music Society

NEBRASKA

Music Publishers
Lari-Jon Publishing

Record Companies
Lari-Jon Records
Redemption Records

Record Producers
Blue Planet Music
Lari-Jon Productions

Managers & Booking Agents
Lari-Jon Promotions
Lutz Entertainment Agency, Richard

Advertising, Audiovisual &
Commercial Music Firms
Blumenthal Cady & Associates, Inc.

Classical Performing Arts
Hastings Symphony Orchestra

Contests & Awards
Omaha Symphony Guild International New
    Music Competition

NEVADA

Music Publishers
Platinum Boulevard Publishing
Pollybyrd Publications Limited

Record Companies
Americatone Records International USA
Platinum Boulevard Records

Record Producers
New Horizon Records
Sound Works Entertainment Productions Inc.
Triplitt Production

Managers & Booking Agents
Dale Management, Frankie
Hansen Enterprises, Ltd.

*Advertising, Audiovisual &
Commercial Music Firms*
Izen Enterprises, Inc.

Classical Performing Arts
Carson City Symphony

Organizations
Las Vegas Songwriters Association, The

Workshops & Conferences
Emerging Artists & Talent in Music (EAT'M)
    Conference and Festival

NEW HAMPSHIRE

Record Companies
Kingston Records

Record Producers
Kingston Records and Talent
Reel Adventures

Retreats & Colonies
MacDowell Colony, The

NEW JERSEY

Music Publishers
Black Rose Productions
Cliffside Music Inc.
Gary Music, Alan
Omni 2000, Inc.
T.C. Productions/Etude Publishing Co.

Record Companies
A.P.I. Records
Airplay Label, The
Disc-tinct Music, Inc.
Lucifer Records, Inc.
Music Quest® Entertainment & Television
Omni 2000 Inc.
Presence Records
Ruf Records

Record Producers
Omni 2000 Inc.
Sphere Group One

Tari, Roger Vincent

Managers & Booking Agents
American Artists Entertainment
Atlantic Entertainment Group
Mazur Public Relations
Renaissance Entertainment Group
Ricca, Jr.'s Entertainment Agency, Joey
Scott Entertainment, Craig
Sphere Group One
Westwood Entertainment Group
White Hat Management

*Advertising, Audiovisual &
Commercial Music Firms*
Creative Associates
KJD Advertising & Teleproductions, Inc.
Smith Multimedia, LLC
Sorin Productions Inc.

Classical Performing Arts
Aureus Quartet
Dúo Clásico
Ocean City Pops Orchestra
Opera Festival of New Jersey
Ridgewood Symphony Orchestra

Organizations
Songwriters Guild of America (SGA), The

Workshops & Conferences
Appel Farm Arts and Music Festival

NEW MEXICO

Music Publishers
Pecos Valley Music

Record Companies
SunCountry Records

Managers & Booking Agents
Northern Lights Management

*Advertising, Audiovisual &
Commercial Music Firms*
Power and Associates, Inc., RH

NEW YORK

Music Publishers
ALLRS Music Publishing Co.
Alpha Music Inc.
Better Than Sex Music
Bixio Music Group/IDM Ventures, Ltd.
Black Rose Productions
BMG Music Publishing
Bourne Co. Music Publishers
Bug Music, Inc.
Camex Music
EMI Music Publishing
Famous Music Publishing Companies
Jasper Stone Music/JSM Songs

JPMC Music Inc.
Kozkeeozko Music
Largo Music Publishing
Majestic Control
MCA Music Publishing
Mymit Music Productions, Chuck
PolyGram Music Publishing
Prescription Company
QUARK, Inc.
Rockford Music Co.
Siskatune Music Publishing Co.
Sony Music Publishing
Sunsongs Music
Tops and Bottoms Music

Record Companies
A&M Records
Alyssa Records
Angel/EMI Records
Arista Records
Arkadia Entertainment Corp.
Atlantic Records
audiofile Tapes
Big Rich Major Label, A
Blind Records
Blue Wave
C.P.R.
Capitol Records
Caroline Records, Inc.
Chiaroscuro Records
Chrome Dome Records
Columbia Records
Com-Four Distribution
Creative Improvised Music Projects (CIMP)
    Records
Crescent Recording Corporation (CRC)
deConstruction Records
Dental Records
Elektra Entertainment Group
Epic Records
Evil Teen Records
Fiction Songs
550 Music
Geffen/DGC Records
Gold City Records, Inc.
Gotham Records
GRP Records
Hollywood Records
Hot Wings Entertainment
Interscope Records
Jive Records
Lamar Music Marketing
London Records
MCA Records
Mercury Records
Mighty Records
Motown Records
NPO Records, Inc.
Omega Record Group, Inc.

Paint Chip Records
Polydor Records
Priority Records
Quark Records
Qwest Records
Radical Records
Razor & Tie Entertainment
RCA Records
Regis Records Inc.
Relativity Records
Reprise Records
Robbins Entertainment LLC
Royalty Records
Select Records
Silvertone Records
Tommy Boy Records
Touchwood Zero Hour Entertainment
TVT Records
Universal Records
VAI Distribution
Verve Group, The
Village Records
Virgin Records
Warner Bros. Records
Windham Hill Records
Work Group
Xemu Records

Record Producers
Allyn, Stuart J.
Appell Productions, Inc., Jonathan
Cacophony Productions
Darrow, Danny
Gallway Bay Music
KMA
Prescription Co., The
Rosenman, Mike
Siskind Productions, Mike
Time-Out Productions/Bramla Music
Wilbur Productions
Y-N-A/C.D.T. Productions

Managers & Booking Agents
Anderson Associates Communications Group
Bassline Entertainment, Inc.
Blue Wave Productions
Chucker Music Inc.
Countdown Entertainment
Cycle of Fifths Management, Inc.
Rogue Management
DAS Communications, Ltd.
DCA Productions
DMR Agency
Earth Tracks Artists Agency
Endangered Species Artist Management
Freedman & Smith Entertainment
GMI Entertainment Inc.
Horizon Management Inc.
International Production Management

Retreats & Colonies
Brevard Music Center

NORTH DAKOTA
Record Companies
Makoché Recording Company

Classical Performing Arts
Greater Grand Forks Symphony Orchestra

OHIO
Music Publishers
Alexander Sr., Music
Barkin' Foe the Master's Bone
Bernard Enterprises, Inc., Hal
New Rap Jam Publishing, A

Record Companies
Deary Me Records
Emerald City Records
Rival Records
Spotlight Records
Starfish Records
Strive Music
Strugglebaby Recording Co.

Record Producers
Bernard Enterprises, Inc., Hal
DAP Productions
Eternal Song Agency, The
New Experience Records
Syndicate Sound, Inc.

Managers & Booking Agents
All Star Management
Backstreet Booking
Concept 2000 Inc.
Lowell Agency
Mabry Ministries, Kevin
Umbrella Artists Management, Inc.

*Advertising, Audiovisual &
Commercial Music Firms*
Group X, Inc.
Heywood Formatics & Syndication

Play Producers & Publishers
Ensemble Theatre

Classical Performing Arts
Lakeside Summer Symphony
Lithopolis Area Fine Arts Association

Contests & Awards
International Clarinet Association Composition
   Competition
Rosenthal New Play Prize, Lois and Richard

Organizations
Songwriters and Poets Critique

Workshops & Conferences
Undercurrents

OKLAHOMA
Music Publishers
Branson Country Music Publishing
Furrow Music
Jae Music, Jana
Old Slowpoke Music

Record Companies
Cherry Street Records
Garrett Entertainment, Marty
Lark Record Productions, Inc.

Record Producers
Lark Talent & Advertising
Studio Seven

Managers & Booking Agents
D&R Entertainment
Hupp Enterprises, Joe
Jae Enterprises, Jana
Stay Gold Productions
Williams & Associates, J.R.

Classical Performing Arts
Cimarron Circuit Opera Company

Contests & Awards
Billboard Song Contest

Organizations
Oklahoma Songwriters & Composers
   Association
Songwriters of Oklahoma

OREGON
Music Publishers
Earitating Music Publishing
High-Minded Moma Publishing & Productions
Moon June Music

Record Companies
Flying Heart Records
OCP Publications

Record Producers
Celt Musical Services, Jan

Managers & Booking Agents
Sirius Entertainment

Classical Performing Arts
Oregon Symphony

Contests & Awards
Portland Songwriters Association Annual
   Songwriting Competition

Organizations
Portland Songwriters Association
Songwriters Resource Network

Retreats & Colonies
Sitka Center for Art & Ecology

PENNSYLVANIA
Music Publishers
Allegheny Music Works
Bowman Productions, David, & W. David Music
Coffee and Cream Publishing Company
Delev Music Company
Kaylee Music Group, Karen
Makers Mark Gold
Shawnee Press, Inc.
Shu'Baby Montez Music
Vokes Music Publishing

Record Companies
Allegheny Music Works
CITA Communications Inc.
Golden Triangle Records
Megaforce Worldwide Entertainment
Reiter Records Ltd.
Ruffhouse Records
Vokes Music Record Co.

Record Producers
AMAJ Records
Big Sky Audio Productions
Coffee and Cream Productions
Integrated Entertainment
Makers Mark Music Productions
Philly Breakdown Recording Co.
Shu'Baby Montez Music
Westwires Digital USA

Managers & Booking Agents
BC Productions
Blank & Blank
Clousher Productions
Cooke & Rose Entertainment & Production, Inc.
Countrywide Producers
Golden Guru Entertainment
Hall Entertainment & Events, Bill
Jacobs Management
McDonnell Group, The
Rock Whirled Music Management
Vokes Booking Agency
Zane Management, Inc.

Advertising, Audiovisual &
Commercial Music Firms
Advertel, Inc.
Bowman Productions, David
BRg Music Works
Fredrick, Lee & Lloyd
Tierney & Partners

Play Producers & Publishers
American Music Theater Festival
Wilma Theater, The

Classical Performing Arts
Hershey Symphony Orchestra
Lehigh Valley Chamber Orchestra

Contests & Awards
CRS National Composers Competition
Future Charters
Words By

Organizations
Philadelphia Songwriters Forum, The
Pittsburgh Songwriters Association

Workshops & Conferences
Philadelphia Music Conference

RHODE ISLAND
Record Companies
North Star Music

Managers & Booking Agents
D&M Entertainment Agency
Twentieth Century Promotions

Organizations
Rhode Island Songwriters' Association

TENNESSEE
Music Publishers
Aim High Music Company
Alan Music, Marcus
Alias John Henry Tunes
AlliSongs Inc.
Balmur Entertainment
Barren Wood Publishing
BMG Music Publishing
Brown & Associates Inc., J. Aaron
Bug Music, Inc.
Bugle Publishing Group
Buried Treasure Music
Cornelius Companies, The
Country Rainbow Music
Cupit Music
Denny Music Group
Doss Music, Buster
EMI Christian Music Publishing
ESI Music Group
Famous Music Publishing Companies
Fricon Music Company
Goodland Music Group Inc., The
Hitsburgh Music Co.
Iron Skillet Music
Jolson Black & White Music, Al
Juke Music
MCA Music Publishing
Moody Music Group, Inc.
Nautical Music Co.

Newcreature Music
Peters Music, Justin
SDM
Silver Thunder Music Group
Simply Grand Music, Inc.
Song Farm Music
Sony Music Publishing
Starstruck Writers Group
Stevens Music, Ray
Still Working Music Group
Sun Star Songs
Talbot Music Group
Tower Music Group
Ultimate Peak Music
Universal Music Publishing
Virginia Borden Rhythms

Record Companies
Arista Records
Asylum Records Nashville
Atlantic Records
Brentwood Records
Capitol Records
Columbia Records
Curb Records
Epic Records
Interstate Records (ISR)
Jive Records
Landmark Communications Group
MCA Records
MCB Records
Mercury Records
DreamWorks Records
Orbit Records
Plateau Music
RCA Records
Stardust
TBS Records
Warner Bros. Records
Word Records & Music

Record Producers
Aberdeen Productions
Birthplace Productions
Cupit Productions, Jerry
Daliven Music
DeLory, Al, and Music Makers
Doss Presents, Col. Buster
Interstate Records
Kleanza River Canyon Productions
Landmark Communications Group
Mathes Productions, David
May Music/Swift River Productions
Pierce, Jim
Silver Thunder Music Group

Managers & Booking Agents
All Star Talent Agency
Circuit Rider Talent & Management Co.
Crowe Entertainment Inc.

Doss Presents, Col. Buster
Dream Team Management
Fox Management, Inc., Mitchell
Gurley & Co.
Hardison International Entertainment
    Corporation
Midcoast, Inc.
Nash-One Management Inc.
Riohcat Music
Sound and Serenity Management
Stephany Management, Jim

Play Producers & Publishers
Playhouse on the Square

Classical Performing Arts
Chattanooga Girls Choir
Opera Memphis

Contests & Awards
American Songwriter Lyric Contest
Playhouse on the Square New Play Competition
Song Spree Songwriter Competition

Organizations
American Society of Composers, Authors and
    Publishers (ASCAP)
Black Country Music Association, The
Broadcast Music, Inc. (BMI)
Gospel Music Association
Memphis Songwriters' Association
Nashville Songwriters Association International
SESAC, Inc.
Singer Songwriter Information Line, The
Songwriters Guild of America (SGA), The
Tennessee Songwriters International, The

Workshops & Conferences
Bluestock International Music Convention and
    Festival
Country Music Expo & Showcase
NSAI Spring Symposium

TEXAS
Music Publishers
Amen, Inc.
Bagatelle Music Publishing Co.
BSW Records
Christopher Publishing, Sonny
Earthscream Music Publishing Co.
Flying Red Horse Publishing
Glad Music Co.
Jaelius Enterprises
Kansa Records Corporation
Lollipop Farm Entertainment
Lyrick Studios
Planet Dallas Recording Studios
Raving Cleric Music Publishing/Euro Export
    Entertainment
Silicon Music Publishing Co.
Starbound Publishing Co.

Texas Cherokee Music
Texas Tuff Music Company

Record Companies
Albatross Records
Arista Records
Bagatelle Record Company
BSW Records
Direct Hit Records
Enterprize Records-Tapes
Front Row Records
Groove Makers' Recordings
Heart Music, Inc.
Howdy Records
Jam Down Entertainment, LLC
Joey Records
Ovni
Red Dot/Puzzle Records
Sabre Productions
Southland Records, Inc.
Surface Records
Sweet June Music
Topcat Records
Tropikal Productions

Record Producers
ACR Productions
Corwin, Dano
Dixon III, Philip D., Attorney at Law
Mayfly Record Productions, Ltd.
Planet Dallas
R&D Productions
Sound Arts Recording Studio
Texas Fantasy Music Group
Texas Music Masters
TMC Productions
Trinity Studio, The

Managers & Booking Agents
All Musicmatters
American Bands Management
Atch Records and Productions
Bread & Butter Productions
Crossfire Productions
Direct Management
Kendall West Agency
Kuper Personal Management
Management Plus
Nelson Promotions & Management Co., Lou
Prairie Fire Music Company
Rymkus Management and Promotions, Mike
Smeltzer Productions, Gary
Southern Made Records
SP Talent Associates
Stevens & Company Management
Stewart Music Group
Umpire Entertainment Enterprizes
Universal Music Marketing
WE Records & Management
Wemus Entertainment

Wright Productions

Advertising, Audiovisual & Commercial Music Firms
East Texas Hospitality Centers
Hammond & Associates
Hepworth Advertising Co.
Juniper Music Productions
McCann-Erickson Worldwide
Stewart Advertising, Nate
Wyatt Advertising, Evans

Play Producers & Publishers
Clark Publications, I.E.
Stages Repertory Theatre

Classical Performing Arts
Mesquite Community Band
Moores Opera Center, Moores School of Music

Contests & Awards
All American Songwriter/Composer Contest
I Write the Songs
McLaren Comedy Playwriting Competition
New Folk Concerts for Emerging Songwriters

Organizations
Artists' Legal & Accounting Assistance (ALAA)
Austin Songwriters Group
Center for the Promotion of Contemporary Composers
Country Music Association of Texas
Dallas Songwriters Association
International Country Gospel Music Association
Kerrville Music Foundation Inc.
Southeast Texas Bluegrass Music Association
Southwest Celtic Music Association
Texas Accountants & Lawyers for the Arts
Texas Music Office
Texas Songwriters Association

Workshops & Conferences
Kerrville Folk Festival
South by Southwest Music Conference and Festival

UTAH
Record Companies
Shaolin Film & Records

Advertising, Audiovisual & Commercial Music Firms
Soter Associates, Inc.

Play Producers & Publishers
Encore Performance Publishing

Classical Performing Arts
University of Utah Orchestras

Contests & Awards
Composers Guild Annual Composition Contest

Organizations
Composers Guild

Workshops & Conferences
Manchester Music Festival

VERMONT
Music Publishers
Elect Music Publishing Company

Record Companies
Big Heavy World
LBI Records

Record Producers
Jericho Sound Lab

Managers & Booking Agents
Mayo & Company, Phil
Professional Artist Management, Ltd.

Retreats & Colonies
Dorset Colony House

VIRGINIA
Music Publishers
Cimirron Music
Slanted Circle Music

Record Companies
Cimirron/Rainbird Records
Warehouse Creek Recording Corp.

Managers & Booking Agents
Cody Entertainment Group
Precision Management

Play Producers & Publishers
Barter Theatre
Mill Mountain Theatre
Shenandoah International Playwrights Retreat
   (A Project of Shenan Arts, Inc.)
Theatrevirginia
Virginia Stage Company

Classical Performing Arts
Virginia Opera

Contests & Awards
Aaron Enterprises Summertime Song Festival
Henrico Theatre Company One-Act Playwriting
   Competition

Organizations
Aaron Enterprises Songwriters Group

WASHINGTON
Music Publishers
Corelli's Music Box
Valet Publishing Co.

Record Companies
Kill Rock Stars

Record Producers
Lazy Bones Productions/Recordings, Inc.
Ormsby, John "Buck"/Etiquette Productions

Managers & Booking Agents
T.L.C. Booking Agency

Play Producers & Publishers
Taproot Theatre

Classical Performing Arts
Cascade Symphony Orchestra
Chaspen Opera Theater

Organizations
Pacific Northwest Songwriters Association
Victory Music

WEST VIRGINIA
Music Publishers
McCoy Music, Jim

Record Producers
Blues Alley Records

Play Producers & Publishers
Theatre West Virginia

Contests & Awards
Museum in the Community Composer's Award

WISCONSIN
Music Publishers
M & T Waldoch Publishing, Inc.

Record Companies
Rhetoric Records
Safire Records
Zerobudget Records

Managers & Booking Agents
Ellis International Talent Agency, The
St. John Artists
Tas Music Co./Dave Tasse Entertainment
Tiger's Eye Entertainment Management &
   Consulting

**Advertising, Audiovisual &
Commercial Music Firms**
AGA Communications

Play Producers & Publishers
Northern Lights Playhouse

Organizations
Songwriters of Wisconsin International

WYOMING
Play Producers & Publishers
American Living History Theater

AUSTRALIA
Record Companies
Makeshift Music

Managers & Booking Agents
Cranium Management
Dinwoodie Management, Andrew

Music Man Promotions
RPM Management Services Pty Ltd.
Shute Management Pty. Ltd., Phill
Walker's Company, Mr.

AUSTRIA
Music Publishers
Edition Rossori

Record Producers
WIR (World International Records)

BELGIUM
Music Publishers
Happy Melody
Inside Records/OK Songs
Succes

Managers & Booking Agents
Flinter Music

BERMUDA
Organizations
Bermuda Songwriters Association

CANADA
Music Publishers
Berandol Music Ltd.
Branch Group Music
G-String Publishing
Hickory Lane Publishing and Recording
Lilly Music Publishing
Montina Music
Saddlestone Publishing
Sci-Fi Music
Third Wave Productions Limited
Warner/Chappell Music Canada Ltd.

Record Companies
Arial Records
Gemini Records
Hi-Bias Records Inc.
iHL Records
KSM Records
L.A. Records
Magnum Music Corp. Ltd.
Merlin Productions
Monticana Records
Oak Street Music
Outpost Recordings
P. & N. Records
RA Records
Random Records
Raw Energy
sonic unyon records canada
Third Wave Productions Ltd.
Time Art Records
Worldwide Recordings Limited

Record Producers
"A" Major Sound Corporation
Harlow Sound
JSB Groupe Management Inc.
Kane Producer/Engineer, Karen
Moffet, Gary
Monticana Productions
Pacific North Studios Ltd.
Panio Brothers Label
Poku Productions
Silver Bow Productions
Spiral-Wave
Szawlowski Productions, William, & Ventura
    Music Publishing
Twist Tunes

Managers & Booking Agents
Alert Music, Inc.
Amok Inc.
Ardenne Int'l Inc.
Dunner Talent Management
EAO Music Corporation of Canada
Entercom
Feldman & Associates, S.L.
Kagan International, Sheldon
M.B.H. Music Management
Magnum Music Corporation Ltd.
Management Trust Ltd., The
Merlin Management Corp.
Outlaw Entertainment International
Phil's Entertainment Agency Limited
Siegel Entertainment Ltd.
Silver Bow Management
Strictly Forbidden Artists
T.J. Booker Ltd.
Tenn Artist Management, William

*Advertising, Audiovisual &
Commercial Music Firms*
Fierce Music Group
Moore Compositions, Patrick

Classical Performing Arts
Arcady
Calgary Boys Choir
Canadian Opera Company
Kitchener-Waterloo Chamber Orchestra
Montreal Chamber Orchestra
Vancouver Chamber Choir

Organizations
Associated Male Choruses of America
Association des Professionel.le.s de la chanson
    et de la musique
Canada Council for the Arts/Conseil des Arts du
    Canada
Canadian Academy of Recording Arts &
    Sciences (CARAS)
Canadian Country Music Association
Manitoba Audio Recording Industry Association
    (MARIA)

Pacific Music Industry Association
Society of Composers, Authors and Music
    Publishers of Canada (SOCAN)
SODRAC Inc.
Songwriters Association of Nova Scotia

Workshops & Conferences
New Music West
North by Northeast Music Festival and
    Conference
River's Edge Songwriter's Retreat with Pat
    Pattison

ENGLAND
Music Publishers
Brightly Music Publishing
Brothers, The
Bug Music, Inc.
CTV Music (Great Britain)
Demi Monde Records & Publishing Ltd.
Ever-Open-Eye Music
First Time Music (Publishing) U.K.
R.J. Music
R.T.L. Music

Record Companies
AMP Records & Music
Demi Monde Records and Publishing, Ltd.
E.S.R. Records
First Time Records
Plastic Surgery
Red Sky Records
Red-Eye Records
Rhiannon Records
Satellite Music
3rd Stone Ltd.
Workers Playtime Music Co.
X.R.L. Records/Music

Record Producers
Coppin, Johnny/Red Sky Records
June Productions Ltd.

Managers & Booking Agents
Bamn Management
Barrett Rock 'n' Roll Enterprises, Paul
Circuit Rider Talent & Management Co.
First Time Management
James Management, Roger
Kickstart Music Ltd.
Marsupial Management Ltd.
Poole Agency Limited, Gordon
Prestige Artistes
Rock 'N' Roll Management

Organizations
American Society of Composers, Authors and
    Publishers (ASCAP)
Guild of International Songwriters &
    Composers, The
International Songwriters Association Ltd.

Society for the Promotion of New Music (spnm)

FRANCE
Music Publishers
Pas Mal Publishing Sarl

GERMANY
Music Publishers
BME Publishing
Clevère Musikverlag, R.D.
Heupferd Musikverlag GmbH
Ja/Nein Musikverlag GmbH
Mento Music Group
Sinus Musik Produktion, Ulli Weigel
Transamerika Musikverlag KG

Record Companies
Comma Records & Tapes
Playbones Records
Westpark Music - Records, Production &
    Publishing

HOLLAND
Music Publishers
All Rock Music

Record Companies
Collector Records

IRELAND
Retreats & Colonies
Guthrie Centre, The Tyrone

JAPAN
Managers & Booking Agents
Jampop Ltd.

Contests & Awards
U.S.-Japan Creative Artists Exchange Fellowship
    Program

MEXICO
Contests & Awards
U.S.-Mexico Fund for Culture

NEW ZEALAND
Music Publishers
Pegasus Music

PUERTO RICO
Organizations
American Society of Composers, Authors and
    Publishers (ASCAP)

SCOTLAND
Music Publishers
Brewster Songs, Kitty
Brian Song Music Corp.

Co-Creations Music Publishing
Riverhawk Music

Record Companies
Airtrax
Street Records
Wanstar Group, The

Record Producers
Durr Productions, David

Managers & Booking Agents
Erwin Music

U.S. VIRGIN ISLANDS
Music Publishers
Island Culture Music Publishers

WALES
Record Companies
Boulevard Music & Publishing

Record Producers
Demi Monde Records & Publishing Ltd.

General Index

Use this index to locate specific markets and resources. Also, we list companies that appeared in the 1999 edition of *Songwriter's Market*, but do not appear this year. Instead of page numbers beside these markets you will find two-letter codes in parenthesis that explain why these markets no longer appear. The codes are: **(ED)**—Editorial Decision, **(NS)**—Not Accepting Submissions, **(NR)**—No (or late) Response to Listing Request, **(OB)**—Out of Business, **(RR)**—Removed by Listing's Request, **(UC)**—Unable to Contact.

A

A.A.M.I. Music Group (NR)
"A" Major Sound Corporation 231
A.P.I. Records 140
A&M Records 140
A&R 12, 27-28, 35-38, 40, 52-53, 137-39
A&R Records (UC)
Aaron Enterprises Songwriters Group 412
Aaron Enterprises Summertime Song Festival 395
Abalone Publishing 60
Abba-Tude Entertainment (NR)
Aberdeen Productions 231
ABL Records 140
Academy of Country Music 412
Acadiana Symphony Orchestra 377
Ace Records (NR)
ACR Productions 231
Acting Company, The (NR)
Actors Alley 358
Ad Agency, The 340
Adrian Symphony Orchestra 377
Advertel, Inc. 341
advertising firms 339
Afterschool Publishing Company 274
Afterschool Records, Inc. 141
AGA Communications 341
AGO/ECS Publishing Award in Choral Composition 395
Aim High Music Company 60
Air Tight Management 274
Airplay Label, The 141
Airtrax 141
Airwave Production Group (RR)
AKO Productions 231
Akron City Family Mass Choir, The (NR)
Alabama Songwriter's Guild 413
Aladdin Music Group (ED)
Alan Agency, Mark (NR)
Alan Music, Marcus 60
Albatross Records 141
Alcazar Theatre 359
ALEA III International Composi-

tion Prize 396
Alert Music, Inc. 274
Alexander Sr., Music 61
Alexas Music Productions (ED)
Alexis 61
Alias John Henry Tunes 61
All American Songwriter/Composer Contest 396
All Musicmatters 274
All Rock Music 62
All Star Management 275
All Star Talent Agency 275
Alle Audio (NR)
Allegheny Music Works 62, 142
Allegro Music 341
Allen Entertainment Development, Michael (NR)
Alliance Theatre Company 359
AlliSongs Inc. 62
ALLRS Music Publishing Co. 62
Allyn, Stuart J. 231
Almo Sounds 142
Alpha Music Inc. 63
Alpha Recording Co (ED)
Alphabeat (NR)
Alyssa Records 142
AMAJ Records 232
AMAS Musical Theatre, Inc. 359
Amelia Magazine 373
Amen, Inc. 63
American Artist Records (ED)
American Artists Entertainment 275
American Bands Management 275
American Boychoir, The (NR)
American Classics 275
American Composers Forum (NR)
American Eastern Theatrical Company (NR)
American Heartstring Publishing 63
American Jazz Philharmonic 378
American Living History Theater 359
American Music Center, Inc. 413
American Music Theater Festival 359

American Musical Theatre of San Jose 360
American Opera Musical Theatre Co. 378
American Recordings 142
American Society of Composers, Authors and Publishers (ASCAP) 13, 23, 51-54, 413
American Songwriter Lyric Contest 396
American Songwriters Network (ASN) 414
American Stage Festival (NR)
Americatone International (NR)
Americatone Records International USA 142
Amherst Saxophone Quartet 378
Amiron Music (OB)
Amok Inc. 275
AMP Records & Music 142
Anderson Associates Communications Group 276
Anderson Communications 341
Anderson Symphony Orchestra 379
Angel Films Company 232, 341
Angel/EMI Records 143
Anisette Records 143
Antelope Publishing Inc. 63
Apodaca Promotions Inc. (NR)
Apophis Music (ED)
Appel Farm Arts and Music Festival 435
Appell Productions, Inc., Jonathan 232
Aquarius Publishing/Records (NR)
Aquila Entertainment (NR)
AR Management 276
ARAS Music 63
Arcady 379
Arcady Music Festival 435
Arden Theatre Company (NR)
Ardenne Int'l Inc. 276
Arial Records 143
Ariana Records 143
Ariel Publicity Artist Relations & Booking 276

Companies that appeared in the 1999 edition of *Songwriter's Market*, but do not appear this year, are listed in this General Index with the following codes explaining why these markets were omitted: (ED)—Editorial Decision, (NS)—Not Accepting Submissions, (NR)—No (or late) Response to Listing Request, (OB)—Out of Business, (RR)—Removed by Listing's Request, (UC)—Unable to Contact.

GENERAL INDEX

GENERAL INDEX

Parrott, Karen 448
Pas Mal Publishing Sarl 106
Patty Lee Records 185
Pavement Music, Inc. (NR)
PBM Records (NS)
PC Music (RR)
Pearl Entertainment Inc. (NR)
Pecos Valley Music 106
PeerMusic 106
Pegasus Music 106
Pentacle Records 187
Performers of the World Inc.
  (P.O.W.) 309
performing songwriter 6-7
Permanent Press Recordings/Per-
  manent Wave 188
Peters Music, Justin 106
Philadelphia Music Conference
  440
Philadelphia Songwriters Forum,
  The 427
Philippopolis Music (UC)
Philly Breakdown Recording Co.
  255
Phil's Entertainment Agency
  Limited 309
Phoenix Records, Inc. (NR)
Photo Communication Services,
  Inc. 354
Piccolo Opera Company Inc. 389
Pickwick/Mecca/International
  Records 188
Pierce, Jim 255
Pioneer Drama Service 375
Pittsburgh Songwriters Association
  427
Planet Dallas 255
Planet Dallas Recording Studios
  107
Plastic City America (RR)
Plastic Surgery 188
Plateau Music 188
Platinum Boulevard Publishing 107
Platinum Boulevard Records 189
Platinum Gold Music (NR)
Platinum Groove Entertainment
  189
Platinum Inc. 189
Platinum Plus Records
  International (NR)
play producers 358
play publishers 373
Playback Records 189
Playbones Records 189
Players Press, Inc. 375
Playhouse on the Square 367
Playhouse on the Square New Play

Competition 405
Playwrights' Arena 367
Playwrights Horizons 367
PMG Records 190
Pointblank Records (NR)
Poku Productions 256
Pollard Sound World (ED)
Pollybyrd Publications Limited 107
Polydor Records 190
PolyGram Music Publishing 107
Pomgar Productions (ED)
Poole Agency Limited, Gordon 310
Pop Record Research (NR)
Portage Music 107
Portland Songwriters Association
  427
Portland Songwriters Association
  Annual Songwriting Competi-
  tion 406
Power and Associates, Inc., RH
  355
Power Play Promotions (NR)
Powerhouse Records (RR)
Powerplay Entertainment 310
PPI/Peter Pan Industries (UC)
PPL Entertainment Group 190
Prairie Fire Music Company 310
Pravda Records (NR)
Precision Management 310
Prejippie Music Group 107, 256
Premiere Records (UC)
Prescription Company 108, 256
Presence Records 190
press kit 36-37
Prestige Artistes 310
Prestige Management (NR)
Price Weber Marketing Communi-
  cations, Inc. 355
PriceClub Productions 311
Primary Stages 367
Prime Time Entertainment (NR)
Princeton Chamber Symphony
  (NR)
Priority Records 191
Prism Saxophone Quartet (NR)
Pritchett Publications 108
Private Music (RR)
Pro Star Talent Agency (NR)
Pro Talent Consultants 311
producers
  play 358
  record 230
Professional Artist Management,
  Ltd. 311
Prospector Three D Publishing
  (ED)
provincial grants 451

publishers
  music 57
  play 373
Publishing Central 108
Pulitzer Prize in Music 406

Q
Qually & Company Inc. 355
QUARK, Inc. 108
Quark Records 191
Queens Opera (NR)
query letter 17
Qwest Records 191

R
R.E.F. Records (ED)
R.J. Music 109
R.T.L. Music 109
RA Records 191
Radical Records 191
RadioActive 311
Radioactive Records (NR)
Rags to Records, Inc. (NR)
Rainbow Collection Ltd. 312
Rainbow Recording (NR)
Rampant Records 192
R&D Productions 256
Random Records 192
Rarefaction (NR)
RAVE Records, Inc. 192
Raving Cleric Music Publishing/
  Euroexport Entertainment 109
Raw Energy 192
Raz Management Co. (NR)
Razor & Tie Entertainment 192
RCA Records 193
React Recordings (NR)
record companies 137
record producers 230
Red Ant Entertainment (NR)
Red Dot/Puzzle Records 193
Red Sky Records 193
Redemption Records 193
Red-Eye Records 193
reel 339
Reel Adventures 256
Regis Records Inc. 196
Reiter Records Ltd. 196
Rejoice Records of Nashville (NR)
Relativity Records 196
Ren Zone Music 109
Renaissance Entertainment Group
  312
Reno Chamber Orchestra (NR)
Repertory Theatre of St. Louis, The
  367
reply postcard 16, 32

Silver Bow Management 316
Silver Bow Productions 258
Silver Thunder Music Group 114,
    258
Silver Wave Records 203
Silvertone Records 203
Simmons Management Group
    (NR)
Simply Grand Music, Inc. 114
Sims Records, Jerry 203
Sin Klub Entertainment, Inc. (NR)
Singer Songwriter Information
    Line, The 428
Singermanagement, Inc. 317
Singers Forum 391
Singing Boys of Pennsylvania
    (NR)
Sinus Musik Produktion, Ulli
    Weigel 114
Sire Records 203
Sirius Entertainment 317
Sirocco Productions, Inc. (NR)
Siskatune Music Publishing Co.
    114
Siskind Productions, Mike 258
Sitka Center for Art & Ecology 449
Sizemore Music (NR)
Skorman Productions, Inc., T. 317
Slanted Circle Music 115
Slatus Management 317
Slavesong Corporation, Inc. (NR)
SM Recording/Hit Records
    Network 259
Small Stone Records 203
Smash the Radio Productions (ED)
Smeltzer Productions, Gary 317
Smith Multimedia, LLC 355
Smithsonian Folkways Recordings
    (NR)
Smokin' Cowboys Publishing Co.
    (see Stevie Ray Hansen Music
    Group 87)
Smoky Mountain Recording Com-
    pany, Inc. (NR)
Smut Pedlurz Disks (NR)
S'N'M Recording/Hit Records
    Network (see SM Recording/
    Hit Records Network 259)
Society for the Promotion of New
    Music (spnm) 428
Society of Composers & Lyricists
    428
Society of Composers, Authors and
    Music Publishers of Canada
    (SOCAN) 428
SODRAC Inc. 429
Soli Deo Gloria Cantorum (NR)

Solid Discs 115
Solitaire Music, Inc. (ED)
Solo Records Productions 204
Song Farm Music 115
song shark 24-25, 55, 60
Song Spree Songwriter
    Competition 407
Songs From Out of the Blue (see
    The Mighty Blue Music
    Machine 102)
Songwriters Advocate (TSA), The
    429
Songwriters & Lyricists Club 429
Songwriters and Poets Critique 429
Songwriters Association of Nova
    Scotia 429
Songwriters Association of
    Washington 430
Songwriters Expo 441
Songwriters Guild Foundation, The
    441
Songwriters Guild of America
    (SGA), The 430, 442
Songwriters of Oklahoma 430
Songwriters of Wisconsin
    International 430
Songwriters Playground® 442
Songwriters Resource Network 431
Songwriters Workshop, The (ED)
Sonic Images Records (NS)
Sonic Records, Inc. (NR)
sonic unyon records canada 204
Sony Music Publishing 115
Sorin Productions Inc. 356
Soter Associates, Inc. 356
Sound and Serenity Management
    318
Sound Arts Recording Studio 259
Sound Cellar Music 115
Sound '86 Talent Management
    (ED)
Sound Management (OB)
Sound Management Direction 318
Sound Sound West (NR)
Sound Works Entertainment Pro-
    ductions Inc. 259
Soundboard Studios (UC)
South by Southwest Music Confer-
    ence and Festival (SXSW) 442
South Florida Recording Studios
    (RR)
South Pacific Song Contest, The
    (NR)
Southeast Texas Bluegrass Music
    Association 431
Southeastern Attractions (NR)
Southern Arizona Symphony

Orchestra 391
Southern Made Records 318
Southern Most Publishing
    Company 116
Southern Nights Entertainment
    (NR)
Southern Songwriters Guild, Inc.
    (NR)
Southland Records, Inc. 204
Southwest Celtic Music
    Association 431
Southwest Virginia Songwriters
    Association (NR)
SP Talent Associates 318
Space Coast Pops, Inc. 391
Sphere Group One 259, 318
Sphere Organization, The (NR)
Sphere Productions (see Sphere
    Group One 259, 318)
Spiral-Wave 260
Spiritual Walk Records (NR)
Spotlight Records 204
Spradlin/Gleich Publishing 116
Squad 16 (NR)
Stage One 368
Stages Repertory Theatre 369
Staircase Promotion 319
Standard Music Publishing 116
Stander Entertainment (NR)
Standing Room Only Inc. (ED)
Starbound Publishing Co. 116
Stardust 204
Starfish Records 205
Stargard Records (NR)
Starkravin' Management 319
Star-Scape (NR)
Starstruck Writers Group 116
Startrak Records, Inc. (UC)
state grants 451
Stay Gold Productions 319
Steel-Sax Publishing (UC)
Steinman Management, Obi 319
Stellar Music Industries 117
Stephany Management, Jim 319
Stepping Stone Music (ED)
Sterling Image Entertainment (NR)
Sternberg Management, Harriet
    319
Stevens & Company Management
    320
Stevens Music, Ray 117
Stewart Advertising, Nate 356
Stewart Management, Steve 320
Stewart Music Group 320
Still Working Music Group 117
Stormin' Norman Productions
    (NR)

Companies that appeared in the 1999 edition of *Songwriter's Market*, but do not appear this year, are listed in this General Index with the following codes explaining why these markets were omitted: (ED)—Editorial Decision, (NS)—Not Accepting Submissions, (NR)—No (or late) Response to Listing Request, (OB)—Out of Business, (RR)—Removed by Listing's Request, (UC)—Unable to Contact.

GENERAL INDEX